# Historical Dictionary
# of the British Monarchy

Kenneth J. Panton

The Scarecrow Press, Inc.
Lanham • Toronto • Plymouth, UK
2011

Published by Scarecrow Press, Inc.
A wholly owned subsidiary of The Rowman & Littlefield Publishing Group, Inc.
4501 Forbes Boulevard, Suite 200, Lanham, Maryland 20706
http://www.scarecrowpress.com

Estover Road, Plymouth PL6 7PY, United Kingdom

British Library Cataloguing in Publication Information Available

**Library of Congress Cataloging-in-Publication Data**

Panton, Kenneth J. (Kenneth John), 1945–
  Historical dictionary of the British monarchy / Kenneth J. Panton.
    p. cm.
  Includes bibliographical references.
  ISBN 978-0-8108-5779-7 (cloth : alk. paper) — ISBN 978-0-8108-7497-8 (ebook)
    1. Great Britain—Kings and rulers—Biography—Dictionaries. 2. Queens—Great
Britain—Biography—Dictionaries. 3. Great Britain—Court and courtiers—Biography—
Dictionaries. 4. Monarchy—Great Britain—History—Dictionaries. 5. Great Britain—
History—Dictionaries. I. Title.
  DA28.1.P27 2011
  941.009'9—dc22                                                    2010038859

Printed in the United States of America

*All photographs from the Library of Congress*

For Aderyn-Carol and Hudson

# Contents

# Editor's Foreword

Although in some ways it is just a shadow of its former self, the British monarchy is still the most impressive monarchy around. It is honored and respected at home and even, in various permutations, provides the sovereign of 15 other countries of the Commonwealth. Its remaining responsibilities and privileges are more modest, but certainly easier to perform, and, according to opinion polls, the population is quite satisfied with the results. True, this is little compared to the raw "power" of earlier centuries, and being a constitutional monarch does have its inconveniences. But they are nothing compared to the difficulties of actually running, or trying to run, a country as compact and yet complicated as Great Britain, to say nothing of its vast empire spanning the globe. So a rather extensive look backward is necessary to see where it is coming from. And this leads to an impressive line of sovereigns reaching back to 1917, for the House of Windsor, and further still to 959 for the first English kings, and 843 for the first Scots kings, and, indeed, to 519, if you will, for the first known king, Cerdic.

This *Historical Dictionary of the British Monarchy* is a big book, and inevitably so. The chronology alone has to list hundreds of major events (and overlook thousands of lesser ones) just to give us an overview of who ruled when and bits and snatches of what these persons did. The introduction then brings together numerous threads of this vast tapestry to provide a still limited overview, as it would have taken several volumes to get all the details. And the dictionary section has entries on hundreds and hundreds of persons, royals and lesser nobility, as well as some of their accomplishments and residences, and a bit about the workings of the monarchy. Obviously, there are entries on Henry VIII, Elizabeth I and Elizabeth II, and yes, indeed, Lady Diana and some others easily recognized by the public. But the most interesting in certain ways are countless persons who have since been forgotten but were in their day high and mighty, loved and hated, or just supported until the next ruler came along. Big as this book is, it can really only be a starting point for a serious study of the British monarchy, and thus one of its main contributions is to provide a bibliography which helps readers access further sources of information.

The book is written by Kenneth J. Panton, who has already coauthored the *Historical Dictionary of the United Kingdom* and the *Historical Dictionary of the Contemporary United Kingdom* and alone wrote the *Historical Dictionary of London*. And a good thing it is, one might add, because that provides a very strong foundation for this latest work on the British monarchy. Born in Scotland, Dr. Panton studied at the University of Edinburgh and King's College, London, and then taught at London Guildhall University and next, of all things, at the University of Southern Mississippi. But this is not so unusual when you consider that he served as the head of the British Studies Program, the largest in the United States, and one that sends some 200 students to Great Britain every year for its summer program. Having since retired, Ken is now living in Scotland again and busily working on yet other historical dictionaries. But nothing will exceed this one in scope and presumably also in usefulness.

Jon Woronoff
Series Editor

# Acknowledgments

Any attempt to provide a chronology for, let alone present even limited analysis of, an institution that has developed over more than a millennium must depend more heavily on secondary sources than on primary research, so the contents of this dictionary reflect the distillation of facts, figures, and opinions originally presented in dozens of academic papers, biographies, encyclopedias, and other scholarly works from a variety of disciplines. It is impossible to acknowledge the contribution made by each of the authors on whom I have relied, but all are listed in the bibliography, and I trust they will understand that I have derived enormous pleasure from sifting through their writings. In particular, I am much in debt to Keith A. Cowlard, of the University of Greenwich, who has allowed me to draw on material used in the two-volume *Historical Dictionary of the United Kingdom* and the *Historical Dictionary of the Contemporary United Kingdom* that we compiled for Scarecrow in 1997–1998 and 2008, respectively.

Also, I am grateful to those skilled librarians who so often pointed me in the right direction, thus limiting time-consuming searches and providing access to sources that might otherwise not have been available. Lorna Cheyne of Edinburgh University Library was especially helpful (and lightened the research load through a delightful correspondence), but I also greatly valued the generous help I received from the staffs of Clackmannanshire Council Libraries, the National Library of Scotland (who facilitated electronic access to sources), Redhill Public Library, Stirling Council Libraries, and the library of the University of Southern Mississippi, all of whom gave generously of their time. Don Shewan used his considerable artistic talents to prepare the genealogical diagrams in the appendixes at the end of the book, taking crude drawings and turning them into attractive family trees.

Jon Woronoff has been as acute an editor of this book as he has of earlier publications, massaging an academic ego over two decades by somehow managing to point out weaknesses without appearing to criticize, and Kellie Hagan and April Snider, at Scarecrow's headquarters, have ushered the text through the production process. There is, in addition, a whole army of people—copyeditors, designers, printers, and others—who shape the product that lands on individual and institutional library shelves. They leave me in awe of their abilities, and I do not have the words to thank them adequately.

Another group of people have also had a considerable impact on this book, albeit indirectly. When I retired from full-time university teaching and administration, I took advantage of newfound freedom to move to Scotland, where, while I have been writing, very talented men have been reconstructing an apartment around me, converting a dingy attic into a penthouse study, installing an up-to-date heating system, and refurbishing the structure of the existing property. Without exception, they have been painstaking and patient, making sure they did exactly what was needed and doing it well. Their skills are not those normally associated with the preparation of a manuscript, but nevertheless they had a considerable impact on the working environment, so I unreservedly recommend, and thank, architect Morris Robb; carpenters Sandy Morrow and Wullie Lauder; heating engineers Allan Macfarlane and Jim Walmsley, and their colleagues Alan Wilson, John Hart, and Stevie Morran; multitaskers William McAlpine and Alan Williams; roofer Jim Mullan; and Ian Gow, who masterminded the whole task of loft conversion. In addition, I am much indebted to Christopher Syme, who guided me through the process of acquiring the property and has looked after it during my absences.

Finally, there are personal debts to acknowledge. Paula Mathis, Stacey Ready, and Peggy Varnado, with whom I worked closely at the University of Southern Mississippi's Honors College, were towers of strength then and now and have my heartfelt thanks and admiration, as have Frances and Phil Sudduth (who have been generous with their help for many years), Gary Pace (whose kindness made the transatlantic move so much easier), Clifton Dixon (chair of the Geography Department at Southern Miss), and Dave Davies (my successor as Honors College dean). My wife, Debbie, relocated from a subtropical home on the Gulf of Mexico in order to be with me in somewhat colder, more northerly climes; she has experienced the travails of setting up house in a new country and has endured lengthy periods of solitude in an unfamiliar world while I indulged in the ultimately selfish pleasure of writing— so much so that I cannot find words adequate to express my thanks. Lastly, in every book I have written, I have acknowledged the unstinting support I have received from Mhorbhaine, my daughter, and without any qualification I do so again because it has meant so much.

My life has been enriched because my path crossed those of all these people. Something of each of them is in this book, but the shortcomings are mine and mine alone.

# Notes on Names

Names pose a major problem for authors and readers of dictionaries such as this. The principal difficulties, and the solutions adopted, can be summarized briefly:

1. Some individuals have many names, and others may have numerous spellings of a single name. That is particularly true of earlier monarchs and their relatives, partly because the names were written down by several chroniclers in different ways at a time when literacy was limited, and partly because modern scholars use different approaches to the conversion of Old English (the language of Anglo-Saxon groups) into current English. Thus, for example, the king of England for most of the period from 978 to 1016 is referred to in different works as Aethelred, Athelred, and Ethelred (along with other forms) and his wife is known as Aelfgifu, Aelflaed, Aelgifu, Effleda, Elfreda, and Elgiva. The problem, however, is not confined to the first royal families; the younger son of Charles, prince of Wales, is commonly called Prince Harry, but his birth name is Henry and he is sometimes also identified as Prince Henry (or Prince Harry) of Wales. In a work of this size, it is not possible to list all of the alternative names used for each individual, although an indication of the range is usually noted.

2. Non-English personal and place names have been anglicized because, in most cases, the anglicized form is the normal form used in the English-speaking world. Thus, the man traditionally, but inaccurately, known as the first king of Scots is listed as Kenneth MacAlpin, not as Cináed Mac Ailpin, Coinneach mac Ailpein, or other Scots Gaelic forms of the name.

3. Kings, queens, and other senior members of British royal families do not use surnames. In this dictionary, monarchs are differentiated by their regnal number (for example, Henry I and Henry II). Other people are differentiated by their senior title (which, in some cases, may be a foreign title, as in the cases of Sophia Dorothea, queen of Prussia, and Sophia, electress of Hanover) or by a territorial descriptor (as with

Caroline of Brandenburg-Ansbach and Caroline of Brunswick-Wolfen-büttel). Students should also note that the term "Plantagenet," which is sometimes used by authors as a surname for members of the royal house that ruled England from 1154 until 1485, is, in almost all cases, a retrospective name applied to help identification, and that most of the people to whom the name is applied would not have recognized it as theirs.

4. The Scottish monarchs who reigned from 1371 are usually known as "the Stewarts," but the members of that dynasty who ruled England as well as Scotland from 1603 until 1714 are often termed "the Stuarts." The change of spelling occurred in the mid-16th century when the young Mary, queen of Scots, was sent to France for safety. The French alphabet does not use the letter w, so the spelling of "Stewart," her family name, was changed to "Stuart" to accommodate her hosts and did not revert to its original form after Mary returned to her homeland. In this dictionary, the latter form is used as a surname for Mary's contemporaries and later members of the dynasty, the earlier form for her predecessors.

5. The child of a monarch is formally styled "His (or Her) Royal Highness," along with his or her name and the territorial designation of any peerage. For example, Queen Elizabeth II's second son is His Royal Highness, Prince Andrew, the duke of York. For reasons of space, the prefix and the definite article are omitted throughout the dictionary.

# Chronology

Note: Some of the dates listed below, and particularly those for the Anglo-Saxon period prior to 1066, are the subject of debate by scholars and would not be accepted by all historians.

**495** The *Anglo-Saxon Chronicle* records that "This year came two leaders into Britain, Cerdic and Cynric his son, with five ships."

**519** Cerdic becomes the first king of Wessex.

**534** Cerdic dies and is succeeded as king of Wessex by his son (or possibly his grandson), Cynric.

**787** In the first recorded coronation of an English monarch, Ecgfrith is anointed king of Mercia.

**802** King Egbert secures the throne of Wessex after the death of King Beorhtric.

**829** King Egbert unites the Anglo-Saxon realms in southern Britain under a single ruler, albeit briefly.

**839** **4 February:** King Egbert dies and is succeeded by Aethelwulf, his son.

**843** By tradition, Kenneth MacAlpin, king of Dalriada, defeats his Pictish neighbors in battle and unites the two communities under a single ruler; many modern historians debunk the story but MacAlpin is still widely regarded as the first king of Scots.

**856** In order to prevent civil war, King Aethelwulf cedes Wessex to Aethelbald, the second of his five sons.

**858** Kenneth MacAlpin dies and his brother, Donald, replaces him as the king of Dalriada and the Picts. **13 January:** King Aethelwulf dies and Aethelbald reunites his father's territories under one ruler.

**860** **20 December:** Aethelbald dies and Aethelbert, his younger brother, replaces him as king of Wessex and of Kent.

**862** **13 April:** King Donald I dies and is succeeded by King Constantine I.

**865** Aethelred succeeds his older brother, Aethelbert, as king.

**868** King Alfred the Great marries Ealhswith.

**871 23 April:** King Aethelred dies and is succeeded by his younger brother, Alfred the Great.

**877** King Constantine I is killed by Viking invaders and is succeeded by his younger brother, Áed. Under attack by Viking invaders, King Alfred the Great seeks safety in the marshlands of southwest England.

**878** Áed is assassinated and succeeded as king of the Picts by Giric and, possibly, Eochaid. **May:** King Alfred the Great defeats a Viking army at Edington; as a result of the negotiations that follow the victory, England is divided, with the invaders controlling the area north of the River Thames and the Anglo-Saxons controlling the rest.

**889** Giric, king of the Picts, dies or is deposed, along with Eochaid, and is succeeded by Donald II.

**899 26 October:** King Alfred the Great dies and is succeeded by his son, Edward the Elder, who consolidates Anglo-Saxon control over southern England.

**900** King Donald II is killed and is succeeded by King Constantine II.

**905 5 December:** Ealhswith, consort of King Alfred the Great, dies.

**924 17 July:** King Edward the Elder dies and is succeeded by his son, Aethelstan.

**925 4 September:** Aethelstan is crowned king of the English.

**927** King Aethelstan annexes the Viking kingdom of York, becoming the first monarch to rule an area with boundaries similar to those of present-day England.

**937** King Aethelstan's Anglo-Saxon army routs a force of Norsemen and North Britons at Brunanburh.

**939 27 October:** King Aethelstan dies, childless, and is succeeded by Edmund, his half-brother, who rules England as King Edmund I.

**c943** King Constantine II abdicates the throne of Alba, making way for King Malcolm I.

**946 26 May:** King Edmund I of England dies and is succeeded by his brother, Eadred.

**952** Constantine II, formerly king of Alba, dies at St. Andrews.

**954**  King Malcolm I of Alba is slain and succeeded by Indulf.

**955**  **23 November:** King Eadred dies, unmarried and childless, and is succeeded by his nephew, Eadwig.

**957**  The leaders of Mercia and Northumbria rebel against King Eadwig and invite Edgar, his younger brother, to replace him.

**959**  **1 October:** King Eadwig dies, and Edgar, his brother and ruler of the northern Anglo-Saxon realms, reunites the English people under a single monarch.

**962**  Indulf, king of Alba, is killed by Viking invaders and succeeded by Duff.

**966**  Colin succeeds Duff as king of Alba.

**968**  **25 August:** Edgiva, third wife of Edward the Elder, dies.

**971**  Colin, king of Alba, is murdered and succeeded by Kenneth II.

**973**  **11 May:** Edgar and Aelfthryth are crowned king and queen of the English at Bath, the first occasion on which the consort of a monarch is crowned alongside her husband.

**975**  **8 July:** King Edgar dies at Winchester and is succeeded by his son, Edward (later known as Edward the Martyr).

**978**  **18 March:** King Edward the Martyr is assassinated, and Aethelred the Unready, his half-brother, is chosen as his successor.

**991**  **10 August:** Viking invaders defeat an Anglo-Saxon army in battle at Maldon; King Aethelred the Unready responds by paying them to withdraw from England.

**995**  King Kenneth II is assassinated and succeeded by King Constantine III.

**997**  King Constantine III dies in battle and is succeeded by King Kenneth III.

**1002**  King Aethelred the Unready marries Emma of Normandy, a union that indirectly leads to the invasion of England by William the Conqueror in 1066. **13 November:** Aethelred orders the massacre of all Danes living in England in an effort to reduce the Viking presence in his country.

**1005**  **c25 March:** King Kenneth III is killed in battle by his cousin, who succeeds him as King Malcolm II.

**1013**  **25 December:** Sweyn is proclaimed king of England after his Viking invaders force King Aethelred the Unready into exile.

**1014  3 February:** King Sweyn dies, and King Aethelred the Unready returns to rule England.

**1016  23 April:** King Aethelred the Unready dies in London and is succeeded by his son, who rules as King Edmund II. **18 October:** Anglo-Saxon forces are defeated by an invading Danish army at Assandun, leaving Canute, the leader of the victorious force, in control of all of England north of the River Thames. **30 November:** King Edmund II dies, and the whole of England is united under King Canute.

**1017  2 July:** Emma of Normandy marries King Canute and thus becomes the only woman to be queen consort to two kings of England.

**1034  25 November:** King Malcolm II dies and is succeeded by his grandson, King Duncan I.

**1035  12 November:** King Canute dies and is succeeded by Harthacanute, his only son by Emma of Normandy; King Harthacanute appoints Emma and his half-brother, Harold, as co-regents while he attempts to forestall a Norwegian invasion of Denmark.

**1037**  Harold, son of Canute and Aelfgifu of Northampton, seizes the English throne from Harthacanute, his half-brother, and reigns as King Harold I.

**1040  17 March:** King Harold I dies at Oxford; later in the year, Harthacanute reclaims the English crown. **14 August:** King Duncan I is killed and is succeeded by Macbeth.

**1042  8 June:** King Harthacanute, the last Scandinavian king of England, dies childless and is replaced by King Edward the Confessor, who thus restores the Anglo-Saxon line of succession to the throne.

**1045  23 January:** King Edward the Confessor marries Edith of Wessex.

**1052  7 March:** Emma of Normandy, the only woman to be consort to two English kings, dies.

**c1053**  Duke William of Normandy (later King William I of England) marries Matilda of Flanders.

**1057  15 August:** Macbeth dies and is succeeded as king of Scots by his stepson, Lulach.

**1058  17 March:** Malcolm, son of King Duncan I, kills Lulach (the king of Scots) and takes the crown, reigning as King Malcolm III.

**1066  5 January:** King Edward the Confessor dies and is succeeded by Harold Godwinson, his brother-in-law, who becomes King Harold II. **25 Sep-**

**tember:** The Anglo-Saxon army of King Harold II defeats a 15,000-strong Scandinavian invasion force at Stamford Bridge. **14 October:** William the Conqueror's Norman troops defeat King Harold II's weary army at the Battle of Hastings; according to legend, Harold dies when an arrow pierces his eye. **25 December:** William the Conqueror is crowned William I of England.

**c1070** King Malcolm III marries Margaret of Wessex.

**1075** **19 December:** Edith of Wessex, wife of King Edward the Confessor, dies.

**1083** **2 November:** Matilda of Flanders, wife of William the Conqueror, dies.

**1087** **9 September:** William the Conqueror dies; Robert, his eldest son, inherits Flanders, and William, the second son, inherits the kingdom of England.

**1093** **13 November:** King Malcolm III is killed; his brother, reigning as King Donald III, succeeds him. **16 November:** Margaret, queen consort of King Malcolm III, dies in Edinburgh Castle just three days after her husband is slain.

**1094** **May:** Duncan, son of King Malcolm III, ousts King Donald III and reigns as King Duncan II. **12 November:** King Donald III returns to the Scottish throne after King Duncan II is murdered.

**1097** **October:** King Donald III is removed from the Scottish throne for a second time and is replaced by Edgar of Scotland.

**1100** **2 August:** King William II of England is killed, and his younger brother seizes the throne, reigning as King Henry I. **11 November:** King Henry I marries Matilda of Scotland in a political union that helps to stabilize the northern boundaries of his kingdom.

**1101** **2 August:** Robert Curthose (eldest son of William the Conqueror) relinquishes his claim to the English crown in return for an annual pension from his brother, King Henry I.

**1106** **28 September:** The armies of King Henry I defeat supporters of Robert Curthose at Tinchebrai; the victory puts an end to 30 years of intermittent strife between the brothers and adds Normandy to the English king's realm.

**1107** **8 January:** Edgar of Scotland dies and is succeeded by Alexander I.

**1118** **1 November:** Matilda of Scotland, wife of King Henry I, dies.

**1121   c2 February:** King Henry I marries Adeliza of Leuven in a vain attempt to produce an heir to replace his son, William the Aetheling, who had drowned late the previous year.

**1122   12 or 13 July:** Sybilla of Normandy, consort of King Alexander I, dies.

**1124   c23 April:** King Alexander I dies at Stirling and is succeeded by his younger brother, King David I.

**1125**   Stephen of Blois (later King Stephen) marries Matilda of Boulogne.

**1127   1 January:** King Henry I, lacking an heir, makes his reluctant nobles swear that they will accept his daughter, Matilda, as their sovereign when he dies.

**1128   17 June:** Matilda, the only surviving child of King Henry I, marries Geoffrey of Anjou; 26 years later, Henry, their eldest child, becomes the first Plantagenet king of England.

**1134   10 February:** Robert Curthose, eldest son of William the Conqueror, dies at Cardiff Castle after being kept prisoner for 28 years by his brother, King Henry I.

**1135   1 December:** King Henry I dies of food poisoning, leaving more than 20 illegitimate children but no son to follow him to the throne; Stephen, his nephew, claims the crown, and England plunges into 19 years of civil war as Matilda, Henry's daughter, tries to wrest it from him.

**1141   2 February:** King Stephen is taken captive by Matilda's troops at the Battle of Lincoln. **14 September:** Royalist supporters capture Robert of Gloucester, one of Matilda's principal allies. **1 November:** The warring factions in England release King Stephen and Robert of Gloucester in an exchange of prisoners.

**1149   8 July:** King Alexander II dies.

**1147   31 October:** Robert of Gloucester dies, and Matilda (who claims that the English crown is rightfully hers) retreats to Normandy shortly afterward, leaving the throne to Stephen.

**1151   24 March or 23 April:** Adeliza of Louvain, consort of King Henry I, dies.

**1152   3 May:** The doughty Matilda of Boulogne, wife of King Stephen, dies. **18 May:** Henry of Anjou (later King Henry II) marries Eleanor of Aquitaine.

**1153   6 January:** Henry of Anjou invades England, pursuing his claim to the throne. **24 May:** King David I dies and is succeeded by his grandson, King Malcolm IV. **17 August:** Eustace of Boulogne, the only son of King Stephen, dies suddenly while plundering church estates at Bury St. Edmunds. **6 November:** King Stephen, worn out by war and saddened by the deaths of his wife and son, signs an agreement that Henry of Anjou will succeed him.

**1154   25 October:** King Stephen dies; his grandson, Henry, becomes the first Plantagenet king of England, reigning as King Henry II.

**1165   9 December:** King Malcolm IV dies and is succeeded by his brother, King William I of Scotland.

**1167   10 September:** Matilda, who precipitated a lengthy civil war when she challenged King Stephen for the English throne in 1135, dies in Rouen, having seen her son win the crown as King Henry II.

**1174   12 July:** King William I of Scotland is taken captive at the Battle of Alnwick; in return for his release, he has to accept King Henry I of England as his feudal overlord.

**1183   11 June:** Henry, the young king, technically the co-monarch of England with his father, King Henry II, dies, leaving Richard, his younger brother, heir to the throne.

**1186   5 September:** King William I of Scotland marries Ermengarde de Beaumont.

**1189   6 July:** King Henry II dies at Chinon, in Anjou, and is succeeded by his son, who reigns as King Richard I. **29 August:** John (later King John) marries Isabel of Gloucester.

**1191   12 May:** King Richard I marries Berengaria of Navarre.

**1199   **King John's marriage to Isabel of Gloucester is annulled. **6 April:** King Richard I dies; he is succeeded as king of England by his brother, John.

**1200   24 August:** King John marries Isabella of Angoulême.

**1204   1 April:** Eleanor of Aquitaine, queen consort of King Henry II, dies.

**1209   November:** Pope Innocent III excommunicates King John, who wants to select his own archbishop of Canterbury rather than accept Innocent's choice of Stephen Langton.

**1213   15 May:** In return for the cancellation of an order excommunicating him from the Roman Catholic Church, King John makes England a papal fiefdom.

**1214   27 July:** King John's military campaign to retrieve territories on the European mainland lost to Philip II of France ends in ignominious failure with defeat at the Battle of Bouvines. **4 December:** King William I of Scotland dies and is succeeded by his son, King Alexander II.

**1215   15 June:** English clerics and nobles force King John to sign the Magna Carta, a charter that greatly curtails the monarch's rights but adds to the power of the church and the law courts.

**1216   22 May:** Louis, son of King Philip II of France, arrives in England with an army ready to support barons who have rebelled against King John. **19 October:** King John dies and is succeeded by his nine-year-old son, King Henry III.

**1217   11 September:** After a military defeat at Lincoln and naval defeats in the English Channel, Louis, son of King Philip II of France, agrees to end his efforts to win the English crown and withdraws to France with his army. **14 October:** Isobel of Gloucester, first wife of King John, dies.

**1221   June:** King Alexander II marries Joan, sister of King Henry III of England.

**1230   23 December:** Berengaria of Navarre, queen consort of King Richard I, dies.

**1233   12 February:** Ermengarde de Beaumont, queen consort of King William I of Scotland, dies.

**1236   14 January:** King Henry III marries Eleanor of Provence and incurs his nobles' annoyance by giving her family and friends important positions at the royal court.

**1238   4 March:** Joan, queen consort of King Alexander II, dies.

**1239   15 May:** King Alexander II takes Marie de Coucy as his second wife.

**1246   4 June:** Isabella of Angoulême, former consort of King John, dies.

**1249   6 July:** King Alexander II dies and is succeeded by his son, King Alexander III.

**1251   26 December:** King Alexander III of Scotland marries Margaret, eldest daughter of Henry III of England.

**1254   1 November:** Edward, later King Edward I, marries Eleanor of Castile.

**1255** Prince Edward of England goes to war against Llywelyn ap Gruffydd, prince of Gwynnedd, without the approval of his father, King Henry III, and is roundly defeated.

**1258** **11 June:** King Henry III negotiates the Provisions of Oxford with his barons, receiving contributions to his treasury in return for the concession of significant powers to England's parliament.

**1264** **23 January:** King Louis IX of France is asked to adjudicate on the dispute between King Henry III and his nobles over the Provisions of Oxford (*see* **1258**); his decision in favor of the monarch precipitates the Second Barons' War. **14 May:** Antiroyalist forces, led by Simon de Montfort, capture King Henry III at the Battle of Lewes.

**1265** **4 August:** Royalist troops defeat a rebel army and kill Simon de Montfort at the Battle of Evesham; after the rebels' defeat, King Henry III is released from captivity.

**1272** **16 November:** King Henry III dies and is succeeded by his son, King Edward I.

**1275** **26 February:** Margaret, consort of Alexander III, dies.

**1282** **11 December:** King Edward I's troops kill Llywelyn ap Gruffydd and end Wales's struggle for independence from England.

**1284** **17 January:** Alexander, the only surviving child of King Alexander III, dies, precipitating a succession crisis in Scotland.

**1284 or 1285** Marie de Coucy, second wife of King Alexander II, dies.

**1285** **14 October:** King Alexander III, hoping to sire an heir, marries Yolande de Dreux.

**1286** **19 March:** King Alexander III is thrown from his horse and killed, leaving the throne to his granddaughter, Margaret, maid of Norway.

**1290** **September/October:** Margaret, maid of Norway, dies en route to her coronation in Scotland; 14 men claim her crown. **28 November:** Eleanor of Castile, wife of King Edward I, dies at Harby, near Lincoln; Edward takes her back to London, erecting a stone cross at each overnight resting place.

**1291** **25 June:** Eleanor of Provence, consort of King Henry III, dies.

**1292** **17 November:** King Edward I of England makes John Balliol king of Scotland and thus increases English influence in northern Britain.

**1296  10 July:** King Edward I forces King John of Scotland to abdicate and takes him to London, along with the Stone of Scone, on which Scottish monarchs were seated during their coronation.

**1299  10 September:** King Edward I takes Marguerite of France as his second wife.

**1301  7 February:** King Edward I creates his son, Edward, prince of Wales in order to emphasize English sovereignty over the defeated territory.

**1302**  Robert the Bruce (later King Robert I) marries Elizabeth de Burgh.

**1306  25 March:** King Robert I is crowned king of Scots, occupying a throne that has been vacant since 1296.

**1307  7 July:** King Edward I dies; his son, King Edward II, succeeds him.

**1308  25 January:** King Edward II marries Isabella of France.

**1314  24 June:** The Scots, under Robert I (Robert the Bruce), defeat a large English army at Bannockburn and strengthen their claims to independent nationhood.

**1318  14 February:** Marguerite of France, second wife of King Edward I, dies.

**1322  16 March:** The armies of King Edward II defeat rebel forces at Boroughbridge.

**1326  21 September:** Queen Isabella and her lover, Roger Mortimer, launch an invasion of England in a successful effort to depose King Edward II and kill his unpopular advisors. **16 November:** Supporters of Queen Isabella and Roger Mortimer capture King Edward II near Tonyrefail, in south Wales.

**1327  20 January:** King Edward II is forced to abdicate in favor of his 14-year-old son, who reigns as King Edward III. **26 October:** Elizabeth de Burgh, queen consort of King Robert I, dies.

**1328  24 January:** King Edward III marries Philippa of Hainault at York Minster. **17 March:** At a meeting in Edinburgh, English envoys renounce all claims to sovereignty over Scotland and recognize King Robert I and his successors as the country's rulers. **3 May:** The English parliament, meeting in Northampton, approves the agreement reached in Edinburgh on 17 March. **17 July:** Four-year-old David (son of King Robert I of Scotland) weds seven-year-old Joan of the Tower (daughter of King Edward II of England) in a marriage designed to cement a peace pact between the two countries.

**1329   7 June:** King Robert I dies and is succeeded by his son, King David II.

**1330   29 November:** Roger Mortimer, earl of March and regent of England, is hanged in London, and Queen Isabella of France, his lover, is banished to Castle Rising as the young King Edward III begins to assert his authority.

**1332   24 September:** Edward de Balliol is crowned king of Scots but never finds the support needed to defeat the supporters of King David II. **23 November:** Edward de Balliol formally recognizes King Edward III of England as his feudal superior and thus as overlord of Scotland.

**1333** Despite the misgivings of his parliament, King Edward III of England repudiates the 1328 Treaty of Northampton that recognized Scotland as an independent country.

**1334   May:** David II, Scotland's boy king, and Joan of the Tower (his queen) are sent to the court of Philip VI of France to prevent them from falling into English hands.

**1337   7 March:** King Edward III creates the title "duke of Cornwall" (England's first dukedom) for his son, Edward, the black prince; in modern times, the honor goes to the eldest son of the reigning monarch. **May:** King Philip VI of France confiscates Gascony and Guyenne, which were held by King Edward III of England as feudal fiefdoms. **7 October:** King Edward III asserts his claim to the throne of France.

**1340   24 June:** In the first major engagement of the Hundred Years' War, an English fleet, under the command of King Edward III, destroys the French navy at Sluys.

**1346   26 August:** The English army, led by King Edward III and helped by its longbowmen, inflicts a heavy defeat on the French at Crécy. **17 October:** The English defeat a Scots army, led by King David II, at Neville's Cross; David is taken prisoner and held captive for 11 years.

**1347   22 November:** Pope Clement VII issues a dispensation legitimizing the children of Robert Stewart (later King Robert II) and Elizabeth Mure.

**1355   2 May:** Pope Innocent VI grants a dispensation for the marriage of Eupheme de Ross to Robert Stewart (later King Robert II), whose first wife had died.

**1356   20 January:** Edward de Balliol abdicates the kingship of Scotland in favor of King Edward III of England—an act that means little to the Scottish people, who continue their refusal to recognize English overlordship. **19**

**September:** Edward, the black prince, leads an English army to victory over the French at Poitiers and captures John, the French king.

**1358    22 August:** Isabella of France, consort of King Edward II, dies.

**1360    8 May:** English and French negotiators prepare the Treaty of Brétigny, which details the conditions under which King Edward III will release King John of France, whom he is holding captive. **24 October:** The Treaty of Calais confirms the principles of the Treaty of Brétigny; King John of France will be released from English captivity in return for a ransom of three million gold crowns, and King Edward III will renounce his claim to the French throne but will be compensated by the incorporation into his realm of much of western France, including Calais and Aquitaine.

**1362    7 September:** Joan of the Tower, queen consort of King David II, dies.

**1363 or 1364    King David II marries Margaret Drummond.

**1364    January:** Edward de Balliol, claimant to the Scottish throne, dies.

**1366    13 March:** John Stewart, later King Robert III, marries Annabella Drummond.

**1369    King David II divorces Margaret Drummond. **21 May:** King Charles V of France renounces the Treaties of Brétigny and Calais (*see* **1360**) and resumes the war with England. **c15 August:** Philippa of Hainault, queen consort of King Edward III, dies at Windsor Castle.

**1371    22 February:** King David II dies and is succeeded by his nephew, King Robert II.

**1377    21 June:** King Edward III dies and is succeeded by his 10-year-old grandson, King Richard II.

**1380    27 July (or 5 February 1381):** Henry Bolingbroke (later King Henry IV) marries Mary de Bohun.

**1381    13 June:** King Richard II meets the leaders of peasants who are revolting against conditions in agricultural areas of England and promises them that serfdom will be abolished and that rents will be reduced. **14 June:** Richard II reneges on his promises to the peasants and orders the execution of their leaders.

**1382    20 January:** King Richard II marries Anne of Bohemia.

**1384    November:** King Robert II is deprived of his monarchical authority, which is placed in the hands of his son, John, earl of Carrick.

**1385  6 August:** Edmund of Langley, son of King Edward III, is created "Duke of York," a title that, since 1474, has been conferred on the second son of the reigning monarch.

**1386  July:** John of Gaunt leaves England, determined to assert his right to be king of Castile and Léon. **November:** Parliament asks King Richard II to dismiss his unpopular lord chancellor, Michael de la Pole, who is accused of embezzlement; the king retorts that he would not remove even a servant from his kitchen at parliament's request.

**1387  19 December:** Rebels led by Henry Bolingbroke (later King Henry IV) defeat a royalist army at Radcot Bridge, near Oxford.

**1388  3 February:** Parliament accuses King Richard II's closest advisors of treason; several are executed and others exiled.

**1389** John of Gaunt gives up his claim to the throne of Castile and Léon.

**1390  19 April:** King Robert II dies and is succeeded by his son, John, who reigns as King Robert III.

**1394  7 June:** Anne of Bohemia, queen consort of Richard II, dies. **4 June or 4 July:** Mary de Bohun, wife of Henry Bolingbroke, dies.

**1396  4 November:** King Richard II marries Isabella of Valois, daughter of King Charles VI of France.

**1397  8–9 September:** King Richard II arranges the murder of his uncle, Thomas of Woodstock, duke of Gloucester, as he reasserts his authority over nobles who oppose him.

**1398  28 April:** King Robert III creates the dukedom of Rothesay—the first dignity of its kind in Scotland—for David, his eldest son; the first son of the reigning British monarch now acquires the title at birth.

**1399  3 February:** John of Gaunt dies, and King Richard II, his nephew, appropriates his estates, prompting Henry Bolingbroke (John's heir and later Henry IV) to mount a rebellion. **15 August:** King Richard II surrenders to rebels at Conwy Castle. **29 September:** King Richard II abdicates. **30 September:** Parliament declares Henry Bolingbroke England's new king, reigning as King Henry IV.

**1400  c14 February:** Richard, formerly King Richard II of England, dies in Pontefract Castle, possibly of starvation but perhaps as a result of violence.

**1402  26 March:** David Stewart, duke of Rothesay and heir to the Scottish throne, dies in suspicious circumstances in Falkland Palace. **2 April:** King Henry IV takes Joan of Navarre as his second wife.

**1403  21 July:** King Henry IV's army routs a rebel force, led by Harry Hotspur, at the Battle of Shrewsbury.

**1405  8 June:** King Henry IV ends a rebellion in the north of England by beheading, without trial, two of the leaders—Thomas Mowbray, earl of Norfolk, and Richard le Scrope, archbishop of York.

**1406  4 April:** King Robert III of Scotland dies and is succeeded by his 11-year-old son, King James I, who is being held captive by the English.

**1408  19 February:** Henry Percy, earl of Northumberland, is defeated at the Battle of Bramham Moor by forces loyal to King Henry IV, bringing another rebellion against the monarch to an unsuccessful conclusion.

**1409  13 September:** Isabella of Valois, queen consort of King Richard II, dies.

**1413  20 March:** King Henry IV dies and is succeeded by his son, Hal, who reigns as King Henry V.

**1415  11 August:** King Henry V launches another attempt to retrieve former English territories in France. **25 October:** King Henry's forces defeat the French at Agincourt.

**1419  19 January:** Rouen surrenders to King Henry.

**1420  21 May:** King Charles VI of France makes King Henry V of England his heir and regent. **2 June:** King Henry V marries Catherine of Valois (daughter of King Charles VI of France) in a union designed to ensure that the children of the English monarch will hold the French throne in perpetuity. **1 September:** King Henry V makes a ceremonial entry into Paris.

**1421  10 June:** King Henry V begins another military campaign in France. **6 December:** King Henry decrees that the "first-begotten sons of the kings of England" will, in future, hold the title "duke of Cornwall."

**1422  31 August:** King Henry V dies and is succeeded by his son, King Henry VI. **21 October:** Under the terms of the treaty of Troyes, King Henry VI succeeds to the throne of France on the death of King Charles VI.

**1424  2 February:** King James I of Scotland marries Joan Beaufort.

**1437  3 January:** Catherine of Valois, consort of King Henry V, dies. **20 February:** King James I of Scotland is assassinated and is succeeded by his son, King James II. **9 July (or 10 June):** Joan of Navarre, formerly queen consort of King Henry IV, dies.

**1445   22 April:** King Henry VI marries Margaret of Anjou. **15 July:** Joan Beaufort, widow of King James I of Scotland, dies.

**1449   3 July:** King James II of Scotland marries Mary of Gueldres.

**1455   22 May:** The Wars of the Roses begin at St. Albans with a decisive victory for a rebel army, led by Richard, duke of York, over a Lancastrian force under Edmund, duke of Somerset.

**1460   10 July:** King Henry VI is captured by Yorkist troops at the Battle of Northampton. **3 August:** King James II of Scotland is killed and is succeeded by his son, King James III. **10 October:** Parliament refuses to accept the claim to the throne of England made by Richard, duke of York. **30 December:** Lancastrian supporters kill Richard, duke of York, at Wakefield.

**1461   17 February:** Lancastrian forces defeat a rebel army at St. Albans, releasing King Henry VI from the hands of the Yorkists, who had held him captive since the Battle of Northampton in July 1460. **4 March:** Edward, son of Richard, duke of York, deposes his cousin, King Henry VI, and reigns as King Edward IV. **29 March:** Yorkist soldiers rout a Lancastrian army at Towton in the bloodiest battle ever fought in England; historians estimate that as many as 60,000 men (about 1 percent of the country's population) may have died.

**1463   1 December:** Mary of Gueldres, widow of King James II of Scotland, dies.

**1464   1 May (?):** King Edward IV annoys many of his supporters by marrying Elizabeth Woodville, widow of a Lancastrian enemy, at a time when his advisors were negotiating his wedding to a relative of Louis XI, king of France.

**1465   July:** King Henry VI is captured by Yorkists once again and is imprisoned in the Tower of London.

**1469   13 July:** King James III marries Margaret of Denmark. **27 November:** The Scottish parliament confirms that, in the future, the firstborn son of the reigning monarch will hold the title "duke of Rothesay."

**1470   3 October:** King Henry VI is restored to the English throne, and King Edward IV is driven into exile.

**1471   14 March:** King Edward IV, exiled the previous year, returns to England with an army. **11 April:** Edward IV recaptures Henry VI and imprisons him in the Tower of London. **4 May:** Edward IV's Yorkist troops defeat Henry VI's Lancastrian force at Tewkesbury. **21 May:** King Henry VI dies, probably by violence, in the Tower of London.

**1472**   **12 July:** Richard, duke of Gloucester (later King Richard III), marries Anne Neville.

**1475**   **4 July:** King Edward IV invades France, intent on claiming the French crown and retrieving estates formerly held on the continent of Europe by English monarchs. **29 August:** The Treaty of Picquigny ends the English invasion of France; King Edward IV renounces his claim to the French throne and receives a payment of 75,000 crowns from King Louis XI of France, with a promise of annual sums of 50,000 crowns for the rest of his life.

**1482**   **25 August:** Margaret of Anjou, widow of King Henry VI, dies.

**1483**   **9 April:** King Edward IV dies and is succeeded by his 12-year-old son, King Edward V. **25 June:** Parliament declares that King Edward IV's marriage to Elizabeth Woodville (*see* **1464**) was invalid, a ruling that means King Edward V is illegitimate and therefore not entitled to the throne; King Edward IV's brother, Richard, succeeds as King Richard III. **August:** Former King Edward V and his younger brother, Richard, duke of York, vanish from the Tower of London.

**1485**   **16 March:** Anne, queen consort of King Richard III, dies. **22 August:** Henry Tudor's army kills King Richard III at the Battle of Bosworth Field, and Henry claims the English throne by right of conquest as King Henry VII, ending more than three centuries of Plantagenet rule.

**1486**   **18 January:** King Henry VII marries Elizabeth of York, daughter of King Edward IV, and thus unites the warring families of Lancaster and York. **14 July:** Margaret of Denmark, wife of King James III, dies.

**1487**   **24 May:** Lambert Simnel is crowned King Edward VI in Dublin. **5 June:** A Yorkist army, raised in support of Lambert Simnel's claim to the English crown, crosses the Irish Sea from Ireland to Lancashire. **16 June:** King Henry VII quashes the Yorkist rebellion with a decisive victory in a battle at Stoke Field and condemns Simnel to work in the royal kitchens.

**1488**   **11 June:** King James III is killed at the Battle of Sauchieburn and is succeeded by his son, King James IV.

**1492**   **8 June:** Elizabeth Woodville, widow of King Edward IV, dies.

**1495**   **3 July:** Perkin Warbeck mounts an invasion of England claiming that he is Richard, son of King Edward IV, but his army is easily defeated by King Henry VII's troops.

**1497**   **7 September:** Perkin Warbeck leads another rebellion against King Henry VII but is captured and incarcerated in the Tower of London.

**1499  23 November:** Perkin Warbeck, who led two unsuccessful attempts to unseat King Henry VII, is hanged after attempting to escape from the Tower of London.

**1501  14 November:** Catherine of Aragon marries Arthur, prince of Wales.

**1502  2 April:** Arthur, prince of Wales, dies; his younger brother, Henry (later King Henry VIII) becomes heir apparent.

**1503  11 February:** Elizabeth of York, queen consort of King Henry VII, dies. **8 August:** King James IV marries Margaret Tudor, daughter of King Henry VII.

**1509  21 April:** King Henry VII dies and is succeeded by his son, King Henry VIII. **11 June:** King Henry VIII marries his sister-in-law, Catherine of Aragon.

**1511  13 November:** Against the advice of many of his advisors, King Henry VIII joins the Holy League in an alliance against France.

**1513  16 August:** King Henry VIII invades France and leads his army to victory in the Battle of the Spurs at Guinegate. **9 September:** King James IV—the last British monarch to die in battle—is killed, along with the flower of the Scottish nobility, at Flodden and is succeeded by his one-year-old son, King James V.

**1514  April:** King Henry VIII declares a truce in his war with France.

**1521  11 October:** Pope Leo X confers the title of "Defender of the Faith" on King Henry VIII.

**1527**  King Henry VIII petitions Pope Clement V for the annulment of his marriage to Catherine of Aragon, but the pope procrastinates.

**1533  25 January:** King Henry VIII marries Anne Boleyn. **23 May:** King Henry VIII's marriage to Catherine of Aragon is annulled by an English court convened solely for that purpose. **28 May:** Archbishop of Canterbury Thomas Cranmer announces his approval of Henry's marriage to Anne Boleyn.

**1534  23 March:** Parliament passes legislation that bastardizes Mary (King Henry VIII's daughter by Catherine of Aragon) and makes Elizabeth (his daughter by Anne Boleyn) heiress apparent. **11 November:** Parliament passes legislation making King Henry VIII "supreme head in earth of the Church of England."

**1535  31 August:** Pope Paul III excommunicates King Henry VIII, depriving him of the title "Defender of the Faith," which was granted in **1521**.

**1536**   **7 January:** Catherine of Aragon, first wife of King Henry VIII, dies; Henry calls for public celebrations. **2 May:** Anne Boleyn, Henry VIII's second wife, is arrested on charges of adultery, incest, and treason. **19 May:** Anne Boleyn, consort of King Henry VIII, is beheaded. **30 May:** Henry VIII marries Jane Seymour. **18 July:** Parliament approves legislation that bastardizes Mary and Elizabeth (Henry VIII's daughters by Catherine of Aragon and Anne Boleyn, respectively) and gives his (as yet unborn) children by Jane Seymour precedence in the line of succession to the throne.

**1537**   **1 January:** King James V marries Madeleine de Valois. **7 July:** Madeleine de Valois, queen consort of King James V, dies. **24 October:** Jane Seymour, consort of King Henry VIII, dies 12 days after giving birth to the son her husband craved.

**1538**   **18 May:** King James V and Mary of Guise marry by proxy.

**1540**   **6 January:** King Henry VIII marries Anne of Cleves. **9 July:** King Henry VIII's marriage to Anne of Cleves is annulled. **28 July:** King Henry VIII marries Catherine Howard.

**1541**   **18 October:** Margaret Tudor, consort of King James IV of Scotland, dies.

**1542**   **13 February:** Catherine Howard, queen consort of King Henry VIII, is executed after being found guilty of adultery, a treasonable offense. **14 December:** King James V of Scotland dies and is succeeded by his six-day-old daughter, Mary, queen of Scots.

**1543**   **1 July:** Representatives of the Scottish and English crowns meet at Greenwich to sign a peace treaty that betroths Mary, queen of Scots, to Edward, King Henry VIII's son and heir. **12 July:** King Henry VIII takes Catherine Parr as his sixth and last wife. **11 December:** Scotland's parliament refuses to ratify the treaty signed at Greenwich on 1 July.

**1544**   **29 March:** Parliament reinstates Henry VIII as "Defender of the Faith."

**1547**   **28 January:** King Henry VIII dies and is succeeded by his only surviving son, King Edward VI.

**1548**   **7 August:** Five-year-old Mary, queen of Scots, is dispatched to safety in France. **5 September:** Catherine Parr, the last of King Henry VIII's six wives and the most oft-married of English queens, dies.

**1553**   **6 July:** King Edward VI dies and is succeeded, briefly, by Lady Jane Grey. **19 July:** Mary, Edward VI's half-sister, enters London and is proclaimed Queen Mary I; Jane Grey is imprisoned. **13 November:** A court finds Jane Grey and her husband, Guildford Dudley, guilty of treason.

**1554    25 January–8 February:** Thomas Wyatt leads a short-lived rebellion against Queen Mary I. **12 February:** Lady Jane Grey and her husband are beheaded. **18 March–19 May:** Elizabeth (King Henry VIII's daughter by Anne Boleyn) is imprisoned in the Tower of London, suspected of complicity in Wyatt's rebellion. **25 July:** Ignoring the advice of many of her advisors, Queen Mary I marries Prince Philip of Spain.

**1555    4 February:** John Rogers, a preacher and translator of the Bible, is burned at the stake in London—the first of some 270 Protestants to die as Queen Mary I attempts to enforce Roman Catholic worship on England.

**1557    7 July:** Queen Mary I declares war on France in support of her husband, King Philip II of Spain. **16 July:** Anne of Cleves, the fourth—and longest lived—of Henry VIII's six wives, dies.

**1558    7 January:** The French recapture Calais, which had been a possession of the English crown since 1347 and was England's last toehold on the European mainland. **24 April:** Mary, queen of Scots, marries Francis, heir to the throne of France. **17 November:** Queen Mary I dies and is succeeded by her half-sister, Queen Elizabeth I.

**1559    29 April:** Parliament passes an Act of Supremacy, recognizing Queen Elizabeth I as the supreme governor of the Church of England and paving the way for development of the church on Protestant lines.

**1560    11 June:** Mary of Guise, consort of King James V, dies. **5 December:** Francis II of France dies, leaving Mary, queen of Scots, a widow at the age of 18.

**1561    19 August:** Mary, queen of Scots, returns to her homeland after 13 years in France.

**1565    29 July:** Mary, queen of Scots, marries Henry Stuart, lord Darnley.

**1567    9 February:** Lord Darnley, consort of Mary, queen of Scots, is murdered. **24 April:** Mary, queen of Scots, is "abducted" by James Hepburn, earl of Bothwell. **15 May:** Mary, queen of Scots, marries the earl of Bothwell. **24 July:** Mary, queen of Scots, is forced to abdicate and is succeeded by her son, King James VI.

**1568    16 May:** Mary, queen of Scots, flees to England but is imprisoned by Queen Elizabeth I.

**1570    25 February:** Queen Elizabeth I is excommunicated by Pope Pius V.

**1582    22 August:** King James VI is abducted by Presbyterian nobles and held captive until July 1583.

**1587    8 February:** Mary, queen of Scots, is executed.

**1589    20 August:** King James VI marries Anne of Denmark by proxy.

**1598** King James VI of Scotland publishes *The Trew Law of Free Monarchie*, which expounds the doctrine of the divine right of kings. **13 February:** King Philip II of Spain, former consort of Queen Mary I, dies.

**1603    24 March:** Queen Elizabeth I dies, ending the line of Tudor monarchs in England; James VI of Scotland (her closest male relative) succeeds her as James I of England, uniting the two countries under a single crown.

**1619    2 March:** Anne of Denmark, consort of King James VI and I, dies.

**1625    27 March:** King James VI and I dies; his son, who reigns as King Charles I, succeeds him. **11 May:** King Charles I makes an unpopular marriage, by proxy, with Henrietta Maria of France.

**1649    30 January:** King Charles I is executed. **19 May:** Parliament declares England a republic.

**1651    1 January:** At the last coronation to be held in Scotland, Charles II is made king of Scots. **3 September:** Defeat at the Battle of Worcester brings a temporary end to King Charles II's attempt to restore the English monarchy.

**1660    8 May:** Charles II is declared king of England, restoring the country's monarchy after an 11-year flirtation with republicanism. **3 September:** James, duke of York (later King James VII and II), marries Anne Hyde.

**1662    21 May:** King Charles II marries Catherine of Braganza.

**1669    10 September:** Henrietta Maria, queen consort of King Charles I, dies.

**1671    31 March:** Anne Hyde, wife of James, duke of York (later King James VII and II), dies.

**1673    30 September:** James, duke of York (later King James VII and II), marries Mary of Modena.

**1677    4 November:** Mary, daughter of James, duke of York, and later Queen Mary II, marries William, prince of Orange (later King William III of England and II of Scotland).

**1682    21 November:** George of Brunswick-Lüneburg (later King George I) marries his first cousin, Sophia Dorothea of Celle.

**1683** **28 July:** Anne Stuart (later Queen Anne) marries George, prince of Denmark.

**1685** **6 February:** King Charles II dies; the crowns of England and Scotland pass to his brother, who reigns as King James VII of Scotland and II of England. **20 May–15 July:** James Scott, duke of Monmouth, and Archibald Campbell, earl of Argyll, lead rebellions intended to depose King James VII and II; both men are caught and beheaded.

**1688** **5 November:** William of Orange lands at Torbay with a 12,000-strong army and begins his efforts to claim the throne from King James VII of Scotland and II of England. **23 December:** King James VII and II flees to France.

**1689** **12 February:** The English parliament decides that King James II has abdicated. **13 February:** The English parliament confirms that James II will be replaced by co-monarchs, Mary II and her husband, William of Orange (William III). **12 March:** King James VII and II, supported by an army supplied in part by King Louis XIV of France, lands at Kinsale in southern Ireland, hoping to win back his crowns. **11 April:** The Scottish parliament concurs with the English decision of 12 February, accepting Mary II and William II (William III of England) as co-monarchs. **16 April:** John Graham, viscount Dundee, mounts a rebellion in support of King James VII and II. **27 July:** Viscount Dundee's troops win a battle with the government army at Killiecrankie, but he is killed and the rebellion begun in April peters out. **16 December:** A Bill of Rights establishes the supremacy of parliament over the monarch in England.

**1690** **1 July 1690:** The attempts of King James VII and II to retrieve his thrones come to naught with his defeat at the Battle of the Boyne.

**1691** **3 October:** Jacobite rebels in Ireland sign a peace treaty with King William III and II.

**1694** **28 December:** George of Brunswick-Lüneburg (later King George I) divorces his wife, Sophia Dorothea of Celle, on grounds of adultery; Sophia is imprisoned for the rest of her life. Queen Mary II dies, leaving King William III and II to rule on his own for another eight years.

**1701** **12 June:** The Act of Settlement—legislation designed to ensure that no Roman Catholic will ever wear the English crown—receives royal assent. **5 September:** The exiled King James VII and II dies.

**1702** **8 March:** King William III and II dies; he is succeeded by Queen Anne, the last of the Stuart monarchs.

**1705** **22 August:** George, duke of Cambridge and later King George II, marries Caroline of Brandenburg-Ansbach. **31 December:** Catherine of Braganza, queen consort of King Charles II, dies.

**1707** **1 May:** England and Scotland unite as a single country under Queen Anne.

**1708** **28 October:** George, prince of Denmark and consort of Queen Anne, dies.

**1714** **1 August:** Queen Anne, the last of the Stuart monarchs, dies and is succeeded by King George I of the House of Hanover.

**1715** **6 September:** John Erskine, earl of Mar, mounts a rebellion designed to return the Stuarts to the English and Scottish thrones. **14 November:** Mar's rebellion peters out after defeat at the Battle of Preston. **22 December:** James Stuart, the Old Pretender, lands at Peterhead, too late to influence the rebellion mounted earlier in the year in his name by John Erskine, earl of Mar.

**1718** **7 May:** Mary of Modena, queen consort of King James VII and II, dies.

**1726** **13 November:** Sophia Dorothea of Celle, former consort of King George I, dies after more than 30 years of imprisonment.

**1727** **11 June:** King George I dies and is succeeded by his son, King George II.

**1737** **20 November:** Caroline of Brandenburg-Ansbach, queen consort of King George II, dies.

**1743** **27 June:** King George II becomes the last British monarch to lead his armies in battle, defeating the French at Dettingen.

**1745** **23 July:** Charles Edward Stuart (Bonnie Prince Charlie), grandson of King James VII and II, lands at Eriskay, beginning the ill-fated '45 rebellion that was intended to return the Stuarts to the English and Scottish thrones. **17 September:** Charles Edward Stuart enters Edinburgh and proclaims his father King James VIII of Scotland. **4 December:** Prince Charlie's army reaches Derby, but English reinforcements fail to appear and his generals order a retreat.

**1746** **16 April:** Bonnie Prince Charlie's army is routed at Culloden, ending Jacobite attempts to reclaim the English and Scottish thrones for the House of Stuart.

**1760** **25 October:** King George II dies; he is succeeded by his grandson, King George III.

**1761   8 September:** King George III marries Charlotte of Mecklenburg-Strelitz.

**1788–89**   King George III suffers a bout of mental illness, precipitating a political crisis as parliamentarians bicker over the powers to be given to a regent.

**1795   8 April:** George, prince of Wales (later King George IV), marries Caroline of Brunswick-Wolfenbüttel.

**1811   7 February:** Parliament appoints the prince of Wales (later King George IV) regent, with power to rule in place of his father, King George III, who is suffering from mental illness.

**1816   6 November:** Princess Charlotte Augusta, King George III's only grandchild, dies, leaving her three unmarried uncles to chase brides to produce an heir to the throne.

**1818   11 July:** William, duke of Clarence (later King William IV), marries Adelaide of Saxe-Meiningen. **17 November:** Charlotte of Mecklenburg-Strelitz, wife of King George III and the longest-serving queen consort in British history, dies.

**1820   29 January:** King George III dies, nearly a decade after mental illness prevented him from continuing monarchical duties, and he is succeeded by his son, who reigns as King George IV.

**1821   7 August:** Caroline of Brunswick-Wolfenbüttel, queen consort of King George IV, dies.

**1830   26 June:** King George IV dies; he is succeeded by his brother, reigning as King William IV.

**1834   14 November:** King William IV dismisses his prime minister, viscount Melbourne—the last occasion on which a monarch will dispense with the services of a prime minister of whom he disapproves.

**1837   20 June:** King William IV dies and is succeeded by his niece, Queen Victoria.

**1840   10 February:** Queen Victoria marries Albert of Saxe-Coburg and Gotha.

**1848   18 March:** Queen Victoria is given chloroform to help her give birth to Princess Louise—the first time the procedure has been used by the royal family.

**1849**  **2 December:** Adelaide of Saxe-Meiningen, consort of King William IV, dies.

**1861**  **14 December:** Albert of Saxe-Coburg and Gotha, consort of Queen Victoria, dies; Victoria blames her son, Albert Edward, prince of Wales, for the death and sends him abroad for six months.

**1863**  **10 March:** Albert Edward, prince of Wales and heir apparent to the throne, marries Alexandra of Denmark; lady guests at the ceremony wear dark dresses because the court is still in mourning for Queen Victoria's consort, Prince Albert, who died 15 months earlier.

**1871**  **21 March:** Princess Louise, daughter of Queen Victoria, weds John Campbell, marquess of Lorne—the first time a member of the royal family has married a commoner in more than 300 years.

**1893**  **6 July:** George, duke of York (later King George V), marries Princess Mary of Teck.

**1901**  **22 January:** Queen Victoria dies; she is succeeded by her eldest son, King Edward VII.

**1910**  **6 May:** King Edward VII dies; he is succeeded by his eldest surviving son, King George V.

**1917**  **26 June:** As World War I reaches a decisive stage, King George V drops the royal family's German family names; Saxe-Coburg and Gotha is changed to Windsor, and Battenberg becomes Mountbatten.

**1923**  **26 April:** Prince Albert (later King George VI) marries Elizabeth Bowes-Lyon.

**1925**  **20 October:** Alexandra of Denmark, consort of King Edward VII, dies.

**1926**  **21 April:** A first child (later Queen Elizabeth II) is born to Prince Albert (later King George VI) and his wife, Elizabeth.

**1930**  **21 August:** Elizabeth, wife of Prince Albert (later King George VI), gives birth to Princess Margaret, her second child.

**1936**  **20 January:** King George V dies and is succeeded by his son, King Edward VIII. **11 December:** Edward VIII abdicates in order to marry Wallis Simpson, a twice-divorced American citizen; his younger brother succeeds him as King George VI.

**1937    3 June:** Edward, duke of Windsor (formerly King Edward VIII), marries Wallis Simpson, the American divorcee for whom he had abdicated the throne the previous year.

**1947    20 November:** Princess Elizabeth (later Queen Elizabeth II) marries Lieutenant Philip Mountbatten (now Prince Philip, duke of Edinburgh).

**1948    14 November:** Princess Elizabeth (later Queen Elizabeth II) gives birth to Charles, her first child.

**1950    15 August:** Princess Elizabeth (later Queen Elizabeth II) gives birth to Princess Anne, her second child. **25 December:** Four students steal the Stone of Scone from Westminster Abbey and smuggle it back to Scotland, more than 600 years after Edward I had taken it south (*see* **1296**).

**1952    6 February:** King George VI dies and is succeeded by his daughter, Queen Elizabeth II.

**1953    24 March:** Mary of Teck, consort of King George V, dies.

**1958    26 July:** Queen Elizabeth II confers the title "Prince of Wales" on Charles, her eldest son.

**1960    8 February:** Queen Elizabeth II announces that all of her agnatic descendants with the title "Prince" or "Princess" and using the style "Her (or His) Royal Highness" will be members of the House of Windsor; other agnatic descendants will use the surname "Mountbatten-Windsor." **19 February:** Queen Elizabeth gives birth to Prince Andrew, the first child born to a reigning monarch in 103 years.

**1964    10 March:** Queen Elizabeth II gives birth to Prince Edward, her fourth child.

**1969    1 July:** At a ceremony at Caernarfon, Queen Elizabeth II invests Charles, her eldest son, "Prince of Wales"; the ceremony carries implications of English overlordship and is resented by many Welsh people.

**1972    28 May:** Edward, duke of Windsor (formerly King Edward VIII), dies.

**1973    14 November:** Princess Anne marries Lieutenant Mark Phillips.

**1977    15 November:** Princess Anne gives birth to Peter Phillips, her first child.

**1978    30 June:** Prince Michael of Kent gives up his place in the line of succession to the throne in order to marry Baroness Marie-Christine von Reibnitz, a practicing Roman Catholic.

**1979**  **27 August:** An Irish Republican Army bomb kills Lord Louis Mountbatten of Burma, uncle of Prince Philip, duke of Edinburgh. **23 November:** Thomas McMahon is sentenced to life imprisonment for his part in the murder of Lord Mountbatten.

**1981**  **15 May:** Princess Anne gives birth to Zara Phillips, her second child. **29 July:** Charles, prince of Wales, marries Lady Diana Spencer.

**1982**  **21 June:** Diana, princess of Wales, gives birth to Prince William, her first child.

**1984**  **15 September:** Diana, princess of Wales, gives birth to Prince Henry (or Harry), her second child.

**1986**  **24 April:** Wallis, duchess of Windsor, for whom King Edward VIII gave up his throne (*see* **1936**), dies. **23 July:** Prince Andrew marries Sarah Ferguson.

**1987**  **13 June:** Queen Elizabeth II announces that her daughter, Anne, will be known as "Princess Royal" in recognition of her work for charities.

**1988**  **8 August:** Sarah, duchess of York, gives birth to her first child, Princess Beatrice.

**1990**  **23 March:** Sarah, duchess of York, gives birth to her second child, Princess Eugenie.

**1992**  **23 April:** Princess Anne and Mark Phillips divorce. **20 November:** Fire damages more than 100 rooms at Windsor Castle. **12 December:** Princess Anne takes Commander Timothy Laurence as her second husband.

**1994**  **14 January:** Katharine, duchess of Kent, becomes the first member of the royal family for more than three centuries to leave the Church of England and take communion as a Roman Catholic.

**1996**  **30 May:** Prince Andrew and Sarah, duchess of York, divorce. **28 August:** Charles, prince of Wales, and Diana, princess of Wales, divorce. **30 November:** The Conservative Party government returns the Stone of Scone to Scotland (*see* **1296**); public reaction is distinctly muted.

**1997**  **31 August:** Diana, princess of Wales, is killed in a car accident in Paris.

**1999**  **19 June:** Prince Edward marries Sophie Rhys-Jones.

**2002**  **9 February:** Princess Margaret, countess of Snowdon, dies. **30 March:** Elizabeth, the queen mother, dies.

**2003   8 November:** Sophie, countess of Wessex, has her first child (Lady Louise Windsor).

**2004   29 October:** Princess Alice, duchess of Gloucester and the longest-lived member of any British royal family, dies just eight weeks before her 103rd birthday.

**2005   9 April:** Charles, prince of Wales, takes Camilla Parker Bowles as his second wife.

**2007   17 December:** Sophie, countess of Wessex, has her second child (James, viscount Severn).

# Introduction

The monarch is the United Kingdom's head of state, exercising powers that are circumscribed by common law, convention, and statute law. Nowadays, many of the sovereign's functions are ceremonial, but in the past the balance between ceremony and decision making was very different. The foundations of the modern monarchy were laid more than a millennium ago, in Anglo-Saxon and Celtic Britain, so its modern form is a stage in an evolution that has been shaped by attitudes toward divorce, the changing role of women, the democratization of society, dynastic intermarriage, financial demands, religious convictions, struggles for economic and political power, and territorial aggrandizement.

## THE EARLY ENGLISH MONARCHIES

At the beginning of the 5th century, much of Britain was occupied by Roman legions. By 410, however, those troops had left, and the land was infiltrated by agriculturalists from the North German Plain who gradually gained dominance over the native Britons. By the mid-7th century, most of the territory was occupied by a motley collection of small Anglo-Saxon groups, headed by leaders who exerted purely local control. Gradually, however, these groups coalesced into larger kingdoms, the mergers resulting partly from conquest, partly from military and political alliances, and partly from intermarriage among leading families. By the 8th century, Wessex — in the south of what is now England — was emerging as the most powerful of the new monarchies, and leaders such as Alfred the Great were creating centralized systems of government, with legal codes that maintained group cohesion, and were encouraging cooperation against external threats from Scandinavian marauders.

Aethelstan (Alfred's grandson) united England under one ruler in 927, albeit only for a few years, and — through the marriages of his half-sisters — forged alliances with powerful groups on the European mainland, starting a political trend that was to last into the 20th century. King Edgar, during a 16-year reign from 959 until 975, was able to establish a power base that prevented further fragmentation into lesser monarchies, and for this reason he is often considered the first king of England. However, even though his realm was relatively secure internally, it was still subject to attacks from outsiders, notably from Ireland, Scandinavia, and Scotland. For a generation, from 1014, the Anglo-Saxons lost control of much of England to the Danes, and although they regained authority under Edward the Confessor, who succeeded the highly unpopular Harthacanute in 1042, it was only two decades before the arrival of the Normans fundamentally altered the source of monarchical power and the way in which that power was exercised.

William the Conqueror's invasion of England was not a simple land grab. King Edward the Confessor had spent most of his youth in Normandy, safe from the Danes, and William believed that this second cousin once removed had promised him the English throne. However, when Edward died early in 1066, the royal council of advisors chose King Harold II as his successor. So, with the approval of Pope Alexander II, William gathered his forces, sailed across the English Channel, defeated Harold at the Battle of Hastings, and on Christmas Day was crowned king, as William I, in Westminster Abbey.

The new monarch made London the capital of his realm, a status the city has retained ever since. Moreover, he stamped his authority on the country by establishing heavily fortified regional bases and by enforcing control through the punishment of even minor offenses against his rule by way of heavy fines and, on occasion, mutilation of offenders. The feudal system of landholding, common in Normandy, was used to prevent opposition. All of England became the property of the crown but was divided up among the Norman nobles in return for promises of military support. The estates received by each noble were widely spread geographically, making it difficult for any individual to raise an army that could topple the king, but the large number of landholders ensured that the sovereign always had soldiers at his disposal—a source of power that supported future monarchies until England's standing army was placed under the control of parliament in the late 17th century.

However, when William I died in 1087, the succession to the throne created difficulties, as it was to do on numerous occasions until a stable system was established by parliament in 1701. Normandy was left to Robert, William's eldest son, and England to King William II, the third son (the second son—Richard—having been killed some years earlier while hunting deer), but this division posed problems for landholders who had estates in both places, particularly so because the siblings were constantly at odds.

Diplomatic difficulties were resolved temporarily in 1106, when King Henry I (William II's successor and younger brother) captured and imprisoned Robert, but they resurfaced 30 years later as the country was wracked by civil war while Matilda (Henry's daughter) and Stephen (his nephew) contested control. William the Aetheling, Henry's only son, drowned in

1120, and the monarch had failed to produce another heir. So, in 1127, the king made his nobles swear that they would accept Matilda as their sovereign when he died. The oath was taken reluctantly, however. No queen had ever ruled England alone, and many at the royal court argued that a woman could not lead them in battle, which was then one of the chief requirements of a ruler. So, after Henry succumbed to food poisoning in 1135, some of the most powerful men in the realm turned to Stephen, the son of Adela, Henry's sister.

For 18 years, families were divided by conflict as King Stephen's armies struggled with those who believed Matilda was the rightful sovereign, but eventually, in 1153, Matilda's son, Henry (later King Henry II), won a promise that he would succeed to the throne on Stephen's death. The young man did not have long to wait because the king, worn out by war and by grieving for both his son and his wife, died the following year.

## PLANTAGENETS AND TUDORS

Henry II was the first of the Plantagenet monarchs, the name given because his father allegedly had a habit of putting a sprig of the common broom plant, whose Latin name is *Planta genista*, in his cap. The dynasty maintained its grip on the English crown until King Richard III was supplanted by Henry Tudor in 1485. However, although the succession remained secure (albeit by passing through different branches of the family), the boundaries of the realm and the extent of the monarch's authority underwent great change. Henry II reestablished the control over the nobles that had been lost during the civil war of King Stephen's reign, he restored law and order, he took territories in the north from the Scots, and he added Ireland to his kingdom (where it remained until the early 20th century). However, his sons were less skillful tacticians. King John lost much of the land his father had held in France and faced rebellion at home, where, by signing the Magna Carta in 1215, he became the first English sovereign to accept specified restrictions to his power. This began the process that eventually led to the modern democracy of the United Kingdom, where legislative authority is in the hands of a parliament that acts independently of the monarchy, and an independent judiciary imposes sanctions on lawbreakers.

John's monarchical successors struggled to regain the estates conceded to the French but failed. By 1453, only Calais was left, and by 1558, even that last toehold on the European mainland was gone. Welsh opposition to English occupation was subdued, however, and Wales was absorbed within the English realm, not to regain its separate identity until an assembly with limited influence in shaping the economy and other aspects of Welsh life was created in 1999. Attempts to push northward were less successful, though, as the Scots fought to preserve their independence, often making common cause with France in their resistance to English invasion.

Then, in the last years of the 14th century, the succession to the throne again became an issue. In 1399, King Richard II—unpopular because of his arrogance and greed—was forced to abdicate, leaving no son to succeed him. Henry Bolingbroke, indisputably the most powerful baron in the land, took the crown and, with the approval of parliament, ruled as King Henry IV. He was followed by his son, King Henry V, and his grandson, King Henry VI, but the latter was a deeply religious man who failed to provide strong military leadership. As he succumbed to bouts of mental instability, social order disintegrated, and funds in the royal treasury diminished as officials lined their own pockets.

Opposition to the weak monarch was led by Richard, duke of York, who, given the tradition of succession by male primogeniture that had been established under Norman rule, had a strong claim to the crown. He was descended from Lionel of Antwerp (the third son of King Edward III), whereas Henry VI was descended only from John of Gaunt, duke of Lancaster (the fourth son). The latter occupied the throne because his grandfather, Henry IV, had asserted his right to it—as a result of military strength rather than heredity—after King Richard II's abdication. York initially proffered loyalty to the king and in 1453 was made "protector of the realm" by parliament when Henry suffered one of his bouts of insanity. However, Margaret of Anjou, Henry's doughty queen, opposed the appointment, recognizing that the duke's designs on the crown would usurp the inheritance of her only son, Edward of Lancaster. Thus, when her husband recovered his faculties in 1455, she persuaded him to rescind the decision.

York then turned to force, beginning what novelist Sir Walter Scott termed "the wars of the roses" between the House of Lancaster (which sported a red rose as its emblem) and the House of York (which sported a white rose). The conflict began with the Battle of St. Albans on 22 May 1455 and continued for 30 years until Lancastrian Henry Tudor killed King Richard III (York's youngest son) at Bosworth Field on 22 August. Henry then claimed the crown by right of conquest and (because his father's ancestral roots were in the island of Anglesey) introduced Welsh blood into the royal line by founding a dynasty that was to rule England until the Stuarts gained the crown by less violent means in 1603.

Under the Tudors, the monarchy was to experience further changes as the implications of marriage and divorce, relations with the church, and women's rights to the succession caused much debate. Initially the controversies centered on King Henry VIII, who failed to get papal approval for his divorce from Catherine of Aragon, his former sister-in-law. In 1533, in order to achieve this end by other means, Henry convened a special court that annulled the marriage and thus gave legitimacy to his union with Anne Boleyn, through whom he hoped to sire a son and heir. Then, the following year, he arranged for parliament to pass legislation that broke the links to the Roman Catholic Church that had been forged in 597 when Augustine arrived in England as an emissary of Pope Gregory the Great. The Church of England thus became an independent entity, with Henry as its supreme head on earth.

Queen Mary I, Henry's only child by Catherine, attempted to reverse this religious tide, often brutally. However, after her death in 1558, her half-sister, Queen Elizabeth I (Henry's daughter by Anne Boleyn) diplomatically supported the Protestant cause but called herself Supreme Governor (a title still held by the British monarch today), partly because some nobles were unhappy at the prospect of a woman terming herself the head of an organization previously dominated by men (though partly, too, because many royal advisors argued that Jesus Christ was the supreme head of the church).

Elizabeth's 45-year reign, from 1558 to 1603, was later regarded as a golden age, providing a lengthy period of domestic peace between the religious persecutions of Mary's rule and the upheavals of the 17th century. The sovereign still held much power because parliament was not yet strong enough, or confident enough, to challenge monarchical authority, but the economy strengthened, literary arts flourished, and new trade routes opened up to Africa, the Americas, and the East. Nevertheless, courtiers were concerned about the future of the English monarchy. Elizabeth did not marry, and as she grew older it was clear that even if she did find a partner late in life, she would not be able to produce an heir. Moreover, her closest kin—her half-sister Mary and her half-brother King Edward VI—were both dead and had left no children.

In 1543, parliamentary legislation gave Henry VIII the right to bequeath the succession in his will, and he specifically stipulated that the crown should go to the heirs of his younger sister, Mary Tudor, queen of France, if his own children died without leaving any issue. Given this criterion, the most senior line of descent lay through Lady Catherine Grey, Mary's granddaughter. However, in 1560, Catherine secretly married Edward Seymour, earl of Hertford (and brother of Jane Seymour, the third of King Henry's six wives), without seeking Queen Elizabeth's approval, so she was accused of treason and was cast into the Tower of London. The marriage was annulled in 1562, so both of the sons born as a result of the match were considered illegitimate and were thus not entitled to the throne. Had the marriage been approved, the older boy—Edward Seymour, viscount Beauchamp—would have been heir presumptive under the terms of Henry's will, and the English monarchy would have taken a very different direction.

With Lord Beauchamp ruled out because of his suspect legitimacy, the heiress presumptive was Anne Stanley, countess of Castlehaven. The countess was Mary Tudor's great-great-granddaughter, but she was in her early twenties and was still unmarried as Queen Elizabeth approached the end of her life. Had she taken the throne, uncertainties about the succession would have remained. Arbella Stuart—the daughter of Margaret Tudor, Henry's older sister—was a candidate, but Henry had implicitly excluded Margaret's descendants from any right to the crown by designating the heirs of Mary Tudor, the younger sister, as his preferred successors. And in any case, Arbella was also unmarried.

Faced with these unsatisfactory options, Elizabeth chose to ignore her father's will and decided—never explicitly, but influenced by the machinations of Robert Cecil, her principal advisor—that her successor on the English throne would be her closest male relative, her first cousin (once removed), King James VI of Scotland.

## THE SCOTTISH MONARCHY

Traditionally, Kenneth MacAlpin is regarded as the first king of Scots because in 843 he united his Celtic kingdom of Dalriada with the kingdom of the Picts. This is regarded as no more than a folktale by modern historians, but there is little dispute that MacAlpin founded a dynasty strong enough to provide leaders of the emerging Scottish kingdom until well into the 11th century. From the reign of King Malcolm III—particularly after his marriage to Margaret of Wessex in 1070—the Scottish court became increasingly anglicized, with English replacing Gaelic as the medium of conversation and children being given Anglo-Saxon names rather than Celtic ones. This acceptance of cultural innovation from the south did not mean, however, that the Scots were willing to accept political domination by England. As the Norman and Plantagenet kings attempted to expand their territorial control over the whole of the British Isles, Scotland resisted and as a result suffered periods of invasion and occupation by foreign troops that lasted into the 18th century. For long periods—such as from 1174 to 1189, when King William I was held captive and forced to accept King Henry II of England as his overlord, and again from 1292 until 1306, when John Balliol functioned as a client king of Edward I of England and then went into exile—Scotland was either without a resident monarch or was governed by a king whose powers of maneuver were limited by an English superior.

The difficulties posed by the aggressiveness of a powerful neighbor were exacerbated by internal problems. Scotland's mountainous and forested landscape was ideal for guerilla warfare against invaders, as William Wallace and King Robert I showed in the late 13th and early 14th centuries, but it was unable to provide the wealth that the more productive lands of England could yield. Moreover, from the early 15th century, seven successive monarchs from the House of Stewart were children when they came to the throne—James I at the age of 11 in 1406; James II at the age of six in 1437; James III at the age of eight or nine in 1460; James IV at the age of 15 in 1488; James V at the age of 1 in 1513; Mary, queen of Scots, at the age of just six days in 1542; and James VI at one month after his first birthday in 1567. Regents were appointed to govern until the children were old enough to make decisions for themselves, but often these regents were more concerned with their own interests than with those of the sovereign whom they supposedly served, so frequently the most powerful people in the land were at loggerheads as they fought for power.

The Stewarts also seemed dogged by tragedy. King James I spent 20 years as a prisoner in England. He then returned to find Scotland in a shambles and attempted to restructure the governmental and financial system. However, he was murdered by kinsmen from a different branch of the family that felt it had a better claim to the throne. King James II was killed by a cannon that exploded while he was attempting to prize an English garrison from Roxburgh Castle. King James III—hugely unpopular because he pursued a policy of détente with England—was killed while fighting against an army that included his own son; King James IV led his country to a disastrous defeat at the Battle of Flodden in 1513; King James V collapsed and died at the age of 30 after a defeat at the Battle of Solway Moss; and Mary, queen of Scots, suffered both from an injudicious choice of partners and from the pursuit of a claim to the English throne that led to her execution.

## ONE SOVEREIGN

On 8 August 1503, 13-year-old Margaret Tudor, the eldest daughter of King Henry VII of England, was married to 30-year-old King James IV of Scotland in a match intended to buy off Scottish support for Perkin Warbeck, a claimant to Henry's crown. Only one of their six children reached adulthood, and he succeeded to the Scottish throne as King James V, who sired at least nine illegitimate progeny by a covey of mistresses, and three legitimate offspring by Frenchwoman Mary of Guise. Of these three, only a daughter survived infancy, becoming Mary, queen of Scots.

Mary succeeded to her father's throne when she was just a week old, so her mother sent her to France, where she would be safe from the clutches of ambitious Scottish nobles and marauding English armies. The French, who have no letter *w* in their alphabet, had trouble with her royal surname, so to help out, she changed the spelling from "Stewart" to "Stuart."

In 1558, at the age of 15, Mary married Francis, the sickly heir to the throne of France, in an alliance that meant she was destined to become queen of her adopted country, but which was also clearly intended to lead to a situation in which Scotland could unite with its continental ally under one sovereign. However, Mary believed she also had a claim to the English crown. Her paternal grandmother, Margaret Tudor, was the elder sister of King Henry VIII, whose only son to survive infancy (King Edward VI) had died childless and whose three brothers (Arthur, prince of Wales; Edmund Tudor; and Edward Tudor) had also left no issue. In his will, Henry had decreed that the succession should pass to his children, but there were several English nobles—notably those who held to the Roman Catholic faith—who felt that Henry's divorce from Catherine of Aragon was legally invalid and that, as a result, his marriage to Anne Boleyn, the mother of Queen Elizabeth I, was bigamous. In their view, Elizabeth was illegitimate, so Mary, queen of Scots and of France, was the rightful queen of England. Moreover, she was the closest legitimate relative in a direct line of descent from King Henry VII after the death of Queen Mary I in 1558.

Francis died in 1560, so in August 1561, Mary—seeing no future on the European mainland—accepted an invitation from Scottish nobles to return to her native country, where on 29 July 1565 she married her cousin, Henry Stuart, lord Darnley. This second marriage produced a single child who in 1567 became king of Scotland, as King James VI, and inherited his mother's desire for the English throne. James was fortunate in that he had a committed supporter in Robert Cecil, Queen Elizabeth's chief minister, who paved the way with the aging English monarch, advising the Scots' king on how to curry favor with the queen. As a result, the succession was smooth, and Cecil, for his part, retained his position of power during the early years of James's rule, holding the reins of government on the king's behalf.

Over the next 22 years, there were critics—James annoyed his Scottish subjects by attempting to make them adopt English church practices, by discriminating against those Roman Catholics who refused to take an oath of allegiance that rejected any papal authority over them, by dismissing parliament several times because it refused to do what he wanted, and by scandalizing courtiers who believed he was homosexual—but the sovereign was much mourned when he died in 1625. And he continued to influence the monarchy even after his death because his eldest son, King Charles I, inherited his belief that kings had a God-given right to rule. As a result, he precipitated a conflict with the English parliament in 1642, which tipped the country back into civil war.

The 17th-century English parliament had evolved from the Great Councils the Norman monarchs had used as advisory bodies. Although there were times when it differed with the king, usually over demands to increase taxes, it was relatively compliant for most of its history. Charles changed that. His marriage to a French princess, Henrietta Maria, only months after his accession caused initial concern because it raised the prospect of Roman Catholics following him on the throne. Attempts to introduce more ceremony into the services of the Church of England simply added to the worries. He also needed funds to pursue war on the European mainland, and, war being expensive, parliament was unwilling to give him what he wanted. Believing that he had a divine right to exercise authority and that his subjects should obey even if they fundamentally disagreed with a command, he dismissed parliament altogether in 1629 and for the next 11 years ruled as an autocrat, attempting to raise funds without parliament's approval.

The straw that broke the camel's back was his insistence that the Church of Scotland should adhere to English religious practices, notably by having bishops and by using a prayer book modeled on England's Book of Common Prayer. The Scots were having none of it and rebelled, so Charles had to recall the English parliament in 1640 in order to raise the funds needed to pay for an army that would quell the uprising. Not surprisingly, the members of that parliament were less than conciliatory, passing laws that prevented the monarch both from dissolving it and from imposing taxes without its consent. Charles, in response, tried to arrest five of the members on charges of treason.

Throughout the realm, as opinions solidified for or against the king, tempers flared, scuffles were superseded by large-scale fighting, and by the fall of 1642 the country was in the grip of civil war. In 1646 Charles was taken prisoner, and in 1649 he was tried for treason and beheaded. His son was crowned king of Scots (as Charles II) in 1651 but spent most of the next nine years in France while Oliver Cromwell—king in all but title—ruled an England that had become a republic.

It was Cromwell's death in 1658 that precipitated a return to monarchy. His son and successor as "Lord Protector of England, Scotland, and Ireland," Richard Cromwell, could not exert the same control as his father, and the country slipped once again toward anarchy. Charles II issued a declaration that if he was offered the throne he would not seek revenge against his enemies, and on 8 May 1660, parliament, considering that his return provided the best prospect for political stability, declared that he had been England's lawful king since Charles I's execution.

Charles's reign started well, with many of the repressive measures imposed during the interregnum repealed, but it was not all plain sailing. By the 1670s, squabbles with parliament broke out again as Protestants protested the king's leniency toward Roman Catholics and his willingness to join a military alliance with Catholic France. Also, Charles's consort, Catherine of Braganza (a Roman Catholic), had not produced a child despite many years of marriage. This rendered Charles's younger brother James, duke of York, heir apparent, and he was known to have converted to Catholicism. As a result, the circumstances surrounding James's accession to the throne in 1685, as King James VII of Scotland and II of England, were less than auspicious.

Trouble broke out early as the new king appointed Catholics to positions of command in the army and to senior offices of state. He then issued a proclamation suspending the laws that discriminated against those of his English subjects who preferred not to worship in the Anglican fold. The announcement in 1687 that Mary of Modena, James's Catholic queen, was pregnant raised the prospect, horrifying to Protestants, of a line of Catholic successors to the throne. This pushed James's opponents into action. They contacted William of Orange, the husband of James's Protestant daughter Mary by his first wife, Anne Hyde, and asked him to intervene. William answered the call, landing with an army in southwest England in late 1688. James, finding that his own officers were deserting him, fled with his family to France, and on 12 February the following year, the English parliament declared that he had abdicated. In April, the Scots concurred.

William III of England and II of Scotland was accepted as James's successor, ruling jointly with his wife, Queen Mary II, but England's Protestant parliament, now in a position to exert power over the sovereign, prepared a Bill of Rights that meant the joint rule was not unfettered—neither the king nor the queen could dispense with laws passed by the parliament, impose taxes without parliamentary consent, interfere with elections, or maintain a standing army without parliament's approval—measures that, in effect, freed citizens from the kind of arbitrary authority that the doctrine of the divine right of kings implied, and paved the way for the establishment of parliament as the legislative branch of government, independent of the executive.

In 1694, Mary died childless. Under the terms of the Bill of Rights, the crown would go to Anne, her younger sister, when William too passed away. However, in 1700, Anne's only surviving child—William, duke of Gloucester—succumbed to an illness that was probably smallpox, and it seemed unlikely that his mother, in poor health after 13 miscarriages, would bear another child. The following year, England's parliament, intent on maintaining a Protestant monarchy and unwilling to see the throne pass to James Stuart, the Roman Catholic son of the exiled King James VII and II and Anne's successor if the long-accepted principles of inheritance by primogeniture were followed, approved an Act of Settlement that named Sophia, granddaughter of King James VI and I and the staunchly Protestant electress of Hanover, heiress apparent. When she died, the right of succession would pass to "the heirs of her body being Protestants," unless those heirs married Catholics. The legislation, which overlooked the rights of more than 50 Roman Catholics who had closer blood links to the crown than Sophia, also specified that the monarch "shall join in communion with the Church of England," thus ensuring that the link between church and state remained intact.

James Stuart and his son, Charles Edward Stuart (often known as "Bonnie Prince Charlie"), refused to accept the loss of their claims to the throne and mounted invasions in 1715 and 1745, but neither succeeded, the Stuart cause (and the Roman Catholic cause) dying on the battlefield at Culloden in April 1746, along with hundreds of its Jacobite supporters. In the weeks that followed, the rebels were ruthlessly hunted down in a campaign that effectively ended any prospect of future uprisings by others but which stabilized the state politically and provided a firm platform for economic growth.

By the time the Jacobite rebellions were mounted, England and Scotland had formed a single parliament, the two countries merging as one state on 1 May 1707. The Act of Settlement raised Scottish hackles because the Scots saw no reason why an English assembly should insist on conditions for the succession of a monarch who would also be their sovereign. Scotland was still an independent country; it wanted to choose its own ruler and said so. Unfortunately, by 1707 the Scots were nearly bankrupt, their finances drained by an ill-considered attempt to develop a colony in Central America, so when England threatened to ban all imports from Scotland (and thereby cut off about half of Scotland's export trade) unless the Scots parliament pursued plans for union, there seemed little alternative. Robert Burns, the Scottish poet, wrote that his countrymen were "bought and sold for English gold," but many modern historians argue that they had little option, doing well to retain their country's distinctive educational, financial, and legal institutions after the merger.

Anne was the first monarch to rule over a united Great Britain. When she died in 1714, predeceased by the electress, the throne passed to Sophia's son, King George I, the first monarch from the House of Hanover. George, who spoke German and made little effort to learn the language of his new subjects, was never popular and quarreled regularly with his son, who became King George II in 1727. However, despite the dynastic bickering, the suppression of the Stuart uprisings meant that by midcentury the monarchy was more stable than it had been for 50 years. King George III's periods of insanity were later to cause worries, and King George IV—financially extravagant, promiscuous, and reactionary—was little loved, but the Hanoverian right to the kingship was unquestioned.

When Victoria came to the throne in 1837, she established Buckingham Palace as the monarch's principal London residence, but she was as distant as her predecessors from the great majority of the people she ruled, living a life of comparative luxury and, despite parliament's legislative freedom, wielding great influence because of her position. By the time she died in 1901, however, her daughters had begun the work with charitable organizations that characterizes all members of the modern royal family. Within a few decades, cinema newsreels were showing moving pictures of royalty fulfilling official state engagements, radio was broadcasting an annual Christmas message from the sovereign to the people, and the sons of monarchs were being educated in schools with other boys (albeit well-endowed private schools rather than state-funded institutions), greatly changing the public's image of the institution of the monarchy.

## THE MODERN MONARCH

By the early years of the 20th century, the functions and funding of the monarchy were clearly defined. In 1761, King George III had surrendered the income from the crown estate—the private property of the monarch, which, at the time, added only a limited amount to his coffers—to the government in return for an annual sum that would cover the cost of fulfilling his official duties. This arrangement continues, though now the annual revenue from the estate amounts to well over £200 million, and the annual payment to the sovereign (known as the civil list) is less than £8 million.

The boundaries of the realm were established in their present form in 1921, when most of the island of Ireland, predominantly Roman Catholic in religious conviction, became self-governing, leaving six contiguous counties that had a Protestant majority as part of a United Kingdom of Great Britain and Northern Ireland. However, as colonial territories freed themselves from British control, particularly after World War II, many decided to retain the United Kingdom's monarch as their own head of state. As a result, by the first years of the 21st century, the British sovereign was head of state of 16 independent countries.

The political role of the monarch, though not defined in a single document, is more limited than in the past. The accepted position, as Walter Bagehot wrote in *The English Constitution* in 1867, is that he or she has "three rights—the right to be consulted [by government], the right to encourage [or advise], the right to warn," but parliament has control over legislation, including fiscal policy, and the judiciary determines the extent of punishment for those who break the law.

Many of the powers that remain to the sovereign are more apparent than real. The monarch must give assent to a bill before it becomes law, but that assent has not been withheld since 1708, when Queen Anne refused to sign a bill "For Settling the Militia of That Part of Great Britain Called Scotland" on the grounds that any army raised in that part of the country might prove disloyal. The monarch also appoints the country's prime minister (the head of the government), but in practice this post always goes to the leader of the majority party in the House of Commons (the lower chamber in the United Kingdom's bicameral parliament). The monarch can also dismiss a prime minister, but this has not been done since 1834, when King William IV got rid of William Lamb, viscount Melbourne, but then had to invite him back. Even as supreme governor of the Church of England, rights are limited because the occupants of the most important ecclesiastical posts are chosen by clerics and politicians. Some significant powers remain, but these are only exercised in very unusual circumstances, as in 1963 when Prime Minister Harold Macmillan resigned, leaving no obvious successor. Queen Elizabeth II consulted widely with leading politicians before replacing him with Alec Douglas-Home.

The difficulties faced by the monarchy in modern times stem from social rather than political issues. In 1936, King Edward VIII gave up his throne rather than give up his mistress, the American-born Wallis Simpson, when his advisors told him that she would not make a suitable consort. The problem was neither that Mrs. Simpson was American (the British royal family had been marrying foreigners for a millennium) nor that she was a commoner (in 1871, Princess Louise, Queen Victoria's daughter, had wed John Campbell, marquess of Lorne, who had no royal blood in his veins). The difficulty was that Wallis Simpson was divorced, and the Church of England, of which the king was secular head, refused to marry divorcees, believing that marriage should last until the death of one of the partners. A similar position arose in the 1950s, when Princess Margaret, the younger daughter of King George VI, was dissuaded from marrying Group Captain Peter Townsend even though he was the wronged party in the divorce action.

Within a few decades, however, attitudes had changed. Princess Anne, Queen Elizabeth II's daughter, was divorced from Mark Phillips, her first husband, in 1992, and later that year she married Timothy Laurence in the Church of Scotland, which took a more compassionate view of the remarriage of divorcees. Then, in 2005, Prince Charles, the heir to the throne, wed Camilla Parker Bowles, his previously married mistress, at a civil ceremony in Windsor.

The royal family has also suffered because modern technology allows photographers and journalists to follow its members' every move and report on their activities to an international audience. In 1992, the *Daily Mirror*, a tabloid newspaper, published details of a sexually explicit telephone conversation between Prince Charles and Camilla. In the same year, the same newspaper printed photographs of Sarah, duchess of York and wife of Prince Andrew, Queen Elizabeth's second son, as she sat topless while John Bryan, her financial advisor, sucked her toes. Then, in 1997, Queen Elizabeth was pilloried as cold and unfeeling when she failed to make any public statement of sorrow in the immediate aftermath of the death of her former daughter-in-law, Diana, princess of Wales.

The behavior of younger members of the House of Windsor has also elicited much negative comment, as in 2005, when Prince Harry (Prince Charles's younger son) turned up at a birthday party wearing a Nazi uniform and the London *Times* condemned his association with "a group of self-indulgent young men, who are apparently content with a life of pointless privilege."

Some politicians, such as Labour Party members of parliament Tony Banks and Anthony Wedgwood Benn, have argued that the monarchy should be abolished, and opinion polls consistently show that a hard core of British voters agree with them, but it is unlikely to happen. The institution remains an important cornerstone of government, and despite the public gaffes, the senior members of the royal family are regarded with much affection, with images of Queen Elizabeth shedding tears during a memorial service for people killed in the terrorist attacks in the United States on 11 September 2001 helping to counteract the more negative stories of reserve and distance.

**ADA DE WARENNE (c1120–c1178).** Ada, mother of King **Malcolm IV** of Scotland and King **William I of Scotland**, was the daughter of William de Warenne, earl of Surrey, and Elizabeth of Vermandois (a granddaughter of King Henry I of **France**). She married **Henry, earl of Northumberland** and only surviving son of King **David I**, in 1139, possibly as part of King **Stephen**'s efforts to make peace with England's Scottish neighbors and earn their support in his struggle with **Matilda** for the English throne. Stephen had earlier confirmed Henry's right to the earldom of Huntingdon, which he inherited through his mother, and gave him Northumberland as well.

Ada and her husband had at least six children before his death in 1152, then she played a significant role as advisor at the royal court after Malcolm, only 11 or 12 years old, succeeded David the following year. William of Newburgh, a contemporary chronicler, reports that she was frustrated by her deeply religious son's insistence on celibacy and even encouraged an attractive young woman into his bed in an effort to encourage him to sire an heir. Ada was also noted for her piety, however, founding a Cistercian nunnery at Haddington (20 miles east of **Edinburgh**). She died c1178, but her burial place is unknown.

David—Ada's third son, born in about 1144—became, like his father, earl of Huntingdon. One daughter (Matilda) died in 1152 while still very young, but at least two others reached maturity. Ada (who was born c1142 and lived until about 1206) married Floris, count of Holland, in 1162, and together they had nine children, one of whom (also named Floris) was appointed bishop of Glasgow in 1202. Margaret, born c1140, was married first to Conan, duke of Brittany, and then to Humphrey de Bohun, earl of Hereford. Constance—a daughter by the first marriage—became the wife of **Geoffrey, duke of Brittany**, son of King **Henry II** of England. Some sources indicate that there was a fourth daughter—Isabel or Isabella—who married Robert de Ros, one of the English barons appointed to ensure that King **John** observed the requirements of the **Magna Carta**.

**ADELA, COUNTESS OF BLOIS (c1062–1137).** Adela, daughter of **William I of England** (William the Conqueror) and **Matilda of Flanders**, was the mother of **Stephen**, who, in 1135, became the last English king from the **House of Normandy** (or, according to some genealogists, the only king from the **House of Blois**). In about 1080, at a wedding that was followed by a much more lavish ceremony in Chartres Cathedral the following year, she married **Stephen Henry**, who succeeded his father as count of Blois in 1089. The count was very wealthy, and Adela proved to be a capable spouse, ably administering his estates while he was absent on crusades in the Holy Land. She also took an interest in church matters, encouraging ecclesiastical leaders to replace the wooden cathedral at Chartres with a place of worship built of stone, and she ensured that her children received a sound education.

There is little doubt that Adela approved of her husband's participation in the First Crusade in 1095, and also little doubt of her disapproval when he returned in 1099, tainted by charges of cowardice at the siege of the Muslim city of Antioch the previous year. Embarrassed, she persuaded him to campaign again, and he died fighting the Egyptians at Ramleh, near Jerusalem, in 1102. By that time, Adela had borne at least 6, and possibly as many as 12, children. She looked after her husband's properties until 1109, then handed the responsibility over to Theobald, one of her five sons, and retired to the Cluniac Priory at Marcigny-sur-Loire, living out the rest of her life as a nun but still playing an active part in church and public politics. She died in 1137, probably on 8 March, and was buried at the Abbey aux Dames in Caen, close to her mother and to **Cecilia of Normandy**, her sister.

**ADELAIDE OF SAXE-MEININGEN, PRINCESS (1792–1849).** The death, on 6 November 1817, of **Princess Charlotte Augusta**—the daughter of George, **prince of Wales** (later King **George IV**)—caused much concern in court circles because, although **George III** was on the throne (albeit suffering from insanity) and had a large family to succeed him, none of his sons or daughters had children, so the **House of Hanover**'s grasp on the crown was assured only for one more generation. In order to sire an heir and thus be sure of long-term retention of the British throne, the king's unmarried sons hastened to find wives, and William, duke of Clarence (later King **William IV**), settled on Adelaide, daughter of George, duke of Saxe-Meiningen, and his wife, Louisa Eleanora. The choice of bride was governed by circumstances; Saxe-Meiningen was of little political import to Britain, but Adelaide (only 25 years old) was young enough to bear children (William was 53), other possible partners had rejected his approaches, and the **prince** was in a hurry.

The wedding was held at **Kew Palace** on 11 July 1818 (the duke's brother, **Edward, duke of Kent and Strathearn**, was wed to **Princess Victoria**

**of Saxe-Coburg-Saalfield** at the same ceremony), and soon afterward the couple moved to Hanover, where they could live more cheaply than in **London**—an important consideration in view of William's debts. Adelaide conceived within weeks of the marriage, but the child—**Princess Charlotte of Clarence**—survived her birth on 21 March 1819 by only a few hours. A second daughter—**Princess Elizabeth of Clarence**—was born on 10 December 1820 but died the following March, and two boys were stillborn on 8 April 1822.

Despite the dynastic setbacks and the age difference, the duke and duchess seemed happy, and Adelaide was successful at curbing the less attractive aspects of her husband's personality, calming his outbursts, limiting his curses, and reining in his spending. A pious and generous woman, she also accepted the duke's 10 illegitimate children by Irish actress Mrs. Dorothy Jordan, gave liberally to charitable causes, and attempted to restrain the often open hostility between William and his sister-in-law, Victoria, duchess of Kent and Strathearn. However, she was implacably opposed to political change at a time when there was much agitation for parliamentary reform and was accused of using her influence as **queen consort** to stiffen William's resistance to proposals that would extend the franchise.

When the monarch's health deteriorated in 1837, Adelaide helped care for him, staying at his bedside, except for a brief trip to Germany following her mother's death on 30 April. He died in her arms on 20 June, and the rigors of those weeks seemed to affect the queen's own constitution because her own health very quickly declined and, despite spending much time in the Mediterranean seeking vitality from the sunny climate, she passed away on 2 December 1849 at Bentley Priory, a home close to London that she had rented the previous year. She was buried, like her husband, in **St. George's Chapel** at **Windsor Castle**. Adelaide, the capital city of South Australia, is named after her.

**ADELIZA OF LOUVAIN (c1103–1151).** In 1120, **William the Aetheling**—the only legitimate son of King **Henry I**—drowned in the English Channel. **Matilda of Scotland**, the **queen consort**, had died two years earlier, so Henry desperately sought a new wife who could provide him with an heir. On 24 January 1121, only some 10 weeks after William's accident, he married Adeliza, daughter of Godfrey, count of Lower Lorraine and duke of Brabant, and his wife, Ida of Namur. Adeliza was in her late teens (and therefore Henry's junior by more than 30 years), but the union failed to produce the child the king needed. Therefore, in 1127, he made his reluctant barons swear that they would accept **Matilda**, his daughter, as their sovereign when he passed away. By the time of his death in 1135, there was still no son, and the nobles, unwilling to work with a female monarch (and particularly Matilda), accepted the claim to the throne made by **Stephen**, Henry's nephew. In doing so, they committed England to a lengthy civil war.

Adeliza made little effort to interfere in political matters while her husband was alive, and when he died, she retired to mourn in the Benedictine convent at Wilton, which was established in about 800 by Alburga, daughter of **Ealhmund** of Kent and sister of King **Egbert**. She emerged by 1139 to marry William d'Aubigny, earl of Arundel, and (after a barren 14-year marriage to Henry) gave birth to their seven children who survived to adulthood. Her last years were spent at the Abbey of Affligham, near Brussels, where she died on 24 March 1151 according to some sources, and on 23 April 1151 according to others. There is similar uncertainty about her burial place, which may be either at Affligham or at Reading Abbey, close to Henry.

**ADELIZA OF NORMANDY (c1055–?).** Sources from the 11th and 12th centuries agree that Adeliza (also known as Adelaide, Adelida, Adelisa, and Alice) was the daughter of **William I of England** (William the Conqueror) and **Matilda of Flanders**, but data on her life is contradictory. Some writers claim that she was the eldest daughter in the family, others that she was the third or fourth. There are also suggestions that she was betrothed to Harold Godwinson (later King **Harold II**) before her father invaded England in 1066, but not all texts agree, and it is possible that she is being confused with her sister, **Agatha of Normandy**. The monk Orderic Vitalis, writing in the first half of the 12th century, records that Adeliza was "a most fair maiden [who] vowed herself to God when she reached marriageable age and made a pious end." She died as a nun on 7 December, possibly as early as 1065, but perhaps as late as 1113.

**ADOLPHUS, PRINCE, DUKE OF CAMBRIDGE (1774–1850).** Adolphus, born at **Buckingham Palace** on 24 February 1774, was the seventh and, according to some writers, the favorite son of King **George III** and **Charlotte of Mecklenburg-Strelitz**. Like most of his brothers, he pursued a military career, receiving injuries in Flanders (where he served under his older sibling, **Prince Frederick, duke of York and Albany**, in 1793) and campaigning in the Netherlands (1794–95) and Germany (1805). He made no effort to intervene in British political processes, but from 1816 to 1837 he acted as viceroy of his father's German realm in Hanover and proved a capable administrator. Particularly toward the end of his life, he took a considerable interest in medical charities.

On 7 May 1818 (at Cassel, in Germany) and on 1 June (at **Kew Palace**), Adolphus married his second cousin, Augusta, granddaughter of **Princess**

**Mary, landgravine of Hesse-Cassel** and great-granddaughter of King **George II**. They had three children—George (born in 1819 and the successor to his father's dukedom), Augusta (born in 1822), and Mary Adelaide (born in 1833 and mother of **Mary of Teck**, queen consort of King **George V**). The **prince** died at Cambridge House, his **London** home, on 8 July 1850 after suffering from gastric fever. He was initially buried at Kew, but his remains were later reinterred at **St. George's Chapel** in **Windsor Castle**.

**ÁED (?–878).** In 877, Áed succeeded his older brother, **Constantine I**, as leader of the realm that their father—**Kenneth MacAlpin**—had begun to form in north Britain some three decades earlier by uniting Pictish communities with the kingdom of Dalriada. There are few contemporary records available to scholars, but it is likely that the kingdom was in some turmoil at the time as a result of serious Scandinavian invasions in 875–876, and the unrest may have led opponents to challenge the new monarch. He survived for only a few months before being assassinated, with one source noting that he was "killed by his associates" and another reporting that "the shortness of his reign has bequeathed nothing memorable to history." Some writers suggest that **Giric**, who succeeded Áed as leader, may have been the murderer. There is a tradition that Áed was buried at Inverurie in northeast Scotland, but it is also possible that his remains were interred on the island of **Iona**. In 900, one of his sons, **Constantine II**, became king of the same territory, by then known as **Alba**, and some writers have argued that Donald, a second son, ruled the neighboring kingdom of Strathclyde. *See also* CONSTANTINE III.

**AELFFLAED (c878–c920).** When **Edward the Elder** succeeded his father, **Alfred the Great**, as king of **Wessex** in about 899, he discarded **Ecgwynn**, his first wife (or perhaps mistress) and replaced her with Aelfflaed, the daughter of a man named Aethelhelm and a woman named Aethelglyth. It is not known why Edward proved disloyal to his partner, but the reasons may have been political. When Alfred became king in 871, he followed his brother Aethelred to the throne. Aethelred had left two sons—Aethelwald and Aethelhelm—but they were considered too young to lead a people in battle, and Wessex was under threat from Viking invaders. When Alfred died, however, the boys had become men, and Aethelwald promoted his own claim to the kingship by allying with Scandinavians in Northumbria and mounting a military campaign against Edward. Aethelhelm took no part in the fighting, and some writers suggest that Aelfflaed was his daughter, arguing that Edward married her in order to prevent her father from taking arms against him.

Aelfflaed bore at least seven children. **Aelfweard** was born in 904 and might have succeeded his father as king of Wessex, but he died, or was killed, before being crowned. According to the ***Anglo-Saxon Chronicle***, Edwin, his brother, drowned at sea in 933, and historians speculate that **Aethelstan**, Aelfweard's successor and Edward's son by his first wife, may have been implicated in both deaths.

After Aethelstan became king, he cemented relationships between the Wessex royal house and noble families on the European mainland by arranging marriages for several of Aelfflaed's daughters. Eadhild was wed to Hugh the Great, duke of the Franks, in 926, and in 929, Aedgyth (or Edith) and Aldiva (or Algiva) were sent to Germany to meet Otto, later Holy Roman Emperor and king of Germany and Italy. Otto was offered either lady as his wife and he selected Aedgyth. Algiva's fate is not clear; some scholars suggest that she married Boleslaus II of Bohemia, others that she may be the same person as another daughter known as Eadgifu, Edgiva, or Edgifa, who married Charles III of **France** (though that marriage took place in 919) and gave birth to their son who became Louis IV, and yet others say that her husband was Conrad, duke of Burgundy. Two other daughters—Aethelhild and Eadflaed—led lives devoted to religion, the former as a lay recluse, the latter as a nun.

Most authorities believe that Aelfflaed had already died before 920, when Edward took a third wife (**Edgiva** or Eadgifu), but some maintain that she outlived him.

**AELFGIFU (?–944).** In about 940, **Edmund I** took Aelfgifu (also known as Edgira and Elgira) as his first wife. They had two sons who were destined to follow their father as kings of England—**Eadwig** (born c941) and **Edgar of England** (born c943)—but she died on 18 May 944, long before they succeeded to the throne, and was buried at Shaftesbury Abbey. Her parentage is uncertain, though her mother was probably Wynflaed, a lay sister at Shaftesbury. William of Malmesbury, writing of Aelfgifu in the early 12th century, describes her as a pious woman who cared for condemned men and for the poor. He also says that she endured physical pain with great stoicism, but he does not give any indication of the cause of her suffering. She became revered as a saint after several visitors to her grave were cured of infirmities.

**AELFGIFU OF NORTHAMPTON (c995–c1044).** Aelfgifu was the "handfast" wife of King **Canute**, who ruled England from 1016 to 1035. (In handfast wedding ceremonies, the couple's wrists were tied together to symbolize union, but the Roman Catholic Church did not recognize the "marriages" because no priest was present). She was the daughter of Aelfhelm, ealdorman of south Northumbria, who, according to some sources, was killed by supporters of King **Aethelred the Unready** in 1006. It is not known how she met Canute or when she married him, but they certainly had two sons—**Svein**

**of Norway** and Harold (later **Harold I**, king of England from 1035 to 1040). It is probable that both boys were born in 1015–16. Although Canute later married **Emma of Normandy** in more conventional fashion, he maintained the relationship with Aelfgifu and in 1030 sent her to rule Norway with Svein, but their regime of harsh taxation led to rebellion, and they were forced to flee in 1035.

Aelfgifu was determined that Harold, her other child, would become king of England, even though Canute had named **Harthacanute**—his son by Emma—as his heir, and, given that goal, she was fortunate that Harthacanute was in Denmark preparing for war with Magnus I of Norway when her "husband" died on 12 November 1035, because, according to some scholars, that gave her an opportunity to bribe members of the **witan** (the council of advisors to the monarch) to appoint Harold **regent** during his half-brother's absence. The following year, she may have been implicated in an assault that led to the death of **Aelfred Aetheling**, Emma's son by King Aethelred (her first husband) and a claimant to the crown. In 1037, Harold was made king in his own right, but some scholars believe that his mother was the power behind the throne until his death on 17 March 1040. Harthacanute returned to England three months later, and Aelfgifu's influence over affairs terminated. The date of her death is not known.

**AELFGIFU OF YORK (c963–1002).** Although Aelfgifu bore at least nine children to **Aethelred the Unready**, king of England, between 986 and 1002, details of her life are little known. Several historians believe she was born in about 963 to Thored (an ealdorman, or senior official in the Anglo-Saxon community) and Hilda, his wife, but some maintain that her father's name may have been Aethelbert. She married Aethelred sometime between 980 and 985 and together they had possibly seven sons. Aethelstan, the eldest, was born in about 986 but died c1012–15 from wounds received while attempting to repel Viking invaders. Ecberht (born in about 987) probably died in about 1005, leaving Edmund, the third born and later **Edmund II**, to succeed his father as king in 1016. The other boys barely reached maturity. Edward (born between 988 and 1002) had died by 1004, Eadred (born between 987 and 1002) and Edgar (born between 987 and 1002) by c1012–15. After Edmund's death in 1016, only a single son—Eadwig (born between 989 and 1002)—remained as a focus of opposition to King **Canute**, who had wrested the kingdom from Edmund's hands in 1016, and the Viking ruler solved that problem by arranging for the young man's murder the following year.

Details on the daughters are even sparser. In about 1009, Edith married Eadric Streona, who was one of Aethelred's most trusted supporters but later defected to the Viking camp (*see* ASSANDUN, BATTLE OF) and then, in

1017, was executed by Canute as an example to any other of his nobles who were considering a change of allegiance. Her second husband was Thorkell Havi, a Scandinavian who fought for the English against the Vikings in 1013 and then, like Eadric, aligned himself with Canute. According to one 12th-century source, in 1021 Edith was accused of killing Thorkell's son by an earlier marriage, was found guilty, and was banished to Denmark with her husband.

In about 1015, Aelfgifu, another daughter, married Uchtred, earl of Northumbria, with whom she had a daughter, Ealdgyth, who married into the Scottish royal house through a union with Maldred, brother of **Duncan I**. Some sources report that after Uchtred was murdered in 1016, probably with Canute's knowledge, Aelfgifu took Aelfgar of Mercia as a second husband and had several children with him.

The marriage between Aethelred and Aelfgifu of York may have produced still more offspring. For example, it is probable that a woman named Wulfhild, probably born c998 and married to Ulfcytel Snillingr, a leader of Aethelred's subjects in East Anglia, was their child, though there is no confirmation in contemporary records. (Ulfcytel died fighting the Vikings at Assandun, one victim of Eadric Streona's perfidy.) The *Anglo-Saxon Chronicle* also makes passing reference to an unnamed daughter who became abbess at Wherwell (a nunnery founded by **Aelfthryth**, Aethelred's mother, in 986) and in 1051 provided sanctuary for **Edith of Wessex** when **Edward the Confessor** attempted to banish her from his court and exile her family. Additionally, it mentions a man named Aethelstan, who was "the king's son-in-law" and was thus married to another, still unknown, daughter.

A number of sources note that Aelfgifu (who was also known as Aelflaed, Aelgifu, Effleda, Elfreda, and Elgiva) died at **Winchester** in 1002, the year in which Aethelred married **Emma of Normandy**.

**AELFRED AETHELING (c1003–1036).** Aelfred, son of the Anglo-Saxon King **Aethelred the Unready** and his second wife, **Emma of Normandy**, spent most of his life in Normandy, where his father had taken refuge after much of England was overrun by Viking invaders in 1013. When King **Canute**, the Scandinavian leader, died in 1035, his son and designated heir, **Harthacanute**, was in Denmark preparing for battle with Magnus I of Norway, so the **witan** (the council of advisors to the monarch) named Harold (Harthacanute's half-brother and later King **Harold I**) **regent**, despite protests from Emma, whom Canute had married after Aethelred's death in 1016, partly in order to prevent Emma's Norman relatives from attempting to unseat him and place Aelfred or his brother Edward (afterward **Edward the Confessor**) on the throne.

In 1036, or possibly 1037, Aelfred returned to England. According to some contemporary sources, he was enticed by a letter from Harold which told him that the Anglo-Saxon community would prefer Aelfred or Edward, not Harthacanute, as their king, but it is also possible that Emma had sought his support in her quarrels with Harold. As he rode toward Guildford from his landing place on the south coast, he was intercepted by **Godwin, earl of Wessex** and Harold's father, who, according to the *Anglo-Saxon Chronicle*, took him to Ely in East Anglia and gouged out his eyes. Aelfred died of his wounds, probably on 5 February 1036, and was buried at the abbey, where he was molested. *See also* AELFGIFU OF NORTHAMPTON.

**AELFTHRYTH (c944–c1000).** Aelfthryth (also known as Alfrida and Elfrida) was the first consort of a king of England to be crowned as queen. William of Malmesbury, a 12th-century historian, records that when King **Edgar of England** (who reigned from 959 until his death in 975) heard of her beauty, he sent Aethelwald, one of his senior administrators, to check on her looks and offer her the king's hand in marriage if she was as pretty as the reports suggested. Aethelwald, however, was smitten; he married her himself and told Edgar that the stories of her attractions had been greatly exaggerated. Edgar, learning of the deception, decided to visit the lady himself, and Aethelwald attempted to hold on to his bride by getting her to make herself look plain. The ruse failed because she did exactly the opposite, making every effort to beguile the king, who killed her husband and took her as his second wife in 964 or 965. Politically, the match was certainly attractive because Aelfthryth's family connections were in **Wessex**, one of the most powerful regions in the Anglo-Saxon realm, and Edgar's roots were in similarly powerful Mercia.

When Edgar's **coronation** was held in Bath on 11 May 973, Aelfthryth was crowned alongside him. They had two sons—Edmund (who was born in 966) and **Aethelred the Unready** (born in about 968)—but the elder boy died while still very young, probably in 970. Edgar also had a son (**Edward the Martyr**) by his first wife, **Aethelflaed Eneda**, and the half-brothers were candidates for the vacant throne when he died in 975. Aelfthryth, understandably, supported her own child's claims and resented the decision of the **witan** (the council of advisors to the king) to choose Edward, who was some six years older than Aethelred.

In 978, when her stepson called at Corfe Castle where she was living, Aelfthryth offered him a glass of mead, and then she or one of her retine stabbed him while he was drinking, mortally wounding him. Aethelred became king, but, because he was so young, Aelfthryth served as **regent** for six years. However, her authority was undermined because she was widely believed to have been party to Edward's death, and in 984 the young monarch forced her to leave his court. At some point, though, she suffered from remorse, and in penitence she founded abbeys at Amesbury in 980 and Wherwell in 986. She became the first abbess at Wherwell, in Hampshire, where she died on 17 November 999, 1000, or 1001.

**AELFWEARD (904–924).** The **succession to the throne** following the death of **Edward the Elder** on 17 July 924 is unclear. Some documents indicate that the kingdom was divided, with **Aethelstan** (a son by Edward's first marriage, to **Ecgwynn**) appointed ruler of Mercia and Aelfweard (a son by Edward's second marriage, to **Aelfflaed**) getting **Wessex**. Others, however, suggest that Aethelstan ruled the whole realm. If Aelfweard—who is described as a recluse in a number of texts and as a married man with children in others—ever was a monarch, he had little time to make an impact because he died in Oxford on 2 August, only 16 days after his father's death, and Aethelstan reunited the realm. Some writers suggest that the older brother may have conspired in the death of the younger one. Others claim that, because Aethelstan was not crowned until 4 September the following year, Edwin (Aelfflaed's other son by Edward) may have succeeded Aelfweard for a period and then been ousted.

**AETHELFLAED ENEDA (?–?).** King **Edgar of England**, who reigned from 959 until 975, appears to have taken Aethelflaed as his spouse in 961 or 962. The daughter of Ordmaer (a senior official in Anglo-Saxon society) and his wife, possibly named Ealda, she bore Edgar a son, later known as **Edward the Martyr**, whose appearance may have preceded the wedding. Thereafter, Aethelflaed disappears from the historical record, though historians speculate that she may have died in childbirth or that Edgar, whose youthful interest in women was fickle, may have cast her aside in favor of somebody else. In 964 or 965, he married **Aelfthryth**, with whom he had two sons, thereby setting the stage for conflict over the **succession to the throne** after his death. The name *Eneda*, meaning "swan" and referring to fair skin, was coined by the late 11th- and early 12th-century monk, Florence of Worcester. *See also* WULFTHRYTH.

**AETHELFLAED OF DAMERHAM (?–?).** In about 944, **Edmund I** of England took Aethelflaed, daughter of Aelfgar (a high-ranking official in **Wessex**), as his second wife following the death of **Aelfgifu**. However, the marriage was short lived and childless because the king was killed in a brawl at Pucklechurch, Gloucestershire, on 26 May 946. Aethelflaed remarried, but some sources record that she later became a nun at Shaftesbury Abbey and died sometime after 975.

**AETHELING.** In Anglo-Saxon England, an aetheling was a person of noble birth (and usually a member of the ruling family who might succeed to the kingship). The word (often spelled as "aethling," "atheling," "etheling," or "ethling") is derived from the Old English *aethel* (which meant "noble") and the suffix *-ing* (meaning "belonging to"). The term was used only occasionally after the **Norman** invasion of 1066, most notably in the case of **William the Aetheling**, the son and heir of King **Henry I**.

**AETHELRED THE UNREADY (c968–1016).** Aethelred (also known as Ethelred) is usually depicted as an ineffectual ruler because he failed to prevent Danish invaders from subjugating the English people. His nickname— "the Unready"—comes from *unraed*, an Old English word that means "poorly counseled," and is, in part, a pun on his own name, which derives from *aethel raed* (or "noble counsel").

The son of King **Edgar of England** and **Aelfthryth** (Edgar's second wife), he was rejected as successor to the throne in 975, when his father died, because he was still a child, the **witan** (the king's council of advisors) favoring Edward, his older half-brother, later known as **Edward the Martyr**. However, three years later, Edward was murdered, possibly by Aelfthryth, and Aethelred was appointed in his stead. He was anointed at Kingston-upon-Thames on 4 May 979, with his mother acting as **regent** for the first years of his reign.

The new king's youth, Edward's violent death, and suspicions that Aelfthryth had assassinated her stepson combined to produce a climate of uncertainty in England, and the Danes were quick to take advantage, mounting a series of raids from 980 and strengthening the attacks from 991. When the Anglo-Saxon army was defeated at the Battle of Maldon on 10 August that year, Aethelred was persuaded that, rather than continue to fight apparently superior foes, it would be better to pay a tribute (known as **danegeld**, or "Dane gold") of 10,000 pounds of silver in an effort to persuade them to leave. The ploy worked, but it also taught the Danes that it was worth coming back and asking for more. In 994, they returned, concentrating on **London**. Again, they were paid to go away, and the pattern was repeated in 1002, 1007, and 1012, by which time the price of peace was 48,000 pounds of silver.

Not all of the invaders left when the payments were made. Some settled, mainly in towns, and Aethelred, his patience exhausted, attempted to extract revenge by massacring them on 13 November 1002 (*see* ST. BRICE'S DAY

MASSACRE). The effort proved futile because, by 1013, England was being ruled by the Danish King **Sweyn**, and Aethelred had sought safety in Normandy. Aethelred returned following Sweyn's death in 1014, but his position was never secure, and while he was dying in London on 23 April 1016, his shores were again under siege, this time by **Canute**, Sweyn's son.

Until the mid-20th century, historians depicted Aethelred as a cowardly, incompetent monarch who achieved very little. More recently, students of Anglo-Saxon England have been more sympathetic, stressing the problems he faced in dealing with persistent attacks by a strong enemy and questioning the quality of the advice he received from his courtiers. These historians also suggest that the repeated payments of danegeld indicate that he had devised an efficient monetary system, and they point out that the last years of the millennium, in particular, were characterized by an increase in church building and by a flowering of scholarship in the monasteries.

Aethelred married twice, siring at least nine sons and three daughters. **Aelfgifu of York**, his first wife, gave birth to seven boys, one of whom—Edmund—succeeded him as **Edmund II** (or Edmund Ironsides). Margaret, Edmund's daughter, married **Malcolm III**, King of Scots (*see* MARGARET, ST.), and so, through her, Aethelred's bloodline merged with that of Scotland's royal house, but the monarch's second match—to **Emma of Normandy**—proved to have greater consequences for the English nation. There were three children, two sons and a daughter, with Edward (the elder boy, now known as **Edward the Confessor**) becoming king in 1042. More importantly, however, the marriage provided one rationale for the claim by Emma's grandnephew, William, duke of Normandy and later **William I**, that he was entitled to the throne when William the Confessor died in 1066—a claim that he pursued through a successful invasion, altering the course of British history. *See also* AELFRED AETHELING; EDITH OF EAST ANGLIA; GODGIFU.

**AETHELSTAN (c895–939).** Aethelstan (also known as Aethelstan the Glorious, Athelstan, and Ethelstan) was the first monarch to win effective control over the area approximating to present-day England. The son of **Edward the Elder** and his first wife, **Ecgwynn** (of whom nothing is known except her name), he was born in about 895, succeeded to the thrones of Mercia and **Wessex** in 924, and was crowned king of all the English the following year. He added York, a Viking kingdom, to his realm in 927, and in succeeding years he forced rulers of territories on his northern and western borders to pay him homage. Inevitably, his strength created jealousies, but he successfully repelled all threats to his throne, most notably in 937, when he routed an army of Norsemen and Scots at the **Battle of Brunanburh**.

Despite the difficulties of travel at the time, Aethelstan maintained contact with powerful families on the European mainland, creating alliances by marrying his half-sisters to leading nobles. For example, he sent Aedgyth (or Edith) and Aldiva (or Algiva) to Germany and invited Otto, duke of Saxony and later king of the Germans and Holy Roman Emperor, to choose whichever he preferred; Otto chose Aedgyth, who bore him a daughter and a son (*see also* AELFFLAED).

Aethelstan also imposed a series of laws on his subjects; historians disagree about the extent to which these were written and applied throughout the realm, but there is evidence of efforts to prevent theft, limit corruption, and show some compassion for the poor. Six mints produced coins for use in trade, which was largely confined to major settlements, thus encouraging the growth of towns in a strongly agricultural society. The church, too, benefited from his donations of art and money and from his support of learning. Aethelstan died childless on 27 October 939 and was buried at Malmesbury Abbey. He was succeeded by **Edmund I**, his half-brother by Edward the Elder and **Edgiva** (or Eadgifu), Edward's third wife. *See also* AELFWEARD.

**AETHELWULF (c795–858).** From 839 until 855, Aethelwulf, father of **Alfred the Great**, led the Saxon kingdom of **Wessex** in resistance to attacks by Viking invaders. The son of **Egbert**, who in 829–30 had briefly united the Anglo-Saxon realms under a single ruler, he had been at the forefront of his father's campaigns in southeast England in 825 and with him had virtually guaranteed a smooth succession to the Wessex throne through generous grants of land to the cathedrals of Canterbury and **Winchester** in 838. After Egbert's death in 839, he faced a series of attacks by Viking (primarily Danish) marauders, winning a particularly bloody victory at Acleah (probably Ockley, in Surrey) in 851.

In 852 or 853, Aethelwulf formed an alliance with Burgred, king of Mercia, to defeat the Britons in north Wales, but shortly afterward he left on a pilgrimage to Rome. In his absence, Aethelbald, one of his five sons, seized the opportunity to build support for his own claim to the leadership and presented Aethelwulf with the possibility of rebellion when he returned to Wessex in 856. Rather than weaken his realm through internecine warfare, the now aging monarch ceded the western—and, politically, the most important—part to Aethelbald, keeping the eastern section under his own wing.

Aethelwulf died on 13 January 858 and was buried at Steyning, but his remains were later moved to Winchester, the most important settlement in Wessex and the burial place of many of the kingdom's leaders. Aethelwulf is also known as Ethelwulf. *See also* ELGIVA; JUDITH OF FLANDERS; OSBURGA.

**AETHLING.** *See* AETHELING.

**AGATHA (?–?).** Agatha was the wife of **Edward the Exile** and the mother of **Edgar Aetheling** (the last **Anglo-Saxon monarch** to rule England, albeit in name only) and **St. Margaret**, wife of King **Malcolm III** of Scotland, but little is known either of her background or of her life. Many scholars believe she was of central or eastern European origin and that she met Edward while he was living in either Hungary or Kiev. She traveled to England with her husband and children in 1057, when Edward was declared **heir apparent** to the throne by **Edward the Confessor**, but she was widowed when he died only days after the family's arrival, possibly at the hands of other aspirants to the kingship. She fled to Scotland when William, duke of Normandy (*see* WILLIAM I OF ENGLAND), ended Anglo-Saxon rule of England in 1066, but it is not known how long she survived. Some sources suggest she may have passed away soon after 1070, others that she may have lived until about 1090.

**AGATHA OF NORMANDY (c1064–c1080).** Agatha (also known as Elgiva and Margaret) is mentioned by the 12th-century monk and chronicler Orderic Vitalis as one of the younger members of the family of **William I of England** (William the Conqueror) and **Matilda of Flanders**. Orderic records that she was betrothed to Harold Godwinson (later King **Harold II**), but scholars have pointed out that he also writes of an engagement between Harold and Agatha's sister, **Adeliza of Normandy**. The same source notes that Agatha was promised in marriage to Alfonso VI, king of Galicia and Léon, but she passed away while on her way to meet her prospective husband and was buried in the cathedral at Bayeux. The cause of her death is not clear, but some writers claim she may have resisted the match and died of a broken heart.

**AIR TRAVEL.** In 1936, King **Edward VIII** became the first British monarch to travel by air, but it was hardly a new experience for him because, as **prince of Wales**, he had learned to fly in **France** during World War I. A King's Flight of airplanes for use on royal trips was formed in 1936, was disbanded during World War II, was reformed in 1946, was named the Queen's Flight on the accession of Queen **Elizabeth II** in 1952, and was merged with 32 Squadron of the Royal Air Force in 1995. None of 32 Squadron's aircraft is capable of traveling farther than Eastern Europe without refueling, and in any case planes are made available for royal use only if they are not required for military purposes. So, in recent years, Queen Elizabeth has usually chartered jets for longer journeys. Where possible, other members of the **royal**

**family** travel by scheduled services, but a helicopter is available for short trips. The crown equerry, who is based in the lord chamberlain's Department of the **Royal Household**, coordinates all travel.

Since Edward VIII's days, several other royals have learned to fly, including **Prince Andrew, duke of York** (who served with the Royal Navy as a helicopter pilot during the Falklands War with Argentina in 1982); **Charles, prince of Wales**; and his father, **Prince Philip, duke of Edinburgh**. The United Kingdom is unusual in that it does not have a dedicated aircraft for its head of state, but proposals to provide a suitable airplane have fallen foul of criticisms over costs. Also, members of the royal family have frequently been pilloried in parliament and in the press for using chartered aircraft to transport relatively small groups at considerable expense and to the detriment of the environment. *See also* ROYAL TRAIN; ROYAL YACHT; STATE COACHES.

**ALBA.** The Gaelic term "Alba" originally applied to the whole island of Great Britain, but after c900, it was particularly used with reference to the kingdom created from about 843 when **Kenneth MacAlpin** united Dalriada (in the west of modern Scotland) with the territory of the Picts (north of the River Forth). By the 11th century, the same territory was more commonly referred to by the Latin word "Scotia," and monarchs called themselves *rex scottorum* or "king of Scots." That medieval kingdom evolved into modern Scotland, which is still called *Alba* in Scots Gaelic. The dukedom of Albany derived its name from Alba; the title, created by King **Robert III** in 1398, was conferred in 1660 on James, son of King **Charles I**, and later on King **James VII and II**, for whom Albany—the capital of New York State—is named.

**ALBERT OF SAXE-COBURG AND GOTHA, PRINCE (1819–1861).** **Prince** Albert was husband to Queen **Victoria**, playing a significant role in advising his wife on affairs of state throughout a 21-year marriage. Born on 26 August 1819 at the Rosenau, the family residence near Coburg in Bavaria, he was the second son of Ernest, duke of Saxe-Coburg-Saalfield, and his young wife, Louise of Saxe-Coburg-Altenburg. A restructuring of the duchies in 1826 gave Ernest the territory of Saxe-Coburg and Gotha, a name which his son assumed. Albert's marriage to Victoria, his first cousin, was plotted by King Leopold I of Belgium, the widower of **Princess Charlotte Augusta**, daughter of King **George IV**. (In 1818, Leopold had persuaded his older sister, **Victoria of Saxe-Coburg-Saalfield**, to marry **Prince Edward, duke of Kent and Strathearn**, the fourth son of King **George III**; Queen Victoria was the sole product of that union.)

Albert—an awkward, insecure young man, his maturity blunted by his parents' unhappy marriage and the departure of his mother when he was only five years old—was presented to the 16-year-old **princess** in **London** on 18 May 1836, and Victoria thought him "extremely good-looking." They corresponded over the next three years, and then, with the relationship flourishing, he returned to Britain on 10 October 1839. Five days later, the young queen (very much in love but also under pressure to find a husband who would provide dispassionate political advice and sire the son who would secure the **succession to the throne**) proposed. They married on 10 February 1840 at **St. James's Palace**, and Victoria noted in her diary that "we did not sleep much" that night.

Albert was regarded with suspicion by many people—he was a foreigner and an intellectual—and although he won over a significant number of his critics as a result of his hard work, his obvious devotion to the queen, and his diligent attempts to learn about the political and economic issues that dominated debate in his adopted country, he never completely dispelled the unease. At first, Victoria was adamant that her husband should have no say in government, but after some six months, on the advice of the prime minister, Viscount Melbourne, he was permitted to view dispatches and then to attend meetings between the queen and her ministers. Gradually, his role grew, and in succeeding years the queen learned from Albert the need for order in her dealings with advisors and the benefits of self-discipline and diligent attendance to papers and responsibilities.

On many occasions, Victoria took her husband's advice, to good effect. For example, in 1861, during the American Civil War, the U.S. government stopped the British ship *Trent* during its passage to England and abducted the two confederate envoys who were on board. At that time, the monarch played a large part in Britain's dealings with foreign nations, and Victoria responded angrily. However, Albert persuaded her to tone down her reaction in order to give the United States room to maneuver, and as a result, conflict between the two countries was avoided. After his death, Victoria continued to make decisions based on what she felt her husband would have done in the same situation.

Beyond the realm of politics, Albert took a particular interest in the **Royal Household** and **royal residences**. By 1842, he had in effect become Victoria's private secretary. By 1844, he had completely reorganized the household, and by the 1850s he had enabled the queen to pay off her father's debts, purchase **Osborne House** on the Isle of Wight (off the southern coast of England), and buy **Balmoral Castle** (in Scotland), where they spent many happy times together. Despite great opposition, the prince was the major force behind the Great Exhibition, which showed Britain's industrial might to the world in 1851 and produced a financial surplus that was used to develop the complex of museums (including the Victoria and Albert Museum) and other cultural institutions in the South Kensington area of **London**.

The couple had nine children, born between 1840 and 1857. In 1861, while visiting his eldest son (later King **Edward VII**) in Cambridge, Albert contracted typhoid. Complications followed, and on 14 December he died at **Windsor Castle**. His name is remembered in a multitude of British buildings—notably the Albert Memorial and the Albert Hall in London—and in numerous other ways, including the city of Prince Albert and Prince Albert National Park (both in Saskatchewan, Canada), Lake Albert (on the border between Uganda and the Democratic Republic of Congo, in Africa), four British army regiments, and the Albert Medals (one still awarded by the Royal Society of Arts for contributions to scientific and social advance, the other formerly given in recognition of gallantry in saving someone's life). Queen Victoria, bereft and desolated by his passing, spent many years in mourning. Forty years later, she was buried beside him in a mausoleum at **Frogmore**.

Benjamin Disraeli, who later became prime minister and developed a close friendship with the widowed queen, commented at the time of the prince's death that "we have buried our sovereign"—a reference to the considerable part that Albert had played in national life. Contemporary biographers were understandably sycophantic, but 20th-century writers were much more critical, as Victorianism became unfashionable. However, more recent studies have been sympathetic, painting a picture of a man who exerted considerable influence for the public good and who died too soon. *See also* ALFRED, PRINCE, DUKE OF EDINBURGH AND SAXE-COBURG AND GOTHA; ALICE, PRINCESS, GRAND DUCHESS OF HESSE; ARTHUR, PRINCE, DUKE OF CONNAUGHT AND STRATHEARN; BEATRICE (OR HENRY) OF BATTENBERG, PRINCESS; CHRISTIAN OF SCHLESWIG-HOLSTEIN, PRINCESS; LEOPOLD, PRINCE, DUKE OF ALBANY; LOUISE, PRINCESS, DUCHESS OF ARGYLL; VICTORIA, PRINCESS ROYAL, GERMAN EMPRESS.

**ALBERT VICTOR, PRINCE, DUKE OF CLARENCE AND AVONDALE (1864–1892).** Albert Victor—known as "Eddy" within the **royal family**—was second in the line of **succession to the throne** after his father, but he suffered an untimely death that was considered fortuitous by several commentators. The eldest of six children in the family of Albert Edward, **prince of Wales** (later King **Edward VII**), and **Alexandra of Denmark**, he was born, two months prematurely, at **Frogmore** House on 8 January 1864. Like the **prince** of Wales, he was a poor scholar, though the educational process may have been affected by a deafness he inherited from his mother and by his early birth (because a high proportion of premature babies exhibit learning difficulties). In 1877, he was sent with his younger brother, George (who eventually reigned as King **George V**), for experience with the Royal Navy and then, from 1879, on a three-year visit to Britain's colonial territories, including Aden, Australia, the Falkland Islands, the Pacific Ocean islands, Singapore, and South Africa. An unproductive period at Cambridge University from 1883 to 1885 was followed by a spell in the army with the 10th Hussars, but Albert Victor had no commitment to a military career and left in 1891.

Two years earlier, the royal court had been awash with rumors that the prince was a frequent visitor to a homosexual brothel in **London**. Nothing was ever proven (and biographers still debate the nature of his sexuality), but a visit to India the following year produced further scandal because Margery Hadden—the wife of a civil engineer—later claimed that Albert Victor had fathered her son, Clarence. Mrs. Hadden was a mentally disturbed alcoholic and had not a shred of evidence to support her assertions, but the prince's attorneys nevertheless admitted that there had been "some relations" between the lady and their client. (In 1933, Clarence attempted to make King George V pay him to keep quiet about his parentage but was charged with demanding money with menaces. Documents produced at his trial showed that he was born at least two years before the prince set foot in India). Albert Victor's name has also been advanced—purely speculatively—as the likely identity of Jack the Ripper, who murdered five women in the Whitechapel area of London in 1888 (in practice, he could not have been responsible because he was known to be elsewhere on each occasion, including at **Balmoral Castle** in Scotland at the time of two of the killings). Still other authors have asserted that he was blackmailed by prostitutes and that he contracted venereal diseases.

Queen **Victoria**, who did not believe the young man had a character appropriate to a future sovereign, and the prince of Wales determined to find the prince a bride with a personality strong enough to curb his waywardness. Several possibilities were considered, and eventually, on 7 December 1891, his suit was accepted by **Mary of Teck**. The wedding was scheduled for 27 February the following year, but, while the plans were being made, Prince Albert Victor fell victim to the Asian influenza epidemic that was sweeping Britain, developed pneumonia, and died at **Sandringham House** on 14 January. He was buried in **St. George's Chapel** at **Windsor Castle**. Alexandra was grief stricken, turning the room where he died into a shrine, but Victoria took advantage of the situation to arrange a betrothal between Mary of Teck and George. Some biographers considered the prince's death "a merciful act of providence" because it paved the way for the much more conventional

George to follow Victoria and Edward to the throne, but recent writers have been less condemnatory, pointing out that there is no proof of Albert Victor's homosexuality or of many of his alleged misdemeanors and suggesting that he was a personable man whose education was affected by physical disabilities and poor teachers. *See also* LOUISE, PRINCESS ROYAL, DUCHESS OF FIFE.

**ALEXANDER I (c1080–1124).** Alexander, son of King **Malcolm III** and his second wife, Margaret of **Wessex** (later **St. Margaret**), ruled Scotland from 1107 to 1124, succeeding his brother, **Edgar of Scotland**. Throughout his reign, David, the youngest of Malcolm and Margaret's children, controlled much of the southern area of the realm (in accordance with Edgar's wishes) and eventually succeeded Alexander to the throne as **David I**. Alexander was a devout man, founding Augustinian priories at **Scone** (the traditional **coronation** site of Scottish kings) and on Inchcolm island, near the mouth of the River Forth. He also resisted attempts by English clerics to persuade Scots churchmen to submit to their authority. However, he was also a warrior of repute, supporting **Henry I** of England in campaigns against the **Welsh princes** and hunting down opponents who tried to kill him while his court was based at Invergowrie, on the north shore of the River Tay, west of Dundee. In about 1107, he married **Sybilla of Normandy**, one of some five illegitimate children born to Henry and Lady Sybilla Corbet, but the union was childless. Alexander died at **Stirling** c23 April 1124 and was buried at **Dunfermline Abbey**.

**ALEXANDER II (1198–1249).** Alexander, the only son of **William I of Scotland** and **Ermengarde de Beaumont**, was born at Haddington on 24 August 1198 and succeeded to the throne on his father's death in 1214. The year after his accession, he supported the English nobles in their revolt against King **John** (*see* FIRST BARONS' WAR), anticipating that if he helped them to oust the unpopular monarch they would reward him with Northumbria, which William had spent his life trying to retrieve for the Scottish crown. The efforts came to naught, however, and John exacted revenge by sending an army to ravage the southern regions of Alexander's realm.

In 1221, five years after John's death, the Scots king took a different tack, marrying **Joan of England (1210–1238)**, sister of King **Henry III**, partly in the hope that the English monarch would give the bride Northumbria as a dowry. That ploy was as unsuccessful as his military efforts had been, and the issue became a source of resentment to both rulers until 1237, when, after negotiations at York, they agreed that the border between the kingdoms would run from the Solway Firth in the west to the River Tweed in the east—a line that has survived, with only minor alterations, to the present day. In return for giving up his claim to Northumbria, Alexander received other estates in England.

At home, Alexander attempted to exert his authority over areas which his predecessors had had difficulty controlling. Much of his attention was devoted to the Outer Hebrides, a chain of islands off Scotland's western coast where a strong Scandinavian heritage meant that local leaders allied with Norwegian kings. In 1249, he mounted an expedition to annex the isles, but on 8 July he died while his galley sailed close to Kerrera. He was buried at Melrose Abbey (a Cistercian settlement founded by his great-grandfather, King **David I**) and was succeeded by **Alexander III**, his son by a second marriage to **Marie de Coucy**, who came from a powerful French family that continued to support Scots causes long after Alexander's death. *See also* ROXBURGH CASTLE; STIRLING.

**ALEXANDER III (1241–1286).** Alexander, the only son of King **Alexander II** and his second wife, **Marie de Coucy**, ruled Scotland from 1249 until his death, presiding over a period of growing trade, peace with England, and expansion of the realm. He was born at **Roxburgh Castle** on 4 September 1241 and was only seven years old when his father died. So, during the early part of his reign, government was in the hands of **regents**.

At the age of 21, Alexander took control himself and determined to complete the task, begun by his father, of adding the Western Isles to his kingdom. The archipelago lies off the west coast of Scotland but had a strong Scandinavian heritage and so owed more loyalty to Norwegian than to Scottish monarchs. In July 1263, King Haakon IV sailed to the island of Arran, intending to defend his country's rights to the islands, but Alexander shrewdly extended negotiations so that battle was delayed until autumn storms began in October. The Norwegian fleet was battered by wind as it lay in the Firth of Clyde. Then, after an indecisive conflict at Largs, Haakon, worried about the onset of winter, decided to return home, but he died at Kirkwall, in Orkney, during the journey. The following year, Alexander's army occupied the islands and subdued the local leaders. In 1266, Haakon's successor, Magnus VI, conceded sovereignty over the disputed territories in return for a lump sum payment and an annuity.

While the king of Scots was contemplating expansion of his authority over Norwegian-held lands, King **Henry III** of England was planning to take Scotland under his wing. In 1251, he made arrangements for Alexander to marry Margaret, his eldest daughter and later **Margaret, queen of Scots**, at York, and he took the opportunity to invite his new son-in-law to pay homage to him. However, Alexander—either through a shrewdness that belied his years or because he had been well prepared by advisors—told him that he had come south to get married, not to deal with difficult political matters, and that he would have to talk to his counselors before taking such an important step. The two countries then remained at peace for the rest of the Scottish monarch's reign. However, the English kings did not give up their claims to overlordship, and the centuries after Alexander's death were scarred by conflict as Scots rulers asserted their right to independence.

Margaret and Alexander had two sons and a daughter, but by 1283 she and all three children were dead. In an effort to produce an heir to the throne, Alexander took French-born **Yolande de Dreux** as his second wife late in 1285. On 19 March the following year, after a meeting at **Edinburgh** Castle and against advice, he decided to brave a stormy night and ride to Kinghorn, where his pregnant bride was living. Somehow, near the end of his journey, he fell from his horse and was killed. Yolande's baby was stillborn, so the throne passed to Alexander's three-year-old granddaughter, **Margaret, maid of Norway**. When she died, uncrowned, in 1290, Scotland stumbled into a crisis over the succession which lasted until **John of Scotland** (also known as John Balliol) was installed as a puppet king under English control in 1292. Alexander was buried, close to several of his predecessors, in **Dunfermline Abbey**. *See also* ALEXANDER OF SCOTLAND; DAVID OF SCOTLAND; MARGARET, QUEEN OF NORWAY.

**ALEXANDER JOHN, PRINCE (1871).** Alexander John was the sixth and last addition to the family of Albert Edward, **prince of Wales** (later King **Edward VII**) and **Alexandra of Denmark**. Born prematurely at **Sandringham House** on 6 May 1871, the baby survived only for a day and was buried nearby in the graveyard at the Church of St. Mary Magdalene.

**ALEXANDER OF SCOTLAND (1264–1284).** As the elder son of King **Alexander III** and **Margaret, queen of Scots**, Alexander was expected to follow his father to the Scottish throne. He was born at Jedburgh on 21 January 1264 and on 14 November 1282 was married at **Roxburgh Castle** to Margaret, daughter of Guy of Dampierre, count of Flanders, and his second wife, Isabelle of Luxembourg. However, on 17 January 1284, before the union produced any children, the young man died at Lindores Abbey on the south bank of the River Tay. He was buried in **Dunfermline Abbey**, and his widow returned to the European mainland where, in about 1290, she married Raymond, count of Gueldres, and together they had three daughters and a son.

Alexander's death caused a crisis in Scotland because **David of Scotland**, his younger brother, had died in 1281, and **Margaret, queen of Norway**, his elder sister, died two years later. Thus there was no heir to the throne, and his father was a widower. The king responded by marrying **Yolande de Dreux**, and he persuaded parliament to accept **Margaret, maid of Norway**—his granddaughter—as queen if he died before he fathered any more children. Early in 1286, while his wife was pregnant, the king was thrown from his horse and killed. Yolande's child was stillborn later that year, and in 1290 the maid of Norway died while traveling to her **coronation**. Several claimants to the throne appeared, so the Scots submitted their petitions for adjudication to **Edward I** of England, who chose **John of Scotland** (often known as John Balliol). He also attempted to assert overlordship of Scotland and thus paved the way for centuries of conflict between the two kingdoms.

**ALEXANDRA OF DENMARK (1844–1925).** Alexandra—the popular but long-suffering consort of King **Edward VII**, a playboy monarch—was born on 1 December 1844 at the Yellow Palace in Copenhagen, the eldest daughter of Prince Christian of Schleswig-Holstein-Sonderburg-Glücksburg (later King Christian IX of Denmark) and Princess Louise of Hesse-Cassel. Her family was not wealthy (as a child, Alexandra sewed her own clothes), so she was an unlikely choice of bride for the **heir apparent** to the British throne. Moreover, Denmark and Prussia both claimed sovereignty over Schleswig-Holstein, and while Alexandra's family was pro-Danish, the sympathies of Edward's parents were with the Prussians because **Prince Albert of Saxe-Coburg and Gotha** was born in Germany and Queen **Victoria** had a German mother (**Victoria of Saxe-Coburg-Saalfield**). However, the **prince of Wales** refused to consider a marriage simply because it cemented an alliance with a powerful family, the 1701 **Act of Settlement** ruled out a Roman Catholic partner for an heir apparent to the throne, and there were few Protestant princesses available. Also, Alexandra was considered a great beauty—a matter of some import given Edward's roving eye. The wedding ceremony was held at **St. George's Chapel** in **Windsor Castle** on 10 March 1863, with many of the female guests wearing dark dresses because the court was still in mourning for **Prince** Albert, who had died 15 months earlier.

Queen Victoria was not impressed by the young couple's lavish, partygoing lifestyle, which contrasted markedly with the somber tenor of her own life, but she was somewhat mollified by the birth of a grandchild in January 1864. (**Prince Albert Victor, duke of Clarence and Avondale**, and his five brothers and sisters were all born prematurely, but some writers have suggested that Alexandra may have misled Victoria about the likely dates of the births on the grounds that she did not want her mother-in-law around when she went into labor.) At first, Edward played the part of devoted husband, but before long he was keeping the company of other good-looking women. Alexandra seemed willing to tolerate his affairs, preferring to spend time with her growing family at **Sandringham** in East Anglia or at **Osborne House** on the Isle of Wight, all the more so as she became increasingly deaf (a result of otosclerosis, an ear condition inherited from her mother) and a bout of rheumatic fever in 1867, which complicated her pregnancy with **Louise, princess royal, duchess of Fife**, left her with a pronounced limp.

By 1901, when Victoria died and Edward became king, Alexandra was enjoying a quiet life with her grandchildren and living apart from her husband for several months at a time. However, she took her role as queen seriously, playing little part in political matters (allegedly, Edward carefully kept government papers on international affairs well away from her eyes because of her strong anti-German sentiments) but—like several of her sisters-in-law (*see, for example,* ALICE, PRINCESS, GRAND DUCHESS OF HESSE, *and* CHRISTIAN OF SCHLESWIG-HOLSTEIN, PRINCESS)—devoting much effort to charity work. Nowadays, she is best remembered for Alexandra Rose Day (an annual event first held in 1912 that raises money for more than 250 groups that care for the disabled, the hungry, the needy, and the sick), but she also established Queen Alexandra's Imperial Nursing Service, took the chair at the inaugural meeting of the Red Cross Society in 1902, and was a regular visitor to medical centers, including the **London** Hospital, which is located in the city's deprived east end and to which she was particularly attached.

Never careful with money, Alexandra continued to spend even after the king's death in 1910, though much of that expenditure went to charitable causes. However, with her health failing, her deafness total, and her eyesight severely impaired, her mobility was increasingly limited. She died at Sandringham on 20 October 1925 after suffering a heart attack and was buried beside her husband in St. George's Chapel. *See also* ALEXANDER JOHN, PRINCE; GEORGE V; MARLBOROUGH HOUSE; MARY, PRINCESS, LANDGRAVINE OF HESSE-CASSEL; MAUD, PRINCESS, QUEEN OF NORWAY; QUEEN MOTHER; VICTORIA, PRINCESS.

**ALEXANDRA, PRINCESS (1936– ). Princess** Alexandra—the only daughter and second child of **Prince George, duke of Kent**, and **Princess Marina, duchess of Kent**—is one of the more active members of the **royal family**, carrying out about 120 engagements each year. She was born on Christmas Day, 1936, at 3 Belgrave Square, her parents' **London** home, but she grew up at Coppins, their country house at Iver, not far from **Windsor Castle**, and spent the World War II years at Badminton (in the rural west of England) with her paternal grandmother, **Mary of Teck**, widow of King **George V**.

The first British princess to be educated at a school rather than at home, Alexandra attended Heathfield, a girls' boarding school near Ascot, which merged in 2006 with St. Mary's, Wantage, where her niece, **Lady Helen Taylor**, was taught. After a period at Mademoiselle Anita's finishing school in Paris (where she had been sent to learn appropriate dress codes by her fashion-conscious mother), she studied nursing at Great Ormond Street Children's Hospital in London. From her late teens, she took an increasingly public role, earning a reputation as a popular and accessible member of the royal family, and it was soon clear that she would help to fashion the image of the monarchy in the late 20th century.

On several occasions, the princess has represented Queen **Elizabeth II** at events abroad, beginning with visits to Australia (where she attended Queensland's centenary celebrations in 1959) and Nigeria (where in 1960 she took part in the events marking the country's independence from Britain); more recently, she has traveled to Rome, Oman, and Hungary (in 1998); Gibraltar (1999); the Falkland Islands and Norway (2000); and Thailand and Burma (2003). At home, she is best known for her work with medical and welfare charities, particularly with organizations that care for people afflicted with diseases of the eye. Like other members of the royal family, she also has several military commitments, acting as colonel-in-chief of a number of army regiments.

On 24 April 1963 at **Westminster Abbey**, Princess Alexandra married **Angus Ogilvy**, son of the earl of Airlie, in a ceremony watched by 200 million television viewers around the world. They had two children—**James Ogilvy** (born in 1964) and **Marina Ogilvy** (born in 1966 and later to cause her parents much heartbreak when she rebelled against them). Ogilvy refused Queen Elizabeth's offer of an earldom, but he combined a business career with royal duties until his death in 2004. The princess's home is the six-bedroom Thatched House Lodge in southwest London; the 17th-century property was enlarged in 1771, became the home of U.S. General Dwight D. Eisenhower during World War II, and was leased by Sir Angus when the couple married. *See also* ST. JAMES'S PALACE.

**ALFONSO, EARL OF CHESTER (1273–1284).** The fourth son in the family of **Edward I** and **Eleanor of Castile**, Alfonso was born in Gascony on 24 November 1273 and was named after his maternal uncle, Alfonso X of Castile, who had renounced his claims to the Gascon territories when Eleanor and Edward married in 1254. When he was less than a year old, **Henry Plantagenet**, his older brother, passed away, leaving the infant as heir to the English throne, but he never reached maturity, dying at **Windsor Castle** on 19 August 1284. Thus the fifth son, Edward (later **Edward II**), claimed the crown when their father died in 1307.

**ALFRED, PRINCE (1780–1782).** Alfred, the ninth son and fourteenth child of King **George III** and **Charlotte of Mecklenburg-Strelitz**, was born at **Windsor Castle** on 22 September 1780 but failed to survive childhood, dying at Windsor on 20 August 1782, a month before his second birthday. The **prince** was initially buried in **Westminster Abbey**, but his remains were transferred to **St. George's Chapel** in 1820. Arthur was the first of George's children to die, and the king, much attached to his sons and daughters, was grief stricken. After the monarch succumbed to his last bout of madness in 1811, he apparently held imaginary conversations with the boy and with four-year-old **Prince Octavius**, who died in the spring of the following year after contracting smallpox.

**ALFRED, PRINCE, DUKE OF EDINBURGH AND SAXE-COBURG AND GOTHA (1844–1900).** A shy, retiring man, **Prince** Alfred was nevertheless a talented naval officer and the first member of the British **royal family** to travel extensively beyond Europe. Born at **Windsor Castle** on 6 August 1844, the second son and fourth child of Queen **Victoria** and **Prince Albert of Saxe-Coburg and Gotha**, he entered the Royal Navy of his own volition in 1856, commanded the English Channel fleet in 1883–84 and the Mediterranean Fleet in 1886–89, and became admiral of the fleet in 1893, earning the admiration of fellow officers because of his tactical abilities.

In 1862, having deposed King Otto, the Greek people offered Alfred their throne after he won 95 percent of the vote in a national referendum to elect a new monarch, but the British government demurred, arguing that his appointment was contrary to the terms of a protocol, signed in 1830, that guaranteed Hellenic independence. Alfred, therefore, continued with his naval career but also made a series of visits to British colonies around the world, becoming the first prince to visit Cape Colony, now part of South Africa, in 1860, Australia (1867), Hong Kong (1868), India (1868), and New Zealand (1869). On 12 March 1868, while picnicking on a Sydney beach, he was shot in the back by Henry James O'Farrell, a mentally ill alcoholic; the prince recovered, but O'Farrell was hanged.

On 23 January 1874, Alfred married the Grand Duchess Maria Alexandrovna of Russia at the Winter Palace in St. Petersburg, a union unpopular with many Britons because political relations with Russia were tense and because Maria was a member of the Russian Orthodox Church. They had four daughters and a son, but the grand duchess never fared well with her in-laws, believing some of their spouses to be social inferiors. As a result, she was considered arrogant, causing tensions that, after the birth of their last child (**Princess** Beatrice, in 1884), pushed the couple into increasingly separate lives.

The prince, an enthusiastic if technically unskilled violinist, was (with his older brother, later King **Edward VII**) instrumental in founding the Royal College of Music in **London**, built up a large collection of ceramics and glass, and is considered one of the founders of the **Royal Philatelic Collection**. However, he also drank heavily and by 1900 was suffering from cancer of the throat and tongue. He died on 30 July at Castle Rosenau, his summer home near Coburg in Bavaria, and was buried nearby in Glockenburg Cemetery.

Alfred, the prince's only son, contracted syphilis and committed suicide in 1899, but his sisters took British royal blood around Europe. Alexandra married Queen Victoria's grandnephew, Maximilian, prince of Hohenlohe-Langenburg; Beatrice found a partner—Alfonso, duke of Galliera—in the Spanish royal house; Marie became **queen consort** to King Ferdinand I of Romania; and Victoria took Ernest, grand duke of Hesse, as her first husband and Grand Duke Cyril Vladimirovich of Russia as her second. Prince Alfred's travels are commemorated in sites around the world. In Australia, the Royal Prince Alfred Hospital in Sydney and Prince Alfred College in Adelaide are named after him, as are Prince Alfred Park (in Port Elizabeth, South Africa) and Edinburgh of the Seven Seas (the principal township on Tristan da Cunha). Also, in 1874, the Peek Freans bakery in London created a new type of cookie to celebrate the prince's wedding. Round and flavored with vanilla, it is known as a Marie biscuit because the bride's name was printed on top; still enormously popular, it is sold around the world, particularly in tea-drinking countries. *See also* CHRISTIAN OF SCHLESWIG-HOLSTEIN, PRINCESS; CLARENCE HOUSE.

**ALFRED THE GREAT (c849–c899).** In a reign lasting from 871 until about 899, Alfred organized a system of urban defense works that protected his kingdom from Viking invaders, reformed the legal code, restructured his navy, and did much to encourage the spread of literacy. The son of **Aethelwulf**, king of **Wessex**, and (probably) **Osburga**, Aethelwulf's first wife, he was an unlikely candidate for kingship, even allowing for the disturbed conditions of the period, because he had four older brothers. His siblings all predeceased him, however, and he came to the throne as a seasoned warrior, having fought nine battles against Scandinavian (primarily Danish) marauders during 871 alone. In one of these engagements—the Battle of Merton on 23 April—his brother, Aethelred, was killed. Aethelred left young sons named Aethelhelm and Aethelwald, but both were considered too young to provide leadership at a time of military crisis, so Alfred succeeded him as king.

For five years, the new monarch was able to maintain peace, but in 876 the Danes attacked again, and early the following year Alfred was forced to flee to safety deep in near-impenetrable marshlands. There is an almost certainly apocryphal story that he was given shelter in a peasant home by a woman who, not recognizing her king, asked him to keep watch on some cakes she was baking so that they would not burn. Absorbed by military problems, he let the cakes blacken and consequently was berated by one of the poorest of his subjects. Whatever the truth of the tale, Alfred was able to regroup and defeat the Vikings decisively at Edington in 878. As a result, southern Britain was divided, with the Vikings controlling an area that became known as the **Danelaw**, located north of the River Thames, and with Alfred's Saxons controlling the rest.

Alfred used the ensuing peace to build up his navy so that ships carrying Scandinavian forces could be intercepted before they reached land, and he created a standing army that could be mobilized quickly, thus enabling him to resist invading forces before they moved far inland. In addition, he organized the construction of a network of fortified, defensible settlements that provided places of safety for his people as well as bases for trade. The legal system was restructured, too, with greater protection given to subjects who did not wield great political power, and literacy was encouraged throughout the kingdom. The Saxons believed that the destruction wrought in their land by the Danes was God's punishment because they had sinned. Alfred argued that education would bring the sagacity needed to ensure a return to righteousness, so he learned Latin, invited scholars to his court, decreed that young men should learn to read, and translated texts himself. Modern historians have reason to be grateful because the writing of the ***Anglo-Saxon Chronicle***, one of the principal sources of information about England from the 5th to the early 12th century, began during Alfred's reign, probably because of the intellectual climate he created.

As a result of Alfred's military and strategic initiatives, Wessex maintained its independence. The Vikings returned in about 885 and repeated their assaults intermittently for a decade, but they failed to overpower the Saxon armies and ultimately left the kingdom in peace. According to the *Anglo-Saxon Chronicle*, Alfred died on 26 October 901, but many writers believe his passing actually occurred in 899. He was initially buried at the New Minster in **Winchester**, but when the monks moved to Hyde Abbey in 1110, they took his remains with them. This tomb, however, was destroyed during the construction of a jail in 1788. John Mellor, a local antiquarian, claimed to have discovered the king's bones at the Hyde Abbey site and to have reburied them in 1866, but his story was much questioned. Modern archaeologists using more sophisticated techniques believed they had found the site of the royal grave during excavations in the 1990s, along with the resting places of Alfred's wife (**Ealhswith**) and their son (**Edward the Elder**), but there were no human remains that could be dated to the late 9th or early 10th century to authenticate the discovery. *See also* CROWN JEWELS OF THE UNITED KINGDOM.

**ALICE, PRINCESS, DUCHESS OF GLOUCESTER (1901–2004).** **Princess** Alice was the longest-lived member of any British **royal family**. The fifth child, and third daughter, of John Scott, duke of Buccleuch and of Queensbury, and his wife, Margaret Alice, she was born at Montagu House (the Buccleuchs' **London** home) on Christmas Day 1901 and could trace her descent through James, duke of Monmouth (*see* MONMOUTH RE-BELLION), from the Scottish monarchs of the **House of Stuart**. Unusual for a girl of aristocratic stock, she was educated at a boarding school—St. James's in West Malvern—but she spent her vacations in family mansions in Northamptonshire and Scotland, developing an interest in the outdoors that considerably exceeded her interest in London's social life, which she found "pointless and boring."

Demonstrating a sense of adventure unusual in young women of the period, Alice (who described herself as "a pre-beatnik") traveled to Africa in 1924, visited Lord Francis Scott—an uncle who farmed in Kenya—and fell in love with the continent. She also ruffled diplomatic feathers by disguising herself as a boy and entering an area of Afghanistan then barred to females. The adventures were recorded in watercolor paintings and photographs good enough to provide an income that helped to finance future trips.

Alice's father was a good friend of King **George V**, so when she was in Britain, she moved in circles that frequently brought her into contact with the royal family. The monarch's son—**Prince Henry, duke of Gloucester**— shared her interest in country life and served with the 10th Hussars, the same army regiment as her brother, Lord William Scott, so their decision to marry came as no surprise. The wedding was initially scheduled for **Westminster Abbey** on 6 November 1935, but Buccleuch's death on 19 October resulted in a change of arrangements, and a low-key ceremony was held at **Buckingham Palace**.

Princess Alice was, in some ways, a reluctant royal, preferring to shun the limelight and the crowds, but she had a strong sense of duty and accepted the new commitments that marriage to the son of a king entailed. During World War II, she worked hard to support the Nursing Corps, the Red Cross, the St. John's Ambulance Brigade, and the Women's Auxiliary Air Force. She also traveled to cities (such as Belfast and Coventry) that had suffered greatly from bombing, in an effort to raise morale. From 1945 to 1947, the princess helped her husband with his commitments as **governor-general** of Australia, and then, from her return until she was well into her nineties, she resumed her program of public engagements and support for charitable organizations, with a notable preference for hospitals and other medical groups.

In January 1965, Princess Alice was injured in a car accident while returning from Sir Winston Churchill's funeral, breaking her arm and requiring more than 50 stitches in facial wounds. Her husband seemed less physically affected, but the incident was followed by a period of deteriorating health until he died in 1974. The princess continued to live at Barnwell Manor (her Northamptonshire country mansion) until 1995, when financial circumstances forced the family to lease the property and move her to accommodations in **Kensington Palace**, where she passed away on 29 October 2004, just eight weeks before her 103rd birthday. She was interred at the royal burial ground at **Frogmore**, close to her husband. Princess Alice had two children; **Prince William of Gloucester** (born on 18 December 1941) was killed in a flying accident on 28 August 1972, so **Prince Richard of Gloucester** (born on 26 August 1944) succeeded to his father's dukedom.

**ALICE, PRINCESS, GRAND DUCHESS OF HESSE (1843–1878).** Alice—the third child, and second daughter, of Queen **Victoria** and **Prince Albert of Saxe-Coburg and Gotha**—gained a reputation as a thoughtful, caring woman with a genuine concern both for her family and for those living in less fortunate circumstances. She was born at **Buckingham Palace** on 25 April 1843 and developed a strong bond with her older brother, "Bertie" (later King **Edward VII**), often interceding on his behalf during his frequent disputes with their parents. In 1861, when her father was terminally ill, she summoned Bertie to his bedside, even though her mother would have preferred her son to stay away, and after Albert's death, she became the primary channel of communication between the queen and the outside world, including government ministers.

On 1 July 1862, at **Osborne House**, Alice was married to Prince Louis of Hesse (later Louis IV, grand duke of Hesse). The union strengthened monarchical links with the German states (Victoria's mother—**Victoria of Saxe-Coburg-Saalfield**—was German, Albert was German, and Alice's older sister, **Victoria, princess royal**, had also found a German husband), but George Villiers, earl of Clarendon and secretary of state for foreign affairs on three occasions during Victoria's reign, doubted that the **princess** would find happiness, lamenting that she was "going with a dull boy to a dull family in a dull country." His assessment proved accurate because Alice, although fond of the spouse chosen for her, never felt at ease with the conservatism and parochialism of Louis's court at Darmstadt. She threw herself into charitable work, caring for soldiers wounded in the Austro-Prussian War of 1866 and the Franco-Prussian War of 1870–71, establishing a training program for nurses, promoting educational opportunities for women, and raising funds for a hospice for people suffering from mental illness. However, the stresses of these tasks, coupled with seven pregnancies in the 11 years from 1863 to 1874, took a toll on her health, and in 1873, the death of her hemophiliac three-year-old son, **Prince** Frederick, added to her worries.

In the early winter of 1878, Louis and five of Alice's children took ill with diphtheria. The grand duchess attempted to nurse all of them, but, already weak, she fell victim herself and died at Darmstadt on 14 December, a month after the death of her youngest daughter, Princess May. She was buried in the ducal mausoleum at Rosenhöhe. Two of her daughters—Princess Elisabeth and Princess Alix—married into the Russian tsarist aristocracy and were murdered during the Bolshevik revolution in 1918. Prince Ernest, her eldest son, succeeded his father as grand duke but lost his throne when Germany became a republic after World War I, and her elder daughter, Princess Victoria, married Prince Louis of Battenburg, becoming the maternal grandmother of **Prince Philip, duke of Edinburgh** and consort of Queen **Elizabeth II**. *See also* CHRISTIAN OF SCHLESWIG-HOLSTEIN, PRINCESS; MOUNT-BATTEN, LOUIS, EARL MOUNTBATTEN OF BURMA.

**ALPIN, HOUSE OF.** Modern historians often refer to **Kenneth MacAlpin** and his descendants, who ruled a large tract of northern Britain for most of the period from the mid-9th until the mid-11th century, as the House of Alpin. The origins of the dynasty are obscure, but it seems likely that MacAlpin may have been a leader of the kingdom of Dalriada who inherited the throne of the Picts in about 843. The first three rulers of the united realm—Kenneth (who reigned from c843 to 859) and his sons, **Constantine I** (862–77) and **Áed** (877–78)—were known as kings of the Picts, but from about 889, when **Donald II** began an 11-year period on the throne, the monarchs were termed "king of **Alba**." For more than a century from 877, descendants of Constantine and Áed competed for the crown, and many of those who won it came to a violent end as members of the other branch of the family attempted to wrest it from them.

**Constantine III** (995–97) was the last king from Áed's line, and direct male descent from Constantine I ended with the death of **Malcolm II** (1005–34), who left no heirs. Malcolm was succeeded by the first king from the **House of Dunkeld—Duncan I** (1034–40), the son of **Bethóc** (Malcolm's eldest daughter) and **Crinan**, the abbot of Dunkeld. Through Bethóc, modern British monarchs can trace their ancestry to the earliest Scottish rulers. The rulers from the House of Alpin, in addition to those mentioned above, were **Colin** (966–71), **Constantine II** (900–43), **Duff** (962–66), possibly **Eochaid** (879–89), **Indulf** (954–62), **Kenneth II** (971–95), **Kenneth III** (997–1005), and **Malcolm I** (943–54). Kenneth MacAlpin's brother ruled as **Donald I** from 859 to 862, and his nephew, **Giric**, may have ruled with Eochaid from 879 to 889, but neither is normally considered a member of the house of Alpin.

**AMELIA, PRINCESS (1711–1786).** The second daughter (and third child) of King **George II** and **Caroline of Brandenburg-Ansbach**, Amelia (often called Emily) was born in Hanover at the Palace of Herrenhausen on 30 May 1711 and moved to **London** with her parents in 1714. Although **Sophia Dorothea, queen of Prussia** and the only daughter of King **George I**, plotted a marriage between Amelia and Sophia's son, Prince Frederick (later known as Frederick the Great), the scheme foundered on the rocks of European politics, and the **princess** remained unmarried throughout her life, though some writers have suggested that she may have been the mother of composer Samuel Arnold as a result of a liaison with a commoner named Thomas Arnold.

Contemporary writers describe Amelia as clever but opinionated and arrogant. She also developed a strong sense of ownership. In 1751, she caused outrage when she attempted to prevent all but a few of her friends from entering Richmond Park near London. In 1758, following a series of court cases, she had to concede access to the public. She died of erysipelas (a skin infection) at her Cavendish Square home in London on 31 October 1786 and was buried in **Westminster Abbey**. In the United States, Amelia County in Virginia and Amelia Island in Florida are named after her. *See also* KEW PALACE; WHITE LODGE.

**AMELIA, PRINCESS (1783–1810).** Amelia, the 15th and last child of King **George III** and **Charlotte of Mecklenburg-Strelitz**, was born at the **Royal Lodge** on the **Windsor Castle** estate on 7 August 1783. Perhaps because she was the youngest in a large family, perhaps because her birth came soon after the deaths of two of her brothers, **Prince Alfred** and **Prince Octavius**, she was her father's favorite. Never a robust girl, Amelia developed tuberculosis at the age of 15 and was sent to Weymouth, on the southern coast of England, in the hope that the sea air would improve her health. However, her condition continued to decline, and in 1810 she contracted erysipelas, a skin infection that also afflicted her brother, **Prince Augustus Frederick, duke of Sussex**, and her namesake, **Princess Amelia (1711–1786)**, the third child of King **George II**.

At Weymouth, the **princess** developed an attachment to Charles FitzRoy, the son of Charles, baron of Southampton. George's daughters, raised in an environment that restricted contact with males outside of the immediate family, often fell in love with the king's equerries (*see* AUGUSTA

SOPHIA, PRINCESS; SOPHIA, PRINCESS), and Amelia certainly hoped she would be able to marry, even though FitzRoy was not of royal blood and was more than 20 years her senior. However, despite the attentive nursing of her sister, **Princess Mary, duchess of Gloucester and Edinburgh**, she became increasingly immobile. By 25 October 1810, she was bedridden, and on 2 November she died at Augusta Lodge, Windsor. She was buried in **St. George's Chapel** at Windsor Castle. Amelia's death had a profound impact on the king, so much so that, according to some writers, it caused the onset of his last lengthy bout of insanity the following year.

**AMLAÍB (?–977).** Little is known of Amlaíb, who is named Olaf in some sources and may have overthrown **Kenneth II** and then ruled as king of **Alba** for a short period c977. Like his father (**Indulf**) and his brother (**Colin**), he met a premature end; according to the 12th–14th-century *Annals of Tigernach*, Kenneth was able to kill him and retrieve the crown.

**ANDREW, PRINCE, DUKE OF YORK (1960– ).** Andrew—the second son, and third child, of Queen **Elizabeth II** and **Prince Philip, duke of Edinburgh**—was born at **Buckingham Palace** on 19 February 1960, the first child born to a reigning monarch since Queen **Victoria** gave birth to **Princess Beatrice of Battenberg** in 1857. He was educated at Heatherdown Preparatory School in Ascot before following in the footsteps of his father and his brother, **Charles, prince of Wales**, to Gordonstoun School in Scotland. Then, after a period at Lakefield College in Ontario, Canada, he entered the Royal Naval College Dartmouth. The **prince** gained his helicopter pilot's wings in 1981 and flew missions from the aircraft carrier *Invincible* during the Falklands War between the United Kingdom and Argentina in 1982.

While he was in his late teens and early twenties, the prince earned a reputation as a playboy with a string of girlfriends (notably Koo Stark, who had been an actress in erotic movies), but on 23 July 1986, he married Sarah Ferguson (*see* SARAH, DUCHESS OF YORK) in **Westminster Abbey**, London. The couple had two daughters—**Princess Beatrice of York** (born on 8 August 1988) and **Princess Eugenie of York** (born on 23 March 1990)—but by the time of Eugenie's birth, the press was reporting rumors that the marriage was in trouble, and on 20 and 21 August 1992, the *Daily Mirror* newspaper published photographs, taken clandestinely, that showed the duchess enjoying herself in the company of John Bryan, her American financial advisor. On 19 March the following year, the Yorks announced that they were separating, and on 30 May 1996 they divorced.

Despite the problems, the couple remained close (the year after the divorce, Sarah and her children moved back into the family home at **Sunninghill**

**Park**), and stories of an impending remarriage surfaced regularly but never had a fairy-tale ending. Andrew, widely considered the wronged party in the marital dispute, continued his active Royal Navy career until 1997 when he took a desk job at the Ministry of Defence. In 2001, to the astonishment of the press, he was made a roving ambassador for British Trade International, a government body that promotes exports and investment in the United Kingdom by foreign interests. The surprise resulted from the prince's apparent return to a playboy lifestyle (earlier in the year, for example, he had incurred his mother's wrath after being photographed surrounded by topless women while sunbathing on a boat off the coast of Thailand). However, since then, he has visited many parts of the world on tours designed to showcase British goods and services. He has also served as honorary colonel-in-chief of army regiments in the United Kingdom and Canada and is patron or supporter of over 100 charitable organizations, including the British Deaf Association, the City Ballet of **London**, and the National Maritime Museum. A fair, and enthusiastic, golfer, he plays off a handicap of six. *See also* DUKE OF YORK; ROYAL LODGE.

**ANGEVIN DYNASTY.** *See* ANJOU, HOUSE OF.

*ANGLO-SAXON CHRONICLE.* The *Chronicle* is the principal—and in some cases the only—source of information on **Anglo-Saxon monarchs**. The original version, a year-by-year account of events from 60 BC, was probably written in **Wessex** during the reign of **Alfred the Great** (871–c899) and then copied and distributed to monasteries across England. The monks at the various sites updated their copies individually, so several versions survive, one (from Peterborough) dating from as late as 1155. Historians use the *Chronicle* with caution, questioning some of the dates, noting contradictions, identifying transcription errors, and suggesting that individual scribes built their biases into the text. Genealogies, for example, are suspect because, for political reasons, recorders attempted to show that all of Wessex's rulers were related to **Cerdic**, who arrived in the British Isles in c495 and founded the royal house. On the other hand, most scholars believe that the annals provide an important chronology for the period, particularly for the late 10th and early 11th centuries and for the century following the **coronation** of **Edward the Confessor** in 1042.

**ANGLO-SAXON MONARCHS.** From the middle of the 5th century, groups of Germanic people from mainland Europe colonized much of the British Isles, and by the end of the 6th century they were collectively known as Anglo-Saxons. With agricultural rather than urban economies and with no system of hereditary rule, they elected leaders at regional assemblies and fought with each other for dominance. The kings' primary role was to protect their people, so many of them died in battle. As a result, kingdoms were unstable, their continued existence depending on a new ruler's ability to stave off the attacks of rival claimants to their lands. It was not until the 9th century that **Aethelstan**, from the royal house of **Wessex**, united an area approximating to present-day England under one monarch, but even then control was never secure. A true sense of unity did not develop until the reign of King **Edgar of England**, from 959 to 975, which brought the establishment of a common currency and the introduction of a system of local government that survived the Norman conquest in 1066 (*see* NORMANDY, HOUSE OF).

The Anglo-Saxon king's power was absolute, but he was advised by a group of senior civil and ecclesiastical officials, known as the **witan** or witenagemot, who met irregularly at the request of the monarch and whose most crucial task was to select a successor when the king died. Decisions were based partly on a candidate's place in a royal line but also on his military prowess, so men were preferred over boys, and a deceased king's brother, rather than his young son, would frequently be favored. However, the witan's decision was not necessarily the end of the story, because in societies where a community's survival depended on armed might, the lack of clear rules for determining succession meant that there were frequent squabbles between the supporters of opposing claimants, the most notable occurring after the death of **Edward the Confessor** in 1066, when William of Normandy took umbrage at the choice of **Harold II** as successor, raised an army, defeated the Anglo-Saxons at the **Battle of Hastings**, and claimed the English crown for himself, ruling as **William I of England**.

This dictionary includes entries on Aethelstan, his successors as king of England, and other Anglo-Saxon leaders who made a contribution to the emerging monarchy. *See* AELFRED AETHELING; AELFWEARD; AETHELRED THE UNREADY; AETHELWULF; ALFRED THE GREAT; CEAWLIN; CEOL; CEOLWALD; CERDIC; COENRED; CUTHWINE; CUTHWULF; CYNRIC; DANEGELD; EADRED; EADWIG; EAFA; EALHMUND; EDGAR AETHELING; EDMUND I; EDMUND II; EDWARD THE ELDER; EDWARD THE EXILE; EDWARD THE MARTYR; EGBERT; EOPPA; HAROLD I; HAROLD II; INGILD; ROYAL PECULIAR; WINCHESTER.

**ANJOU, HOUSE OF.** The Angevin monarchs followed those of the **House of Normandy** to the English throne. In 1127, King **Henry I** had required his nobles to swear an oath that they would accept his daughter, **Matilda**, as their queen if he left no heir. The following year, Matilda married **Geoffrey, count**

**of Anjou**, but when Henry died in 1135, still without a son, the barons turned their backs on their promise and installed his nephew, **Stephen**, as their sovereign. Rather than accept the situation meekly, Matilda invaded England in 1139 and plunged the country into a civil war that continued until 1153, when Stephen—tired of conflict and depressed by the loss of his wife (**Matilda of Boulogne**) and his heir (**Eustace, count of Boulogne**)—agreed that Henry of Anjou, the eldest son of Geoffrey and Matilda, should succeed him. Henry did not have to wait long because Stephen died on 25 October the following year, and Henry was crowned **Henry II** on 19 December.

Many historians refer to those representatives of the House of Anjou who occupied the English throne as the "Angevin dynasty," but use of the phrase can be confusing. Some writers apply the term only to Henry (who ruled from 1154 until 1189) and his sons, **Richard I** (1189–99) and **John** (1199–1216), because the estates in Anjou were lost during John's reign. Others apply it to the monarchs who ruled from 1154 until 1399, when Henry Bolingbroke deposed **Richard II** and claimed the throne (as King **Henry IV**) for the **House of Lancaster**, and a third group use the term with reference to all 14 of the **House of Plantagenet** monarchs, from Henry II to **Richard III** (who reigned from 1483 to 1485), on the grounds that all were Henry II's direct descendants through the male line.

Anjou lies in the valley of the River Loire in **France**. Under the feudal system of land tenure, the English monarchs who ruled the area were vassals of the French kings, so, in 1202, Philip II of France summoned England's King John to answer a charge that he had abducted and married **Isabella of Angoulême** even though she was betrothed to Hugh of Lusignan, who also owed allegiance to the French sovereign. John's refusal to attend prompted Philip to confiscate Anjou and other English-held lands in 1204, and efforts to retrieve them were terminated by defeat at the Battle of Bouvines in 1214. King **Henry III** formally relinquished English control through the treaty of Paris in 1259, and although efforts were made to recapture the territory during the **Hundred Years' War**, King **Edward III** ceded all authority to the French monarchy when he approved the treaties of Brétigny and **Calais** in 1360. *See also* AQUITAINE; EDMUND, EARL OF LANCASTER; FONTEVRAULT ABBEY; GEOFFREY, COUNT OF NANTES; HENRY V; HENRY, THE YOUNG KING; MARGARET OF ANJOU.

**ANNE (1665–1714).** Queen Anne reigned during a critical period of British history, with the **union of the English and Scottish parliaments** in 1707 making her the first monarch to rule Great Britain. She was born at **St. James's Palace** on 6 February 1665, the second daughter of James, **duke of York** (later King **James VII and II**), and his first wife, **Anne Hyde**. On 28

July 1683 at St. James's, she married **George, prince of Denmark** (a brother of King Christian V of Denmark and her first cousin once removed). Then, in 1689, the English parliamentarians' **Bill of Rights** stipulated that she would follow **William III of England and II of Scotland** and **Mary II** as sovereign if none of Mary's children survived. At the time, Mary was childless (though she had miscarried twice), and she never conceived during the remaining five years of her life. So, in 1702, when William died, Anne succeeded as queen of England and of Scotland.

Historians have often regarded Anne as a weak monarch, diverted from administrative duties by illness and allowing her judgment to be more influenced by people than by principle, so that over her 12-year reign, parliament gradually gained power at the expense of the crown. Also, 13 miscarriages or stillbirths and the early deaths of the five children who survived birth raised doubts about the **succession to the throne**, and strained political nerves were further tautened by an expensive war against European rivals that lasted for almost the entire period Anne was on the throne.

On the other hand, even though Anne was a female head of state in difficult political times, she attempted to impose her belief in moderation by including both of the main parliamentary factions—the Tories and the Whigs—in her governments, and she made no effort to resurrect her father's contentious argument that kings had a **divine right** to rule as absolute monarchs. Also, Britain's empire expanded during her reign (notably in North America), science and literature flourished (though she was little interested in either), and her armies gained several important victories (particularly that at Blenheim in 1704, when troops led by John Churchill, duke of Marlborough, defeated the forces of **France** and Bavaria, heightening her realm's international influence).

Anne, the last monarch from the **House of Stuart**, died at **Kensington Palace** on 1 August 1714, her body so swollen that she had to be placed in a coffin that was almost square before being buried beside her husband (who had predeceased her in 1708) at **Westminster Abbey**. The settlements of Annapolis and **Princess** Anne, both in Maryland, are named after her, as are Queen Anne's County (also in Maryland) and Princess Anne County in Virginia. Anne was succeeded by King **George I**, the first British monarch from the **House of Hanover**. *See also* OLDENBURG, ANNE SOPHIA; OLDENBURG, GEORGE; OLDENBURG, MARY (1685–1687); OLDENBURG, MARY (1690); ROYAL ASCOT; ROYAL ASSENT; SECURITY, ACT OF; SETTLEMENT, ACT OF; WILLIAM, DUKE OF GLOUCESTER.

**ANNE, COUNTESS OF SURREY (1475–1511).** Anne, born in the **Palace of Westminster** on 2 November 1475, was the seventh of 10 children in the family of **Edward IV** and **Elizabeth Woodville**. In 1479, her father arranged for her to marry Philip, son of Maximilian I, archduke of Austria, in a deal designed to bolster English political alliances; Maximilian was the son of Frederick III of Habsburg, the Holy Roman Emperor, and of Mary, duchess of Burgundy, who owned extensive estates in **France** and had considerable influence in European royal courts. However, Edward's death in 1483 made the match much less desirable to the archduke, so on 4 February in either 1494 or 1495, Anne was wed to Thomas Howard, earl of Surrey, at the **Palace of Placentia**.

The match produced one son who survived infancy (Thomas, born c1496), but the union was an unhappy one. Young Thomas died in 1508, and there are indications that two other boys failed to survive infancy, one child was stillborn, the couple was straitened financially, the earl turned to Bess Holland (his wife's maid) for sexual comforts, and the countess suffered from ill health. Anne died c23 November 1511 and was buried at Thetford Priory, a 12th-century Cluniac foundation in Norfolk, but her remains were later removed to the Church of St. Michael at Framlingham, one of the Howard family's principal estates, which was once owned by **Thomas of Brotherton**, son of King **Edward I** and **Marguerite of France**. Thomas Howard remarried, distinguished himself as a military commander, and became a leading politician during the reign of King **Henry VIII**, but he quarreled with the monarch over the execution of **Catherine Howard** (Thomas's niece and Henry's fifth wife). He was condemned to death for treason, but Henry died the day before the execution was due to be carried out, and the sentence was commuted to life imprisonment. Released in 1553 by Queen **Mary I**, who needed his support for her efforts to reestablish the Roman Catholic faith in England, he played a large part in suppressing **Wyatt's Rebellion** the following year, but he died shortly afterward.

**ANNE OF BOHEMIA (1366–1394).** Anne—daughter of Charles IV, king of Bohemia and Holy Roman Emperor, and his fourth wife, Elizabeth of Prague (also known as Elizabeth of Pomerania)—was the first **queen consort** of King **Richard II**. The wedding, held in **Westminster Abbey** on 20 January 1382, was shaped by politics. At the time, there were competing claimants for the papacy. The French, whom the English were opposing in the **Hundred Years' War**, supported Clement VII, but the Bohemians favored Urban VI, so the marriage cemented an alliance against a common enemy. On the other hand, the union was not popular with Richard's advisors because Anne's family was poor and unable to provide a rich dowry, so she brought no financial benefit to the realm.

Chroniclers writing during the period are often critical of the bride (one refers to her as "a tiny scrap of humanity"), but she earned the soubriquet

"Good Queen Anne" from her subjects because of her gentleness, her patronage of religious foundations, and her willingness to intercede on behalf of men condemned to death. The relationship did not yield any children, but Richard seems to have been genuinely fond of his wife (an emotion not always apparent in the arranged marriages common among European nobility in medieval times) and was greatly upset when she succumbed to bubonic plague at **Sheen Palace** on 7 June 1394. Anne's remains were interred in Westminster Abbey, but when her tomb was opened in 1871, many of her bones were missing, having been removed by souvenir hunters over the centuries. *See also* EDMUND OF LANGLEY, DUKE OF YORK.

**ANNE OF CLEVES (1515–1557).** The fourth wife of King **Henry VIII**, Anne was born at Düsseldorf on 22 September 1515, the second daughter of John, duke of Cleves, and his wife, Mary. Her brief union with the English king was a purely political affair. Henry was afraid that the Roman Catholic powers in Europe would combine against him and was advised by Thomas Cromwell, his chief counselor, that an alliance with German Protestants could stave off the attack. The marriage to Anne at the **Palace of Placentia** on 6 January 1540 was negotiated as part of that alliance, but it soon became clear that neither **France** nor the Holy Roman Empire had any intention of invading England. Henry, finding his bride unattractive (he complained that her breasts drooped), unsophisticated (her exposure to music and literature had been very limited), and with a poor command of English, quickly decided that the union should be terminated. Anne was banished from the royal court on 24 June, and on 9 July the marriage was annulled, partly on the grounds that it had not been consummated, and partly because Anne had previously been betrothed, as a child, to Francis, heir to Antoine, duke of Lorraine. The former queen remained in England, became good friends with the king, and lived in comfort at Bletchingley Place in Surrey and at **Sheen Palace**. She died at Chelsea Old Palace in **London** on 16 July 1557 and was buried in **Westminster Abbey**, never having remarried.

**ANNE OF DENMARK (1574–1619).** Until comparatively recently, historians have treated Anne—the **queen consort** of King **James VI and I**—with ill-disguised contempt, describing her as a woman of few intellectual gifts and little political influence who enjoyed extravagant displays of wealth that drained her husband's coffers. More recently, however, scholars have been less critical, emphasizing her importance as a patron of the arts and suggesting that she had greater diplomatic skill than earlier commentators have suggested.

Anne was born on 12 December 1574 at Skanderborg to King Frederick II of Denmark and his wife, Sophia of Mecklenburg. She married James by proxy on 20 August 1589 and then sailed for Scotland, but her ship was forced by storms and a series of accidents to take shelter in Oslo. The Scots king, hearing of his bride's troubles, journeyed to Norway to collect her and accompanied her to **Edinburgh** in what David Harris Wilson, a 20th-century biographer, has described as "the one romantic episode of [the monarch's] life." She gave birth to the first of her seven children—**Henry Frederick Stuart**, duke of Rothesay and later **prince of Wales**—on 19 February 1594, but the event, even though much welcomed because it provided Scotland with a male successor to the crown, exacerbated the friction that by then character-ized the royal relationship. James insisted that his son should be placed in the care of John Francis, earl of Mar, whose family were the traditional wards of the heirs to the Scottish throne, but the queen wanted the child looked after in her own household and was so distressed at James's persistent refusal to let her see the boy that she suffered miscarriages in 1595 and again in 1603. Ul-timately, however, she prevailed. When the king moved his court to England (*see* UNION OF THE CROWNS), she refused to go with him unless she was given custody of Henry, and James conceded defeat.

Anne's unhappiness was deepened by the antagonism of hard-line Scottish Protestant reformers, who condemned much of her behavior as frivolous, but in **London** she was more free to indulge herself, staging dances, masques (in which she often performed herself), and plays, and patronizing architects, artists, and musicians. Nevertheless, she and her husband grew further and further apart, arguing over religion, over James's choice of advisors, and over the selection of her ladies-in-waiting. Henry Frederick's death in 1612 made matters worse, but, even so, and despite failing health, she continued to perform her public duties without making any undiplomatic criticism of the monarch. She died of edema (or dropsy) at **Hampton Court Palace** on 2 March 1619 and was buried in **Westminster Abbey**. James, also ill, was un-able to attend her funeral. *See also* CHARLES I; DUNFERMLINE ABBEY; ELIZABETH OF BOHEMIA; QUEEN'S HOUSE, GREENWICH; SOM-ERSET HOUSE; STUART, MARGARET; STUART, MARY (1605–1607); STUART, ROBERT, DUKE OF KINTYRE; STUART, SOPHIA.

**ANNE, PRINCESS ROYAL (1709–1759).** Anne, the eldest daughter of King **George II** and **Caroline of Brandenburg-Ansbach**, played a signifi-cant role in Dutch politics while she acted as regent for her young son from 1751 to 1759. Born at the Leine Palace in Hanover on 2 November 1709, she was named after Queen **Anne** (who, distancing herself from the Hanoveri-ans destined to be her successors as a result of the 1701 **Act of Settlement**, showed little interest in the child) and moved to **London** with her parents in 1714. Her marriage to William, prince of Orange, at **St. James's Palace** on

14 March 1734 was an entirely political arrangement, designed to strengthen an alliance with a Dutch dynasty that was supportive of Britain rather than **France**.

After her husband's death in 1751, Anne was appointed governor of the United Provinces of the Netherlands because their son, also William, was only three years old and unable to rule in his own right. She pursued a course of neutrality in foreign policy, annoying the British because she was unable to engineer military help from the Dutch, and annoying the Dutch because she failed to prevent the British navy from boarding Dutch ships that were suspected of trading with France. She died of edema (then known as dropsy) at the Binnenhof (the focus of the Dutch court and government) in The Hague on 12 January 1759 and was buried beside her husband in the Nieuwe Kerk (the Orange family burial place) at Delft.

**ANNE, PRINCESS ROYAL (1950– ).** Anne is the second child, and only daughter, of Queen **Elizabeth II** and **Prince Philip, duke of Edinburgh**. Born in **Clarence House**, London, on 15 August 1950, she was educated at Benenden School in Kent and accompanied her parents on several public engagements before undertaking duties on her own. An accomplished horse-woman, the **princess** was a member of the British equestrian team in the early 1970s, winning the European Three Day Event in 1971, earning silver medals in individual and team events at the same competition in 1975, and taking part in the Montreal Olympic Games the following year. **Mark Phillips**, her first husband, was a fellow competitor in many of the events. They married on 14 November 1973 and had two children—**Peter Phillips** (born on 15 November 1977) and **Zara Phillips** (born on 15 May 1981)—but the press carried increasingly frequent stories of discord in the relationship during the 1980s, and in 1989 the couple separated. Divorce followed in 1992; then, on 12 December the same year at **Crathie Church** near **Balmoral Castle**, Anne married her second husband, Commander **Timothy Laurence**, a naval officer and former royal equerry.

As a young woman, the princess earned an unenviable reputation for having a short temper and for her brusqueness in dealing with the media, but she gained much respect for her calmness during an abortive attempt to kidnap her while she drove through **London** with her husband in 1974 (when the kidnapper told her to get out of her car, she told him, "Not bloody likely"), and more recently, she has been considered one of the most hardworking members of the **royal family**. President or patron of over 200 charitable organizations, she carries out some 500 engagements every year and is par-ticularly active on behalf of the Save the Children Fund. In 2002, the public engagement that attracted the most attention was her appearance in court when she was charged with allowing one of her dogs to attack two boys in Windsor Great Park. She was fined £500 and ordered to train the dog better, but, the following year, one of the Queen's corgis had to be destroyed after another of Anne's pets savaged it. *See also* GATCOMBE PARK; PRINCESS ROYAL; ST. JAMES'S PALACE.

**AQUITAINE.** Aquitaine, now a region of southwestern **France**, came under the control of the English royal house in 1152, when **Eleanor of Aquitaine** (who had inherited the estates on the death of her father, Duke William X, in 1137) married Henry of Anjou (later King **Henry II**). At the time, the province was the most wealthy in France, but over the next 400 years its extent varied as territorial fortunes waxed and waned, sometimes amounting to a relatively small strip of land stretching from the Pyrenees to the mouth of the Garonne River, and sometimes expanding to include Gascony, Limousin, Poitou, and Saintonge.

Eleanor maintained a court at Poitiers, one of the principal settlements in the area, especially in the years immediately after her estrangement from Henry in 1167, and her son, **Richard I**, spent more of his life there than in his English kingdom. Under the feudal system of landholding, however, the English crown ruled all of its possessions on the European mainland as vassals of the French king, and in 1337, at a time when tensions between the two countries were high, Philip VI of France attempted to regain control of the area, an action that precipitated the **Hundred Years' War**. The treaties of Brétigny and **Calais** in 1360 made **Edward III** of England absolute sovereign of Aquitaine, but Charles V of France repudiated those pacts nine years later, and by the beginning of the 15th century, English dominance was confined to little more than a strip of land along the coast from Bayonne to Bordeaux. In 1453, that territory also was lost as English interests focused increasingly on domestic concerns. *See also* EDWARD, THE BLACK PRINCE; HENRY V; NORMANDY, HOUSE OF.

**ARMSTRONG-JONES, ANTONY, EARL OF SNOWDON (1930– ).** Although he is best known as the former husband of **Princess Margaret, countess of Snowdon** and sister of Queen **Elizabeth II**, Armstrong-Jones has also earned a considerable reputation as a society photographer specializing in informal portraiture. Born in **London** on 7 March 1930, the only son of barrister Ronald Armstrong-Jones and his wife Anne, Snowdon was educated at Eton College and at Cambridge University, where he studied architecture and in 1950 coxed the winning crew in the annual boat race against Oxford University. As his photography career flourished, he began to take pictures of royal subjects (including, in 1957, Queen Elizabeth II and **Prince Philip,**

duke of Edinburgh), and while working in those circles, he met **Princess Margaret**, who was attracted both by his extroverted personality and by his circle of friends in the arts world. They married at **Westminster Abbey** on 6 May 1960; at the time, Armstrong-Jones declined a title, but the following year, as advisors expressed concern about the daughter of a monarch having children who bore no title, he was created earl of Snowdon, the name carrying associations with the **Welsh princes** who fought against English domination in the 12th and 13th centuries and recognizing his own Welsh ancestry.

The couple had two children—**David Armstrong-Jones, viscount Linley**, born on 3 November 1961, and Lady Sarah Armstrong-Jones (*see* CHATTO, LADY SARAH), born on 1 May 1964—but even in its early years, the marriage was under strain and soon began to fall apart, partly because Snowdon spent much time on his work, neglecting the princess, and partly because he was a serial philanderer. Increasingly, Armstrong-Jones and Margaret went their separate ways, and eventually, in 1978, the union was dissolved by the divorce courts. On 15 December that year, Snowdon married Lucy, the daughter of film director Michael Lindsay-Hogg. They had one daughter—Frances, born on 17 July 1979—but divorced in 2000 after Armstrong-Jones fathered a son (Jasper, born on 30 April 1998) by Melanie Cable-Alexander, an editor with *Country Life* magazine. Some sources suggest that he is also the father of a daughter, Polly, who was born to Camilla Fry on 28 May 1960, just three weeks after he married Princess Margaret.

Snowdon codesigned the aviary at London Zoo and has published a lengthy list of books containing his photographs. In 2001, a major exhibition of his studies was held at the National Portrait Gallery, London, and at the Yale Center for British Art. He suffered from polio as a child (neither his father nor his mother visited him during his six months' hospitalization) and has been a strong supporter of charities for physically disabled people, who have been the subjects of many of his photographs. In 2006, when Viscount Linley and Lady Chatto auctioned some of their mother's jewelry and other possessions, ostensibly to meet inheritance taxes, the earl was unhappy that certain items were being included in the sale and wrote to Christie's, the auction house (of which his son was a director), questioning his children's right to dispose of the property.

**ARMSTRONG-JONES, DAVID, VISCOUNT LINLEY (1961– ).** Viscount Linley, the elder child of **Princess Margaret, countess of Snowdon**, and **Antony Armstrong-Jones, earl of Snowdon**, was born at **Clarence House**, London, on 3 November 1961 and educated at Bedales School, Petersfield, which has a particular reputation for teaching arts subjects and where he was able to develop an interest in working with wood. From 1982, after two years at the Parnham House School for Craftsmen in Dorset, he has built up a business crafting bespoke furniture using neoclassical designs and inlaid wood. The high-quality workmanship is targeted at wealthy clients (such as television hostess Oprah Winfrey, for whom he made a desk).

Linley joined the board of Christie's auction house in 2005 and was appointed chairman of the United Kingdom branch of the company the following year. On 8 October 1993, he married Serena Stanhope, whom he met when her father, Charles Stanhope, viscount Petersham, commissioned furnishings from him. They have a son (Charles, born on 1 July 1999) and a daughter (Margarita, born on 14 May 2002). In 2006, Armstrong-Jones and his sister, **Lady Sarah Chatto**, upset Lord Snowdon by selling some of their mother's jewelry and other possessions through Christie's because, they said, the money was needed in order to meet death duties. Two years later, foreign media alleged that two men had demanded £50,000 from him in return for video footage showing him having sex and snorting cocaine with a male member of the **Royal Household**.

**ARTHUR, PRINCE, DUKE OF CONNAUGHT AND STRATHEARN (1850–1942).** Arthur, the seventh—and longest-lived—child of Queen **Victoria** and **Prince Albert of Saxe-Coburg and Gotha**, was born at **Buckingham Palace** on 1 May 1850. As his father, who died in 1861, had wished, he opted for a military career, graduating as a lieutenant from the Royal Military College, Woolwich, in 1868 and serving in Canada, Egypt, India, Ireland, and South Africa as he worked his way up the ranks. The promotions undoubtedly owed much to Arthur's royal birth, but they were not entirely unearned because in 1882 he led a brigade with distinction in Egypt, becoming the last British **prince** to command troops in action. In 1904 he was given the task of ensuring that proposed reforms of army administration were properly implemented, but his critical reports annoyed politicians as well as senior officers, who moved him to a post as commander-in-chief in the Mediterranean, based at Malta, where he felt that he was doing little of value and so resigned.

The resignation brought a premature end to life with the army, but soon afterward Connaught was offered a new direction. On 13 October 1911, he was sworn in as **governor-general** of Canada, a position occupied some 30 years earlier by his brother-in-law, John Campbell, husband of **Princess Louise, duchess of Argyll**. In that capacity, he traveled much of northern North America, performing ceremonial duties across the dominion, and though when World War I broke out in 1914 he quarreled with Samuel Hughes, the Canadian minister of militia, over munitions, he worked hard to improve standards of military training so that troops would be ready for combat. After returning to Britain in 1916, he carried out numerous public engagements at home and abroad (including opening India's new legislative assembly in 1921), he served as ceremonial head of several army regiments, and he gave his support to the Boy Scouts Association and other charities, but from 1928, at the age of 78, he handed over most of these duties to others. The prince died at **Bagshot Park**, his country home near **London**, on 16 January 1942 and was buried at **Frogmore**.

On 13 March 1879, Arthur married Princess Louise Margaret, daughter of Prince Frederick Charles of Prussia, at **St. George's Chapel** in **Windsor Castle**. They had three children. The eldest, **Princess** Margaret (born in 1882) wed Prince Gustaf Adolf of Sweden and became the grandmother of King Carl XVI Gustaf of Sweden, Queen Anne-Marie of Greece, and Queen Margarethe II of Denmark. Prince Arthur (born in 1883) married Alexandra, the elder daughter of **Louise, princess royal, duchess of Fife**, and became governor-general of South Africa, and Princess Patricia (born in 1886) eschewed matches with foreign royals to marry a British commoner, Commander Alexander Ramsay, an aide-de-camp to her father, who at the outbreak of World War II was head of Britain's Naval Air Services. *See also* FORT BELVEDERE.

**ARTHUR, PRINCE OF WALES (1486–1502).** Arthur was the eldest son of King **Henry VII** and **Elizabeth of York** but did not live long enough to inherit his father's throne. He was born at St. Swithin's Priory in **Winchester**, the capital of late Anglo-Saxon England, on 19 or 20 September 1486 and— because his father, whose claim to the English throne was genealogically dubious, wanted to emphasize the family's links to past monarchs—was named after the semimythical figure who had summoned knights to a round table.

Although Henry had ousted his predecessor, King **Richard III**, as a result of victory on the battlefield, he was always more of a diplomat than a warmonger, preferring to achieve his ends by treaty rather than by military campaign. One of those treaties—that of Medina del Campo, framed in 1489—strengthened economic and political ties with Spain and included a provision that Arthur, then only two years old, would marry **Catherine of Aragon**, the youngest daughter of Ferdinand II of Aragon and Isabella I of Castile. The wedding was held in **London** on 14 November 1501 at St. Paul's Cathedral, but soon after the ceremony the young couple traveled to Ludlow, close to the Welsh border. There, the bridegroom fell ill and died on 2 April 1502, possibly of the mysterious sweating disease that struck Europe in epidemic waves between 1485 and 1551, but possibly also of diabetes, a genetic disorder, overexertion in the bedroom, plague, or tuberculosis.

Even before the **prince** was buried in the cathedral at Worcester, courtiers raised doubts about whether his marriage had ever been consummated. Although Arthur had allegedly called for water on the morning after his wedding, claiming that he was thirsty after spending the night in Spain, Catherine was later to deny that intercourse had ever occurred, then or at any other time, and in 1509 she was given dispensation by Pope Julius II to marry her brother-in-law, King **Henry VIII**. Nearly two decades later, while Henry was trying to get his own bonds to Catherine loosened, he paraded bloodstained bed sheets before his courtiers, alleging that they were evidence that Arthur and Catherine really did have sexual congress. In 2002, archaeologists used ground-penetrating radar to determine the exact location of the prince's grave in Worcester Cathedral.

**ASHINGDON, BATTLE OF.** *See* ASSANDUN, BATTLE OF.

**ASSANDUN, BATTLE OF (18 October 1016).** On 18 October 1016, an army led by **Canute** defeated King **Edmund II**'s forces at a site in southeast England. The victory led to a division of the country, with Edmund ruling the land south of the River Thames and Canute ruling the rest. A clause in the agreement provided that if either monarch died, the other would inherit his lands, so when Edmund conveniently passed away (or, according to some writers, was murdered by the invaders) on 30 November, Canute became monarch of the whole realm. The location of the battle is not known for certain, though many scholars believe it was fought close to Ashingdon, south of the River Crouch and about 35 miles east of **London**; for that reason, it is sometimes referred to as the Battle of Ashingdon. According to the ***Anglo-Saxon Chronicle***, Edmund's defeat was due in part to the treachery of Eadric Streona, one of his followers, who deserted the English host and allied with Canute. *See also* AELFGIFU OF YORK.

**ATHELSTAN (c895–939).** *See* AETHELSTAN.

**AUGUSTA OF SAXE-GOTHA, PRINCESS OF WALES (1719–1772).** Augusta—mother of King **George III**—plotted a difficult course through the maze of 18th-century royal politics and was pilloried in later life for allegedly attempting to exert undue influence over her son, but she undoubtedly prepared the boy for his monarchical responsibilities. The 13th child of Frederick, duke of Saxe-Gotha, and his wife, Magdalena Augusta, she was born in Gotha on 19 November 1719. At the age of 16, she made a very favorable impression on King **George II**, who was under pressure to find a bride for his son and heir, **Frederick, prince of Wales**, so a wedding was arranged at **St. James's Palace** on 17 April 1736.

The groom was 12 years older than the bride, who initially spoke no English, but the union was a happy one, producing nine children during the 15-year-long marriage. Augusta deferred to her husband on most matters, won praise for her efforts to mix with courtiers and citizens despite the language difficulty, and attempted to remain on speaking terms with her in-laws while Frederick feuded with his father (when the **princess** of Wales went into labor with her first child on 31 July 1737, she was at **Hampton Court Palace**, so Frederick hustled her into a coach and took her back to St. James's so that the baby would not be born in his parents' home).

When Frederick died in the early spring of 1751, George (the second child and first son) was only 12 years old. Augusta immediately set about training him for the role he would play when his grandfather, King George II, died. She shielded him from the influence of her brother-in-law, **William Augustus, duke of Cumberland**, who had been one of her husband's fiercest political opponents, and attempted to prevent him from coming in contact with young women (who might divert him from the straight and narrow moral path). Also, she employed John Stuart, earl of Bute and a former colleague of her husband, to teach the young **prince** the principles of government. However, stories of a sexual liaison between the dowager princess and the earl soon began to circulate in court as Bute's influence over George became increasingly evident and resentment of that influence mounted.

Augusta, the subject of virulent abuse as critics claimed that she was attempting to control her son, virtually retired from public life after George celebrated his 18th birthday, but she invested much time and money in improvements to the botanic garden that she had developed with Frederick at Kew. She died of throat cancer at **Carlton House** on 8 February 1772 and was buried in **Westminster Abbey**.

**AUGUSTA SOPHIA, PRINCESS (1768–1840).** King **George III** doted on his daughters, so much so that he was unwilling to see them leave home as they matured, and after his mental breakdown in 1788–89, **Charlotte of Mecklenburg-Strelitz**, his **queen consort**, refused to discuss their marriage prospects with him in case the conversation might provoke another bout of insanity. Augusta, the couple's second girl and sixth child, was born at **Buckingham Palace** on 8 November 1768. An outgoing, fun-loving young woman, she became aware, as she grew older, that her parents were rejecting the tentative approaches of prospective husbands and were limiting her contacts with eligible bachelors. With a limited circle of male associates, she developed a strong attraction to Major General Sir Brent Spencer, an Irish-born army officer who was attached to the **Royal Household** as an equerry of the king; as news of her feelings spread, rumors of a clandestine marriage circulated, but there is no evidence to support the tales.

In 1812, Augusta and her three surviving unmarried sisters wrote to Charlotte, requesting more freedom, and—although shocked at the prospect—the queen bowed to the advice of her eldest son (later King **George IV**) and permitted a less restricted regime. By that time, however, Augusta was in her early forties and unlikely to have children, so she was less of an attraction to suitors. She cared for her aging mother and took a close interest in the activities of her brothers and sisters but remained a spinster until the end of her days, dying at **Clarence House** in **London** on 22 September 1840. She was buried in **St. George's Chapel** at **Windsor Castle**.

**AUGUSTUS FREDERICK, PRINCE, DUKE OF SUSSEX (1773–1843).** By far the least conventional of the nine sons of King **George III** and **Charlotte of Mecklenburg-Strelitz**, Augustus Frederick was born at **Buckingham Palace** on 27 January 1773. Afflicted with asthma, he was unable to follow his brothers into military service, so he spent most of his teens and twenties traveling on the European mainland. On 4 April 1793 (at the Hotel Sarmiento in Rome) and again on 5 December (at the fashionable St. George's Church in Mayfair, **London**), he married 31-year-old Lady Augusta Murray, the daughter of John, earl of Dunmore. The wedding contravened the **Royal Marriages Act** of 1772 because the **prince** had failed to seek his father's approval of the union, so in 1794 the courts ruled it void, but the couple simply ignored the decision and had two children—a son, Augustus Frederick, who was born in 1794, and a daughter, Augusta Emma, who was born in 1801, the year in which the "marriage" broke up.

The prince then turned his attention to the arts and sciences, building up a 50,000-volume library and holding the posts of president of the Society of Arts from 1816 until his death, and president of the Royal Society (the world's oldest learned society for scientists) from 1836 to 1838. However, he continued to annoy his father and his conservative brothers with his vociferous support for political change, arguing for the abolition of the slave trade, for improvements in the rights of Jews and Roman Catholics, and for reform of parliament. When his brother, William, succeeded to the throne as King **William IV** in 1830, Augustus Frederick was partially rehabilitated by his family and was made chief ranger and keeper of the royal parks, but on 2 May 1831, he once again ignored the marriage legislation and wed Lady Cecilia, widow of Sir George Buggin. Because the union was not lawful, Lady Cecilia was unable to call herself Duchess of Sussex or to sit beside her husband at formal functions, though in 1840 Queen **Victoria** (who was fond of her uncle and had asked him to give her away at her wedding to **Prince Albert of Saxe-Coburg and Gotha**) created her duchess of Inverness (Augustus Frederick had become earl of Inverness in 1801).

The couple, who had no children, lived at **Kensington Palace** until the duke's death from erysipelas—a skin infection that also claimed his sister, **Princess Amelia (1783–1810)**—on 21 April 1843. Unlike most members of the **royal family**, he eschewed burial in **Westminster Abbey**, preferring a grave at Kensal Green Cemetery in northwest **London** so that his wife could be laid beside him when she passed away 30 years later. *See also* SOPHIA, PRINCESS.

# B

**BAGSHOT PARK.** Bagshot, an 88-acre estate some 11 miles south of **Windsor**, is the country home of **Edward, earl of Wessex**, the youngest child of Queen **Elizabeth II**, and his family. The first building on the site, designed by Inigo Jones, was erected for King **Charles I** in 1631–33. In the 19th century, after much remodeling, it was occupied by William, duke of Clarence (later King **William IV**), and then by **Prince** William Frederick (a nephew of **George III** and great-grandson of **George II**) and his wife, **Princess Mary, duchess of Gloucester and Edinburgh** (the 11th of George III's 15 children), but the structure was demolished in 1877–79, and a new 120-room residence was erected for Queen **Victoria**'s son, **Prince Arthur, duke of Connaught and Strathearn**.

When Arthur died in 1942, the Royal Army Chaplains' Department took over the premises, remaining there until 1996. Edward moved in the following year after the property had been extensively and expensively refurbished. The prince converted the stables into a base for his television company, Ardent Productions, but was much mocked for establishing a headquarters far from any useful media contacts. He has also been criticized by journalists who claim that the rent he is charged by his landlord, the **crown estate**, is well below the market rate, but his supporters point out that he took a dilapidated edifice of historical significance and turned it into a business enterprise and home. Opinion on the building itself is divided, with some architects condemning it as ugly while others praise the Indian influences on the interior.

**BALDWIN OF BOULOGNE (c1126–1135).** Baldwin—the son of King **Stephen** and **Matilda of Boulogne**—was born in about 1126 but failed to reach maturity, dying at the **Tower of London**, then a **royal residence**, by early December 1135. He was buried in **London** at the Priory of the Holy Trinity, Aldgate.

**BALLIOL, EDWARD (c1282–1364).** *See* EDWARD DE BALLIOL.

**BALLIOL, HOUSE OF.** The House of Balliol produced two Scottish monarchs—**John of Scotland** (who ruled from 1292 to 1296) and **Edward de Balliol** (who was crowned in 1332 but had control only over southern and eastern areas of the country). The dynasty is named after Guy de Balliol, a Norman baron who fought with William the Conqueror (**William I of England**) in 1066 and, in about 1093, received a grant of lands in Northumbria from **William II of England**. In 1233, **John de Balliol** married **Dervorguilla**, the daughter of Alan, lord of Galloway, and Margaret of Huntingdon, who was a descendant of King **David I**. The death of **Margaret, maid of Norway**, in 1290 left Scotland with no obvious successor to the kingship, so the Scots nobles asked **Edward I** of England to adjudicate the claims of 14 candidates. On grounds of primogeniture, he chose John of Scotland, son of John de Balliol and Dervorguilla, and then treated him as a client king who owed feudal allegiance to the English monarch. Unwilling to accept their lack of independence, the Scots formed a military alliance with **France**, England's bitter enemy, in 1295, and Edward responded with an invasion that forced John to abdicate. For a decade—until the **coronation** of **Robert I** (Robert the Bruce) brought a representative of the **House of Bruce** to the throne in 1306—Scotland had no monarch, and the English tried to impose their authority on the country.

In 1332, and with the support of **Edward III** of England, Edward de Balliol—John's son—attempted to take by force the crown that he regarded as his birthright. He landed with an army on the coast of Fife and won control of much of east and south Scotland at a time when **regents** were governing the country on behalf of **David II**, Robert the Bruce's eight-year-old son and successor. He was crowned king of Scots at **Scone** on 24 September but was no more popular than his father, recognizing Edward III as his feudal superior but frequently having to take refuge from his rebellious "subjects" in England. In 1338, he left the country for the last time, and in 1356 he "abdicated," giving his crown to the English sovereign, who was holding David II, Scotland's other king, captive. In return, Edward de Balliol received a pension. He died childless at Wheatley (Yorkshire) eight years later.

**BALLIOL, JOHN (?–1268).** *See* JOHN DE BALLIOL.

**BALLIOL, JOHN (c1250–c1314).** *See* JOHN OF SCOTLAND.

**BALMORAL CASTLE.** Since the mid-19th century, the **royal family** has used Balmoral, close to the River Dee in Aberdeenshire, as its summer home, spending much of August and September there every year. The 50,000-acre estate was bought by **Prince Albert of Saxe-Coburg and Gotha**, consort of Queen **Victoria**, in 1848, and the neo-Gothic, granite castle, which he designed, was constructed from 1853 to 1856, replacing a smaller 15th-century building, which was demolished. Victoria loved the place, spending much time there after Albert's death in 1861 and referring to it as "my dear paradise in the highlands." Other wealthy visitors followed, spawning a still-important tourist trade, with the area marketed as "Royal Deeside" (but with some critics using "Balmorality" as a negative descriptive term for Scotland's heather and tartan image).

When Victoria died in 1901, the property passed to her eldest son, King **Edward VII**, and since then it has been owned by each of his monarchical successors (though King **George VI** had to buy it from his elder brother, King **Edward VIII**, in order to ensure that it remained a residence for the sovereign). Most of the land around the castle is mountainous and thus unsuitable for crop growing, so it is devoted to deer forest and grouse moor, with an emphasis on wildlife conservation. The castle ballroom and gardens attract some 85,000 visitors each year, and several tens of thousands of hikers roam the surrounding hills, occasionally intruding unwittingly on royal picnics. Birkhall, in the Balmoral grounds, was used as a summer home by **Elizabeth, the queen mother**, and is now a base for **Charles, prince of Wales**, who spent part of his first honeymoon there and found that his wife, **Diana, princess of Wales**, was less fond of rural solitude than he was. *See also* CRATHIE CHURCH.

**BANNOCKBURN, BATTLE OF (24 June 1314).** The victory plotted by **Robert I** (Robert the Bruce) at Bannockburn confirmed both his status as king of Scots and—at least temporarily—his realm's freedom from the overlordship of English monarchs. Over the previous seven years, Bruce had conducted a campaign of guerilla warfare, gradually winning back Scottish castles that were under English control. The one remaining focus of resistance was **Stirling**, which had held out against his siege. King **Edward II** determined to hold on to the fortress, marching an army of some 20,000 men into Scotland in an effort to relieve his beleaguered supporters, but he had neither the tactical skill nor the guile of his father and predecessor, **Edward I**. Bruce, with a force of about one-third the size, used the marshy terrain of the Bannock Burn (or stream), which flowed a few miles south of the castle, to crowd his opponents into a relatively small area where they had difficulty maneuvering and then attacked, taking advantage of the English disorganization. Edward escaped the slaughter, fleeing to Dunbar (on Scotland's east coast) and then sailing home, but thousands of his followers—including many of the nobility—were killed. With his kingdom free from English control, Robert used the remaining years of his rule to consolidate his position and develop a governmental infrastructure, holding meetings of parliament and augmenting the royal exchequer, but he had to wait until 1328 before England's monarchs would recognize his right to govern an independent country (*see* NORTHAMPTON, TREATY OF).

There is a story, much told to Scottish schoolchildren, that on the day before the Battle of Bannockburn, Sir Henry de Bohun (an English knight) saw Bruce astride a small pony, carrying only a battleaxe and without any armor. Henry spurred his charger, intending to kill the king, and Bruce watched as the warhorse and its rider bore down on him, lance at the ready. When the Englishman was only a few feet away, Bruce moved his agile pony a few steps sideways and then cleft the helmet and head of the knight as he galloped past. Allegedly, he then expressed regret that he had broken his ax.

**BARONS' WARS.** *See* FIRST BARONS' WAR (1215–1217); SECOND BARONS' WAR (1264–1267).

**BEATRICE, DUCHESS OF BURGUNDY (1242–1275).** As the second daughter of King **Henry III** and **Eleanor of Provence**, Beatrice (also known as Beatrice of England), born on 25 June 1242, was much sought after as a bride by scions of aristocratic European families. Although alliances with the royal houses of **France** and Norway were considered, she was married on 22 January 1260 to John, son and heir of John, duke of Brittany, and Blanche of Navarre. They had four sons and three daughters, all of whom survived childhood, though Henry, the second boy, died at the age of about 20, in 1284, while campaigning with King **Edward I**—his uncle—in Wales. Beatrice predeceased all of her family, dying in **London** on 24 March 1275, possibly while giving birth to Alice (also known as Eleanor), who later became abbess at **Fontevrault**. She was buried in Greyfriars Church at Greenwich. Her husband, who never remarried, inherited the dukedom in 1286 and was killed on 18 November 1305 when a wall collapsed on him while he was leading Pope Clement V on horseback through Lyon.

**BEATRICE (OR HENRY) OF BATTENBERG, PRINCESS (1857–1944).** Beatrice was the ninth and (by four years) the youngest child of Queen **Victoria** and **Prince Albert of Saxe-Coburg and Gotha**. She was born at **Buckingham Palace** on 14 April 1857 and—partly because of the age difference between her and her siblings, and partly because **Prince Leopold, duke of Albany**, the next oldest child, suffered from ill health—spent much of her childhood without playmates, growing up to be a shy and somewhat introspective adult. As her sisters married, Beatrice became her mother's preferred companion, accepting, throughout her life, the restrictions imposed by the queen's need to have her nearby. After **Princess Louise, duchess of Argyll** and the last to find a husband, left the parental home in 1871, the **princess** became Victoria's personal assistant, diligently writing out journal entries to the queen's dictation, preparing much of the sovereign's correspondence, and communicating with government ministers.

Although at times it seemed that Beatrice would sacrifice marital happiness in order to fulfill the role of dutiful daughter, numerous possible suitors were considered, including Louis, widower of the princess's sister, **Alice, grand duchess of Hesse**, who died of diphtheria in 1878. Eventually, Beatrice herself made a choice—Prince Henry of Battenberg, whom she met at a wedding in Darmstadt, Germany, in April 1884. Victoria was not amused. For more than six months, she refused to speak to her daughter, but eventually she relented on condition that Henry resign his commission in the Prussian army and agree that he and his wife would set up home with her. The wedding ceremony was held on 23 July 1885 at St. Mildred's, Whippingham, the church where members of the **royal family** worshipped when staying at **Osborne House**, the home that Victoria and Albert had bought on the Isle of Wight off England's southern coast.

Henry managed to escape from his possessive mother-in-law several times (though there was one occasion when he slipped off to Corsica and she sent a Royal Navy warship to fetch him back), but in 1899, given reluctant monarchical permission to volunteer for service in a military campaign against the Ashanti people of West Africa, he contracted malaria and died on board the ship that was carrying him home. After his death, Beatrice continued to carry out secretarial duties for Victoria until the queen passed away in 1901; then she set about the task of editing her mother's journals, which dated from 1831 (when Victoria was 12) and numbered some hundreds of volumes. In the years following World War I, she limited her public engagements, and on 26 October 1944, at the age of 87, she died at Brantridge Park, her country home south of **London**. Initially, she was buried in **St. George's Chapel** at **Windsor Castle**, but in August 1945 her remains were reinterred, as she had wished, beside those of her husband at Whippingham.

Beatrice (who was known as Princess Henry of Battenberg after her marriage) had four children. All three of her sons fought during World War I: Alexander (born in 1886) earned a mention in dispatches; Maurice (born in 1891) was killed in action at Ypres, Belgium, in 1914; and Leopold (who was born in 1889 and inherited the hemophilia that plagued so many of Victoria's descendants) survived only to die during knee surgery in 1922. Their sister, Victoria Eugenie (born in 1887 and known as Ena), married King Alfonso III of Spain—a match that annoyed King **Edward VII** because it necessitated the princess's conversion to Roman Catholicism. Ena proved unpopular with her husband's subjects, not least because she brought hemophilia into the Spanish royal house, the eldest (Alfonso) and youngest (Gonzalo) of her four sons suffering from the illness.

**BEATRICE OF YORK, PRINCESS (1988– ).** Beatrice—the elder daughter of **Prince Andrew, duke of York**, and **Sarah, duchess of York**—spent most of her childhood outside the spotlight but received much more media attention as she reached her late teens and early twenties. Born at the Portland Hospital in **London** on 8 August 1988, she was educated at Upton House School in Windsor, Coworth Park School in Surrey (where she accidentally broke another girl's tooth as she flung her coat around her head), and St. George's School in Ascot. In 2008, after a "gap year" (part of which she spent working as a personal shopper for wealthy customers at Selfridges department store in London) and despite suffering from dyslexia, she registered at Goldsmith's College (one of the colleges of the University of London) to study for a degree in history and the history of ideas.

Given her position in the **royal family** and her parents' lifestyle and divorce, press interest in **Princess** Beatrice was inevitable, but she has accepted that it "comes with the territory." In 2006, she was much criticized for spending £500,000 on her 18th birthday party celebrations and for consorting with Paolo Luizzo, an American convicted of assault after a fight in which another man died. Then, in 2008, she was also embarrassed by photographs showing her ample bosom and chubby figure enclosed in only a skimpy bikini while she vacationed in the Caribbean. However, she learned from the experiences, dropped Luizzo, slimmed down, and celebrated her 21st birthday quietly with her mother and younger sister (**Princess Eugenie of York**). The princess has appeared with her mother at charity events and, according to observers, is soon expected to carry out similar commitments on her own. She also had a cameo role as a **lady-in-waiting** in the 2009 movie *The Young Victoria*.

**BEAUFORT, JOAN (c1404–1445).** Joan, daughter of John Beaufort, earl of Somerset, and his wife, Margaret, was consort of King **James I of Scotland** and, as a granddaughter of **John of Gaunt**, had blood links to the English **royal family**. The couple met while James was being held captive in England, but their marriage on 2 February 1424 at the Church of St. Mary Overy (now Southwark Cathedral) suited the **regents** ruling on behalf of two-year-old King **Henry VI** because James had been thoroughly anglicized during his 18 years of enforced exile, and union with an Englishwoman would be an additional factor favoring the maintenance of peace between the country where he was born and the country where he had grown up. Over the next 13 years,

Joan and her husband had twin sons (one of whom succeeded his father as King **James II**) and six daughters (five of whom married into noble families on the European mainland). On 21 February 1437, she was with him when he was murdered in Perth, and in the weeks that followed, she took a leading part in ensuring that the killers were tracked down, brutally tortured, and then executed (*see* STEWART, WALTER, EARL OF ATHOLL).

The king's death precipitated a contest for power in Scotland because his heir was only six years of age and was thus unable to rule in his own right. As Sir William Crichton and Sir Alexander Livingstone disputed control of the country, Joan took the boy to **Stirling** Castle for safety and married Sir James Stewart, the "Black Knight of Lorne," in an effort to protect both herself and her family. However, on 3 August 1439, Livingstone imprisoned Stewart, releasing him only after Joan had signed an agreement that Livingstone would have custody of the child, that her marriage dowry would pay for the boy's upkeep, and that he would live at Stirling. After that, the **queen dowager**'s political influence was limited, though she and her second husband had three sons who held influential posts (Andrew was bishop of Moray from 1482 until 1501, John was created earl of Atholl c1457, and James became earl of Buchan, high chamberlain of Scotland, and Scottish ambassador to **France**). Joan died at Dunbar Castle on 15 July 1445 and was buried beside her first husband at the Carthusian monastery he had founded in Perth. Her niece, **Margaret Beaufort**, was the mother of King **Henry VII**. *See also* STEWART, ALEXANDER, DUKE OF ROTHESAY; STEWART, ANNABELLA, COUNTESS OF HUNTLY; STEWART, ELEANOR, ARCHDUCHESS OF AUSTRIA; STEWART, ISABELLA, DUCHESS OF BRITTANY; STEWART, JOAN, COUNTESS OF MORTON; STEWART, MARGARET, DAUPHINE OF FRANCE; STEWART, MARY, COUNTESS OF GRANDPRÉ.

**BEAUFORT, MARGARET, COUNTESS OF RICHMOND (1443–1509).** Margaret, a great-granddaughter of **John of Gaunt**, was the mother of King **Henry VII**, bearing the baby when she was only 13 years old. She was born at Bletsoe Castle in Bedfordshire on 31 May 1443, the only child of Margaret Beauchamp and John Beaufort, who was created duke of Somerset by **Henry VI** just three months later and died, possibly by suicide, the following year. At the age of six, she was married to John de la Pole (the son of William, duke of Suffolk, and her senior by only a few months), but the union was dissolved by the king, who wed her to his half-brother, **Edmund Tudor, earl of Richmond** (one of about six children born to **Owen Tudor** and queen dowager **Catherine of Valois**) at Bletsoe on 1 November 1455. Edmund died a year later while being held prisoner in Carmarthen Castle by supporters of the **House of York** who wanted to oust the monarch, but he left his young wife pregnant, and Henry was born the following January. Margaret was to remarry twice—first (in about 1462) to Henry Stafford, the eldest son of Humphrey, duke of Buckingham, and then, after Stafford's death in 1471, to Thomas Stanley, earl of Derby, whose duplicity helped his stepson to victory over **Richard III** at the **Battle of Bosworth Field** in 1485. Both of the later marriages were childless.

Margaret was protective of her status after Henry claimed the throne by right of conquest, signing herself as Margaret R.; the letter *R* is an abbreviation for the Latin *Regina*, which means "Queen," and the form is normally used by **queens regnant** (that is, queens who rule in their own right) rather than by the mothers of kings. Also, although she had colluded with **Elizabeth Woodville** (later Henry's mother-in-law) to ensure the success of her son's rebellion against Richard, she made sure that the lady was banished from the court afterward so that there would be no influence over the monarch through his wife.

On the other hand, Margaret also earned a reputation for piety and for furthering education, founding Christ's College at the University of Cambridge in 1505 and leaving funds in her will both for the establishment of St. John's College (also at Cambridge) and for the building of a free school (now known as Queen Elizabeth's School) for the public at Wimborne in Dorset. Lady Margaret Hall, the first college for women at Oxford University, was named in her honor in 1878. She died in the abbot's house at **Westminster Abbey** on 29 June 1509, just two months after her son, and, like him, was buried in the building. **Joan Beaufort**, Margaret's aunt, was the consort of King **James I of Scotland**.

**BEHEADING.** In England, from the time of the Norman invasion in 1066 (*see* WILLIAM I OF ENGLAND) until the middle of the 18th century, beheading was the usual form of execution for people of royal or noble status who were found guilty of serious crimes, such as treason (an offense that could involve incurring the monarch's displeasure as well as rebelling against the sovereign or betraying state secrets). The sentence could be carried out with a sword (in which case the victim stood or knelt so that the implement could be swung properly) or with an axe (in those circumstances the condemned individual knelt and placed his or her head on a block). The Scots used a maiden (a form of guillotine), first employing it in 1561.

The only monarchs to die by these methods were **Mary, queen of Scots** (who was condemned by Queen **Elizabeth I** in 1587) and **Charles I** (who was executed in 1649 after failing to convince a court that nobody had the right to put a king on trial). Some historians, however, would add **Lady Jane**

Grey, who in 1553 was proclaimed queen but was deposed after nine days, was never crowned, and was beheaded in 1554. In addition, two of King **Henry VIII**'s **queens consort**—**Anne Boleyn** and **Catherine Howard**—were decapitated (in 1536 and 1542, respectively), and **Guildford Dudley**, Jane's husband, was executed shortly before her in 1554. Nobles who were beheaded included Edward Seymour, duke of Somerset (1552); his successor as **regent**, John Dudley, duke of Northumberland (1553); and James Douglas, earl of Morton and regent of Scotland (1581). The last to suffer was 80-year-old Simon Fraser, Lord Lovat, who was charged with supporting **Charles Edward Stuart**'s Jacobite cause and was put to death on 9 April 1747; 20 spectators died with him when a viewing area collapsed.

Decapitation was a cheap and simple form of punishment, usually bringing a quick death that was preferable to the suffering experienced by commoners accused of similar wrongdoing (women were normally burned at the stake, and men were hung from a scaffold until almost dead, were then drawn—their internal organs were cut from them and shown to them while they were still alive—and then their torso was hacked into four pieces). However, beheading was never very common so executioners lacked practice, and sometimes (as with Mary, queen of Scots) several swings of the sword or axe were required before the head was completely severed. The last forms of beheading as a form of capital punishment were abolished by parliament in 1870.

**BERENGARIA OF NAVARRE (c1164–c1230).** Berengaria, consort of **Richard I** (also known as Richard the Lionheart), was the only queen of England who never set foot in the country. Although she had a noble pedigree—she was one of six children in the family of King Sancho VI of Navarre and Sancha of Castile—she was not the first choice of bride for the young monarch. In 1169, his father, **Henry II**, had arranged his betrothal to Alys, daughter of Louis VII of **France**. However, the marriage was delayed amidst rumors that Alys had become Henry's mistress, and in 1190, shortly after assuming the throne, Richard withdrew from the arrangement, claiming that she had borne Henry's child.

The following year, while journeying to the Holy Land on crusade, Richard asked his mother, **Eleanor of Aquitaine**, to bring Berengaria to him. Some writers have suggested that he had met her some years earlier and that there was a romantic attachment, but others, alleging homosexuality, believe the attachment was to her brother, Sancho (later Sancho VII of Navarre). They met up in Sicily, where the king put Berengaria on board a boat for Palestine accompanied by his sister, **Joan, queen of Sicily**, whom he had recently released from captivity. Unfortunately, the vessel was shipwrecked off Cyprus, and Isaac Komnenos, the island's ruler, held the women captive. Richard, learning of their fate, took his army to their rescue, imprisoned Isaac, and married Berengaria in the Chapel of St. George at Limassol on 12 May 1191.

From Cyprus, the couple traveled to the Holy Land, but they returned on different ships, and Richard, blown off course, fell into the hands first of Leopold V of Austria and then of Henry VI, the Holy Roman Emperor, both of whom kept him prisoner. Berengaria joined Eleanor and others in raising money for the ransom demanded in return for his freedom, but after his release in 1194, he concentrated on military campaigns against Philip II of France rather than on domestic matters—so much so that he was ordered by Pope Celestine III to show more devotion to his wife.

On 11 April 1199, Richard succumbed to wounds received while laying siege to the castle of Chaluz in the Limousin region of **France**. Berengaria retired to Le Mans and founded a Cistercian nunnery at L'Epau, where she died, according to some sources, on 23 December 1230, having outlived Richard by more than 30 years and having struggled to get King **John**, his successor, to pay the pension to which she was entitled. The couple had no offspring. Some writers have alleged that the marriage was never consummated, some that the queen was unable to have children, some that the king was more interested in his own sex than in women, and some that Richard regarded the marriage as no more than a political arrangement, whatever Berengaria may have felt.

**BETHÓC (c984–?).** Bethóc was the eldest daughter of **Malcolm II**, ruler of **Alba** (the realm from which the kingdom of Scotland evolved). According to some writers, she married **Crinan**, the abbot of Dunkeld, in about 1000, though others report dates closer to 1010. Because she had no brothers, her elder son had a strong claim to the throne and, in 1034, succeeded his grandfather as **Duncan I**, with a number of authorities suggesting that Malcolm may have paved the way by eliminating possible competitors. Maldred, Bethóc's younger son, was killed in 1045 while attempting to avenge Duncan's murder by **Macbeth**. The date of her own death is not known.

**BETHÓC (?–?).** The daughter of King **Donald III**, Bethóc married Uchtred de Tyndale. Hextilda, their daughter, was wed to Richard Comyn, a Scottish noble, in 1145, and through the female line their grandchild, John Comyn of Badenoch, became one of several claimants to the Scottish throne after the death of **Margaret, maid of Norway**, in 1290. Details of Bethóc's birth and death, and the name of her mother, are not recorded.

**BILL OF RIGHTS (1689).** On 16 December 1689, following the **Glorious Revolution** that resulted in the flight of the Roman Catholic King **James VII**

**and II** to **France** and his replacement by the Protestant King **William III and II** and his wife, Queen **Mary II**, the new monarchs gave their assent to parliamentary legislation that curtailed their powers and laid the foundations of modern parliamentary government in the United Kingdom. The provisions prevented the sovereign from dispensing with laws passed by parliament, from imposing taxes without the consent of parliament, from interfering with elections for parliament or with elected members' right to free speech, and from maintaining a standing army without parliamentary consent. Moreover, it barred Catholics from succeeding to the throne of England because "it hath been found by experience that it is inconsistent with the safety and welfare of this Protestant kingdom to be governed by a papist prince." William and Mary were to be succeeded by Mary's children or, if she had none, by her sister, Anne (later Queen **Anne**), or her descendants. All future monarchs would be required, at their **coronation**, to promise to defend the Protestant faith. The legislation, which attempted to provide citizens with freedom from the arbitrary government that could be exercised by an absolute monarch, with established principles of free elections and with regular meetings of parliament as a law-making body, effectively paved the way for parliamentary sovereignty and is still occasionally cited in court actions. *See also* CLAIM OF RIGHT.

**BIRGITTE, DUCHESS OF GLOUCESTER (1946– ).** Birgitte, the wife of **Prince Richard, duke of Gloucester** and grandson of King **George V**, was born in Odense, Denmark, on 20 June 1946 to attorney Asger Henrikson and his wife, Vivian. She met the **prince** while she was attending finishing school in Cambridge and he was taking undergraduate classes in architecture at Cambridge University, but she went back to Denmark to complete a three-year program of commercial studies before returning to Britain in 1971 to work with the Danish Embassy. The couple married at St. Andrew's Church near the Gloucester country home at Barnwell in Northamptonshire on 8 July 1972.

Less than two months later, **Prince William of Gloucester**—Prince Richard's elder brother—was killed in a flying accident. Moreover, the young men's father—**Prince Henry, duke of Gloucester**—was in poor health, so Prince Richard had to abandon his embryonic architectural career and assume responsibility both for the management of the Barnwell estate and for the royal duties that the family was expected to undertake. Birgitte accompanied her husband to the celebrations marking the 70th birthday of King Olav V of Norway in 1973, and since then she has visited more than 20 countries on official visits, sometimes with the prince, sometimes on her own. She carries out about 150 engagements each year, many of them associated with the long list of charities (notably, educational, medical, and music organizations) that she supports. She and Prince Richard have three children—**Alexander Windsor, earl of Ulster** (born on 24 October 1974), **Lady Davina Lewis** (born on 19 November 1977), and **Lady Rose Gilman** (born on 1 March 1979).

**BIRKHALL.** *See* BALMORAL CASTLE.

**BLANCHE, DUCHESS OF LANCASTER (1345–1369).** As wife of **John of Gaunt** and mother of King **Henry IV**, Blanche (often known as Blanche of Lancaster) had a considerable impact on the direction of English history despite her short lifespan. She was born on 25 March 1345, the younger of two daughters in the family of Henry Grosmont, duke of Lancaster, and his wife, Isabella (or Isabel) de Beaumont. Lancaster died in 1361 (or, according to some sources, in 1360), leaving no heir, and his elder daughter (Matilda, or Maud) died in 1362 without any children, so Blanche inherited the vast family estates in northern England. These lands provided a power base for John of Gaunt, whom she had married at Reading Abbey on 13 May 1359, and allowed him to maintain influential positions at the court of his father, King **Edward III**, and Edward's successor, **Richard II**.

The marriage, although undoubtedly arranged for financial and political reasons (Henry Grosmont was one of King Edward's most senior advisors), was apparently a happy one, yielding three daughters and four sons. Four of the children died before reaching adulthood, but Philippa (born in 1360) became **queen consort** of Portugal by marrying King John I; Elizabeth (born in 1363 or 1364) married three times (one husband, John Holland, duke of Exeter, was a half-brother of Richard II and remained loyal to him as other support dwindled); and Henry (born in 1366 or 1367) deposed King Richard in 1399. Blanche succumbed to bubonic plague at Bolingbroke Castle, a Lancaster stronghold in Lincolnshire, on 12 September 1369 and was interred in St. Paul's Cathedral, **London**. Thirty years later, her husband, who had taken two other wives, was buried beside her, but the locations of the graves are no longer known. *See also* LANCASTER, HOUSE OF.

**BLANCHE, ELECTRESS PALATINE (1392–1409).** The first daughter, and sixth child, of King **Henry IV** and his first wife, **Mary de Bohun**, Blanche (sometimes known as Blanche Plantagenet) was born at Peterborough Castle in the spring of 1392. On 6 July 1402, she was married to Louis (or Ludwig), elector palatine and son of King Rupert of Germany, the Holy Roman Emperor, at Cologne Cathedral. The couple had a stillborn son in

1407, and then, on 22 May 1409, Blanche died at Neustadt, in Alsace, while giving birth to another boy, named Rupert.

**BLOIS, HOUSE OF.** Some writers consider that King **Stephen**, who reigned for most of the period from 1135 until 1154, was the sole representative from the House of Blois to rule England. Others consider that he was the last representative of the **House of Normandy**. The disagreement arises because he was the son of **Adela, countess of Blois** (daughter of **William I of England**), and **Stephen Henry** of Blois, so his descent from the first Norman king of the country was through the female rather than the male line. Adela's marriage to Stephen was conditioned by politics. Blois and Normandy, two of four major dynasties that ruled northern **France** in the 11th and 12th centuries, shared a common boundary, so an alliance made strategic sense and the marital union of members of the ruling families cemented the political pact.

**BLOODLESS REVOLUTION (1688–1689).** *See* GLORIOUS REVOLUTION.

**BOLEYN, ANNE (c1500–1536).** Anne was the second wife of King **Henry VIII** and the mother of Queen **Elizabeth I**. Her father was Sir Thomas Boleyn (who became one of the monarch's most trusted foreign envoys), and her mother was Elizabeth Howard (a daughter of the duke of Norfolk and a direct descendant of King **Edward I**). She was probably born in about 1500 at either Blickling Hall in Norfolk or Hever Castle in Kent, but details of her early life are uncertain, although it is known that she spent much of her childhood on the European mainland and returned to England in 1521 to become **lady-in-waiting** to **Catherine of Aragon**, the king's first wife. At some point, Henry (who had previously taken Mary, Anne's elder sister, as a mistress) fell in love with her, but she initially refused his sexual advances.

Anne's refusals fueled Henry's infatuation, adding to his determination to rid himself of Catherine, who, despite six pregnancies, had failed to produce an heir to the throne. He petitioned Pope Clement VII to annul the marriage on the grounds that Catherine had previously been married to his elder brother, **Arthur, prince of Wales**; that marriage, he claimed, had been consummated, and the law did not allow a man to wed his sister-in-law. However, Catherine denied any sexual contact with Arthur, and the pope delayed making a decision, in large part because of pressure from Charles V, the Holy Roman Emperor and Catherine's nephew. So Henry took matters into his own hands. He married Anne in secret on 25 January 1533 (without papal dispensation and while still married to Catherine) and then convened a special court that on 23 May ruled his first wedding invalid. Five days later,

Thomas Cranmer, the recently appointed archbishop of Canterbury and thus head of the English church, approved the second union.

Anne was crowned **queen consort** on 1 June, becoming only the second woman of nonroyal birth to attain the position (the first was **Elizabeth Woodville**, wife of King **Edward IV**). On 7 September, she gave birth for the first time, but the child was a girl (later Queen **Elizabeth I**) and Henry was bitterly disappointed—a disappointment that grew over the years as she failed to produce a son (though historians suggest that one boy was still-born in 1534 and another miscarried in 1536). Moreover, her arrogance, her animosity toward Catherine, and her financial extravagances were making enemies at court.

As early as 1534, Henry was exploring means of discarding Anne. On 2 May 1536 (by which time he had transferred his affections to **Jane Seymour**), he had her arrested on charges of adultery (then a treasonable offense for a queen) and incest with her brother, George. The allegations were almost certainly groundless, but even so, George and four other men were executed on 17 May. Anne was **beheaded** two days later and buried in the Chapel of St. Peter ad Vincula at Tower Hill in **London**. On 30 May, Henry took Jane as his third wife.

**BONNIE PRINCE CHARLIE.** *See* STUART, CHARLES EDWARD.

**BOSWORTH FIELD, BATTLE OF (22 August, 1485).** The battle between the armies of King **Richard III** and Henry Tudor near the village of Market Bosworth (some 12 miles west of Leicester) ended both control of the English throne by the House of Plantagenet and the **Wars of the Roses** between the rival dynasties of the **House of Lancaster** and the **House of York**. Henry took advantage of disaffection with Richard's rule to mount a rebellion that was outnumbered by the royalist force but prevailed because of dissembling and deception within the monarch's camp. Many of the details of the battle are unclear (including its precise location), but it seems certain that, at one point, the king called on Henry Percy, earl of Northumberland, to commit his supporters to the fray. Percy refused, as did Thomas Stanley, earl of Derby and Henry's stepfather. Then William, Thomas's younger brother, changed sides, attacking Richard's flank, and the king's troops began to slip away to safety. Richard himself preferred to stand his ground and became the last English king to die in battle, with even his enemies agreeing that he fought bravely. Immediately after his victory, Henry claimed the crown by right of conquest, ruling as **Henry VII** for the next 24 years.

**BOYNE, BATTLE OF THE (1 July 1690).** In 1688, King **James VII and II** was deposed from his English and Scottish thrones, primarily because of his Roman Catholic beliefs. He fled to **France**, where, with the help of King Louis XIV, he gathered an army that he hoped would enable him to win back his crowns. Landing at Kinsale in southern Ireland on 12 March 1689, he found much support among the predominantly Catholic population, but on 1 July the following year, he faced battle with a royalist army commanded by his successor, **William III and II**, on the banks of the River Boyne near Drogheda. Forced to retreat, James returned to France even though his troops had suffered few casualties. The campaign struggled on without him for another year, but the defeat at the Boyne, and James's subsequent flight, effectively ended his hopes of reclaiming his kingdoms. Several modern scholars downplay the religious element of the conflict (pointing out, for example, that James found support among Protestants who felt that his ousting was unconstitutional), but William's victory is still celebrated every year by many Protestants in Northern Ireland, with marches led by flute bands, often adding to the friction between religious communities in Belfast and other urban centers.

**BRIDGET OF YORK (1480–c1517).** Bridget, born at **Eltham Palace** on 10 November 1480, was the 10th and youngest child in the family of King **Edward IV** and **Elizabeth Woodville**. At the age of about seven, she was committed to the care of nuns at Dartford Priory, about 15 miles southeast of central **London**, where she spent the rest of her life. The cause of her death, and the exact date, are unknown.

*BRITANNIA,* **HER MAJESTY'S YACHT.** *See* ROYAL YACHT.

**BRUCE, HOUSE OF.** The Bruce family, which gave Scotland two kings—**Robert I** (Robert the Bruce) and **David II**—during the 14th century, takes its name from the Brix area of Normandy. In 1066, Robert de Brus was among the Norman nobles who accompanied William the Conqueror (later **William I of England**) on his invasion of the British Isles. His son, also named Robert, supported King **David I** as he attempted to make Scotland a single realm after the death of **Alexander I** and was rewarded with estates in the southwest of the country. In 1219, another Robert married Isobel, niece of **William I of Scotland**, in a union that allowed their son (again, Robert) to make an unsuccessful claim for the Scottish crown following the death of **Margaret, maid of Norway**, in 1290, and allowed their great-grandson to take the throne for himself in 1306, after a decade during which it had been empty following King **John of Scotland**'s enforced abdication and imprisonment in England.

Despite initial setbacks, Robert I was able to release the English stranglehold on his country, retaking the castles they held and defeating King **Edward II**'s army at the **Battle of Bannockburn** in 1314. Eventually, in 1328, England recognized Scotland's independence (*see* NORTHAMPTON, TREATY OF), but that recognition was withdrawn after only a few years, and David II, Robert's son and successor, spent much of his reign either in exile, attempting to avoid capture by the English, or under the watchful eye of English jailers. His efforts to make King **Edward III** of England, or one of Edward's sons, heir to the Scottish throne were rejected by the Scots parliament, and when he died, childless, the crown passed to his nephew, **Robert II**, the first monarch from the House of Stewart (*see* STUART, HOUSE OF). Because Robert II was the child of **Marjorie Bruce**, Robert I's daughter, the Bruce bloodline has passed into the present British **royal family** along with that of the Stewarts. The surname, too, has continued, with the earls of Elgin heading the modern Bruce family.

**BRUCE, JOHN (c1324–c1327).** John, the second son of King **Robert I** and **Elizabeth de Burgh**, failed to survive childhood. Some sources record that he was born at **Dunfermline** in March 1324 and that he lived only for some two years, others that he was born in October 1327 and was buried at Restennet Priory, an Augustinian settlement founded by King **David I** near Forfar. Had John reached maturity, he (rather than **Robert II**, the son of Bruce's daughter, **Marjorie Bruce**, by his first wife, **Isabella of Mar**) would have succeeded to the throne on the death of **David II** (John's older brother) in 1371.

**BRUCE, MARGARET, COUNTESS OF SUTHERLAND (c1317–1346).** One of two daughters born to King **Robert I** and his second wife, **Elizabeth de Burgh**, Margaret was married to William de Moravia, earl of Sutherland, in the summer of 1345. She died in 1346 or 1347 while giving birth to John, her first child, who survived only until his midteens. Soon after her death, her husband married Joan Menteith (daughter of Sir John Menteith), who gave birth to two more sons, one of whom (Robert) succeeded to the earldom.

**BRUCE, MARJORIE (c1296–1316).** The only child of Robert the Bruce (later **Robert I**) and **Isabella of Mar**, Marjorie had a short and unhappy life, but she cofounded the House of Stewart (*see* STUART, HOUSE OF) and thus is ancestress of all monarchs of Scotland, Great Britain, and the United Kingdom since 1371. When England's King **Edward I**, who claimed overlordship of Scotland, heard of Robert's **coronation** in 1306, he sent his armies north, forcing the Bruces to flee. Marjorie was captured, along with **Elizabeth de Burgh** (Bruce's second wife) and other females, and was then held prisoner for eight years in the care of nuns at Watton, a Gilbertine priory near Beverley in Yorkshire. She was released in 1314, probably in exchange for English knights taken by the Scots at the **Battle of Bannockburn**, and the following year she was married to **Walter Stewart (c1293–1326)**, one of her father's principal counselors and military commanders.

On 2 March 1316, heavily pregnant, Marjorie was riding near Paisley when her horse took fright and threw her. As a result of the shock, she went into labor and gave birth to a son (later **Robert II**) but died soon afterward. She was buried in Paisley Abbey. Some sources record that Robert was born by caesarian section and that Marjorie's last words were a prophecy that her son would be king, but many scholars consider these claims dubious. The reputed site of the accident, at the junction of Dundonald Road and Renfrew Road in Paisley, about a mile north of the abbey, is now marked by a cairn.

**BRUCE, MATILDA (c1316–1353).** Matilda, daughter of King **Robert I** and his second wife, **Elizabeth de Burgh**, was probably born in Dunfermline in about 1316 after her parents were reunited following a separation that lasted from 1306 (when her father went into hiding and her mother was taken captive by King **Edward I** of England) until prisoners were exchanged in the wake of the Scots' victory over an English army at the **Battle of Bannockburn** in 1314. She and her husband, Thomas Isaac, had four daughters between 1335 and 1339, and after her death at Aberdeen on 20 July 1353, she was buried in **Dunfermline Abbey**, the favored burial place of Scottish royalty from the late 11th century.

**BRUNANBURH, BATTLE OF (c937).** At an unknown site in northern England in about 937, **Aethelstan**, king of the English, defeated an army led by Norseman Olaf Guthfrithson, king of Dublin, whose father had held the throne of York until Aethelstan forced him to submit in 927. **Constantine II**, king of Scotland, and Owain, king of Strathclyde, supported the Viking force, but according to the *Anglo-Saxon Chronicle*, "The host from the ships fell doomed . . . the whole day the West Saxons with mounted companies kept in pursuit of the hostile peoples. Grievously they cut down the fugitives from behind with their whetted swords." The victory confirmed the **Anglo-Saxon monarchs'** control of the southern territories of the British Isles, confining Celtic and Scandinavian influences to the north and west. *See also* EALHSWITH.

**BUCKINGHAM PALACE.** Buckingham Palace, in central **London**, has been the principal residence of the **royal family** since Queen **Victoria**'s accession to the throne in 1837. Throughout the preceding century, **Kensington**

**Palace** and **St. James's Palace** had been the homes of Britain's monarchs. In 1702–5, John, duke of Buckingham, built a mansion on a site at the western end of St. James's Park. The building was purchased in 1762 by King **George III**, who intended to use the property as a private dwelling (11 of his 15 children were born there), but his eldest son, who succeeded him (as King **George IV**) in 1820, decided to convert it into a palace and, moreover, insisted that architect John Nash should be responsible for the design. Parliament, though unhappy about the costs, allocated £200,000 to the project, and Nash produced plans for a courtyard enclosed on all sides except the east. George, however, demanded Carrara marble, Bath stone, and other expensive building materials, which pushed up the cost of construction, so Nash was twice called before parliament to explain why the bills were three times greater than the funds apportioned. In the end, the government's patience ran out. After the king died in 1830, Nash was dismissed, and Edward Blore was commissioned to complete the work.

When Victoria moved in, the place was hardly fit for servants, let alone a queen. Bells would not ring, doors would not close, windows would not open, and many fittings (such as sinks) had not been installed. Nevertheless, by 1843 she was able to write, "I have been so happy here," a sentiment echoed by all later monarchs, with the exception of King **Edward VIII**, who hated the place and spent only a few nights there during his short reign. In 1913, during the reign of King **George V**, the eastern frontage was replaced by a facade of Portland stone designed by Sir Ashton Webb. In addition, considerable renovation and refurbishment were carried out after World War II (during which, parts of the structure, including the chapel, were badly damaged by bombs).

The present building has about 600 rooms, most of which are used as offices or as accommodations for the staff. Queen **Elizabeth II** and her husband, **Philip, duke of Edinburgh**, occupy 12 rooms in the north wing, facing the 40-acre gardens. The state apartments—including the Ball Room, Music Room, and Throne Room—are reserved for events such as banquets honoring foreign dignitaries and ceremonies conferring knighthoods on the great and the good. Since 1993, they have been open to the public from August until early October while the royal family is at **Balmoral** in Scotland; the admission charges contribute to the cost of rebuilding the parts of **Windsor Castle** that were damaged by fire in November 1992. **Charles, prince of Wales**, was born at Buckingham Palace (1948), as were his brothers **Prince Andrew, duke of York** (1960), and **Prince Edward, earl of Wessex** (1964). Their sister—**Anne, princess royal**—was born at **Clarence House** in 1950. *See also* CHANGING OF THE GUARD.

# C

**CALAIS.** Calais was captured by King **Edward III**'s army in 1347, after an 11-month siege during the **Hundred Years' War**, and was assigned to the English monarchs in perpetuity (along with neighboring Guînes and Marck) by the treaties of Brétigny and Calais in 1360. It became a staple port in 1363, acting as a gateway for cloth, lead, tin, and wool (known as staples), as well as other merchandise sent from England for sale in Europe. By 1372, the settlement was sending representatives to parliament, but English authority in the area depended on the construction and maintenance of expensive defense systems because the town was regularly attacked by armies of the king of **France** and the duke of Burgundy. Eventually, on 7 January 1558, the forces of Francis, duke of Guise, overran the garrison, and Calais returned to French rule. *See also* ANJOU, HOUSE OF; AQUITAINE; HENRY VI; MARY I; NORMANDY, HOUSE OF; PHILIPPA OF HAINAULT.

**CAMBUSKENNETH ABBEY.** Cambuskenneth, the burial place of King **James III** and his queen, **Margaret of Denmark**, lies in a meander of the River Forth east of **Stirling**. Founded for Arrouaisian monks by **David I** in about 1140, but later administered by Augustinians, it benefited greatly from the patronage of Scotland's medieval royal families, who were often in residence at Stirling's castle, but it was also the target of invading English armies. As the Protestant Reformation spread during the 16th century, the abbey fell into disuse, and much of the stone was carted away for buildings elsewhere. However, excavations by William Mackison in 1864 uncovered bones that were believed to be James's and Margaret's remains. At the command of Queen **Victoria**, these were reinterred on the site of the former choir. The abbey ruins are now managed by Historic Scotland (a government agency charged with the maintenance of buildings of national importance) and are open to visitors.

**CAMILLA, DUCHESS OF CORNWALL (1947– ).** The long-time companion and confidante, and then wife, of **Charles, prince of Wales**, Camilla Parker Bowles was born in **London** on 17 July 1947 to Major Bruce Shand

and his wife, Rosalind. Raised on a country estate in the County of Sussex (where she developed a passion for fox hunting), she was educated at Queen's Gate School in London and then attended finishing schools in Switzerland and **France**—an upbringing that honed self-confidence in an environment of wealth and privilege. She met the shy, somewhat retiring **prince** at a polo match in 1971 and, by all accounts, took the initiative in developing the relationship. She is a descendant of Alice Keppel, who had an affair with King **Edward VII**, Charles's great-great-grandfather. Apparently, during a dance in a night club, Camilla said to the prince, "My great-grandmother was your great-great-grandfather's mistress, so how about it?" They were seen together regularly until 1973, when, according to some accounts, Charles decided to concentrate on his naval career and, according to others, Camilla became convinced that he would never propose. While the prince was in the Caribbean and South America, she accepted an offer of marriage from Andrew Parker Bowles, an army officer, and had two children with him—Tom (born in 1975) and Laura (born in 1979).

In 1981, Charles married Diana Spencer (*see* DIANA, PRINCESS OF WALES), but the friendship with Camilla continued. As his marriage soured, he increasingly turned to Mrs. Parker Bowles for support, but by that time her relationship was also in trouble and her husband had taken a mistress. Diana, who referred to Camilla as "the rottweiler," publicly accused her of enticing Charles away, claiming in a television interview in 1995 that "there were three of us in this marriage so it was a bit crowded." On the other hand, Charles's supporters claim that Diana became paranoid about his friendship with Camilla and that there was no impropriety until the marriage had irretrievably broken down. Whatever the truth of the matter, Charles admitted in 1994 that he had committed adultery. Mr. and Mrs. Parker Bowles divorced the following year, and Charles and Diana, who had formally separated in 1992, began divorce proceedings in 1996.

A public that wanted to believe in a fairy-tale **princess** pilloried Camilla as a selfish, devious hussy, but she maintained a decorous silence, refusing to add to salacious gossip by telling her side of the story. Following Diana's death in 1997, she kept a low profile, and despite much pressure from official and unofficial advisors, Charles made clear that he would not give her up. By 1998, the prince's publicity staff was working hard to ensure a more favorable press coverage for Camilla, and in 1999, at a carefully staged event, the couple was photographed leaving the Ritz Hotel in London after attending a birthday party. Media reports suggest that **Prince William of Wales**, Charles's eldest son, made the moves toward family reconciliation by inviting Camilla to tea. After **Elizabeth, the queen mother**, died in 2002, the prince moved into her former home in **Clarence House**, London, and Camilla

Parker Bowles moved with him. Their relationship condoned, though not necessarily approved of, by Queen **Elizabeth II**, they eventually married in Windsor Guildhall on 9 April 2004, with Camilla taking the title "duchess of Cornwall" and beginning a formal program of royal duties that has included visits to Egypt and to the United States. *See also* CAMILLAGATE.

**CAMILLAGATE.** In 1974, Richard Nixon was forced to resign the presidency of the United States following an investigation into wiretapping at the Democratic Party's National Committee headquarters in the Watergate Hotel in Washington, D.C. Since then, journalists in the United Kingdom, as well as in the United States, have used the suffix *-gate* as a shorthand way of referring to a political scandal. The Camillagate episode began in 1992, when the *Daily Mirror*, a tabloid newspaper, was given a tape recording of a sexually explicit telephone conversation between **Charles, prince of Wales**, and Camilla Parker Bowles (now **Camilla, duchess of Cornwall**), which had taken place on 18 December 1989. The paper printed extracts from the tape on 13 November, and on 9 December, Charles and his wife, **Diana, princess of Wales**, announced that they would separate. The full text of the conversation was published around the world on 13 and 14 January the following year, but the source of the tape was never revealed. The *Mirror*'s editors claimed that they received it from "a very ordinary member of the public," but columnists in other newspapers suggested that the security service was involved, and some journalists speculated that an amateur radio enthusiast had made a chance interception of a cell phone conversation.

**CANMORE, HOUSE OF.** Some historians and genealogists prefer to use House of Canmore, rather than **House of Dunkeld**, as a genealogical means of categorizing Scotland's 11th- to 13th-century monarchs. The descriptor is derived from **Malcolm III**, who was nicknamed "Canmore," a term derived from the Gaelic *ceann* (meaning "head" or "chief") and *mor* (meaning "great" or "large") and thus indicating either a man with a big head or a great chief. Most writers include 11 monarchs in the House, although **Donald III** was a brother (rather than a descendant) of Malcolm, and **Margaret, maid of Norway**, is excluded from some lists because she was never crowned. The period—more than 200 years—over which the dynasty presided was significant because (apart from the time of Donald's brief reign from 1093 to 1097) it was characterized by the anglicization of the Scottish royal court. Those kings who married all had English (rather than Gaelic) names, took English wives, and organized society on the feudal lines introduced to the British Isles by **William I of England** and his Norman supporters. The classification is, however, a modern construct because the monarchs claimed their descent not from Malcolm III but from Fergus Mór ("Big Fergus" or "Fergus the Great"), a quite possibly legendary king of Dalriada in western Scotland.

The monarchs from the House of Canmore, in addition to those mentioned above, are **Duncan II** (1094), **Edgar of Scotland** (1097–1107), **Alexander I** (1107–24), **David I** (1124–53), **Malcolm IV** (1153–65), **William I of Scotland** (1165–1214), **Alexander II** (1214–49), and **Alexander III** (1249–86). The House of Dunkeld normally includes, in addition, **Duncan I**, who was Malcolm III's father.

**CANUTE (c995–1035).** Canute, although sometimes ruthless, brought England a welcome 20 years of political peace and commercial growth after the uncertainties and conflicts of **Aethelred the Unready**'s reign. He was the son of **Sweyn** Forkbeard, who led a successful Viking (and largely Danish) invasion of England in 1013, but his mother's antecedents, his birth date, and details of his early life are largely unknown. He certainly accompanied his father on the campaign in 1013 and was in command of the fleet when Sweyn died early the following year. The Danes chose Canute to succeed his father as king of England, but the **witan** (the royal council of advisors) preferred to restore the Anglo-Saxon line and invited the exiled Aethelred to return from Normandy. Canute retired to Denmark, where he raised another fleet and then attempted a reconquest of his father's territories. **Edmund II** led the opposition, but after succumbing to the Danes at the **Battle of Assandun** in October 1016, he was forced to accept a treaty that gave Canute control of all the land north of the River Thames. A clause to the agreement provided that if either monarch died, his realm would revert to the survivor, so with Edmund's demise only a month later (there are suggestions that he was killed by Danes), Canute became king of all of England.

The new monarch made short shrift of his political opponents, executing many of the leading Anglo-Saxon nobility (including, in 1017, Eadwig, Edmund's brother) and distributing their lands among his followers. However, within a few years, his court was dominated by native Englishmen, many of the laws introduced during the reign of King **Edgar of England** were being reinstated, and Canute was making generous donations to the church. It is unclear whether the change of tack reflected a mellowing in the former warrior or whether it was politically motivated (for example, the funding given to religious institutions was reflected in support from the Roman Catholic leadership, which had a strong influence on the common people), but it undoubtedly initiated a lengthy period of peace, during which markets flourished, the currency strengthened, and trade with Scandinavia burgeoned.

In either 1004 or 1016, Canute "married" **Aelfgifu of Northampton** in a handfast ceremony. These unions, which involved tying the couple's wrists together, were not normally recognized by the Roman Catholic Church because they were carried out in the absence of a priest, but in the king's case, the Catholic authorities appear to have turned a blind eye. The match produced two sons, **Svein of Norway** and Harold (later **Harold I**), both born c1015–16. However, Aethelred's sons—Edward (later known as **Edward the Confessor**) and **Aelfred Aetheling**—were living in exile in Normandy and were clearly a threat to the Danish succession to the English throne. Canute attempted to solve the problem by marrying Aethelred's widow, **Emma of Normandy**, in the conventional manner and siring another son—**Harthacanute**—who was named heir. When Canute died at a monastery in Shaftesbury on 12 November 1035, Harthacanute was in Denmark preparing to wage war against Magnus I of Norway, so the following year, the witan appointed Harold and Emma as co-**regents**. Within months, Harold had driven Emma out of the court and was ruling alone, though probably greatly influenced by his mother.

Canute is probably best known from the legend that recounts his efforts to hold back the advancing tide. As the ruler of a vast empire that included England, Denmark, Norway, and parts of Sweden, he was the subject of much flattery by courtiers. In order to put their adulation into context, he is said to have arranged for his throne to be placed on the shoreline. Seated there, he told the waves to recede; then, as they rolled in over his feet, he pointed out to his followers that the power of an earthly king was significantly less than the power of God. Canute was buried in **Winchester**, the ancient capital of **Anglo-Saxon monarchs**, but the chest that contained his remains was disturbed during the 17th century, and his bones were scattered among other tombs. *See also* EDITH OF EAST ANGLIA; GUNHILDA OF DENMARK; WULFTHRYTH.

**CARLTON HOUSE.** Carlton House, formerly located in the St. James's area of central **London**, was a **royal residence** for much of the 18th and early 19th centuries. Built for politician Henry Boyle (later Baron Carleton) from 1700, it was acquired by **Frederick, prince of Wales**, in 1732. After his death in 1751, his widow—**Augusta of Saxe-Gotha**—remained in the accommodation until she, too, passed away in 1772. In 1783, when George, **prince of Wales** (later the much disliked King **George IV**), reached the age of 21, Carlton House became his London home. Parliament approved expenditure of £60,000 on renovations, with a similar sum allocated 12 years later as costs (and the **prince**'s debts) mounted. French craftsmen lavishly refurbished the building, which was remodeled to designs prepared by architect Henry Holland, and the walls were hung with paintings by Thomas Gainsborough, Joshua Reynolds, and other contemporary artists whom George patronized.

Despite the investment of effort and funds, when the prince succeeded to the throne in 1820, he decided that Carlton House was too small for his monarchical needs and opted to enlarge **Buckingham Palace**, which had been the home of his mother, **Charlotte of Mecklenburg-Strelitz**, prior to her death in 1818. The building was demolished in 1827, and two white-stuccoed rows known as Carlton House Terrace were erected on the site, with the income from the lease of the properties devoted to the cost of building at Buckingham Palace. George, who died in 1830, never saw his new residence completed, but the houses constructed on the site of his old home remain part of the **crown estate**.

**CAROLINE ELIZABETH, PRINCESS (1713–1757).** Caroline was the third daughter, and fourth child, of King **George II** and **Caroline of Brandenburg-Ansbach**. She was born at the Palace of Herrenhausen in Hanover on 30 May 1713, exactly two years after **Princess Amelia (1711–1786)**, her older sister, and moved to **London** with her parents in 1714. She never developed Amelia's eccentricities but, like her, never married. As she grew older, Caroline suffered increasingly from ill health and died, aged just 44, at **St. James's Palace**, London, on 28 December 1757. She was buried in **Westminster Abbey**. *See also* KEW PALACE.

**CAROLINE OF BRANDENBURG-ANSBACH (1683–1737).** Caroline, **queen consort** of King **George II**, had considerable intellectual ability and a diplomatic skill that allowed her to exercise much influence over her husband. The daughter of Johann, margrave of Brandenburg-Ansbach, and his second wife, Eleanore, she was born at the palace of Ansbach in Germany on 1 March 1683. As a teenager, she was considered a suitable partner for Charles, the second son of Leopold I, Holy Roman Emperor, but she turned down the prospect of marriage in order to preserve her Protestant faith, and on 22 August 1705, she was wed to George at a ceremony in Hanover.

An attractive and intelligent young woman, Caroline corresponded regularly with Gottfried Leibniz, the mathematician and philosopher who developed the binary system of numbers utilized by modern computer systems, and although she admitted that she had trouble learning English, she earned the respect of British courtiers, many of whom believed that she was the power behind George's throne. Her political influence, though sometimes overstated both by contemporaries and by modern apologists, was undoubtedly considerable, stemming partly from good relations cultivated with Robert Walpole, who is often considered Britain's first prime minister, and partly from the strength of her marriage. George certainly demonstrated considerable faith in her abilities, discussing national issues with her, leaving her as **regent** on the four occasions when he visited his homeland, and giving her considerable power in prickly matters of ecclesiastical politics, such as the appointment of bishops.

Caroline and her husband had nine children together, one of whom was stillborn but seven of whom survived to adulthood. She died of a ruptured womb at **St. James's Palace** on 20 November 1737 and was buried in **Westminster Abbey**. George, devastated, never remarried, although he took several mistresses. *See also* AMELIA, PRINCESS (1711–1786); ANNE, PRINCESS ROYAL (1709–1759); CAROLINE ELIZABETH, PRINCESS; FREDERICK, PRINCE OF WALES; GEORGE WILLIAM, PRINCE; KEW PALACE; LOUISA, QUEEN OF DENMARK AND NORWAY; MARY, PRINCESS, LANDGRAVINE OF HESSE-CASSEL; WHITE LODGE; WILLIAM AUGUSTUS, DUKE OF CUMBERLAND.

**CAROLINE OF BRUNSWICK-WOLFENBÜTTEL (1768–1821).** Caroline was married to King **George IV** for 26 years, lived with him for only a few months, and quarreled with him until her death. The second female child born to Charles, duke of Brunswick-Wolfenbüttel, and **Princess** Augusta, the daughter of **Frederick, prince of Wales**, she was born at Brunswick on 17 May 1768. Her marriage was arranged because George, then **prince of Wales**, was heavily in debt and needed a wife so that parliament would increase his allowance. Caroline was probably chosen partly because she was available (there were few eligible Protestant princesses at the time); partly because Britain was at war with **France**, and Brunswick—although small—was a useful ally in Central Europe; and partly because Augusta was a favorite sister of King **George III**, the prospective father-in-law. The **prince**, for his part, did not much care who was selected as a bride, commenting that "one damned German frau is as good as another." The wedding ceremony was held at **St. James's Palace** on 8 April 1795, but neither principal was impressed; Caroline thought her new husband "very fat," and George claimed that he had to "overcome the disgust of her person" in order to climb into bed with her. A daughter—**Princess Charlotte Augusta**—was born in January the following year, but the couple were already living apart.

Caroline was garrulous, uncouth, and not renowned for her personal hygiene, but she was by no means unpopular, described by a sympathetic press as a wife wronged by a husband who lavished his affection and his money on mistresses. However, she took a string of lovers herself, at one point facing **Privy Council** charges of bearing a son by another man. When George became king in 1820, Caroline attempted to claim her share of the limelight. She had left Britain six years earlier and was living in an almost certainly adulterous relationship with Bartholomew Pergami, an Italian whom she had originally hired as a servant, but she immediately prepared a return to **London** as **queen consort**. The government attempted to stave off trouble by offering to increase her allowance from £35,000 to £50,000 if she stayed away, but the gesture was refused, and when she reached England on 5 June, she was greeted by widespread public celebration. Parliament halfheartedly debated legislation intended to end the marriage, but in the face of popular support for her cause and widespread dissatisfaction with the reactionary king, there was little chance that it would be approved, and on 10 November the prime minister, Robert Jenkinson, Lord Liverpool, announced that he did not intend to proceed with the bill.

On 19 July 1821, Caroline was refused admission to her husband's **coronation** at **Westminster Abbey**. She took ill shortly afterward, and on 7 August she died in London. She had expressed a wish to be buried beside her father, and the British government, surprised by her passing but happy to accede, arranged for her remains to be carried to the family mausoleum at Brunswick. Her sudden death has never been satisfactorily explained; at the time, rumors of poisoning circulated around the court, but doctors diagnosed an intestinal obstruction, and some writers have suggested that the real cause was stomach cancer. Whatever the truth, Caroline's departure was a profound relief for the king because she had become a figurehead for opposition to his rule in a country increasingly annoyed by his intransigence over parliamentary reform and his unwillingness to increase the civil rights of Roman Catholics.

**CASKET LETTERS.** In 1567, James Douglas, earl of Morton, claimed that on 20 June he was handed a silver casket containing eight letters and several sonnets that **Mary, queen of Scots**, had written to her lover, **James Hepburn, earl of Bothwell**. If the documents were authentic, they confirmed the monarch's complicity in the murder of her second husband, **Henry Stuart, lord Darnley**. They were certainly influential in turning opinion against the young and headstrong queen, both in Scotland and in England, where she claimed the throne of **Elizabeth I**, but contemporary debates about their authenticity have continued through the centuries. The modern consensus is that they were forgeries, but it is impossible to be sure because the originals, written in French and allegedly in the queen's handwriting, disappeared after 1584, when William Ruthven, earl of Gowrie and the last person known to possess them, was executed for treason. Some writers speculate that they may have been acquired and destroyed by Mary's son, King **James VI and I**.

**CASTLE OF MEY.** The Castle of Mey, some 15 miles east of Thurso, was the principal Scottish residence of **Queen Elizabeth, the queen mother**. It was built in the second half of the 16th century by George Sinclair, earl of

Cathness, and was in a much dilapidated state when the queen mother purchased it from Captain F. B. Imbert-Terry soon after the death of her husband, King **George VI**, in 1952. Over the next four decades, a considerable sum was invested in restoration and refurbishment (including the installation of electricity) and in improvements to the gardens and to Longoe Farm, which occupies 100 hectares of the estate and has a prizewinning herd of Aberdeen Angus cattle. In 1996, the queen mother placed the property in the hands of a trust, which has opened some of the 38 rooms to the public during the summer months each year since her death in 2002. The castle attracts some 30,000 visitors annually despite its remoteness and even though it is usually closed for two weeks in July and August when **Charles, prince of Wales**, and his wife, **Camilla, duchess of Cornwall**, visit the area.

**CATHERINE OF ARAGON (1485–1536).** Catherine was the first wife of King **Henry VIII** and the mother of Queen **Mary I**. Henry's efforts to annul their marriage were instrumental in promoting the Protestant Reformation through the creation of a **Church of England** that was independent of the Roman Catholic hierarchy in the Vatican.

The youngest child of Ferdinand II of Aragon and Isabella I of Castile, Catherine (also known as Catalina, Catarina, Caterina, Catharine, Katherine, and Katharine) was born on 16 December 1485 in the archbishop's palace at Alcalá de Henares, northeast of Madrid. Under the terms of the treaty of Medina del Campo, which strengthened political and economic ties between England and Spain in 1489, she was acknowledged as the future wife of **Arthur, prince of Wales**, the son of **Henry VII** and **Elizabeth of York**. They married at St. Paul's Cathedral in **London** on 14 November 1501 but had little opportunity to enjoy wedded life because Arthur died at Ludlow on 2 April the following year. Soon afterward, Catherine was betrothed to Henry, Arthur's younger brother, but the marriage was postponed until 11 June 1509, partly because of political differences between the two fathers and partly because of arguments over the extent of the dowry.

A union between brother-in-law and sister-in-law required papal dispensation, but Catherine claimed that her first marriage had never been consummated, so Pope Julius II approved the match. The early years of the relationship appeared to be happy, with Henry sufficiently confident in his wife's political skills to appoint her **regent** while he was on military campaigns against the French in 1513–14, but as time wore on, the lack of an heir caused problems. In the nine years from 1510 to 1518, the **queen consort** gave birth to six babies, but four were either stillborn or lived for only a few hours, and **Henry, duke of Cornwall**, born on New Year's Day in 1511, survived only until 22 February. The one child who reached adulthood was a daughter (later Mary I), and—apart from the possible exception of **Matilda** in the early 12th century—England had no experience with a female ruler. Moreover, the pregnancies had taken their toll on Catherine's health, and it was unlikely that she would have another child.

Anxious to avoid problems over the **succession to the throne**, intent on siring a son, and increasingly enamored of **Anne Boleyn** (who was rejecting his sexual advances), Henry petitioned Pope Clement VII for annulment of the marriage in 1527, arguing that Catherine's previous union with Arthur had been consummated, so his own wedding was invalid. Catherine disputed the claim, and Gregory procrastinated, unwilling to annoy either the powerful king or the equally powerful Charles V, Holy Roman Emperor and Catherine's nephew, who was, in effect, holding him captive. In July 1531, Catherine was banished from the English court, and two years later, Henry, having broken with Rome in exasperation over the delay in getting a ruling from the pope, married Anne. Then, on 23 May 1533, an English court, convened solely for the purpose, annulled the king's first marriage.

For the remainder of her life, Catherine was kept in near isolation, unable to see even her daughter, at Kimbolton Castle in Cambridgeshire, where the damp fenland climate undoubtedly hastened the decline of her already weakened body. She died on 7 January 1536, still maintaining that she was Henry's lawful wife and refusing to recognize Anne. Her remains were buried in Peterborough Cathedral, but there are stories that her ghost still haunts Kimbolton.

**CATHERINE OF BRAGANZA (1638–1705).** Because of her devotion to the Roman Catholic beliefs in which she had been raised, Catherine was an unpopular consort for King **Charles II**. The daughter of John, duke of Braganza (and later King John IV of Portugal), and his wife, Luiza Maria de Guzmán, she was born at the Vila Viçosa in Alentejo, Portugal, on 25 November 1638 and, according to a contemporary report, was "bred hugely retired," rarely leaving the family homes. Her marriage partner was chosen by Luiza, who acted as **regent** of her country following John's death in 1656 and who settled for Charles after being turned down by Louis XIV of **France**. For Portugal, the match ensured that the country had an ally in wars with Spain. For the English king, it provided a huge financial dowry at a time when he was attempting to reestablish a royal court in London after the **restoration of the monarchy**. Also, that dowry included the important trading ports of Tangier (in North Africa) and Bombay (in India); the English were forced to abandon the former in 1679, forced out by Sultan Moulay Ismail of Morocco, but Bombay became an important gateway to British domination of India.

Charles and Catherine wed on 21 May 1662 in Portsmouth, with a secret Roman Catholic ceremony preceding a public **Church of England** event. The king was unimpressed by his bride's looks—he referred to her as a bat—and very quickly turned to more attractive female companions. Moreover, as time passed and Catherine had three miscarriages, it seemed more and more unlikely that the queen would bear an heir. Royal advisors urged the monarch to seek a divorce, hoping that the new wife would be a Protestant, but Charles refused. In 1678, the counselors alleged that the queen had been involved in a plot to poison the monarch, but despite his initial lack of gallantry and his attentions to other ladies, the king voiced his belief in her innocence even as the House of Commons, the lower chamber in Britain's bicameral parliament, called for her to be banished from the realm.

Catherine played little active part in politics during her husband's reign (although she undoubtedly figured in the schemes of others), but she had a considerable impact at court, introducing the Portuguese habit of tea drinking to England, influencing fashion trends by shortening her skirts so that her feet showed, and playing cards on Sunday despite the criticism by Protestants for not observing the Sabbath. After her husband's death in 1685, she set up a home in **Somerset House**, but in 1692 she returned to Portugal, and in 1704–5 she acted as regent while her brother, Peter II, was unwell. She died on 31 December 1705 at the Palace of Bemposta in Lisbon and was buried at the Hieronymite monastery in that city. Catherine looked back on her life with little pleasure, writing in 1687 that she was sacrificed in the interests of Portugal and the House of Braganza.

**CATHERINE OF VALOIS (1401–1437).** Catherine was **queen consort** of King **Henry V**, mother of King **Henry VI**, and grandmother of King **Henry VII** (the first of England's five monarchs from the **House of Tudor**). She was born in Paris on 27 October 1401, the daughter of Charles VI of **France** and Isabeau (or Isabelle) of Bavaria, and her marriage was arranged to meet the needs of international diplomacy. Less than two weeks before the wedding, Catherine's mentally unstable father had made Henry V his **regent** and heir (*see* TROYES, TREATY OF), and the wedding—held on 2 June 1420 at Troyes Cathedral on the River Seine, about 90 miles southeast of Paris—underscored a clause in the agreement that the English king's children would hold the French throne in perpetuity. However, although on 6 December 1421, the couple had a son who later became Henry VI, the boy was not destined to receive the inheritance his father had intended for him. Henry V died when the child was less than nine months old, and Charles VI followed some seven weeks later. Charles's son (also named Charles) repudiated the treaty, and by the time the young monarch reached adulthood, the French had reclaimed most of the territory they had earlier lost to English armies.

When her husband died, Catherine, still in her early twenties, retired to **Wallingford Castle**, where she succumbed to the attractions of **Owen Tudor**, a senior member of the **Royal Household**. It is possible that she married him, but there are no records of any ceremony, and even if there were, the union may not have been legal because, in 1428, parliament passed legislation that prevented **queens dowager** from remarrying without royal approval. Their children included three sons—Owen Tudor (who was born in 1429 and became a monk at **Westminster Abbey**); **Edmund Tudor, earl of Richmond** (born in 1430 and father of King Henry VII); and Jasper, duke of Bedford (born in 1431 and guardian of his nephew in the early years of the young king's reign). There were also at least four girls—Mary (born in 1432), Jacina (1433), Margaret (1437), and a daughter, born in 1435, whose name is not known and who became a nun. Catherine died on 3 January 1437 at Bermondsey Abbey in **London** shortly after giving birth to the last of her daughters. She was buried in Westminster Abbey. *See also* ISABELLA OF VALOIS.

**CATHERINE OF YORK (1479–1527).** Catherine, the ninth of 10 children in the family of King **Edward IV** and **Elizabeth Woodville**, outlived her three brothers and six sisters by more than a decade. She was born at **Eltham Palace** on 14 August 1479 and betrothed to Juan of Aragon, heir to the Spanish throne, while still an infant. However, the details of the marriage agreement were still being worked out when her father died in 1483 and were not pursued by his successors. Instead, a second contract, binding her to **James Stewart, duke of Ross** and son of King **James III** of Scotland, was proposed by King **Henry VII** in an effort to cement peaceful relations between England and its northern neighbor, but the Scottish king was killed in 1488 before the wedding could take place. A little over a year after that, however, Margaret wed William Courtney and they had two sons (Henry, born c1496, and Edward, born c1497) and a daughter (Margaret, born c1499). Courtney was imprisoned from 1503 to 1509, accused of plotting against the king, and he died two years after his release. His widow, although still in her early thirties, took an oath of celibacy. She died on 15 November 1527 at Tiverton Castle in southwest England.

**CEAWLIN (c535–593).** The scribes who wrote the text of the *Anglo-Saxon Chronicle* recorded that Ceawlin, son of **Cynric**, ruled **Wessex** from 560 until 592, but other sources suggest that his reign may have lasted for as little as seven years. Whatever the disagreements, modern scholars believe that, under his leadership, Wessex expanded its boundaries considerably, particularly to the east (as a result of a victory in 568 over the armies of Aethelberht of Kent at Wibbandun, a site still unidentified) and to the northwest (in 577, the defeat of a British force at Deorham—now Dyrham—won him control of the settlements at Bath, Cirencester, and Gloucester, opening the lands along the lower reaches of the River Severn to Saxon farmers and dividing the Britons in Wales from those in southwest England).

In spite of these successes, Ceawlin (also known as Cealin and Caeulin) was forced from the throne in 592, probably by his nephew **Ceol**, after a bloody battle at Woden's Barrow near the village of Alton Priors in present-day Wiltshire. He died, or was killed, the following year, leaving (according to some records) two sons named Cutha and **Cuthwine**. Although genealogies for the period have inaccuracies, there is some evidence that Ceawlin's line was restored to the kingship through Cuthwine's descendants after Centwine, the last king from Ceol's house, died c685.

**CECILIA OF NORMANDY (c1054–1126).** Cecilia was probably the first daughter born to **William I of England** (William the Conqueror) and his wife, **Matilda of Flanders**. Her entire life seems to have been centered on the church, because by the time her father led the Norman conquest of England in 1066, she was a nun at the Abbey aux Dames, which her parents had founded in Caen, Normandy, and where her mother was later buried. Cecilia was abbess from 1112 until her death on 30 July 1126.

**CECILY, VISCOUNTESS WELLES (1469–1507).** Cecily (also known as Cecilia and as Cecily of York) was the third daughter of **Edward IV** and **Elizabeth Woodville**, born at the **Palace of Westminster** on 20 March 1469. Plans to marry her to **James III** of Scotland's eldest son (also named James and later to become King **James IV**) came to naught as traditional rivalries between the English and the Scots turned into conflict, and a later scheme to wed her to the ambitious **Alexander Stewart, duke of Albany** and James III's brother, suffered a similar fate when the noble succumbed to wounds received in a jousting contest in Paris in 1485.

Two years before Albany's accident, the English king had died, and his brother had taken the throne as **Richard III**. According to some writers, in c1485 the new monarch forced Cecily into marriage with Ralph Scrope of Upsall, a relatively minor landowner. The match of a king's daughter with a man who had no royal blood was intended to lower the young woman's status, but the union was annulled in 1486, and **Henry VII**, Richard's successor, arranged another wedding (on a date and at a place still unknown) to John, viscount Welles, his uncle and staunch supporter. Cecily and her husband had two daughters together (Elizabeth, born in 1498, and Anne, born in 1499) before he died; then, probably sometime between the spring of 1502 and early 1504, she married Thomas Kyme and settled with him on the Isle of Wight. Henry, who was not informed, took his revenge by banishing her from the court and confiscating much of her estate.

There is little information about Cicely's remaining years, though it seems she had two more children (Richard and Margaret, whose birth dates are not recorded). She died on 24 August 1507, but her burial place is not certain, some writers believing that she was laid to rest at Quarr Abbey on the Isle of Wight, others that she is buried at **Hatfield** in Hertfordshire. *See also* PHIL-LIPS, PETER.

**CEOL (?–597).** Little is known of Ceol except that he was probably the son of Cutha, brother of **Ceawlin**, and that, in 592, he ousted his uncle from his position as king of **Wessex** after a battle at Woden's Barrow, which lies some six miles west of Devizes near the village of Alton Priors, and where, the *Anglo-Saxon Chronicle* records, there was "great slaughter." Ceol's family ruled Wessex, with only brief interruptions, until c685. Also, some scholars believe that his bloodline was evident in the royal house of Mercia, another Anglo-Saxon kingdom, as late as the 9th century.

**CEOLWALD (?–?).** Ceolwald is listed in some genealogies as the son of **Cuthwulf** and the great-grandson of **Ceawlin**, who may have ruled **Wessex** from 560 to 592. Some scholars suggest that he was born before 597, and most agree that he left a son, **Coenred**, who was born c640. If those details are correct, Ceolwald is an ancestor of the present British **royal family**, but several writers have questioned the reliability of the sources on which studies of this period of Anglo-Saxon history are based.

**CERDIC (?–534).** According to some genealogists, Cerdic, who founded the Saxon dynasty in **Wessex**, is the ancestor of all English and, since the **union of the crowns** in 1603, British monarchs except **Canute** and **Harthacanute** (both of whom were of Danish blood), **Harold I** (who was of Danish and Mercian ancestry), and **William I of England** (who was from the **House of Normandy**). The *Anglo-Saxon Chronicle* records that he traveled from the mainland of Europe, landed on the southern coast of Britain in 495, defeated the local rulers, and became the first king of Wessex in 519. He then added the Isle of Wight to his domains and, after his death in 534, was succeeded by his son, or grandson, **Cynric**. However, many modern scholars question the accuracy of the data in the *Chronicle*, suggesting that his reign began in 538, and a few claim that he may never have existed at all.

**CHANGING OF THE GUARD.** The ceremonial changing of the guard at **Buckingham Palace**, the monarch's central **London** residence, is a major tourist attraction. Usually, the guard (known as "The Queen's [or King's] Guard") is mounted by one of the British Army's five regiments of foot (the Coldstream Guards, the Grenadier Guards, the Irish Guards, the Scots Guards, and the Welsh Guards) in full dress uniform, but other regiments may be used when, for example, the foot regiments are stationed abroad. Sometimes, too, the guard may consist of troops from the **commonwealth realms**, of which the British monarch is also sovereign.

Led by a corps of drums, a detachment of the "Old Guard"—the soldiers who have been on duty—marches from **St. James's Palace** to Buckingham Palace, where it joins the men who have been on guard there. The "New Guard," which will take over the responsibilities, marches into the palace forecourt behind a military band that continues to play throughout the ceremony. After both groups have presented arms, the captain of the Old Guard receives the keys to the palace from the outgoing captain. The incoming sentries (four if the monarch is in residence, two if not) then go to their posts, and the Old Guard marches back to the barracks. The ceremony, which takes about 30 minutes, is held at 11:30 every day from May until July, and every second day for the rest of the year. Similar ceremonies are conducted at Horse Guards Parade in London and at **Windsor Castle**.

**CHARLES I (1600–1649).** Charles followed his father, King **James VI and I**, to the thrones of England, Ireland, and Scotland, adopting an authoritarian approach to government that led to clashes with subjects throughout his realms and ultimately to his execution. A devout man, he was attracted to the ceremony of the **Church of England** but had little interest in politics and little diplomatic skill.

The fifth of **Anne of Denmark**'s nine children, Charles was born at **Dunfermline** on 19 November 1600 and took the crown because his elder brother—**Henry Frederick Stuart, prince of Wales**—died in 1612. A sickly child, he was considered too ill to travel south in 1603 when James (who had been king of Scotland since 1567) moved his court to **London** (*see* UNION OF THE CROWNS), but he rejoined his parents the following year and acquired a sound education, reading widely and learning French, Italian, and Spanish. As he grew older, however, he became more aware of his stammer and his short stature, regarding them as embarrassments, and those perceived shortcomings, coupled with Henry's death in 1612 and the departure of his only surviving sibling, **Elizabeth of Bohemia**, to her wedding in 1613, left him lonely and withdrawn.

Troubles with the English parliament surfaced soon after Charles became king in 1625, partly because that body was largely Puritan and was suspicious of the monarch's preference for ecclesiastical ceremony, but also because of the mounting cost of pursuing wars with **France** and Spain. In 1628, legislators passed resolutions condemning arbitrary imprisonment and taxation; then, the following year, they raised objections to the revival of "popish practices" in the church and to the levying of customs duties without their consent. Stung by this opposition, the king ruled on his own from then until 1640—a period still known as "the eleven years' tyranny."

North of the border as well, dissent simmered as the new monarch attempted to enforce land ownership reforms, introduced additional taxes, and tried to make the Calvinist Church of Scotland more like the Anglican institution he favored. Opposition to the policies mounted over the years and flared into open resistance in 1637, when Charles told the Scots clerics to adopt a new liturgy based on the English Book of Common Prayer. In 1639, after leading churchmen and nobles signed a covenant to defend their Presbyterian beliefs while maintaining loyalty to their sovereign, the monarch elected to impose the changes by force, but his army, faced by experienced Scottish generals, opted not to fight. A truce was agreed to at Berwick, with the king promising to summon a Scottish parliament and hold a General Assembly of the Church of Scotland, but both sides knew that the peace was unlikely to be permanent.

Following this campaign, Charles reconvened his English parliament in April 1640, seeking approval for taxes that would raise money to support his army, but the majority of members refused to help, so the body was promptly dissolved again, precipitating yet more argument about the rights of the monarch and the rights of his subjects. The war was resumed, but the Scots army was able to advance well into England before agreeing to go no further. Shocked by the ease of its advance, Charles summoned another parliament in November of 1640; to his dismay, it continued to oppose his policies and impeached several of his ministers for treason.

Anxious to placate his critics and build support, the king agreed to a measure that would prohibit any further dissolutions of parliament without its consent, and in Scotland he accepted the full establishment of Presbyterianism, but those and other concessions failed to stem the tide. On 23 November 1641, the London parliament issued a "Grand Remonstrance" listing all of the monarch's mistakes since his accession, and attitudes on both sides became increasingly entrenched. Fighting broke out all over England in the summer of 1642, and soon the country was divided by civil war. During its early phases, the royalist cause prospered and there were rumors of disagreements within the parliamentarian ranks, but defeat at the Battle of Naseby on 14

June 1645 led to a turning of the tide. In the spring of 1646, Charles escaped in disguise from Oxford, which was surrounded by parliamentary troops, and surrendered to the Scottish army, which was encamped at Newark. He accompanied the Scottish army northward to Newcastle-upon-Tyne, but in 1647, the Scots came to terms with the English rebel forces and marched home, leaving the king to his fate.

After several attempts at conciliation, Charles was charged with high treason and was brought before the courts on 20 January 1649. He refused to recognize the legality of the proceedings on the grounds that "a king cannot be tried by any superior jurisdiction on earth" (*see* DIVINE RIGHT OF KINGS), but he was found guilty nonetheless and on 27 January was sentenced to death. He was **beheaded** at **Whitehall Palace** three days later, despite the protests of the Scots that an English court had no authority to murder their sovereign, and was buried in **St. George's Chapel** at **Windsor Castle**. For the next 11 years, England was ruled as a republic (*see* COMMONWEALTH OF ENGLAND), but the Scots recognized Charles's eldest surviving son as their king and crowned him **Charles II** at **Scone** on 1 January 1651 in the last **coronation** to be held in their country.

In 1663, three years after the **restoration of the monarchy** in England, King Charles II granted eight of his supporters the right to develop territory on the east of the North American continent and named the colony "Carolina" after his father (the name is taken from *Carolus*, the Latin for "Charles"); the area, divided into North Carolina and South Carolina, later became part of the United States. *See also* BAGSHOT PARK; HENRIETTA ANNE, DUCHESS OF ORLÉANS; HENRIETTA MARIA OF FRANCE; JAMES VII AND II; LINLITHGOW PALACE; MAGNA CARTA; MARY HENRIETTA, PRINCESS ROYAL, PRINCESS OF ORANGE; OATLANDS PALACE; PLACENTIA, PALACE OF; PRINCESS ROYAL; STATE OPENING OF PARLIAMENT; STUART, ANNE; STUART, ELIZABETH; STUART, HENRY, DUKE OF GLOUCESTER.

**CHARLES II (1630–1685).** Charles, king of Scotland from 1650 and of England and Ireland from 1660, much preferred pleasure to the hard work of government, but he managed to hold his realms together after a period of near chaos. He was born at **St. James's Palace**, London, on 29 May 1630, to King **Charles I** and **Henrietta Maria of France** and was educated at his father's court until the outbreak of civil war disrupted the learning process in 1642, forcing him to seek refuge, with his mother, in **France** and the Netherlands. Following the execution of Charles I in 1649, England became a republic (*see* COMMONWEALTH OF ENGLAND), but the youthful exile was determined to restore the country's monarchy (and, he believed, his birthright).

Thus, in 1650 he moved from the European mainland to Scotland (where his kingship was accepted) and, against the advice of many royalists, accepted that allowing the Scots their independence in matters of religious worship (rather than attempting to impose the practices of the **Church of England**, as his father had done) was the price to be paid for his northern subjects' help in achieving his English ends.

The initial results of his efforts were inauspicious. Gathering an army, Charles invaded England, but defeat at Worcester on 3 September 1651 forced him into exile again, and he eventually fled to France after narrowly escaping capture on several occasions (he later told diarist Samuel Pepys that at one point he had been hiding in an oak tree in Boscobel Wood, not far from the battle site, when an enemy soldier walked underneath the branches). Prospects did not immediately improve after the death of Oliver Cromwell, the rebel leader and de facto ruler of England, in 1658, partly because neither France nor Spain was willing to back Charles's cause with men and arms. However, Cromwell's successor—his son, Richard—lacked the strong power base that was needed to hold the numerous Puritan factions together, let alone control the royalists, so England gradually slipped toward anarchy. Support for the **restoration of the monarchy** was not great, but to many military and political leaders, it seemed the best way of reestablishing order. Contacts between the king and his opponents led, on 4 April 1660, to the Declaration of Breda, in which Charles expressed his belief in freedom of conscience and promised to declare a general amnesty, to ensure that soldiers received arrears of pay, and to negotiate equitable settlements of land disputes. On 8 May he was proclaimed king, and on 29 May—his 30th birthday—he returned to **London**.

Popularly known as "the Merry Monarch," Charles earned a reputation for extravagant living and the company of ladies (he left a string of illegitimate offspring), but he was plagued by debt and regularly sought parliamentary funds for the upkeep of the army, navy, and diplomatic service. **Dunkirk** was sold to France in 1662, partly to raise money and partly because the royal forces were too weak to defend overseas possessions properly. War with Holland depleted the coffers further, adding to the gloom of a nation already weakened by the ravages of bubonic plague in 1665 and by the devastation of the great fire of London in 1666 and leading to frequent spats with parliament. By the late 1670s, partly because of the king's willingness to permit freedom of religious expression, rumors of a Roman Catholic insurrection were rife, and Charles came under pressure to exclude his brother James (later King **James VII and II**), who had converted to Catholicism in 1668 or 1669, from the succession, but he refused to bend and dissolved parliament in 1681, ruling as an absolute monarch for the rest of his life.

Despite his political limitations and his profligacy, the king was a considerable patron of the arts and sciences. He was instrumental in founding the Royal Society, which is still one of the world's leading scientific organizations, and in establishing a Royal Observatory at Greenwich so that the study of astronomy could be advanced. Also, he helped further the architectural career of Christopher Wren, who prepared the designs for the rebuilding of many London churches, including St. Paul's Cathedral, after the great fire, and he granted theater licenses that allowed women to act on the stage for the first time. Charles died at **Whitehall Palace** on 6 February 1685 after suffering a stroke; he was buried in **Westminster Abbey**. He had married **Catherine of Braganza** in 1662, but they had no children so the crown went to James. *See also* CROWN JEWELS OF THE UNITED KINGDOM; HAMPTON COURT PALACE; HOLYROOD PALACE; MONMOUTH REBELLION; ST. JAMES'S PALACE.

**CHARLES, PRINCE OF WALES (1948– ). Prince** Charles is the eldest child of Queen **Elizabeth II** and **Prince Philip, duke of Edinburgh**. Heir to the United Kingdom throne (as well as to those of Australia, Canada, and other **commonwealth realms**), he was born at **Buckingham Palace** on 14 November 1948. Much of his early life was spent apart from his parents, as his father pursued a naval career and his mother undertook tours abroad, so his grandmother, **Queen Elizabeth, the queen mother**, played a central role in his life, forming a bond that lasted until her death in 2002.

At the age of eight, the prince was sent to Hill House School in **London**, becoming the first **heir apparent** to be educated alongside children from families outside the royal circle. From there he went, as a boarder, to Cheam School in Berkshire west of London (1957–62), and later to Gordonstoun School in Scotland (1962–67). A sensitive and introverted child, he hated being away from his parents, suffered from homesickness, and was bullied by more robust classmates, but a period at Timbertop School in Australia from January to September 1966 seemed to give him some confidence, and he did sufficiently well in examinations to justify places at Cambridge University and University College of Wales, Aberystwyth. His studies were interrupted in 1969 when he was invested **prince of Wales** at a ceremony in Caernarfon Castle, but he returned to his anthropology and archaeology lectures soon afterward, earning a bachelor's degree the following year. His formal education completed, Charles spent periods at the Royal Air Force College Cranwell and the Royal Naval College Dartmouth before entering the Royal Navy in 1971. By 1976, when he left the service so that he could devote himself wholly to his civilian duties, he was in command of a coastal mine hunter.

A thoughtful, contemplative man, the prince has frequently courted criticism because of his outspoken comments—as when, in 1984, he condemned a proposed extension to London's National Gallery as "a monstrous carbuncle on the face of a much loved and elegant friend"—but, through the Prince's Trust (a charity that he founded in 1976), he has helped over 400,000 young people in poor inner-city areas to get job training and set up businesses. Also, he has used his high profile to promote Britain and British firms on international tours and has done much to encourage environmental conservation and organic farming.

In 1977, Charles met Lady Diana Spencer (*see* DIANA, PRINCESS OF WALES), and by the summer of 1980, the media were speculating on the possibility of a wedding. As the press comment grew, the duke of **Edinburgh** told his son to make a decision quickly because a delay would damage Diana's reputation. Charles, uncertain of his feelings but pressured into making a choice between marriage and ending the friendship, chose the altar. He proposed on 24 February 1981, and the couple married in St. Paul's Cathedral, London, on 29 July the same year. Within weeks, courtiers were talking of problems.

When the new husband and wife returned from their Mediterranean honeymoon, they went straight to the royal home at **Balmoral Castle** in Scotland, where the prince seemed happier alone in the countryside than in the company of his bride. Their first child, **Prince William of Wales**, was born on 21 June 1982 and their second, **Prince Henry of Wales** (usually known as Prince Harry), on 15 September 1984, but the appearance of a family did nothing to prevent marital disintegration. Diana became increasingly unhappy, suffering from eating disorders, and suspecting that Charles was conducting a clandestine affair with his old friend Camilla Parker Bowles (*see* CAMILLA, DUCHESS OF CORNWALL). Husband and wife drifted apart, with tabloid newspapers regularly chronicling their differences by the late 1980s, and in 1992 they separated. Divorce followed in 1996. Then, on 30 August the following year, Diana was killed in a car accident in Paris.

Opinion polls at the time of Diana's death showed that many people blamed the prince for the breakup of the marriage, but in the years that followed, views mellowed, and the **royal family**'s press officers worked hard to improve Charles's image, concentrating on his role as a single father and his deep affection for Camilla. In 1999, the heir to the throne and Ms. Parker Bowles were photographed leaving a birthday party at the Ritz Hotel in London, and after that they were seen together with increasing regularity. They were married in Windsor Guildhall on 9 April 2005, with Camilla taking the title "duchess of Cornwall." *See also* CAMILLAGATE; CHURCH OF ENGLAND; CLARENCE HOUSE; DEFENDER OF THE FAITH; DUKE OF

CORNWALL; DUKE OF ROTHESAY; HIGHGROVE; REGENCY ACTS; ROYAL STANDARD; ROYAL WARRANT.

**CHARLOTTE AUGUSTA, PRINCESS (1796–1817).** Charlotte, born at **Carlton House** in **London** on 7 January 1796, was the only child of the unhappy union between George, **prince of Wales** (later King **George IV**), and **Caroline of Brunswick-Wolfenbüttel**. Her parents, married in the spring of the previous year, were already leading separate lives by the time of her birth, and her father, in particular, took little interest in her upbringing. As a result, the **princess** grew up with mixed feelings about both, writing that "My mother was wicked but she would not have turned so wicked had not my father been much more wicked still."

In 1813, George arranged a marriage between Charlotte and Prince William of Orange. At the time, however, the princess was second in the line of **succession to the throne**, after her father, and she felt that she could not be queen of one country and live in another with her husband. So, after initially agreeing to the match, she terminated the arrangement, much to the prince of Wales's annoyance. A second engagement—to Prince Leopold of Saxe-Coburg-Saalfield (later King Leopold I of Belgium)—proved more attractive, and on 2 May 1816 the couple married at Carlton House. On 5 November the following year, after 50 hours in labor, Charlotte gave birth to a stillborn son. She died early the next day and was buried at **St. George's Chapel** in **Windsor Castle** while gossip ascribed responsibility for her death to the failings of her doctor, Sir Richard Croft, who was so distraught that he killed himself.

Charlotte's sudden passing raised problems for the **House of Hanover** because, not only did **Prince** George have no other legitimate offspring, but neither did any of his 11 surviving brothers and sisters. With the dynasty's hold on the crown appearing tenuous, the eligible bachelors—**Prince Adolphus, duke of Cambridge**; **Prince Edward, duke of Kent and Strathearn**; and Prince William, duke of Clarence (later King **William IV**)—hastened to find brides and produce an heir. Edward succeeded, marrying Leopold's sister, **Victoria of Saxe-Coburg-Saalfield**, the following year and, on 24 May 1819, siring a daughter who became Queen **Victoria**. *See also* MARLBOROUGH HOUSE.

**CHARLOTTE OF CLARENCE, PRINCESS (1819).** Charlotte was the first child born to King **William IV** (who was duke of Clarence at the time of her birth) and **Adelaide of Saxe-Meiningen**. Her parents had married the previous year after William and his unmarried brothers had made a hasty search for brides so they could produce heirs who would ensure that the British throne remained with the **House of Hanover** (see CHARLOTTE

AUGUSTA, PRINCESS). Adelaide conceived soon after the wedding but developed pleurisy during the seventh month of her pregnancy and gave birth to Charlotte prematurely at the Fürstenburg Palace in Hanover on 29 April 1819. The baby lived for only a few hours, dying the same day. A second daughter (**Princess Elizabeth of Clarence**, born on 10 December 1820) lived for just three months, and twin boys were stillborn on 8 April 1822.

**CHARLOTTE OF MECKLENBURG-STRELITZ (1744–1818).** Charlotte's marriage to King **George III** was arranged for political reasons, like most royal weddings of the time, but, even so, the union was a happy one, producing 15 children and lasting for nearly 60 years. The future **queen consort** was born on 19 May 1744 at the Mirow Castle in northeast Germany, the eighth child in a family of five sons and five daughters raised by Duke Charles Louis Frederick of Mecklenburg-Strelitz and Elizabeth-Albertina of Saxe-Hildeburghausen. Although her background was aristocratic rather than regal and she was plain rather than pretty, she met many of the criteria that George and his advisors had specified as necessities for the bride of a monarch, as she was of good reputation, she was healthy, and she was a Protestant, with a willingness to adapt her Lutheran beliefs to those of the **Church of England**. So the two were married at **St. James's Palace** on 8 September 1761 only a few hours after meeting. Their first child (who succeeded his father as King **George IV**) was born in August the following year, and their last in the same month of 1783.

As queen consort, Charlotte played little part in politics, but she was a considerable patron of the arts (she sang with composer Wolfgang Amadeus Mozart, for example, and supported painter Thomas Gainsborough). She also worked with numerous charitable organizations, notably those for women, and, no intellectual slouch, she became an accomplished botanist (the *Strelitzia reginae*—a southern African plant—is named after her) while building up a multilingual, 4,000-volume library and maintaining a correspondence with Queen Marie Antoinette, the wife of King Louis XVI of **France**.

George's period of insanity during the winter of 1788–89 placed great stress on Charlotte, particularly so because the king, in his ravings, accused her (quite falsely) of adultery and because some politicians claimed that she was using her husband's illness to acquire power for herself. In 1811, when the symptoms manifested themselves again and parliament decided that the king could no longer continue to carry out monarchical duties, he was committed to her care once more, but his descent into madness was so complete that it is unlikely he was aware of her death at **Kew Palace** (then known as Dutch House) on 17 November 1818.

Charlotte was buried in **St. George's Chapel** at **Windsor Castle**, having been consort for longer than any other British queen. Her name is commemorated in numerous administrative areas and landscape features, including the city of Charlotte in North Carolina, Charlottetown on Prince Edward Island, and the Queen Charlotte Sound in New Zealand. *See also* ADOLPHUS, PRINCE, DUKE OF CAMBRIDGE; ALFRED, PRINCE; AMELIA, PRINCESS (1783–1810); AUGUSTA SOPHIA, PRINCESS; AUGUSTUS FREDERICK, PRINCE, DUKE OF SUSSEX; CARLTON HOUSE; CHARLOTTE, PRINCESS ROYAL, QUEEN OF WURTEMBURG; EDWARD, PRINCE, DUKE OF KENT AND STRATHEARN; ELIZABETH, PRINCESS, LANDGRAVINE OF HESSE-HOMBURG; ERNEST AUGUSTUS, KING OF HANOVER; FREDERICK, PRINCE, DUKE OF YORK AND ALBANY; FROGMORE; GEORGE IV; MARY, PRINCESS, DUCHESS OF GLOUCESTER AND EDINBURGH; OCTAVIUS, PRINCE; SOPHIA, PRINCESS.

**CHARLOTTE, PRINCESS ROYAL, QUEEN OF WURTEMBURG (1766–1828).** Charlotte, the eldest daughter and fourth child of King **George III** and **Charlotte of Mecklenburg-Strelitz**, was born at **Buckingham Palace** on 29 September 1766. George was devoted to his daughters and was unwilling to see them leave home, so, after his mental breakdown in 1788–89, the queen refused to discuss their marriage prospects with him, fearing that the topic might precipitate a further bout of insanity. As a result, the **princess royal** did not find a husband until she was in her early thirties, when Prince Frederick of Wurtemburg proposed. Frederick's first wife had left him because of his abusive behavior (and had died giving birth to an illegitimate baby), but even so, the prince's proposal was accepted, and the couple, both greatly overweight, married in **St. James's Palace** on 18 May 1797.

Despite these inauspicious circumstances, the marriage was a happy one (though it produced only one, stillborn, child). In 1805, Frederick infuriated his father-in-law by lending military support to **France** and Napoleon Bonaparte in return for recognizing him as king of Wurtemburg, but he returned to the British fold in 1813. In periods of sanity during the breach, George refused to recognize Charlotte as queen of Wurtemburg, but after her husband's death in 1816, her brothers and sisters were able to visit her at the Ludwigsburg Palace near Stuttgart, and in 1827, when she returned to England seeking treatment for edema (then known as dropsy), she dined at **Windsor Castle** with her eldest sibling, who had become King **George IV.** Charlotte died at Ludwigsburg on 5 October the following year, following a bout of apoplexy.

**CHATTO, LADY SARAH (1964– ).** The younger child, and only daughter, of **Princess Margaret, countess of Snowdon**, and **Antony Armstrong-Jones, earl of Snowdon**, Lady Sarah was born at **Clarence House**, London, on 1 May 1964. She was educated at Bedales (the Hampshire school, with a strong reputation for arts teaching, that her brother—**David Armstrong-Jones, viscount Linley**—also attended) and then studied at Middlesex Polytechnic and Camberwell College of Arts before establishing a career as an artist good enough to exhibit at the Royal Academy. On 14 July 1994, in St. Stephen's Walbrook Church, **London**, she married Daniel Chatto, a television and film actor turned painter. They have two sons—Samuel (born on 28 July 1996) and Arthur (born on 5 February 1999). In 2006, Lady Sarah and her brother annoyed their father by auctioning much of their mother's jewelry, ostensibly to raise the funds necessary to pay death duties on her estate.

**CHRISTIAN OF SCHLESWIG-HOLSTEIN, PRINCESS (1846–1923).** Queen **Victoria**'s third daughter—a boisterous tomboy as a child—caused family ructions over her marriage but devoted much of her life to charitable work, notably in connection with medical causes. The fifth of nine children in the family of the queen and her consort, **Prince Albert of Saxe-Coburg and Gotha**, Helena was born at **Buckingham Palace** on 25 May 1846. When she was in her midteens, a flirtation with a royal librarian, Carl Ruland, resulted in the official's dismissal but focused Victoria's attention on potential marriage partners for the **princess**. The choices were limited, partly because the queen was adamant that her daughter should live close to her, partly because Helena was no beauty, and partly because eligible bachelors in European royal houses preferred the prestige of union with elder daughters rather than younger ones. Prince Christian of Schleswig-Holstein met with the monarch's approval but divided the family.

Denmark (which formed the northern portion of the Jutland peninsula) claimed sovereignty over both Holstein and Schleswig (which formed the southern portion), but the prince had fought against the Danish armies, so Danish-born **Alexandra of Denmark**, princess of Wales, protested vigorously when plans for the match were mooted. Alexandra, the daughter of King Christian XI of Denmark, enlisted the support of her husband, Albert Edward, **prince of Wales** (later King **Edward VII**), and **Princess Alice, grand duchess of Hesse** (who was very close to her brother), lent weight to the opposition, as did **Alfred, duke of Edinburgh and Saxe-Coburg and Gotha**. On the other hand, **Victoria, princess royal**, had long been friends with Christian and his family, so she was enthusiastic about the proposals, and Helena herself, fond of the prince even though he was 15 years her senior, wanted the marriage to go ahead. Despite the protests, the queen insisted on having her own way, so the wedding was celebrated at **Windsor Castle** on 5 December 1865.

Helena was not a healthy woman (she suffered from rheumatism, had lung problems, and regularly took both laudanum and opium), so it was perhaps understandable that she should take an interest in nursing, heading the Royal British Nurses' Association and often bickering with Florence Nightingale over administrative matters. She also established a holiday home for deprived children, helped to found the Red Cross, lent her influence to the Society for the Prevention of Cruelty to Children, raised funds to provide free meals for unemployed people in Windsor, and was the first president of the School of Art Needlework (which provided jobs for women). Known after her marriage as Princess Christian of Schleswig-Holstein, she had five children (and, in 1877, a stillborn son). Only one of her offspring—Princess Marie Louise, born in 1872—married (briefly, unhappily, and without issue). **Prince** Christian Victor (born in 1867) died of enteric fever while serving with the 60th King's Royal Rifles in the Boer War, Prince Albert (born in 1869) was raised in Germany but refused to fight against his mother's country in World War I, and Prince Harold (born in 1876) survived for little more than a week. Princess Helena Victoria (born in 1870) followed her mother's example and devoted much effort to medical charities, as did Marie Louise.

Princess Christian died at Schomberg House, her **London** home, on 9 June 1923, after contracting influenza. She was buried in **St. George's Chapel** at Windsor Castle, but her remains were moved to the royal burial ground at **Frogmore** in 1928. Mount Helena, in British Columbia, is named after her.

**CHURCH OF ENGLAND.** The relationship between the British monarch and the Anglican Church is governed by legislation passed by the English parliament in the 16th and 18th centuries. In particular, the **Act of Supremacy**, approved in 1534, confirmed King **Henry VIII** as "Supreme Head" of the church, a title changed to "**Supreme Governor**" in 1559. Also, in 1544, parliament conferred the title "**Defender of the Faith**" on Henry's son, King **Edward VI**, and in 1701, during the reign of **William III and II**, the Act of Settlement specified that an individual could only become sovereign if he or she was in full communion with the Church of England. Parish priests are still required to swear an oath of allegiance to the monarch, who exercises the **royal prerogative** of making appointments to senior posts in the church (though in practice the people recommended are selected by the prime minister after discussion with clerics and laity). The clergy also officiate at **coronation** ceremonies, anointing the new king or queen with oil, placing the crown on the monarch's head, and administering Holy Communion.

Although the links between ruler and religious establishment are now largely formal, they have been the subject of considerable debate in recent years, with **Charles, prince of Wales**, suggesting that the sovereign should be considered "Defender of Faith," rather than "Defender of the Faith," because that title would be more appropriate in a multicultural society. Also, some commentators have argued that the laws requiring the British sovereign to be in communion with the Church of England should be relaxed. *See also* EDWARD VIII; GLORIOUS REVOLUTION; KATHARINE, DUCHESS OF KENT; MARGARET, PRINCESS, COUNTESS OF SNOWDON; MARY I; ROYAL PECULIAR; ST. GEORGE'S CHAPEL.

**CIVIL LIST.** The civil list is the funds, raised through taxation, that are used to finance the monarch's duties as head of state, covering the cost of garden parties, official receptions, and similar expenses. The arrangement dates from the 17th century but took its present form in 1761, when King **George III** agreed to surrender the revenues from the **crown estate** in return for an annual grant from parliament.

From 1990 to 2000, the civil list amounted to £7.9 million each year, with £359,000 going to **Prince Philip, duke of Edinburgh**, and the remainder to Queen **Elizabeth II**. Low rates of inflation over the decade, coupled with administrative savings, allowed a surplus of £35.3 million to be carried forward into the new millennium, so in 2001 the government confirmed that the yearly payments would continue at the same level until 2010, but by mid-decade, annual expenses had risen to £11.2 million (about 70 percent of them on wages), necessitating transfers from the earlier surplus. (Over the same period, annual income from the **crown estate** amounted to some £225 million.) Smaller allowances are also made to other members of the **royal family** from parliamentary funds, but the queen reimburses these from her own resources.

The total cost of maintaining the monarchy (including, for example, government contributions toward the cost of maintenance to **royal residences** as well as funds committed to the civil list) amounted to £40 million (about 66 pence for every member of the British population) in 2007. In 2010, the government announced that the civil list would be replaced, in 2013, by a payment, called the Sovereign Support Grant, that would be funded entirely by the crown state. *See also* PRIVY PURSE; ROYAL HOUSEHOLD.

**CLAIM OF RIGHT (1689).** On 4 April 1689, following the **Glorious Revolution** in England and the flight of King **James VII and II** to **France**, Scotland's parliament (the Convention of Estates), declared that the exiled monarch had forfeited the country's crown. A week later, it approved a "Claim of Right" that listed James's shortcomings (in particular, his conversion of the kingdom "from a legal limited monarchy to an arbitrary despotic power" and his "subversion of the Protestant religion" by placing "papists in the positions of greatest trust, civil and military"). The document also spelled out principles that were enacted in the **Bill of Rights** passed by the English parliament later in the year—that laws could not be suspended by royal command, that members of the Estates had a right to freedom of speech, that Roman Catholics were to be excluded from the line of **succession to the throne**, and that taxes could not be levied without the Estates' approval.

On the same day, the convention offered the crown jointly to William of Orange and his wife, Mary, James's sister, who ruled as William II of Scotland (*see* WILLIAM III OF ENGLAND AND II OF SCOTLAND) and **Mary II**. Many Scots clearly expected the new king and queen to treat the Claim of Right as a contract between the monarchs and their subjects and to simply approve what the Convention wanted. However, William was quick to disenchant them, taking issue, for example, with the Scots' efforts to outlaw the Episcopal Church and establish Presbyterianism as the only acceptable form of religious belief.

**CLARENCE HOUSE.** The southwest suite of rooms in **St. James's Palace**, London, is joined by a passage to Clarence House, designed by John Nash and built for William, duke of Clarence (later King **William IV**), who felt that the accommodation available in St. James's was too cramped after his marriage to **Princess Adelaide of Saxe-Meiningen** in 1818. The original structure was completed in 1828, but considerable enlargement and restoration work was carried out in the 1870s under the supervision of Queen **Victoria**'s second son, **Prince Alfred, duke of Edinburgh and Saxe-Coburg and Gotha**, and then again in the late 1940s, when the extensive bomb damaged incurred during World War II was repaired. For part of that war, the building was an operational headquarters for the Red Cross and St. John's Ambulance Brigade, but for most of its history Clarence House has been a home for members of the **royal family**.

**Princess** Elizabeth (now Queen **Elizabeth II**) made the residence her home from 1949 to 1952, after her marriage to **Prince Philip, duke of Edinburgh**; their daughter, **Anne, princess royal**, was born in the house in 1950. Queen **Elizabeth, the queen mother**, moved in following the death of her husband, King **George VI**, in 1952, and after she died in 2002, a £4.5 million refurbishment was undertaken while plans were made for **Charles, prince of Wales**, and his sons, **Prince William of Wales** and **Prince Henry—or Harry—of Wales**, to make Clarence House their official London base.

**COACHES.** *See* STATE COACHES.

**COENRED (c640–?).** Coenred (also known as Cenred) was the son of **Ceolwald** and possibly the great-great-grandson of **Ceawlin**, who ruled **Wessex** from 560 until his nephew, Ceol, overthrew him in 592. Some scholars dispute the accuracy of details of Coenred's ancestry reported in the *Anglo-Saxon Chronicle*, but if those details are accurate, he is one element of the direct male line from **Cerdic** (traditionally regarded as the founder of the Saxon Wessex dynasty) to **Egbert** (sometimes considered the first king of England) and thus is an ancestor of the present British **royal family**.

Coenred had at least three children by an unknown partner or partners. Ine, born about 670, was king of Wessex from 688 to 726, losing much of the territory won by Caedwalla, his predecessor, but introducing one of the first Saxon legal systems and overseeing a considerable expansion of trade. Cuthburg (or Cuthburga), whose birth date is not known, married Aldfrith, king of Northumbria, and had at least one son, but she later renounced sexual intercourse and became the first abbess of the nunnery at Wimborne Minster, which she founded in about 705. The line to the modern monarchy was continued through **Ingild**, who was born c672. Information about Coenred's influence on Wessex is sketchy, with some documents suggesting that he was a co-ruler with Ine and others indicating that he helped his son formulate laws for the territory. The date and location of his death are not known.

**COLIN (?–971).** Colin (the son of **Indulf** and also known as Cuilén and Culen) was king of **Alba** from 966 to 971. Some writers believe that he gained his position by arranging the murder of his predecessor, **Duff**, who had earlier defeated him in battle. In 971, he died at the hands of Amdarch (a military leader from the neighboring kingdom of Strathclyde), perhaps as revenge for the rape of his daughter, and may have been buried at **Iona**. He was succeeded by **Kenneth II**, son of **Malcolm I**, but his own son reigned briefly as **Constantine III** in 995–996 following Kenneth's murder.

**COMMONWEALTH OF ENGLAND.** On 19 May 1649, less than four months after the execution of King **Charles I**, parliament declared England a "commonwealth" (in effect, a republic), with power formally residing in a Council of State whose first meeting was chaired by Oliver Cromwell, but with the army and the parliamentary assembly exerting considerable influence. Although royalists in Ireland and Scotland fiercely opposed the regicide, by 1651 Cromwell had sent troops to end the resistance and bring the whole of the British Isles under Commonwealth control. On 16 December 1653, he was appointed lord protector, and from then until his death on 3 September 1658, he ruled with all the authority of an uncrowned sovereign. Richard Cromwell succeeded his father as lord protector (the period of the two Cromwells' administrations is often known as "the protectorate"), but, unable to exert authority over the army or unite disputing factions within the Commonwealth, he resigned on 25 May 1659. As the country slipped toward anarchy, military and political leaders agreed that a **restoration of the monarchy** was the only way of reestablishing stable government, so, on 8 May 1660, Charles's son was proclaimed King **Charles II**. *See also* CROWN JEWELS OF THE UNITED KINGDOM.

**COMMONWEALTH REALM.** Independent countries, including the United Kingdom, that recognize Britain's monarch as their own head of state are known as commonwealth realms. Those states (with the year in which they joined the group in parentheses) are Antigua and Barbuda (1981), Australia (1942), the Bahamas (1973), Barbados (1966), Belize (1981), Canada (1931), Grenada (1974), Jamaica (1962), New Zealand (1947), Papua New Guinea (1975), St. Kitts and Nevis (1983), St. Lucia (1979), St. Vincent and the Grenadines (1979), the Solomon Islands (1978), and Tuvalu (1978). With the exception of Papua New Guinea (which is a union of two territories controlled by Australia), all are former British colonies. A further 18 nations, once commonwealth realms, have changed their political status and become republics.

The multiple monarchy arrangement can create constitutional anomalies, as in 1939, when Britain declared war on Germany before Canada took the same action; because **George VI** was king of both countries, he was, even though only for seven days, technically both at war with Germany and at peace with Germany at the same time. Problems can also arise when, for example, the monarch makes a speech that conflicts with the policy of one of his or her governments, as occurred when Australia's political leaders took issue with aspects of an address made by Queen **Elizabeth II** in Jordan in 1984, even though she was acting in her capacity as British monarch and expressing the views of the British government. Partly as a result of such complications, and because of a desire for complete independence, republican sentiments are regularly expressed in several commonwealth realms, but for many people, the concept of a politically neutral head of state remains attractive.

In each realm, apart from the United Kingdom, the monarch is represented by a **governor-general**, appointed on the advice of the country's prime minister (and, in some cases, its legislature), who carries out ceremonial and constitutional duties on behalf of the sovereign. *See also* QUEEN'S (OR KING'S) BIRTHDAY HONOURS LIST; *also* QUEEN'S (OR KING'S) OFFICIAL BIRTHDAY; ROYAL STANDARD; SETTLEMENT, ACT OF (1701).

**CONSTANCE, DUCHESS OF BRITTANY (c1057–1090).** By some accounts, Constance (also known as Constance of Normandy) was the most talented of the daughters born to **William I of England** (William the Conqueror) and his wife, **Matilda of Flanders**. In 1086, when nearly 30, she was married to Alain Fergant (Alan the Younger), duke of Brittany, after her father had invaded his lands and forced him into submission. Stories of the childless union differ. William of Malmesbury, writing in the early 12th century, claims that Constance was unpopular because of her "sever and conservative manner" and alleges that her husband had his servants poison her. On the other hand, Orderic Vitalis, who was penning his *Historia Ecclesiastica* at the same time, paints a picture of a caring, considerate woman, whose death on 13 August 1090 was a great loss to the Breton people.

**CONSTANTINE I (?–877).** In 862, Constantine succeeded his uncle, **Donald I**, as king of the territory that was formed in the north of the British Isles when, some two decades earlier, his father, **Kenneth MacAlpin**, began the process of uniting Pictish communities with the kingdom of Dalriada. Most of his 15-year reign was devoted to defending his realm against Viking attacks; In 866 and in 870–871, for example, the Scandinavians ravaged the Picts' homeland and took away many slaves. Then, in 875, Halfdan (the Danish king of York) inflicted a heavy defeat on their forces at Dollar, nine miles east of **Stirling**. Eventually, in 877, Constantine was killed while attempting to resist their incursions, possibly on the Fife coast in eastern Scotland. According to one source, he was buried on the island of **Iona** and was succeeded by his younger brother, **Áed**. His son later took the throne, as **Donald II**, in 889.

**CONSTANTINE II (?–952).** For 43 years, from 900 until 943, Constantine, the son of Áed, ruled **Alba** (the precursor of modern Scotland)—a singular achievement, at a time of great unrest in northern Britain, that provided a stable foundation for the evolution of the medieval Scottish state. Danish invaders had killed his predecessor, **Donald II**, but Constantine managed to defeat a Viking force at Strathearn (Perthshire) in 904 and then, for the most part, was able to preserve peace through diplomacy and intermarriage (one of his daughters was wed to Olaf Cuaran, the Norse king of Dublin, for example). He also engineered the election of his brother, Donald, to the kingship of neighboring Strathclyde and promoted major developments within the church. Eventually, however, he faced the might of **Aethelstan**, who was expanding the English state northward. In 937, Constantine, then more than 60 years old, allied with the kingdoms of Dublin and Strathclyde to invade England but was routed at the **Battle of Brunanburh**. Unlike many of his colleagues (including Cellach, his son), he escaped with his life, but some six years later he abdicated the throne (possibly unwillingly) in favor of his cousin, **Malcolm I**, and retired to a Culdean monastery at St. Andrews, where he died in 952. **Indulf**, another of his sons, succeeded to the throne on Malcolm's death in 954.

**CONSTANTINE III (?–997).** Constantine succeeded **Kenneth II** as king of **Alba**, ruling for only about 18 months. The son of **Colin**, who led the fledgling Scottish state from 967 to 971, he was, according to some sources, implicated in his predecessor's assassination in 995 and died in battle at Rathinveramond, an unidentified site probably located close to Perth. According to one source, he was buried at **Iona**. Constantine left no children, thus ending the monarchical line that claimed descent from **Kenneth MacAlpin**'s son, **Áed**, who was monarch for a similarly brief period in 877–878. His probable killer, **Kenneth III**, succeeded him.

**CORONATION.** It is not known when the practice of crowning kings began in Britain, though there are reports of Celtic anointings dating from the 5th century and of Anglo-Saxon rituals in which a helmet was placed on the new leader's head. In Scotland, early coronations were held at **Scone**, near Perth, with the king sitting on the **Stone of Scone**. After King **Edward I** took the Stone to England in 1296, these ceremonies took place either in Scone Abbey or at **Stirling** Castle, the last being that for **Charles II** at Scone in 1651. In England, all coronations since that of King **Harold II** in 1066 have been held in **Westminster Abbey**, broadly following a ritual designed by St. Dunstan for King **Edgar of England** in 973.

In modern coronation ceremonies, the sovereign processes through the abbey and then sits on a "chair of estate" while the archbishop of Canterbury (the leader of the **Church of England**) asks other members of the assembly to affirm that they are willing to pay homage to their king or queen. Having received the necessary assurance, the cleric asks the monarch to swear an oath confirming that he or she will govern according to the law and "maintain . . . the Protestant reformed religion." The promises made, and the gift of a Bible accepted, the sovereign moves to King Edward's Chair, where the archbishop anoints her or him with holy oil and presents spurs, the sword of state, an orb, and scepters before placing the St. Edward's Crown on the new ruler's head. Senior clergy and nobility pay homage, and Holy Communion is administered before the sovereign exchanges the St. Edward's Crown for the less weighty Imperial State Crown and leaves the church while the congregation sings the national anthem. If the monarch is married, the consort may be crowned at the same ceremony.

In the United Kingdom, there is no break in kingship, a new monarch succeeding as soon as the predecessor dies, so the coronation ceremony confirms power rather than confers it and may take place several months after the accession because of the planning involved. *See also* BILL OF RIGHTS; CROWN JEWELS OF THE UNITED KINGDOM; HONOURS OF SCOTLAND; STATE COACHES; WINCHESTER.

**COUNSELLOR OF STATE.** *See* REGENCY ACTS.

*COURT CIRCULAR.* The *Court Circular* is a daily report of the official activities of members of the **royal family**. It first appeared in 1785 when King **George III** decided to issue his own summary of public engagements because coverage by the press was often inaccurate and misleading. Nowadays, the monarch's private secretary prepares the text, which is approved by the sovereign and then faxed to the *Daily Telegraph*, *Scotsman*, and *Times* newspapers each evening. Those papers publish the document without making any editorial changes, even though it is couched in very formal language and is little more than a record of distinguished visitors received and functions attended by members of the royal family, in the United Kingdom and abroad. Announcements are listed according to the individual's place in the order of precedence (thus those relating to the monarch always come first) and are identified by the appropriate official residence (those of the sovereign usually appear under a "**Buckingham Palace**" heading, for example).

Despite the lack of commentary and the emphasis on protocol, the *Court Circulars* are a valuable indicator of the changing demands on the monarchy over the past two centuries, detailing an increasing involvement with charitable and community activities and (as a result of vastly improved transport) a much larger number of engagements carried out annually. All circulars prepared since 1998 are archived on the monarchy's media center website at http://royal.gov.uk/output/Page3759.asp.

**COURT OF ST. JAMES'S. St. James's Palace** was built by King **Henry VIII** from 1531 on the site of the medieval leper hospital of St. James in **London** and remained a principal residence of the royal court until Queen **Victoria** settled in **Buckingham Palace** in 1837. Foreign ambassadors and high commissioners, numbering over 150, are still accredited to the Court of St. James's and are assisted by some 3,000 diplomatic staff, although, for convenience, most audiences with the monarch are held at Buckingham Palace.

**CRATHIE CHURCH.** When members of the **royal family** are staying at **Balmoral Castle**, they regularly join the Church of Scotland congregation in the village of Crathie for Sunday morning worship in their small, granite building, erected in 1895 on a site used by Christian communities since the 9th century. The south transept is reserved for the royal visitors. King **Ed-**

ward VII presented the church with two marble medallions in memory of his father (**Prince Albert of Saxe-Coburg and Gotha**); King **George V** presented the marble communion table in memory of King Edward (his father); **Princess Beatrice of Battenberg** (Queen **Victoria**'s youngest child) donated the four bells that still hang in the bell tower; Queen **Elizabeth II** donated a bible; **Victoria, princess royal and German Empress** (Queen Victoria's eldest child), gifted the organ; and Queen Victoria herself paid for two of the stained glass windows. In 1992, **Anne, princess royal (1950– )**, married her second husband, **Timothy Laurence**, at Crathie because the Church of Scotland had a more charitable attitude toward the remarriage of divorcees than did the **Church of England**.

**CRINAN (?–1045).** Crinan, a lay abbot at Dunkeld (one of the principal Scottish monastic centers during the 11th century), was the father of **Duncan I** and founder of the **House of Dunkeld**, whose members were kings of Scots from 1034 to 1040 and from 1058 to 1286. At some time between 1000 and 1010, Crinan married **Bethóc**, the eldest daughter of King **Malcolm II**. Duncan, their son, succeeded Malcolm in 1034 but was killed by **Macbeth** six years later, and Crinan, too, fell victim to the usurper, being slain in 1045 while leading an uprising that was intended to put his grandson, Malcolm (later **Malcolm III**), on the throne.

**CROWN ESTATE.** From the time of the Norman Conquest and the accession of King **William I of England** to the throne in 1066, monarchs acquired large estates, using the income to fund the costs of governing the kingdom, pursuing military campaigns abroad, and sustaining their often lavish lifestyles. In 1761, however, King **George III** exchanged the revenues from his own lands for a guaranteed annual payment from parliament, an arrangement formalized in 1777 through the **Civil List** Act. Nowadays, that royal estate includes some 300,000 acres of agricultural property, 29 quarries, and a lengthy list of urban sites, including, for example, much of Regent Street, a prime retail area in central **London**. In addition, it owns the rights to all gold and silver mined in the United Kingdom and to all minerals (except hydrocarbons) taken from the continental shelf that surrounds the country. The total value of the portfolio was about £6 billion in 2009, with annual returns exceeding £225 million, all of which still accrues to the government. The estate, which provides employment for about 400 people, is managed by a board of up to eight commissioners, who are appointed by the sovereign and are expected to maintain and enhance the value of the holdings while giving due regard to requirements of good management. *See also* BAGSHOT PARK; CARLTON HOUSE; FORT BELVEDERE; ROYAL ASCOT.

**CROWN JEWELS OF SCOTLAND.** *See* HONOURS OF SCOTLAND.

**CROWN JEWELS OF THE UNITED KINGDOM.** Most of the British crown jewels date from the mid-17th century because earlier versions were either lost in 1216 (when they were carried away by a tide in the Wash while King **John** was transporting them around the country as he retreated from his nobles and their French allies during the **First Barons' War**) or were melted down between 1649 and 1660, during the **Commonwealth of England** (when England was a republic under the control of Oliver Cromwell and his son, Richard). The principal items in the collection are as follows:

- Armills (gold bracelets) that symbolize security and wisdom;
- The crowns of **queens consort**, the earliest used by **Mary of Modena** during the reign of **James VII and II** (1685–88) and the most recent designed for **Elizabeth, the queen mother**, consort of King **George VI**, in 1937 and incorporating the Koh-i-Noor diamond, which, when it was acquired by Britain in 1849, was believed to be the largest in the world;
- The **George IV** State Diadem, which has 1,333 diamonds, was made for the **coronation** of King George IV in 1821, and was worn by Queen **Victoria** at her coronation in 1838 and by Queen **Elizabeth II** at **state openings of parliament**;
- The gold Ampulla and Spoon, dating from the 12th century, that are used to anoint the monarch with holy oil during the coronation ceremony;
- The Imperial Crown of India, used when King **George V** visited India as emperor in 1911 and made because the other crown jewels cannot be taken abroad;
- The Imperial State Crown, which was made in 1937 for King George VI's coronation, is lighter than the St. Edward's Crown (which is used to crown new monarchs at coronation ceremonies), and contains more than 2,800 diamonds, one of which—the Cullinan II or Second Star of Africa—is the fourth largest in the world;
- The Jeweled Sword of Offering, made for the coronation of King George IV in 1821 and presented to the new sovereign during the coronation ceremony;
- The Ring, made for King **William IV**'s coronation in 1831;
- The Scepter with the Cross, which is held in a monarch's right hand while he or she is being crowned, was made for King **Charles II**'s coronation in 1661, and was altered in 1910 to include the Cullinan I (or Great Star of Africa), the world's largest flawless cut diamond;
- The Scepter with the Dove, a bejeweled gold rod, also designed in 1661, which is held in the monarch's left hand during the crowning ceremony;

- The Small Orb, topped by a cross, which was made for the coronation of Queen **Mary II** in 1689;
- The Sovereign's Orb, a hollow gold sphere manufactured in 1661 for King Charles II's coronation;
- The St. Edward's Crown, designed in 1661 for the coronation of King Charles II and reputed to contain gold from the crown of **Alfred the Great**;
- The Sword of Mercy, which, according to legend, was broken by an angel to prevent a killing;
- The Sword of Spiritual Justice, which may have been made for the coronation of King **Charles I** in 1626, though it is not known how it escaped Cromwell's depredations;
- The Sword of State, the largest of the five swords among the crown jewels, carried in front of the monarch at coronation ceremonies and at the state opening of parliament; and
- The Sword of Temporal Justice, possibly made (like the Sword of Spiritual Justice) for Charles I's coronation.

The crown jewels have been housed in the **Tower of London** since 1303, except during World War II, when, according to some sources they were hidden at **Windsor Castle**, and according to others they were taken to Canada for safekeeping. *See also* HONOURS OF THE PRINCIPALITY OF WALES; HONOURS OF SCOTLAND.

**CULLODEN, BATTLE OF (16 April 1746).** Culloden—the last major set-piece battle fought on British soil—ended both the second **Jacobite rebellion** and the **House of Stuart**'s efforts to regain the crowns lost by King **James VII and II** in the **Glorious Revolution** of 1688–89. Seven thousand exhausted, hungry supporters of **Charles Edward Stuart** (Bonnie **Prince** Charlie) faced a 9,000-man Hanoverian army led by **William Augustus, duke of Cumberland**, on ground near Inverness that none of the Jacobite advisors believed could be protected. With sleet driving into their faces, the rebels were routed within 40 minutes, sacrificing 1,000 men in the battle or shortly afterward. Cumberland lost only 50 soldiers but took vicious reprisals, bayoneting the wounded, hanging fugitives, and burning the homes of those believed to be harboring adherents of the Stuart cause. The prince escaped, spending five months skulking in caves and huts before fleeing to the European mainland, but he failed to find political or financial support for another attempt to retrieve his grandfather's thrones.

**CURIA REGIS.** The body of advisors to England's Norman (*see* HOUSE OF NORMANDY) and early **House of Plantagenet** kings was known as the Curia Regis (Latin for "King's Council"). Introduced by **William I**, it replaced the **witan**, which had performed a similar function for **Anglo-Saxon monarchs**, and consisted of senior clerics and tenants-in-chief (nobles who had been granted their estates by the sovereign). Initially, the king's rule was absolute, and the Curia Regis was consulted only when the monarch felt that advice was necessary or that discussion was politically desirable. However, the barons gradually gained more power (*see, for example,* MAGNA CARTA; PROVISIONS OF OXFORD), and by the mid-14th century the Curia Regis had evolved into a body more closely resembling the modern British parliament. *See also* PRIVY COUNCIL.

**CUTHWINE (?–?).** Cuthwine is a shadowy figure in Anglo-Saxon history, known largely from genealogies, some of which place him in the line of descent from **Cerdic** (founder of the kingdom of **Wessex**) to the present British **royal family**. According to the *Anglo-Saxon Chronicle*, he was the son of **Ceawlin**, who ruled Wessex from 560 to 592. He fought with his father at the Battle of Deorham (now Dyrham) in 577, winning a victory that added the settlements of Bath, Cirencester, and Gloucester to the Saxon realm and divided the Britons in southwest England from those in Wales. A number of sources claim that he predeceased his father, dying in 584. Others suggest that he lived until about 597 but did not succeed to the throne because Ceawlin was deposed by **Ceol**, Cuthwine's cousin, in 592. Cuthwine may have left three sons—Cynebald, Cedda, and **Cuthwulf**—and there is evidence that Cedda's line regained the throne through Caedwalla, Cuthwine's great-grandson, when Centwine, the last of Ceol's house, died in about 685. The line of descent to modern monarchs, however, is supposedly through Cuthwulf, though there is continued scholarly debate about whether Cuthwine and Cuthwulf were the same person.

**CUTHWULF (?–?).** Cuthwulf (also known as Cutha) features in some genealogies that link **Cerdic**—the founder of the kingdom of **Wessex**—to the modern British **royal family**, but very little is known about him. Some scholars believe that he was the son of **Cuthwine** and grandson of **Ceawlin** (who ruled Wessex from 560 to 592), but others suspect that Cuthwine and Cuthwulf were the same person. His birth date is sometimes given as 560 but sometimes as late as 592. The year of his death is unknown, but he apparently left one son, **Ceolwald**.

**CYNRIC (c495–560).** Cynric ruled **Wessex** from 534 to 560. The *Anglo-Saxon Chronicle* notes that he traveled from the European mainland with **Cerdic**, whom it lists in one place as his grandfather and in another as his father, and landed on the southern shores of the British Isles in 495. After he became king, he consolidated the boundaries of Saxon territory with victories over the native Britons at Searobyrig (near Salisbury) in 552 and at Beranburh (south of Swindon) in 556. Some scholars suggest, however, that certain of the dates cited in the *Chronicle* may be wrong and that Cynric actually reigned from 554 to 581. His son, **Ceawlin**, succeeded him.

# D

**DANEGELD.** In the last years of the first century AD, **Anglo-Saxon monarchs** attempted to buy peace by paying Viking raiders not to pillage their lands. The first recorded tribute, known as danegeld (or "Dane gold"), was handed over in 856, but the word is most usually applied to the series of payments made during the reign of King **Aethelred the Unready** from 978 to 1016. Modern writers suggest that as much as 100 tonnes of silver were handed over, but the policy of appeasement proved expensive because the Danes quickly learned that they could get more by threatening to invade than they could by actually invading. As a result, every few years they returned with increased demands. The term is still in use in modern English with reference to payments, such as ransom money, that are made under coercion but may fail to achieve the desired end.

**DANELAW.** The Danelaw was the area of central, eastern, and northern England colonized by Viking (and predominantly Danish) settlers during the 9th and 10th centuries. Boundaries between the Anglo-Saxon and Danish realms were agreed upon by **Alfred the Great** and Guthrum (the Viking leader) in two treaties drawn up between 878 and 890, but peace was never assured. The relative wealth of the Danelaw meant that other Viking groups constantly threatened it, but many of its resources were used up in squabbles with the neighboring Anglo-Saxon kingdoms of Mercia and **Wessex**. Reconquest of the area began under **Edward the Elder** from 910 and was completed during the reign of his son, **Eadred**, who drove Eric Bloodaxe out of Northumbria in 954. During the period of occupation, society in the Danelaw was governed by Danish legal principles, and there is a modern legacy in place names (for example, the suffix *-by* is common in settlement names in eastern England and derives from the Old Norse word for "village").

**DAVID I (c1082–1153).** The youngest son of **Malcolm III** and **St. Margaret**, David was king of Scotland from 1124 until his death and used his comparatively lengthy reign to modernize his country by establishing law and order, supporting the Roman Catholic Church, and improving administrative efficiency. He spent several years of his youth at the court of **Henry I** of England and, while there, imbued Norman values that later influenced the manner in which he governed his own kingdom. Also, he encouraged the settlement of noble Norman families, including the Bruces and the Stewarts, who were later to exert great influence over Scottish affairs. (*See* BRUCE, HOUSE OF; STUART, HOUSE OF.)

From 1113, Scotland was divided between David and his brother, **Alexander I**, the former being responsible for the southern half of the country and the latter for the north. When Alexander died in 1124, David inherited the whole territory, though even with Henry's military assistance it took him a decade to establish his rule and repel challenges from Malcolm, Alexander's illegitimate son. The feudal system of land tenure, which David introduced to Scotland, undoubtedly enhanced his power (as well as that of later monarchs) and brought considerable cohesion to a previously divided kingdom. His wealth—one of the keys to authority—was augmented by the establishment of a series of royal burghs, such as **Edinburgh** and **Stirling**, that were given trading rights in return for cash payments to the monarch. A standard coinage was developed, and a uniform series of weights and measures was imposed. The church, with its strong influence on David's subjects through its literacy and learning, as well as its theology, was supported by large grants (for example, during his reign, **Holyrood**, Jedburgh, Kelso, Melrose, and some dozen other abbeys were all established on the continental European model), and much of its structure was reorganized.

Progress was periodically interrupted by rebellion at home and by war with England (he initially sided with his niece, **Matilda**, in her struggle against **Stephen** but willingly agreed to a truce if it could bring him grants of land). However, when he died at Carlisle on 24 May 1153, he left a kingdom more united than at any time in its history and extending further south than it had ever done before. David was buried at **Dunfermline Abbey** and was succeeded by his grandson, King **Malcolm IV**. *See also* CAMBUSKENNETH ABBEY; HENRY, EARL OF NORTHUMBERLAND; LINLITHGOW PALACE; MAUD, COUNTESS OF HUNTINGDON; ROXBURGH CASTLE.

**DAVID II (1324–1371).** David was king of Scots for more than 40 years but spent 7 of them in exile and a further 11 as a prisoner of King **Edward III** of England. Born at the royal palace in **Dunfermline** on 5 March 1324, he was the only male child of **Robert I** (Robert the Bruce) and **Elizabeth de Burgh** to survive childhood, and he succeeded to his father's crown on 7 June 1329, at the age of five. By that time, he was married, because the **Treaty of Northampton**, which was signed in 1328 and which temporarily ended hostilities between England and Scotland, contained a provision that Bruce's son would wed **Joan of the Tower**, Edward's younger sister. The ceremony was held at Berwick on 17 July the same year.

Because David was still a boy when he succeeded to the throne, government was placed in the hands of **regents** (known as **Guardians of Scotland**). However, they failed to repel the challenge of **Edward de Balliol**, son of King **John of Scotland**, who had been forced to abdicate in 1296. With the support of Edward III and the nobles who had been disinherited by the young king's father, Balliol brought an army from **France**, defeated a Scots force at Dupplin Moor (Perthshire) on 12 August 1332, was crowned king on 24 September, and in late November recognized the English monarch as his overlord.

In 1333, Edward III repudiated the Northampton agreement, which had recognized Scotland as an independent state and disavowed English monarchs' claims to suzerainty, so in May of the following year, David was sent to **France** for safety. He remained there until the summer of 1341, by which time his supporters had chased Edward de Balliol out of the kingdom. His return was not permanent, however. In 1346, he led troops into England, offering support to King Philip VI of France who was attempting to repel an invasion by Edward's army. On 17 October, David was defeated at the **Battle of Neville's Cross**, near Durham, was taken prisoner, and was held at various locations in England for 11 years until ransom arrangements could be agreed upon.

David was released late in 1357, but the price of his freedom turned out to be more than his treasury could find. During his period of captivity, he had developed a good relationship with Edward III, so in 1363 he proposed that, in lieu of the ransom money, the English king or one of his sons should follow him on the Scottish throne. The Scots parliament refused to accept this plan, but David continued to plot secretly until he died, suddenly and childless, at **Edinburgh** Castle on 22 February 1371. He was buried in **Holyrood** Abbey, Edinburgh, and was succeeded by his nephew, **Robert II**, the first monarch from the House of Stewart (*see* STUART, HOUSE OF).

David has had bad press from scholars, who have stressed his apparent willingness to surrender Scotland's hard-won independence, the expensive military conflicts that punctuated his reign, and his financial profligacy in later years. However, his father was a hard act to follow, Edward de Balliol's invasion took place while he was still a minor, and his capture by the English was due as much to the desertion of colleagues as to bad judgment. In an effort to redress the critical balance, some writers have stressed that he extended representation in parliament by giving seats to burgesses (previously, nobles alone had been entitled to attend), that by the time of his death he was exerting firm control over a lawmaking body that had previously exhibited a decided propensity to squabble, and that his plans for the future of the crown may have been a pragmatic effort to bring peace to a poor country threatened by a wealthier, more powerful neighbor. *See also* DRUMMOND, MARGARET; STEWART, MARJORIE, COUNTESS OF MORAY.

**DAVID OF SCOTLAND (1273–1281).** David, the younger son of King **Alexander III** and **Margaret, queen of Scots**, was born on 20 March 1273 but failed to survive boyhood, dying at **Stirling** Castle in June 1281. He was buried close to his mother at **Dunfermline Abbey**. *See also* ALEXANDER OF SCOTLAND.

**DEFENDER OF THE FAITH.** Perhaps ironically in view of later events (*see, for example,* SUPREMACY, ACT OF [1534]), Pope Leo X granted King **Henry VIII** the title of *Fidei Defensor* (Defender of the Faith) on 11 October 1521 because the monarch had written a text entitled *Assertio Septem Sacramentorum* (Defense of the Seven Sacraments) that opposed reformist Protestant views by affirming papal authority over the church and the sacramental nature of marriage ties. Pope Paul III withdrew the honor in 1535 after Henry's rift with the Roman Catholic Church, but the king continued to use the title, and it was formally reinstated by the English parliament on 29 March 1544. Neither Oliver nor Richard Cromwell used it from 1653, when Britain was governed by a lord protector rather than a hereditary sovereign, but it was adopted again with the **restoration of the monarchy** in 1660 and has been used by all kings and queens of England, Britain, and the United Kingdom since then.

The abbreviations "Fid. Def." and "F.D." have been engraved on coins since the reign of King **George I** (1714–27); in 1849, the Royal Mint's decision to issue a new florin piece without either caused such an outcry that the coin had to be withdrawn and redesigned. In 1994, **Charles, prince of Wales**, the **heir apparent**, suggested that the title should be changed to "Defender of Faith," a proposal that some commentators felt would be appropriate in Britain's multicultural society but which was attacked by critics who argued that some faiths should not be defended and by traditionalists who believed that the sovereign's role as **supreme governor of the Church of England** should not be changed.

**DERVORGUILLA (c1209–1290).** Dervorguilla (or Devorguilla) was the mother of King **John of Scotland**. Through her own mother (Margaret of Huntingdon), she was related to King **David I**, and through her father (Alan, lord of Galloway), she inherited the large estates that made her a rich woman from 1234. Much of that wealth was devoted to patronage of religious communities, including the Dominican friary at Wigtown and the Franciscan friaries at Dumfries and Dundee. Also, she provided considerable funding for the college that her husband, **John de Balliol**, had founded at Oxford University. Dervorguilla married John in 1233 and had at least four sons and four daughters, outliving all but one of them. When John died in 1268, she had his heart encased in an ivory container and then carried it with her wherever she went. She passed away at Buittle Castle, near Dalbeattie, on 28 January 1290 and was buried, with the casket on her breast, at Sweetheart Abbey, a Cistercian monastery that she had established in 1275. John of Scotland, the only child to survive Dervorguilla, became king in 1292, basing his claim to the throne on his mother's descent from the Scottish royal house.

**DETTINGEN, BATTLE OF (27 June 1743).** Dettingen was the last battle at which a British monarch commanded troops in the field. King **George II** had allied Britain with Hanover, Hesse, and others in a war against the French and the Prussians, ostensibly over the rights of succession to the Austrian throne, but in practice over the distribution of power in Europe. On 27 June 1743, nearly 60 years old, he won a notable victory over the French at Dettingen in Bavaria and was much praised for his courage, but his strategy was strongly criticized (John Dalrymple, earl of Stair—the king's principal general—resigned shortly afterward, complaining that the monarch had ignored his advice) and he was accused of favoring his Hanoverian troops at the expense of British forces.

**DIANA, PRINCESS OF WALES (1961–1997).** Diana, late wife of **Charles, prince of Wales**, was born on 1 July 1961 at Park House, on the **Sandringham** estate in Norfolk. The third child of Edward Spencer, viscount Althorp, and his wife, Frances, she became Lady Diana when her father succeeded to the Spencer earldom in 1975. Lady Diana was educated at Riddlesworth Hall (Thetford), at West Heath School (Sevenoaks), and in Chateau d'Oex in Switzerland but never distinguished herself academically. For a time after leaving school, she worked at a London kindergarten, but her social activities brought her into regular contact with the **royal family**, and romance with the **prince** blossomed. The couple were engaged on 24 February 1981 and were married in St. Paul's Cathedral, **London**, on 29 July. Their first son (**Prince William of Wales**) was born on 21 June 1982 and their second (**Prince Henry—or Harry—of Wales**) on 15 September 1984.

During the 1980s, Diana became widely known for her charity work. Support for victims of AIDS was a major interest (in 1987, when many people believed that the disease could be spread by casual contact, she was photographed holding the hand of a sufferer), and several observers claim that her well-publicized campaign against the use of landmines led to the international ban signed in 1994. However, while the **princess** worked on behalf of others, her personal life became increasingly anguished. She suffered from depression after the birth of Prince William and reportedly made several attempts at suicide. Also, she developed *bulimia nervosa*, a dietary disorder, and grew further and further apart from her husband, whom she believed was uncaring and more in love with Camilla Parker Bowles, his longtime confidante (*see* CAMILLA, DUCHESS OF CORNWALL), than with her. Diana herself became sexually involved with other men, notably James Gilbey and James Hewitt.

On 14 August 1992, *The Sun*, a tabloid newspaper, printed what it purported to be extracts from a telephone conversation between Diana and Gilbey, and on 9 December, **Buckingham Palace** announced that she and the prince would separate. Their divorce was finalized in August 1996, but even after that she was pursued relentlessly by the press, and on 31 August the following year she was killed in a Paris car accident, along with Dodi Al-Fayed (the son of Mohammed Al-Fayed, the owner of Harrods department store), while trying to escape the attentions of photographers. The full details of the incident were never revealed, but French investigators believe that her driver, Henri Paul, was drunk and was exceeding the speed limit when the vehicle crashed. A three-year investigation, led by Lord Stevens (a former commissioner of London's Metropolitan Police) and published in 2006, supported that conclusion and debunked the conspiracy theories that had been advanced as alternative explanations. The princess was buried at Althorp, the Spencer family's Northamptonshire home, on 6 September. Mohammed Al-Fayed has contended that the deaths of Diana and of his son were planned, rather than caused by accident, but has produced no convincing evidence in support of his case. *See also* ELIZABETH II; HER (OR HIS) ROYAL HIGHNESS; HIGHGROVE; KENSINGTON PALACE; PHILIP, PRINCE, DUKE OF EDINBURGH.

**DIVINE RIGHT OF KINGS.** From the medieval period until the late 17th century, many courtiers throughout Europe held to a doctrine that monarchs were ordained by God to rule and were accountable to Him and not to their subjects. Citizens had a duty to obey their sovereign, no matter how much they disagreed with an order; dissent was allowed only if the instruction contradicted God's own commands, but even then the dissenter had to accept, without objection, any punishment that was meted out by the king. In essence, the belief functioned as a means of social control and was supported by churchmen and nobles who sought preferment.

The British monarch most strongly identified with the philosophy was **James VI and I**, who, in 1598, published *The Trew Law of Free Monarchies*, arguing that the divine right of kings (with its implications of hereditary **succession to the throne**) was analogous to the concept of apostolic succession, which traces the line of bishops back to Jesus Christ's 12 disciples. James told his English parliament in 1610 that "Kings are . . . God's lieutenants upon earth and sit on God's throne," but that view—held also by his successors, **Charles I** (James's son) and **Charles II** and **James VII and II** (his grandsons)—was contested by many in a country that had been curbing the power of the monarch since King **John** was forced to accept the limitations to his powers specified by the **Magna Carta** in 1215. Also, as the Protestant Reformation swept through Europe, the rights of rulers were being challenged on several fronts, and in Scotland, **Mary, queen of Scots**, was forced to abdicate her throne in 1567.

The dissent mounted during the reign of Charles I, leading to his execution and to the abolition of the English monarchy in 1649. When kingship was restored in 1660, the doctrine of divine right was resurrected as well, outlined in treatises such as Sir Robert Filmer's *Patriarcha* in 1680, but by that time the advocates of absolute monarchy were in a minority, and their voice was little heard after 1688, when, in the **Glorious Revolution**, James VII and II was deposed in an anti-Catholic coup.

**DONALBANE/DONALDBANE (c1033–c1099).** *See* DONALD III.

**DONALD I (?–862).** Donald followed his brother, **Kenneth MacAlpin**, as ruler of the united kingdom of Dalriada and the Picts in 858. Little is known of his reign, though some sources suggest that he may have introduced a series of laws (possibly relating to the church, grants of privileges, and inheritance) and that he was a noted military leader. He died on 13 April 862, possibly at Rathinveramond (a location still unidentified but probably in Perthshire), and according to one source he was buried on the island of **Iona**. His nephew succeeded him as King **Constantine I**.

**DONALD II (?–900).** Donald, son of **Constantine I**, is the first monarch referred to in a contemporary record as king of **Alba** (the territory, north of the River Forth, from which present-day Scotland evolved). His reign, from 889 to 900, was marked (like that of his father) by repeated Scandinavian incursions. Unlike Constantine, he seems to have had some success in holding back the invaders, but even so, it is probable that he was killed during a struggle with them at Dunottar (a coastal site some 14 miles south of Aberdeen). One source indicates that Donald was buried on the island of **Iona**, the last resting place of many early Scottish rulers. His cousin, **Constantine II**, succeeded him, and his son later became king as **Malcolm I**. *See also* GIRIC.

**DONALD III (c1033–c1099).** After King **Malcolm III** married Margaret of Wessex (later **St. Margaret**) in c1070, the Scots' royal court became increasingly anglicized, with English displacing Gaelic in conversation and children of royal birth being given Anglo-Saxon, rather than traditional Celtic, names. The innovations were not universally popular, however, so in 1093, when Malcolm and **Edward of Scotland**, his eldest son and likely heir, were killed on one of their periodic forays into northern England, the supporters of the old ways took the opportunity to reassert themselves, led by Malcolm's brother, Donald. Accounts of the succession differ, but it is clear that Donald became king and banished the English from his court. In May 1094, Malcolm's son by his first marriage, to **Ingibiorg Finnsdottir**, managed to oust Donald with the aid of an Anglo-Norman army and rule as **Duncan II**, but his grip on the crown was always uncertain. Within weeks, a revolt by his new subjects forced him to send his foreign troops home, and on 12 November of the same year, he was murdered by Donald's supporters.

Donald returned to the throne for a further three years, but in 1097 **Edgar Aetheling**, Margaret's brother, arrived with an army of English soldiers, deposed him again, and placed **Edgar of Scotland** on the throne in his stead. Accounts of Donald's fate differ; the *Anglo-Saxon Chronicle* records that he was expelled from the kingdom, but other sources report that he was blinded and then imprisoned at Rescobie, near Forfar, until he died. He was initially buried either at **Dunfermline Abbey** or at Dunkeld Abbey but was later reinterred on the island of Iona. The three kings of Scots who followed Donald (Edgar of Scotland, **Alexander I**, and **David I**) were all sons of Malcolm and Margaret and were aware of their Anglo-Saxon heritage, so with his passing, Celtic customs and manners at the Scottish court became less and less important. Donald was also known as Donalbane and Donald Bane, the latter part of the name being an anglicization of the Gaelic *bán*, meaning "fair." *See also* BETHÓC (?–?); EDMUND OF SCOTLAND.

**DOWAGER QUEEN.** *See* QUEEN DOWAGER.

**DRUMMOND, ANNABELLA (c1350–c1401).** Annabella, wife of King **Robert III** and mother of King **James I of Scotland**, made unavailing efforts to prevent her brother-in-law, **Robert Stewart, duke of Albany (c1340–1421)**, from extending his influence over the government of her husband's realm. The eldest daughter of Sir John Drummond and, probably, Mary Montefichet, she married the future monarch (then known as John Stewart) in 1366 or, more probably, 1367, but it was another 11 years before she gave birth to a son—**David, duke of Rothesay**—who would survive to adulthood and become heir to the throne. By 1394, four years after Robert's accession, she was corresponding with King **Richard II** of England about the possibility of a marriage between one of his relatives and one of her own children, and apparently she earned the respect of advisors to the English monarchs, since when **Henry IV** invaded Scotland in 1400, he reportedly told his commanders to spare the countryside around **Edinburgh** from devastation because he admired Robert's queen.

Robert III, lame and depressive, was ruler in little more than name because Albany, a much stronger personality, could dominate the Scottish nobles, but Annabella was concerned about the duke's growing power and was one of the leading figures behind a decision to transfer his responsibilities to David in 1399. However, her death at **Scone** in late 1401 or early 1402 provided opportunities for Albany to regain his position and carry out all the functions of a sovereign until he died in 1420. Annabella—described by John of Fordun, a contemporary chronicler, as "faire, honorabil, and pleasand"—was buried in **Dunfermline Abbey**, where a stained glass window depicts her **royal coat of arms**. *See also* STEWART, EGIDIA (?–?); STEWART, ELIZABETH (?–c1411); STEWART, MARGARET, COUNTESS OF DOUGLAS; STEWART, MARY, COUNTESS OF ANGUS; STEWART, ROBERT (?–c1393).

**DRUMMOND, MARGARET (c1340–c1375).** Margaret, daughter of Sir Malcolm Drummond and his wife, Margaret, was King **David II**'s second consort. In 1328, David was married, at the age of five, to **Joan of the Tower**, the youngest child of King **Edward II**, in a dynastic tie that was intended to cement peace between England and Scotland (*see* NORTHAMPTON, TREATY OF). However, the international harmony was brief. The two countries were soon at war again, and in 1346, David was captured after the **Battle of Neville's Cross** and was held prisoner by King **Edward III** for 11 years. Joan moved back to her homeland and died on 7 September 1362 without having borne any children.

When David was released in 1357, he returned to Scotland and took Margaret Drummond as a mistress. She had previously been married to Sir John Logie, giving birth to their son who was named after his father. The Drummonds were an influential family that were at odds with Robert Stewart, David's nephew and later King **Robert II**, so some scholars speculate that the monarch's growing relationship with Margaret may have led Stewart to join a short-lived rebellion against the king in 1363. Within months of Joan's death, and possibly as early as April of 1363, Margaret and David were wed at Inchmurdo in Fife. Andrew of Wyntoun, a cleric and chronicler, wrote of the bride's "desirable appearance," but after five years, the monarch was still without an heir, so in 1369 or 1370 he divorced her. Refusing to accept the decision, the former queen attempted to win a papal reversal, but the matter was still undecided when David died, unexpectedly and still childless, on 22 February 1371. Margaret embarked on a pilgrimage to Rome and died during the journey, probably in 1375.

**DUDLEY, GUILDFORD (c1536–1554).** Guildford (or Guilford) Dudley was the husband of **Jane Grey**, queen of England for nine days—the shortest reign of any of the country's monarchs. The youngest child of John Dudley, duke of Northumberland, and his wife, Jane Guildford (or Guilford), he was sacrificed to his father's quest for power.

When King **Henry VIII** died in 1547, **Edward VI** (the old sovereign's only surviving son) was crowned king in his stead, but because the new ruler was only nine years old and was considered unable to take decisions on matters of state, a council of **regents** was appointed to govern on his behalf. From the autumn of 1549, John Dudley was the leader of that council and was so powerful that he was king in all but name. However, Edward fell ill during the winter of 1552–53, and as the months passed it became clear that he was unlikely to live for long. In an effort to preserve his position, the duke married Guildford to Jane (the daughter of Henry Grey, one of his supporters) at Durham House in **London** on 21 May 1553. Then Northumberland persuaded the young king to make a declaration that the throne should pass to Jane and her male heirs, not (as specified by the **Succession to the Crown Act of 1543**) to Mary, King Henry's daughter by **Catherine of Aragon**.

Edward was easily manipulated because he was strongly committed to the Protestant reforms instituted by his father and had no wish that they should be cast aside by the very pro-Roman Catholic Mary, so after his death on 5 July 1553, Northumberland duly proclaimed Jane queen.

This proclamation was a political miscalculation. Over the previous four years, the duke had made many enemies while he acted virtually as a dictator, adding to his own coffers while rigorously imposing Protestant forms of worship. These enemies opposed his blatant attempt to maintain control of the country, as did citizens who believed that parliamentary legislation should take precedence over royal decree, most Roman Catholics, and people who felt that Mary was being deprived of her rightful inheritance. As a result, Mary was able to enter London and take the throne as **Mary I**. Guildford and Jane were charged with treason and, on 13 November, were found guilty by the courts and condemned to death. Initially, Mary spared their lives (although she kept them confined in the **Tower of London**), but Henry Grey's participation in **Wyatt's Rebellion** in January 1554 convinced her that she had to get rid of possible foci of future revolts. Guildford—who had played no part in the resistance to Mary and had simply followed his father's instructions by marrying Jane—was **beheaded** on 12 February 1554, aged 17. Jane followed shortly afterward, and the two were buried in the chapel of St. Peter ad Vincula in the Tower of London.

**DUFF (?–966?).** Duff (also known as Dub and Dubh) succeeded **Indulf** as king of **Alba** in 962. Little is known of him other than that he was the son of **Malcolm I**, that he defeated **Colin** (Indulf's son) in battle, and that he reigned for some five years. One report suggests that he was eventually forced out of the realm, but others indicate that he was murdered (possibly by Colin's supporters) near Forres and that his body was carried to the island of **Iona** for burial. One of his sons later became king of Alba as **Kenneth III**, and some sources claim that another (Malcolm) became king of Strathclyde. Later descendants were earls of Fife.

**DUKE OF CORNWALL.** The dukedom of Cornwall—granted by King **Edward III** to his son **Edward, the black prince**, on 7 March 1337—was the first created in England. When his first child, Henry (later King **Henry VI**), was born on 6 December 1421, King **Henry V** decreed that the title would in future be held by "the first-begotten sons of the kings of England," so the present holder is **Charles, prince of Wales**, eldest son of Queen **Elizabeth II** and **heir apparent** to the throne. The duchy (the territory to which the title is attached) covers some 54,600 hectares, most of it in southwest England. The duke is not allowed to dispose of the capital but receives the income, which is used for charitable work and to cover the cost of public engagements.

When **Prince** Charles becomes king (or dies if that occurs before he succeeds to the throne), the title will pass to **Prince William of Wales**, his eldest son. It cannot be held by a female (**Camilla, duchess of Cornwall**, is the wife of Charles, **prince of Wales** and duke of Cornwall, so she does not hold the title in her own right); thus it lapses if a monarch has no male children. However, King Henry's decree has not always been interpreted strictly. For example, in 1502, when **Arthur, prince of Wales**, the 15-year-old son of King **Henry VII**, died without leaving any heirs, the title transferred to his younger brother, who ascended the throne as King **Henry VIII** in 1509, and, more recently, Prince Charles was accorded the title even though he is the son of a queen rather than a king. *See also* DUKE OF ROTHESAY; DUKE OF YORK; PRINCE OF WALES.

**DUKE OF ROTHESAY.** The **heir apparent** to the throne is usually known as the duke of Rothesay, rather than by any of his other titles, when he is in Scotland. King **Robert III** created the dignity—the first Scottish dukedom—on 28 April 1398 for David, his eldest son (*see* DAVID STEWART, DUKE OF ROTHESAY). The tradition that it would pass to the firstborn son of the monarch was confirmed by the Scottish parliament on 27 November 1469, with the legislation also including the subsidiary titles of baron Renfrew, earl of Carrick, great steward of Scotland, and **lord of the isles**. The title, which is currently held by **Charles, prince of Wales**, lapses if the holder dies before succeeding to the throne. Moreover, there is no provision for it to go to the eldest daughter of a sovereign. In the late 14th century, Rothesay, on the Isle of Bute, was an important stronghold held by the **House of Stuart** on the western coast of Scotland. Now it is better known as a seaside tourist destination, but unlike the duchy of Cornwall (*see* DUKE OF CORNWALL), it does not bring any income to the duke. *See also* DUKE OF YORK; PRINCE OF WALES; PRINCESS ROYAL.

**DUKE OF YORK.** King **Edward III** created the dukedom of York on 6 August 1385 for his son, Edmund of Langley (*see* EDMUND OF LANGLEY, DUKE OF YORK). In 1474, **Edward IV** conferred the title on Richard, his second son by **Elizabeth Woodville**, and since then, when granted, it has been held by the second sons of reigning monarchs of England (and, later of Great Britain and the United Kingdom). Curiously, every one of the 12 dukes from Richard onward has either become king or died without leaving a male heir. **Prince Andrew**, the current holder of the title, is no exception, having two daughters (**Princess Beatrice of York** and **Princess Eugenie of York**). When the dukedom was created, York was a major ecclesiastical and market center in northeast England. Nowadays, however, the title brings no income from estates. *See also* DUKE OF CORNWALL; DUKE OF ROTHESAY; FREDERICK, PRINCE, DUKE OF YORK AND ALBANY; PRINCE OF WALES; PRINCESS ROYAL; WAKEFIELD, BATTLE OF; YORK, HOUSE OF.

**DUNCAN I (?–1040).** When **Malcolm II**, king of Scots, died in 1034, he left no heirs, so the crown went to Duncan, the son of **Bethóc** (the monarch's eldest daughter) and **Crinan** (the abbot of Dunkeld), in a succession notable because it was uncontested, perhaps indicating that Malcolm had taken measures to eliminate other possible claimants. According to some writers, the late king's maneuvers had placed his grandson on the throne of Strathclyde in 1018 after Owen, the previous ruler, was killed in battle at Carham, near Coldstream. However, Duncan proved to be an ineffective commander, suffering two defeats in conflicts with his cousin, Thorfinn, earl of Orkney, and retreating ignominiously from Durham after an unsuccessful siege in 1039. In 1040, he invaded the territory of Moray, where **Macbeth** ruled, and was killed at Pitgaveny (near Elgin), possibly on 14 August. One source reports that he was buried on the island of **Iona**.

Duncan may have married a relative of Sigurd, earl of Northumberland. Two of his sons (**Malcolm III** and **Donald III**) also occupied the throne, and it is possible that a third (Máel Muire, earl of Atholl) survived into his nineties. William Shakespeare's play *Macbeth* focuses on Duncan's death and its aftermath but misrepresents many of the historical circumstances, for example by portraying Duncan as an elderly man even though he was still young and vigorous.

**DUNCAN II (?–1094).** Duncan—the son of King **Malcolm III** by his first marriage to **Ingibiorg Finnsdottir**—ruled Scotland briefly in the latter half of 1094. In 1072, he was taken hostage by King **William I of England** in an effort to ensure that Malcolm would refrain from attacking northern England, but the Scottish monarch seems to have made no attempt to obtain his child's release. Duncan, therefore, grew up at the **London** court imbibing the Normans' values and learning the customs they had brought from the European mainland. In 1093, Malcolm was killed while laying siege to the town of Alnwick in Northumbria, and his brother claimed the throne as **Donald III**. The following spring, Duncan invaded Scotland with an Anglo-Norman army and ousted his uncle, but he soon found that his English supporters were not welcome to a people determined to assert Celtic traditions, and facing a rebellion by his new subjects, he was forced to send his supporters home. Thus weakened, he was easy prey for Donald, who arranged his murder at Mondynes, some five miles southwest of Stonehaven, on 12 November 1094, and returned to the throne for another three years. Duncan's remains were interred at **Dunfermline Abbey** according to some sources, and on the island of **Iona** according to others. *See also* EDMUND OF SCOTLAND; FITZDUNCAN, WILLIAM; OCTREDA OF NORTHUMBRIA.

**DUNDONALD CASTLE.** Dundonald, located in southwest Scotland near Kilmarnock, was one of the favorite residences of the first kings from the **House of Stuart**. The site had been occupied for some 3,000 years before a timber motte and bailey fortification was constructed in the mid-12th century, probably by Walter FitzAlan, the first **high steward of Scotland**. Alexander Stewart, the fourth high steward, built a stone fortress late in the 13th century, and from 1371 King **Robert II** erected a third structure in the form of a tower house, probably as a celebration of his accession to the throne. For 200 years, Dundonald was a popular base for the **royal family**. Robert II died there in 1390, as did his son, **Robert III**, in 1406, but King **James III** sold the estate in 1482, and by the late 17th century the castle was in ruins. The building, now in the care of Historic Scotland (a government agency responsible for the upkeep of important monuments), is open to visitors.

**DUNFERMLINE ABBEY.** From the late 11th century until the early 15th century, the royalty of Scotland were buried at Dunfermline. The site was a religious center as early as AD 800, but its importance grew from about 1070, when it became a favored location for the court of King **Malcolm III** and his wife, Margaret of **Wessex** (later **St. Margaret**). Margaret invited a group of Benedictine monks—the first in the country—to erect a priory, and **David I**, her youngest son, raised the building to abbey status, building a new church between 1128 and 1150. **Edward I** of England, recognizing the psychological significance of the place to his Scots adversaries, destroyed much of the structure in 1303–4, but **Robert I** (Robert the Bruce) helped to finance a restoration project. Protestant militants caused further damage in 1560, but the nave survived and was incorporated within the present Church of Scotland in 1821. In 1933, a stained glass window was installed, commemorating the wedding of Margaret and Malcolm, which may well have been held in Dunfermline.

Apart from the island of **Iona**, which was the last resting place of many earlier monarchs, Dunfermline was the burial ground for more members of the **royal family** than anywhere else in Scotland. Margaret and Malcolm, who died a few days apart in 1093, lie there (though some writers believe that the king's remains are still in Tynemouth, where he was originally interred). Nearby, graves were dug for **Duncan II** (1094), **Edgar of Scotland** (1107), **Alexander I** (1124), David I (1153), **Malcolm IV** (1165), **Alexander III** (1286), and Robert I (1329), as well as for several of their consorts. The last adult interments included those of **Annabella Drummond** (wife of **Robert III** and mother of **James I**, who was buried in 1401) and **Robert Stewart, duke of Albany** (a son of **Robert II**, who was **regent** during the reigns of his father, Robert III, and James I and who died in 1420), but the abbey's royal associations lasted almost until the **union of the crowns** because **Robert Stuart, duke of Kintyre**, the infant son of King **James VI** and **Anne of Denmark**, was laid to rest there in 1602.

The abbey complex included rooms suitable for royal visitors, including **David II**, James I, and **Charles I**, who were born there in 1324, 1394, and 1600, respectively. The area was refurbished by **James IV** in about 1500 and given by **James VI** as a wedding present to his wife, **Anne of Denmark**, in 1589, but after the union of the crowns in 1603, the royal court moved to **London**, so the palace was abandoned and little more than ruins of the kitchens and cellars remain.

**DUNKELD, HOUSE OF.** Some historians use the term "House of Dunkeld" as a means of categorizing, genealogically, the monarchs who ruled Scotland from 1034 to 1040 and from 1058 to 1286. King **Malcolm II**, who died in

1034, was the last ruler from the **House of Alpin**. He left no male offspring and so made preparations for the throne to pass through the female line to his grandchild, **Duncan I**, the son of **Bethóc** (his elder daughter) and **Crinan** (the lay abbot of Dunkeld). In 1040, **Macbeth** killed Duncan, interrupting the dynastic succession, but in 1058 Macbeth was in turn killed by Duncan's son, who returned the crown to the Dunkeld line, ruling as **Malcolm III** from 1058 to 1093.

In 1069 or 1070, Malcolm married Margaret of **Wessex** (later **St. Margaret**), sister of **Edgar Aetheling**—the last (and uncrowned) **Anglo-Saxon monarch** of England—and to please her, he introduced many southern practices into his court. These innovations were not universally welcomed, but over the decades, several survived, and, in particular, the monarchical succession gradually became based on the principles of male primogeniture that had been introduced to England by **William I** and his Norman invaders rather than on the traditional Scots-Irish principles of **tanistry**. The dynasty ended with **Alexander III**, who reigned for 37 years until 1286, when he fell from his horse and was killed, leaving no sons alive to succeed him. The Scots nobles and churchmen decided that his granddaughter, **Margaret, maid of Norway**, should be queen, but she died in 1290 while making the journey to her realm, leaving a host of claimants to compete for the crown she had never worn.

In addition to the rulers mentioned above, the kings from the House of Dunkeld were **Alexander I** (who reigned from 1107 to 1124), **Alexander II** (1214–49), **David I** (1124–53), **Donald III** (1093–97), **Duncan II** (1094), **Edgar of Scotland** (1097–1107), **Malcolm IV** (1153–65), and **William I of Scotland** (1165–1214). *See also* CANMORE, HOUSE OF.

**DUNKIRK.** Dunkirk, a port in northwest **France**, was captured from the Spanish by Oliver Cromwell's troops, in alliance with the French, on 15 June 1658. On 17 October 1662, King **Charles II**, badly needing funds to pay his army and support an expensive lifestyle, sold the city to King Louis XIV of France for £500,000 (though only about £300,000 was paid).

# E

**EADRED (c922–955).** For much of his nine-year reign as king of England, Eadred's principal concern was the retention of the Northumbrian territories that lay on the northeastern frontier of the Anglo-Saxon realm. **Aethelstan**, his half-brother, had wrested the area from Viking control in 927, but the Scandinavians were uncowed, and **Edmund I**, his predecessor and older brother, had struggled to hold on to the area. Eadred's contribution to the shaping of the English state was to end, for a time, Norse efforts to add the land to their empire.

The son of **Edward the Elder** and **Edgiva**, his third wife, Eadred became king in 946 when Edmund was killed in a brawl. Initially, the leaders of Northumbria assured them of their loyalty, but they quickly changed their minds and transferred their allegiance from the Anglo-Saxons to the Vikings, acknowledging Eric Bloodaxe, son of Harald I of Norway, as their ruler. Eadred took his revenge by ravaging the countryside, forcing Eric to flee in 948, and demanding reparation from the Northumbrians, who again accepted him as their king, and then, the following year, rejected him for a second time, turning once more to the Norse. In 954, however, they turned against Eric and reverted to Eadred. Eric was slain, and with his death, Scandinavian interest in England petered out, if only temporarily.

Eadred was a devout Christian who did much to support the church, but he also suffered a wasting disease that often prevented him from digesting his food and ultimately killed him on 23 November 955, while he was still a young man. He was buried at **Winchester**, where many other Anglo-Saxon rulers were interred, and left £16,000 in his will so that his subjects could buy relief from famine or from heathen armies, if needed. He never married and had no children, so the **witan** (the council of royal advisors) chose his nephew, **Eadwig**, the eldest son of **Edmund I**, as his successor. *See also* DANELAW.

**EADWIG (c941–959).** When **Eadred**, king of the English, died in 955, he left no children, so the **witan** (the council of royal advisors) chose Eadwig, his nephew, to succeed him. The elder son of **Edmund I** and his first wife,

**Aelfgifu**, Eadwig (also known as Edwy) was still a child when his father died and so was considered too young to be a leader. Even on his accession, he was still in his midteens and demonstrating the lapses of judgment characteristic of that age group. On the day in 956 when he was consecrated as king, his nobles met to discuss matters of state, but the monarch failed to turn up. Eventually, Dunstan, abbot of Glastonbury and one of the leaders of the church, found him in the company of two ladies, a young woman named **Elgiva** and her mother, Aelfgifu. Eadwig was not impressed by the efforts to make him forsake the pleasures of female company, and he exacted revenge the following year, forcing Dunstan to flee from the royal court. The king eventually wedded Elgiva, but relations with churchmen were not improved in 958, when Archbishop Odo of Canterbury annulled the marriage on the grounds that the partners—third cousins once removed—were too closely related.

The historical evidence suggests that Eadwig was a weak king, granting privileges too readily to his sycophants while removing critics from his circle and confiscating the estates of landowners who had displeased him. Eventually the people of Mercia and Northumbria rebelled, claiming that he was favoring the inhabitants of **Wessex**, and in 957 they invited **Edgar of England** (Eadwig's younger brother) to lead them. Some writers suggest that the two men met in battle at Gloucester and that Eadwig was defeated, others that nobody had any heart for a civil war so the two sides agreed to divide the country, with Eadwig retaining the area south of the River Thames and Edgar ruling the rest. This experience seemed to mellow the young king, because for the next two years he displayed greater political aptitude than had been evident earlier and made several generous donations to the church. However, he died suddenly on 1 October 959, and his people pledged their allegiance to Edgar, reuniting England once again.

**EAFA (c730–?).** Although very little is known about him, Eafa (who is also called Eaba and Eoffa) is listed in some genealogies as an ancestor of the modern British **royal family**. The son of **Eoppa** and grandfather of **Egbert**, who is often considered to be the first king of England, Eafa was born c730, a scion of the royal house of **Wessex**. With a woman whose name is not recorded, he sired a son, **Ealhmund**, who became king of Kent. Some sources suggest that he may have reigned during the last decade of the 8th century.

**EALDGYTH OF MERCIA (?–?).** Ealdgyth was the consort of **Harold II**, who had previously had at least seven children during a lengthy relationship with **Edith Swan-Neck** that was not recognized by the church. The daughter of Aelfgar, earl of Mercia, and his wife, Aelfgifu, Ealdgyth (also known as

Aldgyth and Edith) had first married Gruffydd ap Llywelyn, who ruled much of Wales from 1055 and resisted incursions by Harold's Anglo-Saxon armies until he was killed by his own people in 1063. They had two sons—Maredudd (born in 1055) and Idwal (born in 1057)—and possibly a daughter named Nesta. Both boys died in battle in 1070 attempting to win back parts of their father's realm, but Nesta may have survived to bear children of her own.

Harold married Ealdgyth before he became king of England in January 1066, probably fathering a son, Harold, born in November 1066. However, he never saw the child because he was killed by the Norman army of William the Conqueror (later **William I of England**) at the **Battle of Hastings** on 14 October the same year. Ealdgyth initially fled for safety to her brothers, Edwin, earl of Mercia, and Morcar, earl of Northumberland, but her ultimate fate is unknown, though some scholars speculate that she went into exile on the European mainland with other members of Harold's family.

**EALHMUND (c745–827).** Ealhmund was the son of **Eafa**, whose ancestry can be linked both to **Cerdic** (the founder of the kingdom of **Wessex**) and to members of the present British **royal family**. He married a woman of royal birth whose name is unknown but who is often assumed to be a daughter of King Aethelbert of Kent, who ruled from 725 to 762. The *Anglo-Saxon Chronicle* records that Ealhmund was king of Kent in 784 but gives no details of his reign other than that, in that year, he made a grant of land to the monks of Reculver, on the estuary of the River Thames near Herne Bay. In all probability, he was subject to the overlordship of Offa, the powerful king of Mercia. Ealhmund left two children. Alburga, his daughter, married Wulfstan of Wiltshire. Wulfstan founded a college of secular priests in Wilton, near Oxford, but after his death in about 800, Alburga converted it into a Benedictine nunnery and became the abbess. She died on Christmas Day in 810. **Egbert**, Ealhmund's son, was king of Wessex from 802 to 839 and is sometimes considered the first king of England.

**EALHSWITH (c852–905).** Much less is known of Ealhswith (who is also known as Ealhswitha) than of her husband, **Alfred the Great**. The daughter of Aethelred Mucus, she had links to the royal house of Mercia (one of the Anglo-Saxon kingdoms) through her mother, Eadburh, and married Alfred in 868, three years before he became king of **Wessex**. They had at least five children, including **Edward the Elder**, who succeeded to the throne on his father's death, which probably occurred in 899.

Aethelflaeda, the eldest daughter, was born c869 and married Aethelred of Mercia in about 886 as part of a political pact arranged by her father in recognition of Mercian help in resisting the Viking invaders. She proved to be a formidable leader, earning recognition for her military prowess and for administrative abilities that led to the redesign of the settlement of Gloucester. Aethelflaeda died in 918. Aelfthryth, Aethelflaeda's youngest sister, was born c877 and in 884 was married to Count Baldwin II of Flanders, also as part of an anti-Viking alliance. They had four children, including a son, Arnulf, whose line, some five generations later, would lead to **Matilda of Flanders**, wife of Duke William of Normandy, who led the Norman conquest of England in 1066 and ruled the country as **William I**. Aelfthryth died in 929, 11 years after her husband.

Aethelgifu, a third daughter, born in about 875, spent most of her brief life in a convent. In 880, Alfred ordered the rebuilding of the town of Shaftesbury, which had a site defensible against Viking attacks, and installed her as the first abbess of a new nunnery. She died c896. Aethelweard, the younger son, was born in about 880, and according to Asser, who prepared a biography of Alfred in 893, he "was given over to training in reading and writing under the attentive care of teachers." He had three boys, all of whom died without issue, two of them as a result of wounds received in the **Battle of Brunanburh** in 937. Aethelweard died on 26 October 922. Some sources suggest that Alfred and Ealhswith may also have had a son named Edmund who was born in about 870 but died young. After her husband's death, Ealhswith became a nun at the Nunnaminster (later St. Mary's Abbey), which she founded in **Winchester** in 903. She died on 5 December 905 and was buried beside her husband in the city's New Minster. *See also* EDGIVA.

**ECGWYNN (?–?).** Almost nothing is known of **Edward the Elder**'s first wife except her name. Some sources suggest that she was a lady of nobility, others that she had a humble background, perhaps as the daughter of a shepherd. It is also possible that she was a mistress, rather than a spouse, although several writers postulate a marriage c893. Scholars of the period agree, however, that Ecgwynn bore two of Edward's 14 children. **Aethelstan**, born in about 895, succeeded his father as king of England and in 926 arranged for his sister, Edith, to marry Sihtric (the Viking king of York) in an effort to extend his influence in territory far from his **Wessex** base. The attempt proved short lived, however, because the new husband died the following year. Ecgwynn was apparently superseded by **Aelfflaed** when Edward succeeded his father, **Alfred the Great**, as king of **Wessex** in c899.

**EDGAR AETHELING (c1051–c1126).** Edgar was the last Anglo-Saxon king of England, succeeding **Harold II**, who died at the **Battle of Hastings** while attempting to prevent Duke William of Normandy (later **William I of England**) from claiming his realm. The only son of **Edward the Exile** and his wife, **Agatha** (whose antecedents are unclear), he was named **heir apparent** by **Edward the Confessor** after the Exile died in 1057. However, when the Confessor himself passed away in 1066, Edgar, his great-nephew, was still a teenager and was considered too young to lead a country in a time of war, so Harold Godwinson (who ruled as Harold II) was preferred as the country's sovereign. After Harold fell at Hastings, the **witan** (the council of royal advisors) did proclaim Edgar king, but he was never crowned and, after only a few weeks, had to promise obedience to the invaders.

In 1068, Edgar joined an unsuccessful rebellion against William; then, fearing for his life, he fled for safety to the court of **Malcolm III** of Scotland. Malcolm agreed to support Edgar's claim to the English throne, and in alliance with Sweyn II, king of Denmark, he sent an army south the following year. The combined force captured York, but then the Danes went home, bought off by William's gold, and Edgar had to return to Scotland empty-handed. Six years later, he pledged allegiance to William for a second time and in 1086 led a Norman army into Apulia (in southern Italy), but he harbored dreams of greater power.

When William died in 1087, his younger surviving son inherited the English realm and ruled as **William II**, but the Norman lands went to **Robert Curthose**, his eldest son. Edgar joined Robert in an effort to recombine the kingdom, but that project proved fruitless too, and he had to seek refuge in Scotland yet again. In 1097, reconciled with William II, the Aetheling helped to overthrow **Donald III** (a committed opponent of the Normans) and place Malcolm's son, **Edgar of Scotland**, on the Scottish throne, but by 1106 he was back in alliance with Duke Robert attempting to oust Henry (another of William I's sons), who had succeeded to the English throne as King **Henry I** on his brother's death in 1100. Eventually, in 1106, Edgar was taken captive by Henry's troops at the **Battle of Tinchebrai**. After receiving a pardon, he spent the remainder of his days quietly on his estates and, possibly, in Scotland.

**EDGAR OF ENGLAND (c943–975).** Edgar's lengthy and, for the times, peaceful reign is considered by many historians to be the high point of Anglo-Saxon kingship. The younger son of **Edmund I** and his first wife, **Aelfgifu**, he was born in 943 or 944 and so was considered too young to lead his people when his father died in 946. **Eadwig**, his older brother, succeeded his uncle **Eadred** as king of the English in 955 but proved unpopular, so in 957 the leaders of Mercia and Northumbria rebelled and invited the 14-year-old Edgar to replace him. England was divided, with Edgar controlling the area north of the River Thames and Eadwig retaining the rest, but two years later Eadwig died, and Edgar reunited the country without any conflict.

In 957, while ruler of only part of the country, Edgar recalled Dunstan, a senior churchman who had been banished from his brother's court, and approved his appointment as Bishop of Worcester. The following year, Dunstan was made Bishop of **London**; then, in 960, he became archbishop of Canterbury and thus the leader of the Roman Catholic Church in England. The impact of the relationship between the two men proved far reaching because, in many ways, Dunstan was the power behind the throne, shaping the young king's policies, particularly those that affected the church. Monastic principles had become corrupted, with offices bought and sold, the rule of celibacy widely ignored, and positions awarded through patronage rather than merit. Edgar and Dunstan encouraged acceptance of the strictures of the Benedictine order, with its emphasis on chastity, communal life, and poverty. In addition, new monasteries were founded, and parish priests were expected to become educators as well as savers of souls. The social and cultural effects wrought by the new order are still debated by historians, but there was certainly a revival of interest in monasticism, an increase in missionary work, and the development of a tradition of detailed, scholarly study by monks.

The period was also marked by a lack of any major war or civil disruption, though a report, in the *Anglo-Saxon Chronicle*, that the island of Thanet (in the River Thames) was ravaged on Edgar's orders in 969 suggests that the peace may have been due to the threat of military retribution rather than because the king's subjects were law abiding. Whatever the reason, the lack of violence facilitated the introduction of new laws (such as penalties for failure to pay the tithes due to the church), the promotion of trade, and a reorganization of the way justice was administered in the courts. The northern borders of the kingdom were secured through negotiations that involved the ceding of Lothian to **Kenneth II** of Scotland, and areas that had been strongly influenced by the Vikings were allowed to retain their own customs.

Edgar was not crowned until 973, the ceremony marking the achievements of the reign rather than the beginning of it. The event, held at Bath Abbey, became the template for future **coronations** of England's monarchs and was followed by a gathering at Chester, where rulers of subject kingdoms gathered to pay homage. However, only two years later, on 8 July 975, Edgar died at **Winchester**, and the succession was disputed. **Aelfthryth** (or Elfrida), the king's second wife, promoted the cause of **Aethelred the Unready**, her seven-year-old son, but Dunstan successfully engineered the accession of **Edward the Martyr**, who was born in 962 to Edgar and his first wife, **Aethelflaed Eneda**, with the birth possibly preceding the marriage. *See also* ANGLO-SAXON MONARCHS; WULFTHRYTH.

**EDGAR OF SCOTLAND (c1074–1107).** Edgar, who ruled Scotland for the decade from 1097, was the son of **Malcolm III** and Margaret of **Wessex** (later **St. Margaret**) and thus was the first Scottish king to have Anglo-Saxon blood in his veins. After Malcolm's death in 1093, **Donald III** claimed the crown and attempted to reverse the anglicization of the royal court. Edgar fled with his brothers to safety in England, but in the spring of 1097, his uncle, **Edgar Aetheling**, led an army north, deposed Donald, and made Edgar king. The new monarch undoubtedly exerted authority more as a vassal of King **William II of England** and of King **Henry I** than as the independent leader of a sovereign state, so even if he had objected, he would have been unable to prevent Henry from taking his sister Edith for his wife (*see* MATILDA OF SCOTLAND) or from arranging the marriage of **Mary, countess of Boulogne**, another sister, to Eustace III, count of Boulogne. He did cede the Hebridean islands and the Kintyre peninsula to Magnus, king of Norway (though this was largely a recognition of political realities because the Scandinavians had been raiding the area and Edgar did not have the resources to defend them) and gave much support to the church—so much so that Aelred of Rievaulx, an English monk, compared his generosity to that of **Edward the Confessor**. Edgar died in **Edinburgh** Castle, unmarried and childless, on 8 January 1107 and was buried at **Dunfermline Abbey**. His brother, **Alexander I**, succeeded him.

**EDGIVA (?–968).** In about 920, **Edward the Elder**, king of England, took Edgiva (also known as Eadgifu) as his third wife. The daughter of Sigehelm (an ealdorman, one of the leading noblemen in Anglo-Saxon society), she bore four children in the five years before her husband died in 925. Edmund (later **Edmund I**) was born in 921 or 922 and followed **Aethelstan** as king of England in 939. **Eadred**, his younger brother, born c922 and plagued for much of his life by ill health, succeeded him. Their sister, Eadburh (or, alternatively, Eadburga), was born in about 920 and devoted herself to a religious life, becoming a nun (and possibly abbess) at the Nunnaminster, a monastery founded in 903 by **Ealhswith**, her grandmother and wife of **Alfred the Great**. Eadburh died on 15 June 960 and initially was buried in **Winchester**, but her remains were transferred to Pershore Abbey in Worcestershire after her canonization in 972. Eadgifu, a second daughter, was married to Louis II of Provence in accordance with the policy of King **Aethelstan** (Edward the Elder's son by his first wife, **Ecgwynn**, and his successor) to build alliances with major European families by wedding his half-sisters into them (*see also* AELFFLAED). Edgiva survived her husband by more than four decades, dying on 25 August 968.

**EDINBURGH.** As Scotland's capital city, Edinburgh is the principal focus for official royal engagements in northern areas of the United Kingdom. The site has been settled for over 3,000 years, favored initially because the volcanic plug known as Castle Rock provided a defensible location that commanded the surrounding plain. It was first used extensively as a base for the **Royal Household** during the reign of **Malcolm III** from 1058 to 1093 and was designated a royal burgh in about 1127 by Malcolm's son, **David I**, who also established an Augustinian religious community at nearby **Holyrood** in 1128. King **Robert I** confirmed the burghal designation in 1329, but the trading privileges that it conferred were not fully developed until the periodic conflicts with England, and consequent occupation by English armies, had declined in the second half of the 14th century. By the reign of **James III** (1460–88), Edinburgh was the most important settlement in the country and was widely regarded as the capital of the kingdom. **James IV** began construction of Holyroodhouse, now the sovereign's official residence in Scotland, in about 1498, and leading nobles built imposing homes nearby.

As the town grew in importance, the land between Holyrood and the castle was built over (the street connecting the two foci is known now as the Royal Mile). Administration, commerce, education, government, and the law all needed space on the cramped site, so walkways (known as wynds) were narrow, and housing expanded upward rather than outward. That growth continued even though the royal court moved to **London** after King **James VI** succeeded to the English throne, as James I, in 1603 (*see* UNION OF THE CROWNS) and parliament followed when England and Scotland were united under a single administration in 1707 (*see* UNION OF PARLIAMENTS). **Charles Edward Stuart**'s troops occupied Edinburgh during the second **Jacobite rebellion** of 1745–46, but shortly after the revolt was crushed, a new town (called New Town) was constructed to the north of the old one, laid out in gridiron Georgian fashion, with street names emphasizing the dominance of the **House of Hanover**.

During the 20th century, the city earned a growing reputation as a cultural and financial center, and after the reestablishment of a Scottish parliament in 1999, it experienced an administrative renaissance as well, with the monarch spending at least a week of each year at Holyrood, presiding at formal functions and holding meetings with leading Scottish politicians. Also, government and private bodies have invested heavily in conservation efforts, so the architectural heritage and annual events such as the Edinburgh Festival and the Hogmanay (New Year's Eve) street party attract nearly 4 million tourists each year. At the time of the 2001 census, the city had a population of 448,000. *See also* HONOURS OF SCOTLAND; ROYAL YACHT.

**EDINBURGH, TREATY OF (17 March 1328).** *See* NORTHAMPTON, TREATY OF (1 May 1328).

**EDITH OF EAST ANGLIA (?–1017).** In 1015, **Aethelred the Unready**, king of England, ordered the murder of Sigeferth, an East Anglian nobleman and supporter of his son Edmund (later **Edmund II**), with whom he was enmeshed in a power struggle. Sigeferth's widow—whose name is not recorded in the *Anglo-Saxon Chronicle* but who is thought by some historians to be Aldgyth, Ealdgyth, Eldgyth, or, in modern English, Edith—was confined to a monastery after her husband's death, but Edmund, very much against Aethelred's wishes, removed her and married her himself. They had two sons—**Edward the Exile** (born in 1016) and Edmund (born either in the same year or the following one)—but the marriage was brief because Edmund died in November 1016, just seven months after succeeding to the throne. King **Canute** took control of Edmund's lands and sent the infant boys to his half-brother, Olaf, king of Sweden, on the understanding that they would be killed. However, Olaf moved them to Kiev, where Ingigerd, his daughter, was queen, and from there they went to Hungary. Edmund eventually married Hedwig, daughter of Stephen I, King of Hungary, but died without leaving any issue. Edward returned to England in 1057 and, some scholars say, was probably murdered just two days after his arrival, possibly by members of the Godwin family, who may have wanted to ensure that the throne fell into their hands rather than the Exile's when the reign of **Edward the Confessor**, Edward's uncle, came to an end. It is not known where or when Edith died, although some scholars speculate that she may have left England with her children.

**EDITH OF SCOTLAND (c1080–1118).** *See* MATILDA OF SCOTLAND.

**EDITH OF WESSEX (c1029–1075).** Edith was **queen consort** of **Edward the Confessor**, king of England from 1042 until 1066. She was one of 10 children born to **Godwin, earl of Wessex** and the most powerful noble in the country, and **Gytha Thorkelsdóttir**, his second wife, who according to some scholars was a descendant of the Danish and Swedish royal houses. For Godwin, the marriage, which took place on 23 January 1045, was undoubtedly a political alliance promoted in the hope of establishing a royal dynasty, but it produced no offspring. Edith, in *Vita Edwardi Regis* (her account of her life with the king), claimed that she was childless because her husband had taken a vow of celibacy, but historians have also suggested that one of the partners may have been infertile or that there may even have been no intercourse because of Edward's antipathy toward the Godwins, whom he attempted to banish from his realm in 1051.

When her family was exiled, Edith was dispatched to the nunnery at Wherwell, which had been founded by **Aelfthryth**—a previous royal consort—some seven decades earlier, but she returned to Edward's side when her father forced the monarch to restore the family estates the following year. Then, while Edward was funding the construction of **Westminster Abbey**, his queen ("in pious rivalry" according to some sources) provided money for rebuilding the church at Wilton Abbey, a Benedictine foundation, in stone rather than wood.

When Edward died in 1066, he was succeeded by Edith's brother, Harold (*see* HAROLD II), but the Godwins' rule was short lived. Edith lost one brother (Tostig) at the **Battle of Stamford Bridge** on 25 September and three others (Harold, Gyrth, and Leofwine) at the **Battle of Hastings** on 14 October. She herself had to hand the keys of **Winchester**, the ancient Anglo-Saxon base, to William the Conqueror (*see* WILLIAM I OF ENGLAND) as he made his way across his new realm. William allowed her to keep her considerable properties, so she remained in Winchester until her death on 19 December 1075. She was buried close to her husband in Westminster Abbey.

**EDITH SWAN-NECK (c1025–?).** Edith (also known as Aldgyth, Ealdgyth, and Edith Swanneshals) was the common-law wife of **Harold II**, who ruled England from January to October 1066. Much of her life is unrecorded, but most sources suggest that she was born sometime between 1020 and 1035 and that she "married" Harold in a handfast ceremony in about 1045. These handfast weddings, involving the tying of the couple's hands together, were not recognized by the church because they were carried out in the absence of a priest, but the laity seems to have considered Harold and Edith's seven or eight offspring legitimate. Edith is best remembered because she walked through a field of bloody bodies after the **Battle of Hastings** on 14 October 1066 and identified Harold's mutilated remains by marks on his chest. After that, she vanishes from the pages of history. Scholars speculate that she may have died in the violence that followed William the Conqueror's victory at Hastings (*see* WILLIAM I OF ENGLAND), may have been sheltered by supporters in Ireland, or may have taken refuge in a nunnery.

Little is known of Edith's children. However, Gytha, one of her daughters, escaped to the court of King Sweyn of Denmark after Harold's death and later married Waldemar Monomakh, grand prince of Kievan Rus. One of her descendants—**Isabella of France**—became **queen consort** of King **Edward II** in 1308, reintroducing Harold's Anglo-Saxon bloodline to the English royal house.

**EDMUND I (c921–946).** King of England from 939 until his murder in 946, Edmund was the son of **Edward the Elder** and **Edgiva**, his third wife. Known as Edmund the Deed-Doer, Edmund the Elder, Edmund the Just, and Edmund the Magnificent, he assumed the throne in 939 on the death of **Aethelstan**, his half-brother, with whom he had defeated an alliance of Norsemen and Scots at the **Battle of Brunanburh** two years earlier, and had to devote much time and effort to retaining the northern outposts of his kingdom. Olaf Guthfrithson, king of Dublin, who had led the Viking force at Brunanburh, took the opportunity presented by Aethelstan's death to overrun Northumbria and the East Midlands, and Edmund did not regain all of the lost territories until 944. Then, in 945, he successfully invaded Strathclyde, entrusting its rule to **Malcolm I**, king of the Scots, in return for military aid. The decision was an astute move designed to secure stable northern borders and peaceful coexistence with neighbors who had greatly troubled Aethelstan, but, according to some scholars, it was also an implicit recognition that Northumbria was the northernmost extension of the English kingdom.

Edmund, however, had little opportunity for further success because, according to the *Anglo-Saxon Chronicle*, he was killed in a fight with a robber named Leofa at his home in Pucklechurch (now in Gloucestershire, in the west of England) on 26 May 946 and was buried at Glastonbury Abbey. He had two sons by **Aelfgifu**, his first wife. Both were still children at the time of his death, so he was succeeded by **Eadred**, his younger brother. However, the boys were destined to follow in their father's footsteps, **Eadwig** (the first-born) reigning as king of England from 955 to 957 and as ruler of Kent and Wessex from 957 to 959, and **Edgar of England** (the younger child) acting as ruler of Mercia and Northumbria from 957 and of England from 959 to 975. *See also* AETHELFLAED OF DAMERHAM.

**EDMUND II (c989–1016).** Edmund, who ruled parts of England for a few months in 1016, earned his nickname—Ironsides—as a result of his ultimately unavailing efforts to prevent the Danes from overrunning his kingdom. Probably the third son born to King **Aethelred the Unready** and his first wife, **Aelfgifu of York**, he became heir to the throne when his older brothers, Ecberht (born c987) and Aethelstan (born c986), died c1005 and 1012–15, respectively. By 1014–15, Edmund was at odds with his father, who arranged for the murder of Sigeferth, one of his son's supporters. **Edith of East Anglia**, Sigeferth's wife, was banished to a nunnery, but Edmund retrieved her, married her himself, and occupied some of Aethelred's lands. Nevertheless, when **Canute** invaded England with a Danish army in 1015, Edmund rallied to his father's cause and continued the fight when he succeeded to the throne in April the following year.

Initially, Edmund had some success in his struggles with the Norsemen, but on 18 October 1016, he was decisively beaten in battle at **Assandun** in Essex. The ensuing peace settlement left Canute in control of all the lands north of the River Thames, with Edmund holding on only to his **Wessex** homeland in the south. A clause in the agreement provided that, if either king should die, the other would succeed to his domains, so when Edmund passed away only a month later, on 30 November, the country was reunited under Canute. Some sources suggest that the death was due to natural causes, but there is a legend that a group of Canute's followers hid beneath a lavatory and pushed a sword up Edmund's anus while he was relieving himself.

Edmund and Edith had two sons (**Edward the Exile** and Edmund), both of whom were born in 1016 (or, in Edmund's case, possibly in 1017). Canute sent the infants to Sweden to be killed, but they survived, and **Edgar Aetheling**, Edward's son, ruled England, in name if not in practice, for a few weeks after William the Conqueror (*see* WILLIAM I OF ENGLAND) led the Norman invasion in 1066. Margaret (later **St. Margaret**), Edward's daughter, had greater impact, marrying **Malcolm III** of Scotland and bearing eight children, four of whom were to succeed to their father's throne.

**EDMUND, EARL OF LANCASTER (1245–1296).** The second son of King **Henry III** and **Eleanor of Provence**, Edmund was born in **London** on 16 January 1245. King **John**, Edmund's grandfather, had lost most of the French territories held by the English kings as a result of their descent from the royal **House of Anjou**, and Henry, spurred on by his wife and her relatives, was anxious both to retrieve them and to add other lands to his empire. In 1254, as part of that policy, he made a pact with Pope Innocent IV that Edmund would be made king of Sicily (then part of the Norman empire) in return for financial support to invade the territory and incorporate it within the area over which the head of the Roman Catholic Church had civil as well as spiritual jurisdiction. Innocent fulfilled his part of the bargain, but the English barons were unwilling to provide financial resources for a military campaign, seeing little benefit to themselves in the venture, so Henry had to make major concessions over the government of his kingdom in return for the funds he needed (*see* PROVISIONS OF OXFORD). In the end, the invasion did not take place; Pope Alexander IV (Innocent's successor) withdrew Edmund's monarchical title in 1258, and Edmund himself stopped using it in 1263, but the project did much to sour the already acid relations between Henry and his nobles.

For Edmund, however, other honors were to follow. In 1265, he was made earl of Leicester after Simon de Montfort, the previous holder of the title and leader of the opposition to Henry's rule, was killed at the Battle of Evesham (*see* SECOND BARONS' WAR). Two years later, he was created earl of Lancaster, founding a dynasty that was eventually to occupy the throne for six decades in the 15th century (*see* LANCASTER, HOUSE OF). In 1271–72, he took part in the ninth (and last) crusade to the Holy Land; some historians suggest that his nickname—Crouchback—stems from that time and is a reference to the cross that the crusaders wore on the back of their tunics rather than an indication that he was a hunchback. He also supported his brother's campaigns against the Scots and the Welsh.

Edmund married twice. His first wedding, on 8 April 1269, was to the 11-year-old Aveline de Forz, countess of Holderness and daughter of William, count of Aumale, and Isabel de Reviers, but she died four years later, possibly in childbirth. The second was to Blanche, the widow of Henry, king of Navarre, on or about 3 February 1276. The couple spent most of their time at their French properties but returned to England in 1293, when Philip IV of **France** declared that **Edward I** (king of England and Edmund's older brother) had forfeited Gascony by failing to visit the French court and pay him homage in his role as duke of **Aquitaine**. They had three sons and a daughter, with the eldest two boys (Thomas and Henry) succeeding to the earldom in 1296 and 1322 respectively. Edmund died on 5 June 1296 after an unsuccessful attempt to capture Bordeaux for Edward. His body was carried back to England and buried in **Westminster Abbey**. Blanche survived him for six years.

**EDMUND IRONSIDES (c989–1016).** *See* EDMUND II.

**EDMUND OF LANGLEY, DUKE OF YORK (1341–1402).** Edmund, the fifth son of King **Edward III** and **Philippa of Hainault**, was the founder of the **House of York**, which provided three English monarchs (**Edward IV**, **Edward V**, and **Richard III**) from 1471 to 1485. Born on 13 November 1341 at Kings Langley (an estate, now in Hertfordshire, that had been acquired by **Eleanor of Castile**, consort of **Edward I**, in about 1276), he spent much of his life on military campaigns in **France**, Portugal, and Scotland, but he also acted as guardian of the realm in 1394 while **Richard II** was absent in Ireland and represented England's interests in many international negotiations, including those leading to Richard's marriage to **Anne of Bohemia** in 1382. Edmund was created **duke of York** on 6 August 1385 but withdrew from the court in 1399 when **Henry IV**, son of **John of Gaunt**, Edmund's older brother, became the first representative of the **House of Lancaster**, later the Yorkists' archenemies, to occupy the throne. He died at Kings Langley on 1 August 1402 and was buried at the Dominican church there.

Edmund married twice. His first wife, whom he wed in 1372, was Isabella of Castile, daughter of King Peter of Castile, who had once been betrothed to **Joan Plantagenet (c1333–1348)**, Edmund's younger sister. The previous year, Constance, Isabella's sister, had married John of Gaunt, so Edmund's union emphasized the connections between two of Europe's most powerful families. The couple had three children—Edward (who was born in 1373 and died at the Battle of Agincourt, during the **Hundred Years' War**, in 1415); Richard (born in 1375 and executed for treason by King **Henry V** in 1415); and Constance (who was born c1374, whose husband—Thomas le Despenser—supported Richard II against her uncle, **Thomas of Woodstock**, and who died in 1416). In 1393, the year after Isabella's death, Edmund married his cousin, Joan de Holland, but the match produced no offspring.

**EDMUND OF SCOTLAND (?–?).** Edmund was one of six sons and two daughters born to King **Malcolm III** and **St. Margaret**. When Malcolm was killed in 1093, his brother, Donalbane, succeeded to the throne as **Donald III**, and Edmund fled with his brothers to safety in England. The following year, Edmund's half-brother was able to oust the new monarch and take the crown for himself as **Duncan II**, but he too was slain only a few months later, with some chroniclers (including 12th-century historian William of Malmesbury) alleging that Edmund and Donalbane were responsible. It is not clear why Edmund would ally with his uncle, though it is possible that Donald, who had no sons and was probably well over 50 years old, may have designated him as his preferred heir. The older man reclaimed the throne after Duncan's murder but was overthrown again in 1097, this time by **Edgar Aetheling** (Margaret's brother), who supported the claims to the crown of **Edgar of Scotland**, Edmund's younger sibling. The victors forced Edmund to become a monk at Montacute Abbey, a Cluniac foundation in Somerset, where he died. A number of sources list Edmund as a king or co-king of Scotland from 1094 to 1097, but there is no evidence that he ever ruled. The dates of his birth and death are not known.

**EDMUND OF WOODSTOCK, EARL OF KENT (1301–1330).** Traditionally, historians have portrayed Edmund—the younger son of King **Edward I** and his second wife, **Marguerite of France**—as a weak half-brother of **Edward II**, vacillating between support for the monarch and aid to the rebels who opposed his rule. However, more recent scholarship has tended to burnish, rather than tarnish, his reputation. Born at **Woodstock Palace**, a royal hunting lodge near Oxford, on 5 August 1301, he led England's forces in Gascony (the last major English possession on the European mainland) in 1324–25. Then, while assuring Edward II that he had no malicious intent, he journeyed to Paris for meetings with Queen **Isabella of France** (the king's estranged wife) and **Roger Mortimer** (her lover), who were plotting an invasion designed to depose the allegedly homosexual sovereign and get rid of his unpopular advisors. In 1328–29, however, Edmund changed sides again, joining Henry, earl of Lancaster (son of **Edmund, earl of Lancaster**, and grandson of King **Henry III**), in an unsuccessful effort to overthrow Mortimer, who was ruling the country as **regent** after capturing Edward in 1327 and, it was widely assumed, arranging his murder.

Apparently believing that his half-brother was still alive and incarcerated in Corfe Castle, Edmund continued to campaign for the king's release and ultimately was brought before parliament at **Winchester**, where he was found guilty of treason. He was **beheaded** on 19 March 1330, but only after a condemned criminal offered to carry out the execution in return for his freedom because nobody else would accept the task. Until comparatively recently, students of the period have accepted the evidence that Edward died in 1327 and was buried in Gloucester Cathedral. As a consequence, Edmund has been characterized as something of a fool for continuing to believe that his sovereign was still alive. However, in recent years, researchers have suggested that the king may have survived well into the 1330s and that Edmund's actions in agitating for his release were wholly understandable. Edmund was buried at the church of the Dominican Friars in Winchester and probably achieved more in death than he had in life. Public outrage at the judicial murder of a king's son fueled opposition to Mortimer, and in autumn, Henry of Lancaster persuaded **Edward III**, the son of Edward II, to exert authority and rid the realm of the regent.

In 1325, Edmund had married Margaret Wake, Mortimer's cousin. They had two sons—Edmund (born c1326) and John (born in 1330). Also, there were two daughters—Margaret (born in 1327) and **Joan, countess of Kent** (who was born in 1328; married **Edward, the black prince**, the son of **Edward III**; and became the mother of King **Richard II**).

**EDWARD I (1239–1307).** King of England from 1272 until 1307 (and known as "Longshanks" because of his height), Edward was the eldest son of **Henry III** and **Eleanor of Provence**. He was born in the **Palace of Westminster** on 17 June 1239 and for much of his youth and early manhood was a source of considerable trouble to his father. In 1255, without Henry's support, he attacked Llewelyn ap Gruffydd, prince of Gwynnedd, following a dispute over the administration of royal estates in Wales, and was soundly defeated. Then, in 1259, he supported the nobles' campaign for restrictions on the king's powers (*see* PROVISIONS OF OXFORD; PROVISIONS OF WESTMINSTER; SECOND BARONS' WAR). Later, Edward deserted the rebels and was forgiven by his father, but he was sent to Gascony in the hope that he could be kept out of mischief. That hope was misplaced because, when he returned in 1263, he resumed his former headstrong ways. At the Battle of Lewes, in 1264, his impetuosity contributed to the capture of both father and son by the dissident barons. The following year, however, he escaped and gained his revenge, leading the army that routed the antiroyalists at Evesham.

Henry died on 16 November 1272, while his son was returning from a crusade to the Holy Land, and Edward, despite his tempestuous past, became king with the full support of the English nobility. By that time, although still autocratic and intolerant of opposing views, he was somewhat older and wiser and was demonstrating considerable political skill. It was clear that feudal revenues could no longer meet all the demands made on the monarch, particularly with respect to the administration of justice. Money was needed from the growing merchant class, and the only realistic way to get it was through parliamentary levies, so Edward regularly called the knights and representatives of the towns to meet and advise him on important issues, using their support to underpin royal authority. As a result, parliament increasingly became accepted as the established means of running the country, particularly from 1297, when it gained the right to vote on taxes. Reforms of the judicial system initiated by **Henry II**, Edward's great-grandfather, were also developed, a court of chancery was created to provide redress for circumstances in which no other court was appropriate, and other courts were given their own staff to improve their efficiency. In addition, measures were taken to limit the power of the clergy and maintain social order.

However, Edward's love of action helped drain his coffers and offset much of the good he did in other spheres. In 1277, he invaded Wales and starved Llywelyn ap Gruffydd into submission. Five years later, faced with a rebellion, he invaded again, and on 11 December 1282, he killed the Welshman, thus ending the struggle for Welsh independence from England and beginning the imposition of government on English lines. He also attempted to incorporate Scotland into his kingdom, but those efforts met with less success. Although his puppet king, **John of Scotland**, paid him homage, the Scots nobles and the common people were less obeisant. In an attempt to compel submission, Edward invaded the country in 1296 and captured the **Stone of Scone**, on which Scottish kings were traditionally crowned, removing it to London. Even so, the opposition continued, led by William Wallace, and Edward was unable to bring the northerners to heel. In addition to these conflicts, Edward warred with **France** from 1297 to 1299 as a result of attempts by King Philip IV to acquire the English-held lands in Gascony.

Edward died at Burgh by Sands, near Carlisle, on 7 July 1307, while on his way north with an army, and was buried at **Westminster Abbey** in a tomb that bears the Latin inscription *Edwardus primus Scottorum malleus hic est* (Here lies Edward, the Hammer of the Scots). His son, **Edward II**, succeeded him. *See also* ALFONSO, EARL OF CHESTER; DUNFERMLINE ABBEY; EDMUND OF WOODSTOCK; ELEANOR, COUNTESS OF BAR; ELEANOR CROSSES; ELEANOR OF CASTILE; ELIZABETH, COUNTESS OF HEREFORD; JOAN OF ACRE; MARGARET, DUCHESS OF BRABANT; MARGARET, MAID OF NORWAY; MARGUERITE OF FRANCE; PLANTAGENET, ALICE; PLANTAGENET, BEATRICE; PLANTAGENET, BERENGARIA; PLANTAGENET, BLANCHE (1290); PLANTAGENET, ELEANOR; PLANTAGENET, HENRY (1267–1274); PLANTAGENET, ISABELLA; PLANTAGENET, JOAN (1265); PLANTAGENET, JOHN (1266–1271); PLANTAGENET, JULIANA; PLANTAGENET, MARY; PRINCE OF WALES; THOMAS OF BROTHERTON, EARL OF NORFOLK; TOWER OF LONDON.

**EDWARD II (1284–1327?).** Although Edward was the first child of a monarch to be created **prince of Wales** and the first king to found colleges at Cambridge and Oxford universities, he is remembered primarily for his feuds with the English nobles and for the uncertainty surrounding his death. The fourth son and one of about 16 children in the family of King **Edward I** and **Eleanor of Castile**, Edward was born on 25 April 1284 amidst the construction works at Caernarfon Castle in Wales and succeeded to the throne on his father's death in July 1307. A man of limited intellectual ability who scandalized court circles because of his homosexual affairs, he sought friends outside the normal group of royal contacts and thus antagonized those who would normally have acted as his advisors. Conflict developed, particularly over Piers Gaveston, a Gascon knight who was exiled by Edward I but recalled by his son, even before Edward's **coronation** on 25 February 1308, and made earl of Cornwall, a title originally intended for **Thomas of Brotherton**, a child of Edward I by his marriage to **Marguerite of France**. In 1311, Gaveston's unpopularity led a faction of nobles to demand that the king should renew his exile and, in addition, agree to a limitation of **royal prerogatives** on appointments to the court, declarations of war, and financial matters. Initially Edward had to accept the demands, but he worked to draw supporters to his cause and soon had Gaveston's second banishment annulled. Stung by the rebuke, the barons kidnapped the favorite and arranged for his murder on 19 June 1312, an action that Edward never forgave despite an apparent reconciliation with the rebels the following year.

Wars with Scotland rubbed salt into the sores. England's kings claimed overlordship of the Scots, but the independence movement, led by **Robert I** (Robert the Bruce), had successfully occupied all of the major strongholds in the country except that at **Stirling**, which was placed under siege. Edward led a large army north to repair the situation but was soundly beaten at the **Battle of Bannockburn** on 24 June 1314. He retreated to lick his wounds, leaving Bruce to raid England's northern frontier and further reduce the English monarch's standing with his nobility, many of whom had lost sons and brothers in the fruitless Scottish campaign. With his freedom of action limited, the king had to concede control of his realm to his cousin, Thomas of Lancaster, who by 1321 was rousing antiroyalist opinion in the north of England. By that time, Edward was able to raise an army to subdue him, and the two sides met at Boroughbridge on 16 March 1322. Thomas was soundly defeated and executed six days later.

With newfound confidence, and with the help of Hugh Despenser the Elder and his son, Hugh the Younger, Edward began to reorganize the administration of his country in order to augment his private income. However, the Despensers aroused antagonism as they filled their own coffers and, in particular, fueled the fury of Edward's queen, **Isabella of France**, whose estates were seized in 1324. In 1325, Isabella moved to Paris, where she gathered a group of disaffected nobles around her and announced her intention to remove the Despensers. With her lover, **Roger Mortimer**, baron Wigmore and later earl of March, she invaded England in 1326. Edward, unable to muster any support, fled with his advisors, but all three were captured, the Despensers were killed, and the king was imprisoned at Kenilworth.

Roger and Isabella called a meeting of parliament on 7 January 1327, declared Edward unfit to govern, and decreed that his 14-year-old son, also Edward, would be the new sovereign (*see* EDWARD III). Representatives of the assembly called on the imprisoned monarch and forced him to abdicate, making the announcement on 20 January. His fate after this is unclear. The long-held belief is that he was moved to Berkeley Castle, near Gloucester, where he was murdered on Roger's orders on 21 September (some accounts record that he was strangled, others that he was suffocated, and others that a red-hot length of copper was pushed up his rectum). Recent scholars have questioned this story, however, suggesting that he may have been alive in 1330 or even later. *See also* EDMUND OF WOODSTOCK; ELEANOR, COUNTESS OF GUELDRES; ELTHAM PALACE; JOAN OF THE TOWER; JOHN OF ELTHAM, EARL OF CORNWALL; MARGARET, MAID OF NORWAY.

**EDWARD III (1312–1377).** The son of King **Edward II** and his queen, **Isabella of France**, Edward was born at **Windsor Castle** on 13 November

1312 and ruled England for half a century. His reign began on 25 January 1327 following his father's enforced abdication, though in the early years his mother and her lover, **Roger Mortimer**, governed in his name.

In 1330, Edward took control himself, executing Mortimer and ending Isabella's influence by banishing her to Castle Rising in Norfolk. He immediately attempted to reestablish the prestige that England had lost under his father's inept leadership. Aiming to reverse recognition of Scotland's independence (*see* NORTHAMPTON, TREATY OF), he supported an invasion of the country, making **Edward de Balliol** a puppet king. Also, when Charles IV of **France** died in 1328 without leaving any male heirs, Isabella, acting as **regent**, advanced her son's claim to the French throne on the grounds that he was the only living male descendant of her father, Philip IV, who had been king from 1285 to 1314. The French were unwilling to acquiesce, however, pointing out that Edward's descent was through the female line and preferring Philip's brother's son, who ruled as Philip VI. For England, there were considerable economic implications—the crown wanted to retain control of Gascony (partly because of the profitable wine trade through Bordeaux) as well as facilitate trade between English wool merchants and markets in Flanders (at the time, the Flemish burghers were at odds with their French overlord)—so Edward continued to pursue the claim after he became king in his own right, a decision that led to the **Hundred Years' War** between the two powers.

The conflict ended, albeit temporarily, in 1360 when, under the Treaty of **Calais**, Edward added **Aquitaine** to his possessions in return for surrendering his rights to the whole of **France**. Six years later, he formally rejected papal assertions to feudal overlordship of England (assertions that stemmed from King **John**'s homage to Pope Innocent III in 1213), but by that time domestic stability was threatened by the costs of war and by the ravages of bubonic plague, which was known as the Black Death and which may have killed as much as 40 percent of the English population from 1348 to 1351. The need for funds led to attacks on the wealth of the church and to frequent requests to parliament for financial support that was granted reluctantly only after much bargaining by the nobles and churchmen for greater rights and more privileges.

Increasingly, as the king aged, he left military matters in the hands of his sons, **Edward, the black prince**, and **John of Gaunt**, particularly after war with France was renewed in 1368. Ultimately Aquitaine was lost, and a new truce was signed in 1375, leaving Edward with only Bayonne, Bordeaux, Brest, and Calais on the continental mainland. England itself was divided by a power struggle between the two brothers that was resolved only by the death of the black prince in 1376.

Edward died at **Sheen Palace**, near **London**, on 21 June 1377 after suffering a stroke while supervising improvements to the building. He never achieved the aims he set for himself, largely because ambition outran resources. Nevertheless, he had overseen a period of major social and political change, because by the end of his reign parliament had been divided into two houses (a division that has been retained into the 21st century) and had increased its role in the government of the realm, English had replaced French as the language of the law courts, and Protestantism was beginning to win converts from the Roman Catholic faith. International ambitions had come to naught, but Edward had held his country together in a time of strife and had reintroduced a self-confidence that favored the development of trade and industry. *See also* ANJOU, HOUSE OF; DAVID II; DUKE OF CORNWALL; DUKE OF YORK; EDMUND OF LANGLEY, DUKE OF YORK; ISABELLA DE COUCY; KENNINGTON PALACE; LIONEL OF ANTWERP; MANN, KINGS OF; MARGARET, COUNTESS OF PEMBROKE; MARY, DUCHESS OF BRITTANY; PHILIPPA OF HAINAULT; PLANTAGENET, BLANCHE (1342); PLANTAGENET, JOAN (c1333–1348); PLANTAGENET, THOMAS; PLANTAGENET, WILLIAM (1337); PLANTAGENET, WILLIAM (1348); ST. GEORGE'S CHAPEL; THOMAS OF WOODSTOCK.

**EDWARD IV (1442–1483).** King of England from 1461 to 1470 and from 1471 to 1483, Edward was a much more efficient military leader than his predecessor, **Henry VI**, but he became greedy and autocratic toward the end of his reign. The son of **Richard, duke of York (1411–1460)**, and **Cicely Neville**, he was born at Rouen in **France** on 28 April 1442. When York was killed by royalist forces at the **Battle of Wakefield** in 1460, Edward gathered an army, defeated Henry's troops at Mortimer's Cross on 2 February 1461, and then marched on **London** and was acclaimed king on 4 March.

The early part of his reign was marked by the continuation of the dynastic struggle between the **House of Lancaster** and the **House of York** (*see* WARS OF THE ROSES), but Edward's secret wedding to **Elizabeth Woodville** (the widow of a Lancastrian) in 1464 alienated many of his fellow Yorkists, particularly Richard Neville, earl of Warwick, who was attempting to end war with France through a peace treaty that would have been sealed by the king's marriage to a sister-in-law of King Louis XI. Warwick responded by allying with **Margaret of Anjou** to free Henry VI (her husband) from captivity and return him to the throne in the autumn of 1470.

Edward fled to Holland, but with support from his brother-in-law, Charles, duke of Burgundy, he returned to England in March 1471. Landing at Ravenspur, on the River Humber, he turned south, took London, and slew Warwick at Barnet on 14 April. A further success at the **Battle of Tewkesbury** on 4 May made the throne secure, and with domestic opposition subdued, he turned his attention to a revival of previous monarchs' claims to territories in **France**. In 1475, he took a large army across the English Channel but met French forces that were well prepared and were willing to reach an accommodation. Under the terms of the Treaty of Picquigny, the English monarch agreed to withdraw in return for a sum of 75,000 gold crowns and an annual tribute of 50,000 gold crowns for as long as he and Louis survived. These payments released Edward from dependence on parliament for his income and augmented coffers he was already filling through a reorganization of his estates, trade on his ships, and other measures. With his money, he patronized William Caxton, funding his innovative printing methods, and established a library of illuminated Flemish manuscripts. The reign was also characterized by administrative innovations that improved law and order and therefore promoted trade, but by his last years, the king was becoming increasingly avaricious, cruel, and promiscuous. He died at the **Palace of Westminster** on 9 April 1483, possibly of pneumonia but perhaps worn out by overeating and lack of exercise, while still only 40. His 12-year-old son succeeded him, briefly, as King **Edward V**.

Scholars still debate whether Edward was the legitimate son of Richard of York. Skeptics point out that, at the likely week of conception, the duke was distant from his wife on a military campaign and that the child's christening was a very private affair, whereas the celebrations for the birth of Edmund, their next son, were much more flamboyant, perhaps because they both had cause for joy. On the other hand, it is possible that York had returned for a visit to his wife nine months before Edward was born or that the boy was born prematurely. Whatever his parentage, he would have had a strong claim to the throne through right of conquest and also by law, because a child born to a married woman was considered legitimate unless the husband denied paternity, which Richard never did.

On 25 June 1483, parliament declared Edward's marriage to Elizabeth invalid because, according to a clergyman—possibly Ralph Shaa (a theologian) or Robert Stillington (bishop of Bath and Wells)—he had previously wed Lady Eleanor Butler, a tryst that made the later union with Elizabeth bigamous. Edward's brother argued that, as a result, the deceased king's children were illegitimate and thus he was the true heir. He took the throne as **Richard III**, but the parliamentary declaration was repealed in 1485 so that **Henry VII** could marry **Elizabeth of York**, Edward's eldest daughter. There is, in any case, no documentary evidence that the first "marriage" ever happened. *See also* ANNE, COUNTESS OF SURREY; BRIDGET OF YORK; CATHERINE OF YORK; CECILY, VISCOUNTESS WELLES;

DUKE OF YORK; EDWARD V; GEORGE, DUKE OF BEDFORD; MAR-
GARET OF YORK; MARY OF YORK; NORTHAMPTON, BATTLE OF;
PLACENTIA, PALACE OF; RICHARD, DUKE OF YORK (1473–1483?);
TOWTON, BATTLE OF; WARBECK, PERKIN.

**EDWARD V (1470–1483?).** Twelve-year-old Edward became king of England when his father, **Edward IV**, died on 9 April 1483, but he did not live
long enough to have any influence on his realm. He was born on 2 November
1470 in **Westminster Abbey**, where his mother, **Elizabeth Woodville**, had
sought sanctuary after her husband fled the country to escape the clutches of
**Margaret of Anjou** and her allies in the **House of Lancaster**, who struggled
to keep the mentally unstable **Henry VI** on the throne (*see* WARS OF THE
ROSES). By the following year, however, the exile had returned and reclaimed the crown. He proclaimed his son **prince of Wales** on 25 June 1471
and sent him to Ludlow, located close to the English border with the principality, which was not yet completely subdued.

The boy spent most of his childhood in the Shropshire town but set out
for **London** shortly after his father's death. During the journey, he was intercepted by his uncle Richard, duke of Gloucester, who had been appointed
protector of the realm by parliament and was intent on removing the young
monarch from the control of the Woodvilles. The duke then escorted the new
king to the **Tower of London**, and his mother fled to Westminster Abbey
once again.

For reasons not entirely clear, but certainly influenced both by threats and
by cajoling, Elizabeth allowed **Richard, duke of York (1473–1483?)**, her
other son, to leave the sanctuary on 16 June and join his brother. Nine days
later, an assembly of nobles and others, meeting at Westminster, upheld a
claim that Edward IV's marriage to Elizabeth was invalid on the grounds
that he had previously agreed to wed Eleanor Butler, daughter of the earl of
Shrewsbury. As a result of the ruling, the children of the marriage were declared illegitimate, and Richard of Gloucester was deemed to be the rightful
king of England. He was crowned **Richard III** the next day, ending Edward's
brief reign.

For some weeks after that, the young brothers were seen playing on the
tower's grounds, but in August they vanished. Modern historians tend to
believe that they were murdered on Richard's orders, but there were other
possible culprits, including Henry Stafford, duke of Buckingham and one
of Richard's staunchest allies, and Henry Tudor, who was later to claim
the throne as **Henry VII** and may have wanted to eliminate rivals. Nearly
200 years later, in 1674, workmen in the tower discovered a wooden chest
containing the remains of two children. At the instigation of King **Charles**

**II**, the bones were put in an urn and placed in Westminster Abbey. The urn was reopened in 1933, and the forensic experts who examined the material concluded that one child was aged 12 to 13 and the other 9 to 11. However, there was insufficient evidence for them to conclude that the skeletons were those of the **princes**.

**EDWARD VI (1537–1553).** Edward—the first English king to be raised as a Protestant and the only son of King **Henry VIII** to survive infancy—was born at **Hampton Court Palace** on 12 October 1537. His mother, **Jane Seymour** (Henry's third **queen consort**), died of puerperal fever 12 days later. In July 1543, Edward was betrothed to the infant **Mary, queen of Scots**, as part of his father's campaign to unite England with its neighbor to the north, but the Scottish parliament rejected the proposals later in the year; Henry reacted with characteristic fury, initiating a series of punitive military expeditions that continued well after his death (*see* GREENWICH, TREATY OF).

Edward was just nine years old when he succeeded to the throne in January 1547. His father's will had declared that a council of **regents** should be appointed to rule the country until the new king reached the age of 18, but Edward Seymour, duke of Somerset and Jane's brother, very quickly maneuvered himself into a position of power as "lord protector of the realm" and made the major decisions himself, pursuing the war with Scotland at considerable expense and attempting to quell social unrest at home. Inevitably, his actions annoyed other ambitious nobles, so in the fall of 1549 he was arrested, and early the following year he was replaced at the head of the regency council by John Dudley, earl of Warwick, who was as corrupt and greedy as his predecessor but who nevertheless restored some stability to government while continuing to pursue a vigorous program of religious reform, bolstered by Edward's strong support for Protestantism.

Some historians believe that during this period the young monarch was in poor health, but others contend that he was a strong, active young man. Whatever the truth of the matter, he undoubtedly fell ill during the winter of 1552–53, possibly with tuberculosis, and, influenced by Dudley, schemed to ensure that neither of his half-sisters—later **Mary I** and **Elizabeth I**—would succeed him if he died. (Essentially, the plot, clearly in conflict with the provisions of the **Succession to the Crown Act of 1543**, was hatched to ensure that the staunchly Roman Catholic Mary would not have the power to reverse the direction of religious change, so the reasons for the exclusion of Elizabeth are not known.) Lady **Jane Grey**—Edward's first cousin once removed and the wife of Dudley's son, **Guildford (or Guilford) Dudley**—was named as the successor to the throne, to be followed by her male heirs.

Edward died at the **Palace of Placentia** on 6 July 1553, having had little opportunity to stamp his authority on the realm, and was buried in **Westminster Abbey**. Jane was proclaimed queen, unwillingly, four days later, precipitating a power struggle between supporters of her father-in-law and those—including Dudley's enemies, nobles supporting the legality of the parliamentary legislation, and many Roman Catholics—who felt that the crown belonged to Mary. After only nine days, it was evident that Mary's supporters were in the majority; Dudley and Jane were both **beheaded**, leaving Mary to begin her efforts to return the English church to the papal fold. *See also* CHURCH OF ENGLAND; ELTHAM PALACE.

**EDWARD VII (1841–1910).** "Bertie" acquired a deserved reputation for his devotion to gambling, wine, and women, but in a short nine-year reign, he nevertheless endeared himself to a people weary of the austerity of his maternal predecessor. His birth at **Buckingham Palace** on 9 November 1841, as the eldest son of Queen **Victoria** and **Prince Albert of Saxe-Coburg and Gotha**, made him the first **heir apparent** born to a reigning monarch since King **George III**'s consort, **Charlotte of Mecklenburg-Strelitz**, produced a son (later King **George IV**) in 1762. **Prince** Albert was intent on giving the boy an education that would prepare him for kingship, but the child was not interested in books and quickly fell behind his sisters in the royal classroom, though later periods at **Edinburgh** and Oxford universities in 1859 and at Cambridge University in 1861 demonstrated that he had a quick mind and an interest in many aspects of learning. Moreover, in 1860, a visit to North America that included a three-day stay with U.S. president James Buchanan clearly indicated that the young prince had considerable social charm and an ability to mix with all classes of society.

As he entered his twenties, Edward, who loved parades and uniforms, expressed a wish to pursue a career in the army. This was considered much too risky an occupation for an heir to the throne, but he did spend the summer of 1861 with the Grenadier Guards at a camp in Ireland, where actress Nellie Clifton was smuggled into his bed by officer friends. Nellie and the conspirators were less than circumspect in descriptions of her experience, so by early winter the story had reached the ears of Edward's parents, and Albert, unwell but shocked, set off for Cambridge, where his son was living, in order to remonstrate with him. Then, or soon afterward, the prince consort contracted typhoid and, on 14 December, died at **Windsor Castle**. Victoria, who spent the rest of her life in mourning, blamed her son and wrote to his sister, **Victoria, princess royal**, that "I never can or shall look at him without a shudder."

Wishing him well out of her way, the queen dispatched Edward to the Near East for six months and then, on his return, pursued arrangements for him to marry **Alexandra of Denmark**, whose father later became King Christian IX. The wedding was held in **St. George's Chapel** at Windsor on 10 March 1863; the marriage produced six children (including Edward's successor, King **George V**), but the marital state did nothing to detract from the prince's playboy lifestyle, as he developed a series of close friendships with attractive women, including actresses Sarah Bernhardt and Lillie Langtry, Lady Randolph Churchill (mother of Sir Winston Churchill), and socialite Alice Keppel (the great grandmother of **Camilla, duchess of Cornwall**). As he presided at parties and traveled overseas, becoming (in 1875–76) the first heir apparent to visit India, Alexandra kept in the background, preferring to spend time with her young family at **Sandringham** or at **Osborne House** rather than at balls or in the **London** theaters.

Victoria prevented Edward from taking any significant role in public life until just before her death in 1901, but even so, he clearly developed something of a social conscience, associating with Jews despite the strong anti-Semitic sentiment of many of his aristocratic friends, deploring the "rude and rough" way in which colonial officials treated the Indian people, and visiting slums in disguise in an effort to find out about housing conditions in the poorest parts of Britain's cities. These views were, in many ways, liberal for the time, but Bertie was no radical, and he argued against voting rights for women and opposed proposals to give Ireland home rule.

By the time the prince succeeded to the throne, he was nearly 60 years old, overweight, and a grandfather, but he still approached his duties with the same energy that he had earlier invested in his socializing, livening up the court (by introducing continental-style Sundays, for instance), refurbishing residences, and reorganizing royal finances. He was never greatly interested in politics, but he had decided views on many domestic issues (for example, he condemned food taxes as unjust because they had a disproportionate effect on the least wealthy of his subjects) and worked hard to strengthen his country's diplomatic power in Europe. Fluent in both French and German, he used his linguistic skills to good effect in speeches abroad, furthering a new sense of cooperation between Britain and **France**, and fostering good relations with tsarist Russia. However, his indulgent lifestyle told against him as, from 1906, his health began to fail, and he developed bronchitis as a result of heavy smoking. On 9 March 1910, while staying with Alice Keppel at Biarritz in southern France, he collapsed, and his decline continued after his return to **London**. The king died at Buckingham Palace on 6 May and was buried in St. George's Chapel, ending a reign that is now regarded both as a flamboyant reaction to the somberness of the late Victorian era and as the last hurrah of a wealthy European aristocratic culture that was ended by World War I. *See also* ALBERT VICTOR, PRINCE, DUKE OF CLARENCE AND

AVONDALE; ALEXANDER JOHN, PRINCE; ALFRED, PRINCE, DUKE OF EDINBURGH AND SAXE-COBURG AND GOTHA; ALICE, PRINCESS, GRAND DUCHESS OF HESSE; BEATRICE (OR HENRY) OF BATTENBERG, PRINCESS; CHRISTIAN OF SCHLESWIG-HOLSTEIN, PRINCESS; LOUISE, PRINCESS, DUCHESS OF ARGYLL; LOUISE, PRINCESS ROYAL, DUCHESS OF FIFE; MARLBOROUGH HOUSE; MARY, PRINCESS, LANDGRAVINE OF HESSE-CASSEL; MAUD, PRINCESS, QUEEN OF NORWAY; QUEEN'S (OR KING'S) OFFICIAL BIRTHDAY; REGNAL NAME; SAXE-COBURG AND GOTHA, HOUSE OF; VICTORIA, PRINCESS; WHITE LODGE.

**EDWARD VIII (1894–1972).** The only British monarch to abdicate a throne voluntarily, Edward reigned for just 11 months in 1936. Born at **White Lodge** in Richmond, southwest of **London**, on 23 June 1894, he was the eldest of the six children of George, **duke of York** (later King **George V**), and **Mary of Teck**. From childhood, he was exposed to the experiences deemed necessary for a future king, attending naval college from 1907 to 1911, serving briefly as a midshipman, being invested as **prince of Wales** in 1911, and attending Oxford University (without distinguishing himself academically) from 1912 to 1914. At the outbreak of World War I in 1914, he joined the Grenadier Guards but was refused permission to fight (because the capture of the **heir apparent** by the enemy would have been a considerable political embarrassment) and was given staff duties instead. Even so, he visited the front line on several occasions, earning the respect of combatants through his willingness to face danger and maintaining the **royal family**'s high wartime profile.

In the years that followed the cessation of hostilities in 1918, the prince made several visits to territories within the British Empire but also to Europe and to the United States. However, he also developed a taste for dancing, dining, and married women, conducting several affairs that made his father, and most of his advisors, doubt whether he had the character appropriate to a king. Their concerns seemed justified because, when he did succeed to the throne after George V's death on 20 January 1936, he showed little interest in the papers sent to him by his ministers and he appeared to have a favorable view of Adolf Hitler's Germany, which was out of kilter with the more critical approach adopted by the government. Moreover, he made it clear that he intended to marry Mrs. Wallis Simpson (*see* WALLIS, DUCHESS OF WINDSOR), the daughter of a Pennsylvania family who had divorced her first husband—Lieutenant Earl Winfield Spencer, Jr.—in 1927 and was in the process of divorcing her second (Ernest Simpson, a London businessman).

The political problem raised by the proposed union was not that Mrs. Simpson was an American citizen (British kings had long found foreign brides), nor that she was a commoner (from the late 19th century, several members of the **royal family** had found partners who had no royal blood), but that the lady was a divorcee, and Edward, as king, was **supreme governor of the Church of England**, which took the view that marriage was for life and refused to wed individuals who had been granted divorces by the courts. Edward considered a morganatic marriage (implying that he would remain king, but his wife would not be known as queen), but Prime Minister Stanley Baldwin and other parliamentarians deemed that unacceptable. Baldwin, in effect, gave his sovereign three choices—to give up Mrs. Simpson, to ignore political advice and marry her in a nonconformist church or at a civil ceremony, or to abdicate. Edward was not prepared to give up his mistress and was well aware that all his ministers would resign if he married, creating a constitutional crisis of major proportions, so on 11 December he abdicated. That night, he told the British people in a radio broadcast that he "found it impossible to carry the heavy burden of responsibility and to discharge my duties as king as I would wish to do without the help and support of the woman I love."

Edward was replaced by his brother, King **George VI**, who created the former sovereign duke of Windsor but would not permit any of his family to attend his brother's wedding, celebrated at the Chateau de Candé, near Tours in central **France**, on 3 June 1937. He also refused to allow the duke's wife to be known as "**her royal highness**," a decision that Windsor considered an insult and that caused much ill feeling. Queen Mary, for her part, felt that her son's abdication was the greatest humiliation of her life and would not meet the woman she believed had caused it, while, according to some writers, Queen Elizabeth (*see* ELIZABETH, QUEEN MOTHER), King George's consort, never forgave Mrs. Simpson for an action that made her shy husband monarch, a position he never wanted.

At the beginning of World War II, the Windsors fled to Spain and then to Portugal before the duke was made governor of the Bahamas, a post that enabled the British government to prevent him from giving any support to Nazi Germany. Although he attempted to reduce poverty on the islands, he never enjoyed his administrative role—the Bahamas, he considered, were "a third-class British colony"—and when the war ended in 1945, he returned to France with the duchess. For several years, the couple commuted between Paris and the United States, becoming minor celebrities in both places (they were entertained at the White House by American president Dwight D. Eisenhower in 1955, for instance, and appeared on Ed Murrow's *Person to Person* television show the following year), but by the 1960s Edward's health was in decline, his condition exacerbated by heavy smoking. In 1965, he had an eye operation to prevent him from going blind, by 1971 he was suffering from throat cancer, and early in 1972 he underwent a hernia operation. On 28 May 1972, the duke died at his Paris home in the Rue du Champ d'Entraînement. His body was returned to the United Kingdom, and after a funeral service attended by Queen **Elizabeth II** and other members of the royal family, he was buried at **Frogmore**. Windsor's critics had believed that his marriage would not last, but the duke and duchess spent 35 years together, never having any children but apparently devoted to each other. When the duchess died in 1986, she was laid to rest beside him. *See also* AIR TRAVEL; BALMORAL CASTLE; BUCKINGHAM PALACE; FORT BELVEDERE; HONOURS OF THE PRINCIPALITY OF WALES; MARY, PRINCESS ROYAL, COUNTESS OF HAREWOOD.

**EDWARD DE BALLIOL (c1282–1364).** On 24 September 1332, Edward, son of King **John of Scotland** and **Isabella de Warenne**, was crowned king of Scots, but he had insufficient following to impose himself on those countrymen who considered that eight-year-old **David II** was the realm's lawful sovereign. When John was forced to abdicate in 1296, Edward went with him to imprisonment in England and then moved to **France**, harboring ambitions to occupy a Scottish throne that he believed to be his birthright. In 1332, with the support of **Edward III** of England and accompanied by a group of nobles who had been disinherited by King **Robert I** (David's father), he landed at Kinghorn (on the coast of Fife) with a small army, routed a Scots force at Dupplin Moor (in Perthshire) on 12 August, and marched to a **coronation** at **Scone**. On November 23, he formally recognized the English monarch as his feudal superior, and therefore as overlord of the kingdom of Scotland.

The Scots, however, were less willing than Balliol to cede their independence. On 16 December, David's supporters surprised Edward at Annan while he was asleep and chased him and the remnants of his army over the border into England. Despite this setback, Edward III was unwilling to give up his efforts to bring Scotland under his heel, so on 19 July 1333, at Halidon Hill (near Berwick), he led his own army to another victory. The military success was enough to establish Balliol's authority over much of the eastern side of the country, and it forced his enemies to take David to France for safety. However, large areas of Scotland still lay outside his control, and sentiment against him grew as knowledge spread of territorial concessions made to the English king.

In September 1334, Balliol was forced to flee again, but once more Edward III intervened, sending another army north in 1335 in an effort to consolidate the English grip on the lands initially occupied two years earlier. The invasion yielded little, and further attempts the following year were no more successful. By 1338, the Scots had won back nearly all they had lost and had chased Balliol south yet again. Also, the political climate had changed because Edward III was expressing greater interest in pursuing a claim to the French throne (*see* HUNDRED YEARS' WAR) than in supporting an aspirant Scottish king who was clearly not acceptable to most of his intended subjects. Edward de Balliol made a last foray into Scotland in 1347 and then, on 20 January 1356, "abdicated" in favor of Edward III, claiming that age and the Scots' rebelliousness combined to prevent him from imposing his rule over the country. He died, unmarried, at Wheatley, Yorkshire, in January 1364.

**EDWARD LONGSHANKS (1238–1307).** *See* EDWARD I.

**EDWARD OF LANCASTER, PRINCE OF WALES (1453–1471).** Edward (also known as Edward of Westminster and Edward Plantagenet) is often cited as the one **prince of Wales** who perished in battle, although the circumstances of his death are in fact unclear. The only child of King **Henry VI** and **Margaret of Anjou**, he was born at the **Palace of Westminster** in **London** on 13 October 1453. At the time, there was much gossip about his birth because many courtiers believed that the mentally unstable Henry was incapable of siring a child, but although several possible alternative fathers were suggested (including Edmund Beaufort, duke of Somerset, and James Butler, earl of Wiltshire), the rumors were never supported by evidence. Edward was invested as **prince** of Wales at **Windsor Castle** in 1454 and, as the only son of the monarch, would normally have followed his father to the throne. However, England was in a state of turmoil, partly as a result of the sovereign's weak leadership (*see* WARS OF THE ROSES), and in 1460 Henry was forced by parliament to declare that **Richard, duke of York (1411–1460)**, would be his heir.

The young prince's mother responded to her son's disinheritance by seeking military support in the north of England, Scotland, and Wales and ultimately found a powerful ally in Richard Neville, earl of Warwick, who had initially supported the Yorkist cause but had become disaffected after Edward, Richard's son, deposed Henry and ruled as King **Edward IV**. Unfortunately for the Lancastrians, Warwick was killed at the Battle of Barnet on 14 April 1471. With Edmund Beaufort as their only experienced military commander, Margaret and her 17-year-old son had to take responsibility for much of their army's strategy themselves, but they were unable to match their opponents' guile and were routed at the **Battle of Tewkesbury** on 4 May. It is unclear whether Edward of Lancaster died fighting or whether he was later executed on Edward's command (there are unsubstantiated reports that he was taken prisoner by Richard, duke of Gloucester, who later ruled as

**Richard III**, and that he was killed because he insulted the king). He was buried in Tewkesbury Abbey, where the victorious Yorkists cut down some of his supporters after the battle, and Margaret was imprisoned until King Louis XI of **France** paid for her release in 1475. The prince's death also ended Lancastrian hopes of winning back the throne and presaged a period of peace that lasted until 1485, when **Henry VII** deposed the unpopular Richard III. *See also* NEVILLE, ANNE; WAKEFIELD, BATTLE OF.

**EDWARD OF MIDDLEHAM, PRINCE OF WALES (c1473–1484).** Edward was the only son of King **Richard III** and **Anne Neville**, the **queen consort**. He was born, possibly in December 1473 but perhaps later, at Middleham Castle (a stronghold close to York that became the royal couple's principal base in northern England) and was created **prince of Wales** on 24 August 1483, some two months after his father had been declared king. According to the *Croyland Chronicle* (a contemporaneous document written at Croyland Abbey, a Benedictine religious house in Lincolnshire) the boy was taken ill while at Nottingham with his parents early in 1484 and died at Middleham, either on 31 March or on 9 April. The same source records that Richard and his wife were overcome with grief but that the monarch's enemies were inclined to interpret the child's death as divine retribution for Richard's implication in the murder of his young predecessor, King **Edward V**. The boy—probably buried in the church of St. Helen and the Holy Cross at the village of Sheriff Hutton, which lay on his mother's family estates north of York—is supposedly the only **prince** of Wales to be interred outside **London**.

The bereavement created a constitutional crisis because it left the sovereign with no legitimate heir and with a queen who was in ill health and was unlikely to produce another child. Richard responded by naming his nephew, Edward, earl of Warwick, his preferred successor (probably as a result of Anne's influence) and then (after Anne's death) changing his mind and nominating John de la Pole, earl of Lincoln and son of Elizabeth, the king's older sister. In the end, neither got the crown because, in 1485, Richard died at the **Battle of Bosworth Field**, and Henry Tudor claimed the throne by right of conquest, ruling as King **Henry VII**.

**EDWARD OF SCOTLAND (?–1093).** The eldest son of King **Malcolm III** and **St. Margaret**, Edward died on 13 November 1093 from wounds received in a skirmish with forces attempting to relieve a Scottish siege of Alnwick Castle. Malcolm was killed in the same struggle, and Margaret died three days later when news of the deaths reached the royal court at **Edinburgh** Castle. *See also* DONALD III.

**EDWARD, PRINCE, DUKE OF KENT (1935– ).** The elder son of **Prince George, duke of Kent**, and **Princess Marina, duchess of Kent**, Prince Edward was born at his parents' **London** home in Belgrave Square on 9 October 1935. He succeeded to his father's title on 25 August 1942, at the age of six, when **Prince** George was killed in an aircraft accident in northern Scotland. The young duke was educated at Ludgrove Preparatory School (Berkshire), at Eton College, and then (partly because his mother felt that the mountain air would help to alleviate his asthma) at the Institut Le Rosey in Switzerland before entering the Royal Military Academy Sandhurst. After graduating in 1955, he served with the army for more than 20 years, his postings including spells in Hong Kong (1962–63) and Cyprus (where he was part of a United Nations peacekeeping force in 1970). He also represented his cousin, Queen **Elizabeth II**, at several international events, including the ceremonies in Sierra Leone (1961), Uganda (1962), the Gambia (1965), and Guyana (1965) with which the United Kingdom's former colonies marked their first days as independent states. (In 2007, the prince participated in Ghanaian celebrations on the 50th anniversary of the country's independence from Britain, half a century after his mother had attended the events marking the colonial power's withdrawal from its West African colony.)

At home, after ending his military career in 1976, the duke became vice chairman of British Trade International, acting as a roving ambassador for British manufacturing industries and commercial services until 2001, when he handed the task to **Prince Andrew, duke of York**. He still carries out some 200 public engagements each year, serving as president of the All England Lawn Tennis and Croquet Club (a post previously held by **Princess** Marina) and as grand master of the United Grand Lodge of Freemasons, England, as well as lending support to numerous military and charitable organizations, including the Boy Scout movement, the Commonwealth War Graves Commission, and the Royal National Lifeboat Institution.

On 8 June 1961, Prince Edward married Katharine, daughter of Sir William Arthrington Worsley, at York Minster (*see* KATHARINE, DUCHESS OF KENT). They have two sons (**George Windsor, earl of St. Andrews**, who was born in 1962, and **Lord Nicholas Windsor**, born in 1970) and one daughter (**Lady Helen Taylor**, born in 1964). None of the children carries out public engagements on behalf of the **royal family**.

**EDWARD, PRINCE, DUKE OF KENT AND STRATHEARN (1767– 1820).** Edward—father of Queen **Victoria** and pursuer of an expensive lifestyle, the cost of which considerably outstripped his means—was the fourth son, and fifth child, of King **George III** and **Charlotte of Mecklenburg-Strelitz**. He was born at **Buckingham Palace** on 2 November 1767 and, from 1785, pursued a career in the army, serving mainly in North America (where he was commander-in-chief of the British forces in 1799–80) and in Gibraltar. Unfortunately, a rigorous approach to military discipline that made him thoroughly unpopular with his men led, in 1802, to a mutiny that ended his career. He was recalled to Britain, promoted from general to field marshal, and given a nominal post as keeper of the park at **Hampton Court Palace**.

A fun-loving **prince**, Edward spent lavishly on entertainment and on his French-born mistress, Thérèsa-Bernardine Mongenet, but did not marry until he was in his early fifties. By the second decade of the 19th century, 12 of George III's 15 children were still alive, but none had any surviving legitimate children, and the youngest female (**Princess Sophia**) was nearing the end of her childbearing years. As a result, the **House of Hanover**'s grip on the crown was slackening, so, in a bid to produce a successor to the throne, on 29 May 1818 at Schloss Ehrenburg in Bavaria and then on 11 July at **Kew Palace**, Edward wed **Princess Victoria of Saxe-Coburg-Saalfield**, the 31-year-old widow of Emich Carl, prince of Leiningen, who had died four years previously. (The second wedding was a double event, with Edward's brother, William, duke of Clarence and later King **William IV**, marrying **Adelaide of Saxe-Meiningen** at the same ceremony). Victoria—their only child—was born on 24 May 1819, but while she was still an infant, the duke developed pneumonia and passed away on 23 January 1820 at Woodbrook Cottage, a property he had leased at Sidmouth in southwest England. He was buried in **St. George's Chapel** at **Windsor Castle**. Prince Edward Island, the smallest of the Canadian provinces, was named in his honor in 1798.

**EDWARD, PRINCE, EARL OF WESSEX (1964– ). Prince** Edward is the fourth, and youngest, child of Queen **Elizabeth II** and **Prince Philip, duke of Edinburgh**. Born at **Buckingham Palace** on 10 March 1964, he was educated at Heatherdown Preparatory School near Ascot and then (like his father and **Charles, prince of Wales**, his eldest brother) at Gordonstoun School in Scotland before going to Cambridge University, where he studied anthropology, archaeology, and history. After graduating in 1986, he joined the Royal Marines but resigned his commission after a year, claiming that he was no Rambo, and joined Andrew Lloyd Webber's Really Useful Theatre Company as a production assistant. In 1993, he formed his own firm—Ardent Productions—but despite completing a popular television series dealing with the **royal family**, the venture was never a financial success.

While he was preparing to launch himself into the business world, the prince met Sophie Rhys-Jones (now **Sophie, countess of Wessex**), a public relations consultant. In the spring of 1994, tabloid press reports revealed that Sophie had moved into Edward's apartments at Buckingham Palace, apparently with the Queen's approval (commentators suggested that she had acquiesced because she felt that the arrangement might help to prevent the problems that had bedeviled the marriages of the prince's brothers and sister). The couple eventually married at **St. George's Chapel** in **Windsor Castle** on 19 June 1999, with the queen recognizing the change in her son's status by creating him earl of **Wessex**. They have two children—Lady Louise Windsor (born on 8 November 2003) and James, viscount Severn (born on 17 December 2007).

The prince and his wife were regularly criticized in the press for exploiting their royal connections to promote their businesses, and in 2002 they gave up their jobs. Since then, they have concentrated on royal duties, with Edward accepting tasks that, in the past, would have fallen to his father. In particular, he has worked to promote the Duke of **Edinburgh**'s Award Scheme, a community service and outdoor activity program for young people.

**EDWARD, THE BLACK PRINCE (1330–1376).** The eldest son of **Edward III** and **Philippa of Hainault**, Edward was heir to the English throne and was one of the commanders most feared by the French during the **Hundred Years' War**. He appears to have earned his nickname because he wore black armor, but there are no contemporary sources that confirm the habit; in his lifetime, he was known as Edward of Woodstock (after **Woodstock Palace**, his birthplace), the soubriquet only appearing in 1569, when Richard Grafton coined it in his *Chronicle of England*.

Born on 15 June 1330, Edward was created earl of Chester in 1333, **duke of Cornwall** in 1337, and **prince of Wales** in 1343. He fought with his father at the Battle of Crécy in 1346 and won his most famous victory at Poitiers on 19 September 1356, when he captured the French king, John II, and took him back to England.

Under the terms of the Treaty of **Calais**, which set out the conditions for the monarch's release in 1360, **Aquitaine** was ceded to England and Edward was appointed duke, but the black prince's prowess as a soldier considerably exceeded his skill as a governor. He antagonized the nobles and peasantry in his new duchy, partly through the heavy taxes that he imposed in order to support his luxurious lifestyle and partly because he helped Peter the Cruel win back the throne of Castile, from which he had been deposed by an alliance that included King Charles V of **France**. Edward won a major victory in Peter's cause at Najera on 3 April 1367, but the campaign broke both his treasury and his health. Summoned to explain himself to the French parliament in May 1369, he retorted that he would appear with 60,000 men at his back. However, despite the boasting, he was dependent for control of Aquitaine on an army he could not pay, so in 1371 he returned to England.

The details of the remainder of Edward's life are not clear, but as his health declined, he clearly realized that he was likely to predecease his father, so he worked hard to ensure that his son, Richard (later **Richard II**), would take preference over his younger brothers in the **succession to the throne**. He also supported parliament at a time of political discontent, providing the focus of opposition to the administration of **John of Gaunt**.

Edward died on 8 June 1376 and was buried at Canterbury Cathedral, leaving only the one child. His marriage in 1361 to **Joan, countess of Kent** (daughter of **Edmund of Woodstock, earl of Kent**), had caused some controversy, partly because the bride had a somewhat unusual marital history (her first wedding had been held in secret and her second union had been annulled), partly because the two were cousins and so needed papal dispensation for the match, and partly because many nobles felt that marriage to a foreigner would have been preferable because it would have offered the possibility of a political and military alliance with another European power. Despite the criticisms, Edward and Joan were apparently very fond of each other and spent much time together in Aquitaine. Apart from Richard, they had one son—Edward—who was born in 1365 but failed to survive childhood. Joan died in August 1385 at **Wallingford Castle** and was buried at Greyfriars Church in Stamford. *See also* KENNINGTON PALACE; PRINCE OF WALES'S FEATHERS.

**EDWARD THE CONFESSOR (c1002–1066).** Edward was the last of a long line of men from **Wessex** to rule England. The son of **Aethelred the Unready** and **Emma of Normandy**, he was born at Islip (now in Oxfordshire) in about 1002–5 but spent most of his youth at his mother's family home on the European mainland, safe from the predations of the invaders from Denmark who had occupied his father's realm. He returned in 1041 while **Harthacanute**, his half-brother, was on the throne.

Edward was Harthacanute's preferred successor and, according to the *Anglo-Saxon Chronicle*, was chosen as king by "all the people . . . in **London**" when Harthacanute died the following year. He was crowned at **Winchester** Cathedral on 3 April 1043, and one of his first acts was to deprive his mother of her lands on the grounds that she had neglected him while he was a child (and she had certainly preferred the claims of Magnus of Norway to the English throne over those of her own son).

It was Edward's misfortune that he was appointed at a time when much of England was controlled by powerful nobles, notably Godwin, earl of Wessex, and his son Harold (later **Harold II**). In 1051, Edward attempted to outlaw the Godwins, but his preference for Norman advisors annoyed some of the other courtiers, and the exiles were able to capitalize on the discontent, raising such a large army that the king had little option but to restore the family's estates.

Edward's inability to control the nobles has led some writers to regard him as a weak king, but there is much evidence to suggest that his was a successful reign. Trade flourished, helped by the maintenance of friendly relations with the Scots and a series of campaigns that subdued the Welsh. Civil administration (such as the collection of taxes and the circulation of coinage) was well organized, courts of law were respected, monasteries became renowned for the quality of the illuminated manuscripts they produced, and **Westminster Abbey** was rebuilt in stone rather than wood. However, there is no doubt that the political and military power of the monarch declined in the face of the nobles' strength and that the connections with Normandy presaged the end of Anglo-Saxon control of England.

The **succession to the throne** following Edward's death on 5 January 1066 was bitterly contested because he had no legitimate children who could step into their father's shoes. Norman sources claimed that he had promised the crown to William, duke of Normandy (later **William I of England**, usually known as William the Conqueror and Edward's second cousin once removed). They say that the king sent Harold Godwinson to Normandy in 1064 to confirm the arrangement and that Harold swore an oath to support the claim. However, English reports suggest that, on his deathbed, Edward pointed at Harold—who was undoubtedly the most powerful man in England—and some of the nobles present assumed that he was indicating his preference for the succession. In addition, **Edgar Aetheling** (or **prince**), who was Edward's great-nephew and thus was closer kin than either of the other candidates, also had his supporters, and Harald Hardråde, king of Norway, believed that he too was entitled to be the next monarch (*see* STAMFORD BRIDGE, BATTLE OF). In any event, the royal council of advisors chose Harold, a decision that enraged William to the extent that he mounted an invasion later in the year and took the crown by force (*see* HASTINGS, BATTLE OF).

Edward was canonized in 1161 and designated Edward the Confessor (a term that indicates he died a natural death) to distinguish him from **Edward the Martyr**, who had been made a saint in 1008. He was buried in Westminster Abbey, but his remains were moved within the building on several occasions, and their location was only confirmed in 2005 during conservation work on the medieval pavement around the high altar. *See also* EDITH OF WESSEX; EDWARD THE EXILE; ST. GEORGE'S CHAPEL; WESTMINSTER, PALACE OF.

**EDWARD THE ELDER (c870–924). Alfred the Great** consolidated the Anglo-Saxon kingdom of **Wessex**'s control over southern England, resisting the recurring attempts of Viking invaders to wrest the territories from him. Edward, his son, built on those foundations, extending the realm northward. His **succession to the throne** was not assured, however. Alfred had followed his brother, Aethelred, to the Wessex throne because Aethelred's sons were both too young to lead a people in battle. However, by the time Alfred died, probably in 899, the boys were young men, and Aethelwald, the elder sibling, contested Edward's right to take command. With military support from Vikings in Northumbria, who acknowledged him as king, he harassed the Saxons until he lost his life at the Battle of Holme in 901.

Edward's program of expansion began in 909, when he defeated another Northumbrian force at Tettenhall (which has since been absorbed by Wolverhampton), and continued with the seizure of territory around **London** and Oxford in 911. By 918, while adding to Wessex's fortifications, he had taken control of all land south of the Humber estuary that had been controlled by the Scandinavians, and in addition he had asserted his authority over Mercia, another Anglo-Saxon kingdom. In 920, according to the *Anglo-Saxon Chronicle*, the Northumbrians, the Scots, and the rulers of Strathclyde (now part of southwest Scotland) acknowledged Edward as "father and lord," but scholars doubt whether he was actually able to impose his will on areas north of the Humber, so true unification of England was only achieved by **Aethelstan**, his son and successor.

Edward died at Farndon, east of Wrexham, on 17 July 924 while attempting to put down a rebellion by Mercian and Cambrian dissidents. He was buried in the New Minster, a monastery in **Winchester** whose construction he had ordered in 901. In 1110, his remains were reinterred at Hyde Abbey, but the grave was disturbed during the construction of a prison in 1788 and his bones were lost. From the later 10th century, Edward was given the designation "the Elder" to distinguish him from **Edward the Martyr**, who ruled England from 975 to 978. *See also* AELFFLAED; EADRED; EALHSWITH; ECGWYNN; EDGIVA; EDMUND I.

**EDWARD THE EXILE (1016–1057).** Edward (also known as Edward **Aetheling**) was the son of King **Edmund II** and his wife, **Edith of East Anglia**. He spent most of his life outside England, hence his soubriquet, but even so his own son, **Edgar Aetheling**, became the last Anglo-Saxon king of England, albeit only for a few weeks, and his daughter, **St. Margaret**, married **Malcolm III**, king of Scotland.

When Danish invaders, led by **Canute**, conquered England in 1016, Edward was exiled (along with his brother, Edmund), and after traveling much of northern and central Europe, he eventually settled in Hungary. In 1057, however, with Anglo-Saxon rule reinstated, **Edward the Confessor** summoned him back to his homeland. The aging king was childless, so there was no obvious heir to the English throne. Harold Godwinson (later King **Harold II**) was one of the most powerful men in England and was staking a claim, as were William, duke of Normandy (*see* WILLIAM I OF ENGLAND), and Harald Hardråde, king of Norway (*see* STAMFORD BRIDGE, BATTLE OF). Edward the Exile was a scion of **Anglo-Saxon monarchs** and so had a strong and legitimate case for the succession that, if accepted, might preserve the nation's peace. However, he died only a few days after his return, and there are scholarly suspicions that he was murdered, with the Godwinson family the chief suspects. *See also* AGATHA.

**EDWARD THE MARTYR (c962–978).** Edward's brief, three-year reign as king of the English was marked by growing opposition to the monasteries and ended in violence. Scholars agree that he was the son of King **Edgar of England**, but they are less certain about his legitimacy and about his mother, who was probably **Aethelflaed Eneda**, whom Edgar later married. He was chosen as the new ruler when his father died in 975, but the accession was contested by **Aelfthryth** (or Elfrida), Edgar's second wife, who advanced the cause of Aethelred, her own seven-year-old child, later known as **Aethelred the Unready**. Although the decision in favor of the older boy was made by the **witan** (the king's group of advisors), Aelfthryth refused to accept defeat and allied herself with men who opposed her late husband's policy of granting land to religious bodies, primarily because they wanted it for themselves. Edward sided with the church and appeared to be popular with his people, but he was only 13 when he succeeded to the throne, and there is little doubt that the inexperience of youth was reflected in some of his judgments.

On 18 March 978, during a hunting expedition, the king called at Corfe Castle, where Aelfthryth and Aethelred were living. His stepmother offered him mead, and while he was drinking, she or one of her retinue stabbed him. He rode off, mortally wounded, but slumped from his horse; his foot caught in a stirrup and he was dragged into a bog, where, according to legend, the location of his body was revealed to searchers by a pillar of light. The *Anglo-Saxon Chronicle* recorded that "There has not been among the Angles a worse deed than this was, since first they sought Britain," and Aelfthryth was apparently so struck by remorse that she founded a nunnery at Amesbury in 980 and an abbey at Wherwell (where she died) in 986. Edward was buried at Wareham, but his remains were moved to Shaftesbury Abbey in 981 after several miracles were attributed to him.

In 1931, the bones of a young man were found in a casket during an archaeological investigation at Shaftesbury, and forensic examinations concluded that they had injuries similar to those Edward had received. After years of negotiation, the relics were laid to rest again in 1988, this time at a site in Brookwood, near **London**, that was owned by the Russian Orthodox Church Abroad, which, along with the **Church of England** and the Roman Catholic Church, recognizes Edward as a saint. The land is now in the care of the St. Edward the Martyr Orthodox Brotherhood, and the miracles are still said to occur. *See also* WULFTHRYTH.

**EDWY (c941–959).** *See* EADWIG.

**EGBERT (c770–839).** Some historians argue that Egbert (also known as Ecgberht and Ecgbryh) was the first king of England because he united the disparate Anglo-Saxon realms under one ruler, albeit briefly. The son of **Ealhmund** and an unknown woman who was probably the daughter of Aethelbert of Kent, he was forced into exile in Francia, probably in 789, in order to escape the depredations of Offa, the powerful ruler of Mercia. The support of Emperor Charlemagne, the Frankish leader, was probably instrumental in helping Egbert win the throne of **Wessex** when King Beorhtric died in 802, but little is known of the early years of his reign, though it seems likely that he managed to maintain Wessex's independence. In 825, Egbert defeated the Mercians in battle at Ellendun, four miles southeast of Swindon, and followed up the victory by establishing control of southeast England and East Anglia. By 829, he had conquered Mercia and, according to the *Anglo-Saxon Chronicle*, subdued Northumbria, thus extending Wessex's influence over the whole area of Anglo-Saxon dominance.

By 830, however, it was clear that the reins were loosening. Possibly because the Franks had to withdraw their soldiers in order to quell troubles at home, Mercia regained its independence, as did East Anglia. However, Egbert maintained overlordship of England south of the River Thames, extending his influence into the native British kingdom of Dumnonia, in the southwest peninsula of Great Britain, and defeating Viking invaders at Hingston Down in 838. He died on 4 February the following year and was buried at **Winchester**, having changed the political landscape of Anglo-Saxon England, and was succeeded by his son, **Aethelwulf**. *See also* RAEDBURH.

**ELEANOR, COUNTESS OF BAR (c1264–1298).** The daughter of King **Edward I** and **Eleanor of Castile**, Eleanor (also known as Eleanor of England and Eleanor Plantagenet) was born at **Windsor Castle**, west of **London**, her birth date noted by some sources as 17 June 1264 and by others as 18

June 1269. She was betrothed to Alfonso III, King of Aragon, and married him in a proxy ceremony at **Westminster Abbey** on 15 August 1290, but he died in June the following year. On 20 September 1293, she wed for a second time, taking Henry, count of Bar, as her husband. The union was political; Eleanor's father needed allies in case of war with King Philip IV of France, and Henry, whose estates bordered the territories in Champagne held by the French royal house, was bolstered by the support of the powerful English monarch. The match produced three children—Edward (born in 1284) succeeded his father as count, Eleanor (born in 1285) married Llewelyn ap Owain (a Welsh noble), and Joan (born in 1295) had a short-lived marriage with John de Warenne, earl of Surrey. Eleanor senior died on 12 October 1298 at Ghent in Belgium. Her husband was killed in battle in Italy four years later.

**ELEANOR, COUNTESS OF GUELDRES (1318–1355).** Eleanor, born at **Woodstock Palace** on 18 June 1318 and sometimes known as Eleanor of Woodstock, was the elder of two daughters in the family of **Edward II** and **Isabella of France**. In May 1332, she was married to Reinoud, count of Gueldres, who was later to become a close ally of **Edward III** in his wars with **France**. Eleanor bore two children—Reinoud (born in 1334) and Edward (born in 1336)—but the union was not happy. In 1338, her husband expelled her from his court and then attempted to annul the marriage, claiming that she had leprosy, but Eleanor, determined to counter the deception, took off her clothes before judges in order to prove that she was not diseased, and Reinoud had to take her back. After the count's death in 1343, she acted for a time as regent in Gueldres but later quarreled with both of her sons. On 22 April 1355, she died in poverty at Deventer Abbey, a Cistercian nunnery that she had founded near Nijmegen.

**ELEANOR, COUNTESS OF LEICESTER (1215–1275).** Eleanor (also known as Eleanor of England and Eleanor Plantagenet) was the last of five children born to King **John** and **Isabella of Angoulême**. On 23 April 1224, at the age of 9, she was married to 34-year-old William, earl of Pembroke and one of the most powerful nobles in England. When he died in 1231, before the birth of any children, Eleanor took an oath of chastity, witnessed by Edward Rich, the archbishop of Canterbury, but before long she fell in love with French nobleman Simon de Montfort, who held the title of earl of Leicester, and on 7 January 1238 they wed in secret.

The archbishop protested at the breaking of the oath; the nobles objected that the monarch's sister was tied to a foreigner of little rank; **Richard, earl of Cornwall** (Eleanor's brother), mounted a rebellion and had to be pacified with a large payment; and King **Henry III** (John's successor and Eleanor's older brother) was later to claim that he had allowed the wedding to go ahead only because Simon had seduced the young woman. Despite the opposition, the union survived, with Eleanor bearing five sons and two daughters over the 20 years from 1238, but Henry and his brother-in-law became increasingly bitter enemies, and in 1264 Simon was killed fighting the royalist army at the Battle of Evesham. Eleanor fled for safety to the nunnery at Montargis Abbey in **France** and died there on 13 April 1275. *See also* SECOND BARONS' WAR (1264–1267).

**ELEANOR CROSSES.** After **Eleanor of Castile**, **queen consort** of King **Edward I**, died at Harby, near Lincoln, on 28 November 1290, her husband carried her remains to **London**, erecting a decorated stone cross at each of the 12 places where the cortege rested overnight. Originally, the structures stood at the Gilbertine priory near Lincoln (where the queen's body was embalmed), Grantham, Stamford, Geddington, Hardingstone, Stony Stratford, Woburn, Dunstable, St. Albans, Waltham (now known as Waltham Cross), Westcheap (now Cheapside, in the City of London), and Charing (now Charing Cross, in central London). The only crosses still standing are those at Geddington, Hardingstone, and Waltham, though small sections of those from the priory, Stamford, Westcheap, and Charing are preserved in museums. The original site of the Charing cross, on the south side of Trafalgar Square, is now occupied by a statue of King **Charles I**. A modern replacement was erected in front of Charing Cross railroad station in 1865.

**ELEANOR OF AQUITAINE (c1122–1204).** Eleanor, consort of King Louis VII of **France** and then (for nearly 35 years) of King **Henry II** of England, was one of the most powerful women in Europe during the late 12th century. The daughter of William, duke of **Aquitaine**, and his wife, Aenor de Châtellerault, she inherited Aquitaine from her father in 1137 and, only months later, was married to Louis. Within days of the wedding, Louis's father, Louis VI, had died, and the 15-year-old Eleanor was queen, exercising considerable influence over a husband who seemed to idolize her. The young man's initial ardor cooled, however, amidst rumors (never proven) that his wife was conducting an affair with her uncle, Raymond of Antioch, and the relationship deteriorated further while the two were participating in the second crusade to the Holy Land in 1145–49. Eventually, in 1152 and after initial doubts, Pope Eugenius III agreed to annul the marriage on grounds of consanguinity (Louis and Eleanor were third cousins, once removed).

Single and wealthy, the former queen was at some risk because it was not unusual at the time for powerful men to kidnap women whom they felt would make desirable brides (*see, for example,* MARIE, COUNTESS OF

BOULOGNE). In order to avoid this fate, she allegedly took the bull by the horns and asked Henry (then only a claimant to the English throne) to marry her even though he was her junior by 11 years and was reputed to be a philanderer (he eventually fathered at least nine illegitimate children). Henry agreed, attracted as much by the estates of Aquitaine as by Eleanor's undoubted charms, and the wedding ceremony was held in Poitiers, capital of Poitou, on 18 May 1152.

Over the next 13 years, the couple had five sons and three daughters, but by the time John, the youngest and later King **John**, was born in 1166, the marriage was under strain, partly because of Henry's dalliances with other women. They separated the following year, with Eleanor moving her court to Poitiers, where she became renowned for her patronage of the arts. However, when three of her sons rebelled against their father in 1173, she supported the uprising, a decision that proved disastrous because she was taken captive by Henry and kept in custody for the next 16 years, moved from place to place at her husband's behest until his death in 1189. Later, while Richard (her son and, as **Richard I**, her husband's successor as king) was on crusade, she acted as his **regent**, ruling England on his behalf and raising taxes to pay the ransom required following his capture by Leopold V of Austria.

Eleanor outlived Richard, seeing his brother, John, take the throne in 1199, but she died—either at **Fontevrault Abbey**, in **Anjou**, or in Poitiers—on 1 April 1204 and was buried in the abbey beside her husband. The marriage to Henry had been tempestuous, but even so, she claimed that it had been much happier than the one to Louis. *See also* GEOFFREY, DUKE OF BRITTANY; HENRY, THE YOUNG KING; JOAN, QUEEN OF SICILY; ELEANOR (OR LEONORA), QUEEN OF CASTILE; MATILDA, DUCHESS OF SAXONY AND OF BAVARIA; WILLIAM, COUNT OF POITIERS; WOODSTOCK PALACE.

**ELEANOR OF CASTILE (c1241–1290).** The first consort of King **Edward I**, Eleanor was the daughter of Ferdinand III, king of Castile, and Jeanne, countess of Ponthieu, his second wife. The marriage, which took place in the Abbey of Las Huelgas in Burgos, Spain, on 1 November 1254, was one element of a political power game involving the Castilians and King **Henry III**, Edward's father. Alfonso, Eleanor's half-brother by her father's first marriage to Elisabeth of Hohenstaufen, had resurrected long-held but legally dubious claims to Gascony, the last significant territory held by the English crown in **France**. Henry pondered military action but eventually reached a peaceful settlement, with Alfonso renouncing all interest in the area and Henry agreeing that Edward, his eldest son, would marry Eleanor. The English nobles were less than happy with the arrangement, however, fearing that the young bride's relatives would descend on the royal court in **London** and never leave, much as **Eleanor of Provence**'s family had done when she married Henry 18 years earlier.

Despite its inauspicious start, the union proved strong. After Edward succeeded to the throne in 1272, he allowed his queen very little influence over political decision making, but she encouraged the development of the literary arts and helped to found several priories for Dominican monks. Moreover, although she annoyed many of the king's subjects by an aggressive policy of land acquisition that often involved foreclosure on estates pledged for debts, she pleased her husband because she built a considerable portfolio that meant she did not have to draw on the national treasury for financial support.

Eleanor also accompanied her husband on many of his military campaigns, traveling with him to the Holy Land in 1270–71 and to Wales in 1284, giving birth to Edward (their fourth son and later **Edward II**) amidst the construction work at Caernarfon Castle. She died at Harby, near Lincoln, on 28 November 1290 and was carried to **Westminster Abbey**, in London, for the funeral service. At each overnight stop along the route, a distraught Edward erected a cross to mark the place where she lay (*see* ELEANOR CROSSES). After the queen's death, Edward's behavior became increasingly arbitrary and erratic, frustrating courtiers, who attributed it to his grief, although exasperation at the younger Edward's inability to behave like an heir to the throne undoubtedly added to the monarch's concerns. It is unclear how many children the couple had, though most sources list 11 to 13 daughters and four or five sons. Only six survived beyond their teenage years. *See also* ALFONSO, EARL OF CHESTER; ELEANOR, COUNTESS OF BAR; ELIZABETH, COUNTESS OF HEREFORD; JOAN OF ACRE; MARGARET, DUCHESS OF BRABANT; PLANTAGENET, ALICE; PLANTAGENET, BEATRICE; PLANTAGENET, BERENGARIA; PLANTAGENET, BLANCHE (1290); PLANTAGENET, HENRY (1267–1274); PLANTAGENET, ISABELLA; PLANTAGENET, JOAN (1265); PLANTAGENET, JOHN (1266–1271); PLANTAGENET, JULIANA; PLANTAGENET, MARY.

**ELEANOR OF PROVENCE (c1223–1291).** For more than 30 years, Eleanor staunchly supported her husband, King **Henry III**, but the monarch's willingness to indulge the queen's relatives contributed greatly to the conflict between sovereign and barons that dominated the reign (*see* PROVISIONS OF OXFORD; PROVISIONS OF WESTMINSTER; SECOND BARONS' WAR).

The second of four daughters in the family of Raymond Berengar, count of Provence, and Beatrice of Savoy, Eleanor was probably born in 1223. The wedding, held in Canterbury Cathedral on 14 January 1236, was attended by many of the bride's cousins and other family members, several of whom remained at the royal court afterward and were given posts of considerable influence, much to the annoyance of the English nobles, who coveted the positions for themselves. Moreover, once they were established in London, the Provençals added to the tensions by encouraging Henry's ambitions to recover French lands lost by his father, King **John**, and supporting his expensive—and ultimately unsuccessful—invasion plans.

Eleanor also made herself very unpopular by promoting a project to win the crown of Sicily for **Edmund of Woodstock, earl of Lancaster**, her second son, because the barons believed that the costly scheme would involve them in a war that would bring them no benefit. On the other hand, the queen worked hard to bring troops from **France** to augment the royalist army in 1264 while it battled with rebel forces led by Simon de Montfort (though her efforts were thwarted by storms that prevented her fleet from leaving their base at Sluys in Flanders).

The couple probably had five children, though some sources list as many as nine. The first—Edward (later King **Edward I**)—was born on 17 June 1239, with the others following by 1253 (or possibly 1256). After Henry's death in 1272, Eleanor helped to raise her grandchildren but then retired to the nunnery at Amesbury Abbey, in Wiltshire, where she died on c25 June 1291. *See also* BEATRICE, DUCHESS OF BURGUNDY; MARGARET, QUEEN OF SCOTS; PLANTAGENET, HENRY (c1257); PLANTAGENET, JOHN (c1250–c1256); PLANTAGENET, KATHERINE; PLANTAGENET, RICHARD; PLANTAGENET, WILLIAM (c1251–c1256).

**ELEANOR (OR LEONORA), QUEEN OF CASTILE (1162–1214).** Eleanor, born in Domfront Castle, Normandy, on 13 October 1162, was the sixth child of **Henry II** and **Eleanor of Aquitaine**. In September 1176, she was married to Alfonso VIII of Castile at Burgos Cathedral; the prenuptial negotiations resulted in her politically astute father gaining control of Gascony, which stretched his empire to the Pyrenees, providing a buffer between the mountains and the vast estates of **Aquitaine**.

Alfonso had succeeded to the throne at the age of three and spent much of his adult life quelling strife within his realm, negotiating boundaries, and resisting invasion by Muslim groups as well as by neighboring monarchs. Leonora was an able supporter and advisor—so much so that Alfonso specified in his will that she should rule alongside the son that succeeded him. As a result of her mother's influence, she also promoted the arts at the Castilian court.

The marriage was a happy one, so when Alfonso passed away on 5 October 1214, Eleanor (who called herself "Leonora" after her marriage) was broken-hearted and survived her husband by less than a month, dying on 31 October.

She had borne 12 children between 1180 and 1204; six of the offspring pre-deceased her, but Henry, the youngest son, succeeded his father on the throne of Castile, and rulers of other kingdoms married four of the daughters, with Blanche (born on 4 March 1188) inheriting her mother's diplomatic skills and becoming a doughty consort for the powerful King Louis VIII of **France**.

**ELGIVA (c943–959).** Late 18th- and early 19th-century artists and writers were fascinated by the story of Elgiva and King **Eadwig**, commemorating it with paintings by Joanne Boyce, Edwin F. Holt, Emanuel Gottlieb Leutze, and others, as well as by an admittedly disastrous performance of a play by Fanny Burney in 1796. Eadwig succeeded his uncle **Eadred** to the throne of England in 955. However, on the day of his **coronation** the following year, the king slipped away from meetings with his courtiers and was found by Dunstan, the powerful abbot of Glastonbury, closeted in a room with the youthful Elgiva and her mother, Aelfgifu, who some writers have claimed was his mistress. Dunstan thought women were instruments of the devil, so he may have seen what he wanted to see, but according to William of Malmesbury, writing in the early 12th century, "Regardless of royal indigna-tion, [he] dragged the lascivious boy from the chamber."

Although Eadwig married Elgiva shortly afterward, the incident clearly soured relations, and Dunstan was forced to flee to Flanders. However, Ead-wig was not a popular leader and counted senior churchmen among his prin-cipal opponents, one of whom—Odo, archbishop of Canterbury—annulled the marriage on the grounds of consanguinity (the couple were third cousins once removed, both descended from **Aethelwulf**, king of **Wessex**). The ra-tionale was tenuous but, given the climate of the times, a sufficient excuse for action. Elgiva was taken from her husband, branded on the face with hot irons, and exiled to Ireland. Either by escaping her captors or with the help of Irish sympathizers, she returned to England in September 959, but her entou-rage was intercepted near Gloucester, and she was mutilated by swordsmen, allegedly employed by Dunstan and Odo. She died of her wounds and was buried at **Winchester**, still in her teens. Eadwig followed her to the grave shortly afterward, little loved by his people.

**ELIZABETH I (1533–1603).** Queen of England from 1558 to 1603, Eliza-beth was born at the **Palace of Placentia** on 7 September 1533, the only child of **Henry VIII** and his second wife, **Anne Boleyn**. When she was just two years old, her mother was found guilty of very dubious charges of adultery and was **beheaded**.

The **Succession to the Crown: Marriage Act**, passed by parliament in 1536, made Elizabeth illegitimate and thus unable to succeed to the throne, giving precedence to Henry's children by **Jane Seymour**, his third wife. Her legitimacy was never formally reestablished, but the provisions of the **Succession to the Crown Act of 1543** placed her back in the line of succession after her half-brother, Edward (later **Edward VI**), and her half-sister, Mary (later **Mary I**). As a child, she received the usual education for the daughter of a monarch, becoming an accomplished linguist (she spoke French, Italian, and Spanish) and showing considerable musical ability. She seems also to have been happy in the company of Edward and Mary, though she saw little of her father, who died when she was 13. At times, however, her life was in danger because of her Protestant upbringing, as when she was imprisoned in the **Tower of London** in 1554, suspected of involvement in **Wyatt's Rebellion** against Mary, who was a staunch Roman Catholic.

When Mary died on 17 November 1558, Elizabeth became queen, to the acclaim of a people disheartened by setbacks in the war with **France** and the persecution of individuals who espoused Protestantism at a time when Roman Catholicism was being enforced rigorously. Although her personal beliefs are unknown, she tackled the religious differences within her realm immediately, confirming the **Church of England**'s development on Protestant lines in 1559 (albeit with Catholic overtones, as in the vestments worn by priests). In 1570, Pope Pius V excommunicated her and ruled that her subjects were absolved of all allegiance to her. That papal bull effectively made it impossible for any loyal English man or woman to be a Roman Catholic and led many adherents of the Church of Rome to claim that Elizabeth's Catholic cousin, **Mary, queen of Scots**, was their country's true sovereign. Elizabeth held Mary captive for nearly 20 years from 1568, reluctant to take any action because of the implications of executing the crowned monarch of a neighboring state. Nevertheless, Mary's presence in England provoked a series of assassination attempts, and Elizabeth reluctantly agreed to have her beheaded in 1587.

That event, coupled with fines and imprisonment for those who sought to put a Catholic monarch on the throne, did much to contain revolt by the supporters of Rome. Elizabeth, however, was no more enamored of the Protestant extremists, clashing with Puritan members of parliament who attacked the principle of episcopacy and called for the reorganization of the Church of England on Presbyterian lines. Unlike her predecessor, though, she did not persecute her opponents, and by the last decade of her reign, many Roman Catholics were willing to accept her secular authority if a way of preserving their spiritual allegiance to the pope could be found.

Elizabeth's control of foreign policy was just as tight as that over ecclesiastical matters, although it was exerted with some caution. Within a few months of her accession to the throne, she brought the war with France to an end. Between 1559 and 1562, she took action against Scotland to protect England's northern border, but throughout her life she detested military conflict, preferring to achieve her aims by diplomatic means. The peace maintained by these tactics allowed England to build its naval strength and ultimately to beat off the invasion threatened by the Spanish Armada in 1588. Moreover, the lengthy peace during the early part of her reign also allowed her to gain control of an economy that was on the brink of disaster.

Commerce was promoted by regulations that directed surplus labor from the cloth-making industry into farming, and a tax on property owners was introduced so that the unemployed could receive support. Also, the sovereign encouraged commerce with other nations and backed Sir Walter Raleigh's journeys to the Americas. (The colony of Virginia was named after Elizabeth, the virgin queen). Much of her success was a result of her skill in appointing advisors on the basis of ability rather than noble birth. Her only serious mistake was Robert Devereux, earl of Essex, who was a confidant for 13 years but ultimately plotted against her and was executed in 1601.

The peace and prosperity that the country experienced over much of the second half of the 16th century was reflected in a cultural renaissance that became known as the Elizabethan era—Francis Bacon was publishing his essays, William Shakespeare was writing plays (as were Ben Jonson and Christopher Marlowe), and Edmund Spenser composed *The Faerie Queen*, a narrative poem dedicated to Elizabeth and portraying her as the eternally youthful Gloriana. In the monarch's last years, however, war with Spain led to problems. Poor trading prospects and a series of bad harvests caused much poverty as prices rose and landowners protested against high taxes. In addition, Elizabeth's decision not to marry (despite offers from numerous suitors and much pressure from her advisors) caused considerable heart searching as she aged. The two principal candidates for the crown on her death were Edward Seymour, lord Beauchamp (the great-great grandson of **Mary Tudor, queen of France**, and the successor under the terms of Henry VIII's will), and **James VI** of Scotland (the son of Mary, queen of Scots, and the successor by hereditary descent). Robert Cecil, the leader of Elizabeth's government, coached James on how to ingratiate himself with the sovereign, and eventually she accepted him as her heir, although never through an explicit statement.

When the queen died at **Sheen Palace** on 24 March 1603 (some medical authorities suggest blood poisoning or cancer of the blood), she brought to an end the line of five monarchs from the **House of Tudor**, and James united England and Scotland under a single crown for the first time. Elizabeth's remains were interred in **Westminster Abbey**. *See also* HAMPTON COURT PALACE; HATFIELD PALACE; SOMERSET HOUSE; SUPREMACY, ACT OF (1559); UNION OF THE CROWNS; WOODSTOCK PALACE.

**ELIZABETH II (1926– )**. Queen Elizabeth was born at 17 Bruton Street, **London**—her maternal grandparents' city home—on 21 April 1926, the elder daughter of the duke and duchess of York (later King **George VI** and Queen **Elizabeth, the queen mother**). Educated by Marion Crawford (her governess) and by private tutors, she spent most of her teenage years at **Balmoral Castle** (in Scotland) and at **Windsor Castle** (near Reading) while her parents endured the rigors of World War II life in the capital. In **Westminster Abbey** on 20 November 1947, she married Lieutenant Philip Mountbatten (now **Prince Philip, duke of Edinburgh**), whom she had first met some eight years earlier while he was in training at the Royal Naval College Dartmouth. **Charles, prince of Wales**, their first child, was born on 14 November 1948. **Anne, princess royal**, followed on 15 August 1950; **Prince Andrew, duke of York**, on 19 February 1960; and **Prince Edward, earl of Wessex**, on 10 March 1964.

In 1952, Elizabeth became queen on her father's death. She was crowned on 2 June 1953 and almost immediately embarked on a series of overseas tours, visiting Australia, Ceylon, New Zealand, the West Indies, and Uganda on lengthy journeys that indicated she intended to take her duties to the **commonwealth realms**, of which she was also head of state, as seriously as she took her duties to the United Kingdom. The same concern led to an outburst of anger in 1982, when the United States invaded Grenada (one of those realms) without notifying her of its intentions.

Formally, the British monarch is expected to remain aloof from party politics, but as sovereign, Queen Elizabeth has twice had to choose a successor when a prime minister resigned. The first occasion was in 1957, when Anthony Eden gave up office in the wake of the Suez crisis. After seeking the views of leading political figures, she selected Harold Macmillan rather than Rab Butler, who had deputized when Eden was ill. When Macmillan gave up the job for health reasons in 1963, she chose Alec Douglas-Home. More recently, she apparently was at odds with Margaret Thatcher; on 20 July 1986, the *Sunday Times*, a respected broadsheet newspaper, reported that the queen believed that her prime minister's policies were "uncaring, confrontational and socially divisive." These claims were denied by spokesmen for the **royal family**, but nevertheless they were widely considered to be accurate.

Informally, the queen exercises considerable influence on political decision making. She has received weekly reports from a succession of prime ministers over the past half century and has developed very cordial friendships with a galaxy of world leaders, so she is extremely well informed and has no qualms about expressing her views in private conversations with her political advisors. At times, she will go further when she feels that her intervention is advantageous, as in 1993 when she invited Mary Robinson, the president of the Republic of Ireland, to tea at **Buckingham Palace**; the tête-à-tête was the first official meeting between the heads of state of the two countries.

In the United Kingdom, opinion polls suggest that support for the concept of monarchy has declined in recent decades, but the queen herself has remained popular apart from a period in late 1997, when she was perceived as cold and unfeeling as she failed to make any public statement of grief in the immediate aftermath of the death of her former daughter-in-law, **Diana, princess of Wales**. In 2002, the golden jubilee of her reign was celebrated with parties, concerts, and parades throughout the country, and she undertook a strenuous program of engagements despite her age. Rumors that she may abdicate in favor of **Prince** Charles surface periodically but appear to have no foundation. *See also* CLARENCE HOUSE; FRANCE; GATCOMBE PARK; MICHAEL OF KENT, PRINCESS; ROYAL CYPHER; ROYAL STANDARD; TROOPING THE COLOUR CEREMONY.

**ELIZABETH, COUNTESS OF HEREFORD (1282–1316).** One of the younger daughters of **Edward I** and **Eleanor of Castile**, Elizabeth was born on 7 August 1282 at Rhuddlan Castle in Wales (and, for that reason, is sometimes known as Elizabeth of Rhuddlan). In January 1297, she was married to the 13-year-old John, count of Holland, who had been raised at her father's court but who succumbed to dysentery on 10 November 1299, leaving her childless. On 14 November 1302, she took Humphrey de Bohun, earl of Hereford and one of the most powerful nobles in England, as a second husband; they had 10 or 11 children over the next 14 years. She died in childbirth on 5 May 1316. Humphrey, who was much affected by her passing, was killed while leading a rebel army against royalist forces at Boroughbridge on 16 March 1322.

**ELIZABETH DE BURGH (?–1327).** Consort of King **Robert I** (also known as Robert the Bruce), Elizabeth was one of 10 children in the family of Richard de Burgh, earl of Ulster, and his wife, Margaret. Neither the date nor the place of her birth is recorded, but it was probably in northern Ireland at some time between 1280 and 1289. The Bruce family had extensive estates in Ireland, so there is a possibility that the couple first met there. However, Richard was a strong supporter of **Edward I** of England and a regular visitor to **London** with his family, so the initial encounter may well have occurred at the royal court while Robert, who had pledged allegiance to Edward, was also in the city. They married in 1302 at a ceremony held, according to some writers, at Writtle, the Bruce family home near Chelmsford in southeast England.

Bruce claimed the Scottish throne in 1306 (apparently he behaved so immaturely at his **coronation** that Elizabeth chided him for merely "playing at kings and queens") and, by doing so, thoroughly upset Edward, who asserted suzerainty over the country. Elizabeth was forced to flee but was captured by William, earl of Ross and no friend of her husband, and then held prisoner at various English locations (including **Windsor Castle**) for eight years before being released following negotiations over an exchange of captives after Robert defeated Edward's army at the **Battle of Bannockburn** in 1314. The couple's enforced separation meant that there were no male children to succeed the king until 1323, when (18 years after her wedding) Elizabeth produced a son, who was eventually to succeed his father as **David II**. After she died at Cullen Castle, a **royal residence** near Elgin, on 26 October 1327, having given birth to another male child (**John Bruce**) and two daughters (**Margaret Bruce, countess of Sutherland**, and **Matilda Bruce**), she was buried in the choir at **Dunfermline Abbey**, where, less than two years later, her husband's body was also interred after his heart had been removed and preserved.

**ELIZABETH OF BOHEMIA (1596–1662).** Elizabeth (or Elisabeth), daughter of King **James VI of Scotland and I of England** and **Anne of Denmark**, is an ancestress of all British monarchs from **George I**, providing, through her marriage, an important genealogical link between the royal dynasties of the **House of Stuart** and the **House of Hanover**. She was born at **Falkland Palace** on 19 August 1596 and was named after Queen **Elizabeth I**, whom James was anxious to succeed on the English throne. The **union of the crowns** in 1603 greatly enhanced Elizabeth's marital prospects, so she was pursued by several eligible European bachelors, including King Philip III of Spain, whose suit her mother favored, but James insisted on a match with Frederick V, the elector palatine, because he wanted to strengthen alliances with the Protestant families who ruled Germany. The wedding was held on 14 February 1613, and the first of the couple's 13 children was born early the next year.

In 1619, Frederick accepted an invitation to become king of Bohemia, anticipating that his father-in-law would help him to subdue Roman Catholic opposition to his rule. That assumption proved unfounded because, when a Catholic coalition mounted an attack against him within months of his **coronation**, James refused to intervene, despite his daughter's pleadings and pressure from his counselors. Elizabeth, forced to take refuge in Holland with her husband and family, spent the rest of her life in straitened financial circumstances, prevented from returning to England by civil war and rejected by her second son, Charles Louis, who in 1648 was restored to the palatinate (albeit in a less powerful position than that held by his father, who died in 1632). In 1661, however, she was able to travel to **London**, where she died on 13 February the following year. She was buried in **Westminster Abbey**.

Elizabeth is sometimes nicknamed "the winter queen" because her husband's reign in Bohemia lasted for a single winter. She is also known as "the queen of hearts"; according to some writers, she earned the soubriquet because, as a young woman, she had many suitors, but other scholars suggest that the descriptor reflects her popularity with her subjects. In 1701, the English parliament, through the **Act of Settlement**, declared Elizabeth's youngest daughter, **Sophia, electress of Hanover**, heiress presumptive to Queen **Anne**, her first cousin once removed. Sophia died before she could succeed to the throne, but the crown eventually went to her son, who ruled as King **George I**. *See also* ERNEST AUGUSTUS, ELECTOR OF HANOVER.

**ELIZABETH OF CLARENCE, PRINCESS (1820–1821). Princess** Elizabeth, born at **St. James's Palace** on 10 December 1820, was the second child of King **William IV** (who was duke of Clarence at the time of her birth) and **Adelaide of Saxe-Meiningen**. Her elder sister, **Princess Charlotte of Clarence**, had been born in Hanover the previous year but had lived for only a few hours, so the new baby was third in line to the throne after her uncle—George, **prince of Wales** (later King **George IV**), whose only child (**Princess Charlotte Augusta**) had died in 1817—and her father. Initially, she seemed healthy, but on 4 March 1821 she developed convulsions and died at the palace, doctors ascribing her sudden passing to bowel problems. Elizabeth was buried at **St. George's Chapel** in **Windsor Castle**, and her parents remained childless (though twin boys were stillborn in 1822), so William was eventually succeeded on the throne by his niece, Queen **Victoria**.

**ELIZABETH OF YORK (1466–1503).** Elizabeth (who is also known as Elizabeth Plantagenet) has the unique distinction of having been daughter, mother, niece, sister, and wife to kings of England. She was born at the **Palace of Westminster** on 11 February 1466, the first of 10 children in the family of King **Edward IV** and **Elizabeth Woodville**. After her father's death in 1483, her paternal uncle had her and her siblings declared illegitimate so that he could claim the throne for himself, as **Richard III**. That move was not universally popular, however, particularly after Edward's sons, **Edward V** (who had followed his father to the throne) and **Richard, duke of York (1473–1483?)**, vanished while under Richard's care in the **Tower of London**. As a result, the **queen dowager** was able to negotiate a pact with **Margaret Beaufort**, mother of Henry Tudor, that—in addition to combining the two women's powerful supporters in one military unit—would result in the marriage of their children if Henry mounted a successful attempt to oust the monarch. Because Elizabeth was a scion of the **House of York** and Henry of the **House of Lancaster**, the union would also have the political advantage of ending the **Wars of the Roses** that had divided the two dynasties for more than 30 years.

The ploy worked. On 22 August 1485, Richard was killed in battle at **Bosworth Field**, on 30 October his victor was crowned king as **Henry VII**, and on 18 January 1486 the couple wed at **Westminster Abbey**. Henry never allowed his consort to interfere in political matters, but the relationship was close nonetheless, and together they had eight children between 1486 and 1503. She died at the Tower of **London** on 11 February 1503—her 37th birthday—as a result of an infection contracted while giving birth to **Katherine Tudor**, her fourth daughter, and was buried in Westminster Abbey.

Henry survived for a further 6 years but never remarried. One son succeeded him as King **Henry VIII**, and a daughter, **Margaret Tudor**, married **James IV** of Scotland—a match that led to the **union of the English and Scottish crowns** in 1603. **Mary Tudor, queen of France**, Margaret's younger sister, briefly joined the French royal family as consort of Louis XII. Some writers believe that Elizabeth of York, who had a reputation for caring and for generosity, was the inspiration for the design of the queen of hearts in packs of playing cards. *See also* ARTHUR, PRINCE OF WALES; TUDOR, EDMUND, DUKE OF SOMERSET; TUDOR, EDWARD; TUDOR, ELIZABETH.

**ELIZABETH, PRINCESS, LANDGRAVINE OF HESSE-HOMBURG (1777–1840).** Elizabeth was the third of six daughters (and the seventh of 15 children) in the family of King **George III** and **Charlotte of Mecklenburg-Strelitz**. She was born at **Buckingham Palace** on 22 May 1770 and was raised in a fairly strict environment that became increasingly repressive after her father's first bout of mental illness in 1788–89. George, very attached to his daughters, was as unwilling as his wife to see them leave home, so Charlotte refused to discuss their marriage prospects with him in case the discussions might lead to another period of insanity. Elizabeth's potential suitors were simply rejected, as in 1808 when Louis-Philippe, duke of Orléans and later king of **France**, was sent packing (though, even in more propitious circumstances, his Roman Catholicism would undoubtedly have been a problem for the staunchly Protestant British monarchy).

In 1812, the **princess** won a degree of freedom after she and her unmarried sisters wrote to the queen, outlining their grievances, and George, their older brother (who became King **George IV**), interceded on their behalf. She bought a property near **Windsor Castle**, escaping from the confines of "the Nunnery," as the female accommodation at **St. James's Palace** had become known, and in 1814 met Prince (and later Landgrave) Frederick of Hesse-Homburg at a royal ball. The prince proposed, and Charlotte, after much procrastination, agreed to a wedding in St. James's on 7 April 1818. The union was very much a matter of convenience for both bride and groom— Elizabeth won independence from parental control; Frederick gained a wife who, though too old to have children, brought funds sufficient to refurbish his palace at Homburg; and the match proved happy. Frederick lived until 1829, after which Elizabeth enjoyed herself at European spas until she passed away in Frankfurt on 10 January 1840. She was buried at Homburg.

**ELIZABETH, THE QUEEN MOTHER (1900–2002).** Elizabeth, consort of King **George VI**, is credited with many of the initiatives that brought the **royal family** closer to the people of the United Kingdom. Born at St. Paul's Waldenbury in Hertfordshire on 4 August 1900, she was ninth of the 10 children of Claude Bowes-Lyon (Earl of Strathmore and Kinghorne) and his wife, Nina Cecilia. She spent much of her childhood at Glamis Castle, the family home in Scotland, and worked with nurses to care for wounded servicemen when the building was used as a convalescent home for repatriated troops during World War I.

Elizabeth met her future husband (then **Prince** Albert) in 1920 and married him in **Westminster Abbey** on 26 April 1923 after he proposed for the third time. Their first child, **Princess** Elizabeth (later Queen **Elizabeth II**), was born on 21 April 1926, and their second, **Princess Margaret, countess of Snowdon**, on 21 August 1930. The couple attended the public engagements and undertook the foreign tours that were required of members of the royal family, but there was no expectation that they would occupy **Buckingham Palace**, because the prince's older brother, Edward, was heir to the throne. However, when King **George V** died in 1936, Edward reigned for only 11 months, as King **Edward VIII**, before announcing his intention to abdicate because he wanted to marry Wallis Simpson, an American divorcee (*see* WALLIS, DUCHESS OF WINDSOR). The new King George VI was devastated. A shy, retiring man who preferred the quiet of family life to the glare of the spotlight, he approached monarchical responsibilities with dread, and, according to some writers, Elizabeth never forgave either Edward or his new wife. Biographers claim that it was she who was responsible for the decision not to grant Mrs. Simpson the title "**her royal highness**," and even at Edward's funeral, in 1972, the two women did not talk to each other.

During the 1930s, Queen Elizabeth was an ardent supporter of Prime Minister Neville Chamberlain's efforts to appease Adolf Hitler, but after World War II broke out, she and the king spent most of their days in **London** visiting families who had lost their homes to German bombs and working to keep morale high (so much so that Hitler claimed that she was the woman he most feared in the whole of Europe). Then, when the conflict was over, she resumed her schedule of engagements, performing many of them on her own during the king's illness in 1951 and 1952. After George's death on 6 February 1952, she spent a lengthy period in mourning, much of it in Scotland at the **Castle of Mey**, her favorite home, but she did attend her daughter's **coronation** in 1953 and then visited Rhodesia, Canada, and the United States.

As the **queen mother** aged, the number of commitments was reduced, but she appeared in public regularly until shortly before her death. Newspapers satirized her love of gin and tonic, her fondness for horse racing, and her addiction to large hats with lots of netting, but the satire did little to dent her public image. She was also known to have a wicked sense of humor. Most of her male courtiers were gay. On one occasion, she was ascending a staircase to attend a gala occasion, with her footmen lining the route and the avowedly homosexual playwright Noel Coward at her side. Noting the playwright's admiring glances at the attendants, she told him, "I wouldn't if I were you, Noel. They count them before they put them out."

The queen mother died at the **Royal Lodge** near **Windsor Castle** in the early hours of 30 March 2002, only days after attending the funeral of Princess Margaret and four months short of her 102nd birthday. She was laid to rest in **St. George's Chapel**, close to her husband. *See also* BALMORAL CASTLE; CHARLES, PRINCE OF WALES; CLARENCE HOUSE; CROWN JEWELS OF THE UNITED KINGDOM; QUEEN DOWAGER.

**ELTHAM PALACE.** Eltham, built south of the River Thames and close to the road that led from **London** to the ports on the English Channel, was a popular **royal residence** from the 14th to the 16th century and is one of few medieval palaces that have not been demolished. Originally a manor house, it was acquired in 1305 by King **Edward II**, who regularly spent Christmas there hunting deer. **Edward VI** added the great hall with its large hammerbeam roof in the 1470s, and **Henry VIII** spent much of his childhood at the property. However, the court's interest in Eltham declined as the expanding **Palace of Placentia** at Greenwich became increasingly popular, and during the civil wars of the 1640s it fell into disrepair. From the mid-17th century, the land was farmed (with the great hall used as a barn), but in 1933 Sir Stephen and Lady Virginia Courtauld—whose family had made its fortune from the textile industry—leased the estate and built a large house, in art deco style, that incorporated much of the earlier structure. After they left in 1944, the Royal Army Educational Corps took up residence, but since 1995, English Heritage (a government body responsible for protecting historic sites) has managed the property, which is open to visitors and has become a popular location for film and television productions.

**EMMA OF NORMANDY (c985–1052).** Emma, the wife of **Aethelred the Unready** and later of **Canute**, is the only woman to have been **queen consort** to two English monarchs. The daughter of Richard, count of Rouen, and Gunnora, his Danish-born second wife, she wed for political reasons on both occasions. Normandy had strong Scandinavian connections and was a base for the Viking fleets that regularly invaded England. For Aethelred, the union with Emma in 1002 was intended as a means of reducing the threat. It produced two sons—Edward (born c1004 and now usually known as **Edward the Confessor**) and **Aelfred Aetheling** (born sometime after Edward and before 1012)—but did not achieve the ends that Aethelred sought, because in 1013 the family was forced to flee to Emma's homeland to escape the ravages of the Danes, led by Canute.

Emma returned to England with her husband when he reclaimed his throne in 1014, but it is unclear whether she remained in the country or returned to Normandy when he died two years later. Some writers believe that she and her boys went back to her father but that Canute persuaded her to marry him, partly in order to provide a semblance of continuity with Aethelred's regime, and partly in an effort to prevent Duke Richard from attempting to topple him and place one of Emma's sons on the throne. Other scholars suggest, however, that she remained in England and that Canute—knowing that the Normans were unlikely to invade a country where one of their own people was queen—wooed her with a promise that any son of their own would be guaranteed the kingship.

Emma may have acquiesced to the wedding, held on 2 July 1017, because it provided security and an opportunity to exert influence over the course of political affairs, but she may also have decided that a place in the court of the strong monarch would provide protection for her sons, both of whom could be murdered if Canute felt that they were Anglo-Saxon threats to Danish rule. In the end, however, Canute's hopes for the succession were confounded because when he died in 1035, Harthacanute (his only son by Emma) was in Denmark, preparing to resist an invasion by Norway and Sweden, so the **witan** (the council of advisors to the monarch) named Harold (later King **Harold I**), a child by his first, "handfast," marriage to **Aelfgifu of Northampton**, as co-**regent** with his stepmother.

Harold and Emma were constantly at odds—so much so that Harold eventually hounded his stepmother out of the kingdom—and even after Harthacanute regained control in 1040, a few months after Harold's death, Emma's problems were not over. Because he was childless, Harthacanute named Edward (Emma's older son and his half-brother) as his preferred successor, but, on becoming king in 1043, Edward deprived his mother of all her property, claiming that she had neglected him while he was a child (and there is certainly some evidence that she may have preferred the claim of Magnus of Norway to the English crown over that of her own son). Emma eventually regained her position at court but died in **Winchester** on 7 March 1052, leaving the *Encomium Emmae Reginae*, a self-serving account of her life that makes no reference whatsoever to Aethelred. Edward passed away in 1066 leaving no legitimate heirs, so the **succession to the throne** was contested. The witan appointed Harold Godwinson king (as **Harold II**), but William, duke of Normandy (later **William I of England**), led a successful invasion in the late summer, justifying this action in part on the grounds that, as Emma's grandnephew, he was entitled to the throne. *See also* GODGIFU; GUNHILDA OF DENMARK.

**EOCHAID (?–?).** Eochaid is a shadowy figure who, some scholars suggest, was king of the Picts jointly with **Giric** for 11 years after **Áed**'s death in 878. However, other writers believe that Giric ruled alone or as a **regent** for Eochaid, who, according to some sources, was the grandson of **Kenneth MacAlpin** by a daughter whose name is not known. After **Donald II** became king in 889, Eochaid vanished from the historical record, with one source suggesting that he and Giric were banished from the kingdom.

**EOPPA (c706–?).** Eoppa was the son of **Ingild** and nephew of Ine, king of **Wessex** from 688 to 726. Details of his life are scant, but it is known that he had a son, **Eafa**, who was born c730 and, according to some genealogies, continued the direct line of succession from **Cerdic**, the founder of Wessex, to the present British **royal family**.

**ERMENGARDE DE BEAUMONT (c1170–1233/34).** On 5 September 1186, **William I of Scotland** took Ermengarde as his **queen consort**. It was not an arrangement chosen by either party. In 1174, William had been captured by King **Henry II** of England, taken to Falaise (in Normandy), and forced to sign an agreement accepting the English monarch as his feudal overlord. Until his death 15 years later, Henry humiliated his Scottish counterpart at every opportunity, including choosing his bride. William had asked to marry Matilda, Henry's eldest daughter (*see* MATILDA, DUCHESS OF SAXONY AND OF BAVARIA), but was refused and instead was given Ermengarde, daughter of a minor noble, Richard, viscount of Beaumont-sur-Sarthe, and, possibly, Constance FitzRoy, one of **Henry I**'s numerous illegitimate offspring. Moreover, in order to emphasize his superiority, Henry ensured that the wedding ceremony was held in England, at **Woodstock Palace**, and—in recognition of the occasion—he returned **Edinburgh** Castle (one of the Scots' principal fortresses, which the English had occupied) to William on condition that he give it to his new wife.

In spite of this inauspicious start to the union, there is some evidence that Ermengarde played an important role in Scottish affairs. For example, records from **Dunfermline Abbey** show that she acted in a formal judicial capacity, hearing a dispute over ecclesiastical issues, and one chronicler records that when her husband met King **John** of England in 1212, she "acted as a mediator, an extraordinary woman, gifted with a charming and witty eloquence." The couple had four children, including a son who succeeded his father as King **Alexander II** in 1214. Ermengarde died on 12 February 1233 and was buried at Balmerino Abbey, a Cistercian monastery that she had founded on the south bank of the River Tay in Fife. *See also* ISABELLA, COUNTESS OF NORFOLK; MARGARET, COUNTESS OF KENT; MARJORIE, COUNTESS OF PEMBROKE.

**ERNEST AUGUSTUS, ELECTOR OF HANOVER (1629–1698).** Ernest Augustus, father of King **George I** (the first British monarch from the **House of Hanover**), was born at Herzberg am Hartz Castle in Lower Saxony on 20 November 1629, one of seven children in the family of George, duke of Brunswick-Lüneburg, and his wife, Anne Eleonore. As the fourth son, Ernest was expected to receive only a small portion of the family estate on his father's death, so in 1562, in order to augment his income, his relatives appointed him Protestant bishop of Osnabrück. However, two older brothers died without leaving male heirs—Christian in 1665 and Johann in 1679—so ultimately he inherited the area of his father's duchy known as Calenberg, which merged with Lüneberg-Celle to form Hanover in 1705. In 1692, as a reward for supporting the Holy Roman Empire, he was appointed prince-elector by Emperor Leopold I—a prestigious appointment allowing him to participate in the vote that would select his patron's successor but one that was not well received by critics who saw no need to expand the electoral college.

On 30 September 1658 in Heidelberg, Ernest married Sophia of the Palatinate (*see* SOPHIA, ELECTRESS OF HANOVER), the youngest of five daughters born to his second cousin, **Elizabeth of Bohemia** (daughter of King **James VI of Scotland and I of England**), and her husband, Frederick V, elector palatine of the Rhine. As a result of the distrust of Roman Catholicism that forced King **James VII and II** into exile following the **Glorious Revolution** of 1688–89, the match determined the succession to the British monarchy, as outlined by the **Act of Settlement** in 1701. In 1683, Ernest decreed that, in order to prevent subdivision of his lands, his entire estate would pass to George, his eldest son, who was born in 1660. He died at Herrenhausen Castle on 23 January 1698, and George succeeded to the British throne 16 years later. *See also* SOPHIA DOROTHEA OF CELLE.

**ERNEST AUGUSTUS, KING OF HANOVER (1771–1851).** Dogged by controversy throughout his life, Ernest—described as "the black sheep" by his brother **Frederick, duke of Kent and Strathearn**—was much disliked in Britain but extremely popular in his Hanoverian realm. The fifth son, and eighth child, of King **George III** and **Charlotte of Mecklenburg-Strelitz**, he was born at **Buckingham Palace** on 5 June 1771 and seemed destined for a military career until injuries sustained in Flanders, **France**, and the Netherlands during a campaign in 1793–95 left his face permanently disfigured. Turning to politics, he displayed a barbed wit and an implacable opposition to change that made him many enemies and led to scurrilous stories about his private life, among them a tale that he had sired a son by **Princess Sophia**, his younger sister.

On 31 May 1810, the death of Joseph Sellis, Ernest's valet, added to the tittle-tattle. Sellis's throat had been cut, but the **prince**, who had a head wound, claimed that his servant had committed suicide after making an unsuccessful attempt to murder him. This account of the event, which was greeted with raised eyebrows at the time, is still doubted by several historians. Five years later, Ernest caused further upset by marrying the twice-widowed Princess Frederica of Mecklenburg-Strelitz against his mother's wishes. The bride (a daughter of the queen's older brother, Charles) was suspected of poisoning Prince Frederick of Solms-Braunfels, her second husband, prompting Charlotte both to stay away from the wedding and to tell her son to leave Britain.

When King **William IV** died on 20 June 1837, the prince succeeded him as king of Hanover, and **Victoria** succeeded as sovereign of Great Britain, Hanoverian law explicitly forbidding female succession. The two monarchs squabbled at formal occasions for years over ownership of Charlotte's jewelry and the extent of Ernest's precedence, if any, over **Prince Albert of Saxe-Coburg and Gotha**, Victoria's husband. However, the Hanoverians greatly admired their ruler, who supported initiatives to build suburbs, develop the economy through the construction of railroads, improve sanitation, and introduce gas lighting. He died at the Altes Palais in Hanover on 18 November 1851 and was buried in the Herrenhausen mausoleum, leaving one son (George, who succeeded him).

**ETHELDREDA OF NORTHUMBRIA (?–?).** *See* OCTREDA OF NORTHUMBRIA.

**ETHELING.** *See* AETHELING.

**ETHELRED OF DUNKELD (?–?).** *See* ETHELRED OF SCOTLAND.

**ETHELRED OF SCOTLAND (?–?).** Of the eight children born to King **Malcolm III** and **St. Margaret**, Ethelred has received the least attention from historians, probably because he had the most limited impact on affairs of state. He was almost certainly named after **Aethelred the Unready**, his maternal great-great-grandfather, and (like **Crinan**, his paternal great-grandfather) became the lay abbot of Dunkeld, one of the richest and most prestigious religious settlements in Scotland. Earlier writers have claimed that he was mormaer (or earl) of Fife, but modern scholars are more skeptical, suggesting that such assertions are based on misinterpretations of documentary sources. It is not clear why Ethelred never became king although his three younger brothers succeeded to the throne as **Edgar of Scotland**, **Alexander I**, and **David I**, but it is possible that, influenced by his pious mother, he deliberately opted for church rather than politics. The dates of his birth and death are not recorded, and his place of burial is unknown, though some authors speculate that his remains may lie in **Dunfermline** or St. Andrews. He is sometimes known as Ethelred of Dunkeld.

**ETHELSTAN (c895–939).** *See* AETHELSTAN.

**ETHLING.** *See* AETHELING.

**EUGENIE OF YORK, PRINCESS (1990– ).** The younger daughter of **Prince Andrew, duke of York**, and **Sarah, duchess of York**, Eugenie was born in the Portland Hospital, **London**, on 23 March 1990 and educated (like her sister, **Princess Beatrice of York**) at Upton House School in Windsor, Coworth Park School in Surrey, and St. George's School in Ascot. She then attended Marlborough College, a coeducational establishment in Wiltshire, where she was reported dancing naked on the grounds with other girls to celebrate the end of examinations. Although the **princess** has acquired something of an extroverted reputation (her father has described her as "a bit of a tearaway"), she has also appeared with the duchess at a number of royal events and opened a Teenage Cancer Unit at St. James's Hospital, Leeds, in 2008. She spent much of 2008–9 traveling (while she was in Phnom Pen, Cambodia, a friend's purse was snatched while they were walking along a street together) and then registered to study English and art history at Newcastle University, which has a considerable reputation as a party school. Eugenie elected to live in an undergraduate dorm with other students, unlike her sister, who had a four-bedroom apartment at **St. James's Palace** refurbished at a cost of £250,000 before she began her studies at Goldsmith's College, London.

**EUPHEMIA DE ROSS (?–c1389).** Euphemia (or Eupheme), daughter of Hugh, earl of Ross, and his wife, Margaret, was the second wife but only **queen consort** of King **Robert II**. She was married first to John Randolph, earl of Moray, who was killed at the **Battle of Neville's Cross** on 17 October 1346, leaving his wife childless. Euphemia remained a widow until, on 2 May 1355, Pope Innocent VI issued a dispensation approving a match with Robert Stewart, whose first spouse (**Elizabeth Mure**) had died. Such approval by the Roman Catholic Church was necessary because the couple were first cousins once removed and were therefore within prohibited degrees of consanguinity.

Euphemia never played a major role in politics, but the union cemented an allegiance between Robert (then **heir presumptive** to the throne) and the Rosses, who were a political thorn in the side of King **David II** after his release from English captivity in 1357. Also, the marriage may have allowed Stewart to claim control of Badenoch, which had been part of Randolph's estate; in 1371, when he assumed the throne, Robert gave the lordship of Badenoch to **Alexander Stewart, wolf of Badenoch**, his son by Elizabeth, but he failed to deal with the abuses of power that followed. The couple had two boys and two girls who, according to several critics, had greater entitlement to the throne than Elizabeth's children, who were born out of wedlock. The date and place of Euphemia's death are uncertain, some sources contending that she died in 1386, others that she may have lived until the early weeks of 1389. *See also* STEWART, DAVID, EARL OF CAITHNESS; STEWART, EGIDIA (?–?); STEWART, ELIZABETH, COUNTESS OF CRAWFORD; STEWART, KATHERINE; STEWART, WALTER, EARL OF ATHOLL.

**EUSTACE, COUNT OF BOULOGNE (c1130–1153).** As the oldest surviving son of King **Stephen** and his wife, **Matilda of Boulogne**, Eustace was expected to follow in his father's footsteps and occupy the English throne. In 1140, he was married to Constance, younger sister of Louis VII of **France**, in an alliance that linked two of the major European monarchies, and in 1152, Stephen persuaded some of his nobles to accept Eustace as the heir to the crown. However, allies of the daughter of King **Henry I**, another **Matilda**, who had long contested Stephen's own right to the kingship, made clear that the young man was not acceptable, and churchmen voiced ecclesiastical opposition, anxious to see an end to the civil war that had engulfed England as the claimants' armies fought each other for nearly two decades. Moreover, Eustace himself was unpopular, pilloried in the *Anglo-Saxon Chronicle* as "an evil man" who "did more harm than good wherever he went," levying high taxes on the families that farmed his lands and threatening clerics who disagreed with him.

Events favored Stephen's opponents. On 17 August 1153, Eustace died while laying waste to church estates at Bury St. Edmunds. The king, devastated by the loss of his son and by the death of his wife the previous year, had no heart for continued conflict and entered into negotiations with Henry of Anjou, Matilda's son, which ended with an agreement that Stephen would retain the throne until his death but that Henry would succeed him as King **Henry II**.

# F

**FALKLAND PALACE.** Falkland, in central Fife, was a favorite residence of the monarchs of the House of Stewart (*see* STUART, HOUSE OF). Built as a castle by the 13th-century earls of Fife, it was acquired for the crown by King **James I** and transformed into a Renaissance palace during the reigns of **James IV** and **James V**. For Scotland's kings, Falkland was a comfortable base for hunting and falconry, but inevitably it had a role in the darker side of the country's history. **David Stewart, duke of Rothesay** and heir to the throne of **Robert III**, perished there in 1402 (allegedly starved to death by his uncle, **Robert Stewart, duke of Albany [c1340–1420]**), and James V died at the palace in 1542 only a few days after hearing of the birth of his daughter and heiress, **Mary, queen of Scots**.

After the **union of the crowns** in 1503, **James VI and I**, **Charles I**, and **Charles II** all visited the estate, but the structure was partially destroyed by fire while Oliver Cromwell's troops were based there in 1654, and by the early 19th century it was largely derelict under the care of a nonresident keeper. Restoration began in 1887, when John Crichton-Stuart, marquess of Bute, purchased the keepership, and it has continued under the direction of the National Trust for Scotland, which assumed responsibility for care and maintenance in 1952. The palace, its gardens, and its real (or royal) tennis court, built in 1541, are all open to visitors throughout the year. *See also* ELIZABETH OF BOHEMIA.

**FINDLÁECH OF MORAY (?–c1020).** Findláech (also known as Findláech mac Ruaidrí and Findláech MacRory) was the father of **Macbeth**, who was king of Scots from 1040 to 1057. He probably controlled Moray—an area of northern Scotland—before 1014 and was killed in 1020, perhaps by his nephews (Gille Coemgáin and Malcolm). His wife's name is unknown, but she may have been a daughter of **Kenneth II**, **Kenneth III**, or **Malcolm II**.

**FINNSDOTTIR, INGIBIORG (?–c1069).** Ingibiorg was the first wife of King **Malcolm III**. Their eldest son ruled Scotland as **Duncan II** for a few months in 1094, and it is likely that they had at least one other male child

(Donald, who died in 1085). Ingibiorg also had two boys—Paul and Erlend— by an earlier marriage to Thorfinn Sigurdsson, earl of Orkney; both took part in Harald Hardråde's invasion of England in 1066 but were guarding the Vikings' fleet while their seniors fought at **Stamford Bridge**. Possibly the daughter of Finn Arnesson (a nobleman at the court of King Olaf II of Norway) and Bergljot Halvansdottir (a niece both of Hardråde and of Olaf), she was probably dead by 1069–70, when Malcolm married Margaret of **Wessex** (later **St. Margaret**), and may even have passed away before her second husband killed **Lulach** and claimed the Scots' crown in 1058.

**FIRST ACT OF SUCCESSION (1534).** *See* SUCCESSION TO THE CROWN ACT (1534).

**FIRST BARONS' WAR (1215–1217).** Although King **John** appended his seal to the **Magna Carta** in 1215, the document's restrictive clauses circumscribed his freedom so much that he failed to honor the agreement. The English barons, determined to prevent him from reintroducing a regime of heavy taxes and ill-led military campaigns, sought help from Louis, heir to King Philip II of **France**, who (despite his father's disapproval) brought an army to help the dissidents, arriving on 22 May 1216. The invaders easily took control of **London** (where Louis was widely welcomed) and captured most of the castles in southern England, though the king's supporters held on to the fortresses at Dover and **Windsor**.

John's unexpected death from dysentery on 18 or 19 October changed the political climate. His nine-year-old son, who later ruled as **Henry III**, was too young to control the country, so William Marshall was appointed **regent**. Promising that his decisions would be guided by the principles embodied in the Magna Carta, he gradually weaned the rebels away from Louis, who wanted to claim the throne for himself. The two sides continued to struggle for another year, but in 1217, a military defeat at Lincoln and naval defeats in the English Channel ended the Frenchman's dreams. On 11 September, he agreed to withdraw to France in return for a payment of 10,000 marks and amnesty for the nobles who had supported him. Some modern scholars suggest that, as Louis controlled much of the country, including the capital, for many months, he should be listed among the monarchs of England, even though he was never crowned. *See also* ALEXANDER II; CROWN JEWELS OF THE UNITED KINGDOM.

**FIRST SUCCESSION ACT (1534).** *See* SUCCESSION TO THE CROWN ACT (1534).

**FITZDUNCAN, WILLIAM (c1094–c1154).** William was the only known child of King **Duncan II** and **Octreda of Northumbria**. It seems likely that he spent his childhood in England after the murder of his father in 1094 and that he returned to Scotland during the reign of **Alexander I**, his half-uncle. As the only son of a king who had been ousted from the throne, he clearly had a claim to the crown, but he appears not to have asserted his rights even though he became a noted military leader, routing an English force at Clitheroe in Yorkshire on 10 June 1138. It is possible that Alexander and his successor, **David I**, designated William as their heir for a portion of their reigns and arranged for him to receive the title of mormaer (or earl) of Moray when David's son, **Henry, earl of Northumberland**, reached an age at which he could succeed to the throne if his father died. William also controlled large estates in the north of England. He married at least twice, leaving several legitimate and illegitimate children, and he died by 1154.

**FLODDEN, BATTLE OF (9 September 1513).** In the early summer of 1513, King **James IV** of Scotland responded to a request for help from King Louis XII of **France**, who was under attack by the armies of King **Henry VIII** of England. Against the advice of many of his counselors, he launched a military campaign against the English, leading a force of 30,000 men over the border into Northumbria, where on 9 September he faced 25,000 troops led by Thomas Howard, earl of Surrey, at Branxton, north of Flodden Edge. In a two-hour struggle, the Scots were cut to pieces and James was killed, along with at least 10,000 of his men, three bishops, nine earls, and 13 barons (the dead are the "Flowers o' the Forest" in the haunting lament written to commemorate the loss). The effects were far reaching because James was succeeded by his son, **James V**, who was only one year old, and Scotland suffered a lengthy period of political instability while **regents** controlled the government.

**FONTEVRAULT ABBEY.** Fontevrault is the burial place of several leading members of the royal **House of Anjou**, including King **Henry II**, **Eleanor of Aquitaine** (Henry's wife); **Isabella of Angoulême** (Henry's daughter-in-law and the second wife of King **John**); **Joan, queen of Sicily** (Henry's daughter); and King **Richard I** (Henry's son). Founded in 1099 by Robert of Arbrissel, an itinerant preacher, it now lies in the village of Fontevraud-L'Abbaye, near Chinon in western **France**. The complex, which initially consisted of a group of religious houses for nuns as well as monks, benefited from the patronage of the monarchs of the House of Anjou after Matilda, Henry's aunt, became its second abbess. Later, the Bourbon family lent their support, but in 1792, after the French revolution, the royal tombs were desecrated and the building was turned into a prison. Reconstruction work, begun in 1860, was completed in 1906, and the site, now owned by the state, is used as a cultural center. The coffins that contained the royal remains have been lost, but effigies mark the spots where archaeologists believe the burials took place. *See also* BEATRICE, DUCHESS OF BURGUNDY.

**FORT BELVEDERE.** Fort Belvedere, in Windsor Great Park, close to **Windsor Castle**, was a **royal residence**, albeit intermittently, for most of the period from 1755 (when it was built for **Prince William Augustus, duke of Cumberland** and second son of King **George II**) until 1976 (when it was vacated by **Gerald Lascelles**, the younger son of **Mary, princess royal and countess of Harewood**). Initially used as a summer house, it was converted into a hunting lodge (with a very fortlike appearance and 31 cannons) for King **George IV** in 1828 and then, in 1911, into a country home for the use of Queen **Victoria**'s third son, **Prince Arthur, duke of Connaught and Strathearn** and **governor-general** of Canada. In 1929, King **George V** gave it to Edward, **prince of Wales** (later King **Edward VIII**), who supervised extensive refurbishment and entertained the married ladies (including **Wallis, duchess of Windsor**) with whom he had a string of affairs.

The building housed government offices during World War II but then lay empty until Lascelles took the lease of the rather run-down house in 1956, restored the gardens, added a tennis court and swimming pool, and played host to celebrities from the worlds of jazz and motor racing. Since his departure, the property has been occupied by private individuals; however, it remains part of the **crown estate**, so the rental income augments government coffers.

**FRANCE.** For nearly 500 years, from the first half of the 14th century to the early 19th century, monarchs of England (and, after the **union of parliaments** in 1707, sovereigns of Great Britain) styled themselves king or queen of France. Connections between the two powers had been strong since 1066, when William the Conqueror led a successful invasion of England, deposing the Anglo-Saxon leaders and ruling the country as **William I**. William was duke of Normandy, a large territory in northwestern France. Later marriages were to add extensive areas in northern France (notably Anjou) and also in the southwest (particularly **Aquitaine**) to the sphere of English influence. However, after King **John**'s defeat at the Battle of Bouvines on 27 July 1214, Philip II of France was able to place many of those estates under his own authority, and English control was confined to a coastal strip of Aquitaine stretching from the Pyrenees to Bordeaux and the northern banks of the Garonne River.

Until that point, all of the English crown's properties on the European mainland had been held under feudal arrangements that made the English king a vassal of whoever occupied the French throne. However, when Charles IV of France died in 1328 without leaving a male heir, **Isabella of France**, co-**regent** of England along with her lover **Roger Mortimer**, claimed that her son, **Edward III**, was Charles's closest male relative and was therefore entitled to the French throne. The French disagreed, preferring Philip, count of Valois, who was descended through the male line and ruled as Philip VI. From 1337, Edward asserted his right to the crown militarily (*see* HUNDRED YEARS' WAR), and from 1340, by styling himself king of the country. However, acquisition of land was more important to the English king than monarchical ambition, so in 1360, under the terms of the treaties of Brétigny and **Calais**, he renounced his claim to the French kingdom in return for freehold, rather than feudal rights, in Calais and Aquitaine. That arrangement, always fragile because of political tensions, lasted for nine years before Charles V of France repudiated it and Edward retaliated by resurrecting his claim that he, rather than Charles, was the rightful king of France. A further pact was negotiated in 1420, when, at a time of English military strength, **Henry V** of England was married to **Catherine of Valois**, daughter of Charles VI of France, and was thus recognized as Charles's heir. Then, in 1422, Henry and Charles died within two months of each other, leaving Henry's 10-month-old son (**Henry VI**) as the first sovereign of both countries.

The infant's status did not go unchallenged. English authority in France was restricted to the northern region, with Charles VII (Charles VI's son) controlling the south. Over the next 30 years, England's power had eroded, and by 1453 Henry was king of France in name alone, holding on only to Calais. By 1558, even that small area had gone, but English (and then British) monarchs still accorded themselves the empty title of king or queen of France until **George III** gave up the usage in 1801.

The Scottish monarchy's relationship with France was very different. Often known as the auld (or old) alliance and shaped by the recognition that England was an enemy of both countries, it began with a formal treaty signed in Paris in 1295 and lasted into the 16th century. Over the period, the two nations regularly provided each other with military support. For example, during the Hundred Years' War, the Scots made a significant contribution to the English defeat at the Battle of Baugé in 1421 and helped Joan of Arc break the siege of Orléans in 1429. The link was also cemented through marriage between royal and noble families, as when King **James V** wed **Madeleine de Valois** (daughter of King Francis I of France) in 1537 and then, in 1538, **Mary of Guise** (daughter of Claude, duke of Guise). Mary acted as regent of Scotland from 1554 to 1560, and her only female child, **Mary, queen of**

**Scots**, was married to **Francis II of France**, son of King Henry II of France and, at the time of the wedding in 1558, heir to the French throne. Shortly afterward, the Scottish parliament made Francis king of Scotland, and in 1559, when Henry died, Mary became **queen consort** of France. Any son born to the couple would have been king of both countries, but Francis died in 1560 before Mary conceived, and with the union of the English and Scottish crowns in 1603, the auld alliance petered out.

Possibilities of a merger between the British and French states were raised again in the 20th century. In June 1940, when France was under attack by Germany, the British government proposed full integration of France and the United Kingdom, with common citizenship, but the French capitulated before the plan could be investigated in detail. Then, in 1956, when both countries were responding to Egypt's nationalization of the Suez Canal, Guy Mollet, the anglophile French prime minister, suggested a merger of Britain and France, with Queen **Elizabeth II** as head of state. The British government would not entertain the idea, which caused consternation in Paris as well as **London** when papers relating to the discussion were publicized in 2007. *See also* ANJOU, HOUSE OF; BALLIOL, HOUSE OF; BEATRICE, DUCHESS OF BURGUNDY; BERENGARIA OF NAVARRE; BLOIS, HOUSE OF; DUNKIRK; EDWARD IV; EDWARD, THE BLACK PRINCE; ELEANOR OF AQUITAINE; ELEANOR OF CASTILE; ELEANOR OF PROVENCE; EMMA OF NORMANDY; FIRST BARONS' WAR; GEOFFREY, COUNT OF ANJOU; GEOFFREY, COUNT OF NANTES; HENRIETTA ANNE, DUCHESS OF ORLÉANS; HENRIETTA MARIA OF FRANCE; HENRY II; HENRY VIII; HENRY, THE YOUNG KING; HERLEVA; ISABELLA OF ANGOULÊME; JOAN OF NAVARRE; JOHN OF LANCASTER, DUKE OF BEDFORD; MARGARET OF ANJOU; MARGUERITE OF FRANCE; MARIE DE COUCY; MARIE, COUNTESS OF BOULOGNE; NORMANDY, HOUSE OF; PHILIPPA OF HAINAULT; PRINCESS ROYAL; RICHARD I; ROBERT I, DUKE OF NORMANDY; STEPHEN HENRY, COUNT OF BLOIS; STEWART, MARGARET, DAUPHINE OF FRANCE; STUART, HOUSE OF; TINCHEBRAI, BATTLE OF; TROYES, TREATY OF; TUDOR, MARY, QUEEN OF FRANCE; WINDSOR, TREATY OF; YOLANDE DE DREUX.

**FRANCIS II OF FRANCE (1544–1560).** Francis, king of **France** for a few months in 1559–60, was the first husband of **Mary, queen of Scots**. The eldest son of Henry II of France and Catherine de' Medici, he was born at Fontainebleau on 19 January 1544. The marriage, proposed by Henry (*see* GREENWICH, TREATY OF) in a move designed to unite the French and Scots states under one monarch, took place at Notre Dame Cathedral in Paris on 24 April 1558, when Mary was 15 years old and Francis 13. They had grown up together at the French court and, according to the groom's father, had gotten along well even though Francis was sickly and very short, with a pronounced stutter, and Mary was tall and articulate. Francis succeeded to the throne on 10 July 1559, when his father died from wounds sustained in a jousting tournament, but was too young and too much of an invalid to assert himself as ruler, so the reins of power in the realm lay in the hands of relatives of his mother-in-law, **Mary of Guise**. He died at Orléans on 5 December 1560 when an ear infection deteriorated and led to an abscess in his brain. Francis's younger brother, Charles IX, took the crown, and Mary returned to Scotland.

**FREDERICK, PRINCE, DUKE OF YORK AND ALBANY (1763–1827).** Frederick—the second son of King **George III** and **Charlotte of Mecklenburg-Strelitz**—was born at **St. James's Palace**, London, on 16 August 1763 and, according to some writers, inspired the nursery rhyme about the grand old **duke of York** who "marched his men to the top of the hill and marched them down again." He married Princess Frederica of Prussia at ceremonies in Berlin on 29 September 1791 and at **Buckingham Palace** on 23 November, but the union was unhappy; the couple separated before any children were born, and the young **prince** enjoyed himself with a series of willing mistresses.

At the king's behest, Frederick pursued a career as a soldier. He served bravely in Flanders in 1793–95, and in 1798, despite having demonstrated a lack of talent either for leadership or for strategy, he was appointed commander-in-chief of the army. In 1799, he led a contingent of troops that, allied with a Russian force, was supposed to drive the French out of Holland, but, as in the Flanders campaign, he was compelled to withdraw. The prince was well aware, though, that the defeats were not entirely due to his own shortcomings. Using his considerable influence, he founded a military academy at Woolwich, near **London**, in an effort to improve officer training, he attempted to prevent the scions of wealthy families from purchasing commands (thus making merit, rather than money, the means of entry to senior posts), and he raised the standard of clothing supplied to lower ranks. However, his efforts were compromised by the activities of his mistress, Mary Anne Clark, who promised officers promotion in return for payment. In 1809, parliament acquitted the prince of wrongdoing, but he was forced to resign his post (though he was reinstated two years later, despite the protests of critics).

Throughout his life, Frederick enjoyed wine, women, and gambling. As a result, he accrued debts, estimated at over £400,000, that were not covered by the sale of his assets after his death at the home of John, duke of Rutland, in

Arlington Street, London, on 5 January 1827. He was buried in **St. George's Chapel** at **Windsor Castle** as his creditors waited in vain for their money. The nursery rhyme mockery of the duke's military skills may be unjustified because, although many writers claim that he is the commander vilified in the verses, the lines may refer either to **Richard, duke of York (1411–1460)**, who died at the **Battle of Wakefield** after a strategic misjudgment, or to **James VII of England and II of Scotland**, who had been **duke of York** before his accession to the throne and had, in 1688, marched his troops from London to meet the advancing army of William of Orange (later King **William III of England and II of Scotland**) but then sent them home again without giving battle. Fredericton, the capital of New Brunswick, is named after the prince, as are many of the Canadian settlements known as York.

**FREDERICK, PRINCE OF WALES (1707–1751).** Frederick, the eldest son of King **George II** and **Caroline of Brandenburg-Ansbach**, was born in the Leine Palace, Hanover, on 20 January 1707. He proved to be a large thorn in his father's flesh for many years but died before he could succeed to the throne. When George and Caroline moved to Britain in 1714, they left the young **prince** behind to serve as the family representative in the homeland and were not reunited with him until 1727, by which time they had produced another son (**William Augustus, duke of Cumberland**) who was given more of the political limelight because he was born in **London**.

After the freedoms—and particularly the financial freedoms—of life in Germany, Frederick resented his more restricted life at the British court, so relations between parents and son soured speedily as the young man attempted to assert his independence. Marriage, in 1736, to **Princess Augusta of Saxe-Gotha** brought an increase in his allowance, but, still dissatisfied, he made an unsuccessful appeal to parliament for even more funding and in 1738 moved his heavily pregnant wife from **Hampton Court** to **St. James's Palace** so that his first child would not be born in the house where his mother and father were living. Thoroughly insulted, George and Caroline refused to communicate with Frederick and banned court officials from conversing with him. Reconciliation with the king in 1742 lasted only briefly; Frederick was refused permission to lead royalist forces against the armies of **Charles Edward Stuart** in the **Jacobite rebellion** of 1745–46 and afterward became a significant figure in the opposition to his father's government.

In addition to his political activities, the prince took a keen interest in the arts (he acquired a large collection of paintings), industry (he helped to found the British Herring Industry Company), and sport (he was a keen cricketer). He also devoted much time to his family, but preparations for kingship came to naught. His health suddenly declined early in 1751, and on 20 March he died at Leicester House in London, his passing ascribed by doctors to a burst lung abscess that may have formed as a result of a cricket injury. He was buried in **Westminster Abbey**, leaving nine children, the second of whom succeeded to the throne as King **George III** in 1760. *See also* CARLTON HOUSE; CAROLINE OF BRUNSWICK-WOLFENBÜTTEL; LOUISA, QUEEN OF DENMARK AND NORWAY.

**FROGMORE.** The 33-acre Frogmore estate, near **Windsor Castle**, was acquired by the **royal family** in 1792, when King **George III** purchased it as a country retreat for his queen, **Charlotte of Mecklenburg-Strelitz**, and his unmarried daughters. Since the mid-19th century, it has become a favored burial place for his descendants. The residence, which dates from 1680–84, became the home of Queen **Victoria**'s mother, **Princess Victoria of Saxe-Coburg-Saalfield, duchess of Kent and Strathearn**, who died there in 1861 and is buried in a mausoleum that was designed as both her summer house and her last resting place. From 1866 to 1873, **Princess Christian of Schleswig-Holstein**, the queen's third daughter, lived in the property with her family, and King **George V** often brought his wife, **Mary of Teck**, from 1902 until he succeeded to the throne in 1910. Now, however, although it is still visited occasionally by royalty and the grounds are sometimes used for receptions, it is no longer a permanent home.

Queen Victoria and her consort, **Prince Albert of Saxe-Coburg and Gotha**, deliberately decided to eschew burial in **Westminster Abbey** or **Windsor Castle**, where many of their royal predecessors had been interred, and lie together in a mausoleum located close to that of the duchess. Shaped like a Greek cross, the structure is flamboyantly typical of the era, with walls made of Portland Stone and granite brought from around Britain, a roof of Australian copper, two bronze angels at the entrance, and an interior decorated with marble imported from three continents. The sarcophagus is a single piece of granite, reputedly the world's largest flawless block of the stone.

The mausoleum is surrounded by the graves of other members of the royal family, including **Princess** Christian (interred in 1928) and two of Victoria's other eight children—**Prince Arthur, duke of Connaught and Strathearn** (1942), and **Princess Louise, duchess of Argyll** (1939)—as well as **Princess Victoria** (1935); **Prince George, duke of Kent** (1968), and **Princess Marina, duchess of Kent** (1968); **Prince William of Gloucester** (1972); King **Edward VIII** (1972) and **Wallis, duchess of Windsor**, the American-born divorcee for whom he gave up the throne (1986); and **Prince Henry, duke of Gloucester** (1974), and **Princess Alice, duchess of Gloucester** (2004).

Frogmore House and its grounds are opened to the public a few days every year, usually in August, but access is not available to the interior of the duchess of Kent's mausoleum or to the graves in the royal burial ground. *See also* ALBERT VICTOR, PRINCE, DUKE OF CLARENCE AND AVONDALE; MOUNTBATTEN, LOUIS, EARL MOUNTBATTEN OF BURMA; OGILVY, SIR ANGUS.

# G

**GATCOMBE PARK.** Gatcombe Park, near the village of Minchinhampton, in Gloucestershire, is the country home of **Anne, princess royal (1950– )**, and her husband, Vice-Admiral **Timothy Laurence**. The house, built of Bath stone, was erected in 1771–74 and has nine bedrooms, four reception rooms, a billiard room, a library, and a conservatory as well as staff quarters. The 730-acre estate also includes farmland and extensive wooded areas. Queen **Elizabeth II** purchased the property from Lord Rab Butler of Saffron Walden for a reported £5 million in 1976 and then gave it to the **princess** and Captain **Mark Phillips**, her first husband. The couple had a joint interest in horse trials and, even after their separation in 1989, cooperated in the organization of competitions on the grounds, notably the Festival of British Eventing, held in August. Captain Phillips and his American-born second wife, Sandy Pflueger, live in Aston Farm, which was added to the estate in 1978, and his children by the princess—**Peter Phillips** and **Zara Phillips**—have cottages nearby. **Highgrove**, the country home of **Charles, prince of Wales**, lies some six miles to the south.

**GEOFFREY, COUNT OF ANJOU (1113–1151).** As father of King **Henry II**, Geoffrey of Anjou was the founder of the Plantagenet dynasty that ruled England from 1154 to 1485 (*see* PLANTAGENET, HOUSE OF). He was born on 24 August 1113 to Fulk V of Anjou and Eremburga of La Flèche and on 17 June 1128 wed **Matilda**, daughter of **Henry I**, in a union that was designed to seal a peace agreement between the two fathers. Matilda was more than 10 years older than Geoffrey and had a reputation for haughtiness, so the prospects for a harmonious marriage were not great. Even so, although there are records of arguments and separations, the couple produced three sons—Henry in 1133; **Geoffrey, count of Nantes**, in 1134; and **William, count of Poitou**, in 1136.

In 1127, Henry I, whose only son (**William the Aetheling**) had drowned seven years earlier, forced his barons to take an oath that they would recognize Matilda as his successor. When he died in 1135, they broke that promise and accepted the claims of **Stephen**, grandson of **William I of**

**England** (William the Conqueror), crowning him king at a ceremony in **Westminster Abbey** on 26 December. Matilda, however, chose to pursue her inheritance, mounting an invasion of England in 1139 and plunging the country into civil war.

Despite their differences, Geoffrey supported his wife's stance. In 1135, he was faced with a rebellion by his own nobles in Anjou, and continued troubles there limited his ability to send armies to join her, as did conflict with his brother, Elias, over family estates in Maine. Nevertheless, by 1144 he had conquered Normandy, which initially had recognized Stephen as duke, and in 1149 (jointly with Matilda) ceded it to his eldest son.

Geoffrey died suddenly at the Château-du-Loir, in the Pays de la Loire region of **France**, on 7 September 1151 and was buried in Le Mans Cathedral, three years before his son became king of England, inheriting a country near anarchy but ruling for more than three decades and making himself one of the most powerful monarchs in Europe. There are various stories about how Geoffrey earned the nickname "Plantagenet," all associated with the yellow flower of the common broom plant (*Planta genista* in Latin and *genet* in French), which still grows in Anjou. Some writers suggest that he wore a sprig in his hat, others that he encouraged its spread as cover for birds and animals on land that he used for hunting. *See also* ANJOU, HOUSE OF.

**GEOFFREY, COUNT OF NANTES (1134–1158).** Geoffrey was the second son of **Matilda** (daughter of King **Henry I**) and her husband, **Geoffrey, count of Anjou**. His birth, on 1 June 1134, was a difficult one—so much so that his mother nearly died—and he caused other problems in later life. When his father passed away in 1151, Geoffrey inherited the castles of Chinon, Loudon, and Mirebeau, but he also claimed that he was entitled to all of the family estates in Anjou when, three years later, Henry, his elder brother, won the throne of England, succeeding King **Stephen** and ruling as **Henry II**. Geoffrey attempted to take his inheritance by force, but the new monarch's armies were too strong, so he was forced to concede a defeat that required him to accept Henry's control of Anjou in return for an annual pension. He did not live long to enjoy the payments, however, dying unmarried and childless at Nantes on 26 July 1158. Geoffrey is also known as Geoffrey of Anjou and (because his mother's first husband was Henry V, Holy Roman Emperor) as Geoffrey FitzEmpress. *See also* WILLIAM, COUNT OF POITOU.

**GEOFFREY, DUKE OF BRITTANY (1158–1186).** The fourth son of King **Henry II** and **Eleanor of Aquitaine**, Geoffrey was born on 23 September 1158 and became duke of Brittany in 1181 through his marriage to Constance of Penthièvre, who had inherited the title from her father, Conan of Brittany, and whose mother, Margaret of Huntingdon, was the daughter of **Ada de Warenne** and granddaughter of **David I** of Scotland. The couple had been betrothed several years earlier—the price paid by Conan for Henry's help in suppressing a revolt by his nobles (a revolt that Henry may actually have provoked)—and after the wedding Geoffrey allowed his wife little say in the administration of her vast estates.

In 1173–74, Geoffrey allied with his brothers, **Henry, the young king**, and Richard (later **Richard I**), in a rebellion against their father and almost succeeded in toppling the monarch. They were later reconciled, but other squabbles followed, not only with the king but also between the siblings—so much so that Geoffrey earned a considerable reputation for treachery. Also, his habit of plundering monasteries in order to raise funds for his military campaigns invoked the wrath of churchmen. However, though he had made many enemies, his death on 19 August 1186 was unexpected. According to some reports, his horse trampled him during a jousting tournament at the Paris court of his friend, King Philip II of **France**. On the other hand, one record suggests that he passed away after complaining of abdominal pains.

Geoffrey left three children, all of whom led unhappy lives. Arthur, the only son, was born on 29 March 1187. When Geoffrey died, Arthur took his place as second in line to the English throne after Richard. However, Richard—who succeeded Henry II in 1189—named **John**, his younger brother, as his heir, giving him precedence over his nephew. Philip of France supported Arthur's cause, but in 1202, supporters of King John, who had taken the crown in 1199, imprisoned the boy at Rouen. The youngster's fate is unknown, but rumors circulating at the time suggest that John himself may have murdered him. Eleanor, Arthur's older sister, was born c1184 and was captured at the same time as her brother. She spent her entire life in prison at Corfe Castle in southern England, dying on 10 August 1241, possibly as a result of starvation. Maud, the third child, was born c1185 but died while still very young. Constance married twice more and died in Nantes on 5 September 1201, perhaps after contracting leprosy but perhaps of complications following the birth of twin girls.

**GEORGE I (1660–1727).** When **William, duke of Gloucester**—the only surviving child of Anne, princess of Denmark and later Queen **Anne**—died in 1700, England's parliament took steps to ensure that the country's monarchy would remain Protestant rather than pass to **James Francis Edward Stuart**, the Roman Catholic son of King **James VII and II**, who had been deposed by the **Glorious Revolution** of 1688–89. Under the terms of the **Act of Settlement**, which received **royal assent** in 1701, the crown would pass, on Anne's death, to **James VI and I**'s granddaughter **Sophia, electress**

**of Hanover**, or her descendants. Sophia predeceased Anne by less than two months, so George, her eldest son, became king of Great Britain when the queen died on 1 August 1714.

George was born on 28 May 1660 at Osnabrück, then part of the Holy Roman Empire. His father, **Ernest Augustus (1629–1698)**, who was elector of Brunswick-Lüneburg (and was later appointed elector of Hanover), raised him as heir to the family estates as well as to those of Ernest's three childless brothers. In 1682, marriage to his first cousin, **Sophia Dorothea of Celle**, added even more territories and thus greatly augmented both his prestige and his power.

An unpopular ruler who had little taste for the trappings of royalty, George made no serious effort to learn the language of his British subjects. Some historians have been critical of his diplomatic skills, but in 1717–18, he had enough guile to negotiate a military alliance with **France**, the Holy Roman Empire, and the Netherlands which helped guarantee political stability in northern Europe. And although he was never at ease with parliament, he learned to accommodate and work with ministers who frequently disagreed with him. His rule, however, was dogged by stories of cruelty to his wife (he divorced her in 1694 and then kept her imprisoned until her death in 1726) and by long-running quarrels with his son, who aligned himself with the sovereign's political opponents and later succeeded him as King **George II**. Also, an economic crisis in 1721 weakened his already poor reputation, leaving him reliant on his chief minister, Sir Robert Walpole (who had earlier attempted a reconciliation between the monarch and his son), to prevent his indiscreet financial transactions from being revealed in parliament.

George returned to Hanover several times and died at Osnabrück on 11 June 1727 after suffering a stroke during his sixth journey home. He was buried near his mother in the chapel at Leineschloss, but the building was much damaged during World War II, so in 1957 his remains were transferred (along with those of other members of his family) to the Berggarten in Hanover. *See also* DEFENDER OF THE FAITH; GEORGE WILLIAM, PRINCE; KENSINGTON PALACE; SOPHIA DOROTHEA, QUEEN OF PRUSSIA.

**GEORGE II (1683–1760).** George, monarch of Great Britain from 1727 until 1760, was the only son of King **George I** and **Sophia Dorothea of Celle**. He was born at Herrenhausen, in lower Saxony, on 30 October 1683 but was raised by his paternal grandparents (**Ernest Augustus, elector of Hanover, and Sophia, electress of Hanover**), never seeing his mother after her divorce and imprisonment in 1694. As a young man, George rebelled against his father, in large part because he felt that the treatment of Sophia was unjust, so his home in **London** became a regular meeting place of the monarch's political opponents. The pair was never reconciled, and there were clear echoes of the relationship in George II's quarrels with his own son, **Frederick, prince of Wales**.

As a soldier, George showed considerable courage, fighting with distinction against the French in the Battle of Oudenarde in 1708, and in 1743, at nearly 60 years of age, becoming the last British sovereign to lead his army into battle, where he won a decisive victory against the same foe at **Dettingen**. However, his political judgment was sometimes more suspect. When he succeeded to the throne in 1727, he intended—more out of pique than considered judgment—to replace most of the ministers who had advised his father, but he was persuaded to listen to the diplomatic advice of his astute wife, **Caroline of Brandenburg-Ansbach**, and in the end made few changes. As sovereign, he followed domestic and foreign affairs with considerable interest but tended to leave decision making to others, notably to Sir Robert Walpole, who, as a consequence, developed considerable power and is often considered Britain's first prime minister, even though the title was not used at the time.

After Walpole resigned in 1742, having failed to prevent war with Spain, George conferred most closely with John, baron Carteret, who was considered arrogant and was much disliked by many parliamentarians. For two years, king and peer pursued a foreign policy that was greatly criticized because it seemed to take more account of the monarch's Hanoverian priorities than those of his British realm. Inevitably the criticism mounted, led by William Pitt the Elder, and in 1744 became so strong that the king was left with no choice other than to dispense with Carteret's services.

George despised Pitt and did his utmost to keep him out of office, but in 1746, faced with a mass resignation of ministers, he relented, and for the remaining years of his reign, Pitt dominated the political scene. The king retained his organized, militaristic approach to his household, but for the rest of his life he took little interest in government even though his ministers were aggressively acquiring colonies in Africa, the Caribbean, India, and North America. On 25 October 1760, he suffered an aneurism of the aorta and died at **Kensington Palace**. He was buried at **Westminster Abbey** and was succeeded by his grandson, who ruled as King **George III**. The last British monarch to be born outside the country, George II had presided over a period that saw Britain become a world (rather than simply a European) power. Parliament had continued to increase in influence at the expense of the monarch, but by the time George died in the middle years of the 18th century, the **House of Stuart**'s hopes of retrieving the thrones it had lost in the **Glorious Revolution** of 1688–89 had been dashed (*see* JACOBITE REBELLIONS;

STUART, CHARLES EDWARD), so the monarchy itself was more stable than it had been when he first sat on the throne.

There is a story that the king once got so excited during a performance of George Frideric Handel's *Messiah* oratorio that he stood up during the Hallelujah chorus. Because the monarch was on his feet, the audience had to stand as well. Since then, there has been a tradition that audiences rise from their seats during the chorus. Scholars debunk the tale, saying that George had little interest in music, but some writers point out that his estranged son, Frederick, **prince of Wales**, was a considerable patron of the arts and may be the real founder of the practice. *See also* AMELIA, PRINCESS (1711–1786); ANNE, PRINCESS ROYAL (1709–1759); CAROLINE ELIZABETH, PRINCESS; GEORGE WILLIAM, PRINCE; LOUISA, QUEEN OF DENMARK AND NORWAY; MARY, PRINCESS, LANDGRAVINE OF HESSE-CASSEL; ROYAL MARRIAGES ACT (1772); WHITE LODGE; WILLIAM AUGUSTUS, DUKE OF CUMBERLAND.

**GEORGE III (1738–1820).** King George III reigned for nearly 60 years— more than any other British monarch except Queen **Victoria**—and presided over major agricultural and industrial change in his realm, but he is probably best remembered for his bouts of insanity and for being the king who was on the throne when Britain lost the colonies that became the United States of America. Born on 24 May 1738 at Norfolk House (his parents' home in St. James's Square, **London**), he was the eldest son of **Frederick, prince of Wales**, and **Princess Augusta of Saxe-Gotha**, succeeding to the throne in 1760 because his father had predeceased his grandfather, King **George II**.

The early years of the reign were marked by considerable political instability, largely precipitated by differences over war with Austria, **France**, and Russia, but partly also resulting from George's political inexperience and personality clashes with his ministers. Although the cost of the war in Europe caused financial problems, and attempts to tax settlers in the American colonies met considerable resistance, the king insisted that parliament had sovereignty over British possessions in the New World and committed further resources in an effort to suppress the transatlantic revolution. As France, Holland, and Spain lent support to the rebels, domestic support for continued conflict waned, but the government seemed unable to prevent escalation of the dispute, and the king's popularity reached such a low ebb that he was tempted to abdicate.

In 1783, however, an unusually authoritative show of monarchical authority brought a change of fortune. Frederick, lord North (George's prime minister), and Charles Fox (a politician whom the king believed to be untrustworthy) produced a parliamentary bill designed to reform the East India

Company, which had monopoly trading rights with the East Indies. The proposals aroused fears that the two men intended to enhance their own power and wealth, so George made it clear that anyone who supported the scheme would be considered his enemy. The bill failed, George was considered to have preserved the nation's interests, North resigned, and William Pitt the Younger was made prime minister. There were no more unilateral royal interventions, however, and Pitt gradually grew in political strength as George's influence on government declined, continuing a long-term waning in the powers of the monarchy.

In the fall of 1788, the king suffered a prolonged bout of mental illness (now believed to be porphyria), and the attack caused a parliamentary crisis as members squabbled over the powers that should be granted to the **prince of Wales** (later King **George IV**) if he was appointed **regent**. George's recovery early in 1789 put an end to the dispute and initiated a period of administrative calm that lasted until 1795, when Pitt supported calls for Irish Catholics to be allowed to sit in parliament. With the enforced exile of the Roman Catholic King **James VII of Scotland and II of England** little more than a century old, George objected furiously, pointing out that he was expected to uphold the concept of a Protestant state—a view that was widely held in the country at the time. Pitt resigned, and the king opposed further attempts to reduce the severity of the laws against Catholics in 1806–7, but by that time he was going blind and his mind was failing again. On 7 February 1811, parliament made the **prince** of Wales regent, and on 29 January 1820, George—the first monarch from the **House of Hanover** to be born in Britain—died at **Windsor Castle**.

Nineteenth-century historians were critical, often painting George as a tyrant opposed to reform, but recent writers have been more kind, presenting him as a well-meaning man weakened by illness and by the uncertain politics of the times. *See also* ADOLPHUS, PRINCE, DUKE OF CAMBRIDGE; ALFRED, PRINCE; AMELIA, PRINCESS (1783–1810); AUGUSTA SOPHIA, PRINCESS; AUGUSTUS FREDERICK, PRINCE, DUKE OF SUSSEX; CHARLOTTE OF MECKLENBURG-STRELITZ; CHARLOTTE, PRINCESS ROYAL, QUEEN OF WURTEMBURG; CIVIL LIST; *COURT CIRCULAR*; EDWARD, PRINCE, DUKE OF KENT AND STRATHEARN; ELIZABETH, PRINCESS, LANDGRAVINE OF HESSE-HOMBURG; ERNEST AUGUSTUS, KING OF HANOVER; FRANCE; FREDERICK, PRINCE, DUKE OF YORK AND ALBANY; FROGMORE; HAMPTON COURT PALACE; KEW PALACE; MARY, PRINCESS, DUCHESS OF GLOUCESTER AND EDINBURGH; OCTAVIUS, PRINCE; QUEEN'S HOUSE, GREENWICH; ROYAL MARRIAGES ACT (1772); SOPHIA, PRINCESS; WILLIAM IV.

**GEORGE IV (1762–1830).** One of the least-loved of British monarchs, George was the eldest son of King **George III** and **Charlotte of Mecklenburg-Strelitz.** He was born at **St. James's Palace,** London, on 12 August 1762 and, as a young man, demonstrated a profoundly hedonistic personality, admitting while still a teenager that he was "rather too fond of women and wine." The **prince** had several mistresses before falling in love with Maria Anne Fitzherbert, an attractive and twice-widowed Roman Catholic. Maria refused to become his paramour, so the couple secretly participated in a marriage ceremony on 15 December 1785 at the bride's **London** home. In practice, the match was never recognized because the **Royal Marriages Act** of 1772 prohibited members of the **royal family** under the age of 25 from marrying without the monarch's consent, and had George persisted, it would have placed his future in jeopardy because the 1701 **Act of Settlement** debarred the husband of a Roman Catholic from succeeding to the throne.

As "Prinny" (a nickname derived from "prince") pursued his expensive lifestyle, debts mounted, but the king and queen, who thoroughly disapproved of his behavior, refused to provide any financial help. So, in order to extract an increased allowance from parliament, he denied that there was any union with Mrs. Fitzherbert and agreed to marry his cousin, **Caroline of Brunswick-Wolfenbüttel,** the daughter of Charles, duke of Brunswick-Wolfenbüttel, and Augusta, King **George III**'s older sister. The match, solemnized at St. James's Palace on 8 April 1795, was entirely loveless—Caroline thought the prince "very fat," and George wrote that he found it difficult to "conquer my aversion and overcome the disgust of her person" on their wedding night—but a child (**Princess Charlotte Augusta**) was born in January the following year. By that time, though, the couple had separated.

In 1811, after the death of his youngest child, **Princess Amelia (1783–1810),** George III began his final, lengthy descent into insanity, and on 7 February the following year, the prince was appointed **regent.** By the time the king died on 29 January 1820, his son had assumed all the trappings of sovereignty. Caroline, technically now the **queen consort,** wanted her share of those trappings. In June 1820, she returned to Britain after spending six years in Italy, but George succeeded in having her excluded from his coronation ceremony and encouraged Robert Jenkinson, lord Liverpool and prime minister, to introduce parliamentary legislation designed to dissolve the marriage and deprive her of her title. However, Caroline died on 7 August 1821, relieving the new monarch of a major problem.

Enormously unpopular with his subjects because of his reputation for extravagance and promiscuity, the new king inflamed political opponents as a result of his opposition to parliamentary reform and his unwillingness to consider improving the civil rights of Catholics, who were excluded from public office. Moreover, his overindulgence was leading to obesity and declining health, so his reign lasted only a decade. He died at **Windsor Castle** on 26 June 1830 and was buried at **St. George's Chapel**, unlamented by his country. In its obituary, the *Times* newspaper did not pull any punches, recording that "there never was an individual less regretted by his fellows than this deceased king," and that view appears to have persisted over the years, because in a poll conducted by English Heritage in 2008, George was voted the country's "most useless monarch." A man of considerable intelligence and an acknowledged patron of the arts (he supported architect John Nash and recognized Walter Scott's literary genius with a baronetcy, for example), he was unable to control the coarser elements of his personality and eventually alienated most of his acquaintances and his government ministers. Charlotte Augusta, his only legitimate child, died in 1817, so he was succeeded as sovereign by his brother William, duke of Clarence, who ruled as King **William IV**. *See also* AUGUSTA SOPHIA, PRINCESS; BUCKINGHAM PALACE; CARLTON HOUSE; CROWN JEWELS OF THE UNITED KINGDOM; ELIZABETH, PRINCESS, LANDGRAVINE OF HESSE-HOMBURG; FORT BELVEDERE; PRINCE REGENT; ROYAL LODGE.

**GEORGE V (1865–1936).** King George V—although sometimes considered a dull, conventional sovereign when compared with his father, **Edward VII**—introduced an element of informality to the British monarchy and dealt adroitly with the series of crises that punctuated his 26-year reign. He was born at **Marlborough House** (his parents' **London** home) on 3 June 1865, the second son of Albert Edward (then **prince of Wales**) and **Alexandra of Denmark**. As a younger child, he was not expected to succeed to the throne, so in 1877 he embarked on a naval career that took him to British colonies around the world and by 1890 saw him in command of a gunboat.

The **prince**'s promotions were earned rather than simply being a concomitant of royal status, but in 1890, with the sudden death of his older brother (**Prince Albert Victor, duke of Clarence and Avondale**), he became **heir apparent** and had to change direction, preparing for duties as king. On 6 July 1893, at **St. James's Palace**, he married **Mary of Teck** (who had earlier been betrothed to Albert Victor) in a union that ended concerns about the future **succession to the throne** (*see* LOUISE, PRINCESS ROYAL, DUCHESS OF FIFE). In 1900 he went to Australia to open the new parliament (visiting several other British territories, such as Canada, New Zealand, and South Africa, during the trip); from 1901 (when his father became king) he was privy to government papers; and in 1905 and 1908 he traveled abroad again (to India and Canada respectively).

The prince was no intellectual giant but was reasonably experienced in domestic and international diplomacy (and, unlike his father, was untainted by scandal) when he became king in 1910. He had to draw on that experience almost immediately. In 1909, the unelected House of Lords (the upper chamber in Britain's bicameral parliament) was dominated by the Conservative Party and had thrown out the budget prepared by Liberal Party ministers and approved by the House of Commons (the lower house). Angered, the Liberals sought to introduce a bill that would curb the Lords' power and asked the new monarch to create additional members of the upper house in numbers that would ensure the legislation's passage. The request posed a constitutional problem for the king. To deny it would mean rejecting the advice of the country's democratically elected government, but to accept it would mean overriding the will of the Lords, whose duty was to prevent the Commons from taking actions that the country might consider unreasonable. In the end, George reluctantly acceded—but only if the government called an election, as a means of testing public opinion, and won. The Liberals duly gained their election victory in December 1910, but the extra peers were not needed because the threat of their creation was enough to convince the Lords to pass the bill.

World War I, which began in 1914, caused further problems. As a result of the 19th-century propensity for members of Britain's **royal family** to seek Protestant marriage partners in Europe, George numbered several close relatives among his realm's German enemies. Kaiser Wilhelm II was his first cousin, the son of Queen **Victoria**'s eldest daughter, **Victoria, princess royal**; and Charles Edward, the only son of his uncle, **Prince Leopold, duke of Albany**, had enlisted with the German army. Moreover, the sovereign's own father-in-law (Prince Francis of Teck) was of German extraction, and the combination of family members aligned against Britain was enough to make some people question George's commitment to the nation's cause. On 17 July 1917, he responded to the doubters by changing his family name from the German-sounding "Saxe-Coburg and Gotha" to "Windsor" and persuaded family members who were British subjects but had Germanic names to change them too (so, for example, the Battenbergs became the Mountbattens). Supporters of Germany who held British titles had those titles withdrawn, and George himself did much to support the war effort, conferring awards for bravery, touring munitions factories and shipyards, visiting hospitals, and bolstering the morale of troops. (On 21 October 1915, during a visit to the western front, his horse threw him, and he broke his pelvis, an injury from which he never fully recovered.)

In the years after the war, the king maintained his interest in politics, expressing his concern about the violence with which the British government was attempting to suppress demands for home rule in Ireland and voicing his sympathy for participants in the series of strikes that paralyzed the country in 1926. However, his involvement led to strains on his health, as did his heavy smoking, and from 1928, his eldest son, Edward (later King **Edward VIII**) assumed many of his responsibilities. Early in 1936, a cold complicated his chest complaints, and on 20 January, he died at **Sandringham**. His doctor, Lord Penrose of Penn, later admitted to easing the sovereign's passing with an injection of cocaine and morphine. King George V was buried in **St. George's Chapel** at **Windsor Castle**. *See also* CRATHIE CHURCH; CROWN JEWELS OF THE UNITED KINGDOM; FORT BELVEDERE; FROGMORE; GEORGE VI; GEORGE, PRINCE, DUKE OF KENT; HENRY, PRINCE, DUKE OF GLOUCESTER; JOHN, PRINCE; MARY, PRINCESS ROYAL, COUNTESS OF HAREWOOD; PRINCESS; QUEEN'S (OR KING'S) BIRTHDAY HONOURS LIST; ROYAL PHILATELIC COLLECTION; WINDSOR, HOUSE OF.

**GEORGE VI (1895–1952).** George—shy and reserved by nature, with a pronounced stammer—was a reluctant monarch who succeeded to the throne because his older brother, King **Edward VIII**, opted to abdicate rather than give up the woman he loved. He was born at York Cottage on the **Sandringham House** estate on 14 December 1895, the second of six children in the family of George, **duke of York** (later King **George V**), and **Mary of Teck**. Although baptized Albert Frederick Arthur George (the first name chosen to mollify his great-grandmother, Queen **Victoria**, who was annoyed because it had not been given to Edward) and known as "Bertie" within the **royal family**, he chose his last name as his **regnal name** when he became king in 1936, partly because it provided an element of continuity with his father's reign and partly because he felt that sense of continuity might help to restore public confidence in the monarchy after Edward's abdication.

**Prince** Albert was educated at home until 1907, when he joined the Royal Naval College and proved to be a less-than-stellar student, finishing 68th in a class of 68 cadets. Commissioned as a midshipman in 1913, he fought at the Battle of Jutland in 1916 but had to withdraw from further frontline action during World War I as intestinal problems took their toll on his health (his appendix was removed in 1914 and a duodenal ulcer was diagnosed in 1916). After one year with the Royal Air Force, and a further year studying civics, economics, and history at Cambridge University, he began to assume the duties of a royal prince, with a particular preference for tours of dockyards, railways, and other industrial sites.

When King George V died early in 1936, Edward, his eldest son, followed him on the throne but quickly found that his intention to marry American-born divorcee Wallis Simpson (*see* WALLIS, DUCHESS OF WINDSOR) was politically unpalatable, so on 11 December he abdicated, leaving the crown to George VI, who cried when he realized what awaited him and complained (somewhat unfairly) that he had not been trained for a monarchical role. As Britain negotiated with an increasingly militant Germany in the spring and early summer of 1939, the new king traveled to Canada and the United States, the itinerary choreographed to dilute North America's self-imposed isolation from events in Europe. Then, when World War II began in early September, George remained in **London** to face bombing raids with his subjects rather than retreat to a safer, rural location. That decision, coupled with his acceptance of food rationing and other wartime austerities, made him enormously popular, as did his institution of the George Cross and the George Medal as civilian awards for gallantry; his journeys to talk to troops in **France**, Malta, and North Africa; and his willingness to visit cities and factories that had suffered attacks.

The immediate postwar years were marked by the initiation of a process leading toward the independence of most of Britain's colonial dependencies, preparations for a resumption of peacetime manufacturing and trade, and the election of a Labour Party government determined to make radical changes to arrangements for the provision of education, health care, housing, and other aspects of social welfare. Although the king was unsympathetic to many aspects of his ministers' welfare-state programs, he refrained from intervention and concentrated on cementing new relationships with former colonial territories. However, the stresses of his wartime activities, coupled with his heavy smoking, told on his health. In 1950, he was diagnosed with lung cancer and on 6 February 1952 he died in his sleep at Sandringham. His remains were interred at **St. George's Chapel** in **Windsor Castle**.

On 26 April 1923, George—then duke of York—married Elizabeth Bowes-Lyon (*see* ELIZABETH, THE QUEEN MOTHER) in **Westminster Abbey**. They had two daughters—**Princess** Elizabeth (who succeeded her father as Queen **Elizabeth II**) and **Princess Margaret, countess of Snowdon**. As monarch, George VI reigned in abnormal times, but he died a much respected man because he made little effort to influence political processes and much effort to associate himself with his people's wartime sufferings. *See also* BALMORAL CASTLE; COMMONWEALTH REALM; CROWN JEWELS OF THE UNITED KINGDOM; ROYAL LODGE; WHITE LODGE.

**GEORGE, DUKE OF BEDFORD (1477–1479).** George, the youngest of the three sons of **Edward IV** and **Elizabeth Woodville**, was born at **Windsor Castle** in March 1477 but died just two years later, probably of bubonic plague. He was buried within the castle walls, in **St. George's Chapel**.

**GEORGE, PRINCE, DUKE OF KENT (1902–1942). Prince** George was the fourth son and fifth child of George, **duke of York** (later King **George V**) and **Mary of Teck**. A tearaway in his youth, he settled down somewhat after marriage but died an untimely death in an aircraft accident. Born at York Cottage, on the **Sandringham** estate, he—with his brother, **Prince Henry, duke of Gloucester**—was the first member of the **royal family** to be educated at school (St. Peter's Court, in Broadstairs, Kent) rather than by private tutors, and proved intelligent but lacking in diligence. Three years at naval college (1917–20) were followed by seven on board ship, principally with the Royal Navy's Mediterranean fleet, but for some time after that, the young prince had no permanent focus as he visited Europe and Canada and then worked as a civil servant in the Foreign Office and the Home Office. A handsome man with wealth and status, he inevitably attracted admirers and had numerous affairs, some of them homosexual, with partners who allegedly included entertainer Jessie Matthews and Indira Raje (the maharani of Cooch Behar) as well as art historian Anthony Blunt, who was exposed as a Russian agent in 1979.

The prince also became addicted to cocaine and morphine, but his marriage in **Westminster Abbey** on 29 November 1934 to **Princess Marina**, daughter of Prince Nicholas of Greece and Denmark, provided some stability. He inherited Coppins, a country home near Iver, west of **London**, from his aunt, **Princess Victoria**, who died in 1935; made it his home; raised two sons (**Prince Edward, duke of Kent**, and **Prince Michael of Kent**) and a daughter (**Princess Alexandra**); augmented his considerable collection of artwork; and carried out a number of public duties. When World War II began in 1939, plans to make the duke **governor-general** of Australia were abandoned, and he returned to naval duties. He transferred to the Royal Air Force the following year, but on 25 August 1942, he was killed when a flying boat in which he was a passenger crashed into a hillside at Dunbeath in northern Scotland. Several authors have advanced conspiracy theories to explain the "accident," suggesting that it was planned by British intelligence services, who believed that Kent wanted to seek peace with Germany, but there is no firm evidence to support any of the claims. The duke was initially buried in **St. George's Chapel** at **Windsor Castle**, but in 1968 his remains were reinterred in the royal burial ground at **Frogmore** beside those of his wife.

**GEORGE, PRINCE OF DENMARK (1653–1708).** George, consort of Queen **Anne**, was a chronic asthmatic with few intellectual gifts, but he and his wife were devoted to each other. He was born in Copenhagen on 2 April 1653, the sixth child of King Frederick III of Denmark and his wife, Sophie Amalie. When he married Anne at **St. James's Palace** on 28 July 1683, there was no expectation that she would ever be queen because her uncle, King

**Charles II**, was on the throne, and her father, James, **duke of York** (later King **James VII of Scotland and II of England**), was **heir apparent**. Moreover, she had an older sister who was ahead of her in the line of **succession to the throne** and later became Queen **Mary II**. The wedding, however, was well received by King Louis XIV of **France** because, as Denmark and France were allies against the Netherlands, it helped to counterbalance the political implications of Mary's marriage to William of Orange (later **William III of England and II of Scotland**).

When James became king in 1685, he added George to the ranks of his closest political advisors, but that did not prevent his son-in-law from defecting to William's camp during the **Glorious Revolution** of 1688–89. (There is a story that when news of a defection reached James's court, George would look astonished and say, "*Est-il possible?*" ["Is it possible?" in French]. When he heard that George, too, had changed his allegiance, James allegedly commented, "So, '*Est-il possible*' has gone as well.") The Danish prince was rewarded for his fickleness with the dukedom of Cumberland, but the accord with William, the new monarch, was short lived because the two men soon differed over financial matters, differences made all the greater because William—not of royal blood—was undoubtedly jealous of George's status in the European dynastic hierarchy.

At times after Anne's accession, there were suggestions that George should be made king so that the two could rule in a joint monarchy, much as William and Mary had done. However, the plans were never pursued with much enthusiasm, and although he held many high offices, notably that of lord high admiral, most of the positions were almost entirely symbolic and his influence was limited (although he did participate in parliamentary debates and votes). His wife's failure to produce an heir is also often considered a result of his deficiencies. She conceived 18 times but had 13 miscarriages or stillbirths, and none of the children who survived birth reached adulthood, possibly because George had syphilis, but possibly, too, because Anne suffered from lifelong illness. In the fall of 1708, George's asthma deteriorated, and on 28 October he died in **Kensington Palace**. He was buried in **Westminster Abbey**. *See also* OLDENBURG, ANNE SOPHIA; OLDENBURG, GEORGE; OLDENBURG, MARY (1685–1687); OLDENBURG, MARY (1690); WILLIAM, DUKE OF GLOUCESTER.

**GEORGE WILLIAM, PRINCE (1717–1718).** George William lived for only three months but had a considerable impact on British politics. The fifth child of King **George II** (then **prince of Wales**) and **Caroline of Brandenburg-Ansbach**, he was born at **St. James's Palace**, London, on 3 November 1717. Much to the prince's annoyance, his father, King **George**

I, insisted that one of the royal advisors—Thomas Pelham-Holles, duke of Newcastle and later prime minister—should be made the child's godfather. When tempers flared after the christening service on 28 November, the monarch ordered his son to move out of the palace, leaving the children behind. The Waleses set up home at Leicester House, establishing an alternative court that became a focus of opposition to the king's rule. George William, the first member of the **House of Hanover** to be born in Britain, died at **Kensington Palace** on 6 February the following year and was buried in **Westminster Abbey**. His passing simply fueled the animosity between father and son, with the younger man claiming that the child's death was a result of the enforced separation from his parents.

**GILMAN, LADY ROSE (1980– ).** Lady Rose is the younger daughter, and youngest of three children, in the family of **Prince Richard, duke of Gloucester**, and **Birgitte, duchess of Gloucester**. Born on 1 March 1980 in St. Mary's Hospital, **London** (where her brother, **Alexander Windsor, earl of Ulster**, and sister, **Lady Davina Lewis**, were also delivered), she was educated at St. George's School, Ascot (which Lady Davina also attended), and then took the first steps toward a career in the movie industry, working as an art assistant; sharp-eyed film buffs will find her as Rose Windsor among the credits for the 2007 production of *Harry Potter and the Order of the Phoenix*. On 19 July 2008 at **St. James's Palace**, Lady Rose married George Gilman, the son of a property developer and former director of the Leeds United Football Club. Like her siblings, she is not required to carry out royal duties and prefers to keep out of the press limelight, apparently rejecting a lucrative bid by *Hello!* magazine to cover her wedding.

**GIRIC (?–c889).** Some scholars suggest that, in 878, Giric killed **Áed** (the king of the Picts) and took the throne for himself. However, nothing certain is known of Giric's parentage, and other writers claim that he may have been acting as a **regent** for **Eochaid**, the grandson of **Kenneth MacAlpin**, who united the Pictish communities with the kingdom of Dalriada in c843. There are also reports that Giric extended his control southward into areas of Cumbria and Northumberland (both now in northern England) and that he made several concessions to the church in order to win popularity. One source records that he was banished from the kingdom soon after a solar eclipse in 885, without identifying a reason for the exile, but another source records that he died in 889 and was buried at Iona. For reasons still not evident, chroniclers in the 12th through the 16th century refer to him as Gregory the Great, painting an entirely fictitious picture of extensive conquests in England and Ireland. **Donald II** succeeded Giric as king.

**GLORIOUS REVOLUTION (1688–1689).** The "Glorious Revolution" that resulted in the ousting of King **James VII of Scotland and II of England** finally established the supremacy of parliament over monarchy in England. James succeeded to the throne in 1685 on the death of his older brother, King **Charles II**, because Charles left no legitimate children, but many of his subjects had doubts about the accession because the new monarch was a Roman Catholic married to a Roman Catholic queen consort (**Mary of Modena**). These doubts increased as James gave Catholics positions of command in his expanded army and then, in 1687, attempted to suspend the laws discriminating against individuals who refused to worship in the **Church of England**. Matters came to a head in April the following year, when James commanded all clerics to read an edict in their churches regarding freedom of worship. Many of the priests objected because there was no guarantee that the Anglican Church would remain the national church, and seven bishops who asked the king to withdraw the measure were prosecuted for seditious libel (but were acquitted by the courts). Then, in June 1688, Mary gave birth to her first son—an event suggesting to the dissidents that the monarch's religious policies would be continued by the generation that followed him.

A group of leading nobles and churchmen wrote to William of Orange (the husband of James's daughter Mary by his earlier marriage to **Anne Hyde**) and asked him for help. William, considered the champion of the Protestant faith in Europe, was more than willing to respond, hoping that his assistance would lead to English support in his dispute with **France**, and arrived at Torbay with an army on 5 November. As the invaders advanced, James's followers melted away—even his daughter, Anne (later Queen **Anne**), dissociated herself from his policies—and in December he fled to France. Parliament, after considerable debate, decided that his action meant he had abdicated, and on 13 February 1689, the crown passed jointly to William and Mary, who ruled as **William III** and **Mary II**. Scotland had taken no part in the rebellion, but in April, that country's parliament, too, declared its throne vacant, and on 11 May, William and Mary accepted their invitation to rule as William II and Mary II.

The English offer to the new king and queen was not made without conditions. In December 1689, parliament passed a **Bill of Rights** that severely circumscribed the monarch's powers, barred Roman Catholics from the line of **succession to the throne**, and forbade the sovereign from suspending laws that had been passed legally. Since then, the power of the monarchy has declined further, and the power of parliament has increased. By the early 21st century, the rights retained by the monarch were very limited.

The events of 1688–89 are sometimes referred to as "the revolution of 1688" (because that phrase avoids the value judgments implicit in the use of

"Glorious") and sometimes as "the Bloodless Revolution" (because conflict in England was limited). Most modern historians conclude that the results were positive, spelling an end to absolute monarchy (*see* DIVINE RIGHT OF KINGS) and opening the way to parliamentary democracy. Some, however, take the view that James was wronged and that William was an opportunist. The latter view was certainly common at the time, particularly in Scotland, so it was only after the defeat of James's grandson, **Charles Edward Stuart** (Bonnie **Prince** Charlie) at **Culloden** in 1746 that the exiled monarch's descendants finally gave up military efforts to retrieve the crowns. *See also* CLAIM OF RIGHT; JACOBITE REBELLIONS.

**GODGIFU (c1004–c1049).** By her first husband (Drogo—or Dreux—count of Amiens and the Vexin), Godgifu (or Goda), the only daughter of **Aethelred the Unready** and **Emma of Normandy**, had two sons—Ralph, earl of Hereford, and Walter, who succeeded to his father's titles. A second marriage, to Eustace, count of Boulogne, in 1016 (the year after Drogo died while on a pilgrimage to Jerusalem) was childless, but Eustace used the union to cement military alliances with Godgifu's sons and with her brother, **Edward the Confessor**. The date of Godgifu's death is not known, but it had certainly occurred by 1049, when Eustace married Ida of Lorraine in yet another effort to shore up his power.

**GODWIN, EARL OF WESSEX (c1001–1053).** Godwin (or Godwine), father of King **Harold II**, was one of the most powerful magnates in England during the second quarter of the 11th century. Believed by some historians to be the son of Wulfnoth Cild, an Anglo-Saxon thegn (or nobleman), he initially helped King **Edmund II** to resist Danish incursions into England but eventually allied with King **Canute**, became one of his principal advisors, and married his sister, Thyra Sveinsdóttir.

In the unsettled political conditions that followed Canute's death in 1035, Godwin was implicated in the death of **Aelfred Aetheling**, one of several claimants to the throne. Then, in 1045, he married **Edith of Wessex**, his elder daughter, to **Edward the Confessor**, who had been made king the previous year, and over the remainder of the decade he continued to extend his power base in southern England. The earl's growing influence inevitably created political tensions that came to a head in 1051, when he refused to obey an order from the monarch to "carry war into Kent" because the people of Dover had attacked Eustace, count of Boulogne and husband of Goda, Edward's sister.

Edward responded by expelling Godwin and his sons by his second wife (**Gytha Thorkelsdóttir**) from the kingdom, but the nobleman's following was so strong that the exiles (who included Harold) were able to return the following year. Godwin died suddenly on 12 April 1053, some reports suggesting that he suffered a stroke while attending a banquet, others less plausibly that he choked on a piece of bread. He was buried at **Winchester**, and Harold succeeded to the earldom.

**GODWINSON, HAROLD (c1020–1066).** *See* HAROLD II.

**GOVERNOR-GENERAL.** In **commonwealth realms** (the 16 members of the Commonwealth of Nations that recognize the British monarch as their head of state), the sovereign is represented by a governor-general. Appointments are made by the crown after receiving advice from the realm's prime minister, and the individual selected performs all of the monarch's ceremonial and constitutional functions within the territory. Until the 1920s, governors-general were British citizens, but nowadays they are more likely to be distinguished public servants from the country where they carry out their duties. Members of the **royal family** who have held the post include John Campbell, marquess of Lorne and husband of **Princess Louise, duchess of Argyll** (Canada, 1878–83); **Prince Arthur, duke of Connaught and Strathearn** (Canada, 1911–16) and his son, also **Prince** Arthur (South Africa, 1920–23); and **Prince Henry, duke of Gloucester** (Australia, 1945–47).

**GREENWICH PALACE.** *See* PLACENTIA, PALACE OF.

**GREENWICH, TREATY OF (1543).** On 1 July 1543, representatives of England and Scotland, meeting in the **Palace of Placentia** at Greenwich, signed a treaty that was intended to ensure peace between the two countries, in part by betrothing **Mary, the infant queen of Scots**, to Edward (later King **Edward VI**), the five-year-old heir to England's King **Henry VIII**. Henry had long wanted to unite the independent kingdoms, partly in order to expand his realm, partly in order to put an end to centuries of finance-consuming war with his northern neighbor, and partly to destroy the Scots' military alliance with **France**, another of England's ancient enemies. In the summer of 1543, the tide appeared to be running in his favor because several Scottish noblemen, taken captive at the Battle of Solway Moss in November the previous year, were willing to support the agreement in return for their freedom.

However, the monarch's ambitions foundered on the rocks of Scottish distrust of English intentions. Although the provisions of the Greenwich treaty allowed the Scots to retain their distinctive legal system, there were many influential nobles and churchmen who believed that Henry's ultimate aim was the imposition of English interests over Scottish affairs, so on 11

December 1543, the Scottish parliament refused to ratify the agreement. Henry sought to impose his will through a process that novelist Walter Scott termed "the rough wooing," launching hundreds of cross-border raids, ransacking southern Scotland, destroying villages, and killing livestock in a campaign that continued, with greater intensity, after his death in 1547. Mary's mother—**Mary of Guise**—turned to her native France, Scotland's long-term ally, for help, agreeing to a proposal from King Henry II that her daughter should be betrothed to his son (later **Francis II**), with the clear intention that the two countries should eventually be united under a single monarch. After Mary, queen of Scots, was dispatched to the French court in August 1548, her countrymen, with French military aid, were able to resist efforts to subdue them until, in 1551, the English agreed to a peace (through the Treaty of Norham), even though their aspirations for political and marital unions were still unfulfilled.

**GREY, JANE (1536/7–1554).** Jane Grey was "queen" of England for nine days in 1553—the shortest reign of any of the country's monarchs. The eldest of the three daughters of Henry Grey, marquess of Dorset, and his wife, Frances Brandon, she was born at Bradgate Park (Leicestershire), probably in October 1537, but perhaps earlier in the year or in 1536. An intelligent child, she became an accomplished linguist, able to read Greek and Latin and acquiring a working knowledge of Arabic, Chaldee, and Hebrew as well as of French and Italian.

At the age of nine, Jane was sent to live with **Catherine Parr**, who had married King **Henry VIII** in 1543. After Henry's death in 1547, the **queen dowager** took a previous love—Thomas, lord Seymour (brother of **Jane Seymour**, Henry's third wife and the mother of King **Edward VI**)—as her fourth husband, but she died the following year only days after giving birth to a daughter. Thomas proposed a marriage between Jane and Edward, but the plan was abandoned after Seymour was **beheaded** for treason in 1549.

In October 1551, the staunchly Protestant Henry Grey was created duke of Suffolk, a reward for supporting John Dudley, duke of Northumberland, who was the de facto ruler of England, exercising considerable influence over the young Edward and making major decisions on his behalf. During the winter of 1552–53, the king fell ill, and as his health declined, the two nobles (with the enthusiastic approval of Frances Brandon) negotiated a marriage between Jane and **Guildford (or Guilford) Dudley**, the duke's youngest child, that was designed primarily to enhance their own power. Henry VIII had left a will, given legislative authority through the **Succession to the Crown Act of 1543**, which declared that if Edward died childless and with no brothers or half-brothers, the throne would go to Mary, his half-sister. However, Edward was a convinced Protestant, and Mary was an equally convinced Roman Catholic.

Jane and Guildford wed at Durham House (the former **London** residence of the bishops of Durham) on 21 or 25 May 1553. The 15-year-old king, probably acting on Northumberland's advice, then prepared a will that attempted to overturn his father's wishes by declaring that the line of succession should be through the descendants of his paternal aunt, **Mary Tudor, queen of France**—a declaration that effectively nominated his cousin, the staunchly Protestant Jane Grey, as the next monarch of England because Henry Brandon, Mary Tudor's only son, had died unmarried in 1834, and Frances, his younger sister, was Jane's mother.

The role was one that Jane did not seek, and when told the news of Edward's death on 6 July and of her own future, she fainted and needed much persuasion before she would agree to become sovereign. John Dudley, pursuing his own interests, proclaimed her queen four days later, but there were many influential citizens who opposed the move. Some believed that the laws of parliament (specifically the Succession to the Crown Act) should be observed, some felt that the wishes of Henry VIII should be respected, some simply sympathized with Mary, and others sympathized with her religious convictions. As support for Henry's daughter grew, even Jane's father declared her the rightful queen (as **Mary I**), and she entered London in a triumphal procession on 19 July, taking Jane and the Dudleys captive. Northumberland was executed on 21 August. Jane and Guildford were tried on charges of treason in November and found guilty. Initially their lives were spared, but Suffolk's participation in Thomas **Wyatt's rebellion** against the new sovereign early the following year sealed their fate, and they were beheaded on 12 February 1554, Jane still only 16 or 17 and her husband just a few months older.

**GRUOCH (?-?).** Gruoch was the wife of **Macbeth** (king of Scots from 1040 to 1057) and mother of **Lulach** (who ruled for a few months in 1057–58). The daughter of Boite (also known as Boedhe and Bodhe), son of either King **Kenneth II** or King **Kenneth III**, she was first married to Gille Coemgáin, the mormaer (or earl) of Moray, with whom she had Lulach. In 1020, Gille Coemgáin may have been responsible for the death of **Findláech of Moray**, Macbeth's father, and in 1032 was trapped in a building and burned alive, along with about 50 of his supporters. The likely culprits were **Malcolm II** (attempting to eliminate a rival) and Macbeth (avenging his father's death). Shortly after the mass murder, Macbeth married Gruoch, possibly to protect the widow of a kinsman but possibly also because she was of royal blood. The second marriage yielded no children.

Gruoch's reputation as the scheming Lady Macbeth is based solely on the play written by William Shakespeare in the early 17th century because contemporary writings give no indication of her behavior or her personality. The dates and locations of her birth and death are unknown.

**GUARDIANS OF SCOTLAND.** From 1286 to 1290 (while **Margaret of Norway** was too young to rule), from 1290 to 1292 (while the **succession to the throne** was disputed after her death), from 1329 to 1341 (during the minority and exile of King **David II**), and from 1346 to 1357 (during David's imprisonment in England), representatives of Scotland's senior churchmen and nobles ruled the country as **regents** and were known as Guardians of Scotland. From 1296 to 1306, while **Edward I** attempted to incorporate Scotland within his English kingdom, the leaders of the resistance movement—including William Wallace and Robert the Bruce (later **Robert I**)—were given the same title, as, frequently, were the regents who controlled the territory during the minorities of other monarchs.

**GUNHILDA OF DENMARK (c1020–1038).** Gunhilda was the daughter of King **Canute** (who ruled England from 1016 to 1035) and **Emma of Normandy**, his second wife. On 10 June 1036, she was married at Nijmegen to Henry (later Henry III of Germany and Holy Roman Emperor) as part of a pact in which Conrad II, the Holy Roman Emperor, ceded strategically important areas of Schleswig and Pomerania to her father. The couple had one child—Beatrice, born in 1037—but the union was short lived because Gunhilda (who was known as Kunigunde after her wedding) took ill and died on Italy's Adriatic coast on 16 or 18 July 1038 while accompanying her husband and father-in-law on a military campaign.

# H

**HAMPTON COURT PALACE.** When Thomas Wolsey, archbishop of York, began building Hampton Court Palace in 1514, he intended that it would be the finest residence in England. Located on the north bank of a meander in the River Thames, about 12 miles southwest of central **London**, it became famous throughout Europe both for the splendor of its architecture and for the sumptuousness of its furnishings. Initially, it had about 280 rooms, but King **Henry VIII** (to whom Wolsey gifted the property in 1529 in a vain attempt to regain the status lost by his failure to plot the monarch's divorce from **Catherine of Aragon**) added a library and additional kitchens as well as replacing the great hall and refurbishing the chapel. Such was the haste to get the work done that carpenters were employed night and day, working by candlelight after dark. Gardens were laid out, trees were planted, and deer were introduced to the surrounding parkland.

**Edward VI** (Henry's only son to survive infancy) spent most of his 15 years at Hampton Court, and Queen **Mary I** (Edward's half-sister) pined there for four years while she hoped for a child. **Elizabeth I** (another half-sister) conducted affairs of state at the palace but also turned it into a place for festivity and entertainment, with balls, banquets, and hunts to keep her guests amused. **James VI and I**, her successor, continued the tradition but also, more seriously, held a Conference of Divines in 1604 in a fruitless effort to resolve theological differences between the Puritans and the **Church of England** (one of the results of that meeting was the authorized version of the Bible).

Between 1651 and 1658, when England was a republic (*see* COMMONWEALTH OF ENGLAND), Oliver Cromwell lived in the palace, but his simple tastes appealed little to **Charles II** who, after the **restoration of the monarchy** in 1660, acquired lavish furnishings, changed the layout of the gardens, and provided accommodation for his string of courtesans. From 1689, **William III and II** and **Mary II** carried out another extensive building program, commissioning Christopher Wren to redesign the property in accordance with late 17th-century taste by incorporating the French renaissance style. Construction and refurbishment continued until **George III** came to the throne in 1760. He broke with tradition by staying away from Hampton Court (allegedly because he harbored a grudge about being chastised there while he was a child), and his successors followed suit.

Since Queen **Victoria**'s reign, the public has been allowed increasing access to the building. Visitors can now visit many of the rooms, including the enormous Tudor kitchens; Henry VIII's great hall (with a hammer-beam roof over a chamber 97 feet long, 40 feet wide, and 60 feet high); and the state apartments (which contain works of art by Pieter Brueghel, Tintoretto, and others). The grounds contain lawns and formal flower beds, an astronomical clock designed by Nicholas Oursian in 1540, a maze laid out for William III, and a vine planted by landscape gardener Capability Brown in 1768 which still produces grapes. In 1986, fire damaged part of Wren's south wing, but it was restored over the next four years. *See also* ANNE OF DENMARK; AUGUSTA OF SAXE-GOTHA, PRINCESS OF WALES; MARY HENRIETTA, PRINCESS ROYAL, PRINCESS OF ORANGE; PARR, CATHERINE; SEYMOUR, JANE; WINDSOR, LORD FREDERICK.

**HANOVER, HOUSE OF.** The Hanoverians, a German dynasty, occupied the British throne from 1714 to 1901, winning the crown because England was determined that its sovereigns would be staunch Protestants, and losing it because they failed to sire sons. During their two centuries of rule, Britain evolved from an agrarian to an industrial society, and a monarchy that had played an important role in government decision making at the beginning of the period had become a largely ceremonial institution by the end of it.

At the start of the 18th century, **William III of England and II of Scotland** was king but had no children, and his likely successor, later Queen **Anne** (the last monarch from the **House of Stuart**), was in poor health after suffering 13 miscarriages. If both died childless, as seemed likely, and the principles of male primogeniture were followed, the crown would pass to Anne's half-brother, **James Francis Edward Stuart**, son of the exiled King **James VII of Scotland and II of England**. However, like his father, James Stuart was a Roman Catholic, and most Englishmen in positions of power had no desire for Catholic rule, so in 1701 parliament passed an **Act of Settlement** that made **James VI and I**'s granddaughter, **Sophia, electress of Hanover**, the **heiress presumptive**, with the right of succession passing on her death to "the heirs of her body being Protestant."

Sophia predeceased Anne, so when the queen died, she was succeeded by the electress's son, who reigned as King **George I** from 1714 to 1727. He was followed by **George II** (1727–60), **George III** (1760–1820), **George IV** (1820–30), **William IV** (1830–37), and **Victoria** (1837–1901). None of the kings was much loved. The first two were born in Germany and were considered foreigners by many of their subjects, George III suffered from bouts of madness and was held responsible for the conduct of the unpopular war in North America, George IV had a deserved reputation for extravagance and promiscuity, and William IV (also a profligate) was opposed to reforms that would increase parliamentary representation of the growing industrial areas of the country.

William left no legitimate offspring to succeed him—nor did either of his older brothers, King George IV and **Prince Frederick, duke of York and Albany**—so on his death in 1837, the crown passed to his niece, Victoria, the daughter of **Edward, duke of Kent and Strathearn** (King George III's fourth son, born two years after William). Victoria, who restored dignity to the monarchy and was thus much more admired than her predecessors, became the symbol of Britain's 19th-century growth and prosperity. In 1840, she married **Prince Albert of Saxe-Coburg and Gotha**, so when she died in 1901 after the longest reign of any British monarch, the throne passed to her second child and eldest son, King **Edward VII**, who—because he took his father's name—was the first monarch from the **House of Saxe-Coburg and Gotha**.

**HAREFOOT, HAROLD (c1015–1040).** *See* HAROLD I.

**HAROLD I (c1015–1040).** Harold ruled England from 1035 to 1040, initially as co-**regent** for Harthacanute, his half-brother, but then in his own right after he seized the throne. When King **Canute** died on 12 November 1035, Harthacanute (his son by **Emma of Normandy**, whom he had married according to Christian rites in 1017) was declared his heir by the **witan** (the royal council of advisors). However, at the time, the new monarch was occupied with preparations to resist an invasion of his Danish lands by the kings of Norway and Sweden, so he appointed Emma and Harold to act as his regents.

Harold was Canute's son by a "handfast" marriage to **Aelfgifu of Northampton** (handfast ceremonies were non-Christian trysts that involved tying the couple's wrists together, a practice that gave rise to the modern saying that a bride and groom are "tying the knot"). In 1036, while the two regents bitterly disputed control of the realm, Harold's followers blinded **Aelfred Aetheling**—Emma's son by **Aethelred the Unready**, her previous husband—to ensure that he would not attempt to usurp the crown. Aelfred died from the wounds, and the following year, Emma, fearing for her life, fled to Bruges on the European mainland. Harold seized control of the country's treasury and, according to the ***Anglo-Saxon Chronicle***, "was everywhere chosen king."

Little is known of the new monarch's reign except that he earned the nickname "Harefoot" because of his fleetness of foot and that he protected

England against incursions from Scotland and Wales. He died in Oxford on 17 March 1040, but the cause of his passing remains uncertain, some writers believing that he suffered a stroke, others that he was murdered. At the time, Harthacanute was raising an army to invade England and reclaim his kingdom. When he arrived a few weeks later, he took Harold's body from its burial place at Westminster, cut the head off, and threw the corpse into the marshes alongside the River Thames. However, Harold's followers retrieved the remains and reburied them in St. Clement Danes Church, which now lies in the heart of **London**.

**HAROLD II (c1020–1066).** Harold succeeded **Edward the Confessor** as king of England in 1066 but ruled for only nine months before succumbing to the superior military power of Duke William of Normandy (*see* WILLIAM I OF ENGLAND). The second of about 10 children born to **Godwin, earl of Wessex**, the strongest and most influential of the country's noblemen, and **Gytha Thorkelsdóttir**, his second wife, he played a large part in subduing Welsh resistance to English overlordship in 1062–63 and helped quell rebellion in Northumberland in 1065.

There were long-running tensions between Edward and the Godwins (the king had tried to banish the family from his realm in 1051 but was forced to return its forfeited estates the following year), but in 1064, according to some sources, the monarch sent Harold to Normandy with a message indicating that Edward was nominating William, his second cousin once removed, as his preferred successor. In practice, there may have been other reasons for the journey—Harold may have been attempting to negotiate the release of family members who were being held hostage or he may have been assessing support for his own claim to the throne—but whatever the rationale, his ship was wrecked at Ponthieu on the Normandy coast and he was taken prisoner. Some writers suggest that William then made Harold agree to support Edward's nomination, others that the men made a pact that Wulfnoth, Harold's younger brother who was being held captive by the duke, would be freed if William became king.

Two years later, as Edward lay on his deathbed, he pointed to Harold, and several of the nobles in the chamber interpreted this as a sign that he was indicating his choice of successor. Although other claimants, including **Edgar Aetheling** (Edward's great-nephew) and Harald Hardråde, king of Norway, had their supporters, Harold was chosen and was crowned in **Westminster Abbey** on 6 January 1066 at the first **coronation** ceremony to be held in the building. Although Duke William clearly interpreted Harold's acceptance of the throne as a sign of a broken oath, the Norwegian monarch was the first to take action. Allying with Tostig, another of Harold's brothers, and promising him a third of the kingdom in return for support, he mounted an invasion with a 15,000-man army, but after some initial success both men were killed by Harold's troops at the **Battle of Stamford Bridge** on 25 September.

Meanwhile, William was taking advantage of the diversion to gather his own invasion force. Three days after Stamford Bridge, he landed at Pevensey on the unfortified southern coast of England with around 7,000 soldiers ferried across the English Channel on 600 ships. Harold was forced to march his army some 250 miles, from Stamford Bridge to the south coast where William was encamped, and on 14 October, his tired, battle-weary followers were routed by the fresher Norman archers, cavalry, and infantry (*see* HASTINGS, BATTLE OF).

According to tradition, Harold died when an arrow pierced his eye, but there is no way of confirming this tale. Norman reports suggest that he was buried in a grave overlooking the sea, but other sources indicate that he may have been interred at Waltham Abbey, which he had refounded in 1060 (there are stories that he had been cured of a form of paralysis after praying at the site). However, in 1954, a Saxon-built stone sarcophagus containing a body with its head and part of a leg missing were found at Bosham, Harold's birthplace. Some scholars believe the relics may be Harold's remains, but in 2004 the chancellor of the Diocese of Chichester refused to sanction a forensic examination on the grounds that DNA testing would be futile and that "the vast preponderance of academic opinion" pointed to Harold being buried at Waltham. *See also* ADELIZA OF NORMANDY; EALDGYTH OF MERCIA; EDITH OF WESSEX; EDITH SWAN-NECK; ISABELLA OF FRANCE.

**HARRY, PRINCE (1984– ).** *See* HENRY OF WALES, PRINCE.

**HARTHACANUTE (c1018–1042).** Harthacanute, who reigned from 1040 to 1042, was the last **Viking monarch** of England. The only son of King **Canute** and **Emma of Normandy**, he was named heir by his father but was in Denmark preparing for war with Norway when the monarch died in 1035. On the advice of the English nobles, he appointed Emma co-**regent** in his absence along with Harold (later **Harold I**), his half-brother as a result of Canute's liaison with **Aelfgifu of Northampton**. That arrangement lasted for only a few months, however, because the pair squabbled incessantly, and in 1037 Emma fled to safety in Flanders, leaving Harold to assume the throne.

By 1039, the Norwegian threat to Denmark had been averted, so Harthacanute began amassing an invasion force and turned his attention to the task of regaining his English crown. The warriors were not needed, though, because Harold died on 17 March 1040, before the invasion could be mounted, and

England's leaders invited Harthacanute to return, greeting him at Sandwich on the southeast coast on 17 June.

Reactions to the new ruler were not uniformly positive. Harthacanute undoubtedly pleased many of his subjects by inviting Edward (later **Edward the Confessor**), Emma's son from her first marriage to **Aethelred the Unready**, to return from exile in Normandy and join his household. On the other hand, he certainly annoyed supporters of his predecessor by taking Harold's body from its resting place in **Westminster Abbey** and throwing it into the marshes alongside the River Thames. Moreover, he taxed his people very heavily in order to provide funds for his navy, and the *Anglo-Saxon Chronicle* reports that "he never accomplished anything kingly," so his death on 8 June 1042 at Lambeth, a settlement on the south bank of the Thames, was almost certainly greeted with relief in many quarters. Harthacanute was buried at **Winchester**, where his father lay and where his mother was to join him a decade later, and because he left no son to succeed him, Edward took the throne, restoring the Anglo-Saxon (and principally **Wessex**) line of succession.

Harthacanute is also known as Hardecanute, Hardicanute, and Harthacnut. In addition to ruling England, he was king of Denmark from 1035 to 1042. *See also* STAMFORD BRIDGE, BATTLE OF.

**HASTINGS, BATTLE OF (14 October 1066).** William the Conqueror's victory at the Battle of Hastings on 14 October 1066 sealed his campaign to secure the English crown and changed the course of British history.

Just before **Edward the Confessor**, England's king, died on 5 January that year, he had named Harold Godwinson (later **Harold II**)—his brother-in-law and the most powerful man in the realm—as his heir. Approval was not unanimous. Some influential nobles supported **Edgar Aetheling**, grandson of King **Edmund II**, even though he was still a child, and William himself claimed that Edward had promised him the position several years earlier. While Harold was distracted by raids mounted against England's east coast by his brother, Tostig, and Harald Hardråde, king of Norway, William gathered an army in Normandy, sailed his troops across the English Channel, and landed at Pevensey on 28 September.

Harold heard of the invasion just after a bloody battle at **Stamford Bridge** near York, in which Tostig and Harald were slain. He marched 250 miles south to Hastings, where William was encamped, and arrived late on 13 October, his troops mentally and physically exhausted. The following morning, before the English force had fully organized itself for conflict, the Normans attacked. Initially Harold's lines held, but William's better-trained archers and cavalry eventually wore them down. Late in the day, Harold himself was killed—felled, according to legend, by an arrow to the eye—and the invading force moved on to occupy **London**, where on 25 December William was crowned as **William I of England**. His **coronation** initiated a period of strong Norman rule (*see* NORMANDY, HOUSE OF) that replaced the Anglo-Saxon regime and lasted until the 13th century, when it in turn was replaced by the **House of Plantagenet**.

**HATFIELD PALACE.** Queen **Elizabeth I** grew up at Hatfield, which had been built by John Morton, bishop of Ely, in the last years of the 15th century and acquired by King **Henry VIII** when he appropriated church properties from 1536. She held her first meeting with her ministers in the building after she succeeded to the throne in 1588, but her successor, **James VI and I**, was less enamored of the place and in 1607 exchanged it for **Theobalds House**, the home of Robert Cecil, earl of Salisbury and his principal advisor. Cecil demolished most of the palace and used the stone to build another residence, which is still the Salisbury family home. The house, which contains many mementoes of Elizabeth's reign, and its extensive gardens are open to the public. *See also* PLANTAGENET, WILLIAM (1337).

**HEIR (OR HEIRESS) APPARENT.** The heir apparent to the throne is the person who cannot be displaced in the line of succession. Because the line is based on primogeniture, with male children taking priority over females, the heir apparent is normally the monarch's eldest son. However, the term would also be applied to the eldest surviving son or to the eldest daughter of a monarch too old to give birth to a son. The present heir apparent is **Charles, prince of Wales**. When he becomes king, the heir apparent will be his son, **Prince William of Wales**. If William should then die before succeeding to the throne and without having children, **Prince Henry (or Harry) of Wales**, his younger brother, would become heir. *See also* DUKE OF CORNWALL; DUKE OF ROTHESAY; HEIR (OR HEIRESS) PRESUMPTIVE; HIGH STEWARD OF SCOTLAND; LORD OF THE ISLES; PRINCE OF WALES; TANISTRY.

**HEIR (OR HEIRESS) PRESUMPTIVE.** The heir or heiress presumptive to the throne is the person who is next in line to the throne but who could be displaced. Succession to the British throne is based on primogeniture, with priority given to males, so the daughter of a reigning monarch would be the heiress presumptive if she was the firstborn child. A brother born after her would become the **heir apparent**. Thus when the unmarried Princess **Victoria** became queen in 1837, her nearest male relative—**Ernest Augustus, king of Hanover** (her father's younger brother)—became heir presumptive.

However, in 1840, she married **Albert of Saxe-Cobourg-Gotha**, and when their first child (**Victoria, princess royal**) was born at the end of that year, the appellation passed to the infant. Then, when the first son, Albert Edward (later King **Edward VII**), was born in 1841, he became the heir apparent, and the "presumptive" descriptor lapsed.

**HELENA, PRINCESS (1846–1923).** *See* CHRISTIAN OF SCHLESWIG-HOLSTEIN, PRINCESS.

**HENRIETTA ANNE, DUCHESS OF ORLÉANS (1644–1670).** Henrietta (also known as Henrietta of England, Henriette, and, familiarly, Minette) was the ninth child of King **Charles I** and **Henrietta Maria of France** and the youngest of the seven who survived infancy. She was born at Bedford House, Exeter, on 16 June 1644 while the city was under siege from Oliver Cromwell's parliamentarian forces and England was rent by civil war, but she was raised at the French court, where her mother eventually found refuge. In 1661, the year after the **restoration of the monarchy** had confirmed her brother, **Charles II**, on the English throne, Anne was married to Philippe, duke of Orléans, at the Palais Royale in Paris.

Philippe, although he initially professed great love for his wife, preferred males for sexual companionship, so Anne looked elsewhere for affection and formed a close attachment to Louis XIV, king of **France** and her husband's elder brother. Charles, also, was very fond of his young sister, so her role as a confidante of two powerful monarchs made her a significant figure in international politics. In particular, she played an important part in negotiations over the Treaty of Dover, signed in 1670, which provided for Anglo-French military action against the Dutch. However, shortly after returning to France, the duchess complained of a pain in her side, and she died on 30 June at the Château de Saint-Cloud, a royal residence west of Paris. She was buried beside her mother in the basilica at Saint-Denis, the traditional place of interment for France's monarchs and their families.

At the time, there was a widespread belief that Anne had been poisoned by one of her husband's associates, but historians now discount these claims, suggesting that peritonitis or a ruptured appendix were more likely the cause of her sudden passing. Despite her differences with her husband, she had three children who survived infancy—Marie Louise (born in 1662), Philippe Charles (1664), and Anne Marie (1669). Contemporary court rumors credited Louis with the fatherhood of both girls. Philippe lived for only two years, and Marie Louise died childless in 1689, but from 1714 to 1720, Anne Marie was, according to supporters of the deposed **House of Stuart**, the **heiress presumptive** to the British crown. After Cardinal **Henry Benedict Stuart**, the last male descendant of King **James VII and II**, died in 1807, scholars traced Jacobite claimants to the throne through Anne Marie, although few of those individuals argued their case themselves. Also, through her marriage to Victor Amadeus, duke of Savoy, Anne Marie became the ancestress of King Louis XV of France and of monarchs of Sardinia and Spain.

**HENRIETTA MARIA OF FRANCE (1609–1669).** Henrietta Maria married King **Charles I** in 1625. Two of her sons (**Charles II** and **James VII and II**) followed their father on the thrones on England, Ireland, and Scotland, and through her youngest daughter (**Henrietta Anne, Duchess of Orléans**), she became the ancestress of monarchs of **France**, Sardinia, and Spain.

The daughter of King Henry IV of France and his second wife, Maria de' Medici, Henrietta Maria was born at the Louvre Palace in Paris on 25 or 26 November 1609 and was wed to Charles at the age of 15 (the ceremony was held by proxy on 11 May 1625 and in person at St. Augustine's Church in Canterbury on 13 June). It was an unpopular match because the French princess was a practicing Roman Catholic, and many of Charles's advisors felt that she would persuade the monarch to relax the penalties on those of his subjects who refused to worship in the Protestant **Church of England**. She also crossed swords frequently with George Villiers, duke of Buckingham, who was one of the king's confidants, but after he was murdered in 1628, husband and wife became much closer, and as civil war approached in 1642, she worked hard to raise funds for his cause.

The money was welcome, but Henrietta Maria's intervention was much resented by the king's Puritan opponents because she invested much of her persuasive effort on Roman Catholic sources, notably her French relatives and Pope Urban VIII. In February 1643, she landed on England's eastern coast, bringing soldiers and arms from Holland, and set about drumming up royalist support in the north of the country. However, in July the following year, as the rebels gained the ascendancy, she had to seek refuge in France, never seeing her husband again before his execution in 1649.

Henrietta Maria returned to England after the **restoration of the monarchy** in 1660 and lived for a few years at **Somerset House** in **London**, but she went back to France in 1665 and spent her last years in the Convent of Visitation that she had founded at Chaillot, west of Paris. She died at the Château de Colombes, near Paris, on 10 September 1669, and her remains were interred at the Cathedral of St. Denis, the traditional burial place of French royalty. She and her husband had nine children together, two of whom were stillborn, a son in 1629 and a daughter in 1639. In 1632, King Charles granted Caecilius Calvert, baron Baltimore, a charter to develop a colony, to be named Maryland after Henrietta Maria, on the east coast

of North America; the territory joined the United States in 1788. *See also*
MARY HENRIETTA, PRINCESS ROYAL, PRINCESS OF ORANGE;
QUEEN MOTHER; QUEEN'S HOUSE, GREENWICH; STUART, ANNE;
STUART, CHARLES, DUKE OF CAMBRIDGE (1660–1661); STUART,
ELIZABETH; STUART, HENRY, DUKE OF GLOUCESTER.

**HENRY I (c1068–1135).** Although Henry could be harsh, his 35-year reign
was marked by administrative, legal, and political change that undoubtedly
benefited his subjects. The fourth, and youngest, son of King **William I of
England** (William the Conqueror) and **Matilda of Flanders**, he was also
known as Henry Beauclerc (the word is derived from the Norman French for
"fine scholar").

As a child with three older brothers, it seemed unlikely that Henry would
ever succeed to his father's throne—a career in the church would have been
a more likely future—but throughout his life he demonstrated a quickness of
wit that ultimately allowed him to win, and hang on to, the kingship. When
the Conqueror died in 1087, his estates were divided, with **Robert Curthose**
(the oldest boy) getting the duchy of Normandy and William (the third son)
getting the kingdom of England and ruling as **William II**. The second son—
**Richard, duke of Bernay**—had been gored by a deer and had bled to death
c1081. In 1096, Robert led his armies on a crusade to the Holy Land, and on
2 August 1100, William was killed while hunting. The two older sons had
agreed that each would be the other's heir, but Henry, who some scholars
believe had a hand in William's death, took advantage of Curthose's absence, seized the royal treasury at **Winchester**, and arranged to have himself
crowned at **Westminster Abbey**, London, just three days after William died.

Robert attempted to claim his inheritance by invading England in 1101, but
Henry managed to talk him into withdrawal in return for an annual payment
of silver that was undoubtedly welcome to a man recently returned from an
expensive military campaign in the eastern Mediterranean and whose financial affairs were in disarray. However, the arrangement lasted only a few
years because Beauclerc, concerned by the extent to which the payments were
diminishing his funds, took his troops across the English Channel in 1106 and
on 28 September captured his brother at the **Battle of Tinchebrai** and then
kept him in prison for the remaining 28 years of his life. The victory reunited
Normandy and England under a single ruler and ended two decades of strife
between the English king and the duchy.

Seven years earlier, as he assumed the crown, Henry had quelled unrest at
home by approving a charter of liberties that purported to cut levels of taxation, end William II's practice of appropriating church revenues, and ensure
that important ecclesiastical offices no longer went to men prepared to pay

for the privilege of holding the post. A series of judicial reforms, notably to the courts, also pleased his supporters because although they undoubtedly added to the authority of the central government and included the installation of Henry's allies as judges, they nevertheless stressed firm and fair sentencing and reduced abuses of power. In addition, financial innovations radically improved the auditing of royal income and expenditures.

Henry also stabilized the northern boundary of his kingdom by marrying Edith, daughter of King **Malcolm III** of Scotland (*see* MATILDA OF SCOTLAND). This union of a Norman to a woman who could trace her ancestry to the kings of **Wessex** pleased his Anglo-Saxon subjects but annoyed the Norman nobles who wanted to keep the bloodline from mainland Europe pure. So, in an effort to appease them, Edith changed her name to Matilda (the name of Henry's mother) when she became queen.

Matilda gave birth to a daughter (**Matilda**, born in 1102) and a son (**William the Aetheling**, born the following year). William was expected to succeed to the throne on his father's death but drowned while still in his teens, creating a crisis for a society in which the ruler was expected to exert military as well as political leadership.

Early in 1121—some two years after Edith's death—Henry, then in his early fifties, took the youthful **Adeliza of Louvain** as his second wife, hoping that she would produce a male heir. After six years, the marriage was still childless (though Beauclerc left more than 20 illegitimate offspring by a string of mistresses), so in 1127 the king made his nobles swear allegiance to his daughter and promise to accept her as monarch when he died. Most, however, later chose to forget that oath. Henry fell victim to food poisoning on 1 December 1135 while visiting his grandchildren in Normandy, but his body was returned to England and buried at Reading Abbey. For the next 18 years, his kingdom was racked by civil war as Matilda and her cousin, **Stephen** of Blois, vied for the monarchy. *See also* ERMENGARDE DE BEAUMONT; MAUD, COUNTESS OF HUNTINGDON; SYBILLA OF NORMANDY; WOODSTOCK PALACE.

**HENRY II (1133–1189).** When in 1154 Henry became the first king from the **House of Plantagenet** to rule England, his country was in a state of near anarchy, weakened by a lengthy civil war and by dissensions stemming from the inability of **Stephen**, his predecessor, to keep a firm grip on the activities of the nobles. However, by the time he died in 1189—and despite spending less than half of his 35-year reign in the realm—he had revolutionized the legal system, restructured the army, and made himself one of the most powerful men in Europe.

Henry, also known as Henry of **Anjou** and Henry Curtmantle (meaning "short cloak"), was born in Le Mans (then part of the county of Maine in northern **France**) on 5 March 1133. His mother, **Matilda**, was the daughter of **Henry I** and, supported by her husband, **Geoffrey, count of Anjou**, claimed that the English throne was rightfully hers after her father's death in 1135, even though the barons preferred Stephen, her cousin. Henry supported her in a failed invasion during 1147 and returned in 1153. Stephen had lost his indomitable wife (**Matilda of Boulogne**) in 1152, and **Eustace, count of Boulogne**, his son and heir, died suddenly only months after Henry's arrival. Depressed by the deaths and ground down by years of conflict, he was in no mood to fight and meekly agreed that Anjou would be his successor.

The young man did not have to wait long for the crown after the pact was sealed because Stephen passed away on 25 October the following year. Almost immediately, Henry set about establishing his authority and restoring order. He demolished fortresses that nobles had built without the king's consent, he raised new taxes from landholders to pay his army, and he reestablished the court system. In the north, he regained Cumberland, Northumberland, and Westmorland, which Stephen had lost to the Scots. In 1171, he annexed Ireland, and in 1174 he captured King **William I of Scotland** at Alnwick and forced him to accept English overlordship.

Attempts to curb the powers of the church were less successful and led to repeated clashes with archbishop of Canterbury Thomas Becket. In the mid-12th century, about 1 in 50 of the population was a cleric. Henry wanted any of those people who were convicted of crimes to be handed over to the secular courts for punishment, but Becket refused to accept such a limitation on the church's jurisdiction and was forced to flee to France for safety. He returned in 1170 but was murdered in Canterbury Cathedral by four of the king's knights on 29 December. Four years later, when he faced attacks on two fronts—from the Scots and from Flanders—Henry did penance for the killing and his military prospects improved, but his policies on ecclesiastical matters were never wholly implemented.

The king's other problems stemmed from relationships with his wife, **Eleanor of Aquitaine**, and his children. Some scholars have argued that the traditional inability of Plantagenet monarchs to control their offspring contributed to their downfall, and Henry was no exception. His marriage to Eleanor in 1152 had given him control of Aquitaine and Gascony, adding to his own estates in Anjou, Normandy, and Maine. The acquisition of the English crown and the annexation of Ireland had contributed further territory, so by the last quarter of the 12th century, he dominated an enormous empire stretching from the Scottish border to the Pyrenees.

Henry attempted to rule by dividing much of the empire among his sons while retaining administrative power for himself, but the spirited youngsters resented their lack of authority. In 1173, while their father was still tainted by his association with the murder of Thomas Becket, three of the boys—Henry (known as **Henry, the young king**); **Geoffrey, duke of Brittany**; and Richard (later **Richard I** and also known as Richard the Lionheart)—rebelled, winning support from Eleanor and from many of the English nobles as well as from the Scots and from Louis VII of France. The alliance was crushed, but trouble flared again in 1181, 1184, and 1189, with Henry ultimately forced to concede much of his land in northern France to Richard. Supported only by one of his illegitimate children, Geoffrey, archbishop of York, he is reported by some sources as claiming that his legitimate sons were the "real bastards."

The constant friction took its toll on the aging monarch, who died in the castle at Chinon, one of the major Anjou settlements, on 6 July 1189. He was buried nearby at **Fontevrault Abbey** and was succeeded by two of his recalcitrant sons—**Richard I** (who reigned from 1189 to 1199) and **John** (who reigned from 1199 to 1216). *See also* BERENGARIA OF NAVARRE; ERMENGARDE DE BEAUMONT; GEOFFREY, COUNT OF NANTES; JOAN, QUEEN OF SICILY; ELEANOR (OR LEONORA), QUEEN OF CASTILE; LASCELLES, GEORGE, EARL OF HAREWOOD; MALCOLM IV; MATILDA, DUCHESS OF SAXONY AND OF BAVARIA; ROYAL COAT OF ARMS; WILLIAM, COUNT OF POITIERS; WILLIAM, COUNT OF POITOU; WINDSOR CASTLE; WOODSTOCK PALACE.

**HENRY III (1207–1272).** Henry was the first child to occupy the English throne since **Aethelred the Unready** nearly 250 years earlier, but despite the turbulent times, he held on to the crown for more than half a century. The son of King **John** and his second wife, **Isabella of Angoulême**, he was born in **Winchester** on 1 October 1207. When his father died on 19 October 1216, the nobles appointed a council of **regents**, headed by William, earl of Pembroke, to rule until he was able to take up the reins himself. At the time, England was in a state of civil war, with Louis (son of King Philip II of **France**) attempting to unseat the **House of Plantagenet** (*see* FIRST BARONS' WAR), and although Pembroke's judicious diplomacy ultimately brought the strife to an end, Henry's reign was marked both by conflict between groups of nobles and by conflict between nobles and the king.

In 1234, Henry began to rule in his own right, initiating a period of weak government that ultimately led to rebellion. In part the problems stemmed from his marriage to **Eleanor of Provence** in 1236 because the monarch's tendency to appoint his new Provençal relatives to positions of authority at the royal court inevitably annoyed ambitious English lords. Also, he adopted an autocratic approach to decision making, he angered his clerics by giving many important church offices to Italians in recompense for papal support during the regency, he issued several decrees discriminating against Jews, and he levied heavy taxes (partly to refill the coffers emptied by his father, partly to finance his military campaigns, and partly to fund his expensive lifestyle).

A lack of military skill added to his problems. Eager to recover the French lands lost by his father, Henry attempted to force King Louis IX of France from Poitou in 1242 but was humiliatingly defeated at the Battle of Saintes. His political skills were equally suspect. In 1254, he made a bargain with Pope Innocent IV to finance the conquest of Sicily in return for the appointment of **Edmund, earl of Lancaster**, his younger son, as king of the island. By 1258, when Pope Alexander IV, Innocent's successor, demanded that Henry meet his financial obligations and threatened him with excommunication if he failed to comply, the royal finances were in a state of shambles, so the pious monarch, threatened with rejection by the church he loved, had to turn to his barons for help. They, however, would agree to cooperate only if the king conceded to a series of major governmental reforms, including the establishment of a **Privy Council** that would act as an advisory body to the sovereign and would consist of 15 people selected by the leading families in the realm (*see* PROVISIONS OF OXFORD; PROVISIONS OF WESTMINSTER).

Increasingly, however, the barons split over the implementation of the changes. Henry added his weight to the conservatives, and Louis IX, called on to mediate, annulled the Oxford agreement. The radical faction, led by Simon de Montfort (who was married to Henry's sister, **Eleanor, countess of Leicester**), refused to accept the decision and went to war (*see* SECOND BARONS' WAR), capturing the king and Edward, his elder son (who was later to rule as **Edward I**), at the Battle of Lewes in 1264. Edward escaped from confinement the following year and raised an army that defeated and killed Simon at Evesham in August 1265. Following the victory, the king too was freed, and from that time on he handed over power to his son, exercising his monarchical duties in name only.

Henry died on 16 November 1272 in **London** and was buried in **Westminster Abbey**. A sensitive, cultured man, he had no aptitude whatsoever for leadership, but he was a great patron of the arts and particularly of church architecture. During his reign, Westminster Abbey was rebuilt, and the plain Norman style of construction was superseded by the flying buttresses and lancet windows of the early English style. *See also* ALEXANDER III; ANJOU, HOUSE OF; BEATRICE, DUCHESS OF BURGUNDY;

EDMUND, EARL OF LANCASTER; ELEANOR OF CASTILE; JOAN OF ENGLAND (1210–1238); MARGARET, QUEEN OF SCOTS; PLANTAGENET, HENRY (c1257); PLANTAGENET, JOHN (c1250–c1256); PLANTAGENET, KATHERINE; PLANTAGENET, RICHARD; PLANTAGENET, WILLIAM (c1251–c1256); WINDSOR CASTLE.

**HENRY IV (c1366–1413).** Son of **John of Gaunt** and his wife, **Blanche, duchess of Lancaster**, Henry was the first member of the **House of Lancaster** to occupy the English throne, ruling from 1399 to 1413. He was born, probably in April 1366, at Bolingbroke Castle in Lincolnshire and was known as Henry Bolingbroke until his accession. His first significant foray into politics occurred in 1387 when, with other nobles, he accused King **Richard II**'s advisors of treason. In 1398, he was exiled after quarrelling with Thomas Mowbray, duke of Norfolk, and seeking to solve the dispute by means of a duel, but he returned the following year to reclaim the family lands that Richard had confiscated after John of Gaunt's death. Richard was extremely unpopular at the time—a result of his policies of high taxation and his disregard for the views of parliament—so Henry was able to rally a great deal of support, and in September 1399, he forced the king to abdicate. Parliament declared its approval and proclaimed Henry sovereign in his stead.

The reign was fraught with rebellion. Determined to preserve as much power as possible for the monarchy, Henry quickly made enemies of those knights who wanted authority for themselves. Some of his opponents argued that he had usurped the throne and that the true king should be Edmund Mortimer, earl of March, who was descended from **Lionel of Antwerp**, Henry's father's older brother. Others rallied to the flag of the Percy family, who were unhappy that lands and money promised in return for protecting England's frontier with Scotland had not materialized. Also, Owain Glyndr led opposition to English rule in Wales.

As tensions rose, Harry Hotspur, the eldest son of Henry Percy, earl of Northumberland, withdrew his allegiance to the king, and on 21 July 1403, he met the royalist army in battle at Shrewsbury, only to die on the field in a defeat that turned into a rout. Then, in 1405, a rebellion in the north of England ended with the **beheadings**, without trial, of Thomas Mowbray, earl of Norfolk, and Richard Scrope, Archbishop of York. By 1406, however, the most serious uprisings in Wales had been quashed (though the troubles continued for the rest of Henry's reign), and in 1408, Henry Percy (Hotspur's father) was killed in the Battle of Bramham Moor, ending his efforts to depose the king. Even so, the monarch's health was deteriorating, and he found himself under attack from parliament over the cost of his government, a cost that was inevitably increased by the problems of keeping the peace. Moreover, his son, Hal (later King **Henry V**), was adding his voice to the chorus of criticism, demanding a greater say in the way the country was being run, and by 1410 he had succeeded in winning seats for several of his allies on the king's council of advisors.

Hal's influence declined after 1411, but he did not have long to wait for real power because Henry died at the home of the abbot of Westminster on 20 March 1413 and was buried (uniquely for an English monarch) in Canterbury Cathedral. A literate and energetic ruler, he had brought an element of stability to his kingdom despite the constant threat of civil upheaval, the perfidy of his son, and the debilitating effects of a disease that scholars believe may have been leprosy or syphilis. *See also* BLANCHE, ELECTRESS PALATINE; HUMPHREY, DUKE OF GLOUCESTER; ISABELLA OF VALOIS; JOAN OF NAVARRE; JOHN OF LANCASTER, DUKE OF BEDFORD; MANN, KINGS OF; MARY DE BOHUN; PHILIPPA, QUEEN OF DENMARK, NORWAY, AND SWEDEN; PLANTAGENET, EDWARD; THOMAS OF LANCASTER, DUKE OF CLARENCE.

**HENRY V (1387–1422).** The eldest son of **Henry IV** and his first wife, **Mary de Bohun**, Henry was king of England from 1413 until his death in 1422 and earned a reputation as a military leader of great accomplishment even though the war he pursued with **France** brought his country few long-term benefits. Born at Monmouth Castle (one of his father's favorite residences) on either 9 August or 16 September in 1386 or 1387, he was commanding part of his father's army at the age of 15 as he attempted to subdue followers of Owain Glyndŵr, who was leading a rebellion against English rule in Wales. From 1408, he was increasingly involved in government affairs as the king's health declined, and from 1410, he was in effect administering the realm even though his policies often differed from those advocated by the reigning monarch.

When Henry succeeded to the throne after his father's death in 1413, he made a concerted effort to regain territories formerly held by England in Anjou (*see* ANJOU, HOUSE OF), **Aquitaine**, and Normandy (*see* NORMANDY, HOUSE OF) and to add other regions of France to his empire. His experience in Wales stood him in good stead. The victory at the Battle of Agincourt in 1415 demonstrated his ability to use a relatively small army with great effect against numerically superior forces, and the Battle of the Seine the following year showed his strong grip on the principles of maritime control.

The reconquest of Normandy, by a long process of attrition from 1417 until early 1419, led to the **Treaty of Troyes** (1420), which recognized Henry as the heir to the French throne, but he never tasted the full fruits of his victory because he died at Bois de Vincennes, near Paris, on 31 August 1422 after contracting dysentery. A hard, stern man, he was often ruthless in his

treatment of opponents (in 1401, for example, he authorized the burning of religious heretics at the stake), but his organizational skills and his bravery were widely recognized. In a comparatively short reign, he took England to a place among the leading nations of Europe. However, it is unlikely that the Treaty of Troyes would have been accepted in the areas of France that remained unconquered, so, had he lived, he would have had to seek additional funds from parliament in order to continue the **Hundred Years' War** and the process of territorial aggrandizement. It is quite likely that such a request would have been turned down because the conquest was taking much longer, and was thus becoming much more expensive, than anticipated. *See also* CATHERINE OF VALOIS; DUKE OF CORNWALL; HENRY VI; JOAN OF NAVARRE; SHEEN PALACE.

**HENRY V, KING OF GERMANY AND HOLY ROMAN EMPEROR (1086–1125).** Henry was the first husband of **Matilda**, who contested the English crown with **Stephen** from 1141 until 1147. The couple married at Worms on 6 or 7 January 1114, cementing a military alliance that Matilda's father, King **Henry I**, hoped would discourage the French from attempting to annex his estates in Normandy. One source suggests that the marital union produced one child, but if so the baby did not survive beyond infancy.

Henry—the second son of Henry IV, holy Roman emperor, and Bertha of Savoy (also known as Bertha of Turin)—was born on 11 August 1086 and crowned king of Germany on 6 January 1099. Six years later, he forced his father to abdicate but bickered with Vatican authorities over church reforms and so was not invested as emperor until he took his armies to Rome and forced Pope Paschal II to preside over an investiture in 1111. Although he was a skillful (and unscrupulous) politician, Henry also had trouble establishing his authority in Germany, where several nobles opposed his rule. With the support of his father-in-law, he attempted to exert control over Flanders and in 1124 unsuccessfully invaded France. Matilda, who had occasionally acted as his **regent**, returned to the English court after his death in Utrecht on 23 May 1125 and three years later, at the age of 26, was married to the 14-year-old **Geoffrey, count of Anjou**, in yet another attempt by her father to ensure a successful political pact.

**HENRY VI (1421–1471).** The **House of Lancaster**'s 72-year hold on the English crown ended, as it had begun, with a civil war that culminated in the death of a monarch. King Henry VI reigned from 1422 to 1461 and from October 1470 to May 1471, when Edward, son of **Richard, duke of York (1411–1460)**, deposed him, just as **Henry IV** (Henry VI's grandfather) had begun Lancastrian rule by deposing **Richard II** in 1399. He was born at **Windsor Castle** on 6 December 1421, the only child of King **Henry V** and

**Catherine of Valois**, succeeding to the English throne after his father's death on 31 August 1422 and to the French throne (*see* TROYES, TREATY OF) after the death of Charles VI, his maternal grandfather, on 21 October the same year.

Because the new monarch was still an infant, parliament formed a council of **regents** to rule in his name, but by 1437 he was considered old enough to govern for himself. He proved to be a weak and ineffectual head of state, subject to mental breakdowns (possibly a genetic inheritance from Charles VI, who faced similar problems) and with a strong dislike for military conflict. The French territories that his father had acquired were gradually lost, so by 1453, when the **Hundred Years' War** ended, he was left with **Calais** alone. At home, government was delegated to advisors, who were often inefficient and were frequently more concerned with their own aggrandizement than with their country's interests. Moreover, many members of the royal court exploited the king's natural generosity, draining his resources.

Together, the weak monarch, the decline in national prestige that accompanied the loss of the French territories, policy differences between leading nobles, poor leadership, and the sovereign's growing poverty combined to provoke civil upheaval as opposing factions, led by the royalist Edmund Beaufort, duke of Somerset (and grandson of **John of Gaunt**), and the rebel Richard, **duke of York** (Henry's cousin), engaged in a struggle for superiority that culminated in the **Wars of the Roses**. The first battle was fought at **St. Albans** on 22 May 1455, but trouble flared intermittently throughout the years that followed, and on 10 July 1460, Henry himself was taken prisoner at **Northampton**.

With the monarch under his control, York claimed the crown, but parliament refused to give its approval, though the members did force Henry to recognize the powerful duke as his heir. On 30 December, Richard was killed in a struggle with Lancastrian forces at the **Battle of Wakefield**, but his son, Edward, pursued his cause, deposed Henry on 4 March 1461, and ruled as **Edward IV**. Henry fled to Scotland for safety but returned in 1464 to support an abortive Lancastrian rising that failed to make any headway. For the next year he lived in hiding, but in July 1465 he was captured again and was confined within the **Tower of London**.

By the end of the decade, the tide had turned in the monarch's favor. Edward had quarreled with Richard Neville, earl of Warwick and his principal advisor, who allied with **Margaret of Anjou** (Henry's politically astute consort), drove Edward into exile, and restored the king to his throne on 3 October 1470. The peace did not last, however. Edward returned to England with an army in March 1471, captured the monarch, defeated the royalist forces at **Tewkesbury** on 4 May, and again imprisoned Henry in the tower, where he was murdered on 21 May, an act that virtually extinguished the male Lancaster line and thus the opposition to the Yorkist king. Some writers suggest that the killer may have been Richard, duke of Gloucester and later King **Richard III**, but there is no evidence to support this allegation.

Henry was initially buried in Chertsey Abbey, but his remains were reinterred at **St. George's Chapel**, Windsor, in 1485. Although by temperament wholly unsuited to kingship in an age when strong leadership was necessary, he left a positive legacy through the foundation of Eton College in 1440, still one of Britain's most prestigious schools, and King's College in 1441, now a distinguished college of the University of Cambridge. Every year, on the anniversary of his death, representatives of both institutions lay flowers on the altar that marks the place where he was killed. *See also* EDWARD OF LANCASTER, PRINCE OF WALES; PLACENTIA, PALACE OF.

**HENRY VII (1457–1509).** Henry, who claimed the English throne by right of conquest after defeating King **Richard III** at the **Battle of Bosworth Field** in 1485, was the first of five monarchs from the **House of Tudor**, founding a dynasty that ruled the country until the **union of the English and Scottish crowns** in 1603. The only son of **Edmund Tudor, earl of Richmond**, and **Margaret Beaufort**, he was born at Pembroke Castle in Wales on 28 January 1457, nearly three months after his father had died and while his mother was still only 13. Margaret was the great-granddaughter of **John of Gaunt**, whose children by Catherine Swynford were born before the couple married. King **Richard II** legitimized the family, and the legitimization was confirmed by **Henry IV**, but with the stipulation that the Beaufort line be excluded from any right to kingship. Thus, while Henry Tudor's claim to being the rightful sovereign of England was very weak, it was the best that the **House of Lancaster** could muster in opposition to **Edward IV**, Richard III, and the **House of York**.

Henry spent most of his childhood in Brittany, where he was relatively safe from Yorkist hands and was thus able to provide a focus for the Lancastrian cause. The widespread dissent in England after Richard usurped the crown in 1483, as well as the rumors surrounding his part in the death of his predecessor, King **Edward V**, drew additional support to Henry's side. Thus, in 1485, supported by Charles VIII of **France** who resented Richard's claim to the French throne, he was able to land in Pembrokeshire and march an army of 5,000 men toward **London**. On 22 August, at Bosworth Field in Leicestershire, he confronted the royal troops, killed the king, and claimed the throne. Then, on 18 January the following year, he married **Elizabeth of York** (the eldest child of King **Edward IV**), uniting the rival families and ending the **Wars of the Roses**.

The early years of the new monarch's reign were marked by a series of attempts to remove him. In 1486, a poorly organized revolt by Francis, viscount Lovell, was easily put down, but a rebellion led by **Lambert Simnel** was crushed only after the hard-fought **Battle of Stoke Field** in 1487, and **Perkin Warbeck** (with support at various times from Austria, France, the Netherlands, and Scotland) led two invasions before being captured in 1497.

However, despite these distractions, Henry proved to be an able administrator. One of his principal aims was the restoration of order after a long period of civil war, so judges were given additional powers and arrangements were made for the poor to present cases for adjudication. Royal finances had to be improved in order for the court to maintain its dignity and the respect of citizens, so fiscal obligations were enforced rigorously, new foreign markets were sought for English products (Henry helped John Cabot finance his voyages of discovery to North America in 1496, for example), and revenue from customs dues was increased through the encouragement of exports.

Foreign policy, pursued through diplomacy rather than war because it was less expensive, stressed peace with European neighbors. Treaties were signed with France in 1492, with the Netherlands in 1496, and with Scotland in 1499 and were cemented by marriage; **Arthur, prince of Wales** (Henry's eldest son), and, after his death, **Henry VIII** (the second son) were wed to **Catherine of Aragon**; **Margaret Tudor** (the eldest daughter) was married to King **James IV** of Scotland; and **Mary Tudor, queen of France** (the fifth child), was betrothed to Charles of Castile, who was later to become Holy Roman Emperor. In addition, these political and dynastic links were enhanced by trade as commercial treaties with the governments of Denmark, Florence, the Netherlands, Spain, and others greatly benefited the country's economy.

Henry died on 21 April 1509 at **Sheen Palace** (some writers suggest that he never recovered from the loss of his eldest son in 1502 and his wife in 1503) and was buried in **Westminster Abbey**. He had made England one of the richest and most powerful states in Europe, though his success as a ruler was probably as much a reflection of popular desire for strong leadership after a long period of insecurity as of his obsessive attention to detail and his firm control of finances. *See also* CATHERINE OF YORK; CECILY, VISCOUNTESS WELLES; MARY, QUEEN OF SCOTS; PLACENTIA, PALACE OF; STUART, HENRY, LORD DARNLEY; TUDOR, EDMUND, DUKE OF SOMERSET; TUDOR, EDWARD; TUDOR, ELIZABETH; TUDOR, KATHERINE; WINDSOR CASTLE.

**HENRY VIII (1491–1547).** Although he was, in many ways, a despotic, selfish ruler, Henry is one of the best known English monarchs, largely because of his disagreements with the Roman Catholic hierarchy which led to the formation of the **Church of England**, his disputes with such skilled political advisors as Thomas More, his efforts to sire an heir and thus avoid arguments over the **succession to the throne**, and his six marriages. The son of King **Henry VII** and **Elizabeth of York**, he was born at Greenwich Palace (*see* PLACENTIA, PALACE OF) on 28 June 1491. In his youth, he became an accomplished linguist, musician, and sportsman, but as a younger son, he would not have followed his father as sovereign if his older brother, **Arthur, prince of Wales**, had not died in 1502 while still in his teens.

During the first years of his kingship, from 1509, Henry seemed happy to leave most affairs of state to others. In 1511, and against the advice of most of his court, he joined the Holy League (an anti-French alliance formed by Pope Julius II) and two years later invaded **France**, ostensibly in support of papal authority though primarily in search of territorial gain. But this act was something of an exception, because until about 1527, Thomas Wolsey, the lord chancellor, was undoubtedly in charge of the government in England. Eventually, though, the need to produce an heir encouraged the monarch to take more interest in the details of politics.

Shortly after becoming king, Henry married **Catherine of Aragon**, Arthur's widow. Although she produced a healthy daughter (later Queen **Mary I**) in 1516, Catherine suffered four stillbirths, and as her body grew weaker, it became increasingly unlikely that she would bear a son strong enough to survive into adulthood (in 1511, she had given birth to a boy—**Henry, duke of Cornwall**—but he lived for less than two months). With the possible exception of Empress **Matilda** in the 12th century, England had never had a queen rule as head of state (all of the earlier queens had been consorts of kings), so there was no guarantee that Mary would be acceptable to many of the noble families in the land, and Henry feared dynastic strife if he failed to leave an obvious male successor. Concerned that his country might be torn apart by families fighting for the crown as had happened in the previous century with the **Wars of the Roses**, Henry sought to discard Catherine and replace her with **Anne Boleyn**, who had refused to yield to his sexual advances unless he married her.

The king petitioned Pope Clement VII to annul his marriage, claiming that Catherine and Arthur had actually consummated their union and that the wedding binding him to his sister-in-law was therefore invalid. With Catherine denying this claim, the pope delayed making a decision—not least, perhaps, because he was being held captive by Charles V, the Holy Roman Emperor and Catherine's nephew, and did not want to make a greater enemy of either powerful ruler. Wolsey, who was considered guilty of dereliction of duty because he had failed to persuade Clement to act in Henry's favor, was deprived both of his post and of his estates, even though he had made significant contributions to the realm through improvements to the court system which gave poorer members of society more access to justice, through international diplomacy, and through a restructuring of fiscal measures that included the introduction of a form of income tax.

Initially, Thomas More (Wolsey's successor as lord chancellor) supported the king's case for annulment, but increasingly he too found himself at odds with a monarch apparently ready to challenge the pope's authority, and in 1535 he was executed for treason after allegedly denying that Henry was the legitimate head of the English Church. On or around 25 January 1533, the king married Anne Boleyn in secret, even though legally he was still Catherine's husband. Then, on 23 May 1533, a special court convened solely to consider Henry's first marriage ruled that it was invalid, and five days later Thomas Cranmer (the newly consecrated archbishop of Canterbury) approved the union with a second bride.

On 7 September 1533, the new queen gave birth to a baby girl (later **Elizabeth I**) who was named after Elizabeth of York, her paternal grandmother. In 1534, a **Succession to the Crown Act** formally declared Henry's child by Catherine a bastard, thus making Elizabeth **heiress presumptive**, but by that time the infant's parents were squabbling frequently and the king was still concerned about the lack of an heir. By the end of the year, Henry was considering the possibility of finding yet another wife, and in 1536 Anne was **beheaded**, allegedly guilty of adultery with five men, including George Boleyn, her brother.

Less than two weeks later, Henry married **Jane Seymour**, who died 12 days after giving birth to the male child (later **Edward VI**) the monarch so much wanted. Then, in January 1540, the king married **Anne of Cleves**, sister of the Protestant William, duke of Cleves, who the sovereign's advisors considered would be a useful ally if Europe's Roman Catholic powers launched an attack on England. However, Henry found his new bride unattractive and again sought annulment. Anne was happy to oblige, asserting that the marriage had never been consummated, and the match was dissolved after only seven months.

Within days, the king had found a fifth wife in **Catherine Howard**, a Roman Catholic. However, the Protestant Cranmer feared the influence Howard had on the king and told him stories of Catherine's amoral activities both before and after the marriage, so in 1542 she was beheaded too. In 1543, **Catherine Parr** became Henry's last wife and survived long enough to outlive him.

Perhaps inevitably, Henry's marital exploits have overshadowed other aspects of his reign. He did not intend to launch a campaign for religious change, but his efforts to rid himself of Catherine of Aragon were instrumental in determining the direction of the reformation in England and in leading to the establishment of the Church of England, which is still closely linked to the monarchy (*see* SUPREME GOVERNOR OF THE CHURCH OF ENGLAND). Moreover, Henry's anticlerical policies, including the breakup of the great monastic estates, received a considerable measure of support from a population dissatisfied by corruption among the clergy. In addition, his grants of church land to supporters helped ensure loyalty and thus maintain public order.

Henry also brought Wales into full legal union with England between 1534 and 1536, successfully quelled unrest in Ireland, and created an efficient, effective navy that was later to challenge Spain's dominance of the high seas. On the other hand, he had a large ego and a fiery temper, his decision making was influenced by a belief that his good was England's good and that failings (including the initial failure to produce an heir) were failings of those around him rather than shortcomings of his own, and his supremacy over the church was enforced harshly.

Obese (some reports suggest that he weighed as much as 420 pounds in later life) and suffering from boils, Henry died at **Whitehall Palace**, London, on 28 January 1547 and was buried in **St. George's Chapel** at **Windsor Castle**. The son he had so much desired succeeded him, but Edward was sickly and occupied the throne for only six years, never reaching an age at which he could exert authority over the powerful nobles and churchmen who competed for power at the royal court. *See also* ANNE, COUNTESS OF SURREY; DEFENDER OF THE FAITH; ELTHAM PALACE; GREENWICH, TREATY OF; HAMPTON COURT PALACE; MARY OF GUISE; MARY, QUEEN OF SCOTS; NONSUCH PALACE; OATLANDS PALACE; ST. JAMES'S PALACE; SUCCESSION TO THE CROWN ACT (1543); SUCCESSION TO THE CROWN: MARRIAGE ACT; SUPREMACY, ACT OF (1534); UNION OF THE CROWNS; WINDSOR, TREATY OF.

**HENRY BEAUCLERC (c1068–1135).** *See* HENRY I.

**HENRY BOLINGBROKE (c1366–1413).** *See* HENRY IV.

**HENRY CURTMANTLE (1133–1189).** *See* HENRY II.

**HENRY, DUKE OF CORNWALL (1511).** Henry was the second child borne by **Catherine of Aragon** to King **Henry VIII**, following a stillborn daughter in 1510. The boy was born at **Sheen Palace**, near **London**, on 1 January 1511 but died suddenly in the same building on 22 February and was buried in **Westminster Abbey**. Had he survived, the course of British history may have been very different because Catherine's failure to give her husband an heir led both to the annulment of the royal couple's marriage and to a break with Vatican religious authorities that hastened the Protestant Reformation in England.

**HENRY, EARL OF NORTHUMBERLAND (c1114–1152).** As the only surviving son of **David I** and **Maud, countess of Huntingdon**, Henry was expected to succeed to the throne of Scotland when his father died. Named after his paternal uncle, **Henry I** of England, who had been David's patron, he married **Ada de Warenne**, daughter of the earl of Surrey and great-grand-daughter of Henry I of **France**, in 1139 but died on 12 June 1152, predeceasing the monarch by less than a year. He was buried at Kelso Abbey, one of his father's foundations.

Henry and Ada had at least six children, two of whom were to rule their country as **Malcolm IV** and **William I of Scotland**. A third son, David (born c1144), became, like his father, earl of Huntingdon. One daughter (Matilda) died in 1152 while still very young, but others reached maturity. Ada (who is known to have lived until at least 1206) married Floris, count of Holland, in 1162 and had nine children with him, one of whom (also named Floris) was made bishop of Glasgow in 1202. Margaret, born c1140, was married first to Conan, duke of Brittany, and then to Humphrey de Bohun, earl of Hereford; Constance (a daughter by the first marriage) became the wife of **Geoffrey, duke of Brittany**, son of King **Henry II** of England. Some sources indicate that there was a fourth daughter—Isabel or Isabella—who married Robert de Ros, one of the English barons appointed to ensure that King **John** observed the requirements of the **Magna Carta**.

**HENRY OF ANJOU (1133–1189).** *See* HENRY II.

**HENRY OF BATTENBERG, PRINCESS (1857–1944).** *See* BEATRICE (OR HENRY) OF BATTENBERG, PRINCESS (1857–1944).

**HENRY OF WALES, PRINCE (1984– ). Prince** Henry—who is invariably known as "Harry"—is the younger son of **Charles, prince of Wales**, and **Diana, princess of Wales**. He is third in the line of **succession to the throne**, following his father and his elder brother, **Prince William of Wales**.

Harry was born in St. Mary's Hospital, **London**, on 15 September 1984 and was educated (like his brother) at Ludgrove School in Berkshire and at Eton College. After a "gap year" working on a cattle ranch in Australia and at an orphanage in Lesotho, he trained as an army officer at the Royal Military Academy Sandhurst. Then, in 2007, he spent some time on the front line in Afghanistan, until newspapers printed stories of his presence, raising the possibility that he would be targeted by the Taliban and thus put his comrades in danger.

Like all members of the **royal family**, the prince has been under intense media scrutiny throughout his life, with regular press speculation about how his mother's death would affect him. A sportsman with particular enthusiasms for polo, rugby, and skiing and with much youthful energy, he made his teenage mistakes in the glare of the spotlight. In 2002, for example, tabloids carried reports that he had smoked marijuana (his father responded by taking him to a drug rehabilitation center), and in 2004 he allegedly pushed a photographer who was watching him leave a London nightclub. Then, in

2005, he turned up at a fancy dress party wearing a Nazi uniform, prompting the London *Times* to condemn both his choice of clothing and his association with "a group of self-indulgent young men who are apparently content with a life of pointless privilege." The gaffes continued after Harry joined the army; in 2009, he was forced to apologize after the *News of the World* acquired video footage of the prince referring to a Pakistani fellow officer as a "Paki" and another soldier as a "raghead," terms widely considered racist in the United Kingdom.

Apparently, Prince Harry wanted to pursue a career as a professional polo player, but Prince Charles insisted that he must forgo that idea and prepare for a future more useful to his country. He has since undertaken training as a military helicopter pilot. *See also* CLARENCE HOUSE; HIGHGROVE.

**HENRY, PRINCE, DUKE OF GLOUCESTER (1900–1974).** Prince Henry—born on 31 March 1900 at York Cottage on the **Sandringham House** estate in Norfolk—was the third of five sons, and the fourth of six children, in the family of Prince George, **duke of York** (later King **George V**) and **Mary of Teck**. In 1910, his parents broke with royal tradition by sending him (and his brother, **Prince George, duke of Kent**) to St. Peter's Court School in Broadstairs, Kent, where he was educated with other boys, rather than arranging for private tutoring at home. After three years, he transferred to Eton College and then, in 1918, registered for 12 months of training at the Royal Military Academy Sandhurst before studying for a year at Cambridge University. For most of the next quarter century, the prince served with the army but was often frustrated by cautious administrators who refused to let him see active duty because of his royal status.

Prince Henry's military career was interrupted temporarily by the abdication of his older brother, King **Edward VIII**, because he was appointed **regent** designate should King **George VI** (Edward's successor) die and leave his teenage daughter, **Princess** Elizabeth (later Queen **Elizabeth II**), as a very young monarch. However, when World War II began in 1939, he returned to duty, acting as a liaison officer between British and French forces. This post offered more excitement; he was wounded when his car was attacked by enemy aircraft in 1940, he was appointed deputy commander of the 20th Armoured Brigade in 1941, and he was sent on a series of morale-boosting visits to military units in places as far flung as India and North Africa. In 1945, shortly before the war ended, Gloucester was appointed **governor-general** of Australia, a position he occupied for two years with mixed success, his lack of social skills and self-confidence limiting his diplomatic effectiveness but his genuine interest in agriculture commending him to many in the farming community.

From the later 1920s, the prince had juggled royal duties with military commitments. Those duties continued into the early 1960s as he represented

Queen Elizabeth II at domestic and overseas engagements, but in 1965, while he was returning from Sir Winston Churchill's funeral service, his car overturned, causing few physical injuries but initiating a period of declining health. Two strokes in 1968 made matters worse, and on 10 January 1974 he died at Barnwell Manor, his country home in Northamptonshire. He was interred in the royal burial ground at **Frogmore**.

On 6 November 1935, at the Chapel Royal in **St. James's Palace**, the prince married Lady Alice Montagu-Douglas-Scott (*see* ALICE, PRINCESS, DUCHESS OF GLOUCESTER). They had two sons—**Prince William of Gloucester** (who was born on 18 December 1941 and was killed in a flying accident on 28 August 1972) and **Prince Richard of Gloucester** (who was born on 26 August 1944 and succeeded to his father's dukedom).

**HENRY, THE YOUNG KING (1155–1183).** Henry, born on 28 February 1155, was the second eldest of five sons in the family of King **Henry II** and **Eleanor of Aquitaine**. In 1156, on the death of his brother **William, count of Poitiers**, he became heir to his father's extensive estates in England and on the European mainland, a position that was emphasized by his **coronation** as King Henry III on 14 June 1170. Theoretically, he ruled jointly with his father, but the 15-year-old boy was never likely to be given authority by an experienced monarch who wanted to maintain strict control over his nobles and territories.

On 2 November 1160, Henry was married to Marguerite, daughter of King Louis VII of **France**. Marguerite's dowry was the Vexin, an area of northern France that bordered Normandy, which was part of Henry II's realm but had long been a battleground between the French royal house and the **House of Anjou**. In practice, the marriage did nothing to solve the political problem as the area continued to be a source of contention between two powerful dynasties.

By the time he reached his late teens, the younger Henry was at odds with his father, possibly because he was frustrated by his powerlessness, but perhaps, too, because he disagreed with the king's policies and because he needed funds to pay for an expensive lifestyle that allowed him to travel with his knights around Europe, from jousting tournament to jousting tournament. In 1173, the frustrations led to a rebellion supported by his mother and his brothers, **Geoffrey, duke of Brittany**, and Richard (later **Richard I** and also known as Richard the Lionheart). The conflict nearly unseated the monarch, but after 18 months of struggle, the two generations reached a settlement, which included a large increase in the younger Henry's finances.

For the next seven years, Henry continued to participate in tournaments, but by 1182 he was at war with Richard over lands in Poitou. The following year, while laying waste monasteries in the Limousin region of northern France in an effort to raise money to pursue the war, he contracted dysentery, and on 11 June he died in the castle at Martel, near Limoges. Initially he was buried at Le Mans, but his remains were moved a few weeks later to the cathedral at Rouen. Henry and Marguerite had only one child, a son (William), who was born on 19 June 1177 and survived for just three days.

**HEPBURN, JAMES, EARL OF BOTHWELL (c1535–1578).** Hepburn—the third husband of **Mary, queen of Scots**—was the only son of Patrick, earl of Bothwell, and his wife, Agnes. In 1560, he met Mary in Paris and clearly made an impression, because when the young queen set up court in Scotland the following year, Bothwell (who had succeeded to his father's title in 1556) was appointed to her **Privy Council**. An allegation by James Hamilton, earl of Arran, that he had plotted to kidnap the sovereign led to his imprisonment in **Edinburgh** Castle in March 1562, but he escaped after five months and fled to **France**.

In 1565, Bothwell was recalled to Scotland to help suppress a rebellion led by Mary's half-brother, James Stewart, earl of Moray, and shortly afterward he married Jean, the daughter of George Gordon, earl of Huntly. During the rebellion and the crisis that followed the murder of the queen's secretary, David Rizzio, on 9 March 1566, Bothwell proved wholly loyal to his sovereign and gradually became her chief advisor, acquiring titles and property that made him one of the most powerful nobles in the country. However, there was also a growing affection between the two, and the earl clearly wanted to find a way of making the relationship more formal. On the morning of 10 February 1567, Mary's husband—**Henry Stuart, lord Darnley**—was found strangled after an explosion had wrecked the Edinburgh house where he was staying. Public opinion held Bothwell responsible, but on 12 April, he was cleared at a trial that was clearly biased in his favor.

Twelve days later, the earl intercepted Mary's entourage while she was traveling to Edinburgh and carried her off to his castle at Dunbar, ostensibly to ensure her safety. Then, early in May, Jean was persuaded to divorce him on the grounds that he had committed adultery with one of her maids. On 15 May, he married the queen at **Holyrood Palace**. At the time, Mary was pregnant (almost certainly by Bothwell), but the union lasted for only one month. The match encouraged Protestant and Roman Catholic lords, who were usually at loggerheads, to unite against the pair, and on 15 June the opposing sides met at Carberry Hill. The royal troops refused to give battle, and Mary surrendered on condition that her husband be allowed to flee. He escaped to Scandinavia but was eventually imprisoned at Dragsholm Castle in Denmark, where he died, insane, on 14 April 1578. *See also* CASKET LETTERS.

**HER (OR HIS) ROYAL HIGHNESS.** In 1864, Queen **Victoria** decreed that **princes** and **princesses** were entitled to be styled "Royal Highness," but the practice can be varied. For example, **Prince Philip, duke of Edinburgh**, was known as "His Royal Highness" from the date of his wedding to Princess Elizabeth (later Queen **Elizabeth II**) in 1947 but was not made a **prince** for a further decade. Since 1996, men and women who have the right to the style as a result of marriage must relinquish it if they divorce—a rule that affected **Diana, princess of Wales**, and **Sarah, duchess of York**. *See also* ELIZABETH, THE QUEEN MOTHER; WALLIS, DUCHESS OF WINDSOR; WINDSOR, HOUSE OF.

**HERLEVA (c1003–c1050).** The parentage of the mother of **William I of England** (William the Conqueror) is not known, some writers suggesting that she was the daughter of a merchant, others that she was the child of a tanner in Falaise, Normandy. There is a story, wholly unconfirmed by documentary evidence, that **Robert I, duke of Normandy**, watched her from the walls of his castle as she lifted her skirts to stamp on clothes that had been put in baths for dyeing. The duke, overcome by youthful desire, told his servants to smuggle Herleva into the building by a side entrance, but she refused, saying that she would arrive by the main gate or not at all. Robert accepted the demand, and William was born in 1027 or 1028, with a daughter, Adelaide, probably following in 1030.

The difference in social status between the lovers made marriage impossible, so in 1031, Duke Robert arranged for his mistress to wed Herluin de Conteville, one of his closest advisors. That match produced two sons (Odo and Robert) and two daughters (Emma and Muriel), all four of whom reached maturity. The date of Herleva's death, and her burial place, are uncertain, though one source records that she passed away in about 1050 and was buried in the Benedictine Abbey of Grestain, which was founded by her husband. She is also known by several other names, including Arlette, Arletta, and Herleve.

**HIGH STEWARD OF SCOTLAND.** "High Steward of Scotland" is one of the subsidiary titles held by the **duke of Rothesay**. The title, first awarded in about 1150 to Walter FitzAlan (one of the principal administrative aides to King **David I**), was made hereditary in 1157. FitzAlan's grandson (another Walter) adopted Steward as a surname, which over time changed to Stewart and then to Stuart (*see* STUART, HOUSE OF). In 1398, King **Robert III** granted both the dukedom and the stewardship to his son, **David Stewart, duke of Rothesay**. Since then, the titles have been held by the **heir apparent** to the Scottish, British, and United Kingdom thrones.

**HIGHGROVE.** Highgrove, near Tetbury in Gloucestershire, is the country home of **Charles, prince of Wales**, and **Camilla, duchess of Cornwall**. The Georgian mansion, with nine bedrooms and four reception rooms, was built in 1796–98 and was acquired by the Duchy of Cornwall (*see* DUKE OF CORNWALL) from member of parliament Maurice Macmillan in 1980, fueling newspaper speculation that the **prince** was considering marriage. After completing a refurbishment program, Charles moved into the house with his first wife, **Diana, princess of Wales**, the following year. Then, in 1988, he carried out a number of alterations to the exterior of the building and constructed an annex for his staff.

From 1985, the prince experimented with organic farming techniques on the 37-acre estate, and in 1996 he converted to fully biologically sustainable crop growing and animal rearing (he has a herd of pedigree Aberdeen-Angus beef cattle). The gardens have also been replanned to include a formal layout, a walled plot for vegetables, and a wild area. Highgrove was the early home of Prince Harry (*see* HENRY OF WALES, PRINCE) and **Prince William of Wales**, who were often seen shopping with their mother in local towns. The rooms are not open to the public, and only organized groups can view the gardens. *See also* GATCOMBE PARK.

**HIS ROYAL HIGHNESS.** *See* HER (OR HIS) ROYAL HIGHNESS.

**HOLYROOD PALACE.** Holyrood—formally known as the Palace of Holyroodhouse—is the British monarch's official residence in Scotland, located in **Edinburgh**, a mile east of the castle, next to the ruins of an Augustinian abbey founded by King **David I** in 1126. Visiting royalty stayed in the abbey guesthouse until the late 15th century, when **James IV** ordered the construction of a palace. **James V**, his son and successor, supervised additions in 1528–36, but the building was destroyed by fire while Oliver Cromwell's troops occupied it in 1650. Cromwell arranged for the structure to be rebuilt, but **Charles II** had that edifice replaced in 1671–79 with the one designed by Sir William Bruce, which still stands.

Although the palace has been the focus of several important events in Scottish monarchical history—it was a base for **Charles Edward Stuart** (Bonnie **Prince** Charlie) when he occupied Edinburgh in 1745 during his attempt to wrest the crown from the **House of Hanover**, for example—it is best known for its associations with **Mary, queen of Scots**, who made it her home when she returned from the European mainland after the death of her first husband, **Francis II of France**, in 1560 and married **Henry Stuart, lord Darnley**, in the abbey in 1565. The following year, she saw him murder David Rizzio (her secretary) in her rooms, and in 1567 she was wed to **James Hepburn, earl of Bothwell**, at Holyrood, possibly under duress. Nowadays, the palace is used for garden parties and other state events, particularly in the early summer, but it is open to visitors when no members of the **royal family** are in residence. *See also* DAVID II; JAMES II OF SCOTLAND; MADELEINE

DE VALOIS; MARGARET OF DENMARK; MARY OF GUELDRES; ROYAL PECULIAR; STEWART, JAMES, DUKE OF ROTHESAY (1540–1541); TUDOR, MARGARET.

**HONOURS OF SCOTLAND.** The Scottish crown jewels—also known as the Scottish Regalia—consist of the crown, scepter, and sword of state that were used at the **coronations** of **Mary, queen of Scots**, in 1543; King **James VI** in 1567; King **Charles I** in 1633; and King **Charles II** in 1651. The crown, designed in 1540 and therefore older than any of the crowns in the collection of the **crown jewels of the United Kingdom**, is made from Scottish gold and contains precious stones taken from the previous crown as well as 94 Scottish freshwater pearls. The gold scepter (presented to King **James IV** by Pope Alexander VI in 1494 and lengthened in 1536) is topped by a rock crystal and a pearl, and the sword (presented to James by Pope Julius II in 1507) has representations of St. Paul and St. Peter etched on the blade.

When James VI moved his court to **London** in 1603 (*see* UNION OF THE CROWNS), the Honours of Scotland remained in **Edinburgh**, the Scottish capital, where they were displayed as symbols of the monarchy at meetings of the Scots' lawmaking body until the parliaments of England and Scotland were combined in 1707 *(see* UNION OF PARLIAMENTS). After that, they languished for a century until in 1819, at the instigation of novelist Sir Walter Scott, they were placed on public view in Edinburgh Castle, where they remain. The crown is still used at the opening of each session of the Scottish parliament, which was reestablished in 1999. *See also* HONOURS OF THE PRINCIPALITY OF WALES.

**HONOURS OF THE PRINCIPALITY OF WALES.** The Honours of Wales are the regalia used at the investiture of a **prince of Wales**. The insignia of the earliest **Welsh princes** have not survived, but in 1911 a new set—a coronet (symbolizing rank), a ring (symbolizing duty), a robe, a rod (symbolizing government), and a sword (symbolizing justice)—was designed for the investiture of **Prince** Edward (eldest son of King **George V** and later, briefly, King **Edward VIII**) and incorporated gold from the Clogau mine in the northeast of the principality. The dragon that features on the Welsh flag was engraved on the ring, rod, and sword.

The regalia, now on display at the National Museum of Wales in Cardiff, were last used for the investiture of Queen **Elizabeth II**'s eldest son, **Charles, as prince of Wales** at Caernarfon in 1969, but a new coronet (similar in design to the Imperial State Crown and the St. Edward's Crown in the **crown jewels of the United Kingdom**) had to be fashioned because Edward

VIII took the earlier one with him when he abdicated. *See also* HONOURS OF SCOTLAND.

**HOWARD, CATHERINE (c1521–1542).** Catherine—whom historian Alison Weir has described as an "empty-headed wanton"—was the fifth wife of King **Henry VIII** and daughter of Lord Edward Howard and his wife, Joyce Culpeper. The date and place of her birth are uncertain, but it is known that she was brought up in the household of Agnes Howard, her step-grandmother and the second wife of Thomas, duke of Norfolk. While there, she had several lovers, including Thomas Culpeper (her cousin), Francis Dereham (who referred to her as his wife), and Henry Mannock or Manox (her music teacher). In 1540, the duke obtained her a post as **lady-in-waiting** to **Anne of Cleves**, Henry's new queen, but the king was much more attracted by Catherine's charms than by those of his bride.

Just 19 days after the king's marriage to Anne was annulled on 9 July 1540, Henry and Catherine (also known as Katherine and Katheryn) were married at **Oatlands Palace** in Surrey. The monarch seemed happy, but it is possible that his wife was less enamored; she was a girl 15 to 20 years old with few intellectual gifts wedded to a husband who was nearly 50, grossly overweight, and suffering from several medical conditions, including an evil-smelling ulcer on his thigh. Under the circumstances, it seems possible— though unproven—that she at least flirted with young men at the court, and she certainly employed Dereham and Mannock in her household.

Late in 1541, Thomas Cranmer, the archbishop of Canterbury, heard of Catherine's real and alleged sexual indiscretions and reported the details to the king, who was flabbergasted by the tales. Cranmer was not acting out of friendship; the Howards were Roman Catholic, and the archbishop, heading an infant Protestant **Church of England**, greatly feared their influence. Henry eventually accepted the cleric's assurances that the stories were true, so Catherine was arrested on 12 November. On 21 January the following year, parliament passed legislation declaring that an unchaste woman who married a sovereign was committing treason, and on 13 February, the former queen—probably still a teenager—was **beheaded** at the **Tower of London** and then buried in an unmarked grave at the Church of St. Peter ad Vincula, where the remains of **Anne Boleyn** (Henry's second wife) had been interred after her execution in 1536.

Modern scholars concur that Catherine was of relatively minor political importance, but they differ over their assessment of her character and behavior, some (like Weir) criticizing her conduct, but others (such as Antonia Fraser) adopting a less condemnatory stance, pointing out that Catherine and her supposed lovers all denied adultery.

**HUMPHREY, DUKE OF GLOUCESTER (1390–1447).** Humphrey, born on 3 October 1390, was the fifth son of King **Henry IV** and his first wife, **Mary de Bohun**. He was created duke of Gloucester by his older brother, King **Henry V**, in 1414; fought in the Battle of Agincourt (*see* HUNDRED YEARS' WAR) the following year; and was appointed **regent** when his infant nephew succeeded to the throne as King **Henry VI** in 1422. In 1428, he built Bella Court at Greenwich, now part of southeast **London**; in later years, the building would become known as the **Palace of Placentia** and be the birthplace of King **Henry VIII**, **Mary I**, and Queen **Elizabeth I**. Also, the collection of manuscripts he donated to Oxford University in 1435–37 is still an important part of the Bodleian Library, much used by scholars of the late medieval period.

By early 1422, Gloucester was married to Jacqueline, countess of Hainault and Holland, by whom he had a stillborn child in 1424. From 1425, the couple lived apart, and in 1428, Pope Martin V decreed that Jacqueline was still married to a previous husband, John, duke of Brabant and Limburg. Humphrey turned to Eleanor Cobham, who had been both a member of Jacqueline's household and his mistress for some years. They married, probably in 1428, but in 1441 Eleanor was found guilty of practicing witchcraft against Henry VI and was imprisoned for the rest of her life at Peel Castle on the Isle of Man. Gloucester incurred the wrath of Henry VI's consort, **Margaret of Anjou**, and was arrested on charges of treason in 1447. On 23 February, before facing trial, he died at Bury St. Edmunds, possibly as a result of a stroke but possibly, also, by violence.

**HUNDRED YEARS' WAR.** For much of the 14th century and the first half of the 15th, the kings of England warred with the French house of Valois for control of **France**. Conventionally, historians date the start of the hundred years' war from 1337, when **Edward III** began a military campaign in pursuit of his claim to the French throne, and consider that it ended with the defeat of an English force at Castillon, near Bordeaux, in 1453. In practice, however, the feuding had begun in the 12th century and animosities continued long after the armies had withdrawn.

In 1328, Charles IV of France died, leaving no male heir. Edward's assertion that he was the legitimate successor was based on the argument that he was the only living male descendant of his maternal grandfather, Philip IV, who had been king of France from 1285 to 1314. However, the French, who had no desire to be ruled by a foreign sovereign, preferred Philip's brother's son (who ruled as Philip VI) because he was descended through the male line. The conflict did not stem solely from monarchical egos, though. The English kings had held estates in France for nearly 300 years (*see, for example,* AN-

JOU, HOUSE OF; AQUITAINE; NORMANDY, HOUSE OF), and although much of that territory had been lost, notably during the reign of King **John**, important areas remained under their control, including Gascony, where Bordeaux was the focus of a profitable wine trade. In a society in which land was the basis of status and power, the English crown wanted to hold on to its possessions on the European continent, and, additionally, many of the barons felt that an effort should be made to recapture the regions that had been relinquished. Moreover, English merchants had significant investments in the wool industry of Flanders (which, at the time, was controlled by France), and the French were providing support for the Scots, England's old enemy on its northern border.

Initially, the English had the upper hand, though events moved slowly. The French fleet was almost totally destroyed at Sluys in 1340, longbowmen won a convincing victory at Crécy in 1346, **Calais** was captured the following year, and King John II (who had succeeded Philip as king of France in 1350) was captured at Poitiers in 1356. On 8 May 1360, the Treaty of Brétigny recognized the English successes. In return for a payment of three million gold crowns, John would be released and Edward would renounce his claim to the French crown but be confirmed as owner of much of southwest and northwest France. The two kings agreed to the pact at a meeting in Calais on 24 October the same year, but after John's death in 1364, his successor, Charles V, repudiated the arrangements, and the conflict began again.

This time, the French, who recaptured Poitiers in 1372 and Bergerac in 1377, made the advances, but the deaths of Edward (also in 1377) and Charles (in 1380) led to another truce that lasted until August 1415, when England's King **Henry V** once again launched a campaign to expand his country's influence on the continental mainland, winning an important victory at Agincourt on 25 October. By 1422, in alliance with Philip the Good, duke of Burgundy, he controlled Aquitaine and all of the settlements north of the River Loire, including Paris, but Philip defected to the French in 1435, Normandy was lost in 1450, and Aquitaine fell in 1453, leaving **Henry VI** (Henry V's successor) with Calais alone.

By 1455, England was divided by civil war (*see* WARS OF THE ROSES), and international aggrandizement was less important than internal strife. Moreover, the long war had proved expensive, virtually bankrupting the royal treasury, and future monarchs showed little interest in paying for further efforts to regain former estates in France. *See also* EDWARD, THE BLACK PRINCE; MARGARET, COUNTESS OF PEMBROKE.

**HYDE, ANNE (1637–1671).** Anne, the wife of James, **duke of York** and later King **James VII and II**, was the last commoner to marry an heir to the throne until Diana Spencer (*see* DIANA, PRINCESS OF WALES) wed **Charles, prince of Wales**, in 1981. The daughter of Sir Edward Hyde and his second wife, Frances Aylesbury, she was born in Windsor on 12 March 1637 and joined the household of **Mary Henrietta, the princess royal**, in 1655. She first met James the following year in Paris, where several of the **royal family** had taken refuge from the civil war that was ravaging England, and by the early summer of 1660 she was pregnant by him. James was very much in love with Anne, but with the **restoration of the monarchy** in England that year, he had become **heir presumptive** to the throne because his brother, King **Charles II**, had no children, and the prospect of a man in his position marrying a commoner appalled many royal advisors. Even Anne's father counseled against a wedding, but Charles eventually approved the arrangement, and the ceremony was held in secret on 3 September.

Most 17th-century commentators, including diarist Samuel Pepys, wrote that Anne was a plain woman, but that, apparently, was par for the course for James, whose numerous mistresses seemed, according to Gilbert Burnet, a Scottish theologian and historian, to have been given to him by his priests as a penance. She was, however, a witty, intelligent lady who remained devoted to her husband despite his dalliances. They had eight children; only two survived to adulthood, but those two both became monarchs as Queen **Mary II** and Queen **Anne**.

Unusual for the age, James spent much time with his family, and it seemed to several observers that his wife, who looked after household finances, ruled the domestic roost (Samuel Pepys wrote in his diary on 30 October 1668 that "in all things but in his codpiece, [James] is led by the nose by his wife"). A pious woman, Anne converted from the Anglican faith to Roman Catholicism in 1668 or 1669 (as did James), but the details were kept secret because neither England nor Scotland wanted a Catholic monarchy. By that time, Anne was also gaining weight, and it was soon evident that she was seriously ill. She gave birth to **Catherine Stuart**, her last child, on 9 February 1671 and died at **St. James's Palace** on 31 March, probably a victim of breast cancer. Anne was buried in **Westminster Abbey**, and two years later, James married **Mary of Modena**, who was to give him another 12 children, only two of whom survived beyond childhood. *See also* STUART, CHARLES, DUKE OF CAMBRIDGE (1660–1661); STUART, CHARLES, DUKE OF KENDAL; STUART, EDGAR, DUKE OF CAMBRIDGE; STUART, HENRIETTA; STUART, JAMES, DUKE OF CAMBRIDGE.

# I

**INDULF (?–962).** Indulf—the son of **Constantine II** and, possibly, a daughter of Eadulf, ruler of Northumbria—was king of **Alba** from 954 to 962, succeeding **Malcolm I**. He consolidated extensions of his realm south of the River Forth and resisted Viking incursions but was probably killed by Danish raiders at Invercullen in 962. One source indicates that he was buried on the island of **Iona** beside other early Scottish rulers. Indulf had three sons, two of whom—**Colin** (or Cuilén) and **Amlaíb** (or Olaf)—also became kings and (like their brother, Eochaid, and their father) met premature ends.

**INGILD (c672–718).** Ingild was the son of **Coenred** and the younger brother of Ine, king of **Wessex** from 688 to 726. Little is known of his life (some sources date his birth as late as 680), but most scholars agree that he died in 718, leaving a son, **Eoppa**, who continued the line of descent from **Cerdic** (founder of Wessex) to the present British **royal family**.

**IONA.** A tiny island covering little more than five square miles and lying off the west coast of Scotland, Iona was the traditional burial ground of the earliest Scottish kings. In about 563, St. Columba arrived from Ireland, established a monastery, and began to convert to Christianity the peoples who lived on the neighboring mainland and in offshore communities. A series of Viking invasions from 795 to 986 resulted in the destruction of the monastery, but the Reilig Odhráin (the graveyard to the southwest of the church) remained the last resting place for Scotland's monarchs until well into the 11th century, with a document from 1549 reporting that four Irish, eight Scandinavian, and 48 Scottish kings are buried there, including **Kenneth MacAlpin** (who is traditionally regarded as the first king of Scots), **Macbeth** (the subject of William Shakespeare's play), and **Duncan I** (murdered by Macbeth in the drama).

In 1938, George MacLeod established the Iona Community in an attempt to intermesh spiritual and material aspects of the Christian faith, as Columba had done. His leadership led to the restoration of many of the buildings on the island, including the abbey. *See also* ÁED; COLIN; CONSTANTINE

261

I; CONSTANTINE III; DONALD I; DONALD II; DONALD III; DUFF; DUNCAN II; DUNFERMLINE; GIRIC; INDULF; KENNETH III; LULACH; MALCOLM I; MALCOLM II; MALCOLM III.

**ISABEL OF GLOUCESTER (c1160–1217).** Isabel, daughter of William, earl of Gloucester, and his wife, Hawise de Beaumont, was the first wife of King **John**. The couple married in Marlborough Castle on 29 August 1189, while **Richard I** held the crown. A decade later, after Richard's death and John's **succession to the throne**, the new monarch successfully petitioned Pope Boniface VIII for a divorce on the grounds that he and his wife were second cousins and were therefore within the Roman Catholic Church's prohibited degrees of consanguinity. Isabel and John had no children, and in 1214 she married Geoffrey, earl of Essex, who died two years later. In September 1217, she took a third husband—Hubert, earl of Kent—but she had only days to enjoy the new relationship, passing away on 14 October. She was buried in Canterbury Cathedral.

**ISABELLA, COUNTESS OF NORFOLK (c1195–?).** Isabella (also known as Isabel and as Isabella of Scotland) was the second daughter of **William I of Scotland** and **Ermengarde de Beaumont**. In 1209, under the terms of the Treaty of Norham, which forced William to make concessions that would prevent an invasion of his realm by King **John**, she and her elder sister, Margaret (later **Margaret, countess of Kent**), were taken to **London** so that they could be married into the English royal house. Nothing came of the plan, however, so Isabella returned home in 1223 and then, in May 1225, was married at Alnwick to Roger Bigood, who was probably about 20 years younger than she and still a minor. The couple lived in Scotland at the court of King **Alexander II**, Isabella's brother, until 1233, when Bigood succeeded to the earldom of Norfolk. Thirty years later, he was one of the nobles who attempted to force King **Henry III** to relinquish some of his power (*see* SECOND BARONS' WAR).

In 1245, the earl attempted to have his childless marriage annulled on grounds of consanguinity, but he failed to get the approval of Pope Innocent IV and arranged a reconciliation with his wife in 1253. The date of Isabella's death is not known, though records show that she was alive in 1263.

**ISABELLA DE COUCY (c1332–1382).** The second child of **Edward III** and **Philippa of Hainault** was born at **Woodstock Palace** on 16 June 1332 and was named after her paternal grandmother, **Isabella of France**. Several writers suggest that she was Edward's favorite daughter and that she was much indulged, becoming something of a tearaway as she grew up. Her parents considered several potential husbands (including Peter of Castile, who was later betrothed to **Joan Plantagenet [c1333–48]**, Isabella's younger sister) before she married Enguerrand VII, lord of Coucy, in **Windsor Castle** on 27 July 1365. Enguerrand had arrived in England as a captive in 1360, during the **Hundred Years' War**, but he was befriended by the king, who persuaded the Frenchman to become one of his subjects. At the time of the wedding, extensive English estates that had formerly belonged to the bridegroom's family were restored to him, and in 1366 he was created earl of Bedford. According to some sources, the couple had two daughters—Marie (born in 1366) and Philippa (born in 1367). Other authorities believe that there was a third child, named Isabel, whose birth date is unknown but who died in 1411.

Enguerrand attempted to balance responsibilities to his English and French sovereigns, spending time with his family in both countries. However, when Edward died in 1377, Enguerrand gave up all of his English lands, left his wife, and returned to **France**. Isabella died in **London**, possibly in April 1379 but perhaps between 17 June and 5 October 1382. She was buried at Greyfriars Church in Greenwich alongside others of the **House of Plantagenet** dynasty. Her husband survived until 1397, when he contracted bubonic plague after being taken captive by Turks during a crusade to the Holy Land. The marriage was the last between a daughter of the royal house and one of her father's subjects until Queen **Victoria**'s daughter, Louise, married John, duke of Argyll, in 1871 (*see* LOUISE, PRINCESS, DUCHESS OF ARGYLL).

**ISABELLA DE WARENNE (c1253–?).** Isabella was the wife of King **John of Scotland** and the mother of **Edward de Balliol**, who attempted to take the crown for himself in 1332–36. Her father (John, earl of Surrey) was a rich and distinguished English nobleman who served both King **Henry III** and King **Edward I**, but her mother, Alice de Lusignan, came from a much poorer background even though she was a daughter of **Isabella of Angoulême**—the widow of King **John** of England—and therefore Henry's half-sister. The younger Isabella probably married John of Scotland in 1280 or 1281 and, although some writers refer to her as his queen, may have died before he was crowned in 1292. Edward is the only child known for certain to stem from the union, but there may have been at least one other son (named Henry) and possibly two or more daughters.

**ISABELLA, HOLY ROMAN EMPRESS (1214–1241).** Isabella (sometimes known as Isabella of England) was the fourth child, and second daughter, in the family of King **John** and **Isabella of Angoulême**. She was wed to Frederick II, Holy Roman Emperor, on 15 or 20 July 1235 at Worms Cathedral in the German Rhineland. The marital union was designed to cement a political allegiance that would counterbalance French antipathy toward England, which at the time was ruled by Isabella's brother, King **Henry III**. While her husband conducted military campaigns and argued with popes Gregory IX and Innocent IV, Isabella was kept in seclusion, isolated from all male company except the eunuchs who attended her. She had, with Frederick, four (or possibly five) children but died while giving birth to the last baby in December 1241.

**ISABELLA OF ANGOULÊME (c1188–1246).** On 24 August 1200, only a year after casting off his first wife (**Isabel of Gloucester**), King **John** married Isabella, the daughter of Count Aymer Taillefer of Angoulême and Alice de Courtney. The groom was in his early thirties; the bride was about 12.

The marriage proved disastrous for John—and not simply because his young wife tended to lose her temper easily. Isabella had been betrothed to Hugh of Lusignan, and John had in effect kidnapped her. The Lusignans took up arms in defense of their honor and were supported by Philip II of **France**, who confiscated all of the English king's continental estates with the exception of Gascony. John's attempts to retrieve the territory ended in a heavy military defeat that upset his nobles and contributed to the discontent that led, in 1215, to the **Magna Carta**, which circumscribed his rights as king.

Despite the emotional turmoil and political problems, Isabella bore five children, including a son, Henry, who succeeded to his father's throne, ruling as King **Henry III**. After John succumbed to dysentery in 1216, Isabella returned to France and married Hugh, with whom she had another five sons and four daughters. She died at **Fontevrault Abbey** in Anjou on 4 June 1246, having fled to the nunnery for safety after facing accusations that she had plotted against Louis IX, king of France. *See also* ANJOU, HOUSE OF; ELEANOR, COUNTESS OF LEICESTER; ISABELLA DE WARENNE; ISABELLA, HOLY ROMAN EMPRESS; JOAN OF ENGLAND (1210–1238); RICHARD, EARL OF CORNWALL.

**ISABELLA OF FRANCE (c1295–1358). Queen consort** of King **Edward II**, Isabella ultimately turned against her husband and his homosexual advisors, leading a revolt that forced him to abdicate in favor of his teenage son, who was crowned as **Edward III**. The daughter of King Philip IV of **France** and Jeanne of Navarre, she married in Boulogne Cathedral on 25 January 1308, the long-planned union designed to cement peace between the English and the French, who had been warring over the ownership of estates in Gascony and elsewhere on the European mainland. Edward, however, showed more interest in his male friends than in his young bride, and though at times

Isabella attempted to intercede in arguments between the sovereign and his barons, the couple grew further and further apart.

In 1325, Edward sent his wife to the French court with instructions to negotiate a further agreement on the status of Gascony, but her presence in Paris provided a focus for the nobles who were opposed to the monarch. Encouraged by their support, she announced that she would not return to **London** until the king told his confidants to leave. Edward refused; Isabella took **Roger Mortimer**, baron Wigmore and later earl of March, as a lover; and the dissidents (helped by William, count of Hainault, who provided eight warships) led an army of mercenaries to England on 21 September 1326.

With few allies left, the king fled to south Wales but was captured on 16 November and was forced to give up his throne early the following year. His son was crowned as Edward III on 1 February 1328 but was only 15 years old, so Isabella and Wigmore ruled as **regents** until the youthful monarch began to assert authority on his own account at about the time of his 18th birthday in the early winter of 1330. That authority was decisive because Wigmore was hanged on 29 November, and Isabella was forced to retire to Castle Rising (near Kings Lynn, in Norfolk). The queen joined the Franciscan Order of St. Clare (also known as the Poor Clares) in later life and died on 22 August 1358.

Most sources note that Isabella and her husband had three children in addition to Edward—**John of Eltham, earl of Cornwall** (born in 1316); **Eleanor, countess of Gueldres** (1318); and **Joan of the Tower** (1321). Through her mother, a daughter of King Philip IV of France and Isabel of Aragon, Isabella was a descendant of **Harold II** and thus reintroduced the bloodline of the **Anglo-Saxon monarchs** to the English royal house. *See also* EDITH SWAN-NECK; NORTHAMPTON, TREATY OF; SHEEN PALACE.

**ISABELLA OF MAR (?–c1297).** Isabella (or Isabel) married Robert the Bruce in about 1295 but did not live to see him become king of Scots as **Robert I**. Little of her life is documented, though she was probably born in about 1277. Her father, Donald, was earl of Mar (a territory in northeast Scotland) and was a strong supporter of the Bruces' unsuccessful claim to the Scottish throne after the death of **Margaret, maid of Norway**, in 1290. Some sources suggest that her mother, Helen (or Ellen), may have had a Welsh heritage, but there is no certain evidence to support this claim.

Isabella's marriage was undoubtedly arranged for political reasons, emphasizing a relationship between two powerful families, but reputedly there was a strong emotional attachment between her and her new husband. They had little time to enjoy their relationship, however. In 1296, Isabella gave birth to a daughter, **Marjorie Bruce**, but died soon afterward (certainly by 1302, when her husband took **Elizabeth de Burgh** as his second wife). Her burial place is not known. Marjorie married **Walter Stewart (c1293–1326), high steward of Scotland**, in 1315, and their son, as **Robert II**, became the first monarch from the House of Stewart (*see* STUART, HOUSE OF). Isabella is, therefore, an ancestress of all monarchs of Scotland, Great Britain, and the United Kingdom since the late 14th century.

**ISABELLA OF VALOIS (1389–1409).** Isabella was the second **queen consort** of King **Richard II**. The daughter of King Charles VI of **France** and Isabella of Bavaria, she was born in Paris on 9 November 1389. Her wedding to Richard at St. Nicholas's Church in **Calais** on 4 November 1396 was a matter of political expediency. **Anne of Bohemia**—Richard's first wife—had died in 1394, leaving the king without an heir. The monarch, who was little interested in military matters, also wanted to end a lengthy conflict with the French (*see* HUNDRED YEARS' WAR) and saw marriage to Isabella as a way both of cementing peace and of ensuring the birth of a son who would succeed to his throne. In fact, he had little time with his child bride because in 1399 he surrendered to opponents of his rule, and early the following year he died in Pontefract Castle. King **Henry IV**, William's successor, tried to marry Isabella to his own son (also named Henry and later **Henry V**), but she refused and returned to France, where, in 1406, she wed Charles, duke of Orléans. She died in childbirth at the Château of **Blois** on 13 September 1409. King Henry, spurned, married his heir to **Catherine of Valois**, Isabella's younger sister.

# J

**JACOBITE REBELLIONS (1689–1746).** The **Glorious Revolution** that replaced the Roman Catholic King **James VII and II** with the Protestant King **William III and II** in 1688 caused little bloodshed in England, but the repercussions in Ireland and Scotland were more violent. James had considerable support in Ireland, where the population was overwhelmingly Catholic, so he was welcomed when he landed at Kinsale on 12 March 1689 with an army supplied largely by King Louis XIV of **France** and intent on regaining his thrones. Defeat at the **Battle of the Boyne** on 1 July the following year encouraged him to return to safety on the European mainland, but many of his followers fought on until heavy losses to William's troops at Aughrim on 12 July 1691 and failure to withstand a siege at Limerick led to a peace agreement, signed on 3 October.

In Scotland, John Graham of Claverhouse, viscount Dundee, also raised an army in support of the deposed king, drawing heavily on men from the Roman Catholic highland clans. Although his troops won an important victory at Killiecrankie on 27 July 1689, Claverhouse was killed in the battle, and without his leadership the rebellion petered out. Twenty-six years later, John Erskine, earl of Mar, attempted another rising (often called the first Jacobite rebellion). Declaring **James Francis Edward Stuart** (James VII and II's son) the lawful sovereign of Scotland, he summoned support from men willing to fight for "the relief of our native country from oppression and a foreign yoke," but he lacked talent for military leadership, and a campaign that began with high hopes at Braemar on 6 September 1715 ended with surrender to the government army at Preston on 14 November.

In the years following "the Fifteen," Jacobites continued to plot, but there was no further serious military attempt to regain the crown until 1745, when **Charles Edward Stuart** (grandson of James VII and II and son of James Stuart) landed at Eriskay, in the Outer Hebrides, on 23 July. With an army of highland clansmen augmented by contingents from France, Ireland, and the Scottish lowlands, he headed south, taking **Edinburgh** and Carlisle before reaching Derby—just 125 miles from **London**—on 4 December. However, Charles found few reinforcements in England, so his commanders ordered a retreat, and on 16 April 1746 his troops were routed at **Culloden**, near Inverness.

"Bonnie **Prince** Charlie" escaped to France, but there was no more support for invasion. The Holy See had recognized James Francis Edward Stuart as King James VIII of Scotland and III of England, but when he died in 1766, there was no such honor for his son, who had become an embittered, violent alcoholic. **Henry Benedict Stuart**, Charles's younger brother, styled himself Henry IX of England and I of Scotland from 1788, but in that year Scottish Catholics, and Anglicans who felt that James VII and II had been unconstitutionally deposed, swore allegiance to King **George III**, and the Jacobite cause died. The term "Jacobite" is derived from *Jacobus*, the Latin for "James." *See also* STUART, HOUSE OF; WILLIAM AUGUSTUS, DUKE OF CUMBERLAND.

**JAMES I OF ENGLAND (1566–1625).** *See* JAMES VI OF SCOTLAND AND I OF ENGLAND.

**JAMES I OF SCOTLAND (1394–1437).** James was born at **Dunfermline** in 1394 (some sources claim that the date was in late July, others 10 December) and became king of Scotland on the death of his father, **Robert III**, in 1406, but by that time he was in the hands of the English, who held him captive for the next 18 years. His mother, **Annabella Drummond**, had died in late 1401 or early 1402, and his older brother, **David Stewart, duke of Rothesay**, died shortly thereafter. Robert, lame and ill, decided to send his only surviving son to **France** for safety, but the 11-year-old boy's ship was intercepted, and he was taken prisoner. The Scots monarch died within weeks of hearing the news, and James remained in England while his devious and acquisitive uncle, **Robert Stewart, duke of Albany (c1340–1420)**, controlled the government of the realm.

However, the young man's enforced absence from his kingdom was not entirely unproductive—he was educated well (learning several languages); he developed a taste for poetry (*The Kingis Quair*, a long narrative work, is usually considered to be his composition); he experienced the strengths and weaknesses of the English administrative system at first hand; and he gained military experience in France with King **Henry V**.

When terms for James's release were finally agreed upon in 1424, he returned to Scotland with a bride (**Joan Beaufort**, granddaughter of **John of Gaunt**) and with the determination to restore royal authority to a kingdom that had lacked firm government since the death of his great-great-grandfather, King **Robert I**, in 1329. He rounded up nobles who seemed unwilling to concede power (including Murdoch, Albany's son) and executed them, adding their estates to his own. The realm's financial administration was reorganized in an effort to reduce graft, and changes to the judicial system were designed to give the poorest subjects a fairer hearing before the courts. Also, learning was encouraged, parliament was remodeled on English lines, and a series of social changes (including efforts to curb excessive consumption of alcohol) were introduced.

In practice, many of the measures had little effect, but they did promote the image of a monarch intent on reform and on the maintenance of firm rule. Inevitably, however, James's emphasis on change made enemies, and on 20 February 1437, he was murdered at Blackfriars Priory in Perth by a group of conspirators led by Sir Robert Graham and including **Walter Stewart, earl of Atholl** and son of King **Robert II** by his marriage to **Euphemia de Ross**. The monarch was buried at the Carthusian monastery he had founded in 1429 in the town where he was killed, and his seven-year-old son followed him to the throne as **James II**, leaving Scotland in the hands of **regents** once again. The assassins, who had hoped to see Walter get the crown but who received little support, were brutally tortured and then executed. *See also* FALKLAND PALACE; LINLITHGOW PALACE; STEWART, ALEXANDER, DUKE OF ROTHESAY; STEWART, ANNABELLA, COUNTESS OF HUNTLY; STEWART, ELEANOR, ARCHDUCHESS OF AUSTRIA; STEWART, ISABELLA, DUCHESS OF BRITTANY; STEWART, JOAN, COUNTESS OF MORTON; STEWART, MARGARET, DAUPHINE OF FRANCE; STEWART, MARY, COUNTESS OF GRANDPRÉ.

**JAMES II OF ENGLAND (1633–1701).** *See* JAMES VII OF SCOTLAND AND II OF ENGLAND.

**JAMES II OF SCOTLAND (1430–1460).** Born at **Holyrood Palace** in **Edinburgh** on 16 October 1430, James became king of Scotland at the age of six, when his father, **James I**, was murdered in Perth. Attempts by his mother, **Joan Beaufort**, to keep him under her guardianship failed, and in 1439 he was handed over to Sir Alexander Livingstone, who kept a watchful eye on the boy in **Stirling** Castle.

It was not until 1449, after his marriage to **Mary of Gueldres**, that James began to wrest control of his country from the nobles who had squabbled over the reins of power during his minority. He attempted to follow many of the policies introduced by his predecessor in an effort to increase prosperity and reduce lawlessness. The estates of barons whose loyalty was suspect were forfeited, judicial practices were reviewed, a new coinage was issued, and offices of state were no longer treated as hereditary entitlements. At home, he imposed his authority on the most powerful lords, and notably on the Douglas family (in 1452, he killed William, earl of Douglas, in a quarrel at Stirling). Abroad, he tightened links to **France**, a traditional ally of the Scots, and opposed Norway's claims to the Orkney and Shetland islands at the northern outpost of the kingdom. He also led attacks on English-held fortresses in Scotland in an effort to secure the state's boundaries.

As a result, despite the inauspicious start to his reign, by the time he died on 3 August 1460, James had a firm hold on his country's affairs. His death, at the age of 29, was a tragedy for Scotland. He was killed when a cannon exploded beside him during a siege of **Roxburgh Castle**, and the crown passed to his son, **James III**, a significantly less effective leader who allowed the realm to descend, once again, into near anarchy. James II—sometimes known as "Fiery Face" because of his bright birthmark—was buried at Holyrood. *See also* STEWART, ALEXANDER, DUKE OF ALBANY; STEWART, DAVID, EARL OF MORAY; STEWART, JOHN, EARL OF MAR (c1457–1479); STEWART, MARGARET (c1459–c1514); STEWART, MARY, COUNTESS OF ARRAN.

**JAMES III (1451 or 1452–1488).** Traditionally, scholars have described James as a weak monarch, but some recent studies have suggested that he was more of a tyrant than a wimp. The son of **James II** and **Mary of Gueldres**, he was born either on 10 or 20 July 1451 at **Stirling** Castle, or in May 1452 at St. Andrews. Because his elder brother, born on 19 May 1450, survived for only a few hours, James became king when his father was killed by an exploding cannon while supervising a siege of **Roxburgh Castle** on 3 August 1460. Mary tried to protect the boy from the predations of ambitious nobles, but in 1466 he fell into the hands of the Boyd family (*see* STEWART, MARY, COUNTESS OF ARRAN) and remained under their control until 1469, when he married **Margaret of Denmark** and took command of government himself.

In many ways, the early years of James's rule were very successful. As a result of his marriage, he won full sovereignty over the Orkney and Shetland islands because Christian I, king of Denmark, Norway, and Sweden, was unable to find the promised financial dowry for his daughter and conceded territory instead. Also, James was able to extend his authority over much of the Scottish highlands when John MacDonald, **lord of the isles**, was forced to submit to him in 1476.

However, much of his reign was marred by feuds with family and nobles. In 1474, he negotiated a marriage between his son (later King **James IV**) and Cecily, daughter of King **Edward IV** of England (*see* CECILY, VISCOUNTESS WELLES); the match never happened, but the possibility of such a link to a longtime enemy caused much apprehension among the Scots lords (as did the prospect of the taxes they would be required to pay for the wedding). Moreover, some sources indicate that James was more interested in music and other arts than in such manly pursuits as hunting and honing his military skills, and that he cultivated commoners at the expense of lords. One brother (**Alexander Stewart, duke of Albany**) led a series of rebellions against him, and another (**John Stewart, earl of Mar [1457–1479]**) died under mysterious circumstances after being imprisoned, possibly on entirely false charges that he had used witchcraft against the king.

In 1482, an English force led by Richard, duke of Gloucester (later King **Richard III**), and including Alexander, advanced on Scotland. James led an army to meet them but was taken captive by disaffected nobles and was confined to **Edinburgh** Castle while several of his courtiers were hanged. By the end of the year, the king had bribed many of the most important rebels to change sides, and Alexander was forced to flee. However, problems continued to mount, with a series of bad harvests, coupled with rising prices and increased lawlessness, promoting a hostile mood that was exacerbated by James's unwillingness to travel outside Edinburgh.

Eventually, in 1488, dissatisfaction flared into a rebellion that included the teenage **heir apparent** to the throne among its figureheads. The two sides met at Sauchieburn, near Stirling, on 11 June, and James's army was cut to pieces. There is a legend that he fled the field and was thrown from his horse. Injured, he asked a peasant woman to find him a priest, but the man who arrived drew a knife and stabbed him. Historians discount the tale, preferring the evidence that James fell from his horse during the battle and either died as a result of the fall or was killed by the rebels. He was buried nearby at **Cambuskenneth Abbey** (the monument that now marks his grave was built with funds provided by Queen **Victoria**) and was succeeded by his son, James IV, who for the rest of his life wore a heavy iron chain around his waist at Lent in penance for his contribution to his father's death. *See also* DUNDONALD CASTLE; STEWART, JAMES, DUKE OF ROSS; STEWART, JOHN, EARL OF MAR (c1479–1503); STEWART, MARGARET (c1459–c1514).

**JAMES IV (1473–1513).** James—the last British monarch to die in battle—is variously described as arrogant, extravagant, and promiscuous, but even so he is usually considered one of the most popular of Scotland's rulers. He was born, probably at **Stirling**, on 17 March 1473, the first of the three sons of **Margaret of Denmark** and King **James III**, and he succeeded to the throne in 1488 after supporting a rebellion that led to his father's death at the Battle of Sauchieburn.

The new king was little more than 15 years old at the time of his coronation, and initially many senior positions in the realm were occupied by older and more experienced fellow rebels. However, over the years, he increasingly involved himself in the government, augmenting his navy, beginning the manufacture of cannons in **Edinburgh**, establishing a university at Aberdeen, expanding the system of peripatetic judges, granting a **royal charter** to the Royal College of Surgeons of Edinburgh, providing patronage for the arts (by aiding poets Gavin Douglas and William Dunbar, for example), supporting the introduction of Scotland's first printing press, and initiating building projects at **Falkland Palace**, **Holyrood Palace**, **Linlithgow Palace**, and Stirling Castle.

James's domestic policies were greatly aided by an extended period of peace with England. Relationships with Scotland's southern neighbor were difficult at first, with a series of border forays and skirmishes as the Scots supported **Perkin Warbeck**'s pretensions to the English crown, but a seven-year truce signed in 1497, and the king's marriage to **Margaret Tudor**, the elder surviving daughter of King **Henry VII**, provided security for both countries. (This marriage had enormous significance because in 1603 it led to the **House of Stuart**'s accession to the English throne and the **union of the crowns** of England and Scotland.) The peace ended, however, when **Henry VIII** became king of England in 1509. His attitude toward the Scots was more aggressive than that of his predecessor, and when in 1513 he invaded **France**, James found himself under pressure to support Scotland's continental ally. Several advisors counseled caution, but after Henry declared that he owned Scotland, James gathered his army and marched south. He met the English force, led by Thomas Howard, earl of Surrey, in the **Battle of Flodden** on 9 September 1513 and was utterly routed, falling on the field along with nine of his own earls and many other Scottish nobles and clan chiefs.

The dead king's body was carried south to **Sheen Palace** where it lay in a room for several years before being buried in an unmarked grave at the Carthusian monastery founded nearby by **Henry V** in 1414, or possibly in St. Paul's Cathedral in **London**. A cultured man, James spoke several languages and was an able administrator. Wherever he went—and he traveled widely— he spent money on all social classes, and at his court he gathered musicians and acrobats as well as political advisors. His love affairs were numerous and his gambling energetic, but he had great personal charm and presided over a reign that gave Scotland improved standards of living, a lengthy period of relative freedom from internecine strife, and a place of some importance in Renaissance Europe. Mid-20th-century historians argued that his approaches to international diplomacy were unrealistic, but recent assessments have been more generous, sometimes even condoning the decisions that led to the carnage at Flodden. James was succeeded by his 17-month-old son, **James V**, condemning Scotland to yet another lengthy period of government by **regents** and squabbling among nobles. *See also* DUNFERMLINE ABBEY; HON-

OURS OF SCOTLAND; LORD OF THE ISLES; STEWART, ALEXAN-
DER, DUKE OF ROSS; STEWART, ARTHUR, DUKE OF ROTHESAY;
STEWART, JAMES, DUKE OF ROTHESAY (1507–1508).

**JAMES V (1512–1542).** James, the third son of **James IV** and **Margaret
Tudor**, was born at **Linlithgow Palace** 10 April 1512. His older brothers
(**Arthur Stewart, duke of Rothesay,** and **James Stewart, duke of Rothesay [1507–1508]**) had both failed to survive infancy, so he succeeded to the
throne, at the age of 17 months, on 9 September 1513, when his father died at
the **Battle of Flodden**. For the next 15 years, Scotland was ruled by **regents**,
initially the **queen dowager**; then John Stewart, duke of Albany (and son of
**Alexander Stewart, duke of Albany**); and later Archibald Douglas, earl of
Angus, whom James's mother had married in 1514. From 1525, Angus held
the young man captive in **Edinburgh**, but in 1528 the teenage king managed
to escape, on the simple pretext that he was going hunting, and he took control of government himself.

To emphasize his authority, the monarch traveled through the Douglas
strongholds along the realm's border with England, subduing leaders who opposed him, and in the highlands and Western Isles, he forced rebel clan chiefs
to submit to his rule. He also made strenuous efforts to increase his income
in order to support his extravagant lifestyle, which included investments in
expensive building projects at his palaces at **Holyrood**, **Falkland**, Linlithgow, and **Stirling**. And he augmented his coffers (and cemented Scotland's
lengthy alliance with **France**) through judicious marriages to **Madeleine de
Valois** and **Mary of Guise**.

James earned the staunch support of clerics because he refused to countenance the Protestant reforms that were being pursued by King **Henry VIII** of
England, but his resistance to change gained him enemies as well. Opponents
of Roman Catholicism were put to death, leading those nobles who sympathized with their cause to distance themselves from the king. Moreover, many
of the lords were offended by the monarch's apparent willingness to rely on
ecclesiastical officers for advice rather than on secular counselors. This unwavering attachment to the Catholic Church and the continued alliance with
France annoyed Henry, who allowed the annoyance to foam into war after
Margaret Tudor (his sister) died in 1541. The following year, he sent troops
north, and on 24 November he routed a dispirited and disaffected Scottish
army at Solway Moss. James—the victim, according to some writers, of a
nervous breakdown—retreated to Falkland, where he learned that his queen
had given birth to a daughter rather than to the son and heir he so much desired. Exhausted, he died on 14 December, only 30 years old, and was buried
at Holyrood, leaving the week-old **Mary, queen of Scots**, to succeed him.

Although James could be cruel, he was admired by many of his subjects, not least because he sometimes adopted a disguise and, as "the Gude (or Good) Man of Ballengeich," walked out of Stirling Castle to mix with the townspeople, though he probably fooled few of them. He also, apparently, had a talent for prediction. After hearing of Mary's birth, and just before he died, he allegedly claimed that "It cam' [or came] wi' a lass and it will gang [or go] wi' a lass." The words were a reference to the **House of Stuart**, which had gained the throne through the marriage of **Marjorie Bruce** (daughter of King **Robert I**) to **Walter Stewart (c1293–1326)**, one of her father's principal advisors. The dynasty did indeed end with a woman, albeit not with Mary, but two centuries later with Queen **Anne**. *See also* LORD OF THE ISLES; STEWART, JAMES, DUKE OF ROTHESAY (1540–1541); STEWART, ROBERT, DUKE OF ALBANY (1541).

**JAMES VI OF SCOTLAND AND I OF ENGLAND (1566–1625).** The first monarch to rule the whole of the British Isles, James was born in **Edinburgh** Castle on 19 June 1566, the only child of **Mary, queen of Scots**, and her second husband, **Henry Stuart, lord Darnley**. He was proclaimed king on 24 July 1567 after his mother was forced to abdicate.

For most of his minority, James lived at **Stirling** Castle, where he developed interests in languages and theology, acquiring a love of learning that lasted a lifetime. Although notionally governing in his own right from the age of 12, he was initially buffeted by counselors more experienced in the intricacies of Scottish politics. Then, in August 1582, he was seized by William Ruthven, earl of Gowrie, and held until June the following year, when he escaped and began to pursue his own political course.

It was clear that James's twin aims were to diminish the power of his nobles and to establish a claim to succeed to the throne of England on the death of **Elizabeth I**. The first was achieved by avoiding head-on collisions, balancing opposing groups, and gradually excluding powerful political figures from his government, replacing them with his own appointees—tactics which ensured that, by 1597, factional disputes between powerful families had become rare and that Scotland had entered a lengthy period of domestic peace.

The second aim was achieved on 24 March 1603, when Elizabeth died childless and James was proclaimed king of England (*see* UNION OF THE CROWNS). The joint monarchy offered much potential, both domestically and on the European stage, and many of the new king's policies initially bore fruit despite his lack of familiarity with the English political system. The war with Spain was ended the year following his accession, law and order were established on the border between England and Scotland, trade between English and Scottish merchants was encouraged, and attempts were made to place colonists in Ulster and Nova Scotia.

However, despite these secular successes, James was in conflict with Presbyterian churchmen in Scotland. With an unwavering belief that he had a **divine right** to rule, he attempted to subject the church to his personal authority, an authority that the increasingly democratic theologians were unwilling to accept. Through its sermons and its hold on the education system, the church had significant influence on the minds of the people and so was a considerable threat to the king's power. James's solution was to attempt to impose bishops, a move that was much resented by a population that felt it was an anglicization of their worship. Further reforms, including a new liturgy and changes in ceremony (such as the obligation to kneel for communion), were similarly resisted and provoked resentment against a monarch who appeared to have abandoned his native country, earning him the title of "the wisest fool in Christendom."

In England, too, he had problems. His success in dealing with political factions was not repeated south of the border, partly because of his limited understanding of the English parliamentary system, partly because his habit of lecturing assemblies on the rights of kings made his hearers wary, partly because he frequently took the law into his own hands (he summoned parliament only once between 1611 and 1621), and partly because his extravagances greatly added to the country's debt.

Moreover, his foreign policy showed considerable disdain for English public opinion. In particular, he developed a scheme to unite warring Protestant and Catholic nations through marriage; his daughter, **Elizabeth of Bohemia**, was wedded to the Protestant Prince Frederick V, elector palatine of the Rhine, and his heir, Charles (later King **Charles I**), was intended for Maria Anna, daughter of the Catholic King Philip III of Spain, even though the Spanish were occupying Frederick's lands and the majority of James's English subjects wholeheartedly supported Elizabeth's husband. However, if that policy was to be implemented, James would need money, and money meant having a parliament that could raise funds. Parliament, though, resented the sovereign, so when it was summoned in 1621, it launched an attack on his government and claimed the right to dictate foreign policy. Despite the rebuff, Charles was sent to Spain in 1623, but he returned with no prospect of marriage. James, by this time an aging figure taking less and less interest in politics, reversed his previous strategy and capitulated to parliament the following year. Suffering from dysentery, he died on 27 March 1625 at **Theobalds House**, a Hertfordshire residence he had acquired in 1607, and was buried in **Westminster Abbey**.

Historians have tended to be critical of James VI and I, but there were mitigating circumstances, and some recent studies have offered more generous assessments. In England, he had the misfortune of following a popular monarch whose period of rule was frequently depicted later as one of the most glorious in English history. Also, he was a newcomer, unused to the intricacies of English politics and the English parliamentary system, and he was succeeded by a politically inept son who compounded his faults. In addition, his physical impediments—his shambling walk and constantly dribbling mouth—gave him a most unkingly appearance and made his lectures on divine rights difficult to accept, but he took Scotland from domestic discord to lasting peace, fostered the arts, had an unshakable belief in his calling, and used considerable political skill to keep both of his kingdoms out of expensive international wars. His vision was often narrow, but in many ways he was one of the more able members of the **House of Stuart**. *See also* ANNE OF DENMARK; CASKET LETTERS; DUNFERMLINE ABBEY; HAMPTON COURT PALACE; HATFIELD PALACE; LINLITHGOW PALACE; NONSUCH PALACE; STUART, HENRY FREDERICK, PRINCE OF WALES; STUART, MARGARET; STUART, MARY (1605–1607); STUART, ROBERT, DUKE OF KINTYRE; STUART, SOPHIA; TOWER OF LONDON; WHITEHALL PALACE.

**JAMES VII OF SCOTLAND AND II OF ENGLAND (1633–1701).** The last of Britain's Roman Catholic kings, James was deposed in the **Glorious Revolution**, which confirmed the power of parliament over the monarchy. He was born to King **Charles I** and **Henrietta Maria of France** at **St. James's Palace**, London, on 14 October 1633 and succeeded to the throne on 6 February 1685 because his older brother, **Charles II**, had died without leaving any legitimate offspring (though there were more than a dozen who were illegitimate).

After his father was executed in 1649, James fled to the Netherlands and then joined his mother in **France**. He returned to England with the **restoration of the monarchy** in 1660 and was made lord high admiral, a post for which he was well suited after serving with the French and the Spanish forces. In 1668 or 1669, James secretly joined the Roman Catholic Church. When this became public knowledge in 1672, it caused much anxiety because at the time Catholicism was associated widely with royal absolutism and was seen as the root of all evil. The concern forced him to resign his naval position, and it increased in 1673 when he married the Roman Catholic **Mary of Modena** (his first wife, the Protestant **Anne Hyde**, whom he had wed in 1660, had died two years earlier). Charles II's advisors put much pressure on him to exclude James from the succession, but he refused, and in practice James remained favorably disposed toward the **Church of England**, cultivated its leaders, and gradually won the approval of many of its more conservative elements.

As a result of his temperate approach to differences in belief, James initially met little opposition from the clerics when he became king. However, rebellions by James Scott, duke of Monmouth (*see* MONMOUTH REBELLION), and Archibald Campbell, earl of Argyll, during the summer of 1685, although unsuccessful, led to disputes between the monarch and his English parliament, largely because James gave Roman Catholic officers posts of influence in the army. Then, in 1686, Catholics were appointed to the **Privy Council** and to high offices of state, and the religious opposition to his rule began to mount again.

In 1687, the king issued a proclamation (usually known as the Declaration of Indulgence) that suspended laws discriminating against Roman Catholics and others who preferred not to worship in the Anglican fold, and in November of the same year he announced that his queen was pregnant, raising the specter of a Catholic successor to the throne. Anglicans, worried by the trends and fearful of the implications, talked increasingly of ousting him and handing the crown to William of Orange (later **William III of England and II of Scotland**), the husband of James's elder daughter, Mary (later **Mary II**). The breaking point came in the spring of 1688, when James reissued his declaration, ordering that it should be read in all churches on 4 May. Seven clerics, including the archbishop of Canterbury (the Church of England's senior bishop), petitioned him to withdraw the order and were charged with seditious libel. The courts acquitted the priests on 30 June, but on the same day, a group of leading Englishmen sent a letter to William asking him to come with an army and call a free parliament.

William answered the call, landing with his troops at Torbay on 5 November and preparing to face the royalist forces, but James's Protestant officers deserted in large numbers, and he felt unable to commit himself to battle. Then Anne (later Queen **Anne**), his younger daughter, defected as well, and, seeing his support slipping away, he escaped to France on 23 December. On 12 February 1689, the English parliament declared that he had abdicated. The Scots reached a similar decision on 11 April.

James plotted in vain to win back his throne. In 1689, he landed in Ireland, and a parliament summoned in Dublin acknowledged him as king, but his army, composed largely of Frenchmen and Irishmen, was defeated at the **Battle of the Boyne** on 1 July 1690. James returned to exile in France and died of a brain hemorrhage at the Chateau of St. Germain-en-Laye, west of Paris, on 5 September 1701. Having by that time acquired something of a reputation as a holy man, his body was cut up, and pieces were given to those who might appreciate them, the brain going to the Scots College in Paris and the bowels to the English College at St. Omer. The rest of his corpse was interred in the church of the English Benedictines, but the tomb was disturbed during the French Revolution and his remains were scattered.

Historians have differed in their assessments of James, some characterizing him as a bigoted tyrant, others seeing him as a genuine believer in religious liberty who was out of tune with the times. *See also* ALBA; DIVINE RIGHT OF KINGS; PRINCESS ROYAL; STUART, CATHERINE; STUART, CATHERINE LAURA; STUART, CHARLES, DUKE OF CAMBRIDGE (1660–1661); STUART, CHARLES, DUKE OF CAMBRIDGE (1677); STUART, CHARLES, DUKE OF KENDAL; STUART, CHARLOTTE MARIA; STUART, EDGAR, DUKE OF CAMBRIDGE; STUART, ELIZABETH; STUART, HENRIETTA; STUART, ISABELLA; STUART, JAMES, DUKE OF CAMBRIDGE; STUART, JAMES FRANCIS EDWARD; STUART, LOUISA MARIA THERESA.

**JOAN, COUNTESS OF KENT (1328–1385).** The mother of King **Richard II** and wife of **Edward, the black prince** (heir to the English throne until his death in 1376), had a checkered domestic career. The daughter of **Edmund of Woodstock, earl of Kent** (son of King **Edward I**), and his wife, Margaret Wake, Joan (sometimes known simply as Joan of Kent) was born c20 September 1328. In 1339 or 1340, at the age of about 12, she secretly married 19-year-old Thomas de Holland (later earl of Kent) without getting the required approval from the reigning monarch, **Edward III**. Shortly afterward, while Thomas was involved in military campaigns in **France** (*see* HUNDRED YEARS' WAR), Joan's parents arranged for her to wed William Montacute, son of the earl of Salisbury, and she took her vows without revealing anything of the earlier match. When Thomas returned and learned of his wife's bigamous relationship, he successfully petitioned Pope Clement VI for an annulment of the second marriage. Joan supported the petition, much to Montacute's displeasure, and in 1349 she returned to her first husband, with whom she had four (or possibly five) children.

In 1361, a year after Thomas's death, Joan is said by some sources to have participated in another clandestine wedding, this time with Edward, the black prince, whom she had known since childhood. The secrecy may have been necessary because the two were cousins and were therefore within the degrees of consanguinity prohibited by the Roman Catholic Church, but the king, who had initially opposed the union, persuaded Pope Clement to grant a dispensation that would allow them to marry openly. The ceremony was held on 10 October 1361 in **Windsor Castle**.

In 1362, Edward was created prince of **Aquitaine**, so the couple moved court to southwest France, where their children—Edward (who did not survive childhood) and Richard—were born. They returned to England in 1371, with the black prince's resources depleted and his health in decline after a long period of warfare in France and Castile. After her husband's death in 1376, Joan exerted considerable influence over her young son during the early years of his kingship. She died at **Wallingford Castle**, probably on 7 or 8 August 1385, while pleading with him not to execute John Holland, a son by her first marriage who had killed Ralph Stafford and incurred the displeasure of **Anne of Bohemia**, the **queen consort**. John was spared, and Joan—often known as "the Fair Maid of Kent" because of her beauty—was buried, at her request, in Greyfriars Church at Stamford, beside Thomas, her first husband, even though the black prince had prepared a chapel at Canterbury Cathedral for her remains.

**JOAN OF ACRE (1272–1307).** When Edward, duke of Gascony and later **Edward I**, went on crusade to the Holy Land in 1271, he took his young wife, **Eleanor of Castile**, with him. Eleanor gave birth to two daughters during the journey. The first (**Juliana Plantagenet**) died after only a few weeks, but Joan, born at Acre (in western Galilee) in April 1272, survived into adulthood. While still a child, she was betrothed to Hartmann, the second son of King Rudolf I of Germany, but he drowned before the marriage could take place, so on 30 April 1290 she was wed to Gilbert de Clare, earl of Hertford and earl of Gloucester, at **Westminster Abbey**. The union—the first occasion on which a daughter of England's royal house married one of her father's subjects—was designed to benefit the king's coffers. Gilbert, 30 years older than his bride, was one of the wealthiest barons in England, and Edward approved the match only when the bridegroom agreed that all of his estates would be inherited by one of Joan's direct descendants, even if that descendant was the offspring of a later marriage.

Over the next five years, the couple had a son (Gilbert), who succeeded to his father's titles, and three daughters (Eleanor, Elizabeth, and Margaret) who inherited the family lands when their brother died fighting the Scots at the **Battle of Bannockburn** in 1314. However, Gilbert senior died at Monmouth Castle on 7 December 1295, and two years later Joan secretly married Ralph de Monthermer, who had been an attendant in her household. Furious that his daughter would consider such a low-born husband, Edward threw Ralph into prison but later relented and made him a baron. Joan had another two sons and two daughters but died at Clare, in Suffolk, giving birth to a fifth child, stillborn, and was buried at the Augustinian priory there on 23 April 1307.

For a time, there were reports that visitors to her grave were miraculously cured of toothaches and other ailments. Ralph survived until 1325 and did not remarry.

**JOAN OF ENGLAND (1210–1238).** As the eldest daughter of King **John** of England and his wife, **Isabella of Angoulême**, Joan—also known as Joanna and born on 22 July 1210—was considered a potential bride by many of the noble families of Europe seeking partners for their sons. After advances by Philip II of **France** were spurned, Joan was betrothed to Hugh X of Lusignan in an effort to compensate him for the loss of Isabella, whom he had been planning to marry when John kidnapped her. However, after the king's death in 1216, the **queen dowager** decided to take Hugh as a second husband. Subsequently, **Henry III**, the new monarch, dispatched envoys to Scotland with instructions to arrange a match between Joan and King **Alexander II**.

The union was attractive to both rulers. Alexander believed that he could convince Henry to give Joan Northumbria (which the Scot had long coveted) as a dowry, and Henry believed that the wedding would help to cement the fragile peace between the two countries. The couple married at York Minster in June 1221 (the date is given by various sources as 18 June, 19 June, 21 June, and 25 June). At the time, Joan was 9 years old and Alexander was 21. The pair regularly visited the English court, and Joan remained there through the autumn and early winter of 1237 after making a pilgrimage to Canterbury. Early in 1238, she was taken ill at Havering-atte-Bower, a favorite **royal residence** northeast of **London**, and on 4 March she died, still childless, cradled in Henry's arms. She was buried, according to legend, in a golden coffin at Tarrant Abbey, a Cistercian nunnery in Dorset.

**JOAN OF NAVARRE (c1368–1437).** Nine years after **Mary de Bohun** died, King **Henry IV** took Joan (or Joanna) of Navarre, widow of John, duke of Brittany, as his **queen consort** and second wife. They were married on 7 February 1403 at **Winchester** Cathedral in a union that was not popular with many of Henry's subjects because Joan was French, and England had recently been involved in a lengthy conflict with her countrymen (*see* HUNDRED YEARS' WAR). In 1413, the king died and was succeeded by his son, who ruled as **Henry V** and needed funds to pursue military campaigns in **France**. The **queen dowager** refused to provide any resources, partly because her own children were still on the European mainland and, in some cases, had declared their allegiance to Charles V, the French king. Henry, furious at the rejection, took advantage of rumors that Joan had dabbled in necromancy, accused her of trying to kill him by sorcery, had her imprisoned in Pevensey Castle from 1419 to 1422, and confiscated her estates so that he could use the income to supplement his war chest. After her release, she retired to the royal manor at Havering-atte-Bower, northeast of **London**, and died there on 9 July (or, according to some sources, 10 June) 1437. Her remains were interred near those of Henry IV in Canterbury Cathedral, but her ghost is said to appear regularly at Pevensey.

**JOAN OF THE TOWER (1321–1362).** The youngest child of King **Edward II** and **Isabella of France**, Joan (also known as Joan of England and Joanna of England) was born in the **Tower of London** on 5 July 1321. The circumstances of her birth were inauspicious; rain drained through the roof of the room where the queen lay in labor, and soon after the birth Isabella pleaded unavailingly with her husband to rid the court of his unpopular advisors, whom she hated. Matters did not improve. On 17 July 1328, at the age of seven, Joan was married to four-year-old David, son of King **Robert I** of Scotland and later King **David II**, at Berwick-upon-Tweed as part of a peace arrangement between the English and the Scots (*see* NORTHAMPTON, TREATY OF).

Robert died the following year, and in 1334, with the two countries again at war, the children were sent to the court of Philip VI of **France** in an effort to ensure their safety. They returned in 1341, when David was considered able to govern his people himself, but in 1346 the Scottish king was taken prisoner by the armies of **Edward III** and was held in captivity for 11 years because his countrymen could not afford the ransom that was demanded. The couple never lived together again. Joan moved back to England and died at Hertford Castle, near **London**, on 7 September 1362, never having borne children. Like many other members of the **House of Plantagenet**, she was buried at Greyfriars Church in Greenwich.

**JOAN, QUEEN OF SICILY (1165–1199).** The seventh child, and third daughter, of **Henry II** and **Eleanor of Aquitaine**, Joan was born at Angers Castle, Anjou, in October 1165. On 13 February 1177, she was married to William, king of Naples and Sicily, in the cathedral at Palermo, but after her husband died in 1189, she was imprisoned by his successor, Tancred, and held for several months until her brother, **Richard I**, forced her captor to release her and return the dowry paid to William on her marriage. Richard put Joan on a ship and sailed for the Holy Land, where he attempted to marry her to Al-Adil, the younger brother of Saladin, leader of the Muslim community. Both parties declined, and a later plan that she should marry Philip II of **France**, Richard's close ally, also came to naught, but eventually, in October 1196, she took Raymond of Toulouse as her second husband. Three years later, however, Joan, heavily pregnant, fled to her mother's court at Rouen in order to escape an uprising by Raymond's nobles, and on 4 September she died in childbirth at **Fontevrault Abbey**, where her father lay buried.

Joan had one child with William, but the boy failed to survive infancy, so her husband's death brought the Hauteville dynasty, the Sicilian branch of the **House of Normandy**, to an end. With Raymond, she had two sons and a daughter; one son, also named Raymond, lived to succeed his father as count of Toulouse. *See also* BERENGARIA OF NAVARRE.

**JOHN (1167–1216).** King John was undoubtedly one of the more unpopular English monarchs, losing much of the territory formerly held by the **House of Anjou** in **France**, warring with his nobles, and reducing his realm to civil war. He is sometimes known as John Lackland (a reference both to his limited inheritance as the youngest of five sons and to his sacrifice of the French estates) or John Softsword (a nickname earned as a result of his lack of skill at warfare).

Most writers agree that John was born in Beaumont Palace, near Oxford, on 24 December 1167 to King **Henry II** and **Eleanor of Aquitaine**, though some suggest that the birth was actually a year earlier. By the time Henry died in 1189, his three eldest boys had predeceased him, so Richard, the fourth son, took the throne as **Richard I**. The new king created John count of Mortain, confirmed the lordship of Ireland that was originally conferred on him in 1177, and granted him extensive estates but required him to stay away from England while the monarch was on crusade in the Holy Land. John willingly accepted the titles and the lands, but his acquiescence to exile ended after only a few months when Richard recognized Arthur, son of **Geoffrey, duke of Brittany** (his older brother), as his heir. Then, when news arrived of Richard's capture by Leopold V of Austria in 1193, John paid homage to King Philip II of France and made arrangements for the dispersal of many of Richard's continental holdings. When the king was released in 1194, John was initially punished by banishment and forfeiture of his properties, but within a few weeks the brothers were reconciled, some of the territories were returned, and in 1197 John was recognized as the new heir to the throne. He was crowned in **Westminster Abbey** on 27 May 1199, following Richard's death the previous month.

In many ways, John's reign was a disaster for England. Unrest in his continental estates led to war with Philip, who was keen to take advantage of any signs of rebellion and annex the territories for himself. By 1206, Anjou, Maine, Normandy, and much of Poitou were lost. Determined to reverse his fortunes, the king tried to increase his tax revenues in order to finance a campaign against the French, only to see his problems multiply as a result of conflict with the church. In 1206, Pope Innocent III appointed Stephen

Langton to the See of Canterbury following the death of Hubert Walter. John insisted that, as king, he could name his own archbishop, and the argument escalated to the extent that John was excommunicated in 1209. However, by that time, the quarrel was seriously diverting him from his efforts to regain his lands in France, so in 1212 he agreed to accept both Langton and the pope's terms for his return to the ecclesiastical fold. On 15 May 1213, he surrendered his kingdom to Innocent III, receiving it back as a vassal paying annual tribute.

The long-delayed campaign against Philip began in February 1214 and ended in failure on 27 July, when John and his allies were decisively defeated at the Battle of Bouvines without regaining any of the former estates. In England, this failure added to the discontent that was simmering as a result of erosion in national prestige, heavy taxes, and resentment at the monarch's efforts to curb the nobles' power. In May 1215, the anger boiled over into civil war, and John was forced to accept the provisions of the **Magna Carta**, which gave the church the right to choose its own officials, emphasized the power of the courts by decreeing that no freeman would be punished except according to the law, and limited the possibilities for extortion by stating that the king could not extract money from feudal tenants without their consent.

Shortly afterward, John appealed to Pope Innocent III, who annulled the agreement, but the nobles reacted by inviting Prince Louis of France (later King Louis VIII) to bring an army in aid of their cause (*see* FIRST BAR-ONS' WAR). John still had the support of many leading families and strenuously resisted the rebellion, but he contracted dysentery and died at Newark on 19 October 1216 (or possibly on the previous day), before the conflict was over. His death brought peace, ensuring the withdrawal of the French force and the succession, as King **Henry III**, of his eldest son by **Isabella of Angoulême**.

John was buried in Worcester Cathedral and since then has been cast as the archetypal evil king. However, though deceitful and callous, he made many donations to the church and promoted several important administrative innovations. He was never as politically or militarily isolated as some histories have suggested, and modern scholars claim that the Magna Carta was a document of enormous importance, greatly influencing the evolution of the legal process in England. In 2006, the British Broadcasting Corporation's *History Magazine* named John the 13th century's worst Briton, but Winston Churchill, the United Kingdom's prime minister during World War II, was less critical, suggesting that "the English-speaking world [owes] more to the vices of John than to the labours of virtuous sovereigns." *See also* ALEX-ANDER III; CROWN JEWELS OF THE UNITED KINGDOM; ELEANOR, COUNTESS OF LEICESTER; ISABEL OF GLOUCESTER; ISABELLA,

HOLY ROMAN EMPRESS; JOAN OF ENGLAND; RICHARD, EARL OF CORNWALL; WALLINGFORD CASTLE.

**JOHN DE BALLIOL (?–1268).** In the mid-13th century, John, the father of King **John of Scotland**, was one of the richest men in Britain. He was of Norman descent, the son of Hugh de Balliol, lord of Barnard Castle (in England) and Bailleul-en-Vimeu (in **France**), and his wife, Cecilia de Fontaines. Hugh, a committed supporter of King **John** of England, probably named his son after the monarch.

In 1233, John de Balliol married **Dervorguilla**, who inherited large parts of the extensive estates owned by her father, Alan, lord of Galloway, when he died the following year. Command of these resources gave John much power, allowing him to serve as an advisor to King **Henry III** of England from 1258 to 1265 and to act as guardian to King **Alexander III** of Scotland during his minority. He supported Henry during the **Second Barons' War** but was captured at the Battle of Lewes on 12 May 1264 and suffered both a period of imprisonment and temporary confiscation of his lands.

In 1263, John became involved in a dispute about feudal rights with Walter Kirkham, bishop of Durham. He lost the argument and as a penance was required to found a college for poor students at Oxford University. Balliol College still survives and, in terms of applications for undergraduate admissions, is the most popular in the institution. He and Dervorguilla had eight children, including three sons who predeceased their brother, leaving John junior to pursue the successful Balliol claim to the throne after the death of **Margaret, maid of Norway**, in 1290. John senior died c25 October 1268.

**JOHN LACKLAND (1167–1216).** *See* JOHN.

**JOHN OF ELTHAM, EARL OF CORNWALL (1316–1336).** The second son of **Edward II** and **Isabella of France**, John was born in **Eltham Palace**, a royal home located southeast of **London** near the road that linked the capital to ports along the English Channel. Some sources give 15 August 1316 as his birth date, while others note 25 August. Several possible marital partners were considered, but on 13 September 1336, before any plans could be finalized, John died at Perth while serving with the English army in Scotland. Prior to his creation as earl of Cornwall in 1328, he was known as John of Eltham, after his birthplace.

**JOHN OF GAUNT, DUKE OF LANCASTER (1340–1399).** The fourth son of **Edward III** and **Philippa of Hainault**, John was the de facto ruler of England during his father's last years, and he continued to exercise power in the realm's governing councils while **Richard II**, Edward's successor, was too young to make decisions himself. He was born in Ghent (which the English knew as Gaunt) on 6 March 1340 and on 19 May 1359 married his third cousin, Blanche (*see* BLANCHE, DUCHESS OF LANCASTER), in a union that led to his acquisition of the estates and title of the duchy of Lancaster (*see* LANCASTER, HOUSE OF).

John allied with Edward's mistress, Alice Perrers, to run the country while his father became increasingly senile, but the administration was not particularly successful, partly because his support for John Wycliffe and other leaders of the Protestant movement annoyed orthodox Roman Catholic churchmen and partly because the corruption of many of his officials was widely resented. On the accession of 10-year-old Richard II in 1377, John became the leading figure in the councils to which government was entrusted, and during the early 1380s, he increasingly played the role of peacemaker between one faction of nobles that were loyal to the king and another (led by John's brother, **Thomas of Woodstock, duke of Gloucester**) that took issue with the young monarch's choice of advisors and his policies for conducting the **Hundred Years' War** with **France**.

However, John was also interested in gaining a crown for himself. Blanche died in 1369, a victim of the bubonic plague that was sweeping the country, and two years later he married Constance, daughter of Peter I of Castile and Léon. Peter had also died in 1369, murdered by his brother Henry, without leaving an heir, so by 1372, John of Gaunt was styling himself "king of Castile and Léon." In 1386, intent on confirming his right to the title, he attempted an invasion of Castile, but it failed dismally, forcing him to withdraw with a payment of £100,000 and an annual pension in return for renouncing his rights to the kingship.

During John of Gaunt's absence from England, the political climate deteriorated drastically, primarily because no other noble was able to exert a moderating influence as attitudes toward Richard hardened. However, after the duke's return, the king gradually regained his authority, and in 1397 he was able to carry out a purge of his enemies that included the murder of Thomas of Woodstock, apparently with John's approval. Lancaster was poorly rewarded for this loyalty to the sovereign. After his death at Leicester Castle on 3 February 1399, Richard confiscated his estates, thus providing an excuse for Henry Bolingbroke, John's heir, to mount a rebellion, depose him, and rule as King **Henry IV**.

John of Gaunt's marriage to Blanche produced three daughters (including Philippa, the eldest, who became queen of Portugal through marriage with King John I in 1387) and four sons (including Henry). His union with Constance produced a son (John, who died in infancy) and a daughter (Katherine, who married King Henry III of Castile in 1393). Two years after Constance's death in 1394, and to the surprise of many courtiers, John married Katherine Swynford, who had been his mistress for more than 20 years. Pope Boniface IX legitimized their four illegitimate children, all adults by the time of the wedding. Philippa, Katherine's sister, was the wife of poet Geoffrey Chaucer, who is best known for his descriptions of late-14th-century England in his *Canterbury Tales* but who also commemorated John's first wife in *The Book of the Duchess* (which is also known as *The Deth of Blaunche*). *See also* BEAUFORT, JOAN; BEAUFORT, MARGARET, COUNTESS OF RICHMOND; EDMUND OF LANGLEY, DUKE OF YORK.

**JOHN OF LANCASTER, DUKE OF BEDFORD (1389–1435).** The fourth son of King **Henry IV** and **Mary de Bohun**, John acted as **regent** in **France** for six years from 1422, while **Henry VI** was too young to rule England's possessions there, and he was responsible for the execution of Joan of Arc. He was born on 20 June 1389 and was created the first duke of Bedford by his older brother, **Henry V**, in 1414. A military commander of considerable skill, he won several notable victories during the **Hundred Years' War** in alliance with John, duke of Brittany, and Philip, duke of Burgundy, but his attempts to further English interests were constantly hampered by a lack of resources and by political problems at home. He resigned the regency after a seven-month siege of Orléans (a strategic settlement on the River Loire) ended in failure, but he retained control of Normandy, where he arranged for the trial and execution of Joan of Arc in 1431, effectively making her a martyr to the French cause.

In 1423, Bedford married Anne, daughter of his ally Philip of Burgundy, but she died in childbirth nine years later. So, in 1433, the duke took Jacquetta of Luxembourg, daughter of Peter, count of St. Pol, Brienne, and Conservan, as his second wife. This choice of bride was designed to strengthen relations between England and the Holy Roman Empire because Jacquetta was a cousin of Sigismund, who was crowned Holy Roman Emperor in the same year, but it also strengthened the resolve of the French, partly because France and the Empire had a long history of disagreement and partly because it was Joan's uncle, John of Luxembourg, who had captured Jacquetta and sold her to the English.

In 1435, the duke of Burgundy changed sides, and on 14 September Bedford died, dejected, in Rouen. However, despite his failure to expand English territorial possessions in Europe, he left a significant legacy, having founded the University of Caen in 1432. Bedford was also an important patron of the arts, commissioning several illuminated manuscripts, including a lavishly decorated book of hours, now held by the British Library, that was prepared for his first wedding and shows the duke and Anne in their formal court dress.

**JOHN OF SCOTLAND (c1250–c1314).** When **Margaret, maid of Norway**, died in the Orkney Islands in 1290 en route to her **coronation**, she left no clear successor to the Scottish throne. Fourteen claimants stepped forward, so in order to avoid civil war, the **regents** governing the country invited King **Edward I** of England to act as adjudicator. Edward seized this opportunity to demand that, in return for his services, the Scots would recognize him as their overlord. The nobles pointed out that without a king there was nobody in the realm that had power to make such a concession. Nevertheless, most of the competitors for the crown willingly agreed to the deal, and on 17 November 1292, Edward's committee announced that John, son of **John de Balliol** and his wife, **Dervorguilla**, was the successful candidate.

Much of the new monarch's early life is unknown, but, as the great-great-great-grandson of King **David I**, he undoubtedly had the strongest case in terms of primogeniture, which, over the previous two centuries, had become the established method of choosing rulers. It soon became clear, however, that Edward intended to enforce his overlordship, refusing to accept Scottish claims to independence and insisting that John owed him feudal allegiance. In 1294, the Scottish king was summoned to **London**, where he was told to provide an army that would support an English invasion of Gascony. The pliant monarch agreed, but his readiness to assist was not shared by the Scottish nobles, who promptly appointed a 12-member council of advisors that took over the management of government; then, on 23 October 1295, they asserted Scottish sovereignty by formalizing an alliance with Philip IV of **France**.

Edward reacted by invading Scotland, pushing further and further northward as castle after castle fell to his army, and eventually, on 10 July 1296 at Stracathro, near Brechin, he demanded Balliol's abdication. With the arms of Scotland torn from his clothing, John was later known as "Toom Tabard" or "empty coat." He was imprisoned in the **Tower of London** until 1299, when he was allowed to leave for France, where he died in about 1314, though neither the precise date nor the place of his burial is known. Twenty years later, **Edward de Balliol**, his son by **Isabella de Warenne**, mounted his own challenge for the crown.

Despite John's unpopularity, the Scots argued that his abdication was invalid because it had been achieved by force and that, even after being imprisoned in London, he was the country's rightful king. The military campaigns against the English that were led in 1297 by William Wallace—hero of the *Braveheart* movie—were mounted in his name, but in effect, from the time of his removal from Scotland until the **coronation** of **Robert I** (Robert the Bruce) in 1306, his country was without a monarch. *See also* BALLIOL, HOUSE OF; REGNAL NAME.

**JOHN, PRINCE (1905–1919).** **Prince** John, the youngest child of King **George V** and **Mary of Teck**, suffered from epilepsy and spent his short life far from the public gaze. Born at **Sandringham House** on 12 July 1905, he first showed signs of the illness when he was four years old, and from the age of 11, as his seizures became more frequent, he was cared for at Wood Farm on the royal estate, where he had few playmates but, according to several reports, seemed happy. He died there on 18 January 1919 after a particularly severe seizure and was buried nearby at the Church of St. Mary Magdalene. In recent years, some commentators have claimed that the **royal family** saw the prince as an embarrassment and so shut him away and forgot about him. Other observers dispute these assertions, pointing out that early 20th-century medicine offered no treatment for epilepsy and that, in the austere conditions of British life during World War I, some special accommodation was necessary for the child. There is little doubt, however, that John's parents and siblings heard of his death with mixed feelings. Queen Mary described it as "a great release" for her son's "restless soul," and his older brother, Edward (later King **Edward VIII**), referred to it as "the greatest relief imaginable."

**JOHN SOFTSWORD (1167–1216).** *See* JOHN.

**JUDITH OF FLANDERS (c844–870).** In 855, **Aethelwulf**, king of **Wessex** and father of **Alfred the Great**, embarked on a pilgrimage to Rome. On the return journey, he stopped at the court of Charles II, king of West Francia, and formed an alliance that was sealed by his marriage to Judith, Charles's daughter. The wedding ceremony was held at Verberie sur Oise on 1 October 856, when the bride was about 12 years old and the groom about 60. Unusual for the Wessex Saxons, who normally referred to their leader's consort simply as "the wife of the king," Judith was given the style of "queen," probably in recognition of her high status at the Frankish court. The couple had no children.

When Aethelwulf died two years later, Judith wed Aethelbald, one of his five sons by an earlier marriage to **Osburga**, but the union was quickly annulled on the grounds of consanguinity. She then returned to Francia and in 861, and much to her father's annoyance, eloped with Baldwin, count of Flanders, with whom she had three sons. She died in 870, still in her twenties.

# K

**KATHARINE, DUCHESS OF KENT (1933– ).** In 1994, the duchess of Kent became the first member of the **royal family** for more than three centuries to desert the **Church of England** and take holy communion as a Roman Catholic. The only daughter of Sir William Arthrington Worsley (an army officer and cricketer) and his wife, Joyce, she was born at Hovingham Hall (the family home in Yorkshire) on 22 February 1933 and was educated at Queen Margaret's School (near York) and at Runton Hill School (Norfolk). She met **Edward, duke of Kent**, in 1956 while he was based at the Catterick army barracks, not far from her home, and married him at York Minster on 8 June 1961. They have three children—**George Windsor, earl of St. Andrews** (born on 26 June 1962); **Lady Helen Taylor** (born on 28 April 1964); and **Lord Nicholas Windsor** (born on 25 July 1970)—none of whom performs royal duties.

Despite a long history of illness (in 1999, she told the *Daily Mail* newspaper that she suffered from celiac disease, but other sources have suggested that she is also a victim of chronic fatigue and depression), the duchess has taken a considerable interest in children's charities, visiting poorer areas of the world on behalf of the United Nations International Children's Fund in an effort to publicize problems of poverty. This work enhanced her compassionate image—an image strengthened in 1993 when television viewers around the world watched her put a comforting arm around Jana Novotna, who dissolved into tears after losing to Steffi Graf in the final of the Wimbledon tennis championships. An accomplished musician who plays the piano, organ, and violin, she has also devoted time to helping young instrumentalists, cofounding Future Talent in 2004, a charity that nurtures the musical skills of children from deprived backgrounds.

In 1994, the duchess decided to worship with the Roman Catholic Church rather than with the Church of England, in which she had been raised—a radical step because the **Act of Settlement**, passed by the English parliament in 1701, had banned heirs to the throne from being, or marrying, a Catholic, and her husband, a cousin of Queen **Elizabeth II**, was 18th in the line of succession. She admitted that the decision was "long-pondered" and explained that it was made because the "Catholic Church offers you guidelines," but several prominent Anglicans suggested that the Church of England's willingness to depart from long-standing traditions (by ordaining woman priests, for example) may have caused concern and precipitated the move. Since then, her younger son, Lord Nicholas, has joined her in the Catholic fold, as have two of the earl of St. Andrews' children—Edward, lord Downpatrick, and Lady Marina-Charlotte Windsor. Since 2002, the duchess has limited her public commitments and has made little use of her formal title ("**her royal highness** the duchess of Kent"), preferring to be known as Katharine Kent. She still teaches music in a Hull school.

**KENNETH I (?–c858).** *See* MACALPIN, KENNETH.

**KENNETH II (?–995).** Kenneth, son of **Malcolm I**, succeeded **Colin** as king of **Alba** in 971. He raided the neighboring kingdom of Strathclyde and plundered as far south as Northumbria, but in 973 he was one of several leaders who accepted **Edgar of England** as overlord, getting control of Lothian (the territory between the River Forth and the River Clyde) in return. It is also possible that Colin's brother, **Amlaíb**, dethroned him for a short period but that Kenneth was able to kill the usurper and win back the crown.

Some sources suggest that—at the expense of descendants of former kings **Duff** and **Indulf**—Kenneth attempted to change the laws of **succession to the throne** in favor of his son, who became **Malcolm II** in 1005; if so, the moves would undoubtedly have led to disputes within the kin group from whom leaders of the kingdom were chosen. Kenneth was assassinated in 995, probably in northeast Scotland at Fettercairn, with some sources suggesting that a woman named Finnguala, whose only son Kenneth had murdered, plotted his death. In addition to Malcolm, Kenneth may have left two other children—Dúngal and his brother Boite (who may actually have been the son of **Kenneth III** and was the father of **Macbeth's** wife, **Gruoch**).

**KENNETH III (?–1005).** In 997, Kenneth, son of **Duff**, followed in his father's footsteps by becoming king of **Alba** when he or one of his supporters killed **Constantine III** in battle at Rathinveramond, an unidentified location probably close to Perth. Constantine died childless, so the victory ended a feud over the kingship that had lasted for over a century and involved the branches of the family descended from **Áed** and **Constantine I**, the sons of **Kenneth MacAlpin**, who had formed the kingdom by uniting the territory of Dalriada (in the west of Scotland) with Pictish lands north of the River Forth in about 843.

Little is known of Kenneth III, but it is clear that familial strife continued because on about 25 March 1005 he was killed in battle at Monzievaird (in the Vale of Strathearn some 15 miles west of Perth) by his cousin, who succeeded to the throne as King **Malcolm II**. One source claims that the deposed monarch was interred on the island of **Iona**, the traditional burial ground of early Scottish kings. Kenneth may have left three sons—Gille Coemgáin (who, according to some sources, was killed in about 999); Giric (reported as dying with his father at Monzievaird); and Boite (who was also known as Bodhe and Boedhe, and who may have been the son of King Kenneth II and the father of **Gruoch**, wife of **Macbeth**).

**KENNINGTON PALACE.** In 1337, King **Edward III** gave the manor of Kennington (now part of the **London** Borough of Lambeth) to **Edward, the black prince**, who built a large palace on the site now bounded by Cardigan Street and Sancroft Street. The building was the location for meetings of parliament in 1340 and 1342 and often hosted important visitors, including **Richard II** and **Catherine of Aragon**, but it was torn down in 1531 so that the stone could be used in **Henry VIII**'s new palace at **Whitehall**. The area is now occupied primarily by housing, but the land is still part of the royal property estate, owned by the Duchy of Cornwall (*see* DUKE OF CORNWALL). The local pub is the Duchy Arms.

**KENSINGTON PALACE.** Originally a country mansion, Kensington Palace, which now stands at the southwest corner of Kensington Gardens in central **London**, has experienced several phases of development. The first building on the site was erected early in the 17th century by Sir George Coppin and was purchased in 1689 by King **William III of England and II of Scotland**, who instructed architect Christopher Wren to supervise an extension. Following the death of his wife, Queen **Mary II**, at the house in 1694, the king (who disliked central London, where the air pollution exacerbated his asthmatic condition) became increasingly attached to the property, lavishing much attention on the landscaping of the gardens. After suffering serious injuries when he fell from his horse at **Hampton Court Palace** in 1702, he begged to be taken back so that he too could die there.

In 1714, Queen **Anne**—William's sister-in-law and successor—also passed away at Kensington (a result of apoplexy caused by overeating). She had treated the residence as a pleasant rural escape, but **George I** wanted greater comfort, and a building more in keeping with his royal status, with new state rooms, improved kitchen facilities, and additional courtyards, was built in 1718. **George II** made Kensington his main residence, but **George**

**III**, who succeeded him in 1760, preferred a home nearer the corridors of power and favored **St. James's Palace**.

Since that time, no reigning monarch has lived at Kensington Palace, but it has been much used by other members of the **royal family**. Queen **Victoria** was born in a ground-floor room in 1819 and held her first **Privy Council** meeting in the Red Saloon in 1837. In 1867, Princess Mary Adelaide gave birth to a daughter, also Mary (*see* MARY OF TECK), who was to become the consort of King **George V**, and in recent years, **Charles, prince of Wales**, and **Diana, princess of Wales**; **Princess Alice, duchess of Gloucester**; **Princess Margaret, countess of Snowdon**; **Prince Richard, duke of Gloucester**, and **Birgitte, duchess of Gloucester**; and **Prince Michael of Kent** and **Princess Michael of Kent** have all had accommodations there.

Victoria opened the state apartments (designed by Colen Campbell and decorated by William Kent) to the public in 1889, and access to other rooms (including the young Victoria's bedroom and nursery) was granted in 1933. Visitors can view an exhibition of court dress and see numerous mementos of Victoria's reign. *See also* AUGUSTUS FREDERICK, PRINCE, DUKE OF SUSSEX; GEORGE, PRINCE OF DENMARK; GEORGE WILLIAM, PRINCE; LEWIS, LADY DAVINA; LOUISE, PRINCESS, DUCHESS OF ARGYLL; MARINA, PRINCESS, DUCHESS OF KENT.

**KEW PALACE.** Kew—the smallest of the British royal palaces—stands in the Royal Botanic Gardens in southwest **London**. The four-story, red brick building, erected by merchant Samuel Fortey in about 1631, was originally known as the "Dutch House" because its gabled frontage looked more typical of buildings in the Low Countries than of those in southern England. It was first used by the **royal family** in 1728, when **Caroline of Brandenburg-Ansbach**, consort of King **George II**, leased it as a home for her three eldest daughters, **Anne, princess royal (1709–1759)**; **Princess Amelia (1711–1786)**; and **Princess Caroline Elizabeth (1713–1757)**.

**George III** eventually bought the property in 1781, intending it to be a temporary base while a larger palace was erected nearby, but as his family grew (he had nine sons and six daughters), the space was needed for children, so it became a permanent home. On several occasions, the king retired to Kew while he was suffering from his bouts of insanity; three of his sons— **Prince Adolphus, duke of Cambridge**; **Prince Edward, duke of Kent and Strathearn**; and **Prince** William, duke of Clarence (later King **William IV**)—married there in 1818; and his queen, **Charlotte of Mecklenburg-Strelitz**, died in one of the rooms just four months later.

George's plans for a more commodious residence were never completed, and 19th-century royal families were much less enamored of the small building than their 18th-century predecessors had been. When Queen **Victoria** succeeded to the throne in 1837, she gifted the gardens to the nation, and in 1898, as her reign was drawing to a close, she opened the palace to a curious public. A decade-long, £6.6 million restoration program was completed in 2006, just before **Charles, prince of Wales**, hosted an 80th birthday party for his mother, Queen **Elizabeth II**, in the building. *See also* OCTAVIUS, PRINCE.

**KING CONSORT.** A king consort is a male who has married a queen rather than a male who has succeeded to the throne. The term has been used only twice in Britain—for the husband of **Mary I** of England (Philip, heir to the Spanish throne and later **Philip II of Spain**) and **Henry Stuart, lord Darnley**, the second husband of **Mary, queen of Scots**. Consorts of other **queens regnant** have been styled "**prince**," as in the case of **Prince Philip, duke of Edinburgh**, husband of Queen **Elizabeth II**. *See also* KING REGNANT; QUEEN CONSORT.

**KING REGNANT.** A king who has succeeded to the throne, rather than married a queen, is known as a king regnant. The term is very rarely used in the British context because consorts of reigning queens are usually styled "**prince**" (thus the husband of Queen **Victoria** was **Prince Albert of Saxe-Coburg and Gotha**, not King Albert). By implication, all kings are kings regnant, so the descriptor is dropped. *See also* KING CONSORT; QUEEN CONSORT; QUEEN DOWAGER; QUEEN REGNANT.

**KING'S BIRTHDAY HONOURS LIST.** *See* QUEEN'S (OR KING'S) BIRTHDAY HONOURS LIST.

**KING'S OFFICIAL BIRTHDAY.** *See* QUEEN'S (OR KING'S) OFFICIAL BIRTHDAY.

# L

**LADY-IN-WAITING.** Ladies-in-waiting act as personal aides to female members of the **royal family**. In the past, they were often close relatives, who were more likely than strangers to be trustworthy (**Anne Boleyn**, the second wife of King **Henry VIII**, had her sister, Mary, as lady-in-waiting, for example). Nowadays, however, the women, who are not considered servants and do not carry out menial duties, are usually members of aristocratic families or close friends. Those who attend a queen are properly known as women of the bedchamber or, if they are wives or widows of peers ranked earl or higher, as ladies of the bedchamber. The former normally work for two or three weeks at a time, and the latter attend ceremonial events.

Ladies-in-waiting receive no remuneration, performing their tasks simply for the honor or because they are acquaintances of the queen. The most senior of the attendants is known as the mistress of the robes and since 1830 has always been a duchess. Formerly, her duties primarily involved care of clothes, but in the modern **Royal Household**, she arranges the rota of ladies-in-waiting and accompanies the queen or **queen consort** to important ceremonies of state.

**LADY OF THE BEDCHAMBER.** *See* LADY-IN-WAITING.

**LANCASTER, HOUSE OF.** The Lancastrian kings of England—**Henry IV** (who reigned from 1399 to 1413), **Henry V** (1413–22), and **Henry VI** (1422–61 and 1470–71)—were members of the **House of Plantagenet** dynasty who could trace their ancestry through **John of Gaunt**, duke of Lancaster and fourth son of King **Edward III**. The Lancaster name dates from 1267, when **Henry III** created his youngest son, **Edmund, earl of Lancaster**—a title that John of Gaunt was to acquire through marriage to Edmund's great-granddaughter (*see* BLANCHE, DUCHESS OF LANCASTER) in 1359. John was elevated to the dukedom by his father in 1362.

The family ruled for more than 60 years, but its hold on the crown was eventually pried loose at the **Battle of Tewkesbury** in 1471, when its supporters were defeated by the armies of the **House of York**, which claimed the throne by descent from **Lionel of Antwerp**, John of Gaunt's older brother. Despite this setback, the bloodline reappeared at the royal court in 1485 because **Margaret Beaufort**, John of Gaunt's great-granddaughter, was the mother of **Henry VII**, the first English king from the **House of Tudor**. Also, Margaret's descendants carried the Lancastrian line into the **House of Stuart** when **Margaret Tudor**, her granddaughter, married King **James IV** of Scotland and became the grandmother of **Mary, queen of Scots**. *See also* ANJOU, HOUSE OF; BOSWORTH FIELD, BATTLE OF; EDWARD OF LANCASTER, PRINCE OF WALES; ELIZABETH OF YORK; JOHN OF LANCASTER, DUKE OF BEDFORD; ST. ALBANS, FIRST BATTLE OF; ST. ALBANS, SECOND BATTLE OF; TOWTON, BATTLE OF; WAKE-FIELD, BATTLE OF; WARS OF THE ROSES.

**LASCELLES, GEORGE, EARL OF HAREWOOD (1923– ).** George Lascelles—the elder son of **Mary, princess royal and countess of Harewood**, and **Henry Lascelles, earl of Harewood**—was born at Chesterfield House (his parents' **London** home) on 7 February 1923 and was educated at Ludgrove School (in Wokingham, Berkshire) and at Eton College. During World War II, he served with the Grenadier Guards in Italy but was taken captive in June 1944. He was then sent to Germany and imprisoned in Colditz Castle until it was liberated by the 1st United States Army in April the following year. After his release, he worked for a year as a personal secretary to his great-uncle, Alexander Cambridge, earl of Athlone, who was **governor-general** of Canada, and then followed a course of undergraduate study at Cambridge University, completing a bachelor of arts degree in 1948.

Lascelles succeeded to his father's earldom in 1947 and soon afterward began to carve out what became a very distinguished career as an administrator in the arts. Among other posts, he was director of the Royal Opera House at Covent Garden, London, from 1951 to 1953 and from 1969 to 1972; an innovative director for the English National Opera from 1972 to 1985 and chairman of its board from 1986 to 1995; and director of the festivals at Leeds (1958–64), **Edinburgh** (1961–65), and Adelaide (1988). He was also a governor of the British Broadcasting Corporation (1985–87), president of the Football Association (1963–72), and president of the Board of Film Classification (1985–96).

Harewood married twice, first (at St. Mark's Church in Mayfair, London, on 29 September 1946) to Austrian concert pianist Marion Stein and then (in New Canaan, Connecticut, on 31 July 1967, following his divorce earlier the same year) to Australian violinist Patricia Tuckwell. He has three sons by Stein. David, his heir, born on 21 October 1950, runs Harewood House, the family home in Yorkshire, as a tourist attraction and, like his father, has married twice, initially (in 1979) to Margaret Messenger, whom he divorced in 1989, and then (in 1990) to Diane Howse. He has four children by Messenger—Emily (born in 1976), Benjamin (1978), Alexander (1980), and Edward (1982).

James Lascelles, Harewood's second son, born on 5 October 1953, has built a career as a musician in the popular and ethnic music industries. He has married three times—to Frederica Duhrrsen of Newport, Maine, in 1973 (divorce followed in 1985); to Lori "Shadow" Lee of New Mexico in 1985 (with the divorce in 1996); and to Nigerian actress Joy Elias-Rilwan (whose stage name is Joy Lemoine) in 1999. He has two children by Duhrrsen (Sophie, born in 1973, and Rowan, born in 1977) and two by Lee (Tanit, a daughter, born in 1981, and Tewa, a son, born in 1985). Jeremy Lascelles, the third son (born on St. Valentine's Day in 1955), is a music publisher, and he too has married twice, first (in 1981) to Julyie Bayliss and then (in 1999) to Catherine Bell; he has three children by Bayliss (Thomas, Ellen, and Amy, born in 1982, 1984, and 1986, respectively) and one (Tallulah, born in 1985) by Bell.

Lord Harewood also has a son—Mark, born in 1965—by Tuckwell. In 1992, Mark married radiographer Andrea Kershaw, by whom he has three daughters—Charlotte (born in 1996), Imogen (1998), and Miranda (2000).

**LASCELLES, GERALD (1924–1998).** Lascelles—the younger son of **Mary, princess royal and countess of Harewood**, and her husband, **Henry Lascelles, earl of Harewood**—was born at Goldsborough Hall, one of the family's country homes in Yorkshire, on 21 August 1924. He served with the Rifle Brigade during World War II, but after his elder brother—**George Lascelles, earl of Harewood**—was taken prisoner by the Germans in 1944, he was refused permission to travel abroad because of his relatively high position (8th at birth) in the line of **succession to the throne**.

When the conflict ended, Lascelles was able to pursue his interest in fast cars, acting as the president of the British Racing Drivers' Club from 1964 to 1991 and playing an important role in developing Silverstone, on the border of Berkshire and Northamptonshire, as one of Britain's most important motor-sport circuits. On 15 July 1952, at St. Margaret's Church in Westminster, **London**, he married Angela Dowding, whom he had met at a party hosted by John "Johnny" Wodehouse, earl of Kimberly (and husband to six women from 1945 to 1982). Dowding was an actress—at the time, a decidedly unconventional partner for a member of the **royal family**—and the match, subject to the **Royal Marriages Act** of 1772, required Queen **Elizabeth II**'s approval, which was only given after considerable pleading by the groom's mother.

The couple acquired the much run-down **Fort Belvedere** in Surrey—where Edward, **prince of Wales** (later King **Edward VIII**), had plotted assignations with his mistress, American divorcee Wallis Simpson (*see* WALLIS, DUCHESS OF WINDSOR), prior to his abdication—and turned it into a comfortable home, entertaining celebrities such as Jack Brabham and Jim Clark from the world of motor racing and Louis Armstrong and Duke Ellington from the world of jazz. However, Lascelles had an extramarital dalliance with Elizabeth Colvin, another actress, and in 1978 divorced his wife in order to marry his paramour at a ceremony in Vienna on 17 November the same year. They settled in **France** in 1991, and he died at Sigoules, in the Dordogne, on 27 February 1998.

Lascelles left a son by each wife. Henry, born on 19 May 1953 to Angela Dowding, was educated at Eton College and married Alexandra Morton in 1979. They have one son (Maximilian, born in 1991) but divorced in 1999. Martin, who was born illegitimately to Elizabeth Colvin on 9 February 1962, changed his surname to Lascelles when his parents married in 1978. He was educated at Bryanston School in Blandford, Dorset, and pursued a career as a musician; he is a gifted performer on the keyboard and now lives in France. He has one child (Alexandre, born in 2002) by Charmaine Eccleston, whom he married in 1999, and another (Georgina, born in 1988) as a result of a relationship with singer Carol Douet.

**LASCELLES, HENRY, EARL OF HAREWOOD (1882–1947).** Lascelles, the husband of **Mary, princess royal and countess of Harewood** and the only daughter of King **George V**, was born at 43 Belgrave Square, **London** (the home of Orlando Bridgeman, his maternal grandfather), on 9 September 1882, the eldest of three children in the family of Henry Lascelles, earl of Harewood, and his wife, Lady Florence. He was educated at Eton College before entering the Royal Military Academy Sandhurst.

Despite his army training, Lascelles initially set out on a political career, acting as personal secretary to Earl Albert Grey, **governor-general** of Canada, from 1907 to 1911 and attempting, unsuccessfully, to become the member of parliament for Keighley in 1913. However, the outbreak of World War I in 1914 took him back to soldiering, which he performed with some gallantry, suffering wounds on three occasions and winning both the Distinguished Service Order from Britain and the Croix de Guerre from **France**.

In 1916, Henry inherited the large estates of his paternal uncle, Hubert de Burgh-Canning, remembered as one of the most callous of the English landholders in Ireland. The income allowed him to indulge his artistic tastes in furniture and painting and his sporting interests in horse racing; it also made him an attractive partner for Mary, the **princess royal**. Some sources have alleged that the **princess** was pressured into marriage by her parents even though she had no love for a man who was 15 years her senior. Others have suggested that Lascelles extended his offer of marriage in order to win a bet, but their elder son—**George Lascelles, earl of Harewood**—has maintained that they were happy together. After the wedding, held in **Westminster Abbey** on 28 February 1922, Lascelles accompanied his wife on many of her royal engagements but also made his own contribution to public life (he was a chancellor of Sheffield University, a **lord lieutenant** of West Yorkshire, a magistrate, a president of the Royal Agricultural Society, and a trustee of the British Museum, for example). Following his death on 23 May 1947, much of his property had to be sold to meet inheritance taxes, but Harewood House in Yorkshire is still owned by the family, and the rooms are open to visitors. *See also* LASCELLES, GERALD.

**LAURENCE, VICE-ADMIRAL TIMOTHY (1955– ).** Laurence, the second husband of **Anne, princess royal (1950– )**, was born on 1 March 1955 in Camberwell, **London**, to Guy Laurence (a marine engine salesman) and his wife, Barbara. He was educated at New Beacon School in Kent and then at Sevenoaks School before studying at the University of Durham, where he graduated with a geography degree in 1976. Then, after training at the Royal Naval College Dartmouth, he served on a series of ships (including *Britannia*, the **royal yacht**) before taking up a post as equerry to Queen **Elizabeth II** in 1986.

While carrying out his duties, Laurence met **Princess** Anne, whose first marriage—to **Mark Phillips**—was under severe strain. The new relationship blossomed, and on 12 December 1992, the year of Anne's divorce, they married at **Crathie Church**, close to **Balmoral Castle**, choosing a Church of Scotland ceremony because the **Church of England** was unwilling to marry divorcees. After the wedding, Laurence (who did not take a title) continued with his naval career, holding staff posts from 1992 to 1995 and then commanding the frigates *Cumberland* and *Montrose* for two years before taking a desk job at the Ministry of Defence. In 2007, he was promoted to vice-admiral and made chief executive of Defence Estates, which is responsible for the management of the ministry's property portfolio, covering about 1 percent of Britain's landmass.

Although the media have sometimes suggested that Laurence's marriage is under stress and that some members of the **royal family** treat him as though he is still an equerry, he is widely regarded as a modest, unassuming man who has built a substantial professional reputation by dint of talent and hard work rather than by using his royal connections. *See also* GATCOMBE PARK.

**LEOPOLD, PRINCE, DUKE OF ALBANY (1853–1884).** Leopold, the fourth son and eighth child of Queen **Victoria** and **Prince Albert of Saxe-Coburg and Gotha**, was the first member of the **royal family** whose birth was assisted by the administration of chloroform, which was used by Victoria while she was in labor and thus, according to some writers, encouraged wider acceptance of the procedure by aristocratic mothers.

Born at **Buckingham Palace** on 7 April 1853, the **prince** was a scholar of some ability, studying at Oxford University from 1872 to 1876, but throughout his life he was dogged by hemophilia and epilepsy. Attempting to disregard the limiting effects of ill health, he tried to lead a vigorous life, adopting new clothing fashions, making speeches in support of the expansion of technical education, supporting the Royal Society of Literature (he was elected president in 1878) and the Society of Arts (where he became vice president in 1879), traveling to Europe and (in 1880) to Canada and the United States, and lending influence to numerous charities, including the Royal Institution in Aid of the Deaf and Dumb.

Victoria would have much preferred her son to lead a sheltered existence, but he was determined to be independent, and that included finding a wife. The task was not easy because his illnesses discouraged potential partners, but eventually the queen (who had considered several of Leopold's suggested brides wholly unsuitable and rejected any possibility of a Roman Catholic) arranged an introduction to Princess Helen of Waldeck-Pyrmont, a tiny German principality. They married in **St. George's Chapel** at **Windsor Castle** on 27 August 1882, and in February of the following year, much to her mother-in-law's surprise, Helen produced a healthy daughter (Princess Alice, countess of Athlone, who was later to have a son—Rupert—who would inherit his grandfather's hemophilia). Shortly afterward, Leopold asked to be considered for the post of **governor-general** of Canada, which was being vacated by his brother-in-law, John Campbell (marquess of Lorne and husband of **Princess Louise, duchess of Argyll**), but his mother rejected the idea out of hand.

Early in 1884, with his wife pregnant again, the prince was advised by his doctors to escape the rigors of the **London** winter and spend some weeks in the more benign climes of southern **France**. On 27 March, he slipped on a staircase in the Cannes Yacht Club after dinner and died early the next morning. Leopold was buried in St. George's Chapel, just four months before his wife gave birth to their second child, Prince Charles Edward (who was healthy, because hemophilia cannot be passed from father to son).

Helen never remarried, devoting much of her energy to charitable organizations. Alice took Prince Alexander of Teck (the younger brother of **Mary of Teck**, consort of King **George V**) as her partner and traveled with him when he acted as **governor-general** of South Africa in 1924–30 and of Canada in

1940–46. At Queen Victoria's insistence, Charles Edward inherited the duchy of Saxe-Coburg and Gotha from his uncle **Alfred, duke of Edinburgh and Saxe-Coburg and Gotha**, and joined the German army at the outset of World War I, a decision that resulted in the loss of his British titles. Sibylla, his elder daughter, became the mother of King Carl XVI Gustaf of Sweden, and his three sons fought for Adolf Hitler's forces during World War II. Princess Alice, visiting Germany in an effort to trace Charles after the conflict ended, found him searching through garbage for food.

**LEWIS, LADY DAVINA (1977– ).** Lady Davina—the elder daughter, and second child, of **Prince Richard, duke of Gloucester**, and **Birgitte, duchess of Gloucester**—was born, like her older brother (**Alexander Windsor, earl of Ulster**) and her younger sister (**Lady Rose Gilman**), at St. Mary's Hospital in Paddington, **London**. Early education at Kensington Preparatory School in Notting Hill was followed by classes at St. George's School, Ascot, which her sister also attended, as, some years later, did **Princess Beatrice of York**, the elder daughter of **Prince Andrew, duke of York**. From there, she went to the University of the West of England, where she graduated with a degree in media studies.

On 31 July 2004, at **Kensington Palace**, Lady Davina married New Zealander (and former sheep shearer turned property renovator) Gary Lewis, whom she had met four years earlier while on holiday in Bali, Indonesia. Apparently, without initially revealing her family background, she went to New Zealand and lived with him for over a year in Grey Lynn, a working-class suburb of Auckland, before returning to the United Kingdom. Lewis, who has a son (Ari, born in 1992) by a previous partner, is the first person of Maori descent to marry into the **royal family**. Neither Lady Davina nor her husband, both of whom try to keep a low profile, is required to carry out public engagements.

**LINE OF SUCCESSION TO THE THRONE.** *See* SUCCESSION TO THE THRONE.

**LINLITHGOW PALACE.** Linlithgow—the birthplace of King **James V** in 1512 and **Mary, queen of Scots**, in 1542—stands beside a small loch almost midway between the royal castles at **Edinburgh** and **Stirling**. King **David I** erected a residence on the site during the 12th century, and English troops occupied the building for much of the period from 1296 to 1314, following the invasion led by King **Edward I** ("the hammer of the Scots"). However, most of the present structure dates from the decades after 1424, when **James I of Scotland** began a program of reconstruction and expansion that was continued, in particular, during the reigns of **James III**, **James IV**, and James V. The palace fell into disrepair during the tempestuous years of the late 16th century, and although King **James VI and I** rebuilt the north range and King **Charles I** continued refurbishment, much of their work was destroyed by royalist armies as they chased **Charles Edward Stuart**'s retreating Jacobite troops in January 1746. The ruins are now maintained by Historic Scotland (a government agency charged with the conservation of buildings of national importance) and are open to visitors. *See also* STUART, MARGARET.

**LIONEL OF ANTWERP, DUKE OF CLARENCE (1338–1368).** Lionel, the third son of King **Edward III** and **Philippa of Hainault**, was born on 29 November 1338 in Antwerp, and on 9 September 1342, in the **Tower of London**, he married Elizabeth de Burgh, heiress to extensive family estates in Ireland. Styled earl of Ulster from 1347, he was made chief governor of Ireland in 1361 and then, in 1365, was created duke of Clarence (the name is derived from Elizabeth's properties in Suffolk).

Through his wife's inheritance, Lionel administered large territories of Connacht, Munster, and Ulster in north, west, and southwest Ireland. Thus, as a member of the **royal family**, he had a vested interest in curbing the tendency of English barons on the island to hold only a tenuous loyalty to the monarch and identify themselves increasingly as Irish. In 1366, he encouraged a parliament at Kilkenny to pass statutes that prohibited marriage between native Irish people and English settlers, required the immigrants to use English rather than Irish Gaelic as a means of communication, and prevented the adoption of Irish dress, customs, and sports. The legislation had little impact, however, because Clarence had neither the funds nor the manpower to enforce it, and the following year, frustrated, he returned to England.

Elizabeth died in Dublin in 1363, so on 28 May 1368, Lionel married Violante, the teenage daughter of Galeazzo Visconti, lord of Pavia, who promised a large dowry. By 17 October, Lionel was dead, allegedly poisoned in Alba (Italy) by his new father-in-law, though that was never proven. He left one child—Philippa, born to Elizabeth on 16 August 1355—who became the great-great-grandmother of King **Edward IV** and King **Richard III**. *See also* HENRY IV; WARS OF THE ROSES.

**LONDON.** London, the capital of the United Kingdom, has had royal associations since late Anglo-Saxon times, when **Edward the Confessor** built **Westminster Abbey**, where every English monarch has been crowned since his successor, King **Harold II**, in 1066, and every British monarch since King **George I** in 1714. **William I of England** (William the Conqueror) made the city his base from 1066, building the **Tower of London** both as a fortress and as a means of impressing his subjects. With the royal court in London, noble families erected homes nearby, and a considerable civil service developed as parliament increased its powers.

The monarch's principal residence is at **Buckingham Palace**, in the heart of the city, though foreign ambassadors are still accredited to the **Court of St. James's** because **St. James's Palace** was the hub of royal decision making from the 16th to the 19th century as the country became a European and then a world power. Other members of the **royal family** also occupy accommodations (such as **Clarence House** and **Kensington Palace**) in the city center, which is the location for the country's most important ceremonial occasions, including banquets for foreign dignitaries, royal weddings, state funerals, the **state opening of parliament**, and the **trooping of the colour** that marks the **queen's (or king's) official birthday**. *See also* ALBERT OF SAXE-COBURG-GOTHA, PRINCE; CARLTON HOUSE; CHANGING OF THE GUARD; CROWN ESTATE; ELTHAM PALACE; HAMPTON COURT PALACE; KENNINGTON PALACE; KEW PALACE; MARLBOROUGH HOUSE; NONSUCH PALACE; PLACENTIA, PALACE OF; ROYAL PECULIAR; SHEEN PALACE; SOMERSET HOUSE; UNION OF PARLIAMENTS; WESTMINSTER, PALACE OF; WHITEHALL PALACE; WHITE LODGE.

**LORD LIEUTENANT.** A lord lieutenant is appointed by the monarch to act as his or her representative in areas (usually counties) of the United Kingdom. The post dates from the 16th century, when the holder's duties related primarily to the organization of local defense and the maintenance of civil order. In more modern times, the holder of the office maintains links with local bases of the armed forces and with ambulance, fire, and police services, but the duties are largely ceremonial, involving tasks such as supervising arrangements for royal visits and representing the sovereign at funerals and other significant events.

**LORD OF THE ISLES.** The lordship is one of the subsidiary titles held by the **duke of Rothesay**. It was first used in the 12th century by rulers of the islands along Scotland's west coast and parts of the adjacent mainland. The first lords were immensely powerful, governing virtually as independent monarchs, but their successors gradually lost authority to the Scottish kings until, in 1493, King **James IV** stripped John MacDonald, the last nonroyal lord, of the title. MacDonald's descendants made several unsuccessful efforts to regain the dignity, but King **James V** reserved it for the crown in 1540 and gave it, along with the dukedom, to his short-lived son, James (*see* STEWART, JAMES, DUKE OF ROTHESAY [1540–1541]). Since then, both titles have been granted to the **heir apparent** to the Scottish, British, and United Kingdom thrones.

**LOUISA, QUEEN OF DENMARK AND NORWAY (1724–1751).** Louisa, the youngest of **Caroline of Brandenburg-Ansbach** and King **George II**'s nine children, was born at Leicester House in **London** on 7 December 1724. On 10 November 1743, in Hanover, she was married by proxy to Frederick, son of Christian VI, king of Denmark and Norway, with her brother— **William Augustus, duke of Cumberland**—standing in for the groom (a service he had also performed at the wedding of Louisa's older sister, **Princess Mary, landgravine of Hesse-Cassel**, three years earlier). On 1 December, a second ceremony was held at Christiansborg Castle in Copenhagen, with both principals present.

The union was arranged solely for political reasons (King George's ministers wanted Danish support in disputes with Prussia), but the couple seemed happy, and Louisa, who encouraged performances by actors and musicians, was a popular figure at court even though she never exerted significant influence over her husband's decision making. She bore five children but died at Christiansborg on 19 December 1751, at the age of 37, following complications during her pregnancy with the sixth child, and was buried in Roskilde Cathedral. In 1766, Christian, her second son (the older boy, who carried the same name, died just before his second birthday), further cemented the relationship between the British and Danish royal houses by marrying his cousin, Princess Caroline Matilda, the youngest child of **Frederick, prince of Wales**, and sister of King **George III**.

**LOUISE, PRINCESS, DUCHESS OF ARGYLL (1848–1939). Princess** Louise Caroline Alberta, the sixth child and fourth daughter of Queen **Victoria** and **Prince Albert of Saxe-Coburg and Gotha**, was the first member of a British **royal family** in more than 300 years to marry a commoner. Born at **Buckingham Palace** on 18 March 1848, she grew up to be an artistically talented, attractive teenager who had little time for the conservative ways of Victoria's court or for the queen's insistence on a lengthy period of mourning after **Prince** Albert's death in 1861. Various eligible bachelors from the royal houses of Europe were considered as potential husbands, but Louisa wanted none of them, preferring instead John Campbell, marquess of Lorne and heir to George, duke of Argyll. Albert Edward, **prince of Wales** (later King **Edward VII**), objected to the proposed match on the grounds that royal blood should not be diluted, but Victoria overruled him, considering that the Argylls were "no lower in rank than minor German royalty," and her subjects greeted the news with considerable fervor. The wedding, held at **St. George's Cha-**

pel in **Windsor Castle** on 21 March 1871, was the first occasion on which a princess had married outside of royalty since **Mary Tudor, queen of France**, defied her brother—King **Henry VIII**—to marry Charles Brandon, duke of Suffolk, in 1515 and **James Hepburn, earl of Bothwell**, abducted **Mary, queen of Scots**, and forced her to become his wife in 1567.

Louise's marriage started well, but relations later deteriorated, partly because the union remained childless and possibly because the marquess may have been homosexual. Moreover, the news of Lorne's appointment as **governor-general** of Canada in 1878 was not well received by those Canadians who saw no reason why the British crown should interfere with the running of their country, and though Campbell and his wife did much to encourage development, particularly in the arts, Louise was often homesick after moving to North America. On 14 February 1880, both were injured in a sledging accident, and the following year, Louise returned to Britain. Campbell followed in 1833 and pursued a political career.

With her marriage under increasing strain, the princess spent much time improving her artistic skills and socializing with artists. Skillful in several fields, she exhibited in prestigious company at the Society of Painters in Watercolour and carved a marble statue of Queen Victoria that still stands in Kensington Gardens, **London**. She also lent support to campaigns that aimed to improve women's rights (much to her mother's annoyance), formally opened numerous buildings on behalf of the aging queen, and squabbled with her sisters (partly over family jealousies, and partly over rumors—never substantiated—of affairs with artist friends). However, from 1911, Campbell's health worsened as he became more and more senile, and, after spending lengthy periods apart, the couple grew closer as Louise looked after him.

When Lorne died in May 1914, Louise suffered a nervous breakdown but threw herself into charity work, initially for men injured during World War I and then with hospitals (she was president of 25 medical institutions and often visited them unannounced). By the 1930s, though, her own health was deteriorating, and on 3 December 1939, she died at **Kensington Palace**, aged 91, the *Times* declaring in its obituary that she was "the least bound by convention and etiquette of any of the Royal Family." The princess was cremated, and her ashes were initially interred at **St. George's Chapel** but were moved to the royal burial ground at **Frogmore** the following year. The Canadian province of Alberta is named after her; originally, the territory was to be called "Louise," but the princess wanted her father to be honored, so her third given name was chosen instead.

**LOUISE, PRINCESS ROYAL, DUCHESS OF FIFE (1867–1931).** Louise—the eldest daughter, and third child, of Albert Edward, **prince of Wales**

(later King **Edward VII**), and **Alexandra of Denmark**—was born at **Marlborough House**, London, on 20 February 1867. She was accorded the style "**princess royal**" by her father in 1905. Shy and retiring, Louise nevertheless accepted a proposal of marriage from William Duff, earl of Fife, in 1889 and wed at **Buckingham Palace** on 27 July. Duff was created duke of Fife in recognition of his new status as consort to the eldest daughter of a future monarch, but the union was to cause Queen **Victoria** some concern when Louise's older brother, **Albert Victor, duke of Clarence and Avondale**, died unexpectedly and unmarried early in 1892.

Clarence (as the eldest son of the **heir apparent**) had been second in line to the throne after the **prince** of Wales, and Albert Edward had only one other son, George (who later reigned as King **George V**). If George also died without leaving any issue, Louise (as Albert Edward's eldest daughter) would succeed him as sovereign (or succeed her father if George predeceased him), but her children were commoners, and that created the possibility that someone not of purely royal stock could occupy the throne. In any event, George's marriage in 1893 to Princess **Mary of Teck** (who had earlier been betrothed to Albert Victor) and the birth of their children solved the monarch's problem.

In 1911, the duke and duchess of Fife set sail with their teenage daughters on a visit to Egypt, but their vessel, the *Delhi*, ran aground off the Moroccan coast. The whole family survived and traveled on to Cairo, but Fife contracted pneumonia and died at Aswan on 29 January 1912. Although the **princess** royal carried out a number of public duties after that date—she became colonel-in-chief of the 7th Dragoon Guards (the Princess Royal's Own) in 1914, for example—she much preferred to avoid the limelight, living quietly at her home in Portman Square, **London**, where she died on 4 January 1931. She was initially buried in **St. George's Chapel** at **Windsor Castle**, but her remains were later placed beside those of her husband at Mar Lodge, a property they had built in the Cairngorm Mountains in 1895–98.

The Fifes had two daughters and, in 1890, a stillborn son. Alexandra, the elder girl, born in 1891, inherited her father's dukedom as a result of a decree made by Queen Victoria in 1900. She married a first cousin once removed, Prince Arthur of Connaught (the son of **Prince Arthur, duke of Connaught and Strathearn**), in 1913 and worked as a nurse in London during World War I. From 1920 to 1923, she lived in South Africa with her husband while he was **governor-general**. Maud, the younger child, was born in 1893. She married Charles, lord Carnegie (later earl of Southesk) in 1923 and managed a farm with him in northeast Scotland.

**LULACH (?–1058).** Lulach was appointed king of Scots by followers of **Macbeth** after that monarch was killed by Malcolm, the son of **Duncan I**, in August 1057. The son of Gille Coemgáin, the mormaer (or earl) of Moray, and his wife, **Gruoch** (who married Macbeth after her first husband was burned to death, possibly by Macbeth himself), he was a weak ruler with a reputation as a simpleton, surviving only until March the following year, when Malcolm assassinated him too and took the throne as **Malcolm III**. Some sources indicate that Lulach was buried on the island of **Iona**, the last resting place of many of Scotland's early monarchs. He left a son (Máel Snechtai), who seems to have challenged Malcolm's right to the crown, and a daughter, whose name is not recorded and whose son, Angus, was known as king (rather than merely mormaer) of Moray.

**MACALPIN, KENNETH (?–c858).** Traditionally, Kenneth MacAlpin (also known as Kenneth I) is regarded as the king of Dalriada who defeated his Pictish neighbors in 843 and united the two territories into a single realm that covered Britain north of the River Clyde and the River Forth. Many modern scholars dispute this tale, however, suggesting that Kenneth was never the ruler of Dalriada, that he became chief of the Picts through inheritance rather than battle, and that fusion of the two societies occurred over a period of decades rather than in a single year so that his status as the first king of Scots is more legend than fact.

Little is known of Kenneth, although he may have made raids into the lands south of the Forth and undoubtedly was faced with encroachments by Scandinavian invaders. There is little dispute, though, that he founded a dynasty, now termed the **House of Alpin**, that provided leaders of the emerging Scottish kingdom until the mid-11th century. Two of his sons—**Áed** and **Constantine I**—were also to become kings. One daughter (whose name is unknown) married Run, king of Strathclyde, and a second (Máel Muire) was twice married into leading Irish families, initially to Aed Finliath and then to Flann Sinna. After his death, possibly at Forteviot on 8 February 858, and burial (on the island of **Iona**, according to some sources), Kenneth was succeeded by his brother, who ruled as **Donald I**.

**MACBETH (c1005–1057).** Macbeth, king of Scots from 1040 to 1057, has had bad press ever since William Shakespeare wrote his eponymous play in the early years of the 17th century. However, far from being an evil murderer, he rid his country of an ineffective military commander, was regarded by contemporary sources as a legitimate monarch, supported religious communities, and introduced laws that give daughters the same inheritance rights as sons.

The son of **Findláech of Moray** and, possibly, a daughter of **Kenneth II**, **Kenneth III**, or **Malcolm II**, Macbeth succeeded his cousin, Gille Coemgáin, as mormaer (or earl) of Moray in 1032 and confronted King **Duncan I** when that monarch attempted a foray into his territory in 1040. Shakespeare portrays Duncan as an elderly man assassinated while he lay asleep in Macbeth's castle, but in fact he was a youthful and incompetent military leader who died on the battlefield at the hands of his opponent's supporters.

Macbeth's accession to the throne after Duncan's death was widely welcomed and was followed by a lengthy period of peace, broken only by a rebellion in 1045, when **Crinan** (Duncan's father) led an uprising designed to install his grandson (later **Malcolm III**) on the throne. There was also, apparently, considerable prosperity, because in 1050, during a pilgrimage to Rome, the king "scattered alms like seed corn," according to one chronicler. However, on 15 August 1057, Malcolm, with English support, avenged his father's death, mortally wounding Macbeth in a conflict at Lumphanan, some 25 miles west of Aberdeen. Macbeth, according to one source, was buried on the island of **Iona**, and his stepson, **Lulach**, succeeded him but survived for only a few months before he too was killed, leaving Malcolm to claim the throne. *See also* GRUOCH; MORAY, HOUSE OF.

**MADELEINE DE VALOIS (1520–1537).** For a few months in 1537, Madeleine—the daughter of King Francis I of **France** and Claude, daughter of King Louis XII—was **queen consort** of King **James V**. The Scottish monarch had been anxious to find a bride who would both enhance his international standing and augment his treasury through a handsome dowry, but Francis initially proved unwilling to sanction a match with one of his children, partly because he had no wish to annoy **Henry VIII** of England, who had earlier attempted to extend his possessions in the north of the French realm. Madeleine, born at St. Germain-en-Laye on 10 August 1520, was Francis's fifth child and third daughter by his consort Claude.

Never a healthy girl, the Scots king's bride had spent much of her youth in the relatively congenial climate of the River Loire valley. Her father felt that exposure to Scotland's much harsher weather would do nothing to help her condition, but, aware that she and James had fallen for each other, he eventually capitulated to her pleadings that she should be allowed to marry. The couple wed at Notre Dame Cathedral in Paris on 1 January 1537 and sailed for Scotland in May, but Madeleine, who had contracted tuberculosis, became increasingly unwell and died in James's arms in **Edinburgh** on 7 July. The king buried his bride in **Holyrood** Abbey and almost immediately began a search for a second wife, marrying **Mary of Guise** less than a year later.

**MAGNA CARTA.** By appending his seal to the Magna Carta, King **John**, who reigned from 1199 to 1216, became the first English monarch to submit to demands for a detailed limitation to the powers of the sovereign. During the first years of the 13th century, John's policies had led to the loss of long-held estates in northern **France**, eliminating an important source of his nobles' wealth. Also, his arguments with the church (over matters such as the right to appoint archbishops of Canterbury) resulted in a decline in national pride as England became a fiefdom of the pope, and the imposition of heavy taxes (to fund the army) added to a simmering discontent that boiled over into rebellion in 1215. On June 15, in return for promises of loyalty, John met his barons and clerics at Runnymede, on the banks of the River Thames southwest of **London**, and agreed to provisions, outlined in a lengthy manuscript, that would greatly curtail his authority. An amended version was approved four days later, and a formal record of the understanding was prepared by the royal chancery on 15 July. Revised versions of the document, known as the Magna Carta (Latin for "Great Charter" or "Great Paper"), were issued in 1216, 1217, 1225, 1264, and 1297.

The 63 clauses in the Magna Carta covered many aspects of life dealing with the church, landholding arrangements, the legal system, royal appointments, urban trade, and means by which the monarch could be held to the agreement. Most focused on the circumstances of the time and are of little importance to modern society, but three still have legal force. Clause 1 of the 1297 charter guaranteed that "the **Church of England** shall be free," clause 9 confirmed the ancient "liberties and customs" of the City of London, and clause 29 declared that "No freeman shall be taken or imprisoned, or be disseised [dispossessed] of his freehold, or liberties, or free customs, or be outlawed, or exiled, or any other wise destroyed; nor will we . . . condemn him, but by lawful judgment of his peers, or by the law of the land."

Centuries later, the document became a basis of efforts to improve civil liberties, as in 1628, when parliament addressed a petition of right to King **Charles I**, seeking redress for perceived failings by the monarch that included imprisonment contrary to the provisions of the Magna Carta. Its legacy is also evident in the United States' Bill of Rights, which echoes the principles of clause 29 by emphasizing that "No person shall be . . . deprived of life, liberty, or property without due process of law."

Four copies of the 1215 manuscript survive, one in the British Library, one in the House of Lords, one in Lincoln Castle, and one in Salisbury Cathedral. In 2007, Sotheby's auction house in New York auctioned a copy of the 1297 version, owned by the Perot Foundation. It was bought for $21.3 million by David Rubenstein, cofounder (with Stephen L. Norris) of the Carlyle Group, an American-based private equity company, so that it would remain in North America. The Perot Foundation invested the proceeds in provision of assistance to wounded soldiers, improvements to public education, and support for medical research. *See also* FIRST BARONS' WAR.

**MALCOLM I (?–954).** Malcolm succeeded his cousin, **Constantine II**, as king of **Alba** in about 943, possibly by forcing the aging monarch to abdicate. He adopted an aggressive military policy, leading an army northward into Moray, raiding southward into Northumbria, and apparently winning control over the kingdom of Strathclyde in return for an alliance with **Edmund I**, king of England. In 954, he was killed, either at Dunottar or at Fetteresso (both near Aberdeen), by rebels attempting to avenge their earlier defeat in Moray. One source records that he was buried on the island of **Iona**, where many other early Scottish kings were interred, but there are legends that his remains lie underneath a mound on the Fetteresso Castle estate. *See also* DONALD II; DUFF; KENNETH II.

**MALCOLM II (c980–1034).** Malcolm claimed the crown of **Alba** in 1005 after killing his cousin, **Kenneth III**, in a battle fought at Monzievaird, some 15 miles west of Perth. The son of King **Kenneth II**, he was the first monarch to exert authority over a territory broadly similar in extent to that of modern mainland Scotland outside the Highlands.

In 1018, Malcolm defeated the forces of King **Canute** at Carham, on the River Tweed near Coldstream, and thus strengthened (or perhaps won) control over Lothian in southeast Scotland. According to some sources, King Owen of Strathclyde, in southwest Scotland, died in the struggle, and Malcolm was able to replace him with his grandson, Duncan, thus consolidating his influence over that realm as well. Skillfully negotiated marriages also facilitated the extension of power. In about 1008, the monarch wed Donalda, one of his daughters, to Sigurd, earl of Orkney. Their son, Thorfinn, was raised at Malcolm's court, and when Sigurd was killed in battle in 1014, the five-year-old boy became titular ruler of Orkney and Caithness, relying on his maternal grandfather for the military support needed to thwart threats of invasion by Olaf Haraldsson, king of Norway. (Donalda may previously have married **Findláech of Moray** and given birth to a boy—**Macbeth**—who was also destined to become king.)

Malcolm died in 1034 (on 25 November, according to one source), but accounts of his last hours conflict, some reporting that he passed away quietly at Glamis (near Forfar), and others that he was murdered. His burial place is similarly uncertain, with one source claiming that he lies on the island of **Iona**, but local legend asserts that he was interred at Glamis, where a large, flat stone is alleged to be his grave slab. Duncan followed him, as **Duncan I**, in an uncontested **succession to the throne**, so it is possible that Malcolm, well before his death, had taken measures to dispose of potential competitors for the crown. *See also* ALPIN, HOUSE OF; BETHÓC; GRUOCH.

**MALCOLM III (c1031–1093).** Malcolm III ruled Scotland for 35 years, introducing Anglo-Saxon customs that, despite the protests of significant factions among his subjects, were to end many of the Celtic traditions at the royal court. He was taken to safety, probably in England, after **Macbeth** killed his father, **Duncan I**, and assumed the crown in 1040. In 1057, however, he returned, avenged Duncan's death, and then, on 17 March the following year, assassinated **Lulach**, who had been placed on the throne by Macbeth's followers.

By the time Malcolm claimed the kingship, it is possible that he had married **Ingibiorg Finnsdottir**, widow of Thorfinn of Orkney. They may have had three sons, the eldest of whom was later to become **Duncan II**, but by 1069 she was dead, so Malcolm took Margaret of **Wessex** (later **St. Margaret**) as his second wife. In the company of her mother (**Agatha**, wife of **Edward the Exile**) and her brother (**Edgar Aetheling**, the last **Anglo-Saxon monarch** of England), Margaret had fled to Scotland to find refuge from William the Conqueror (**William I of England**) and his Norman invaders. Malcolm was captivated by the young woman and willingly acquiesced to her wishes, conversing in English (rather than Gaelic) at the royal court, extending contacts with the European mainland, giving their children southern names, and introducing ecclesiastical reforms that she favored.

Inevitably, the welcome accorded to Margaret and her family meant that other Anglo-Saxons sought safety in Scotland, and the Normans, equally inevitably, were concerned that the growing concentration of dissidents would be a threat to their security. William marched an army north in 1072, and Malcolm, rather than meet a superior force in battle, accepted him as overlord, giving his son, Duncan (later Duncan II), as hostage to ensure that he would keep his promise. Several times in the past, however, Scots monarchs had given English kings similar assurances and then ignored them, and Malcolm maintained this tradition, raiding south of the border on several occasions. There is little doubt that the Normans could have crushed him had they wished, but it seems likely that William tolerated the invasions because he feared that any successor would reverse the anglicization of the Scottish court and adopt a much more aggressive anti-England policy (and, in practice, those fears were justified by events after Malcolm's death).

In 1093, Malcolm ravaged Northumbria but was killed in a skirmish at Alnwick on 13 November. **Edward of Scotland**, his eldest son by Margaret, died with him, and Margaret herself, already ill, passed away three days later when she heard the news. Malcolm was buried nearby at Tynemouth Priory, but there are reports that his remains were later reinterred in **Dunfermline Abbey** or on the island of **Iona**. Some sources refer to him as Malcolm Canmore; the soubriquet is derived from the Gaelic *ceann* (meaning "head" or "chief") and *mor* (meaning "great" or "large") and so could indicate either a man with a big head or a great chief. *See also* ALEXANDER I; CANMORE, HOUSE OF; CRINAN; DAVID I; EDGAR OF SCOTLAND; EDINBURGH; EDMUND OF SCOTLAND; ETHELRED OF SCOTLAND; MARY, COUNTESS OF BOULOGNE; MATILDA OF SCOTLAND.

**MALCOLM IV (1141–1165).** King **David I** of Scotland was predeceased by both of his male offspring, so when he died in 1153, he was succeeded by his grandson, Malcolm, the child of **Henry, earl of Northumberland**, and **Ada de Warenne**. Malcolm, only 11 or 12 years old, faced problems both at home and in England, where he had inherited large estates in Cumbria and Northumbria. By a combination of diplomacy and armed might, Scottish claimants to his crown were either defeated or persuaded to accept his rule, but **Henry II** was a more difficult opponent. The English king refused to allow him to keep the lands in northern England, offering instead the earldom of Huntingdon (which, arguably, Malcolm held by right of succession from his father) but requiring Malcolm to pay him homage as feudal overlord.

These arrangements were unpopular with the Scots, who did not like to see their king paying homage to anybody, but even so, Malcolm fought alongside Henry in **France** and took part in a siege of Toulouse in 1159. Sources suggest, however, that he was never a healthy man and that he may have suffered from Paget's disease, which causes enlargement and deformation of the bones. He died at Jedburgh Abbey (one of his grandfather's foundations) on 9 December 1165 and was buried at **Dunfermline Abbey**. Malcolm—sometimes known as "the Maiden" because he lived a celibate life, possibly by choice because he was a deeply religious monarch—never married and so left no heirs. His brother, **William I of Scotland**, succeeded him. *See also* SCONE.

**MALCOLM CANMORE (c1031–1093).** *See* CANMORE, HOUSE OF; MALCOLM III.

**MALCOLM THE MAIDEN (c1141–1165).** *See* MALCOLM IV.

**MANN, KINGS OF.** From 1079, the rulers of the Isle of Man (which lies in the Irish Sea between the coasts of the Republic of Ireland and the United Kingdom) were known as the kings of Mann and the Isles, exercising their power as vassals of the kings of Norway. In 1266, however, the Scandinavians ceded the islands off Britain's northwestern shores to the Scots, and Mann became an independent unit. As control was disputed by England and Scotland, the territory changed hands several times until 1333, when King

**Edward III** renounced all his claims and recognized the island's sovereignty under King William Montacute, earl of Salisbury. King **Henry IV**, Edward's successor, reannexed Mann as an English fiefdom in 1399 but allowed the local rulers to style themselves "king," a title that continued in use until 1504, when Thomas Stanley, earl of Derby, adopted "lord of Mann." Successive rulers have maintained this usage. In 1765, Charlotte Murray, baroness Strange, sold her overlordship rights to the British government, and the title was vested in the crown. Since then, the reigning monarch of the United Kingdom has also been lord of Mann.

**MARGARET, COUNTESS OF KENT (c1193–1259).** Margaret was the first child of **William I of Scotland**, born some seven years after his marriage to **Ermengarde de Beaumont**. In 1209, under the terms of the Treaty of Norham, which prevented an invasion of Scotland by King **John**, William was forced to send her and her sister Isabella (later **Isabella, countess of Norfolk**) to **London** for marriage into the English royal house. However, that plan was never fulfilled because on 19 June 1221, in York, she became the third wife of Hubert de Burgh, who was the most important English noble of the time, acting, in effect, as **regent** for the 13-year-old King **Henry III**. The couple had one child, Margaret (or Megotta), who was born in c1222 and was married at the age of about 10 to Richard de Clare, earl of Hertford and of Gloucester, but lived for only one more year. Hubert, who was created earl of Kent in 1227, died in 1243, but his wife survived until 1259. Her remains were interred at Blackfriars Church in London, close to those of her husband and her sister, **Marjorie, countess of Pembroke**.

**MARGARET, COUNTESS OF PEMBROKE (1346–1361).** The daughter of **Edward III** and **Philippa of Hainault**, Margaret was born at **Windsor Castle** on 20 July 1346. She was married to John Hastings, earl of Pembroke and a friend through much of her early childhood, in May 1359, but she died late in 1361 before having children. Margaret (who is sometimes known as Margaret of Windsor or Margaret Plantagenet) was buried at Abingdon Abbey, where her older sister, **Mary, duchess of Brittany**, was interred shortly afterward. In 1372, during the **Hundred Years' War**, Hastings commanded the English fleet that was soundly defeated at the Battle of La Rochelle. He was taken prisoner by the French and Castilian navies and died in captivity three years later.

**MARGARET, DUCHESS OF BRABANT (1275–c1333).** One of about 12 daughters in the family of **Edward I** and **Eleanor of Castile** (and one of the few to reach adulthood), Margaret was born at **Windsor Castle** on 11

September 1275. She married John, duke of Brabant, in **Westminster Abbey** on 8 July 1290, just a few weeks after one sister, **Joan of Acre**, had wed Gilbert de Clare, and before another, **Eleanor, countess of Bar**, had been united by proxy with Alfonso, king of Aragon. The couple had one son, John, who was born in 1300, succeeded to his father's titles, and became a staunch supporter of the English crown. Margaret (who is also known as Margaret of England and Margaret Plantagenet) died in Brussels in about 1333, her husband in 1312.

**MARGARET, MAID OF NORWAY (1283–1290).** When King **Alexander III** fell from his horse and was killed in March 1286, leaving no surviving children, the Scots nobles kept a promise, originally made to the monarch on 5 February 1284, that they would recognize Margaret, his granddaughter, as successor to the throne. Margaret was the only child of **Margaret, queen of Norway** (who died on 9 April 1283, either while giving birth or soon afterward) and Eric II, king of Norway. Her right to the crown was not unchallenged because Robert Bruce, lord of Annandale and a great-great-grandson of King **David I**, mounted a rebellion in an effort to win the realm for himself, but by 1289 the **regents** who governed Scotland were negotiating with King **Edward I** of England for a marriage between his son (later **Edward II**) and the "maid of Norway."

The English king was in a position of some power because three-year-old Margaret was with her Norwegian father, who could arrange a match whether the Scots liked it or not, and Edward took full advantage of the situation, promising Scotland its independence but demanding control of its castles. The Scottish negotiators were understandably reluctant to accept these conditions, but on 6 November 1289 all parties agreed that Margaret would travel to Scotland before 1 November the following year and that a final decision about marriage would not be made until after her arrival. She sailed in September or early October 1290 but fell ill during the journey. She died on the Orkney Islands and was taken back to Bergen, where she was buried in Christ's Kirk beside her mother.

Although most historians have recognized Margaret's position as queen, some have demurred, pointing out that she was known at the time as "Lady of Scotland," that she was never crowned, and that she never set foot in her kingdom. With her passing, Scotland was plunged into political crisis. When a host of candidates claimed the throne, the Scots asked Edward I to choose one of them, and, in an attempt to ensure English overlordship of his northern neighbors, he selected the pliant John de Balliol (*see* JOHN OF SCOTLAND), a move that led to decades of war between the two countries.

**MARGARET OF ANJOU (1430–1482).** Margaret—**queen consort** of King **Henry VI** of England—was ambitious, politically astute, and militaristic, differing greatly in personality from her pious, mentally unstable husband, who hated war. The daughter of René, duke of Anjou, and Isabelle, duchess of Lorraine, she was born (probably at Pont-à-Mousson in **France**) on 23 or 24 March 1430. Her marriage to Henry at Titchfield Abbey on 22 April 1445 was intended to cement a 21-month truce in the **Hundred Years' War** between England and France and was unpopular with those nobles, including **Richard, duke of York (1411–1460)**, who wanted to see the conflict pursued with greater vigor so that lands lost to the French could be regained. Other critics felt that Margaret, the niece of Charles VII of France, was too distantly related to the French king to be an appropriate bride for the sovereign of England and complained that she had brought no dowry with her. The arrangements for the marriage were spelled out in the Treaty of Tours, which was signed by both sides on 22 May 1444 and included an understanding that **Anjou** and Maine, both of which were still under English control, would be returned to the French. Parliament was not informed of the territorial concessions, so when the matter became public knowledge in 1446, the news inflamed the Yorkist prowar faction even though Henry ultimately refused to give up Maine.

On 13 October 1453, Margaret gave birth to a son, **Edward of Lancaster**, but many in court circles doubted that Henry (who had already suffered from bouts of insanity) could be the father and suggested that the boy was the result of a clandestine relationship with one of the king's close allies, possibly Edmund Beaufort, duke of Somerset, or James Butler, earl of Wiltshire. Increasingly, Margaret feared for her son's life as York defeated royalist armies in the **Wars of the Roses** and then, in 1460, asserted his right to the crown after taking Henry prisoner. Determined to protect the interests of her husband and her son, the queen traveled to the north of England, Scotland, and Wales to find support for her cause, and her commanders won significant military victories at **Wakefield** on 30 December 1460, when York was killed, and at the **Second Battle of St. Albans** on 17 April the following year, when she gained her husband's release.

However, despite these successes, York's son Edward continued to provide a focus of opposition to the monarchy, and, winning the support of **London**, he seized the throne on 4 March 1461, ruling as **Edward IV**. In July 1465, he captured Henry again, and Margaret fled to France, where she made an ally of Richard Neville, earl of Warwick, who had earlier been one of the Yorkists' staunchest allies. Their combined forces were able to return Henry to the throne in 1470, but the success was short lived. Warwick was killed at the Battle of Barnet on 14 April 1471. Then, at **Tewkesbury**, on May 4, the Lancastrians were routed, and Edward, the queen's cherished son, was slain. Henry died (probably by violence) in the **Tower of London** shortly afterward.

Margaret was kept in custody at **Wallingford Castle** and the Tower of London until 1475, when King Louis XI of France paid for her release. She died at the Château de Dampierre in Saumur, Anjou, on 25 August 1482 and was buried in St. Maurice's Cathedral at Angers, but her tomb was destroyed during the French Revolution in 1789–99 and her remains were lost. *See also* TOWTON, BATTLE OF.

**MARGARET OF DENMARK (1456–1486).** Margaret, consort of King **James III**, was born on 23 June 1456, the fourth child and only daughter of King Christian I of Denmark, Norway, and Sweden, and his wife, Dorothea. The wedding, negotiated on behalf of the Scottish monarch by Robert and Thomas Boyd (*see* STEWART, MARY, COUNTESS OF ARRAN), was held at **Holyrood Palace** on 13 July 1469 when the bride was just 13 years old. Her father had promised a dowry of 60,000 Rhenish florins, with 10,000 florins to be paid before Margaret left home and the Orkney Islands pledged as security for the remainder. However, the impoverished Christian could raise only 2,000 florins, so the Shetland Islands had to be pledged as well. And, as the full dowry was never paid, both territories—which had long been a source of contention between the Scots and the Scandinavians—became possessions of the Scottish crown.

Giovanni Sabadino, writing shortly after Margaret's death, credited the queen with greater administrative ability than her husband and pointed out that James avoided her from 1483 until her death. The king had been taken captive by rebels in 1482, and while he was being held, Margaret discussed the education of her three sons—James, born in 1473 (and later King **James IV**); **James Stewart, duke of Ross** (born three years later); and **John Stewart, earl of Mar (born c1479)**—with his brother, **Alexander Stewart, duke of Albany**, who had attempted to win the throne for himself. These conversations may have been enough to make the monarch distrust his wife for the rest of their marriage.

Margaret died at **Stirling** on 14 July 1486 and was buried before the high altar at **Cambuskenneth Abbey**, where her husband was interred two years later. James's enemies claimed, unjustly, that she had been murdered, and the king tried, unsuccessfully, to have her canonized.

**MARGARET OF YORK (1472).** Margaret, the fifth child of **Edward IV** and **Elizabeth Woodville**, was named after the duchess of Burgundy, her paternal aunt. She was born at **Winchester** on 10 April 1472 but failed to survive infancy, dying on 11 December, and was buried in **Westminster Abbey**.

**MARGARET, PRINCESS, COUNTESS OF SNOWDON (1930–2002).** **Princess** Margaret's principles prevented her from marrying the man she loved, but the politics surrounding the affair, and the lifestyle she adopted afterward, meant that the press took a close interest in her activities for the rest of her life. The younger daughter of **Prince** Albert, **duke of York** (later King **George VI**) and Elizabeth Bowes-Lyon (*see* ELIZABETH, THE QUEEN MOTHER), she was born at Glamis Castle, her maternal grandparents' Scottish home, on 21 August 1930 and received a basic education from her governess, Marion Crawford, later complaining that she had not been stretched intellectually because her mother saw little point in providing scholarly opportunities for women.

In 1952, the princess fell in love with Group Captain Peter Townsend, an equerry in the **Royal Household**, but the provisions of the **Royal Marriages Act of 1772** required the approval of the monarch (her sister, Queen **Elizabeth II**) in order to wed, and it was made clear to the sovereign that the government was opposed to the match because Townsend was a divorcee. On 31 October 1955, after much deliberation, Margaret announced that there would be no nuptials. At the time, several commentators suggested that she had made the decision because she did not want to give up the trappings of royalty as her uncle, King **Edward VIII**, had done in 1936 when he abdicated in order to marry Mrs. Wallis Simpson (*see* WALLIS, DUCHESS OF WINDSOR), but more recent study of archival sources suggests that she had, undoubtedly reluctantly, accepted the **Church of England**'s teaching that "Christian marriage is indissoluble" and that she did not wish to compromise Queen Elizabeth's position as **supreme governor** of the church.

Five years later, on 6 May 1960, Princess Margaret married photographer Antony "Tony" Armstrong-Jones (*see* ARMSTRONG-JONES, ANTONY, EARL OF SNOWDON) in **Westminster Abbey**. They had two children— **David Armstrong-Jones, viscount Linley**, born on 3 November 1961, and Lady Sarah Armstrong-Jones (*see* CHATTO, LADY SARAH), born on 1 May 1964—but, although they were often together in public and were regulars at society parties, the match did not take long to fall apart. Biographers have suggested numerous reasons for the discord—Snowdon had little interest in keeping his mind active, he may have resented the restraints that royal status placed on his behavior, he spent much time away from home on photographic work, and he was undoubtedly promiscuous, whereas Margaret, who was very fond of books, was considered possessive and was subject to bouts of depression. She, too, had affairs, linked to—among others—wine merchant Anthony Barton, Mick Jagger of the Rolling Stones, and actor Peter Sellers. In 1976, when she was photographed by the *News of the World* newspaper at her holiday home on the Caribbean island of Mustique with baronet and landscape gardener Roddy Llewellyn, 17 years her junior, members of parliament condemned her as "a royal parasite," and on 11 July 1978 her marriage was finally dissolved.

For the rest of her life, the princess was the subject of negative press comment, although she continued to support many charities, was popular with her office staff, and was one of the few members of the **royal family** to support **Diana, princess of Wales**, who also faced marital problems. Inevitably, the party-going lifestyle had an effect on her health, as well as on her public image, as alcohol and tobacco exacted their toll. In January 1985 she underwent an operation to remove part of her left lung, in January 1995 she was hospitalized with pneumonia, in 1998 she had a stroke, in 1999 she scalded her feet (permanently impairing her mobility), and in 2001 further strokes paralyzed her left side and affected her sight. Despite these problems, Princess Margaret appeared at her mother's 101st birthday celebrations in August 2001 and at the events marking the 100th birthday of her aunt, **Princess Alice, duchess of Gloucester**, in December of the same year. In early 2002 she suffered another stroke, and on 9 February she died at the King **Edward VII** Hospital in **London**. The princess was cremated, and her ashes were placed in her father's tomb in **St. George's Chapel** at **Windsor Castle**.

**MARGARET, QUEEN OF NORWAY (1261–1283).** Margaret—the eldest of three children in the family of King **Alexander III** and **Margaret, queen of Scots** (the eldest daughter of **Henry III** of England and **Eleanor of Provence**)—was born on 28 February 1261 at **Windsor Castle**, where her mother had celebrated Christmas with her parents. On or about 31 August 1281, she was married in Bergen to King Eric II of Norway, whose father—Magnus VI—had ceded sovereignty over the Hebrides to Alexander in 1266.

On 9 April 1283 (or possibly on 27 or 28 February), Margaret gave birth to a daughter—**Margaret, maid of Norway**—who at the age of three was named "queen of Scots" after Alexander was thrown from his horse and killed. However, either during childbirth or shortly afterward, the queen died. She was buried at Christ's Kirk, Bergen, and 10 years later, Eric took Isabel Bruce, a sister of King **Robert I** of Scotland, as his second wife. *See also* ALEXANDER OF SCOTLAND.

**MARGARET, QUEEN OF SCOTS (1240–1275).** Margaret (also known as Margaret of England) was the eldest daughter of King **Henry III** of England and **Eleanor of Provence**. She was born at **Windsor Castle** in September or early October 1240 and was married to King **Alexander III** of Scotland at York Minster on 26 December 1251. Her father had hoped to use the match as a way of encouraging Alexander to accept him as overlord, but the Scottish monarch was too wily, paying the homage due for his English estates but telling his new father-in-law that he had no authority to make any concessions about Scotland without consulting his council of advisors. Margaret bore a daughter—**Margaret, queen of Norway**—and two sons (**Alexander of Scotland** and **David of Scotland**) but died at Cupar Castle on 26 February 1275. She was buried in **Dunfermline Abbey**, where her husband and sons were later interred.

**MARGARET, ST. (c1045–1093).** Medieval **queens consort** often had very little political or cultural impact on their husbands' realms, but King **Malcolm III** of Scotland was devoted to his wife, allowing her to introduce innovations that resulted in the anglicization of the Scottish court and ended many Celtic traditions. Margaret was the daughter of **Edward the Exile** (son of **Edmund II of England**) and **Agatha** (whose origins are obscure). She was probably born at Castle Réka in Mecseknádasd, Hungary, where her father had taken refuge after being forced out of England by King **Canute**'s Viking invaders in 1016. Edward returned in 1057 but was dead within days, probably as a result of foul play, and after the Norman victory at the **Battle of Hastings** in 1066, Agatha and her children were forced to move again, seeking safety with Malcolm.

The Scots monarch, a widower since the death of **Ingibiorg Finnsdottir**, was fascinated by the pious Margaret and married her (possibly at **Dunfermline Abbey**) in about 1070. He sought her advice on matters of state, welcomed other southerners to his realm, and, at her request, developed closer links between the Scottish church and the Church of Rome while encouraging Benedictine monks to establish their first religious community in his country. Margaret also introduced the Scots nobility to continental fashions, which in turn promoted trading links with the European mainland. Increasingly, too, she gained a reputation for charitable work, building hostels for the poor, caring for the sick, and patronizing the arts and education. She and Malcolm had six sons, three of whom were to become king (as **Edgar of Scotland**, **Alexander I**, and **David I**). One daughter (Edith, later known as **Matilda of Scotland**) married **Henry I** of England, and the other (**Mary, countess of Boulogne**) was wed to Eustace III, count of Boulogne. All of the children had Anglo-Saxon, rather than Celtic, names.

Margaret died at **Edinburgh** Castle on 16 November 1093, just three days after her husband and her eldest son, **Edward of Scotland**, were killed on one of their periodic forays into Northumbria. She was canonized by Pope

Innocent IV in 1250 and is remembered in the names of Queen Margaret Academy (a high school in Ayr), Queen Margaret College (a girls' school in Wellington, New Zealand), and Queen Margaret University (which was founded as an Edinburgh cookery school in 1875 and became a degree-granting institution in 2007). St. Margaret's Chapel, the oldest surviving structure in Edinburgh Castle, was built by King David I as a private chapel for the royal family dedicated to his mother. *See also* EDMUND OF SCOTLAND; ETHELRED OF SCOTLAND.

**MARGUERITE OF FRANCE (c1279–c1317).** Marguerite (also known as Margaret) was the second **queen consort** of King **Edward I**. In 1293, three years after the death of **Eleanor of Castile**, his first wife, Edward entered negotiations for the hand of Blanche, daughter of Philip III of **France** and Marie of Brabant. The French king accepted the match provided that Edward gave up his estates in Gascony, the last extensive territory held by the English monarch on the European mainland. Edward agreed to the condition but then discovered that Blanche had also been promised to Rudolph of Bohemia. Furious, he rejected Philip's offer of Marguerite, Blanche's younger sister, as a replacement and launched a war that lasted for five years, ending with Edward's acceptance of Marguerite in return for financial and territorial concessions by her father.

The wedding was held at Canterbury Cathedral on 10 September 1299. The groom was in his sixties, the bride in her late teens or early twenties, but despite the age difference, the couple appears to have been happy. Marguerite became close friends with **Mary Plantagenet** and Edward (later **Edward II**), the king's children by his first wife, and she greatly pleased her husband by joining him on military campaigns, just as Eleanor had done. It appears, too, that she exerted some influence over him, persuading him to tone down certain of the more harsh punishments he had intended to inflict on wayward subjects.

Marguerite bore three children—**Thomas of Brotherton, earl of Norfolk** (born in 1300); **Edmund of Woodstock, earl of Kent** (1301); and **Eleanor Plantagenet** (1306). Although she was still a young woman when Edward died in 1307, she never remarried, retiring to Marlborough Castle, where she passed away on 14 February 1318. She was buried at Greyfriars Church in Greenwich.

**MARIE, COUNTESS OF BOULOGNE (1136–1182).** Like many females born to noble families in medieval England, Marie, daughter of King **Stephen** and **Matilda of Boulogne**, seemed destined for a life of devotion to the church. By 1148, she was living at Higham Priory (also known as Lillechurch Priory), a Benedictine foundation in the southeast of the country, but she spent her teenage years at Romsey Abbey in Hampshire. In 1159, **William of Blois**, her only surviving brother, died, leaving her an heiress to the extensive family estates in Boulogne. With no near male relatives to protect her, she was forcibly removed from the nunnery by Matthew of Alsace, whom she married in 1160 and who became count of Boulogne as a result of the union. They had two children—Ida, born c1160, and Matilda, born some two years later—but the union was never happy, and they were divorced in 1170. Marie returned to convent life at St. Austrebert in Montreuil and died there in 1182. Her former husband administered the Boulogne properties until, on his death in 1173, Ida inherited them. Marie's English holdings went to Matilda.

**MARIE DE COUCY (c1218–c1285).** The year after the death of **Joan of England (1210–1238)**, King **Alexander II** took Marie de Coucy as his second wife. Marie, born in Picardy, was the daughter of Enguerrand, lord of Coucy, and Marie de Montmirel-en-Brie, his third wife. The couple married at **Roxburgh Castle** on 15 May 1239, and on 4 September 1241, at the same place, Marie gave birth to a son, later **Alexander III**, who proved to be the only child of her husband's two marriages. Diplomatically, as well as dynastically, the match was advantageous to the Scots king. Marie's father was one of the most influential nobles in **France** and a great-grandson of King Louis VI, so the union brought both prestige and a military alliance. Marie, however, appears to have had little influence on government while her husband was alive, and although, in 1258, she was appointed to the regency council that ruled Scotland during her son's minority, she played no part in decision making. After Alexander's death in 1249, she returned to Picardy and wed Jean de Brienne, a high-ranking French official, but she continued to visit Scotland regularly. She died in 1284 or 1285 and, according to some sources, was buried at Newbattle Abbey, a Cistercian monastery near **Edinburgh**.

**MARINA, PRINCESS, DUCHESS OF KENT (1906–1968).** For two decades after the end of World War II, the tall, willowy duchess of Kent set fashion standards for female members of the **royal family**. The youngest of three daughters born to Prince Nicholas of Greece and Denmark and Grand Duchess Elena Vladimirovna of Russia, she was born in Athens on 13 December 1906 and spent her early childhood in Greece but was forced into exile, with her father, mother, and sisters, when the pro-German King Constantine I of Greece abdicated his throne in 1917. Apart from a brief return in 1921, she spent the rest of her life outside her homeland.

On 29 November 1934, at **Westminster Abbey**, the princess married **Prince George, duke of Kent**, the drug-addicted, bisexual son of King **George V**. They settled at Coppins, a country house in the village of Iver, near **Windsor Castle**, and at Belgrave Square, in **London**, where they became the focus of a lively and diverse social circle that included acquaintances from the arts world as well as from the voluntary organizations that they supported. On 25 August 1942, however, the duke was killed when the flying boat in which he was a passenger crashed in northern Scotland. The duchess, left in the middle of World War II with three young children and in straitened financial circumstances that were relieved only by the sale of part of her husband's collection of art and furniture, responded by investing much energy in the Women's Royal Naval Service and by supporting groups that were attempting to alleviate the worst effects of war on the British people.

After the conflict ended, Princess Marina represented Queen **Elizabeth II** at several foreign engagements, including Ghana's independence celebrations in 1957 and those of Botswana and Lesotho in 1966. In the United Kingdom, she took particular interest in mental health charities, and as president of the All-England Lawn Tennis and Croquet Club, she was in regular attendance at the annual Wimbledon tennis championships. The last foreign-born princess to marry into the royal family during the 20th century, she had made many of her own clothes as a young woman. The interest in fashion continued after her marriage, so her regular public appearances earned her a reputation for elegance that had a considerable impact on the dress—and notably the hats—of other royal women in the 1950s and 1960s. She died at **Kensington Palace** on 27 August 1968, the victim of a brain tumor. As she had wished, her remains were interred beside those of her husband in the royal burial ground at **Frogmore**. *See also* ALEXANDRA, PRINCESS; EDWARD, PRINCE, DUKE OF KENT; MICHAEL OF KENT, PRINCE.

**MARJORIE, COUNTESS OF CARRICK (?–c1292).** Marjorie (or Margaret), mother of King **Robert I** (Robert the Bruce), was the only daughter (and therefore heiress to the estates) of Niall, earl of Carrick and **regent** during the minority of King **Alexander III**, and his wife, Margaret (the second daughter of Walter, **high steward** and justiciar—or senior legal officer—of Scotland). She was wed, first, to Adam of Kilconquhar, who was killed on crusade to the Holy Land in 1270, leaving her childless. According to John Fordun, the 14th-century chronicler of Scottish history, she went hunting with **Robert de Bruce, lord of Annandale**, soon after hearing of her husband's death and was so entranced by him that she held him captive until, in 1271 or 1272, he agreed to marry her.

The match, which united Anglo-Norman and Celtic bloodlines because Marjorie was descended from King **Henry I** of England and Robert from **Malcolm III** of Scotland, took place without the consent of Alexander III, who confiscated the bride's estates until she paid a fine in order to retrieve them. Over the next 15 years, the couple produced some 12 children. Robert (born on 11 July 1274) was to become king of Scotland, and Edward, his brother, was declared king of Ireland in an act of defiance against **Edward I** of England, who claimed overlordship of the island. Three other sons—Neil, Thomas, and Alexander (who was considered the best scholar of his time at Cambridge University)—reached adulthood but were captured by the forces of King Edward of England and executed, Neil in 1306 and his brothers in 1307.

In 1293, Isabel, the eldest daughter, became the second wife of King Eric II of Norway, whose first consort—**Margaret, queen of Norway**, daughter of King **Alexander III** and **Margaret, queen of Scots**—had died giving birth to **Margaret, maid of Norway**, a decade earlier. Other daughters married into Scotland's noble families, though Mary, one of the younger sisters, suffered greatly before she was able to wed. Taken captive by Edward I soon after her brother was crowned king of Scots in 1307, she was confined for two years in a cage at **Roxburgh Castle**, prohibited from speaking to anyone except the woman who brought her food. She was then moved to more civilized accommodations in Newcastle, but even so, she remained in English hands until she was exchanged for English knights captured at the **Battle of Bannockburn** in 1314.

Marjorie inherited her father's title and estates in 1256. She died by the end of 1292, but her husband survived until 1304.

**MARJORIE, COUNTESS OF PEMBROKE (c1200–1244).** Marjorie (sometimes known as Marjorie of Scotland) was the youngest of four children born to King **William I of Scotland** and **Ermengarde de Beaumont**. **Richard, earl of Cornwall**, the sometimes renegade brother of **Henry III**, visited the Scottish court in an effort to secure her as a bride, but neither Henry nor his prospective parents-in-law approved of the plan, so on 1 August 1235, in Berwick, Isabel married Gilbert Marshal, earl of Pembroke. They had no offspring before he was thrown from his horse and killed while taking part in a tournament in 1241. Marjorie, who survived until 17 November 1244, was buried in Blackfriars Church, **London**, where her elder sister, **Margaret, countess of Kent**, was interred 15 years later.

**MARLBOROUGH HOUSE.** Marlborough House, located on Pall Mall, close to **St. James's Palace** in central **London**, was a **royal residence** for much of the 19th and early 20th centuries. The red brick building was erected in 1709–11 for Sarah, duchess of Marlborough, and was acquired by the **royal family** in 1817 as a home for **Princess Charlotte Augusta** (the only child of George, **prince of Wales** and later King **George IV**), who had married

Prince Leopold of Saxe-Coburg-Saalfield the previous year. Charlotte died in November 1817 following a difficult childbirth, but Leopold remained in the house until 1831, when he became King Leopold I of the Belgians. The property then passed to Queen **Adelaide of Saxe-Meiningen**, consort of King **William IV**, who lived there from the time of the monarch's death in 1837 until she too passed away in 1849.

From 1853 to 1861, the mansion was used as an art gallery and as accommodations for a design school, but in 1863, after a large extension was added, another **prince** of Wales, Albert Edward, moved in with his bride, **Alexandra of Denmark**, raised a family, and turned Marlborough House into the pivot of social London. When the prince succeeded Queen **Victoria** on the throne as King **Edward VII** in 1901, he transferred to rooms in **Buckingham Palace**, and the residence became a home for his son, George, **duke of York**. At Edward's death in 1910, George became King **George V**, and the house was occupied by **queen dowager** Alexandra until 1925. The last royal resident— George's consort, **Mary of Teck**—used the property from the time of her husband's death in 1936 until she passed away in 1953. Six years later, Queen **Elizabeth II** made the building available for use by the Commonwealth of Nations, a grouping of some 50 independent states, most of which were once British colonies. It now houses the organization's secretariat. *See also* LOUISE, PRINCESS ROYAL, DUCHESS OF FIFE; MAUD, PRINCESS, QUEEN OF NORWAY; VICTORIA, PRINCESS.

**MARY I (1516–1558).** The only child of King **Henry VIII** and **Catherine of Aragon** to survive infancy, Mary (also known as Mary Tudor) was—with the possible exception of Empress **Matilda** in the 12th century—the first woman to rule England. She reigned from 1553 to 1558, riding an early wave of popular support but soon becoming feared and reviled by many of her subjects.

Mary was born in the **Palace of Placentia** on 18 February 1516 and, like many royal children of her time, very quickly became a pawn in the chess game of European political alliances. At the age of two, she was betrothed to the dauphin Francis, heir to the throne of **France**. However, three years later, that engagement was broken, so in 1522, under the terms of the **Treaty of Windsor**, she was matched with Charles V, the Holy Roman Emperor. In 1525, Charles withdrew from the agreement, but two years later another marital deal was struck linking her either to Francis I of France (the dauphin's father) or to Henry, Duc d'Orléans (Francis's second son). That, too, came to naught.

From 1527, King Henry pursued a campaign to get papal consent for a divorce from Catherine, and from 1531, he kept Mary apart from her mother. In **1534, an Act of Succession** recognized **Anne Boleyn**, Henry's second consort, as England's queen, and her daughter, Elizabeth (later **Elizabeth I**), as heiress to the throne. It also formally annulled Henry's marriage to Catherine and declared Mary illegitimate. Mary refused to acknowledge this status; in reprisal, her household was broken up, and she was dispatched to act as **lady-in-waiting** to the infant who had replaced her in the line of succession. Her health deteriorated, but even then Henry refused to allow her mother to visit her, and when Catherine died in 1536, Mary was forbidden to attend the funeral.

Undoubtedly, the enforced separation from her mother and the stigma of illegitimacy embittered the young woman, but in the spring of 1536, Anne Boleyn was **beheaded**, and Mary was encouraged to seek reconciliation with her father. The terms were humiliating—she had to renounce the Roman Catholic Church, recognize Henry as the supreme religious authority in England, and admit her illegitimacy by accepting that the king's marriage to Catherine was "incestuous and unlawful." The reconciliation did restore many of her privileges, but after Henry's death in 1547, she was subject to further pressure while his successor, **Edward VI** (her half-brother), was on the throne. In spite of her public renunciation of Catholicism, Mary had retained her faith, and though Edward was kind to her, his advisors were aggressively promoting Protestantism. Inevitably there were clashes with royal counselors, as for example when Mary tried to gain permission for a Latin mass to be held in her private chapel even though services in English were being imposed throughout the realm.

Just before Edward died in 1553, he prepared a will that was manipulated to ensure that the **succession to the throne** passed to the Protestant Lady **Jane Grey** and her heirs rather than to Mary. Lady Jane did rule for nine days, but the mood of the country was very much on Mary's side, and she became queen to popular acclaim on 19 July. However, shortly after her accession, she announced her engagement to Philip of Spain (*see* PHILIP II OF SPAIN), because even though she was in her late thirties, she wanted to produce a Roman Catholic heir who would prevent Elizabeth, her half-sister, from succeeding her under the terms of the **1543 Act of Succession**. As Spain was England's major trading competitor, this match proved unpopular. Parliament advised her to cancel the wedding, but she refused, sparking a rebellion by Sir Thomas Wyatt in 1554 (*see* WYATT'S REBELLION).

Undaunted, Mary went ahead with her plans and married at **Winchester** Cathedral on 25 July 1554. She then set about a program of ecclesiastical change, stirring up opposition by abolishing the **Church of England**, reestablishing papal authority, and reviving the laws of heresy. Her decision, in 1557, to allow England to be drawn into war with France as an ally of Spain further alienated many of her subjects because, the following year, she suffered the ignominy of losing **Calais**, her country's last foothold on the mainland of Europe.

Protestants responded to the banishing of their religion by holding services in secret and circulating anti-Catholic pamphlets. Over the four years from 1554, Mary—convinced that hers was the only true faith—acquiesced to the burning of nearly 300 of her opponents at the stake, including Thomas Cranmer (the archbishop of Canterbury) and John Hooper (the bishop of Gloucester). The executions continued until her death from influenza at **St. James's Palace**, London, on 17 November 1558, earning her the soubriquet "Bloody Mary." Deserted by her husband, she left no children. Historians have chastised her for the harshness of her rule, but she showed much kindness to the poor and, at the start of her reign, clemency to many in the Jane Grey faction. Her unhappy childhood seems to have strengthened her religious zeal, leading her to believe that strict treatment of heretics was necessary in order to save souls. Mary was buried in **Westminster Abbey** despite her wish that she be interred beside her mother in Peterborough Cathedral. She was succeeded by her half-sister, Elizabeth I, who—for entirely political reasons—returned the Church of England to Protestant forms of government. See also DUDLEY, GUILDFORD; HAMPTON COURT PALACE; SEYMOUR, JANE; SUCCESSION TO THE CROWN: MARRIAGE ACT; SUPREMACY, ACT OF (1534); WOODSTOCK PALACE.

**MARY II (1662–1694).** The elder daughter of King **James VII and II** by his first wife, **Anne Hyde**, Mary ruled with her husband, **William III of England and II of Scotland**, from 1689 until her death in 1694. Born at **St. James's Palace**, London, on 30 April 1662, she was raised as a Protestant, and on 4 November 1677, she was married to her cousin, William of Orange, in her bedchamber at the palace.

James had converted to Roman Catholicism in the late 1660s, and after his accession to the throne in 1685, he increasingly antagonized his subjects by attempting to grant Catholics freedom of worship and by appointing them to senior posts in government and the army. In 1688, when **Mary of Modena**, James's second wife, produced a son and heir (see JAMES FRANCIS EDWARD STUART), fears of a permanent Catholic monarchy led several influential English noblemen and clerics to invite William to raise an army in Holland and invade England in defense of the Protestant faith. The king's daughter supported the invasion, partly because she felt it to be her duty both to her husband and to her religious beliefs, but also because she suspected that there had been some deception over the birth of her half-brother, her stepmother having previously had several miscarriages. William landed at Torbay in November 1688, and James fled to **France** the following month. Mary, who joined her husband in **London** in February 1689, rejected all suggestions that she should become queen of England by herself, but she accepted a proposal that the crown should be held jointly. The Scots made a similar deal.

While William was at home, Mary happily left politics to him, but she governed by herself when he was absent with his troops in Ireland or on the European mainland. As a monarch, she was popular with her people and proved to be an effective politician, taking responsibility for many ecclesiastical matters in an age when religion was the cause of much tension. She also supervised extensive building works at **Kensington Palace** and at **Hampton Court Palace** and established the Greenwich Hospital for Seamen. However, she was constantly worried by the estrangement from her father and from her sister, Anne (later Queen **Anne**).

On 19 December 1694, Mary was struck by smallpox, and nine days later she died, childless, at Kensington. She was buried in **Westminster Abbey**, with James's supporters interpreting her passing—at the age of 32—as divine retribution for abandoning her father. *See also* BILL OF RIGHTS; CLAIM OF RIGHT; CROWN JEWELS OF THE UNITED KINGDOM.

**MARY, COUNTESS OF BOULOGNE (c1082–1116).** Mary, the daughter of King **Malcolm III** and **St. Margaret**, spent most of her childhood in the company of her sister, **Matilda of Scotland** (later **queen consort** of King **Henry I**), in the care of nuns at Romsey Abbey. In 1101 or 1102, she married Eustace III, count of Boulogne, and in about 1103 she gave birth to their only child, **Matilda of Boulogne**, who married **Stephen** of Blois in 1125 and gave him unflinching support after he became king of England 10 years later. Mary (who is sometimes known as Mary of Scots) died on 31 May 1116 and was buried at Bermondsey Abbey in **London**. Her husband survived until 1125 but did not remarry. *See also* EDGAR OF SCOTLAND.

**MARY DE BOHUN (c1369–1394).** Mary was the first wife of Henry Bolingbroke but died five years before he deposed King **Richard II** and, with the approval of parliament, succeeded him as King **Henry IV**. The daughter of Humphrey de Bohun, earl of Hereford, and his wife, Joan Fitz-Alan, she may have married Henry on 27 July 1380 at Arundel Castle, her mother's family home, or on 5 February 1381 at Rochford Hall, one of her father's residences in Essex. A son (**Edward Plantagenet**), born in 1382, survived for only four days, but five years later Mary gave birth to another male child, who followed his father to the English throne as **Henry V**. Three more sons—**Thomas of Lancaster, duke of Clarence**; **John of Lancaster, duke of Bedford**; and **Humphrey, duke of Gloucester**—followed in 1388, 1389, and 1390, respectively, and a daughter (**Blanche, Electress Palatine**) in 1392. However, Mary died at Peterborough Castle, possibly on 4 June or 4 July 1394, while giving birth to a second female child (**Philippa, Queen of Denmark, Norway, and Sweden**). She was buried in the Church of St. Mary of the Newarke in Leicester, but her remains were later reinterred at the chapel of Trinity Hospital.

**MARY, DUCHESS OF BRITTANY (1344–c1362).** Mary, daughter of **Edward III** and **Philippa of Hainault**, was born on 10 October 1344 at Bishops Waltham, where Henry of Blois, bishop of **Winchester** and brother of King **Stephen**, had built a palace in 1135. In 1361, she was married at **Woodstock Palace** to John, duke of Brittany, who had grown up at her father's court, but she died shortly afterward without leaving any children and was buried close to her sister, **Margaret, countess of Pembroke**, at Abingdon Abbey. Her husband remarried twice and survived until 1399. Mary is sometimes known as Mary of Waltham, after her birthplace.

**MARY HENRIETTA, PRINCESS ROYAL, PRINCESS OF ORANGE (1631–1660).** Mary—the eldest daughter of King **Charles I** and **Henrietta Maria of France**—was the mother of King **William III of England and II of Scotland**. She was born at **St. James's Palace** in **London** on 4 November 1631 and was married to William, heir to Frederick, prince of Orange (*see* WILLIAM, PRINCE OF ORANGE), at **Whitehall Palace** on 2 May 1641. The match was not what Mary's parents had wanted—her father would have preferred a powerful dynastic alliance with a son of King Philip IV of Spain, and her mother would have been much happier if her daughter had found a husband in a more staunchly Roman Catholic state—but political realities in an England uneasy about Charles's Catholic consort, and increasingly divided by conflict between monarch and parliament, made a Protestant husband more acceptable.

Just 10 years old on her wedding day, Mary (who is sometimes known as Mary of Orange) remained in London until 1644 and then journeyed to Holland, but she was always unpopular with a people who sided with Oliver Cromwell and the Puritan parliamentarians instead of the royalist cause which incorporated Charles's belief in the **divine right of kings**. Despite these problems in her new home, the **princess royal** urged her father to join her rather than risk his life while civil war ravaged England. She also offered help to those of his supporters who had to flee their homeland, but in the early winter of 1650, while she was in the late stages of pregnancy, her husband contracted smallpox. He died on 6 November, just eight days before William, his only child, was born.

For the 11 years that followed Charles's execution in 1649, England was a republic, governed by the Cromwell faction, but after the **restoration of the monarchy** in 1660, Mary's son was fifth in the line of **succession to the throne**, and she became somewhat more popular in her adopted country. However, when she returned to London for a visit, she too contracted smallpox and died at Whitehall Palace on 24 December 1660. She was buried, at her request, beside her brother, **Henry Stuart, duke of Gloucester**, who had succumbed to the same disease only three months earlier and was interred in **Westminster Abbey**.

Mary was the first princess royal. She was given this form of address because her mother wanted the eldest daughter of the English monarch to be recognized in a manner similar to that in her native **France**, where the firstborn daughter of a king was known as "Madame Royale." In November 1647, when King Charles I fled from **Hampton Court Palace** to escape from his parliamentarian captors, he left orders that a picture of Mary, painted by Anthony Van Dyke when she was six years old, should be taken from the chamber where he had been confined and sent to Holland under the care of Katherine, lady Aubigny, one of his supporters. It remained in mainland European collections until 1967, when it was acquired by Sir Oliver Millar, an authority on the artist. In 2009, it was returned to Hampton Court under a scheme that permits items of historic or artistic value to be given to the nation in lieu of inheritance tax.

**MARY OF GUELDRES (c1434–1463).** Mary, daughter of Arnold, duke of Gueldres (or Guelders), and his wife, Catherine, was married to King **James II of Scotland** at **Holyrood** Abbey, **Edinburgh**, on 3 July 1449 in a union designed to further Scots commercial interests in the coastal areas around the mouth of the River Rhine (*see also* STEWART, MARY, COUNTESS OF GRANDPRÉ). Over the next decade, she and King James had seven children, including an heir who would succeed him as **James III**, and she acted as **regent** after he was killed in 1460 when a cannon exploded while he was laying siege to **Roxburgh Castle**. Despite her youth, she showed considerable diplomatic skill as she negotiated with **Margaret of Anjou** (the redoubtable consort of King **Henry VI**) to free Berwick from English control in return for augmenting the **House of Lancaster**'s army with Scots mercenaries but then adroitly changed sides and sought a peace with **Edward IV** and the **House of York**.

An attractive, politically powerful woman in her twenties, Mary was romantically involved with Adam Hepburn, master of Hailes (who abducted her son in 1466), and with Henry Beaufort, duke of Somerset (one of the principal Lancastrian military commanders), but she did not remarry before her sudden death on 1 December 1463 at Ravenscraig Castle, which her husband had been building for her at the time of his accident. Mary was buried in the Trinity College Church, Edinburgh, that she had founded in James's memory, but her remains were reinterred at Holyrood in 1848 when the building was demolished to provide land for the construction of Waverley railroad station. *See also* STEWART, ALEXANDER, DUKE OF ALBANY; STEWART, DAVID, EARL OF MORAY; STEWART, JOHN, EARL OF MAR (c1457– 1479); STEWART, MARGARET (c1459–c1514); STEWART, MARY, COUNTESS OF ARRAN.

**MARY OF GUISE (1515–1560).** For a turbulent five years, from 1554 to 1559, Mary—**queen consort** of King **James V** and mother of **Mary, queen of Scots**—acted as **regent** of Scotland, ruling on behalf of her daughter. She was born at Bar-le-Duc in Lorraine on 20 November 1515, the eldest child of Claude, duke of Guise (and one of the most powerful men in **France**), and Antoinette de Bourbon. On 4 August 1534, she married Louis, duke of Longueville, but he died after only three years, leaving her a widow in her early twenties. She had no intention of remarrying, but only a few weeks after her bereavement, she received an instruction from King Francis I of France to wed the Scottish monarch, whose first wife, **Madeleine de Valois**, had succumbed to tuberculosis in July. Soon afterward, King **Henry VIII** of England tossed his hat into the marital ring, saying that he needed a big wife. Mary, well aware of the English ruler's propensities, retorted that although she was big her neck was small and consented to James's proposal—a decision that both augmented the Scottish king's coffers and strengthened his country's alliance with France against English aggression.

The couple married by proxy at Notre Dame Cathedral in Paris on 18 May 1538 and in person at St. Andrews on 18 June. **James Stewart, duke of Rothesay (1540–1541)**, a son and heir, was born on 22 May 1540 but lived only until 21 April 1541, and a second son, **Robert Stewart, duke of Albany (1541)**, survived for only a few days before dying within hours of his brother. Then, on 7 or 8 December 1542, Mary was born, but her father, depressed by defeat at the Battle of Solway Moss and by the news that his new child was a girl rather than a male heir, passed away at **Falkland Palace** on 14 December, leaving his week-old daughter queen of the realm.

James Hamilton, earl of Arran, was appointed **regent**, primarily because, as great grandson of King **James II**, he was James V's closest male relative and was thus next in line to the throne after the newborn baby. However, Hamilton failed to take a consistent position within either the pro-English or the pro-French factions in Scottish politics, and in 1554 he resigned in favor of the **queen dowager**. As regent, Mary of Guise initially adopted a position of religious tolerance at a time of growing support for Protestantism, but the appointment of members of the Roman Catholic Guise family to positions of power at her court eroded support among the Scottish nobles. In the spring of 1559, apparently under pressure from France, she abandoned conciliation and embarked on a campaign to suppress the new faith. This decision led to civil disorder and ultimately, on 21 October 1559, to the lords' decision to depose her. She survived only until 11 June the following year, dying of edema (or dropsy) at **Edinburgh** Castle. (John Knox, one of the principal leaders of the reformation in Scotland, celebrated her passing in a manner that, according to historian Jenny Wormald, "made clear why charity has not been thought a notable feature of Scottish Calvinism.") Mary's body was taken to Rheims and buried at the Convent of St. Pierre, where her sister, Renée, was abbess.

Mary is sometimes known as Mary of Lorraine after her birthplace in northeast France. *See also* GREENWICH, TREATY OF.

**MARY OF LORRAINE (1515–1560).** *See* MARY OF GUISE.

**MARY OF MODENA (1658–1718).** On 30 September 1673, at the ducal palace in Modena, Italy, James, **duke of York** (later King **James VII of Scotland and II of England**), took Mary of Modena as his second wife. The 14-year-old bride was not happy—she had wanted to enter a nunnery—and many of the groom's countrymen were displeased because she was a devout Roman Catholic. At the time, **Charles II** was monarch of England and Scotland, and it seemed increasingly unlikely that his consort, **Catherine of Braganza**, would give him an heir. James was **heir presumptive**, so it was probable that he would become king and that his sons, the future rulers, would be raised in the Catholic faith. For Charles, the wedding was politically important; Mary's family were strong supporters of Louis XIV of **France**, so the match helped to cement an Anglo-French alliance. However, Louis too was Catholic, and there had long been enmity between France and England, so that also caused concern for many citizens of the realms.

Over the next 12 years, Mary conceived on 11 occasions, but every pregnancy ended either in a miscarriage or with the child dying while still very young, so when James succeeded to the throne in 1685, he still had no issue (at the time, some people claimed that the problems were a result of his venereal disease). However, on 10 June 1688, the **queen consort** at last gave birth to a son (**James Francis Edward Stuart**) who seemed likely to survive. The event was met by disbelief, with rumors circulating that the baby had been stillborn and that a replacement had been smuggled into the birth room in a warming pan. Such a substitution would have required the cooperation of many people because advisors and courtiers, as well as doctors and midwives, attended royal births, but James had to call two meetings so that members of his **Privy Council** could hear testimonies that Mary really had given birth to the child.

The infant's arrival had another effect. By the time it was born, knowledge that James had become a Roman Catholic had been widespread for many years, and the prospect of a long-term Catholic monarchy was the spur that encouraged William of Orange (later **William III of England and II of Scotland**) to respond to pleas from noblemen and church leaders by leading an army that would defend the Protestant cause in England. On 5 November, he landed with his troops at Torbay, and on 11 December Mary disguised herself as a laundry maid and fled to France, where her husband joined her shortly afterward. They never returned. Louis XIV gave them the royal palace at St. Germain-en-Laye, near Paris, as a residence, and the queen spent the rest of her life there, often praying at the nearby Convent of the Visitation at Chaillot.

Mary was born at the ducal palace in Modena on 5 October 1658 to Alfonso, duke of Modena, and his wife, Laura. She lived to see her son lead an uprising against the **House of Hanover** in 1715 (*see* JACOBITE REBELLIONS) but died of inflammation of the lungs, complicated by an operation for breast cancer, at St. Germain on 7 May 1718 and was buried at Chaillot. Many historians have treated her sympathetically, depicting her life as a series of unhappinesses and tragedies (an approach adopted by biographers of other Stuart queens), but several have suggested, too, that both she and her husband lacked the political skill that would have allowed them to keep their crowns. *See also* CROWN JEWELS OF THE UNITED KINGDOM; STUART, CATHERINE LAURA; STUART, CHARLES, DUKE OF CAMBRIDGE (1677); STUART, CHARLOTTE MARIA; STUART, ISABELLA; STUART, LOUISA MARIA THERESA.

**MARY OF TECK (1867–1953).** Mary of Teck was consort to King **George V**, playing a considerable role in helping the monarchy make a transition from the distant formality of late Victorian times to the more open, socially concerned style of the late 20th and early 21st centuries. She was born at **Kensington Palace** on 26 May 1867 and was always known as May by her family because of her birth month. Her father (Prince Francis of Teck) and mother (Princess Mary Adelaide of Cambridge) were not wealthy, and her royal blood was diluted because her paternal grandfather, Duke Louis of Würtemburg (brother of King Frederick I of Würtemburg), had married a commoner, Claudine Rhédey von Kis-Rhéde. Both of these circumstances reduced Mary's desirability as a bride, but she was a favorite of Queen **Victoria**, whose own daughter, **Princess Louise, duchess of Argyll**, was, in 1871, the first member of a British **royal family** to marry a nonroyal for more than three centuries.

Victoria felt that Mary, who had a strong sense of duty and considerable self-discipline, would help to keep her somewhat louche grandson and **heir apparent** to the throne, **Prince Albert Victor, duke of Clarence and Avondale**, on the straight and narrow, so an engagement was arranged. In January 1892, the **prince** contracted influenza and died, but, undaunted, the queen advocated a betrothal to George, Albert Victor's younger brother and the new heir apparent, because he and Mary had gotten to know each other well in the aftermath of Clarence's death. Both parties agreed, probably more out of a sense of duty than because of any great mutual affection, so the wedding was held at **St. James's Palace** on 6 July 1893. Despite the unlikely beginnings (and despite George's apparent inability to express emotion other than in letters), the union was a great success, the couple producing six children (including two future kings—**Edward VIII** and **George VI**) and writing to each other every day they were apart.

By the time George succeeded his father, King **Edward VII**, in 1910, he had earned a reputation as a dull but worthy individual. Mary's public image was very similar, but she was no fool. Aware of the growing politicization of Britain's urban working classes, she set about the task of shoring up the monarchy at a time when republicanism was much in vogue throughout Europe. Initially, considerable energy was invested in visits to industrial areas and in meetings with coal miners and textile mill workers, but after the outbreak of World War I in 1914, while the loyalties of the **queen consort** and her husband were being questioned because of their German ancestry, she visited injured combatants in hospitals, coordinated the work of numerous charities, and collected food and clothing for distribution to needy families. Then, as recession followed conflict, she continued her charitable efforts, differing fundamentally with the growing socialist ethos in Britain but attempting to keep a high profile by providing help to the parts of the country worst hit by unemployment and by holding tea parties for labor militants. As a result, at the time of the king's death in 1936, the monarchy remained popular, even among the poor.

Mary was greatly affected by the decision of her eldest son (and her husband's successor), King Edward VIII, to abdicate the throne in order to marry American divorcee Wallis Simpson (*see* WALLIS, DUCHESS OF WINDSOR), calling it the most humiliating experience of her life. She could never understand how Edward could turn his back on what she felt was his duty to his country, and she refused to have anything to do with Mrs. Simpson after their marriage. In later years, the **queen dowager** acquired much material for the **Royal Collection** of artwork, notably material relating to the royal family, and—though she is often criticized for paying over the odds for pieces she wanted—she did much to promote conservation of artifacts and to trace items that had gone astray. She outlived her second son, King George VI, and died at **Marlborough House**, her **London** residence, on 24 March 1953, just a few weeks before the **coronation** of her granddaughter as Queen **Elizabeth II**. Her body was interred beside that of her husband in **St. George's Chapel** at **Windsor Castle**. *See also* ADOLPHUS, PRINCE, DUKE OF CAMBRIDGE; FROGMORE; GEORGE, PRINCE, DUKE OF KENT; HENRY, PRINCE, DUKE OF GLOUCESTER; JOHN, PRINCE; LOUISE, PRINCESS ROYAL, DUCHESS OF FIFE; MARY, PRINCESS, LANDGRAVINE OF HESSE-CASSEL; MARY, PRINCESS ROYAL, COUNTESS OF HAREWOOD; QUEEN MOTHER; VICTORIA, PRINCESS.

**MARY OF YORK (1467–1482).** Mary, the second child of **Edward IV** and **Elizabeth Woodville**, was born at **Windsor Castle** on 11 August 1467. According to some sources, her father intended to marry her to Hans, the eldest surviving son of Christian I, king of Denmark and Norway, but the scheme never came to fruition, and she died, unwed, at the **Palace of Placentia** on 23 May 1482.

**MARY, PRINCESS, DUCHESS OF GLOUCESTER AND EDINBURGH (1776–1857).** Mary, the longest-lived of the 15 children of King **George III** and **Charlotte of Mecklenburg-Strelitz**, was born at **Buckingham Palace** on 25 April 1776. Like her sisters, she was raised in an environment that discouraged contact with males other than those in her immediate family, but in 1796 she became attached to William George Frederick, the son of William, prince of Orange, and marriage seemed likely until, in 1799, the young suitor took ill and died. In 1801, Mary and her sisters wrote to Queen Charlotte, complaining of their lack of independence. The move brought an increased freedom that led, on 22 July 1816, to a wedding at Buckingham Palace to her first cousin, **Prince** William, duke of Gloucester and **Edinburgh**, the only son of Prince William Henry, her father's younger brother. By that time, Mary was 40, so the union—unhappy because the duke was an autocratic husband whose radical views annoyed the duchess's conservative brothers—produced no children. William died in 1834, but Mary survived until 30 April 1857, a week after her 81st birthday. She died at Gloucester House, her **London** home, and was buried in **St. George's Chapel** at **Windsor Castle**. *See also* AMELIA, PRINCESS (1783–1810); BAGSHOT PARK; WHITE LODGE.

**MARY, PRINCESS, LANDGRAVINE OF HESSE-CASSEL (1723–1772).** Mary—the eighth child and fourth daughter of King **George II** and **Caroline of Brandenburg-Ansbach**—was born at Leicester House (her parents' **London** home) on 22 February 1723. On 8 May 1740, at the age of 17, she was married by proxy to Frederick, son of William, landgrave of Hesse-Cassel (now part of Germany), with her brother—**William Augustus, duke of Cumberland**—standing in for the groom. A second ceremony was held at Cassel on 28 June, with both principals present. The match was a political union that brought a return to the British crown in 1745–46, when Frederick led 6,000 Hessian soldiers in support of Cumberland's efforts to prevent **Charles Edward Stuart** from regaining the throne for the **House of Stuart**. Mary, however, was desperately unhappy, bearing four sons (the first of whom died in infancy) but suffering much physical abuse at the hands of her husband. The couple separated in 1755, but rather than return to her father's court in England, the **princess** opted to remain on the continent and look after her children. Her supportive father-in-law provided her with a residence at Hanau, where she remained—estranged but not divorced—until she died on 14 January 1772 after a lengthy period of ill health. She was buried nearby in the Marienkirche.

In 1760, Frederick succeeded his father as landgrave (in effect, as a count exercising sovereign rights over a territory but owing feudal homage to the Holy Roman Emperor). He took a second wife the year after Mary's passing but had no further children, dying in 1785. **Alexandra of Denmark** and **Mary of Teck**, descendants of Mary's youngest son, Frederick, later married back into the British **royal family** as **queens consort** of King **Edward VII** and King **George V**, respectively. *See also* ADOLPHUS, PRINCE, DUKE OF CAMBRIDGE.

**MARY, PRINCESS ROYAL, COUNTESS OF HAREWOOD (1897–1965).** **Princess** Mary—the only daughter and third of six children in the family of George, **duke of York** (later King **George V**), and **Mary of Teck**—spent her adult life improving her husband's country estate and fulfilling royal commitments. Born at York Cottage in the grounds of **Sandringham House** on 25 April 1897, she was educated by governesses even though her younger brothers (**Prince Henry, duke of Gloucester**, and **Prince George, duke of Kent**) were sent to school with other children. During World War I, the young princess worked with several of the charities that assisted servicemen and their families; then, in 1918, she went to work as a trainee nurse at Great Ormond Street Children's Hospital in **London**.

On 28 February 1922, in **Westminster Abbey**, Princess Mary married Henry, viscount Lascelles (later **Henry Lascelles, earl of Harewood**). The wedding helped to dispel an element of Britain's postwar gloom, but some sources have suggested that the bride was unhappy because her parents were pressuring her into a match with a man for whom she had no feelings and despite the objections of her brother Edward (later King **Edward VIII**), to whom she was particularly close and who understood her concerns. Later, rumors circulated of Lascelles's abusiveness toward his wife, but their elder son—**George Lascelles, earl of Harewood**—rejected tales that the marriage was unhappy, writing that his mother and father got along well together.

As countess of Harewood, Mary was able to pursue her interests in cattle breeding (on which she became an authority), horse racing, interior decoration, and landscaping, but she also carried out a program of public engagements. Several of these were military obligations (she was colonel-in-chief of the Royal Scots regiment, for instance), but she was never happy with parade-ground inspection of ranks of soldiers, a task she felt was more appropriate for a man. Her shyness made many events something of a trial, but even so, she was conscientious, devoting much time to such groups as the Girl Guides and the Red Cross, as well as representing Queen **Elizabeth II** at functions abroad, as in 1964, when she visited Lusaka for the celebrations when Northern Rhodesia gained its independence from the United Kingdom and was renamed Zambia. Princess Mary died after suffering a heart attack while walking in the grounds of her home on 28 March 1965. She was buried on the estate. *See also* LASCELLES, GERALD; PRINCESS ROYAL.

**MARY, QUEEN OF SCOTS (1542–1587).** Mary is one of the more romantic figures in the pageant of Scottish history, her life usually depicted as a series of sorrows and tragedies borne with dignity and courage. Born at **Linlithgow Palace** on 7 or 8 December 1542, she was just one week old when she became queen on the death of her father, King **James V**. Five years later, her mother—**Mary of Guise**—sent her to **France** while nobles struggled for power and English troops attacked villages and religious houses in the southern parts of her realm (*see* GREENWICH, TREATY OF). She was raised at the French court, becoming a skilled linguist and a noted musician but apparently failing to acquire much political acumen.

In 1558, at the age of 15, Mary married Francis, the sickly dauphin of France (and later **Francis II**), in an alliance that meant she was destined to become queen of her adopted country, but which was also clearly intended to lead to a situation in which Scotland could unite with its continental ally under one sovereign. However, the exiled Scottish monarch believed that she also had a claim to the English crown. Her paternal grandmother, **Margaret Tudor**, was the elder sister of King **Henry VIII**, whose only son to survive infancy (**Edward VI**) had died childless and whose three brothers (**Arthur, prince of Wales**; Ed-

**ward Tudor**; and **Edmund Tudor, duke of Somerset**) had also left no issue. In his will, Henry had decreed that the succession should pass to his children, but there were several English nobles—notably those who held to the Roman Catholic faith—who felt that Henry's divorce from **Catherine of Aragon** was legally invalid and that, as a result, his marriage to **Anne Boleyn**, the mother of **Elizabeth I**, was bigamous. In their view, Elizabeth was illegitimate, so Mary, queen of Scots and of France, was the rightful queen of England too, because she was the closest legitimate relative in a direct line of descent from King **Henry VII** after the death of Queen **Mary I** in 1558.

Francis died in 1560, and in August 1561, Mary—seeing no future on the European mainland—accepted an invitation from the Scottish nobles to return to her native country. Initially—and partly as a result of a policy of religious tolerance in a country sharply divided between Protestant and Roman Catholic factions—her rule was accepted, but marriage to her cousin, **Henry Stuart, lord Darnley**, on 29 July 1565, raised hackles. The Protestant James Stewart, earl of Moray and one of several children of King James V born on the wrong side of the blanket, was his half-sister's closest counselor, but he took umbrage at the Catholic Darnley's rise to power, rebelled against the queen, and ultimately was declared an outlaw. Moreover, the wedding, undoubtedly a love match, further annoyed Elizabeth, who took no joy in seeing a claimant to her throne marrying another Tudor (Margaret Tudor was a grandmother of Darnley as well as of Mary).

However, the couple was soon estranged as Mary turned from her arrogant and jealous husband to other admirers. Unwilling to tolerate her philandering, Darnley led a group of conspirators into his wife's apartments at **Holyrood Palace** on 9 March 1566 and murdered David Rizzio, her Italian secretary and favored companion. Mary, six months pregnant, never forgave him either for the humiliation or for endangering her unborn child. A brief reconciliation, during which her son (later **James VI of Scotland and I of England**) was born, was followed by an affair with **James Hepburn, earl of Bothwell**. Darnley became an embarrassment, threatening to cause scandal by leaving Scotland, and toward the end of 1566, Mary discussed with her advisors the possibility of freeing herself from her marital ties.

In January the following year, Darnley fell ill, so Mary took him to **Edinburgh**, ostensibly to nurse him. He was lodged in the upper floor of a house in Kirk o' Field, with the queen occupying a room below. On the night of 9 February, while Mary was attending a wedding festival, the building was blown up. Darnley was found later in the grounds, along with his valet. Both were unmarked by the explosion and strangled. At a trial held in May, Bothwell was acquitted of complicity in the murder; shortly afterward, he divorced his wife and, on 15 May 1567, married Mary at Holyrood.

Universally disparaged, the queen now found herself even more deeply enmeshed in conflict with the nobles, who resented Bothwell's power. She was taken prisoner and held first in Edinburgh and then at Loch Leven Castle, where, on 24 July 1567, she was forced to sign a deed of abdication that handed the throne to her son. She escaped from captivity on 2 May 1568 and rallied loyal supporters, but after her troops were defeated at the Battle of Langside on 13 May, she fled to England. For Elizabeth, this posed a difficult problem. Mary's death would eliminate the major Roman Catholic threat to her Protestant crown but might unite Catholic forces against her and lead to her downfall. For 19 years, Mary was held prisoner; then, in October 1586, she was brought to trial at Fotheringhay Castle, charged with colluding with Bothwell in Darnley's murder. The evidence was questionable, and Mary conducted her defense with a dignity that aroused much sympathy and admiration. However, she was found guilty and on 8 February 1587 was executed in the building's great hall. Elizabeth had taken three months to authorize the death warrant and in the end had insisted that the paper should be placed innocently among other documents for her signature. Mary had played for high stakes and had lost, but she had shown great courage and determination. In many ways, her downfall was due to her inability to control her sexual relationships; despite her charm, she—like so many members of the **House of Stuart**—had a personality that included a self-destruct mechanism.

After Mary was **beheaded**, her body was embalmed. It remained at Fotheringhay, unburied, for a year and then was taken to Peterborough Cathedral. In 1612, her son ordered that it should be exhumed and reburied in **Westminster Abbey**, but occasionally some Scots have argued that the queen's remains should be returned to her native land. In February 2008, the library of the archbishop of Canterbury paid £72,485 for a copy of Mary's death warrant and then in April presented it to Blairs Museum, Aberdeenshire, which displays artifacts related to Scotland's Roman Catholic heritage, among them a full-length memorial painting of Mary dressed as she was when she walked to her execution. *See also* CASKET LETTERS; HONOURS OF SCOTLAND; STIRLING.

**MATILDA (1102–1167).** The daughter of King **Henry I** and **Matilda of Scotland**, Matilda (also known as Maud to distinguish her from other women with the same name) claimed that she was the rightful queen of England after her father's death in 1135 and, attempting to take the throne by force, pitched her country into a destructive civil war. As she grew up, she was groomed for marriage into the European nobility but believed that **William the Aetheling**, her younger brother, would succeed Henry as king. However, the young man's death in a drowning accident in 1120, coupled with the aging monarch's failure to produce another heir, changed both the English political landscape and her own prospects.

Matilda was born c2 February 1102, probably at Sutton Courtenay (Oxfordshire), and at the age of 7 she was betrothed to **Henry V, king of Germany**, in an alliance that her father believed would cement opposition to French designs on his estates in Normandy. By the time of the marriage at Worms in 1114, Henry V was Holy Roman Emperor, but he died 11 years later, leaving his wife with no surviving children (although one source mentions a baby that did not live beyond infancy). Matilda returned to England, where in 1127 her father made his nobles swear that in the absence of an heir they would accept her as their monarch when he died. The barons took their oaths with much reluctance, though—partly because England had never had a queen who had ruled alone, and partly because monarchs were supposed to lead armies in battle, and that, they considered, was no task for a female. Opposition hardened the following year when Matilda was married to **Geoffrey, count of Anjou**, her second husband, because Henry had not sought any advice from the great landholders before making the arrangement, which was designed to seal a peace treaty between the English and Norman realm and Anjou.

The birth of a son, who was named after his maternal grandfather, led to hopes that the succession problem might be solved, but when the king died in 1135, the child was only two years old. Turning their backs on the promise they had made eight years earlier, the nobles rejected Matilda and invited **Stephen**—son of **Adela, countess of Blois** and daughter of **William I of England**, and **Stephen Henry, count of Blois**—to take the crown. The great majority of the most powerful men in the land supported Stephen's accession, as did the principal churchmen, but Matilda had influential backing from King **David I** of Scotland and from Robert of Gloucester (her half-brother and the eldest of King Henry's numerous illegitimate offspring). She mounted an invasion in 1139 and for a time was besieged in Arundel Castle, but Stephen, ever chivalrous, failed to press home his advantage and provided her with an escort to Gloucester's fortress at Bristol, which became a center of antiroyalist activity in the west of England.

Matilda's fortunes reached their peak in February 1141, when Stephen was taken prisoner at Lincoln. With the king deposed, she marched on **London**, where the citizenry were ready to crown her queen, but she showed the same lack of political sense as her cousin, refusing to cut taxes and offending nobles who could have provided arms. So when she arrived, she found that the gates to the settlement were barred against her. Then, in September, Robert of Gloucester was taken captive, and against Matilda's wishes, Stephen was released in exchange for his return. England collapsed into civil war once again, and in 1142 Matilda was trapped in Oxford, escaping, according to legend, only because she donned a white cloak that concealed her as she crossed the snow-covered fields around the town. In 1147, Robert, her most loyal follower, died, and she sought safety in Normandy. Then, six years later, when **Eustace, count of Boulogne**, Stephen's heir, passed away, the king agreed that Henry of Anjou, Matilda's son, would succeed to his throne as King **Henry II**.

Matilda bore two other children—**Geoffrey, count of Nantes**, and **William, count of Poitou**, both of whom died childless while still young men. She passed away at the Abbaye de Notre-Dame des Près, near Rouen, on 10 September 1167 and was buried at the Abbaye du Bec, though her remains were later moved to Rouen Cathedral, where her epitaph reads, "Great by birth, greater by marriage, greatest in her offspring, here lies Matilda, the daughter, wife and mother of Henry." *See also* WALLINGFORD CASTLE.

**MATILDA, COUNTESS OF HUNTINGDON (c1074–c1130).** *See* MAUD, COUNTESS OF HUNTINGDON.

**MATILDA, DUCHESS OF SAXONY AND OF BAVARIA (1156–1189).** The eldest of three daughters born to King **Henry II** and **Eleanor of Aquitaine**, Matilda (also known as Matilda of England and as Maud) seemed destined for a wedding with one of the sons of Frederick I, the Holy Roman Emperor, but negotiations broke down, and on 1 February 1168 she became the second wife of Henry the Lion, duke of Saxony and of Bavaria; she was 12 years old and he was 39. During the early years of the marriage, Matilda, despite her youth, often administered her husband's extensive properties while he was absent, but in 1174, Henry refused to assist Frederick in an invasion of Normandy, so when the campaign ended disastrously, the emperor blamed the Lion's lack of support for the failure. Declaring that imperial law took priority over other laws, he tried the duke in his absence, declared him an outlaw, and then in 1182 forced him to flee with Matilda to the safety of Henry II's court at Argentan in Normandy.

After three years, the couple were able to return to Saxony, but they were exiled again in 1188. The constant insecurities, coupled with the rigors of childbearing, took their toll on Matilda, who died at Brunswick, Germany, in 1189 and was buried in St. Blaise Church (also known as Brunswick Cathedral), the date of her death variously given as 8 June, 28 June, and 13 July. She and Henry had at least six children who reached maturity, including a son, Otto, who became Holy Roman Emperor and a supporter of her brother, King **Richard I**.

**MATILDA OF BLOIS (c1134–c1137).** Matilda, one of five children born to King **Stephen** and his consort, **Matilda of Boulogne**, was betrothed at the age of about two to Waleran, count of Meulan, but died while still very young and was buried at the Priory of the Holy Trinity in Aldgate, **London**.

**MATILDA OF BOULOGNE (c1103–1152).** In 1125, Matilda of Boulogne married **Stephen** of Blois, who ruled England from 1135 until 1154. She proved to be one of his closest allies and a formidable political force, playing a large part in designing the strategy that led to the capture of Dover Castle in 1138 and in the negotiations that resulted, the following year, in the signing of a treaty with her uncle, King **David I** of Scotland, which helped to maintain peace on the country's northern boundaries while civil war gripped the south. In February 1141, when Stephen was taken captive by his cousin **Matilda**, who claimed his throne, his wife rallied his forces and, in September, captured Robert of Gloucester, one of Matilda's principal supporters, with her own troops. Gloucester was exchanged for the imprisoned Stephen, a move that ultimately allowed the monarch to regain his kingdom.

Matilda of Boulogne was the only child of Eustace, count of Boulogne, and his wife, **Mary, countess of Boulogne** (daughter of **King Malcolm III** of Scotland and **St. Margaret**). In the year of Matilda's wedding, Eustace, by then a widower, retired to a monastery, leaving her and her husband to administer the extensive family estates. She and Stephen had five children, two of whom—**Baldwin of Boulogne**, born c1126, and **Matilda of Blois**, born c1134—died before reaching maturity. The eldest surviving child, **Eustace, count of Boulogne**, was born c1130 and was expected to succeed his father as king but predeceased him. **William of Blois**, born c1137, would normally have taken his brother's place as heir to the crown, but his father, tired of the drawn-out conflict with Matilda, agreed that her own son, Henry of Anjou (later **Henry II**), would occupy the throne when he died. **Marie, countess of Boulogne**, sister to the three boys, was born in 1136, bore two daughters in an unhappy marriage with Matthew of Alsace, and then entered a nunnery, where she remained until her death in 1182.

Matilda of Boulogne died on 3 May 1152 and was buried at the Cluniac Faversham Abbey, which she had founded with her husband in 1147. Stephen, severely affected by her death and by that of Eustace the following year, survived only until the autumn of 1154.

**MATILDA OF FLANDERS (c1031–1083).** Diminutive Matilda, only four feet two inches tall, was the wife of William the Conqueror, who ruled England as **William I** from 1066 to 1087. The second child of Count Baldwin

V of Flanders and his wife, Adela, daughter of King Robert II of **France**, she spurned William's advances initially, claiming that because she was descended from **Alfred the Great**, she was too highborn to marry a bastard, but eventually she succumbed and they wed, probably in 1053. She then acted as **regent** in his Normandy duchy when he was in England, and in England when he was in Normandy. Scholars believe that William and Matilda had at least nine children, including William Rufus and Henry Beauclerc, who succeeded their father on the English throne as King **William II** and King **Henry I**, respectively.

Matilda died on 2 November 1083 and was buried in the choir of the Abbaye aux Dames (Abbey of Women) which she had founded with her husband in Caen. Following her death, the monarch apparently became increasingly despotic—a trait that some writers have suggested reflected his sorrow at her passing, even though she had provided financial support for their eldest son, **Robert Curthose**, when he rebelled against his father in 1077. *See also* ADELA, COUNTESS OF BLOIS; ADELIZA OF NORMANDY; AGATHA OF NORMANDY; CECILIA OF NORMANDY; CONSTANCE, DUCHESS OF BRITTANY; EALHSWITH; RICHARD, DUKE OF BERNAY.

**MATILDA OF SCOTLAND (c1080–1118).** Like most highborn women of her time, Matilda, consort of King **Henry I** (also known as Henry Beauclerc), was married for political reasons, but even so, she had a considerable influence on the English court, providing funds for the church, relief for the poor, and support for the arts. The daughter of **Malcolm III** of Scotland and his wife, **St. Margaret**, and granddaughter of **Edward the Exile**, she was born in **Dunfermline** in about 1080, christened Edith, and spent much of her childhood in the Benedictine nunnery at Romsey, where Cristina, her mother's sister, was abbess.

William of Malmesbury, a 12th-century chronicler, notes that Henry had "long been attached" to Matilda, but the interest was almost certainly also influenced by affairs of state. Henry was Norman, and Edith, through her mother, could trace her ancestry to the **Anglo-Saxon kings** of England, so marriage would cement relationships with the native peoples who formed the vast majority of his subjects. Also, a union with the daughter of the Scottish monarch would help guarantee peace on England's northern frontier. However, there was a problem, because if Edith had taken her vows as a nun, she could not marry. Anselm, archbishop of Canterbury, and his council of bishops questioned her, listened to her denial that she had ever intended to devote her life to the church, and gave their support to the union, which took place on 11 November 1100 at **Westminster Abbey**. At some point after the ceremony, Edith changed her name to Matilda (Henry's mother's name), probably to placate those Norman barons who disapproved of their king's marriage to a non-Norman.

Matilda and Henry had two children—**Matilda**, born in 1102, and **William the Aetheling**, born the following year. William was drowned in the English Channel in 1120, but Matilda survived to marry Henry V, the Holy Roman Emperor, and become the mother of King **Henry II** of England by a second marriage to **Geoffrey, count of Anjou**. Matilda of Scotland died on 1 May 1118 and was buried in Westminster Abbey. Three years later, her husband sought a youthful bride in **Adeliza of Louvain**, hoping—vainly—that he would produce an heir to succeed him. *See also* MARY, COUNTESS OF BOULOGNE.

**MAUD (1102–1167).** *See* MATILDA.

**MAUD, COUNTESS OF HUNTINGDON (c1074–c1130).** Maud (also known as Matilda) was **queen consort** of **David I** of Scotland. The daughter of Waltheof, earl of Northumbria (who was **beheaded** after taking part in a rebellion against **William I of England** in 1075) and his wife, Judith of Lens (who betrayed her husband to William, her uncle), she first married Simon de St. Liz, earl of Huntingdon and Northampton, in about 1090 and they had three children—Matilda (whose second husband, Saer de Quincy, was one of the barons who forced King **John** to agree to the provisions of the **Magna Carta**); Simon (who fought for King **Stephen** against **Matilda**'s armies); and Waltheof (who became abbot at Melrose Abbey, which was founded by his stepfather). Maud was widowed in 1109, and her marriage to David was arranged in 1113 by **Henry I** of England. Henry had wed David's sister, **Matilda of Scotland**, some years earlier, and as Maud was heiress to large estates in northern England, he clearly saw the match as advantageous because it made his brother-in-law (and supporter) one of the most powerful noblemen in the country. They had two daughters and a son—Claricia, Hodierna, and Malcolm—all of whom died young. A second boy—**Henry, earl of Northumberland**, born c1114—was expected to succeed his father to the Scottish throne but predeceased him. One source records that Maud herself died in 1130 and was buried at **Scone**, but another suggests that she was still alive in 1147.

**MAUD, PRINCESS, QUEEN OF NORWAY (1869–1938).** Maud—**queen consort** of King Haakon VII of Norway—was born at **Marlborough House** (her parents' **London** home) on 26 November 1869, the third daughter and fifth child of Albert Edward, **prince of Wales** (later King **Edward VII**), and **Alexandra of Denmark**. Alexandra was in no hurry to see any of her daughters marry, but on 22 July 1896, Maud wed her cousin, Prince Carl, the second son of Crown Prince Frederick of Denmark (and later King Frederick VIII). For the next five months, she lived at Appleton House, a property on the **Sandringham** estate that was given to her by her father as a wedding present. Unhappy at the thought of leaving Britain, she had to be persuaded of her wifely responsibilities by Alexandra. She moved reluctantly to Denmark but never felt at home there. In 1905, however, Norway ended its union with Sweden, and its parliament, after considering several candidates from the royal houses of Europe, offered the country's throne to Prince Carl, primarily because he could trace his ancestry to earlier Norwegian monarchs. Carl insisted that the proposal should be confirmed by a nationwide referendum. When that was satisfactorily completed (79 percent of those who voted favored the appointment), Carl gave up his naval career and assumed the title of King Haakon VII (on the grounds that the name had been used by previous Norwegian rulers).

Maud, perhaps surprisingly given her previous unwillingness to leave home, adapted to her new country enthusiastically, learning the language, lending her influence to charitable organizations, setting the scene for fashion as she kept an informal court, and supporting the arts. Norway's neutrality during World War I was difficult for her as she found herself more isolated from family in Britain, but she invested much effort in fundraising for groups that cared for needy Norwegians buffeted by the disruption to normal trade. The 1920s and 1930s were also hard, as the death of her mother in 1925, followed by those of **Louise, princess royal, duchess of Fife** (1931) and **Princess Victoria** (1935) and King **George V** (1936), left her with neither parents nor siblings. Her own health declined, bronchitis and neuralgia taking their toll as her heart weakened, and on 20 November 1938 she died while on a shopping trip in London. She was buried in the royal mausoleum at Akershus Castle in Oslo. Queen Maud Land, in the sector of Antarctica claimed by Norway, was named in her honor by polar explorer Roald Amundsen, as were the Queen Maud Mountains. Maud's only child was born at Appleton House in 1903. Christened Alexander but known as Olav from the time his father assumed the Norwegian throne, he succeeded Haakon as King Olav V in 1957 and reigned until 1991.

**MICHAEL OF KENT, PRINCE (1942– ). Prince** Michael is the youngest of the three children in the family of **Prince George, duke of Kent**, and **Princess Marina, duchess of Kent**. He was born at Coppins (the family home at the village of Iver, west of **London**) on 4 July 1942, only a few weeks before his father was killed in an aircraft accident in northern Scotland. The prince was educated at Sunningdale (a small and exclusive Berkshire school that Ian Fleming, author of the James Bond novels, also attended) then went to

Eton College before entering the Royal Military Academy Sandhurst. From 1963 to 1981, he served in the army, based in Cyprus (where he was part of a United Nations peacekeeping force in 1971), Germany, and Hong Kong, as well as at postings in the United Kingdom. For much of that time, he was attached to the Defence Intelligence Staff, making use of his linguistic skills (he speaks French and German fluently and has a lesser command of Italian).

More recently, Prince Michael has acted as a business consultant—taking groups representing British firms to China and India, for example—and has provided support for a diverse range of nonprofit organizations, including the David Shepherd Wildlife Foundation, the Institute of Road Safety Officers, and the Royal Life Saving Society. He receives no government funding for royal duties but in recent years has carried out about 200 engagements annually and has represented Queen **Elizabeth II** on several occasions, attending the events marking Belize's independence from the United Kingdom in 1981 and the coronation of 18-year-old King Mswati III of Swaziland in 1986. In his youth, he was also an accomplished sportsman, good enough to act as reserve for the British bobsled team at the Sapporo Winter Olympics in 1972 and to drive in car rallies at the international level.

On 30 June 1978, Prince Michael married Baroness Marie-Christine von Reibnitz (*see* MICHAEL OF KENT, PRINCESS) at a civil ceremony in Vienna. Because his bride was a Roman Catholic, under the terms of the **Act of Settlement** passed by the English parliament in 1701, the prince had to give up his place (then 15th) in the line of **succession to the throne**. The couple has two children—**Lord Frederick Windsor**, born on 6 April 1979, and **Lady Gabriella Windsor**, born on 23 April 1981. At times, the prince and **princess** have been accused of using their royal status for commercial gain, newspapers occasionally referring to them as the "Rent-a-Kents" because of their willingness to attend events in return for payment. Also, in 2002, following complaints by members of parliament that they were not being charged a commercial rent for their rooms in **Kensington Palace**, Queen Elizabeth was forced to come to their defense by indicating that she was meeting the costs from her own funds "in recognition of the royal engagements and work for various charities which Prince and Princess Michael of Kent have undertaken at their own expense, and without any public funding." However, she noted, that arrangement would end in 2010, and from then they would have to find the money themselves.

**MICHAEL OF KENT, PRINCESS (1945– ). Princess** Michael—known as "Princess Pushy" by some sections of the press—is the wife of **Prince Michael of Kent**, a grandson of King **George V** and cousin of Queen **Elizabeth II**. At her birth on 15 January 1945 at Karlovy Vary (now part of the Czech Republic but then known as Carlsbad and located in German-occupied

Sudetenland), she was named Marie-Christine. As the Russian army advanced into the area toward the end of World War II, her parents (Baron Günther Hubertus von Reibnitz—an active supporter of the Nazi Party—and his second wife, Countess Maria) were forced to flee. Later they divorced, so Marie-Christine was raised in Australia, attending Rose Bay Convent School in Sydney while her mother managed a hairdressing salon. After finishing her education, she traveled to Africa to visit her father, who was living in Mozambique, and then moved to **London**, where she established an interior design business and met banker Thomas Troubridge, whom she married on 14 September 1971. They separated after two years and divorced in 1977, before having any children. The following year, the union was annulled by the Roman Catholic Church without any reason being made public.

Marie-Christine met **Prince** Michael through contacts in Troubridge's social circle and married him on 30 June 1978 at a civil ceremony in Vienna that was attended by only a few members of the **royal family**. Because, under the terms of the 1701 **Act of Settlement**, heirs to the throne are not permitted to marry Roman Catholics, Prince Michael had to give up his 15th place in the line of succession as a result of the wedding. The couple has two children—**Lord Frederick Windsor** (born on 6 April 1979) and **Lady Gabriella Windsor** (born on 23 April 1981).

The princess has accompanied her husband on several official engagements (such as the coronation of King Mswati III of Swaziland in 1986) but has never been popular with the press. In 2002, she and the prince were criticized for failing to pay a commercial rent for their apartment in **Kensington Palace**. Queen Elizabeth II came to their defense, indicated that she was meeting the bills on their behalf because they undertook royal duties and gave support to charities at no cost to public funds, but she made clear that the arrangement would end in 2010. Newspapers have also reported that the "Princess Pushy" title was conferred by **Anne, princess royal (1950– )**, and that Princess Michael both dismissed **Diana, princess of Wales**, as "that silly girl next door" and suggested that the queen's corgi dogs should be shot. In 2004, she apparently told a group of African American diners in a New York restaurant to "go back to the colonies," and there have been several stories, which the princess has denied, of extramarital affairs with men such as Texas oil tycoon J. Ward Hunt and actress Elizabeth Taylor's former husband, John Warner. However, her supporters point out that she is an intelligent woman (she has published several books on historical themes), that she made no attempt to court public sympathy when she was diagnosed with skin cancer in 2008, and that other members of the royal family—including Queen Elizabeth's husband, **Prince Philip, duke of Edinburgh**, and her son, **Charles, prince of Wales**—also have a habit of speaking their mind.

**MIDDLETON, CATHERINE "KATE" (1982– ).** In October 2010, **Prince William of Wales** (second in line to the British throne after his father, **Charles, prince of Wales**) proposed to Kate Middleton, whom he had dated since 2003. The daughter of Michael Middleton (formerly an airline dispatch officer) and his wife, Carole (a flight attendant), Kate was born at the Royal Berkshire Hospital in Reading on 9 January 1982 and educated at St. Andrew's School in Pangbourne and at Marlborough College in Wiltshire. The couple met at St. Andrews University, where both were studying the art history (though the prince eventually switched to geography).

After graduating in 2005, Middleton found a job with Jigsaw, a clothing chain, but soon left to help with her parents' internet-based business selling supplies for children's parties. The press followed her on- and off-again relationship with William closely, praising her fashion sense but dubbing her "Waity Katy" because she failed to embark on a career and appeared to be marking time until the prince decided to marry her. In 2005 and again in 2007, reports of a split made headline news in the tabloid papers and gossip columnists portrayed Carole Middleton as something of a social bulldozer and a bit classless (on one occasion, television viewers saw her chewing gum while sitting close to members of the royal family).

While claiming that they were "just good friends," the couple rekindled their relationship, shrugged off the press coverage, and were seen together regularly from June 2007 on. William eventually proposed during a vacation to a wildlife sanctuary in Kenya, giving his fiancée the ring that his mother, **Diana, princess of Wales**, had worn because that, he said, was his way of "keeping her close to it." The wedding was arranged for 29 April 2011 in **Westminster Abbey**.

**MISTRESS OF THE ROBES.** *See* LADY-IN-WAITING.

**MONMOUTH REBELLION (1685).** In 1685, the Protestant James Scott, duke of Monmouth, led a rebellion designed to stop the Roman Catholic brother of King **Charles II** from succeeding to the thrones of England and Scotland as King **James VII and II**. Four years earlier, Anthony Ashley Cooper, earl of Shaftesbury, had unsuccessfully tried to get parliament to pass legislation that would prevent James from being crowned. At the time, one group of the bill's supporters argued that if Charles died without leaving any children, then Monmouth—an illegitimate son that Charles had sired by Lucy Walter, the daughter of one of his Welsh supporters—should be the next monarch, his religious convictions being more important than his parentage. At the time, there were claims that Charles had married Lucy, but there is little evidence for these assertions; the king accepted that the boy was his (and placed the child in the care of his own mother, **Henrietta Maria of**

**France**) but denied that he had been married at any time before his wedding to **Catherine of Braganza** in 1662.

On 11 June 1685, Scott, who had been living in Holland, landed at Lyme Regis on England's south coast with a small army of some 80 men. His "invasion" was coordinated with a rising in Scotland led by Archibald Campbell, earl of Argyll, but neither rebellion was successful. Argyll was unable to raise a force sufficiently large to threaten the royal troops and was taken prisoner; then, on 30 June, he was executed in **Edinburgh**. Monmouth gathered recruits to his cause as he marched through southwest England, and even declared himself king, but his untrained farmworkers were easily overcome when they attempted a night attack on James's standing army at Sedgemoor on 6 July. Monmouth was **beheaded** nine days later (some sources report that as many as eight blows of the axe were needed), and hundreds of his followers were hanged or transported to England's Caribbean colonies. James took advantage of his victory to increase the size of his army and to appoint several Roman Catholic commanders. He then dissolved parliament when its members objected. *See also* ALICE, PRINCESS, DUCHESS OF GLOUCESTER.

**MORAY, HOUSE OF.** The rulers who controlled the area of Moray, in northern Scotland, are sometimes grouped genealogically as the House of Moray. Two became king of Scots—**Macbeth** (who killed **Duncan I** in 1040 and then reigned until 1057) and his stepson, **Lulach**, who succeeded him but was killed only seven months later.

**MORTIMER, ROGER, EARL OF MARCH (1287–1330).** For more than three years, from early 1327 until the autumn of 1330, Roger Mortimer ruled England with **Isabella of France**, the estranged **queen consort** of King **Edward II**. The son of Edmund Mortimer and his wife, Margaret de Fiennes, he was born at Wigmore Castle in the west of England on 25 April 1287. Through his marriage in 1301 to Joan de Geneville, he acquired large tracts of land in Ireland and numerous other properties on home soil, including the strategically important castle at Ludlow on the border with Wales, but by 1318 he was counted among the nobles opposed to Edward's rule.

In 1322, Mortimer was imprisoned in the **Tower of London** after refusing a summons to appear before his sovereign, but he drugged his captors and fled to **France**. By that time, Isabella was already at odds with her bisexual husband and his advisors. Some writers believe that she helped Mortimer escape from the tower, although there is no evidence to support this claim. There is, however, no doubt that they lived openly together after she arrived in Paris in 1324. With the support of her brother, King Charles IV of France, they were able to raise an army of mercenaries that was augmented by the supporters of several nobles when it landed in eastern England on 21 September 1326. Edward fled but was captured in Wales on 16 November and was forced to abdicate on 24 January the following year.

Edward and Isabella's son was crowned **Edward III** on 1 February, but as the new monarch was only 14 years old, his mother and her lover, acting as **regents**, were the powers behind the throne. The young man's relationship with Mortimer was not good. The queen's companion was considered a good military strategist by many courtiers, and although he had rid the country of an unpopular king, he had a reputation as an arrogant, greedy man who used his position to increase his own wealth. When in March 1330 he ordered the execution of **Edmund of Woodstock, earl of Kent**, Edward II's inoffensive half-brother, many of his supporters were appalled, and the teenage monarch decided to take matters into his own hands. On 19 October, he had Mortimer seized, and on 29 November had him hung, drawn, and quartered, despite Isabella's pleas for clemency. Isabella was spared but was banished to Castle Rising in Norfolk, and Joan (Mortimer's wife) was pardoned only after spending six years in prison. *See also* NORTHAMPTON, TREATY OF.

## MOUNTBATTEN, LOUIS, EARL MOUNTBATTEN OF BURMA (1900–1979).

Lord Mountbatten—an uncle of **Prince Philip, duke of Edinburgh**, and confidant of **Charles, prince of Wales**—was the only close kinsman of the **royal family** to be murdered by the Irish Republican Army during its campaign of terrorism in the last three decades of the 20th century. Born at **Frogmore** House on 25 June 1900, he was the second son of Prince Louis of Battenberg and Princess Victoria, the eldest daughter of **Princess Alice, grand duchess of Hesse**, Queen **Victoria**'s third child. In 1917, while he was serving with the Royal Navy during World War I, he renounced his German-sounding title (Prince Louis of Battenberg) and adopted the more English surname "Mountbatten."

In 1922, Mountbatten married heiress Edwina Ashley, but the union was unhappy, and by the 1930s both were admitting to having taken other lovers. Mountbatten, however, pursued his naval career and in 1939, just before the outbreak of World War II, became captain of the destroyer *Kelly*. The vessel was sunk in the Mediterranean in May 1941, and he survived only by swimming away from the ship as it turned over. The following year, he was made chief of combined operations (a post that involved planning commando raids) and then, in 1943, was appointed supreme allied commander in Southeast Asia. In 1945, Mountbatten accepted the formal surrender of the Japanese at Singapore and in 1947 was made viceroy of India, with the task of partitioning Britain's colony on the subcontinent into the independent states of India and Pakistan. That job completed, he returned to **London**, where in 1952 he resumed naval duties as commander-in-chief of the Mediterranean fleet. Promotions continued until 1965, when he retired after six years as chief of the defense staff, having united the administration of the British Army, the Royal Air Force, and the Royal Navy under the umbrella of the Ministry of Defence.

In his later years, the earl invested much time in charitable work, particularly in organizations dealing with young people. He also acted as a mentor and confidant to **Prince** Charles, who called him "Honorary Grandfather," with the mentorship including an offer to make his home available if the young man wanted to entertain a girlfriend discreetly. Every year, he vacationed at Classiebawn Castle in northwest Ireland, and on 27 August 1979 he went out in a fishing boat to collect lobster pots. The vessel was destroyed by an Irish Republican Army bomb that killed Mountbatten and three companions—Nicholas Knatchbull (the 15-year-old son of his daughter, Patricia); 83-year-old Doreen Knatchbull, Baroness Brabourne (his daughter's mother-in-law); and 15-year-old Paul Maxwell, who was crewing the boat. Before the earl was buried in Romsey Abbey, Hampshire, Gerry Adams, a leader of the republican movement in Ireland, justified the killing, claiming that what the Irish Republican Army did to Mountbatten "is what Mountbatten had been doing all his life to other people" and that as a result of the attack "people started paying attention to what was happening in Ireland." On 23 November 1979, Thomas McMahon was sentenced to life imprisonment for the murder, but he was released in 1998 under terms of the peace agreement that ended the terrorism.

**MOWATT, MARINA (1966– ).** *See* OGILVY, MARINA.

**MURE, ELIZABETH (?–c1355).** Elizabeth—the daughter of Ayrshire landowner Sir Adam Mure of Rowallan and his wife, Janet (or Joan)—was the mother of King **Robert III** and the mistress and wife of Robert Stewart, earl of Atholl (later **Robert II**). She had maintained a relationship with Stewart for more than a decade before Pope Clement VI issued a dispensation legitimizing their numerous children on 22 November 1347. John of Fordun, a contemporary priest and chronicler, records that the couple were married in 1349, but historians suggest that there may have been an earlier, less formal ceremony in the mid-1330s, when **David II** (the king of Scots) was exiled in **France** and Stewart was heir to the throne. Elizabeth died c1355 and was buried in the church of the Blackfriars in Perth, many years before her husband followed David as Scotland's sovereign. She gave birth to four boys, and probably six girls, her eldest son succeeding his father as King Robert III despite misgivings among many of the Scots nobility. *See also* STEWART, ALEXANDER, WOLF OF BADENOCH; STEWART, ELIZABETH (?–?); STEWART, ISABELLA, COUNTESS OF DOUGLAS; STEWART, JOANNA; STEWART, KATHERINE; STEWART, MARGARET (c1342–c1410); STEWART, MARJORIE, COUNTESS OF MORAY; STEWART, ROBERT, DUKE OF ALBANY (c1340–1420); STEWART, WALTER (c1340–c1362).

# N

**NEVILLE, ANNE (1456–1485).** Like most highborn women of her time, Anne—the **queen consort** of King **Richard III**—had very limited control over her own destiny. The second child of Richard, earl of Warwick, and Anne Beauchamp, she was born at Warwick Castle on 11 June 1456. At that time, her father was a strong supporter of the **House of York**, helping to place his cousin on the throne as **Edward IV** in 1461 and acting as the power behind that throne for some time afterward. However, as the two men differed increasingly, the earl changed allegiance and allied with the **House of Lancaster** and **Margaret of Anjou**, wife of the dethroned **Henry VI**. To cement the new political relationship, Anne was married to **Edward of Lancaster, prince of Wales**, Henry's son, c13 December 1470, but the young man died the following May. Either during the **Battle of Tewkesbury** or shortly afterward, his 14-year-old widow went to live with Isabel, her older sister, and George, duke of Clarence (Isabel's husband).

Events after that are not clear, but it is likely that Clarence attempted to prevent Anne from remarrying so that he could acquire control of her inheritance. Anne, for her part, appears to have run off, quite willingly, with the politically ambitious Richard, then duke of Gloucester, for whom her inheritance was a considerable attraction. They were married on 12 July 1472 at **Westminster Abbey** after the two dukes had agreed on a partition of her estates. She bore one child—**Edward of Middleham**—in December the following year, but little is known of the couple's married life between that time and the boy's death on 31 March or 9 April 1484.

After their bereavement, rumors circulated that Richard intended to seek a divorce and marry his niece, **Elizabeth of York** (the eldest daughter of King Edward IV), because Anne, probably suffering from tuberculosis, was in poor health and was unlikely to produce another son and heir. The tales were never substantiated, however, because the queen died at the **Palace of Westminster** on 16 March the following year. She was buried in the abbey at Westminster, close to the high altar, and Richard's death at the **Battle of Bosworth Field** five months later brought an end to the **House of Plantagenet** rule of England that had lasted since 1154.

**NEVILLE, CICELY, DUCHESS OF YORK (1415–1495).** Cicely, wife of **Richard, duke of York (1411–1460)**, was the mother of King **Edward IV** and King **Richard III**. The daughter of Ralph Neville, earl of Westmorland, and his wife, Joan Beaufort, she was born on 3 May 1415 at Raby Castle, County Durham. She was betrothed to York at the age of 10 and was married by 1437 (though some sources date the wedding earlier). Historians believe that the couple had at least five daughters and eight sons between 1438 and 1455, but some argue that Edward may have been illegitimate because Richard was on a military campaign at the likely time of conception. Skeptics point out, however, that the duke may have taken time from soldiering to visit Rouen, where his wife was staying, or that the baby may have been born prematurely.

Cicely played an active role in furthering the cause of the **House of York** in its struggles with the **House of Lancaster** (*see* WARS OF THE ROSES), interceding with King **Henry VI** and his queen consort (**Margaret of Anjou**) on behalf of her husband after he had rebelled against the monarch and the royal coterie of Lancastrian advisors. She also attempted to effect reconciliation when George, her sixth son, threw his weight behind Edward's opponents in an effort to win the crown for himself in 1469–70. In her last years, the duchess devoted much of her time to prayer, and on 31 May 1495 she died at Berkhamstead Castle in Hertfordshire, predeceased by all but two of her children. She was buried at the Collegiate Church of Fotheringhay in Northamptonshire alongside her husband and her son Edmund, who was killed with his father at the **Battle of Wakefield** on 30 December 1460.

**NEVILLE'S CROSS, BATTLE OF (17 October 1346).** During the summer of 1346, King **Edward III** made preparations for an invasion of **France**. Philip VI, the French monarch, sent repeated requests for help to King **David II**, whom he had sheltered for seven years while Scotland was under attack from English forces. Eventually, in early October, David led a 12,000-man army into northern England, expecting to find the territory easy prey while Edward concentrated on France. However, English strategists had anticipated the move and had stationed men in readiness. The two sides met west of Durham, and as the English gained the upper hand, Scots commanders (including Robert Stewart, who was no friend of David but succeeded him as **Robert II**) fled the field, leaving the king to his own devices. Eventually the monarch too was forced to retreat.

The defeat was a disaster for the Scots. David was taken prisoner (there are tales, perhaps apocryphal, that he tried to avoid his pursuers by hiding under a bridge) and was held captive for 11 years while the English took advantage of their success and occupied all of Scotland south of the rivers

Forth and Clyde. Eventually he was released, but the Scots could not find the ransom money, so David, to the considerable annoyance of his parliament, offered Edward the Scottish crown in lieu of the funds. *See also* EUPHEMIA DE ROSS.

**NONSUCH PALACE.** Nonsuch was one of three **royal residences** built south of **London** during medieval times (the others were **Eltham Palace** and the **Palace of Placentia**). In 1538, King **Henry VIII** cleared the population from Cuddington Village, near Cheam, and built a hunting palace that was named Nonsuch because it was without equal. The building was small by the standards of the time but opulently decorated in Renaissance style, with stucco reliefs along the south front and around the inner of two courtyards. Ornate towers surmounted by cupolas were erected at each end of the 150-yard-long structure, and gardens were laid out with the studied formality required by Tudor taste. King **James VI and I** continued to use the palace as a base for hunting, but his grandson, King **Charles II**, presented it to a mistress, Barbara, countess of Castlemaine, who sold it to Lord Berkeley in 1682 because she needed money to repay gambling debts. Shortly afterward, the new owner demolished the structure, using some of the stone to erect another property in nearby Epsom. The location of the building was lost until 1959, when excavations allowed archaeologists to reconstruct its ground plan. The land is now used as a public park.

**NORMANDY, HOUSE OF.** Normandy, now a region of northern **France**, played a significant political and cultural role in Europe from the 10th to the 13th century, extending its influence as far south as Sicily and as far east as Byzantium, on the borders of Asia. Connections with England were cemented by marriage in 1002, when **Emma of Normandy** was wed to **Aethelred the Unready**, a match that was to provide one element of the claim to the English throne made by William, duke of Normandy, who became King **William I of England** and is usually known as William the Conqueror. The claim was backed up by an invasion that resulted in the defeat of **Harold II**'s troops at the **Battle of Hastings** on 14 October 1066 and the replacement of the **Anglo-Saxon kings** of **Wessex** by the House of Normandy.

Once the base in southern England was consolidated, the Norman armies attempted to extend their control into the north of the country, as well as into Ireland, Scotland, and Wales. Arriving as conquerors and behaving as rulers of an occupied country, they spoke a regional dialect of French and expected the vanquished people to learn it in order to communicate with them. They looked to mainland Europe as the focus of political and social innovation, they introduced new cultural styles (for example, in church architecture and land tenure), and they maintained control by armed might, building castles to protect themselves from insurrection.

Most writers consider that they produced three monarchs of England. William I ruled from 1066 until 1087. He was followed by his third son, **William II of England** (who was widely considered a tyrant by the time he died in 1100), and then by his fourth son, **Henry I** (whose 35-year reign was less controversial than his brother's and was more marked by social and economic advance, though it was plagued in its later stages by the lack of an heir). Some scholars add **Stephen**, Henry's much-derided successor, to the list, but others consider him the sole English monarch from the **House of Blois** because he was descended from the Conqueror through the female line rather than the male line. Similarly, some include **Matilda**, Henry's daughter, on the grounds that she held Stephen captive from April to November 1141, but others exclude her on the grounds that she was never crowned. The dynasty ended with Stephen, whose only son (**Eustace, count of Boulogne**) predeceased him and who was succeeded by King **Henry II**, Matilda's son and the first of the rulers from the **House of Plantagenet**.

From 1066 to the early 13th century, Normandy remained a possession of the English crown. However, under the feudal system of land tenure, monarchs of England held their territories on the European mainland only as vassals of the French king. In 1202, therefore, Philip II of France was able to summon King **John** to his court to address a series of charges, including the claim that he had kidnapped and married **Isabella of Angoulême**, who was betrothed to another of his vassals, Hugh of Lusignan. John refused to attend, so Philip confiscated Normandy in 1204 and confirmed ownership by defeating English troops at the Battle of Bouvines in 1214. **Henry III** formally recognized French authority in the area in 1259, but his successors made a series of attempts to win the lands back, holding them from 1346 to 1360 and then from 1415 to 1450 (*see* HUNDRED YEARS' WAR), so French control was not confirmed until the mid-15th century. *See also* BRUCE, HOUSE OF; EDWARD THE CONFESSOR; HENRY V; ROBERT I; ROBERT CURTHOSE, DUKE OF NORMANDY; TINCHEBRAI, BATTLE OF.

**NORTHAMPTON, BATTLE OF (10 July 1460).** The Battle of Northampton was one of the more significant encounters in the **Wars of the Roses** because it resulted in the capture of King **Henry VI** by his Yorkist enemies. After earlier defeats, Edward, son of **Richard, duke of York (1411–1460)**, had fled to **France** along with his ally and advisor Richard Neville, earl of Warwick. There they regrouped, and on 26 June 1460, while Henry and his consort, **Margaret of Anjou**, were away from **London**, they returned to England with their army. They entered the capital, where they received much support, on 2 July and then headed north, prepared to meet the Lancastrian force at Northampton.

The conflict, fought eight days later, was over quickly. Henry's troops had taken up defensive positions in the grounds of Delapre Abbey, a Cluniac nunnery, but they were heavily outnumbered, and heavy rain reduced the effectiveness of their cannons. Lord Grey of Ruthin, leading the royalist right flank, ordered his men not to do battle, with the result that the Yorkists quickly overran the abbey. The king, who appeared to have suffered a mental breakdown, was taken prisoner, and on 10 October the victorious Richard of York invited parliament to accept his claim to the English throne. The request was refused, so Henry kept his crown, but he was required to nominate the duke as his heir. After Richard's death at the **Battle of Wakefield** on 30 December, his son continued to espouse the York family cause, ultimately deposing Henry and ruling as King **Edward IV**.

**NORTHAMPTON, TREATY OF (1 May 1328).** Under the terms of the Treaty of Northampton, England recognized Scotland as an independent country with **Robert I** (Robert the Bruce) as its king. Throughout the decade from 1296, when King **Edward I** of England took King **John of Scotland** prisoner, Scotland was occupied by English troops. But gradually, from 1307, Bruce regained control of his country's fortresses, and his victory at the **Battle of Bannockburn** on 24 June 1314 resulted in the complete expulsion of the invading forces. In the years that followed, Scots raiding parties regularly ventured deep into northern England, until eventually **Isabella of France** and **Roger Mortimer, earl of March**, who were acting as **regents** for **Edward III**, the teenage English king, sought a formal peace, preferring this to an expensive war.

The contract (also known as the Treaty of **Edinburgh** because it was signed in that city by King Robert on 17 March 1328) included provisions that England would renounce all claims to sovereignty over Scotland and that the boundary between the two countries would be as it had been during the reign of King **Alexander III** (and much as it is now). Robert was accepted as the rightful king, and the pact was to be sealed by the marriage of his son (later **David II**) to **Joan of the Tower** (Isabella's youngest daughter by King **Edward II**). The wedding was held on 17 July 1328. However, many English nobles found the negotiations demeaning, so in 1333, Edward III, after taking the government into his own hands, repudiated the treaty, once again attempting to subjugate the Scots, who continued to assert their right to independence under their own king.

**OATLANDS PALACE.** Oatlands, favored by monarchs of the **House of Tudor** and their successors from the **House of Stuart**, stood on the south bank of the River Thames in Surrey, close to Weybridge. King **Henry VIII** acquired a mansion house on the site in 1537, and, using stone from nearby Chertsey Abbey which had fallen into disuse as a result of his break with the Roman Catholic Church, he built an imposing residence for **Anne of Cleves**, his fourth wife. Anne may never have visited the palace, but on 28 July 1540, less than three weeks after having that marriage annulled, Henry married **Catherine Howard** in the building. **Elizabeth I** and **James VI and I** visited regularly, and in 1647, **Charles I** was held prisoner there by Oliver Cromwell's parliamentarian forces. In 1650, the year after Charles's execution, the palace was demolished, and in succeeding decades the estate passed through several hands. For a short period at the end of the 18th century, the property was leased to Frederick, **duke of York** and second son of King **George II**, but in 1794 it was badly damaged by fire. Then, in 1856, the estate was subdivided into several lots and sold off. The grounds of the former **royal residence** are now occupied by social housing and by a country house hotel. *See also* STUART, HENRY, DUKE OF GLOUCESTER.

**OCTAVIUS, PRINCE (1779–1783).** Octavius was the last member of the British **royal family** to suffer from smallpox. He was born at **Buckingham Palace** on 23 February 1779, the thirteenth child and eighth son (hence his name) of King **George III** and **Charlotte of Mecklenburg-Strelitz**. The **prince** contracted the disease (which had also afflicted his father) in 1783, shortly after his fourth birthday. He died at **Kew Palace** on 3 May, a few days after being inoculated in an effort to reduce the impact of the infection, and was buried in **Westminster Abbey**; his remains were transferred to **St. George's Chapel** at **Windsor Castle** in 1820. The king, who was very attached to his children, was inconsolable, saying that "There will be no heaven for me if Octavius is not there" and holding imaginary conversations with the boy after his final bout of madness descended in 1811.

**OCTREDA OF NORTHUMBRIA (?–?).** Octreda, daughter of Gospatric, earl of Dunbar and Northumbria, was the wife of **Duncan II**, who occupied the Scottish throne for a few months in 1094. Gospatric—a great-grandson of King **Malcolm II**—proposed a betrothal that was initially spurned but later was accepted because Duncan needed military support for his efforts to take the crown from **Donald III**. The couple had one son—**William FitzDuncan**—who became a supporter of King **David I** and a noted military commander. The dates of Octreda's birth and death, and the name of her mother, are unknown, but there are records of her burial at **Dunfermline Abbey**. She is also known as Etheldreda and as Uctreda.

**OGILVY, SIR ANGUS (1928–2004).** Sir Angus, husband of **Princess Alexandra**, developed a successful business career, tainted by political scandal, while helping his wife with her royal duties. Born in **London** on 14 September 1928, the second son of David Ogilvy, earl of Airlie, and his wife, Lady Alexandra, he received his early education at Heatherdown Preparatory School, near Ascot (an establishment later attended by **Prince Andrew, duke of York**, and **Prince Edward, earl of Wessex**, as well as by other members of the **royal family**), and then went to Eton College and Oxford University.

From 1950, after graduating with a degree in philosophy, politics, and economics, Ogilvy pursued a career in the City of London, specializing in real estate. In 1961, however, his employer sent him to Africa to rejuvenate the London and Rhodesia Mining and Land Company (later known as Lonrho). Ogilvy handed management of the firm to R. W. "Tiny" Rowland, an Anglo-German businessman whose assertive style and questionable ethics annoyed many of his associates. During the late 1960s, rumors began to spread that Lonrho had broken the economic sanctions placed on Rhodesia by the British government after Ian Smith, the head of the country's all-white government, unilaterally declared independence from the United Kingdom in 1965. Prime Minister Edward Heath condemned Rowland's entrepreneurial tactics as the "unpleasant and unacceptable face of capitalism," and in 1976 a report by officers from the Department of Trade and Industry criticized the firm's practices. Ogilvy immediately resigned all of his directorships and, though he was later cleared of any wrongdoing, changed the direction of his interests.

On 24 April 1963, Ogilvy married **Princess** Alexandra, a granddaughter of King **George V**, in **Westminster Abbey**, turning down the offer of an earldom from Queen **Elizabeth II** because he wanted to look after his wife by dint of his own efforts and not through titles or royal connections. The couple had two children—**James Ogilvy** (born in 1964) and **Marina Ogilvy** (born in 1966 and later to cause her parents much sorrow as a rebellious young woman)—and undertook many public engagements together, including several overseas. Although the Lonrho affair ended Ogilvy's full-time career in commerce, he remained a highly respected figure in the business community and was offered places on the boards of several large companies, including Sotheby's, the auction firm, for which he acted as a "roving ambassador." He also turned his attention to working with charities, in particular helping organizations connected with health care (despite his addiction to tobacco, he was president of the Imperial Cancer Research Fund) and with providing opportunities for young people. Much of his time was devoted to fund-raising, rather than simply acting as a figurehead who turned out at formal engagements, and in 1988 alone he raised £80 million for the Prince's Youth Business Trust, a group (headed by **Charles, prince of Wales**) that provides financial assistance to unemployed young people keen on launching their own companies.

Sir Angus, who was knighted in 1988, tolerated ill health for much of his life, suffering greatly from back pain (from which he tried to win relief by cycling through London to his office). He died in Kingston-upon-Thames Hospital on 26 December 2004 after contracting throat cancer and was interred in the royal burial ground at **Frogmore.**

**OGILVY, JAMES (1964– ).** James Ogilvy—the only son, and elder child, of **Princess Alexandra** and **Sir Angus Ogilvy**—followed his father into commerce and made a successful career as a publisher. He was born on 29 February 1964 at Thatched House Lodge, the family home at Richmond in southwest **London**, and was educated at Eton College before going to St. Andrews University, where he graduated with a master of arts degree in art history. On 30 June 1988, he married fellow student Julia Rawlinson, the daughter of a businessman, at Saffron Walden in Essex. They have two children—Flora (born on 15 December 1994) and Alexander (born on 12 November 1996).

In 1996, Ogilvy, who is not required to carry out public engagements on behalf of the **royal family**, launched *Luxury Briefing*, a monthly periodical targeted at companies that sell fashion, food, interior design, and other goods to very wealthy clients. His wife was managing director of jeweler Hamilton & Inches, winning the Scottish Businesswoman of the Year award in 2001 for turning around the nearly moribund company. However, the death of two children of close friends prompted a change of direction. In 2005, she founded ProjectScotland, which works with nonprofit organizations to provide volunteer opportunities for 16- to 25-year-olds; the success of the venture earned her the Scotland Ernst & Young Social Entrepreneur of the Year award in 2007.

**OGILVY, MARINA (1966– ).** Marina, the only daughter and younger child of **Princess Alexandra** and **Sir Angus Ogilvy**, caused her parents much embarrassment when, as a young woman, she rebelled against her upbringing. Born on 31 July 1966 at Thatched House Lodge, the family home at Richmond on the southwestern outskirts of **London**, and named after her maternal grandmother, **Princess Marina**, she was educated at St. Mary's, Wantage, a **Church of England** school for girls that her cousin, **Lady Helen Taylor**, also attended. However, when she was in her twenties, Marina became increasingly estranged from her parents as she flouted royal protocols (for example, by appearing on the cover of the *Skin Two* fetish magazine wearing a jump suit and a crown, draped across a throne and with corgi dogs at her feet). In 1989, she told the tabloid press that she was pregnant by her boyfriend, fashion photographer Paul Mowatt; that she had no intention of getting married; and that her parents (who, she claimed, put duty to the country before duty to their family) wanted her to have an abortion.

When Marina changed her mind about marriage, **Princess** Alexandra and her husband attempted to support her by attending the wedding at St. Andrew's Church in Ham, Surrey, on 2 February 1990, even though she had sold exclusive coverage to *Today* newspaper. A baby girl (Zenouska) was born on 26 May 1990, and a son (Christian Alexander) on 4 June 1993, but the union was stormy, with some sources suggesting that Mowatt physically abused his wife. The couple divorced in 1997, and Marina has since kept a low profile, registering for a music degree at the University of London and attending some royal occasions (such as the wedding of **Prince Edward, earl of Wessex**, in 1999), but being noticeably absent from others. In 2003, she was the subject of much speculation about her finances when newspapers revealed that she was receiving funds from government welfare agencies. She has indicated that she prefers to be known as Marina Ogilvy rather than by her former married name.

**OLD PRETENDER.** *See* STUART, JAMES FRANCIS EDWARD.

**OLDENBURG, ANNE SOPHIA (1686–1687).** In 1684—the year after her marriage to **George, prince of Denmark** and a member of the Oldenburg dynasty—Anne (later Queen **Anne**), the daughter of James, **duke of York**, suffered a miscarriage. The following year, shortly after her father succeeded to the throne as King **James VII of Scotland and II of England**, she gave birth to a daughter, **Mary Oldenburg**; then, on 12 May 1686, at **Windsor Castle**, she delivered another girl, Anne Sophia. Early in 1687, the infant took ill with smallpox, which killed her on 2 February. Her older sister died six days later. Both girls were buried in **Westminster Abbey**.

**OLDENBURG, GEORGE (1692).** Anne, daughter of King **James VII and II** and later Queen **Anne**, conceived on 18 occasions during her marriage to

**George, prince of Denmark**, a scion of the Oldenburg dynasty which produced several monarchs in North Germany and Scandinavia. Only five of the 18 pregnancies resulted in live births, and George was the last. He was born at Syon House in Brentford (where Anne was staying with Charles Seymour, duke of Somerset, and his wife, Elizabeth) on 17 April 1692 but lived for only a few minutes. A series of eight stillbirths followed over the next eight years.

**OLDENBURG, MARY (1685–1687).** Mary was born at **Whitehall Palace** on 2 June 1685 to Anne (later Queen **Anne**)—the daughter of King **James VII and II**—and her husband, **George, prince of Denmark**, whose family name was Oldenburg. In 25 years of marriage, Anne conceived 18 children, but only five survived birth and none reached maturity. Mary lived for less than two years, contracting smallpox and dying at **Windsor Castle** on 8 February 1687, just six days after the death of her younger sister, **Anne Sophia Oldenburg**. Both girls were buried in **Westminster Abbey**.

**OLDENBURG, MARY (1690).** On 14 October 1690, at **St. James's Palace**, Anne (later Queen **Anne**)—daughter of the exiled King **James VII and II** and consort of **George, prince of Denmark**—gave birth to a daughter, Mary. Only five of Anne's pregnancies resulted in live infants, and none of the children lived to maturity. Mary survived for only about two hours and was buried in **Westminster Abbey**, where her older sisters, **Anne Sophia Oldenburg** and another **Mary Oldenburg (1685–1687)**, had been interred after succumbing to smallpox three years earlier.

**ORANGE, HOUSE OF.** The House of Orange is an aristocratic European dynasty that has played an important role, in particular, in the development of the Netherlands. Its only representative on the British thrones was **William III of England and II of Scotland**, who ruled both countries from 1689 to 1702.

In 1677, William of Orange married his cousin, Mary, the daughter of James, **duke of York** (later King **James VII of Scotland and II of England**), and his first wife, **Anne Hyde**. James was a convert to Roman Catholicism, and **Mary of Modena**, his second wife, was raised as a Catholic, so when a son (**James Francis Edward Stuart**) was born in 1688, many English nobles and churchmen were concerned that the monarchy would owe allegiance to the Church of Rome for several generations. These dissidents invited William, then seen as the military champion of the Protestant cause in Europe because of his opposition to King Louis XIV of **France**, to bring an army in defense of the faith, and he willingly accepted the call, landing at Torbay on 5 November 1688. James fled, leaving William to be crowned joint sovereign with his wife (*see* MARY II) the following year. The Scots had more doubts about the legality of the invasion but followed the English lead.

Widely considered a cold, arrogant foreigner, William was never popular with his English and Scottish subjects and was little mourned when he died as a result of a riding accident in 1702, but he gave the English parliament a more assured role in government than had been the case under his predecessors, effectively quashed rebellions in Ireland and Scotland, and promoted religious tolerance. He is remembered particularly in Northern Ireland, where the Orange Lodge—a Protestant organization—is named after him and annually celebrates his victories over James's Roman Catholic supporters on the island. The family gets its name from its origins in the Orange region of southwest France. *See also* ANNE, PRINCESS ROYAL (1709–1759); CHARLOTTE AUGUSTA, PRINCESS; GLORIOUS REVOLUTION; MARY HENRIETTA, PRINCESS ROYAL, PRINCESS OF ORANGE; WILLIAM, PRINCE OF ORANGE.

**OSBORNE HOUSE.** Osborne, on the Isle of Wight off England's southern coast, was a favorite residence of Queen **Victoria**, who claimed that it was "impossible to imagine a prettier spot." She and her husband, **Prince Albert of Saxe-Coburg and Gotha**, bought the property from Lady Isabella Blachford in 1845, intending to use it as a country retreat. The prince immediately started a program of expansion and remodeling, employing Thomas Cubitt, an innovative **London** builder, to erect and furnish a family home in flamboyant Italian Renaissance style. Most of the work was completed by 1851, but in 1854 a "cottage" was dismantled in Switzerland and reerected in the Osborne House grounds as the queen's gift to her children on her 35th birthday, and additions were made to the main building as late as 1891, when a new wing incorporated the Durbar Room, decorated by Indian architect Bhai Ram Singh and used for elaborate state functions.

After Albert's death in 1861, Victoria spent much time at Osborne, making little change to her private apartments before her death there on 22 January 1901 and ensuring that her late husband's shaving equipment was laid out every morning as if he were alive. Her sons and daughters, however, were much less enamored of the place. Victoria had requested that the house, which she had bought and furnished with her own resources, should remain within the family, but nobody wanted it. So King **Edward VII**, her successor, presented it to the nation.

From 1903 to 1921, part of the property housed a training school for the Royal Navy, and during World War I, rooms were converted into a convalescent home for officers from all branches of the armed forces (A. A. Milne, author of *Winnie the Pooh*, recovered there after contracting trench fever while serving with the Royal Warwickshire Regiment). The estate is now owned by English Heritage, a government agency charged with the maintenance of buildings of historic importance, and is open to the public, who can also rent a holiday cottage that once served as the naval college's cricket pavilion. *See also* ALEXANDRA OF DENMARK; ALICE, PRINCESS, GRAND DUCHESS OF HESSE; BEATRICE (OR HENRY) OF BATTENBERG, PRINCESS.

**OSBURGA (?–?).** Osburga (or Osburh) was the first wife of **Aethelwulf**, king of **Wessex**, and, probably, the mother of **Alfred the Great**. She was the daughter of Oslac, a member of Aethelwulf's court, but her mother's name is unknown.

Some writers speculate that Osburga was born in about 810 and died before 856 (the year in which Aethelwulf married **Judith of Flanders**), but there is no documentary record of either event. Most historians of the period assume that she and Aethelwulf were the parents of Alfred's older brothers and his sister. Aethelstan, the eldest son, was made king of Kent by his father in 839 but had probably died by 856. Aethelbald, the second son, forced his father to divide his realm in 856, giving the younger man Wessex, but he died after ruling for only four years and was succeeded by Aethelbert, his younger brother.

When Aethelbert died, childless, in 865, Aethelred, the fourth brother, became king in his stead, leading his people for six years before dying in battle. Viking invaders constantly plagued all four monarchs, but there was little effective Anglo-Saxon resistance to Scandinavian incursions until Alfred's reign (871–c899). A sister, Aethelswith, was married to Burgred, king of Mercia, in c853, when he made an alliance with Aethelwulf to fight the Britons in north Wales. In 874, however, the Vikings forced Aethelswith and her husband into exile in Italy, and she died in Pavia in 888, apparently without ever having children.

Queen Elizabeth I in youth, middle age, *and maturity. Three photo engravings after paintings by (1) school of Holbein, (2) F. Zucchero, and (3) Marc Garrard the Elder.*

Mary, Queen of Scots. *Photograph of portrait created by G. W. Wilson & Co. in the late 19th century.*

King Charles I. *Reproduction of painting, published by the Detroit Publishing Co., c1907.*

King William III, Prince of Orange. *Hand-colored lithograph originally published by Currier & Ives, c1880.*

Queen Victoria and Members of the Royal Family. Wood engraving by J. M. Ridley, published in Frank Leslie's Illustrated Newspaper, 14 July 1877.

*Queen Victoria Arrives in London for the Celebrations of the 60th Anniversary of Her Coronation, 28 June 1897.*

Victoria, Queen of Great Britain and Ireland. *Steel engraving.*

His Royal Highness Prince Albert. *Painted by John Lucas, engraved by Henry S. Sadd, originally published in 1847.*

*King Edward VII Bids Farewell to Captain Scott on Board the Discovery, 5 August 1901.*

*King George V and His Consort, Mary of Teck, Leave St. George's Chapel, Windsor Castle, after the Investiture of Edward, Prince of Wales, with the Order of the Garter, 10 June 1911.*

Edward, Prince of Wales, at the White House, November 1919. *National Photo Company collection.*

King George VI. *Created 1940–1946. Part of the G. Eric and Edith Matson Photograph Collection.*

King George VI and Queen Elizabeth with Princess Elizabeth and Princess Margaret. *Undated print in the G. Eric and Edith Matson Photograph Collection.*

Queen Elizabeth, the Queen Mother. *Part of the G. Eric and Edith Matson Photograph Collection.*

The Christening of Her Royal Highness Princess Elizabeth. *From the Bain News Service Collection.*

*Caernarvon Castle. Published c1910–1915. From the Bain Collection.*

Holyrood Palace. *Print originally published by the Detroit Publishing Co., c1895.*

The Throne Room, Buckingham Palace. *Untitled photograph published by Bain News Service.*

The Tower of London. *Originally published c1890–1900.*

Westminster Abbey. *Photomechanical print originally published by the Detroit Publishing Co., 1905.*

# P

**PALACE OF HOLYROODHOUSE.** *See* HOLYROOD PALACE.

**PALACES.** *See* ROYAL RESIDENCES.

**PARR, CATHERINE (1512–1548).** Catherine (or Katherine) was the sixth and last wife of King **Henry VIII**. The daughter of Sir Thomas Parr (a descendant of King **Edward III**) and his wife, Maud Green, she was born, probably in the summer of 1512, at Kendal Castle (a family home in northwest England). In 1529, she married Sir Edward Borough, who died in late 1532 or early 1533, and then, in 1534, she wed John Neville, lord Latimer. Neville's death in 1543 left her a wealthy widow, wooed by Thomas Seymour (the brother of **Jane Seymour**, Henry's third queen), but the king, too, was interested. On 12 July 1543, she married the monarch at **Hampton Court Palace** and for the remainder of his life exercised a stabilizing influence on him, acting as **regent** while he campaigned in **France** from July to September 1544, developing good relationships with his children—Mary (later **Mary I**), Elizabeth (later **Elizabeth I**), and Edward (later **Edward VI**)—and showing sympathy to Protestant reformers despite her Roman Catholic upbringing.

After Henry's death early in 1547, Catherine returned to Seymour and married him in the spring of the same year. In August 1548, she gave birth to a daughter named Mary—the only child of her four marriages—but contracted puerperal fever (or possibly puerperal sepsis) and died on 5 September at Sudeley Castle, her husband's property in Gloucestershire. The castle was reduced to ruins during the civil war of 1642–51, but her grave was rediscovered in the chapel in 1728, and her remains were reinterred in 1817. Thomas was executed for treason in 1549. Nothing is known of Mary after 1550; most historians believe that she failed to reach maturity, but some writers speculate that she may have survived into adulthood, either in Ireland or as the wife of a courtier of **Anne of Denmark**, consort of King **James VI of Scotland and I of England**.

**PHILIP II OF SPAIN (1527–1598).** Philip's marriage to Queen **Mary I** of England was not greeted with universal acclaim by her majesty's subjects. After succeeding to the throne in 1553, at the age of 37 and still unmarried, Mary cast around for a suitable Roman Catholic husband so that she could produce the heir who would keep the crown in Catholic hands, reversing the moves to Protestantism initiated by her father (King **Henry VIII**) and half-brother (King **Edward VI**). Philip—the only son of Charles V, king of Spain and Holy Roman Emperor, and Isabella of Portugal—was a decade younger than Mary but had already been married to Maria Manuela, a daughter of King John III of Portugal. Manuela had died in 1545, just one month after giving birth to a baby boy, so a union with Mary made political sense to the Spanish royal house because Philip was destined to inherit the Netherlands, with which England had a mutual defense treaty. However, the match caused considerable concern in England, where some nobles resented the reestablishment of a Catholic monarchy and others believed that their country would become no more than a Spanish colony, foreseeing—rightly—that it would be sucked into a war between Spain and **France**.

Despite the protests, the wedding ceremony was held at **Winchester** Cathedral on 25 July 1554, and Philip was officially declared "King of England." However, although he guided efforts to restore papal authority over the **Church of England**, the new monarch was always more interested in events on the European mainland than in domestic matters, and moreover, he exercised authority behind the scenes, preferring to persuade his wife rather than exert control himself. Mary's willingness to acquiesce to her consort's wishes was to have considerable consequences for her country. In late August 1555, Philip left to take command of his armies in Flanders, remaining abroad until March 1557, when he returned to ask his wife to pledge English support for Spain in its war with France. This prospect inflamed opposition to a queen already under attack for her repression of Protestant sympathizers. War was expensive, so taxes would have to be levied to pay for the campaign; trade would be disrupted; and the Scots—longtime allies of France—were likely to open a second front on England's northern border. Even so, Mary agreed to Philip's request. But her troops failed to dominate the battlefield, so in 1558, England lost **Calais**, its last territorial toehold on the European continent.

Philip left England on 6 July 1557, never to return, and Mary was left to lament that when she died, "Philip" and "Calais" would be found inscribed on her heart. And her death was not long in coming. The queen passed away on 17 November 1558, and Philip remarried twice—to Elisabeth of Valois (a daughter of King Henry II of France and thus a sister-in-law of **Mary, queen of Scots**) in 1559, and to Anna of Austria (his niece) in 1570. He became king of Spain when his father abdicated in 1556 and made his country a major international power, but he never managed to impose Catholicism throughout his territories. Philip died in the Escorial (the residence of Spanish monarchs) on 13 September 1598 from a combination of edema, fever, and gout.

**PHILIP, PRINCE, DUKE OF EDINBURGH (1921– ).** The consort of Queen **Elizabeth II**, Philip was born at Mon Repos (Corfu) on 10 June 1921, the son of Prince Andrew of Greece and Denmark and of Princess Alice of Battenburg, whose maternal grandmother—**Princess Alice, grand duchess of Hesse**—was the second of Queen **Victoria**'s five daughters. At the time of his birth, the Greek royal family was in exile, so Philip was educated at Cheam (in England), at Baden (in Germany), and at Gordonstoun (in Scotland). After training at the Royal Naval College Dartmouth, he served with the Mediterranean Fleet and with the British Pacific Fleet during World War II, taking part in the action at Cape Matapan (1941) and in the landings at Sicily (1943). In the spring of 1947, he became a British citizen, renounced his claims to the Greek and Danish thrones, and adopted the surname Mountbatten. Then, in **Westminster Abbey** on November 20 the same year, he married **Princess** Elizabeth, whom he had first met when he was tasked with escorting her around Dartmouth eight years earlier.

Philip continued to follow his naval career, commanding the frigate *Magpie*, until his wife's accession to the throne on 6 February 1952. From then, he has shared many of the queen's official engagements and in addition has carried out his own schedule of commitments. He was created a **prince** of the realm in 1957 but has frequently courted controversy because of his outspoken views and unprincely offensive remarks. In 1995, for example, the prince invited a Scottish driving instructor to explain how he managed to "keep the natives off the booze long enough to get them through the test," and in 2002, he asked an Australian aborigine, "Do you still throw spears at each other?"

Critics have also suggested that the Duke of **Edinburgh**'s passion for hunting was incompatible with his presidency of the Worldwide Fund for Nature; that he bullied **Charles, prince of Wales**, into marrying **Diana, princess of Wales**, in 1981; that he was unduly critical of Diana after her divorce from Prince Charles; and that his role in bringing up his children has contributed to the family's dysfunctionality (his daughter and two of his sons have suffered broken marriages). On the other hand, he has received much credit for founding, in 1956, the Duke of Edinburgh's Award Scheme, which links community service and development of skills to a sense of adventure and now has branches in more than 100 countries.

Prince Philip and Queen Elizabeth have four children—Prince Charles (born on 14 November 1948); **Anne, princess royal** (15 August 1950); **Prince Andrew, duke of York** (19 February 1960); and **Prince Edward, earl of**

**Wessex** (10 March 1964). *See also* BUCKINGHAM PALACE; CIVIL LIST; CLARENCE HOUSE; HER (OR HIS) ROYAL HIGHNESS; PRINCE; REGENCY ACTS; ROYAL STANDARD; ROYAL TRAIN; ROYAL WARRANT; SARAH, DUCHESS OF YORK; WINDSOR, HOUSE OF.

**PHILIPPA OF HAINAULT (1311–1369). Queen consort** of King **Edward III**, Philippa was probably born in Valenciennes (now in northern **France**) on 24 June 1311, the daughter of William, count of Hainault, and Jeanne of Valois. She married Edward at York Minster on 24 January 1328 and, through the union, reintroduced the bloodline of **Stephen** (king of England from 1135 to 1154) to the **royal family**. The alliance assured the young monarch of the influential support of Philippa's relatives in his struggles with the French, but, unlike such predecessors as **Eleanor of Provence**, she did not antagonize her new subjects by finding positions for her family at her new court. The queen often traveled with her husband on his military campaigns and exercised considerable influence over him, most famously at **Calais** in 1346, when she persuaded him not to kill six of the town's burghers who had offered themselves for execution on condition that the lives of other citizens be spared. She also did much to help local economies by promoting coal mining in northeast England and weaving in Norwich.

Philippa bore five or six daughters and eight sons. None of her offspring would occupy the throne, but several—notably **Edward, the black prince** (born in 1330); **Lionel of Antwerp, duke of Clarence** (1338); **John of Gaunt** (1340); **Edmund of Langley, duke of York** (1341); and **Thomas of Woodstock, duke of Gloucester** (1355)—would greatly influence the development of the English monarchy and its relationships with European neighbors. A popular consort (her chaplain, Robert de Eglesfield, had founded Queen's College at Oxford University in her honor in 1341), she was much mourned on her death c15 August 1369 in **Windsor Castle**. Philippa was interred in **Westminster Abbey**, leaving her husband to pursue a relationship with Alice Perrers, her former **lady-in-waiting**. *See also* ISABELLA DE COUCY; MARGARET, COUNTESS OF PEMBROKE; MARY, DUCHESS OF BRITTANY; PLANTAGENET, BLANCHE (1342); PLANTAGENET, JOAN (C1333–1348); PLANTAGENET, THOMAS; PLANTAGENET, WILLIAM (1337); PLANTAGENET, WILLIAM (1348).

**PHILIPPA, QUEEN OF DENMARK, NORWAY, AND SWEDEN (1394–1430).** Philippa's birth at Peterborough Castle on 4 June 1394 was not easy, causing complications that led to the death of her mother, **Mary de Bohun**, first wife of Henry Bolingbroke (later King **Henry IV**). In 1401, two years after he had deposed King **Richard II**, Henry sought an alliance with the Scandinavian countries, hoping that they would provide support for England in its conflict with **France** (*see* HUNDRED YEARS' WAR). The Nordic leaders refused to get involved but were willing to approve a defense treaty that would be sealed by Philippa's marriage to Eric, son of Wartislaw, duke of Pomerania, and later king of Denmark, Norway, and Sweden. When the couple married at Lund, in Sweden, on 26 October 1406, Philippa (sometimes known as Philippa of England) became the first daughter of an English sovereign to wear a white outfit at her wedding. She was unconventional in other ways too, taking important roles in the government of her husband's domains by acting as regent in Sweden in 1420 and in Denmark and Norway from 1423 to 1425. Also, she successfully organized the defense of Copenhagen when it was attacked, in 1428, by the Hanseatic League, which perceived the city as a threat to its trading monopoly in the Baltic Sea. Shortly afterward, however, Eric physically abused her when her navy lost a sea battle, the baby she was carrying was stillborn, and she retired to the convent at Vadstena, in southern Sweden, where she died on 5 January 1430.

**PHILLIPS, MARK (1948– ).** Phillips, the first husband of **Anne, princess royal (1950– )**, was born in Tetbury on 22 September 1948, the only son of Major Peter Phillips and his wife, Anne. He was educated at Marlborough College and the Royal Military Academy Sandhurst; then, in 1969, he joined the 1st Queen's Dragoon Guards, serving with them until 1974, when he returned to Sandhurst as a company instructor. In 1977–78, he was a member of the Ministry of Defence's Army Training Directorate. An accomplished horseman, Phillips was a regular member of the British equestrian team from 1970 to 1976, winning world, European, and Olympic championships in 1970, 1971, and 1972 respectively. He also took the badminton three-day event title in 1971, 1972, 1974, and 1981. These sporting links brought him in contact with **Princess** Anne, who rode with the British team at the Montreal Olympics in 1976, and a relationship blossomed. They married on 14 November 1973 and had two children—**Peter Phillips** (born on 15 November 1977) and **Zara Phillips** (born on 15 May 1981)—but tabloid rumors of discord during the 1980s proved accurate, and the troubles led to a parting in 1989. Divorce followed three years later.

In 1991, Phillips attracted more unwanted publicity when Heather Tonkin, a New Zealand art teacher, demonstrated in court that he was the father of Felicity, her six-year-old daughter. After this revelation, the press periodically reported romantic attachments, and in February 1997, he married Sandy Pflueger, an American whom he had met on the equestrian circuit and who had been a member of the United States' dressage team in 1984. They have one daughter, Stephanie, who was born on 2 October 1997. Despite the diversions, Phillips has continued his sporting career with considerable success, serving as head of the United States' eventing team; running an equestrian center at Gleneagles (in Scotland); and, with Princess Anne, organizing annual horse trials at **Gatcombe Park**, the home given to him and the princess as a wedding present by Queen **Elizabeth II**.

**PHILLIPS, PETER (1977– ).** Phillips—the only son and elder child of **Anne, princess royal (1950– )**, and **Mark Phillips**, her first husband—was born in St. Mary's Hospital, **London**, on 15 November 1977, the first legitimate grandchild of a monarch not to hold a title since Anne and Elizabeth Welles, the children of **Cecily, viscountess Welles**, daughter of King **Edward IV**, in the latter years of the 15th century. He was educated at Port Regis School in Shaftesbury and then (like his maternal grandfather, **Prince Philip, duke of Edinburgh**, and his uncle, **Charles, prince of Wales**) attended Gordonstoun School in Scotland, where he honed his rugby skills and played at international level for the Scottish Schools team during the 1995–96 season. (There is a story, possibly apocryphal, that on one occasion when he was captaining his school, the referee, before tossing the coin at the start of the game, asked him to choose "Grandmother or tails.") After school, he went to Exeter University, graduated in 2000 with a degree in sports science, and then worked for the Jaguar automobile company as corporate hospitality manager and for the Williams motor racing team as sponsorship accounts manager before moving to the Royal Bank of Scotland.

While with Williams at the Canadian Grand Prix in 2003, Phillips met Autumn Kelly, a management consultant and daughter of an electricity company executive; she later said that she had no idea about his royal background until, six weeks later, she saw him on television news coverage of **Prince William of Wales**'s 21st birthday. They married at **St. George's Chapel** in **Windsor Castle** on 17 May 2008, so Phillips, the firstborn of Queen **Elizabeth II**'s grandchildren, also became the first of her grandchildren to wed. Although he has managed to avoid the negative publicity sometimes given to such royal cousins as **Princess Eugenie of York** and **Prince Henry (or Harry) of Wales**, the wedding provoked much media interest, partly because the bride had to renounce her Roman Catholic faith so that, under the terms of the 1701 **Act of Settlement**, her husband could retain his place in the line of **succession to the throne**, and partly because the couple reportedly received £500,000 from *Hello!* magazine for photographic rights. Their first child and Queen Elizabeth's first great-grandchild, Savannah, was born in Gloucestershire Royal Hospital, Gloucester, on 29 December 2010. *See also* GATCOMBE PARK.

**PHILLIPS, ZARA (1981– ).** Zara Phillips—the younger child and only daughter of **Anne, princess royal (1950– )**, and her first husband, **Mark**

**Phillips**—inherited her mother's equestrian talents, winning the world eventing championship at Aachen, Germany, in 2006. Born in St. Mary's Hospital, **London**, on 15 May 1981, she carries no title, apparently at her parents' wish. She was initially educated at Beaudesert Park School in Gloucestershire and then (like her similarly nontitled brother, **Peter Phillips**) went to Port Regis School near Shaftsbury and to Gordonstoun School in Scotland. After a "gap year," much of it spent in Australia and New Zealand, she qualified at Exeter University as a physiotherapist in 2002, but a sponsorship deal with Cantor Index, a betting firm, has allowed her to concentrate on her horsemanship.

Like several other young royals (but unlike her brother), Zara Phillips provided lurid press headlines as a teenager, reportedly turning up at a 50th birthday party for **Charles, prince of Wales**, with a tongue stud in 1995, holding an Ann Summers sex party in 1996, and wearing provocative dresses. A tempestuous three-year relationship with jockey Richard Johnson ended in 2003, but later that year, while in Australia, she met England rugby player Mike Tindall, who is credited with calming her down and helping her to focus on her sporting activities. The couple announced their engagement in December 2010 and are expected to marry the following year. Zara Phillips does not undertake royal engagements, but she does support numerous charities, with a particular preference for organizations caring for children and for injured riders. *See also* GATCOMBE PARK.

**PLACENTIA, PALACE OF.** For more than two centuries, Placentia (or Pleasaunce) was a favorite residence of England's monarchs, particularly those from the **House of Tudor**, which ruled from 1485 to 1603. The building, initially known as Bella Court, was erected in 1428 by **Humphrey, duke of Gloucester** and brother of King **Henry V**, who made provision for a large library (the first to be built up by an individual rather than an institution) that became one of the foundations on which Oxford University developed the Bodleian Library after his death. **Henry VI** acquired the property after Gloucester's death in 1447, renaming it Placentia (derived from the Old French *plaisir*, the word indicates "a pleasant place"). **Edward IV** and **Henry VII** both spent considerable funds on expansion and renovation.

**Henry VIII**, who was born in the palace in 1491, greatly enjoyed hunting in the extensive grounds and grew very fond of the residence, adding a banqueting hall, armories, and a tiltyard for jousting. His daughters, Mary (later **Mary I**) and Elizabeth (later **Elizabeth I**), were also born there; Mary was never greatly enamored of the place, but Elizabeth spent many summers there after she became queen (during one visit, Walter Raleigh allegedly spread his cloak in a puddle so that she would not get her dainty shoes dirty, and during another, she signed the warrant sending **Mary, queen of Scots**, to her death after asking that it be hidden among other documents so that she would not know what she was doing).

Following the execution of **Charles I** in 1649, Oliver Cromwell's parliamentarian supporters tried to sell the palace but, in grimly Puritan England, could find no purchaser. Instead, they turned it into a biscuit factory, then, in 1653–54, into a prisoner of war camp for captives taken during the war with Holland. After the **restoration of the monarchy** in 1660, **Charles II** undertook some rebuilding work, but his successors, **William III of England and II of Scotland** and **Mary II**, had little interest in the house, preferring **Hampton Court Palace** and **Kensington Palace**. So, in 1694, the building was demolished and a Royal Naval Hospital was erected in its place. The Trinity School of Music and the University of Greenwich now occupy the site.

The former residence is now almost always referred to as Greenwich Palace rather than by either of its earlier names. *See also* ANNE, COUNTESS OF SURREY; ANNE OF CLEVES; ELTHAM PALACE; GREENWICH, TREATY OF; MARY OF YORK; QUEEN'S HOUSE, GREENWICH; STUART, MARY (1605–1607); STUART, SOPHIA; TUDOR, EDMUND, DUKE OF SOMERSET; TUDOR, MARY, QUEEN OF FRANCE.

**PLANTAGENET, ALICE (1279–c1291).** Some sources list Alice (also known as Alice of England) as one of the younger daughters of **Edward I** and **Eleanor of Castile**, noting that she was born on 12 March 1279 at **Woodstock Palace**, a royal hunting lodge near Oxford. The child failed to reach adulthood, dying in about 1291. *See also* PLANTAGENET, ISABELLA.

**PLANTAGENET, BEATRICE (c1286–?).** Beatrice (also known as Beatrice of England) was, according to some sources, one of the youngest children in the large family of **Edward I** and **Eleanor of Castile**, born either in Gascony or in **Aquitaine**. She did not reach maturity, but details of the date and place of her death are unknown.

**PLANTAGENET, BERENGARIA (c1277–c1279).** Berengaria (also known as Berengaria of England) was one of several children in the family of **Edward I** and **Eleanor of Castile** who died well before reaching adulthood. She was born in 1276 or 1277 (on 1 May, according to some sources) but lived for no more than three years and was buried in **Westminster Abbey**.

**PLANTAGENET, BLANCHE (1290).** Blanche (sometimes known as Blanche of England) was the youngest of 17 or more children in the family of **Edward I** and **Eleanor of Castile**, born in 1290, the year of her mother's death. Like many of her brothers and sisters, she failed to reach adulthood.

**PLANTAGENET, BLANCHE (1342).** The third daughter of **Edward III** and **Philippa of Hainault**, Blanche was born at the **Tower of London** in March 1342 but died the same month and was buried in **Westminster Abbey**.

**PLANTAGENET, EDWARD (1382).** Edward, the first child of Henry Bolingbroke (later King **Henry IV**) and **Mary de Bohun**, was born in April 1382 but survived for less than a week and was buried at Monmouth Castle.

**PLANTAGENET, ELEANOR (1306–1311).** Eleanor (also known as Eleanor of England) was born in **Winchester** on 6 May 1306, the youngest of three children in the family of King **Edward I** and his second wife, **Marguerite of France**. She died in 1311 at Amesbury Abbey in Wiltshire and was buried at Beaulieu Abbey, Hampshire.

**PLANTAGENET, HENRY (c1257).** Henry is listed in some sources as the last child born to King **Henry III** and **Eleanor of Provence**. The precise dates of his birth and death are unknown, but it is suggested that he was born in late 1256 or early 1257 and survived for only a few weeks.

**PLANTAGENET, HENRY (1267–1274).** The second son in the large family of **Edward I** and **Eleanor of Castile**, Henry was born at **Windsor Castle** on 13 July 1267, when his father was still duke of Gascony and earl of Chester. **John Plantagenet**, Edward's elder sibling, died in 1271, and Edward became king the following year, so Henry (sometimes known as Henry of England) was heir to the throne at the age of five. However, on 14 October 1274, he too passed away, leaving his infant brother, **Alfonso, earl of Chester**, as **heir apparent**.

**PLANTAGENET, HOUSE OF.** From 1154 (when King **Henry II** took the throne) until 1485 (when **Richard III** was killed at the **Battle of Bosworth Field**), England was ruled by a succession of 14 Plantagenet kings. The dynasty allegedly got its name because its founder, **Geoffrey, count of Anjou**, had a habit of putting a sprig of common broom, whose Latin species name is *Planta genista*, in his cap. However, the term was not used as a surname until the late 15th century, so it is not hereditary and is employed principally to identify Geoffrey's descendants.

In 1128, Geoffrey married **Matilda**, daughter of King **Henry I** of England. The previous year, Henry had forced his nobles to swear that they would accept Matilda as their queen if he died without leaving an heir, but when he passed away in 1135, they preferred the claims to the crown advanced by his nephew, **Stephen**. Matilda, however, attempted to claim her inheritance, and England was wracked by nearly two decades of civil war before the king overlooked his only surviving son, **William of Blois**, and agreed that Henry, the eldest child of Matilda and Geoffrey, would be his successor, ruling as Henry II.

Use of the term "Plantagenet" can be confusing because, although the dynasty is usually considered to consist of three royal houses—the **House of Anjou**, the **House of Lancaster**, and the **House of York**—which ruled successively, some writers employ the term "Angevin" (the adjective from "Anjou") as a synonym, applying it to all of the Plantagenet monarchs, regardless of the house from which they came. The Plantagenet monarchs (with the years of their reigns in parentheses) were Henry II (1154–89), **Richard I** (1189–99), **John** (1199–1216), **Henry III** (1216–72), **Edward I** (1272–1307), **Edward II** (1307–27), **Edward III** (1327–77), **Richard II** (1377–99), **Henry IV** (1399–1413), **Henry V** (1413–22), **Henry VI** (1422–61 and 1470–71), **Edward IV** (1461–70 and 1471–83), **Edward V** (1483), and Richard III (1483–85). Richard III was succeeded by **Henry VII**, the first king from the **House of Tudor**.

The legitimate male Plantagenet line was extinguished when Edward, earl of Warwick, was executed for treason in 1499, and the legitimate female line ended when his older sister, Margaret, was **beheaded**, also for treason, in 1541 at the age of 67. However, an illegitimate line survives, descended from Henry Beaufort, duke of Somerset (1436–1464), with the male head of the family inheriting the dukedom of Beaufort. *See also* CURIA REGIS; WARS OF THE ROSES.

**PLANTAGENET, ISABELLA (1279).** Some sources indicate that Isabella was a twin sister of **Alice Plantagenet**, born at **Woodstock**, near Oxford, to **Edward I** and **Eleanor of Castile** on 12 March 1279. Alice survived until she was about 12 years old, but Isabella died as an infant and was buried in **Westminster Abbey**.

**PLANTAGENET, JOAN (1265).** One of the first children in the large family of **Edward I** (then Edward, duke of Gascony) and his wife, **Eleanor of Castile**, Joan (also known as Joan of England) was born in Paris but failed to survive infancy. Some sources suggest that she was born in January, others that she arrived in June, but there is agreement that she had died by 7 September.

**PLANTAGENET, JOAN (c1333–1348).** Joan (sometimes known as Joan of England or as Joanna) was the second daughter, and third child, in the family of **Edward III** and **Philippa of Hainault**. She was probably born in February 1333, but possibly in 1334 or 1335, at either **Woodstock Palace** or the **Tower of London**. In 1345, she was betrothed to Peter, the son of King Alfonso XI of Castile and León, in a political match designed to unite two of the most powerful families in Europe. Three years later, Joan set off on the journey to her wedding, sailing initially to Bordeaux, one of the foci of English power in **Aquitaine**. When she arrived, her entourage was warned that bubonic plague had reached epidemic proportions in the area, but her guardians chose to ignore advice that they should move to a safer part of the province. Soon, several of her companions fell ill, and eventually Joan herself succumbed, dying on 2 September 1348. On October 25, Edward sent a mission to Aquitaine to retrieve his daughter's body, but there is no record of her remains being returned to England, and it is not known where she was buried.

Some historians suggest that Joan's death affected the course of the **Hundred Years' War**—even though two of her brothers (**Edmund of Langley, duke of York**, and **John of Gaunt**) would later find Castilian wives—because it prevented an alliance between dynasties in the early years of the conflict. Others have stressed that it made the English leaders aware of the likely impact of the plague at a time when the disease was just beginning to spread through the kingdom. *See also* ISABELLA DE COUCY.

**PLANTAGENET, JOHN (c1250–c1256).** John (who is also known as John of England) is listed in some sources as the fourth son born to King **Henry III** and **Eleanor of Provence**. There is no contemporary record of his existence, but later chroniclers record that, like **Richard Plantagenet** (a possible older brother), **William Plantagenet (c1251–c1256)** and **Henry Plantagenet** (younger brothers), and **Katherine Plantagenet** (his sole younger sister), he failed to survive childhood and was buried in **Westminster Abbey**, where his father, Katherine, and his brothers were also laid to rest.

**PLANTAGENET, JOHN (1266–1271).** As the eldest son of **Edward I** and **Eleanor of Castile**, John, born in July 1266 (some sources give the date as 10 July, others as 13 July), would have succeeded to the English throne if he had survived, but he died on 3 August 1271 and was buried in **Westminster Abbey**. He is sometimes known as John of England.

**PLANTAGENET, JULIANA (1271).** **Eleanor of Castile** accompanied her husband, Edward, duke of Gascony and later **Edward I**, on many of his military campaigns, giving birth to two daughters while she was with him on crusade in the Holy Land. Juliana, the elder child, was born in 1271 but survived for only a few weeks. Some sources suggest that she was born on 28 May and died on 5 September; others indicate that she was born early in the year and died on 28 May. The child's name, too, is uncertain, with a number of authorities indicating that she may also have been known as Katherine. *See also* JOAN OF ACRE.

**PLANTAGENET, KATHERINE (1253–1257).** Katherine (named Katherine of England by some writers) was born on 25 November 1253, the youngest daughter in the family of King **Henry III** and **Eleanor of Provence**. Deaf and possibly also mute, she survived only until 3 May 1257 and was buried in **Westminster Abbey**.

**PLANTAGENET, MARY (c1278–c1332).** One of several daughters in the family of **Edward I** and **Eleanor of Castile**, Mary, born in 1278 or 1279 at **Woodstock Palace**, is sometimes known as Mary of England or as Mary of Woodstock. She joined the Benedictine nunnery at Amesbury (which had been founded by **Aelfthryth**, wife of King **Edgar of England**, as an act of penance in 980) and died there, probably in the spring or early summer of 1332, some sources noting 29 May as the date of her death, others indicating that she had passed away by 8 July. *See also* MARGUERITE OF FRANCE.

**PLANTAGENET, RICHARD (c1247–c1256).** There is no contemporary 13th-century record of Richard's existence, but a 14th-century source notes that he was the third son born to King **Henry III** and **Eleanor of Provence**. The dates of his birth and death are unknown, but it is clear that, if he ever did exist, he never reached maturity.

**PLANTAGENET, THOMAS (1347–c1348).** The sixth son, and eleventh child, of **Edward III** and **Philippa of Hainault**, Thomas (sometimes known as Thomas of England) was born at **Windsor Castle** but lived for only a few months. He was buried at the Dominican church at Kings Langley in Hertfordshire, where **Edmund of Langley, duke of York**, his older brother, was also interred.

**PLANTAGENET, WILLIAM (c1251–c1256).** William is recorded in some sources as a fifth son and seventh child of **Henry III** and **Eleanor of Provence** who survived infancy, died while still a child, and was buried in **London** at the Church of the Knights Templar. His father had initially requested that his own burial be at the same site, but he changed his mind and asked that his remains be laid to rest in **Westminster Abbey**, which had been extensively renovated during his reign. Some historians question William's existence and suggest that the records may misidentify a nephew of William de Valence, the king's maternal half-brother.

**PLANTAGENET, WILLIAM (1337).** The second son of King **Edward III** and **Philippa of Hainault**, William was born at **Hatfield**, where the bishops of Ely had built a palace during the 12th century. He survived for only a few weeks, sources recording that his birth took place before 16 February 1337, and his death either before 3 March at Hatfield or before 8 July in York. William is also known as William of England and, after his birthplace, as William of Hatfield.

**PLANTAGENET, WILLIAM (1348).** William was the seventh son of **Edward III** and **Philippa of Hainault**. He was born at **Windsor Castle** on 24 June 1348 but failed to survive infancy and was buried in St. Edmund's Chapel, **Westminster Abbey**, on 5 September. The child is sometimes known as William of Windsor, after his birthplace, to distinguish him from his older brother of the same name, who died in 1337.

**PRINCE.** Sons of monarchs were not normally referred to as princes until the reign of King **George I** (who introduced the practice from Germany), although there were some exceptions, such as the **prince of Wales** (the English sovereign's eldest boy) and King **John** (who is sometimes known as Prince John). During the 18th and 19th centuries, the usage became increasingly common and was extended to grandsons and great-grandsons of the sovereign in the male line, as well as to the eldest surviving son of the eldest son of the prince of Wales, but, because the title is a gift of the monarch, it can be granted to others, as in 1957, when Queen **Elizabeth II** created her husband (**Prince Philip, duke of Edinburgh**, who had family roots in Denmark and Greece) a prince of the United Kingdom. Sons of monarchs are styled "his royal highness," along with their name and the territorial designation of their peerage (for example, Queen Elizabeth II's second son is His Royal Highness, the **Prince Andrew, the duke of York**). Grandchildren and great-grandchildren do not use the definite article (thus the youngest grandson of King **George V** is His Royal Highness, **Prince Richard, duke of Gloucester**). *See also* HER (OR HIS) ROYAL HIGHNESS; KING CONSORT; PRINCESS; WINDSOR, HOUSE OF.

**PRINCE OF WALES.** Since 1301, the title "**Prince** of Wales" traditionally has been granted to the eldest living son of the reigning monarch of England,

and later of Great Britain and the United Kingdom. Prior to that date, Wales was divided into several competing territories, with the strongest of the rulers known as prince of Wales. However, when King **Edward I** of England defeated the Welsh toward the end of the 13th century, he gave the honor to his own son, Edward (later **Edward II**), in order to emphasize English control of the area. (According to legend, the king told the subjugated Welsh people that he would give them a prince who had been born in Wales and did not speak a word of English; then he produced the infant Edward, who had been born in Caernarfon Castle and was too young to speak anything.)

The title, which is conferred by the monarch rather than automatically acquired at birth, is currently held by **Charles, prince of Wales**, who was accorded the honor by his mother, Queen **Elizabeth II**, on 26 July 1958. The investiture at Caernarfon on 1 July 1969, much resented by many Welsh people because of its continued overtones of English overlordship, was marred by the deaths of two members of Mudiad Amddiffyn Cymru (a Welsh nationalist group), who were killed in an attempt to bomb the **royal train** on its way to the ceremony. *See also* DUKE OF CORNWALL; DUKE OF ROTHESAY; HEIR APPARENT; HONOURS OF THE PRINCIPALITY OF WALES; PRINCE; PRINCE OF WALES'S FEATHERS; PRINCESS ROYAL; WELSH PRINCES.

**PRINCE OF WALES'S FEATHERS.** The heraldic badge of the **prince of Wales** consists of three white feathers rising through a coronet of alternate crosses and fleurs-de-lys that is usually studded with emeralds and rubies. Underneath, the words "*Ich Dien*" (German for "I Serve") are inscribed on a dark blue ribbon.

The origin of the device is not known. There is a legend that **Edward, the black prince**, saw it being used by an enemy soldier at the Battle of Crécy in 1346 and adopted it because it would make him identifiable by his soldiers in future conflicts, but, less romantically, historians of heraldry believe that the plumes may have been incorporated at an earlier date into the badges of relatives of his mother, **Philippa of Hainault**. The source of the motto is also not documented.

The feathers are used, often in modified form, by army regiments with which **princes** of Wales have had an association, by Welsh national rugby league and rugby union teams, and by the Surrey County Cricket Club (whose **London** pitch—the Oval—is on land owned by the prince). In 2007, **Charles, prince of Wales**, attempted to prevent several jewelers from using the feathers in commercial forms that he considered inappropriate, but in practice they are widely employed on a variety of goods, and the name is given to such diverse phenomena as a species of amaranthus (a grain producing plant), a geyser in the Rotorua volcanic region of New Zealand's North Island, and scores of public houses. A minority of Welsh people object to use of the feathers in any circumstances because they carry implications of English overlordship of Wales.

**PRINCE REGENT.** George, **prince of Wales**, was known as the prince **regent** while he carried out monarchical duties during the illness of his father, King **George III**, from 1811 to 1820. The period was characterized by innovations in architecture and the decorative arts, now known as the regency style, with much emphasis on classical Greek and Roman design in buildings, the use of Egyptian and Chinese motifs as embellishments, and a pronounced French influence on furnishings. When the incapacitated king died, having spent the last decade of his life insane, the **prince** succeeded him as King **George IV**.

Also, in 1741, **James Francis Edward Stuart**—the son of the exiled King **James VII and II** and a claimant to the British throne—named **Charles Edward Stuart** prince regent.

**PRINCES IN THE TOWER.** *See* EDWARD V; EDWARD OF MIDDLEHAM, PRINCE OF WALES; RICHARD III; RICHARD, DUKE OF YORK (1473–1483?).

**PRINCESS.** Until the 18th century, nearly all daughters of English and Scottish monarchs were known as "Lady" rather than as "Princess." The exceptions were the wife of the **prince of Wales** (the eldest son of the English sovereign) and **Mary Henrietta** (the daughter of **Charles I** and **Henrietta Maria of France**), who was designated "**Princess Royal**" because her mother wanted to adopt the French practice of according special distinction to the king's eldest daughter. However, King **George I** introduced Hanoverian customs after he succeeded to the throne in 1714, and the usage became more common. In 1917, it was formalized by King **George V**, who decreed that the daughters of a sovereign, the daughters of the sovereign's sons (but not daughters of daughters), and women who marry a **prince** are all entitled to be addressed as "Princess." Nevertheless, the practice is not unvarying; for example, Camilla Parker Bowles, the second wife of **Charles, prince of Wales**, is known as the duchess of Cornwall rather than as the princess of Wales (*see* CAMILLA, DUCHESS OF CORNWALL; DUKE OF CORNWALL).

The daughter of a sovereign (other than a princess royal) is styled "**Her Royal Highness**, the Princess . . ." followed by her name (thus, Queen **Elizabeth II**, prior to her accession to the throne in 1952, was known as "Her Royal Highness, the Princess Elizabeth"). Daughters of the sovereign's sons adopt the format of their father's senior peerage and drop the definite article, so the elder daughter of **Prince Andrew, duke of York**, is "Her Royal Highness, **Princess Beatrice of York**." A woman who weds the son of a sovereign, or who weds a grandson through the male line, takes his first name in her formal title (so Baroness Marie-Christine von Reibnitz became Her Royal Highness **Princess Michael of Kent** when she married in 1978). *See also* WINDSOR, HOUSE OF.

**PRINCESS ROYAL.** The term "**Princess** Royal" is a form of address (rather than a title) that may be granted by the monarch to his or her eldest daughter. It is held for life and cannot be inherited.

**Anne, princess royal**, Queen **Elizabeth II**'s only daughter, was accorded the honor on 13 June 1987 in recognition of her charitable work. She has six predecessors—**Mary Henrietta, princess royal** (daughter of King **Charles I**); **Anne, princess royal** (daughter of King **George II**); **Charlotte, princess royal, queen of Wurtemburg** (daughter of King **George III**); **Victoria, princess royal** (daughter of Queen **Victoria**); **Louise, princess royal, duchess of Fife** (daughter of King **Edward VII**); and **Mary, princess royal** (daughter of King **George V**). Also, King **James VII and II** gave the title to his daughter, **Louisa Maria Theresa Stuart**, but by the time she was born, he had been deposed and was living in exile in **France**.

The form was introduced for Mary Henrietta in 1642 because **Henrietta Maria of France**, her mother and **queen consort** of Charles I, wanted to distinguish the eldest daughter of the English monarch in a similar way to that adopted in her native country, where the firstborn princess was known as Madame Royale. *See also* DUKE OF CORNWALL; DUKE OF ROTHESAY; DUKE OF YORK.

**PRIVY COUNCIL.** The Privy Council acts as a body of advisors to the monarch, tracing its ancestry to the **Curia Regis**, which counseled England's Norman kings. In those days, membership of the body was a prized position, conferring much power because the sovereign's rule was absolute, but with the growth of parliamentary democracy since the 17th century, the council's role in government has declined, so nowadays its business is entirely formal.

Appointments, although technically the privilege of the sovereign, are made by the government as a reward for political or public service. Members—who include all present and former cabinet ministers, senior judges, senior members of the **royal family**, two archbishops, and British ambassadors—number well over 500, although only four or five are called to the monthly meetings, at which everybody (including the monarch) stands throughout the session in order to keep meetings short. The agenda items include the granting of **royal charters** (which give special status to bodies such as professional organizations), the making of orders in council (a form of secondary legislation, drafted by the government), and other detailed matters.

In the past, the council also served as the final court of appeal from the legal jurisdictions of the British Empire, but as colonies have gained their independence, this role has become less important. The appeals that remain are heard by a judicial committee, consisting of senior judges, who may also consider cases sent by some special courts in the United Kingdom, including those of the **Church of England**. Members are entitled to be styled "The Right Honourable," and a peer or peeress of the realm who serves may use the letters "P.C." after his or her name. Their work is coordinated by an office within the Ministry of Justice. There is a separate Queen's (or King's) Privy Council for Canada.

**PRIVY PURSE.** The monarch's private income is known as the privy purse, which for ceremonial purposes takes the form of an embroidered bag. The keeper of the privy purse is responsible for the financial management of the **Royal Household**, a task that includes oversight of expenditures on such disparate matters as buildings, the royal stables, the royal stamp collection, and salaries. In practice, much of the income to the privy purse is used to cover the expenses incurred by members of the **royal family**, other than the monarch and his or her consort, in undertaking official engagements. *See also* CIVIL LIST.

**PROTECTORATE.** *See* COMMONWEALTH OF ENGLAND.

**PROVISIONS OF OXFORD (1258).** In 1258, King **Henry III** faced excommunication by Pope Alexander IV unless he fulfilled his promise to finance an invasion of Sicily. Desperate to raise funds, he agreed to meet his barons in Oxford and attempt to negotiate contributions in return for concessions over the way England was governed. A pact, reached on 11 June, brought the donations he needed but resulted in a significant transfer of power from the monarch to the nobles. In the future, Henry would rule in conjunction with a 15-member council that would review many of his decisions. Moreover, parliament would meet three times a year both to consider the actions of the council and to discuss additional reforms. The arrangements were superseded by the **Provisions of Westminster** the following year but are considered by many historians to be England's first written constitution and a significant stage in the growth of parliamentary government at the expense of the rights of the sovereign.

**PROVISIONS OF WESTMINSTER (1259).** For some of King **Henry III**'s nobles, the concessions to parliament made through the **Provisions of Oxford** did not go far enough, so in the autumn of 1259, they attempted to strengthen that agreement with a new set of Provisions that added conditions relating to the conduct of the courts, inheritance of property, and taxation. Initially, Henry indicated agreement, but two years later, as the barons squabbled over implementation of the reforms, he was able to persuade Pope Alexander IV to issue a papal bull allowing him to renege. The nobles turned to King Louis IX of **France** for arbitration, but he annulled the arrangement, a decision that precipitated the **Second Barons' War**.

# Q

**QUEEN CONSORT.** The queen consort is the wife of a reigning king. She has no constitutional powers but can exert considerable informal influence over the monarch and may be appointed **regent** if he is absent from his realm or if he is incapacitated (for example, the Regency Act of 1728 gave **Caroline of Brandenburg-Ansbach** authority to deputize for her husband, King **George II**, while he was in his Hanover duchy). Queens consort, unlike queens who reign in their own right, do not have numbers affixed to their names, so historians tend to identify them by using a geographical descriptor or their name before marriage. Thus, King **Henry VIII**'s first wife is usually known as **Catherine of Aragon**, and his second wife as **Anne Boleyn**. *See also* KING CONSORT; KING REGNANT; QUEEN DOWAGER; QUEEN REGNANT.

**QUEEN DOWAGER.** A **queen consort** who survives her husband may be known as the queen dowager (or, sometimes, the dowager queen), though the widow herself may decline to use the term. Because women tend to outlive men, queens dowager have been a common feature of the British monarchy. Some have been politically active after their husband's death (for example, **Margaret Tudor** was **regent** in Scotland after King **James IV** was killed at the **Battle of Flodden** in 1513 and continued to influence her son, **James V**, following parliament's decision, in 1524, that the young man was old enough to make decisions himself). Others made an impact through later relationships (**Catherine of Valois**, wife of **Henry V**, was an ancestor of the **House of Tudor** because **Henry VII**—her grandson as a result of a liaison with **Owen Tudor**—deposed **Richard III** in 1485). However, several queens dowager (such as **Marguerite of France**, consort of **Edward I**) retired to nunneries or secluded **royal residences**, playing little part in public life during the reign of the next monarch.

The most recent queen dowager was **Elizabeth, the queen mother**, wife of King **George VI**. It is unlikely that there will be another for some time because the heir to the throne—**Charles, prince of Wales**—will become king only when his mother, Queen **Elizabeth II**, dies (and even if she abdicated, she would not be a queen dowager because she is a **queen regnant** rather than a queen consort). Charles's second wife, **Camilla, duchess of Cornwall**, will not be queen dowager if he predeceases her after the succession, because even though she will legally be queen, she will be known as "**Her Royal Highness, the Princess** Consort." On Charles's death, he will be succeeded by his elder son, **Prince William of Wales**, whose mother (**Diana, princess of Wales**) died in 1997. The next possible queen dowager would, therefore, be the wife of **Prince** William, assuming that he becomes king, dies before his spouse, and has at least one child who survives him. *See also* QUEEN MOTHER.

**QUEEN MOTHER.** A former **queen consort** who is the mother of the reigning monarch is known as the queen mother. The title has been applied to only four women since the "**union of the crowns**" of England and Scotland in 1603—**Henrietta Maria of France**, wife of King **Charles I** and mother of **Charles II** (diarist Samuel Pepys wrote, on 29 June 1665, of "the Queene-mother setting out for France this day"); **Alexandra of Denmark** (wife of King **Edward VII** and mother of King **George V**); **Mary of Teck** (wife of George V and mother of **George VI**); and **Elizabeth, the queen mother** (wife of George VI and mother of Queen **Elizabeth II**). Neither Alexandra nor Mary wanted to be addressed as "queen mother," but the style was one of the formal titles held by Elizabeth, who was often informally termed "the queen mum" by press and public.

It is unlikely that there will be another queen mother for many years. **Charles, prince of Wales**—the heir to the throne—will probably succeed only on the death of his mother (Elizabeth II), and even if she abdicates in his favor, there is no precedent for a **queen regnant**, rather than a queen consort, becoming queen mother. When Charles dies, he will be succeeded by **Prince William of Wales**, his elder son, whose mother (**Diana, princess of Wales**) was killed in a car accident in 1997. If the usual order of **succession to the throne** is followed, the next possible queen mother would therefore be William's wife, assuming that he succeeds to the throne and has at least one child who survives him. *See also* QUEEN DOWAGER.

**QUEEN REGNANT.** Females who succeed to the throne and rule in their own right are known as queens regnant. In England, they include **Mary I** (who reigned from 1553 to 1558) and her successor, **Elizabeth I** (who reigned from 1558 to 1603). Some writers would add **Matilda** (who was never crowned but held King **Stephen** in captivity for several months in 1141) and Lady **Jane Grey** (who was proclaimed queen on 10 July 1553 but was deposed nine days later). In Scotland, **Mary, queen of Scots**, was queen regnant from 1542 to 1567, and the style is sometimes also accorded to **Margaret, maid of Norway**, who died in 1290 while traveling from Scandinavia for her **coronation**.

After the union of the English and Scottish crowns in 1603, **Mary II** was co-sovereign of both countries with her husband (King **William III of England and II of Scotland**) from 1689 to 1694, and **Anne** ruled in her own right from 1702. Following the **union of parliaments**, which created a single realm in 1707, Anne remained on the throne as queen of Great Britain until 1714. Queen **Victoria** was sovereign of Great Britain (and Ireland) from 1837 to 1901, and **Elizabeth II**, the present monarch, became queen of the United Kingdom on the death of her father, King **George VI**, in 1952. *See also* KING CONSORT; KING REGNANT; QUEEN CONSORT; QUEEN DOWAGER; QUEEN'S (OR KING'S) BIRTHDAY HONOURS LIST; QUEEN'S (OR KING'S) OFFICIAL BIRTHDAY; TROOPING THE COLOUR CEREMONY.

**QUEEN'S (OR KING'S) BIRTHDAY HONOURS LIST.** Each June, a list of individuals who are to be honored for contributions to the arts, business, education, entertainment, the law, local communities, sports, or other aspects of British life is published to mark the **queen's (or king's) official birthday**. Most recipients are awarded membership in the Most Excellent Order of the British Empire, which was founded in 1917 by King **George V** as a means of recognizing contributions made by noncombatants during World War I. The order has five classes, with the people appointed to the highest ranks receiving knighthoods. A government-appointed committee sifts candidates, who are nominated by employers, colleagues, or others knowledgeable about an individual's efforts. Those who are successful receive a badge and ribbon from the monarch (or his or her representative) at a formal investiture ceremony. Separate lists are issued for several of the **commonwealth realms**, which recognize the British sovereign as their head of state.

**QUEEN'S HOUSE, GREENWICH.** In 1616, **Anne of Denmark** (consort of King **James VI and I**) commissioned Inigo Jones to build her a house close to Greenwich Palace (which was formerly known as the **Palace of Placentia**). Jones, who had made contributions to the masques Anne staged at the royal court, produced a structure, on classical lines, that was revolutionary for the times. The work was completed in 1629, by which time King **Charles I**, James's son, was on the throne, and the building was being used by his wife, **Henrietta Maria of France**. Her occupancy was interrupted by the civil war that ravaged England from 1642 to 1660, but she returned in 1662 and lived there for some months before moving to **Somerset House**, on the north bank of the River Thames. The residence, little visited by the **royal family** after that time, was gifted by King **George III** to the Royal Naval Asylum (a charity that cared for orphaned children of seamen) in 1805. Since 1934, it has provided accommodation for the National Maritime Museum, which has furnished part of the upper floor to represent a mid-17th-century **royal residence** and displays part of its extensive art collection in the rooms.

**QUEEN'S (OR KING'S) OFFICIAL BIRTHDAY.** Official celebrations of the sovereign's birthday are held on a Saturday in June rather than on the day he or she was born. The practice began during the reign of King **Edward VII**, whose birthday was in November, when the British weather is not at its most clement. In the United Kingdom, a **queen's (or king's) birthday honours list** is published, recognizing the contributions made by citizens to the arts, business, education, entertainment, sports, and other aspects of life. Also, flags are flown on government buildings, and the monarch takes the salute at a **"trooping the colour" ceremony** held at Horse Guards Parade in **London**.

Several **commonwealth realms**, which recognize the British monarch as their head of state, also have official birthday celebrations, but not on the same date as the United Kingdom. In Canada, for example, the Monday on or before 24 May is a public holiday, known as Victoria Day, when several cities hold parades or fireworks displays to celebrate the birthdays of Queen **Victoria** and the current monarch. There, the events are often considered the beginning of summer, but in Australia (where the birthday is marked with a public holiday on the second Monday in June) and New Zealand (where the holiday is on the first Monday of the same month), they are the start of the snow season. In Fiji (which is a republic, but where Queen **Elizabeth II** has the title of paramount chief), the 2006 celebrations were used to mark the country's first world rugby seven-a-side title, but in Bermuda (where Queen Elizabeth is head of state), the last official birthday celebrations were held in 2008.

# R

**RAEDBURH (?–?).** Some historians believe that **Egbert**, who briefly united the Anglo-Saxon kingdoms in 829–30, was married to a woman named Raedburh or Redburga, but detail of her life is so scanty and contradictory that several scholars doubt she ever existed. In about 789, Egbert was forced to flee England to escape possible death at the hands of Offa, the powerful king of Mercia, and he sought sanctuary on mainland Europe at the court of Charlemagne. The Frankish emperor probably provided military support to help him return to his homeland as king of **Wessex** in 802 and may have arranged his marriage to Raedburh, who, records suggest, may have been Charlemagne's sister, sister-in-law, or other close relative. Egbert certainly sired a son, **Aethelwulf**, who succeeded him as ruler of Wessex.

**REGENCY ACTS.** For much of England's history, monarchs appointed **regents** to rule in their stead if they were unable to carry out their duties (as when they were abroad on military campaigns), and sometimes groups of nobles were designated as temporary leaders (when, for example, a king died suddenly and his heir was too young to lead armies or make political decisions). In Scotland, regents were chosen either by a council (which could include the sovereign as well as nobles and churchmen) or by parliament.

Since the two countries combined as a single unit in 1707, the selection process has been a matter for statutory regulation by the parliament of Great Britain (and, later, of the United Kingdom), which, until the early 20th century, passed legislation every time a regent was required. The first Regency Act, given **royal assent** in 1728, allowed **Caroline of Brandenburg-Ansbach** to act for her husband, **George II**, while he was in Hanover. Then, in 1751, when **Frederick, prince of Wales** and heir to the throne, died and George, his eldest son, was only 12 years old, parliament approved a Minority of Successor to Crown Act, decreeing that, if necessary, **Princess Augusta of Saxe-Gotha** (Frederick's wife) could rule with the help of a council of regency if the king (**George II**) died before the boy reached the age of majority. The child eventually succeeded his grandfather in 1760, ruling as **George III**. He married the following year, and in 1765 parliament took the precautionary measure of passing a Minority of Heir to the Crown Act so that, if necessary, his mother or his consort (**Charlotte of Mecklenburg-Strelitz**) could act as regent until his heir (the eldest surviving son) came of age.

The onset of George's mental illness in 1789 caused a crisis because the British monarch has to give royal assent to legislation before it can become law, but an insane king would be unable to perform this duty properly. Thus any regency act passed by parliament could not reach the statute books, and there was no previously agreed upon method for appointing a regent in such circumstances. The solution—asking the lord chancellor, guardian of the great seal of the realm, to approve a Regency Bill that would allow Prince George (George III's eldest son and his eventual successor as King **George IV**) to fulfill monarchical duties during his father's indisposition—was not approved by everybody, so it was fortunate that the king recovered before the action had to be taken. Later, the ailing monarch indicated his approval of the proposed procedure, so a similar approach was adopted for the Care of King during His Illness, etc. Act when he was again incapacitated in 1811.

Three further bills followed during the 19th century. In the 1830 Regency Act, provision was made for **Princess Victoria of Saxe-Coburg-Saalfield** to act as regent in the event of the death of King **William IV**, her childless brother-in-law, until her daughter (also **Victoria**) reached adulthood. In 1837, the unmarried, 18-year-old Victoria became queen, but her closest male relative, **Ernest Augustus, king of Hanover**, lived abroad, so the Lord Justices Act provided that, if the sovereign died without having a family, lord justices would be appointed to govern for the short period until he could travel to Britain. Early in 1840, however, Victoria wed **Albert of Saxe-Coburg and Gotha**, and a further Regency Act, passed in the same year, gave him power to act as regent if she died before any of their children reached adulthood.

The 1910 Regency Act permitted **Mary of Teck**, consort of King **George V**, to carry out similar duties if her husband died leaving young children, but rather than continue to legislate for specific circumstances, parliament decided in 1937 to frame a bill that would meet all future needs. The Regency Act passed in that year decreed that a regent must be the person next in the line of **succession to the throne** who is over the age of 21, a British subject living in the United Kingdom (a provision that disqualified descendants of previous monarchs who were members of royal houses on the European mainland), and qualified under the **Act of Settlement** of 1701 (thus Roman Catholics and anyone who married a Roman Catholic were excluded).

The act also approved the appointment of "counsellors of state," who could act for a sovereign unable to fulfill responsibilities for short periods. The counsellors would be the monarch's consort and the first four individuals in the line of succession to the throne who were over 21. In addition, they would have to meet the qualifications required of regents. Amendments in 1943 and 1953 made provision for **Prince Philip, duke of Edinburgh** and husband of Queen **Elizabeth II**, to act as regent if the sovereign died before their eldest child reached the age of 18 (under the terms of the 1937 act, **Princess Margaret** would have been regent in such circumstances). It also reduced the minimum age of a regent from 21 to 18 and reinstated **Elizabeth, the queen mother**, as a counsellor of state (a position she had lost when her husband, King **George VI**, died in 1952).

Under the current regulations, **Charles, prince of Wales** and **heir apparent** to the throne, would act as regent if his mother, Elizabeth II, was unable to continue with her duties. The counsellors of state are normally **Prince** Philip (unless he is absent from the country with the queen); Prince Charles; **Prince William of Wales** (Prince Charles's elder son and second in line to the throne); **Prince Henry of Wales** (Prince Charles's younger son, third in line to the throne and usually known as Prince Harry); and **Prince Andrew, duke of York** (the queen's second son and fourth in line to the throne). *See also* PRINCE REGENT.

**REGENCY STYLE.** *See* PRINCE REGENT.

**REGENT.** When monarchs are incapacitated, out of the country, or too young to make political decisions, regents are appointed to govern on their behalf. For example, in post–Anglo Saxon England, they were appointed from 1216 to 1227, from 1327 to 1330, from 1422 to 1437, in 1483, and from 1547 to 1553, during the minorities of King **Henry III**, King **Edward III**, King **Henry VI**, King **Edward V**, and King **Edward VI**, respectively. Also, regents ruled for various periods between 1189 and 1199 while **Richard I** was in prison or undertaking military campaigns, from 1454 to 1458 while Henry VI suffered a mental breakdown, in August and September 1714 between the death of Queen **Anne** and the arrival of **George I** from Germany, and during **George III**'s insanity from 1811 until his death in 1820.

For much of the period from the late 13th century to the latter 16th century, Scotland was plagued by a succession of child monarchs, necessitating the appointment of regents there for the periods 1286–90, 1329–34, 1437–49, 1460–69, 1488–94, 1513–28, 1542–61, and 1567–81, during the reigns of **Margaret, maid of Norway**; **David II**; **James II**; **James III**; **James IV**; **James V**; **Mary, queen of Scots**; and **James VI**, respectively. In addition, there were periods of regency from 1290 to 1292 (while 13 candidates competed for the throne), from 1334 to 1341 and from 1346 to 1357 (while David II was in France and then while he was held captive in England), from 1388 to 1390 (due to the infirmity of **Robert II**), and from 1399 to 1424 (as a result of the disability of **Robert III**, who had been kicked by a horse, and the imprisonment of **James I** in England). The Scots, therefore, were ruled by ambitious regents for almost half of the two centuries before the "**union of the crowns**" in 1603, when **James VI of Scotland** also became **James I of England**. *See also* GUARDIANS OF SCOTLAND; PRINCE REGENT; REGENCY ACTS.

**REGNAL NAME.** The monarch's regnal name is the name used during his or her period of rule. In most cases, sovereigns choose to use their first baptismal name, but there have been four exceptions. King **Robert III** was baptized as John but changed his name to that of his father when he succeeded to the Scottish throne in 1390 in order to avoid associations with the much-derided **John of Scotland**. Queen **Victoria** was christened Alexandrina Victoria but from childhood was known as Victoria by her family, so she chose to use that name when she succeeded to the throne in 1837. When her son, **Prince** Albert Edward (*see* EDWARD VII), followed her in 1901, he too elected to use his second name, much against his late mother's wishes (she had wanted the name of her husband—**Albert of Saxe-Coburg and Gotha**—to be used by British kings in perpetuity). Then, in 1936, **George V**'s son, Prince Albert Frederick Arthur George, opted to rule as King **George VI** in order to emphasize the continuity of the monarchy after the abdication of his elder brother, King **Edward VIII**.

The monarch's regnal name is followed by a number that reflects the ruler's position in the line of sovereigns with the same name; thus King **Henry I** can be distinguished from King **Henry VIII**. A king or queen with a unique name in the line of monarchs has no number, so for example, Queen **Anne** is never referred to as Queen Anne I. These conventions raised political problems following the death of King George VI in 1952. His eldest child chose to rule in her own name and is widely known as Queen **Elizabeth II**, but that numbering caused some upset in Scotland, which had never had a Queen **Elizabeth I** because that queen was queen of England alone. Two Scottish attorneys took the issue to court but lost their case because the judges ruled that the men had no title to sue the crown and that the choice of number was a **royal prerogative** and was therefore a matter for the monarch alone. The problem will not arise if **Charles, prince of Wales** and **heir apparent**, succeeds to the throne on his mother's death, but it could become an issue on the accession of his son, Prince William, because England has had four King Williams and Scotland only three.

**RESERVE POWER.** By convention, certain political powers are reserved for use at the monarch's discretion in unusual circumstances. These include the right to decline a prime minister's request that parliament be dissolved (allegedly King **George V** threatened such action in 1910); the right to dismiss a prime minister (King **William IV**, who removed William Lamb, viscount Melbourne, from office in 1834, was the last sovereign to take advantage of this rule); and the right to refuse **royal assent** to a bill passed by parliament (a power last exercised by Queen **Anne** in 1708).

In modern times, the most important reserve power is the right to appoint a prime minister. Normally the post goes to the leader of the majority party in the House of Commons (the lower house in the British parliament), so exercise of the power is purely nominal, but if no party commands an overall majority, the monarch can select the individual most likely to form a government that will command support. In such cases, the decision is made after consultation with senior statesmen, as in 1963, when Harold Macmillan resigned and Queen **Elizabeth II** talked to leading politicians before replacing him with Alec Douglas-Home. Some writers consider that the reserve powers are simply a holdover from the days when the sovereign's rule was absolute, but others argue that they remain important because they allow the state to deal with governmental crises.

**RESTORATION OF THE MONARCHY (1660).** Soon after his **succession to the throne** in 1625, King **Charles I** became involved in a series of squabbles with his English parliament, partly because he believed that he had a divine right to rule (*see* DIVINE RIGHT OF KINGS) and thus had absolute authority within his realm, and partly because the Puritan parliamentarians were wary both of his liking for ecclesiastical ritual and of his marriage to **Henrietta Maria of France**, a Roman Catholic. In 1642, the tensions flared into civil war, and in 1649, as the troubles escalated, Charles was **beheaded**, his **queen consort** fled into exile, and England became a republic. However, the death in 1658 of Oliver Cromwell, the parliamentarian leader, left the state rudderless, lacking any central authority that could rely on the support of the army and so ensure that opposing factions would work together. On 4 April 1660, as the country slipped toward anarchy, Charles's eldest surviving son, **Charles II**, issued a statement (known as the Declaration of Breda after the Dutch city where it was made) that if he was offered the throne he would not seek revenge against his enemies, that land disputes would be settled equitably, that soldiers would be paid the arrears they were due, and that there would be no attempt to impose religious uniformity. In response, on 8 May, parliament decided that Charles had been the lawful king of England ever since his father's execution, so the "merry monarch" returned to **London** on 29 May (his 30th birthday) and established a court that was, in many ways, the antithesis of Puritan austerity, with theaters reopened, women allowed to act on the stage for the first time, and drama characterized by its bawdiness. *See also* COMMONWEALTH OF ENGLAND; ROYAL YACHT.

**REVOLUTION OF 1688.** *See* GLORIOUS REVOLUTION.

**RICHARD I (1157–1199).** The son of **Henry II** and **Eleanor of Aquitaine**, Richard ruled England from 1189 to 1199 but spent only some six months in the country. For much of the remainder of the time, he was involved in European military campaigns and in the third crusade to the Holy Land, winning a reputation as a warrior that made him the hero of innumerable stories told throughout the continent and earning the nickname "Lionheart."

Richard was born on 8 September 1157 at Beaumont Palace, which had been built by his great-grandfather, **Henry I**, close to the royal hunting grounds at Woodstock, near Oxford. He was invested as duke of **Aquitaine** in 1168 and count of Poitou three years later, but his aspirations lay well beyond those limited French horizons, so in 1173–74 he joined his brothers, **Henry, the young king**, and **Geoffrey, duke of Brittany**, in a rebellion against their father that seriously threatened the monarchy. The king and his sons were eventually reconciled, but squabbles continued until 1189, when, in alliance with Philip II of **France**, the ambitious heir to the throne turned on the aging king again. On 6 July, in the midst of that campaign, Henry died and Richard inherited the crown.

The new monarch immediately turned his attention to the Holy Land, hoping to recapture Jerusalem, which Saladin, the Muslim leader, had taken in 1187. In order to raise money for the venture, he sold the rights to many offices of state, freed King **William I of Scotland** from his oath of subservience to the English monarch in return for a payment of 10,000 marks, raised taxes, and dug deeply into his treasury. His kingdom was viewed solely as a source of revenue—so much so that, according to some sources, he even said that he would sell **London** if a buyer could be found.

In 1190, Richard set off for Palestine, wintering in the Mediterranean, where he set his sister, **Joan, queen of Sicily**, free from captivity and then captured Cyprus. The following year, he joined the siege of Acre, in western Galilee, retrieving it from Muslim hands, but after the victory, he allowed the brutal side of his nature to control his judgment, killing 2,500 of Saladin's supporters whom he had taken prisoner rather than allow them to slow down his army's movements and use up resources.

After Acre, the king took the fortress at Arsuf and then marched on Jerusalem, but the European coalition was beginning to crack as its leaders quarreled over policy. Some of the commanders, including Leopold V of Austria and Philip II of **France**, turned for home, leaving Richard in undisputed charge of the crusade. However, the depleted army was unable to drive the Muslims from the Holy City, so in 1192 he negotiated a truce that allowed Christian pilgrims free access to their sacred sites even though Saladin remained in control of the settlement.

On 9 October, Richard started on the return trip to Europe, but his ship was blown ashore near Venice during a storm. Leopold, his former ally, held him in prison, suspecting that he had murdered Conrad of Montferrat, Leopold's cousin, who had been elected king of Jerusalem by the crusaders despite Richard's opposition. Leopold eventually passed Richard on to Henry VI, the Holy Roman Emperor, who kept him in confinement and moved him from castle to castle so that he could not be traced. According to legend, Blondel, the royal musician, foiled this plan by traveling from fortress to fortress playing his master's favorite tunes; eventually he heard Richard respond on his harp, and Henry agreed to release his prisoner in return for a payment of 150,000 marks—a sum that gives some indication of England's wealth at the end of the 12th century.

After Richard was released in 1194, he spent most of the remainder of his life at war with Philip of France. He died on 6 April 1199 while laying siege to the castle at Châlus, in Limousin, and was buried in the abbey at **Fontevrault** in Anjou, close to his father. The Lionheart's exploits brought great honor to England, enormously increasing the country's prestige in Europe, but he was fortunate that domestic affairs had been left in the hands of capable administrators who were able to maintain prosperity and order in the absence of a monarch.

In 1191, Richard married **Berengaria of Navarre**, but he died without leaving any legitimate issue. Modern scholars argue about his sexuality, some concluding that he was gay, others (partly on the basis that he may have had two illegitimate children) that he was a philanderer. **John**, his younger brother, who had schemed against him during his years outside the kingdom, followed him to the throne.

**RICHARD II (1367–1400).** King of England from 1377 to 1399, Richard was the son of **Edward, the black prince**, and **Joan, countess of Kent**. He was born on 6 January 1367 in Bordeaux, one of the major settlements in his father's duchy of **Aquitaine**, and he inherited the crown because his grandfather, **Edward III**, outlived the black prince (the heir to the throne) by just over a year, dying on 21 June 1377. At the time, Richard was only 10 years old, so responsibility for governing the realm was initially placed in the hands of councils of nobles, with **John of Gaunt** (the king's uncle) particularly influential. Then, in 1381, despite his tender years, the young monarch persuaded a group of peasants, who were complaining about conditions in agricultural areas and had destroyed several properties in **London**, that their requests for improvements would be approved. This promise was not honored, however. Instead, Richard had the leaders of the revolt executed, demonstrating a duplicity that became increasingly evident as he grew older and adding to a growing reputation for arrogance, unwillingness to accept criticism, and lack of judgment in choice of advisors, many of whom became renowned for their greed and expensive lifestyles.

Unsurprisingly, tensions between sovereign and subjects escalated. For a time, John of Gaunt provided a moderating influence, but matters came to a head after that diplomat left England in 1386 to pursue his claim to the throne of Castile and Léon. Parliament accused Michael de la Pole, earl of Suffolk and the king's lord chancellor, of embezzlement. Richard came to his official's defense, saying that if parliament asked him to remove even a lowly kitchen boy he would refuse. But in the end the pressures were too great, and Suffolk was dismissed. Then, in 1387, the monarch's opponents—who included another of his uncles, **Thomas of Woodstock**, **duke of Gloucester**—demanded the arrest of several other favorites, notably Robert de Vere, earl of Oxford and Richard's closest friend. The king allowed his allies to escape the clutches of his critics, but the following year they were impeached by parliament and found guilty of treason. Several were hanged and **beheaded**, others exiled.

John of Gaunt's return in 1389 brought an apparent reconciliation between the two sides, but Richard used the uneasy peace to garner new support. A military expedition to Ireland in 1394–95 enhanced his prestige in some quarters, as did the signing of a truce with **France** in 1396. In 1397, he felt sufficiently powerful to attack his opponents openly: Gloucester was murdered; Richard FitzAlan, earl of Arundel, was beheaded; and Thomas de Beauchamp, earl of Warwick, was exiled to the Isle of Man. Then, with the opposition weakened, the mercenary monarch embarked on a policy of high taxation to support a luxurious court. Even those who had been loyal to him suffered from his need for funds, because when John of Gaunt, for years a peacemaker in a country divided into feuding factions, died in 1399, the king confiscated his estates. This, however, was the straw that broke the camel's back. Henry Bolingbroke, John's son and later **Henry IV**, rebelled, finding much support in a land tired of oppressive fiscal measures and of the continual disregard of the rights of individuals and of parliament. On August 15, Richard conceded defeat. On 29 September, parliament was told that he was willing to abdicate (though that was probably a distortion of the truth), and he was incarcerated in Pontefract Castle, where he died in February 1400, probably of starvation but perhaps by violence. Initially he was buried at the Dominican church at Kings Langley, north of London, but in 1413 his remains were reinterred in **Westminster Abbey**.

The last of the monarchs from the **House of Anjou**, Richard was a sensitive man who, while often considered effete and foppish, supported literature and the arts, patronizing such writers as Geoffrey Chaucer (author of *The Canterbury Tales*) and providing funds for a new ceiling at Westminster Hall in the **Palace of Westminster**. He is also sometimes credited with the first use of handkerchiefs because the royal accounts record the purchase of small pieces of fabric "for the lord King to wipe and clean his nose," but he was uninterested in military matters, and that, as much as anything, alienated him from leading nobles during his youth. Later, his self-interest and malice made him enemies, and his reign collapsed quickly after the death of John of Gaunt, who had worked tirelessly and with much skill to prevent confrontation.

Richard was married twice, first to **Anne of Bohemia** and then to **Isabella of Valois**, but he left no children by either. *See also* SHEEN PALACE; WARS OF THE ROSES.

**RICHARD III (1452–1485).** Richard, the last king of England from the **House of York** and the last to die in battle, was reviled by historians for many years because he plotted to remove his nephew, **Edward V**, from the throne, and allegedly he arranged for the child's murder in the **Tower of London**. More recently, however, scholars have rehabilitated him somewhat, stressing his abilities as an administrator and as a military commander. The youngest son of **Richard, duke of York (1411–1460)**, and **Cicely Neville**, he was born at Fotheringhay Castle on 2 June 1452 and was created duke of Gloucester in 1461. As a teenager, he served in the Yorkist armies during the **Wars of the Roses** and may have been involved in the murder of **Henry VI** in 1471. He later led English armies in invasions of **France** and Scotland.

In 1483, King **Edward IV**—Richard's brother—died, leaving a young son who succeeded him as Edward V. The boy had been brought up by the Nevilles, but Richard, wary of the family's influence, took him to the Tower of **London** while **Elizabeth Woodville**, the **queen dowager**, sought protection for herself and the rest of her family in **Westminster Abbey**. On 25 June 1483, parliament decreed that Edward's marriage to Elizabeth was invalid on the grounds of an earlier contract with Eleanor, daughter of the earl of Shrewsbury. Their children were declared illegitimate, and Richard was acknowledged as the rightful king. Some weeks later, Elizabeth was persuaded to allow her other son, **Richard, duke of York (1473–1483?)**, to join his brother in the tower. In August, they disappeared, and although there is no evidence to show that the monarch was involved, it was widely believed at the time that the children were murdered on his orders.

Richard proved to be an efficient manager, building churches, introducing a series of financial reforms, promoting trade, and supporting learning, but he had alienated so many of the nobility with his machinations that his power base was limited. Henry Tudor (later King **Henry VII**) provided a rallying point for the opposition, building an army that met the royalist troops at **Bosworth Field** on 22 August 1485. Richard died in the fighting, ending a reign that lasted just two years, and was buried at Leicester, probably either at the Greyfriars Church or at the Newarke (the Church of the Annunciation of Mary the Virgin). *See also* CECILY, VISCOUNTESS WELLES; EDWARD OF LANCASTER, PRINCE OF WALES; EDWARD OF MIDDLEHAM, PRINCE OF WALES; ELIZABETH OF YORK; NEVILLE, ANNE; SIMNEL, LAMBERT.

**RICHARD, DUKE OF BERNAY (1054–c1081).** Richard—the second son of **William I of England** (William the Conqueror) and **Matilda of Flanders**—was born in Normandy. He died, childless, after being gored by a stag while hunting in the New Forest and was buried in **Winchester** Cathedral. The date of the accident is not known for certain, with some authorities placing it as early as 1069. Conspiracy theorists suggest that Richard's death, no mishap, was planned by Henry, William's fourth son (and later King **Henry I**), because he wanted to improve his chances of sitting on the English throne.

**RICHARD, DUKE OF YORK (1411–1460).** Richard's efforts to win the English throne were unavailing, pushing the country into the lengthy "**Wars of the Roses**" between the **House of Lancaster** and the **House of York**. The second child of Richard of Conisburgh, earl of Cambridge, and his wife, Anne de Mortimer (who died giving birth), he fought in **France** during the **Hundred Years' War** at a time when King **Henry VI** was still a child and government was increasingly falling under the control of the powerful Beaufort family, which was dissatisfied with the military operations. Richard threw his weight behind the Beauforts' opponents, so in 1447 he was moved to Ireland as lieutenant, a post that was intended as an exile but in which he earned much praise. He returned to England in 1450 and then, as well as in 1452, attempted to remove Henry's chief minister, Edmund Beaufort, duke of Somerset, by armed force. The king, now old enough to rule without **regents**, rebuffed these efforts, but in 1453 he had a mental breakdown.

Parliament appointed York "protector of the realm" during the monarch's incapacity, but the decision was opposed bitterly by **Margaret of Anjou**, Henry's **queen consort**, who rightly believed that Richard, despite his expressions of loyalty to the king, wanted the throne for himself and thus was a rival to her son, **Edward of Lancaster, prince of Wales**. In practice, the duke's claims had a strong basis because he was descended from **Lionel of Antwerp, duke of Clarence**, the third son of King **Edward III**, whereas Henry was descended from the fourth son (**John of Gaunt, duke of Lancaster**). As tensions rose, Henry recovered his faculties and, succumbing to Margaret's pleas, restored Somerset to favor, relieving York of his role as protector. Richard responded by raising an army that met Beaufort's troops at St. Albans on 22 May 1455 (*see* ST. ALBANS, FIRST BATTLE OF). In the skirmishing, Somerset was killed, so York—now the most powerful noble in the land—was able to take control of government. The queen, however, continued her opposition, rebuilding her army, and further conflict seemed inevitable.

In 1459, Richard fled to Ireland because his soldiers refused to fight against troops led by the king himself, but on 10 July 1460, York's son, Edward, defeated the royal force at the **Battle of Northampton** and took Henry prisoner. With the monarch under his control, the duke returned from Ireland and claimed that he was the rightful king of England. Parliament demurred but, albeit with some qualms, required Henry to designate York as his heir. In response, Margaret raised yet another force, and York marched north to meet it. On 30 December 1460, showing an uncharacteristic lack of strategic judgment, he left his secure base in Sandal Castle with a small company and was killed (*see* WAKEFIELD, BATTLE OF). His head, bearing a paper crown, was displayed in York until his son removed it after the **Battle of Towton** on 29 March the following year.

The duke's remains were finally interred at Fotheringhay in 1476. His efforts to become king had come to nothing, but his descendants had a profound effect on the development of the British monarchies. His second son, **Edward IV**, reigned from 1461 to 1470 and from 1471 to 1483, and his eighth son, **Richard III**, reigned from 1483 to 1485. Also, a grandson (**Edward V**) ruled for a few weeks in 1483, and a great-grandson (**Henry VIII**) from 1509 to 1547. **Margaret Tudor**, a great-granddaughter who married King **James IV** of Scotland, was the mother of **James V** and grandmother of **Mary, queen of Scots**. *See also* FREDERICK, PRINCE, DUKE OF YORK AND ALBANY; NEVILLE, CICELY, DUCHESS OF YORK.

**RICHARD, DUKE OF YORK (1473–1483?).** Richard, the second son of King **Edward IV** and **Elizabeth Woodville**, died with his older brother, **Edward V**, in circumstances that have never been satisfactorily explained. He was born at the Dominican Friary in Shrewsbury on 17 August 1473 and was created **duke of York** on 28 May the following year; since then, the dukedom has traditionally been awarded to the second son of the English monarch (and, later, to the second sons of monarchs of Great Britain and of the United Kingdom). On 15 January 1478, he was married at the **Palace of Westminster** to five-year-old Anne de Mowbray, heiress to the rich estates of her father, John, duke of Norfolk.

Edward IV died on 9 April 1483. Shortly afterward, parliament heard testimony that, prior to his wedding with Elizabeth, he had promised to make Eleanor Butler, widow of Sir Thomas Butler, his wife. In the late 15th century, such promises precluded unions with any other woman, so although there was no documentary evidence of a betrothal, the late king's children were declared illegitimate, Edward V was deprived of the succession, and Richard, duke of Gloucester (Edward IV's brother), was crowned **Richard III**.

The new monarch immediately placed both of his nephews in the **Tower of London**, and though the events that followed are not known for certain, it seems likely that the children were murdered by the end of the year. Many historians believe that their uncle was responsible, killing the boys to ensure that they would not provide a focus for rebellion by dissident nobles, but a number of other historians have pointed out that there were other possible culprits, including **Henry VII**, who (assuming that the boys survived until he became king in 1485) may have wanted to eliminate potential claimants of his crown. In 1674, workmen discovered the remains of two children in a box buried in the Tower. King **Charles II**, the monarch at the time, ordered the skeletons to be placed in an urn and interred in **Westminster Abbey**. Forensic examiners, in 1933, could not find sufficient evidence to conclude that the bones were those of Richard and Edward. *See also* WARBECK, PERKIN.

**RICHARD, EARL OF CORNWALL (1209–1272).** The younger son of King **John** and **Isabella of Angoulême**, Richard was born in **Winchester** Castle on 5 January 1209. As a young man, he was often at odds with his brother, Henry, who succeeded his father as **Henry III** in 1216, rebelling against him on three occasions and winning large estates in return for promises to desist. Later, however, he proved to be one of the king's staunchest supporters, leading his armies in an effort to retrieve lands lost by King John in Brittany and Poitou and spending over a year in prison after being taken captive by rebels at the Battle of Lewes in 1247. Also, the younger brother acted as **regent** when the elder was abroad, and he played a large part in changing the English coinage. In 1240, he joined the sixth crusade to the Holy Land, using his negotiating skills to win the release of prisoners and his strategic talents to rebuild the coastal fortress at Ascalon.

In 1247, Richard was crowned king of the Romans (in effect, emperor-elect of the Holy Roman Empire), but he had used his considerable wealth to buy the votes of the electorate and he visited his "kingdom" on only four occasions, so the title was little more than nominal. He married three times. His first wife, Isabel Marshal, widow of Gilbert de Clare, earl of Gloucester, had four children, three of whom died in infancy. Henry, the only surviving son, lived only to be murdered in 1271, at the age of 35, by his cousins during mass at the Cathedral of St. Nicholas in Viterbo, Italy. Isabel died in childbirth in 1240, and three years later Richard took a second wife, Sanchia, daughter of Raymond Berenger, the count of Provence. He and Sanchia had two sons, one of whom (also named Richard) reached maturity and succeeded his father as earl of Cornwall. In 1269, eight years after Sanchia's death, Richard—at the age of 60—wed Beatrice, the 16-year-old daughter of Dietrich, count of Falconburg. He died at Berkhamsted Castle on 2 April 1272, and Beatrice, childless, survived him by only five years. *See also* ELEANOR, COUNTESS OF LEICESTER; WALLINGFORD CASTLE.

**RICHARD, PRINCE, DUKE OF GLOUCESTER (1944– ). Prince** Richard, the youngest of King **George V**'s nine grandchildren, succeeded to his father's dukedom because his elder brother (**Prince William of Gloucester**) was killed in a flying accident in 1971. He was born to **Prince Henry, duke of Gloucester**, and **Princess Alice, duchess of Gloucester**, on 26 August 1944—like William, by caesarian section and at Lady Almira Carnarvon's Nursing Home, which had moved to Hadley Common, Hertfordshire, from **London** at the start of World War I—and attended Wellesley House School in Broadstairs, Kent, and Eton College before going to Cambridge University, where he graduated with a bachelor's degree in architecture in 1966.

Prince Richard had taken only the first steps toward developing a career as an architect before the death of his elder brother, and his father's declining health, forced him to change direction and concentrate on the management of Barnwell Manor, the country home in Northamptonshire that his parents had purchased in 1938, as well as on royal duties. He supports the work of more than 100 nonprofit organizations, several concerned with architectural interests, and undertakes some 300 public engagements each year in such capacities as chancellor of the University of Worcester and as commissioner with English Heritage (the government body charged with maintaining the historic character of England's built environment). In 2005, however, he had to resign his presidency of the Institute of Advanced Motorists after receiving four speeding tickets in three years and being banned from driving for six months by the courts. The prince also holds numerous honorary military posts (though he has never served with British forces) and has represented Queen **Elizabeth II** on several occasions overseas, as at the funeral of King Taufa'ahau Tupou IV of Tonga in 2006.

On 8 July 1972, Prince Richard married Birgitte van Deurs (*see* BIRGITTE, DUCHESS OF GLOUCESTER) at St. Andrews Church in Barnwell. They have three children—**Alexander Windsor, earl of Ulster** (born on 24 October 1974); **Lady Davina Lewis** (born on 19 November 1977); and **Lady**

**Rose Gilman** (born on 1 March 1980). None of their children carries out royal duties. *See also* KENSINGTON PALACE.

**RICHARD THE LIONHEART (1157–1199).** *See* RICHARD I.

**RICHMOND PALACE.** *See* SHEEN PALACE.

**ROBERT I (1274–1329).** Robert (often known as Robert the Bruce) was king of Scots from 1306 to 1329, repulsing English attempts to establish overlordship of his kingdom and ultimately winning an assurance of independence. The son of **Robert de Bruce, lord of Annandale**, and his wife, **Marjorie (or Margaret), countess of Carrick**, he was born on 11 July 1274 into a family whose original home had been at Brieux in Normandy but which had acquired estates in Scotland during the early 12th century. His grandfather, also named Robert, was one of the candidates for the crown awarded to **John of Scotland** after the death of **Margaret, maid of Norway**, in 1290.

Little is known of the future monarch's early life, with even his birthplace the subject of scholarly debate, some writers suggesting that Turnberry Castle in Ayrshire was the most likely site but others indicating that the family estate at Writtle, near Chelmsford in southern England, is more probable. He seems to have changed political allegiance several times during his teens and early twenties, sometimes supporting King **Edward I** of England but often aligning with groups committed to ensuring Scotland's sovereignty. From 1298 to 1300, he was one of the **Guardians of Scotland**, acting as **regent** while John of Scotland was held prisoner in **London**, but he increasingly found himself at odds with John Comyn, the most powerful noble in the country and — as nephew of John of Scotland — a contender for the vacant throne. On 10 February 1306, the two men met inside the Franciscan church at Dumfries. Bruce attacked Comyn, injuring him, and then fled, but two friends went back inside the building to make sure the wounded man would die.

In the weeks that followed, Bruce asserted his claims to a throne that had been empty since King Edward had imprisoned John of Scotland in 1296, and on 25 March he was crowned at **Scone**. Monarch largely in name only, his kingdom was divided by civil war, with Comyns and Bruces at each other's throats. Moreover, his troops were defeated by English forces at Methven on 19 June 1306 and near Tyndrum on 11 August; his wife (**Elizabeth de Burgh**) was taken prisoner; and three of his brothers — Alexander, Neil, and Thomas — were executed. According to legend, Robert, now a fugitive in his own realm, took refuge in a cave, possibly on Rathlin Island off the coast of Northern Ireland, but perhaps on Arran or one of the other islands lying along Scotland's west coast. There, say the storytellers, he watched a spider spin its web. Twice the spider tried to secure the strands of the web to a rock, and twice it failed, but the third attempt was successful. Bruce, having twice failed to defeat English forces, determined, like the spider, not to give up, so he returned to the mainland. His chances of success were undoubtedly bolstered by the death of Edward I on 7 July 1307. Edward's son and successor, **Edward II**, was a much less accomplished commander and strategist, so Bruce, by a process of guerilla warfare, was able to retake English-held castles one by one and then, on 24 June 1314, win a major set-piece encounter at the **Battle of Bannockburn**, near **Stirling**.

Over the next 14 years, the Scots mounted repeated raids into northern England and invaded Ireland in an effort to engage English troops on a second front, but Robert's energies were largely devoted to consolidation of his position at home. The estates of nobles who had supported the English occupation were forfeited—many of those barons, known as "the disinherited," moved to **France** and allied with **Edward de Balliol**, who attempted to usurp the crown in 1332—and their lands were given to the king's men. Parliament met on several occasions, and a basic administrative structure was developed for the realm, providing income for the royal exchequer.

It was not until 1328 that England recognized Scotland's independence and Bruce's kingship (*see* NORTHAMPTON, TREATY OF). By then, however, his health was failing, and on 7 June the following year he died at Cardross, near Dumbarton, of what some chroniclers describe as an "unclean ailment," which later writers suggest may have been leprosy, strokes, syphilis, or even motor neurone disease. His body was buried at **Dunfermline Abbey**, but Sir James Douglas carried his heart on a crusade against the Moors in Spain. Although Douglas was killed, the heart was returned to Scotland and buried in an unmarked location at Melrose Abbey. In 1996, newspapers speculated that a casket unearthed during construction work on the building might once have contained the organ.

Robert I was succeeded by his five-year-old son, **David II**, who was to undo much of what his father had achieved. *See also* BRUCE, JOHN; BRUCE, MARGARET, COUNTESS OF SUTHERLAND; BRUCE, MARJORIE; BRUCE, MATILDA; ISABELLA OF MAR.

**ROBERT I, DUKE OF NORMANDY (1000–1035).** Robert—the father of King **William I of England** (often known as William the Conqueror)—was one of six children born to Richard II, duke of Normandy, and his wife, Judith of Brittany. On Richard's death in 1027, Robert's older brother (also named Richard) inherited their father's title, but he survived only a few more months, possibly dying as a result of poisoning instigated by Robert.

Robert supported King Henry I of France in the monarch's conflicts with his brother (Robert, duke of Burgundy) and mother (Constance of Arles), winning control of the Vexin area of northeast France as a reward for his loyalty, but apparently he never married; William was born illegitimate, the result of a liaison with **Herleva** of Falaise, whose parentage is not known.

In 1035, before setting off on a pilgrimage to Jerusalem, Robert named William—his only son—as his heir, so when he died at Nicaea, in Turkey, on 2 July 1035, during the return journey, the bastard boy (only seven or eight years old) became a duke. Robert is sometimes referred to as "Robert the Devil" (because of his alleged murder of his brother) and sometimes as "Robert the Magnificent" (because of his love of fine clothes and furnishings).

**ROBERT II (1316–1390).** Robert, the first monarch from the House of Stewart (*see* STUART, HOUSE OF), was **heir presumptive** to the Scottish throne for much of his life, but after his accession, he had limited impact on the course of political affairs. The son of **Marjorie Bruce**, daughter of King **Robert I**, and her husband, **Walter Stewart (c1293–1326)**, he was born prematurely on 2 March 1316 after his mother fell from her horse while riding near Paisley. Some writers have suggested that the birth was caesarean, but this claim has been much contested.

For more than 50 years, Robert was king-in-waiting. From 1316 until the birth of Robert I's first son, David (later **David II**), in 1324, he was heir presumptive to his paternal grandfather, and from 1326 until his **succession to the throne** in 1371, he was heir presumptive to David. He served as **Guardian of Scotland** (in effect, as **regent**) during periods when David was in exile in **France** from 1334 to 1341 and again while he was held prisoner by the English from 1346 to 1357. In 1346, he fought at the **Battle of Neville's Cross** but ran away, leaving the king exposed, when the English troops gained the upper hand, and in 1363 he joined a rebellion against David, perhaps because the king appeared willing to designate **Edward III** of England or one of his sons as the **heir apparent** to the Scottish throne, or perhaps because the monarch was planning to marry **Margaret Drummond**, a member of a family with which the Stewarts were feuding.

Robert eventually became king, at the age of 54, when David died unexpectedly in 1371. The first decade of his reign was marked by improvements in the country's finances, partly because of a prosperous trade in wool and partly because of the termination of payments to the English crown that had been promised in return for David's release from captivity. However, differences with one son (John, earl of Carrick) over military strategies, and an unwillingness to deal with the despotic administrative policies of another (**Alexander Stewart, wolf of Badenoch**), led to a palace revolution in 1384, with Carrick taking control of government and leaving his father as king in little more than name. Robert never regained control and died on 19 April 1390 at **Dundonald Castle**, which he had built as a **royal residence** in Ayrshire. He was buried at **Scone** and was succeeded by Carrick, who ruled as **Robert III** (rather than John) in order to avoid associations, if only through nomenclature, with the oft-disparaged King **John of Scotland**.

Traditional assessments of Robert II's reign have concluded that he had passed his intellectual and physical peaks by the time he became king and so was a weak monarch who failed to provide direction and leadership for a divided country. Some more modern views are less critical, however, suggesting that he adopted a pragmatic approach to war with England and that he attempted to maintain control at home through strategic marriages that linked his daughters to politically important nobles as well as by dispensing patronage in the form of payments derived from customs revenues—a low-profile form of leadership out of kilter with the age. *See also* EUPHEMIA DE ROSS; MURE, ELIZABETH; STEWART, DAVID, EARL OF CAITHNESS; STEWART, EGIDIA (?–?); STEWART, ELIZABETH (?–?); STEWART, ELIZABETH, COUNTESS OF CRAWFORD; STEWART, ISABELLA, COUNTESS OF DOUGLAS; STEWART, JOANNA; STEWART, KATHERINE; STEWART, MARGARET (c1342–c1410); STEWART, MARJORIE, COUNTESS OF MORAY; STEWART, ROBERT, DUKE OF ALBANY (c1340–1420); STEWART, WALTER (c1340–c1362); STEWART, WALTER, EARL OF ATHOLL.

**ROBERT III (c1337–1406).** Robert was king of Scotland in name only. The eldest surviving son of King **Robert II** and **Elizabeth Mure**, he was born c1337, before his parents were recognized as married by the Roman Catholic Church, but was legitimized (along with his brothers and sisters) by dispensation of Pope Clement VI on 22 November 1347. In 1384, as dissatisfaction with his father's rule mounted, he was made lieutenant of the kingdom, a title that gave him command of government. However, about three years later he was made lame by a kick from a horse, and in 1388 the powers were transferred to his younger brother, **Robert Stewart, later duke of Albany (c1340–1420)**.

Robert III was baptized as John but changed his name when he succeeded to the throne in 1390 to avoid associations, even if only in nomenclature, with the still derided **John of Scotland**, who had been king a century earlier but had had his powers removed by Scottish nobles who disliked his willingness to acquiesce with the wishes of **Edward I** of England. In practice, partly because of the new monarch's physical disabilities and partly because of his age and lack of strong allies, control of government remained in Albany's hands until 1399, when **David Stewart, duke of Rothesay** and heir to the throne, was named lieutenant of the realm. Rothesay proved rash and headstrong, however, and he made enemies because he broke a promise of marriage to Elizabeth, daughter of the earl of March, and took Marjorie, daughter of the earl of Douglas, as his bride because she brought a larger dowry.

In 1402, Albany confined David in **Falkland Palace**, where, according to rumor, he allowed the young man to starve to death. Inevitably, the loss led to concern for the safety of James (later King **James I of Scotland**), Robert's only surviving son and thus heir apparent to Scotland's throne. In 1406, the 11-year-old boy set sail for France, but his ship was intercepted by English sailors, who may well have been given details of the plans by Albany, and for the next 18 years he was kept prisoner by **Henry IV**, **Henry V**, and **Henry VI**. When Robert heard the news, his health declined further, and he told his wife, **Annabella Drummond**, that he should be buried under a "midden" (or dunghill), identified by a notice reading, "Here lies the worst of kings and the most miserable of men." He died on 4 April 1406 at **Dundonald Castle** in Ayrshire and was interred in Paisley Abbey. *See also* DUKE OF ROTHESAY; STEWART, EGIDIA (?–?); STEWART, ELIZABETH (?–c1411); STEWART, MARGARET, COUNTESS OF DOUGLAS; STEWART, MARY, COUNTESS OF ANGUS; STEWART, ROBERT (?–c1393).

**ROBERT CURTHOSE, DUKE OF NORMANDY (c1054–1134).** The eldest son of King **William I of England** (William the Conqueror) and **Matilda of Flanders**, Robert spent much of his life squabbling with his father and brothers, ultimately failing to win the English crown, which he coveted. Allegedly the rebellions began in 1077 when the sovereign neglected to chastise two other sons—William and Henry—after they had soaked Robert in a deluge of stinking water. Robert responded by laying siege to his father's castle at Rouen, in **Normandy**, and ravaging large areas of the Norman countryside in a campaign of destruction that only ceased when Matilda negotiated a reconciliation in 1080.

On Matilda's death three years later, Robert left his father's court and traveled Europe until he inherited the dukedom of Normandy when the Conqueror himself died in 1087. Curthose and his brother, William, who had inherited their father's English kingdom and ruled as **William II of England**, agreed that each would be the other's heir, but only a year later Robert was backing an unsuccessful attempt to unseat the new monarch. Then, when William died in 1100, Henry ignored his brothers' pact and seized the crown as King **Henry I**, taking advantage of Robert's absence on a crusade to the Holy Land.

Curthose responded by forming an army and mounting an invasion of England in 1101, but he was easily beaten back, and in 1105 Henry demonstrated his opportunism again by leading his own troops into Normandy at a time when Robert's mismanagement of the family estates had led to much unrest. The brothers met in battle at **Tinchebrai** on 28 September 1106, the struggle lasting for only an hour before Robert was taken prisoner (along with **Edgar Aetheling**, the last Anglo-Saxon king of England, who had transferred his support from the rebels to the monarchists and back again). Curthose—his nickname is taken from the Norman French *court*, meaning "short," and *heuse*, meaning "hose" or "stockings"—remained in captivity for the next 28 years. He died at Cardiff Castle on 10 February 1134 and was buried in the abbey church of St. Peter on the site now occupied by Gloucester Cathedral.

**ROBERT DE BRUCE, LORD OF ANNANDALE (1243–1304).** Robert, father of King **Robert I**, was probably born in July 1243 to Robert de Bruce (or Brus), lord of Annandale, and his first wife, Isabella (or Isobel) de Clare, a daughter of the earl of Gloucester. The family was of Norman background but had extensive estates and considerable political influence in Scotland, where Robert senior was one of the candidates for the throne after the death of **Margaret, maid of Norway**, in 1290.

In 1271 or 1272, at Turnberry Castle, the younger Bruce married **Marjorie (or Margaret), countess of Carrick**, without the consent of King **Alexander III**, who confiscated the bride's estates until she paid a fine. On several occasions, he pledged allegiance to **Edward I** of England, recognizing him as overlord of Scotland and providing soldiers for English armies attempting to subdue Scotland and Wales, but he changed sides after the English king took King **John of Scotland** prisoner in 1296 and fought with the Scots, who resisted Edward's claims to suzerainty, at the Battle of **Stirling** Bridge the following year. In 1302, however, Robert changed his mind again, possibly because he felt that continued attempts to gain John's release were futile, but perhaps because the monarch's return would spell the end of his son's aspirations for the throne. He died in March 1304 and was buried at Holm Cultram Abbey in Cumbria.

**ROBERT THE BRUCE (1274–1329).** *See* ROBERT I.

**ROXBURGH CASTLE.** Roxburgh was a favorite residence of Scottish royalty during the 12th and 13th centuries. It is first mentioned in documentary sources in 1107 as a home of the earls of Northumberland but soon afterward was acquired by King **David I**, who began its transformation into a large fortress. **Alexander II** married **Marie de Coucy** at the castle in 1239, **Alexander III** (his only son) was born there in 1241, and **Alexander of Scotland** (son of Alexander III) married there in 1282. However, the stronghold's location close to Scotland's border with England made it strategically important, so it was regularly attacked and occupied by one side or the other. For two years from 1307, **Edward I** of England confined **Robert I**'s sister, Mary, in a cage at Roxburgh, forbidding her to speak to anyone except the woman who brought her food, and in 1460 **James II** was laying siege to the castle when a cannon exploded and killed him. **Mary of Gueldres**, James's wife, ordered the destruction of the building soon after it had been retaken by the Scots, so visitors can now see only the ruined remains that stand in the grounds of Floors Castle, seat of the duke of Roxburghe.

**ROYAL ASCOT.** The annual horse races at Ascot in mid-June have long had an important place in Britain's social calendar. The course, located some six miles from **Windsor Castle** and now owned by the **crown estate**, was developed at Queen **Anne**'s request in 1711 and until 1945 was used for only one week each year. Since then, other events have been added, but the June meeting is still the only one regularly attended by the **royal family**.

The dress code for race goers who have passes to the royal enclosure is strict. Men must wear morning dress, including a waistcoat, and bring a top hat (singer Rod Stewart had neither pass nor hat when he tried to enter in 2002 and was turned away). Ladies have been allowed to wear trouser suits since 1999, but by 2008 the meeting organizers felt that female dress standards were falling and banned bare midriffs, dresses that had straps less than an inch wide, halter necks, off-the-shoulder tops, and short skirts. Hats (or "significant fasteners") are obligatory and include many works of fantasy as well as more understated creations by fashionable designers. Outside the royal enclosure, standards are less strict, but many of the 300,000 visitors who attend the weeklong meeting conform to the dress code nonetheless. The principal event is the Ascot Gold Cup, a two-and-a-half-mile flat race for thoroughbreds of four years or more that is traditionally held on the Thursday (Ladies' Day).

**ROYAL ASSENT.** The granting of royal assent is the final stage in the legislative processes of the United Kingdom's parliament. When a bill has been approved by parliament, it is sent to the sovereign, who, by signing the document, makes the provisions law. In the past, monarchs could withhold their consent, but nowadays kings and queens act on the advice of government ministers, who command the support of a majority of elected representatives, so the proceedings are a formality. Royal assent has not been refused, against ministerial advice, since 1708, when Queen **Anne** declined to approve a Scottish Militia Bill because she believed that any militia that was formed could not be trusted.

Assent can be granted in person, with the sovereign attending the House of Lords (the upper chamber in the British parliament), but that method was last used by Queen **Victoria** in 1854. Alternatively, the monarch may appoint three or more commissioners who are members both of the Lords and of the **Privy Council** to represent her at the ceremony. The most usual approach, however, is to signify approval through the issue of letters patent, a simple documentary procedure that was introduced by the Royal Assent Act of 1997. Royal assent is also necessary before legislation passed by the National Assembly for Wales, the Northern Ireland Assembly, or the Scottish Parliament becomes law. *See also* REGENCY ACTS; RESERVE POWER.

**ROYAL CHARTER.** In the past, royal charters were the only means by which cities, companies, and institutions could be incorporated. Over the years, other forms of legitimization, such as acts of parliament, have evolved, but the grant of a charter remains a **royal prerogative**, is the gift of the sovereign, and is used as a means of according status to professional bodies and other organizations. Recipients include the University of Cambridge, which was chartered in 1231; the **London** Hospital (1758); the British Broadcasting Corporation (1926); the Institute of Bankers (1987); and Brighton and Hove Borough Council (1997).

**ROYAL COAT OF ARMS.** Coats of arms were initially used by noble warriors so that they could be identified in battle. They were adopted during the 12th century by King **Henry II** in England and by King **William I of Scotland** but have changed over the years, partly to suit individual whims, and partly to represent the acquisition and loss of territory.

The present royal arms have a shield quartered identically with the **royal standard**. Above it, a helmet supports a crown and a standing lion. To the right (or dexter) side of the bearer, there is a lion, wearing a crown and representing England; to the left (or sinister) side, there is a unicorn (chained because it is a dangerous animal) that represents Scotland. The motto *Honi Soit Qui Mal Y Pense* ("Shamed Be Whoever Thinks Ill Of It") surrounds the shield on a blue ribbon, and *Dieu Et Mon Droit* ("God And My Right") appears underneath, also on a blue scroll.

In the Scottish version of the coat of arms, the shield is quartered in the manner used on the form of royal standard used in Scotland, and the crest is a red lion holding a sword and scepter. The lion and the unicorn are on different sides of the shield, wearing the crowns and carrying the flags of their kingdoms, and there is a single motto—the Latin *Nemo Me Impune Lacessit*, which translates into English as "Nobody Touches Me With Impunity" and is normally rendered in Scotland as "Wha Daur Meddle Wi' Me" (or "Who Dares Meddle With Me").

The arms are used by the monarch and by government for official purposes (for example, on coins and passports). They are also displayed in courtrooms because the sovereign is considered the fount of justice, and judges are considered the representatives of the king or queen. *See also* ROYAL CYPHER; ROYAL WARRANT.

**ROYAL COLLECTION.** Over the years, British monarchs have amassed a large collection of artwork, including ceramics, furniture, manuscripts, and maps, as well as paintings and prints. Most have been acquired since the **restoration of the monarchy** in 1660 because the possessions of earlier kings and queens were destroyed, given to other owners, or stolen while England was a republic. Even so, the present holdings have an estimated value of £10 billion. They include pictures by Canaletto, Leonardo da Vinci, Rembrandt, Michelangelo, and Titian, as well as Gobelins tapestries and one of the world's largest accumulations of Sèvres pottery. All are owned by the sovereign but held in trust for the nation, so items are regularly on display at museums and in **royal residences** that are open to visitors. Since 1987, their care has been the responsibility of the Royal Collection Department of the **Royal Household**. *See also* MARY OF TECK; ROYAL PHILATELIC COLLECTION.

**ROYAL CYPHER.** Government papers, and other state documents, may be authenticated by a cipher that includes the monarch's initials. The same marks may be placed on buildings as an alternative to the **royal coat of arms** and have been employed since the 16th century as a means of identifying the sovereign. The form adopted by Queen **Elizabeth II** contains the notation EIIR surmounted by a crown (the E and R are abbreviations for *Elizabeth Regina*, and *regina* is Latin for "queen"). *See also* ROYAL STANDARD.

**ROYAL FAMILY.** There is no formal legal definition of the term "royal family," so different writers ascribe membership in different ways. Most, however, include the sovereign and his or her spouse, siblings, children and their spouses, grandchildren (though some commentators include only male grandchildren), and surviving parents. The present royal family would thus consist of the following:

- Queen **Elizabeth II** and her husband, **Prince Philip, duke of Edinburgh**.

- **Charles, prince of Wales** (the queen's eldest son); **Camilla, duchess of Cornwall** (his wife); and **Prince William of Wales** and **Prince Henry (or Harry) of Wales** (his children by his first wife, **Diana, princess of Wales**).
- **Anne, princess royal** (the queen's only daughter); her husband, **Vice-Admiral Timothy Laurence**; and **Peter Phillips** and **Zara Phillips** (her children by her first marriage to **Mark Phillips**).
- **Prince Andrew, duke of York** (the queen's second son), and his children, **Princess Beatrice of York** and **Princess Eugenie of York**.
- **Prince Edward, earl of Wessex** (the queen's youngest child); **Sophie, countess of Wessex** (his wife); and their children, **Lady Louise Windsor** and **James, viscount Severn**.

In addition, first cousins, and the wives of first cousins in the male line, are frequently added to the list, extending membership of the royal family to the following:

- **Prince Richard, duke of Gloucester**, and **Birgitte, duchess of Gloucester**.
- **Prince Edward, duke of Kent**, and **Katharine, duchess of Kent**.
- **Prince Michael of Kent** and **Princess Michael of Kent**.
- **Princess Alexandra**.
- **Kate Middleton**, after her marriage to **Prince William of Wales**.

*See also* CIVIL LIST; PRIVY PURSE.

**ROYAL HOUSEHOLD.** Monarchs have always had a corps of officials and servants to look after their affairs and their well-being. In the modern era, the Royal Household numbers some 1,200 people, grouped into five departments. The private secretary's office is the primary artery of communication between the sovereign, the government, and the media, managing the monarch's program of official duties and advising on political matters. The officers working for the keeper of the **privy purse** administer the public funds allocated to the sovereign for the upkeep of official **royal residences** and the performance of official duties. The master of the household is responsible for all catering, hospitality, and housekeeping arrangements (a task that includes everything from preparing guest lists to managing wine cellars and supervising the preparation of food and the repair of upholstery), and the director of the **Royal Collection** oversees the conservation and display of the sovereign's artworks.

The work of these departments is coordinated by the lord chancellor's office, which also organizes major ceremonial events (such as the **state**

**opening of parliament**) and maintains contact with the 150 or so foreign embassies in the United Kingdom. In addition, there are several members of the household with specifically Scottish duties (for example, the Royal Company of Archers, which forms the monarch's ceremonial bodyguard in Scotland), and there are a number of primarily honorific posts, such as astronomer royal, poet laureate, and warden of the swans. Other members of the **royal family** who undertake public duties have their own households; these, like that of the monarch, are funded through parliament, but the monarch returns an equivalent amount to government coffers from her or his own funds. *See also* AIR TRAVEL; CIVIL LIST; LADY-IN-WAITING; ROYAL PHILATELIC COLLECTION; ROYAL TRAIN; ROYAL WARRANT; STATE COACHES.

**ROYAL LODGE.** Royal Lodge, in the grounds of Windsor Great Park and close to **Windsor Castle**, is the official home of **Prince Andrew, duke of York** and second son of Queen **Elizabeth II** and **Prince Philip, duke of Edinburgh**. The original building on the site dated from the mid-16th century and was first used by the **royal family** in 1812, when George, **prince of Wales** (later King **George IV**), adopted it as a residence. King **William IV** demolished most of the structure in the 1830s, replacing it with accommodation for members of the **Royal Household**, and since then it has been enlarged, by a gradual process of accretion, to a structure with about 30 rooms, including seven bedrooms.

In 1931, Royal Lodge became a country residence for the duke and duchess of York, later King **George VI** and Queen **Elizabeth, the queen mother**. Queen Elizabeth continued to use the house after her husband's death in 1952, but in 2004, two years after her passing, **Prince** Andrew vacated **Sunninghill Park** and moved in, embarking on a £7.5 million refurbishment program that he funded with a loan from his mother, promising repayment when Sunninghill was sold. (This arrangement caused much speculation in the press when an unknown buyer paid £3 million more than Sunninghill's £12 million asking price and then allowed the building to deteriorate as it remained unoccupied.)

The Royal Lodge's 90-acre grounds include the Royal Chapel of All Saints, which Queen Elizabeth II uses for Sunday worship when she is at Windsor because it affords greater privacy than the larger **St. George's Chapel**, which is within the castle walls but open to the public. *See also* AMELIA, PRINCESS (1783–1810).

**ROYAL MARRIAGES ACT (1772).** In 1771, **Prince** Henry Frederick, duke of Cumberland, married Anne Horton even though his brother, King

**George III**, disapproved of the match because the lady was not of royal blood. In response, the monarch persuaded parliament to pass a Royal Marriages Act that required all descendants of King **George II** (excluding descendants of the **princesses** who wed into foreign families) to get the sovereign's approval before marrying. Those aged over 25 who were refused permission could marry a year after giving the **Privy Council** notice of their intention provided that parliament did not pass legislation prohibiting the match.

The measure has been used on a number of occasions, as in the 1950s when **Princess Margaret** (later countess of Snowdon) was told that she could not marry Group-Captain Peter Townsend, who was divorced from his first wife in 1952. On the other hand, it has sometimes been flouted, as in 1793, when **Prince Augustus Frederick, duke of Sussex**, married Lady Augusta Murray in Rome without seeking permission from his father, King George III. The English courts annulled the union the following year, but in 1831 the **prince** broke the rules for a second time by marrying Lady Cecilia Buggin and continued to live with her in **Kensington Palace** even though the wedding was technically invalid. The act has never been repealed or modified, so with each generation, the number of descendants who have to get permission for a wedding increases. *See also* GEORGE IV; LASCELLES, GERALD.

**ROYAL MISTRESSES.** Until comparatively recently, royal marriages were arranged for financial or political reasons, designed to augment coffers or cement dynastic alliances. Affection between the principals was unimportant because the primary function of the female consort was to give her husband an heir. In such circumstances, mistresses were the norm as kings sated their physical passion with partners who were either more attractive or more companionable than their own wives. Such paramours could exert considerable influence over a monarch, but the position was fraught with risk and was usually temporary because lovers could easily be replaced by other women who were attracted by royal power and wealth.

The most obvious historical evidence of these relationships is illegitimate offspring who were acknowledged by the monarch (King **Henry I** had some 20, King **Charles II** 14) and often given titles although they could not succeed to the throne. In modern times, affairs are usually discreet, but in 1936 King **Edward VIII**—who as **prince of Wales** formed several associations with married ladies—abdicated the throne rather than give up his mistress, American-born divorcee Wallis Simpson (later **Wallis, duchess of Windsor**), and 60 years later, **Charles, prince of Wales**, declared that his love for Camilla Parker Bowles (later **Camilla, duchess of Cornwall**) was "non-negotiable" when aides suggested that the public would not accept her as his partner when he became king.

**ROYAL PECULIAR.** Anglican churches that are administratively responsible to the sovereign, rather than to a bishop of the **Church of England**, are
known as royal peculiars. Their "peculiar" jurisdiction dates from the days
of **Anglo-Saxon monarchs**, when individual places of worship could declare
allegiance to a secular ruler rather than to ecclesiastical officials. Only about a
dozen survive, most of them—like **St. George's Chapel** (at **Windsor Castle**)
and **Westminster Abbey**—on, or close to, royal estates. With the exception
of the chapel at **Holyrood Palace**, Edinburgh, all are located in southern
England, particularly around **London**. In 2001, a review group appointed
by Queen **Elizabeth II** under the aegis of the government's Department of
Constitutional Affairs recommended that the royal peculiars' independence
be maintained.

**ROYAL PHILATELIC COLLECTION.** The Royal Philatelic Collection
is the world's most comprehensive accumulation of postal material relating
to Britain and the Commonwealth of Nations. Begun by **Alfred, duke of
Edinburgh and Saxe-Coburg and Gotha**, and expanded by King **George
V**, it is particularly strong in material for 1839–41 (the period when stamps
were first used on mail) and contains airmail covers, proofs, and examples
of prepaid letters as well as stamps. Many of the items are unique, so the
collection cannot be accurately valued. There is a story that, in 1904, a member of the **Royal Household** asked George V whether he knew that "some
damned fool" had paid £1,400 for a single stamp. "Yes," said the king. "I
was the 'damned fool.'" Examples of that rarity—the Mauritius two pence
blue—now fetch over $1 million at auction. The collection is maintained by
a staff based at **St. James's Palace**, but it is not open to public view. *See also*
ROYAL COLLECTION.

**ROYAL PREROGATIVE.** As Britain has become more democratic, the
rights enjoyed by monarchs have been eroded. Those powers that remain are
known as "royal prerogatives." Because they are enshrined in common law,
rather than statute law, there is no definitive list of them, but they include the
power to appoint or dismiss government ministers (including the prime minister), to appoint the head of the British Broadcasting Corporation, to appoint
the senior hierarchy of the **Church of England**, and to award honors, create
new universities, declare war, give **royal assent** to bills, open and dissolve
parliament, and make treaties with foreign states. However, these privileges
are more apparent than real.

The appointment of a prime minister is normally a formality because the
post always goes to the leader of the majority party in the House of Commons
(the lower, elected chamber in the British parliament), and the individual cho-

sen selects the other appointees, including those who will occupy ecclesiastical posts. With the exception of the Order of the Garter, the Order of Merit, the Order of the Thistle, and the Royal Victorian Order, all knighthoods, peerages, and similar honors are likewise conferred on the advice of the prime minister. Royal assent to a bill has not been withheld since 1708. The choice of a date for the dissolution of parliament is made by the government, and the opening of a parliament is a purely ceremonial event. By implication, occasions when a monarch could exercise the use of the prerogative by making an independent decision are likely to arise only in emergencies. *See also* BILL OF RIGHTS; CLAIM OF RIGHT; EDWARD II; ELIZABETH II; wMAGNA CARTA; REGNAL NAME; ROYAL CHARTER.

**ROYAL RESIDENCES.** *See* ALEXANDRA, PRINCESS; BAGSHOT PARK; BALMORAL CASTLE; BUCKINGHAM PALACE; CARLTON HOUSE; CASTLE OF MEY; CLARENCE HOUSE; DUNDONALD CASTLE; DUNFERMLINE ABBEY; ELTHAM PALACE; FALKLAND PALACE; FORT BELVEDERE; FROGMORE; GATCOMBE PARK; HAMPTON COURT PALACE; HATFIELD PALACE; HIGHGROVE; HOLYROOD PALACE; KENNINGTON PALACE; KENSINGTON PALACE; KEW PALACE; LINLITHGOW PALACE; MARLBOROUGH HOUSE; NONSUCH PALACE; OATLANDS PALACE; OSBORNE HOUSE; PLACENTIA, PALACE OF; QUEEN'S HOUSE, GREENWICH; ROXBURGH CASTLE; ROYAL LODGE; SANDRINGHAM HOUSE; SCONE; SHEEN PALACE; SOMERSET HOUSE; STIRLING; ST. JAMES'S PALACE; SUNNINGHILL PARK; THEOBALDS HOUSE; TOWER OF LONDON; WALLINGFORD CASTLE; WESTMINSTER, PALACE OF; WHITEHALL PALACE; WHITE LODGE; WINDSOR CASTLE; WOODSTOCK PALACE.

**ROYAL STANDARD.** The royal standard is the official flag flown by the monarch. It has two forms, one flown in Scotland and one flown elsewhere. In both versions, the flag is divided into four quadrants. In England, Northern Ireland, Wales, and most territories outside the United Kingdom, the sections on the upper left and lower right represent England, with three gold lions, passant guardant (that is, each lion has three paws raised and is facing toward the viewer); the animals are placed vertically on a red field. The section on the upper right has a red lion rampant on a gold field, representing Scotland, and the section on the lower left has a gold harp on a blue field, representing Ireland. There is no representation for Wales, which, from the 16th century, was considered an integral part of England. In the Scottish version of the standard, the lion rampant occupies the upper left and lower right quadrants, the three gold lions occupy the upper right, and the lower left has the gold harp on the blue field. The flags, which in their present forms date from the reign of Queen Victoria, are flown on buildings where the monarch is resident or visiting and on vehicles or aircraft in which he or she is traveling.

Other members of the **royal family** use variations of the standard, but **Prince Philip, duke of Edinburgh**, has a quite different flag that incorporates heraldic references to his ancestry in Denmark and Greece, and **Charles, prince of Wales**, has four standards that are used when he acts in his capacity as **duke of Cornwall**; as **duke of Rothesay** and **lord of the isles**, heir apparent to the king of Scots; and as **prince of Wales**, with a fifth standard for other occasions. There is also a royal standard of Scotland depicting a red lion rampant, with blue tongue and claws, surrounded by a red double border on a yellow field; theoretically it may be flown only by the sovereign's representatives in Scotland and on Scottish **royal residences** when the monarch is absent, but in practice it is much in evidence at international sporting events and has been adopted, in particular, by the "tartan army" that follows Scotland's football team around the globe.

In addition, there are separate royal standards for use in Australia, Barbados, Canada, Jamaica, and New Zealand, which independently recognize the monarch of the United Kingdom as their own sovereign (*see* COMMONWEALTH REALMS). Queen **Elizabeth II** also uses a personal flag with the letter *E* in gold, surmounted by a gold crown and surrounded by a garland of gold roses, on a dark blue field. It was devised at her request in 1960 and symbolizes her role as head of the Commonwealth of Nations. *See also* ROYAL COAT OF ARMS; ROYAL CYPHER; ROYAL WARRANT.

**ROYAL TRAIN.** Queen **Victoria** was the first British monarch to travel by train, making the 17-mile journey from Slough to Paddington Station, **London**, in 23 minutes, at a speed (of 44 miles an hour) that her husband, **Prince Albert of Saxe-Coburg and Gotha**, felt was excessive. The carriages for the modern, claret-liveried royal train were introduced in 1977, when Queen Elizabeth celebrated her silver jubilee on the throne with visits to communities around the United Kingdom. They are pulled by two diesel locomotives, named *Queen's Messenger* and *Royal Sovereign*, that are used on the country's main line rail services when not required by the **royal family**. The queen and her husband, **Prince Philip, duke of Edinburgh**, have individual saloons, each fitted with a bathroom, bedroom, and sitting room. The train is used primarily for overnight travel, which is organized by the crown equerry, an official of the **Royal Household** based in the lord chamberlain's department. *See also* AIR TRAVEL; PRINCE OF WALES; ROYAL YACHT; STATE COACHES.

**ROYAL TRANSPORT.** *See* AIR TRAVEL; ROYAL TRAIN; ROYAL YACHT; STATE COACHES.

**ROYAL WARRANT.** Queen **Elizabeth II**; **Prince Philip, duke of Edinburgh**; and **Charles, prince of Wales**, can each grant a warrant to businesses that have supplied them with goods or services for at least five consecutive years. The recipients may then display the **royal coat of arms** on their products and other material (such as stationery), accompanied by the text "By appointment to [followed by the name of the patron and an indication of the commodity or service provided]." The warrants are granted on the advice of the lord chamberlain (a senior member of the **Royal Household**), are valid for five years, and are renewable but can be revoked at any time. Firms can hold warrants from each of the three grantors but may not hold more than one from any individual.

The first royal warrants were issued in the 15th century (one of the earliest went to printer William Caxton). Now there are more than 800 suppliers, with about 25 being added and the same number deleted each year. Some of the vendors, who charge for their products, have international markets, including Bentley (which supplies cars to Queen Elizabeth and **Prince** Charles), Burberry (which supplies both with clothing), and Land Rover (which supplies vehicles to Prince Philip). Others are small or local concerns, such as Aboyne and Ballater Flowers (which provides fruit and vegetables to Prince Charles when he is at Birkhall, on the **Balmoral Castle** estate).

**ROYAL YACHT.** The first royal yacht was the *Mary*, which was presented to King **Charles II** by the Netherlands to celebrate the **restoration of the monarchy** in 1660. She has had more than 80 successors, including the *Fubbs* (built at Greenwich, on the River Thames, in 1682 and given Charles's pillow name for one of his mistresses, Louise, duchess of Portsmouth); the *Royal Caroline* (which in 1716 carried **Charlotte of Mecklenburg-Strelitz** toward marriage to King **George III** and was renamed *Royal Charlotte* in her honor); the *Alexandra* (built in 1907–8, sold to a Norwegian shipping firm in 1925, and sunk by German aircraft in 1940); and three vessels named *Victoria and Albert* (used in 1843–55, 1855–1900, and 1901–37, respectively).

The most recent in the line of vessels was *Britannia*, which served as a floating base for members of the **royal family** from 1954 to 1997, allowing them to visit remote island communities and seaports around the world. Built at the John Brown shipyard on the River Clyde and weighing 5,769 gross tons, *Britannia* (whose name was chosen by Queen **Elizabeth II**) was commissioned in 1954. She covered over 1 million nautical miles on royal duty, visiting areas such as the Caribbean, Russia, South Africa, and the South

Pacific with a complement of 217 Royal Navy crew and 19 officers, who issued their orders by hand signals and written instructions, not by voice, in order not to disturb their passengers.

In 1997, the newly elected Labour Party government announced that the ship would be withdrawn from service later in the year and that no replacement would be built because money for construction would have to come from the defense budget, which was needed for more important purposes. Queen Elizabeth, who rarely shows emotion in public, was seen to weep as she left the yacht when it was decommissioned on 1 December. It is now a tourist attraction and a venue for corporate entertainment, docked in the redeveloped harbor at Leith, **Edinburgh**'s port. *See also* AIR TRAVEL; ROYAL TRAIN; STATE COACHES.

# S

**SANDRINGHAM HOUSE.** Sandringham, in Norfolk, is the **royal family**'s Christmas home and is a regular base for shooting parties. The estate (then covering some 7,000 acres but now stretching to 20,000) was purchased for £22,000 in 1863 by Queen **Victoria** as a residence for her eldest son, later King **Edward VII**, and the Jacobean-style, two-story, red brick mansion, designed by A. J. Humbert, was completed in 1870. **Diana, princess of Wales**, was born in the grounds at Park House in 1961, and Queen **Alexandra of Denmark** (Edward's consort) died at Sandringham in 1925, as did her son, King **George V** (who described the property as "the place I love better than anywhere else in the world"), in 1936 and her grandson, King **George VI**, in 1952.

Edward opened the gardens to the public in 1908, and Queen **Elizabeth II** has allowed visitors to tour the first-floor rooms of the house itself since 1977. The property includes a country park, extensive apple orchards, a museum (with an eclectic collection of exhibits that includes the clock used to time Queen Elizabeth's racing pigeons), and a racehorse stud farm. *See also* ALBERT VICTOR, PRINCE, DUKE OF CLARENCE AND AVONDALE; ALEXANDER JOHN, PRINCE; GEORGE, PRINCE, DUKE OF KENT; HENRY, PRINCE, DUKE OF GLOUCESTER; JOHN, PRINCE; MARY, PRINCESS ROYAL, COUNTESS OF HAREWOOD.

**SARAH, DUCHESS OF YORK (1959– ).** The duchess of York, former wife of **Prince Andrew, duke of York**, is the daughter of Major Ronald Ferguson (who can count King **Charles II** among his ancestors) and Susan, his first wife. She was born in the Welbeck Nursing Home in **London** on 15 October 1959, played with the children of the **royal family** while she was growing up because she came into contact with them regularly at her father's polo events, and became an accomplished horse rider. Never distinguishing herself academically, she had several jobs after leaving Queen's Secretarial College (London) at the age of 18, working with a public relations firm, an art gallery, and a publisher. She also led an exuberant social life, and the **prince** was clearly attracted by her flamboyant, extroverted personality. The two developed an intimate relationship from 1985, when they attended a party at **Windsor Castle**, and were married in **Westminster Abbey** on 23 July the following year. They have two daughters—**Princess Beatrice of York** (born on 8 August 1988) and **Princess Eugenie of York** (born on 23 March 1990).

Initially, the couple seemed happy, and Sarah was a popular public figure, seen as a youthful antidote to the traditionally distant, stuffy image of royalty. However, the prince's naval duties took him away from home for lengthy periods, and for security reasons his wife could not travel with him. To occupy her time, she involved herself in charity work, learned to fly a helicopter, and wrote a series of children's books, but inevitably she was often lonely. The press noted that she was putting on weight; criticized her clothes sense, comparing her unfavorably to **Diana, princess of Wales**; and speculated about the expenses generated by her jet-setting lifestyle. Frequently, too, she was seen in male company. It was clear that the marriage was under pressure, and it was no surprise when Sarah and Andrew separated in March 1992. They divorced in 1996, and Sarah lost the right to use the title "**her royal highness**."

In the years that followed, the duchess attempted to rebuild her life and regain the public's respect. She worked to pay off debts that allegedly amounted to £4 million, acted as a spokesperson for the American branch of WeightWatchers, took part in a publicity campaign for a personal finance company, and made several television appearances, including a stint deputizing for Larry King on CNN. She also continued to do much work for children's charities, and both she and Andrew have remained good friends, sharing the custody of their daughters. After the divorce, Sarah remained at **Sunninghill Park**, where she had lived with the prince, while she tried to rebuild her finances. In 2004, however, Prince Andrew moved to **Royal Lodge** (Queen **Elizabeth, the queen mother**'s former residence, in the grounds of **Windsor Castle**), and in 2007, when Sunninghill was sold, the duchess bought Dolphin House, next door to her former husband's home. In 2004, Sarah watched a polo match with Andrew, Beatrice, and Queen **Elizabeth II**—the first signs of a reconciliation with her former mother-in-law. Press rumors suggest that **Prince Philip, duke of Edinburgh**, is unwilling to forgive his former daughter-in-law for her peccadilloes, but even so, in 2008 the duchess spent a weekend at **Balmoral Castle** as the queen's guest. However, rumors of money worries continue to dog her and in 2010 she was filmed, clandestinely, by the *News of the World*, as she promised a journalist, posing as a businessman, that she could get him an introduction to her former husband in return for £500,000.

**SAXE-COBURG AND GOTHA, HOUSE OF.** The House of Saxe-Coburg and Gotha (sometimes known as Saxe-Coburg-Gotha) succeeded the **House of Hanover** as the royal house of British monarchs. In 1840, Queen **Victoria**, the last of the Hanoverian sovereigns, married **Albert of Saxe-Coburg and Gotha**. As succession to the crown is determined by patrilineal descent, their eldest son, Albert Edward, became (as **Edward VII**) the first king from the dynasty when his mother died in 1901. In 1910, he was succeeded by his second son, reigning as King **George V**, because his firstborn (**Albert Victor, duke of Clarence and Avondale**) had succumbed to influenza in 1892. In the early years of World War I, George's German heritage led to doubts about his loyalties, so on 17 July 1917, he changed the name of the royal house from the German-sounding "Saxe-Coburg and Gotha" to the more anglicized "Windsor."

**SCONE.** Until the 17th century, **coronation** ceremonies for Scottish monarchs were held on the Moot Hill at Scone, close to the town of Perth. The site developed as a meeting place for leaders of the Pictish kingdom of **Alba**, from which Scotland evolved, and as a focus for Celtic religious rituals. Then, between 1114 and 1122, King **Alexander I** founded an Augustinian monastery that **Malcolm IV** raised to abbey status in 1163 or 1164, because by that time Scone was "the principal seat in our kingdom." The abbey housed the **Stone of Scone**—on which kings were crowned, until **Edward I** of England carted it south in 1296—and also served as a **royal residence** and a meeting hall for the country's parliaments.

In medieval Scotland, however, the king was constantly on the move, traveling from one part of his realm to another, and as monarchs spent increasing amounts of time in such larger, fortified settlements as **Edinburgh** and **Stirling**, Scone's importance declined. The destruction of the abbey by Protestant reformers in 1559 was a further blow to its prestige, but the crowning rituals continued until 1651, when **Charles II** succeeded to the Scottish throne. In 1803, the earl of Mansfield decided to construct a new home on the site and moved the villagers to a location about a mile away. The red sandstone palace that he built is now an important tourist attraction, lying amid extensive landscaped gardens and containing a large collection of furniture and porcelain. *See also* DRUMMOND, ANNABELLA; EDWARD DE BALLIOL; MAUD, COUNTESS OF HUNTINGDON; ROBERT I; ROBERT II; STEWART, JOANNA.

**SCOTTISH REGALIA.** *See* HONOURS OF SCOTLAND.

**SECOND ACT OF SUCCESSION (1536).** *See* SUCCESSION TO THE CROWN: MARRIAGE ACT (1536).

**SECOND BARONS' WAR (1264–1267).** The lengthy reign of King **Henry III** was marked by conflict between the monarch and the English barons. In part, the problems were a result of financial demands because Henry enjoyed an expensive lifestyle but had to finance military campaigns on the European mainland as well, so taxes were high. Also, however, the nobles sought to gain more governmental influence and end the tradition of absolutist rule by the sovereign. In addition, there were personal animosities; Simon de Montfort, who led the dissidents, had married Henry's sister, **Eleanor, countess of Leicester**, in secret and had angered the king as a result.

In 1258 and 1259, through the **Provisions of Oxford** and the **Provisions of Westminster**, the two sides had negotiated an agreement that gave Henry the funds he needed in return for significant concessions to parliament. However, in 1261 the monarch withdrew from the pact, and early in 1264 King Louis IX of **France**, who had been asked to arbitrate, annulled the arrangement. Stung by the loss of their privileges, the barons went to war. Although heavily outnumbered, they captured the king and his son, Edward (later **Edward I**), at the Battle of Lewes on 14 May 1264 and placed them under house arrest. Simon embarked on a series of administrative reforms, which included the election of county and borough representatives to parliament, but several influential supporters, disagreeing with the nature and pace of change, drifted away. Then, in 1265, Edward escaped from custody, formed an army, and outwitted his opponents at Evesham on 4 August, killing Simon and most of the rebels who still rallied to his cause. However, a group of antiroyalists took refuge in Kenilworth Castle and defied all efforts to move them until 1267, when the sides agreed to terms for an end to the struggle. *See also* EDMUND, EARL OF LEICESTER; ELEANOR OF PROVENCE; JOHN DE BALLIOL.

**SECOND SUCCESSION ACT (1536).** *See* SUCCESSION TO THE CROWN: MARRIAGE ACT (1536).

**SECURITY, ACT OF (1703).** In 1701, the English parliament approved the **Act of Settlement**, which provided that if King **William III of England and II of Scotland** and his sister-in-law, Anne (who was expected to succeed him as Queen **Anne**), both died childless, the crown would pass to **Sophia, electress of Hanover** and granddaughter of King **James VI of Scotland and I of England**, or to her Protestant heirs. The Scots were not consulted about the legislation. Piqued, the Scottish parliament passed the Act of Security, which asserted that, unless Scotland's sovereignty and security were ensured, the successor to Queen Anne would not be the same person as the monarch of England, with the implication that the choice could be the Roman Catholic **James Francis Edward Stuart**, only son of the exiled King **James VII and II**. Anne declined to give **royal assent** to the act, so the Scots refused to grant her funding until she acquiesced in 1704. England retaliated the following year with the Alien Act, which called for the repeal of the Act of Security and the suspension of all trade with Scotland, thus aggravating the political sparring that continued until the **union of the parliaments** in 1707.

**SETTLEMENT, ACT OF (1701).** The Act of Settlement, which received **royal assent** on 12 June 1701, is the legal basis on which the **succession to the throne** of the United Kingdom is determined, its passage through the English parliament prompted by the death of **William, duke of Gloucester**, the previous year. Queen **Mary II** had died childless in 1694, and her husband, King **William III of England and II of Scotland**, had never remarried. Gloucester's mother, Anne (daughter of the exiled King **James VII of Scotland and II of England**), was expected to succeed William as Queen **Anne**, but she had suffered 13 miscarriages, had no surviving children, and was in poor health. If she died, leaving no heir or heiress, and the normal principles of male primogeniture were followed, the crown would go to **James Francis Edward Stuart**, James VII and II's son by **Mary of Modena**, but that would mean reversing the results of the **Glorious Revolution** and reinstating a Roman Catholic monarchy that would be abhorrent to most Protestants.

Parliament's solution was the creation of legislation that named **Sophia, electress of Hanover**, daughter of **Elizabeth of Bohemia** and granddaughter of King **James VI and I**, heiress apparent. When she died, the right of succession would pass to "the heirs of her body being Protestant," unless those heirs married Catholics. The act also specified that the monarch "shall join in communion with the **Church of England**" (another measure designed to prevent communicants with the Church of Rome from wearing the crown) and that if the sovereign was not a native of England, he or she could not, without parliamentary consent, require English armies to fight wars in defense of "any dominions or territories which do not belong to the crown of England." Other clauses prevented a king or queen from traveling abroad without parliamentary approval and from dismissing judges.

Sophia was certainly the highest-ranking Protestant in the line of succession to the throne, but in selecting her, the act overlooked the claims of 57 Catholics who had closer blood relations to the crown. In recent years, some individuals have voluntarily excluded themselves from the succession in order to marry Catholics, notably **Prince Michael of Kent** (who was 15th in line prior to his wedding to Baroness Marie-Christine von Reibnitz [**Princess Michael of Kent**] in 1978) and **George Windsor, earl of St. Andrews** (who was 25th when he married Sylvana Tomaselli [Sylvana Windsor, countess of St. Andrews] 10 years later). George Windsor's mother, **Katharine, duchess of Kent**, converted to Catholicism in 1994, but her husband—**Prince Edward, duke of Kent** and first cousin of Queen **Elizabeth II**—was not excluded from the succession because she was an adherent of the Church of England when they took their marriage vows in 1961.

Proposals to repeal the Act of Settlement are made periodically on the grounds that they discriminate against a specific religious group. Cardinal Cormac Murphy-O'Connor, the leader of the Roman Catholic community in England, complained in 2002 that **Prince William of Wales**, elder son of **Charles, prince of Wales**, the **heir apparent**, "can marry by law a Hindu, a Buddhist, anyone, but not a Roman Catholic" and argued for change, but others make a case for the status quo. In particular, constitutionalists point out that the pope, as head of the Catholic Church, claims a universal authority, so a British Roman Catholic monarch would owe allegiance to a superior earthly power, and that would imply a loss of the country's sovereignty. Moreover, a Roman Catholic could not act as supreme governor of the Church of England or be crowned at a Church of England **coronation** (so church and state would have to be separated), and the 15 independent countries that recognize the British sovereign as their own head of state (*see* COMMONWEALTH REALM) would have to approve any action that could affect their own constitutions. *See also* GEORGE I; PHILLIPS, PETER; SECURITY, ACT OF; STUART, HOUSE OF; WINDSOR, LORD NICHOLAS.

**SEYMOUR, JANE (1508 or 1509–1537).** As King **Henry VIII** tired of **Anne Boleyn**, he turned to Jane Seymour, who became his third wife but died soon after giving birth to the son and heir (later King **Edward VI**) that the monarch craved. The eldest daughter of Sir John and Lady Margaret Seymour, she was born in 1508 or 1509 and became a **lady-in-waiting** at the royal court, initially to **Catherine of Aragon** (Henry's first wife) and then to Anne. Henry may have become interested in her potential as a consort when he visited her parents' home at Wolf Hall in Wiltshire in 1535. Apparently she resisted his sexual overtures, and scholars still debate whether that resistance was part of a deliberate plot to ensure the departure of a queen from whom Henry was already estranged. In May 1536, Anne was charged with adultery, incest, and treason. On May 19, she was **beheaded**, and on the following day, Henry and Jane were betrothed. They married at **Whitehall Palace** in **London** on May 30.

Jane made little effort to influence political affairs, but she enforced much greater formality on her household than her predecessor had done, eliminating the flamboyance and extravagance that had characterized Anne's lifestyle. She appears, also, to have been popular with the English people and to have effected a reconciliation between Henry and Mary (later **Mary I**), his daughter by Catherine. By the spring of 1537, she was pregnant, and on 12 October, she gave birth to the boy who her husband believed would ensure an orderly **succession to the throne**. However, Jane fell ill with puerperal fever and died at **Hampton Court Palace** only 12 days later; she was buried in **St. George's Chapel** at **Windsor Castle**. Her husband was laid beside her in 1547. Over that decade after Jane's passing, Henry continued to favor his former queen's family; one brother, Edward Seymour, ultimately became Lord Protector (in effect, **regent**) after Henry's death, and another, Thomas, married **Catherine Parr**, the king's sixth and last wife. *See also* SUCCESSION TO THE CROWN: MARRIAGE ACT (1536).

**SHEEN PALACE.** Sheen, located to the southwest of the present-day **London** metropolitan area, was a popular **royal residence** from the early 14th century to the middle of the 17th century. In 1327, King **Edward III** gave the building to his mother, **Isabella of France**. In 1383, **Richard II** made it his principal home, but 12 years later, distraught at the death of his wife, **Anne of Bohemia**, he razed it to the ground. **Henry V** began a rebuilding program in 1414, but fire destroyed most of the structure in 1497, so **Henry VII** rebuilt again, naming the new edifice Richmond Palace after Richmond Castle, a favorite base in Yorkshire.

In 1502, **Margaret Tudor** was betrothed to King **James IV** of Scotland at Richmond, and in 1509, Henry VII died there. **Anne of Cleves**, the fourth wife of **Henry VIII**, acquired the palace when she was divorced from the king in 1540, and **Princess** Elizabeth (later **Elizabeth I**) was held captive there in 1554 (later, she spent much time on the estate voluntarily, hunting the deer that roamed the grounds). John Harington installed a flush toilet in 1596, but the queen refused to use it because of the noise. After **Charles I**'s execution in 1649, most of the building was torn down, though the gatehouse and some other parts of the structure can still be seen. *See also* HENRY, DUKE OF CORNWALL; STUART, ANNE; STUART, CHARLES, DUKE OF KENDAL; STUART, EDGAR, DUKE OF CAMBRIDGE; STUART, JAMES, DUKE OF CAMBRIDGE; TUDOR, MARY, QUEEN OF FRANCE.

**SIMNEL, LAMBERT (c1475–c1535).** Simnel was the unfortunate focus of efforts to unseat King **Henry VII**. Little is known of his background (even his name is not confirmed by historians), but it is clear that, at the age of about 12, he fell under the influence of a priest named Richard Symonds or Roger Simon. Symonds claimed that the boy was Edward, earl of Warwick and **Edward IV**'s nephew, whom **Richard III** had named as his **heir apparent** in 1484 but who was rumored to have died after being incarcerated by Henry in the **Tower of London** the following year. Simnel was taken to Ireland, where opposition to Henry was strong, and was crowned King Edward VI in Dublin on 24 May 1487. With the support of Flemish mercenaries recruited by Margaret of York (daughter of Richard, **duke of York** [1411–1460]) and troops raised in Ireland, rebels fighting in his name brought an army to England, landing in Lancashire on 5 June. They were heavily defeated by royalist troops at the **Battle of Stoke Field** 11 days later, but Henry condemned Simnel only to menial work in his kitchens, apparently realizing that the child was an innocent puppet of men with political motives. The date of his death is unknown but was probably sometime between 1525 and 1535. *See also* WARBECK, PERKIN.

**SIMPSON, WALLIS (1896–1986).** *See* WALLIS, DUCHESS OF WINDSOR.

**SOMERSET HOUSE.** Somerset House, now in central **London**, was a popular **royal residence**—particularly with England's queens—from 1552 to 1692. In its initial form, it was built from 1547 to 1551 by Edward Seymour, duke of Somerset and elder brother of **Jane Seymour** (King **Henry VIII**'s third wife). It was acquired by the crown when Somerset was executed for treason in 1552. **Elizabeth I** stayed in the property regularly before she became queen (though she was probably more attached to **Hatfield Palace**), and while she was on the throne, she used it to accommodate visiting diplomats. **Anne of Denmark**, consort of King **James VI and I**, established court there, entertaining in lavish style and participating in many of the masques that she staged. She also employed architect Inigo Jones to extend the property, forming a three-sided courtyard, the construction of which caused her husband considerable financial headaches.

By the time Anne died in 1619, the building was known as Denmark House, and it retained that name while it was occupied by **Henrietta Maria of France**, consort of **Charles I**. She too extended the building, notably adding a richly decorated chapel where she could say mass and which, because it was a place for Roman Catholic worship in a royal palace in staunchly Protestant England, did nothing to help the king's popularity. Christopher Wren supervised further expansion and refurbishment in 1685, when **Catherine of Braganza** made it her principal home following the death of her husband, King **Charles II**. After she left in 1692, it was little used by the **royal family**, and by the first quarter of the 18th century, it was becoming derelict. In 1775, however, parliament passed legislation authorizing construction of a new Somerset House for use as public offices, and Sir William Chambers was employed to design the building that presently stands on the site, providing a focus for the visual arts in London.

**SOPHIA DOROTHEA OF CELLE (1666–1726).** King **George I**'s treatment of his wife, Sophia Dorothea, did much to contribute to his unpopularity after his accession to the British throne in 1714. She was born at Celle Castle, in lower Saxony, on 15 September 1666 to George William, duke of Brunswick-Lüneburg, and his mistress, French-born Eléonore Desmier d'Olbreuse. Her parents had committed themselves to a form of legal union the previous year and eventually married in 1676.

Sixteen-year-old Sophia's wedding to George, her cousin, on 21 November 1682 at Celle, was no love match, negotiated between her father and his brother (her future father-in-law, **Ernest Augustus, elector of Hanover**) as a way of ensuring that the Celle estates would remain in family hands. When Sophia first heard of the scheme, she apparently retorted that she would not marry that "pig snout," but she had little option, and her apprehension was justified. The two argued regularly and quickly sought escape in the arms of others. Sophie turned to Count Philip Christophe von Königsmark, initially undoubtedly in a platonic friendship, though later letters (which may have been forged) suggest that the relationship became more physically intimate as the two planned to escape Hanover and live together.

On 1 July 1694, in circumstances that are still unclear, the count vanished, and on 28 December, George was granted a divorce. Politically, however, the Hanoverians faced problems. There was a real possibility that Sophia would attempt to malign her former husband's character, and if she was successful, her criticisms would provide support for the Roman Catholic supporters of King **James VII and II**, who had been deposed in 1688–89 but whose descendants still claimed the crowns of England and Scotland (*see* JACOBITE REBELLIONS). In order to prevent her from making public comments, her father and father-in-law confined her to a house at Ahlden. Even after her former husband became king of Great Britain in 1714, she remained in prison and eventually died there (scholars have suggested gall stones, a heart attack, liver failure, or stroke as the cause) on 13 November 1726 after more than 30 years of confinement. She was buried in the church at Celle.

Sophia left two children. Her son, who became King **George II**, resented the treatment meted out to his mother and sided with his father's political opponents as a result. Her daughter, **Sophia Dorothea, Queen of Prussia**, married Frederick William I of Prussia and was the mother of Frederick the Great.

**SOPHIA DOROTHEA, QUEEN OF PRUSSIA (1687–1757).** Sophia, the only daughter and younger child of King **George I** and **Sophia Dorothea**

**of Celle**, was born in Hanover on 16 March 1687. On 28 November 1706, she married Crown Prince Frederick William of Prussia, merging two of the great dynasties of Protestant Europe. She became queen of Prussia when her husband succeeded to the throne in 1713, the year before her father, as a result of the **Act of Settlement** (1701), took the British crown.

From 1707 until 1739, Sophia and Frederick had 14 children, 10 of whom survived to adulthood, including Frederick (who was born in 1712, succeeded his father in 1740, and is often known as Frederick the Great) and Louisa Ulrika (who was born in 1720, married Adolf Frederick of Sweden—later King Adolf Frederick—in 1744, and gave birth to their three sons, two of whom followed their father to the throne). Sophia died on 28 June 1757 and was buried at Potsdam. *See also* AMELIA, PRINCESS (1711–1786).

**SOPHIA, ELECTRESS OF HANOVER (1630–1714).** Sophia, mother of King **George I**, was born in The Hague on 4 October 1630. Her father, Frederick V, was elector palatine, so his daughter is sometimes known as Sophia of the Palatinate. Her mother, **Elizabeth of Bohemia**, was the eldest daughter of **James VI of Scotland and I of England**, who had arranged the match with Frederick in a deliberate effort to strengthen ties between his own realm and the Protestant communities in northern Europe. On 30 September 1658, Sophia (having been rejected by her cousin, later King **Charles II**) married **Ernest Augustus, elector of Hanover**, in Heidelberg and over the next 16 years they had seven children who survived to reach adulthood.

On 30 July 1700, **William, duke of Gloucester**—the last surviving child of Anne, princess of Denmark, **heiress apparent** to the English and Scottish thrones and later Queen **Anne**—died suddenly at **Windsor Castle**. Anne, in poor health and having suffered many miscarriages, was unlikely to bear another son, so in 1701 the English parliament, determined to keep the throne securely in Protestant hands, passed an **Act of Settlement** that named Sophia **heiress presumptive** and gave the rights of succession, on her death, to "the heirs of her body being Protestant," unless those heirs married Roman Catholics.

The electress was undoubtedly the first Protestant in the line of **succession to the throne**, her 11 older brothers and sisters having predeceased her, but the legislation overlooked the claims of 57 Catholics with closer blood relations to the crown, including **James Francis Edward Stuart**, the son of the deposed King **James VII and II**. From the time of Anne's accession to the throne, Sophia took a close interest in English affairs—too close for Anne's liking—but Sophia collapsed and died at Herrenhausen on 28 May 1714 at the age of 83, after running to escape a downpour of rain, so she never became queen. When Anne passed away just two months later, on 1 August, the British crown went to Sophia's eldest son, who ruled as King **George I**, the first of five monarchs with sovereignty over both Britain and Hanover. Other than George, none of the electress's sons had children, but through Sophia Charlotte, her only daughter, she also became the ancestress of kings of Prussia.

**SOPHIA OF THE PALATINATE (1630–1714).** *See* SOPHIA, ELECTRESS OF HANOVER.

**SOPHIA, PRINCESS (1777–1848).** Sophia, born at **Buckingham Palace** on 2 November 1777, was the fifth daughter (and the twelfth of 15 children) in the family of King **George III** and **Caroline of Mecklenburg-Strelitz**. The king and queen raised their girls in an environment that restricted contact with males outside the **Royal Household**, conditions that almost guaranteed rumors of illicit liaisons and sexual scandal. In the last years of the 18th century, Sophia developed an attachment to Thomas Garth, the king's chief equerry and more than twice the **princess**'s age. On 11 August 1800, she gave birth to a son who was named Thomas and was raised by Garth in Dorset. However, at the same time, rumors were circulating of an incestuous affair involving Sophia and her older brother, **Ernest Augustus, king of Hanover**. It is not known whether the tales were scurrilous inventions by Ernest's numerous political enemies, but inevitably historians have speculated on whether he was the boy's father.

Some 30 years later, young Garth, then an army captain, attempted to blackmail members of the **royal family** in an effort to get his considerable debts paid off and to acquire payment in return for silence about his origins, but Sophia never publicly revealed details about her lover and never married. She became blind during the last decade of her life and died at her home in Vicarage Place, **London**, on 27 May 1848. In accordance with her wishes, she was buried at Kensal Green Cemetery, in the northwest of the city, so that she could be near her brother, **Prince Augustus Frederick, duke of Sussex**, who was one of her closest confidants. Later, investigations revealed that much of her wealth had been stolen by Sir John Conroy, her financial advisor, who also caused the royal family headaches as a result of his influence on **Princess Victoria of Saxe-Coburg-Saalfield**, Queen **Victoria**'s mother.

**SOPHIE, COUNTESS OF WESSEX (1965– ).** Sophie—the wife of **Prince Edward, earl of Wessex** and the youngest of Queen **Elizabeth II**'s four children—was born on 20 January 1965 at the Radcliffe Infirmary, Oxford, to tire salesman Christopher Rhys-Jones and his secretary wife, Mary. She was educated at Dulwich College Preparatory School and Kent College for Girls, in

Pembury, before taking secretarial classes at West Kent College in Tonbridge and then developing a career in public relations. She met the **prince** in 1993, when they were both involved in planning a charity real tennis event, and married him in **St. George's Chapel** at **Windsor Castle** on 19 June 1999.

The couple has two children—Lady Louise Windsor (born on 8 November 2003) and James, viscount Severn (born on 17 December 2007). Both births were by caesarian section, the first a month premature after an emergency operation when the placenta separated from the countess's uterus.

Sophie, although widely considered as making a positive contribution to the **royal family**'s sometimes tarnished image, has not been entirely successful at avoiding tabloid headlines. In 1999, just weeks before her wedding, the *Sun* printed a decade-old photograph of television presenter Chris Tarrant lifting her bikini top and exposing her breasts; the **Buckingham Palace** press office described the publication as "premeditated cruelty," and public outrage forced the newspaper to issue an apology. Then, in 2001, a *News of the World* reporter obtained recordings of her criticizing Prime Minister Tony Blair and appearing to use her royal connections as a means of obtaining clients for the public relations company that she co-owned. The same paper also quoted her denial of persistent rumors that Prince Edward was gay. In 2002, the earl and countess both gave up their business interests to concentrate on royal duties. In addition to a program of visits, the countess has supported numerous charitable organizations, particularly those that care for children, physically disabled individuals, and people with communication problems.

**ST. ALBANS, FIRST BATTLE OF (22 May 1455).** The opening conflict of the **Wars of the Roses** ended with a resounding victory for **Richard, duke of York (1411–1460)**, who was able to capture King **Henry VI**. Henry's troops had occupied the town of St. Albans, some 20 miles north of **London**, but were caught by surprise when York's army attacked. Several leading members of the ruling **House of Lancaster**—including Edmund, duke of Somerset, and Henry Percy, earl of Northumberland—were killed, so the Yorkists were able to keep the monarch in captivity for several months while Richard took control of government.

**ST. ALBANS, SECOND BATTLE OF (17 February 1461).** As a result of her victory at St. Albans on 17 February 1461, queen consort **Margaret of Anjou** was able to release her husband, King **Henry VI**, from the hands of his Yorkist captors, but her army failed to capitalize on its success and was soon on the defensive again. The **Wars of the Roses** between Henry (of the **House of Lancaster**) and **Richard, duke of York (1411–1460)** (of the **House of York**), had begun some six years earlier. Henry was taken prisoner on 10 July 1460 at the **Battle of Northampton**. Then, five months later, on 30 December, Richard was killed at **Wakefield**, and the Lancastrians, hoping for further success, marched toward **London**. A Yorkist force, commanded by Richard Neville, earl of Warwick, advanced to meet them at St. Albans, 20 miles north of the capital, but was outflanked, taken by surprise, and forced to retreat. Henry, who was subject to frequent bouts of mental illness, was apparently found sitting under a tree, singing. Rather than continue on to London, where they were undoubtedly unpopular, the Lancastrians withdrew, and on 4 March the citizens in the capital proclaimed Edward, Richard's son, king (as **Edward IV**). Little over a month later, he routed the Lancastrians at **Towton**, forcing Henry and Margaret to flee to Scotland for safety.

**ST. BRICE'S DAY MASSACRE (13 November 1002).** In the final years of the first century AD, Anglo-Saxon England was regularly subjected to attacks from Viking invaders. **Aethelred the Unready**, the English king, believed that Scandinavian (and primarily Danish) settlers were helping these raiders as they marched through the country, so he ordered that "all the Danish men who were in England" should be killed on St. Brice's Day (13 November), 1002. Most scholars accept that it would be impossible to carry out such an edict fully, but there is little doubt that many people died in towns where the Danes had congregated. In Oxford, for example, a church where Scandinavians had taken refuge was burned down. Aethelred's policy of extermination proved counterproductive, however. Gunhilde, the sister of King **Sweyn** of Denmark, was one of those who died in the Oxford flames, and Sweyn sought revenge, ultimately taking the English crown and forcing Aethelred into exile in 1013.

**ST. GEORGE'S CHAPEL.** St. George's, the church in **Windsor Castle**, is used regularly as a place of worship. Unusually for modern British religious sites, it is both collegiate (that is, services are organized by a college of canons) and a **royal peculiar** (making it responsible directly to the monarch rather than to a bishop of the **Church of England**).

The College of St. George was founded by King **Edward III** in 1348, and its chapel (originally dedicated to **Edward the Confessor**) became the spiritual base of the Order of the Garter, the senior community of knights. The building was much expanded from 1475 to 1528, during the reigns of **Edward IV**, **Henry VII**, and **Henry VIII**, but it was plundered by antiroyalist troops in 1642–43 and required extensive refurbishment after **Charles II** became king in 1660 (*see* RESTORATION OF THE MONARCHY). Under Queen **Victoria**'s supervision, a ceremonial entrance was erected, and a royal mausoleum was constructed underneath the choir.

Several of Victoria's children and grandchildren were married in St. George's, including King **Edward VII**, who wed **Alexandra of Denmark** on 10 March 1863. More recently, wedding ceremonies were held for **Prince Edward, earl of Wessex** and the youngest child of Queen **Elizabeth II**, and Sophie Rhys-Jones (*see* SOPHIE, COUNTESS OF WESSEX) on 19 June 1999, and for **Peter Phillips**, the only son of **Anne, princess royal (1950– )**, and Canadian-born Autumn Kelly on 17 May 2008.

The lengthy list of monarchs and other members of the **royal family** interred in the building includes kings Edward IV and Edward VII (buried at the altar in 1483 and 1910, respectively); Henry VIII and **Charles I** (in the choir in 1547 and 1649); **George III, George IV**, and **William IV** (in the royal vault in 1820, 1830, and 1837), **George V** (near the west door in 1936), and **George VI** (in the memorial chapel named after him in 1952). **Princess Margaret, countess of Snowdon**, and **Elizabeth, the queen mother**, were laid to rest beside George VI in 2002. *See also* ADELAIDE OF SAXE-MEININGEN, PRINCESS; ADOLPHUS, PRINCE, DUKE OF CAMBRIDGE; ALBERT VICTOR, PRINCE, DUKE OF CLARENCE AND AVONDALE; ALFRED, PRINCE; AMELIA, PRINCESS (1783–1810); ARTHUR, PRINCE, DUKE OF CONNAUGHT AND STRATHEARN; AUGUSTA SOPHIA, PRINCESS; CHARLOTTE AUGUSTA, PRINCESS; CHARLOTTE OF MECKLENBURG-STRELITZ; EDWARD, PRINCE, DUKE OF KENT AND STRATHEARN; ELIZABETH OF CLARENCE, PRINCESS; FREDERICK, PRINCE, DUKE OF YORK AND ALBANY; GEORGE, DUKE OF BEDFORD; HENRY VI; LEOPOLD, PRINCE, DUKE OF ALBANY; LOUISE, PRINCESS, DUCHESS OF ARGYLL; MARY OF TECK; MARY, PRINCESS, DUCHESS OF GLOUCESTER; OCTAVIUS, PRINCE; ROYAL LODGE; SEYMOUR, JANE; STATE COACHES; TAYLOR, LADY HELEN.

**ST. JAMES'S PALACE.** Standing at the western end of Pall Mall in central **London**, St. James's is located on the site of a medieval leper hospital. King **Henry VIII** bought the property in 1531, gave the inmates a pension, demolished the buildings, and erected a residence in their place. It has been much used by royalty ever since. **Elizabeth I** slept there while the Spanish Armada sailed up the English Channel in 1588, **Charles I** stayed there in 1649 the night before he was executed, **Charles II** made it his main home (refurbishing it so that he could provide rooms for his several mistresses), and **William III of England and II of Scotland** employed Christopher Wren (the architect of St. Paul's Cathedral) to design new apartments of state. Queen **Anne** and her successors (**George I, George II**, and **George III**) spent much time there, and George III's son (the future **George IV**) was married there in 1795 (his bride, **Caroline of Brunswick-Wolfenbüttel**, reported that he was so drunk after the wedding celebrations that he collapsed, stupefied, into a fireplace and lay there until morning).

From 1698 (when **Whitehall Palace** was destroyed by fire) until 1837 (when Queen **Victoria** moved into **Buckingham Palace**), the building was the principal **royal residence** in Britain, which is why foreign ambassadors are accredited to the **Court of St. James's**. It is now the London base for **Anne, the princess royal (1950– )**, and for **Princess Alexandra**. It also houses the **royal philatelic collection** and provides office facilities for many of the administrators required to keep the monarchy functioning.

With the exception of the Chapel Royal (where services are held on Sunday mornings from October until Good Friday) and the Queen's Chapel (where they are held from Easter Sunday until the end of July), none of the rooms—which contain fine carvings by Grinling Gibbons (who also worked on the choir stalls, thrones, and organ screens in St. Paul's), door cases by William Kent (*see also* KENSINGTON PALACE), and tapestries woven for Charles II—are open to the public. *See also* ANNE, PRINCESS ROYAL (1709–1759); AUGUSTA OF SAXE-GOTHA, PRINCESS OF WALES; CAROLINE ELIZABETH, PRINCESS; CAROLINE OF BRANDENBURG-ANSBACH; CHARLOTTE OF MECKLENBURG-STRELITZ; CHARLOTTE, PRINCESS ROYAL, QUEEN OF WURTEMBURG; CLARENCE HOUSE; ELIZABETH OF CLARENCE, PRINCESS; FREDERICK, PRINCE, DUKE OF YORK AND ALBANY; FREDERICK, PRINCE OF WALES; GEORGE V; GEORGE, PRINCE OF DENMARK; GEROGE WILLIAM, PRINCE; GILMAN, LADY ROSE; HENRY, PRINCE, DUKE OF GLOUCESTER; HYDE, ANNE; JAMES VII OF SCOTLAND AND II OF ENGLAND; MARY I; MARY HENRIETTA, PRINCESS ROYAL, PRINCESS OF ORANGE; MARY OF TECK; OLDENBURG, MARY; STUART, CATHERINE; STUART, CATHERINE LAURA; STUART, CHARLES, DUKE OF CAMBRIDGE (1660–1661); STUART, CHARLES, DUKE OF CAMBRIDGE (1677); STUART, CHARLES, DUKE OF KENDAL; STUART, EDGAR, DUKE OF CAMBRIDGE; STUART, HENRIETTA; STUART, HENRY FREDERICK, PRINCE OF WALES; STUART, JAMES FRANCIS EDWARD; VICTORIA, PRINCESS ROYAL, GERMAN EMPRESS; WINDSOR, ALEXANDER, EARL OF ULSTER.

**STAMFORD BRIDGE, BATTLE OF (25 September 1066).** The Scandinavian army's defeat by Anglo-Saxon forces at Stamford Bridge, Yorkshire, ended Viking efforts to add England to an already extensive empire. In 1038 or 1039, **Harthacanute**—who ruled England from 1040 to 1042—agreed with Magnus I of Norway that if either of them died the other would be his successor. Magnus outlived Harthacanute, so two decades later Harald Hardråde, king of Norway and Magnus's uncle, cited the agreement as the basis of a claim to the English throne when **Edward the Confessor** died in 1066, but the **witan** (the royal council of advisors which elected English monarchs) preferred Harold Godwinson, who ruled as **Harold II**.

Incensed, Harald offered Tostig, Harold's brother, a one-third share in the kingdom in return for his support, and the two men launched an invasion, landing 15,000 men on the east coast of England in September 1066. Initially they made progress, destroying the coastal town of Scarborough and successfully overcoming an Anglo-Saxon force led by a group of northern nobles at Fulford, two miles south of York, on 20 September. Harold, however, was determined to hold on to his realm. He gathered an army in **London** and marched it 200 miles north in just four days, taking the Scandinavian commanders by surprise at Stamford Bridge and killing both Harald and Tostig. The Vikings who survived the conflict were allowed to return home, but Harold was given no respite because his southern shores were being threatened by William, duke of Normandy (later **William I of England**). Marshalling his troops again, he led them back south to Hastings, where he died less than three weeks later during an unsuccessful struggle to resist the challenge of an invader much mightier than Hardråde (*see* HASTINGS, BATTLE OF).

**STATE COACHES.** Over 100 coaches, carriages, and cars ferry members of the **royal family** and other participants to ceremonial events and on official business. The gold state coach, first used by King **George III** at the **state opening of parliament** in 1762, is the oldest. Entirely covered in gold leaf and richly decorated with cherubs, lions, palm trees, and other symbols, it is almost 12 feet high, weighs nearly four tons, and requires eight horses to pull it. It has been used at every **coronation** since that of King **George IV** in 1821. The blue and black Irish state coach, built for Benjamin Guinness, the first elected mayor of Dublin, in 1852, usually provides the monarch's transport to modern state openings of parliament. Queen **Victoria** saw the carriage when she visited Ireland in 1852, liked it, and bought it for £700.

In Scotland, the most usual form of transport is the Scottish state coach, which was built in 1830 for **Prince Adolphus, duke of Cambridge**, the favorite son of King George III, and was extensively refurbished in 1968–69. The more modern Australian state coach was gifted to Queen Elizabeth II in 1988 by the people of Australia to celebrate the country's bicentenary. With the comfort of air conditioning and electric windows, it was first seen at the state opening of parliament in that year. In 2007, state coach *Britannia* was added to the fleet. Built in Australia by J. W. Frecklington, who was also responsible for the Australian state coach, it incorporates material from many historic British ships and buildings, including **Edinburgh** Castle, **St. George's Chapel**, **Westminster Abbey**, and the *Mary Rose*, King **Henry VIII**'s flagship.

The coaches are serviced in the Royal Mews at **Buckingham Palace**, along with other carriages, 34 horses (mainly Cleveland Bays and Windsor Greys), and eight claret-colored limousines—three Daimlers, three Rolls-Royces (the oldest a Phantom IV dating from 1950), and two Bentleys. The work of the 38 chauffeurs, coachmen, and grooms is coordinated by the crown equerry, an official of the **Royal Household** attached to the lord chamberlain's office. The Mews, originally built in 1825 to designs by John Nash but much changed since then, are opened to the public for most of the period from April to October. *See also* AIR TRAVEL; ROYAL TRAIN; ROYAL YACHT.

**STATE OPENING OF PARLIAMENT.** The opening session of the British parliament, in October or November, is a major event in the royal calendar, marked by much ceremony. At the beginning of the day, a representative of the sovereign formally takes a member of parliament hostage as a means of guaranteeing his or her safety (a reminder of the days when ruler and ruled were frequently at odds). The monarch then drives from **Buckingham Palace** to the **Palace of Westminster**, usually in the horse-drawn Irish **state coach**, and, wearing the imperial state crown (one of the **crown jewels of the United Kingdom**), walks to the throne in the House of Lords, parliament's upper chamber. (Since 1642, when King **Charles I** entered the House of Commons in an attempt to arrest five of its members, lawmakers have observed a convention that the sovereign is not admitted to the lower chamber.)

When the royal procession is over and the sovereign is seated, the gentleman usher of the black rod makes his way from the Lords to the Commons. The doors there are slammed shut, refusing him entry in an act that symbolizes the freedom of members of parliament from royal control, but after knocking three times, he is admitted and announces that the monarch "commands this honourable House to attend [her or his] majesty immediately in the house of peers." The elected representatives of the monarch's subjects then walk in pairs (casually, rather than in formal procession) to the Lords, where they bow to the sovereign, who reads a "speech from the throne," prepared by ministers and written on vellum, that outlines the government's program for the coming session. When the address—delivered in a monotone in order to emphasize the head of state's political neutrality—is over, members of parliament bow for a second time and then walk back to the Commons, where they will spend several days debating the legislative proposals. After the monarch has left the Lords to make the return journey to Buckingham Palace, the peers, too, discuss the plans that were presented to them.

The pageantry and ceremony associated with the event, apart from being a considerable tourist attraction, are important because they emphasize continuity over time and heighten the impression of stable administration. However, the symbolism, too, is significant because the state opening of parliament is one of the few occasions when the three branches of government—the executive (represented by the monarch), the judiciary (represented by the senior judges), and the lawmakers (the members of both chambers of Britain's bicameral parliament)—are gathered in one place, thus stressing that each has an important role to play in maintaining an ordered society.

**STEPHEN (c1096–1154).** Often considered the last king of England from the **House of Normandy**, Stephen succeeded **Henry I** to the throne in 1135 but spent much of his 19-year reign embroiled in civil war as he attempted to prevent his cousin, **Matilda**, from taking his crown.

Henry and his wife, **Matilda of Scotland**, had produced two children—Matilda (born in 1102) and **William the Aetheling** (born the following year). William was expected to succeed his father as king but drowned in 1120. As Henry aged and failed to produce another heir, he made his nobles swear that they would accept Matilda as their queen, but they took their oaths reluctantly. When he died in 1135, they welcomed Stephen's assertion that the monarch had changed his mind on his deathbed and had named his nephew, rather than his daughter, as successor. The nobles' decision to renege on their promise was understandable. Neither the kingdom of England nor the duchy of Normandy had ever had a queen or duchess who ruled other than as consort of a king or duke. Moreover, rulers were expected to lead their armies in battle, and that was not a task traditionally undertaken by women. Also, Matilda had originally been married to **Henry, king of Germany and Holy Roman Emperor**, and had spent all her teenage years at his court, speaking German and absorbing German manners. Stephen, on the other hand, had been raised in **Blois**, which bordered Normandy, and had been reared at Henry's court in **London**, so he understood Norman customs. In addition, many of the barons distrusted Matilda's second husband, **Geoffrey, count of Anjou**, who was regarded more as an enemy than an ally.

Stephen, the son of **Adela, countess of Blois** (daughter of **William I of England**, also known as William the Conqueror), and **Stephen Henry, count of Blois**, was a popular, charming man, strongly supported by the church, but he proved to be a political disaster, unable either to control the nobles or to maintain law and order. His weaknesses became evident soon after his **coronation** in December 1135 because within months he had conceded much of northern England to an invading Scottish army even though he had a large force at his command. Then, in 1137, he failed to take advantage of unrest in Normandy to wrest the duchy from Matilda. In 1138, Robert of Gloucester, having initially pledged allegiance to Stephen but became frustrated by the king's ineptitude, changed sides and openly supported Matilda's claim to the throne. Others followed, and, encouraged, Matilda traveled to England the following year. Stephen, instead of imprisoning her, courteously provided her with an escort to Robert's castle at Bristol, which speedily became a focus of antiroyalist activity as the country slipped into civil war, with nobles exercising authority over their own lands and often failing to keep the peace.

Early in 1141, it seemed as though the situation would be resolved because Stephen was taken prisoner and his cousin prepared for her coronation in London. However, Matilda's arrogance offended many of her supporters, and her refusal to reduce Londoners' taxes turned many potential allies against her. She arrived to find the gates of the city barred against her entrance. Shortly afterward, Robert of Gloucester was captured and was only returned to Matilda in exchange for Stephen's release. A lengthy period of stalemate followed, with neither side able to gain the upper hand, but in 1147 Robert died, and Matilda, deprived of her strongest ally, retreated to Normandy.

That retreat did not imply an end to the struggle, however. In 1153, Matilda's son, Henry of Anjou (later King **Henry II**) invaded England with a small army, determined to claim his inheritance. By that time, Stephen had no heart for a fight. His barons were warring with each other, his wife (**Matilda of Boulogne**) had died the previous year, and his elder surviving son (**Eustace, count of Boulogne**), who was being groomed as his heir, had passed away a few months after Henry's arrival.

In November 1153, king and claimant reached an agreement that Stephen would retain the throne until his death and that Henry would be recognized as his heir. The young man did not have long to wait. Stephen died at Dover Priory less than a year later, on 25 October 1154, and was buried beside his wife and son at Faversham Abbey, which he and Matilda of Boulogne had founded in 1147. The *Anglo-Saxon Chronicle* recorded that "In the days of this King there was nothing but strife, evil and robbery," so "never did a country endure greater misery." A brave, chivalrous, and kindhearted man, Stephen never had the ruthlessness to rule a Norman nobility bent on self-aggrandizement. *See also* ADA DE WARENNE; BALDWIN OF BOULOGNE; MARIE, COUNTESS OF BOULOGNE; MATILDA OF BLOIS; PHILIPPA OF HAINAULT; TOWER OF LONDON; WILLIAM OF BLOIS.

**STEPHEN HENRY, COUNT OF BLOIS (c1045–1102).** Stephen Henry was the father of King **Stephen**, who ruled England for a turbulent 19 years from 1135 to 1154 with the exception of a few months in 1141, when he was imprisoned by **Matilda**, his cousin and competitor for the throne. The son of Thibault III of **Blois** and Gundrada, his second wife, Stephen Henry was married in about 1080 (and again the following year in a lavish ceremony at

Chartres Cathedral) to **Adela, countess of Blois**, daughter of **William I of England** (William the Conqueror). The union made political sense for both families because William's Normandy estates adjoined those of Thibault's Blois in northern **France**. It was also prolific, producing 12 children over a period of some two decades.

Stephen Henry succeeded his father as count in 1089 and joined his brother-in-law, **Robert Curthose, duke of Normandy**, in the first crusade to the Holy Land in 1095. During the campaign, he wrote often and lovingly to his wife, who was administering his extensive lands during his absence, but she was undoubtedly unhappy when he returned after four years, tainted by cowardice at the siege of Antioch in 1098. Embarrassed and annoyed, Adela forced him to take up arms again in 1101, along with others who had dubious records of bravery, and he died fighting Egyptian forces at the Battle of Ramleh, near Jerusalem, on 19 May 1102.

Of his offspring, other than Stephen, Henry, born in 1101, had the most significant impact on the English monarchy. He was made Abbot of Glastonbury and then bishop of **Winchester** (the richest see in the country) by King **Henry I**, he supported his brother's claim to the throne in 1135, and, apart from a brief defection to Matilda in 1141, he was an influential advisor throughout Stephen's reign.

**STEWART, ALEXANDER, DUKE OF ALBANY (c1454–1485).** Alexander, the third son of King **James II** of Scotland and **Mary of Gueldres**, rebelled against his only surviving brother, the unpopular **James III**, but failed to oust him from the throne. The troubles began in 1479, when Albany was suspected of plotting against the king and was accused of conducting raids into England even though such expeditions were explicitly banned by the terms of an understanding, reached five years earlier, that the future **James IV** would marry Cecily (*see* CECILY, VISCOUNTESS WELLES), daughter of **Edward IV**, the first English monarch from the **House of York**. Albany fled to **France**, but King Louis XI refused to help him unseat his sibling. He then moved on to England, where Edward agreed to recognize him as king of Scotland, and Alexander agreed to become a vassal of the English crown.

With Richard, duke of Gloucester (later King **Richard III**), Albany led an army of 20,000 men north in 1482. The English troops occupied the border town of Berwick-upon-Tweed, but then the Scottish nobles persuaded Alexander to accept James as king in return for the restoration of the lands he had forfeited when he fled. In addition, he would be created earl of Mar and Garioch and be made lieutenant-general of the realm. Despite these inducements, Alexander made another attempt to unseat James early the following year, but Edward's death on 9 April 1483 destroyed his power base, and he was forced to flee again. A second invasion with a much smaller force (in 1484) and possibly a third (in 1485) ended in failure, so Albany went back to France, where he was killed, by a splinter from a lance, in a jousting tournament on 7 August 1485. He was buried in the choir of the Church of the Celestines in Paris. John, Albany's son by his marriage to French-born Anne de la Tour d'Auvergne, inherited the duchy and acted as **regent** in Scotland from 1514 to 1524, during the minority of King **James V**. *See also* MARGARET OF DENMARK.

**STEWART, ALEXANDER, DUKE OF ROSS (1514–1515).** Alexander, the fourth son of King **James IV** and **Margaret Tudor**, was born at **Stirling** Castle on 30 April 1514, seven months after his father had died at the **Battle of Flodden**. Like two of his older brothers (**Arthur Stewart, duke of Rothesay**, and **James Stewart, duke of Rothesay [1507–1508]**), he failed to survive infancy, dying at Stirling on 18 December 1515. He was buried at **Cambuskenneth Abbey** near his paternal grandparents, King **James III** and **Margaret of Denmark**.

**STEWART, ALEXANDER, DUKE OF ROTHESAY (1430).** Alexander was the fifth child, but first son, of **James I of Scotland** and **Joan Beaufort**. He was born at **Holyrood Palace** in **Edinburgh** on 16 October 1430 but failed to survive infancy, so his younger twin brother became king (as **James II** of Scotland) when their father died in 1437.

**STEWART, ALEXANDER, WOLF OF BADENOCH (c1343–c1405).** Alexander, the fourth and youngest son of Robert Stewart (later King **Robert II**) and **Elizabeth Mure**, earned his nickname because of the ruthlessness with which he governed northern Scotland. At the time of his birth, his parents were not considered married, but, along with his brothers and sisters, he was legitimized by a dispensation of Pope Urban V dated 11 July 1370. After his father's accession to the throne in 1371, he was made lord of Badenoch, but in 1382 a judicious marriage to Eupheme, countess of Ross, greatly expanded the territory under his control. Robert's unwillingness to rein in Alexander, who let the north of Scotland descend into lawlessness, led to a palace revolution in 1384, with John (Alexander's older brother and later King **Robert III**) given authority to run the kingdom and curb excesses that had led to conflicts with churchmen and other nobles.

By 1389, Eupheme had failed to produce any children, so Alexander, who fathered some 40 illegitimate offspring, sought a divorce, but his petition was turned down by the bishop of Moray. In retaliation, Alexander sacked the town of Forres, then pillaged the Benedictine Pluscarden Abbey, and burned Elgin, destroying the cathedral. It is still unclear whether the violence was simply a search for revenge or whether it was an attempt to extend his power during the inevitable period of political uncertainty in the weeks after the physically impaired Robert III's **succession to the throne**. If the latter, it failed, because in the aftermath, much of Alexander's lands were lost and his power was curbed.

The date of the Wolf's death is uncertain, with some sources reporting dates in c1395 but others suggesting that he survived until 1405 or 1406. There is a legend that, the evening before he died, a visitor dressed in black arrived at Ruthven Castle, one of Alexander's residences, and challenged him to a game of chess. A storm lashed the fortress throughout the night, and in the morning, the Wolf of Badenoch was found lifeless in his banqueting hall, the nails torn from his boots. He was buried in Dunkeld Cathedral.

**STEWART, ANNABELLA, COUNTESS OF HUNTLY (c1433–?).** Like most of her sisters, Annabella—daughter of King **James I of Scotland** and his wife **Joan Beaufort**—was married into a noble European family, but the union did not last. On 14 December 1447, she was wed, at **Stirling** Castle, to Louis, count of Savoy, when she was about 14 years old and her bridegroom about 11. In 1455, she traveled to join her husband in Savoy, but the French king, Charles VII, intervened, and three years later, before any children were born, the marriage was annulled.

In 1459, Louis took Queen Charlotte of Cyprus as his second wife. Annabella married George Gordon, earl of Huntly, with some sources suggesting that she produced as many as 10 children over the next decade, but on 24 July 1471, he obtained an annulment on the grounds that she was so closely related to his first wife (Elizabeth Dunbar, daughter of James, earl of Moray) the marriage was prohibited by the Roman Catholic Church. The earl then promptly wed his mistress, Elizabeth Hay, but Annabella apparently remained single for the rest of her life. The date of her death is not known, but records suggest that she was alive in 1509.

**STEWART, ARTHUR, DUKE OF ROTHESAY (1509–1510).** Arthur, born at **Holyrood Palace** on 20 October 1509, was the second son of King **James IV** and **Margaret Tudor**. He was named after his maternal uncle— **Arthur, prince of Wales**—and, like him, was heir to a throne, his older brother (**James Stewart, duke of Rothesay [1507–1508]**) having failed to survive infancy, but he died at **Edinburgh** Castle on 14 July 1510 and was buried in Holyrood Abbey, leaving his parents to wait two more years for another son, who eventually took the crown as King **James V**.

**STEWART, DAVID, DUKE OF ROTHESAY (1378–1402).** David, the first **duke of Rothesay**, was born on 24 October 1378 and was heir to the Scottish throne from 1390 (when his father, King **Robert III**, succeeded to the crown) until his death in still unexplained circumstances in 1402. Robert, ill and lame, was a weak monarch content to leave decision making in the hands of his brother (*see* STEWART, ROBERT, DUKE OF ALBANY [c1340–1420]). **Annabella Drummond**, David's mother, concerned at the concentration of power in the hands of her ambitious and politically astute relative, enlisted the help of nobles to have the young man created duke in 1398 (the first time the title had been granted in Scotland) and, the following year, to name him lieutenant of the realm, a post that made him head of the government.

Soon afterward, David was betrothed to Elizabeth Dunbar, daughter of George, earl of March, but Archibald, earl of Douglas and March's rival, persuaded Rothesay to refute the contract and (through the promise of a large dowry) marry his own daughter, Marjorie. March responded by renouncing his allegiance to Robert III and pledging himself to King **Henry IV** of England. Henry invaded Scotland in 1400 in support of his new adherent, and though he retreated without giving battle, the incursion undoubtedly provided fuel for David's critics, who had condemned him for abandoning Elizabeth and were slighted by his unwillingness to consult the nobles before making important decisions.

Seizing the initiative, Albany and Archibald Douglas (who had succeeded to the earldom on his father's death in 1400 and was offended by Rothesay's lack of fidelity to his sister) seized the duke and confined him in Falkland Palace, where he died on 26 March 1402. He was buried at Lindores Abbey, a Tironensian foundation at Newburgh in Fife, where Alexander of Scotland, an earlier heir to the throne, had died in 1284. Rumors circulated that Albany and Douglas had starved David to death, and though a parliamentary enquiry cleared both men, several modern historians suspect that the stories were accurate. *See* STEWART, MARGARET, COUNTESS OF DOUGLAS.

**STEWART, DAVID, EARL OF CAITHNESS (c1357–c1386).** David was the eldest son of King **Robert II** and **Euphemia de Ross**, his second wife. The male children of Robert's first wife — **Elizabeth Mure** — took precedence over those of Euphemia in the line of **succession to the throne**, even though by some measures they had been born illegitimate. Even so, David was a powerful man. He was created earl of Strathearn soon after his father became king in 1371, he was granted the barony of Urquhart later the same year, and he was given the earldom of Caithness c1375. He married a daughter (whose name is unknown) of Sir Alexander Lindsay and left one child (Euphemia) who inherited his estates when he died, probably in 1386.

**STEWART, DAVID, EARL OF MORAY (c1456–1457).** David was the fourth son born to King **James II of Scotland** and **Mary of Gueldres**. He was created earl of Moray on 12 February 1456, probably soon after his birth, but he died by 18 July the following year.

**STEWART, EGIDIA (?–?).** According to the *Liber Pluscardenis* (a chronicle written during the 15th century at Pluscarden Abbey, near Elgin), Egidia, the daughter of King **Robert II** and **Euphemia de Ross**, was much renowned for her beauty, which attracted several suitors. In about 1387, she married Sir William Douglas of Nithsdale, who had distinguished himself at a siege of Carlisle Castle in 1385, and together they had a son (William) and a daughter (Egidia). Douglas was killed in a fight with English knights at Danzig (now Gdańsk) c1392, but the date of Egidia's death is not known.

**STEWART, EGIDIA (?–?).** Egidia, the daughter of King **Robert III** and **Annabella Drummond**, failed to survive to adulthood, unlike her three sisters (Lady **Elizabeth Stewart [?–c1411]**; **Margaret Stewart, countess of Douglas**; and **Mary Stewart, countess of Angus**). The dates of her birth and death are not known.

**STEWART, ELEANOR, ARCHDUCHESS OF AUSTRIA (1433–1480).** Eleanor, daughter of King **James I of Scotland** and **Joan Beaufort**, lived at the court of Charles VII in **France** after her mother's death in 1445, and in 1448 she was married to Sigismund, ruler of Tirol and later archduke of Austria. A gifted linguist, she inherited her father's interest in literature, translating (or supervising the translation of) *Ponthus et al Belle Sidoine*, a French romance, into German as *Pontus und Sidonia*. The work proved so popular that it was still being reprinted in the late 17th century. Eleanor was also a skilled politician, taking over the administration of her husband's estates—and raising funds, guns, and mercenaries for his army—during his absence from 1455 to 1458 and again in 1467. She had no children and died in Innsbruck on 20 November 1480.

**STEWART, ELIZABETH (?–?).** One of at least six daughters born to Robert Stewart and **Elizabeth Mure**, Elizabeth was married to Thomas de la Haye by 7 November 1372. The union was shaped by political ends because Thomas was lord high constable of Scotland, an office that made him second-in-command of the Scots army and the judge responsible for dealing with serious crimes committed within four miles of the king—roles that made him a useful ally for Elizabeth's father, who had succeeded to the throne as **Robert II** in 1371. The couple had four children—two sons (William and Gilbert) and two daughters (Elizabeth and Alice). The dates of Elizabeth's birth and death are not known, but it is likely that she was born before her parents were legally married and that she was legitimized, along with her brothers and sisters, by a dispensation of Pope Urban V dated 11 July 1370.

**STEWART, ELIZABETH (?–c1411).** One of four daughters born to King **Robert III** and **Annabella Drummond**, Elizabeth had married James Douglas, lord of Dalkeith, by 1387. Together they had three sons—William (the firstborn, who predeceased his father); James (who inherited the lordship but was declared insane in 1441); and Henry. She had died by 1411.

**STEWART, ELIZABETH, COUNTESS OF CRAWFORD (?–?).** At some time c1380–84, Elizabeth—the daughter of King **Robert II** and **Euphemia de Ross**—married David Lindsay, who was created earl of Crawford in 1398 and held a series of important offices during the reigns of kings Robert II and **Robert III**, notably lord high admiral of Scotland and Scottish ambassador to England. They had seven children, including Alexander, who was born c1387, succeeded to his father's earldom, and was held hostage by King **Henry VI** of England on several occasions from 1406 to 1427. The dates and locations of Elizabeth's birth and death are not known.

**STEWART, HOUSE OF.** *See* STUART, HOUSE OF.

**STEWART, ISABELLA, COUNTESS OF DOUGLAS (?–c1410).** Isabella, daughter of Robert Stewart, earl of Atholl, and **Elizabeth Mure**, was married—like her sisters—for political reasons. In 1371, her father succeeded **David II** as king of Scots (*see* ROBERT II), and soon afterward Isabella was wed to James, heir to the earldom of Douglas and Mar. The Douglases were the most powerful family on the Scottish border with England, so the union provided an important strategic and dynastic link for the new monarch. However, the couple were still childless when James died at the Battle of Otterburn in 1388. By early 1390, Isabella had taken Sir John Edmonston, a member of her father's court, as her second husband, bringing an estate at Edenham (or Ednam), near **Roxburgh Castle**, as a dowry. She had one son (David) before she died c1410.

**STEWART, ISABELLA, DUCHESS OF BRITTANY (c1426–1494).** Isabella was one of six daughters born to King **James I of Scotland** and **Joan Beaufort**. Like her sister **Margaret, dauphine of France**, she was married into French nobility at a time when a lengthy peace between Scotland and England had broken down and the Scots felt that closer ties with **France** were politically expedient. With the enthusiastic support of Charles VII, the French monarch, Isabella wed Francis I, duke of Brittany, at the Château d'Auray, on the Brittany coast, on 30 October 1442. (John, Francis's father, had sent envoys to Scotland to meet the young woman, and they had reported that she was beautiful but not very bright. Supposedly John commanded them to confirm the wedding arrangements because "clever women do more harm than good.") The couple had two daughters—Marguerite (who was born in 1443 and married her cousin, Francis, who had succeeded to her father's dukedom) and Mary (born the following year and married to John, viscount of Rohan). Isabella died in 1494, surviving her husband by 44 years and never remarrying despite pressure from her brother, King **James II**, to consider suitors.

**STEWART, JAMES, DUKE OF ROSS (1476–1504).** James, born in March 1476, was the second of three boys that **Margaret of Denmark** had with King **James III**. He was given the same name as his older brother (who became King **James IV**), leading some writers to suggest that the firstborn son (and heir to the Scottish throne) may have been seriously ill and was considered unlikely to live long, but there is no strong evidence to support this idea.

The younger James was undoubtedly the apple of his father's eye; he, rather than the firstborn, was the subject of negotiations relating to a possible marriage to **Catherine of York**, daughter of **Edward IV** of England, and, in 1486, he was created duke of Ross. The obvious favoritism annoyed the senior brother so much that, in 1488, he joined a group of nobles in a rebellion that led to the monarch's death at the Battle of Sauchieburn. Possibly in order to ensure that he had an ally among the senior clerics, but perhaps also to sideline a possible focus of opposition to his rule, **James IV** nominated Ross for the position of archbishop of St. Andrews (one of the most important ecclesiastical offices in the country) in 1497, even though the nominee was much younger than the 30 years required for consecration. Then, in 1502, the younger James was made chancellor of Scotland, but he played little part in affairs of state before his death on 12 January 1504. He was buried in the chancel of St. Andrews Cathedral at a site marked by a tombstone he had bought in Bruges in 1488.

**STEWART, JAMES, DUKE OF ROTHESAY (1507–1508).** James, born to King **James IV** and **Margaret Tudor** at **Holyrood Palace** on 21 February 1507, was heir to the throne of Scotland but survived for little over a year, dying at **Stirling** Castle on 27 February 1508. Margaret and James would later have five other children, only one of whom (**James V**) survived to adulthood.

**STEWART, JAMES, DUKE OF ROTHESAY (1540–1541).** James, born to King **James V** and **Mary of Guise** at St. Andrews on 22 May 1540, was the monarch's eldest son and thus was expected to inherit the throne, but the child died on 21 April the following year, a month short of his first birthday and three days before the birth of his brother **Robert Stewart, duke of Albany (1541)**, who survived for only a few days. Both boys were buried at **Holyrood** Abbey.

**STEWART, JOAN, COUNTESS OF MORTON (c1428–c1486).** Joan, daughter of King **James I of Scotland** and **Joan Beaufort**, was born deaf. At the age of about 13, she was betrothed to her cousin, James Douglas, earl of Angus, but he died before the wedding ceremony could be held, so in 1445, shortly after her mother's death, she was sent to **France** with her sister, **Eleanor Stewart**, for education in a nunnery. In 1459, Joan (who is sometimes known as Joan of Scotland) married another James Douglas, who was raised to the peerage as earl of Morton before the wedding. They had four children, including a son, John, who succeeded to his father's title in 1493. The countess and her husband were both buried in the choir at the Collegiate Church of St. Nicholas Buccleuch in Dalkeith. Joan's tomb is marked by an effigy that is the earliest known sculpture of a deaf person.

**STEWART, JOANNA (c1351–c1404).** Joanna (or Jean), daughter of Robert Stewart, earl of Atholl (and later King **Robert II**), and **Elizabeth Mure**, married three times into noble Scottish families, creating important dynastic alliances for her father. The first union, in 1373 or 1374 with Sir John Keith, whose family had held the title "marischal of Scotland" since the reign of **Malcolm IV** in the 12th century, was brief, ending with her husband's death in 1375, and soon afterward, in the summer or early autumn of 1376, she was wed to Sir John Lyon, one of Robert's most trusted advisors. Lyon was made royal chamberlain in recognition of his status as husband of a sovereign's daughter, but after siring an heir (also named John), he was killed in a quarrel with Sir James Lindsay of Crawford on 4 November 1382. Finally, in late 1384 or the first months of 1385, Joanna married Sir James Sandilands of Calder, giving birth to their son (James) as well. The circumstances of Joanna's birth are not known, but it is probable that she was born before her parents were legally married and that she was legitimized, along with her brothers and sisters, by a dispensation of Pope Urban V dated 11 July 1370. She died sometime after 1404 and was buried at **Scone** Abbey.

**STEWART, JOHN, EARL OF MAR (c1457–1479).** John, the youngest son of King **James II of Scotland** and **Mary of Gueldres**, was probably born by July 1547. His father had been involved in a lengthy disagreement with Robert, lord Erskine, (and later with Robert's son, Thomas) over rights to the earldom of Mar, but in 1457 he won a court decision that they belonged to the crown and he bestowed the title and lands on John. When James was killed in 1460, he was succeeded on the throne by **James III**, his eldest surviving son. Until recently, historians have reported that the new king was extremely superstitious. He was at odds with many of the nobles and, aware of possible challenges to his rule, was thus easily convinced by his confidant, Robert Cochrane, that Mar was conspiring against him and plotting his death through witchcraft.

In 1479, John was confined in Craigmillar Castle, a Preston family residence near **Edinburgh**, and he died in somewhat mysterious circumstances. The official story was that he contracted a fever and was being bled by doctors, but once when he was left alone he became delirious, tore off his bandages, and succumbed to a loss of blood. Cochrane was given John's estates, and a number of supposed accomplices of the dead earl were burned—the first recorded cases of witchcraft executions in Scotland. Several modern historians are inclined to believe that Mar's death really was a result of illness, but others suggest that he may have been murdered on Cochrane's orders (possibly with James's acquiescence), some argue that there is no evidence that Cochrane was involved in any way whatsoever (claiming that his supposed role was entirely the invention of later writers), and another group believes that the earl was killed because James feared he might provide a focus of opposition to a rule that was causing much dissension.

**STEWART, JOHN, EARL OF MAR (c1479–1503).** John was the youngest of the three sons of King **James III** and **Margaret of Denmark**. He was born between July 1479 and July 1480 and was created earl of Mar in 1486. He died unmarried on 11 March 1503 without making a significant impact on affairs of state.

**STEWART, KATHERINE (?–?).** King **Robert II** ensured that his daughters were married to noblemen who controlled strategically important areas of Scotland, using the dynastic links to build political alliances. Katherine was no exception, wed to Sir Robert Logan, whose family estates included the port of Leith, which was located close to **Edinburgh** and from which ships carried goods across the North Sea to trading partners on the European mainland. In 1400, **Robert III** made Logan lord high admiral of Scotland. The marriage apart, little is known of Katherine. Her birth and death dates are not recorded, and some sources list her mother as **Elizabeth Mure** (Robert II's first wife), although others suggest that she was the child of **Euphemia de Ross** (his second wife).

**STEWART, MARGARET (c1342–c1410).** Long before Robert Stewart succeeded **David II** as king of Scots in 1371 (*see* ROBERT II), he was using family links to forge diplomatic alliances. On 18 July 1350, Margaret (his daughter by **Elizabeth Mure**) was wed to John Macdonald, **lord of the isles**. Macdonald had to divorce Amy MacRuari, his first wife, in order to make the match, but he was a skilled politician, preferring negotiation to war and seeing a pact with the Stewarts as the most likely source of prosperity for his territory on Scotland's western seaboard. Robert, for his part, welcomed the association with a powerful noble who controlled a fractured landscape difficult to subdue by force.

Margaret, who was probably born c1342, and her husband had nine children. But the five sons, and their descendants, failed to inherit John's political acumen, so by the 16th century the lordship of the isles was in the hands of the crown. John died in 1387, but his wife survived until about 1410. Margaret was probably born to Robert while Elizabeth was his mistress, rather than his wife. She was legitimized, along with her brothers and sisters, by a dispensation grant by Pope Clement VI in 1347.

**STEWART, MARGARET (c1459–c1514).** Margaret was one of the five children of King **James II** and **Mary of Gueldres** who survived infancy. She had a daughter, Margaret, and possibly a son, James, by William, lord Crichton of Auchingoul, but it is not certain that they were married. William joined **Alexander Stewart, duke of Albany**, in an unsuccessful revolt against King **James III**, Margaret Stewart's brother, in 1482. Unconfirmed reports suggest both that he joined the rebels because the monarch had seduced his first wife, Marion Livingstone, and that he, in turn, seduced Margaret as a means of exacting revenge. Their daughter married George, earl of Rothes, who was acquitted of involvement in the murder of Cardinal David Beaton at St. Andrews in 1546. The precise dates of Margaret Stewart's birth and death are not known.

**STEWART, MARGARET, COUNTESS OF DOUGLAS (c1372–c1456).** One of four daughters born to King **Robert III** and **Annabella Drummond**, Margaret was married, c1390, to Archibald Douglas, later earl of Douglas, who in 1402 was cleared by parliament of conspiring—along with **Robert Stewart, duke of Albany (c1340–1420)**—to murder her brother, **David Stewart, duke of Rothesay**, who was married to Douglas's sister, Marjorie. For much of their married life, Archibald was fighting the English, negotiating with them, or being held captive by them, but she gave bith to their three sons—Archibald (who succeeded to the earldom); James (who died with his father at the Battle of Verneuil, in Normandy, on 17 August 1424); and William—along with three daughters (Helen, Margaret, and Mary). Margaret died at Threave Castle, a Douglas stronghold in southwest Scotland in about 1456 and was buried at Lincluden Collegiate Church, near Dumfries.

**STEWART, MARGARET, DAUPHINE OF FRANCE (c1424–1445).** Margaret, daughter of King **James I of Scotland** and his wife, **Joan Beaufort**, was married to Louis, eldest son of Charles VII, king of **France**, at Tours Cathedral on 24 June 1436 in a match designed to emphasize the lengthy alliance between Scotland and France. Contemporary chroniclers write of the bride's beauty, and Charles doted on her. But she never felt at ease in the French court. Charles and Louis were constantly at odds, and Margaret frequently sided with her father-in-law while her husband's coterie of friends plotted against her. She was desperately afraid of becoming pregnant and on 16 August 1445 died at Châlons-sur-Marne (now Châlons-en-Champagne) while giving birth to her first child.

Initially Margaret was buried at Châlons Cathedral, but her remains were later reinterred at the Abbey of St. Laon de Thouars in Poitou. Allegedly her last words were, "Fie on life! Speak no more of it to me."

**STEWART, MARJORIE, COUNTESS OF MORAY (?–c1417).** Marjorie was one of at least six daughters born to Robert Stewart (later King **Robert II**) and **Elizabeth Mure** between 1336 and 1355. On 11 July 1370, Pope Urban V granted her a dispensation to marry John Dunbar, who was made earl of Moray two years later. The dispensation was needed because the bride and groom were cousins. Also, given the tangled politics of the time, it is possible that King **David II** (Robert's uncle) was behind the match because the Dunbars were a powerful family and the monarch (having divorced **Margaret Drummond**) was planning to wed Agnes, John's sister, in the hope of producing a son (at the time, Robert was **heir apparent**).

Over the next 20 years, Marjorie gave birth to two or three sons and one or two daughters. Then, in about 1403, some 10 years after Dunbar's death, she married Sir Alexander Keith (a member of an influential dynasty based in the northeast of Scotland) and they had a daughter as well. The dates of Marjorie's birth are not known, but it is likely that she was born before her parents were legally married and that she was legitimized, along with her brothers and sisters, by a dispensation of Pope Urban V dated 11 July 1370. She died sometime after May 1417.

**STEWART, MARY, COUNTESS OF ANGUS (?–c1458).** Mary, daughter of King **Robert III** and **Annabella Drummond**, married four times, carrying the House of Stewart (*see* STUART, HOUSE OF) bloodline into many of Scotland's noble families. Her first husband—George Douglas, earl of Angus—was an illegitimate son of William, earl of Douglas, and Margaret, dowager countess of Mar and countess of Angus. The wedding, held on 24 May 1397, owed much to the countess's influence with the **royal family**

because she had been married to Thomas, earl of Mar, her lover's brother-in-law, so George was considered not just a bastard but also the result of an incestuous relationship and therefore an unusual mate for a child of a sovereign. Mary and George had two children, Elizabeth and William. Through William, their descendants included Margaret Douglas, who was born in 1515 and was the mother of **Henry Stuart, lord Darnley**, and grandmother of King **James VI and I**.

George Douglas died while being held captive by the English after the Battle of Homildon Hill, fought in 1402, so Mary married Sir James Kennedy the Younger of Dunure, probably the following year, and had a daughter (Mary) and three sons (Gilbert, James, and John); through Gilbert, Mary Stewart became the ancestress of the marquesses of Ailsa, hereditary chiefs of Clan Kennedy. After Sir James's death in a fight with Gilbert, his illegitimate half-brother, sometime before 8 November 1408, Mary took Sir William Graham as her third husband and had four more children—Patrick, Robert, William, and Walter; Patrick's grandson (William) became earl of Montrose in 1504 and ancestor of the present duke of Montrose, who is also chief of Clan Graham. Mary's final marriage—in 1425 to Sir William Edmonstone—produced no children. She died c1458 and was buried at Strathblane, north of Glasgow, on estates that had been given to the Edmonstones by her brother, King **James I**.

**STEWART, MARY, COUNTESS OF ARRAN (c1450–c1488).** One of the two daughters that **Mary of Gueldres** had with King **James II of Scotland** (*see also* STEWART, MARGARET [c1459–c1514]), Mary was born in **Stirling** and was married, in 1466 or 1467, to Thomas Boyd, who was later created earl of Arran. The Boyds had supported King **Robert I** (Robert the Bruce) as he struggled to ensure Scotland's independence from English control during the early 14th century and had been rewarded with lands and titles, growing increasingly influential and closer to the centers of power in the realm. In 1466, Robert Boyd (Thomas's father) abducted Mary's brother, **James III**, then in his mid-teens, then persuaded parliament to appoint him sole **regent**, arranged the wedding to Mary, and ensured the grant of the earldom. Father and son also negotiated James's marriage to **Margaret of Denmark**, with some sources crediting Mary with persuading King Christian I, the bride's father, to pledge the Orkney and Shetland islands as security for a dowry that was never paid.

However, the family's self-aggrandizement inevitably aroused opposition, and in 1469 Thomas and Robert were unseated while they were out of the country. There is a story that Mary, hearing of the plot, hastened to Leith, where her husband's ship had been docked on his return to Scotland, told him of the danger, and fled with him to Bruges. However, James lured her home on the pretext of discussing a pardon for Thomas and refused to let her leave.

Mary's marriage to Thomas Boyd was dissolved in 1473, and in 1474 she married James, lord Hamilton, whose first wife (Eupheme Graham) had died in 1468. She had five children. A son (James) with Boyd was killed in a duel at the age of 16, and a daughter (Margaret) married twice but died without issue (her second husband, David Kennedy, earl of Cassillis, was killed at the **Battle of Flodden** in 1513). With Hamilton, Mary had two sons—Robert and James, the latter of whom was a principal negotiator during the discussions that led to the wedding of King **James IV** to **Margaret Tudor**—and a daughter (Elizabeth) who had six children with Matthew Stewart, earl of Lennox. The date of Mary's death is unknown, but most authorities suggest that it occurred around May 1488.

**STEWART, MARY, COUNTESS OF GRANDPRÉ (?–1465).** In 1444, at ter Veere on the former island of Walcheren in Zeeland (now part of the Netherlands), Mary—one of eight children born to King **James I of Scotland** and his English wife, **Joan Beaufort**—was married to Wolfert Borsele, who succeeded to his father's title as count of Grandpré in 1474. At the time, Scots merchants had strong links with the area through the wool trade, so the match both cemented commercial connections and linked the Scottish **royal family** to an important dynasty on the European mainland. Mary bore one son (Charles), who did not survive to adulthood, and died at Sandenburg Castle on 20 March 1465. She was buried at the Grote Kerk in ter Veere, but Scots connections with the area continued until the late 18th century, and there is still a Scottish Houses Museum in the town.

**STEWART, ROBERT (?–c1393).** Robert was the son of King **Robert III** and **Annabella Drummond**. Like his sister, **Egidia Stewart**, he failed to reach adulthood, but the dates of his birth and death are not known, his last mention in contemporary documents occurring on 8 February 1393.

**STEWART, ROBERT, DUKE OF ALBANY (c1340–1420).** At the time of his death in 1420, Stewart, son of Robert Stewart and **Elizabeth Mure**, was the most powerful noble in Scotland, having acted as **regent** during the reigns of his father (King **Robert II**), his brother (King **Robert III**), and his nephew (King **James I**). He was born before his parents were formally married but was legitimized, along with his numerous brothers and sisters, by dispensation of Pope Urban V on 11 July 1370.

While his father was on the throne, Robert earned a considerable reputation as a soldier, leading forays into England, and late in 1388 he was appointed **guardian of Scotland**. He retained this title—and the authority that accompanied it—when his ill, lame brother succeeded in 1390, but in 1399 parliament handed control to **David Stewart, duke of Rothesay** and Robert III's heir. The young man proved unpopular, however, and Albany, with characteristic ruthlessness, took advantage of the situation, imprisoning him at **Falkland Palace**, where he perished in 1402. The official line was that the death was a result of "divine providence," but there is an enduring legend that Robert starved him in order to be rid of a competitor for power.

Four years later, James—Robert III's other surviving son—was captured by the English. The king, apparently overcome with grief, died on 4 April, and Albany was given the task of negotiating the return of the 11-year-old boy—Scotland's new monarch—from English hands. Not surprisingly, given the duke's desire to hold on to the reins of government, the discussions lacked urgency, so James was still languishing in exile when Albany died in **Stirling** Castle on 3 September 1420, aged about 80. He was buried in **Dunfermline Abbey**. Robert's efforts to win and hold on to power were devious and unprincipled, but scholars have given him credit for strong, politically astute rule that held a divided country together and continued a military alliance with **France** in the face of English aggression. *See also* DRUMMOND, ANNABELLA.

**STEWART, ROBERT, DUKE OF ALBANY (1541).** Robert, the second son of King **James V** and **Mary of Guise**, was born at **Stirling** Castle on 24 April 1541, just three days after the death of his infant brother, **James Stewart, duke of Rothesay (1540–1541)**. Robert survived for only a few days and, like James, was buried at **Holyrood** Abbey. In some sources, Robert is named as Arthur. There is also some doubt about whether he was ever formally created duke of Albany.

**STEWART, WALTER (c1293–1326).** Stewart, father of King **Robert II** and founder of the royal **House of Stuart**, was the son of James Stewart and his wife, Cecilia. When James died in 1309, Walter inherited the family estates and the title "**high steward of Scotland**." In 1314, he fought with **Robert I** (Robert the Bruce) against the English army at the **Battle of Bannockburn**; then, the following year, he married **Marjorie Bruce**, Robert's daughter. In March 1316, his wife, heavily pregnant, fell from her horse and died, but the baby survived to succeed **David II** as monarch in 1371. Walter took two other wives from noble families, fathering a daughter (Jean) with Alice Erskine, and a daughter and two sons with Isabel Graham. He spent much of his life in battle, beating off a siege at Berwick by King **Edward II** of England in 1319 and nearly capturing him in Yorkshire in 1322. He died on 9 April 1326 at the now-ruined Bathgate Castle, which had come to him as part of Marjorie's dowry.

**STEWART, WALTER (c1340–c1362).** Stewart, son of Robert Stewart, earl of Atholl (later King **Robert II**), and **Elizabeth Mure**, was born in the late 1330s or early 1340s, while his mother was the mistress of the Scottish monarch. He was legitimized, along with his brothers and sisters, by a dispensation granted by Pope Clement VI in 1347 and married Isabella, countess of Fife, between 21 July 1361 and 21 July 1362. As a result of the match, he was styled "lord of Fife," but the union did not last long; Walter died, childless, in late 1362 or early 1363.

**STEWART, WALTER, EARL OF ATHOLL (c1360–1437).** Walter, the son of King **Robert II** and **Euphemia de Ross**, died a horrible death as punishment for his part in the assassination of King **James I of Scotland**. He had worked hard to effect James's release from imprisonment in England and had acquired titles and estates through marriage and inheritance as well as by way of reward for his service to the crown. However, James, after his return to Scotland in 1424, ruled with a vigor that annoyed some of the nobles, who had acquired much power during his 18-year exile. Walter turned against him, perhaps because he felt that he might lose some of his lands, or perhaps because of family tensions.

James was descended from the line of Stewarts who traced their origin to Robert's liaison with **Elizabeth Mure**, which produced several children before the couple were formally married in 1349, and some Scots believed that the products of Robert's union with Euphemia had a greater right to the throne because there was no doubt that they were legitimate. In company with other dissidents, Atholl plotted to murder the monarch, killing him in Perth on 21 February 1437, but the conspirators were caught and, on 26 March, were executed. Even by the standards of early-15th-century Scotland, Walter's execution was horrific. At an age of more than 70 and after two days of torture, he was disemboweled and then made to watch his entrails being burned. His heart was torn out, he was beheaded, and his torso was cut into four parts that were exhibited around the kingdom as a deterrent to other wrongdoers.

**STIRLING.** From the 13th to the 16th century, the Scottish royal court was regularly based at Stirling. The settlement had existed since prehistoric times, was made a royal burgh (and thus acquired trading privileges) during the reign of King **David I**, and was made a **royal residence** by **Alexander II**. Its importance stemmed from its strategic position on a defensible site above the lowest bridging point on the River Forth and commanding routeways through central

Scotland. The battles of Stirling Bridge and **Bannockburn** were fought nearby in 1297 and 1314, respectively, and the castle, built atop volcanic rocks, was besieged on several occasions from the late 13th century until the early 18th (the last was attempted by **Charles Edward Stuart**'s forces in 1746). King **James V** was crowned in Stirling in 1513; **Mary, queen of Scots**, in 1543; and **James VI** in 1567, probably because it was the safest place in the realm for infant monarchs (the Church of the Holy Rude, where the **coronation** of James VI was held, is the only surviving church in the United Kingdom, apart from **London**'s **Westminster Abbey**, to have hosted a coronation).

Because of the town's importance, leading nobles built grand houses just outside the castle walls, but when James VI succeeded to the English throne in 1603, the royal court moved south, the lords left, and the town's status declined. Nowadays, education, financial services, local government, and tourism are major employers. At the time of the 2001 census, the population numbered 41,200. In 2002, Stirling was awarded city status to celebrate the 50th anniversary of Queen **Elizabeth II**'s accession to the throne. *See also* ALEXANDER I; BEAUFORT, JOAN; CAMBUSKENNETH ABBEY; DAVID OF SCOTLAND; JAMES II OF SCOTLAND; JAMES III; JAMES IV; MARGARET OF DENMARK; STEWART, ALEXANDER, DUKE OF ROSS; STEWART, ANNABELLA, COUNTESS OF HUNTLY; STEWART, MARY, COUNTESS OF ARRAN; STEWART, ROBERT, DUKE OF ALBANY (C1340–1420); STEWART, ROBERT, DUKE OF ALBANY (1541); STUART, HENRY FREDERICK, PRINCE OF WALES; STUART, HENRY, LORD DARNLEY; WILLIAM I OF SCOTLAND.

**STOKE FIELD, BATTLE OF (16 June 1487).** The battle fought near the village of East Stoke in Nottinghamshire is often considered to be the last conflict in the **Wars of the Roses**. Supporters of the **House of York** had rallied to the cause of **Lambert Simnel**, either truly believing that he was the nephew of King **Edward IV** and the rightful king of England or prepared to support the fiction that he was. From an Irish base, they raised an army of Flemish mercenaries, local troops, and dissident Englishmen led by John de la Pole, earl of Lincoln. On the morning of 16 June 1487, their soldiers met a royalist force led by **Henry VII**. They fought strongly for several hours but were eventually cut down in large numbers by their more experienced and better equipped opponents, losing most of their senior commanders. Afterward, Henry condemned Simnel, who was only about 12 years old, to menial work in his kitchens, realizing that he had been a pawn in the hands of conspirators against the crown, that he had never comprehended their aims or their strategies, and that he thus was not deserving of execution.

**STONE OF DESTINY.** *See* STONE OF SCONE.

**STONE OF SCONE.** In 1296, King **Edward I**—determined to impress his authority on the Scots—removed the Stone of **Scone** (on which Scottish monarchs since **Kenneth MacAlpin** had been seated during their **coronation**) from Scone Abbey and carried it to **London**. There, he placed it under a specially constructed coronation chair in **Westminster Abbey** so that the status of future English sovereigns as the overlords of Scotland would be emphasized.

According to legend, the stone, which is also known as the Stone of Destiny, was the pillow on which Jacob laid his head while he had his vision of angels climbing a ladder between earth and heaven. A sandstone block measuring some $66 \times 41 \times 28$ centimeters and weighing about 152 kilograms, it remained at Westminster until, on Christmas Day 1950, four students—Ian Hamilton, Kay Matheson, Alan Stuart, and Gavin Vernon—smuggled it out of the abbey and back to Scotland. There, despite a series of searches ordered by the government, it remained hidden for over a year, eventually reappearing on the altar of the ruined Arbroath Abbey on 11 April 1951.

From Arbroath, the stone was taken back (under guard) to London and replaced beneath the coronation chair, where Queen **Elizabeth II** was crowned in 1953. However, in 1996, Michael Forsyth, Prime Minister Margaret Thatcher's secretary of state for Scotland, announced that it would be returned to its homeland, and on 30 November (the feast day of St. Andrew, Scotland's patron saint), it was moved to **Edinburgh** Castle. The media interpreted the event as a political gesture by an unpopular Conservative Party government in the dying months of its administration, public interest was muted, and stories still circulate in Scotland that the stone left at Arbroath was not the one removed from Westminster.

**STUART, ANNE (1637–1640).** Anne—the third daughter of King **Charles I** and **Henrietta Maria of France**—was born at **St. James's Palace**, London, on 17 March 1637. She survived for only three years, dying at Richmond Palace (*see* SHEEN PALACE) on 8 December 1640, and was buried in **Westminster Abbey**.

**STUART, CATHERINE (1671).** Catherine was the youngest of the eight children that **Anne Hyde** had with her husband, James, **duke of York** (later King **James VII and II**), in 12 years of marriage. She was born at **Whitehall Palace**, London, on 9 February 1671, and her mother, undoubtedly weakened by the pregnancy, died—probably of breast cancer—on 31 March. Catherine's life, like those of all but two of her brothers and sisters, was brief. She passed away at **St. James's Palace** on 5 December, less than 10 months old, and was buried in **Westminster Abbey**.

**STUART, CATHERINE LAURA (1675).** Catherine, the second child of James, **duke of York** (later King **James VII and II**), and **Mary of Modena**, was born in **London** at **St. James's Palace** on 10 January 1675. She was baptized in secret by Mary's Roman Catholic priest, but King **Charles II**, when he found out, insisted on a second, **Church of England**, christening. Like so many of her brothers and sisters, Catherine failed to survive for more than a few months. In the fall of the year, she suffered convulsions at the palace and died on 3 October. Her remains were interred in **Westminster Abbey**. On the day after her death, her mother suffered her third miscarriage.

**STUART, CHARLES, DUKE OF CAMBRIDGE (1660–1661).** Charles was the first of eight children born to James, **duke of York** (later King **James VII and II**), and **Anne Hyde**. He was conceived before his parents married, and if royal advisors and **Henrietta Maria of France** (his paternal grandmother) had had their way, he would have been born illegitimate because his mother was not of royal blood. However, King **Charles II** approved the match, and the wedding was held on 3 September 1660. Anne gave birth at Worcester House in **London** on 22 October, but her baby survived for only a few months, succumbing to smallpox and dying at **Whitehall Palace** on 5 May. The infant was buried in **Westminster Abbey**.

**STUART, CHARLES, DUKE OF CAMBRIDGE (1677). Mary of Modena**, the wife of James, **duke of York** and later King **James VII and II**, gave birth to Charles at **St. James's Palace**, London, on 7 November 1677. At the time, King **Charles II** had no legitimate children, and his queen consort, **Catherine of Braganza**, was nearly 40 years of age, so it seemed likely that York would eventually succeed to the throne. Because all four of the duke's sons by **Anne Hyde**, his first wife, were dead, the newborn baby would then be **heir apparent**—a possibility that caused much concern in England and Scotland because both James and Mary were Roman Catholics, and the majority of citizens wanted a Protestant monarchy. The infant lived for little more than a month, dying at the palace on 13 December, but his parents' beliefs eventually cost them their crowns. The child was buried in **Westminster Abbey**.

**STUART, CHARLES, DUKE OF KENDAL (1666–1667).** The third son and fourth child of James, **duke of York** (later King **James VII and II**), and **Anne Hyde**, his first wife, Charles was born at **St. James's Palace** in

**London** on 4 July 1666. He died at Richmond Palace (*see* SHEEN PALACE) on 22 May 1667, six weeks short of his first birthday and less than a month before the death of his older brother, **James Stuart, duke of Cambridge**. Both boys were buried in **Westminster Abbey**.

**STUART, CHARLES EDWARD (1720–1788).** One of the great romantic heroes of Scottish history, Bonnie **Prince** Charlie (also known as "the Young Pretender") was the last member of the **House of Stuart** to make a serious claim to the British throne. The elder son of **James Francis Edward Stuart** ("the Old Pretender") and Maria Clementina Sobieska, he was born at the Palazzo Muti (the Stuarts' home in Rome) on 31 December 1720. In 1744, his father named him prince regent and sent him to Paris to promote French plans for an invasion of Britain. Faced with bad weather and the threat of a strong British navy presence in the English Channel, King Louis XV of **France** decided to abandon the scheme, so Charles, in the headstrong Stuart tradition, opted to go it alone, setting out from Nantes in June 1745 with 700 men in two ships. One of the vessels turned back, damaged after an encounter with an English man-o-war, but Charles persevered and landed at Eriskay, in the Outer Hebrides, on 23 July.

From there, he sailed to Loch nan Uamh, on the west coast of Scotland, and on 19 August he raised his standard in Glenfinnan, beginning the second **Jacobite rebellion**.

Although some of the Scottish clan chiefs shunned him, as did the bulk of Presbyterians (who deplored his Roman Catholic convictions), within a week he had gathered 2,000 followers. On 20 August, the army set off south, taking **Edinburgh** on 17 September. By 4 December, it had reached Derby, just 125 miles from **London**, but by that time the highlanders were far from home, and many had deserted. Moreover, their officers were divided by personal jealousies, and the promised support from England and France had not materialized.

After much debate, Charles agreed to retreat, and on 6 December he turned north. By April, he had reached Inverness, and despite advice that his depleted band of exhausted, hungry soldiers should be allowed to adopt a strategy of guerilla warfare in the hills, he insisted on facing the forces of the **House of Hanover** in full-scale battle. When the two sides met at **Culloden** on 16 April 1646, the Pretender's ill-prepared, ill-equipped men were cut down in droves by the fitter, better-trained regular soldiers of the crown, and the Stuart cause died with them.

For five months, Charles skulked in caves and glens, with a £30,000 reward on his head. Then, in September, two French ships carried him to safety on the continent. His exploits had earned him a reputation as a folk hero, but as he aged, his vanity, boasting, and drunkenness destroyed the image of the young gallant, and the Catholic powers in Europe saw no political advantage in supporting further efforts to restore the Stuarts to the British throne. In 1772, he married Princess Louise de Stolberg, but the match was childless and unhappy, and she left him in 1780. Alone and ill, he was cared for in his last days by Charlotte, his daughter by a mistress, Clementina Walkinshaw.

Charles died in Rome on 31 January 1788 and was buried at the Cathedral Basilica of St. Peter Apostle in Frascati, where his brother, **Henry Benedict Stuart**, was cardinal. In 1807, his remains were reinterred close to those of his parents at St. Peter's Basilica in the Vatican. A tall, handsome man, Charles spoke four languages, had a tough physique, and could inspire great loyalty, but he was a much better leader when times were good than when he faced adversity. Historians have tended to regard him as a tragic figure—charismatic and intelligent, but with considerable weaknesses of temperament.

**STUART, CHARLOTTE MARIA (1682).** By mid-1682, **Mary of Modena** had been married to James, **duke of York** (later King **James VII and II**), for nearly nine years and had been pregnant six times, but she had suffered three miscarriages and had seen the three children who survived birth die while still very young. Late in 1681, she had a riding accident while expecting another baby, but this time there was no mishap, and the following year her mother— Laura, duchess of Modena—traveled from Italy to be with her at the birth. However, Charlotte Maria, who was born at **St. James's Palace** in **London** on 16 August 1682, also lived for only a short time, dying at the palace on 6 October. She was buried in **Westminster Abbey**.

**STUART, EDGAR, DUKE OF CAMBRIDGE (1667–1671).** The youngest son of James, **duke of York** (later King **James VII and II**), and his first wife, **Anne Hyde**, Edgar was born at **St. James's Palace**, London, on 14 September 1667. Like his three brothers, he failed to survive to adulthood, dying at Richmond Palace (*see* SHEEN PALACE) on 8 June 1671. Edgar was buried in **Westminster Abbey**. In the year of his death, Great Harbour, one of the early settlements at Martha's Vineyard in Massachusetts, was renamed Edgartown in his honor.

**STUART, ELIZABETH (1635–1650).** Elizabeth, the second daughter of King **Charles I** and **Henrietta Maria of France**, spent much of her brief life isolated from her parents as a prisoner of the English parliamentarian faction that in 1649 condemned her father to death. She was born at **St. James's Palace**, London, on 28 December 1635, and when civil war broke out in 1642, she initially was confined there along with her younger brother, **Henry Stuart, duke of Gloucester**, but was later moved to a series of homes in southern England. On two occasions, she was visited by another brother, James (later **James VII and II**), and allegedly helped him escape the clutches of his enemies, dressing him as a woman on one occasion in order to deceive his pursuers.

While her father faced execution, Elizabeth sought permission to join her sister, **Mary Henrietta, the princess royal**, in Holland, but approval was denied and she was moved to Carisbrooke Castle on the Isle of Wight where she developed pneumonia and died on 8 September 1650. She was buried at St. Thomas's Church in Newport, her grave marked by a monument erected on the command of Queen **Victoria**, who purchased **Osborne House** on the island in 1845 and died there in 1901.

**STUART, HENRIETTA (1669).** The seventh of eight children in the family of James, **duke of York** (later King **James VII and II**), and his first wife, **Anne Hyde**, Henrietta was born at **Whitehall Palace** in **London** on 13 January 1669. Like all but two of her brothers and sisters, she failed to survive childhood, dying at **St. James's Palace** on 15 November the same year. She was buried in **Westminster Abbey**.

**STUART, HENRY BENEDICT (1725–1807).** Henry, born on 6 March 1725 at the Palazzo Muti in Rome, was the last member of the **House of Stuart** to lay claim to the English and Scottish thrones. The son of **James Francis Edward Stuart** (sometimes known as "the Old Pretender") and his wife, Clementina Sobieska, he supported the **Jacobite rebellion** led by his elder brother (**Charles Edward Stuart**) in the hope of winning back the crowns lost by their grandfather, King **James VII and II**, in the **Glorious Revolution** of 1688–89, but after the comprehensive defeat at the **Battle of Culloden** on 16 April 1746, he opted for a career in the Roman Catholic Church. Charles was dismayed, believing—rightly—that the decision would harm prospects for a revival of Stuart support in strongly Protestant England, but Henry, unmoved, was made a cardinal by Pope Benedict XIV on 3 July 1747.

Although often at odds with his brother, who became increasingly abusive and alcoholic, and shocked when he learned that Charles's wife, Louisa, was conducting an affair, he was attentive to his ecclesiastical obligations. He also did much to patronize the arts and built up a large library, though his income was much reduced after Napoleon Bonaparte's army occupied Rome in 1798. Known as Cardinal York (the English monarch's second son was normally created **duke of York**), he styled himself Henry IX of England and I of Scotland after the death of his father in 1766 and his brother in 1788. Henry died on 13 July 1807 at the episcopal palace at Frascati, where he had lived for many years. He was buried beside his parents in St. Peter's Basilica, Rome, and Charles's remains were brought from his tomb at the Cathedral Basilica of St. Peter Apostle in Frascati to join them.

**STUART, HENRY, DUKE OF GLOUCESTER (1640–1660).** The youngest son of King **Charles I** and **Henrietta Maria of France**, Henry was born on 8 July 1640 at **Oatlands Palace** in Surrey (and for that reason is sometimes known as Henry of Oatlands). He spent much of his childhood as a captive of the parliamentarian forces that executed his father in 1649.

The boy's wards made sure that he was carefully educated in Puritan Protestant theology, so when he was released in 1552 and joined his Roman Catholic mother who had sought refuge in Paris, the two quarreled bitterly. Unable to settle in the strained environment, where Henrietta clearly did not want him, he joined the Spanish army, fighting with his brother, James (later King **James VII and II**), against the French and distinguishing himself as a soldier even though he was still a very young man.

Henry was created duke of Gloucester in 1659 and, with the **restoration of the monarchy** the following year, returned to **London**, but he contracted smallpox shortly afterward and died at **Whitehall Palace** on 13 September. He was buried in **Westminster Abbey**, where his sister—**Mary Henrietta, the princess royal**—joined him after she too succumbed to the disease only a few weeks later. Had he lived, he would almost certainly have become king when James, a convert to Catholicism, was forced into exile in 1688, but his death meant that the crown was offered to Mary Henrietta's only son, who became **William III of England and II of Scotland**.

**STUART, HENRY, LORD DARNLEY (1545–1567).** Darnley, the second husband of **Mary, queen of Scots**, was born at Temple Newsam, now part of the City of Leeds, on 7 December 1545, to Matthew, earl of Lennox, and his wife, Margaret Douglas. Lennox had claims to the throne of Scotland through descent from King **James II** and Margaret to the throne of England through descent from King **Henry VII** so both parents were anxious that their son should make a match with Mary, who, already queen of Scotland, was considered by the majority of English Roman Catholics to be their rightful sovereign as well. (The Catholic community believed that **Henry VIII**'s divorce from **Catherine of Aragon** was invalid and thus **Elizabeth I**—his daughter by **Anne Boleyn**—illegitimate and not entitled to the crown, which should have gone to descendants of **Margaret Tudor**, grandmother to both Mary and Darnley.)

Darnley first met Mary during a visit to **France** in 1559 and renewed their acquaintance early in 1565, following her return to Scotland after the death of **Francis II**, her first husband. While staying at **Stirling**, he fell ill with measles and was nursed by the young queen, who had fallen passionately in love with him. On 29 July that year, they were wed at **Holyrood Palace** in **Edinburgh**, and the following day the bridegroom was proclaimed king of Scots. The marriage was popular only with the young couple and the groom's family, however; Elizabeth I disapproved because it strengthened Mary's claims to her crown, Scots Protestants disapproved because it was interpreted as a victory for papism, and the Scottish nobility disapproved because they found Darnley ignorant, immature, and vain.

For the queen, the decision to let the heart overrule advisors' advice had calamitous consequences. Her ardor cooled quickly as her husband demanded more and more power, insisting that he should rule Scotland when she died rather than have the succession pass to their children. Mary resisted the pleas, partly because Darnley was unwilling to devote time and effort to the chores of government, so the couple became increasingly estranged and Darnley grew jealous of his wife's increasing reliance on her Italian secretary, David Rizzio. He was deeply involved in a plot to murder Rizzio on 9 March 1566 and for that, despite a brief reconciliation and the birth of their child (later **James VI and I**) on 19 June, Mary was never able to forgive him.

Darnley—now universally despised—fled to his father's house in Glasgow, where he fell ill with what is now believed to be either smallpox or syphilis. Mary visited him, having been told that he intended to capture her infant son and rule Scotland as **regent**. Pretending at reconciliation, she persuaded him to return with her to Edinburgh on 31 January 1567. They stayed at a house in Kirk o' Field, just outside the city wall, rather than at the royal palace, ostensibly because Darnley's sickness might affect James. On the night of 9 February, while the queen was attending a wedding celebration, the building was blown up. Darnley's body was found in the garden the following morning, unmarked by the explosion but showing unmistakable signs of strangulation. The corpse was buried at Holyrood.

The identity of the king of Scots' killers has been a source of debate ever since, though many scholars suspect that **James Hepburn, earl of Bothwell** and Mary's next husband, was responsible. The mystery is one of the most compelling in Scottish history, largely because of its importance in the romance and intrigue surrounding Mary's life. In one sense, however, the hopes of the Lennoxes were realized because every British monarch since James VI and I is descended from their son.

## STUART, HENRY FREDERICK, PRINCE OF WALES (1594–1612).

Henry, the eldest child of King **James VI and I** and **Anne of Denmark**, was born at **Stirling** Castle on 19 February 1594 but contracted typhoid when he was in his late teens and died at **St. James's Palace** in **London** on 6 November 1612. He was buried in **Westminster Abbey**, leaving his younger brother, Charles (later **Charles I**), as heir to the thrones of England and Scotland. Despite his youth, two English schools (one in Evesham and one in Otley) are named after him, as are Cape Henry and Henrico County in Virginia.

**STUART, HOUSE OF.** Stuarts occupied the throne of Scotland almost continuously from 1371 to 1714, and of England from 1603 to 1714. The name is derived from **Walter Stewart (c1293–1326)**, who married **Marjorie Bruce**, daughter of King **Robert I** (Robert the Bruce), in 1315, but the family can trace its ancestry to 11th-century Brittany, where it owed fealty to the counts of Dol. Marjorie's son, born in 1316, who was the first scion of the dynasty to wear the Scottish crown, succeeding **David II** in 1371 and ruling as King **Robert II**. The male line continued through **Robert III**, **James I**, **James II**, **James III**, and **James IV** to **James V**, with all but Robert and James IV becoming king as minors and condemning Scotland to instability as **regents** squabbled for power.

The trend continued in 1542 when James V died leaving his week-old daughter, **Mary, queen of Scots**, as the country's sovereign. Mary was sent to **France** for safety as her nobles quarreled and King **Henry VIII** of England took advantage of the Scots' differences to send troops that would plunder the southern regions of the country. While Mary was in France, the spelling of the family name changed from "Stewart" to "Stuart," an accommodation made because the French language has no *w* in its alphabet. In 1565, she married **Henry Stuart, lord Darnley**, and in 1603 their son, King **James VI and I**, united the English and Scottish kingdoms under a single monarch.

James, who fervently believed that kings had a **divine right** to rule, often had confrontations with his parliament, and those troubles mounted under his son and successor, King **Charles I**, who was executed in 1649. For 11 years, England was a republic, but the monarchy was restored in 1660, with **Charles II** on the throne, and survived relatively unscathed until the **Glorious Revolution** of 1688–89 drove King **James VII and II** into exile, ousted because of his Roman Catholic beliefs. He was replaced by his eldest daughter, Queen **Mary II**, and her husband, **William III and II**, and then by another daughter, Queen **Anne**, who reigned from 1702 to 1714.

Through the **Act of Settlement of 1701**, the English parliament had prepared the way for a Protestant **succession to the throne** on Anne's death by gifting the crown to **Sophia, electress of Hanover**, and her descendants, but the Stuarts refused to surrender thrones that they felt were rightfully theirs. In 1715, **James Francis Edward Stuart**, son of King James VII and II, led a **Jacobite rebellion** against King **George I**, the first sovereign from the

**House of Hanover**, and in 1745 his own son, **Charles Edward Stuart**, led a second rising. Neither was successful, but Charles's brother, **Henry Benedict Stuart**, continued to lay claim to the crowns until his death in 1807.

Charles and Henry both died without leaving legitimate issue, so the male Stuart line ended with them. However, there is a female line of descent through **Henrietta Anne, duchess of Orléans** and the youngest daughter of King **Charles I**, to Franz, duke of Bavaria, who has never made any claim that he is the rightful sovereign of the United Kingdom. The duke is a bachelor, so on his death the headship of the House of Stuart will pass to his younger brother, Prince Max of Bavaria, and then to the prince's elder daughter, Princess Sophie of Liechtenstein. *See also entries under* STEWART *and* STUART.

**STUART, ISABELLA (1676–1681).** Isabella—born on 28 August 1676 at **St. James's Palace**, London, to James, **duke of York** (later King **James VII and II**), and his second wife, **Mary of Modena**—failed to reach adulthood, dying on 2 March 1681. She was buried in **Westminster Abbey**.

**STUART, JAMES, DUKE OF CAMBRIDGE (1663–1667).** James was the second son, and third child, of James, **duke of York** (later King **James VII and II**), and his first wife, **Anne Hyde**. He was born at **St. James's Palace** in **London** on 12 July 1663 and was formally created duke of Cambridge shortly after his first birthday, but he died at Richmond Palace (*see* SHEEN PALACE) on 20 June 1667 and was buried in **Westminster Abbey**.

**STUART, JAMES FRANCIS EDWARD (1688–1766).** James Stuart ("the Old Pretender") was accorded the titles King James VIII of Scotland and III of England by his supporters, but he failed to retrieve the thrones that his father had lost. Born at **St. James's Palace** on 10 June 1688, he was the son of **James VII and II** and **Mary of Modena**. His somewhat unexpected survival—Mary had conceived on 11 previous occasions but had either suffered miscarriages or had seen her children die very young—raised the specter of a Roman Catholic successor to the throne (because his father had converted to the faith some two decades earlier) and proved to be the spark that ignited the **Glorious Revolution** later in the year. At the time, there were rumors that the baby boy was actually an imposter, but tales that he had been smuggled into the **queen consort**'s bed in a warming pan are now discounted by historians.

Some scholars believe that the nursery rhyme "Rock-a-Bye Baby" dates from James's birth, arguing that the phrase "When the wind blows, the cradle will fall" refers to the gusts that blew the crowns of England and Scotland from James VII and II to King **William III and II** and his wife, Queen **Mary**

**II**. The child grew up in France, where his parents had sought refuge after being forced to flee **London** when he was only six months old, and throughout his life he fervently believed that his father had been ousted unjustly, depriving him of his regal birthright. When James VII and II died in 1701, King Louis XIV recognized the young man as the rightful king of England and of Scotland, but there was no hope of recovering the crowns for the **House of Stuart** by political means, so in the spring of 1708, James made a first attempt to take them back by force. Hoping to raise an army, he sailed for Scotland, but although he reached the River Forth, his ship was forced back out to sea by an English fleet and he had to return to France.

For some years after that abortive mission, James fought with the French army, distinguishing himself in battle at Oudenarde in 1708 and at Malplaquet in 1709, but part of the price that Louis had to pay for peace with England in 1713 was an understanding that the claimant to the British thrones would leave France forever. "The king over the water" set out for Scotland again in 1715 when John Erskine, earl of Mar, led the first **Jacobite rebellion**, but by the time he landed at Peterhead on 22 December, the rising was effectively over. Bobbing John Mar was no general, **Edinburgh** and **Stirling** held out against the rebel army, and with little progress being made, the highland soldiers began to head for home. By early 1716, the force had disintegrated, and in February James returned to France once again. This time he was unwelcome—Louis XIV, his long-time protector, had died on 1 September 1715, and the regents ruling on behalf of his son, King Louis XV, saw no political advantage in helping him. So James moved on to Rome, where he was more favorably received by the papal authorities because of his refusal to advance his cause by renouncing Roman Catholicism.

The Old Pretender never returned to the lands he claimed to rule, but he did continue to seek sponsorship for an invasion that would restore his crowns. In 1719, Spain prepared a fleet in support of the Jacobites, but after setting sail from Cadiz, most of the ships were driven back to port by storms in the Bay of Biscay. The small group that did reach Scotland surrendered at Glenshiel. That was the last throw of the dice. For the remainder of his life, James lived in Rome. On 1 September 1719, he married Maria Clementina Sobieska, the granddaughter of King John III of Poland. They had two sons—**Charles Edward Stuart** (Bonnie **Prince** Charlie) in 1720 and **Henry Benedict Stuart** in 1725—but the marriage was as disastrous as most of James's other activities, and Maria retired to a convent from 1725 to 1727. James himself had health problems, and gradually Jacobites began to look to his elder son for leadership. He died on 1 January 1766 and was buried in St. Peter's Church in Rome with all the dignity due to a sovereign, but within days the Holy See had recognized King **George III**, of the **House of Hanover**, as the legitimate ruler of Great Britain. *See also* SECURITY, ACT OF (1703); SETTLE-MENT, ACT OF (1701).

**STUART, LOUISA MARIA THERESA (1692–1712).** Louisa Maria, the last child of **Mary of Modena** and King **James VII and II**, was born on 28 June 1692 at the Chateau of St. Germain-en-Laye, near Paris, where her parents had lived in exile after being deposed from the thrones of England, Ireland, and Scotland in 1688. James—still hoping to win back his crowns and remembering the fuss surrounding the birth of his son, **James Francis Edward Stuart**, when many people refused to believe that Mary, who had suffered many miscarriages, was actually the child's mother—wrote to several noble English ladies (including his daughter, Queen **Mary II**), inviting them to be present when Mary went into labor, but none of them showed up.

Louisa, named after King Louis XIV of **France**, who had given her parents shelter, was known to James's supporters as "the **Princess Royal**." She was raised at the French court, enjoying dancing and opera and helping to fund the education of daughters of families that had followed her parents into exile, but in the spring of 1682, while potential marriage partners were being considered, she contracted smallpox and died at St. Germain. Louisa was buried beside her father in the Church of the English Benedictines in Paris, but the tomb was destroyed during the French Revolution.

**STUART, MARGARET (1598–1600).** Margaret, the daughter of King **James VI and I** and **Anne of Denmark**, lived for little over a year. She was born at Dalkeith Castle, then in the hands of the crown, on 24 December 1598 and died at **Linlithgow Palace** in March 1600. She was buried at **Holyrood** Abbey.

**STUART, MARY (1542–1587).** *See* MARY, QUEEN OF SCOTS (1542–1587).

**STUART, MARY (1605–1607).** Mary, the eighth child of King **James VI and I** and **Anne of Denmark**, was born at Greenwich Palace (also known as the **Palace of Placentia**) on 8 April 1605. She died at Stanwell Park, west of **London**, on 16 September 1607 while in the care of Thomas, Lord Knyvett, who had been granted the manor by the monarch in 1603. Mary was buried in **Westminster Abbey**.

**STUART, ROBERT, DUKE OF KINTYRE (1602).** Robert Bruce Stuart was the fifth child of King **James VI and I** and **Anne of Denmark**. He was born at **Dunfermline** on 18 January 1602, he died there on 27 May, and he was buried in the abbey.

**STUART, SOPHIA (1606).** Sophia was the ninth, and last, child of **James VI and I** and **Anne of Denmark**. She was born at Greenwich Palace (also known as the **Palace of Placentia**) on 22 June 1606, she died the next day, and she was buried in **Westminster Abbey**.

**SUCCESSION TO THE CROWN ACT (1534).** In 1532 (at a secret ceremony) and again in early 1553 (at a more public event), King **Henry VIII** married **Anne Boleyn**. In order to ensure that the couple's children would not have to contest the throne with a rival, on 25 March 1534 parliament passed legislation that in effect bastardized Mary (later Queen **Mary I**), who was Henry's daughter by his previous union with **Catherine of Aragon**. All of the king's subjects could be commanded to swear an oath promising to recognize the new law and could be charged with treason if they refused. The act—sometimes known as the Act of Succession (1534), the First Act of Succession, or the First Succession Act—was superseded by the **Succession to the Crown: Marriage Act** of 1536. *See also* SUCCESSION TO THE CROWN ACT (1543).

**SUCCESSION TO THE CROWN ACT (1543).** By the summer of 1543, after five marriages, King **Henry VIII** had only a single heir—a five-year-old boy who would later become **Edward VI**. The monarch's new bride, **Catherine Parr**, was in her thirties and had previously been married twice without producing children. Moreover, his daughter, Mary (later Queen **Mary I**), who was born to **Catherine of Aragon**, his first wife, had been declared illegitimate by the **Succession to the Crown Act of 1534** but was an aunt of Charles V, the Holy Roman Emperor, with whom the king had formed a military alliance against **France** and who was interceding on her behalf.

With that background, parliament introduced legislation (sometimes known as the Act of Succession [1543], the Third Act of Succession, or the Third Succession Act) that confirmed Edward as **heir apparent** to the throne. Edward was to be followed in the line of succession by his own children and any children resulting from Henry's union with Catherine Parr. Mary and Elizabeth (who had been bastardized by the **Succession to the Crown: Marriage Act in 1536**) were placed next—a move that in effect relegitimized them although legitimate daughters might have been expected to take precedence over any daughters by a sovereign's later marriages. Edward, who died at the age of 15, never married, and his attempt to override the legislation and have Lady **Jane Grey** succeed him was abortive. Also, Henry had no further offspring, so Mary became queen as Mary I in 1553, and her younger half-sister followed her as **Elizabeth I** in 1558. *See also* TUDOR, HOUSE OF.

**SUCCESSION TO THE CROWN: MARRIAGE ACT (1536).** On 30 May 1536, just 11 days after **Anne Boleyn** (his second wife) was executed, King **Henry VIII** married **Jane Seymour**. On 18 July of the same year, in order to ensure that any children by Jane took precedence in the line of **succession to the throne** over the daughters (later Queen **Elizabeth I** and Queen **Mary I**) that Henry had sired by Anne and **Catherine of Aragon**, respectively, parliament passed legislation that made both girls illegitimate. The act, which left the monarch without an heir until his son (later **Edward VI**) was born the following year, is also known as the Act of Succession (1536), the Second Act of Succession, and the Second Succession Act. It was replaced by the **Succession to the Crown Act of 1543**. *See also* SUCCESSION TO THE CROWN ACT (1534).

**SUCCESSION TO THE THRONE.** Succession to the United Kingdom throne is controlled by parliament and based on common law as well as statute law. The basic principles are those of cognatic (or male-preference) primogeniture, which were introduced by the Normans when they invaded England in 1066 (*see* HASTINGS, BATTLE OF; WILLIAM I OF ENGLAND).

When a monarch dies, the crown passes to his or her eldest surviving legitimate son. If there are no sons, it goes to the eldest daughter (as happened when King **George VI** died in 1952 and was succeeded by Queen **Elizabeth II**), and if there are no children, it goes to a brother or sister, following the same rules (as when King **George IV** died in 1830 and the throne passed to his younger brother, William, duke of Clarence, who ruled as King **William IV**). If the new monarch is too young to rule, **regents** are appointed to perform the sovereign's duties until the child reaches majority—a frequent occurrence in Scotland from the late 13th to the 16th century.

Parliamentary legislation such as the **Bill of Rights** (1689) and the **Act of Settlement (1701)** also control the succession, debarring adopted and illegitimate children; individuals who are not legitimate descendants of **Sophia, electress of Hanover** (the mother of King **George I**); and anyone who is (or was) committed to the Roman Catholic faith or who marries a Catholic.

In the past, one of the principal advantages of primogeniture was that it prescribed an orderly process for the designation of a new monarch, preventing conflict between competing claimants. As the Scottish experience showed, however, it can create problems when a young child succeeds to the throne and regents compete for power. In modern times, concern is often expressed at the sexual and religious discrimination explicit in the legislation. However, the national government has refused to back proposals for change, although in 1999 the Scottish parliament unanimously passed a motion, introduced by Michael Russell of the Scottish National Party, that the Act of Settlement should be repealed. *See also* CLAIM OF RIGHT; DIVINE RIGHT OF KINGS; MICHAEL OF KENT, PRINCE; PHILLIPS, PETER; SUCCESSION TO THE CROWN ACT (1534); SUCCESSION TO THE CROWN ACT (1543); SUCCESSION TO THE CROWN: MARRIAGE ACT (1536); TANISTRY; WINDSOR, GEORGE, EARL OF ST. ANDREWS; WINDSOR, LORD NICHOLAS; WITAN.

**SUNNINGHILL PARK.** From 1990 to 2004, the 665-acre Sunninghill estate was the official home of **Prince Andrew, duke of York**, the second son of Queen **Elizabeth II**. For part of World War II, the United States' Ninth Air Force used a building in the park as its European headquarters, but the property was destroyed by fire in 1947. Queen Elizabeth purchased the land in 1988 and erected a two-story, red brick house designed by Sir James Dunbar-Naismith, with six reception rooms and 12 bedrooms, for the **prince** and his wife, **Sarah, duchess of York**, who had married in 1986. Unsurprisingly, given both the look of the structure and Andrew's playboy image, the home quickly became known as "South York" — a reference to the South Fork residence of the wealthy, glamorous, and wayward characters in *Dallas*, an American soap opera popular at the time.

After their separation in 1992 and their divorce in 1996, the couple continued to live at Sunninghill with their daughters, **Princess Beatrice of York** (born in 1988) and **Princess Eugenie of York** (born in 1990), but in 2004 Andrew moved to the **Royal Lodge** at **Windsor Castle**, and the duchess bought a home nearby. Sunninghill was sold in 2007 for £15 million (£3 million more than the asking price) and since then has been allowed to go derelict, with the press speculating on the identity of the new owner (who is believed to be a native of Kazakhstan, which the prince visits frequently) and on the reason for the purchase.

**SUPREMACY, ACT OF (1534).** From 1527, King **Henry VIII** attempted to persuade Pope Clement VII to annul his marriage to **Catherine of Aragon** on the grounds that her previous union with his brother, **Arthur, prince of Wales**, had been consummated and that the monarch could not legally marry his sister-in-law. As the pope demurred, Henry became increasingly enraged and ultimately took the English church out of the Vatican's control. On 11 November 1534, parliament passed legislation declaring that "the king, our sovereign lord, his heirs and successors, shall be . . . the only supreme head in earth of the **Church of England**."

This act provided a means by which Henry could get ecclesiastical approval for the annulment, but it also allowed him to mount a campaign against Roman Catholic institutions in his realm which resulted in dissolution of the monasteries and redistribution of their wealth—a move welcomed by gentry (who acquired new lands) and by critics of the monks' accumulation of wealth but condemned by scholars who saw monastic libraries destroyed and by thousands of lay workers who lost their jobs.

The new laws also made religious belief a political matter, requiring nobles to take an oath recognizing the king's position as head of the church and making refusal a treasonable offence punishable by death. The act was repealed by Queen **Mary I**, Henry's Catholic daughter, in 1554 but was reinstated—more for political reasons than religious ones—in the form of the **Act of Supremacy (1559)** by her half-sister, **Elizabeth I**. *See also* DEFENDER OF THE FAITH; SUPREME GOVERNOR OF THE CHURCH OF ENGLAND.

**SUPREMACY, ACT OF (1559).** Queen **Elizabeth I** succeeded to the English throne at a time of considerable religious upheaval. The country had moved from Roman Catholicism during the early years of the reign of her father, King **Henry VIII**, to separation from Vatican jurisdiction in the 1530s as Henry sought to annul his marriage to **Catherine of Aragon**. However, Henry's other daughter, **Mary I**, had attempted to reinstate the authority of the pope, burning well over 200 Protestant dissenters at the stake from 1553 to 1558, and with many Catholics believing that **Mary, queen of Scots**, not Elizabeth, was the rightful occupant of the throne, it was unsurprising that the new queen's first major political initiative was the reinstatement of the **Act of Supremacy (1534)**, which Mary had repealed in 1554.

The legislation, approved by parliament on 29 April 1559, restored the **Church of England** to its former status as an independent entity subject to the sovereign, who would be known as its **supreme governor** (the 1534 legislation had used the term "supreme head," but several nobles were unhappy at the prospect of a woman with the formal title of head of the church, hence the change of nomenclature). Everyone holding public or ecclesiastical office was required to take an oath of loyalty to the monarch, with persistent refusal to do so considered a treasonable offense (though in practice Elizabeth's reign was marked more by religious tolerance than by persecution).

**SUPREME GOVERNOR OF THE CHURCH OF ENGLAND.** In the United Kingdom, church and state are closely linked, with the clergy participating in major ceremonies of the realm, as at the **coronation** of a new monarch. In 1534, while King **Henry VIII** was severing his ties with Roman Catholicism because Pope Clement VII seemed unwilling to grant a petition for the annulment of his marriage to **Catherine of Aragon**, parliament passed an **Act of Supremacy** which recognized the sovereign as the supreme head of the church in England. Henry's daughter, who reigned as Queen **Mary I** from 1553 to 1558, attempted to return the country to the Catholic fold, repealing the act in 1554, but the legislation was reinstated under **Elizabeth I** five years later, with the words "supreme governor" replacing "supreme head" as a concession to lawmakers who were troubled by the concept of a female head of the religious establishment.

All later monarchs of England, Great Britain, and the United Kingdom have held the title, but nowadays it is largely symbolic. For example, technically the members of the senior hierarchy of the **Church of England** (including the archbishop of Canterbury, who heads the worldwide Anglican communion) are appointed by the sovereign, but in practice the individuals are recommended by the prime minister, who acts on advice received from clergy. *See also* DEFENDER OF THE FAITH; EDWARD VIII; MARGARET, COUNTESS OF SNOWDON; SUPREMACY, ACT OF (1534); SUPREMACY, ACT OF (1559).

**SVEIN OF NORWAY (c1015–1035).** Svein was one of two sons born to King **Canute** (who ruled England from 1016 to 1035) and **Aelfgifu of Northampton**. In 1030, Canute sent him to act as viceroy in his Norwegian territories, but the rule was never a success. Many of the Norwegian nobles resented his presence because they believed that Canute had promised them similar posts. Moreover, Svein was dominated by his mother, who accompanied him and in effect ran the country. Their rule was harsh, with heavy taxation on trade in herring, malt, and other commodities and the introduction of a series of repressive laws (for example, if anybody left the territory without permission, his lands reverted to the monarch).

Inevitably, discontent simmered, encouraging Norwegian leaders to visit Russia in a successful effort to persuade the guardians of 10-year-old Magnus—an illegitimate son of King Olaf II, whom Canute had forced into exile (also at the request of the Norwegian nobles)—to claim the kingdom for their ward. In 1035, Svein was forced to flee to Denmark, where he died shortly afterward. His mother returned to England, where she plotted to put her other son on the throne of her native country as King **Harold I**.

**SWEIN (c960–1014).** *See* SWEYN.

**SWEYN (c960–1014).** Sweyn was the father of King **Canute** and the first **Viking monarch** to rule England. The son of Harald I of Denmark (often known as Harald Bluetooth) and, probably, Gyrid (or Gunnhild) Olafsdottir, he was born in about 960, with some sources suggesting that he was illegitimate. Sweyn rebelled against his father, deposing him in 987, and then added Norway to his empire around 1000. After that, he turned his attention to England, leading raids in 1002–5, 1006–7, and 1009–12. According to some writers, the spur to action was the decision by **Aethelred the Unready**, the English king, to kill every Dane in his realm on 13 November 1002 (*see* ST. BRICE'S DAY MASSACRE). Gunhilde, Sweyn's sister, was one of the victims of the ethnic cleansing, so he determined to exact revenge and in the process received considerable sums in **danegeld**—the payments made by Anglo-Saxon nobles in an effort to persuade the invaders to return home.

In 1013, Sweyn made a more serious, and ultimately successful, effort to add England to his estate, landing initially at Sandwich, on the southeast coast, but then acquiring bases along much of the eastern shore and heading inland. By early winter, he had overcome all resistance, and Aethelred had fled to Normandy. Sweyn (who is referred to in some texts as Swein, Swein I, or Sweyn Forkbeard) was proclaimed king on Christmas Day, but he had little opportunity to enjoy the fruits of his success because he died at Gainsborough on 3 February the following year. Shortly afterward, the Viking force appointed his son Canute as their leader and the new king of England, but the **witan** (the royal council of advisors) opted to restore the Anglo-Saxon line and invited Aethelred to return.

**SYBILLA OF NORMANDY (c1092–1122).** One of about five illegitimate children borne by Lady Sybilla Corbet to King **Henry I**, Sybilla was **queen consort** to King **Alexander I** of Scotland. She was born at Domfront in Normandy in about 1092 and married Alexander c1107, but the match, although apparently affectionate, did not produce any children. Sybilla died on Eilean nam Ban, an island in Loch Tay, on 12 or 13 July 1122. Alexander never remarried.

# T

**TANISTRY.** Early kings of Scotland, as well as those in Ireland and the Isle of Man, were chosen according to the principles of tanistry. The procedures varied from group to group, but usually every man descended through the male line from a common royal ancestor (normally a great-grandfather or great-great-grandfather) was a candidate for the position of heir to the throne. The successful individual was normally nominated by the king but needed the approval of the whole group if he was eventually to rule successfully.

The system had the advantage of ensuring that the head of a political unit was sufficiently mature to make governmental decisions and sufficiently strong to provide leadership in battle. However, ambitious young men were often willing to kill the designated heir in an effort to win the position for themselves or for their close kin, so strife over the succession was common, as among the descendants of **Kenneth MacAlpin** in the 9th and 10th centuries. In Scotland, King **Malcolm II** introduced concepts of hereditary leadership (including the possibility of female rulers) from the early 11th century, though the process was gradual and echoes of the old system were still heard in 1296, when Robert de Bruce (grandfather of King **Robert I**) used it to plead his case for the kingship after the death of **Margaret, maid of Norway**. In Ireland, it was still being used in some forms as late as the early 19th century.

The word *tanistry* is derived from the Irish Gaelic *tánaiste*, meaning "second." *See also* HEIR APPARENT; SUCCESSION TO THE THRONE.

**TAYLOR, LADY HELEN (1964– ).** Lady Helen—the second child and only daughter of **Prince Edward, duke of Kent**, and **Katharine, duchess of Kent**—inherited the fashion sense for which her paternal grandmother, **Princess Marina**, was renowned. Born on 28 April 1964 at Coppins, the Kents' country home at Iver, west of **London**, she was educated at St. Mary's, a **Church of England** school for girls at Wantage, near Oxford, and at Gordonstoun School in Scotland. As a young woman, she earned a reputation for hard partying (and was known as "Melons" because of her physical endowments), but by her own admission, the death of her friend Olivia Channon—the daughter of politician Paul Channon—from a drug overdose in 1986 made her rethink her lifestyle.

While in New York, Lady Helen met art dealer Timothy Taylor, whom she married at **St. George's Chapel** in **Windsor Castle** on 18 July 1992. They have two sons (Columbus, born on 6 August 1994, and Cassius, born on 26 December 1996) and two daughters (Eloise, born on 2 March 2003, and Estella, born on 21 December 2004). Despite the demands of that young family, Helen Taylor worked for several years as a "fashion ambassador" for Italian jewelry company Bulgari (which employed her to wear its products at store openings and society events) and for fashion house Armani (which required her to dress only in its products). By 2010, however, she had forsaken the world of high-society clothing accessories and was helping to run her husband's art gallery in Mayfair, **London**. Although she is involved in the work of CLIC Sargent, Britain's largest children's cancer charity, she is not required to undertake public engagements on behalf of the **royal family**.

In 1998, Timothy Taylor was diagnosed with Hodgkin's Disease, a cancer of the lymph nodes, but the illness is in remission.

**TEWKESBURY, BATTLE OF (4 May 1471).** The conflict at Tewkesbury, in the west of England on 4 May 1471, temporarily ended the **Wars of the Roses** and confirmed King **Edward IV**'s hold on the English throne. Edward had deposed King **Henry VI** for a second time the previous month and had imprisoned him in the **Tower of London**, but **Margaret of Anjou** (Henry's **queen consort**) and **Edward of Lancaster, prince of Wales** (their son), continued to struggle against the usurper even though their military cause became hopeless after Richard Neville, earl of Warwick and their principal commander, was killed at Barnet on 14 April. No match for the king, who was a very able strategist, they were outmaneuvered at Tewkesbury, where, according to some estimates, half of their army died on a site still known today as "Bloody Meadow." Margaret was taken captive, Edward of Lancaster was either killed in the fighting or was executed on the monarch's orders shortly afterward, and Henry was murdered in the tower a few weeks later. The battle is reenacted every year at the Tewkesbury Medieval Festival, with over 2,000 participants.

**THEOBALDS HOUSE.** Theobalds, near Cheshunt (in Hertfordshire), was a **royal residence** during the early 17th century. It was built from 1564 to 1585 for Robert Cecil, Queen **Elizabeth I**'s most influential advisor, but was transferred in 1607 to King **James VI and I** in return for **Hatfield Palace**. James suffered a bout of dysentery and died on 27 March 1625 while staying in the house, which was demolished after his son, King **Charles I**, was executed in 1649. King **William III of England and II of Scotland** gave the estate to William Bentinck, earl of Portland, but in 1763 the property was acquired by George Prescott, a merchant and member of parliament who erected the building known as Theobalds Park that now stands on the site and is used as a conference center and hotel.

**THIRD ACT OF SUCCESSION (1543).** *See* SUCCESSION TO THE CROWN ACT (1543).

**THIRD SUCCESSION ACT (1543).** *See* SUCCESSION TO THE CROWN ACT (1543).

**THOMAS OF BROTHERTON, EARL OF NORFOLK (1300–1338).** Thomas was the first child born to King **Edward I** and his second consort, **Marguerite of France**. Marguerite went into labor with the baby while out hunting near Pontefract Castle in West Yorkshire on 1 June 1300 and was carried to the nearby manor house at Brotherton, where she gave birth. Thomas was created earl of Norfolk in 1312 and was made grand marshal of England four years later, but in 1326 these honors did not prevent him from joining the rebellion against **Edward II**, his half-brother, led by **Isabella of France** (Edward's estranged consort) and **Roger Mortimer**, baron Wigmore and later earl of March. Later, he also rebelled against King **Edward III**, but by 1330 he was back in the royal fold, and in 1333 he commanded a section of the monarch's army in a battle against the Scots at Halidon Hill.

Thomas married twice. Although the dates of the weddings are uncertain, it is known that his first wife—Alice, daughter of Sir Roger Hayles and Alice Skogan—gave birth to a son (Edward) and two daughters (Margaret and Alice). After Alice senior died, probably between 1326 and 1330, Thomas took Mary, widow of Baron Cobham, as his second wife and had another son, John, who became at monk at Ely. Thomas passed away in September 1338 and was interred at Bury St. Edmunds Abbey.

**THOMAS OF LANCASTER, DUKE OF CLARENCE (1388–1421).** Thomas was the third of seven children in the family of Henry Bolingbroke (later King **Henry IV**) and his first wife, **Mary de Bohun**. Born on 29 September 1388 at Kenilworth Castle (which **John of Gaunt**, his paternal grandfather, had acquired through marriage to **Blanche, duchess of Lancaster**), he was created the first duke of Clarence in 1412 and held several senior posts at the royal courts of his father and his older brother (King **Henry V**). He was killed on 21 March 1421 while commanding English troops in a struggle with Franco-Scottish forces at Baugé in northwest **France** during the **Hundred Years' War**. In 1411, Lancaster had married Margaret Holland (widow of John Beaufort, earl of Somerset, and granddaughter of **Joan, countess of Kent** by her marriage to Thomas Holland), but he died without leaving any issue.

**THOMAS OF WOODSTOCK, DUKE OF GLOUCESTER (1355–1397).** Thomas—the eighth, and youngest, son of **Edward III** and **Philippa of Hainault**—was born in **Woodstock Palace** near Oxford on 7 January 1355. After Edward's death in 1377, he supported the new king, **Richard II**, commanding his troops in northern **France** and winning his approval to the extent that, while campaigning in Scotland in 1385, he was made the first duke of Gloucester. However, the two men increasingly differed, partly over Richard's choice of advisors and partly over the conduct of the **Hundred Years' War** with France. In 1388, Thomas led a rebellion that resulted in the execution and exile of the monarch's confidants, but over the next few years the king regained sufficient authority to accuse Gloucester of treason and carry him to imprisonment in **Calais**, where he was murdered—probably on Richard's orders—on 8 or 9 September 1397.

At some time in the period 1374–76, Thomas married Eleanor de Bohun, daughter of Humphrey, earl of Hereford, and Joan FitzAlan. (**Mary de Bohun**, Eleanor's sister, would later marry Henry Bolingbroke, but she died some five years before he ousted King **Richard III** and took the English throne as King **Henry IV**.) Gloucester's title was forfeited after his death and so did not pass to his only son, Humphrey, who was born in 1381 and died of bubonic plague in 1399. Anne, the oldest daughter, was born in 1383 and was married three times, most notably to William Bourchier, through whom her descendants would become earls of Bath from 1536 to 1654. She survived until 1438, but the other girls in the family were less fortunate; Joan (born in 1384) died in 1400 (possibly in childbirth), Isabella (who was born in 1385 or 1386 and became a nun at Minoresses' Convent in **London**) died in 1402, and Philippa (born in 1389) died around the time of her 10th birthday. *See also* JOHN OF GAUNT, DUKE OF LANCASTER.

**THORKELSDÓTTIR, GYTHA (?–?).** Gytha (or Githa)—mother of King **Harold II**—was the daughter of Thorgils Sprakaleg, a Danish nobleman. She married **Godwin, earl of Wessex**, in about 1022 and they had some 10 children, including Harold, **Edith of Wessex** (who became **queen consort** of **Edward the Confessor**), Gyrth and Leofwine (who were killed with Harold at the **Battle of Hastings**), Tostig (who died fighting against Harold at the **Battle of Stamford Bridge**), and Wulfnoth (who spent most of his life as a prisoner, initially of Edward the Confessor and then of King **William I of England**). After the Battle of Hastings, Gytha asked William for permission to take Harold's body for burial—one source reports that he refused, another that he agreed. Shortly afterward, she left England, probably for Flanders and then for the court of her nephew, King Sweyn of Denmark. The place and date of her death are not known.

**TINCHEBRAI, BATTLE OF (28 September 1106).** In late September of 1106, **Henry I**'s army routed supporters of **Robert Curthose** at Tinchebrai, some 35 miles east of Avranches in northwest **France**—a victory that put an end to the older brother's efforts to win the English throne and added Normandy to the king's realm. Allegedly, bickering between the two men dated from 1077, when Henry and another brother, William (later **William II of England**), doused Robert with a deluge of stinking water. Their father—**William I of England** (William the Conqueror)—failed to intervene, so Robert responded by laying siege to the family castle at Rouen. The strife lasted on and off for 30 years, until Henry decided both that it was costing too much and that it was diverting him from other matters.

Taking advantage of civil unrest in Normandy, where Robert's mismanagement of his estates had resulted in near anarchy, the monarch sent his troops across the English Channel in the summer of 1106 and laid siege to the castle at Tinchebrai, a stronghold of William of Mortain, one of Curthose's most loyal allies. Robert attempted to raise the siege, but his force was much smaller than that of his brother and the battle lasted for less than an hour. Robert was taken captive and spent the next 28 years in prison. **Edgar Aetheling**, the last of the **Anglo-Saxon monarchs** of England, was more fortunate, because even though he had fought for Curthose after changing sides more than once, he was pardoned and allowed to go free.

**TOWER OF LONDON.** For nearly 1,000 years, the Tower of **London** has served as astronomical observatory, fortress, mint, prison, record office, royal palace, and tourist attraction. King **William I of England** (William the Conqueror) began construction in about 1078, and the work continued until 1285, when **Edward I** added an outer wall and dug a new moat. The oldest building is the White Tower, which gets its name from the whitewash applied during the 13th century. Probably completed in about 1100, it has walls 90 feet high and 50 feet thick and is now used as a museum of arms and armor. Other structures include the Bloody Tower (by tradition, the place where **Edward V** and his brother, **Richard, duke of York (1473–1483?)**, were murdered (probably on the orders of **Richard III**) in 1483, and the Chapel of St. Peter ad Vincula (under the floor of which lie the bodies of **Anne Boleyn** and **Catherine Howard**, the second and fifth wives of King **Henry VIII**). King **Stephen**, in 1140, was the first monarch to use the place as a **royal residence**; from that time, it was popular with England's kings and queens until **James VI and I** became more interested in **Whitehall Palace**.

Many illustrious prisoners spent time in the tower, even though dungeons and cells were never an integral part of the building. Royal captives, who were placed in whatever rooms were available, include **David II** of Scotland, **Henry VI** of England (who was murdered in the building) and **Margaret of Anjou** (his **queen consort**), John II of **France**, **John of Scotland**, and Queen **Elizabeth I**. Lady **Jane Grey**—queen of England for nine days in July 1553—was executed there, as were George, duke of Clarence and brother of **Edward IV**, and his daughter, Margaret Pole.

The tower, which was designated a world heritage site in 1988, now houses the **crown jewels of the United Kingdom** and attracts more than two million visitors annually. *See also* BALDWIN OF BOULOGNE; ELIZABETH OF YORK; JOAN OF THE TOWER; LIONEL OF ANTWERP, DUKE OF CLARENCE; MORTIMER, ROGER, EARL OF MARCH; PLANTA-GENET, BLANCHE (1342); RICHARD, DUKE OF YORK (1473–1483?); TUDOR, KATHERINE.

**TOWTON, BATTLE OF (29 March 1461).** In the early spring of 1461, Edward, son of **Richard, duke of York (1411–1460)**, deposed King **Henry VI** and assumed the crown of England as **Edward IV**. Henry, subject to frequent bouts of mental illness, was unable to contest matters with the usurper, but his queen consort, **Margaret of Anjou**, pursued her husband's cause and assembled an army of supporters from the **House of Lancaster**. Edward, the first English sovereign from the **House of York**, was determined to eliminate the major focus of opposition to his rule, so the two sides met at Towton, some 12 miles southwest of York, on 29 March. The battle was the bloodiest ever fought in England, with casualties estimated at nearly 60,000 men (about 1 percent of the country's population). Initially, forces were equally matched, but the Lancastrian left flank eventually gave way and its soldiers fled the field. The retreat became a rout, with more men dying as they tried to escape than had died fighting. Margaret and Henry made their way to Scotland and most of their military commanders survived, but the victory left Edward in control of the realm.

**TROOPING THE COLOUR CEREMONY.** Since 1748, the colors of one of the battalions of foot guards have been trooped (or carried before the soldiers in the ranks) to mark the **queen's (or king's) official birthday**, with the Coldstream Guards, Grenadier Guards, Irish Guards, Scots Guards, and Welsh Guards each taking their turn. The guards and the mounted bands wear dress uniform as over 1400 soldiers (including 400 musicians) and 200 horses carry out intricate marching maneuvers with much pageantry in **London**'s Horse Guards Parade. From the beginning of her reign in 1952 until

1987, Queen **Elizabeth II** rode to the ceremony on horseback (even after 17-year-old Marcus Serjeant fired six blank shots at her from a starting pistol in 1981). More recently, she has used a horse-drawn phaeton. The sovereign takes the salute, but several other members of the **royal family** are usually present as well.

**TROYES, TREATY OF (1420).** On 21 May 1420, with English armies and their allies dominating the north of his country, the mentally unstable King Charles VI of **France** approved the Treaty of Troyes, which made **Henry V** of England his **regent**. The agreement also included understandings that Henry would marry **Catherine of Valois** (Charles's daughter), that the king of England would become king of **France** when Charles died, and that Henry's heirs would be the rulers of France in perpetuity.

The treaty was designed to end the conflict that was consuming the resources of both countries (*see* HUNDRED YEARS' WAR) and to fulfill long-held English territorial ambitions on the European mainland. However, southern France remained loyal to Charles's eldest surviving son, also named Charles, even though there were doubts about his legitimacy, and after his father's death in 1422, the young man repudiated the treaty that had disinherited him. Moreover, French morale improved as Joan of Arc raised the siege of Orléans in 1429 and then won back land that had been conquered by the English. On 17 July, Charles was crowned king of France in the recaptured city of Rheims, and by midcentury the French had regained most of the regions they had lost in earlier decades, ending English hopes of uniting the two countries under a single monarch. However, Henry's marriage to Catherine did take place, and this union led to the founding of the Tudor dynasty in England when the **queen consort**'s grandson, one result of a liaison with Welshman **Owen Tudor**, became King **Henry VII** in 1485.

**TUDOR, EDMUND, DUKE OF SOMERSET (1499–1500).** Edward was born to King **Henry VII** and **Elizabeth of York** at the **Palace of Placentia** on 21 February 1499 and was created duke the same day, but he lived for little over a year, dying of unknown causes on 19 June 1500. He was buried in **Westminster Abbey**.

**TUDOR, EDMUND, EARL OF RICHMOND (1431–1456).** Edmund, the father of King **Henry VII**, was born—possibly illegitimately—either at Hadham (in Bedfordshire) or at the palace of the bishops of **London** at Much Hadham (in Hertfordshire) to **Owen Tudor** and **Catherine of Valois** (the widow of King **Henry V**). He was created earl of Richmond by King **Henry VI** (his half-brother) in 1452 and married **Margaret Beaufort**—daughter of John Beaufort, duke of Somerset, and Margaret Beauchamp—at Bletsoe Castle (a Beauchamp family home near Bedford) on 1 November 1455. Henry, their only child, was born on 28 January 1457, but by that time Edmund was dead.

After the initial skirmishes in the **Wars of the Roses** between the **House of Lancaster** and the **House of York**, Edmund attempted to build up Lancastrian support in south and west Wales, but he was taken captive by Yorkist supporters and then succumbed to the plague on 1 November 1456 while languishing in prison at Carmarthen Castle. Initially his remains were interred nearby in the Church of the Greyfriars, but the tomb was later moved to St. David's Cathedral. Margaret, who remarried twice, survived until 1509.

**TUDOR, EDWARD (?–?).** Only four of the children of King **Henry VII** and **Elizabeth of York** survived to reach their teens. Edward was one of those who died young. Little is known of him except that he was buried in **Westminster Abbey**.

**TUDOR, ELIZABETH (1492–1495).** Elizabeth, the second of four daughters in the family of King **Henry VII** and **Elizabeth of York**, was born on 2 July 1492. Plans for her betrothal to Francis (later Francis I of **France**), the only son of Charles d'Angoulême (a cousin of France's Louis XII, who had no male offspring by any of his three wives) and Louise of Savoy, were under discussion when she died of a wasting disease on 14 September 1495. She was buried in **Westminster Abbey**.

**TUDOR, HENRY (1457–1509).** *See* HENRY VII.

**TUDOR, HOUSE OF.** The Tudor dynasty provided England with five monarchs—**Henry VII** (who ruled from 1485 to 1509); his son, **Henry VIII** (1509–47); and his grandchildren, **Edward VI** (1547–53), **Mary I** (1553–58), and **Elizabeth I** (1558–1603).

Toward the end of the second decade of the 15th century, rumors circulated in the royal court that **Catherine of Valois**, the widow of King **Henry V**, was romantically involved with **Owen Tudor**, a Welsh-born member of her household who had served with the English army in **France**. Early in 1428, parliament reacted by passing legislation forbidding **queens dowager** to marry without the monarch's consent, and there is no record of a wedding ceremony. But even so, Catherine and Owen had several children together. **Edmund Tudor, earl of Richmond**, one of their sons, married **Margaret Beaufort** in 1455, and though he died the following November, he fathered one child—Henry—who became the **House of Lancaster**'s strongest candidate for the throne, which was held by the rival dynasty of the **House of York**.

In 1485, Henry took advantage of King **Richard III**'s unpopularity to lead a rebellion that culminated in the death of the monarch at the **Battle of Bosworth Field** and widespread acceptance that Henry should succeed him as King **Henry VII** by right of conquest. Over the next 24 years, despite several efforts to unseat him, he cemented relations with foreign powers through judicious family marriages, improved trade, and reorganized much of the court system, making England one of the strongest economic and political forces in Europe. However, the 50 years that followed his death in 1509 brought much social upheaval as **Henry VIII** broke with the Roman Catholic Church, dissolved the monasteries, established himself as **supreme governor of the** (now Protestant) **Church of England**, and initiated investment that led to the development of an extensive navy.

The religious reforms continued during Edward VI's reign and survived efforts by his half-sister, Mary I, to reestablish the doctrines of the papacy, but they also continued the existing social turmoil. Partly for that reason the Elizabethan peace that contrasted with the contentious persecution of non-Catholics during Mary's rule has sometimes been regarded as a golden age, when the arts flourished (William Shakespeare and Ben Jonson were writing at the time), colonies were established in North America (Virginia was named after the virgin queen), Francis Drake circumnavigated the globe, and the Spanish Armada's efforts to invade the realm came to naught. In practice, though, Elizabeth's reign, despite all its achievements, proved to be simply an oasis between the religious strife of the early 16th century and the struggles that pitted parliament against the king in the 17th century.

The **Succession to the Crown Act of 1543** confirmed Henry VIII's wish, expressed in his will, that he should be succeeded by his children, and that if they died without issue, the crown should go to the offspring of **Mary Tudor, queen of France** (his younger sister), rather than to those of **Margaret Tudor** (his older sister and the wife of **James IV** of Scotland). Elizabeth, who never married and had no children of her own, spent much time pondering her father's request as she mulled over the claims of Edward Seymour, Lord Beauchamp (Mary Tudor's great-great-grandson and the preferred successor according to her father's will), and King **James VI** of Scotland (who was the rightful successor by hereditary descent). On her deathbed, she chose James, replacing the House of Tudor with the **House of Stuart**.

**TUDOR, KATHERINE (1503).** Katherine was born to King **Henry VII** and **Elizabeth of York** at the **Tower of London** on 2 February 1503 but survived for only a few days, dying on about 18 February. The birth proved fatal for her mother, who contracted an infection and died on 11 February.

**TUDOR, MARGARET (1489–1541).** As sister of King **Henry VIII** of England and wife of King **James IV** of Scotland, Margaret played a significant role in international as well as domestic politics, particularly while she acted as **regent** during the minority of her son, **James V**. The eldest daughter of **Henry VII** and **Elizabeth of York**, she was born in the **Palace of Westminster** on 28 November 1489. Her father proposed the marriage to James in the hope that a link to Scotland's royal house would head off Scottish support for **Perkin Warbeck**, who was the figurehead for rebels determined to unseat the English monarch in 1495–97. The couple married at **Holyrood** Abbey in **Edinburgh** on 8 August 1503, and four years later Margaret gave birth to **James Stewart, duke of Rothesay (1507–1508)**, the first of their six children, two of whom were daughters stillborn (on 15 July 1508 and in November 1512) and only one of whom (King James V) reached adulthood.

Despite Henry's hopes, the marital union was insufficient to keep the peace. Throughout his reign, the English king was more of a diplomat than a warmonger, but after his death in 1509, his son—Henry VIII—adopted a different approach to foreign policy, invading **France** in 1513 in a campaign of territorial acquisition. The French sought help from the Scots, hoping to divert English military resources with trouble on a second front, so James led his troops south but perished, with many of the Scottish nobility, at the **Battle of Flodden**. The Scots parliament approved the request, expressed in James's will, that his widow should act as regent while their son was too young to rule on his own. However, although Margaret was an astute politician, her sex and her English associations were weaknesses in a fractious country where many influential voices preferred links with the French. And on 6 August 1514, her marriage at Kinnoull (near Perth) to Archibald Douglas, earl of Angus, raised more hackles, particularly among the powerful Douglas family's enemies.

James IV's will had stated that Margaret should be regent only while she was a widow, so after her wedding she was replaced by the pro-French John Stewart, duke of Albany and a grandson of King **James II**. As feelings rose against the **queen dowager**, she sought refuge at Harbottle Castle in England, where she gave birth to Margaret Douglas, who was later to become the mother of **Henry Stuart, lord Darnley**, husband of **Mary, queen of Scots**. However, as the marriage soured, Margaret allied with the duke of Albany against her husband. Eventually, in 1527, Pope Clement VII sanctioned a divorce, but by the time it was granted Margaret had plotted again. In 1524, with the help of James Hamilton (earl of Arran and no friend of Douglas), she had managed to oust Albany and get her 12-year-old son recognized as a king able to make his own decisions, though in practice she was the power behind the throne until the boy was abducted by his stepfather in 1525.

On 3 March 1528, Margaret married Henry Stewart (a distant relative of her first husband), and in the same year James managed to slip from Douglas's grasp, forcing his former stepfather into exile, and took charge of the country himself. Margaret again gained influence at the Scottish court (James created Stewart lord Methven "for the great love he bore for his dearest mother"), and in 1536 she arranged a meeting between the king of Scots and the king of England, in the vain hope of improving relations between the two realms. However, Stewart proved to be a philanderer, and the wealth of her son's court paled beside the riches available in the court of her brother in **London**, so it is hardly surprising that ultimately she confessed herself "weary of Scotland." Toward the end of her life, Margaret was reconciled with Methven and formed a good relationship with James's wife, **Mary of Guise**, even though both were strong-minded women, but on 18 October 1541, she suffered a stroke and died. Her body was interred at the Carthusian Abbey of St. John in Perth, and 62 years later her great-grandson—**James VI** of Scotland—succeeded to the English throne as James I, uniting the ancient enemies under a single sovereign. *See also* SHEEN PALACE; STEWART, ALEXANDER, DUKE OF ROSS; STEWART, ARTHUR, DUKE OF ROTHESAY; UNION OF THE CROWNS.

**TUDOR, MARY.** *See* MARY I; TUDOR, MARY, QUEEN OF FRANCE.

**TUDOR, MARY, QUEEN OF FRANCE (1496–1533).** Mary—queen of **France** for less than three months—was the youngest of the four children of King **Henry VII** and **Elizabeth of York** to survive into adulthood. She was born in **Sheen Palace** on 18 March 1496 and, at the age of 11, was betrothed to Charles of Castile (son of Philip I and Joanna of Castile) as her father attempted to build a series of alliances between England and other powers. However, Henry's death in 1509 and the shifting sands of European political allegiances resulted in a change of marital course, and on 9 October 1514, at Abbeville Cathedral in France, she was wed to the French monarch, Louis XII.

The partnership was almost certainly not of Mary's choosing because she was much attached to Charles Brandon, duke of Suffolk, but for her brother, King **Henry VIII**, a dynastic match with England's closest continental neighbor made much sense.

Fortunately for Mary, the marriage did not last long. Louis had failed to sire any sons by his two previous wives, and he failed with his English bride as well, dying on 1 January 1515 (according to some reports, as a result of exhaustion from efforts to produce an heir). Before Henry sent Suffolk to collect his sister, he took the precaution of making the duke promise that he would not propose to her, but nonetheless the couple arranged to be wed. The king was furious, threatening Brandon with death because he had committed treason by marrying a monarch's daughter without getting the sovereign's permission. But Brandon and Mary had been close since childhood, so tempers cooled and the pair were officially married at the **Palace of Placentia** on 13 May. They had three children—Henry Brandon (who was born in 1515 or 1516 and died unmarried in 1534); Frances Brandon (the mother of Lady **Jane Grey**, who was queen for a few days in July 1553); and Eleanor Brandon (who was born in 1519 and married Henry Clifford, who succeeded his father as earl of Cumberland in 1542).

Mary tested Henry's patience again when she opposed the annulment of his marriage to **Catherine of Aragon** in 1533, thoroughly disapproving of her brother's new companion, **Anne Boleyn**, who had been a maid of honor at her wedding to Louis. She died at Westhorpe Hall, Suffolk, on 25 June the same year and was buried at the Benedictine abbey at Bury St. Edmunds; her remains were removed to nearby St. Mary's church when the building was ravaged in 1539 during the king's campaign to dissolve the English monasteries. Charles Brandon speedily married Catherine Willoughby, his son's fiancée and a wealthy heiress. *See also* UNION OF THE CROWNS.

**TUDOR, OWEN (c1400–1461).** Although the roots of the **House of Tudor** can be traced back to the 12th-century **Welsh princes**, Owen is usually considered the founder of its fortunes. He was born at Plas Penmynydd, on the island of Anglesey off the northwest coast of Wales, to Maredudd ap Tudur and Margaret ferch Dafydd, but he anglicized his forename (changing Owain to Owen) and adopted his grandfather's surname, discarding the patronymic "ap Maredudd" (son of Maredudd) and using "Tudur" instead. Although little is known of his early life, he appears to have fought in **France** for King **Henry V** and then attached himself to the royal court.

When Henry died in 1422, his 21-year-old widow—**Catherine of Valois**—moved from **London** to **Wallingford Castle**, and Owen probably accompanied her as part of her household. There are several tales surrounding their first meeting. One suggests that the young man fell into her lap during a ball, another that the **queen dowager** saw him swimming naked in the River Thames. Rumors of the relationship were certainly circulating at court by about 1426, and parliament reacted by passing legislation that prohibited former **queens consort** from marrying without the monarch's permission. There is no evidence that a wedding ever took place, but the couple had at least seven children, one of whom—**Edmund Tudor, earl of Richmond**—was the father of Henry Tudor, who defeated **Richard III** in battle at **Bosworth Field** in 1485 and claimed the English crown (as King **Henry VII**) by right of conquest.

After Catherine died in 1437, Owen was imprisoned by **Henry VI** (her son by Henry V), but eventually relations improved and the Welshman once again found employment in the **Royal Household**. He fought for the king against the rebels of the **House of York** in the early skirmishes of the **Wars of the Roses** but was taken prisoner at the Battle of Mortimer's Cross on 2 February 1461 and was **beheaded** shortly afterward. His remains were interred at the Church of the Grey Friars in Hereford.

# U

UCTREDA OF NORTHUMBRIA (?–?). *See* OCTREDA OF NOR-THUMBRIA.

UNION OF PARLIAMENTS (1707). On 1 May 1707, England and Scotland united as a single realm, known as Great Britain. Although proposals that the two countries should form a single state had been voiced on several occasions following the **union of the crowns** (when Scotland's king succeeded to the English throne and ruled as **James VI of Scotland and I of England** from 1603), they had never been popular with the Scots, who feared absorption by their more powerful neighbor. Matters came to a head in 1701, when the English parliament passed an **Act of Settlement** that excluded Roman Catholics from the throne and ensured that the crown, on Queen **Anne**'s death, would pass to **Sophia, electress of Hanover**, or her Protestant heirs.

Scots saw no reason why their monarch should be chosen by a foreign assembly, so in 1703 the Estates (Scotland's parliament) approved a bill providing that if Anne died childless—as was likely—they would offer the crown to a Protestant descendant of earlier Scottish monarchs, but not necessarily Sophia. The legislation (which was widely interpreted as an invitation to **James Francis Edward Stuart**, son of the exiled **James VII and II**, to renounce his Roman Catholic faith and worship as a Protestant) was refused **royal assent** by James Douglas, duke of Queensbury (the queen's personal representative in Scotland), but the Scots persisted, threatening to withdraw troops from armies fighting in continental Europe and to refuse payment of taxes unless their wishes were granted.

Under pressure, the queen's advisors wilted, and the legislation, known as the **Act of Security**, became law in 1704. But the English parliament responded the following year with the Alien Act, which imposed an embargo on the importation of Scottish goods (in effect cutting off about half of Scotland's foreign trade) and categorized Scots resident in England as aliens (a provision that affected the inheritance of property). However, the act contained a clause providing for its repeal if Scotland entered discussions designed to lead to political union.

At the time, the Scottish economy had been almost bankrupted by a rash attempt to develop a colony in Central America, so the nation's leaders had little room to maneuver. Extracting a promise of financial support from England and attracted by the prospect of trade with the English colonies, parliamentarians agreed to a Treaty of Union that made the formerly independent states one country, with one monarch (Anne) and one **London**-based parliament. Writing some years later, Robert Burns, the Scottish poet, described the negotiators as "rogues" and complained that his countrymen were "bought and sold for English gold," but many modern historians adopt a more charitable view, arguing that the economics of the times justified the decision.

**UNION OF THE CROWNS (1603).** When Queen **Elizabeth I** of England died on 24 March 1603, King **James VI** of Scotland inherited her crown, uniting the two states under a single monarch for the first time. A first cousin twice removed, James was Elizabeth's closest male relative, but even so, the politics of the succession were not straightforward. King **Henry VIII** had left three children who ruled England successively as **Edward VI**, **Mary I**, and Elizabeth I, but none had left any surviving issue. Moreover, Henry's brothers — **Arthur, prince of Wales**; **Edmund Tudor, duke of Somerset**; and **Edward Tudor** — had also died before siring offspring, as had two of his sisters (**Elizabeth Tudor** and **Katherine Tudor**). In 1543, parliamentary legislation had granted Henry the right to bequeath the succession in his will, and he had specifically excluded his older sister — **Margaret Tudor**, James's paternal great-grandmother — as well as her descendants by indicating that, if his children died childless, the crown should go to the heirs of their younger sibling, **Mary Tudor, queen of France**.

Given this criterion, the most senior line of descent lay through Lady Catherine Grey, Mary's granddaughter (and younger sister of Lady **Jane Grey**). However, in 1560, Catherine had secretly married Edward Seymour, earl of Hertford (and brother of **Jane Seymour**, Henry VIII's third wife), without seeking Queen Elizabeth's permission and had been cast into the **Tower of London**, accused of treason. The marriage was annulled in 1562, so both of the sons born as a result of the match were considered bastards and were thus not entitled to the throne; had the marriage been approved, after Catherine's death in 1568, her elder boy — Edward Seymour, viscount Beauchamp — would have been **heir apparent** under the terms of Henry's will.

With Beauchamp ruled out because of his suspect legitimacy, the heiress apparent, if Henry VIII's wishes were observed, was Anne Stanley, countess of Castlehaven. The countess was Mary's great-great-granddaughter, but she was still unmarried at the time of Elizabeth's death, so she would have created further succession problems had she taken the throne. Arbella

Stuart (or Stewart)—Margaret Tudor's daughter by her second marriage (to James Douglas, earl of Angus)—was a third candidate, but she too was unmarried and in addition had been the subject of rumors that she intended to marry into the Seymour line without seeking the queen's permission. (After James VI and I succeeded Elizabeth, some plotters hatched a scheme to replace him with Arbella, but when she heard of the plan she told the king of the proposals.)

The decision to ignore Henry VIII's requests and to ensure that James followed Elizabeth at the royal court in **London** was entirely the result of political maneuvering by a group of senior English nobles led by Sir Robert Cecil, who believed that the king would make a more acceptable sovereign than the other claimants. While counseling the queen, Cecil conducted a secret correspondence with the Scots monarch, advising him to treat Elizabeth with respect and kindness but not to press his claim to the English throne strongly. The advice was followed, Elizabeth increasingly accepted James as her likely successor, and within two weeks of her death he had left **Edinburgh** for London, meeting cheering crowds as he made his slow progression south. However, the union of the crowns did not imply a political union. Until 1707, England and Scotland continued to function as independent states even though James assumed the title "king of Great Britain."

**UNION, TREATY OF (1707).** *See* UNION OF PARLIAMENTS.

# V

**VICTORIA (1819–1901).** Victoria's 63-year reign—longer than that of any other British sovereign—shaped the modern monarchy while industrialization transformed the economic landscape of her realm and her subjects built an empire that spanned the globe. She was born at **Kensington Palace** on 24 May 1819, the only daughter of **Prince Edward, duke of Kent and Strathearn**, and **Victoria of Saxe-Coburg-Saalfield**. Her father died when she was only eight months old, so she was raised by her mother and a governess, succeeding to the throne on 20 June 1837 because her immediate predecessor, King **William IV**, had left no surviving children and because she was the only living child born to either of his older brothers, Edward and King **George IV**.

Just 18 years of age and inexperienced in political matters, the young queen was initially much influenced by William Lamb, viscount Melbourne, her prime minister and the leader of the Whig faction in the House of Commons (the lower chamber in Britain's bicameral parliament). Melbourne undoubtedly helped to bolster the young monarch's confidence, but, mature and sophisticated, he also turned her into a Whig, and that led to political crisis. In 1839, Melbourne resigned office because he was having difficulty maintaining a majority in the Commons, so Victoria asked his rival, Sir Robert Peel, the head of the Tory party, to form a government. At the time, appointments to the **Royal Household** were made by the prime minister, but when Peel nominated Tory replacements for the Whig ladies of the bedchamber (the high-ranking **ladies-in-waiting**), the queen took umbrage because several of the women had become her friends as well as her attendants. Digging in her heels, she refused to make the changes that Peel wanted, so he too became stubborn and declined the prime ministerial post. In the end, Melbourne reluctantly returned, but Victoria, when she was much older and significantly wiser, admitted that she had handled the matter badly.

Marriage to **Albert of Saxe-Coburg and Gotha** provided both emotional stability and a more dispassionate advisor. They first met in 1836, but Victoria was happy to remain independent until 1839, when she proposed to him. They were married in **St. James's Palace** on 10 February the following year and produced nine children, eight of whom were to find partners from other royal houses and lead writers to refer to the queen as "the grandmother of Europe." Initially, Victoria tried to prevent her husband from taking any part in government, but gradually his influence increased until he was handling most of the affairs of state. For her part, the queen was happiest when living away from **London** at **Osborne House** on the Isle of Wight or at **Balmoral Castle** in Scotland, but even so, she was a conscientious monarch who, under Albert's guidance, learned how to organize her duties and encourage her ministers to explain issues simply but with sufficient detail for her to understand the problems. As a result, when her consort died in 1861, she was able to pick up the reins by attempting to make decisions she believed he would have made.

Despite her sense of duty, for several years after Albert's death Victoria rarely appeared in public, missing her helpmate greatly. Many of her subjects resented her seclusion, believing that she should display the pomp and majesty appropriate to the head of the world's first industrial nation, with its growing empire. It was another prime minister—Benjamin Disraeli—who encouraged her to emerge from her grieving in the late 1870s. "Dizzy," as she called him, was a staunch advocate of overseas expansion, earning her gratitude when, in 1876, he sponsored parliamentary legislation that named her "Empress of India." Relations with William Gladstone, prime minister on four occasions during her reign, were less cordial. Gladstone held his sovereign in great awe, treated her stiffly, and wrote her ponderous missives about his policies, with which she had little sympathy. In particular, she could not support schemes designed to meet the grievances of the people of Ireland, refusing to establish a residence on the island or to consider plans to give the colony some autonomy over its own affairs.

However, despite such conflicts of view, as Victoria aged she insisted on more and more consultation with her prime ministers, leading Joseph Chamberlain to comment in exasperation that "the queen does interfere constantly." Her lengthy reign gave her considerable experience in the affairs of government, and she took every opportunity to present her advisors with the benefit of that experience.

For the British people, the sovereign ultimately became a symbol of power and progress, despite her idiosyncrasies (every night, Albert's clothes were laid out in his room, even after his death), so there was genuine sadness when she passed away at Osborne on 22 January 1901 after a short illness. She was buried beside her husband at **Frogmore**, not far from **Windsor Castle**, as she had wished. Victoria had ruled with dignity over a monarchy that, at the start of her reign, had fallen into some disrepute as a result of the financial extravagances and sexual peccadilloes of her immediate predecessors, and she had allowed her role to evolve from that of a government decision maker to that of a largely ceremonial head of state who nevertheless had, as Walter Bagehot (a contemporary constitutional analyst) wrote, "the right to be consulted, the right to encourage, the right to warn."

A multitude of statues of the queen were built around the empire, and countless administrative areas, buildings, hospitals, railroad stations, parks, and settlements were named after her, including the capital cities of British Columbia and the Seychelles, Lake Victoria and Victoria Falls in Africa, the state of Victoria in Australia, and the township of Victoria in Lunenburg County, Virginia. *See also* ALBERT VICTOR, PRINCE, DUKE OF CLARENCE AND AVONDALE; ALEXANDRA OF DENMARK; ALFRED, PRINCE, DUKE OF EDINBURGH AND SAXE-COBURG-GOTHA; ALICE, PRINCESS, GRAND DUCHESS OF HESSE; ARTHUR, PRINCE, DUKE OF CONNAUGHT AND STRATHEARN; BEATRICE (OR HENRY) OF BATTENBERG, PRINCESS; CAMBUSKENNETH ABBEY; CHRISTIAN OF SCHLESWIG-HOLSTEIN, PRINCESS; CRATHIE CHURCH; EDWARD VII; KEW PALACE; LEOPOLD, PRINCE, DUKE OF ALBANY; LOUISE, PRINCESS, DUCHESS OF ARGYLL; MARY OF TECK; ROYAL TRAIN; ST. GEORGE'S CHAPEL; VICTORIA, PRINCESS ROYAL, GERMAN EMPRESS; WHITE LODGE.

**VICTORIA OF SAXE-COBURG-SAALFIELD, PRINCESS, DUCHESS OF KENT AND STRATHEARN (1786–1861). Princess** Victoria, the mother of Queen **Victoria**, was born at Coburg in Bavaria on 17 August 1786, the fourth daughter (and sixth child) of Frederick Anton, duke of Saxe-Coburg-Saalfield, and Augusta of Reuss-Ebersdorf. On 21 December 1803, she was married to Emich Charles, prince of Leiningen; they had a son (Charles, born in 1804) and a daughter (Anna, born in 1807). The prince died of pneumonia in 1814, so four years later, on 29 May 1818 in Coburg (according to Lutheran Church rites) and on 11 July at **Kew Palace** (in a **Church of England** ceremony), she took **Prince Edward, duke of Kent and Strathearn** and son of King **George III**, as her second husband.

Leopold, Victoria's younger brother, had been married to **Princess Charlotte Augusta**, who was the only child of George, **prince of Wales** (later King **George IV**), and George III's only living grandchild. Charlotte's death in 1817 sent Wales's unmarried brothers on a hurried search for suitable Protestant wives so that they could produce heirs, thus ensuring that the British crown would remain in the **House of Hanover**'s hands, and Victoria was persuaded by Leopold to marry Edward. On May 1819 she gave birth to a daughter, also named Victoria, who was to become Britain's longest reigning monarch. However, the duke of Kent and Strathearn died the following year, leaving the duchess in considerable financial difficulties that were alleviated only by grants from parliament and by generous help from her brother.

Relations with George's successor, King **William IV**, were also strained, largely because the duchess hired John Conroy, an Irish army officer, as her private secretary and, according to some in court circles, became his lover. Conroy had ambitions; he hoped that William—who was nearly 65 when he became king in 1830—would die and that the duchess would be appointed **regent** until her daughter was of an age to govern by herself, because in those circumstances he would exert considerable influence over court and government. The scheming secretary deliberately exaggerated family conflicts, keeping the younger Victoria isolated from most children except his own daughters and making her sleep with her mother, ostensibly in case she was abducted, but the plans came to naught because the heiress to the throne had reached her 18th birthday (albeit by less than a month) before William passed away in 1837.

Queen Victoria immediately broke many ties with her mother and was only reconciled, probably as a result of the cajolings of her husband, **Prince Albert of Saxe-Coburg and Gotha**, after the birth of her first child (**Victoria, princess royal**) in 1840, by which time Conroy had been induced to leave royal employment. The reconciliation was permanent, so when her mother died of cancer at **Frogmore** House on 16 March 1861, the queen was devastated. The duchess was initially interred at **St. George's Chapel** in **Windsor Castle**, but her remains were removed in August of the same year to a mausoleum on the Frogmore estate.

Some writers have argued that Queen Victoria was not the child of the duke of Kent and Strathearn, implying that his wife was unfaithful at the beginning of their marriage. They point out that porphyria, an illness previously common in the **royal family** (with King George III one of the sufferers), is unknown among Victoria's descendants and that the occurrence of hemophilia, never previously recorded, has become more frequent. Moreover, they allege, the duke had no illegitimate children despite consorting with a series of mistresses and thus may have been infertile. However, other scholars contest the evidence, claiming that Kent and Strathearn may have had a child by Adelaide Dubus (one of his paramours), that hemophilia may occur spontaneously, and that there is evidence that Victoria's granddaughter, Charlotte of Prussia, was a victim of porphyria, as were others who can claim her as an ancestor.

**VICTORIA, PRINCESS (1868–1935).** The quiet, retiring life led by **Princess** Victoria contrasted sharply with the rumor-ridden experiences of her older brother, **Albert Victor, duke of Clarence and Avondale**. The fourth child, and second daughter, of Albert Edward, **prince of Wales** (later King

Edward VII), and **Alexandra of Denmark**, she was born at **Marlborough House**, her parents' **London** home, on 6 July 1868. As she grew up, she developed a close bond with her brother George (later King **George V**), who was less than two years older than she, but was less enamored of his wife (Princess **Mary of Teck**, whom she thought "deadly dull"), and she never found a partner herself, maintaining that she would marry only for love, not for dynastic reasons, but failing to meet the right man.

The princess accompanied her parents on many of their official engagements and then, after Edward died in 1910, cared for her increasingly deaf, frail, and virtually immobile mother until the **queen dowager** too passed away in 1925. Finally freed of family responsibilities, she moved to the village of Iver, west of London, and lived outside of the royal limelight, involving herself in community activities and pursuing her interest in photography. She died at Coppins, her Iver home, on 3 December 1935 and was interred in the royal burial ground at **Frogmore**.

**VICTORIA, PRINCESS ROYAL, GERMAN EMPRESS (1840–1901).** The eldest of nine children in the family of Queen **Victoria** and **Prince Albert of Saxe-Coburg and Gotha**, Victoria was born at **Buckingham Palace** on 21 November 1840 and the following year was created **princess royal** (a form of address sometimes granted to the first daughter of a monarch). For dynastic reasons, both parents were keen to see their child married to German stock (Victoria's mother—**Victoria of Saxe-Coburg-Saalfield**—was German, as was Albert), and the **prince** consort undoubtedly hoped that a union with Prince Frederick of Prussia (later Frederick III, German emperor and king of Prussia) would further his vision of a liberal Europe with Germany at its head. Frederick's father (who was to become Emperor William I of Germany) would have preferred his son to find a bride in tsarist Russia, but his mother—Princess Augusta of Saxe-Weimar—was enthusiastic about the match, so the princess and the prince were wed at **St. James's Palace** on 25 January 1858.

The union was arranged for political reasons, but the young couple were very much in love, producing eight children, six of whom reached adulthood. Despite their mutual affection, however, Victoria—an intelligent, perceptive woman, fluent in three languages—always felt constrained by the conservative ethos of German life and differed regularly with government ministers, notably chancellor Otto von Bismarck, whose authoritarian philosophies made him very resistant to change. Moreover, she became increasingly estranged from William, her eldest (and militaristic) son, as he became more and more inclined to von Bismarck's worldview rather than to that of his more free-thinking parents.

On 9 March 1888, Frederick succeeded his father as emperor, but, suffering from throat cancer, he survived for only 99 days. His early death effectively removed Victoria from any position of political influence, though she continued to support the arts and to channel funds to schools and training colleges for women. She also corresponded regularly with her mother and made frequent visits to Britain. In 1898, during one of those trips, she was diagnosed with breast cancer. The tumor proved inoperable, and on 5 August 1901, in considerable pain, she died near Frankfurt at Castle Friedrichshoff, which she had built as a memorial to her husband. She was buried in the family mausoleum at Friedenskirche in Potsdam, still much distrusted by many powerful Germans.

The princess royal's son, who followed Frederick as emperor, quarreled with the reactionary Bismarck but ultimately, in 1914, led his country into conflict with Britain (though he probably never intended that his efforts to make Germany a world power would lead to the devastation of World War I). Four of his siblings found marriage partners in other aristocratic German families, but one—Princess Sophie—married King Constantine I of Greece and had six children, helping to cement Queen Victoria's reputation as the grandmother of Europe. *See also* CHRISTIAN OF SCHWESLIG-HOLSTEIN, PRINCESS; CRATHIE CHURCH.

**VIKING MONARCHS.** During the last years of the 8th century, marauders from Scandinavia began to appear around British shores. Their arrival was merely one element of a colonization that took Vikings from their homeland eastward into the heart of Europe and westward to Newfoundland. Wales suffered little, and for the most part, Norse influence in Scotland was confined to islands and coastal areas. However, in Anglo-Saxon England, the impact was profound. Most of the invaders arriving in that region of the British Isles came from Denmark, and by the last quarter of the 9th century, they ruled the east, the midlands, and the north of the country, frequently through puppet kings, with only King **Alfred the Great**'s **Wessex** able to resist the incursion.

Reconquest of the Viking-dominated area, known as the **Danelaw**, began during the reign of **Edward the Elder** from 899 to 924 and was completed by his son, **Aethelstan**, with victory at the **Battle of Brunanburh** in 937. However, later **Anglo-Saxon monarchs** had trouble holding their realm together, and security was seriously threatened again from about 1000. Efforts to purchase peace failed (*see* DANEGELD), and in 1013, **Sweyn**, king of Denmark and Norway, landed with a Viking force at Sandwich in southeast England. Rapidly overrunning most of the country, he forced King **Aethelred the Unready** to flee to Normandy, replacing him on the throne on December 25 as England's first Viking ruler. He had little opportunity to stamp his authority on his new subjects, however, because he died on 3 February the following year.

The Norse army declared **Canute**, Sweyn's son, king in his stead, but the **witan** (the council of advisors to the monarch) chose instead to invite Aethelred to return from exile. Canute went back to Denmark, raised another army, and led another Norse conquest in 1016. He ruled for 19 years, maintaining a peace that allowed the economy to flourish, but his successors did not inherit his diplomatic skills. He had named **Harthacanute**, his son by **Emma of Normandy**, as his heir, but when he died in 1035, that young man was in Denmark preparing for war with Norway. Harthacanute was persuaded to appoint his mother co-**regent** with Harold (a half-brother through Canute's liaison with **Aelfgifu of Northampton**), but the two leaders bickered incessantly, and in 1037 Harold claimed the throne for himself as **Harold I**.

By 1039, the Norwegian threat to Denmark had been averted, and Harthacanute was able to turn his thoughts to the task of reclaiming his English territories. He began preparations for an invasion, but the army was not needed because Harold died on 17 March 1040, and Harthacanute was able to return unopposed. He was never widely popular, however, because he taxed his people heavily and, according to the *Anglo-Saxon Chronicle*, "never accomplished anything kingly." So when he died childless on 8 June 1042, the Anglo-Saxon line of kings was restored through **Edward the Confessor**. Harald Hardråde, king of Norway, laid claim to the throne when Edward died in 1066, and Duke William of **Normandy**, who became King **William I of England** after the **Battle of Hastings** in the fall of the same year, had Scandinavian blood in his veins—but even so, Viking interest in a conquest of England waned with Harthacanute's passing.

The term "Viking" is derived from the Old Norse *vikingr*, which means "people of the fiords." *See also* AELFGIFU OF YORK; AETHELWULF; ASSANDUN, BATTLE OF; CONSTANTINE I; CONSTANTINE II; EADRED; EDMUND I; INDULF; IONA; STAMFORD BRIDGE, BATTLE OF; ST. BRICE'S DAY MASSACRE; SVEIN OF NORWAY.

**WAKEFIELD, BATTLE OF (30 December 1460).** The conflict at Wake-field was one of the most significant of about 15 battles fought during the **Wars of the Roses**. On 10 July 1460, forces supporting **Richard, duke of York (1411–1460)** and claimant to the English throne, defeated a royalist army at the **Battle of Northampton**, taking King **Henry VI** prisoner. Three months later, York marched into parliament and asked it to recognize him as the legitimate monarch. The members refused but required Henry to name the duke as his heir. **Margaret of Anjou**, the **queen consort**, refused to accept this decision, which disinherited her 17-year-old son, **Edward of Lancaster**, and gathered her own troops in the north of the country.

Richard, attempting to prevent her from growing in strength, faced her with his own men at Wakefield on 30 December. Details of the military strategies and of the fighting are unclear, but somehow York was encouraged to leave the safety of his base at Sandal Castle and to venture out upon open ground, where he and his son, Edmund, earl of Rutland, were hacked down. Marga-ret's triumph was short lived, however, because Edward, Edmund's older brother, took up their father's cause and proved to be a perceptive military commander, ultimately deposing Henry and ruling as **Edward IV**.

The battle is sometimes quoted as the inspiration for the nursery rhyme about *The Grand Old Duke of York*, but there are several alternative can-didates (*see, for example,* FREDERICK, PRINCE, DUKE OF YORK AND ALBANY).

**WALLINGFORD CASTLE.** For six centuries, Wallingford Castle, south of Oxford, was an important royal fortress and residence at a strategic crossing point on the River Thames. It was built in 1067–71—at the behest of King **William I of England**, according to some sources—and became a base for supporters of **Matilda** who fought the forces of King **Stephen** in the civil war that divided England during the first half of the 12th century. King **John** added to the defenses, as did his son, **Richard, earl of Cornwall**. **William, count of Poitiers** (eldest child of **Henry II** and **Eleanor of Aquitaine**), died there in 1156, as did **Joan, countess of Kent** (wife of **Edward, the black**

**prince**, and mother of King **Richard II**), in 1385. **Catherine of Valois** retired to the building after her husband, King **Henry V**, died in 1422, and followers of **Charles I** occupied it during the struggle with Oliver Cromwell's parliamentarian troops during the 17th century, but in 1652 Cromwell ordered its destruction. A walled park, open to the public, now surrounds the few ruins that remain. *See also* MARGARET OF ANJOU.

**WALLIS, DUCHESS OF WINDSOR (1896–1986).** In 1936, King **Edward VIII**'s insistence that he would marry Wallis Simpson, an American divorcee, precipitated a constitutional crisis that led to the monarch's abdication after only 11 months on the throne. Wallis was born in Blue Ridge Summit, Pennsylvania, on 19 June 1896, the only child of businessman Teackle Wallis Warfield and his wife, Alice Montague. Her father died of tuberculosis when she was only a few months old, so she grew up in some poverty, living in Baltimore and supported financially by her uncle, Solomon Warfield.

In the spring of 1916, 19-year-old Wallis met Earl Winfield Spencer, Jr., a United States Navy pilot, while visiting friends in Florida, and they married on 8 November at Christ Episcopal Church in Baltimore. Legally, the union lasted for 11 years, but the alcoholic husband and unsympathetic wife proved incompatible. They separated and reunited several times before divorcing on 16 December 1927, by which time she was already conducting an affair with Ernest Aldrich Simpson, a British-American shipbroker with his father's firm. They wed at a civil ceremony in **London** on 21 July 1928, and through friends they met Thelma, Lady Furness, whose husband was chairman of the Furness Shipping Company.

On 10 January 1931, Lady Furness introduced Mrs. Simpson to her lover, Edward, **prince of Wales**, who soon became emotionally dependent on the American woman, captivated by her aggressive, dominating personality. However, as he spent more and more time with his new mistress, he spent less and less time on other responsibilities, causing considerable concern among his advisors. Edward became king, as Edward VIII, when his father—King **George V**—died on 20 January 1936. On 27 October, Wallis was granted a divorce from her second husband, and soon afterward the sovereign told Prime Minister Stanley Baldwin that he intended to marry her.

This decision posed a constitutional problem because the United Kingdom's monarch is also **supreme governor of the Church of England**, which contended that marriage was for life and so would not remarry people who had been separated by the divorce courts. As Edward struggled to find a way to keep his woman and his crown, Wallis fled to the south of **France** and pleaded with the king to give her up rather than abdicate. Edward, though, refused to change his mind. He formally renounced his throne on 11 December, and then, in a radio broadcast, he told the nation that he could not discharge his duties as sovereign "without the help and support of the woman I love." They married at the Château de Candé, near Tours in central France, on 3 June 1937, but none of the **royal family** attended, and for many years the bride was ostracized by her British relatives.

When World War II broke out in 1939, Edward (who was created duke of Windsor on relinquishing his crown) moved with his wife to Spain and then to Portugal before, in August 1940, taking up an appointment as governor of the Bahamas. During their five years on the islands, the duchess carried out her duties with a goodwill that surprised many who knew of her abrasiveness, but she heartily disliked the colony, bitterly resented the decision of King **George VI** (her husband's successor as sovereign) not to grant her the style of "**her royal highness**," and was much criticized for spending lavishly during shopping trips to the United States while wartime conditions made life in Britain very austere.

After hostilities ended in 1945, the duke and duchess returned to France. With no permanent responsibilities, they spent much of their time socializing in Paris and North America, but as they aged their health deteriorated. When Edward died in 1972, Wallis was briefly accepted into the royal family's fold, staying at **Buckingham Palace** while in the United Kingdom for the funeral. By 1980, she was unable to speak and was becoming increasingly senile, and before her death on 24 April 1986 at her Paris home, she was bedridden. Several of her royal relatives attended her funeral service at **St. George's Chapel** in **Windsor Castle** and her burial, next to her husband, at **Frogmore**.

In 1987, the sale of the duchess's jewelry raised $45 million for the Pasteur Institute, a nonprofit, Paris-based organization conducting research into the biological causes of disease. In fairy-tale fashion, the girl from a poor background had fallen in love with a **prince**, but the politics and social mores of interwar Britain, and the girl's own personality, had turned the romance into tragedy for many people, even though the duke and duchess lived as a devoted couple through 35 years of marriage, defying predictions that they would soon go their own ways. *See also* ELIZABETH, THE QUEEN MOTHER; FORT BELVEDERE; MARY OF TECK.

**WARBECK, PERKIN (1474?–1499).** Like **Lambert Simnel**, Warbeck was used as a focus for rebellion by opponents of King **Henry VII**. Probably born in Tournai (now in Belgium), he had a physical resemblance to **Edward IV** and was persuaded to masquerade as that king's son, **Richard, duke of York (1473–1483?)**, who had disappeared in mysterious circumstances in the **Tower of London**.

With the support of Edward's sister, Margaret of York, Warbeck mounted an invasion of England, attempting a landing at Deal (on the southeast coast) on 3 July 1495, but he was easily beaten back by Henry's troops and fled to Ireland, then to Scotland, and then back to Ireland before seeking support in Cornwall, where there was great opposition to the king's efforts to raise taxes in order to fund a campaign against the Scots. Within days of his arrival on 7 September 1497, he had amassed an army of some 6,000 men, but, faced with the might of Henry's well-trained force, his courage failed and he sought sanctuary in Beaulieu Abbey where he was captured. For two years he was incarcerated in the Tower of London, but on 23 November 1499 he was hanged after attempting to escape. *See also* JAMES IV; TUDOR, MARGARET.

**WARS OF THE ROSES.** Novelist Sir Walter Scott coined the term "Wars of the Roses" to describe the strife that divided England from 1455 to 1485 as two powerful dynasties—the **House of Lancaster** (which sported a red rose as its emblem) and the **House of York** (which had a white rose)—struggled for control of the crown.

The problems had begun in 1399, when King **Richard II** was forced to abdicate, leaving no son who could succeed him. Henry Bolingbroke, who had led a rebellion against the unpopular monarch and was indisputably the most powerful noble in the land, took the throne, ruled as **Henry IV**, and was followed by his son, **Henry V**, and grandson, **Henry VI**. However, the last of these Lancastrian sovereigns was a deeply religious man who allowed himself to be much influenced by a group of relatives intent on withdrawing from the **Hundred Years' War** with **France**. The resulting lack of strong military leadership led to the loss of much of England's territory on the European mainland. At the same time, law and order began to break down, and the royal treasury was depleted because many of the king's ministers were more interested in lining their pockets than in governing the country. Henry's increasingly evident mental instability added to the administrative inefficiencies and to the decline in international prestige that accompanied his withdrawal from the French estates, so inevitably several nobles became disaffected.

The opposition to the monarch was led by **Richard, duke of York (1411–1460)**, who, given the traditions of **succession to the throne** by male primogeniture, had a strong claim to the crown because he was descended from **Lionel of Antwerp**, the third son of King **Edward III**, whereas King Henry VI was descended from **John of Gaunt**, the fourth son. Initially, York professed loyalty to the king and in 1453 was appointed protector of the realm by parliament when Henry suffered one of his bouts of insanity. Understandably, **Margaret of Anjou**, the **queen consort**, opposed this appointment, believing that Richard was intent on becoming king and thus usurping the inheritance of her son, **Edward of Lancaster**. When her husband recovered his faculties in 1455, Margaret encouraged him to rescind the decision, a move that persuaded the duke that the only way of changing the government was through force of arms.

The first battle, at **St. Albans** on 22 May, was followed by many skirmishes and some 15 large-scale conflicts between Lancastrians and Yorkists over the next three decades. On 10 July 1460, the rebels gained a significant victory at the **Battle of Northampton**, capturing the king. Shortly afterward, York invited parliament to recognize him as sovereign. Although the invitation was declined, Henry was forced to name Richard as his heir, so Margaret continued the struggle, and at **Wakefield** on 30 December her troops killed both him and Edmund, his son. Edward—Edmund's older brother—then took up the Yorkist cause, receiving much support in **London**, where he was declared king as **Edward IV** on 4 March 1461. Determined to emphasize his supremacy, the new monarch marched his forces north to **Towton**, where he routed the Lancastrian army on 29 March, forcing Henry and Margaret to flee to Scotland for safety.

This decisive victory ensured that there would be an uneasy peace for several years, but by 1470 Margaret had forged an alliance with Richard Neville, earl of Warwick, who had defected from the Yorkist camp. They were able to build a large army that left Edward little option but to take refuge in Holland. Henry returned to the throne, but the Lancastrian success was short lived because Warwick was killed in battle at Barnet on 14 April 1471. Deprived of her most experienced commander, Margaret stood little chance of military success against her accomplished opponents. She was captured at **Tewkesbury** on 4 May, and Edward of Lancaster was either killed or executed shortly afterward. Edward IV took the crown again, and Henry was imprisoned in the **Tower of London**, where he was murdered on 21 May.

Edward remained king until his death in 1483, when his 12-year-old son succeeded him as **Edward V**. But he reigned for only a few weeks before being deposed by his uncle, who ruled as **Richard III**. The boy's subsequent disappearance, and that of his younger brother, **Richard, duke of York (1473–1483?)**, caused much apprehension, encouraging many of the nobles, including several leading Yorkists, to turn to Henry Tudor, a Lancastrian, for leadership. With assistance from the French, Henry killed the usurper at the **Battle of Bosworth Field** on 22 August 1485 and won parliamentary approval for his claim to be King **Henry VII**. The following year, he married **Elizabeth of York**, Edward IV's daughter, thus uniting the competing families, and on 16 June 1487, at **Stoke Field**, he crushed a final effort by diehard Yorkists to regain the crown.

Historians disagree about the date when the Wars of the Roses ended, some arguing that Edward IV's successes in 1471 destroyed Lancastrian hopes of kingship, several claiming that Henry VII's accession to the throne in 1485 was the turning point, and others asserting that the king's marriage in 1486 or his victory at Stoke brought the conflict to a close. Richard III's death ended three centuries of **House of Plantagenet** control of the crown and initiated a period in which the nobles' power declined while the monarchy increased in strength, but there is still much debate about the long-term impact of the wars on English society. *See also* ST. ALBANS, SECOND BATTLE OF.

**WELSH PRINCES.** Although Gruffydd ap Llywelyn had united Wales under his rule in 1055, his followers rebelled, killing him in 1063, so when King **William I of England**'s Norman troops pushed into the area after the **Battle of Hastings** in 1066, they were opposed by a variety of local rulers rather than by the single, organized enemy that made their advance in Scotland difficult. From a string of heavily fortified stone castles, the Norman barons were able to subdue the individual princes, despite bitter opposition, and in 1301 King **Edward I** made his infant son (later King **Edward II**) prince of Wales. From then on, Wales became an integral part of England. However, though Welsh soldiers were much used in English armies, there was no Welsh blood in the **royal family** until King **Henry VII**, grandson of **Owen Tudor**, usurped the throne and founded the royal **House of Tudor** in 1485. *See also* ARMSTRONG-JONES, ANTONY, EARL OF SNOWDON; EALDGYTH OF MERCIA.

**WESSEX.** Wessex was one of several kingdoms founded by the Saxons, but it was more successful than the others, expanding its influence so that it ultimately provided many of England's earliest monarchs. The area was located in the south of Britain, focusing initially on the settlement at Dorchester and later at **Winchester**. Its territory included the area covered by the modern counties of Dorset, Hampshire, Somerset, and Wiltshire, though boundaries changed over the centuries as military fortunes waxed and waned. According to the *Anglo-Saxon Chronicle*, it was founded by **Cerdic** and his son (or possibly grandson) **Cynric**, who arrived from the European mainland in 495, but modern scholars suggest that it may also have coalesced around communities in the upper reaches of the River Thames.

During the reign of **Ceawlin** from 560 to 592, Wessex expanded north of the Thames, and although threatened at times by the kingdom of Mercia, it had become the dominant dynasty by the early 9th century. From 835, Viking invaders, most of them Danish, sometimes overran parts of England, but a process of retrenchment and reorganization under **Alfred the Great**, who ruled from 871 to c899, ultimately led to the expulsion of the intruders and the unification of England under **Aethelstan** in 927.

As in later times, marriage between members of leading families was common. In 1070, Margaret, daughter of **Edward the Exile** and later known both as Margaret of Scotland and as **St. Margaret**, married **Malcolm III**, the king of Scots. Edith, their daughter, was wed to **Henry I** of England (*see* MATILDA OF SCOTLAND), and as a result of that match, all monarchs of England and Scotland since the 12th century have been able to claim descent from the house of Wessex.

The **House of Normandy** ended Wessex rule at the **Battle of Hastings** in 1066, but the kingdom's name was popularized during the late 19th and early 20th centuries by novelist and poet Thomas Hardy and is still much used by tourist organizations, transport companies, utility providers, and other groups. In 1999, Queen **Elizabeth II** created her youngest son, **Prince Edward**, **earl of Wessex** when he married Sophie Rhys-Jones (*see* SOPHIE, COUNTESS OF WESSEX) and thus revived a title that had not been used for 900 years. *See also* AETHELWULF; ANGLO-SAXON MONARCHS; CEOL; COENRED; CUTHWULF; CUTHWINE; EADWIG; EAFA; EDITH OF WESSEX; EDWARD THE CONFESSOR; EDWARD THE ELDER; EGBERT; EOPPA; GODWIN, EARL OF WESSEX; INGILD.

**WESTMINSTER ABBEY.** The abbey at Westminster, on the north bank of the River Thames in central **London**, was the location for **coronations** of England's sovereigns from 1066, when **Harold II** and **William I** were crowned. The tradition was continued following parliamentary union with Scotland in 1707 and again after the formation of the United Kingdom in 1922. The only monarchical exceptions were **Edgar Aetheling** (who was appointed king by the Anglo-Saxons after Harold II died at the **Battle of Hastings** but who quickly paid homage to William); **Edward V** (who was declared illegitimate, and thus not entitled to the throne, before he could be crowned); Lady **Jane Grey** (who was deposed after a reign of less than two weeks in July 1553); and **Edward VIII** (who abdicated before a coronation was held). Also, the remains of most English monarchs and several **queens consort** lie in the abbey, though sovereigns who followed **George II** have been buried at **Frogmore** or at **St. George's Chapel** in **Windsor Castle**.

According to legend, a Christian community was established at the site in the early 7th century. **Edward the Confessor** built a stone church, which was consecrated on 28 December 1065 (only a few days before his death) but was demolished in 1245 by King **Henry III**, who constructed the present building in the Gothic style popular in France, though significant additions and refurbishments continued well into the 19th century. In 1579, Queen **Elizabeth I** made the abbey a **royal peculiar** (a church whose officials are responsible to the sovereign rather than to a diocesan bishop) and named it the Collegiate Church of St. Peter.

Poet Geoffrey Chaucer was buried in the abbey, probably in 1400. Since then, many other literary figures, scientists, and prominent citizens have been interred nearby, including politicians Ernest Bevin (1951) and Clement Attlee (1967), missionary David Livingstone (1873), scientists Isaac Newton (1727) and Charles Darwin (1882), and writers Ben Jonson (1637), Samuel Johnson (1784), Charles Dickens (1870), Alfred Tennyson (1892), and Rudyard Kipling (1936). The neighborhood of the abbey, which includes the **Palace of Westminster**, was declared a World Heritage Site by the United Nations Educational, Scientific and Cultural Organization (UNESCO) in 1987.

**WESTMINSTER, PALACE OF.** The site now occupied by the houses of parliament, on the north bank of the River Thames in central **London**, was the principal residence of the English **royal family** during the late medieval period. Some writers suggest that Anglo-Saxon leaders erected the first buildings in the area and that **Canute**, the **Viking monarch** who ruled England from 1017 to 1035, built a palace in the same location. **Edward the Confessor** erected a large home there while he watched workmen toil on **Westminster Abbey**, which he founded c1045, and **William I of England** (William the Conqueror) enlarged that structure. **William II of England** added a "great hall" (now known as Westminster Hall) for banquets and entertainment, but these early monarchs regularly moved from place to place around their realm, so it was not until the reign of King **Henry III** that Westminster became the English kings' major base.

In the same period, parliament began to meet regularly in the palace, and by the last quarter of the 14th century, when **Richard II** was on the throne, it had become the focus of government rather than merely the hub of royal life. By the 15th century, the principal law courts were operating there as well, but fire gutted the king's apartments in 1512, and **Henry VIII** moved to **Whitehall Palace**, which had been the home of the archbishops of York.

Even though the monarchs had departed, parliament continued to meet in the palace, much of which was rebuilt after another fire in 1834, and again after Luftwaffe bombs caused considerable damage during World War II. In the 21st century, it is entirely devoted to government, incorporating the debating chambers of the House of Commons and the House of Lords as well as numerous meeting rooms, but technically it is still a royal palace (even though none of the royal family ever resides there), so anybody who dies on the premises would be entitled to a royal funeral; for this reason, the deceased are transported to nearby St. Thomas's Hospital, where they are registered as "dead on arrival." *See also* ANNE, COUNTESS OF SURREY; CECILY, VISCOUNTESS WELLES; EDWARD I; EDWARD IV; EDWARD OF LANCASTER, PRINCE OF WALES; ELIZABETH OF YORK; NEVILLE, ANNE; RICHARD, DUKE OF YORK (1473–1483?); STATE OPENING OF PARLIAMENT; TUDOR, MARGARET.

**WHITE LODGE.** White Lodge, in Richmond Park on the southwestern fringe of **London**, was a **royal residence** for much of the period from 1727 to 1927. Although built as a hunting lodge for King **George II**, it soon became a favorite home of his consort, **Caroline of Brandenburg-Ansbach**. In 1751, it passed to their daughter, **Princess Amelia (1711–1786)**, who added two wings during her 10-year stay and caused much annoyance as a result of her efforts to keep the public out of the park.

For most of the 80 years after Amelia's departure, the building was occupied by two prime ministers—John Stuart, earl of Bute, and Henry Addington, viscount Sidmouth—but in 1844, Queen **Victoria** gave it to **Princess Mary, duchess of Gloucester and Edinburgh** (the last surviving daughter of King **George III**). On Mary's death in 1857, White Lodge became the home of the youthful Edward, **prince of Wales** (later King **Edward VII**), whose father (Victoria's consort, **Prince Albert of Saxe-Coburg and Gotha**) wanted him in an isolated location where he could concentrate on his studies.

Victoria and Albert occupied the lodge themselves for a time in 1861 after the death of the queen's mother, **Princess Victoria of Saxe-Coburg-Saalfield**. From 1869, it was used by **Princess** Mary Adelaide of Cambridge (the daughter of **Prince Adolphus, duke of Cambridge**) and her recently acquired husband, Prince Francis of Teck, who lived there until in 1883 they fled abroad to escape creditors. In 1893, Princess Victoria Mary—Mary Adelaide's daughter (*see* MARY OF TECK)—married George, **duke of York** (the future King **George V**), and established herself in her childhood home, where the following year she gave birth to her first child, who in 1936 reigned as King **Edward VIII** for less than a year before abdicating. The final royal residents were Albert, **duke of York** (later King **George VI**), and his wife, **Elizabeth, the queen mother**, who made it their home in 1923 but moved out in 1927, frustrated by the cost of upkeep and the lack of privacy. In 1955, the lodge was taken over by the Sadler's Wells Ballet (now the Royal Ballet School), which has undertaken major restoration work, including a museum that details the property's history.

**WHITEHALL PALACE.** In 1529, King **Henry VIII** acquired a **London** property that had previously belonged to Thomas, Cardinal Wolsey, the lord chancellor who was deprived of both his office and his estate because he failed to persuade Pope Clement VII that his monarch's marriage to **Catherine of Aragon** should be annulled. Dissatisfied with his aging **Palace of Westminster**, where fire had badly damaged the royal accommodation in 1512, Henry set about converting the premises into a new residence that he named "Whitehall," probably because it was fashionable at the time to accord that title to any place given over to feasting and celebration, but possibly also because the stonework had a very light color. A 2,000-room warren of corridors and staircases, with gardens, orchards, a real tennis court, a tiltyard for jousting, and a cockpit, it became the fulcrum of social life for the **House of Tudor** and the **House of Stuart**.

Henry celebrated his marriages to **Anne Boleyn** and **Jane Seymour** at Whitehall Palace in 1533 and 1536 respectively, **Elizabeth I** used the Great Hall as a theater, **James VI and I** commissioned architect Inigo Jones to build a banqueting house, **Charles I** acquired an extensive collection of paintings during the second quarter of the 17th century, Oliver Cromwell ruled from Whitehall as lord protector of England from 1653 until his death five years later, **Charles II** installed his mistresses shortly after the **restoration of the monarchy** in 1660, and in 1688 the Roman Catholic **James VII and II** sneaked out of the palace to seek safety in **France** from his Protestant persecutors.

In 1689, however, **William III and II**—believing that air pollution in **London** was affecting his asthma—moved the royal court to **Kensington Palace**. Nine years later, Whitehall Palace burned to the ground, apparently because a servant left clothes drying too close to a fire. The banqueting house is the only major part of the structure that still stands, although other sections have been absorbed into the government offices that now occupy the site. The Whitehall name was given to the road on which these offices are located, and it is often used as a collective noun for the United Kingdom's government administration, including the civil service as well as the executive. *See also* KENNINGTON PALACE; MARY HENRIETTA, PRINCESS ROYAL, PRINCESS OF ORANGE; OLDENBURG, MARY; STUART, CATHERINE; STUART, CHARLES, DUKE OF CAMBRIDGE; STUART, HENRIETTA; STUART, HENRY, DUKE OF GLOUCESTER.

**WILLIAM I OF ENGLAND (c1028–1087).** William's invasion of England from Normandy in 1066 changed the course of British history, strengthening the power of the monarchy, altering social relationships, introducing lifestyles from the European mainland, and reshaping the English language (*see* NORMANDY, HOUSE OF). The son of **Robert I, duke of Normandy**, and his mistress, **Herleva** (who is also known as Arletta, Arlotta, Herleve, and other names), William was born in 1027 or 1028 and was the grandnephew of **Emma of Normandy**, who had married **Aethelred the Unready**, king of the English, in 1002. Robert died at Nicaea (now Iznik, Turkey) in 1035 while returning from a pilgrimage to Jerusalem, so William (who had been nominated as heir because his father had no legitimate offspring) inherited his dukedom while still a child.

As a youth, the new duke met **Edward the Confessor** (the son of Emma and Aethelred), who was exiled in Normandy, and later claimed that this second cousin, once removed, had promised him the throne of England on his death. Norman sources certainly suggest that, in 1064 or 1065, Edward sent Harold, earl of **Wessex** and later King **Harold II**, to Normandy to confirm the arrangement and that Harold, taken prisoner during the excursion, had sworn an oath to support William's right to the crown. Nevertheless, the succession was disputed because, shortly before he died, Edward apparently pointed at Harold from his deathbed, and some of his attendants assumed that the gesture was an indication of his preference for his successor.

Harold was crowned on 6 January 1066, chosen by the **witan** (the monarch's advisory council) because he was the most powerful man in the realm. He had a difficult introduction to kingship. Tostig, his exiled brother, raided England in May; then, four months later, he joined Harald Hardråde, king of Norway, in another attack. This unsettled situation, coupled with doubts about the validity of Harold's accession to the throne, undoubtedly helped William's assertion of his own claim. Gaining support for an invasion from Pope Alexander II, who was concerned about irregularities in English church affairs, William gathered his forces in Normandy, sailed across the English Channel, and landed near Pevensey on 28 September. On 14 October, he defeated Harold at the **Battle of Hastings**, and on Christmas Day he was crowned in **Westminster Abbey**.

Over the next few years, the new ruler consolidated his power with considerable ruthlessness. Minor offenses were often punished by heavy fines, sometimes by mutilation (for example, deer poachers were blinded), and a rebellion in the north of England in 1069 was quelled by devastating the countryside, leaving the population to starve. Modern critics have accused William of cruelty, but the heavy hand undoubtedly dissuaded potential rebels from taking action and helped the invaders to maintain control of the population they had subdued.

Aided by the enforced peace, legal and cultural changes permeated the whole of English society. The feudal system of landholding was introduced from Normandy as all of the conquered territory became the property of the crown and was then divided up among the nobles in return for promises of military support. As a result, the country's new landowning class was almost entirely Norman. Moreover, William was astute enough to ensure that the estates awarded to his followers consisted of parcels in different parts of the country, presenting organizational obstacles to any single individual who wanted to construct an army large enough to threaten the sovereign's power.

The new aristocracy had to swear allegiance to the king and imported the Norman custom of building castles, both to defend itself against uprisings and to emphasize its authority. All of the bishops in the English church were deposed and replaced by men from Normandy, Norman French became the language of the law courts as well as the royal court, and in 1085–86, a survey of the whole country was undertaken in order to establish the extent of the monarch's demesne. The results of this census, reported in the *Domesday Book*, provide scholars with a detailed account of agricultural practices, population, and settlement at the end of the 11th century, but the aim of the exercise was entirely practical, providing a basis for taxation.

From 1072, William spent most of his time in Normandy, leaving the administration of his new kingdom largely to his clerics. In 1087, while attempting to regain territory in the Vexin, west of Paris, that had been appropriated by Philip I of **France**, he put the town of Mantes-la-Jolie to fire, but his horse reared as he made his way through the ruins (some sources say that it trod on a hot cinder, others that it was struck by a falling beam), and he suffered internal injuries. He was taken to Rouen where he died on 9 September, having given his Norman estates to **Robert Curthose**, his eldest son, and England to William (later **William II**), his second surviving son.

Largely uneducated and more feared that loved, William nevertheless gained the approval of an anonymous author of the *Anglo-Saxon Chronicle*, who recorded that he brought peace and order to his kingdom "so that a man of any substance could travel unmolested throughout the country with his bosom full of gold." *See also* ADELA, COUNTESS OF BLOIS; ADELIZA OF NORMANDY; AGATHA OF NORMANDY; CECILIA OF NORMANDY; CONSTANCE, DUCHESS OF BRITTANY; CURIA REGIS; DUNCAN II; HENRY I; MATILDA OF FLANDERS; NORMANDY, HOUSE OF; RICHARD, DUKE OF BERNAY; TOWER OF LONDON; WALLINGFORD CASTLE; WESTMINSTER, PALACE OF; WINDSOR CASTLE.

**WILLIAM I OF SCOTLAND (c1143–1214).** The son of **Henry, earl of Northumberland**, and **Ada de Warenne**, William succeeded his childless elder brother, **Malcolm IV**, to the throne in 1165 and then ruled Scotland for longer than any other monarch except **James VI**, submitting to English overlordship for well over a decade but eventually regaining his country's independence.

Known as "the Lion" because he flaunted a red lion rampant on his **royal coat of arms**, William I extended the feudal system introduced by his grandfather, King **David I**; established additional burghs; and improved the framework for the administration of justice in his realm. He also expanded the kingdom by bringing the north of the country under his control despite strong opposition by the earls of Orkney.

Relations with England were less productive, however. **Henry II** deprived William of the earldom of Northumbria in 1157, and efforts to retrieve the title ended in disaster. In 1173, William allied himself with **Eleanor of Aquitaine**, Henry's wife, and three of her sons—**Geoffrey, duke of Brittany**; **Henry, the young king**; and Richard (later **Richard I**)—in a rebellion against the English monarch. The following year, in support of this revolt (and in the hope of winning back the lost estates), he attempted a raid on Northumbria but was captured on 12 July and was taken to Falaise in Normandy while Henry sent an army of occupation to Scotland. In order to achieve his release, the Scots king had to accept Henry as his feudal overlord and tax his subjects to pay for the cost of the invading troops. The arrangement remained in force until 1189, when Henry's successor, Richard I, released his northern neighbor from his commitments in return for a considerable contribution to the funds he needed to mount a crusade to the Holy Land. Even after that, however, diplomatic contacts between the two states deteriorated, partly because, in 1192, Pope Celestine III decided that the Scottish church owed allegiance only to Rome and thus not to England. Also, William continued to pursue his claims to Northumbria until 1209, when, threatened by another invasion of Scotland, this time under King **John**, he renounced all rights to the area.

William died at **Stirling** Castle on 4 December 1214 and was buried at Arbroath Abbey, which he had founded for Tironensian monks in 1178 in honor of St. Thomas Becket. His only son succeeded him as **Alexander II**, and according to genealogists, U.S. president Barack Obama is numbered among his later descendants. *See also* ERMENGARDE DE BEAUMONT; ISABELLA, COUNTESS OF NORFOLK; MARGARET, COUNTESS OF KENT; MARJORIE, COUNTESS OF PEMBROKE.

**WILLIAM II OF ENGLAND (c1056–1100).** For 13 years, from 1087 to 1100, William ruled England with a ruthlessness that made him heartily despised—so much so that he is remembered more for the nature of his death than for anything he did in life. Known as William Rufus because of his ruddy countenance, he was the third son of **William I of England** (William the Conqueror) and **Matilda of Flanders**.

When the Conqueror died in 1087, he divided his territories between his oldest sons, giving **Robert Curthose**, his eldest boy, the duchy of **Normandy** and William the kingdom of England (**Richard, duke of Bernay**, the second son, would have taken precedence over William had he not died in a hunting accident some six years earlier). This division posed difficulties for nobles who held lands in both places because it is easier to serve one master than two, especially when the two are known to be at odds. In 1088, several of the nobles planned a rebellion, with the intention of reuniting the whole area under Robert, but William bought the allegiance of many of the leaders, Curthose failed to send troops to support the others, and the revolt collapsed.

Three years later, Rufus turned the tables and invaded Normandy, forcing his brother to surrender large areas of his estates. However, he failed to keep promises, given to his English supporters, that taxes would be cut and standards of administration improved, so in 1095 he faced a second domestic uprising, which he quelled easily, using the victory to emphasize his authority through harsh punishment of his foes (William of Aldrie was hanged, for example, and William of Eu was blinded and castrated).

In addition to curtailing Robert's ambitions and controlling his nobles, William attempted to stabilize his northern borders. In the spring of 1091, **Malcolm III** of Scotland marched south in an effort to capture the settlement at Newcastle, but a truce, brokered by Curthose and **Edgar Aetheling** (the last Anglo-Saxon king of England and a refugee at Malcolm's court), resulted in the Scots submitting to English overlordship. Also, constant friction between church and state ultimately led to the exile of Anselm (archbishop of Canterbury and leader of the clerics) in 1097 and to William's acquisition of income from ecclesiastical estates.

On 2 August 1100, William sought escape from political affairs by joining a hunting expedition in the New Forest, close to England's southern coast. During the chase, he and Walter Tyrell, lord of Poix, were separated from the other members of the party, and some hours later the king was found dead with an arrow in his chest. No one has ever proved that he was murdered, but there is a suspicion that the killing was organized by Henry, his younger brother, who took advantage of Robert Curthose's absence on a crusade to the Holy Land and seized the crown, ruling as **Henry I**.

William died unmarried and childless, castigated by the 12th-century monk Orderic Vitalis because he "gave himself up insatiably to obscene fornications" and was "hateful to all his people and odious to God," according to the *Anglo-Saxon Chronicle*. *See also* WESTMINSTER, PALACE OF.

**WILLIAM III OF ENGLAND AND II OF SCOTLAND (1650–1702).** William ruled England, Scotland, and Ireland jointly with his queen, **Mary II**, from 1689 until her death in 1694, and then on his own until 1702. The son of **William, prince of Orange**, and **Mary Henrietta, princess royal** (daughter of King **Charles II**), he was born at the Binnenhof Palace in The

Hague on 14 November 1650 and married his cousin, Mary, daughter of King **James VII of Scotland and II of England**, at **St. James's Palace** on 4 November 1677.

By the time of his wedding, William had built up a considerable reputation as an army commander, organizing his Dutch troops to resist the invasion efforts of Louis XIV of **France**. This feat also enhanced his image as the military champion of the Protestant faith in Europe, so, given his familial ties to the **House of Stuart**, it was natural that English opponents of the Roman Catholic James VII and II would turn to him for aid. These requests for help played into William's hands. He had never been close either to James or to James's brother and predecessor, Charles II, and he viewed the increasing political tensions across the North Sea with much concern, because if England descended into the kind of civil war that had ravaged the country 40 years earlier, it could not effectively counterbalance French military and diplomatic power in Europe.

In 1688, the birth of James's son (**James Francis Edward Stuart**) brought matters to a head because it implied the continuation of a Roman Catholic monarchy. So, at the invitation of a group of English nobles, William set sail with an invasion force, landing at Torbay on 5 November. James, seeing several of his generals defect, fled to France, and on 13 February the following year, parliament offered the crown to William, subject to four conditions — that he would rule jointly with Mary (a nominal measure designed to ensure an element of dynastic succession in the monarchy); that Anne, Mary's sister and later Queen **Anne**, would have rights to the succession before any of William's children other than by Mary (a condition that was intended to overcome objections to the imposition of hereditary rule by foreign incomers); that the king would accept that he was a de facto rather than a de jure sovereign; and that he would consider a statement outlining limitations on his powers. On 11 April, William and his wife were offered the Scottish crown as well.

In England, the **Glorious Revolution** was achieved without significant opposition, but in Scotland there was resistance that continued throughout the reign. For many Scots, the monarchy was a contract between people and ruler. James had been deposed by opponents in England, but his ousting, some claimed, had no legal basis, so William had no rights to the crown. John Graham of Claverhouse, viscount Dundee, raised the highland clans in support of the exiled king and led them to victory over William's troops at Killiecrankie, but his death in the battle ended the rebellion. Also, the Convention of Estates (the Scots parliament) presented William and Mary with a **Claim of Right** that, it believed, circumscribed royal powers, with a goodly number of the convention's members expecting that the new monarchs would simply rubber stamp whatever decisions they made. William quickly disabused them, opposing their efforts to make Presbyterianism the only acceptable version of the Protestant faith, and making enemies as a result. In Ireland, too, insurrection erupted as James landed with an army, largely financed by Louis XIV, in an effort to retrieve his throne. And, although on 1 July 1690 William won a sufficiently decisive victory at the **Battle of the Boyne** to encourage James to return to France, the troubles rumbled on for another year.

Despite his problems in the British Isles, William gave much of his attention to European affairs. He took England into an alliance with Austria, the Netherlands, Spain, and a group of German states against France and spent much time in military campaigns on the European mainland. A peace treaty was signed in 1697, but William was convinced that trouble would soon break out again, a conviction that proved justified, because in 1701, when the exiled James passed away, Louis proclaimed James's son king of England and stoked the flames of English enthusiasm for war. However, before William could respond, he died at **Kensington Palace** on 8 March 1702 following a riding accident. He was buried in **Westminster Abbey**.

William's reputation remains high in Northern Ireland, where the anniversary of the Battle of the Boyne is still a day of celebration in the Protestant community, but scholarly assessments of his rule have been downbeat. Many of his subjects always considered him a foreigner more interested in mainland Europe than in his newly acquired kingdoms. On the other hand, he undoubtedly did much to promote religious tolerance, to enhance trade, and (by giving power to parliament) to ensure political stability after many years of unrest in England. *See also* BILL OF RIGHTS; HAMPTON COURT PALACE; ORANGE, HOUSE OF; PLACENTIA, PALACE OF; ST. JAMES'S PALACE; THEOBALDS HOUSE; WHITEHALL PALACE.

**WILLIAM IV (1765–1837).** William, the third son of King **George III** and **Charlotte of Mecklenburg-Strelitz**, inherited the throne because his older brothers—King **George IV** and **Prince Frederick, duke of York and Albany**—died without leaving legitimate children to survive them. He was born at **Buckingham Palace** on 21 August 1765; he joined the Royal Navy as a junior officer at the age of 13; and, during the American Revolutionary War, he saw service in New York, where British officials thwarted an attempt by George Washington to kidnap him. In 1786, he was based in the West Indies with Horatio Nelson, who reported effusively on his abilities as a seaman, but when Britain went to war with **France** in 1795, he was refused permission to fight, probably because he was politically opposed to the conflict, but perhaps, too, because elements of his behavior raised doubts about his leadership qualities.

William enjoyed the intimate company of ladies, fathering a son in Halifax, Nova Scotia, while commanding the frigate *Andromeda* in 1788. By 1791, he was sharing a home with Irish actress Mrs. Dorothy Jordan (there was no Mr. Jordan, the marital prefix having been assumed at the time of Dorothy's first pregnancy). Mrs. Jordan and William, then duke of Clarence, had 10 children during a 20-year relationship. By the time the affair ended in 1811, he was so heavily in debt (a situation not unknown to the sons of King George III) that he was forced to make efforts to find a wealthy wife. With the death, in 1817, of **Princess Charlotte Augusta**—George III's only grandchild and the **heiress presumptive** to the throne—adding urgency to the search, he eventually secured a willing bride in **Adelaide of Saxe-Meiningen**, a woman just 25 years old and less than half his age. In any event, the marriage proved happy, and Adelaide—though she failed to provide the sons needed to secure the **House of Hanover**'s grip on the crown—did much to improve her husband's financial situation.

When he became king on the death of his brother, George IV, in 1830, William, at 64, was the oldest monarch ever to succeed to a British throne. He proved hard working, attempting to tackle his duties conscientiously, but his interest in public affairs was often interpreted as interference by government ministers, and he showed little sympathy with proponents of parliamentary reform. In 1831, his opposition to change led to a political crisis. The House of Lords (the upper chamber in the British parliament) had rejected proposals to increase representation in the House of Commons (the lower chamber) from the burgeoning industrial areas of the country, preferring to protect the "rotten boroughs," which sent delegates elected by only a handful of voters. The prime minister, Charles, earl Grey, asked the king to create 50 new peers who would be receptive to the plans and would supplement their supporters in the Lords so that the bill could pass. William refused and Grey resigned, but the monarch, unable to find a substitute who would command the support of the Commons, was forced to recall him and agree to his demands. As a result, the Reform Bill became law in 1832, democratizing the electoral process and further reducing the power of the sovereign to control parliament.

When Grey retired in 1834, he was replaced by William Lamb, viscount Melbourne. However, several of Melbourne's ministers were too radical for the king's taste, so on 14 November William dismissed him—this being the last time a British sovereign would remove a prime minister of whom he disapproved. This intervention, though, was no more successful than the attempts to sabotage the Reform Bill. William appointed Sir Robert Peel as Melbourne's replacement, but Peel was forced to resign after suffering a string of Commons defeats, and so the viscount returned on 18 April the following year.

The king made no further attempt to stem the tide of change. His health was declining, and by the spring of 1837, following an unusually severe attack of asthma, it was clear that he did not have long to live, his death at **Windsor Castle** on 20 June coming as no surprise. He was buried in **St. George's Chapel**, and because (like his older brothers) he left no legitimate offspring, he was succeeded by his niece, Queen **Victoria**. *The Spectator* summed up the majority view at the time: William, it said, "was a weak, ignorant, commonplace sort of person [but] a popular sovereign" whose popularity "was acquired at the price of something like public contempt." Modern writers have been somewhat less condemnatory, suggesting that the sovereign was intellectually less able than the leading parliamentarians of the time but that his view of the importance of the role of the monarchy in government was by no means idiosyncratic despite the clamor for reform, that his failings were due largely to an inability to understand and cope with widely disparate views in an era of great change, and that he made serious (albeit largely unsuccessful) efforts to plot a path between political extremes. *See also* BAGSHOT PARK; CHARLOTTE OF CLARENCE, PRINCESS; CLARENCE HOUSE; CROWN JEWELS OF THE UNITED KINGDOM; ELIZABETH OF CLARENCE, PRINCESS; KEW PALACE; ROYAL LODGE; VICTORIA OF SAXE-COBURG-SAALFIELD, PRINCESS, DUCHESS OF KENT AND STRATHEARN.

**WILLIAM AUGUSTUS, DUKE OF CUMBERLAND (1721–1765).** Cumberland—known as "the Butcher" because of his brutal treatment of **Charles Edward Stuart**'s supporters during the **Jacobite rebellion** in 1745–46—was the seventh of nine children (including one stillbirth) that **Caroline of Brandenburg-Ansbach** had with King **George II**. Born at Leicester House in **London** on 15 April 1721, he spent two years with the navy and then transferred to the army in 1742. As commander-in-chief of a force of Austrian, British, Dutch, and Hanoverian soldiers, he directed operations at the Battle of Fontenoy in Belgium on 11 May 1745 but was soundly defeated by the French, whose victory inspired Charles Edward to ignite a rising against the crown later the same year. Cumberland was recalled to lead the royalist forces, defeated the rebels at **Culloden** on 16 April 1746, and showed no quarter after the victory, ensuring that followers of the **House of Stuart** would be wary of supporting another insurrection.

On his reappearance in London, the duke was hailed as the hero who had saved the state (even though his savagery was much criticized). However, a decade later, in 1757, his fortunes changed when, again outmaneuvered by continental foes, he was forced to sign an agreement that allowed the French to occupy areas previously under Hanover's control. Returning to

Britain in disgrace, he resigned all of his posts and never fought again. For some years he became deeply involved in politics, but on 31 October 1765 he suffered a heart attack, probably because he was considerably overweight, and died at his London home. He was buried in **Westminster Abbey**. *See also* AUGUSTA OF SAXE-GOTHA, PRINCESS OF WALES; FORT BELVEDERE.

**WILLIAM, COUNT OF POITIERS (1153–1156).** William was the eldest child of **Henry II** and **Eleanor of Aquitaine**, born on 17 August 1153 (coincidentally, the date on which **Eustace, count of Boulogne**, heir to King **Stephen**, Henry's predecessor and enemy, died while ravaging church estates at Bury St. Edmunds). He was given the title count of Poitiers, an honor traditionally held by his mother's family, but he never reached maturity, dying at **Wallingford Castle**, then a royal stronghold, in 1156 (probably in April) and buried in Reading Abbey beside **Henry I**, his great-grandfather.

**WILLIAM, COUNT OF POITOU (1136–1164).** William, born in Argentan, **Normandy**, on 22 July 1136, was the brother of King **Henry II** of England and was the youngest of three sons born to **Matilda**, whose claims to the throne forced the country into a lengthy civil war, and **Geoffrey, count of Anjou**. He lent support to Henry when the third brother, **Geoffrey, count of Nantes**, attempted to take the family estates by force in 1156 and was rewarded with properties that made him one of the wealthiest landowners in the country. However, a proposed marriage to Isabelle de Warenne, the widow of **William of Blois** and daughter-in-law of King **Stephen**, Henry's predecessor, was prohibited by Thomas Becket, archbishop of Canterbury, because the two were cousins and were therefore within the Roman Catholic Church's proscribed degrees of consanguinity.

William (who is also sometimes known as William FitzEmpress because his mother's first husband was Henry V, Holy Roman Emperor) died, childless, at Rouen on 30 July 1164—of a broken heart, according to some writers—and Henry never forgave the archbishop, who was murdered in 1170, possibly on the king's orders.

**WILLIAM, DUKE OF GLOUCESTER (1689–1700).** Six years after her marriage to **George, prince of Denmark**, Anne—the second daughter of King **James VII and II** and, from 1702, Queen **Anne**—was still childless, having suffered several miscarriages and had seen **Anne Sophia Oldenburg** and **Mary Oldenburg** (the only children who survived birth for more than a few hours) die of smallpox within days of each other. William's safe delivery at **Hampton Court Palace** on 24 July 1689 was therefore an occasion for much rejoicing and was interpreted by many Protestants as a divine reward for the **Glorious Revolution** that, late the previous year, ousted the infant's Roman Catholic grandfather from the thrones of England and Scotland.

The baby boy was second in the line of **succession to the throne**, after his mother, but he was never healthy, suffering from bouts of malaria and unable to walk easily even by the time he was five years old. Nevertheless, his sudden death at **Windsor Castle** on 30 July 1700 (probably, like those of his sisters, a result of smallpox) was a surprise that, after his burial in **Westminster Abbey**, occasioned much debate about the future of the monarchy and led to the **Act of Settlement**, passed by the English parliament in 1701.

**WILLIAM OF BLOIS, EARL WARENNE (c1137–1159).** Although William was the third son born to King **Stephen** and his wife, **Matilda of Boulogne**, he was predeceased by his elder brothers and, given different circumstances, would have succeeded to his father's throne. Before **Henry I** died, leaving no male heir, he had made his nobles swear that they would accept **Matilda**, his daughter, as their queen. However, there was no tradition of queenship in England, and many barons felt that they could not rely on a woman to lead armies in battle. Moreover, Matilda had spent much of her life at the German court of Henry, the Holy Roman Emperor, and had thus absorbed a culture alien to that of Norman England.

For these reasons, most of the leading landholders accepted Stephen's claim to the crown when Henry died in 1135, but Matilda maintained support and gained allies as the new monarch's political ineptitude became increasingly apparent. The country slipped into a civil war that lasted for nearly two decades because, although Matilda retired to Normandy after Robert of Gloucester, her half-brother and one of her most able commanders, died in 1147, her son, Henry of Anjou, took up her cause, leading an invasion in 1153. By that time, Stephen was tired of conflict. His wife, Matilda of Boulogne, an indomitable woman who had supervised much of his military strategy, had died the previous year, and **Eustace, count of Boulogne**, his oldest surviving child, had passed away suddenly only months after Henry's arrival. Listening to the advice of his advisors, Stephen entered negotiations with Henry and, overlooking his remaining son's claim to the throne, reached an agreement that allowed him to remain king until his death but that recognized Henry as his heir.

In 1148, William of **Blois** was married to Isabelle de Warenne—daughter of the earl of Surrey, one of Stephen's principal supporters, who had died on a crusade to the Holy Land earlier in the year. When Henry of Anjou became king (as **Henry II**) after Stephen's death on 25 October 1154, he treated the young man well, allowing him to retain his English estates even though there were allegations that William was involved in a plot to assassinate him. After William died, childless, in Toulouse on 11 October 1159, his wife was betrothed to **William, count of Poitou**, Matilda's youngest son, but Thomas Becket, archbishop of Canterbury, refused to grant the dispensation needed because the two were cousins. In 1164, she married Hamelin Plantagenet, an illegitimate child of **Geoffrey, count of Anjou**, and so half-brother to King Henry. The union lasted until their deaths nearly 40 years later.

**WILLIAM OF GLOUCESTER, PRINCE (1941–1972). Prince** William—a grandson of King **George V** and the elder son of **Prince Henry, duke of Gloucester**, and **Princess Alice, duchess of Gloucester**—was expected to inherit his father's dukedom but died in a flying accident while still a young man. Born by caesarian section at Lady Almira Carnarvon's Nursing Home at Hadley Common, Hertfordshire, he was educated at Wellesley House School in Broadstairs, Kent, and at Eton College before studying history at Cambridge University from 1960 to 1963 and then taking a year to explore economics and political science at Stanford University in California.

Spurning the traditional royal career routes through the army and Royal Navy, Prince William joined the Foreign and Commonwealth Office as a civil servant, working at the British High Commission in Lagos and then at the British Embassy in Tokyo. He inherited his mother's adventurous spirit, undertaking a 12,000-mile journey through Africa in 1963 and developing skills in several outdoor sports, including climbing, flying, and skiing. From 1970, he undertook a series of royal engagements, substituting for his father (whose health had suffered as a result of a car accident in 1965 and two strokes in 1968) and representing Queen **Elizabeth II** at the celebrations marking Tonga's independence from the United Kingdom (1970) and at the funeral of President William Tubman of Liberia (1971). However, on 28 August 1972, while taking part in an air show at Halfpenny Green near Birmingham, the prince's plane struck a tree, and he was killed. His remains were interred in the royal burial ground at **Frogmore**.

In 1968, Prince William was diagnosed with porphyria, a disease that had afflicted several of his ancestors, including King **George III**.

**WILLIAM OF NORMANDY (c1028–1087).** *See* WILLIAM I OF ENGLAND.

**WILLIAM OF ORANGE (1650–1702).** *See* WILLIAM III OF ENGLAND AND II OF SCOTLAND.

**WILLIAM OF WALES, PRINCE (1982– ). Prince** William, the elder son of **Charles, prince of Wales**, and **Diana, princess of Wales**, is second in the line of **succession to the throne**, following his father. He was born at St. Mary's Hospital, **London**, on 21 June 1982 and was educated at Ludgrove School (near Wokingham, Berkshire) and Eton College. After leaving school, he spent a year in South America, occupying part of the time on a training exercise with the British Army and the remainder with Raleigh International, a charity that involves young people from a wide range of social backgrounds in environmental and community projects around the world (the press made much of pictures of the prince cleaning restrooms in Chile). With these experiences behind him, he went to St. Andrews University, where he initially studied art history but found that his interests were changing and in 2005 graduated with a degree in geography.

Prince William is known to dislike many of the restraints on his behavior that stem from **royal family** protocol and tries to avoid the attentions of the media, but he was unable to escape the limelight in July 2005, when he performed his first official solo engagement, representing his grandmother, Queen **Elizabeth II**, at events in New Zealand that marked the 60th anniversary of the end of World War II. He graduated from the Royal Military Academy Sandhurst the following year and then, although unable (because of his position in the royal hierarchy) to see active service, flew to Afghanistan in 2008 to assist in the repatriation of a soldier who had been killed. That same year, he was also part of an operation that captured a cocaine-smuggling vessel in the Caribbean. Early in 2009, he began training as a helicopter pilot with the Royal Air Force's search and rescue team, having become a patron of Mountain Rescue (England and Wales) in order to "highlight the courageous work of our mountain rescue organizations."

In 2003, the prince started dating **Kate Middleton**, the daughter of an airline pilot and fellow undergraduate at St. Andrews. The international press followed the affair with great interest, reporting in 2005, and again in 2007, that the couple had split. However, the ardor survived the tiffs and Prince William formally proposed during a vacation to Kenya on October 2010, with a wedding scheduled for 29 April, 2011, in **Westminster Abbey**.

**WILLIAM, PRINCE OF ORANGE (1626–1650).** William—the son of Frederick Hendrik of Orange and his wife, Amalia—was the father of King **William III of England and II of Scotland**. He was born in The Hague on 27 May 1626 and married **Mary Henrietta, princess royal** and daughter of King **Charles I**, at **Whitehall Palace**, London, on 2 May 1641. When his father died in 1647, the prince became stadtholder (or political and military leader) of the Netherlands, and despite his youth he conducted negotiations with Louis XIV of **France** that were intended to extend his area of influence. He also attempted to provide assistance to Charles, who was involved in a civil war with English parliamentarians, but quarreled with other Dutch leaders who wanted to reduce the size of the army. William contracted smallpox in 1650 and died on 6 November, just 8 days before his son was born.

**WILLIAM RUFUS (c1056–1100).** *See* WILLIAM II OF ENGLAND.

**WILLIAM THE AETHELING (1103–1120).** The death of William the **Aetheling**, the only legitimate son of King **Henry I**, precipitated a crisis over the **succession to the throne** that pitched England into 18 years of civil war. William was born in 1103 to Henry and his first wife, **Matilda of Scotland**. From birth, he was groomed to follow his father, pampered at court and betrothed to Matilda of Anjou at the age of 10. By the time he reached his mid-teens, he was referred to as *rex designatus* or "king designate." However, on 25 November 1120, he left Barfleur, one of the principal ports in Normandy, intending to cross the English Channel in Henry's *White Ship*. Passengers and crew had all been drinking heavily, so navigation was unreliable and the vessel struck a rock, quickly filling with water. William and some of his companions jumped into a dinghy in an effort to escape, but the boat capsized and all on board were drowned.

William's mother had died two years earlier, so in an effort to produce an heir, Henry married **Adeliza of Louvain**. But in 1127, with the union still barren, the king forced the English nobles to swear that they would accept **Matilda**, his daughter, as their queen after his death. Most, however, reneged on this promise when the throne became vacant on 1 December 1135, transferring their allegiance instead to **Stephen**, Henry's nephew. Matilda's supporters attempted to unseat him, and the peace of Henry's reign was replaced with bitter strife.

**WILLIAM THE CONQUEROR (c1028–1087).** *See* WILLIAM I OF ENGLAND.

**WILLIAM THE LION (c1143–1214).** *See* WILLIAM I OF SCOTLAND.

**WINCHESTER.** For nearly 400 years, from about 686 until the Normans invaded in 1066, Winchester was the capital of the kingdom of **Wessex**, which united England under a single ruler during the 10th century. The site, originally occupied by an Iron Age hill fort, was settled by the Romans in

AD 70 and was then taken by Saxons, who conquered the area in 519. The first stone church was constructed for King Cenwealh in 648 and was given cathedral status in 660, but the present structure, erected alongside it, dates from 1079. The buildings were the location for the coronation of **Edward the Confessor** in 1043 as well as for the marriages of King **Henry IV** to **Joan of Navarre** (1403) and Queen **Mary I** to **Philip II of Spain** (1554). They were also the burial place for many of Wessex's leaders, including **Egbert** (who reigned from 802 to 839), **Alfred the Great** (871–c899), **Edward the Elder** (c899–924), and **Eadred** (946–55), as well as for the Scandinavian kings **Canute** (1016–35) and **Harthacanute** (1040–42) and novelist Jane Austen, who spent her last years in the nearby village of Chawton.

Winchester's street pattern still reflects the restructuring of the town by King Alfred, who surrounded it with a defensive wall so that citizens could resist Viking attacks. *See also* AELFGIFU OF YORK; AETHELWULF; ARTHUR, PRINCE OF WALES; EALHSWITH; EDMUND OF WOOD-STOCK, EARL OF KENT; ELGIVA; EMMA OF NORMANDY; GOD-WIN, EARL OF WESSEX; HENRY III; MARGARET OF YORK; PLAN-TAGENET, ELEANOR; RICHARD, DUKE OF BERNAY; RICHARD, EARL OF CORNWALL.

**WINDSOR, ALEXANDER, EARL OF ULSTER (1974– ).** Alexander Windsor is the only son—and the eldest of three children—in the family of **Prince Richard, duke of Gloucester**, and **Birgitte, duchess of Gloucester**. Born at St. Mary's Hospital in Paddington, **London**, on 24 October 1974, he was educated at Eton College, King's College (part of the University of London, where he earned a bachelor's degree in war studies), and the Royal Military Academy Sandhurst. After being commissioned into the King's Royal Hussars in 1995, he pursued a career in the army, seeing service in Iraq and northern Ireland with North Atlantic Treaty Organization troops. He now works with the Transnational Crisis Project, a nonprofit organization that attempts to improve government decision-making processes relating to crime, infectious disease, and terrorism. On 22 June 2002, at **St. James's Palace**, Lord Ulster, who is not required to undertake royal duties, married Claire Booth (a pediatrician and fellow King's College graduate). Their first child—Xan, lord Culloden—was born on 12 March 2007.

**WINDSOR CASTLE.** Windsor—one of the **royal family**'s principal residences—is the largest inhabited castle in the world. Although the site, on the south bank of the River Thames about 25 miles west of central **London**, has been occupied since the 9th century, the present structure dates from about 1070, when King **William I of England** (William the Conqueror) built defenses around an artificial hill. **Henry II** replaced that simple structure with a distinctive round stone tower and added further walls, and then **Henry III** built a chapel and additional barricades. Later monarchs added further embellishments, so the castle now consists of two quadrilateral courtyards (known as wards) that are separated by a round tower.

The eastern (or upper) ward contains the sovereign's private apartments, rooms used on other state occasions (such as banquets for visiting dignitaries), and a library with a collection of drawings by such old masters as Leonardo da Vinci and Michelangelo. On 20 November 1992, while **Prince Andrew, duke of York**, was in residence, fire broke out in this part of the building, affecting more than 100 rooms. The incident occurred at a time when the cost of maintaining the monarchy was the subject of much public debate in Britain, so many people expressed concern that public funds would be used to pay for the repairs. Ultimately, Queen **Elizabeth II** agreed to pay 70 percent of the cost and opened **Buckingham Palace**, her London home, to visitors for the first time in order to recoup part of the expenditure.

In the lower (or western) ward, **St. George's Chapel**, constructed during the later 15th and early 16th centuries, is the burial place of several monarchs and their families, including **Edward IV**, **Henry VI**, **Henry VIII**, **Charles I**, **Edward VII**, and **George V**. Nearby, **George III**, **George IV**, and **William IV** lie in the Albert Memorial Chapel, which was constructed during the reign of **Henry VII** but was much adapted by Queen **Victoria** as a tribute to her husband, **Prince Albert of Saxe-Coburg and Gotha**, who died at Windsor. Victoria and Albert are interred at **Frogmore**, a mausoleum in the 700 hectares of parkland that surround the castle.

Windsor Castle is a major tourist attraction, with about one million visitors paying entry fees each year in the hope of catching a glimpse of Queen Elizabeth and her consort, **Prince Philip, duke of Edinburgh**, who spend most weekends in the apartments. *See also the cross-references for the entries on* FROGMORE *and* ST. GEORGE'S CHAPEL, *and* ALFONSO, EARL OF CHESTER; ALFRED, PRINCE, DUKE OF EDINBURGH AND SAXE-COBURG AND GOTHA; BEATRICE (OR HENRY) OF BATTENBURG, PRINCESS; CHANGING OF THE GUARD; CROWN JEWELS OF THE UNITED KINGDOM; EDWARD OF LANCASTER, PRINCE OF WALES; ELEANOR, COUNTESS OF BAR; ISABELLA DE COUCY; JOAN, COUNTESS OF KENT; LOUISE, PRINCESS ROYAL, DUCHESS OF FIFE; MARGARET, COUNTESS OF PEMBROKE; MARGARET, DUCHESS OF BRABANT; MARGARET, QUEEN OF NORWAY; MARGARET, QUEEN OF SCOTS; MARY OF YORK; MARY, PRINCESS, DUCHESS OF GLOUCESTER AND EDINBURGH; OLDENBURG, ANNE SOPHIA; OLDENBURG, MARY; PLANTAGENET, HENRY (1267–1274); PLANTAGENET, THOMAS; PLANTAGENET, WILLIAM (1348);

WILLIAM, DUKE OF GLOUCESTER; WINDSOR, HOUSE OF; WINDSOR, TREATY OF.

**WINDSOR, GEORGE, EARL OF ST. ANDREWS (1962– ).** The earl of St. Andrews is the elder son of **Prince Edward, duke of Kent**, and **Katharine, duchess of Kent**. (Technically, the earldom is held by the **prince**, but by convention, the elder son of a prince may use one of his father's lesser titles.) George was born at Coppins—a country house near Iver, west of **London**, that was left to his grandfather (**Prince George, duke of Kent** and son of King **George V**) by **Princess Victoria**, a daughter of Queen **Victoria**, when she died in 1935—and educated at Eton College and Cambridge University. On 9 January 1988, at a civil ceremony in **Edinburgh**, the earl married Sylvana Tomaselli, a native of Newfoundland who was previously the wife of John Paul Jones, one of the founders of the Led Zeppelin rock band. They have three children—Edward, lord Downpatrick (born on 2 December 1988); Lady Marina-Charlotte (born on 30 September 1992); and Lady Amelia (born on 24 August 1995).

Because the countess of St. Andrews is a Roman Catholic, the earl is excluded from the line of **succession to the throne** by the 1701 **Act of Settlement**. In 2003, Lord Downpatrick also committed himself to the Roman Catholic faith, so if he survives his father, he will become the first Catholic duke of Kent since the Reformation. The earl is a trustee of SOS Children's Villages UK (a charity caring for orphaned and abandoned young people) and patron of the Association for International Cancer Research but is not required to undertake public engagements on behalf of the **royal family**. His wife is a historian at Cambridge University.

**WINDSOR, HOUSE OF.** In 1840, Queen **Victoria** married **Prince Albert of Saxe-Coburg and Gotha**. Under normal circumstances, the name of the royal house passes down the male line, but on 17 July 1917, Victoria's grandson, King **George V**, issued a proclamation changing it to Windsor, the decision made because, three years into World War I, Saxe-Coburg and Gotha sounded too German for British taste. The choice of Windsor as a new name for the royal house reflected successive monarchs' close association with **Windsor Castle**, but, on hearing of the decision, William II, the German emperor, apparently commented that he looked forward to watching a performance of William Shakespeare's play, *The Merry Wives of Saxe-Coburg and Gotha.*

On King George's death in 1936, the crown passed to his eldest son, **Edward VIII**, who reigned for only 11 months before abdicating so that he could marry Wallis Simpson (later **Wallis, duchess of Windsor**), an American-born divorcee. He was followed, reluctantly, by his younger brother, King **George VI**, and from 1952 by his niece Queen **Elizabeth II**.

In 1947, however, Elizabeth had married **Prince Philip, duke of Edinburgh**, a member of the House of Schleswig-Holstein-Sonderburg-Glücksburg. With anti-German sentiment still running high only two years after the end of World War II, and not wanting to present his wife with the problems that George V had faced, Philip adopted the surname "Mountbatten," which his maternal uncle — **Louis Mountbatten, earl Mountbatten of Burma** — had taken in 1917. On 9 April 1952, the queen announced that her descendants would continue to "bear the name of Windsor" rather than Mountbatten, modifying the arrangement on 8 February 1969 when she declared that those of her agnatic descendants who carried the title "**Prince**" or "**Princess**" and were known as "**her (or his) royal highness**" would be members of the House of Windsor and that other agnatic descendants would use the surname "Mountbatten-Windsor." By implication, unless a later monarch initiates changes, the British royal house will remain the House of Windsor and will not change even if a future queen marries and has issue.

**WINDSOR, LADY GABRIELLA (1981– ).** Lady Gabriella — the only daughter and younger child of **Prince and Princess Michael of Kent** — was born on 23 April 1981 in St. Mary's Hospital, **London**, where her brother (**Lord Frederick Windsor**) had been delivered two years earlier. She was educated at Godstowe School in High Wycombe and then at Downe House, a girls' boarding school in Thatcham, Berkshire, where at the age of 13 she was suspended for a week after sneaking off the premises to buy cigarettes (apparently she intended to sell them rather than smoke them). After a year working with Sotheby's auction house in Madrid, she went to Brown University in Rhode Island and graduated with a bachelor's degree in comparative literature in 2004. Since then, she has earned a living as a journalist, getting her work published in such periodicals as *The Mail on Sunday*, *The Spectator*, and the Spanish edition of *Hello!* magazine under an Ella Windsor byline.

**WINDSOR, LORD FREDERICK (1979– ).** The only son, and elder child, of **Prince and Princess Michael of Kent**, Lord Frederick — a self-confessed user of hard drugs in his youth — was born at St. Mary's Hospital in Paddington, **London**, on 6 April 1979. He attended Wetherby School in Notting Hill (where **Prince William of Wales** and **Prince Henry—or Harry—of Wales**, the sons of **Charles, prince of Wales**, were later educated) and then went on to Sunningdale and to Eton College (his father's old schools) before graduating from Oxford University with a classics degree. He dabbled in modeling (for the Burberry clothing company) and with journalism (for *Tatler* magazine), but in 2006, after telling newspapers that he "couldn't stand anything dull," he joined investment bank J. P. Morgan as a financial analyst managing the investments of its wealthiest clients. On 12 September 2009, in the Chapel Royal at **Hampton Court Palace**, he married actress Sophie Winkleman, whom he had been dating for two years. In 1999, Lord Frederick admitted using cocaine at a party, saying, "It is very difficult to avoid getting into this sort of thing when you move in those circles but I don't blame anybody but myself for the incident."

**WINDSOR, LORD NICHOLAS (1970– ).** Lord Nicholas is the youngest of the three children of **Prince Edward, duke of Kent**, and his wife, **Katharine, duchess of Kent**. He was born at University College Hospital, **London**, on 25 July 1970 and was educated at Westminster School (where he was bullied), Harrow School, and Oxford University, but he never completed his undergraduate studies because he decided to go traveling in Africa instead. In 2001, he followed his mother into the Roman Catholic Church, and by doing so lost his place in the line of **succession to the throne**—at the time he was 27th—because the **Act of Settlement**, passed by the English parliament in 1701, prevents the crown from passing to adherents to the Catholic faith.

In 2006, at a civil ceremony in London (on 19 October) and then in a church ceremony at the Vatican (on 4 November), Lord Nicholas married Paolo Doimi de Lupis Frankopan, the daughter of a Croatian attorney of aristocratic descent, whom he had met at a New York party five years earlier. They have two children—Albert (born on 22 September 2007 and named after **Prince Albert of Saxe-Coburg and Gotha**, the husband of Queen **Victoria**) and Leopold (born on 8 September 2009). As an 18-year-old, Nicholas was pilloried as a "royal wastrel" by the tabloid press after being arrested for possession of cannabis, and some sources have suggested that he suffered from anorexia and depression, but he also carries out much charity work, particularly with children who have special needs, while keeping well away from the public gaze.

**WINDSOR, TREATY OF (1522).** On 16 June 1522, King **Henry VIII** and Charles V, the Holy Roman Emperor, formed a military alliance against **France**, sealing the treaty (known as the Treaty of Windsor because it was signed at **Windsor Castle**) with an agreement that Charles would marry Mary, Henry's only child and later **Mary I**. Using **Calais** (then held by the English) as a base, the monarch carried out a series of somewhat desultory attacks on Brittany and Picardy, but Charles was more aggressive, overwhelming the French troops at Pavia (in Italy) on 24 February 1525 and capturing their king, Francis I. At that point, Henry sensed an opportunity to invade France and seize the throne, long cherished by England's rulers, but his efforts to raise funds for the campaign met with strong resistance, and the scheme had to be abandoned. Charles then demanded that Mary join him in Spain and bring a large dowry with her. The English king, in straitened financial circumstances, was unable to comply, so Charles married Isabella of Portugal, who came with a substantial contribution to his treasury. Henry was furious but powerless to do anything about the situation.

**WITAN. Anglo-Saxon monarchs** ruled with the help of a group of advisors known as the witan. Sometimes the members are known as the witenagemot, a word more correctly applied to a meeting of the witan. Membership was by invitation of the king, and meetings were held at his request, usually at one of the royal manors. The heads of leading families were summoned, along with representatives of the church and the chief officials of the **Royal Household**, and were required to comment on any issues on which the monarch sought opinions, so matters relating to land grants, new laws, and taxation were regular topics. They had no status as judges, however; their deliberations were more concerned with affairs of policy rather than with the administration of justice. Thus, for instance, in 1016 they gave their approval to the division of England, with one part to be ruled by **Edmund II** and the other by **Canute** of Denmark.

Anglo-Saxon England had no tradition of inheriting kingship through family lineages, so the most important function of the witan was to choose a new monarch when the incumbent leader died (in 1066, for example, it selected Harold Godwinson, the most powerful figure in the land, to succeed **Edward the Confessor** as **Harold II**). Sometimes, too, it could take action against unpopular rulers, as in 757, when it deposed Sigebert, king of **Wessex**, because it considered him cruel and corrupt.

The word "witan" is derived from the Old English *wita*, which means "one who knows." *See also* ANGLO-SAXON MONARCHS; CURIA REGIS.

**WOMAN OF THE BEDCHAMBER.** *See* LADY-IN-WAITING.

**WOODSTOCK PALACE.** The forest around Woodstock, northwest of Oxford, was a popular royal hunting ground from Anglo-Saxon times. King **Henry I** constructed a lodge during the early 12th century and added a zoo housing camels, lions, a porcupine, and other exotic fauna for the entertainment of his visitors. **Henry II**, the first of the **House of Plantagenet** monarchs, turned the building into a palace and visited it regularly with Rosamund de Clifford, one of his numerous mistresses (there is a legend, entirely untrue, that Rosamund was poisoned by **Eleanor of Aquitaine**, Henry's jealous wife). **Edmund of Woodstock, earl of Kent** (son of **Edward I**), was born there in 1301 and **Edward, the black prince** (son of **Edward III**) in 1330.

**William I of Scotland** married **Ermengarde de Beaumont** (whose mother, Constance FitzRoy, was one of **Henry I**'s illegitimate daughters) at Woodstock in 1186, and the future Queen **Elizabeth I** was imprisoned in the gatehouse by **Mary I** in 1554–55. However, the structure suffered greatly during the civil war between the supporters of **Charles I** and those of Oliver Cromwell, serving as a royalist garrison in 1646 but then falling to the parliamentarians. By 1704, it was in ruins, and John Churchill, duke of Marlborough, who was given the estate by Queen **Anne** in recognition of his military achievements, built Blenheim Palace on the site. *See also* ELEANOR, COUNTESS OF GUELDRES; ISABELLA DE COUCY; MARY, DUCHESS OF BRITTANY; PLANTAGENET, ALICE; PLANTAGENET, ISABELLA; PLANTAGENET, JOAN (C1333–1348); PLANTAGENET, MARY, THOMAS OF WOODSTOCK, DUKE OF GLOUCESTER.

**WOODVILLE, ELIZABETH (c1437–1492).** Elizabeth Woodville (or Wydeville), the first woman not of royal birth to marry an English king, was an unpopular **queen consort** for King **Edward IV**. Born c1437, she was one of some 16 children in the family of Sir Richard Woodville (or Wydeville) and Jacquetta, dowager duchess of Bedford. At the age of about 19, she was married to Sir John Grey (the eldest son of Edward, lord Ferrers of Groby) and they had two sons (Thomas in 1457 and Richard c1458) before he was killed fighting for King **Henry VI** and the **House of Lancaster** at St. Albans in 1461 (*see* ST. ALBANS, SECOND BATTLE OF).

At the time of her husband's death, Elizabeth was still in her mid-twenties and was much renowned for her beauty. King Edward, who had deposed Henry early in 1461, kept a string of mistresses, but Grey's widow was unwilling to succumb to his advances unless he married her, so the couple wed at Grafton Regis, Elizabeth's Northamptonshire home, in 1464, possibly on 1 May but perhaps in August. The ceremony, conducted in secret, caused an uproar when news of it spread to courtiers. Elizabeth was not a lady of royal rank. Moreover, she was the scion and widow of Lancastrians, with whom Edward and the **House of York** were embroiled in a lengthy conflict for the English throne (*see* WARS OF THE ROSES), and she persuaded Edward to appoint many of her relatives to important offices of state. Richard Neville, earl of Warwick and the strategist behind Edward's successful bid for the crown, was particularly upset, not least because he had been negotiating a marriage between the king and a daughter of the French royal house when Edward made his own choice of bride.

From 1466 to 1480, Elizabeth and Edward had 10 children, including three sons, apparently enough to ensure that his offspring would rule England for many years. However, the queen's low esteem and late-15th-century English politics confounded parental hopes. When Edward died in 1483, he was succeeded by his 12-year-old son, **Edward V**. However, within weeks, a clergyman (possibly theologian Ralph Shaa or Robert Stillington, bishop of Bath and Wells) claimed that Edward IV had been betrothed to Lady Eleanor Butler before the wedding ceremony with Elizabeth Woodville had taken place. At the time, a betrothal promise rendered any later marriage bigamous, so on 25 June—and apparently on no evidence other than the cleric's word—parliament declared the 1461 wedding ceremony invalid. By implication, all of Elizabeth's children were illegitimate and thus were not entitled to rule the country, so Edward's brother Richard was crowned king as **Richard III**.

For reasons that historians have never understood, Elizabeth surrendered her two surviving sons (Edward V and **Richard, duke of York [1473–1483?]**) to the care of the new monarch, who is believed to have ordered their murders in the **Tower of London**. Some years later, again in circumstances that are unclear, Elizabeth retired to Bermondsey Abbey, where she died on 8 June 1492. Her genetic legacy was considerable. Through her marriage to John Grey, she was the great-grandmother of Lady **Jane Grey**, who was queen of England for a few days in July 1553. Also, **Elizabeth of York** (her eldest daughter) was queen consort of King **Henry VII** (a match that brought an end to the Wars of the Roses) and mother of King **Henry VIII**. **Margaret Tudor**, a granddaughter, married **James IV** of Scotland, forming a partnership that ultimately led to the **union of the crowns** of England and Scotland through King **James VI and I** in 1603. *See also* ANNE, COUNTESS OF SURREY; BEAUFORT, MARGARET, COUNTESS OF RICHMOND; BRIDGET OF YORK; CATHERINE OF YORK; CECILY, VISCOUNTESS WELLES; GEORGE, DUKE OF BEDFORD; MARGARET OF YORK; MARY OF YORK.

**WULFTHRYTH (?–c988).** Most scholars of the Anglo-Saxon period agree that Wulfthryth (also known as Wilfrida and Wulfritha) bore a daughter to King **Edgar of England** in 961. There is less agreement about other aspects of the relationship, some writers claiming that the couple were married (perhaps by a "handfast" ceremony in which their hands were tied in the absence of a priest), some suggesting that Wulfthryth had tried to seek sanctuary from the king in Wilton Abbey but had been dragged from the cloisters and raped, and others arguing that she may have retired to the nunnery after the child's birth either to do penance for a relationship conducted outside of marriage or because Edgar's interest in her had waned. She had certainly become abbess at Wilton by 965, probably as a result of the monarch's influence, and apparently lived an exemplary life from then until her death c988, so much so that she became revered as a saint.

The daughter, named Eadgyth (or Edith), spent all her days in the convent and, like her mother, became renowned for her piety. Many miracles were attributed to her, both during her life and after her death in 984, so she too achieved sainthood, with the Viking King **Canute** among those who venerated her. A number of historians have proposed that Wulfthryth may also have been the mother of **Edward the Martyr**, who became king of England in 975, but it is more likely that he was born to **Aethelflaed Eneda**, who was probably Edgar's first wife.

**WYATT'S REBELLION (1554).** During the winter of 1554, Thomas Wyatt—who held large estates in southeast England—led a short-lived rebellion against Queen **Mary I**. Wyatt had visited Spain earlier and had been appalled by the attacks on non-Catholics made by the leaders of the Inquisition there. He had also been a supporter of Lady **Jane Grey**, who had been proclaimed queen of England on 10 July 1553 but was deposed by Mary just nine days later. When, soon after her accession to the throne, Mary announced her intention to marry Prince Philip of Spain (*see* PHILIP II OF SPAIN), Wyatt plotted with other nobles—including Henry Grey, marquess of Dorset and Jane's father—to lead a revolt against the new monarch. On 26 January 1554, his hastily organized army occupied Rochester (on the south bank of the River Thames east of **London**), and then, with a company of 4000 men, he marched on the capital. However, the remaining conspirators failed to raise support, and Wyatt surrendered on 8 February.

It was never clear what the rebel leaders intended to do if London had fallen, but even so, Mary imposed a heavy punishment on them and their supporters. Grey was beheaded on 23 February, Wyatt followed him on 11 April, and some 80 to 100 others were executed and then hung from the gates of the city. Jane Grey and her husband, **Guildford Dudley**, also went to the block, even though they had played no part in the revolt, and Mary's half-sister, Elizabeth (later Queen **Elizabeth I**), was imprisoned in the **Tower of London** for two months because some of the monarch's advisors believed that she had been aware of Wyatt's scheme. Mary, however, refused to respond to calls for her execution. *See also* ANNE, COUNTESS OF SURREY.

# Y

**YOLANDE DE DREUX (c1263–1322?).** On 14 October 1285, at Jedburgh Abbey, King **Alexander III** took Yolande de Dreux as his second wife in the hope of producing an heir to the Scottish throne. An earlier marriage to **Margaret, queen of Scots**, had brought him two daughters and a son, but by 1284, all three, as well as Margaret, were dead. The match was a prestigious one for the monarch because Yolande's father (Robert, count of Dreux) was descended from Louis VI of **France**, and her mother (Beatrix of Montfort) came from a distinguished northern French noble family. The union also had the political advantage of stressing Scotland's independence from England by forming alliances with powers on the European mainland.

The Scots' hopes were unfulfilled, however. On 19 March the following year, Alexander fell from his horse and was killed. Yolande was pregnant, but in November the baby was stillborn (or possibly miscarried), so she went back to France where in about 1292 she married Arthur II, duke of Brittany, and they had at least six children. By that time, the Scots had chosen Alexander's granddaughter—**Margaret, maid of Norway**—as their monarch, but her unexpected death in 1290 plunged the country into a succession crisis that provided England's kings with an opportunity to reassert their claims to overlordship of the realm.

Some sources report that Yolande died in 1322, others that she lived until 1330.

**YORK, HOUSE OF.** The Yorkists provided the last three of the **House of Plantagenet** kings of England, wresting the crown from the **House of Lancaster**. Their dynasty was founded in 1385, when **Edmund of Langley, duke of York**, the fifth son of King **Edward III**, was created **duke of York**, but claims to the throne were not made forcefully until the third duke—**Richard, duke of York (1411–1460)**—reached adulthood. His argument was based on right of descent: Richard's mother was Anne de Mortimer, whose great-grandfather—**Lionel of Antwerp, duke of Clarence**—was Edward's third son; whereas the Lancastrians were descended from **John of Gaunt**, Lionel's younger brother.

Richard's efforts to win the throne by unseating the mentally unstable King **Henry VI** resulted in the lengthy **Wars of the Roses** and led to the duke's death at the **Battle of Wakefield** in 1460. However, his son was acclaimed king as **Edward IV** after defeating Henry's troops at Mortimer's Cross in Herefordshire early the following year, and apart from a brief period in 1470–71 when Henry returned to the throne, he ruled until his death in 1483.

Edward was succeeded by his 12-year-old son, **Edward V**, but after only two months, the new monarch's duplicitous uncle persuaded parliament that their sovereign was born illegitimate and that he was entitled to the throne as King **Richard III**. However, this action, and subsequent rumors that he had arranged Edward's murder, fueled vocal opposition that was led by Henry Tudor, a descendant of John of Gaunt through the female line. The sides met in battle at **Bosworth Field** on 22 August 1485, and Richard was killed. Henry claimed the throne as King **Henry VII** by right of conquest, thus beginning a period of rule by the **House of Tudor** that lasted until the **union of the crowns** of England and Scotland in 1603.

**YOUNG PRETENDER.** *See* STUART, CHARLES EDWARD.

# Appendix 1
# Chronology of British Monarchs

For dates of accession to the throne, dates of coronation, and other information see appendix 2, "British Monarchs, Biographical Summaries."

## MONARCHS OF ENGLAND (959–1707)

### Anglo-Saxon Monarchs

| | |
|---|---|
| Edgar | 959–975 |
| Edward the Martyr | 975–978 |
| Aethelred the Unready (first reign) | 979–1013 |
| Sweyn | 1013–1014 |
| Aethelred the Unready (second reign) | 1014–1016 |
| Edmund II | 1016 |

### Scandinavian Monarchs

| | |
|---|---|
| Canute | 1016–1035 |
| Harthacanute (first reign) | 1035–1037 |
| Harold I | 1037–1040 |
| Harthacanute (second reign) | 1040–1042 |

### Anglo-Saxon Monarchs

| | |
|---|---|
| Edward the Confessor | 1042–1066 |
| Harold II | 1066 |
| Edgar Aetheling | 1066 |

### House of Normandy

| | |
|---|---|
| William I | 1066–1087 |
| William II | 1087–1100 |
| Henry I | 1100–1135 |

| | |
|---|---|
| Stephen | 1135–1154 |
| Matilda | 1141 (disputed) |

## House of Plantagenet

*(a) House of Anjou*

| | |
|---|---|
| Henry II | 1154–1189 |
| Richard I | 1189–1199 |
| John | 1199–1216 |
| Henry III | 1216–1272 |
| Edward I | 1272–1307 |
| Edward II | 1307–1327 |
| Edward III | 1327–1377 |
| Richard II | 1377–1399 |

*(b) House of Lancaster*

| | |
|---|---|
| Henry IV | 1399–1413 |
| Henry V | 1413–1422 |
| Henry VI (first reign) | 1422–1461 |

*(c) House of York*

| | |
|---|---|
| Edward IV | 1461–1470 |

*(d) House of Lancaster*

| | |
|---|---|
| Henry VI (second reign) | 1470–1471 |

*(e) House of York*

| | |
|---|---|
| Edward IV | 1471–1483 |
| Edward V | 1483 |
| Richard III | 1483–1485 |

## House of Tudor

| | |
|---|---|
| Henry VII | 1485–1509 |
| Henry VIII | 1509–1547 |
| Edward VI | 1547–1553 |
| Jane Grey | 1553 |

| | |
|---|---|
| Mary I | 1553–1558 |
| Elizabeth I | 1558–1603 |

## House of Stuart

| | |
|---|---|
| James I | 1603–1625 |
| Charles I | 1625–1649 |
| (Interregnum) | |
| Charles II | 1660–1685 |
| James II | 1685–1689 |
| William III and Mary II | 1689–1694 |
| William III | 1694–1702 |
| Anne | 1702–1707 |

# MONARCHS OF SCOTLAND (C843–1707)

## House of Alpin

| | |
|---|---|
| Kenneth I | c843–c858 |
| Donald I | c858–862 |
| Constantine I | 862–877 |
| Áed | 877–878 |
| Eochaid and Giric | 878–885 or 889 |
| Donald II | 889–900 |
| Constantine II | 900–c943 |
| Malcolm I | c943–954 |
| Indulf | 954–962 |
| Duff | 962–966 |
| Colin | 966–971 |
| Kenneth II | 971–995 |
| Constantine III | 995–997 |
| Kenneth III | 997–1005 |
| Malcolm II | 1005–1034 |

## House of Dunkeld (or Canmore)

| | |
|---|---|
| Duncan I | 1034–1040 |

## House of Moray

| | |
|---|---|
| Macbeth | 1040–1057 |
| Lulach | 1057–1058 |

## House of Dunkeld (or Canmore)

| | |
|---|---|
| Malcolm III | 1058–1093 |
| Donald III (first reign) | 1093–1094 |
| Duncan II | 1094 |
| Donald III (second reign) | 1094–1097 |
| Edgar | 1097–1107 |
| Alexander I | 1107–1124 |
| David I | 1124–1153 |
| Malcolm IV | 1153–1165 |
| William I | 1165–1214 |
| Alexander II | 1214–1249 |
| Alexander III | 1249–1286 |
| Margaret, maid of Norway | 1286–1290 (disputed) |
| (Interregnum) | |

## House of Balliol

| | |
|---|---|
| John | 1292–1296 |
| (Interregnum) | |

## House of Bruce

| | |
|---|---|
| Robert I | 1306–1329 |
| David II | 1329–1371 |

## House of Stewart (later Stuart)

| | |
|---|---|
| Robert II | 1371–1390 |
| Robert III | 1390–1406 |
| James I | 1406–1437 |
| James II | 1437–1460 |
| James III | 1460–1488 |
| James IV | 1488–1513 |
| James V | 1513–1542 |
| Mary, queen of Scots | 1542–1567 |
| James VI | 1567–1625 |
| Charles I | 1625–1649 |
| Charles II (first reign) | 1649–1651 |
| (Interregnum) | |
| Charles II (second reign) | 1660–1685 |
| James VII | 1685–1689 |

| | |
|---|---|
| William II and Mary II | 1689–1694 |
| William II | 1694–1702 |
| Anne | 1702–1707 |

## MONARCHS OF GREAT BRITAIN (1707–1922)
## AND THE UNITED KINGDOM (1922– )

### House of Stuart

| | |
|---|---|
| Anne | 1707–1714 |

### House of Hanover

| | |
|---|---|
| George I | 1714–1727 |
| George II | 1727–1760 |
| George III | 1760–1820 |
| George IV | 1820–1830 |
| William IV | 1830–1837 |
| Victoria | 1837–1901 |

### House of Saxe-Coburg and Gotha

| | |
|---|---|
| Edward VII | 1901–1910 |
| George V | 1910–1917 |

### House of Windsor

| | |
|---|---|
| George V | 1917–1936 |
| Edward VIII | 1936 |
| George VI | 1936–1952 |
| Elizabeth II | 1952– |

# Appendix 2
# British Monarchs, Biographical Summaries

The following list provides brief biographical details of all British monarchs who succeeded Edgar (king of England from 959 to 975) and Kenneth I (traditionally regarded as the first king of Scotland, ruling from c843 to 858).

**ÁED:** *Date of birth:* unknown; *Place of birth:* unknown; *Parents:* Kenneth I and unknown woman; *Date of accession:* 877; *Date of coronation:* unknown; *Place of coronation:* unknown; *Predecessor:* Constantine I; *Relationship to predecessor:* brother; *Reign:* 877–878; *Consort:* unknown; *Date of death:* 878; *Place of death:* Strathallan; *Place of burial:* possibly Inverurie, possibly Iona; *Successor:* Giric; *Relationship to successor:* unknown.

**AETHELRED THE UNREADY:** *Date of birth:* c968; *Place of birth:* unknown; *Parents:* Edgar of England and Aelfthryth; *Date of accession:* c18 March 978; *Date of coronation:* 4 May 979; *Place of coronation:* Kingston-upon-Thames; *Predecessor:* Edward the Martyr; *Relationship to predecessor:* half-brother; *Reign:* (a) c18 March 979–Autumn 1013 (forced into exile), (b) Spring 1014–23 April 1016; *Consorts:* (a) Aelfgifu of York, (b) Emma of Normandy; *Date of death:* 23 April 1016; *Place of death:* London; *Place of burial:* probably St. Paul's Cathedral, London; *Successor:* Edmund II; *Relationship to successor:* unrelated to Sweyn, who succeeded by right of conquest in 1013; father of Edmund II, who succeeded in 1016.

**ALEXANDER I:** *Date of birth:* c1080; *Place of birth:* unknown; *Parents:* Malcolm III and St. Margaret; *Date of accession:* 1107; *Date of coronation:* unknown; *Place of coronation:* unknown; *Predecessor:* Edgar of Scotland; *Relationship to predecessor:* brother; *Reign:* 1107–c23 April 1124; *Consort:* Sybilla of Normandy; *Date of death:* c23 April 1124; *Place of death:* Stirling Castle; *Place of burial:* Dunfermline Abbey; *Successor:* David I; *Relationship to successor:* brother.

**ALEXANDER II:** *Date of birth:* 24 August 1198; *Place of birth:* Haddington; *Parents:* William I of Scotland and Ermengarde de Beaumont; *Date of accession:* 4 December 1214; *Date of coronation:* 6 December 1214; *Place* *of coronation:* Scone; *Predecessor:* William I of Scotland; *Relationship to predecessor:* son; *Reign:* 4 December 1214–8 July 1249; *Consorts:* (a) Joan of England, (b) Marie de Coucy; *Date of death:* 8 July 1249; *Place of death:* Kerrera; *Place of burial:* Melrose Abbey; *Successor:* Alexander III; *Relationship to successor:* father.

**ALEXANDER III:** *Date of birth:* 4 September 1241; *Place of birth:* Roxburgh Castle; *Parents:* Alexander II and Marie de Coucy; *Date of accession:* 8 July 1249; *Date of coronation:* 13 July 1249; *Place of coronation:* Scone; *Predecessor:* Alexander II; *Relationship to predecessor:* son; *Reign:* 8 July 1249–19 March 1286; *Consorts:* (a) Margaret, queen of Scots, (b) Yolande de Dreux; *Date of death:* 19 March 1286; *Place of death:* Near Kinghorn, Fife; *Place of burial:* Dunfermline Abbey; *Successor:* Margaret, maid of Norway; *Relationship to successor:* grandfather.

**ANNE:** *Date of birth:* 6 February 1665; *Place of birth:* St. James's Palace; *Parents:* James VII of Scotland and II of England and Anne Hyde; *Dates of accession:* (a) 8 March 1702 (England and Scotland), (b) 1 May 1707 (Great Britain); *Dates of coronation:* 23 April 1702; *Place of coronation:* Westminster Abbey (never crowned in Scotland); *Predecessor:* William III of England and II of Scotland; *Relationship to predecessor:* sister-in-law; *Reigns:* (a) 8 March 1702–1 May 1707 (England and Scotland), (b) 1 May 1707–1 August 1714 (Great Britain); *Consort:* George, prince of Denmark; *Date of death:* 1 August 1714; *Place of death:* Kensington Palace; *Place of burial:* Westminster Abbey; *Successor:* George I; *Relationship to successor:* second cousin.

**CANUTE:** *Date of birth:* c995; *Place of birth:* unknown; *Parents:* King Sweyn and unknown mother; *Date of accession:* 30 November 1016; *Date of coronation:* 1017; *Place of coronation:* possibly London; *Predecessor:* Edmund II; *Relationship to predecessor:* unrelated (succeeded by right of conquest); *Reign:* 30 November 1016–12 November 1035; *Date of death:* 12 November 1035; *Consorts:* (a) Aelfgifu of Northampton, (b) Emma of Normandy; *Place of death:* Shaftesbury; *Place of burial:* Winchester; *Successor:* Harold I; *Relationship to successor:* father.

**CHARLES I:** *Date of birth:* 19 November 1600; *Place of birth:* Dunfermline; *Parents:* King James VI and Anne of Denmark; *Date of accession:* 27 March 1625; *Dates of coronation:* (a) 2 February 1626 (England), (b) 8 June 1633 (Scotland); *Places of coronation:* (a) Westminster Abbey (England), (b) Holyrood Abbey (Scotland); *Predecessor:* James VI of Scotland and I of

England; *Relationship to predecessor:* son; *Reign:* 27 March 1625–30 January 1649; *Consort:* Henrietta Maria of France; *Date of death:* 30 January 1649; *Place of death:* Whitehall Palace; *Place of burial:* St. George's Chapel, Windsor Castle; *Successors:* (a) Charles II (Scotland), (b) interregnum (England); *Relationship to successor:* (a) father.

**CHARLES II:** *Date of birth:* 29 May 1630; *Place of birth:* St. James's Palace; *Parents:* Charles I and Henrietta Maria of France; *Dates of Accession:* (a) 30 January 1649 (Scotland), (b) 14 May 1660 (England and Scotland); *Dates of coronation:* (a) 1 January 1651 (Scotland), (b) 23 April 1661 (England); *Places of coronation:* (a) Scone (Scotland), (b) Westminster Abbey (England); *Predecessors:* (a) Charles I (Scotland), (b) interregnum (England); *Relationship to predecessor:* (a) son; *Reigns:* (a) 30 April 1649–cSeptember 1651 (Scotland), (b) 8 May 1660–6 February 1685 (England), (c) 14 May 1660–6 February 1685 (Scotland); *Consort:* Catherine of Braganza; *Date of death:* 6 February 1685; *Place of death:* Whitehall Palace; *Place of burial:* Westminster Abbey; *Successor:* James VII of Scotland and II of England; *Relationship to successor:* brother.

**COLIN:** *Date of birth:* unknown; *Place of birth:* unknown; *Parents:* Indulf and unknown mother; *Date of accession:* 966; *Date of coronation:* unknown; *Place of coronation:* unknown; *Predecessor:* Duff; *Relationship to predecessor:* cousin; *Reign:* 966–971; *Consort:* unknown; *Date of death:* 971; *Place of death:* unknown (probably southern Scotland); *Place of burial:* probably Iona; *Successor:* Kenneth II; *Relationship to successor:* cousin.

**CONSTANTINE I:** *Date of birth:* unknown; *Place of birth:* unknown; *Parents:* Kenneth I and unknown mother (possibly of Pictish ancestry); *Date of accession:* 13 April 862; *Date of coronation:* unknown; *Place of coronation:* unknown; *Predecessor:* Donald I; *Relationship to predecessor:* nephew; *Reign:* 13 April 862–877; *Consort:* unknown; *Date of death:* 877; *Place of death:* uncertain (possibly the Fife coast); *Place of burial:* possibly Iona; *Successor:* Áed; *Relationship to successor:* brother.

**CONSTANTINE II:** *Date of birth:* unknown; *Place of birth:* unknown; *Parents:* Áed and unknown mother; *Date of accession:* 900; *Date of coronation:* unknown; *Place of coronation:* unknown; *Predecessor:* Donald II; *Relationship to predecessor:* cousin; *Reign:* 900–c943 (abdicated); *Consort:* unknown; *Date of death:* 952; *Place of death:* St. Andrews; *Place of burial:* St. Andrews or Iona; *Successor:* Malcolm I; *Relationship to successor:* cousin.

**CONSTANTINE III:** *Date of birth:* unknown; *Place of birth:* unknown; *Parents:* Colin and unknown mother; *Date of accession:* 995; *Date of coronation:* unknown; *Place of coronation:* unknown; *Predecessor:* Kenneth II; *Relationship to predecessor:* cousin; *Reign:* 995–997; *Consort:* unknown (possibly none); *Date of death:* 997; *Place of death:* Rathinveramond (as yet unidentified but probably in Perthshire); *Place of burial:* Iona; *Successor:* Kenneth III; *Relationship to successor:* cousin.

**DAVID I:** *Date of birth:* c1082; *Place of birth:* unknown; *Parents:* Malcolm III and St. Margaret; *Date of accession:* April or May 1124; *Date of coronation:* April or May 1124; *Place of coronation:* Scone; *Predecessor:* Alexander I; *Relationship to predecessor:* brother; *Reign:* April or May 1124–24 May 1153; *Consort:* Maud, countess of Huntingdon; *Date of death:* 24 May 1153; *Place of death:* Carlisle Castle; *Place of burial:* Dunfermline Abbey; *Successor:* Malcolm IV; *Relationship to successor:* grandfather.

**DAVID II:** *Date of birth:* 5 March 1324; *Place of birth:* Dunfermline; *Parents:* Robert I and Elizabeth de Burgh; *Date of accession:* 7 June 1329; *Date of coronation:* 24 November 1331; *Place of coronation:* Scone; *Predecessor:* Robert I; *Relationship to predecessor:* son; *Reign:* 7 June 1329–22 February 1371; *Consorts:* (a) Joan of England, (b) Margaret Drummond; *Date of death:* 22 February 1371; *Place of death:* Edinburgh Castle; *Place of burial:* Holyrood Abbey; *Successor:* Robert II; *Relationship to successor:* uncle.

**DONALD I:** *Date of birth:* unknown; *Place of birth:* unknown; *Parents:* father probably Alpin, mother unknown; *Date of accession:* c858; *Date of coronation:* unknown; *Place of coronation:* unknown; *Predecessor:* Kenneth I; *Relationship to predecessor:* brother; *Reign:* c858–13 April 862; *Consort:* unknown (possibly none); *Date of death:* 13 April 862; *Place of death:* uncertain (possibly Rathinveramond, as yet unidentified, probably in Perthshire); *Place of burial:* possibly Iona; *Successor:* Constantine I; *Relationship to successor:* uncle.

**DONALD II:** *Date of birth:* unknown; *Place of birth:* unknown; *Parents:* Constantine I and unknown mother; *Date of accession:* 889; *Date of coronation:* unknown; *Place of coronation:* unknown; *Predecessors:* possibly Eochaid and possibly Giric; *Relationship to predecessors:* cousin of Eochaid, relationship to Giric unknown; *Reign:* 889–900; *Consort:* unknown; *Date of death:* 900; *Place of death:* probably Dunottar; *Place of burial:* probably Iona; *Successor:* Constantine II; *Relationship to successor:* cousin.

**DONALD III:** *Date of birth:* c1033; *Place of birth:* unknown; *Parents:* Duncan I and unknown mother (possibly a relative of Sigurd, earl of Northumberland); *Date of accession:* 1093; *Date of coronation:* unknown; *Place of coronation:* unknown; *Predecessors:* (a) Malcolm III, (b) Duncan II; *Relationship to predecessors:* (a) brother, (b) uncle; *Reigns:* (a) November 1093–May 1094 (deposed); (b) 12 November 1094–1097 (deposed); *Consort:* unknown; *Date of death:* c1099; *Place of death:* Roscobie, Angus; *Place of burial:* Dunkeld (remains possibly reinterred on Iona); *Successors:* (a) Duncan II, (b) Edgar of Scotland; *Relationship to successors:* (a) uncle, (b) uncle.

**DUFF:** *Date of birth:* unknown; *Place of birth:* unknown; *Parents:* Malcolm I and unknown mother; *Date of accession:* 962; *Date of coronation:* unknown; *Place of coronation:* unknown; *Predecessor:* Indulf; *Relationship to predecessor:* cousin; *Reign:* 962–966; *Consort:* unknown; *Date of death:* 966 (possibly 20 July); *Place of death:* Forres; *Place of burial:* Iona; *Successor:* Colin; *Relationship to successor:* cousin.

**DUNCAN I:** *Date of birth:* unknown; *Place of birth:* unknown; *Parents:* Crinan, abbot of Dunkeld, and Bethóc; *Date of accession:* 1034; *Date of coronation:* unknown; *Place of coronation:* unknown; *Predecessor:* Malcolm II; *Relationship to predecessor:* grandson; *Reign:* 1034–1040; *Consort:* unknown (possibly a relative of Sigurd, earl of Northumberland); *Date of death:* 1040; *Place of death:* Pitgaveny, near Elgin; *Place of burial:* possibly Iona; *Successor:* Macbeth; *Relationship to successor:* cousin.

**DUNCAN II:** *Date of birth:* unknown; *Place of birth:* unknown; *Parents:* Malcolm III and Ingibiorg Finnsdottir; *Date of accession:* May 1094; *Date of coronation:* unknown; *Place of coronation:* unknown; *Predecessor:* Donald III; *Relationship to predecessor:* nephew; *Reign:* May 1094–12 November 1094; *Consort:* Octreda of Northumbria; *Date of death:* 12 November 1094; *Place of death:* Mondynes, near Stonehaven; *Place of burial:* possibly Dunfermline Abbey, possibly Iona; *Successor:* Donald III; *Relationship to successor:* nephew.

**EDGAR AETHELING:** *Date of birth:* c1051; *Place of birth:* probably Hungary; *Parents:* Edward the Exile and Agatha; *Date of accession:* 15 October 1066; *Date of coronation:* never crowned; *Predecessor:* Harold II; *Relationship to predecessor:* unrelated (appointed by election); *Reign:* 15 October 1066–17 December 1066; *Consort:* none; *Date of death:* c1126; *Place of death:* unknown; *Place of burial:* unknown; *Successor:* William I of

England; *Relationship to successor:* unrelated (William succeeded by right of conquest).

**EDGAR OF ENGLAND:** *Date of birth:* c943; *Place of birth:* unknown; *Parents:* Edmund I and Aelfgifu; *Date of accession:* 1 October 959; *Date of coronation:* 11 May 973; *Place of coronation:* Bath Abbey; *Predecessor:* Eadwig; *Relationship to predecessor:* brother; *Reign:* 1 October 959–8 July 975; *Consorts:* (a) Aethelflaed Eneda, (b) Aelfthryth; *Date of death:* 8 July 975; *Place of death:* Winchester; *Place of burial:* Glastonbury Abbey; *Successor:* Edward the Martyr; *Relationship to successor:* father.

**EDGAR OF SCOTLAND:** *Date of birth:* c1074; *Place of birth:* unknown; *Parents:* Malcolm III and St. Margaret; *Date of accession:* 1097; *Date of coronation:* unknown; *Place of coronation:* unknown; *Predecessor:* Donald III; *Relationship to predecessor:* nephew; *Reign:* 1097–8 January 1107; *Consort:* unknown (possibly none); *Date of death:* 8 January 1107; *Place of death:* Edinburgh Castle; *Place of burial:* Dunfermline Abbey; *Successor:* Alexander I; *Relationship to successor:* brother.

**EDMUND II:** *Date of birth:* c989; *Place of birth:* unknown; *Parents:* Aethelred the Unready and Aelfgifu of York; *Date of accession:* c23 April 1016; *Date of coronation:* unknown; *Place of coronation:* unknown; *Predecessor:* Aethelred the Unready; *Relationship to predecessor:* son; *Reign:* c23 April 1016–30 November 1016; *Consort:* Edith of East Anglia; *Date of death:* 30 November 1016; *Place of death:* probably London; *Place of burial:* Glastonbury Abbey; *Successor:* Canute; *Relationship to successor:* unrelated (Canute succeeded by right of conquest).

**EDWARD I:** *Date of birth:* 17 June 1239; *Place of birth:* Palace of Westminster; *Parents:* Henry III and Eleanor of Provence; *Date of accession:* 20 November 1272; *Date of coronation:* 19 August 1274; *Place of coronation:* Westminster Abbey; *Predecessor:* Henry III; *Relationship to predecessor:* son; *Reign:* 20 November 1272–7 July 1307; *Consorts:* (a) Eleanor of Castile, (b) Marguerite of France; *Date of death:* 7 July 1307; *Place of death:* Burgh by Sands; *Place of burial:* Westminster Abbey; *Successor:* Edward II; *Relationship to successor:* father.

**EDWARD II:** *Date of birth:* 25 April 1284; *Place of birth:* Caernarfon Castle; *Parents:* Edward I and Eleanor of Castile; *Date of accession:* 7 July 1307; *Date of coronation:* 25 February 1308; *Place of coronation:* Westminster Abbey; *Predecessor:* Edward I; *Relationship to predecessor:* son; *Reign:*

7 July 1307–20 January 1327 (abdicated); *Consort:* Isabella of France; *Date of death:* possibly 21 September 1327; *Place of death:* Berkeley Castle, Gloucestershire; *Place of burial:* Gloucester Cathedral; *Successor:* Edward III; *Relationship to successor:* father.

**EDWARD III:** *Date of birth:* 13 November 1312; *Place of birth:* Windsor Castle; *Parents:* Edward II and Isabella of France; *Date of accession:* 24 January 1327; *Date of coronation:* 1 February 1327; *Place of coronation:* Westminster Abbey; *Predecessor:* Edward II; *Relationship to predecessor:* son; *Reign:* 24 January 1327–21 June 1377; *Consort:* Philippa of Hainaut; *Date of death:* 21 June 1377; *Place of death:* Sheen Palace; *Place of burial:* Westminster Abbey; *Successor:* Richard II; *Relationship to successor:* grandfather.

**EDWARD IV:** *Date of birth:* 28 April 1442; *Place of birth:* Rouen, Normandy; *Parents:* Richard, duke of York, and Cicely Neville, duchess of York; *Dates of Accession:* (a) 4 March 1461, (b) 11 April 1471; *Date of coronation:* 28 June 1461; *Place of coronation:* Westminster Abbey; *Predecessors:* (a) Henry VI, (b) Henry VI; *Relationship to predecessor:* unrelated; *Reigns:* (a) 4 March 1461 (succeeded by right of conquest)–2 October 1470 (deposed), (b) 4 May 1471 (succeeded by right of conquest)–9 April 1483; *Consort:* Elizabeth Woodville; *Date of death:* 9 April 1483; *Place of death:* Palace of Westminster; *Place of burial:* St. George's Chapel, Windsor Castle; *Successors:* (a) Henry VI, (b) Edward V; *Relationship to successor:* (a) unrelated, (b) father.

**EDWARD V:** *Date of birth:* 2 November 1470; *Place of birth:* Westminster Abbey; *Parents:* Edward IV and Elizabeth Woodville; *Date of accession:* 9 April 1483; *Date of coronation:* never crowned; *Predecessor:* Edward IV; *Relationship to predecessor:* son; *Reign:* 9 April 1483–25 June 1483 (throne declared vacant); *Consort:* none; *Date of death:* probably summer 1483; *Place of death:* probably the Tower of London; *Place of burial:* unknown; *Successor:* Richard III; *Relationship to successor:* nephew.

**EDWARD VI:** *Date of birth:* 12 October 1537; *Place of birth:* Hampton Court Palace; *Parents:* Henry VIII and Jane Seymour; *Date of accession:* 28 January 1547; *Date of coronation:* 20 February 1547; *Place of coronation:* Westminster Abbey; *Predecessor:* Henry VIII; *Relationship to predecessor:* son; *Reign:* 28 January 1547–6 July 1553; *Consort:* none; *Date of death:* 6 July 1553; *Place of death:* Palace of Placentia (Greenwich Palace); *Place of burial:* Westminster Abbey; *Successor:* Jane Grey; *Relationship to successor:* first cousin, once removed.

**EDWARD VII:** *Date of birth:* 9 November 1841; *Place of birth:* Buckingham Palace; *Parents:* Prince Albert of Saxe-Coburg and Gotha and Victoria; *Date of accession:* 22 January 1901; *Date of coronation:* 9 August 1902; *Place of coronation:* Westminster Abbey; *Predecessor:* Victoria; *Relationship to predecessor:* son; *Reign:* 22 January 1901–6 May 1910; *Consort:* Alexandra of Denmark; *Date of death:* 6 May 1910; *Place of death:* Buckingham Palace; *Place of burial:* St. George's Chapel, Windsor Castle; *Successor:* George V; *Relationship to successor:* father.

**EDWARD VIII:** *Date of birth:* 23 June 1894; *Place of birth:* White Lodge, Windsor; *Parents:* George V and Mary of Teck; *Date of accession:* 20 January 1936; *Date of coronation:* never crowned; *Predecessor:* George V; *Relationship to predecessor:* son; *Reign:* 20 January 1936–11 December 1936 (abdicated); *Consort:* Wallis, duchess of Windsor; *Date of death:* 28 May 1972; *Place of death:* Paris; *Place of burial:* Frogmore; *Successor:* George VI; *Relationship to successor:* brother.

**EDWARD THE CONFESSOR:** *Date of birth:* c1002; *Place of birth:* probably Islip; *Parents:* Aethelred the Unready and Emma of Normandy; *Date of accession:* After 8 June 1042; *Date of coronation:* 3 April 1043; *Place of coronation:* Winchester; *Predecessor:* Harthacanute; *Relationship to predecessor:* half-brother; *Reign:* after 8 June 1042–5 January 1066; *Consort:* Edith of Wessex; *Date of death:* 5 January 1066; *Place of death:* London; *Place of burial:* Westminster Abbey; *Successor:* Harold II; *Relationship to successor:* brother-in-law.

**EDWARD THE MARTYR:** *Date of birth:* c962; *Place of birth:* unknown; *Parents:* Edward of England and, probably, Aethelflaed Eneda; *Date of accession:* after 8 July 975; *Date of coronation:* unknown; *Place of coronation:* unknown; *Predecessor:* Edgar of England; *Relationship to predecessor:* son; *Reign:* mid-July 975–18 March 978; *Consort:* none; *Date of death:* 18 March 978; *Place of death:* Corfe Castle; *Place of burial:* Shaftesbury Abbey; *Successor:* Aethelred the Unready; *Relationship to successor:* half-brother.

**ELIZABETH I:** *Date of birth:* 7 September 1533; *Place of birth:* Palace of Placentia (Greenwich Palace); *Parents:* Henry VIII and Anne Boleyn; *Date of accession:* 17 November 1558; *Date of coronation:* 15 January 1559; *Place of coronation:* Westminster Abbey; *Predecessor:* Mary I; *Relationship to predecessor:* half-sister; *Reign:* 17 November 1558–24 March 1603; *Consort:* none; *Date of death:* 24 March 1603; *Place of death:* Sheen Palace (Richmond Palace); *Place of burial:* Westminster Abbey; *Successor:* James

VI of Scotland and I of England; *Relationship to successor:* first cousin, twice removed.

**ELIZABETH II:** *Date of birth:* 21 April 1926; *Place of birth:* 17 Bruton Street, London; *Parents:* George VI and Elizabeth, the queen mother; *Date of accession:* 6 February 1952; *Date of coronation:* 2 June 1953; *Place of coronation:* Westminster Abbey; *Predecessor:* George VI; *Relationship to predecessor:* daughter; *Reign:* 6 February 1952– ; *Consort:* Prince Philip, duke of Edinburgh; *Heir:* Charles, prince of Wales.

**EOCHAID:** *Date of birth:* unknown; *Place of birth:* unknown; *Parents:* father unknown, mother possibly a daughter of Kenneth I; *Date of accession:* 878 (possibly co-ruler with Giric); *Date of coronation:* unknown; *Place of coronation:* unknown; *Predecessor:* Áed; *Relationship to predecessor:* possibly nephew; *Reign:* 878–885 or 889 (possibly deposed); *Consort:* unknown; *Date of death:* unknown; *Place of death:* unknown; *Place of burial:* unknown; *Successor:* Donald II; *Relationship to successor:* possibly cousin.

**GEORGE I:** *Date of birth:* 28 May 1660; *Place of birth:* Osnabrück, Hanover; *Parents:* Ernest Augustus, elector of Hanover, and Sophia, electress of Hanover; *Date of accession:* 1 August 1714; *Date of coronation:* 20 October 1714; *Place of coronation:* Westminster Abbey; *Predecessor:* Anne; *Relationship to predecessor:* second cousin; *Reign:* 1 August 1714–11 June 1727; *Consort:* Sophia Dorothea of Celle; *Date of death:* 11 June 1727; *Place of death:* Osnabrück, Hanover; *Place of burial:* Leineschloss Church, Hanover; *Successor:* George II; *Relationship to successor:* father.

**GEORGE II:** *Date of birth:* 30 October 1683; *Place of birth:* Herrenhausen, Lower Saxony; *Parents:* George I and Sophia Dorothea of Celle; *Date of accession:* 11 June 1727; *Date of coronation:* 11 October 1727; *Place of coronation:* Westminster Abbey; *Predecessor:* George I; *Relationship to predecessor:* son; *Reign:* 11 June 1727–25 October 1760; *Consort:* Caroline of Brandenburg-Ansbach; *Date of death:* 25 October 1760; *Place of death:* Kensington Palace; *Place of burial:* Westminster Abbey; *Successor:* George III; *Relationship to successor:* grandfather.

**GEORGE III:** *Date of birth:* 24 May 1738; *Place of birth:* Norfolk House, London; *Parents:* Frederick, prince of Wales, and Princess Augusta of Saxe-Gotha; *Date of accession:* 25 October 1760; *Date of coronation:* 22 September 1761; *Place of coronation:* Westminster Abbey; *Predecessor:* George II;

*Relationship to predecessor:* grandson; *Reign:* 25 October 1760–29 January 1820; *Consort:* Charlotte of Mecklenburg-Strelitz; *Date of death:* 29 January 1820; *Place of death:* Windsor Castle; *Place of burial:* St. George's Chapel, Windsor Castle; *Successor:* George IV; *Relationship to successor:* father.

**GEORGE IV:** *Date of birth:* 12 August 1762; *Place of birth:* St. James's Palace; *Parents:* George III and Charlotte of Mecklenburg-Strelitz; *Date of accession:* 29 January 1820; *Date of coronation:* 19 July 1821; *Place of coronation:* Westminster Abbey; *Predecessor:* George III; *Relationship to predecessor:* son; *Reign:* 29 January 1820–26 June 1830; *Consort:* Caroline of Brunswick-Wolfenbüttel; *Date of death:* 26 June 1830; *Place of death:* Windsor Castle; *Place of burial:* St. George's Chapel, Windsor Castle; *Successor:* William IV; *Relationship to successor:* brother.

**GEORGE V:** *Date of birth:* 3 June 1865; *Place of birth:* Marlborough House, London; *Parents:* Edward VII and Alexandra of Denmark; *Date of accession:* 6 May 1910; *Date of coronation:* 22 June 1911; *Place of coronation:* Westminster Abbey; *Predecessor:* Edward VII; *Relationship to predecessor:* son; *Reign:* 6 May 1910–20 January 1936; *Consort:* Mary of Teck; *Date of death:* 20 January 1936; *Place of death:* Sandringham House; *Place of burial:* St. George's Chapel, Windsor Castle; *Successor:* Edward VIII; *Relationship to successor:* father.

**GEORGE VI:** *Date of birth:* 14 December 1895; *Place of birth:* York Cottage, Sandringham House estate; *Parents:* George V and Mary of Teck; *Date of accession:* 11 December 1936; *Date of coronation:* 12 May 1937; *Place of coronation:* Westminster Abbey; *Predecessor:* Edward VIII; *Relationship to predecessor:* brother; *Reign:* 11 December 1936–6 February 1952; *Consort:* Elizabeth, the queen mother; *Date of death:* 6 February 1952; *Place of death:* Sandringham House; *Place of burial:* St. George's Chapel, Windsor Castle; *Successor:* Elizabeth II; *Relationship to successor:* father.

**GIRIC:** *Date of birth:* unknown; *Place of birth:* unknown; *Parents:* father and mother unknown; *Date of accession:* 878 (possibly co-ruler with Eochaid); *Date of coronation:* unknown; *Place of coronation:* unknown; *Predecessor:* Áed; *Relationship to predecessor:* unknown; *Reign:* 878–885 or 889 (possibly deposed); *Consort:* unknown; *Date of death:* possibly 889; *Place of death:* Dundurn; *Place of burial:* possibly Iona; *Successor:* Donald II; *Relationship to successor:* unknown.

**HAROLD I:** *Date of birth:* c1015; *Place of birth:* unknown; *Parents:* Canute and Aelfgifu of Northampton; *Date of accession:* 1037; *Date of coronation:*

never crowned; *Predecessor:* Harthacanute; *Relationship to predecessor:* half-brother; *Reign:* 1037 (usurped throne)–17 March 1040; *Consort:* possibly Aelfgifu; *Date of death:* 17 March 1040; *Place of death:* Oxford; *Place of burial:* Westminster Abbey (the body was later exhumed and thrown into a marsh); *Successor:* Harthacanute.

**HAROLD II:** *Date of birth:* c1020; *Place of birth:* unknown; *Parents:* Godwin, earl of Wessex, and Gytha Thorkelsdóttir; *Date of accession:* 5 January 1066; *Date of coronation:* 6 January 1066; *Place of coronation:* probably Westminster Abbey; *Predecessor:* Edward the Confessor; *Relationship to predecessor:* brother-in-law; *Reign:* 5 January 1066–14 October 1066; *Consorts:* (a) Edith Swan-Neck, (b) Ealdgyth of Mercia; *Date of death:* 14 October 1066; *Place of death:* Hastings; *Place of burial:* probably Waltham Abbey; *Successor:* Edgar the Aetheling; *Relationship to successor:* unrelated (appointed by election).

**HARTHACANUTE:** *Date of birth:* c1018; *Place of birth:* unknown; *Parents:* Canute and Emma of Normandy; *Dates of Accession:* (a) 12 November 1035, (b) 17 June 1040 (reclaimed throne); *Date of coronation:* after 17 June 1040; *Place of coronation:* possibly London; *Predecessors:* (a) Canute, (b) Harold I; *Relationship to predecessors:* (a) son, (b) half-brother; *Reigns:* (a) 12 November 1035–1037 (deposed), (b) 17 June 1040–8 June 1042; *Consort:* unknown; *Date of death:* 8 June 1042; *Place of death:* Lambeth; *Place of burial:* Winchester; *Successor:* Edward the Confessor; *Relationship to successor:* half-brother.

**HENRY I:** *Date of birth:* 1068 or 1069; *Place of birth:* unknown (possibly Selby, Yorkshire); *Parents:* William I of England and Matilda of Flanders; *Date of accession:* 5 August 1100; *Date of coronation:* 5 August 1100; *Place of coronation:* Westminster Abbey; *Predecessor:* William II of England; *Relationship to predecessor:* brother; *Reign:* 5 August 1100–1 December 1135; *Consorts:* (a) Matilda of Scotland, (b) Adeliza of Louvain; *Date of death:* 1 December 1135; *Place of death:* Lyons-la-Forêt Castle, Normandy; *Place of burial:* Reading Abbey; *Successor:* Stephen; *Relationship to successor:* uncle.

**HENRY II:** *Date of birth:* 5 March 1133; *Place of birth:* Le Mans, France; *Parents:* Geoffrey, count of Anjou, and Matilda; *Date of accession:* 19 December 1154; *Date of coronation:* 19 December 1154; *Place of coronation:* Westminster Abbey; *Predecessor:* Stephen; *Relationship to predecessor:* second cousin, once removed; *Reign:* 19 December 1154–6 July 1189; *Consort:* Eleanor of Aquitaine; *Date of death:* 6 July 1189; *Place of death:*

Chinon Castle, Anjou; *Place of burial:* Fontevrault Abbey; *Successor:* Richard I; *Relationship to successor:* father.

**HENRY III:** *Date of birth:* 1 October 1207; *Place of birth:* Winchester; *Parents:* John, and Isabella of Angoulême; *Date of accession:* 28 October 1216; *Dates of coronation:* (a) 28 October 1216, (b) 17 May 1220; *Places of coronation:* (a) St. Peter's Abbey, Gloucester, (b) Westminster Abbey; *Predecessor:* John; *Relationship to predecessor:* son; *Reign:* 28 October 1216–16 November 1272; *Consort:* Eleanor of Provence; *Date of death:* 16 November 1272; *Place of death:* Palace of Westminster; *Place of burial:* Westminster Abbey; *Successor:* Edward I; *Relationship to successor:* father.

**HENRY IV:** *Date of birth:* probably April 1366; *Place of birth:* Bolingbroke Castle, Lincolnshire; *Parents:* John of Gaunt, duke of Lancaster, and Blanche, duchess of Lancaster; *Date of accession:* 30 September 1399; *Date of coronation:* 13 October 1399; *Place of coronation:* Westminster Abbey; *Predecessor:* Richard II; *Relationship to predecessor:* cousin; *Reign:* 30 September 1399–20 March 1413; *Consorts:* (a) Mary de Bohun, (2) Joan of Navarre; *Date of death:* 20 March 1413; *Place of death:* Abbot's House, Westminster Abbey; *Place of burial:* Canterbury Cathedral; *Successor:* Henry V; *Relationship to successor:* father.

**HENRY V:** *Date of birth:* 9 August or 16 September 1386 or 1387; *Place of birth:* Monmouth Castle; *Parents:* Henry IV and Mary de Bohun; *Date of accession:* 20 March 1413; *Date of coronation:* 9 April 1413; *Place of coronation:* Westminster Abbey; *Predecessor:* Henry IV; *Relationship to predecessor:* son; *Reign:* 20 March 1413–31 August 1422; *Consort:* Catherine of Valois; *Date of death:* 31 August 1422; *Place of death:* Bois de Vincennes, near Paris; *Place of burial:* Westminster Abbey; *Successor:* Henry VI; *Relationship to successor:* father.

**HENRY VI:** *Date of birth:* 6 December 1421; *Place of birth:* Windsor Castle; *Parents:* Henry V and Catherine of Valois; *Date of accession:* 31 August 1422; *Date of coronation:* 6 November 1429; *Place of coronation:* Westminster Abbey; *Predecessors:* (a) Henry V, (b) Edward IV; *Relationship to predecessors:* (a) son, (b) unrelated; *Reigns:* (a) 31 August 1422–4 March 1461 (deposed), (b) 3 October 1470–4 May 1471 (deposed); *Consort:* Margaret of Anjou; *Date of death:* 21 May 1471; *Place of death:* Tower of London; *Place of burial:* Chertsey Abbey (remains later reinterred at St. George's Chapel, Windsor Castle); *Successors:* (a) Edward IV, (b) Edward IV; *Relationship to successor:* unrelated.

**HENRY VII:** *Date of birth:* 28 January 1457; *Place of birth:* Pembroke Castle; *Parents:* Edmund Tudor, earl of Richmond, and Margaret Beaufort; *Date of accession:* 22 August 1485; *Date of coronation:* 30 October 1485; *Place of coronation:* Westminster Abbey; *Predecessor:* Richard III; *Relationship to predecessor:* unrelated (succeeded to throne by right of conquest); *Reign:* 22 August 1485–21 April 1509; *Consort:* Elizabeth of York; *Date of death:* 21 April 1509; *Place of death:* Sheen Palace; *Place of burial:* Westminster Abbey; *Successor:* Henry VIII; *Relationship to successor:* father.

**HENRY VIII:** *Date of birth:* 28 June 1491; *Place of birth:* Palace of Placentia (Greenwich Palace); *Parents:* Henry VII and Elizabeth of York; *Date of accession:* 21 April 1509; *Date of coronation:* 24 June 1509; *Place of coronation:* Westminster Abbey; *Predecessor:* Henry VII; *Relationship to predecessor:* son; *Reign:* 21 April 1509–28 January 1547; *Consorts:* (a) Catherine of Aragon, (b) Anne Boleyn, (c) Jane Seymour, (d) Anne of Cleves, (e) Catherine Howard, (f) Catherine Parr; *Date of death:* 28 January 1547; *Place of death:* Whitehall Palace; *Place of burial:* St. George's Chapel, Windsor Castle; *Successor:* Edward VI; *Relationship to successor:* father.

**INDULF:** *Date of birth:* unknown; *Place of birth:* unknown; *Parents:* Constantine II and unknown mother; *Date of accession:* 954; *Date of coronation:* unknown; *Place of coronation:* unknown; *Predecessor:* Malcolm I; *Relationship to predecessor:* cousin; *Reign:* 954–962; *Consort:* unknown; *Date of death:* 962; *Place of death:* Invercullen (an unidentified site, probably in northeastern Scotland); *Place of burial:* probably Iona; *Successor:* Duff; *Relationship to successor:* cousin.

**JAMES I OF ENGLAND:** *See* JAMES VI OF SCOTLAND AND I OF ENGLAND.

**JAMES I OF SCOTLAND:** *Date of birth:* late July or 10 December 1394; *Place of birth:* Dunfermline; *Parents:* Robert III and Annabella Drummond; *Date of accession:* 4 April 1406; *Date of coronation:* 21 May 1424; *Place of coronation:* Scone; *Predecessor:* Robert III; *Relationship to predecessor:* son; *Reign:* 4 April 1406–20 February 1437; *Consort:* Joan Beaufort; *Date of death:* 20 February 1437; *Place of death:* Blackfriars Priory, Perth; *Place of burial:* Carthusian Priory, Perth; *Successor:* James II of Scotland; *Relationship to successor:* father.

**JAMES II OF ENGLAND:** *See* JAMES VII OF SCOTLAND AND II OF ENGLAND.

**JAMES II OF SCOTLAND:** *Date of birth:* 16 October 1430; *Place of birth:* Holyrood Palace; *Parents:* James I of Scotland and Joan Beaufort; *Date of accession:* 20 February 1437; *Date of coronation:* 25 March 1437; *Place of coronation:* Holyrood Abbey; *Predecessor:* James I of Scotland; *Relationship to predecessor:* son; *Reign:* 20 February 1437–3 August 1460; *Consort:* Mary of Gueldres; *Date of death:* 3 August 1460; *Place of death:* Roxburgh Castle; *Place of burial:* Holyrood Abbey; *Successor:* James III; *Relationship to successor:* father.

**JAMES III:** *Date of birth:* 10 or 20 July 1451 or May 1452; *Place of birth:* Stirling Castle (if 1451) or St. Andrews Castle (if 1452); *Parents:* James II and Mary of Gueldres; *Date of accession:* 3 August 1460; *Date of coronation:* 10 August 1460; *Place of coronation:* Kelso Abbey; *Predecessor:* James II of Scotland; *Relationship to predecessor:* son; *Reign:* 3 August 1460–11 June 1488; *Consort:* Margaret of Denmark; *Date of death:* 11 June 1488; *Place of death:* Sauchieburn, near Stirling; *Place of burial:* Cambuskenneth Abbey, near Stirling; *Successor:* James IV; *Relationship to successor:* father.

**JAMES IV:** *Date of birth:* 17 March 1473; *Place of birth:* probably Stirling Castle; *Parents:* James III and Margaret of Denmark; *Date of accession:* 11 June 1488; *Date of coronation:* 24 June 1488; *Place of coronation:* Scone; *Predecessor:* James III; *Relationship to predecessor:* son; *Reign:* 24 June 1488–9 September 1513; *Consort:* Margaret Tudor; *Date of death:* 9 September 1513; *Place of death:* Flodden, Northumberland; *Place of burial:* Richmond-upon-Thames or St. Paul's Cathedral; *Successor:* James V; *Relationship to successor:* father.

**JAMES V:** *Date of birth:* 10 April 1512; *Place of birth:* Linlithgow Palace; *Parents:* James IV and Margaret Tudor; *Date of accession:* 9 September 1513; *Date of coronation:* 21 September 1513; *Place of coronation:* Stirling; *Predecessor:* James IV; *Relationship to predecessor:* son; *Reign:* 9 September 1513–14 December 1542; *Consorts:* (a) Madeleine de Valois, (b) Mary of Guise; *Date of death:* 14 December 1542; *Place of death:* Falkland Palace; *Place of burial:* Holyrood Abbey; *Successor:* Mary, queen of Scots; *Relationship to successor:* father.

**JAMES VI OF SCOTLAND AND I OF ENGLAND:** *Date of birth:* 19 June 1566; *Place of birth:* Edinburgh Castle; *Parents:* Henry Stuart, lord Darnley, and Mary, queen of Scots; *Dates of Accession:* (a) 24 July 1567 (Scotland), (b) 24 March 1603 (England); *Dates of coronation:* (a) 29 July 1567 (Scotland), (b) 25 July 1603 (England); *Places of coronation:* (a)

Church of the Holy Rude, Stirling, (b) Westminster Abbey; *Predecessors:* (a) Mary, queen of Scots (Scotland), (b) Elizabeth I (England); *Relationship to predecessors:* (a) son, (b) first cousin, twice removed; *Reigns:* (a) 24 July 1567–27 March 1625 (Scotland), (b) 24 March 1603–27 March 1625 (England); *Consort:* Anne of Denmark; *Date of death:* 27 March 1625; *Place of death:* Theobalds House, Hertfordshire; *Place of burial:* Westminster Abbey; *Successor:* Charles I; *Relationship to successor:* father.

**JAMES VII OF SCOTLAND AND II OF ENGLAND:** *Date of birth:* 14 October 1633; *Place of birth:* St. James's Palace; *Parents:* Charles I and Henrietta Maria of France; *Date of accession:* 6 February 1685 (England and Scotland); *Date of coronation:* 23 April 1685 (England; never crowned in Scotland); *Place of coronation:* Westminster Abbey; *Predecessor:* Charles II (England and Scotland); *Relationship to predecessor:* brother; *Reigns:* (a) England: 6 February 1685–12 February 1689 (declared by parliament to have abdicated), (b) Scotland: 6 February 1685–11 April 1689 (declared by parliament to have forfeited the throne); *Consorts:* (a) Anne Hyde, (b) Mary of Modena; *Date of death:* 5 September 1701; *Place of death:* St. Germain-en-Laye, near Paris; *Place of burial:* Church of the English Benedictine Monks in Paris (some body parts distributed to other French sites); *Successors:* William III of England and II of Scotland and Mary II; *Relationship to successors:* (a) father-in-law of William III and II, (b) father of Mary II.

**JANE GREY:** *Date of birth:* probably October 1537; *Place of birth:* Bradgate Park, Leicestershire; *Parents:* Henry Grey, marquess of Dorset, and Frances Brandon; *Date of accession:* 6 July 1553 (disputed); *Date of coronation:* never crowned; *Predecessor:* Edward VI; *Relationship to predecessor:* first cousin, once removed; *Reign:* 6 July 1553–19 July 1553 (disputed); *Consort:* Lord Guildford Dudley; *Date of death:* 12 February 1554; *Place of death:* Tower of London; *Place of burial:* Church of St. Peter ad Vincula, London; *Successor:* Mary I; *Relationship to successor:* first cousin, once removed.

**JOHN:** *Date of birth:* 24 December 1167; *Place of birth:* Beaumont Palace, Oxford; *Parents:* Henry II and Eleanor of Aquitaine; *Date of accession:* 27 May 1199; *Date of coronation:* 27 May 1199; *Place of coronation:* Westminster Abbey; *Predecessor:* Richard I; *Relationship to predecessor:* brother; *Reign:* 27 May 1199–19 October 1216; *Consorts:* (a) Isabel of Gloucester, (b) Isabella of Angoulême; *Date of death:* 19 October 1216; *Place of death:* Newark Castle; *Place of burial:* Worcester Cathedral; *Successor:* Henry III; *Relationship to successor:* father.

**JOHN OF SCOTLAND:** *Date of birth:* c1250; *Place of birth:* unknown; *Parents:* John de Balliol and Dervorguilla; *Date of accession:* 17 November 1292 (appointed by Edward I of England after an adjudication of the claims of candidates for the throne); *Date of coronation:* 30 November 1292; *Place of coronation:* Scone; *Predecessor:* interregnum; *Reign:* 17 November 1292–10 July 1296 (abdicated); *Consort:* Isabella de Warenne; *Date of death:* probably late 1314; *Place of death:* probably Picardy; *Place of burial:* unknown; *Successor:* interregnum.

**KENNETH I:** *Date of birth:* unknown; *Place of birth:* unknown; *Parents:* father probably Alpin, mother unknown; *Date of accession:* possibly 843; *Date of coronation:* unknown; *Place of coronation:* unknown; *Predecessor:* uncertain (possibly Alpin in Dalriada and Urad or Drust in Pictavia); *Relationship to predecessor:* son of Alpin; probably unrelated to Pictish leaders; *Reign:* c843–c858; *Consort:* unknown; *Date of death:* c858 (possibly 8 February 858); *Place of death:* possibly Forteviot, near Perth; *Place of burial:* possibly Iona; *Successor:* Donald I; *Relationship to successor:* brother.

**KENNETH II:** *Date of birth:* unknown; *Place of birth:* unknown; *Parents:* Malcolm I and unknown mother; *Date of accession:* 971; *Date of coronation:* unknown; *Place of coronation:* unknown; *Predecessor:* Colin; *Relationship to predecessor:* cousin; *Reign:* 971–995; *Consort:* unknown (possibly a daughter of one of the Irish kings); *Date of death:* 995; *Place of death:* Fettercairn; *Place of burial:* Iona; *Successor:* Constantine III; *Relationship to successor:* cousin.

**KENNETH III:** *Date of birth:* unknown; *Place of birth:* unknown; *Parents:* Duff and unknown mother; *Date of accession:* 997; *Date of coronation:* unknown; *Place of coronation:* unknown; *Predecessor:* Constantine III; *Relationship to predecessor:* cousin; *Reign:* 997–1005; *Consort:* unknown; *Date of death:* 1005; *Place of death:* Monzievaird (near Perth); *Place of burial:* possibly Iona; *Successor:* Malcolm II; *Relationship to successor:* cousin.

**LULACH:** *Date of birth:* unknown; *Place of birth:* unknown; *Parents:* Gille Coemgáin, mormaer of Moray, and Gruoch; *Date of accession:* 15 August 1057; *Date of coronation:* August 1057; *Place of coronation:* Scone; *Predecessor:* Macbeth; *Relationship to predecessor:* stepson; *Reign:* 1057–1058; *Consort:* Finnghuala; *Date of death:* 17 March 1058; *Place of death:* Essie, Aberdeenshire; *Place of burial:* possibly Iona; *Successor:* Malcolm III; *Relationship to successor:* unrelated.

**MACBETH:** *Date of birth:* c1005; *Place of birth:* unknown; *Parents:* Findláech of Moray and, possibly, a daughter of Kenneth II, Kenneth III, or Malcolm II; *Date of accession:* 1040; *Date of coronation:* unknown; *Place of coronation:* unknown; *Predecessor:* Duncan I; *Relationship to predecessor:* cousin; *Reign:* 1040–1057; *Consort:* Gruoch; *Date of death:* 15 August 1057; *Place of death:* Lumphanan, near Aberdeen; *Place of burial:* possibly Iona; *Successor:* Lulach; *Relationship to successor:* stepfather.

**MALCOLM I:** *Date of birth:* unknown; *Place of birth:* unknown; *Parents:* Donald II and unknown mother; *Date of accession:* c943; *Date of corona-tion:* unknown; *Place of coronation:* unknown; *Predecessor:* Constantine II; *Relationship to predecessor:* cousin; *Reign:* c943–954; *Consort:* unknown; *Date of death:* 954; *Place of death:* Dunottar or Fetteresso; *Place of burial:* probably Iona; *Successor:* Indulf; *Relationship to successor:* cousin.

**MALCOLM II:** *Date of birth:* unknown; *Place of birth:* unknown; *Parents:* Kenneth II and unknown mother (possibly a daughter of one of the Irish kings); *Date of accession:* 1005; *Date of coronation:* unknown; *Place of cor-onation:* unknown; *Predecessor:* Kenneth III; *Relationship to predecessor:* cousin; *Reign:* 1005–1034; *Consort:* unknown; *Date of death:* 25 November 1034; *Place of death:* probably Glamis; *Place of burial:* possibly Iona; *Suc-cessor:* Duncan I; *Relationship to successor:* grandfather.

**MALCOLM III:** *Date of birth:* c1031; *Place of birth:* unknown; *Par-ents:* Duncan I and unknown mother (possibly a relative of Sigurd, earl of Northumberland); *Date of accession:* 17 March 1058; *Date of coronation:* possibly 25 April 1058; *Place of coronation:* Scone; *Relationship to pre-decessor:* unrelated (succeeded to throne by right of conquest); *Reign:* 17 March 1058–13 November 1093; *Consorts:* (a) Ingibiorg Finnsdottir, (b) St. Margaret; *Date of death:* 13 November 1093; *Place of death:* Alnwick; *Place of burial:* Tynemouth Priory (remains possibly reinterred in Dunfermline Ab-bey); *Successor:* Donald III; *Relationship to successor:* brother.

**MALCOLM IV:** *Date of birth:* Between 23 April and 24 May 1141; *Place of birth:* unknown; *Parents:* Henry, earl of Northumberland, and Ada de Warenne; *Date of accession:* 24 May 1153; *Date of coronation:* 27 May 1153; *Place of coronation:* Scone; *Predecessor:* David I; *Relationship to predecessor:* grandson; *Reign:* April or May 1153–9 December 1165; *Con-sort:* none; *Date of death:* 9 December 1165; *Place of death:* Jedburgh Ab-bey; *Place of burial:* Dunfermline Abbey; *Successor:* William I of Scotland; *Relationship to successor:* brother.

**MARGARET, MAID OF NORWAY:** *Date of birth:* cApril 1283; *Place of birth:* Norway; *Parents:* Eric II, king of Norway, and Margaret, queen of Norway; *Date of accession:* November 1286 (disputed); *Date of coronation:* never crowned; *Predecessor:* Alexander III; *Relationship to predecessor:* granddaughter; *Reign:* November 1286–September or October 1290 (disputed); *Consort:* none; *Date of death:* September or October 1290; *Place of death:* Orkney Islands; *Place of burial:* Christ's Kirk, Bergen; *Successor:* interregnum.

**MARY I:** *Date of birth:* 18 February 1516; *Place of birth:* Palace of Placentia (Greenwich Palace); *Parents:* Henry VIII and Catherine of Aragon; *Date of accession:* 19 July 1553; *Date of coronation:* 1 October 1553; *Place of coronation:* Westminster Abbey; *Predecessor:* Jane Grey; *Relationship to predecessor:* first cousin, once removed; *Reign:* 19 July 1553–17 November 1558; *Consort:* Philip II of Spain; *Date of death:* 17 November 1558; *Place of death:* St. James's Palace; *Place of burial:* Westminster Abbey; *Successor:* Elizabeth I; *Relationship to successor:* half-sister.

**MARY II:** *Date of birth:* 30 April 1662; *Place of birth:* St. James's Palace; *Parents:* James VII of Scotland and II of England and Anne Hyde; *Dates of Accession:* (a) 13 February 1689 (England), (b) 11 April 1689 (Scotland); *Date of coronation:* 11 April 1689; *Place of coronation:* Westminster Abbey (never crowned in Scotland); *Predecessor:* James VII and II; *Relationship to predecessor:* daughter; *Reigns:* (a) England: co-sovereign with William III from 13 February 1689 to 28 December 1694, (b) Scotland: co-sovereign with William II from 11 April 1689 to 28 December 1694; *Consort:* William III of England and II of Scotland; *Date of death:* 28 December 1694; *Place of death:* Kensington Palace; *Place of burial:* Westminster Abbey; *Successor:* William III of England and II of Scotland as sole sovereign; *Relationship to successor:* consort.

**MARY, QUEEN OF SCOTS:** *Date of birth:* 7 or 8 December 1542; *Place of birth:* Linlithgow Palace; *Parents:* James V and Mary of Guise; *Date of accession:* 14 December 1542; *Date of coronation:* 9 September 1543; *Place of coronation:* Stirling Castle; *Predecessor:* James V; *Relationship to predecessor:* daughter; *Reign:* 14 December 1542–24 July 1567 (abdicated); *Consorts:* (a) Francis II of France, (b) Henry Stuart, lord Darnley, (c) James Hepburn, earl of Bothwell; *Date of death:* 8 February 1587; *Place of death:* Fotheringhay Castle; *Place of burial:* Peterborough Cathedral (remains later reinterred at Westminster Abbey); *Successor:* James VI of Scotland; *Relationship to successor:* mother.

**MATILDA:** *Date of birth:* c2 February 1102; *Place of birth:* Sutton Courtenay; *Parents:* Henry I and Matilda of Scotland; *Date of accession:* 8 April 1141 (disputed); *Date of coronation:* 8 April 1141 (proclaimed "Lady of the English" but never crowned); *Place of coronation:* proclamation made at Winchester; *Predecessor:* Stephen; *Relationship to predecessor:* cousin; *Reign:* 8 April 1141 (disputed)–February 1148 (left England); *Consorts:* (a) Henry V, king of Germany and Holy Roman Emperor, (b) Geoffrey V, count of Anjou; *Date of death:* 10 September 1167; *Place of death:* Abbey of Notre-Dame des Près, Rouen; *Place of burial:* Abbey of Bec, Normandy (remains later reinterred at Rouen Cathedral); *Successor:* Stephen; *Relationship to successor:* cousin.

**RICHARD I:** *Date of birth:* 8 September 1157; *Place of birth:* Beaumont Palace, Oxford; *Parents:* King Henry II and Eleanor of Aquitaine; *Date of accession:* 3 September 1189; *Date of coronation:* 3 September 1189; *Place of coronation:* Westminster Abbey; *Predecessor:* Henry II; *Relationship to predecessor:* son; *Reign:* 3 September 1189–6 April 1199; *Consort:* Berengaria of Navarre; *Date of death:* 6 April 1199; *Place of death:* Châlus, France; *Place of burial:* Fontevrault Abbey; *Successor:* John; *Relationship to successor:* brother.

**RICHARD II:** *Date of birth:* 6 January 1367; *Place of birth:* Abbey of St. André, Bordeaux; *Parents:* Edward, the black prince, and Joan, countess of Kent; *Date of accession:* 21 June 1377; *Date of coronation:* 16 July 1377; *Place of coronation:* Westminster Abbey; *Predecessor:* Edward III; *Relationship to predecessor:* grandson; *Reign:* 21 June 1377–30 September 1399 (deposed); *Consorts:* (a) Anne of Bohemia, (b) Isabella of Valois; *Date of death:* possibly 14 February 1400; *Place of death:* Pontefract Castle; *Place of burial:* Initially the Dominican Priory at Kings Langley (remains later reinterred at Westminster Abbey); *Successor:* Henry IV; *Relationship to successor:* cousin.

**RICHARD III:** *Date of birth:* 2 June 1452; *Place of birth:* Fotheringhay Castle; *Parents:* Richard, duke of York, and Cecily Neville; *Date of accession:* 26 June 1483; *Date of coronation:* 6 July 1483; *Place of coronation:* Westminster Abbey; *Predecessor:* Edward V; *Relationship to predecessor:* uncle; *Reign:* 26 June 1483–22 August 1485; *Consort:* Anne Neville; *Date of death:* 22 August 1485; *Place of death:* Bosworth Field; *Place of burial:* Leicester (probably the Grey Friars Church); *Successor:* Henry VII; *Relationship to successor:* unrelated.

**ROBERT I:** *Date of birth:* 11 July 1274; *Place of birth:* unknown; *Parents:* Robert de Bruce, lord of Annandale, and Marjorie, countess of Carrick; *Date of accession:* 25 March 1306; *Date of coronation:* 25 March 1306; *Place of coronation:* Scone; *Predecessor:* interregnum; *Reign:* 25 March 1306–7 June 1329; *Consorts:* (a) Isabella of Mar, (b) Elizabeth de Burgh; *Date of death:* 7 June 1329; *Place of death:* Cardross; *Place of burial:* Dunfermline Abbey (heart at Melrose Abbey); *Successor:* David II; *Relationship to successor:* father.

**ROBERT II:** *Date of birth:* 2 March 1316; *Place of birth:* Paisley; *Parents:* Walter Stewart and Marjorie Bruce; *Date of accession:* 22 February 1371; *Date of coronation:* 26 March 1371; *Place of coronation:* Scone; *Predecessor:* David II; *Relationship to predecessor:* nephew; *Reign:* 26 March 1371– 19 April 1390; *Consorts:* (a) Elizabeth Mure, (b) Euphemia de Ross; *Date of death:* 19 April 1390; *Place of death:* Dundonald Castle; *Place of burial:* Scone; *Successor:* Robert III; *Relationship to successor:* father.

**ROBERT III:** *Date of birth:* c1337; *Place of birth:* unknown; *Parents:* Robert II and Elizabeth Mure; *Date of accession:* 19 April 1390; *Date of coronation:* 14 August 1390; *Place of coronation:* Scone; *Predecessor:* Robert II; *Relationship to predecessor:* son; *Reign:* 19 April 1390–4 April 1406; *Consort:* Annabella Drummond; *Date of death:* 4 April 1406; *Place of death:* Dundonald Castle; *Place of burial:* Paisley Abbey; *Successor:* James I of Scotland; *Relationship to successor:* father.

**STEPHEN:** *Date of birth:* c1096; *Place of birth:* unknown; *Parents:* Stephen Henry, count of Blois, and Adela, countess of Blois; *Date of accession:* 22 December 1135; *Date of coronation:* 22 December 1135; *Place of coronation:* Westminster Abbey; *Predecessors:* (a) Henry I, (b) Matilda (disputed); *Relationship to predecessors:* (a) nephew, (b) first cousin; *Reigns:* (a) 22 December 1135–8 April 1141 (deposed), (b) 7 December 1141–25 October 1154; *Consort:* Matilda of Boulogne; *Date of death:* 25 October 1154; *Place of death:* Dover Priory; *Place of burial:* Faversham Abbey; *Successors:* (a) Matilda, (b) Henry II; *Relationship to successors:* (a) first cousin, (b) first cousin, once removed.

**SWEYN:** *Date of birth:* c960; *Place of birth:* unknown; *Parents:* King Harald I of Denmark and, possibly, Gyrid Olafsdottir; *Date of accession:* c30 November 1013; *Date of coronation:* never crowned; *Place of coronation:* never crowned; *Predecessor:* Aethelred the Unready; *Relationship to predecessor:* unrelated (succeeded by right of conquest); *Reign:* c30 November

1013–3 February 1014; *Date of death:* 3 February 1014; *Consort:* unknown; *Place of death:* Gainsborough; *Place of burial:* York (remains later reinterred at Roskilde Cathedral, Denmark); *Successor:* Aethelred the Unready; *Relationship to successor:* unrelated (succession by election).

**VICTORIA:** *Date of birth:* 24 May 1819; *Place of birth:* Kensington Palace; *Parents:* Prince Edward, duke of Kent and Strathearn, and Princess Victoria of Saxe-Coburg-Saalfield; *Date of accession:* 20 June 1837; *Date of coronation:* 28 June 1838; *Place of coronation:* Westminster Abbey; *Predecessor:* William IV; *Relationship to predecessor:* niece; *Reign:* 20 June 1837–22 January 1901; *Consort:* Prince Albert of Saxe-Coburg and Gotha; *Date of death:* 22 January 1901; *Place of death:* Osborne House, Isle of Wight; *Place of burial:* Frogmore; *Successor:* Edward VII; *Relationship to successor:* mother.

**WILLIAM I OF ENGLAND:** *Date of birth:* c1028; *Place of birth:* Falaise, Normandy; *Parents:* Robert I, duke of Normandy, and Herleva; *Date of accession:* 25 December 1066; *Date of coronation:* 25 December 1066; *Place of coronation:* Westminster Abbey; *Predecessor:* Edgar Aetheling; *Relationship to predecessor:* unrelated (succeeded by right of conquest); *Reign:* 25 December 1066–9 September 1087; *Consort:* Matilda of Flanders; *Date of death:* 9 September 1087; *Place of death:* Priory of St. Gervais, Rouen; *Place of burial:* Abbaye aux Hommes, Caen; *Successor:* William II of England; *Relationship to successor:* father.

**WILLIAM I OF SCOTLAND:** *Date of birth:* c1143; *Place of birth:* unknown; *Parents:* Henry, earl of Northumberland, and Ada de Warenne; *Date of accession:* 9 December 1165; *Date of coronation:* 24 December 1165; *Place of coronation:* Scone; *Predecessor:* Malcolm IV; *Relationship to predecessor:* brother; *Reign:* 9 December 1165–4 December 1214; *Consort:* Ermengarde de Beaumont; *Date of death:* 4 December 1214; *Place of death:* Stirling Castle; *Place of burial:* Arbroath Abbey; *Successor:* Alexander II; *Relationship to successor:* father.

**WILLIAM II OF ENGLAND:** *Date of birth:* c1056; *Place of birth:* Normandy; *Parents:* William I of England and Matilda of Flanders; *Date of accession:* 26 September 1087; *Date of coronation:* 26 September 1087; *Place of coronation:* Westminster Abbey; *Predecessor:* William I of England; *Relationship to predecessor:* son; *Reign:* 26 September 1087–2 August 1100; *Consort:* none; *Date of death:* 2 August 1100; *Place of death:* New Forest, Hampshire; *Place of burial:* Winchester; *Successor:* Henry I; *Relationship to successor:* brother.

**WILLIAM III OF ENGLAND AND II OF SCOTLAND:** *Date of birth:* 14 November 1650; *Place of birth:* Binnenhof Palace, The Hague; *Parents:* William, prince of Orange, and Mary Henrietta, princess royal; *Dates of Accession:* (a) 13 February 1689 (England), (b) 11 April 1689 (Scotland); *Date of coronation:* 11 April 1689 (co-ruler with Mary I); *Place of coronation:* Westminster Abbey (never crowned in Scotland); *Predecessor:* James VII of Scotland and II of England; *Relationship to predecessor:* son-in-law; *Reigns:* (a) England: co-sovereign with Mary II from 13 February 1689 to 28 December 1694, then sole sovereign until 8 March 1702; (b) Scotland: co-sovereign with Mary II from 11 April 1689 to 28 December 1694, then sole sovereign until 8 March 1702; *Consort:* Mary II; *Date of death:* 8 March 1702; *Place of death:* Kensington Palace; *Place of burial:* Westminster Abbey; *Successor:* Anne; *Relationship to successor:* brother-in-law.

**WILLIAM IV:** *Date of birth:* 21 August 1765; *Place of birth:* Buckingham Palace; *Parents:* George III and Charlotte of Mecklenburg-Strelitz; *Date of accession:* 26 June 1830; *Date of coronation:* 8 September 1831; *Place of coronation:* Westminster Abbey; *Predecessor:* George IV; *Relationship to predecessor:* brother; *Reign:* 26 June 1830–20 June 1837; *Consort:* Adelaide of Saxe-Meiningen; *Date of death:* 20 June 1837; *Place of death:* Windsor Castle; *Place of burial:* St. George's Chapel, Windsor Castle; *Successor:* Victoria; *Relationship to successor:* uncle.

# Appendix 3
## Royal Consorts, Biographical Summaries

The following list provides brief biographical information about royal consorts from Aethelflaed Eneda (first consort of Edgar, king of England from 959 to 975) and Gruoch (consort of Macbeth, king of Scotland from 1040 to 1057). The main text of the dictionary includes detailed entries for each individual.

**ADELAIDE OF SAXE-MEININGEN**, CONSORT OF WILLIAM IV: *Date of birth:* 13 August 1792; *Place of birth:* Meiningen, Germany; *Parents:* George, duke of Saxe-Meiningen, and Louisa Eleanore of Hohenlohe-Langenburg; *Date of marriage:* 11 July 1818; *Place of marriage:* Kew Palace; *Issue:* 2 daughters (and at least 2 miscarriages); *Other marriages:* none; *Date of death:* 2 December 1849; *Place of death:* Bentley Priory, near London; *Place of burial:* St. George's Chapel, Windsor Castle.

**ADELIZA OF LOUVAIN**, SECOND CONSORT OF HENRY I: *Date of birth:* c1103; *Place of birth:* Louvain, Belgium; *Parents:* Godfrey, count of Lower Lorraine and duke of Brabant, and Ida of Namur; *Date of marriage:* 24 January 1121; *Place of marriage:* Windsor Castle; *Issue:* none; *Other marriage:* William d'Aubigny, earl of Arundel (c1139, 4 sons, 3 daughters); *Date of death:* 24 March 1151 or 23 April 1151; *Place of death:* Affligham Abbey, near Brussels; *Place of burial:* Affligham Abbey or Reading Abbey.

**AELFGIFU OF NORTHAMPTON**, FIRST CONSORT OF CANUTE: *Date of birth:* c995; *Place of birth:* unknown; *Parents:* Aelfhelm, ealdorman of southern Northumbria, and, possibly, Wulfrun; *Date of marriage:* unknown (handfast marriage, disavowed by 1017); *Place of marriage:* unknown; *Issue:* 2 sons (including Harold I); *Other marriages:* unknown; *Date of death:* unknown; *Place of death:* unknown; *Place of burial:* unknown.

**AELFGIFU OF YORK**, FIRST CONSORT OF AETHELRED THE UN-READY: *Date of birth:* unknown, possibly c963; *Place of birth:* unknown; *Parents:* father possibly named Thored or Aethelbert, mother possibly named Hilda; *Date of marriage:* c980–985; *Place of marriage:* unknown; *Issue:* at least 7 sons (including Edmund II) and 2 daughters; *Other marriages:* none; *Date of death:* c1002; *Place of death:* possibly Winchester; *Place of burial:* unknown.

**AELFTHRYTH**, SECOND CONSORT OF EDGAR OF ENGLAND: *Date of birth:* c944; *Place of birth:* possibly Lydford Castle, Devon; *Parents:* Ordgar and unknown mother; *Date of marriage:* 964 or 965; *Place of marriage:* unknown; *Issue:* at least 2 sons (including Aethelred the Unready); *Other marriage:* Aethelwald (c960; issue unknown); *Date of death:* 17 November 999, 1000, or 1001; *Place of death:* Wherwell Abbey; *Place of burial:* Wherwell Abbey.

**AETHELFLAED ENEDA**, FIRST CONSORT OF EDGAR OF ENGLAND: *Date of birth:* unknown; *Place of birth:* unknown; *Parents:* Ordmaer and, possibly, Ealda; *Date of marriage:* unknown; *Place of marriage:* unknown; *Issue:* at least 1 son; *Other marriages:* unknown; *Date of death:* unknown; *Place of death:* unknown; *Place of burial:* unknown.

**ALBERT OF SAXE-COBURG AND GOTHA, PRINCE**, CONSORT OF VICTORIA: *Date of birth:* 26 August 1819; *Place of birth:* Rosenau, near Coburg, Bavaria; *Parents:* Ernest, duke of Saxe-Coburg-Saalfield, and Louise of Saxe-Coburg-Altenburg; *Date of marriage:* 10 February 1840; *Place of marriage:* St. James's Palace; *Issue:* 4 sons (including Edward VII), 5 daughters; *Other marriages:* none; *Date of death:* 14 December 1861; *Place of death:* Windsor Castle; *Place of burial:* Frogmore, Windsor.

**ALEXANDRA OF DENMARK**, CONSORT OF EDWARD VII: *Date of birth:* 1 December 1844; *Place of birth:* Yellow Palace, Copenhagen; *Parents:* Christian IX of Denmark and Princess Louise of Hesse-Cassel; *Date of marriage:* 10 March 1863; *Place of marriage:* St. George's Chapel, Windsor Castle; *Issue:* 3 sons (including George V), 3 daughters; *Other marriages:* none; *Date of death:* 20 October 1925; *Place of death:* Sandringham House; *Place of burial:* St. George's Chapel, Windsor Castle.

**ANNE OF BOHEMIA**, FIRST CONSORT OF RICHARD II: *Date of birth:* 11 May 1366; *Place of birth:* Prague; *Parents:* Charles IV, king of Bohemia and Holy Roman Emperor, and Elizabeth of Pomerania; *Date of marriage:* 20 January 1382; *Place of marriage:* Westminster Abbey; *Issue:* none; *Other marriages:* none; *Date of death:* 7 June 1394; *Place of death:* Sheen Palace; *Place of burial:* Westminster Abbey.

**ANNE OF CLEVES**, FOURTH CONSORT OF HENRY VIII: *Date of birth:* 22 September 1515; *Place of birth:* Düsseldorf; *Parents:* John, duke of Cleves, and Maria of Jülich-Berg; *Date of marriage:* 6 January 1540 (annulled 9 July 1549); *Place of marriage:* Palace of Placentia (Greenwich Palace); *Issue:* none; *Other marriages:* none; *Date of death:* 16 July 1557; *Place of death:* Chelsea Old Palace; *Place of burial:* Westminster Abbey.

**ANNE OF DENMARK**, CONSORT OF JAMES VI OF SCOTLAND AND I OF ENGLAND: *Date of birth:* 12 December 1574; *Place of birth:* Skanderborg Castle, Denmark; *Parents:* Frederick II of Denmark and Norway and Sophia of Mecklenburg; *Dates of marriage:* (a) 20 August 1489 (by proxy), (b) 23 November 1589 (in person); *Places of marriage:* (a) Kronborg Palace, Denmark, (b) Bishop's Palace, Oslo; *Issue:* 3 sons (including Charles I), 4 daughters, and several miscarriages; *Other marriages:* none; *Date of death:* 2 March 1619; *Place of death:* Hampton Court Palace; *Place of burial:* Westminster Abbey.

**BEAUFORT, JOAN**, CONSORT OF JAMES I OF SCOTLAND: *Date of birth:* c1404; *Place of birth:* unknown; *Parents:* John Beaufort, earl of Somerset, and Margaret Holland; *Date of marriage:* 2 February 1424; *Place of marriage:* Southwark Cathedral; *Issue:* 2 sons (including James II of Scotland), 6 daughters; *Other marriage:* Sir James Stewart (probably July 1539; 3 sons); *Date of death:* 15 July 1445; *Place of death:* Dunbar Castle; *Place of burial:* Carthusian Monastery, Perth.

**BERENGARIA OF NAVARRE**, CONSORT OF RICHARD I: *Date of birth:* c1164; *Place of birth:* Navarre; *Parents:* Sancho VI of Navarre and Sancha of Castile; *Date of marriage:* 12 May 1191; *Place of marriage:* Chapel of St. George, Limasol, Cyprus; *Issue:* none; *Other marriages:* none; *Date of death:* possibly 23 December 1230; *Place of death:* L'Epau Abbey, near Le Mans, France; *Place of burial:* L'Epau Abbey.

**BOLEYN, ANNE**, SECOND CONSORT OF HENRY VIII: *Date of birth:* c1500; *Place of birth:* probably Blickling Hall, Norfolk, or Hever Castle; *Parents:* Sir Thomas Boleyn and Elizabeth Howard; *Date of marriage:* 25 January 1533 (annulled 17 May 1536); *Place of marriage:* Palace of Westminster; *Issue:* 1 daughter (Elizabeth I), 2 miscarriages; *Other marriages:* none; *Date of death:* 19 May 1536; *Place of death:* Tower of London; *Place of burial:* Church of St. Peter ad Vincula, London.

**CAROLINE OF BRANDENBURG-ANSBACH**, CONSORT OF GEORGE II: *Date of birth:* 1 March 1683; *Place of birth:* Ansbach Palace, Germany; *Parents:* Johann, margrave of Brandenburg-Ansbach, and Eleanore of Saxe-Eisenach; *Date of marriage:* 22 August 1705; *Place of marriage:* Hanover; *Issue:* 4 sons (including 1 stillbirth), 5 daughters; *Other marriages:* none; *Date of death:* 20 November 1737; *Place of death:* St. James's Palace; *Place of burial:* Westminster Abbey.

**CAROLINE OF BRUNSWICK-WOLFENBÜTTEL**, CONSORT OF GEORGE IV: *Date of birth:* 17 May 1768; *Place of birth:* Brunswick, Germany; *Parents:* Charles II, duke of Brunswick-Wolfenbüttel, and Princess Augusta; *Date of marriage:* 8 April 1795; *Place of marriage:* St. James's Palace; *Issue:* 1 daughter; *Other marriages:* none; *Date of death:* 7 August 1821; *Place of death:* Brandenburg House, London; *Place of burial:* Brunswick Cathedral.

**CATHERINE OF ARAGON**, FIRST CONSORT OF HENRY VIII: *Date of birth:* 16 December 1485; *Place of birth:* Archbishop's palace at Alcalá de Henares, near Madrid; *Parents:* Ferdinand II of Aragon and Isabella I of Castile; *Date of marriage:* 11 June 1509 (annulled 23 May 1533); *Place of marriage:* Greyfriars Church, Greenwich; *Issue:* 1 son, 1 daughter (Mary I), at least 3 miscarriages or stillbirths; *Other marriage:* Arthur, prince of Wales (19 May 1499 by proxy, 14 November 1501 in person; no issue); *Date of death:* 7 January 1536; *Place of death:* Kimbolton Castle; *Place of burial:* Peterborough Cathedral.

**CATHERINE OF BRAGANZA**, CONSORT OF CHARLES I: *Date of birth:* 25 November 1638; *Place of birth:* Vila Viçosa, Alentejo, Portugal; *Parents:* John, duke of Braganza (later King John IV of Portugal), and Luiza Maria de Guzmán; *Date of marriage:* 21 May 1662; *Place of marriage:* Church of St. Thomas à Becket, Portsmouth (and also at a secret Roman Catholic ceremony); *Issue:* none (three miscarriages); *Other marriages:* none; *Date of death:* 31 December 1705; *Place of death:* Palace of Bemposta, Lisbon; *Place of burial:* Belem Monastery, Lisbon (remains later reinterred at the Braganza mausoleum in St. Vincente da Fora, Lisbon).

**CATHERINE OF VALOIS**, CONSORT OF HENRY V: *Date of birth:* 27 October 1401; *Place of birth:* Hôtel St. Pol, Paris; *Parents:* Charles VI of France and Isabeau of Bavaria; *Date of marriage:* 2 June 1420; *Place of marriage:* Troyes Cathedral; *Issue:* 1 son (Henry VI); *Other marriage:* possibly Owen Tudor (date unknown; at least 3 sons and 4 daughters); *Date of* *death:* 3 January 1437; *Place of death:* Bermondsey Abbey; *Place of burial:* Westminster Abbey.

**CHARLOTTE OF MECKLENBURG-STRELITZ**, CONSORT OF GEORGE III: *Date of birth:* 19 May 1744; *Place of birth:* Mirow Castle, Germany; *Parents:* Charles Louis Frederick, duke of Mecklenburg-Strelitz, and Elizabeth-Albertina of Saxe-Hildeburghausen; *Date of marriage:* 8 September 1761; *Place of marriage:* St. James's Palace; *Issue:* 9 sons (including George IV and William IV), 6 daughters; *Other marriages:* none; *Date of death:* 17 November 1818; *Place of death:* Kew Palace; *Place of burial:* St. George's Chapel, Windsor Castle.

**DRUMMOND, ANNABELLA**, CONSORT OF ROBERT III: *Date of birth:* c1350; *Place of birth:* unknown; *Parents:* Sir John Drummond and, probably, Mary Montefichet; *Date of marriage:* 1366 or 1367; *Place of marriage:* unknown; *Issue:* 3 sons (including James I of Scotland), at least 4 daughters; *Other marriages:* none; *Date of death:* 1401 or 1402; *Place of death:* Scone Palace; *Place of burial:* Dunfermline Abbey.

**DRUMMOND, MARGARET**, SECOND CONSORT OF DAVID II: *Date of birth:* c1340; *Place of birth:* unknown; *Parents:* Sir Malcolm Drummond, thane of Lennox, and Margaret de Graham; *Date of marriage:* probably 1363 or 1364 (divorced 1369 or 1370); *Place of marriage:* possibly Inchmurdoch Manor, Fife; *Issue:* none; *Other marriage:* Sir John Logie (date of marriage unknown but prior to marriage with David II; at least 1 son); *Date of death:* probably 1375; *Place of death:* Avignon, while on pilgrimage to Rome; *Place of burial:* probably Avignon.

**DUDLEY, GUILDFORD**, CONSORT OF JANE GREY: *Date of birth:* c1536; *Place of birth:* unknown; *Parents:* John Dudley, duke of Northumberland, and Jane Guildford; *Date of marriage:* 21 May 1553; *Place of marriage:* Durham House, London; *Issue:* none; *Other marriages:* none; *Date of death:* 12 February 1554; *Place of death:* Tower Hill, London; *Place of burial:* Church of St. Peter ad Vincula, London.

**EALDGYTH OF MERCIA**, SECOND CONSORT OF HAROLD II: *Date of birth:* unknown; *Place of birth:* unknown; *Parents:* Aelfgar, earl of Mercia, and Aelfgifu; *Date of marriage:* 1064 or 1065; *Place of marriage:* York; *Issue:* probably 1 son; *Other marriage:* Gruffydd ap Llywelyn, king of Gwynnedd (c1057, at least 1 daughter); *Date of death:* unknown; *Place of death:* unknown; *Place of burial:* unknown.

**EDITH OF EAST ANGLIA**, CONSORT OF EDMUND II: *Date of birth:* unknown; *Place of birth:* unknown; *Parents:* unknown; *Date of marriage:* c1015; *Place of marriage:* possibly Malmesbury; *Issue:* at least 2 sons; *Other marriage:* Sigeferth, date unknown, issue unknown; *Date of death:* 1017; *Place of death:* unknown (possibly abroad); *Place of burial:* unknown.

**EDITH OF WESSEX**, CONSORT OF EDWARD THE CONFESSOR: *Date of birth:* c1029; *Place of birth:* unknown; *Parents:* Godwin, earl of Wessex, and Gytha Thorkelsdóttir; *Date of marriage:* 23 January 1045; *Place of marriage:* unknown; *Issue:* none; *Other marriages:* none; *Date of death:* 19 December 1975; *Place of death:* Winchester; *Place of burial:* Westminster Abbey.

**EDITH SWAN-NECK**, FIRST CONSORT OF HAROLD II: *Date of birth:* c1025; *Place of birth:* unknown; *Parents:* unknown; *Date of marriage:* c1045; *Place of marriage:* unknown; *Issue:* at least 5 children; *Other marriages:* unknown; *Date of death:* unknown; *Place of death:* unknown; *Place of burial:* unknown.

**ELEANOR OF AQUITAINE**, CONSORT OF HENRY II: *Date of birth:* c1122; *Place of birth:* unknown; *Parents:* William, duke of Aquitaine, and Aenor de Châtellerault; *Date of marriage:* 18 May 1152; *Place of marriage:* Poitiers; *Issue:* 5 sons (including Richard I), 3 daughters; *Other marriage:* Louis VII of France (25 July 1137; 2 daughters); *Date of death:* 1 April 1204; *Place of death:* Fontevrault Abbey or Poitiers; *Place of burial:* Fontevrault Abbey.

**ELEANOR OF CASTILE**, FIRST CONSORT OF EDWARD I: *Date of birth:* c1241; *Place of birth:* Castile; *Parents:* Ferdinand III of Castile and Jeanne, countess of Ponthieu; *Date of marriage:* 1 November 1254; *Place of marriage:* Abbey of Las Huelgos, Burgos, Castile; *Issue:* at least 4 sons (including Edward II) and 11 daughters; *Other marriages:* none; *Date of death:* 28 November 1290; *Place of death:* Harby, near Lincoln; *Place of burial:* Westminster Abbey.

**ELEANOR OF PROVENCE**, CONSORT OF HENRY III: *Date of birth:* c1223; *Place of birth:* Provence, France; *Parents:* Raymond Berengar V, count of Provence, and Beatrice of Savoy; *Date of marriage:* 14 January 1236; *Place of marriage:* Canterbury Cathedral; *Issue:* 2 sons (including Edward I), 3 daughters; *Other marriages:* none; *Date of death:* 25 June 1291;

*Place of death:* Amesbury Abbey, Wiltshire; *Place of burial:* Amesbury Abbey.

**ELIZABETH DE BURGH**, SECOND CONSORT OF ROBERT I: *Date of birth:* unknown; *Place of birth:* probably Northern Ireland; *Parents:* Richard de Burgh, earl of Ulster, and Margaret de Burgh; *Date of marriage:* 1302; *Place of marriage:* possibly Writtle, near Chelmsford; *Issue:* 2 sons (including David II), 2 daughters; *Other marriages:* none; *Date of death:* 26 October 1327; *Place of death:* Cullen Castle; *Place of burial:* Dunfermline Abbey.

**ELIZABETH OF YORK**, CONSORT OF HENRY VII: *Date of birth:* 11 February 1466; *Place of birth:* Palace of Westminster; *Parents:* Edward IV and Elizabeth Woodville; *Date of marriage:* 18 January 1486; *Place of marriage:* Westminster Abbey; *Issue:* 4 sons (including Henry VIII), 4 daughters; *Other marriages:* none; *Date of death:* 11 February 1503; *Place of death:* Tower of London; *Place of burial:* Westminster Abbey.

**ELIZABETH, THE QUEEN MOTHER**, CONSORT OF GEORGE VI: *Date of birth:* 4 August 1900; *Place of birth:* St. Paul's Waldenbury, Hertfordshire; *Parents:* Claude Bowes-Lyon, earl of Strathmore and Kinghorne, and Nina Cecilia Cavendish-Bentinck; *Date of marriage:* 26 April 1923; *Place of marriage:* Westminster Abbey; *Issue:* 2 daughters (including Elizabeth II); *Other marriages:* none; *Date of death:* 30 March 2002; *Place of death:* Royal Lodge, Windsor; *Place of burial:* St. George's Chapel, Windsor Castle.

**EMMA OF NORMANDY**, SECOND CONSORT OF AETHELRED THE UNREADY AND SECOND CONSORT OF CANUTE: *Date of birth:* c985; *Place of birth:* unknown; *Parents:* Richard, count of Rouen, and Gunnora; *Dates of marriages:* (a) Aethelred the Unready, 1002; (b) Canute, 2 July 1017; *Places of marriage:* (a) Winchester Cathedral, (b) probably Winchester Cathedral; *Issue:* (a) 2 sons (including Edward the Confessor), 1 daughter; (b) 1 son (Harthacanute), at least 1 daughter; *Other marriages:* none; *Date of death:* 7 March 1052; *Place of death:* Winchester; *Place of burial:* Winchester Cathedral.

**ERMENGARDE DE BEAUMONT**, CONSORT OF WILLIAM I OF SCOTLAND: *Date of birth:* c1170; *Place of birth:* unknown; *Parents:* Richard, viscount of Beaumont-sur-Sarthe, and, possibly, Constance FitzRoy; *Date of marriage:* 5 September 1186; *Place of marriage:* Woodstock Palace;

*Issue:* 1 son (Alexander II), 3 daughters; *Other marriages:* none; *Date of death:* 12 February 1233; *Place of death:* unknown; *Place of burial:* Balmerino Abbey.

**EUPHEMIA DE ROSS**, SECOND CONSORT OF ROBERT II: *Date of birth:* unknown; *Place of birth:* unknown; *Parents:* Hugh Ross, earl of Ross, and Margaret Graham; *Date of marriage:* 2 May 1355; *Place of marriage:* unknown; *Issue:* 2 sons, at least 2 daughters; *Other marriage:* John Randolph, earl of Moray (date unknown; no issue); *Date of death:* 1386–1389; *Place of death:* unknown; *Place of burial:* possibly Dunfermline Abbey.

**FRANCIS II OF FRANCE**, FIRST CONSORT OF MARY, QUEEN OF SCOTS: *Date of birth:* 19 January 1544; *Place of birth:* Fontainebleau Palace; *Parents:* Henry II of France and Catherine de' Medici; *Date of marriage:* 24 April 1558; *Place of marriage:* Notre Dame Cathedral, Paris; *Issue:* none; *Other marriages:* none; *Date of death:* 5 December 1560; *Place of death:* Orléans, France; *Place of burial:* Basilica of St. Denis, Paris.

**GEOFFREY, COUNT OF ANJOU**, SECOND CONSORT OF MATILDA: *Date of birth:* 24 August 1113; *Place of birth:* Anjou; *Parents:* Fulk V, count of Anjou, and Eremburga of La Flèche; *Date of marriage:* 17 June 1128; *Place of marriage:* Le Mans Cathedral; *Issue:* 3 sons (including Henry II); *Other marriages:* none; *Date of death:* 7 September 1151; *Place of death:* Château-du-Loir, France; *Place of burial:* Le Mans Cathedral.

**GEORGE, PRINCE OF DENMARK**, CONSORT OF ANNE: *Date of birth:* 2 April 1653; *Place of birth:* Copenhagen; *Parents:* Frederick III of Denmark and Sophie Amalie of Brunswick-Lüneburg; *Date of marriage:* 28 July 1683; *Place of marriage:* St. James's Palace; *Issue:* 2 sons, 3 daughters; *Other marriages:* none; *Date of death:* 28 October 1708; *Place of death:* Kensington Palace; *Place of burial:* Westminster Abbey.

**GRUOCH**, CONSORT OF MACBETH: *Date of birth:* unknown; *Place of birth:* unknown; *Parents:* unknown; *Date of marriage:* unknown; *Place of marriage:* unknown; *Issue:* none; *Other marriages:* Gille Coemgáin, mormaer of Moray (date unknown but before 1032; at least one son); *Date of death:* unknown; *Place of death:* unknown; *Place of burial:* unknown.

**HENRIETTA MARIA OF FRANCE**, CONSORT OF CHARLES I: *Date of birth:* 25 or 26 November 1609; *Place of birth:* Louvre Palace, Paris; *Parents:* Henry IV of France and Maria de' Medici; *Dates of marriage:* (a) 11

May 1625 (by proxy), (b) 13 June 1325 (in person); *Places of marriage:* (a) Notre Dame Cathedral, Paris, (b) St. Augustine's Church, Canterbury; *Issue:* 2 sons (including Charles II and James VII of Scotland and II of England); *Other marriages:* none; *Date of death:* 10 September 1669; *Place of death:* Château de Colombes, near Paris; *Place of burial:* Cathedral of St. Denis, Paris.

**HENRY V, KING OF GERMANY AND HOLY ROMAN EMPEROR,** FIRST CONSORT OF MATILDA: *Date of birth:* 8 November 1086; *Place of birth:* Germany; *Parents:* Henry IV, king of Germany and Holy Roman Emperor, and Bertha of Savoy; *Date of marriage:* 6 or 7 January 1114; *Place of marriage:* Worms, Germany; *Issue:* possibly 1 child; *Other marriages:* none; *Date of death:* 23 May 1125; *Place of death:* Utrecht; *Place of burial:* Speyer Cathedral, Germany.

**HEPBURN, JAMES, EARL OF BOTHWELL,** THIRD CONSORT OF MARY, QUEEN OF SCOTS: *Date of birth:* 1534 or 1535; *Place of birth:* unknown; *Parents:* Patrick Hepburn, earl of Bothwell, and Agnes Sinclair; *Date of marriage:* 15 May 1567; *Place of marriage:* Holyrood Palace; *Issue:* none; *Other marriage:* Lady Jean Gordon (22 February 1566; divorced 3 May 1567; no issue); *Date of death:* 14 April 1578; *Place of death:* Dragsholm Castle, Denmark; *Place of burial:* possibly Fårevejle Church, near Dragsholm.

**HOWARD, CATHERINE,** FIFTH CONSORT OF HENRY VIII: *Date of birth:* c1521; *Place of birth:* unknown; *Parents:* Lord Edmund Howard and Joyce Culpeper; *Date of marriage:* 28 July 1540; *Place of marriage:* Oatlands Palace; *Issue:* none; *Other marriages:* none; *Date of death:* 13 February 1541; *Place of death:* Tower of London; *Place of burial:* Church of St. Peter ad Vincula, London.

**HYDE, ANNE,** FIRST CONSORT OF JAMES VII OF SCOTLAND AND II OF ENGLAND: *Date of birth:* 12 March 1637; *Place of birth:* Cranbourne Lodge, Windsor; *Parents:* Sir Edward Hyde and Frances Aylesbury; *Date of marriage:* 3 September 1660; *Place of marriage:* Worcester House, London; *Issue:* 4 sons, 4 daughters (including Anne and Mary II); *Other marriages:* none; *Date of death:* 31 March 1671; *Place of death:* St. James's Palace; *Place of burial:* Westminster Abbey.

**INGIBIORG FINNSDOTTIR,** FIRST CONSORT OF MALCOLM III: *Date of birth:* unknown; *Place of birth:* unknown; *Parents:* possibly Finn Arneson and Bergljot Halvansdottir; *Date of marriage:* c1060; *Place of* *marriage:* unknown; *Issue:* 3 sons (including Duncan II); *Other marriages:* possibly Thorfinn Sigurdsson, earl of Orkney (date unknown; possibly 2 sons); *Date of death:* possibly 1069–1070; *Place of death:* unknown; *Place of burial:* unknown.

**ISABEL OF GLOUCESTER**, FIRST CONSORT OF JOHN: *Date of birth:* c1160; *Place of birth:* unknown; *Parents:* William, earl of Gloucester, and Hawise de Beaumont; *Date of marriage:* 29 August 1189 (annulled c1199); *Place of marriage:* Marlborough Castle; *Issue:* none; *Other marriages:* (a) Geoffrey de Mandeville, earl of Essex (20 January 1214; no issue); (b) Hubert de Burgh, earl of Kent (probably September 1217; no issue); *Date of death:* 14 October 1217; *Place of death:* possibly Keynsham Abbey; *Place of burial:* Canterbury Cathedral.

**ISABELLA DE WARENNE**, CONSORT OF JOHN OF SCOTLAND: *Date of birth:* c1253; *Place of birth:* unknown; *Parents:* John de Warenne, earl of Surrey, and Alice de Lusignan; *Date of marriage:* 1280 or 1281; *Place of marriage:* unknown; *Issue:* at least 1 son; *Other marriages:* none; *Date of death:* unknown; *Place of death:* unknown but probably earlier than 1292; *Place of burial:* unknown.

**ISABELLA OF ANGOULÊME**, SECOND CONSORT OF JOHN: *Date of birth:* c1188; *Place of birth:* unknown; *Parents:* Aymer Taillefer, count of Angoulême, and Alice de Courtney; *Date of marriage:* 24 August 1200; *Place of marriage:* Angoulême; *Issue:* 2 sons (including Henry III), 3 daughters; *Other marriage:* Hugh X of Lusignan (April or May 1220; 6 sons, 3 daughters); *Date of death:* 4 June 1246; *Place of death:* Fontevrault Abbey, Anjou; *Place of burial:* Fontevrault Abbey.

**ISABELLA OF FRANCE**, CONSORT OF EDWARD II: *Date of birth:* c1295; *Place of birth:* Paris; *Parents:* Philip IV of France and Jeanne of Navarre; *Date of marriage:* 25 January 1308; *Place of marriage:* Boulogne Cathedral; *Issue:* at least 2 sons (including Edward III) and 2 daughters; *Other marriages:* none; *Date of death:* 22 August 1358; *Place of death:* Hertford Castle; *Place of burial:* Franciscan Church (Christ Church Newgate), London.

**ISABELLA OF MAR**, FIRST CONSORT OF ROBERT I: *Date of birth:* unknown; *Place of birth:* unknown; *Parents:* Donald, earl of Mar, and Helen; *Date of marriage:* c1295; *Place of marriage:* unknown; *Issue:* 1 daughter;

*Other marriages:* none; *Date of death:* c1297; *Place of death:* unknown; *Place of burial:* unknown.

**ISABELLA OF VALOIS**, SECOND CONSORT OF RICHARD II: *Date of birth:* 9 November 1389; *Place of birth:* Louvre Palace, Paris; *Parents:* Charles VI of France and Isabella of Bavaria; *Date of marriage:* 4 November 1396; *Place of marriage:* Church of St. Nicholas, Calais; *Issue:* none; *Other marriage:* Charles, duke of Orléans (29 June 1406; 1 daughter); *Date of death:* 13 September 1409; *Place of death:* Blois Château; *Place of burial:* St. Laumer Abbey, Blois (remains later reinterred at the Church of the Celestines, Paris).

**JOAN OF ENGLAND**, FIRST CONSORT OF ALEXANDER II: *Date of birth:* 22 July 1210; *Place of birth:* unknown; *Parents:* John of England and Isabella of Angoulême; *Date of marriage:* June 1221; *Place of marriage:* York Minster; *Issue:* none; *Other marriages:* none; *Date of death:* 4 March 1238; *Place of death:* Havering-atte-Bower, Essex; *Place of burial:* Tarrant Abbey.

**JOAN OF NAVARRE**, SECOND CONSORT OF HENRY IV: *Date of birth:* c1368; *Place of birth:* probably Evreux, Normandy; *Parents:* Charles II, king of Navarre, and Jeanne de Valois; *Dates of marriage:* (a) 2 April 1402 (by proxy), (b) 7 February 1403 (in person); *Places of marriage:* (a) Eltham Palace, (b) Winchester Cathedral; *Issue:* none; *Other marriages:* John, duke of Brittany (25 August 1386; 4 sons, 5 daughters); *Date of death:* 10 June or 9 July 1437; *Place of death:* Havering-atte-Bower, Essex; *Place of burial:* Canterbury Cathedral.

**JOAN OF THE TOWER**, FIRST CONSORT OF DAVID II: *Date of birth:* 5 July 1321; *Place of birth:* Tower of London; *Parents:* Edward II and Isabella of France; *Date of marriage:* 17 July 1328; *Place of marriage:* Berwick-upon-Tweed; *Issue:* none; *Other marriages:* none; *Date of death:* 7 September 1362; *Place of death:* Hertford Castle; *Place of burial:* Greyfriars Church, Greenwich.

**MADELEINE DE VALOIS**, FIRST CONSORT OF JAMES V: *Date of birth:* 10 August 1520; *Place of birth:* St. Germain-en-Laye, near Paris; *Parents:* Francis I of France and Claude of Brittany; *Date of marriage:* 1 January 1537; *Place of marriage:* Notre Dame Cathedral, Paris; *Issue:* none; *Other marriages:* none; *Date of death:* 7 July 1537; *Place of death:* Holyrood Palace; *Place of burial:* Holyrood Abbey.

**MARGARET OF ANJOU**, CONSORT OF HENRY VI: *Date of birth:* 23 or 24 March 1430; *Place of birth:* probably Pont-à-Mousson, Lorraine; *Parents:* René, duke of Anjou, and Isabelle, duchess of Lorraine; *Date of marriage:* 22 April 1445; *Place of marriage:* Titchfield Abbey; *Issue:* 1 son; *Other marriages:* none; *Date of death:* 25 August 1482; *Place of death:* Château de Dampiere, Anjou; *Place of burial:* St. Maurice's Cathedral, Angers.

**MARGARET OF DENMARK**, CONSORT OF JAMES III: *Date of birth:* 23 June 1456; *Place of birth:* Denmark; *Parents:* Christian I of Denmark, Norway, and Sweden and Dorothea of Brandenburg; *Date of marriage:* 13 July 1469; *Place of marriage:* Holyrood Palace; *Issue:* 3 sons (including James IV); *Other marriages:* none; *Date of death:* 14 July 1486; *Place of death:* Stirling Castle; *Place of burial:* Cambuskenneth Abbey.

**MARGARET, QUEEN OF SCOTS**, FIRST CONSORT OF ALEXANDER III: *Date of birth:* September or early October 1240; *Place of birth:* Windsor Castle; *Parents:* Henry III and Eleanor of Provence; *Date of marriage:* 26 December 1251; *Place of marriage:* York Minster; *Issue:* 2 sons, 1 daughter; *Other marriages:* none; *Date of death:* 26 February 1275; *Place of death:* Cupar Castle; *Place of burial:* Dunfermline Abbey.

**MARGARET, ST.**, SECOND CONSORT OF MALCOLM III: *Date of birth:* c1045; *Place of birth:* possibly Castle Réka, Hungary; *Parents:* Edward the Exile and Agatha; *Date of marriage:* c1070; *Place of marriage:* possibly Dunfermline Abbey; *Issue:* 6 sons (including Alexander I, David I, and Edgar of Scotland), 2 daughters; *Other marriages:* none; *Date of death:* 16 November 1093; *Place of death:* Edinburgh Castle; *Place of burial:* Dunfermline Abbey.

**MARGUERITE OF FRANCE**, SECOND CONSORT OF EDWARD I: *Date of birth:* c1279; *Place of birth:* Paris; *Parents:* Philip III of France and Marie of Brabant; *Date of marriage:* 10 September 1299; *Place of marriage:* Canterbury Cathedral; *Issue:* 2 sons, 1 daughter; *Other marriages:* none; *Date of death:* 14 February 1318; *Place of death:* Marlborough Castle; *Place of burial:* Greyfriars Church, Greenwich.

**MARIE DE COUCY**, SECOND CONSORT OF ALEXANDER II: *Date of birth:* c1218; *Place of birth:* unknown; *Parents:* Enguerrand III, lord of Coucy, and Marie de Montmirel-en-Brie; *Date of marriage:* 15 May 1239; *Place of marriage:* Roxburgh Castle; *Issue:* 1 son (Alexander III); *Other marriage:* Jean de Brienne, butler of France (1257; no issue); *Date of death:*

1284 or 1285; *Place of death:* unknown, probably France; *Place of burial:* unknown, possibly Newbattle Abbey.

**MARY II**, CONSORT OF WILLIAM III OF ENGLAND AND II OF SCOTLAND; *Date of birth:* 30 April 1662; *Place of birth:* Palace of Placentia (Greenwich Palace); *Parents:* James VII of Scotland and II of England and Anne Hyde; *Date of marriage:* 4 November 1677; *Place of marriage:* St. James's Palace; *Issue:* none; *Other marriages:* none; *Date of death:* 28 December 1694; *Place of death:* Kensington Palace; *Place of burial:* Westminster Abbey.

**MARY DE BOHUN**, FIRST CONSORT OF HENRY IV: *Date of birth:* c1369; *Place of birth:* unknown; *Parents:* Humphrey de Bohun, earl of Hereford, and Joan FitzAlan; *Date of marriage:* possibly 27 July 1380 or 5 February 1381; *Place of marriage:* Arundel Castle (1380) or Rochford Hall, Essex (1381); *Issue:* 5 sons, 2 daughters; *Other marriages:* none; *Date of death:* Possibly 4 June or 4 July 1394; *Place of death:* Peterborough Castle; *Place of burial:* St. Mary of the Newarke, Leicester (remains later reinterred at Trinity Hospital Chapel, Leicester).

**MARY OF GUELDRES**, CONSORT OF JAMES II OF SCOTLAND: *Date of birth:* c1434; *Place of birth:* unknown; *Parents:* Arnold, duke of Gueldres, and Catherine of Cleves; *Date of marriage:* 3 July 1449; *Place of marriage:* Holyrood Palace; *Issue:* 4 sons (including James III), 1 daughter, and 1 short-lived child of unknown sex; *Other marriages:* none; *Date of death:* 1 December 1463; *Place of death:* Ravenscraig Castle; *Place of burial:* Trinity College Church, Edinburgh (remains later reinterred at Holyrood Abbey).

**MARY OF GUISE**, SECOND CONSORT OF JAMES V: *Date of birth:* 20 November 1515; *Place of birth:* Bar-le-Duc Castle, Lorraine; *Parents:* Claude, duke of guise, and Antoinette de Bourbon; *Dates of marriage:* (a) 18 May 1538 (by proxy), (b) 18 June 1538 (in person); *Places of marriage:* (a) Notre Dame Cathedral, Paris; (b) St. Andrews Cathedral; *Issue:* 2 sons, 1 daughter (Mary, queen of Scots); *Other marriage:* Louis, duke of Longueville (4 August 1534; 2 sons); *Date of death:* 11 June 1560; *Place of death:* Edinburgh Castle; *Place of burial:* Convent of St. Pierre, Rheims.

**MARY OF MODENA**, SECOND CONSORT OF JAMES VII OF SCOTLAND AND II OF ENGLAND: *Date of birth:* 5 October 1658; *Place of birth:* Ducal Palace, Modena, Italy; *Parents:* Alfonso IV, duke of Modena, and Laura Martinozzi; *Date of marriage:* 30 September 1673; *Place of* *marriage:* Ducal Palace, Modena (by proxy); *Issue:* 2 sons, 6 daughters, several miscarriages; *Other marriages:* none; *Date of death:* 7 May 1718; *Place of death:* St. Germain Castle, near Paris; *Place of burial:* Chaillot Abbey, Paris.

**MARY OF TECK**, CONSORT OF GEORGE V: *Date of birth:* 26 May 1867; *Place of birth:* Kensington Palace; *Parents:* Francis, prince of Teck, and Princess Mary Adelaide of Cambridge; *Date of marriage:* 6 July 1893; *Place of marriage:* St. James's Palace; *Issue:* 5 sons (including Edward VIII and George VI), 1 daughter; *Other marriages:* none; *Date of death:* 24 March 1953; *Place of death:* Marlborough House; *Place of burial:* St. George's Chapel, Windsor Castle.

**MATILDA OF BOULOGNE**, CONSORT OF STEPHEN: *Date of birth:* c1103; *Place of birth:* Boulogne; *Parents:* Eustace III, count of Boulogne, and Mary, countess of Boulogne; *Date of marriage:* 1125; *Place of marriage:* Westminster; *Issue:* 3 sons, 2 daughters; *Other marriages:* none; *Date of death:* 3 May 1152; *Place of death:* Castle Hedingham, Essex; *Place of burial:* Faversham Abbey.

**MATILDA OF FLANDERS**, CONSORT OF WILLIAM I OF ENGLAND: *Date of birth:* c1031; *Place of birth:* Flanders, Belgium; *Parents:* Baldwin V, count of Flanders, and Adela of France; *Date of marriage:* c1053; *Place of marriage:* unknown; *Issue:* 4 sons (including Henry I and William II), at least 5 daughters; *Other marriages:* none; *Date of death:* 2 November 1083; *Place of death:* Caen, Normandy; *Place of burial:* Abbey aux Dames, Caen.

**MATILDA OF SCOTLAND**, FIRST CONSORT OF HENRY I: *Date of birth:* probably 1080; *Place of birth:* Dunfermline; *Parents:* Malcolm III and St. Margaret; *Date of marriage:* 11 November 1100; *Place of marriage:* Westminster Abbey; *Issue:* 1 son, 1 daughter; *Other marriages:* none; *Date of death:* 1 May 1118; *Place of death:* Palace of Westminster; *Place of burial:* Westminster Abbey.

**MAUD, COUNTESS OF HUNTINGDON**, CONSORT OF DAVID I: *Date of birth:* c1074; *Place of birth:* unknown; *Parents:* Waltheof, earl of Northumbria, and Judith of Lens; *Date of marriage:* 1113; *Place of marriage:* unknown; *Issue:* 2 sons, 2 daughters; *Other marriage:* Simon de St. Liz, earl of Huntingdon and Northampton (c1090; 2 sons, 1 daughter); *Date of death:* possibly 1130; *Place of death:* unknown; *Place of burial:* possibly Scone.

**MURE, ELIZABETH**, FIRST CONSORT OF ROBERT II: *Date of birth:* unknown; *Place of birth:* unknown; *Parents:* Sir Adam Mure of Rowallan and Janet Cunningham; *Date of marriage:* 1349 (possibly preceded by a ceremony in the 1330s); *Place of marriage:* unknown; *Issue:* 4 sons (including Robert III), probably 6 daughters; *Other marriages:* none; *Date of death:* c1355; *Place of death:* unknown; *Place of burial:* Blackfriars Church, Perth.

**NEVILLE, ANNE**, CONSORT OF RICHARD III: *Date of birth:* 11 June 1456; *Place of birth:* Warwick Castle; *Parents:* Richard Neville, earl of Warwick, and Anne Beauchamp; *Date of marriage:* 12 July 1472; *Place of marriage:* Westminster Abbey; *Issue:* 1 son; *Other marriage:* Edward, prince of Wales (c13 December 1470; no issue); *Date of death:* 16 March 1485; *Place of death:* Palace of Westminster; *Place of burial:* Westminster Abbey.

**OCTREDA OF NORTHUMBRIA**, CONSORT OF DUNCAN II: *Date of birth:* unknown; *Place of birth:* unknown; *Parents:* Gospatric, earl of Dunbar and Northumberland, and unknown mother; *Date of marriage:* possibly c1090; *Place of marriage:* unknown; *Issue:* at least one son; *Other marriages:* unknown; *Date of death:* unknown; *Place of death:* unknown; *Place of burial:* Dunfermline Abbey.

**PARR, CATHERINE**, SIXTH CONSORT OF HENRY VIII: *Date of birth:* probably 1512; *Place of birth:* Kendal Castle; *Parents:* Sir Thomas Parr and Maud Green; *Date of marriage:* 12 July 1543; *Place of marriage:* Hampton Court Palace; *Issue:* none; *Other marriages:* (a) Sir Edward Borough (1529; no issue); (b) John Neville, lord Latimer (1534; no issue); (c) Thomas Seymour (April or May 1547; 1 daughter); *Date of death:* 5 September 1548; *Place of death:* Sudeley Castle; *Place of burial:* Sudeley Castle.

**PHILIP II OF SPAIN**, CONSORT OF MARY I: *Date of birth:* 21 May 1527; *Place of birth:* Valladolid, Castile; *Parents:* Charles V of Spain and Isabella of Portugal; *Date of marriage:* 25 July 1554; *Place of marriage:* Winchester Cathedral; *Issue:* none; *Other marriages:* (a) Maria Manuela of Portugal (12 November 1543; 1 son); (b) Elizabeth of Valois (1559; 1 son, 2 daughters); (c) Anna of Austria (12 November 1570; 5 sons, 2 daughters); *Date of death:* 13 September 1598; *Place of death:* El Escorial Palace, near Madrid; *Place of burial:* El Escorial Palace.

**PHILIP, PRINCE, DUKE OF EDINBURGH**, CONSORT OF ELIZABETH II: *Date of birth:* 10 June 1921; *Place of birth:* Mon Repos, Corfu;

*Parents:* Prince Andrew of Greece and Denmark and Princess Alice of Battenberg; *Date of marriage:* 20 November 1947; *Place of marriage:* Westminster Abbey; *Issue:* 3 sons (including Charles, prince of Wales and heir to the throne), 1 daughter; *Other marriages:* none.

**PHILIPPA OF HAINAULT**, CONSORT OF EDWARD III: *Date of birth:* probably 24 June 1311; *Place of birth:* Valenciennes, France; *Parents:* William, count of Hainault, and Jeanne of Valois; *Date of marriage:* 24 January 1328; *Place of marriage:* York Minster; *Issue:* at least 8 sons and 5 daughters; *Other marriages:* none; *Date of death:* c15 August 1369; *Place of death:* Windsor Castle; *Place of burial:* Westminster Abbey.

**SEYMOUR, JANE**, THIRD CONSORT OF HENRY VIII: *Date of birth:* 1508 or 1509; *Place of birth:* probably Wolf Hall, Wiltshire; *Parents:* Sir John Seymour and Margery Wentworth; *Date of marriage:* 30 May 1536; *Place of marriage:* Whitehall Palace; *Issue:* 1 son (Edward VI); *Other marriages:* none; *Date of death:* 24 October 1537; *Place of death:* Hampton Court Palace; *Place of burial:* St. George's Chapel, Windsor Castle.

**SOPHIA DOROTHEA OF CELLE**, CONSORT OF GEORGE I: *Date of birth:* 15 September 1666; *Place of birth:* Celle Castle, Lower Saxony; *Parents:* George William, duke of Brunswick-Lüneburg, and Eléonore Desmier d'Olbreuse; *Date of marriage:* 21 November 1682 (divorced 28 December 1694); *Place of marriage:* Celle; *Issue:* 1 son (George II), 1 daughter; *Other marriages:* none; *Date of death:* 13 November 1726; *Place of death:* Ahlden Castle, Hanover; *Place of burial:* Stadtkirche, Celle.

**STUART, HENRY, LORD DARNLEY**, SECOND CONSORT OF MARY, QUEEN OF SCOTS: *Date of birth:* 7 December 1545; *Place of birth:* Temple Newsam, Leeds; *Parents:* Matthew Stuart, earl of Lennox, and Margaret Douglas; *Date of marriage:* 29 July 1565; *Place of marriage:* Holyrood Palace; *Issue:* 1 son (James VI of Scotland and I of England); *Other marriages:* none; *Date of death:* 9 February 1567; *Place of death:* Kirk o' Field, Edinburgh; *Place of burial:* Holyrood Abbey.

**SYBILLA OF NORMANDY**, CONSORT OF ALEXANDER I: *Date of birth:* unknown; *Place of birth:* Domfront, Normandy; *Parents:* Henry I and Lady Sybilla Corbet; *Date of marriage:* unknown, possibly c1107 and probably before 1114; *Place of marriage:* unknown; *Issue:* none; *Other marriages:* none; *Date of death:* 12 or 13 July 1122; *Place of death:* Eilean nam Ban, Loch Tay; *Place of burial:* Dunfermline Abbey.

**WALLIS, DUCHESS OF WINDSOR**, CONSORT OF EDWARD VIII: *Date of birth:* 19 June 1896; *Place of birth:* Blue Ridge Summit, Pennsylvania; *Parents:* Teackle Wallis Warfield and Alice Montague; *Date of marriage:* 3 June 1937; *Place of marriage:* Château de Candé, near Tours; *Issue:* none; *Other marriages:* (a) Earl Winfield Spencer (8 November 1916, divorced 16 December 1927; no issue); (b) Ernest Aldrick Simpson (21 July 1928, divorced 27 October 1936; no issue); *Date of death:* 24 April 1986; *Place of death:* Paris; *Place of burial:* Frogmore, Windsor.

**WILLIAM III OF ENGLAND AND II OF SCOTLAND**, CONSORT OF MARY II: *Date of birth:* 14 November 1650; *Place of birth:* Binnenhof Palace, The Hague; *Parents:* William, prince of Orange, and Mary Henrietta, princess royal; *Date of marriage:* 4 November 1677; *Place of marriage:* St. James's Palace; *Issue:* none; *Other marriages:* none; *Date of death:* 8 March 1702; *Place of death:* Kensington Palace; *Place of burial:* Westminster Abbey.

**WOODVILLE, ELIZABETH**, CONSORT OF EDWARD IV: *Date of birth:* c1437; *Place of birth:* probably Grafton Regis, Northamptonshire; *Parents:* Sir Richard Woodville and Jacquetta, dowager duchess of Bedford; *Date of marriage:* possibly 1 May 1464; *Place of marriage:* possibly Grafton Regis; *Issue:* 3 sons (including Edward V), 7 daughters; *Other marriages:* Sir John Grey (c1456; 2 sons); *Date of death:* 8 June 1492; *Place of death:* Bermondsey Abbey; *Place of burial:* St. George's Chapel, Windsor Castle.

**YOLANDE DE DREUX**, SECOND CONSORT OF ALEXANDER III: *Date of birth:* c1263; *Place of birth:* unknown; *Parents:* Robert IV, count of Dreux, and Beatrix of Montfort; *Date of marriage:* 14 October 1285; *Place of marriage:* Roxburgh Castle; *Issue:* none; *Other marriage:* Arthur II, duke of Brittany (1 son, 5 daughters); *Date of death:* after 1324; *Place of death:* unknown; *Place of burial:* unknown.

# Appendix 4
# The Line of Succession to the British Throne

Places in the line of succession are determined primarily by the provisions of the Act of Settlement, passed by the English parliament in 1701, and by male-preference primogeniture. The 25 individuals listed below occupy the leading positions at the beginning of the second decade of the 21st century, but rankings will change with the birth of children to any of the people identified and with the death either of the monarch or of any person in the line.

1. Charles, prince of Wales, eldest son of Queen Elizabeth II
2. Prince William of Wales, elder son of Charles, prince of Wales
3. Prince Henry of Wales, younger son of Charles, prince of Wales
4. Prince Andrew, duke of York, second son of Queen Elizabeth II
5. Princess Beatrice of York, elder daughter of Prince Andrew, duke of York
6. Princess Eugenie of York, younger daughter of Prince Andrew, duke of York
7. Prince Edward, earl of Wessex, third son of Queen Elizabeth II
8. James, viscount Severn, only son of Prince Edward, earl of Wessex
9. Lady Louise Windsor, only daughter of Prince Edward, earl of Wessex
10. Anne, princess royal, only daughter of Queen Elizabeth II
11. Peter Phillips, only son of Anne, princess royal
12. Savannah Phillips, only child of Peter Phillips
13. Zara Phillips, only daughter of Anne, princess royal
14. David Armstrong-Jones, viscount Linley, only son of the late Princess Margaret, countess of Snowdon, younger sister of Queen Elizabeth II
15. The Honourable Charles Armstrong-Jones, only son of David Armstrong-Jones, viscount Linley
16. The Honorable Margarita Armstrong-Jones, only daughter of David Armstrong-Jones, viscount Linley
17. Lady Sarah Chatto, only daughter of the late Princess Margaret, countess of Snowdon, younger sister of Queen Elizabeth II
18. Samuel Chatto, elder son of Lady Sarah Chatto
19. Arthur Chatto, younger son of Lady Sarah Chatto
20. Prince Richard, duke of Gloucester, first cousin of Queen Elizabeth II

21. Alexander Windsor, earl of Ulster, only son of Prince Richard, duke of Gloucester
22. Xan Windsor, only son of Alexander Windsor, earl of Ulster
23. Lady Davina Lewis, elder daughter of Prince Richard, duke of Gloucester
24. Lady Rose Gilman, younger daughter of Prince Richard, duke of Gloucester
25. Prince Edward, duke of Kent, first cousin of Queen Elizabeth II

# Appendix 5
## Genealogies of Britain's Monarchs

This appendix provides family trees for Britain's kings and queens, show-ing the links between dynasties and the pattern of succession. For reasons of space, some people are excluded, including female consorts who produced no issue and monarchs' siblings who never held the crown, but all sovereigns from Edgar (who ruled England from 959 to 975) and Kenneth I (traditionally regarded as the first king of Scotland) are identified. Some individuals appear on more than one page, allowing the student to trace the descent of Britain's present royal family, generation by generation, from the Anglo-Saxon and Celtic kings who held power more than a millennium ago. Family trees A and B detail the later Anglo-Saxon succession and show how the bloodline became part of the lineage of the Scottish royal house and then, through that connection, reentered the English monarchy as a result of intermarriage with the House of Normandy. Family tree C helps readers trace the complex fam-ily relationships that led the descendants of King Edward III and Philippa of Hainault to struggle against each other during the Wars of the Roses in the later Plantagenet period but to eventually reunite, and family tree D (con-sulted along with the main dictionary entries) helps explain how a Scottish king (James VI) was able to sustain a successful claim to the English throne and become sovereign of both countries in 1603. Family tree E depicts the links between the House of Stuart and its successors from the House of Ha-nover, trees F1 and F2 plot the present royal family's descent from Queen Victoria, and trees G and H focus on Scotland's monarchs but also identify marriages to members of the English royal houses. The years during which monarchs reigned are shown under each sovereign's name. Further details on these monarchs, and on their consorts and issue, are contained in the diction-ary entries for each individual.

Family Tree A

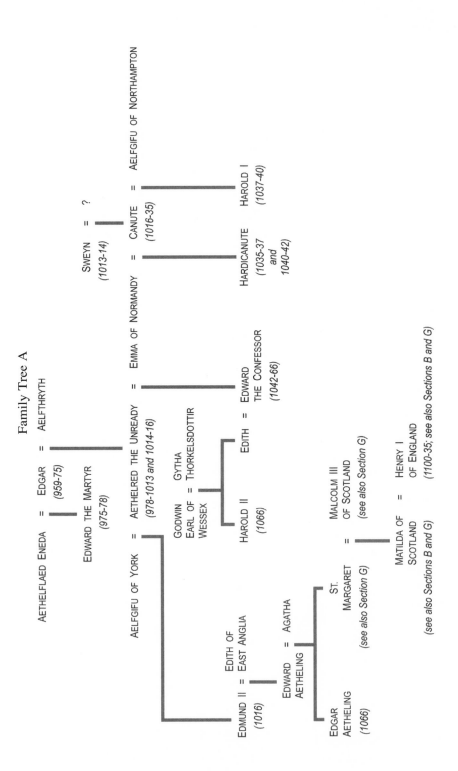

# Family Tree B

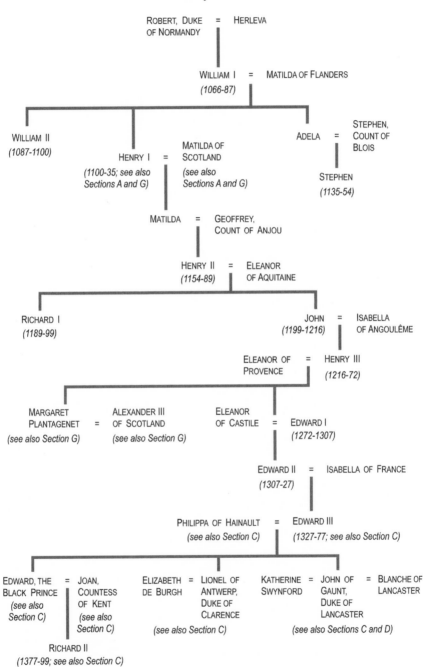

# Family Tree C

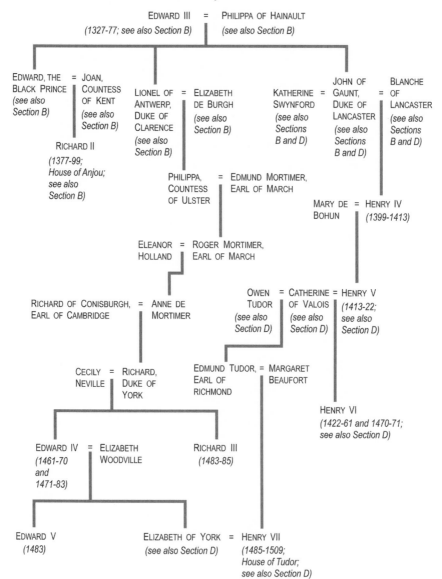

EDWARD III = PHILIPPA OF HAINAULT
*(1327-77; see also Section B)*   *(see also Section B)*

EDWARD, THE = JOAN,
BLACK PRINCE   COUNTESS
*(see also*   OF KENT
*Section B)*   *(see also*
             *Section B)*

RICHARD II
*(1377-99;*
*House of Anjou;*
*see also*
*Section B)*

LIONEL OF = ELIZABETH
ANTWERP,   DE BURGH
DUKE OF    *(see also*
CLARENCE   *Section B)*
*(see also*
*Section B)*

PHILIPPA, = EDMUND MORTIMER,
COUNTESS   EARL OF MARCH
OF ULSTER

ELEANOR = ROGER MORTIMER,
HOLLAND   EARL OF MARCH

KATHERINE = GAUNT, = OF
SWYNFORD   DUKE OF   LANCASTER
*(see also*   LANCASTER   *(see also*
*Sections*   *(see also*   *Sections*
*B and D)*   *Sections*   *B and D)*
            *B and D)*

JOHN OF   BLANCHE

MARY DE = HENRY IV
BOHUN   *(1399-1413)*

RICHARD OF CONISBURGH, = ANNE DE
EARL OF CAMBRIDGE        MORTIMER

OWEN = CATHERINE = HENRY V
TUDOR   OF VALOIS   *(1413-22;*
*(see also*   *(see also*   *see also*
*Section D)*   *Section D)*   *Section D)*

CECILY = RICHARD,
NEVILLE   DUKE OF
          YORK

EDMUND TUDOR, = MARGARET
EARL OF         BEAUFORT
RICHMOND

HENRY VI
*(1422-61 and 1470-71;*
*see also Section D)*

EDWARD IV = ELIZABETH
*(1461-70*   WOODVILLE
*and*
*1471-83)*

RICHARD III
*(1483-85)*

EDWARD V
*(1483)*

ELIZABETH OF YORK = HENRY VII
*(see also Section D)*   *(1485-1509;*
                        *House of Tudor;*
                        *see also Section D)*

# Family Tree D

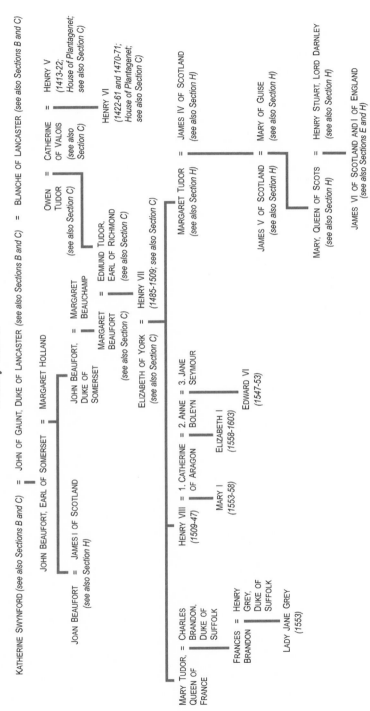

KATHERINE SWYNFORD *(see also Sections B and C)* = JOHN OF GAUNT, DUKE OF LANCASTER *(see also Sections B and C)* = BLANCHE OF LANCASTER *(see also Sections B and C)*

JOHN BEAUFORT, EARL OF SOMERSET = MARGARET HOLLAND

OWEN = CATHERINE = HENRY V
TUDOR   OF VALOIS   *(1413-22;*
*(see also Section C)*   *(see also Section C)*   *House of Plantagenet;*
*see also Section C)*

JOAN BEAUFORT = JAMES I OF SCOTLAND
*(see also Section H)*

JOHN BEAUFORT, = MARGARET
DUKE OF   BEAUCHAMP
SOMERSET

MARGARET = EDMUND TUDOR,
BEAUFORT   EARL OF RICHMOND
*(see also Section C)*   *(see also Section C)*

HENRY VI
*(1422-61 and 1470-71;*
*House of Plantagenet;*
*see also Section C)*

ELIZABETH OF YORK = HENRY VII
*(see also Section C)*   *(1485-1509; see also Section C)*

JAMES IV OF SCOTLAND
*(see also Section H)*

MARGARET TUDOR
*(see also Section H)*

MARY OF GUISE
*(see also Section H)*

JAMES V OF SCOTLAND
*(see also Section H)*

MARY, QUEEN OF SCOTS
*(see also Section H)*

HENRY STUART, LORD DARNLEY
*(see also Section H)*

JAMES VI OF SCOTLAND AND I OF ENGLAND
*(see also Sections E and H)*

HENRY VIII = 1. CATHERINE = 2. ANNE = 3. JANE
*(1509-47)*   OF ARAGON   BOLEYN   SEYMOUR

MARY I
*(1553-58)*

ELIZABETH I
*(1558-1603)*

EDWARD VI
*(1547-53)*

MARY TUDOR, = CHARLES
QUEEN OF   BRANDON,
FRANCE   DUKE OF
SUFFOLK

FRANCES = HENRY
BRANDON   GREY,
DUKE OF
SUFFOLK

LADY JANE GREY
*(1553)*

# Family Tree E

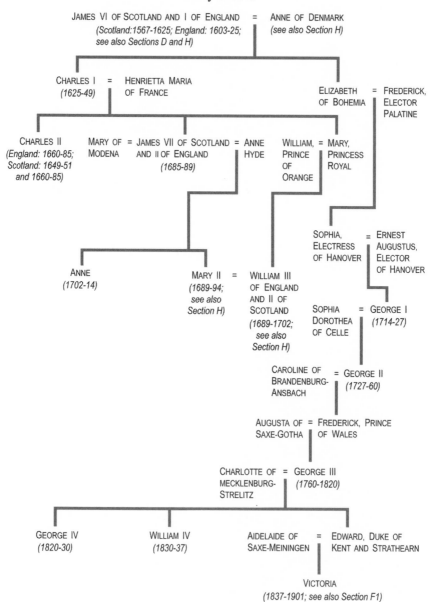

JAMES VI OF SCOTLAND AND I OF ENGLAND = ANNE OF DENMARK
*(Scotland:1567-1625; England: 1603-25;* *(see also Section H)*
*see also Sections D and H)*

CHARLES I = HENRIETTA MARIA
*(1625-49)* OF FRANCE

ELIZABETH = FREDERICK,
OF BOHEMIA ELECTOR
PALATINE

CHARLES II
*(England: 1660-85;*
*Scotland: 1649-51*
*and 1660-85)*

MARY OF = JAMES VII OF SCOTLAND = ANNE
MODENA AND II OF ENGLAND HYDE
*(1685-89)*

WILLIAM, = MARY,
PRINCE PRINCESS
OF ROYAL
ORANGE

SOPHIA, = ERNEST
ELECTRESS AUGUSTUS,
OF HANOVER ELECTOR
OF HANOVER

ANNE
*(1702-14)*

MARY II =
*(1689-94;*
*see also*
*Section H)*

WILLIAM III
OF ENGLAND
AND II OF
SCOTLAND
*(1689-1702;*
*see also*
*Section H)*

SOPHIA = GEORGE I
DOROTHEA *(1714-27)*
OF CELLE

CAROLINE OF = GEORGE II
BRANDENBURG- *(1727-60)*
ANSBACH

AUGUSTA OF = FREDERICK, PRINCE
SAXE-GOTHA OF WALES

CHARLOTTE OF = GEORGE III
MECKLENBURG- *(1760-1820)*
STRELITZ

GEORGE IV
*(1820-30)*

WILLIAM IV
*(1830-37)*

AIDELAIDE OF = EDWARD, DUKE OF
SAXE-MEININGEN KENT AND STRATHEARN

VICTORIA
*(1837-1901; see also Section F1)*

# Family Tree F1

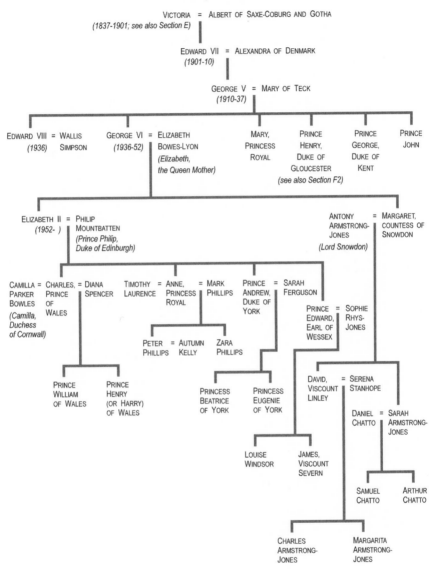

# Family Tree F2

GEORGE V (1910-36; see also Section F1) = MARY OF TECK

# Family Tree G

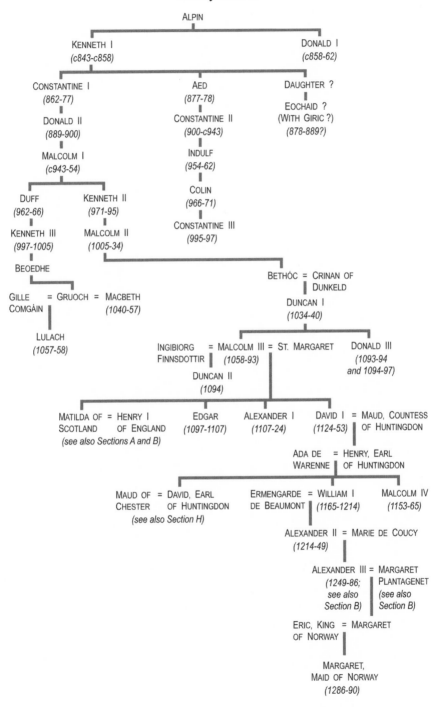

ALPIN

KENNETH I
(c843-c858)

DONALD I
(c858-62)

CONSTANTINE I
(862-77)

AED
(877-78)

DAUGHTER ?

DONALD II
(889-900)

CONSTANTINE II
(900-c943)

EOCHAID ?
(WITH GIRIC ?)
(878-889?)

MALCOLM I
(c943-54)

INDULF
(954-62)

DUFF
(962-66)

KENNETH II
(971-95)

COLIN
(966-71)

KENNETH III
(997-1005)

MALCOLM II
(1005-34)

CONSTANTINE III
(995-97)

BEOEDHE

BETHÓC = CRINAN OF
DUNKELD

GILLE      = GRUOCH = MACBETH
COMGÁIN                (1040-57)

DUNCAN I
(1034-40)

LULACH
(1057-58)

INGIBIORG    = MALCOLM III = ST. MARGARET
FINNSDOTTIR      (1058-93)

DONALD III
(1093-94
and 1094-97)

DUNCAN II
(1094)

MATILDA OF = HENRY I
SCOTLAND     OF ENGLAND
(see also Sections A and B)

EDGAR
(1097-1107)

ALEXANDER I
(1107-24)

DAVID I    = MAUD, COUNTESS
(1124-53)     OF HUNTINGDON

ADA DE    = HENRY, EARL
WARENNE     OF HUNTINGDON

MAUD OF  = DAVID, EARL
CHESTER     OF HUNTINGDON
(see also Section H)

ERMENGARDE = WILLIAM I
DE BEAUMONT   (1165-1214)

MALCOLM IV
(1153-65)

ALEXANDER II = MARIE DE COUCY
(1214-49)

ALEXANDER III = MARGARET
(1249-86;        PLANTAGENET
see also          (see also
Section B)        Section B)

ERIC, KING = MARGARET
OF NORWAY

MARGARET,
MAID OF NORWAY
(1286-90)

# Family Tree H

DAVID, EARL OF HUNTINGDON = MAUD OF CHESTER
*(see also Section G)*

MARGARET OF = ALAN, LORD
HUNTINGDON | OF GALLOWAY

DEVORGUILLA = JOHN BALLIOL

JOHN OF SCOTLAND = ISOBEL DE
*(1292-96)* | WARENNE

EDWARD
BALLIOL

ISOBEL OF = ROBERT BRUCE,
HUNTINGDON | LORD OF
ANNANDALE

ISOBEL OF HERTFORD = ROBERT BRUCE,
AND GLOUCESTER | LORD OF ANNANDALE

ROBERT BRUCE, = MARJORIE,
LORD OF | COUNTESS OF
ANNANDALE | CARRICK

ISOBEL = ROBERT I = ELIZABETH
OF MAR | *(1306-29)* | DE BURGH

MARJORIE = WALTER, HIGH
BRUCE | STEWARD OF
SCOTLAND

DAVID II
*(1329-71)*

ROBERT II = ELIZABETH
*(1371-90)* | MURE

HENRY STUART, = MARY, QUEEN OF SCOTS
LORD DARNLEY | *(1542-67;*
*(see also* | *see also Section D)*
*Section D)*

ANNABELLA = ROBERT III
DRUMMOND | *(1390-1406)*

JAMES VI OF SCOTLAND = ANNE OF
AND I OF ENGLAND | DENMARK
*(Scotland: 1567-1625;*
*England: 1603-1625;*
*see also Sections D and E)*

JAMES I = JOAN BEAUFORT
*(1406-37;* | *(see also Section D)*
*see also Section D)*

JAMES II = MARY OF
*(1437-60)* | GUELDRES

CHARLES I = HENRIETTA MARIA
*(1625-49;* | OF FRANCE
*see also Section E)* | *(see also Section E)*

MARGARET = JAMES III
OF DENMARK | *(1460-88)*

CHARLES II
*(England: 1660-88*
*Scotland: 1649-51*
*and 1660-85;*
*see also Section E)*

MARY OF = JAMES VII = ANNE
MODENA | OF SCOTLAND | HYDE
AND II OF | *(see also*
ENGLAND | Section E)*
*(1685-89;*
*see also Section E)*

MARGARET = JAMES IV
TUDOR | *(1488-1513;*
*(see also* | *see also Section D)*
*Section D)*

JAMES V = MARY OF
*(1513-42;* | GUISE
*see also Section D)* | *(see also Section D)*

MARY II = WILLIAM III
*(1689-94;* | OF ENGLAND
*(see also* | AND II OF
*Section E)* | SCOTLAND
*(1689-1702;*
*see also Section E)*

ANNE
*(1702-14;*
*see also*
*Section E)*

# Bibliography

## CONTENTS

## INTRODUCTION

Students of the United Kingdom's monarchy, and of its English and Scottish predecessors, face no shortage of resources. In order to keep the list of citations in this bibliography within reasonable bounds, entries are restricted to English-language books published since 1980, including reprints of earlier texts. Readers seeking further information on specific topics will find that most of the publications listed include extensive bibliographies. Also, the World Wide Web facilitates searches of the catalogs of the British Library (www.bl.uk), the Library of Congress (www.loc .gov/index.html) and, for a fee, the Bibliography of British and Irish History (www .history.ac.uk/projects/bibh), which is maintained by Brepols Publishers, the Institute of Historical Research, and the Royal Historical Society. All three contain pre-1900 material.

Researchers requiring a general introduction to the history of the monarchy would benefit from Roy Strong's *Coronation: A History of Kingship and the British Monarchy* (London: HarperCollins, 2005) and David Starkey's sometimes opinionated but undoubtedly authoritative two-volume study entitled *The Monarchy of England: The*

*Beginnings* (London: Chatto & Windus, 2004) and *Monarchy: From the Middle Ages to Modernity* (London: HarperPress, 2006). For details on individuals, the most encompassing source is the 61 volumes of the *Dictionary of National Biography*, edited by H. C. G. Matthew and Brian Harrison. The latest print copy of the full dictionary appeared in 2004, but an online version, updated three times each year, is available to subscribers or through membership at some libraries. It does not provide life histories of individuals who are still alive, but its coverage of earlier times is comprehensive and accompanied in many cases by short lists of sources.

Information on the earliest English monarchies is understandably sparser than that on more recent times, but Geoffrey Ashe's *Kings and Queens of Early Britain* (London: Methuen, 2000) and Christopher Brooke's *The Saxon and Norman Kings* (Oxford: Blackwell, 2001) are established texts, the latter also covering the period following the Norman conquest and supplementing M. T. Clanchy's *England and Its Rulers, 1066–1307* (Oxford: Blackwell, 2006). The early Plantagenet period is well covered in Richard Mortimer's *Angevin England* (Oxford: Blackwell, 1994) and Michael Prestwich's *Plantagenet England, 1235–1360* (Oxford: Oxford University Press, 2005), and the later period in Gerald Harriss's *Shaping the Nation: England, 1360–1461* (Oxford: Clarendon, 2005) and John Gillingham's *The Wars of the Roses: Peace and Conflict in 15th Century England* (London: Phoenix, 2001).

Susan Brigden's *New Worlds, Lost Worlds: The Rule of the Tudors, 1485–1603* (New York: Viking, 2001) provides important context for the period that included the break with the Church of Rome and the union of the English and Scottish crowns, and Christopher Hill's *The Century of Revolution, 1603–1714* (London: Routledge Classics, 2002) does so for the turbulent Stuart period that followed. Jeremy Black deals with the House of Hanover in *The Hanoverians: The History of a Dynasty* (London: Hambledon & London, 2004); William M. Kuhn with Queen Victoria and the House of Saxe-Coburg and Gotha in *Democratic Royalism: The Transformation of the British Monarchy, 1861–1914* (New York: St. Martin's, 1996); Piers Brendon and Philip Whitehead with the most recent monarchs in *The Windsors: A Dynasty Revealed* (London: Pimlico, 2000); and Vernon Bogdanor with the current role of the monarchy in *The Monarchy and the Constitution* (Oxford: Clarendon, 1995).

Scholars with an interest in the Scottish monarchy will find much useful material in the five-volume *Scotland: The Making and Unmaking of the Nation, c1100–1707*, edited by Bob Harris and Alan R. MacDonald (Dundee: Dundee University Press in association with the Open University, 2006–2007). A. A. M. Duncan's *The Kingship of the Scots, 842–1292: Succession and Independence* (Edinburgh: Edinburgh University Press, 2002) is a standard (and sometimes provocative) work dealing with the early monarchies, as is *Medieval Scotland: Crown, Lordship and Community; Essays Presented to G. W. S. Barrow*, edited by Alexander Grant and Keith J. Stringer (Edinburgh: Edinburgh University Press, 1998).

In *The Balliol Dynasty, 1210–1364* (Edinburgh: John Donald, 2008), Amanda Beam paints a sympathetic picture of a king usually considered weak, and in *The Early Stewart Kings: Robert II and Robert III, 1371–1406* (East Linton, UK: Tuckwell, 1996), Stephen Boardman examines the legacy of two men who helped to establish Scotland's most enduring royal dynasty. Jenny Wormald continues the Stuart story in *Court, Kirk and Community: Scotland, 1470–1625* (Edinburgh: Edinburgh

University Press, 1991), placing it in the context of the Reformation and cultural change; Leanda de Lisle deals with the clandestine politics that led to the union of the English and Scottish crowns in *After Elizabeth: The Rise of James of Scotland and the Struggle for the Throne of England* (New York: Ballantine, 2005); and John MacLeod details the later history of an independent Scotland's last royal house in *Dynasty: The Stuarts, 1560–1807* (New York: St. Martin's, 2001).

In addition to biographies of individual monarchs, there are many valuable reference books providing details on dynasties, monarchs, and reigns, among them Thomas Cussans's *The Times Kings and Queens of the British Isles* (London: Times Books, 2002), which provides information on Irish kings and Welsh princes as well as the English and Scottish rulers, and Carolly Erickson's *Royal Panoply: Brief Lives of the English Monarchs* (New York: St. Martin's Griffin, 2007), which, despite its title, presents accounts of the lives of all the British monarchs after the union of the crowns as well as of the English monarchs who preceded it.

There are also period-based reference works, such as the *Historical Dictionary of Stuart England, 1603–1689*, edited by Ronald Fritze and William B. Robinson (Westport, Conn.: Greenwood Press, 1996) and *The Plantagenet Encyclopedia: An Alphabetical Guide to 400 Years of English History*, edited by Elizabeth Hallam (New York: Grove Weidenfeld, 1990). The achievements of individual reigns can be gleaned from entries in the *Dictionary of British History*, edited by John Cannon (New York: Oxford University Press, 2009); the two-volume *Historical Dictionary of the United Kingdom*, by Kenneth J. Panton and Keith A. Cowlard (Lanham, Md.: Scarecrow, 1997–1998); and the *Oxford Companion to Scottish History*, edited by Michael Lynch (Oxford: Oxford University Press, 2001).

In addition to the extensive range of book sources, students will find much material on the monarchy in academic journals, including *Court Historian*, the *English Historical Review*, the *Journal of Medieval History*, the *Scottish Historical Review,* and *Transactions of the Royal Historical Society*, as well as in publications of special-interest groups, such as *Ricardian*, the journal of the Richard III Society. Newspaper archives are also an important source of material, particularly for the last two centuries.

American readers can gain access to all of the texts through interlibrary loan services but should also note that many universities have strong collections of material on the monarchy. Current publications can often be purchased through local booksellers or by way of the Internet from Amazon (www.amazon.com). Also, Abebooks (www.abebooks.com) carries a vast selection of used and out-of-print books, many of which can be purchased very cheaply. Researchers in the United Kingdom clearly have a greater range of sources at their disposal. The National Archives at Kew, in southwest London, has original manuscripts and other documents not available elsewhere, and the British Library, also in London, receives copies of all books and journals published in the United Kingdom; both are open to everyone but are best suited, perhaps, to scholars seeking specialized material.

Most British universities—particularly the more established ones—have strong collections of historical studies and make their resources available to serious students, although lending and other privileges are likely to be restricted. However, the Mitchell Library in Glasgow (www.mitchelllibrary.org) houses Europe's most extensive public reference library, and branches of the public library system in other cities concentrate on specific themes, allowing them to build up strength in depth. Scholars in Scotland can seek additional resources, including early newspapers and photographs, at the National Library of Scotland (www.nls.uk).

## ANGLO-SAXON MONARCHIES

Abels, Richard P. *Alfred the Great: War, Culture and Kingship in Anglo-Saxon England*. London: Longman, 1998.

Aelred of Rievaulx. *The Life of Saint Edward, King and Confessor*. Translated by Jerome Bertram. Southampton: St. Austin Press, 1997.

Arnold, C. J. *An Archaeology of the Early Anglo-Saxon Kingdoms*. London: Routledge, 1988.

Ashe, Geoffrey. *Kings and Queens of Early Britain*. London: Methuen, 2000.

Asser, John. *The Medieval Life of King Alfred the Great: A Translation and Commentary on the Text Attributed to Asser*. Translated by Alfred P. Smyth. Basingstoke, UK: Palgrave, 2002.

Barlow, Frank. *Edward the Confessor*. New Haven, Conn.: Yale University Press, 1997.

———. *The Godwins: The Rise and Fall of a Noble Dynasty*. London: Pearson/Longman, 2003.

Baxter, Stephen David. *The Earls of Mercia: Lordship and Power in Late Anglo-Saxon England*. Oxford: Oxford University Press, 2007.

Bede, The Venerable. *Ecclesiastical History of the English People*. London: Penguin, 1990.

Blackburn, Mark A. S., and David N. Dumville, eds. *Kings, Currency and Alliances: History and Coinage of Southern England in the Ninth Century*. Woodbridge, UK: Boydell, 1998.

Bradbury, Jim. *The Battle of Hastings*. Stroud, UK: Alan Sutton, 1998.

Brooke, Christopher. *The Saxon and Norman Kings*. Oxford: Blackwell, 2001.

Brown, Michelle P., and Carol Ann Farr, eds. *Mercia: An Anglo-Saxon Kingdom in Europe*. London: Leicester University Press, 2001.

Campbell, James. *The Anglo-Saxon State*. London: Hambledon & London, 2000.

Campbell, James, Eric John, and Patrick Wormald, eds. *The Anglo-Saxons*. London: Penguin, 1991.

Charles-Edwards, Thomas, ed. *After Rome*. Oxford: Oxford University Press, 2003.

Crouch, David. *The Image of Aristocracy in Britain, 1000–1300*. London: Routledge, 1992.

Davies, Wendy, ed. *From the Vikings to the Normans*. Oxford: Oxford University Press, 2003.

Dumville, David N. *Britons and Anglo-Saxons in the Early Middle Ages*. Aldershot, UK: Variorum, 1993.

———. *Wessex and England from Alfred to Edgar: Six Essays on Political, Cultural and Ecclesiastical Revival*. Woodbridge, UK: Boydell, 1992.

Fletcher, Richard. *Bloodfeud: Murder and Revenge in Anglo-Saxon England*. London: Penguin, 2003.

———. *Who's Who in Roman Britain and Anglo-Saxon England*. London: Shepheard-Walwyn, 1989.

Frantzen, Allen J. *King Alfred*. Boston: Twayne, 1986.

Fry, Fred. *Patterns of Power: The Military Campaigns of Alfred the Great*. Ely, UK: Melrose, 2007.

Gabriel, Ronay. *The Lost King of England: The East European Adventures of Edward the Exile*. Woodbridge, UK: Boydell, 2009.

Greenberg, Janelle Renfrow. *The Radical Face of the Ancient Constitution: St. Edward's "Laws" in Early Modern Political Thought*. Cambridge: Cambridge University Press, 2001.

Hart, Cyril. *The Danelaw*. London: Hambledon, 1992.

Henson, Donald. *The English Elite in 1066: Gone but Not Forgotten*. Hockwold-cum-Wilton, UK: Anglo-Saxon Books, 2001.

———. *A Guide to Late Anglo-Saxon England: From Alfred to Eadgar II*. Norfolk, UK: Anglo-Saxon Books, 1998.

Hibbert, Christopher. *King Arthur*. Stroud, UK: Tempus, 2007.

Higham, Nick. *The Convert Kings: Power and Religious Affiliation in Early Anglo-Saxon England*. Manchester: Manchester Press, 2007.

———. *The Death of Anglo-Saxon England*. Stroud, UK: Alan Sutton, 1997.

———. *An English Empire: Bede and the Early Anglo-Saxon Kings*. Manchester: Manchester University Press, 1995.

———. *King Arthur: Myth-Making and History*. London: Routledge, 2002.

———. *The Kingdom of Northumbria: A.D. 350–1100*. Stroud, UK: Alan Sutton, 1993.

Higham, N. J., and D. H. Hill, eds. *Edward the Elder, 899–924*. London: Routledge, 2001.

Hill, David, and Margaret Worthington, eds. *Aethelbald and Offa: Two Eighth-Century Kings of Mercia*. Oxford: Archaeopress, 2005.

Hill, Paul. *The Age of Aethelstan: England's Forgotten History*. Stroud, UK: Tempus, 2004.

Horspool, David. *Why Alfred Burned the Cakes: A King and His Eleven-Hundred-Year Afterlife*. London: Profile, 2006.

Howarth, David. *1066: The Year of the Conquest*. London: Penguin, 2001.

Humble, Richard. *The Saxon Kings*. London: Weidenfeld & Nicolson, 1980.

Hunter Blair, Peter. *An Introduction to Anglo-Saxon England*. Cambridge: Cambridge University Press, 2003.

Huscroft, Richard. *Ruling England, 1042–1217*. Harlow, UK: Pearson Education, 2004.

James, Thomas Beaumont. *The Palaces of Medieval England, c1050–1550: Royalty, Nobility, the Episcopate and Their Residences from Edward the Confessor to Henry VIII*. London: Seaby, 1990.

John, Eric. *Reassessing Anglo-Saxon England*. Manchester: Manchester University Press, 1996.

Karkov, Catherine E. *The Ruler Portraits of Anglo-Saxon England.* Woodbridge, UK: Boydell, 2004.

Keynes, Simon. *The Diplomas of King Aethelred "the Unready," 978–1016: A Study in Their Use as Historical Evidence.* Cambridge: Cambridge University Press, 1980.

Keynes, Simon, and Alfred P. Smyth, eds. *Anglo-Saxons: Studies Presented to Cyril Roy Hart.* Dublin: Four Courts Press, 2006.

Kirby, D. P. *The Earliest English Kings.* London: Routledge, 2000.

Lapidge, Michael, John Blair, Simon Keynes, and Donald Scragg, eds. *Blackwell Encyclopedia of Anglo-Saxon England.* Oxford: Wiley-Blackwell, 2000.

Lavelle, Ryan. *Aethelred II: King of the English, 978–1016.* Stroud, UK: Tempus, 2002.

———. *Royal Estates in Anglo-Saxon Wessex: Land, Politics and Family Strategies.* Oxford: Archaeopress, 2007.

Loyn, H. R. *The Governance of Anglo-Saxon England, 500–1087.* London: Edward Arnold, 1984.

Mason, Emma. *The House of Godwin.* London: Hambledon & London, 2003.

McLynn, Frank. *1066: The Year of the Three Battles.* London: Jonathan Cape, 1998.

Mortimer, Richard, ed. *Edward the Confessor: The Man and the Legend.* Woodbridge, UK: Boydell, 2009.

Nicolle, David. *Arthur and the Anglo-Saxon Wars.* Oxford: Osprey, 2000.

O'Brien, Bruce R. *God's Peace and King's Peace: The Laws of Edward the Confessor.* Philadelphia: University of Pennsylvania Press, 1999.

O'Brien, Harriet. *Queen Emma and the Vikings: A History of Power, Love and Greed in Eleventh Century England.* London: Bloomsbury, 2005.

Owen-Crocker, Gale R., ed. *King Harold II and the Bayeux Tapestry.* Woodbridge, UK: Boydell, 2005.

Parker, Joanne. *England's Darling: The Victorian Cult of Alfred the Great.* Manchester: Manchester University Press, 2007.

Patterson, Benton Rain. *Harold and William: The Battle for England, 1064–1066.* Stroud, UK: History Press, 2004.

Peddie, John. *Alfred: Warrior King.* Stroud, UK: Alan Sutton, 2005.

Pelteret, David A. E., ed. *Anglo-Saxon History: Basic Readings.* New York: Garland, 2000.

Pollard, Justin. *Alfred the Great: The Man Who Made England.* London: John Murray, 2005.

Pratt, David. *The Political Thought of Alfred the Great.* Cambridge: Cambridge University Press, 2007.

Rex, Peter. *Edgar: King of the English, 959–75.* Stroud, UK: Tempus, 2007.

———. *Harold II: The Doomed Saxon King.* Stroud, UK: Tempus, 2005.

———. *King & Saint: The Life of Edward the Confessor.* Stroud, UK: History Press, 2008.

Reuter, Timothy, ed. *Alfred the Great: Papers from the Eleventh-Centenary Conferences.* Aldershot, UK: Ashgate, 2003.

Ridyard, Susan J. *The Royal Saints of Anglo-Saxon England: A Study of West Saxon and East Anglian Cults*. Cambridge: Cambridge University Press, 1988.

Rollason, David. *Northumbria, 500–1100: The Making and Destruction of a Kingdom*. Cambridge: Cambridge University Press, 2003.

Ronay, Gabriel. *The Lost King of England: The East European Adventures of Edward the Exile*. Woodbridge, UK: Boydell & Brewer, 1989.

Savage, Anne, trans. *The Anglo-Saxon Chronicles*. London: Macmillan, 1984.

Scragg, Donald, ed. *Edgar, King of the English: New Interpretations*. Woodbridge, UK: Boydell, 2008.

Sheppard, Alice. *Families of the King: Writing Identity in the Anglo-Saxon Chronicle*. Toronto: University of Toronto Press, 2004.

Smyth, Alfred P. *King Alfred the Great*. Oxford: Oxford University Press, 1995.

Snyder, Christopher, ed. *The Early Peoples of Britain and Ireland: An Encyclopedia*. 2 vols. Oxford: Greenwood Press, 2008.

Snyder, Christopher. *The World of King Arthur*. New York: Thames & Hudson, 2000.

Stafford, Pauline, ed. *A Companion to the Early Middle Ages: Britain and Ireland, c500–1100*. Oxford: Wiley-Blackwell, 2009.

——. *Queen Emma and Queen Edith: Queenship and Women's Power in Eleventh-Century England*. Oxford: Blackwell, 1997.

——. *Queens, Concubines and Dowagers: The King's Wife in the Early Middle Ages*. London: Leicester University Press, 1998.

——. *Unification and Conquest: A Political and Social History of England in the Tenth and Eleventh Centuries*. London: Edward Arnold, 1989.

Starkey, David. *The Monarchy of England: The Beginnings*. London: Chatto & Windus, 2004.

Stenton, F. M. *Anglo-Saxon England*. Oxford: Oxford University Press, 1989.

Strachan, Isabella. *Emma: The Twice-Crowned Queen: England in the Viking Age*. London: Peter Owen, 2004.

Sturdy, David. *Alfred the Great*. London: Constable, 1995.

Swanton, Michael, trans. and ed. *The Anglo-Saxon Chronicles*. London: Phoenix, 2000.

Walker, Ian W. *Harold: The Last Anglo-Saxon King*. Stroud, UK: Alan Sutton, 2000.

——. *Mercia and the Making of England*. Stroud, UK: Alan Sutton, 2000.

Whittock, Martyn J. *The Origins of England: 410–600*. London: Croom Helm, 1986.

Williams, Ann. *Aethelred the Unready: The Ill-Counselled King*. London: Hambledon & London, 2003.

——. *The English and the Norman Conquest*. Woodbridge, UK: Boydell, 1995.

——. *Kingship and Government in Pre-Conquest England, c500–c1066*. Basingstoke: Macmillan, 1999.

Williams, Ann, Alfred P. Smyth, and D. P. Kirby. *A Biographical Dictionary of Dark Age Britain: England, Scotland and Wales from c500–c1050*. London: Seaby, 1991.

Woods, Douglas, and David A. E. Pelteret, eds. *The Anglo-Saxons: Synthesis and Achievement*. Waterloo, Ontario: Wilfred Laurier University Press, 1985.

Wormald, Patrick. *The Making of English Law: King Alfred to the Twelfth Century; Legislation and Its Limits*. Oxford: Blackwell, 1999.

Yorke, Barbara. *Kings and Kingdoms of Early Anglo-Saxon England*. London: Routledge, 1997.

———. *Nunneries and the Anglo-Saxon Royal Houses*. London: Continuum, 2003.

———. *Wessex in the Early Middle Ages*. London: Leicester University Press, 1995.

## VIKING MONARCHIES

Bolton, Timothy. *The Empire of Cnut the Great: Conquest and the Consolidation of Power in Northern Europe in the Eleventh Century*. Leiden, Netherlands: Brill, 2009.

Crawford, Barbara E. *Scandinavian Scotland*. Leicester: Leicester University Press, 1987.

Davies, Wendy, ed. *From the Vikings to the Normans, 800–1100*. Oxford: Oxford University Press, 2003.

Downham, Clare. *Viking Kings of Britain and Ireland: The Dynasty of Ívarr to AD 1014*. Edinburgh: Dunedin Academic Press, 2007.

Forte, Angelo, Richard Oram, and Frederick Pedersen. *The Viking Empires*. Cambridge: Cambridge University Press, 2005.

Hadley, D. M. *The Northern Danelaw: Its Social Structure*. London: Leicester University Press, 2000.

———. *The Vikings in England: Settlement, Society and Culture*. Manchester: Manchester University Press, 2006.

Howard, Ian. *Swein Forkbeard's Invasions and the Danish Conquest of England, 991–1017*. Woodbridge, UK: Boydell & Brewer, 2003.

Lawson, M. K. *Cnut: England's Viking King*. Stroud, UK: Tempus, 2004.

Loyn, Henry. *The Vikings in Britain*. Oxford: Blackwell, 1995.

O'Brien, Harriet. *Queen Emma and the Vikings: A History of Power, Love and Greed in Eleventh Century England*. London: Bloomsbury, 2005.

Richards, Julian. *Blood of the Vikings*. London: Hodder & Stoughton, 2002.

Rumble, Alexander R., ed. *The Reign of Cnut: King of England, Denmark and Norway*. London: Leicester University Press, 1999.

Sawyer, Peter. *Kings and Vikings: Scandinavia and Europe, 700–1100*. London: Methuen, 1982.

———, ed. *The Oxford Illustrated History of the Vikings*. Oxford: Oxford University Press, 1999.

Stafford, Pauline. *Queen Emma and Queen Edith: Queenship and Women's Power in Eleventh Century England*. London: Blackwell, 1997.

Strachan, Isabella. *Emma: The Twice-Crowned Queen: England in the Viking Age*. London: Peter Owen, 2004.

Trow, M. J. *Cnut: Emperor of the North*. Stroud, UK: Alan Sutton, 2005.

## HOUSE OF NORMANDY

Alexander, Michael V. C. *Three Crises in Early English History: Personalities and Politics during the Norman Conquest, the Reign of King John, and the Wars of the Roses.* Lanham, Md.: University Press of America, 1998.

Barlow, Frank. *The Feudal Kingdom of England: 1042–1216.* London: Longman, 1999.

———. *The Godwins: The Rise and Fall of a Noble Dynasty.* London: Pearson/Longman, 2003.

———. *William Rufus.* New Haven, Conn.: Yale University Press, 2000.

Bartlett, Robert C. *England under the Norman and Angevin Kings, 1075–1225.* Oxford: Clarendon, 2000.

Bates, David. *William the Conqueror.* Stroud, UK: Tempus, 2004.

Bothwell, J. S. *Fall from Grace: Reversal of Fortune and the English Nobility, 1075–1455.* Manchester: Manchester University Press, 2008.

Bradbury, Jim. *The Battle of Hastings.* Stroud, UK: Alan Sutton, 1998.

———. *Stephen and Matilda: The Civil War of 1139–1153.* Stroud, UK: Alan Sutton, 1996.

Brooke, Christopher. *The Saxon and Norman Kings.* Oxford: Blackwell, 2001.

Brown, R. Allen. *The Norman Conquest of England: Sources and Documents.* Woodbridge, UK: Boydell, 1995.

Carpenter. David. *The Struggle for Mastery: Britain, 1066–1284.* Oxford: Oxford University Press, 2003.

Chibnall, Marjorie. *Anglo-Norman England, 1066–1166.* New York: Blackwell, 1987.

———. *The Debate on the Norman Conquest.* Manchester: Manchester University Press, 1999.

———. *The Empress Matilda: Queen Consort, Queen Mother and Lady of the English.* Oxford: Blackwell, 1991.

———. *The Normans.* Oxford: Blackwell, 2000.

Clanchy, M. Y. *England and Its Rulers, 1066–1307.* Oxford: Blackwell, 2006.

Crouch, David. *The Image of Aristocracy in Britain, 1000–1300.* London: Routledge, 1992.

———. *The Normans: The History of a Dynasty.* London: Hambledon & London, 2007.

———. *The Reign of King Stephen, 1135–1154.* Harlow, UK: Longman, 2000.

Dalton, Paul, and Graeme J. White, eds. *King Stephen's Reign (1135–1154).* Woodbridge, UK: Boydell, 2008.

Davies, R. R. *Domination and Conquest: The Experience of Ireland, Scotland and Wales, 1100–1300.* Cambridge: Cambridge University Press, 2006.

Davies, Wendy, ed. *From the Vikings to the Normans, 800–1100.* Oxford: Oxford University Press, 2003.

Davis, R. H. C. *King Stephen, 1135–1154.* London: Longman, 1990.

Davis, R. H. C., and Marjorie Chibnall, eds. and trans. *The Gesta Guillelmi of William of Poitiers.* Oxford: Clarendon, 1998.

Douglas, David C. *William the Conqueror: The Norman Impact upon England.* New Haven, Conn.: Yale University Press, 1999.

Fleming, Robin. *Kings and Lords in Conquest England.* Cambridge: Cambridge University Press, 1991.

Frame, Robin. *The Political Development of the British Isles, 1100–1400.* Oxford: Clarendon, 1995.

Gillingham, John. *The English in the Twelfth Century: Imperialism, National Identity and Political Values.* Woodbridge, UK: Boydell, 2000.

Given-Wilson, Chris, and Alice Curteis. *The Royal Bastards of Medieval England.* London: Routledge, 1988.

Golding, Brian. *The Normans in Britain, 1066–1100.* Basingstoke, UK: Palgrave, 2001.

Green, Judith A. *The Aristocracy of Norman England.* Cambridge: Cambridge University Press, 1997.

———. *Henry I: King of England and Duke of Normandy.* Cambridge: Cambridge University Press, 2006.

Harper-Bill, Christopher, and Elizabeth van Houts, eds. *A Companion to the Anglo-Norman World.* Woodbridge, UK: Boydell, 2003.

Henson, Donald. *The English Elite in 1066: Gone but Not Forgotten.* Hockwold-cum-Wilton, UK: Anglo-Saxon Books, 2001.

Hilliam, Paul. *William the Conqueror: First Norman King of England.* New York: Rosen, 2005.

Hilton, Lisa. *Queens Consort: England's Medieval Queens.* London: Weidenfeld & Nicolson, 2008.

Hollister, C. Warren. *Henry I.* New Haven, Conn.: Yale University Press, 2001.

Howarth, David. *1066: The Year of the Conquest.* London: Penguin, 2001.

Hudson, John. *The Formation of the English Common Law: Law and Society in England from the Norman Conquest to Magna Carta.* London: Longman, 1996.

———. *Land, Law and Lordship in Anglo-Norman England.* Oxford: Oxford University Press, 1984.

Huscroft, Richard. *The Norman Conquest: A New Introduction.* Harlow, UK: Longman, 2009.

———. *Ruling England: 1042–1217.* Harlow, UK: Pearson Education, 2005.

Huneycutt, Lois L. *Matilda of Scotland: A Study in Medieval Queenship.* Woodbridge, UK: Boydell, 2004.

James, Thomas Beaumont. *The Palaces of Medieval England, c1050–1550: Royalty, Nobility, the Episcopate and Their Residences from Edward the Confessor to Henry VIII.* London: Seaby, 1990.

Lack, Katherine. *Conqueror's Son: Duke Robert Curthose, Thwarted King.* Stroud, UK: Alan Sutton, 2007.

Lawson, M. K. *The Battle of Hastings, 1066.* Stroud, UK: Tempus, 2003.

LoPrete, Kimberley A. *Adela of Blois: Countess and Lord (c1067–1137).* Dublin: Four Courts Press, 2007.

Loyn, H. R. *The Norman Conquest*. London: Hutchinson, 1982.

Mason, Emma. *King Rufus: The Life and Mysterious Death of William II of England*. Stroud, UK: History Press, 2008.

Matthew, Donald. *King Stephen*. London: Hambledon & London, 2002.

McLynn, Frank. *1066: The Year of the Three Battles*. London: Jonathan Cape, 1998.

Owen-Crocker, Gale. *King Harold II and the Bayeux Tapestry*. Woodbridge, UK: Boydell, 2005.

Parsons, John Carmi, ed. *Medieval Queenship*. New York: St. Martin's, 1993.

Patterson, Benton Rain. *Harold and William: The Battle for England, 1064–1066*. Stroud, UK: History Press, 2004.

Pool, Austin Lane. *From Domesday Book to Magna Carta, 1087–1216*. Oxford: Oxford University Press, 1993.

Stafford, Pauline, ed. *A Companion to the Early Middle Ages: Britain and Ireland, c500–1100*. Oxford: Wiley-Blackwell, 2009.

Starkey, David. *Monarchy: From the Middle Ages to Modernity*. London: HarperPress, 2006.

Stringer, Keith J. *Earl David of Huntingdon, 1152–1219: A Study in Anglo-Scottish History*. Edinburgh: Edinburgh University Press, 1985.

———. *The Reign of Stephen: Kingship, Warfare and Government in Twelfth-Century England*. London: Routledge, 1993.

Thomas, Hugh M. *The Norman Conquest: England after William the Conqueror*. Lanham, Md.: Rowman & Littlefield, 2008.

Williams, Ann. *The English and the Norman Conquest*. Woodbridge, UK: Boydell, 1995.

Wood, Michael. *In Search of the Dark Ages*. London: Ariel, 1982.

Wormald, Patrick. *The Making of English Law: King Alfred to the Twelfth Century; Legislation and Its Limits*. Oxford: Blackwell, 1999.

## HOUSE OF PLANTAGENET

Alexander, Michael V. C. *The First of the Tudors: A Study of Henry VII and His Reign*. Totowa, N.J.: Rowman & Littlefield, 1980.

———. *Three Crises in Early English History: Personalities and Politics during the Norman Conquest, the Reign of King John, and the Wars of the Roses*. Lanham, Md.: University Press of America, 1998.

Allmand, Christopher. *Henry V*. New Haven, Conn.: Yale University Press, 1997.

———. *The Hundred Years War: England and France at War, c1300–c1450*. Cambridge: Cambridge University Press, 2001.

Ayton, Andrew. *Knights and Warhorses: Military Service and the English Aristocracy under Edward III*. Woodbridge, UK: Boydell, 1994.

Baldwin, David. *Elizabeth Woodville: Mother of the Princes in the Tower*. Stroud, UK: Alan Sutton, 2002.

———. *The Lost Prince: The Survival of Richard of York*. Stroud, UK: Alan Sutton, 2007.

————. *Stoke Field: The Last Battle of the Wars of the Roses*. Barnsley, UK: Pen and Sword Military, 2006.

Barber, Richard. *The Black Prince*. Stroud, UK: Alan Sutton, 2003.

————. *The Devil's Crown: A History of Henry II and His Sons*. Conshohocken, Pa.: Combined Books, 1996.

————. *Henry Plantagenet*. Woodbridge, UK: Boydell, 2001.

Bard, Rachel. *Queen without a Country*. Portland, Ore.: Literary Network, 2001.

Barker, Juliet. *Agincourt: The King, the Campaign, the Battle*. London: Abacus, 2006.

Barlow, Frank. *The Feudal Kingdom of England: 1042–1216*. London: Longman, 1999.

Bartlett, Robert C. *England under the Norman and Angevin Kings, 1075–1225*. Oxford: Clarendon. 2000.

Beem, Charles, ed. *The Royal Minorities of Medieval and Early Modern England*. New York: Palgrave Macmillan, 2008.

Bennett, Michael J. *The Battle of Bosworth*. Stroud, UK: Alan Sutton, 2000.

————. *Lambert Simnel and the Battle of Stoke*. Stroud, UK: Alan Sutton, 1987.

————. *Richard II and the Revolution of 1399*. Stroud, UK: Alan Sutton, 1999.

Bevan, Bryan. *Edward III: Monarch of Chivalry*. London: Rubicon, 1992.

————. *King Richard II*. London: Rubicon, 1990.

Bothwell, J. S., ed. *The Age of Edward III*. York, UK: York Medieval Press and Boydell, 2001.

————. *Edward III and the English Peerage: Royal Patronage, Social Mobility and Political Control in Fourteenth-Century England*. Woodbridge, UK: Boydell, 2004.

————. *Fall from Grace: Reversal of Fortune and the English Nobility, 1075–1455*. Manchester: Manchester University Press, 2008.

Boyle, David. *Blondel's Song: The Capture, Imprisonment and Ransom of Richard the Lionheart*. London: Viking, 2005.

Brand, Paul. *Kings, Barons and Justices: The Making and Enforcement of Legislation in Thirteenth-Century England*. Cambridge: Cambridge University Press, 2003.

Bridge, Antony. *Richard the Lionheart*. London: Grafton, 1989.

Brown, A. L. *The Governance of Late Medieval England, 1272–1461*. London: Arnold, 1989.

Bruce, Marie Louise. *The Usurper King: Henry of Bolingbroke, 1366–99*. London: Rubicon, 1998.

Burley, Peter, Michael Elliott, and Harvey Watson. *The Battles of St. Albans*. Barnsley, UK: Pen and Sword Military, 2007.

Burne, Alfred H. *The Hundred Years War*. London: Penguin, 2002.

Cantor, Norman F. *In the Wake of the Plague: The Black Death and the World It Made*. New York: Free Press, 2001.

————. *The Last Knight: The Twilight of the Middle Ages and the Birth of the Modern Era*. New York: Free Press, 2004.

Carpenter, Christine. *The Wars of the Roses: Politics and the Constitution in England, c1437–1509*. Cambridge: Cambridge University Press, 1997.

Carpenter, David. *The Minority of Henry III*. London: Methuen London, 1990.

——. *The Struggle for Mastery: Britain, 1066–1284.* Oxford: Oxford University Press, 2003.

Chancellor, John. *The Life and Times of Edward I.* London: Weidenfeld & Nicolson, 1981.

Chaplais, Pierre. *Piers Gaveston: Edward II's Adoptive Brother.* Oxford: Clarendon, 1994.

Cheetham, Anthony. *The Wars of the Roses.* London: Cassell, 2000.

Church, S. D., ed. *King John: New Interpretations.* Woodbridge. UK: Boydell, 1999.

Clanchy, M. T. *England and Its Rulers, 1066–1307.* Oxford: Blackwell, 2006.

Crawford, Anne. *The Yorkists: The History of a Dynasty.* London: Continuum, 2007.

Crosland, Margaret. *The Mysterious Mistress: The Life and Legend of Jane Shore.* Stroud, UK: Alan Sutton, 2006.

Crouch, David. *The Image of Aristocracy in Britain, 1000–1300.* London: Routledge, 1992.

Cunningham, Sean. *Richard III: A Royal Enigma.* Richmond, UK: National Archives, 2003.

Curry, Anne. *The Hundred Years War.* Basingstoke, UK: Palgrave Macmillan, 1993.

Danziger, Danny, and John Gillingham. *1215: The Year of Magna Carta.* London: Hodder & Stoughton, 2003.

Davies, R. R. *Domination and Conquest: The Experience of Ireland, Scotland and Wales, 1100–1300.* Cambridge: Cambridge University Press, 2006.

Denholm-Young, N., and Wendy R. Childs, eds. *Vita Edwardi Secundi: The Life of Edward the Second.* Oxford: Oxford University Press, 2005.

Dockray, Keith. *Edward IV: A Sourcebook.* Stroud, UK: Alan Sutton, 1999.

——. *Henry VI and the Wars of the Roses: A Sourcebook.* Stroud, UK: Alan Sutton, 2000.

——. *Richard III: A Sourcebook.* Stroud, UK: Alan Sutton, 1997.

——. *Warrior King: The Life of Henry V.* Stroud, UK: Tempus, 2007.

Dodd, Gwilym, and Douglas Biggs, eds. *Henry IV: The Establishment of the Regime, 1399–1406.* Woodbridge, UK: York Medieval Press in association with Boydell Press, 2003.

Dodd, Gwilym, and Andrew Musson, ed. *The Reign of Edward II: New Perspectives.* Woodbridge, UK: York Medieval Press in association with Boydell Press.

Doherty, Paul. *Isabella and the Strange Death of Edward II.* New York: Carroll & Graf, 2003.

Drewett, Richard, and Mark Redhead. *The Trial of Richard III.* Gloucester: Alan Sutton, 1984.

Falkus, Gila. *The Life and Times of Edward IV.* London: Weidenfeld & Nicolson, 1981.

Fields, Bertram. *Royal Blood: King Richard III and the Mystery of the Princes.* Stroud, UK: Alan Sutton, 2000.

Fletcher, Christopher. *Richard II: Manhood, Youth and Politics, 1377–99.* Oxford: Oxford University Press, 2008.

Flori, Jean. *Richard the Lionheart: King and Knight.* Westport, Conn.: Praeger, 2006.

Frame, Robin. *The Political Development of the British Isles, 1100–1400*. Oxford: Clarendon, 1995.

Gill, Louise. *Richard III and Buckingham's Rebellion*. Stroud, UK: Alan Sutton, 1999.

Gillingham, John. *The Angevin Empire*. London: Edward Arnold, 2001.

———. *The English in the Twelfth Century: Imperialism, National Identity and Political Values*. Woodbridge, UK: Boydell, 2000.

———. *Richard I*. New Haven, Conn.: Yale University Press, 2002.

———. *Richard the Lionheart*. London: Weidenfeld & Nicolson, 1989.

———. *The Wars of the Roses: Peace and Conflict in 15th Century England*. London: Phoenix, 2001.

Given-Wilson, Chris, and Alice Curteis. *The Royal Bastards of Medieval England*. London: Routledge, 1988.

Goodman, Anthony. *John of Gaunt: Exercise of Princely Power in Fourteenth-Century Europe*. Harlow, UK: Longman, 1992.

———. *The Wars of the Roses: Military Activity and English Society, 1452–97*. London: Routledge & Kegan Paul, 1990.

Goodman, Anthony, and James Gillespie, eds. *Richard II: The Art of Kingship*. Oxford: Clarendon, 1999.

Gordon, Dillian, Lisa Monnas, and Caroline Elam, eds. *The Regal Image of Richard II and the Wilton Diptych*. Coventry: Harvey Miller, 1997.

Gregory, Kristiana. *Eleanor of Aquitaine*. New York: Scholastic, 2002.

Griffiths, R. A. *The Reign of King Henry VI*. Stroud, UK: Alan Sutton, 1998.

Haigh, Philip A. *The Battle of Wakefield*. Stroud, UK: Alan Sutton, 1996.

———. *The Military Campaigns of the Wars of the Roses*. Conshohocken, Pa.: Combined Books, 1997.

———. *From Wakefield to Towton: The Wars of the Roses*. Barnsley, UK: Leo Cooper, 2002.

Haines, Roy Martin. *Death of a King: An Account of the Supposed Escape and Afterlife of Edward of Caernarvon, Formerly Edward II, King of England, Lord of Ireland, Duke of Aquitaine*. Scotforth, UK: Scotforth Books, 2002.

———. *King Edward II: Edward of Caernarfon, His Life, His Reign, and Its Aftermath, 1284–1330*. Montreal: McGill-Queen's University Press, 2003.

Hallam, Elizabeth, ed. *The Plantagenet Encyclopedia*. New York: Grove Weidenfeld, 1990.

Hammond, P. W., and Anne F. Sutton. *Richard III: The Road to Bosworth Field*. London: Constable, 1985.

Hancock, Peter A. *Richard III and the Murder in the Tower*. Stroud, UK: History Press, 2009.

Harding, Alan. *England in the Thirteenth Century*. Cambridge: Cambridge University Press, 1993.

Harriss, G. L., ed. *Henry V: The Practice of Kingship*. Stroud, UK: Alan Sutton, 1993.

———. *Shaping the Nation: England, 1360–1461*. Oxford: Clarendon, 2005.

Hibbert, Christopher. *Agincourt*. New York: Cooper Square, 2000.

Hicks, Michael. *Anne Neville: Queen to Richard III*. Stroud, UK: Tempus, 2007.

——. *Edward IV*. London: Hodder Arnold, 2004.

——. *Edward V: The Prince in the Tower*. Stroud, UK: Tempus, 2003.

——. *The Prince in the Tower: The Short Life & Mysterious Disappearance of Edward V*. Stroud, UK: Tempus, 2007.

——. *Richard III*. Stroud, UK: Tempus, 2003.

——. *Warwick the Kingmaker*. Oxford: Blackwell, 1998.

Hilton, Lisa. *Queens Consort: England's Medieval Queens*. London: Weidenfeld & Nicolson, 2008.

Horrox, Rosemary, ed. *Richard III and the North*. Hull, UK: University of Hull, 1986.

Horrox, Rosemary. *Richard III: A Study of Service*. Cambridge: Cambridge University Press, 1989.

Hosler, John D. *Henry II: A Medieval Soldier at War, 1147–1189*. Leiden: Brill, 2007.

Howell, Margaret. *Eleanor of Provence: Queenship in Thirteenth-Century England*. Oxford: Blackwell, 1998.

Hudson, John. *The Formation of the English Common Law: Law and Society in England from the Norman Conquest to Magna Carta*. London: Longman, 1996.

Hughes, Jonathan. *Arthurian Myths and Alchemy: The Kingship of Edward IV*. Stroud, UK: Alan Sutton, 2002.

——. *The Religious Life of Richard III: Piety and Prayer in the North of England*. Stroud, UK: Alan Sutton, 1997.

Huscroft, Richard. *Ruling England: 1042–1217*. Harlow: Pearson/Longman, 2005.

Hutton, William. *The Battle of Bosworth Field*. Stroud, UK: Tempus, 1999.

James, Thomas Beaumont. *The Palaces of Medieval England, c1050–1550: Royalty, Nobility, the Episcopate and Their Residences from Edward the Confessor to Henry VIII*. London: Seaby, 1990.

Johnson, P. A. *Richard, Duke of York, 1411–1460*. Oxford: Clarendon, 1988.

Jones, Michael K. *Agincourt: Battlefield Guide*. Barnsley, UK: Pen and Sword Military, 2005.

——. *Bosworth, 1485: Psychology of a Battle*. Stroud, UK: Tempus, 2002.

Jones, Michael K., and Malcolm G. Underwood. *The King's Mother: Lady Margaret Beaufort, Countess of Richmond and Derby*. Cambridge: Cambridge University Press, 1993.

Kendall, Paul Murray. *Richard the Third*. New York: Norton, 2002.

Kleineke, Hannes. *Edward IV*. London: Routledge, 2009.

Lamb, V. B. *The Betrayal of Richard III*. Stroud, UK: Alan Sutton, 1990.

Laynesmith, J. L. *The Last Medieval Queens: English Queenship, 1445–1503*. Oxford: Oxford University Press, 2004.

Maddicott, J. R. *Simon de Montfort*. Cambridge: Cambridge University Press, 1994.

Maurer, Helen E. *Margaret of Anjou: Queenship and Power in Late Medieval England*. Woodbridge, UK: Boydell, 2003.

McLynn, Frank. *Lionheart and Lackland: King Richard, King John and the Wars of Conquest*. London: Jonathan Cape, 2006.

Meade, Marion. *Eleanor of Aquitaine: A Biography*. London: Phoenix, 2002.

Miller, David. *Richard the Lionheart: The Mighty Crusader*. London: Phoenix, 2005.

Mitchell, Mairin. *Berengaria: Enigmatic Queen of England.* Burwash Weald, UK: A. Wright.

Morris, Marc. *A Great and Terrible King: Edward I and the Forging of Britain.* London: Hutchinson, 2008.

Mortimer, Ian. *The Fears of Henry IV: The Life of England's Self-Made King.* London: Jonathan Cape, 2007.

——. *The Greatest Traitor: The Life of Sir Roger Mortimer, Ruler of England, 1327–1330.* New York: Thomas Dunne, 2006.

——. *The Perfect King: The Life of Edward III, Father of the English Nation.* London: Jonathan Cape, 2006.

Mortimer, Richard. *Angevin England, 1154–1258.* Oxford: Blackwell, 1994.

Munby, Julian, Richard Barber, and Richard Brown. *Edward III's Round Table at Windsor: The House of the Round Table and the Windsor Festival of 1344.* Woodbridge, UK: Boydell, 2007.

Musson, A., and W. A. Ormrod. *The Evolution of English Justice: Law, Politics and Society in the Fourteenth Century.* New York: St. Martin's, 1999.

Neillands, Robin. *The Hundred Years' War.* London: Routledge, 2001.

——. *The Wars of the Roses.* London: Cassell, 1992.

Nelson, Janet L., ed. *Richard Coeur de Lion in History and Myth.* London: King's College, 1992.

Nicholson, Helen J., ed. *The Chronicle of the Third Crusade: A Translation of the Itinerarium Peregrinorum et Gesta Regis Ricardi.* Aldershot, UK: Ashgate, 1997.

Nicolle, David. *Crécy 1346: Triumph of the Longbow.* Westport, Conn.: Praeger, 2005.

Okerlund, Arlene. *Elizabeth Wydeville: England's Slandered Queen.* Stroud, UK: Tempus, 2006.

Ormrod, W. M. *Edward III.* Stroud, UK: Tempus, 2005.

Owen, D. D. R. *Eleanor of Aquitaine: Queen and Legend.* Oxford: Blackwell, 1993.

Packe, Michael. *King Edward III.* London: Routledge & Kegan Paul, 1983.

Parsons, John Carmi. *Eleanor of Castile: Queen and Society in Thirteenth-Century England.* New York: St. Martin's, 1995.

Pollard, A. J. *Richard III and the Princes in the Tower.* Stroud, UK: Alan Sutton, 2002.

——. *The Wars of the Roses.* Basingstoke, UK: Palgrave, 2001.

Pool, Austin Lane. *From Domesday Book to Magna Carta, 1087–1216.* Oxford: Oxford University Press, 1993.

Potter, Jeremy. *Good King Richard?: An Account of Richard III and His Reputation, 1483–1983.* London: Constable, 1983.

Prestwich, Michael. *Edward I.* New Haven, Conn.: Yale University Press, 1997.

——. *Plantagenet England: 1225–1360.* Oxford: Oxford University Press, 2005.

——. *The Three Edwards: War and State in England, 1272–1377.* New York: Routledge, 2003.

——. *War, Politics and Finance under Edward I.* Aldershot, UK: Gregg Revivals, 1991.

Reeves, A. C. *Lancastrian Englishmen*. Washington, D.C.: University Press of America, 1981.

Regan, Geoffrey. *Lionhearts: Saladin and Richard I*. London: Constable, 1998.

Reston, James. *Warriors of God: Richard the Lionheart and Saladin in the Third Crusade*. New York: Doubleday, 2001.

Reuter, Timothy, ed. *Warriors and Churchmen in the High Middle Ages: Essays Presented to Karl Leyser*. London: Hambledon, 1992.

Richardson, Douglas. *Magna Carta: A Study in Colonial and Medieval Families*. Baltimore, Md.: Genealogical Publishing, 2005.

——. *Plantagenet Ancestry: A Study in Colonial and Medieval Families*. Baltimore, Md.: Genealogical Publishing, 2004.

Richardson, H. G., and G. O. Sayles. *The English Parliament in the Middle Ages*. London: Hambledon, 1981.

Rogers, Clifford J. *War Cruel and Sharp: English Strategy under Edward III, 1327–1360*. Woodbridge, UK: Boydell, 2000.

——, ed. *The Wars of Edward III: Sources and Interpretations*. Woodbridge, UK: Boydell, 1999.

Rollason, David, and Michael Prestwich, eds. *The Battle of Neville's Cross*. Stamford, UK: Shaun Tyas, 1998.

Roskell, J. S. *The Impeachment of Michael de la Pole, Earl of Suffolk, in 1386 in the Context of the Reign of Richard II*. Manchester: Manchester University Press, 1984.

Ross, Charles. *Edward IV*. New Haven, Conn.: Yale University Press, 1997.

——. *Richard III*. New Haven, Conn.: Yale University Press, 1999.

Ruvigny and Raineval, Marquis of. *The Plantagenet Roll of the Blood Royal, Being a Complete Table of All the Descendants Now Living of Edward III, King of England*. 4 vols. Baltimore, Md.: Genealogical Publishing, 1994.

Saaler, Mary. *Edward II, 1307–1327*. London: Rubicon, 1997.

Sapet, Kerrily. *Eleanor of Aquitaine: Medieval Queen*. Greensboro, NC: Morgan Reynolds, 2006.

Saul, Nigel. *Richard II*. New Haven, Conn.: Yale University Press, 1997.

——. *The Three Richards: Richard I, Richard II and Richard III*. London: Hambledon & London, 2005.

Seward, Desmond. *A Brief History of the Hundred Years' War: The English in France, 1337–1453*. London: Robinson, 2003.

——. *Henry V as Warlord*. London: Penguin, 2001.

——. *Henry V: The Scourge of God*. New York: Viking, 1988.

——. *Richard III: England's Black Legend*. London: Penguin, 1997.

Smith, Lacey Baldwin. *This Realm of England, 1399–1688*. Boston: Houghton Mifflin, 2001.

Starkey, David, et al. *The English Court: From the Wars of the Roses to the Civil War*. London: Longman, 1987.

——. *Monarchy: From the Middle Ages to Modernity*. London: HarperPress, 2006.

Storey, Robin. *The End of the House of Lancaster*. Stroud, UK: Alan Sutton, 1999.

Stringer, Keith J. *Earl David of Huntingdon, 1152–1219: A Study in Anglo-Scottish History*. Edinburgh: Edinburgh University Press, 1985.

Sumption, Jonathan. *The Hundred Years War: Trial by Battle*. London: Faber & Faber, 1999.

———. *The Hundred Years War II: Trial by Fire*. Philadelphia: University of Pennsylvania Press, 2001.

Sutton, Anne F., and Peter W. Hammond, eds. *The Coronation of Richard III: The Extant Documents*. New York: St. Martin's, 1984.

Sutton, Anne F., and Livia Visser-Fuchs. *The Hours of Richard III*. Stroud, UK: Alan Sutton, 1990.

———. *Richard III's Books: Ideal and Reality in the Life and Library of a Medieval Prince*. Stroud, UK: Alan Sutton, 1997.

Swabey, Ffiona. *Eleanor of Aquitaine, Courtly Love and the Troubadours*. Westport, Conn.: Greenwood Press, 2004.

Tatton-Brown, Tim, and Richard Mortimer, eds. *Westminster Abbey: The Lady Chapel of Henry VII*. Woodbridge, UK: Boydell, 2003.

Taylor, John, and Wendy Childs, eds. *Politics and Crisis in Fourteenth-Century England*. Stroud, UK: Alan Sutton, 1990.

Tittler, Robert, and Norman Jones, ed. *A Companion to Tudor Britain*. Malden, Mass.: Wiley-Blackwell, 2009.

Trindade, Ann. *Berengaria: In Search of Richard the Lionheart's Queen*. Dublin: Four Courts Press, 1999.

Turner, Ralph V. *Eleanor of Aquitaine: Queen of France, Queen of England*. New Haven, Conn.: Yale University Press, 2009.

———. *King John*. New Haven, Conn.: Yale University Press, 1997.

Turner, Ralph, and Richard Heiser. *The Reign of Richard Lionheart: Ruler of the Angevin Empire, 1189–1199*. New York: Longman, 2000.

Underhill, Frances A. *For Her Good Estate: The Life of Elizabeth de Burgh*. New York: St. Martin's, 1999.

Vale, J. *Edward III and Chivalry: Chivalric Society and Its Context, 1270–1350*. Woodbridge, UK: Boydell, 1982.

Walker, Simon. *The Lancastrian Affinity, 1361–1399*. Oxford: Clarendon, 1990.

Warren, W. L. *Henry II*. New Haven, Conn.: Yale University Press, 2000.

———. *King John*. New Haven, Conn.: Yale University Press, 1997.

Watson, Fiona J. *Under the Hammer: Edward I and Scotland, 1286–1306*. East Linton, UK: Tuckwell, 1998.

Watts, John. *Henry VI and the Politics of Kingship*. Cambridge: Cambridge University Press, 1996.

Waugh, Scott L. *England in the Reign of Edward III*. Cambridge: Cambridge University Press, 1991.

———. *The Lordship of England: Royal Wardships and Marriages in English Society and Politics, 1217–1327*. Princeton, N.J.: Princeton University Press, 1988.

Weightman, Christine. *Margaret of York, Duchess of Burgundy, 1446–1503*. Stroud, UK: Alan Sutton, 1993.

Weir, Alison. *Eleanor of Aquitaine: A Life*. New York: Ballantine, 2000.

——. *Isabella: She-Wolf of France, Queen of England.* London: Cape, 2005.

——. *Mistress of the Monarchy: The Life of Katherine Swynford, Duchess of Lancaster.* New York: Ballantine, 2009.

——. *The Princes in the Tower.* New York: Ballantine, 1994.

——. *The Wars of the Roses.* New York: Ballantine, 1995.

Wheeler, Bonnie, and John Carmi Parsons, eds. *Eleanor of Aquitaine: Lord and Lady.* New York: Palgrave Macmillan, 2002.

Williamson, Audrey. *The Mystery of the Princes.* Stroud, UK: Alan Sutton, 2002.

Wolffe, Bertram. *Henry VI.* New Haven, Conn.: Yale University Press, 2001.

Wood, Charles T. *Joan of Arc and Richard III: Sex, Saints and Government in the Middle Ages.* New York: Oxford University Press, 1991.

## HOUSE OF TUDOR

Alford, Stephen. *Burghley: William Cecil at the Court of Elizabeth I.* New Haven, Conn.: Yale University Press, 2008.

——. *The Early Elizabethan Polity: William Cecil and the British Succession Crisis, 1558–1569.* Cambridge: Cambridge University Press, 1998.

——. *Kinship and Politics in the Reign of King Edward VI.* Cambridge: Cambridge University Press, 2002.

Anglo, Sydney. *Images of Tudor Kingship.* London: Seaby, 1992.

——. *Spectacle, Pageantry and Early Tudor Policy.* Oxford: Oxford University Press, 1997.

Arnold, Janet. *Queen Elizabeth's Wardrobe Unlocked: The Inventories of the Wardrobe of Robes Prepared in 1600.* Leeds, UK: Maney, 1988.

Arthurson, Ian. *The Perkin Warbeck Conspiracy, 1491–1499.* Stroud, UK: Alan Sutton, 1994.

Ashdown, Dulcie M. *Tudor Cousins: Rivals for the Throne.* Stroud, UK: Alan Sutton, 2000.

Bacon, Francis. *The History of the Reign of King Henry VII.* London: Hesperus, 2007.

Baldwin, David. *Stoke Field: The Last Battle of the Wars of the Roses.* Barnsley, UK: Pen and Sword Military, 2006.

Beem, Charles, ed. *The Royal Minorities of Medieval and Early Modern England.* New York: Palgrave Macmillan, 2008.

Bennett, Michael J. *Lambert Simnel and the Battle of Stoke.* New York: St. Martin's, 1987.

Bernard, G. W. *The King's Reformation: Henry VIII and the Remaking of the English Church.* New Haven, Conn.: Yale University Press, 2005.

——. *Power and Politics in Tudor England.* Aldershot, UK: Ashgate, 2000.

——. *The Tudor Nobility.* Manchester: Manchester University Press, 1992.

——. *War, Taxation and Rebellion in Early Tudor England: Henry VIII, Wolsey and the Amicable Grant of 1525.* New York: St. Martin's, 1986.

Bernard, G. W., and S. J. Gunn, eds. *Authority and Consent in Tudor England: Essays Presented to C. S. L. Davies.* Aldershot, UK: Ashgate, 2002.

Bevan, Bryan. *Henry VII: The First Tudor King.* London: Rubicon, 2000.

Boehrer, Bruce Thomas. *Monarchy and Incest in Renaissance England: Literature, Culture, Kinship and Kingship.* Philadelphia: University of Pennsylvania Press, 1992.

Brigden, Susan. *New Worlds, Lost Worlds: The Rule of the Tudors, 1485–1603.* New York: Viking, 2001.

Brimacombe, Peter. *All the Queen's Men: The World of Elizabeth I.* New York: St. Martin's, 2000.

Britnell, Richard. *The Closing of the Middle Ages?: England, 1471–1529.* Oxford: Blackwell, 1997.

Buchanan, Patricia Hill. *Margaret Tudor, Queen of Scots.* Edinburgh: Scottish Academic Press, 1985.

Carley, James P. *The Books of King Henry VIII and His Wives.* London: British Library, 2004.

Carlton, Charles, et al., eds. *State, Sovereigns and Society in Early Modern England: Essays in Honour of A. J. Slavin.* New York: St. Martin's, 1998.

Carpenter, Christine. *The Wars of the Roses: Politics and the Constitution in England, c1437–1509.* Cambridge: Cambridge University Press, 1997.

Chapman, Hester W. *Lady Jane Grey: October 1537–February 1554.* London: Grafton, 1985.

——. *The Last Tudor King: A Study of Edward VI (October 12th, 1537–July 6th, 1553).* Bath, UK: Chivers, 1982.

Childs, Jessie. *Henry VIII's Last Victim: The Life and Times of Henry Howard, Earl of Surrey.* London: Jonathan Cape, 2006.

Chrimes, S. B. *Henry VII.* New Haven, Conn.: Yale University Press, 1999.

Coleman, Christopher, and David Starkey, eds. *Revolution Reassessed: Revisions in the History of Tudor Government and Administration.* Oxford: Clarendon, 1986.

Cook, Faith. *Lady Jane Grey: Nine Day Queen of England.* Darlington: Evangelical Press, 2005.

Cross, Claire, et al., eds. *Law and Government under the Tudors: Essays Presented to Sir Geoffrey Elton on the Occasion of His Retirement.* Cambridge: Cambridge University Press, 1988.

Cunningham, Sean. *Henry VII.* London: Routledge, 2007.

Davis, Catherine. *A Religion of the Word: The Defence of the Reformation in the Reign of King Edward VI.* Manchester: Manchester University Press, 2002.

De Lisle, Leanda. *After Elizabeth: The Rise of James of Scotland and the Struggle for the Throne of England.* New York: Ballantine, 2005.

Denny, Joanna. *Anne Boleyn: A New Life of England's Tragic Queen.* Cambridge, Mass.: Da Capo, 2007.

——. *Katherine Howard: A Tudor Conspiracy.* London: Portrait, 2005.

Dickens, Arthur Geoffrey. *The English Reformation.* University Park: University of Pennsylvania Press, 1991.

Doran, Susan. *Monarchy and Matrimony: The Courtships of Elizabeth I*. London: Routledge, 1996.

———. *Queen Elizabeth I*. London: British Library, 2003.

Doran, Susan, and Thomas S. Freeman, eds. *Mary Tudor: Old and New Perspectives*. Basingstoke, UK: Palgrave Macmillan, 2009.

———. *The Myth of Elizabeth*. Basingstoke, UK: Palgrave Macmillan, 2003.

———. *Tudors and Stuarts on Film: Historical Perspectives*. Basingstoke, UK: Palgrave Macmillan, 2009.

Duffy, Eamon, and David Loades. *The Church of Mary Tudor*. Aldershot, UK: Ashgate, 2006.

Dunn, Jane. *Elizabeth and Mary: Cousins, Rivals, Queens*. New York: Knopf, 2004.

Durant, David N. *Bess of Hardwick: Portrait of an Elizabethan Dynast*. London: Peter Owen, 1999.

Edwards, Francis. *Plots and Plotters in the Reign of Elizabeth I*. Dublin: Four Courts Press, 2002.

———. *The Succession, Bye and Main Plots of 1601–1603*. Dublin: Four Courts Press, 2005.

Edwards, Philip. *The Making of the Modern English State, 1460–1660*. Basingstoke, UK: Palgrave, 2001.

Ellis, Steven G. *Tudor Frontiers and Noble Power: The Making of the British State*. Oxford: Clarendon, 1995.

Elton, Geoffrey R. *England under the Tudors*. London: Routledge, 1991.

———. *Great Harry*. London: Dent, 1980.

Erickson, Carolly. *Bloody Mary: The Life of Mary Tudor*. New York: Quill/William Morrow, 1993.

———. *The First Elizabeth*. New York: St. Martin's, 1997.

———. *Mistress Anne*. New York: St. Martin's Griffin. 1998.

Fincham, Kenneth. *Prelate as Pastor: The Episcopate of James I*. Oxford: Clarendon, 1990.

Fraser, Antonia. *The Wives of Henry VIII*. New York: Knopf, 1992.

Fritze, Ronald H., Geoffrey Elton, and Walter Sutton, eds. *Historical Dictionary of Tudor England, 1485–1603*. Westport, Conn.: Greenwood Press, 1991.

George, C. H. L., and Julie Sutherland, eds. *Heroes and Villains: The Creation and Propagation of an Image*. Durham, UK: Centre for Seventeenth Century Studies, 2004.

Given-Wilson, Chris, and Alice Curteis. *The Royal Bastards of Medieval England*. London: Routledge, 1988.

Graves, Michael A. R. *Elizabethan Parliaments, 1559–1601*. New York: Longman, 1996.

———. *Henry VIII: A Study in Kingship*. London: Longman, 2003.

Griffiths, Ralph A., and Roger S. Thomas. *The Making of the Tudor Dynasty*. New York: St. Martin's, 2005.

Gristwood, Sarah. *Arbella: England's Lost Queen*. Boston: Houghton Mifflin, 2005.

———. *Elizabeth and Leicester*. New York: Viking, 2007.

Gunn, S. J. *Early Tudor Government, 1485–1558*. New York: St. Martin's, 1995.

Gunn, S. J., and P. G. Lindley, eds. *Cardinal Wolsey: Church, State and Art.* Cambridge: Cambridge University Press, 1991.

Guth, DeLloyd J., and John W. McKenna, eds. *Tudor Rule and Revolution: Essays for G. R. Elton from His American Friends.* Cambridge: Cambridge University Press, 1982.

Guy, John, ed. *The Reign of Elizabeth I: Court and Culture in the Last Decade.* Cambridge: Cambridge University Press, 1995.

———. *Thomas More.* London: Arnold, 2000.

———. *Tudor England.* Oxford: Oxford University Press, 1988.

———. *The Tudor Monarchy.* London: Arnold, 1997.

———. *The Tudors: A Very Short Introduction.* Oxford: Oxford University Press, 2000.

Haigh, Christopher. *Elizabeth I.* Harlow, UK: Longman, 2000.

———. *English Reformations: Religion, Politics and Society under the Tudors.* Oxford: Clarendon, 1993.

———, ed. *The Reign of Elizabeth I.* Athens, Ga.: University of Georgia Press, 1985.

Hamer, Colin. *Anne Boleyn: One Short Life That Changed the English-Speaking World.* Leominster, UK: Day One, 2007.

Hammer, Paul E. J. *Elizabeth's Wars: War, Government and Society in Tudor England, 1544–1604.* New York: Palgrave Macmillan, 2003.

———. *The Polarisation of Elizabethan Politics: The Political Career of Robert Devereux, 2nd Earl of Essex, 1585–1597.* Cambridge: Cambridge University Press, 2005.

Harrison, G. B., ed. *The Letters of Elizabeth.* Westport, Conn.: Greenwood Press, 1981.

Hibbert, Christopher. *The Virgin Queen: Elizabeth I, Genius of the Golden Age.* Reading, Mass.: Addison-Wesley, 1991.

Hilliam, Paul. *Elizabeth I: Queen of England's Golden Age.* New York: Rosen, 2005.

Hilton, Lisa. *Queens Consort: England's Medieval Queens.* London: Weidenfeld & Nicolson, 2008.

Hoyle, R. W. *The Estates of the English Crown, 1558–1640.* Cambridge: Cambridge University Press, 1992.

———. *The Pilgrimage of Grace and the Politics of the 1530s.* Oxford: Oxford University Press, 2001.

Hudson, Winthrop S. *The Cambridge Connection and the Elizabethan Settlement of 1559.* Durham, N.C.: Duke University Press, 1980.

Hunt, Jocelyn, and Carolyn Hill. *The Mid-Tudor Years.* Harlow, UK: Longman, 2001.

Hunt, Jocelyn, and Carolyn Towle. *Henry VII.* Harlow, UK: Longman, 1998.

Hutchinson, Robert. *The Last Days of Henry VIII: Conspiracy, Treason and Heresy at the Court of the Dying Tyrant.* London: Weidenfeld & Nicolson, 2005.

Ives, Eric Williams. *Henry VIII.* Oxford: Oxford University Press, 2007.

———. *Lady Jane Grey: A Tudor Mystery.* Oxford: Wiley-Blackwell, 2009.

———. *The Life and Death of Anne Boleyn: "The Most Happy."* Malden, Mass.: Blackwell, 2004.

James, Susan. *Catherine Parr: Henry VIII's Last Love*. Stroud, UK: History Press, 2009.

James, Thomas Beaumont. *The Palaces of Medieval England, c1050–1550: Royalty, Nobility, the Episcopate and Their Residences from Edward the Confessor to Henry VIII*. London: Seaby, 1990.

Jones, Michael K. *Bosworth, 1485: Psychology of a Battle*. Stroud, UK: Tempus, 2002.

Jones, Michael K., and Malcolm G. Underwood. *The King's Mother: Lady Margaret Beaufort, Countess of Richmond and Derby*. Cambridge: Cambridge University Press, 1992.

Kinney, Arthur F., and David W. Swain, eds. *Tudor England: An Encyclopedia*. New York: Garland, 2001.

Knighton, C. S., ed. *Calendar of State Papers: Domestic Series of the Reign of Edward VI, 1547–1553, Preserved in the Public Record Office*. London: Her Majesty's Stationery Office, 1992.

———, ed. *Calendar of State Papers: Domestic Series of the Reign of Mary I, 1553–1558, Preserved in the Public Record Office*. London: Public Record Office, 1998.

Laynesmith, J. L. *The Last Medieval Queens: English Queenship, 1445–1503*. Oxford: Oxford University Press, 2004.

Lee, Christopher. *1603: The Death of Elizabeth I and the Birth of the Stuart Era*. London: Review, 2003.

Lindsey, Karen. *Divorced, Beheaded, Survived: A Feminist Reinterpretation of the Wives of Henry VIII*. Reading, Mass.: Addison-Wesley, 1995.

Little, Crawford. *Union of Crowns: The Forging of Europe's Most Independent State*. Glasgow: Neil Wilson, 2003.

Lloyd, Christopher, and Simon Thurley. *Henry VIII: Images of a Tudor King*. Oxford: Phaidon, 1995.

Loach, Jennifer. *Edward VI*. New Haven, Conn.: Yale University Press, 1999.

Loades, David. *The Cecils: Privilege and Power behind the Throne*. London: National Archives, 2007.

———. *Elizabeth I: The Golden Age of Gloriana*. London: Public Record Office, 2003.

———. *Essays on the Reign of Edward VI*. Oxford: Davenant, 2003.

———. *Henry VIII: Court, Church and Conflict*. Kew, UK: National Archives, 2007.

———. *Henry VIII and His Queens*. Stroud, UK: Alan Sutton, 2000.

———. *Intrigue and Treason: The Tudor Court, 1547–1558*. Harlow, UK: Longman/Pearson, 2004.

———. *Mary Tudor: The Tragical History of the First Queen of England*. London: National Archives, 2006.

———. *The Mid-Tudor Crisis*. New York: St. Martin's, 1992.

———. *The Politics of Marriage: Henry VIII and His Queens*. Stroud, UK: Alan Sutton, 1994.

———. *Power in Tudor England*. New York: St. Martin's, 1997.

———. *The Tudor Court*. Bangor, UK: Headstart, 1992.

———. *Tudor Government: Structures of Authority in the Sixteenth Century*. Oxford: Blackwell, 1997.

———. *Tudor Queens of England*. London: Continuum, 2009.

———, ed. *The Tudor Chronicles*. New York: Grove Weidenfeld, 1990.

———, ed. *Chronicles of the Tudor Kings*. Godalming, UK: Bramley, 1996.

———, ed. *Chronicles of the Tudor Queens*. Stroud, UK: Alan Sutton, 2002.

Lockyer, Roger. *Tudor and Stuart Britain, 1485–1714*. New York: Longman/Pearson Education, 2004.

Lockyer, Roger, and Andrew Thrush. *Henry VII*. New York: Addison-Wesley Longman, 1997.

Lovell, Mary S. *Bess of Hardwick: Empire Builder*. New York: Norton, 2006.

Luke, Mary. *The Nine Days Queen: A Portrait of Lady Jane Grey*. New York: William Morrow, 1986.

MacCaffrey, Wallace T. *Elizabeth I: War and Politics, 1588–1603*. Princeton, N.J.: Princeton University Press, 1992.

———. *Queen Elizabeth and the Making of Policy, 1572–1588*. Princeton, N.J.: Princeton University Press, 1981.

MacCulloch, Diarmid. *The Boy King: Edward VI and the Protestant Reformation*. Berkeley, Calif.: University of California Press, 2002.

———, ed. *The Reign of Henry VIII: Politics, Policy, and Piety*. New York: St. Martin's, 1995.

Mackie, J. D. *The Earlier Tudors, 1485–1558*. Oxford: Oxford University Press, 1994.

Marcus, Leah S., et al., eds. *Elizabeth I: Collected Works*. Chicago: University of Chicago Press, 2002.

Marshall, Rosalind K. *Elizabeth I*. Owings Mills, Md.: Stemmer House, 1991.

McCaffrey, Wallace. *Elizabeth I*. London: Edward Arnold, 1993.

McCullough, Peter E. *Sermons at Court: Politics and Religion in Elizabethan and Jacobean Preaching*. Cambridge: Cambridge University Press, 1998.

McDiarmid, John F., ed. *The Monarchical Republic of Early Modern England: Essays in Response to Patrick Collinson*. Aldershot, UK: Ashgate, 2007.

McGurk, John. *The Tudor Monarchies, 1485–1603*. Cambridge: Cambridge University Press, 1999.

McLaren, A. N. *Political Culture in the Reign of Elizabeth I: Queen and Commonwealth, 1558–1585*. Cambridge: Cambridge University Press, 1999.

Morrill, John, ed. *The Oxford Illustrated History of Tudor and Stuart Britain*. Oxford: Oxford University Press, 1996.

Mortimer, Ian. *The Fears of Henry IV: The Life of England's Self-Made King*. London: Jonathan Cape, 2007.

Muhlstein, Anka. *Elizabeth I and Mary Stuart: The Problems of Marriage*. London: Haus, 2007.

Neale, John E. *Queen Elizabeth I*. London: Pimlico, 1998.

Norrington, Ruth. *In the Shadow of the Throne: The Lady Arbella Stuart*. London: Peter Owen, 2002.

Norton, Elizabeth. *Anne Boleyn: Henry VIII's Obsession*. Stroud, UK: Amberley, 2008.

Patterson, Benton Rain. *With the Heart of a King: Elizabeth I of England, Philip II of Spain and the Fight for a Nation's Soul and Crown*. New York: St. Martin's, 2007.

Perry, Maria. *Sisters to the King: The Tumultuous Lives of Henry VIII's Sisters; Margaret of Scotland and Mary of France*. London: Andre Deutsch, 2002.

——, compiler. *The Word of a Prince: A Life of Elizabeth I from Contemporary Documents*. Woodbridge, UK: Boydell, 1990.

Plowden, Alison. *Elizabeth I*. Stroud, UK: Alan Sutton, 2004.

——. *Elizabeth Tudor and Mary Stewart: Two Queens in One Isle*. Totowa, N.J.: Barnes & Noble, 1984.

——. *The House of Tudor*. Stroud, UK: Alan Sutton, 1998.

——. *Lady Jane Grey and the House of Suffolk*. New York: F. Watts, 1986.

——. *Tudor Women: Queens and Commoners*. Stroud, UK: Alan Sutton, 1998.

——. *Two Queens in One Isle: The Deadly Relationship of Elizabeth I & Mary Queen of Scots*. Brighton, UK: Harvester, 1984.

Porter, Linda. *The First Queen of England: The Myth of "Bloody Mary."* New York: St. Martin's, 2008.

Prescott, H. F. M. *Mary Tudor: The Spanish Tudor*. London: Phoenix, 2003.

Randell, Keith. *Elizabeth I and the Government of England*. London: Hodder & Stoughton, 1994.

Rees, David. *The Son of Prophecy: Henry Tudor's Road to Bosworth*. Ruthin, UK: John Jones, 1997.

Rex, Richard. *Elizabeth: Fortune's Bastard?* Stroud, UK: Tempus, 2007.

——. *The Tudors*. Stroud, UK: Tempus, 2002.

Ridley, Jasper. *Bloody Mary's Martyrs: The Story of England's Terror*. New York: Carroll & Graf, 2001.

——. *A Brief History of the Tudor Age*. New York: Carroll & Graf, 2002.

——. *Elizabeth I: The Shrewdness of Virtue*. New York: Fromm International, 1989.

——. *Henry VIII*. New York: Fromm International, 1986.

Ross, Josephine. *The Men Who Would Be King: Suitors to Queen Elizabeth I*. London: Phoenix, 2005.

Routh, C. R. N. *Who's Who in Tudor England*. Mechanicsburg, Pa.: Stackpole Books, 2001.

Scarisbrick, J. J. *Henry VIII*. New Haven, Conn.: Yale University Press, 1997.

Seel, Graham E., and David L. Smith. *Crown and Parliaments, 1558–1689*. Cambridge: Cambridge University Press, 2001.

Simon, Linda. *Of Virtue Rare: Margaret Beaufort, Matriarch of the House of Tudor*. Boston: Houghton Mifflin, 1982.

Skidmore, Chris. *Edward VI: The Lost King of England*. New York: St. Martin's, 2007.

Slavin, Arthur J. *The Tudor Age and Beyond: England from the Black Death to the End of the Age of Elizabeth*. Malabar, Fla.: R. E. Krieger, 1987.

Smith, Lacey Baldwin, ed. *Elizabeth I*. St. Louis, Mo.: Forum, 1980.

——. *The Elizabethan World*. Boston: Houghton Mifflin, 1991.

———. *This Realm of England, 1399–1688*. Boston: Houghton Mifflin, 2001.

Somerset, Anne. *Elizabeth I*. New York: Anchor, 2003.

Starkey, David. *Elizabeth: Apprenticeship*. London: Vintage, 2001.

———. *Henry: Virtuous Prince*. London: HarperPress, 2008.

———. *Henry VIII: A European Court in England*. London: Collins & Brown, 1991.

———. *The Reign of Henry VIII: Personalities and Politics*. London: Vintage, 2002.

———. *Six Wives: The Queens of Henry VIII*. London: Chatto & Windus, 2003.

———, ed. *Rivals in Power: Lives and Letters of the Great Tudor Dynasties*. London: Macmillan London, 1990.

———, et al. *The English Court from the Wars of the Roses to the Civil War*. London: Longman, 1987.

Stater, Victor. *The Political History of Tudor and Stuart England: A Sourcebook*. London: Routledge, 2002.

Steen, Sarah Jayne, ed. *The Letters of Lady Arbella Stuart*. New York: Oxford University Press, 1994.

Stone, Lawrence. *The Causes of the English Revolution, 1529–1642*. London: Ark, 1986.

Strong, Roy. *The Cult of Elizabeth: Elizabethan Portraiture and Pageantry*. Berkeley, Calif.: University of California Press, 1986.

———. *Gloriana: The Portraits of Queen Elizabeth I*. New York: Thames & Hudson, 1987.

———. *Henry, Prince of Wales, and England's Lost Renaissance*. New York: Thames & Hudson, 1986.

———. *The Tudor and Stuart Monarchy: Pageantry, Painting, Iconography*. Vols. 1 (Tudor) and 2 (Elizabethan). Woodbridge, UK: Boydell, 1995.

Stump, Donald, and Susan M. Felch, eds. *Elizabeth I and Her Age: Authoritative Texts, Commentary and Criticism*. New York: Norton, 2009.

Taylor, James D., Jr. *Documents of Lady Jane Grey, Nine Days Queen of England, 1553*. New York: Algora, 2004.

Thompson, Benjamin, ed. *The Reign of Henry VII: Proceedings of the 1993 Harlaxton Symposium*. Stamford, UK: Paul Watkins, 1995.

Thurley, Simon. *The Royal Palaces of Tudor England: Architecture and Court Life, 1460–1547*. New Haven, Conn.: Yale University Press, 1993.

Tittler, Robert. *The Reign of Mary I*. London: Longman, 1991.

Tittler, Robert, and Norman Jones, eds. *A Companion to Tudor Britain*. Malden, Mass.: Wiley-Blackwell, 2009.

Todd, Margo, ed. *Reformation to Revolution: Politics and Religion in Early Modern England*. New York: Routledge, 1995.

Turvey, Roger, and Nigel Heard. *Edward VI and Mary: A Mid-Tudor Crisis? 1540–1558*. London: Hodder & Stoughton, 1991.

Turvey, Roger, and Caroline Rogers. *Henry VII*. London: Hodder Murray, 2005.

Wagner, John A. *Bosworth Field to Bloody Mary: An Encyclopedia of the Early Tudors*. Westport, Conn.: Greenwood Press, 2003.

———. *Encyclopedia of the Hundred Years' War*. Westport, Conn.: Greenwood Press, 2006.

——. *Encyclopedia of the Wars of the Roses*. Santa Barbara, Calif.: ABC-CLIO, 2001.

Warnicke, Retha M. *The Marrying of Anne of Cleves: Royal Protocol in Early Modern England*. New York: Cambridge University Press, 2000.

——. *The Rise and Fall of Anne Boleyn: Family Politics at the Court of King Henry VIII*. New York: Cambridge University Press, 1989.

Watkins, Susan. *Elizabeth I and Her World*. London: Thames & Hudson, 2007.

Weir, Alison. *The Children of Henry VIII*. New York: Ballantine, 2008.

——. *Elizabeth the Queen*. London: Jonathan Cape, 1998.

——. *Henry VIII: The King and His Court*. New York: Ballantine, 2001.

——. *The Life of Elizabeth I*. New York: Ballantine, 2008.

——. *The Six Wives of Henry VIII*. New York: Grove Weidenfeld, 1991.

Wernham, R. B. *The Making of Elizabethan Foreign Policy, 1558–1603*. Berkeley, Calif.: University of California Press, 1980.

Williams, Neville. *The Tudors*. Berkeley, Calif.: University of California Press, 2000.

Williams, Penry. *The Later Tudors: England, 1547–1603*. Oxford: Clarendon, 1995.

Wilson, Derek. *In the Lion's Court: Power, Ambition and Sudden Death in the Reign of Henry VIII*. New York: St. Martin's Griffin, 2003.

——. *The Uncrowned Kings of England: The Black History of the Dudleys and the Tudor Throne*. New York: Carroll & Graf, 2005.

Wooding, Lucy. *Henry VIII*. London: Routledge, 2009.

Woodward, Jennifer. *The Theatre of Death: The Ritual Management of Royal Funerals in Renaissance England, 1570–1625*. Woodbridge, UK: Boydell, 1997.

Wroe, Ann. *Perkin: A Story of Deception*. London: Vintage, 2004.

## HOUSE OF STUART

Alexander, Julia Marciari, and Catherine MacLeod. *Politics, Transgression and Representation at the Court of King Charles I*. New Haven, Conn.: Yale University Press, 2007.

Ashley, Maurice. *Charles I and Oliver Cromwell: A Study in Contrasts and Comparisons*. London: Methuen, 1987.

——. *The Stuarts*. London: Cassell, 2000.

Barratt, John. *Battles for the Three Kingdoms: The Campaigns for England, Scotland and Ireland, 1689–92*. Stroud, UK: Alan Sutton, 2007.

Barroll, Leeds. *Anna of Denmark, Queen of England: A Cultural Biography*. Philadelphia: University of Pennsylvania Press, 2001.

Beauclerk, Charles. *Nell Gwyn: Mistress to a King*. New York: Atlantic Monthly, 2005.

Belloc, Hilaire. *Charles I*. Norfolk, Va.: Gates of Vienna Books, 2003.

Bergeron, David M. *King James & Letters of Homoerotic Desire*. Iowa City: University of Iowa Press, 1999.

——. *Royal Family, Royal Lovers: King James of England and Scotland*. Columbia, Mo.: University of Missouri Press, 1991.

Bevan, Bryan. *King James VI of Scotland and I of England*. London: Rubicon, 1996.

Bingham, Caroline. *James I of England*. London: Weidenfeld & Nicolson, 1981.

Black, Jeremy. *Culloden and the '45*. Gloucester: Alan Sutton, 2000.

Boehrer, Bruce Thomas. *Monarchy and Incest in Renaissance England: Literature, Culture, Kinship and Kingship*. Philadelphia: University of Pennsylvania Press, 1992.

Bongie, L. L. *The Love of a Prince: Bonnie Prince Charlie in France, 1744–1748*. Vancouver: University of British Columbia Press, 1986.

Bucholz, Robert O. *Augustan Court: Queen Anne and the Decline of Court Culture*. Stanford, Calif.: Stanford University Press, 1993.

Burgess, Glenn. *Absolute Monarchy and the Stuart Constitution*. New Haven, Conn.: Yale University Press, 1996.

Burgess, Glenn, Rowland Wymer, and Jason Lawrence. *The Accession of James I: Historical and Cultural Consequences*. Basingstoke, UK: Palgrave Macmillan, 2006.

Callow, John. *James II: The Triumph and the Tragedy*. London: National Archives, 2005.

——. *The King in Exile: James II; Warrior, King and Saint, 1689–1701*. Stroud, UK: Alan Sutton, 2004.

——. *The Making of James II: The Formative Years of a Fallen King*. Stroud, UK: Alan Sutton, 2000.

Carlton, Charles. *Charles I: The Personal Monarch*. London: Routledge, 1995.

——. *Going to the Wars: The Experience of the British Civil Wars, 1638–1651*. London: Routledge, 1992.

——. et al., eds. *State, Sovereigns and Society in Early Modern England: Essays in Honour of A. J. Slavin*. New York: St. Martin's, 1998.

Carpenter, Stanley D. M., ed. *The English Civil War*. Aldershot, UK: Ashgate, 2007.

Carrier, Irene. *James VI and I: King of Great Britain*. Cambridge: Cambridge University Press, 1998.

Childs, John. *The Army, James II and the Glorious Revolution*. New York: St. Martin's, 1980.

Cogswell, Thomas, Richard Cust, and Peter Lake, eds. *Politics, Religion and Popularity in Early Stuart Britain: Essays in Honour of Conrad Russell*. Cambridge: Cambridge University Press, 2002.

Coles, Norman A. *John Ashton's Case for James II as Rightful King of England: Rebellion or Revolution*. Lewiston, N.Y.: Edwin Mellen Press, 1998.

Coote, Stephen. *Royal Survivor: A Life of Charles II*. London: Hodder & Stoughton, 1999.

Corp, Edward. *A Court in Exile: The Stuarts in France, 1689–1718*. Cambridge: Cambridge University Press, 2004.

——. *The Jacobites at Urbino: An Exiled Court in Transition*. Basingstoke, UK: Palgrave Macmillan, 2009.

——, ed. *The Stuart Court in Rome: The Legacy of Exile*. Aldershot, UK: Ashgate, 2003.

Coward, Barry, ed. *A Companion to Stuart Britain*. Malden, Mass.: Wiley-Blackwell, 2009.

Cramsie, John. *Kingship and Crown Finance under James VI and I, 1603–1625*. London: Royal Historical Society, 2002.

Croft, Pauline. *King James*. Basingstoke, UK: Palgrave Macmillan, 2003.

Cruickshanks, Eveline. *The Glorious Revolution*. New York: St. Martin's, 2000.

———, ed. *By Force or by Default: The Revolution of 1688–89*. Edinburgh: John Donald, 1989.

———, ed. *Ideology and Conspiracy: Aspects of Jacobitism, 1689–1759*. Edinburgh: John Donald, 1982.

———, ed. *The Stuart Courts*. Stroud, UK: Alan Sutton, 2000.

Cruickshanks, Eveline, and Edward Corp, eds. *The Stuart Court in Exile and the Jacobites*. Rio Grande, Ohio: Hambledon, 1995.

Cust, Richard. *Charles I: A Political Life*. Harlow, UK: Longman, 2005.

Cust, Richard, and Ann Hughes, eds. *Conflict in Early Stuart England: Studies in Religion and Politics, 1603–1642*. London: Longman, 1989.

Daniels, Christopher W., and John Morrill. *Charles I*. Cambridge: Cambridge University Press, 1988.

De Lisle, Leanda. *After Elizabeth: The Rise of James of Scotland and the Struggle for the Throne of England*. New York: Ballantine, 2005.

Dillon, Patrick. *The Last Revolution: 1688 and the Creation of the Modern World*. London: Jonathan Cape, 2006.

Doelman, J. *King James I and the Religious Culture of England*. Woodbridge, UK: D. S. Brewer, 2000.

Doherty, Richard. *The Williamite War in Ireland, 1688–1691*. Dublin: Four Courts Press, 1998.

Donald, P. *An Uncounselled King: Charles I and the Scottish Troubles, 1637–1641*. Cambridge: Cambridge University Press, 1990.

Doran, Susan, and Thomas S. Freeman, eds. *Tudors and Stuarts on Film: Historical Perspectives*. Basingstoke, UK: Palgrave Macmillan, 2009.

Dougan, David. *To Return a King: Oliver Cromwell to Charles II, 1658–1661*. Bury St. Edmunds, UK: Grove, 2006.

Douglas, Hugh. *The Private Passions of Bonnie Prince Charlie*. Stroud, UK: Alan Sutton, 1998.

Douglas, Hugh, and Michael J. Stead. *The Flight of Bonnie Prince Charlie*. Stroud, UK: Alan Sutton, 2000.

Edwards, Philip. *The Making of the Modern English State, 1460–1660*. Basingstoke, UK: Palgrave, 2001.

Erickson, Carolly. *Bonnie Prince Charlie: A Biography*. New York: William Morrow, 1989.

Fellows, Nicholas. *Charles II and James II*. London: Hodder & Stoughton, 1995.

Fischlin, Daniel, and Mark Fortier, eds. *Royal Subjects: Essays on the Writings of James VI and I*. Detroit: Wayne State University Press, 2002.

Fissel, Mark Charles. *The Bishops' Wars: Charles I's Campaigns against Scotland, 1638–1640*. Cambridge: Cambridge University Press, 1994.

FitzRoy, Charles. *Return of the King: The Restoration of Charles II*. Stroud, UK: Alan Sutton, 2007.

Fraser, Antonia. *Charles I*. London: Phoenix, 2002.

Fritze, Ronald, and William B. Robinson, eds. *Historical Dictionary of Stuart England, 1603–1689*. Westport, Conn.: Greenwood Press, 1996.

Galloway, Bruce. *The Union of England and Scotland, 1603–1608*. Edinburgh: John Donald, 1986.

George, C. H. L., and Julie Sutherland, eds. *Heroes and Villains: The Creation and Propagation of an Image*. Durham, UK: Centre for Seventeenth Century Studies, 2004.

Goldberg, Jonathan. *James I and the Politics of Literature: Jonson, Shakespeare, Donne, and Their Contemporaries*. Baltimore, Md.: Johns Hopkins University Press, 1983.

Goodare, Julian, and Michael Lynch, eds. *The Reign of James VI*. East Linton: Tuckwell Press, 2000.

Gregg, Edward. *Queen Anne*. New Haven, Conn.: Yale University Press, 2001.

Gregg, Pauline. *King Charles I*. London: Dent, 1981.

Grell, Ole Peter, Jonathan I. Israel, and Nicholas Tyacke, eds. *From Persecution to Toleration: The Glorious Revolution and Religion in England*. Oxford: Clarendon, 1991.

Gristwood, Sarah. *Arbella: England's Lost Queen*. Boston: Houghton Mifflin, 2005.

Hanrahan, David C. *Charles II and the Duke of Buckingham: The Merry Monarch and the Aristocratic Rogue*. Stroud, UK: Alan Sutton, 2006.

Harris, Frances. *A Passion for Government: The Life of Sarah, Duchess of Marlborough*. Oxford: Clarendon, 1991.

Harris, Tim. *Politics under the Later Stuarts: Party Politics in a Divided Society*. London: Longman, 1993.

——. *Restoration: Charles II and His Kingdoms, 1660–1685*. London: Penguin, 2006.

——. *Revolution: The Great Crisis of the British Monarchy, 1685–1720*. London: Allen Lane, 2006.

Harris, Tim, Paul Seaward, and Mark Goldie, eds. *The Politics of Religion in Restoration England*. Oxford: Blackwell, 1990.

Hibbert, Christopher. *Cavaliers and Roundheads: The English Civil War, 1642–1649*. New York: Scribner, 1993.

——. *Charles I*. Basingstoke, UK: Palgrave Macmillan, 2007.

Hill, Christopher. *The Century of Revolution, 1603–1714*. London: Routledge, 2002.

Holmes, Clive. *Why Was Charles I Executed?* London: Hambledon Continuum, 2006.

Holmes, Frederick. *The Sickly Stuarts: The Medical Downfall of a Dynasty*. Stroud, UK: Alan Sutton, 2005.

Hook, Michael, and Walter Ross. *The 'Forty-Five: The Last Jacobite Rebellion*. Edinburgh: Her Majesty's Stationery Office, 1995.

Hopkins, Lisa. *Writing Renaissance Queens: Texts by and about Elizabeth I and Mary, Queen of Scots*. Newark: University of Delaware Press, 2002.

Hoppit, Julian. *A Land of Liberty?: England, 1689–1727*. Oxford: Clarendon, 2000.

Houlbrooke, Ralph, ed. *James VI and I: Ideas, Authority and Government*. Aldershot, UK: Ashgate, 2007.

Hoyle, R. W. *The Estates of the English Crown, 1558–1640.* Cambridge: Cambridge University Press, 1992.

Hutton, Ronald. *The British Republic, 1649–1660.* Basingstoke, UK: Macmillan, 2000.

———. *Charles the Second: King of England, Scotland and Ireland.* Oxford: Oxford University Press, 1991.

———. *Debates in Stuart History.* Basingstoke, UK: Palgrave Macmillan, 2004.

———. *The Restoration: A Political and Religious History of England and Wales, 1658–1667.* Oxford: Oxford University Press, 1993.

———. *The Royalist War Effort, 1642–1646.* London: Routledge, 1999.

Israel, Jonathan Irvine, ed. *The Anglo-Dutch Moment: Essays on the Glorious Revolution and Its World Impact.* Cambridge: Cambridge University Press, 2003.

James VI and I. *Letters.* Edited by G. P. V. Akrigg. Berkeley, Calif.: University of California Press, 1984.

———. *Political Writings.* Edited by Johann P. Sommerville. Cambridge: Cambridge University Press, 1994.

Jardine, Lisa. *Going Dutch: How England Plundered Holland's Glory.* London: HarperPress, 2008.

Jones, J. R. *Charles II: Royal Politician.* London: Allen & Unwin, 1987.

———. *The Revolution of 1688 in England.* London: Weidenfeld & Nicolson, 1984.

Keay, Anna. *The Magnificent Monarch: Charles II and the Ceremonies of Power.* London: Continuum, 2008.

Kenyon, J. P., ed. *The Stuart Constitution, 1603–1688: Documents and Commentary.* Cambridge: Cambridge University Press, 1986.

Kenyon, John, and Jane Ohlmeyer, eds. *The Civil Wars: A Military History of England, Scotland and Ireland, 1638–1660.* Oxford: Oxford University Press, 2002.

Kishlansky, Mark. *A Monarchy Transformed: Britain, 1603–1714.* London: Allen Lane, 1996.

Knights, M. *Politics and Opinion in Crisis, 1678–1681.* Cambridge: Cambridge University Press, 1994.

Kybett, Susan Maclean. *Bonnie Prince Charlie: A Biography of Charles Edward Stuart.* New York: Dodd, Mead, 1988.

Lacey, Andrew. *The Cult of King Charles the Martyr.* Woodbridge, UK: Boydell, 2003.

Lagomarsino, David, and Charles T. Wood. *The Trial of Charles I: A Documentary History.* Hanover, N.H.: University Press of New England, 1989.

Lee, Christopher. *1603: The Death of Elizabeth I and the Birth of the Stuart Era.* London: Review, 2003.

Lee, Maurice, Jr. *Government by Pen: Scotland under James VI and I.* Urbana, Ill.: University of Illinois Press, 1980.

———. *Great Britain's Solomon: James VI and I in His Three Kingdoms.* Urbana, Ill.: University of Illinois Press, 1990.

———. *The Road to Revolution: Scotland under Charles I, 1625–37.* Urbana, Ill.: University of Illinois Press, 1985.

——, ed. *The "Inevitable" Union and Other Essays on Early Modern Scotland.* East Linton, UK: Tuckwell, 2003.

Lenihan, Pádraig. *1690: Battle of the Boyne.* Stroud, UK: Tempus, 2003.

Lenman, B. *The Jacobite Cause.* Glasgow: Drew, 1986.

Lindley, David. *The Trials of Frances Howard: Fact and Fiction at the Court of King James.* London: Routledge, 1993.

Little, Crawford. *Union of Crowns: The Forging of Europe's Most Independent State.* Glasgow: Neil Wilson, 2003.

Lockyer, Roger. *The Early Stuarts: A Political History of England, 1603–1642.* New York: Longman, 1999.

——. *James VI and I.* London: Addison Wesley Longman, 1998.

Lord, Evelyn. *The Stuarts' Secret Army: English Jacobites, 1689–1752.* Harlow, UK: Pearson Longman, 2004.

Macinnes, A. I. *Charles I and the Making of the Covenanting Movement, 1625–1641.* Edinburgh: John Donald, 1991.

Maclean, Fitzroy. *Bonnie Prince Charlie.* New York: Atheneum, 1989.

Macleod, John. *Dynasty: The Stuarts, 1560–1807.* New York: St. Martin's, 2001.

Marshall, Alan. *The Age of Faction: Court Politics, 1660–1702.* Manchester: Manchester University Press, 1999.

Marshall, Rosalind K. *Henrietta Maria: The Intrepid Queen.* London: Her Majesty's Stationery Office, 1990.

——. *Mary I.* London: Her Majesty's Stationery Office, 1993.

——. *The Winter Queen: The Life of Elizabeth of Bohemia, 1596–1662.* Edinburgh: National Galleries of Scotland, 1998.

McCullough, Peter E. *Sermons at Court: Politics and Religion in Elizabethan and Jacobean Preaching.* Cambridge: Cambridge University Press, 1998.

McElligott, Jason, ed. *Fear, Exclusion and Revolution: Roger Morrice and Britain in the 1680s.* Aldershot, UK: Ashgate, 2006.

——. *Royalism, Print and Censorship in Revolutionary England.* Woodbridge, UK: Boydell, 2007.

——. *Royalists and Royalism during the English Civil Wars.* Cambridge: Cambridge University Press, 2007.

McLynn, Frank J. *Bonnie Prince Charlie: Charles Edward Stuart.* London: Pimlico, 2003.

——. *The Jacobites.* London: Routledge & Kegan Paul, 1988.

McManus, Clare, ed. *Women and Culture at the Courts of the Stuart Queens.* New York: Palgrave Macmillan, 2003.

Mijers, Esther, and Onnekink, David, eds. *Redefining William III: The Impact of the King-Stadholder in International Context.* Aldershot, UK: Ashgate, 2007.

Miller, John. *After the Civil Wars: Government in the Reign of King Charles II.* New York: Longman, 2000.

——. *Bourbon and Stuart: Kings and Kingship in France and England in the Seventeenth Century.* New York: F. Watts, 1987.

——. *Charles II.* London: Weidenfeld & Nicolson, 1991.

——. *The Glorious Revolution*. London: Longman, 1997.

——. *James II*. New Haven, Conn.: Yale University Press, 2000.

——. *The Restoration and the England of Charles II*. London: Longman, 1997.

——. *The Stuarts*. London: Hambledon & London, 2003.

Monod, Paul Kléber. *Jacobitism and the English People, 1688–1788*. Cambridge: Cambridge University Press, 1989.

Morrah, Patrick. *A Royal Family: Charles I and His Family*. London: Constable, 1982.

Morrill, John, ed. *The Oxford Illustrated History of Tudor and Stuart Britain*. Oxford: Oxford University Press, 1996.

Newton, Diana. *The Making of the Jacobean Regime: James VI and I and the Government of England, 1603–1605*. London: Royal Historical Society, 2005.

Normand, Lawrence, and Gareth Roberts, eds. *Witchcraft in Early Modern Scotland: James VI's Demonology and the North Berwick Witches*. Exeter: Exeter University Press, 2000.

Norrington, Ruth. *In the Shadow of the Throne: The Lady Arbella Stuart*. London: Peter Owen, 2002.

——, commentator. *My Dearest Minette: The Letters between Charles II and His Sister, Henrietta, Duchesse d'Orléans*. London: Peter Owen, 1996.

Ollard, Richard. *The Escape of Charles II after the Battle of Worcester*. London: Constable, 1986.

——. *Image of the King: Charles I and Charles II*. London: Phoenix, 2000.

Oman, Carola. *The Winter Queen: Elizabeth of Bohemia*. London: Phoenix, 2000.

Orr, Clarissa Campbell, ed. *Queenship in Britain, 1660–1837: Royal Patronage, Court, Culture and Dynastic Politics*. Manchester: Manchester University Press, 2009.

Parry, Graham. *The Golden Age Restor'd: The Culture of the Stuart Court, 1603–42*. New York: St. Martin's, 1981.

Patterson, Annabel M. *The Long Parliament of Charles II*. New Haven, Conn.: Yale University Press, 2008.

Patterson, W. B. *King James VI and I and the Reunion of Christendom*. Cambridge: Cambridge University Press, 1997.

Peck, Linda Levy. *Court Patronage and Corruption in Early Stuart England*. London: Routledge, 1993.

——, ed. *The Mental World of the Jacobean Court*. Cambridge: Cambridge University Press, 1991.

Perry, Curtis. *The Making of Jacobean Culture: James I and the Renegotiation of Elizabethan Literary Practice*. Cambridge: Cambridge University Press, 1997.

Pincus, Steven C. A. *England's Glorious Revolution, 1688–1689: A Brief History with Documents*. New York: Palgrave Macmillan, 2006.

Pittock, Murray G. H. *The Invention of Scotland: The Stuart Myth and the Scottish Identity, 1638 to the Present*. London: Routledge, 1991.

——. *Jacobitism*. New York: St. Martin's, 1998.

Plowden, Alison. *Henrietta Maria: Charles I's Indomitable Queen*. Stroud, UK: Alan Sutton, 2001.

———. *The Stuart Princesses*. Stroud, UK: Alan Sutton, 1996.

Reeve, L. J. *Charles I and the Road to Personal Rule*. Cambridge: Cambridge University Press, 1989.

Rhodes, Neil, Jennifer Richards, and Joseph Marshall. *King James VI and I: Selected Writings*. Aldershot: Ashgate, 2003.

Roberts, John L. *The Jacobite Wars: Scotland and the Military Campaigns of 1715 and 1745*. Edinburgh: Polygon, 2002.

Robertson, Geoffrey. *The Tyrannicide Brief: The Story of the Man Who Sent Charles I to the Scaffold*. New York: Anchor Books, 2007.

Rogers, Pat. *Pope and the Destiny of the Stuarts: History, Politics and Mythology in the Age of Queen Anne*. Oxford: Oxford University Press, 2005.

Ross, Stewart. *The Stewart Dynasty*. Argyll, UK: House of Lochar, 1999.

Russell, Conrad. *The Causes of the English Civil War: The Ford Lectures Delivered in the University of Oxford, 1987–1988*. Oxford: Clarendon, 1990.

———. *The Fall of the British Monarchies, 1637–1642*. Oxford: Clarendon, 1991.

Schwoerer, Lois G. *The Revolution of 1688–89: Changing Perspectives*. Cambridge: Cambridge University Press, 1992.

Seaward, Paul. *The Cavalier Parliament and the Reconstruction of the Old Regime, 1661–1667*. Cambridge: Cambridge University Press, 1989.

———. *The Restoration, 1660–1688*. Basingstoke, UK: Macmillan, 1991.

Seel, Graham E. *Regicide and Republic: England, 1603–1660*. Cambridge: Cambridge University Press, 2001.

Seel, Graham E., and David L. Smith. *Crown and Parliaments, 1558–1689*. Cambridge: Cambridge University Press, 2001.

———. *The Early Stuart Kings, 1603–1642*. London: Routledge, 2001.

Sharpe, Kevin. *The Personal Rule of Charles I*. New Haven, Conn.: Yale University Press, 1992.

———. *Politics and Ideas in Early Stuart England: Essays and Studies*. London: Pinter, 1989.

Sharpe, Kevin, and Peter Lake, eds. *Culture and Politics in Early Stuart England*. Stanford, Calif.: Stanford University Press, 1993.

Smith, Lacey Baldwin. *This Realm of England, 1399–1688*. Boston: Houghton Mifflin, 2001.

Smuts, R. Malcolm. *Court Culture and the Origins of a Royalist Tradition in Early Stuart England*. Philadelphia: University of Pennsylvania Press, 1987.

———, ed. *The Stuart Court and Europe: Essays in Politics and Political Culture*. Cambridge: Cambridge University Press, 1996.

Somerset, Anne. *Unnatural Murder: Poison at the Court of James I*. London: Weidenfeld & Nicolson, 1997.

Speck, W. A. *James II*. London: Longman, 2002.

Starkey, David, et al. *The English Court: From the Wars of the Roses to the Civil War*. London: Longman, 1987.

———. *Monarchy: From the Middle Ages to Modernity*. London: HarperPress, 2006.

Stater, Victor. *The Political History of Tudor and Stuart England: A Sourcebook.* London: Routledge, 2002.

Steen, Sarah Jayne, ed. *The Letters of Lady Arbella Stuart.* New York: Oxford University Press, 1994.

Stewart, Allan. *The Cradle King: The Life of James VI and I, the First Monarch of a United Great Britain.* New York: St. Martin's, 2003.

Stone, Lawrence. *The Causes of the English Revolution, 1529–1642.* London: Routledge, 2002.

Strong, Roy. *Henry, Prince of Wales, and England's Lost Renaissance.* London: Pimlico, 2000.

———. *The Tudor and Stuart Monarchy: Pageantry, Painting, Iconography.* Vol. 3 (Jacobean and Caroline). Woodbridge, UK: Boydell, 1998.

Szechi, Daniel. *1715: The Great Jacobite Rebellion.* New Haven, Conn.: Yale University Press, 2006.

———. *The Jacobites: Britain and Europe, 1688–1788.* Manchester: Manchester University Press, 1994.

———. *Jacobitism and Tory Politics, 1710–14.* Edinburgh: John Donald, 1984.

Tapsell, Grant. *The Personal Rule of Charles II, 1681–85.* Woodbridge, UK: Boydell, 2007.

Testa, Ernest. *James II: Bigot or Saint.* Lewes, UK: Book Guild, 1987.

Todd, Margo, ed. *Reformation to Revolution: Politics and Religion in Early Modern England.* New York: Routledge, 1995.

Travers, James. *James I: The Masque of Monarchy.* Richmond, UK: National Archives, 2003.

Trevor, Meriol. *The Shadow of a Crown: The Life Story of James II of England and VII of Scotland.* London: Constable, 1988.

Vallance, Edward. *The Glorious Revolution, 1688: Britain's Fight for Liberty.* London: Little, Brown, 2006.

Waller, Maureen. *Sovereign Ladies, Sex, Sacrifice and Power: The Six Reigning Queens of England.* New York: St. Martin's Griffin, 2008.

———. *Ungrateful Daughters: The Stuart Princesses Who Stole Their Father's Crown.* London: Hodder & Stoughton, 2002.

Webster, Jeremy. *Performing Libertinism in Charles II's Court: Politics, Drama, Sexuality.* New York: Palgrave Macmillan, 2005.

Wedgwood, C. V. *The King's War, 1641–1647.* Harmondsworth, UK: Penguin, 1983.

———. *The Trial of Charles I.* London: Penguin, 2001.

Weil, Rachel Judith. *Political Passions: Gender, the Family and Political Argument in England, 1680–1714.* Manchester: Manchester University Press, 2009.

Weiser, Brian. *Charles II and the Politics of Access.* Woodbridge, UK: Boydell, 2003.

Weston, Corinne Comstock, and Janelle Renfrow Greenberg. *Subjects and Sovereigns: The Grand Controversy over Legal Sovereignty in Stuart England.* Cambridge: Cambridge University Press, 1981.

Wilks, Timothy, ed. *Prince Henry Revived: Image and Exemplarity in Early Modern England.* Southampton: Southampton Solent, 2007.

Wilson, Derek A. *All the King's Women: Love, Sex and Politics in the Life of Charles II*. London: Hutchinson, 2003.

Woodward, Jennifer. *The Theatre of Death: The Ritual Management of Royal Funerals in Renaissance England, 1570–1625*. Woodbridge, UK: Boydell, 1997.

Woosnam-Savage, Robert C., ed. *1745: Charles Edward Stuart and the Jacobites*. Edinburgh: Her Majesty's Stationery Office, 1995.

Young, Michael B. *Charles I*. Basingstoke, UK: Macmillan, 1997.

———. *King James and the History of Homosexuality*. New York: New York University Press, 1999.

Youngson, A. J. *The Prince and the Pretender: Two Views of the '45*. Edinburgh: Mercat, 1996.

## HOUSE OF ORANGE

Barratt, John. *Battles for the Three Kingdoms: The Campaigns for England, Scotland and Ireland, 1689–92*. Stroud, UK: Alan Sutton, 2007.

Bevan, Bryan. *King William III, Prince of Orange: The First European*. London: Rubicon, 1997.

Childs, John. *The British Army of William III, 1689–1702*. Manchester: Manchester University Press, 1987.

———. *The Williamite Wars in Ireland, 1688–91*. London: Hambledon Continuum, 2007.

Claydon, Tony. *William III*. London: Longman, 2002.

———. *William III and the Godly Revolution*. Cambridge: Cambridge University Press, 1996.

Claydon, Tony, and W. A. Speck. *William and Mary*. Oxford: Oxford University Press, 2007.

Cox, B. *The Glorious Revolution*. New York: St. Martin's, 2000.

———. *King William's European Joint Venture*. Assen, Netherlands: Van Gorum, 1995.

Cruickshanks, Eveline, ed. *Ideology and Conspiracy: Aspects of Jacobitism, 1689–1759*. Edinburgh: John Donald, 1982.

Dillon, Patrick. *The Last Revolution: 1688 and the Creation of the Modern World*. London: Jonathan Cape, 2006.

Doherty, Richard. *The Williamite War in Ireland, 1688–1691*. Dublin: Four Courts Press, 1998.

Foord-Kelcey, Jim, and Philippa Foord-Kelcey. *Mrs. Fitzherbert and Sons*. Lewes, UK: Book Guild, 1991.

Garrett, Jane. *The Triumphs of Providence: The Assassination Plot, 1696*. Cambridge: Cambridge University Press, 1980.

Glozier, Matthew. *The Huguenot Soldiers of William of Orange and the Glorious Revolution of 1688: The Lions of Judah*. Brighton, UK: Sussex Academic Press, 2006.

Grell, Ole Peter, Jonathan I. Israel, and Nicholas Tyacke, eds. *From Persecution to Toleration: The Glorious Revolution and Religion in England*. Oxford: Clarendon, 1991.

Harris, Tim. *Revolution: The Great Crisis of the British Monarchy, 1685–1720*. London: Allen Lane, 2006.

Hill, Christopher. *The Century of Revolution, 1603–1714*. London: Routledge, 2002.

Hoak, Dale, and Mordecai Finegold, eds. *The World of William and Mary: Anglo-Dutch Perspectives on the Revolution of 1688–89*. Stanford, Calif.: Stanford University Press, 1996.

Hoftijzer, Paul, and C. C. Barfoot, eds. *Fabrics and Fabrications: The Myth and Making of William and Mary*. Amsterdam: Rodopi, 1990.

Hoppit, Julian. *A Land of Liberty?: England, 1689–1727*. Oxford: Clarendon, 2000.

Israel, Jonathan Irvine, ed. *The Anglo-Dutch Moment: Essays on the Glorious Revolution and Its World Impact*. Cambridge: Cambridge University Press, 2003.

Jardine, Lisa. *Going Dutch: How England Plundered Holland's Glory*. London: HarperPress, 2008.

Kinross, John. *The Boyne and Aughrim: The War of Two Kings*. Moreton-in-Marsh, UK: Windrush, 1997.

Kishlansky, Mark. *A Monarchy Transformed: Britain, 1603–1714*. London: Allen Lane, 1996.

Lenihan, Pádraig. *1690: Battle of the Boyne*. Stroud, UK: Tempus, 2003.

Lenman, B. *The Jacobite Cause*. Glasgow: Drew, 1986.

Lord, Evelyn. *The Stuarts' Secret Army: English Jacobites, 1689–1752*. Harlow, UK: Pearson Longman, 2004.

MacCubbin, R. P., and M. Hamilton-Phillips, eds. *The Age of William and Mary: Power, Politics and Patronage, 1688–1702; A Reference Encyclopedia and Exhibition Catalogue*. Williamsburg, Va.: College of William and Mary, 1989.

Mijers, Esther, and David Onnekink, eds. *Redefining William III: The Impact of the King-Stadholder in International Context*. Aldershot, UK: Ashgate, 2007.

Miller, John. *The Glorious Revolution*. London: Longman, 1997.

Monod, Paul Kléber. *Jacobitism and the English People, 1688–1788*. Cambridge: Cambridge University Press, 1989.

Onnekink, David. *The Anglo-Dutch Favourite: The Career of Hans Willem Bentinck, 1st Earl of Portland (1649–1709)*. Aldershot, UK: Ashgate, 2007.

Orr, Clarissa Campbell, ed. *Queenship in Britain, 1660–1837: Royal Patronage, Court, Culture and Dynastic Politics*. Manchester, Manchester University Press, 2009.

Pincus, Steven C. A. *England's Glorious Revolution, 1688–1689: A Brief History with Documents*. New York: Palgrave Macmillan, 2006.

Rose, Craig. *England in the 1690s: Revolution, Religion and War*. Oxford: Blackwell, 1999.

Schwoerer, Lois G., ed. *The Declaration of Rights, 1689*. Baltimore, Md.: Johns Hopkins University Press, 1981.

———, ed. *The Revolution of 1688–89: Changing Perspectives*. Cambridge: Cambridge University Press, 1992.

Starkey, David. *Monarchy: From the Middle Ages to Modernity*. London: Harper-Press, 2006.

Szechi, Daniel. *The Jacobites: Britain and Europe, 1688–1788*. Manchester: Manchester University Press, 1994.

Troost, Wout. *William III, the Stadholder-King: A Political Biography*. Aldershot, UK: Ashgate, 2005.

Vallance, Edward. *The Glorious Revolution, 1688: Britain's Fight for Liberty*. London: Little, Brown, 2006.

Van der Kiste, John. *William and Mary*. Stroud, UK: Alan Sutton, 2003.

Waller, Maureen. *Sovereign Ladies, Sex, Sacrifice and Power: The Six Reigning Queens of England*. New York: St. Martin's Griffin, 2008.

Weil, Rachel Judith. *Political Passions: Gender, the Family and Political Argument in England, 1680–1714*. Manchester: Manchester University Press, 2009.

## HOUSE OF HANOVER

Aikin, John. *Annals of the Reign of George III*. 2 vols. Stroud, UK: Nonsuch, 2006.

Alexander, Michael, and Sushila Anand. *Queen Victoria's Maharajah: Duleep Singh, 1838–93*. London: Phoenix, 2001.

Ambrose, Tom. *The King and the Vice Queen: George IV's Last Scandalous Affair*. Stroud, UK: Alan Sutton, 2005.

Anand, Sushila. *Indian Sahib: Queen Victoria's Dear Abdul*. London: Duckworth, 1996.

Arnold, Frieda. *My Mistress the Queen: The Letters of Frieda Arnold, Dresser to Queen Victoria*. Edited by Benita Stoney and Heinrich C. Weltzein. London: Weidenfeld & Nicolson, 1994.

Arnstein, Walter L. *Victoria*. Basingstoke, UK: Palgrave Macmillan, 2003.

Aronson, Theo. *Heart of a Queen: Queen Victoria's Romantic Attachments*. London: John Murray, 1991.

Ashdown, Dulcie M. *Victoria and the Coburgs*. London: Hale, 1981.

Baker, Kenneth. *George III: A Life in Caricature*. London: Thames & Hudson, 2007.

———. *George IV: A Life in Caricature*. London: Thames & Hudson, 2005.

Baker-Smith, Veronica P. M. *A Life of Anne of Hanover, Princess Royal*. Leiden, Netherlands: Brill, 1995.

———. *Royal Discord: The Family of George II*. London: Athena, 2008.

Barratt, Corrie Rebora. *Queen Victoria and Thomas Sully*. Princeton, N.J.: Princeton University Press, 2000.

Behrendt, Stephen C. *Royal Mourning and Regency Culture: Elegies and Memorials of Princess Charlotte*. New York: St. Martin's, 1997.

Benson, E. F. *Queen Victoria: An Illustrated Biography*. London: Chatto & Windus, 1987.

Black, Jeremy. *Culloden and the '45*. Gloucester: Alan Sutton, 2000.

——. *George II: Puppet of the Politicians*. Exeter, UK: University of Exeter Press, 2007.

——. *George III: America's Last King*. New Haven, Conn.: Yale University Press, 2006.

——. *The Hanoverians: The History of a Dynasty*. London: Hambledon & London, 2004.

Borman, Tracy. *King's Mistress, Queen's Servant: Henrietta Howard*. London: Pimlico, 2008.

Campbell, Christy. *Fenian Fire: The British Government Plot to Assassinate Queen Victoria*. London: HarperCollins, 2002.

Campbell, Cynthia. *The Most Polished Gentleman: George IV and the Women in His Life*. London: Kudos, 1995.

Cannon, John. *George III*. Oxford: Oxford University Press, 2007.

Chambers, James. *Charlotte and Leopold: The True Story of the Original People's Princess*. London: Old Street, 2007.

Charlot, Monica. *Victoria: The Young Queen*. Oxford: Blackwell, 1991.

Clarke, John, and Jasper Ridley. *The Houses of Hanover and Saxe-Coburg and Gotha*. Berkeley, Calif.: University of California Press, 2000.

Cruickshanks, Eveline, ed. *Ideology and Conspiracy: Aspects of Jacobitism, 1689–1759*. Edinburgh: John Donald, 1982.

Dann, Uriel. *Hanover and Great Britain, 1740–1760: Diplomacy and Survival*. Leicester, UK: Leicester University Press, 1991.

David, Saul. *Prince of Pleasure: The Prince of Wales and the Making of the Regency*. New York: Atlantic Monthly, 1998.

De-la-Noy, Michael. *George IV*. Stroud, UK: Alan Sutton, 1998.

——. *The King Who Never Was: The Life of Frederick, Prince of Wales*. London: Peter Owen, 1996.

——. *Queen Victoria at Home*. London: Constable, 2003.

Ditchfield, G. M. *George III: An Essay in Monarchy*. Basingstoke, UK: Palgrave, 2002.

Donald, Diana. *The Age of Caricature: Satirical Prints in the Reign of George III*. New Haven, Conn.: Yale University Press, 1996.

Downer, Martyn. *The Queen's Knight: The Extraordinary Life of Queen Victoria's Most Trusted Confidant*. London: Bantam, 2007.

Duff, David, ed. *Queen Victoria's Highland Journals*. London: Hamlyn, 1997.

Duffy, Christopher. *The '45*. London: Cassell Military, 2003.

Eilers, Marlene A. *Queen Victoria's Descendants*. New York: Atlantic International, 1987.

Erickson, Carolly. *Her Little Majesty: The Life of Queen Victoria*. New York: Simon & Schuster, 1997.

Feuchtwanger, Edgar. *Albert and Victoria: The Rise and Fall of the House of Saxe-Coburg and Gotha*. London: Hambledon Continuum, 2006.

Fraser, Fiona. *The Six Daughters of George III*. New York: Anchor, 2006.

———. *The Unruly Queen: The Life of Queen Caroline.* New York: Knopf, 1996.

Fulford, Roger, ed. *Beloved Mama: Private Correspondence of Queen Victoria and the German Crown Princess.* London: Evans, 1981.

Gardiner, Juliet. *Queen Victoria.* London: Collins & Brown, 1997.

Gattey, Charles Neilson. *"Farmer" George's Black Sheep: The Lives and Loves of George III's Brothers and Sisters.* Bourne End, UK: Kensal, 1986.

Gregg, Edward. *The Protestant Succession in International Politics, 1710–1716.* New York: Garland, 1986.

Hatton, Ragnhild. *George I.* New Haven, Conn.: Yale University Press, 2001.

Hibbert, Christopher. *The Court of St. James's: The Monarch at Work from Victoria to Elizabeth.* New York: Quill, 1983.

———. *George III: A Personal History.* New York: Basic Books, 1998.

———. *Queen Victoria: A Personal History.* New York: Basic Books, 2000.

———. *Queen Victoria in Her Letters and Journals: A Selection.* New York: Viking, 1985.

Holme, Theà. *Caroline: A Biography of Caroline of Brunswick.* New York: Atheneum, 1980.

Homans, Margaret. *Royal Representations: Queen Victoria and British Culture, 1837–1876.* Chicago: University of Chicago Press, 1998.

Homans, Margaret, and Adrienne Auslander Munich, eds. *Remaking Queen Victoria.* Cambridge: Cambridge University Press, 1997.

Hook, Michael, and Walter Ross. *The 'Forty-Five: The Last Jacobite Rebellion.* Edinburgh: Her Majesty's Stationery Office, 1995.

Hoppit, Julian. *A Land of Liberty?: England, 1689–1727.* Oxford: Clarendon, 2000.

Hudson, Katherine. *A Royal Conflict: Sir John Conroy and the Young Victoria.* London: Hodder & Stoughton, 1994.

Irvine, Valerie. *The King's Wife: George V and Mrs Fitzherbert.* London: Hambledon & London, 2005.

Jaffé, Deborah. *Victoria: A Celebration.* London: Carlton, 2000.

King, Greg. *Twilight of Splendor: The Court of Queen Victoria during Her Diamond Jubilee Year.* Hoboken, N.J.: Wiley, 2007.

Kuhn, William M. *Democratic Royalism: The Transformation of the British Monarchy, 1861–1914.* New York: St. Martin's, 1996.

———. *Henry and Mary Ponsonby: Life at the Court of Queen Victoria.* London: Duckworth, 2002.

Lamont-Brown, Raymond. *John Brown: Queen Victoria's Highland Servant.* Stroud, UK: Alan Sutton, 2002.

Lenman, B. *The Jacobite Cause.* Glasgow: Drew, 1986.

Levy, M. J. *The Mistresses of King George IV.* London: Peter Owen, 1996.

Longford, Elizabeth. *Queen Victoria.* Stroud, UK: Alan Sutton, 2005.

———, ed. *Darling Loosy: Letters to Princess Louise, 1856–1939.* London: Weidenfeld & Nicolson, 1991.

Lord, Evelyn. *The Stuarts' Secret Army: English Jacobites, 1689–1752.* Harlow, UK: Pearson Longman, 2004.

Lowe, Joseph. *A New Most Excellent Dancing Master: The Journal of Joseph Lowe's Visits to Balmoral and Windsor (1852–1860) to Teach Dance to the Family of Queen Victoria.* Edited by Allan Thomas. Stuyvesant, N.Y.: Pendragon, 1992.

Marsden, Jonathan, ed. *The Wisdom of George the Third: Papers from a Symposium at the Queen's Gallery, Buckingham Palace, June 2004.* London: Royal Collection, 2005.

May, John. *Victoria Remembered: A Royal History, 1817–1861, Entirely Illustrated by Commemoratives.* London: Heinemann, 1983.

McDowell, Colin. *A Hundred Years of Royal Style.* London: Muller, Blond & White, 1985.

Millar, Delia. *Queen Victoria's Life in the Highlands, as Depicted by Her Watercolour Artists.* London: P. Wilson, 1985.

Millar, Oliver. *The Victorian Pictures in the Collection of Her Majesty the Queen.* 2 vols. Cambridge: Cambridge University Press, 1992.

Mitchell, Ian R. *On the Trail of Queen Victoria in the Highlands.* Edinburgh: Luath, 2000.

Monod, Paul Kléber. *Jacobitism and the English People, 1688–1788.* Cambridge: Cambridge University Press, 1989.

Mullen, Richard, and James Munson. *Victoria: Portrait of a Queen.* London: British Broadcasting Corporation, 1987.

Munich, Adrienne. *Queen Victoria's Secrets.* New York: Columbia University Press, 1996.

Munson, James. *Maria Fitzherbert: The Secret Wife of George IV.* New York: Carroll & Graf, 2001.

Naftel, W. D. *Prince Edward's Legacy: The Duke of Kent in Halifax; Romance and Beautiful Buildings.* Halifax, Canada: Formac, 2005.

Nash, David, and Antony Taylor, eds. *Republicanism in Victorian Society.* Stroud, UK: Alan Sutton, 2000.

Nelson, Michael. *Queen Victoria and the Discovery of the Riviera.* London: I. B. Tauris, 2001.

Newman, Gerald, ed. *Britain in the Hanoverian Age, 1714–1837: An Encyclopedia.* New York: Garland, 1997.

Newsome, David. *The Victorian World Picture: Perceptions and Introspections in an Age of Change.* New Brunswick, N.J.: Rutgers University Press, 1997.

Oates, Jonathan. *Sweet William or the Butcher?: The Duke of Cumberland and the '45.* Barnsley, UK: Pen and Sword Military, 2008.

Olechnowicz, Andrzej, ed. *The Monarchy and the British Nation: 1780 to the Present.* Cambridge: Cambridge University Press, 2007.

Orr, Clarissa Campbell, ed. *Queenship in Britain, 1660–1837: Royal Patronage, Court, Culture and Dynastic Politics.* Manchester, Manchester University Press, 2009.

Packard, Jerrold M. *Farewell in Splendor: The Passing of Queen Victoria and Her Age.* New York: Dutton, 1995.

——. *Victoria's Daughters.* New York: St. Martin's, 1998.

Parissien, Steven. *George IV: The Grand Entertainment*. London: John Murray, 2001.

Pittock, Murray G. H. *Jacobitism*. New York: St. Martin's, 1998.

Plowden, Alison. *Caroline and Charlotte: Regency Scandals, 1795–1821*. Stroud, UK: Alan Sutton, 2005.

———. *The Young Victoria*. Briarcliff Manor, N.Y.: Stein & Day, 1983.

Plunkett, John. *Queen Victoria: First Media Monarch*. Oxford: Oxford University Press, 2003.

Pocock, Tom. *Sailor King: The Life of King William IV*. London: Sinclair Stevenson, 1991.

Poole, Steve. *The Politics of Regicide in England, 1760–1850*. Manchester: Manchester University Press, 2000.

Potts, D. M., and W. T. W. Potts. *Queen Victoria's Gene: Haemophilia and the Royal Family*. Stroud, UK: Alan Sutton, 1999.

Prebble, John. *Culloden*. London: Pimlico, 2002.

———. *The King's Jaunt: George IV in Scotland, August 1822; "One and Twenty Daft Days."* London: Collins, 1988.

Priestley, J. B. *The Prince of Pleasure and His Regency, 1811–1820*. London: Penguin, 2002.

Ramm, A., ed. *Beloved and Darling Child: Last Letters between Queen Victoria and Her Eldest Daughter, 1886–1901*. Stroud, UK: Alan Sutton, 1990.

Rappaport, Helen. *Queen Victoria: A Biographical Companion*. Santa Barbara, Calif.: ABC-CLIO, 2003.

Rennell, Tony. *Last Days of Glory: The Death of Queen Victoria*. London: Viking, 2000.

Reynolds, K. D., and H. C. G. Matthew. *Queen Victoria*. Oxford: Oxford University Press, 2007.

Roberts, Hugh. *For the King's Pleasure: The Furnishing and Decoration of George IV's Apartments at Windsor Castle*. London: Royal Collection, 2001.

Roberts, Jane, ed. *George III and Queen Charlotte: Patronage, Collecting and Court Taste*. London: Royal Collection, 2004.

Robins, Jane. *The Trial of Queen Caroline: The Scandalous Affair That Nearly Ended a Monarchy*. New York: Free Press, 2006.

Schoch, Richard W. *Queen Victoria and the Theatre of Her Age*. New York: Palgrave Macmillan, 2004.

Simms, Brendan, and Torsten Riotte, eds. *The Hanoverian Dimension in British History, 1714–1837*. Cambridge: Cambridge University Press, 2007.

Sitwell, Edith. *Victoria of England*. London: Cresset Women's Voices, 1987.

Smith, E. A. *George IV*. New Haven, Conn.: Yale University Press, 1999.

———. *A Queen on Trial: The Affair of Queen Caroline*. Stroud, UK: Alan Sutton, 1993.

Smith, Hannah. *Georgian Monarchy: Politics and Culture, 1714–60*. Cambridge: Cambridge University Press, 2006.

Somerset, Anne. *The Life and Times of William IV*. London: Weidenfeld & Nicolson, 1980.

Speck, William Arthur. *The Butcher: The Duke of Cumberland and the Suppression of the '45*. Caernarfon, UK: Welsh Academic, 1995.

Spotto, Donald. *Dynasty: The Turbulent Story of the Royal Family from Victoria to Diana*. London: Simon & Schuster, 1995.

Staniland, Kay. *In Royal Fashion: The Clothes of Princess Charlotte of Wales and Queen Victoria, 1796–1901*. London: Museum of London, 1997.

Starkey, David. *Monarchy: From the Middle Ages to Modernity*. London: Harper-Press, 2006.

St. Aubyn, Giles. *Queen Victoria: A Portrait*. London: Sinclair-Stevenson, 1991.

St-John Nevill, Barry, ed. *Life at the Court of Queen Victoria: Illustrated from the Collection of Lord Edward Pelham-Clinton, Master of the Household, with Selections from the Journals of Queen Victoria*. Exeter, UK: Webb & Bower, 1984.

Strachey, Lytton. *The Illustrated Queen Victoria*. London: Bloomsbury, 1987.

Szechi, Daniel. *1715: The Great Jacobite Rebellion*. New Haven, Conn.: Yale University Press, 2006.

——. *The Jacobites: Britain and Europe, 1688–1788*. Manchester: Manchester University Press, 1994.

Thomas, Peter D. G. *George III: Kings and Politicians, 1760–70*. Manchester: Manchester University Press, 2002.

Thompson, Dorothy. *Queen Victoria: Gender and Power*. London: Virago, 2001.

Tillyard, Stella. *A Royal Affair: George III and His Scandalous Siblings*. London: Chatto & Windus, 2006.

Tomalin, Claire. *Mrs. Jordan's Profession: The Story of a Great Actress and a Future King*. London: Viking, 1994.

Vallone, Lynne. *Becoming Victoria*. New Haven, Conn.: Yale University Press, 2001.

Van der Kiste, John. *Childhood at Court, 1819–1914*. Stroud, UK: Alan Sutton, 2003.

——. *George III's Children*. Stroud, UK: Alan Sutton, 2004.

——. *The Georgian Princesses*. Thrupp, UK: Alan Sutton, 2000.

——. *King George II and Queen Caroline*. Stroud, UK: Alan Sutton, 1997.

——. *Queen Victoria's Children*. Stroud, UK: Alan Sutton, 2003.

——. *Sons, Servants & Statesmen: The Men in Queen Victoria's Life*. Stroud, UK: Alan Sutton, 2006.

Victoria, Queen. *Beloved and Darling Child: Last Letters between Queen Victoria and Her Eldest Daughter, 1886–1901*. Edited by Agatha Ramm. Stroud, UK: Alan Sutton, 1990.

——. *Life at the Court of Queen Victoria, 1861–1901: Illustrated from the Collection of Lord Edward Pelham-Clinton, Master of the Household, with Selections from the Journals of Queen Victoria*. Edited by Barry St-John Nevill. Exeter, UK: Webb & Bower, 1984.

——. *Queen Victoria's Highland Journals*. Edited by David Duff. Phoenix Mill, UK: Alan Sutton, 1997.

Vivian, Frances. *A Life of Frederick, Prince of Wales, 1707–1751, a Connoisseur of the Arts*. Edited by Roger White. Lewiston, N.Y.: Edwin Mellen, 2006.

Waller, Maureen. *Sovereign Ladies, Sex, Sacrifice and Power: The Six Reigning Queens of England*. New York: St. Martin's Griffin, 2008.

Walpole, Horace. *Memoirs of King George II*. Edited by John Brooke. 3 vols. New Haven, Conn.: Yale University Press, 1985.

———. *Memoirs of the Reign of King George III*. Edited by Derek Jarrett. 4 vols. New Haven, Conn.: Yale University Press, 1999.

Wardroper, John. *Wicked Ernest: The Truth about the Man Who Was Almost Britain's King; An Extraordinary Royal Life Revealed*. London: Shelfmark, 2002.

Watkin, David. *The Architect King: George III and the Culture of the Enlightenment*. London: Royal Collection, 2004.

Weintraub, Stanley. *Uncrowned King: The Life of Prince Albert*. New York: Free Press, 1997.

———. *Victoria*. London: John Murray, 1996.

Whittle, Tyler. *Victoria and Albert at Home*. London: Routledge & Kegan Paul, 1980.

Whitworth, Rex. *William Augustus, Duke of Cumberland: A Life*. London: Leo Cooper, 1992.

Williams, D. G. *The Royal Society of Literature and the Patronage of George IV*. New York: Garland, 1987.

Williams, Richard. *The Contentious Crown: Public Discussion on the British Monarchy in the Reign of Queen Victoria*. Aldershot, UK: Ashgate, 1997.

Wolffe, John. *Great Deaths: Grieving, Religion and Nationhood in Victorian and Edwardian Britain*. Oxford: Oxford University Press, 2000.

Woodham-Smith, Cecil. *Queen Victoria: Her Life and Times, 1819–1861*. London: Hamish Hamilton, 1984.

Woosnam-Savage, Robert C., ed. *1745: Charles Edward Stuart and the Jacobites*. Edinburgh: Her Majesty's Stationery Office, 1995.

Wright, Christopher. *George III*. London: British Library, 2005.

York, Sarah, Duchess of. *Victoria and Albert: Life at Osborne House*. London: Weidenfeld & Nicolson, 1991.

Youngson, A. J. *The Prince and the Pretender: Two Views of the '45*. Edinburgh: Mercat, 1996.

Zeigler, Philip. *King William IV*. London: Cassell, 1989.

## HOUSE OF SAXE-COBURG AND GOTHA

Allfrey, Anthony. *Edward VII and His Jewish Court*. London: Weidenfeld & Nicolson, 1991.

Aronson, Theo. *Grandmama of Europe: The Crowned Descendants of Queen Victoria*. London: John Murray, 1984.

———. *The King in Love: King Edward VII's Mistresses; Lillie Langtry, Daisy Warwick, Alice Keppel and Others*. New York: Harper & Row, 1988.

———. *Prince Eddy and the Homosexual Underworld*. London: John Murray, 1994.

———. *Royal Family: Years of Transition*. London: John Murray, 1983.

Ashdown, Dulcie M. *Victoria and the Coburgs*. London: Hale, 1981.

Beatty, Laura. *Lillie Langtry: Manners, Masks and Morals*. London: Chatto & Windus, 1999.

Bentley-Cranch, Dana. *Edward VII: Image of an Era, 1841–1910*. London: Her Majesty's Stationery Office, 1992.

Brendon, Vyvyen. *The Edwardian Age, 1901–1914*. London: Hodder & Stoughton, 1996.

Brooks, Chris, ed. *The Albert Memorial: The Prince Consort National Memorial; Its History, Contexts and Conservation*. New Haven, Conn.: Yale University Press, 2000.

Chomet, Seweryn. *Helena: Princess Reclaimed; The Life and Times of Queen Victoria's Third Daughter*. New York: Begell House, 1999.

Clarke, John, and Jasper Ridley. *The Houses of Hanover and Saxe-Coburg and Gotha*. Berkeley, Calif.: University of California Press, 2000.

Clay, Catrine. *King, Kaiser, Tsar: Three Royal Cousins Who Led the World to War*. New York: Walker, 2007.

Cook, Andrew. *King Eddy: The King Britain Never Had*. Stroud, UK: Tempus, 2006.

Darby, Elisabeth, and Nicola Smith. *The Cult of the Prince Consort*. New Haven, Conn.: Yale University Press, 1983.

David, Saul. *Prince of Pleasure: The Prince of Wales and the Making of the Regency*. New York: Atlantic Monthly, 1998.

Dennison, Matthew. *The Last Princess: The Devoted Life of Queen Victoria's Youngest Daughter*. New York: St. Martin's, 2008.

Dimond, Frances. *Developing the Picture: Queen Alexandra and the Art of Photography*. London: Royal Collection, 2004.

Duff, David. *Alexandra: Princess and Queen*. London: Collins, 1980.

——. *Queen Mary*. London: Collins, 1985.

Dunlop, Ian. *Edward VII and the Entente Cordiale*. London: Constable, 2004.

Edwards, Anne. *Matriarch: Queen Mary and the House of Windsor*. New York: William Morrow, 1984.

Eilers, Marlene A. *Queen Victoria's Descendants*. New York: Atlantic International, 1987.

Farago, Ladislas, and Andrew Sinclair. *Royal Web: The Story of Princess Victoria and Frederick of Prussia*. New York: McGraw-Hill, 1981.

Feuchtwanger, Edgar. *Albert and Victoria: The Rise and Fall of the House of Saxe-Coburg and Gotha*. London: Hambledon Continuum, 2006.

Frankland, Noble. *Prince Henry, Duke of Gloucester*. London: Weidenfeld & Nicolson, 1980.

——. *Witness of a Century: The Life and Times of Prince Arthur, Duke of Connaught*. London: Shepheard-Walwyn, 1993.

Friedman, Dennis. *Darling Georgie: The Enigma of King George V*. London: Peter Owen, 1998.

Fulford, Roger, ed. *Beloved Mama: Private Correspondence of Queen Victoria and the German Crown Princess*. London: Evans, 1981.

Gelardi, Julia P. *Born to Rule: Five Reigning Consorts, Granddaughters of Queen Victoria*. New York: St. Martin's, 2005.

Hannah, Pakula. *An Uncommon Woman: The Empress Frederick, Daughter of Queen Victoria, Wife of the Crown Prince of Prussia, Mother of Kaiser Wilhelm*. New York: Simon & Schuster, 1995.

Hattersley, Roy. *The Edwardians*. New York: St. Martin's, 2005.

Heffer, Simon. *Power and Place: The Political Consequences of King Edward VII*. London: Weidenfeld & Nicolson, 1998.

Hibbert, Christopher. *The Court of St. James's: The Monarch at Work from Victoria to Elizabeth*. New York: Quill, 1983.

———. *Edward VII: The Last Victorian King*. Basingstoke, UK: Palgrave Macmillan, 2007.

Hobhouse, Hermione. *Prince Albert: His Life and Work*. London: Hamilton, 1983.

Hough, Richard. *Edward and Alexandra: Their Private and Public Lives*. London: Coronet, 1994.

James, Robert Rhodes. *Albert, Prince Consort: A Biography*. London: Hamish Hamilton, 1983.

Kuhn, William M. *Democratic Royalism: The Transformation of the British Monarchy, 1861–1914*. New York: St. Martin's, 1996.

Lamont-Brown, Raymond. *Alice Keppel and Agnes Keyser: Edward VII's Last Loves*. Stroud, UK: Alan Sutton, 2005.

Lascelles, Alan. *End of an Era: Letters and Journals of Sir Alan Lascelles, 1887–1920*. Edited by Duff Hart-Davis. London: Hamilton, 1988.

———. *In Royal Service: The Letters and Journals of Sir Alan Lascelles, 1920–1936*. Edited by Duff Hart-Davis. London: Hamilton, 1988.

Longford, Elizabeth, ed. *Darling Loosy: Letters to Princess Louise, 1856–1939*. London: Weidenfeld & Nicolson, 1991.

McDowell, Colin. *A Hundred Years of Royal Style*. London: Muller, Blond & White, 1985.

McLean, Roderick R. *Royalty and Diplomacy in Europe, 1890–1914*. Cambridge: Cambridge University Press, 2001.

Middlemas, K. *The Life and Times of Edward VII*. London: Weidenfeld & Nicolson, 2003.

Morrow, Ann. *Cousins Divided: George V and Nicholas II*. Stroud, UK: Alan Sutton, 2006.

Noel, Gerard. *Ena: Spain's English Queen*. London: Constable, 1999.

Olechnowicz, Andrzej, ed. *The Monarchy and the British Nation: 1780 to the Present*. Cambridge: Cambridge University Press, 2007.

Packard, Jerrold M. *Farewell in Splendor: The Passing of Queen Victoria and Her Age*. New York: Dutton, 1995.

———. *Victoria's Daughters*. New York: St. Martin's, 1998.

Pakula, Hannah. *An Uncommon Woman: The Empress Frederick, Daughter of Queen Victoria, Wife of the Crown Prince of Prussia, Mother of Kaiser Wilhelm*. New York: Simon & Schuster, 1995.

Plumptre, George. *Edward VII*. London: Pavilion, 1995.

Pope-Hennessy, James. *Queen Mary, 1867–1953*. London: Phoenix, 2000.

Potts, D. M., and W. T. W. Potts. *Queen Victoria's Gene*. Stroud, UK: Alan Sutton, 1999.

Price, Harry. *The Royal Tour, 1901; or, The Cruise of H.M.S. Ophir: Being a Lower Deck Account of Their Royal Highnesses the Duke and Duchess of Cornwall and York's Voyage around the British Empire*. Exeter: Webb & Bower, 1980.

Radforth, Ian. *Royal Spectacle: The 1860 Visit of the Prince of Wales to Canada and the United States*. Toronto: University of Toronto Press, 2004.

Rennell, Tony. *Last Days of Glory: The Death of Queen Victoria*. London: Viking, 2000.

Rose, Kenneth. *King George V*. London: Phoenix, 2000.

Sinclair, Andrew. *The Other Victoria: The Princess Royal and the Grand Game of Europe*. London: Weidenfeld & Nicolson, 1981.

Sinclair, David. *Two Georges: The Making of the Modern Monarchy*. London: Hodder & Stoughton, 1988.

Spotto, Donald. *Dynasty: The Turbulent Story of the Royal Family from Victoria to Diana*. London: Simon & Schuster, 1995.

Stamp, Robert M. *Monarchy: From the Middle Ages to Modernity*. London: HarperPress, 2006.

——. *Royal Rebels: Princess Louise and the Marquis of Lorne*. Toronto: Dundurn, 1988.

Van der Kiste, John. *Childhood at Court, 1819–1914*. Stroud, UK: Alan Sutton, 2003.

——. *Crowns in a Changing World: The British and European Monarchies, 1901–1936*. Stroud, UK: Alan Sutton, 1993.

——. *Dearest Vicky, Darling Fritz: The Tragic Love Story of Queen Victoria's Eldest Daughter and the German Emperor*. Stroud, UK: Alan Sutton, 2001.

——. *Edward VII's Children*. Stroud, UK: Alan Sutton, 1991.

——. *Queen Victoria's Children*. Stroud, UK: Alan Sutton, 2003.

Van der Kiste, John, and Bee Jordaan. *Dearest Affie: Alfred, Duke of Edinburgh, Queen Victoria's Second Son, 1844–1900*. Gloucester, UK: Alan Sutton, 1984.

Vickers, Paul H. *"A Gift So Graciously Bestowed": The History of the Prince Consort's Library*. Winchester: Hampshire County Council, 1993.

Victoria, Queen. *Beloved and Darling Child: Last Letters between Queen Victoria and Her Eldest Daughter, 1886–1901*. Edited by Agatha Ramm. Stroud, UK: Alan Sutton, 1990.

Wake, Jehanne. *Princess Louise: Queen Victoria's Unconventional Daughter*. London: Collins, 1988.

Warwick, Christopher, ed. *Queen Mary's Photograph Albums*. London: Sidgwick & Jackson, 1989.

Weintraub, Stanley. *Edward the Caresser: The Playboy Prince Who Became King Edward VII*. New York: Free Press, 2001.

——. *The Importance of Being Edward: King in Waiting, 1841–1901*. London: John Murray, 2000.

——. *Uncrowned King: The Life of Prince Albert*. New York: Free Press, 1997.

Whittle, Tyler. *Victoria and Albert at Home*. London: Routledge & Kegan Paul, 1980.

Wolffe, John. *Great Deaths: Grieving, Religion and Nationhood in Victorian and Edwardian Britain*. Oxford: Oxford University Press, 2000.

York, Sarah, Duchess of. *Victoria and Albert: Life at Osborne House*. London: Weidenfeld & Nicolson, 1991.

Zeepvat, Charlotte. *Prince Leopold: The Untold Story of Queen Victoria's Youngest Son*. Stroud, UK: Alan Sutton, 1998.

——. *Queen Victoria's Family: A Century of Photographs, 1840–1940*. Stroud, UK: Alan Sutton, 2001.

## HOUSE OF WINDSOR

Allen, Martin A. *The Crown and the Swastika: Hitler, Hess and the Duke of Windsor*. London: Hale, 1983.

——. *Hidden Agenda: How the Duke of Windsor Betrayed the Allies*. London: Macmillan, 2000.

Allison, Ronald. *The Queen: 50 Years; A Celebration*. London: HarperCollins, 2001.

Aronson, Theo. *Princess Margaret: A Biography*. Washington, D.C.: Regnery, 1997.

——. *The Royal Family at War*. London: John Murray, 1993.

——. *Royal Family: Years of Transition*. London: John Murray, 1983.

——. *Royal Subjects: A Biographer's Encounters*. London: Sidgwick & Jackson, 2000.

Benson, Ross. *Charles: The Man, the Myths, the Marriage*. London: Gollancz, 1995.

Billig, M. *Talking of the Royal Family*. London: Routledge, 1998.

Birmingham, David. *Duchess: The Story of Wallis Warfield Windsor*. Boston: Little, Brown, 1981.

Blackwood, Caroline. *The Last of the Duchess*. New York: Pantheon, 1995.

Bloch, Michael. *The Duchess of Windsor*. New York: St. Martin's, 1997.

——. *The Duke of Windsor's War: From Europe to the Bahamas, 1939–1945*. New York: Coward-McCann, 1983.

——. *Operation Willi: The Plot to Kidnap the Duke of Windsor, July 1940*. London: Weidenfeld & Nicolson, 1984.

——. *The Reign and Abdication of King Edward VIII*. London: Bantam, 1990.

——. *The Secret File of the Duke of Windsor*. London: Bantam, 1988.

Blundell, Nigel. *The Boy Who Would Be King*. London: Parkgate, 1999.

——. *Windsor v. Windsor*. London: Blake, 1995.

Blundell, Nigel, and Susan Blackhall. *Fall of the House of Windsor*. London: Blake, 1992.

Bogdanor, Vernon. *The Monarchy and the Constitution*. Oxford: Clarendon, 1995.

Bond, Jennie. *Elizabeth: Eighty Glorious Years*. London: Carlton, 2006.

Botham, Noel. *Margaret, the Last Real Princess: The Shockingly Frank and Revealing Account of the Life and Loves of HRH Princess Margaret*. London: Blake, 2002.

——. *The Murder of Princess Diana: Revealed; The Truth Behind the Assassination of the Century*. London: Metro, 2007.

Bousfield, Arthur, and Gary Toffoli. *Fifty Years the Queen: A Tribute to Her Majesty Queen Elizabeth II on Her Golden Jubilee.* Toronto: Dundurn, 2002.

———. *The Queen Mother and Her Century: An Illustrated Biography of Queen Elizabeth, the Queen Mother, on Her 100th Birthday.* Toronto: Dundurn, 2000.

Bradford, Sarah. *Diana.* New York: Viking, 2006.

———. *Elizabeth: A Biography of Her Majesty the Queen.* London: Penguin, 2002.

———. *George VI.* London: Penguin, 2002.

Brandreth, Giles. *Philip and Elizabeth: Portrait of a Marriage.* London: Arrow, 2004.

Brendon, Piers, and Philip Whitehead. *The Windsors: A Dynasty Revealed.* London: Pimlico, 2000.

Brennan, Kristine. *Diana, Princess of Wales.* Philadelphia: Chelsea House, 1999.

Brody, Wendy. *Prince Harry.* New York: Pinnacle, 2000.

Brown, Tina. *The Diana Chronicles.* New York: Doubleday, 2008.

Burchill, Julie. *Diana.* London: Weidenfeld & Nicolson, 1998.

Burgess, Colin, with Paul Carter. *Behind Palace Doors: My Service as the Queen Mother's Equerry.* London: John Blake, 2006.

Burrell, Paul. *A Royal Duty.* New York: Signet, 2004.

———. *The Way We Were: Remembering Diana.* New York: William Morrow, 2006.

Campbell, Judith. *Queen Elizabeth: A Biography.* New York: Crown, 1980.

Cathcart, Helen. *The Queen Herself.* London: Star, 1983.

Clay, Catrine. *King, Kaiser, Tsar: Three Royal Cousins Who Led the World to War.* New York: Walker, 2007.

———. *Princess to Queen.* London: British Broadcasting Corporation, 1996.

Clayton, Tim, and Phil Craig. *Diana: Story of a Princess.* London: Hodder & Stoughton, 2001.

Corby, Tom. *HRH, Princess of Wales: The Public Life.* London: Hale, 1991.

Cornforth, John. *Queen Elizabeth, the Queen Mother, at Clarence House.* London: Michael Joseph, 1996.

Courtney, Nicholas. *Princess Anne: A Biography.* Leicester, UK: Charnwood, 1987.

———. *Queen Elizabeth, the Queen Mother.* London: St. Michael, 1984.

———. *Sisters-in-Law: A Palace Revolution.* London: Futura, 1989.

Crawford, Marion. *The Little Princesses: The Story of the Queen's Childhood, by Her Governess.* London: Orion, 2002.

Culme, John, and Nicholas Rayner. *The Jewels of the Duchess of Windsor.* New York: Vendome, 1987.

Davies, Jude. *Diana: A Cultural History; Gender, Race, Nation and the People's Princess.* Basingstoke, UK: Palgrave, 2001.

Davies, Nicholas. *Diana: A Princess and Her Troubled Marriage.* Secaucus, N.J.: Carol, 1992.

———. *Elizabeth: Behind Palace Doors.* Edinburgh: Mainstream, 2000.

———. *The Princess Who Changed the World.* London: John Blake, 1997.

———. *Queen Elizabeth II: A Woman Who Is Not Amused.* New York: Carol, 1998.

———. *William: The Rebel Prince.* London: John Blake, 2001.

De Courcy, Anne. *Snowdon: The Biography.* London: Weidenfeld & Nicolson, 2008.

De-la-Noy, Michael. *The Queen Behind the Throne.* London: Hutchinson, 1994.

Dempster, Nigel. *Princess Margaret: A Life Unfulfilled.* New York: Macmillan, 1982.

Dempster, Nigel, and Peter Evans. *Behind Palace Doors: Marriage and Divorce in the House of Windsor.* New York: Putnam, 1993.

Denney, Colleen. *Representing Diana, Princess of Wales: Cultural Memory and Fairy Tales Revisited.* Madison, N.J.: Fairleigh Dickinson University, 2005.

Dimbleby, Jonathan. *The Prince of Wales: A Biography.* London: Warner, 1994.

Donnelly, Peter. *Invitation to a Royal Wedding: Edward and Sophie; June 19, 1999.* Godalming, UK: Bramley, 1999.

Duff, David. *Elizabeth of Glamis: The Story of the Queen Mother.* London: Magnum, 1980.

———. *George and Elizabeth: A Royal Marriage.* London: Collins, 1983.

———. *Queen Mary.* London: Collins, 1985.

Edwards, Anne. *Diana and the Rise of the House of Spencer.* New York: St. Martin's, 2000.

———. *Matriarch: Queen Mary and the House of Windsor.* New York: William Morrow, 1984.

———. *Royal Sisters: Elizabeth and Margaret.* London: HarperCollins, 1990.

Edwards, Arthur, and Charles Rae. *The Queen Mum: Her First 100 Years.* London: HarperCollins, 2000.

Fisher, Graham, and Heather Fisher. *Charles and Diana: Their Married Life.* London: Hale, 1984.

———. *Charles: The Man and the Prince.* Long Preston, UK: Magna, 1984.

———. *Consort: The Life and Times of Prince Philip.* London: W. H. Allen, 1980.

———. *Monarch: The Life and Times of Elizabeth II.* London: Hale, 1985.

———. *Prince Andrew.* London: W. H. Allen, 1981.

———. *The Queen's Family.* London: W. H. Allen, 1982.

Flamini, Roland. *Sovereign: Elizabeth II and the Windsor Dynasty.* New York: Delacorte, 1991.

Forbes, Grania. *Elizabeth, the Queen Mother: A Twentieth Century Life.* London: Pavilion, 1999.

———. *My Darling Buffy: The Early Life of the Queen Mother.* London: Headline, 1999.

Frankland, Noble. *Prince Henry, Duke of Gloucester.* London: Weidenfeld & Nicolson, 1980.

Friedman, Dennis. *Darling Georgie: The Enigma of King George V.* London: Peter Owen, 1998.

———. *Inheritance: A Psychological History of the Royal Family.* London: Sidgwick & Jackson, 1993.

Garner, Valerie. *Debrett's Queen Elizabeth, the Queen Mother.* London: Headline, 2002.

Gibbs, Garth, and Sean Smith. *Sophie's Kiss: The True Love Story of Prince Edward and Sophie Rhys-Jones.* London: Blake, 1999.

Goodall, Sarah, and Nicholas Monson. *The Palace Diaries: A Story Inspired by Twelve Years of Life behind Palace Gates.* Edinburgh: Mainstream, 2006.

Graham, Caroline. *Camilla: Her True Story.* London: John Blake, 2003.

——. *Camilla, the King's Mistress: A Love Story*. London: Blake, 1995.

Graham, Tim, and Peter Archer. *William: HRH Prince William of Wales*. London: Simon & Schuster, 2003.

Gregory, Martyn. *The Diana Conspiracy Exposed: The Definitive Account of the Last Days and Death of Diana, Princess of Wales*. Milford, Conn.: Olmstead, 2000.

Greig, Geordie. *Louis and the Prince: A Story of Politics, Intrigue and Royal Friendship*. London: Hodder & Stoughton, 1999.

Grove, Trevor, ed. *The Queen Observed*. London: Pavilion, 1986.

Hall, Phillip. *Royal Fortune: Tax, Money and the Monarchy*. London: Bloomsbury, 1992.

Hall, Unity. *Philip: The Man behind the Monarchy*. London: O'Mara, 1987.

Hall, Unity, and Ingrid Seward. *Royalty Revealed*. London: Sidgwick & Jackson, 1989.

Harewood, George Lascelles, Earl of. *The Tongs and the Bones: The Memoirs of Lord Harewood*. London: Weidenfeld & Nicolson, 1981.

Harris, Kenneth. *The Queen*. New York: St. Martin's, 1995.

Haseler, Stephen. *The End of the House of Windsor: Birth of a British Republic*. London: I. B. Tauris, 1993.

Heald, Tim. *The Duke: A Portrait of Prince Philip*. London: Hodder & Stoughton, 1991.

——. *Princess Margaret: A Life Unravelled*. London: Weidenfeld & Nicolson, 2007.

Hewitt, James. *Love and War*. London: Blake, 1999.

Hibbert, Christopher. *The Court of St. James's: The Monarch at Work from Victoria to Elizabeth*. New York: Quill, 1983.

Higham, Charles. *The Duchess of Windsor: The Secret Life*. Hoboken, N.J.: Wiley, 2005.

——. *Wallis: Secret Lives of the Duchess of Windsor*. London: Sidgwick & Jackson, 1988.

Higham, Charles, and Roy Moseley. *Elizabeth and Philip: The Untold Story of the Queen of England and Her Prince*. New York: Berkley Books, 1993.

Hoey, Brian. *All the Queen's Men: Inside the Royal Household*. London: HarperCollins, 1992.

——. *Anne: The Private Princess Revealed*. London: Sidgwick & Jackson, 1997.

——. *Her Majesty: Fifty Regal Years*. London: HarperCollins, 2001.

——. *Life with the Queen*. Stroud, UK: Alan Sutton, 2006.

——. *Monarchy: Behind the Scenes with the Royal Family*. London: British Broadcasting Corporation, 1997.

——. *Mountbatten: The Private Story*. London: Sidgwick & Jackson, 1994.

——. *Prince William*. Stroud, UK: Alan Sutton, 2003.

——. *Snowdon: Public Figure, Private Man*. Stroud, UK: Alan Sutton, 2005.

——. *Zara Phillips: A Revealing Portrait of a Royal World Champion*. London: Virgin, 2007.

Hogg, James, and Michael Mortimer, eds. *The Queen Mother Remembered: The Intimate Recollections of Her Friends, 1900–2002*. London: British Broadcasting Corporation, 2002.

Holden, Anthony. *Charles: A Biography*. London: Corgi, 1999.

———. *Diana: A Life and a Legacy*. London: Ebury, 1997.

———. *A Princely Marriage: Charles and Diana; The First Ten Years*. London: Bantam, 1991.

———. *The Tarnished Crown: Princess Diana and the House of Windsor*. New York: Random House, 1993.

Hough, Richard. *Born Royal: The Lives and Loves of the Young Windsors*. London: Andre Deutsch, 1988.

———. *Mountbatten: Hero of Our Time*. London: Weidenfeld & Nicolson, 1980.

Howarth, Patrick. *George VI: A New Biography*. London: Hutchinson, 1987.

Hutchins, Chris, and Peter Thompson. *Fergie Confidential: The Full Story*. New York: Pocket, 1993.

James, Paul. *Anne: The Working Princess*. London: Piatkus, 1987.

———. *Margaret: A Woman of Conflict*. London: Sidgwick & Jackson, 1990.

———. *Prince Edward: A Life in the Spotlight*. London: Piatkus, 1992.

———. *Princess Alexandra*. London: Weidenfeld & Nicolson, 1992.

James, Robert Rhodes. *A Spirit Undaunted: The Political Role of George VI*. London: Little, Brown, 1998.

Jay, Antony. *Elizabeth R: The Role of the Monarchy Today*. London: British Broadcasting Corporation, 1992.

Jephson, Patrick. *Portraits of a Princess: Travels with Diana*. New York: St. Martin's, 2004.

———. *Shadows of a Princess: Diana, Princess of Wales, 1987–1996; An Intimate Account by Her Private Secretary*. London: HarperCollins, 2000.

Jobson, Robert. *William's Princess*. London: John Blake, 2006.

Johnson, Richard. *Out of the Shadows*. Exeter, UK: Greenwater, 2002.

Judd, Denis. *King George VI, 1895–1952*. New York: Franklin Watts, 1983.

———. *Prince Philip: A Biography*. London: Sphere, 1991.

Junor, Peggy. *Charles and Diana: Portrait of a Marriage*. London: Headline, 1991.

———. *Charles: Victim or Villain?* New York: HarperCollins, 1998.

———. *Diana, Princess of Wales: A Biography*. London: Sidgwick & Jackson, 1982.

———. *The Firm: The Troubled Life of the House of Windsor*. London: HarperCollins, 2005.

Keay, Douglas. *Elizabeth II: Portrait of a Monarch*. London: Century, 1991.

———. *Queen Elizabeth, the Queen Mother*. London: IPC Magazines, 1980.

———. *Royal Wedding*. London: IPC Magazines, 1981.

Kiggell, Marcus, and Denys Blakeway. *The Queen's Story*. London: Headline, 2002.

King, Greg. *The Duchess of Windsor: The Uncommon Life of Wallis Simpson*. New York: Citadel, 1999.

Kortesis, Vasso. *The Duchess of York, Uncensored*. London: Blake, 1996.

Lacey, Robert. *The Queen Mother's Century*. London: Little, Brown, 1999.

———. *Royal: Her Majesty Queen Elizabeth II*. London: Time Warner, 2002.

Lascelles, Alan. *End of an Era: Letters and Journals of Sir Alan Lascelles, 1887–1920*. Edited by Duff Hart-Davis. London: Hamilton, 1988.

———. *In Royal Service: The Letters and Journals of Sir Alan Lascelles, 1920–1936*. Edited by Duff Hart-Davis. London: Hamilton, 1988.

———. *King's Counsellor: Abdication and War; The Diaries of Sir Alan Lascelles*. Edited by Duff Hart-Davis. London: Weidenfeld & Nicolson, 2006.

Longford, Elizabeth. *Elizabeth R: A Biography*. London: Weidenfeld & Nicolson, 1983.

———. *The Queen Mother*. London: Weidenfeld & Nicolson, 1981.

———. *The Royal House of Windsor*. London: Weidenfeld & Nicolson, 1984.

———. *Royal Throne: The Future of the Monarchy*. London: Coronet, 1993.

Lorimer, David. *Radical Prince: The Practical Vision of the Prince of Wales*. Edinburgh: Floris, 2003.

McDonald, Trevor, with Peter Tiffin. *The Queen and the Commonwealth*. London: Methuen, 1986.

McDowell, Colin. *A Hundred Years of Royal Style*. London: Muller, Blond & White, 1985.

McLeish, K., and V. McLeish, eds. *Long to Reign over Us: Memories of Coronation Day and of Life in the 1950s*. London: Bloomsbury, 1992.

McLeod, Kirsty. *Battle Royal: Edward VIII and George VI, Brother against Brother*. London: Constable, 1999.

Menkes, Suzy. *Queen and Country*. London: HarperCollins, 1992.

———. *The Windsor Style*. London: Grafton, 1987.

Montgomery-Massingberd, Hugh. *Her Majesty, Queen Elizabeth the Queen Mother: Woman of the Century*. London: Macmillan, 1999.

———. *Her Majesty the Queen*. London: Collins, 1985.

Morrow, Ann. *Cousins Divided: George V and Nicholas II*. Stroud, UK: Alan Sutton, 2006.

———. *Princess*. London: Chapmans, 1991.

———. *The Queen*. London: Granada, 1983.

———. *Without Equal: H. M. Queen Elizabeth, the Queen Mother*. Thirsk, UK: House of Stratus, 2000.

Mortimer, Penelope. *Queen Mother: An Alternative Portrait of Her Life and Times*. London: Andre Deutsch, 1995.

Morton, Andrew. *Diana: Her New Life*. London: Michael O'Mara, 1995.

———. *Diana: Her True Story; In Her Own Words*. New York: Simon & Schuster, 1997.

———. *Diana: In Pursuit of Love*. London: Michael O'Mara, 2004.

———. *Diana's Diary: An Intimate Portrait of the Princess of Wales*. New York: Summit, 1990.

———. *Duchess*. Sevenoaks, UK: New English Library, 1989.

———. *Inside Kensington Palace*. London: Michael O'Mara, 1987.

———. *Theirs Is the Kingdom: The Wealth of the Windsors*. London: Michael O'Mara, 1989.

Morton, Andrew, and Mick Seamark. *Andrew, the Playboy Prince*. London: Severn House, 1983.

Morton, James. *Prince Charles: Breaking the Cycle*. London: Ebury, 1998.

Mosley, Diana. *The Duchess of Windsor*. London: Sidgwick & Jackson, 1980.

Mountbatten of Burma, Louis Mountbatten, Earl. *The Diaries of Lord Louis Mount-batten, 1920–1922: Tours with the Prince of Wales*. Edited by Philip Ziegler. London: Collins, 1987.

——. *From Shore to Shore: The Tour Diaries of Earl Mountbatten of Burma, 1953–1979*. Edited by Philip Ziegler. London: Collins, 1989.

——. *Personal Diary of Admiral the Lord Louis Mountbatten, Supreme Allied Commander, South-East Asia, 1943–1946*. Edited by Philip Ziegler. London: Collins, 1988.

Nairn, Tom. *The Enchanted Glass: Britain and Its Monarchy*. London: Vintage, 1994.

Nicolson, Nigel. *The Queen and Us*. London: Weidenfeld & Nicolson, 2003.

Noakes, Michael, and Vivien Noakes. *The Daily Life of the Queen: An Artist's Diary*. London: Ebury, 2000.

Olechnowicz, Andrzej, ed. *The Monarchy and the British Nation: 1780 to the Present*. Cambridge: Cambridge University Press, 2007.

Packard, Jerrold M. *The Queen & Her Court: A Guide to the British Monarchy Today*. New York: Scribner, 1981.

Parker, John. *King of Fools*. London: Macdonald, 1988.

——. *Prince Philip: His Secret Life*. New York: St. Martin's, 1991.

——. *The Princess Royal*. London: Hamilton, 1989.

——. *The Queen*. London: Headline, 1991.

Pearson, John. *Blood Royal: The Story of the Spencers and the Royals*. London: HarperCollins, 1999.

——. *The Ultimate Family: The Making of the Royal House of Windsor*. London: Michael Joseph, 1986.

Picknett, Lynn, et al. *War of the Windsors: A Century of Unconstitutional Monarchy*. Edinburgh: Mainstream, 2003.

Pimlott, Ben. *The Queen: Elizabeth II and the Monarchy*. London: HarperCollins, 2001.

Pope-Hennessy, James. *Queen Mary, 1867–1953*. London: Phoenix, 2000.

Princess Alice, Duchess of Gloucester. *The Memoirs of Princess Alice, Duchess of Gloucester*. London: Collins, 1983.

——. *Memories of Ninety Years*. London: Collins & Brown, 1991.

Prochaska, F. K. *Royal Bounty: The Making of a Welfare Monarchy*. New Haven, Conn.: Yale University Press, 1995.

Pye, Michael. *The King over the Water*. Feltham, UK: Hamlyn, 1982.

Rees-Jones, Trevor. *The Bodyguard's Story: Diana, the Crash and the Sole Survivor*. New York: Warner, 2000.

Richards, Jeffrey, Scott Wilson, and Linda Woodhead, eds. *Diana: The Making of a Media Saint*. London: I. B. Tauris, 1999.

Roberts, Andrew. *The House of Windsor*. London: Cassell, 2000.

Rose, Kenneth. *King George V*. London: Phoenix, 2000.

——. *Kings, Queens & Courtiers: Intimate Portraits of the Royal House of Windsor from Its Foundations to the Present Day.* London: Weidenfeld & Nicolson, 1985.

Saunders, Mark. *Prince Harry: The Biography.* London: John Blake, 2002.

Seward, Ingrid. *Diana.* London: Grafton, 1989.

——. *The Last Great Edwardian Lady.* London: Century, 1999.

——. *Prince Edward.* London: Century, 1995.

——. *The Queen and Di: The Untold Story.* New York: Arcade, 2001.

——. *Sarah: HRH the Duchess of York; A Biography.* London: HarperCollins, 1991.

——. *William and Harry: The Biography of the Two Princes.* London: Headline, 2003.

Shawcross, William. *Queen and Country: The Fifty-Year Reign of Elizabeth II.* New York: Simon & Schuster, 2002.

——. *The Queen Mother: The Official Biography.* New York: Knopf, 2009.

Shute, Nerina. *The Royal Family and the Spencers: Two Hundred Years of Friendship.* London: Hale, 1986.

Sinclair, David. *Two Georges: The Making of the Modern Monarchy.* London: Hodder & Stoughton, 1988.

Smith, Sally Bedell. *Diana in Search of Herself: The Life of a Troubled Princess.* New York: Times Books, 1999.

Smith, Sean. *Royal Racing: The Queen and Queen Mother's Sporting Life.* London: British Broadcasting Corporation, 2001.

Spotto, Donald. *Dynasty: The Turbulent Story of the Royal Family from Victoria to Diana.* London: Simon & Schuster, 1995.

Starkey, David. *Monarchy: From the Middle Ages to Modernity.* London: HarperPress, 2006.

Starkie, Allan. *Fergie: Her Secret Life.* London: Michael O'Mara, 1996.

Swift, Will. *The Roosevelts and the Royals: Franklin and Eleanor, the King and Queen of England, and the Friendship that Changed History.* Hoboken, N.J.: Wiley, 2004.

Talbot, Godfrey. *The Country Life Book of Queen Elizabeth, the Queen Mother.* London: Country Life, 1989.

Taylor, John A. *Diana, Self-Interest and British National Identity.* Westport, Conn.: Praeger, 2000.

Thomas, Gwynne. *King Pawn or Black Knight?* Edinburgh: Mainstream, 1995.

Thomas, James. *Diana's Mourning: A People's History.* Cardiff: University of Wales, 2002.

Thornton, Michael. *Royal Feud: The Dark Side of the Love Story of the Century.* New York: Simon & Schuster, 1985.

Tomlinson, Richard. *Divine Right: The Inglorious Survival of British Royalty.* London: Little, Brown, 1994.

Turnock, Robert. *Interpreting Diana: Television Audiences and the Death of a Princess.* London: British Film Institute, 2000.

Van der Kiste, John. *Crowns in a Changing World: The British and European Monarchies, 1901–1936.* Stroud, UK: Alan Sutton, 1993.

——. *George V's Children.* Stroud, UK: Alan Sutton, 2003.

Varney, Michael. *Bodyguard to Charles*. London: Hale, 1989.

Vickers, Hugo. *Debrett's Book of the Royal Wedding*. London: Debrett's, 1981.

——. *Elizabeth, the Queen Mother*. London: Hutchinson, 2005.

——. *The Private World of the Duke and Duchess of Windsor*. London: Harrods Publishing, 1995.

Walter, Tony, ed. *The Mourning for Diana*. Oxford: Berg, 1999.

Warwick, Christopher. *Abdication*. London: Sidgwick & Jackson, 1986.

——. *Debrett's Queen Elizabeth II*. Exeter: Webb & Bower, 1986.

——. *George and Marina: Duke and Duchess of Kent*. London: Weidenfeld & Nicolson, 1988.

——. *King George VI and Queen Elizabeth: A Portrait*. London: Sidgwick & Jackson, 1985.

——. *Princess Margaret: A Life of Contrasts*. London: Andre Deutsch, 2002.

——, ed. *Queen Mary's Photograph Albums*. London: Sidgwick & Jackson, 1989.

Watson, Sophie. *Marina: The Story of a Princess*. London: Weidenfeld & Nicolson, 1994.

Wharfe, Ken, with Robert Jobson. *Diana: Closely Guarded Secret*. London: Michael O'Mara, 2003.

Whitaker, James. *Settling Down*. London: Quarter, 1981.

Williams, Susan. *The People's King: The True Story of the Abdication*. London: Allen Lane, 2003.

Wilson, A. N. *The Rise and Fall of the House of Windsor*. New York: Fawcett Columbine, 1994.

Wilson, Christopher. *Dancing with the Devil: The Windsors and Jimmy Donahue*. New York: St. Martin's, 2001.

——. *A Greater Love: Prince Charles's Twenty-Year Affair with Camilla Parker Bowles*. New York: William Morrow, 1994.

Windsor, Edward, Duke of. *A King's Story: The Memoirs of HRH the Duke of Windsor, KG*. London: Prion, 1998.

——. *Letters from a Prince: Edward, Prince of Wales, to Mrs Freda Dudley Ward, March 1918–January 1921*. Edited by Rupert Godfrey. London: Warner, 1999.

Windsor, Edward, Duke of, and Windsor, Wallis Warfield, Duchess of. *Wallis and Edward, Letters 1931–1937: The Intimate Correspondence of the Duke and Duchess of Windsor*. Edited by Michael Bloch. New York: Summit, 1986.

Windsor, Wallis Warfield, Duchess of. *The Heart Has Its Reasons: The Memoirs of the Duchess of Windsor*. Bath, UK: Chivers, 1983.

York, Sarah Mountbatten-Windsor, Duchess of. *My Story*. New York: Simon & Schuster, 1996.

Ziegler, Philip. *King Edward VIII: The Official Biography*. Stroud, UK: Alan Sutton.

——. *Mountbatten: The Official Biography*. London: Phoenix, 2001.

## SCOTLAND'S MONARCHIES

Aitchison, Nick. *Macbeth: Man and Myth*. Stroud, UK: Sutton, 2000.

Anderson, Alan Orr. *Early Sources of Scottish History, AD 500–1286*. 2 vols. Edited by Marjorie Anderson. Stamford, UK: Paul Watkins, 1990.

——, ed. *Scottish Annals from English Chroniclers, AD 500 to 1286*. Stamford, UK: Paul Watkins, 1991.

Anderson, Marjorie O. *Kings and Kingship in Early Scotland*. Edinburgh: Scottish Academic Press, 1980.

Ashdown, Dulcie M. *The Stuarts*. London: Cassell, 2000.

——. *Tudor Cousins: Rivals for the Throne*. Stroud, UK: Alan Sutton, 2000.

Barbour, John. *The Bruce*. Translated by A. A. M. Duncan. Edinburgh: Canongate, 1997.

Barnes, Ishbel C. M. *Janet Kennedy, Royal Mistress: Marriage and Divorce at the Courts of James IV and James V*. Edinburgh: John Donald, 2007.

Barratt, John. *Battles for the Three Kingdoms: The Campaigns for England, Scotland and Ireland, 1689–92*. Stroud, UK: Alan Sutton, 2007.

Barrell, A. D. M. *Medieval Scotland*. Cambridge: Cambridge University Press, 2000.

Barrow, G. W. S. *The Anglo-Norman Era in Scottish History*. Oxford: Clarendon, 1980.

——. *The Kingdom of the Scots: Government, Church and Society from the Eleventh to the Fourteenth Century*. Edinburgh: Edinburgh University Press, 2003.

——. *Kingship and Unity: Scotland 1000–1306*. Edinburgh: Edinburgh University Press, 2003.

——. *Robert Bruce and the Community of the Realm of Scotland*. Edinburgh: Edinburgh University Press, 2005.

——, ed. *The Charters of King David I: The Written Acts of David I, King of Scots, 1124–1153, and of His Son, Henry, Earl of Northumberland, 1139–1152*. Woodbridge, UK: Boydell, 1999.

Bath, Michael. *Emblems for a Queen: The Needlework of Mary, Queen of Scots*. London: Archetype, 2008.

Beam, Amanda. *The Balliol Dynasty, 1210–1364*. Edinburgh: John Donald, 2008.

Bergeron, David M. *King James and Letters of Homoerotic Desire*. Iowa City: University of Iowa Press, 1999.

——. *Royal Family, Royal Lovers: King James of England and Scotland*. Columbia, Mo.: University of Missouri Press, 1991.

Bevan, Bryan. *King James VI of Scotland and I of England*. London: Rubicon, 1996.

Bingham, Caroline. *Darnley: A Life of Henry Stuart, Lord Darnley, Consort of Mary Queen of Scots*. London: Constable, 1995.

——. *Robert the Bruce*. London: Constable, 1998.

Boardman, Stephen. *The Early Stewart Kings: Robert II and Robert III, 1371–1406*. East Linton, UK: Tuckwell, 1996.

Bongie, L. L. *The Love of a Prince: Bonnie Prince Charlie in France, 1744–1748*. Vancouver: University of British Columbia Press, 1986.

Broun, Dauvit. *The Irish Identity of the Kingdom of the Scots in the Twelfth and Thirteenth Centuries*. Woodbridge: Boydell Press, 1999.

Brown, Chris. *The Knights of the Scottish Wars of Independence*. Stroud, UK: Tempus, 2008.

——. *Robert the Bruce: A Life Chronicled*. Stroud, UK: Tempus, 2004.

——. *The Second Scottish Wars of Independence*. Stroud, UK: Tempus, 2006.

Brown, Keith M. *Bloodfeud in Scotland, 1573–1625: Violence, Justice and Politics in an Early Modern Society.* Edinburgh: John Donald, 1986.

———. *Kingdom or Province?: Scotland and the Regal Union, 1603–1707.* Basingstoke, UK: Macmillan, 1992.

———. *Noble Society in Scotland: Wealth, Family and Culture from Reformation to Revolution.* Edinburgh: Edinburgh University Press, 2004.

———, general ed. *The History of the Scottish Parliament.* 3 vols. Edinburgh: Edinburgh University Press, 2004.

Brown, Michael. *James I.* Edinburgh: Canongate Academic, 1994.

———. *The Wars of Scotland, 1214–1371.* Edinburgh: Edinburgh University Press, 2004.

Brown, Michael, and Roland Tanner, eds. *Scottish Kingship, 1306–1542: Essays in Honour of Norman Macdougall.* Edinburgh: John Donald, 2008.

Buchanan, George. *A Dialogue on the Law of Kingship among the Scots: A Critical Edition and Translation of George Buchanan's De Jure Regni apud Scotus Dialogue.* Translated by Roger A. Mason and Martin S. Smith. Aldershot, UK: Ashgate, 2004.

Buchanan, Patricia Hill. *Margaret Tudor, Queen of Scots.* Edinburgh: Scottish Academic Press, 1985.

Cameron, Jamie. *James V: The Personal Rule, 1528–1542.* East Linton, UK: Tuckwell, 1998.

Campbell, Jimmy Powdrell. *The Scottish Crown Jewels and the Minister's Wife.* Stroud, UK: Tempus, 2007.

Campbell, Marion. *Alexander III, King of Scots.* Colonsay, UK: House of Lochar, 1999.

Carlton, Charles. *Charles I: The Personal Monarch.* London: Routledge, 1995.

Carrier, Irene. *James VI and I: King of Great Britain.* Cambridge: Cambridge University Press, 1998.

Clark, Ronald W. *Balmoral: Queen Victoria's Highland Home.* London: Thames & Hudson, 1981.

Cogswell, Thomas, Richard Cust, and Peter Lake, eds. *Politics, Religion and Popularity in Early Stuart Britain: Essays in Honour of Conrad Russell.* Cambridge: Cambridge University Press, 2002.

Coote, Stephen. *Royal Survivor: A Life of Charles II.* New York: St. Martin's, 2000.

Corp, Edward. *A Court in Exile: The Stuarts in France, 1689–1718.* Cambridge: Cambridge University Press, 2004.

———. *The Jacobites at Urbino: An Exiled Court in Transition.* Basingstoke, UK: Palgrave Macmillan, 2009.

———, ed. *The Stuart Court in Rome: The Legacy of Exile.* Aldershot, UK: Ashgate, 2003.

Coventry, Martin. *The Castles of Scotland.* Edinburgh: Birlinn, 2006.

Cowan, Edward J., and R. Andrew McDonald, eds. *Alba: Celtic Scotland in the Middle Ages.* East Linton, UK: Tuckwell, 2000.

Cramsie, John. *Kingship and Crown Finance under James VI and I, 1603–1625.* London: Royal Historical Society, 2002.

Crawford, Barbara E. *Scandinavian Scotland*. Leicester: Leicester University Press, 1987.

Croft, Pauline. *King James*. Basingstoke, UK: Palgrave Macmillan, 2003.

Cruickshanks, Eveline, ed. *Ideology and Conspiracy: Aspects of Jacobitism, 1689–1759*. Edinburgh: John Donald, 1982.

———, ed. *The Stuart Courts*. Stroud, UK: Alan Sutton, 2000.

Cruickshanks, Eveline, and Edward Corp, eds. *The Stuart Court in Exile and the Jacobites*. Rio Grande, Ohio: Hambledon, 1995.

Daiches, David. *Bonnie Prince Charlie: The Life and Times of Charles Edward Stuart*. London: Penguin, 2002.

Davies, R. R. *Domination and Conquest: The Experience of Ireland, Scotland and Wales, 1100–1300*. Cambridge: Cambridge University Press, 2006.

De Lisle, Leanda. *After Elizabeth: The Rise of James of Scotland and the Struggle for the Throne of England*. New York: Ballantine, 2005.

Donald, P. *An Uncounselled King: Charles I and the Scottish Troubles, 1637–1641*. Cambridge: Cambridge University Press, 1990.

Donaldson, Gordon. *All the Queen's Men: Power and Politics in Mary Stewart's Scotland*. London: Batsford, 1983.

Donnachie, Ian, and George Hewitt. *The Birlinn Companion to Scottish History*. Edinburgh: Birlinn, 2007.

Doran, Susan. *Mary, Queen of Scots: An Illustrated Life*. London: British Library, 2007.

Douglas, Hugh. *The Private Passions of Bonnie Prince Charlie*. Stroud, UK: Alan Sutton, 1998.

Douglas, Hugh, and Michael J. Stead. *The Flight of Bonnie Prince Charlie*. Stroud, UK: Alan Sutton, 2000.

Duff, David, ed. *Queen Victoria's Highland Journals*. London: Hamlyn, 1997.

Duffy, Christopher. *The '45*. London: Cassell Military, 2003.

Duffy, Seán. *Robert the Bruce's Irish Wars: The Invasions of Ireland, 1306–1329*. Stroud, UK: Tempus, 2002.

Dunbar, John G. *Scottish Royal Palaces: The Architecture of the Royal Residences during the Late Mediaeval and Early Renaissance Periods*. East Linton, UK: Tuckwell, 1999.

Duncan, A. A. M., ed. *The Acts of Robert I, King of Scots, 1306–1329*. Edinburgh: Edinburgh University Press, 1988.

———. *The Kingship of the Scots, 842–1292: Succession and Independence*. Edinburgh: Edinburgh University Press, 2002.

Dunlop, Eileen. *Queen Margaret of Scotland*. Edinburgh: National Museums of Scotland, 2005.

Dunn, Jane. *Elizabeth and Mary: Cousins, Rivals, Queens*. New York: Knopf, 2004.

Dunnigan, Sarah M. *Eros and Poetry at the Courts of Mary, Queen of Scots, and James VI*. Basingstoke, UK: Palgrave Macmillan, 2002.

Erickson, Carolly. *Bonnie Prince Charlie: A Biography*. New York: William Morrow, 1989.

Fellows, Nicholas. *Charles II and James II*. London: Hodder & Stoughton, 1995.

Fischlin, Daniel, and Mark Fortier, eds. *Essays on the Writings of James VI and I*. Detroit: Wayne State University Press, 2002.

Fissel, Mark Charles. *The Bishops' Wars: Charles I's Campaigns against Scotland, 1638–1640*. Cambridge: Cambridge University Press, 1994.

Foster, Sally M. *Picts, Gaels and Scots: Early Historic Scotland*. London: Batsford, 2004.

Frame, Robin. *The Political Development of the British Isles, 1100–1400*. Oxford: Clarendon, 1995.

Franklin, David Byrd. *The Scottish Regency of the Earl of Arran: A Study in the Failure of Anglo-Scottish Relations*. Lewiston, N.Y.: Edwin Mellen, 1995.

Fraser, Antonia. *Mary, Queen of Scots*. New York: Delta, 2001.

Galloway, Bruce. *The Union of England and Scotland, 1603–1608*. Edinburgh: John Donald, 1986.

Goodare, Julian, and Michael Lynch, eds. *The Reign of James VI*. East Linton, UK: Tuckwell Press, 2000.

Goodman, Jean, in collaboration with Sir Iain Moncrieff of that Ilk. *Debrett's Royal Scotland*. New York: Putnam, 1983.

Grant, Alexander, and Keith Stringer, eds. *Medieval Scotland: Crown, Lordship and Community: Essays Presented to G. W. S. Barrow*. Edinburgh: Edinburgh University Press, 1993.

Guy, John. *My Heart Is My Own: The Life of Mary, Queen of Scots*. London: Fourth Estate, 2004.

Hamilton, Duke of. *Maria R: Mary Queen of Scots; The Crucial Years*. Edinburgh: Mainstream, 1991.

Hamilton, Ian R. *Taking of the Stone of Destiny*. London: Corgi, 1992.

Harris, Bob, and Alan R. Macdonald, eds. *Scotland: The Making and Unmaking of the Nation, c1100–1707*. 5 vols. Dundee: Dundee University and the Open University Press, 2006.

Harris, Tim. *Restoration: Charles II and His Kingdoms, 1660–1685*. London: Penguin, 2006.

———. *Revolution: The Great Crisis of the British Monarchy, 1685–1720*. London: Allen Lane, 2006.

Hewitt, George R. *Scotland under Morton, 1572–80*. Edinburgh: John Donald, 1982.

Holmes, Frederick. *The Sickly Stuarts: The Medical Downfall of a Dynasty*. Stroud, UK: Alan Sutton, 2005.

Hook, Michael, and Walter Ross. *The 'Forty-Five: The Last Jacobite Rebellion*. Edinburgh: Her Majesty's Stationery Office, 1995.

Hopkins, Lisa. *Writing Renaissance Queens: Texts by and about Elizabeth I and Mary, Queen of Scots*. Newark: University of Delaware Press, 2002.

Houlbrooke, Ralph, ed. *James VI and I: Ideas, Authority and Government*. Aldershot, UK: Ashgate, 2007.

Hudson, Benjamin T. *Kings of Celtic Scotland*. Westport, Conn.: Greenwood Press, 1994.

———. *The Prophecy of Berchán: Irish and Scottish High-Kings of the Early Middle Ages*. Westport, Conn.: Greenwood Press, 1996.

Hughes, Kathleen. *Celtic Britain in the Early Middle Ages: Studies in Welsh and Scottish Sources*. Edited by David N. Dumville. Woodbridge, UK: Boydell, 1980.

Huneycutt, Lois L. *Matilda of Scotland: A Study in Medieval Queenship*. Woodbridge, UK: Boydell, 2003.

Hutton, Ronald. *Charles the Second: King of England, Scotland and Ireland*. Oxford: Oxford University Press, 1991.

James VI and I. *Letters*. Edited by G. P. V. Akrigg. Berkeley, Calif.: University of California Press, 1984.

———. *Political Writings*. Edited by Johann P. Sommerville. Cambridge: Cambridge University Press, 1994.

Jones, J. R. *Charles II: Royal Politician*. London: Allen & Unwin, 1987.

Kenyon, John, and Jane Ohlmeyer, eds. *The Civil Wars: A Military History of England, Scotland and Ireland, 1638–1660*. Oxford: Oxford University Press, 2002.

Kishlansky, Mark. *A Monarchy Transformed: Britain, 1603–1714*. London: Allen Lane, 1996.

Kybett, Susan Maclean. *Bonnie Prince Charlie: A Biography of Charles Edward Stuart*. New York: Dodd, Mead, 1988.

Laidlaw, James, ed. *The Auld Alliance: France and Scotland over 700 Years*. Edinburgh: Edinburgh University Press, 1999.

Laing, Lloyd, and Jenny Laing. *The Picts and the Scots*. Stroud, UK: Alan Sutton, 1993.

Lamont-Brown, Raymond. *John Brown: Queen Victoria's Highland Servant*. Stroud, UK: Alan Sutton, 2002.

Lane, Alan, and Ewan Campbell. *Dunadd: An Early Dalriadic Capital*. Oxford: Oxbow, 2001.

Lee, Maurice, Jr. *Government by Pen: Scotland under James VI and I*. Urbana, Ill.: University of Illinois Press, 1980.

———. *Great Britain's Solomon: James VI and I in His Three Kingdoms*. Urbana, Ill.: University of Illinois Press, 1990.

———. *The Road to Revolution: Scotland under Charles I, 1625–37*. Urbana, Ill.: University of Illinois Press, 1985.

———, ed. *The "Inevitable" Union and Other Essays on Early Modern Scotland*. East Linton, UK: Tuckwell, 2003.

Lenman, B. *The Jacobite Cause*. Glasgow: Drew, 1986.

Little, Crawford. *Union of Crowns: The Forging of Europe's Most Independent State*. Glasgow: Neil Wilson, 2003.

Lockyer, Roger. *James VI and I*. London: Addison Wesley Longman, 1998.

Lowe, Joseph. *A New Most Excellent Dancing Master: The Journal of Joseph Lowe's Visits to Balmoral and Windsor (1852–1860) to Teach Dance to the Family of Queen Victoria*. Edited by Allan Thomas. Stuyvesant, N.Y.: Pendragon, 1992.

Lynch, Michael, ed. *Mary Stewart: Queen in Three Kingdoms*. Oxford: Blackwell, 1988.

———. *The Oxford Companion to Scottish History*. Oxford: Oxford University Press, 2005.

———. *Scotland: A New History*. London: Barrie & Jenkins, 1991.

Macdougall, Norman. *An Antidote to the English: The Auld Alliance, 1295–1560*. East Linton, UK: Tuckwell, 2001.

———. *James III: A Political Study*. Edinburgh: John Donald, 1982.

———. *James IV: The Stewart Dynasty in Scotland*. Edinburgh: John Donald, 2006.

Macfarlane, Leslie J. *William Elphinstone and the Kingdom of Scotland, 1431–1514: The Struggle for Order*. Aberdeen: Aberdeen University Press, 1985.

Macinnes, A. I. *Charles I and the Making of the Covenanting Movement, 1625–1641*. Edinburgh: John Donald, 1991.

Mackay, James. *In My End Is My Beginning: A Life of Mary, Queen of Scots*. Edinburgh: Mainstream, 1999.

Mackenzie, W. M. *The Battle of Bannockburn: A Study in Medieval Warfare*. Stevenage, UK: Strong Oak Press, 1999.

Mackenzie-Stuart, A. J. *A French King at Holyrood*. Edinburgh: John Donald, 1995.

Maclean, Fitzroy. *Bonnie Prince Charlie*. New York: Atheneum, 1989.

Macleod, John. *Dynasty: The Stuarts, 1560–1807*. New York: St. Martin's, 2001.

Magnússon, Magnús. *Scotland: The Story of a Nation*. London: HarperCollins, 2000.

Marsden, John. *Alba of the Ravens: In Search of the Celtic Kingdom of the Scots*. London: Constable, 1997.

———. *The Tombs of the Kings: An Iona Book of the Dead*. Felinfach, UK: Llanerch, 1994.

Marshall, Rosalind K. *Bonnie Prince Charlie*. Edinburgh: Her Majesty's Stationery Office, 1988.

———. *Mary of Guise: Queen of Scots*. Edinburgh: National Museums of Scotland, 2001.

———. *Queen Mary's Women: Female Relatives, Servants, Friends and Enemies of Mary, Queen of Scots*. Edinburgh: John Donald, 2006.

———. *Queen of Scots*. Edinburgh: Her Majesty's Stationery Office, 1986.

———. *Scottish Queens, 1034–1714*. East Linton, UK: Tuckwell, 2003.

Mary, Queen of Scots. *Bittersweet within My Heart: The Collected Poems of Mary, Queen of Scots*. Translated and edited by Robin Bell. London: Pavilion, 1992.

Mason, Roger A., ed. *Kingship and the Commonweal: Political Thought in Renaissance and Reformation Scotland*. East Linton, UK: Tuckwell, 1998.

McCulloch, John Herries. *The Making of a Monarch: When the Scots Had Home Rule, and the Long Struggle of King James VI of Scotland against Violence and Bigotry*. Glasgow: E. Drew, 2003.

McDonald, R. Andrew. *The Kingdom of the Isles: Scotland's Western Seaboard, c1100–c1336*. East Linton, UK: Tuckwell, 1997.

———. *Outlaws of Medieval Scotland: Challenges to the Canmore Kings, 1058–1266*. East Linton, UK: Tuckwell Press, 2003.

McGladdery, Christine. *James II*. Edinburgh: John Donald, 1990.

McLynn, Frank J. *Bonnie Prince Charlie: Charles Edward Stuart*. London: Pimlico, 2003.

———. *The Jacobites*. London: Routledge & Kegan Paul, 1988.

McNamee, Colin. *The Wars of the Bruces: Scotland, England and Ireland, 1306–1328*. East Linton, UK: Tuckwell, 1997.

McNeill, Peter G. B., and Hector L. MacQueen, eds. *Atlas of Scottish History to 1707*. Edinburgh: University of Edinburgh, 1996.

Merriman, Marcus. *The Rough Wooings: Mary, Queen of Scots, 1542–1551*. East Linton, UK: Tuckwell Press, 2000.

Michael of Albany, His Royal Highness Prince. *The Forgotten Monarchy of Scotland: The True Story of the Royal House of Stewart and the Hidden Lineage of the Kings and Queens of Scots*. London: Vega, 2002.

Millar, Delia. *Queen Victoria's Life in the Highlands, as Depicted by Her Watercolour Artists*. London: P. Wilson, 1985.

Miller, John. *Charles II*. London: Weidenfeld & Nicolson, 1991.

———. *James II*. New Haven, Conn.: Yale University Press, 2000.

———. *The Stuarts*. London: Hambledon & London, 2003.

Mitchell, Ian R. *On the Trail of Queen Victoria in the Highlands*. Edinburgh: Luath, 2000.

Mitchison, Rosalind. *A History of Scotland*. London: Routledge, 2002.

Muhlstein, Anka. *Elizabeth I and Mary Stuart: The Problems of Marriage*. London: Haus, 2007.

Normand, Lawrence, and Gareth Roberts, eds. *Witchcraft in Early Modern Scotland: James VI's Demonology and the North Berwick Witches*. Exeter: Exeter University Press, 2000.

Oates, Jonathan. *Sweet William or the Butcher?: The Duke of Cumberland and the '45*. Barnsley, UK: Pen and Sword Military, 2008.

Oram, Richard. *The Canmores: Kings and Queens of the Scots, 1040–1290*. Stroud, UK: History Press, 2002.

———. *David I: The King Who Made Scotland*. Stroud, UK: Tempus, 2004.

———, ed. *The Kings and Queens of Scotland*. Stroud, UK: Tempus, 2004.

———, ed. *The Reign of Alexander II, 1214–49*. Leiden: Brill, 2005.

Patterson, W. B. *King James VI and I and the Reunion of Christendom*. Cambridge: Cambridge University Press, 1997.

Penman, Michael A. *David II, 1329–71*. Edinburgh: John Donald, 2005.

Perry, Maria. *Sisters to the King: The Tumultuous Lives of Henry VIII's Sisters; Margaret of Scotland and Mary of France*. London: Andre Deutsch, 2002.

Pittock, Murray G. H. *The Invention of Scotland: The Stuart Myth and the Scottish Identity, 1638 to the Present*. London: Routledge, 1991.

———. *Jacobitism*. New York: St. Martin's, 1998.

Plowden, Alison. *Elizabeth Tudor and Mary Stewart: Two Queens in One Isle*. Totowa, N.J.: Barnes & Noble, 1984.

Prebble, John. *Culloden*. London: Pimlico, 2002.

———. *The King's Jaunt: George IV in Scotland, August 1822; "One and Twenty Daft Days."* London: Collins, 1988.

Reese, Peter. *Bannockburn*. Edinburgh: Canongate, 2000.

———. *Flodden: A Scottish Tragedy*. Edinburgh: Birlinn, 2003.

Reid, Norman H., ed. *Scotland in the Reign of Alexander III, 1249–1286*. Edinburgh: John Donald, 1990.

Rhodes, Neil, Jennifer Richards, and Joseph Marshall. *King James VI and I: Selected Writings*. Aldershot: Ashgate, 2003.

Ritchie, Pamela E. *Mary of Guise in Scotland, 1548–1560: A Political Career*. East Linton, UK: Tuckwell, 2002.

Roberts, John L. *The Jacobite Wars: Scotland and the Military Campaigns of 1715 and 1745*. Edinburgh: Polygon, 2002.

———. *Lost Kingdoms: Celtic Scotland and the Middle Ages*. Edinburgh: Edinburgh University Press, 1997.

Russell, Conrad. *The Fall of the British Monarchies, 1637–1642*. Oxford: Clarendon, 1991.

Schaefer, Carol. *Mary, Queen of Scots*. New York: Crossroad, 2002.

Scott, Robert McNair. *Robert the Bruce, King of Scots*. New York: Carroll & Graf, 1996.

Seel, Graham E., and David L. Smith. *The Early Stuart Kings, 1603–1642*. London: Routledge, 2001.

Smyth, A. P. *Warlords and Holy Men: Scotland AD 80–1000*. Edinburgh: Edinburgh University Press, 1989.

Somerset Fry, Plantagenet. *Kings and Queens: A Royal History of Scotland and England*. London: Dorling Kindersley, 1997.

Speck, William Arthur. *The Butcher: The Duke of Cumberland and the Suppression of the '45*. Caernarfon, UK: Welsh Academic, 1995.

Staines, John D. *The Tragic Histories of Mary, Queen of Scots, 1560–1690: Rhetoric, Passions, and Political Literature*. Aldershot, UK: Ashgate, 2009.

Steel, David, and Judy Steel. *Mary Stuart's Scotland: The Landscapes, Life and Legends of Mary Queen of Scots*. London: Weidenfeld & Nicolson, 1987.

Stevenson, David. *King or Covenant?: Voices from Civil War*. East Linton, UK: Tuckwell, 1996.

———. *Scotland's Last Royal Wedding: The Marriage of James VI and Anne of Denmark*. Edinburgh: John Donald, 1997.

Stewart, Allan. *The Cradle King: The Life of James VI and I, the First Monarch of a United Great Britain*. New York: St. Martin's, 2003.

Stringer, Keith J. *Earl David of Huntingdon, 1152–1219: A Study in Anglo-Scottish History*. Edinburgh: Edinburgh University Press, 1985.

———, ed. *Essays on the Nobility of Medieval Scotland*. Edinburgh: John Donald, 1985.

Swain, Margaret. *The Needlework of Mary, Queen of Scots*. Carlton, Australia: Ruth Bean, 1986.

Szechi, Daniel. *1715: The Great Jacobite Rebellion*. New Haven, Conn.: Yale University Press, 2006.

———. *The Jacobites: Britain and Europe, 1688–1788*. Manchester: Manchester University Press, 1994.

———. *Jacobitism and Tory Politics, 1710–14*. Edinburgh: John Donald, 1984.

Tanner, Roland. *The Late Medieval Scottish Parliament: Politics and the Three Estates, 1424–1488.* East Linton, UK: Tuckwell, 2001.

Taylor, Simon, ed. *Kings, Clerics and Chronicles in Scotland, 500–1297: Essays in Honour of Marjorie Ogilvie Anderson on the Occasion of Her Ninetieth Birthday.* Dublin: Four Courts Press, 2000.

Thomson, Duncan, et al. *Dynasty: The Royal House of Stewart.* Edinburgh: National Galleries of Scotland, 1990.

Trevor, Meriol. *The Shadow of a Crown: The Life Story of James II of England and VII of Scotland.* London: Constable, 1988.

Tweedie, David. *David Rizzio and Mary, Queen of Scots: Murder at Holyrood.* Stroud, UK: Alan Sutton, 2006.

Victoria, Queen. *Queen Victoria's Highland Journals.* Edited by David Duff. Exeter, UK: Webb & Bower, 1983.

Walker, Ian W. *Lords of Alba: The Making of Scotland.* Stroud, UK: Alan Sutton, 2006.

Warnicke, Retha M. *Mary, Queen of Scots.* London: Routledge, 2006.

Watkins, Susan. *Mary Queen of Scots.* London: Thames & Hudson, 2001.

Watson, Fiona J. *Scotland: From Prehistory to the Present.* Stroud, UK: Tempus, 2003.

———. *Under the Hammer: Edward I and Scotland, 1286–1306.* East Linton, UK: Tuckwell, 1998.

Weir, Alison. *Mary, Queen of Scots, and the Murder of Lord Darnley.* New York: Ballantine, 2003.

Welander, Richard, David J. Breeze, and Thomas Owen Clancy, eds. *The Stone of Destiny: Artefact and Icon.* Edinburgh: Society of Antiquaries of Scotland, 2003.

Wilkinson, Alexander S. *Mary, Queen of Scots, and French Public Opinion, 1542–1600.* Basingstoke, UK: Palgrave Macmillan, 2004.

Williams, Ann, Alfred P. Smyth, and D. P. Kirby. *A Biographical Dictionary of Dark Age Britain: England, Scotland and Wales from c500–c1050.* London: Seaby, 1991.

Woolf, Alex. *From Pictland to Alba, 789–1070.* Edinburgh: Edinburgh University Press, 2007.

Woosnam-Savage, Robert C., ed. *1745: Charles Edward Stuart and the Jacobites.* Edinburgh: Her Majesty's Stationery Office, 1995.

Wormald, Jenny. *Court, Kirk and Community: Scotland, 1470–1625.* Edinburgh: Edinburgh University Press, 1991.

———. *Mary, Queen of Scots: Politics, Passion and a Kingdom Lost.* London: Tauris Parke, 2001.

———, ed. *Scotland: A History.* Oxford: Oxford University Press, 2005.

Young, Michael B. *King James and the History of Homosexuality.* New York: New York University Press, 1999.

Youngson, A. J. *The Prince and the Pretender: Two Views of the '45.* Edinburgh: Mercat, 1996.

654 • BIBLIOGRAPHY

## ROYAL RESIDENCES, FURNISHINGS, AND COLLECTIONS

Adair, John. *The Royal Palaces of Britain*. London: Thames & Hudson, 1981.

Baldwin, David. *The Chapel Royal: Ancient and Modern*. London: Duckworth, 1990.

Best, David. *The Royal Tennis Court: A History of Tennis at Hampton Court Palace*. Oxford: Ironbark Ronaldson, 2002.

Brown, Sarah, ed. *A History of the Stained Glass of St. George's Chapel, Windsor Castle*. Windsor, UK: Dean and Canons of Windsor, 2005.

Charles, Prince of Wales, and Candida Lycett Green. *The Garden at Highgrove*. London: Weidenfeld & Nicolson, 2000.

Clark, Ronald W. *Balmoral: Queen Victoria's Highland Home*. London: Thames & Hudson, 1981.

Clayton, Martin. *Holbein to Hockney: Drawings from the Royal Collection*. London: Royal Collection, 2004.

Cloake, John. *Palaces and Parks of Richmond and Kew: The Palaces of Shene and Richmond*. Chichester, UK: Phillimore, 1995.

——. *Palaces and Parks of Richmond and Kew: Richmond Lodge and the Kew Palaces*. Chichester, UK: Phillimore, 1996.

Courtney, Nicholas. *The Queen's Stamps: The Authorised History of the Royal Philatelic Collection*. London: Methuen, 2009.

Coventry, Martin. *The Castles of Scotland*. Edinburgh: Birlinn, 2006.

Culme, John, and Nicholas Rayner. *The Jewels of the Duchess of Windsor*. New York: Vendome, 1987.

De-La-Noy, Michael. *Windsor Castle: Past and Present*. London: Headline, 1990.

Dennison, E. Patricia. *Holyrood and Canongate: A Thousand Years of History*. Edinburgh: Birlinn, 2005.

Dunbar, John G. *Scottish Royal Palaces: The Architecture of the Royal Residences during the Late Mediaeval and Early Renaissance Periods*. East Linton, UK: Tuckwell, 1999.

Eaton, Faith. *Dolls for the Princesses: The Story of France and Marianne*. London: Royal Collection, 2002.

Edgar, Donald. *Palace: A Fascinating Behind-the-Scenes Look at How Buckingham Palace Really Works*. London: W. H. Allen, 1983.

Field, Leslie. *The Queen's Jewels: The Personal Collection of Queen Elizabeth II*. London: Weidenfeld & Nicolson, 1987.

Gordon, Sophie. *Noble Hounds and Dear Companions: The Royal Photograph Collection*. London: Royal Collection, 2007.

Groom, Susanne, and Lee Prosser. *Kew Palace: The Official Illustrated History*. London: Merrell, 2006.

Harris, Marion. *The Queen's Windsor*. Bourne End, UK: Kensal, 1985.

Hawkes, Jason, and Jane Struthers. *Royal Britain from the Air*. London: Ebury, 1994.

Healey, Edna. *The Queen's House: A Social History of Buckingham Palace*. London: Michael Joseph, 1997.

Hedley, Olwen. *Windsor Castle*. London: Hale, 1994.

Impey, Edward. *Kensington Palace: The Official Illustrated History*. London: Merrell, 2003.

James, Thomas Beaumont. *The Palaces of Medieval England, c1050–1550: Royalty, Nobility, the Episcopate and Their Residences from Edward the Confessor to Henry VIII*. London: Seaby, 1990.

James, T. B., and A. M. Robinson. *Clarendon Palace: The History and Archaeology of a Medieval Palace and Hunting Lodge near Salisbury, Wiltshire*. London: Society of Antiquaries, 1988.

Leith-Ross, Prudence. *The Florilegium of Alexander Marshal in the Collection of Her Majesty the Queen at Windsor Castle*. London: Royal Collection, 2000.

Lloyd, Christopher. *The Paintings in the Royal Collection: A Thematic Exploration*. London: Royal Collection, 1999.

Lloyd, Christopher, and Vanessa Remington. *Masterpieces in Little: Portrait Miniatures from the Collection of Her Majesty Queen Elizabeth II*. Woodbridge, UK: Boydell, 1996.

Menkes, Suzy. *The Royal Jewels*. London: Grafton, 1988.

Millar, Delia. *The Victorian Watercolours and Drawings in the Collection of Her Majesty the Queen*. London: Philip Wilson, 1995.

Millar, Oliver. *The Victorian Pictures in the Collection of Her Majesty the Queen*. 2 vols. Cambridge: Cambridge University Press, 1992.

Montague-Smith, Patrick, and Hugh Montgomery-Massingberd. *The Country Life Book of Royal Palaces, Castles and Homes, Including Vanished Palaces and Historic Houses with Royal Connections*. London: Country Life, 1981.

Morton, Andrew. *Inside Kensington Palace*. Sevenoaks, UK: New English Library, 1988.

———. *The Royal Yacht Britannia*. London: Orbis, 1984.

Naftel, W. D. *Prince Edward's Legacy: The Duke of Kent in Halifax; Romance and Beautiful Buildings*. Halifax, Canada: Formac, 2005.

Nash, Roy. *Buckingham Palace: The Place and the People*. London: Macdonald, 1980.

Nicolson, Adam. *Restoration: The Rebuilding of Windsor Castle*. London: Michael Joseph, 1997.

Patterson, Stephen. *Royal Insignia: British and Foreign Orders of Chivalry from the Royal Collection*. London: Merrell Holberton, 1996.

Piacenti, Kirsten Aschengreen, and John Boardman. *Ancient and Modern Gems and Jewels in the Collection of Her Majesty the Queen*. London: Royal Collection, 2008.

Plumpre, George. *Royal Gardens*. London: Collins, 1981.

Reynolds, Graham. *The Sixteenth and Seventeenth Century Miniatures in the Collection of Her Majesty the Queen*. London: Royal Collection, 1999.

Richmond, Colin, and Eileen Scarff. *St. George's Chapel, Windsor, in the Late Middle Ages*. Leeds, UK: Maney, 2001.

Roberts, Hugh. *For the King's Pleasure: The Furnishing and Decoration of George IV's Apartments at Windsor Castle*. London: Royal Collection, 2001.

Roberts, Jane, ed. *George III and Queen Charlotte: Patronage, Collecting and Court Taste.* London: Royal Collection, 2004.

——. *Master Drawings in the Royal Collection: From Leonardo da Vinci to the Present Day.* London: Collins Harvill, 1986.

——. *Royal Landscape: The Gardens and Parks of Windsor.* New Haven, Conn.: Yale University Press, 1997.

——. *Royal Treasures: A Golden Jubilee Celebration.* London: Royal Collection, 2002.

Roberts, Jane, Prudence Sutcliffe, and Susan Mayor. *Unfolding Pictures: Fans in the Royal Collection.* London: Royal Collection, 2005.

Robinson, John Martin. *Buckingham Palace: The Official Illustrated History.* London: Royal Collection, 2000.

——. *Windsor Castle: The Official Illustrated History.* London: Royal Collection, 2001.

Salisbury, Marjorie Cecil, Countess of. *The Gardens of Queen Elizabeth, the Queen Mother: A Personal Tour with the Marchioness of Salisbury.* London: Viking, 1988.

Saul, Nigel, ed. *St. George's Chapel, Windsor, in the Fourteenth Century.* Woodbridge, UK: Boydell, 2005.

Strong, Roy. *Cecil Beaton: The Royal Portraits.* New York: Simon & Schuster, 1988.

——. *Royal Gardens.* London: British Broadcasting Corporation, 1992.

Struthers, Jane. *Royal London.* London: New Holland, 2005.

——. *Royal Palaces of Britain.* London: New Holland, 2004.

Thurley, Simon. *Hampton Court: A Social and Architectural History.* New Haven, Conn.: Yale University Press, 2003.

——. *The Royal Palaces of Tudor England: Architecture and Court Life, 1460–1547.* New Haven, Conn.: Yale University Press, 1993.

Vickers, P. H. *"A Gift So Graciously Bestowed": The History of the Prince Consort's Library.* Winchester: Hampshire County Council, 1993.

White, Christopher. *The Later Flemish Pictures in the Collection of Her Majesty the Queen.* London: Royal Collection, 2007.

Whittle, Tyler. *Victoria and Albert at Home.* London: Routledge & Kegan Paul, 1980.

Williams, Neville. *Royal Homes of the United Kingdom.* Ware, UK: Omega, 1984.

Worsley, Lucy, and David Souden. *Hampton Court: The Official Illustrated History.* London: Merrell, 2005.

Wright, Patricia. *The Strange History of Buckingham Palace.* Stroud, UK: History Press, 2008.

York, Sarah, Duchess of. *Victoria and Albert: Life at Osborne House.* London: Weidenfeld & Nicolson, 1991.

## REFERENCE AND GENERAL WORKS

Ailes, Adrian. *The Origins of the Royal Arms of England: Their Development to 1199.* Reading, UK: Reading University, 1982.

Allison, Ronald, and Sarah Riddell, eds. *The Royal Encyclopaedia*. London: Macmillan, 1991.

Ashley, Mike. *A Brief History of British Kings and Queens*. London: Robinson, 2002.

———. *The Mammoth Book of British Kings and Queens*. London: Robinson, 1999.

Barnett, Anthony, ed. *Power and the Throne: The Monarchy Debate*. London: Vintage, 1994.

Beem, Charles. *The Lioness Roared: The Problems of Female Rule in English History*. New York: Palgrave Macmillan, 2006.

———, ed. *The Royal Minorities of Medieval and Early Modern England*. New York: Palgrave Macmillan, 2008.

Bentley-Cranch, Dana. *Royal Faces: From William the Conqueror to the Present Day*. London: National Portrait Gallery, 1990.

Bergeron, David M. *Shakespeare's Romances and the Royal Family*. Lawrence: University of Kansas Press, 1985.

Blair, Claude, et al. *The Crown Jewels: The History of the Coronation Regalia in the Jewel House in the Tower of London*. 2 vols. London: Her Majesty's Stationery Office, 1998.

Bogdanor, Vernon. *The Monarchy and the Constitution*. Oxford: Clarendon, 1995.

Bond, Jennie. *Reporting Royalty: Behind the Scenes with the BBC's Royal Correspondent*. London: Headline, 2001.

Bousfield, Arthur, and Gary Toffoli. *Royal Observations: Canadians & Royalty*. Toronto: Dundurn, 1991.

Brewer, Clifford. *The Death of Kings: A Medical History of the Kings and Queens of England*. London: Abson Books, 2000.

Cannon, John, ed. *Dictionary of British History*. New York: Oxford University Press, 2009.

Cannon, John, and Ralph Griffiths. *The Oxford Illustrated History of the British Monarchy*. Oxford: Oxford University Press, 2000.

Cannon, John, and Anne Hargreaves. *The Kings and Queens of Britain*. Oxford: Oxford University Press, 2001.

Carlton, Charles. *Royal Childhoods*. London: Routledge & Kegan Paul, 1986.

———. *Royal Mistresses*. London: Routledge, 1990.

———. *Royal Warriors: A Military History of the British Monarchy*. Harlow, UK: Pearson/Longman, 2003.

Cavendish, Richard, and Pip Leahy. *Kings and Queens: The Concise Guide*. Newton Abbott, UK: David & Charles, 2007.

Cheshire, Paul. *Kings and Queens: An Illustrated Guide*. London: Star Fire, 2007.

Clark, Anna. *Scandal: The Sexual Politics of the British Constitution*. Princeton, N.J.: Princeton University Press, 2004.

Courtney, Nicholas. *Royal Children*. London: Dent, 1982.

———. *Sporting Royals: Past and Present*. London: Hutchinson, 1983.

Coward, Barry, ed. *A Companion to Stuart Britain*. Malden, Mass.: Wiley-Blackwell, 2009.

Crofton, Ian. *The Kings and Queens of England*. London: Quercus, 2006.

Crystal, David, ed. *Penguin Pocket Kings and Queens*. London: Penguin, 2006.

Cussans, Thomas. *The Times Kings & Queens of the British Isles*. London: Times, 2002.

Dale, John. *The Prince and the Paranormal: The Psychic Bloodline of the Royal Family*. London: W. H. Allen, 1986.

Davies, Norman. *The Isles: A History*. London: Macmillan, 1999.

Davies, Wendy. *Patterns of Power in Early Wales*. Oxford: Clarendon, 1990.

Delderfield, Eric R. *Kings and Queens of England and Great Britain*. Newton Abbot: David & Charles, 1998.

Dewhurst, J. *Royal Confinements*. London: Weidenfeld & Nicolson, 1980.

Dickinson, H. T., ed. *Companion to Eighteenth-Century Britain*. Oxford: Blackwell, 2002.

Doherty, Paul. *The Great Crown Jewels Robbery of 1303: The Extraordinary Story of the First Big Bank Raid in History*. London: Constable, 2005.

Donnachie, Ian, and George Hewitt. *The Birlinn Companion to Scottish History*. Edinburgh: Birlinn, 2007.

Edgar, Donald. *The Royal Parks*. London: W. H. Allen, 1986.

Eilers, Marlene A. *Queen Victoria's Descendants*. New York: Atlantic International, 1987.

Erickson, Carolly. *Royal Panoply: Brief Lives of the English Monarchs*. New York: St. Martin's Griffin, 2007.

Ewan, Elizabeth, and Maureen M. Meikle. *Women in Scotland, c1100–c1750*. East Linton, UK: Tuckwell, 1998.

Fletcher, Richard. *Who's Who in Roman Britain and Anglo-Saxon England*. London: Shepheard-Walwyn, 1989.

Fraser, Antonia, ed. *The Lives of the Kings and Queens of England*. London: Weidenfeld & Nicolson, 1998.

Freeman-Grenville, G. S. P. *The Wordsworth Book of the Kings and Queens of Britain*. Ware, UK: Wordsworth Editions, 1997.

Friedman, Dennis. *Ladies of the Bedchamber: The Role of the Royal Mistress*. London: Peter Owen, 2003.

Fritze, Ronald H., Geoffrey Elton, and Walter Sutton, eds. *Historical Dictionary of Tudor England, 1485–1603*. Westport, Conn.: Greenwood Press, 1991.

Fritze, Ronald H., and William B. Robison, eds. *Historical Dictionary of Late Medieval England, 1272–1485*. Westport, Conn.: Greenwood Press, 2002.

Fritze, Ronald H., William B. Robison, and Walter Sutton, eds. *Historical Dictionary of Stuart England, 1603–1689*. Westport, Conn.: Greenwood Press, 1996.

Fryde, E. B., D. E. Greenway, S. Porter, and I. Roy, eds. *Handbook of British Chronology*. Cambridge: Cambridge University Press, 1996.

Gardiner, Juliet, ed. *The History Today Who's Who in British History*. London: Collins & Brown, 2000.

Gardiner, Juliet, and Neil Wenborn, eds. *The History Today Companion to British History*. London: Collins & Brown, 1995.

Gere, Charlotte, and John Culme, with William Summers. *Garrard: The Crown Jewellers for 150 Years, 1843–1993*. London: Quartet, 1993.

Given-Wilson, Chris, and Alice Curteis. *The Royal Bastards of Medieval England*. London: Routledge & Kegan Paul, 1984.

Golby, J. M., and A. W. Purdue. *Kings and Queens of Empire: British Monarchs, 1760–2000*. Stroud, UK: Alan Sutton, 2000.

Goodman, Jean, in collaboration with Sir Iain Moncrieff of that Ilk. *Debrett's Royal Scotland*. New York: Putnam, 1983.

Grant, Alexander, and K. J. Stringer. *Uniting the Kingdom?: The Making of British History*. London: Routledge, 1995.

Grant, Neil. *Kings and Queens*. London: Collins, 2004.

Gray, Robert. *The King's Wife: Five Queen Consorts*. London: Secker & Warburg, 1990.

Haigh, Christopher, ed. *The Cambridge Historical Encyclopedia of Great Britain and Ireland*. Cambridge: Cambridge University Press, 1985.

Hall, Unity. *The Private Lives of Britain's Royal Women*. London: O'Mara, 1991.

Hall, Unity, and Ingrid Seward. *By Royal Invitation*. London: Sidgwick & Jackson, 1988.

Hallam, Elizabeth, ed. *The Plantagenet Encyclopedia*. New York: Grove Weidenfeld, 1990.

Hamilton, Alan. *The Royal One Hundred: A Who's Who of the First 100 People in Line of Succession to the British Throne*. London: Pavilion, 1986.

Hanrahan, David C. *Colonel Blood: The Man Who Stole the Crown Jewels*. Stroud, UK: Alan Sutton, 2003.

Harper-Bill, Christopher, and Elizabeth van Houts, eds. *A Companion to the Anglo-Norman World*. Woodbridge, UK: Boydell, 2003.

Harris, Bob, and Alan R. MacDonald. *Scotland: The Making and Unmaking of the Nation, c1100–1707*. 5 vols. Dundee: Dundee University Press, 2006–2007.

Hasler, Charles. *The Royal Arms: Its Graphic and Decorative Development*. London: Jupiter Books, 1980.

Hawkes, Jason, and Jane Struthers. *Royal Britain from the Air*. London: Ebury, 1994.

Haywood, Trevor. *The Lives, Deaths and Funerals of British Monarchs*. Kidderminster, UK: El Corvo, 2007.

Heald, Tim. *By Appointment: 150 Years of the Royal Warrant and Its Holders*. London: Queen Anne, 1989.

Herman, Eleanor. *Sex with Kings: 500 Years of Adultery, Power, Rivalry and Revenge*. New York: William Morrow, 2004.

———. *Sex with the Queen: 900 Years of Vile Kings, Virile Lovers and Passionate Politics*. New York: William Morrow, 2006.

Hibbert, Christopher. *The Court at Windsor: A Domestic History*. Harmondsworth, UK: Penguin, 1982.

———. *The Court of St. James's: The Monarch at Work from Victoria to Elizabeth*. New York: Quill, 1983.

Hilliam, David. *Kings, Queens, Bones and Bastards: Who's Who in the English Monarchy from Egbert to Elizabeth II*. Stroud, UK: Alan Sutton, 2004.

———. *Monarchs, Murders and Mistresses: A Calendar of Royal Days*. Stroud, UK: Alan Sutton, 2004.

——. *Who's Who in the British Monarchy: From the Saxon Kings to Elizabeth II.* Bournemouth, UK: Pocket Reference Books, 1996.

Hilton, Lisa. *Queens Consort: England's Medieval Queens.* London: Weidenfeld & Nicolson, 2008.

Hoey, Brian. *All the Queen's Men: Inside the Royal Household.* London: HarperCollins, 1992.

——. *Invitation to the Palace.* London: Grafton, 1989.

——. *Monarchy: Behind the Scenes with the Royal Family.* London: British Broadcasting Corporation, 1997.

——. *The New Royal Court.* London: Sidgwick & Jackson, 1990.

——. *The Royal Yacht Britannia: Inside the Queen's Floating Palace.* Yeovil, UK: Patrick Stephens, 1998.

Holden, Anthony. *Great Royal Front Pages.* London: Collins, 1983.

Inwood, Stephen. *Historic London: An Explorer's Guide.* London: Macmillan, 2008.

——. *A History of London.* New York: Carroll & Graf, 1998.

James, Paul, and Peter Russell. *At Her Majesty's Service.* London: Collins, 1986.

Keay, Douglas. *Royal Pursuit: The Palace, the Press and the People.* London: Severn House, 1983.

Kenyon, J. P., editorial consultant. *Dictionary of British History.* Ware, UK: Wordsworth, 1992.

Kidd, Charles, ed. *Debrett's Book of Royal Children.* London: Debrett's, 1982.

——. *Debrett's Peerage and Baronetage.* Richmond, UK: Debrett's, 2007.

Kinney, Arthur F., and David W. Swain, eds. *Tudor England: An Encyclopedia.* New York: Garland, 2001.

Kuhn, William. *Democratic Royalism: The Transformation of the British Monarchy, 1861–1914.* New York: St. Martin's, 1996.

Laidlaw, James, ed. *The Auld Alliance: France and Scotland over 700 Years.* Edinburgh: Edinburgh University Press, 1999.

Lapidge, Michael, John Blair, Simon Keynes, and Donald Scragg, eds. *Blackwell Encyclopedia of Anglo-Saxon England.* Oxford: Wiley-Blackwell, 2000.

Lee, Min, ed. *Larousse Dictionary of British History.* Edinburgh: Larousse, 1994.

Leese, T. Anna. *Blood Royal: Issue of the Kings and Queens of Medieval England, 1066–1399; The Normans and the Plantagenets.* Bowie, Md.: Heritage Books, 1996.

Leventhal, Fred M., ed. *Twentieth-Century Britain: An Encyclopedia.* New York: Peter Lang, 2002.

Lewis, Brenda Ralph. *Kings & Queens of England: A Dark History; 1066 to the Present Day.* London: Reader's Digest, 2003.

Lloyd, Christopher. *The Paintings in the Royal Collection: A Thematic Exploration.* London: Royal Collection, 1999.

——. *The Queen's Pictures: Royal Collectors through the Centuries.* London: National Gallery, 1991.

——. *The Quest for Albion: Monarchy and the Patronage of British Painting.* London: Royal Collection, 1998.

Loades, David, ed. *Chronicles of the Tudor Kings*. Godalming, UK: Bramley Books, 1996.

Longford, Elizabeth, ed. *The Oxford Book of Royal Anecdotes*. Oxford: Oxford University Press, 1991.

Lynch, Michael, ed. *The Oxford Companion to Scottish History*. Oxford: Oxford University Press, 2005.

———. *Scotland: A New History*. London: Barrie & Jenkins, 1991.

Lyon, Ann. *Constitutional History of the United Kingdom*. London: Cavendish, 2003.

Lyon, Bryce Dale. *A Constitutional and Legal History of Medieval England*. New York: Norton, 1980.

Maccubbin, Robert P., and Martha Hamilton-Phillips, eds. *The Age of William and Mary: Power, Politics and Patronage, 1688–1702; A Reference Encyclopedia and Exhibition Catalogue*. Williamsburg, Va.: College of William and Mary, 1989.

Maclagan, Michael. *Lines of Succession: Heraldry of the Royal Families of Europe*. Hoo, UK: Grange, 2002.

Magnússon, Magnús. *Scotland: The Story of a Nation*. London: HarperCollins, 2000.

Marshall, Rosalind K. *Scottish Queens, 1034–1714*. East Linton, UK: Tuckwell, 2003.

Matthew, H. C. G., and Brian Harrison, eds. *Oxford Dictionary of National Biography*. 61 vols. Oxford: Oxford University Press, 2004.

McDonald, R. Andrew. *Manx Kingship in Its Irish Sea Setting, 1187–1229: King Rognvalder and the Crovan Dynasty*. Dublin: Four Courts Press, 2007.

McNeill, Peter G. B., and Hector L. MacQueen, eds. *Atlas of Scottish History to 1707*. Edinburgh: University of Edinburgh, 1996.

Menkes, Suzy. *The Royal Jewels*. London: Grafton, 1988.

Mercer, Derrik, ed. *Chronicle of the Royal Family*. London: Chronicle Communications, 1991.

Miller, Alan. *The Homosexual Kings of England*. London: Blackie, 2003.

Mitchell, Sally, ed. *Victorian Britain: An Encyclopedia*. New York: Garland, 1988.

Mitchison, Rosalind. *A History of Scotland*. London: Routledge, 2002.

Morgan, Kenneth O. *The Oxford Illustrated History of Britain*. Oxford: Oxford University Press, 2009.

Morrill, John, ed. *The Oxford Illustrated History of Tudor and Stuart Britain*. Oxford: Oxford University Press, 1996.

Mosley, Charles. *Blood Royal: From the Time of Alexander the Great to Queen Elizabeth II; A Golden Jubilee Memoir*. Bournemouth, UK: Smith's Peerage for Ruvigny, 2002.

Nash, David, and Antony Taylor, eds. *Republicanism in Victorian Society*. Stroud, UK: Alan Sutton, 2000.

Newman, Gerald, ed. *Britain in the Hanoverian Age, 1714–1837: An Encyclopedia*. New York: Garland, 1997.

Olechnowicz, Andrzej, ed. *The Monarchy and the British Nation: 1780 to the Present*. Cambridge: Cambridge University Press, 2007.

Oram, Richard, ed. *The Kings and Queens of Scotland*. Stroud, UK: Tempus, 2004.

Ormrod, W. M., ed. *The Kings and Queens of England.* Stroud, UK: Tempus, 2004.

Palmer, Alan. *Crowned Cousins: The Anglo-German Royal Connection.* London: Weidenfeld & Nicolson, 1985.

———. *Kings and Queens of England.* London: Peerage, 1985.

Palmer, Alan, and Veronica Palmer. *The Pimlico Chronology of British History.* London: Pimlico, 1996.

———. *Royal England: A Historical Gazetter.* London: Methuen, 1983.

Panton, Kenneth J. *Historical Dictionary of London.* Lanham, Md.: Scarecrow, 2001.

———. *London: A Historical Companion.* Stroud, UK: Tempus, 2003.

Panton, Kenneth J., and Keith A. Cowlard. *Historical Dictionary of the Contemporary United Kingdom.* Lanham, Md.: Scarecrow, 2008.

———. *Historical Dictionary of the United Kingdom.* 2 vols. Lanham, Md.: Scarecrow, 1997 (vol. 1) and 1998 (vol. 2).

Paxman, Jeremy. *On Royalty.* London: Viking, 2006.

Pearsall, Ronald. *Kings and Queens: A History of British Monarchy.* New York: Todtri, 1999.

Potter, Jeremy. *Pretenders.* London: Constable, 1986.

Prochaska, Frank. *The Eagle and the Crown: Americans and the British Monarchy.* New Haven, Conn.: Yale University Press, 2008.

———. *The Republic of Britain, 1760–2000.* London: Allen Lane, 2000.

———. *Royal Bounty: The Making of a Welfare Monarchy.* New Haven, Conn.: Yale University Press, 1995.

———, ed. *Royal Lives.* Oxford: Oxford University Press, 2002.

Rappaport, Helen. *Queen Victoria: A Biographical Companion.* Santa Barbara, Calif.: ABC-CLIO, 2003.

Roberts, Jane. *Royal Artists: From Mary Queen of Scots to the Present Day.* London: Grafton, 1987.

———. *Royal Treasures: A Golden Jubilee Celebration.* London: Royal Collection, 2002.

Rose, Kenneth. *Intimate Portraits of Kings, Queens and Courtiers.* London: Spring, 1989.

Rose, Tessa. *The Coronation Ceremony of the Kings and Queens of England and the Crown Jewels.* London: Her Majesty's Stationery Office, 1992.

Routh, C. R. N. *Who's Who in Tudor England.* Mechanicsburg, Pa.: Stackpole Books, 2001.

Sawyer, Peter, ed. *The Oxford Illustrated History of the Vikings.* Oxford: Oxford University Press, 1999.

Schama, Simon. *A History of Britain.* 3 vols. New York: Hyperion, 2000–2002.

Seward, Ingrid. *Royal Children of the Twentieth Century.* London: HarperCollins, 1993.

Shahrad, Cyrus. *Secrets of the Royal Family.* London: Arcturus, 2007.

Simmons, Simone, with Ingrid Seward. *Diana: The Last Word.* London: Orion, 2005.

Snyder, Christopher, ed. *The Early Peoples of Britain and Ireland: An Encyclopedia.* 2 vols. Oxford: Greenwood Press, 2008.

Somerset, Anne. *Ladies-in-Waiting: From the Tudors to the Present Day*. London: Phoenix, 2005.

Somerset Fry, Plantagenet. *Kings and Queens: A Royal History of Scotland and England*. London: Dorling Kindersley, 1997.

Starkey, David. *Monarchy: From the Middle Ages to Modernity*. London: HarperPress, 2006.

———. *The Monarchy of England: The Beginnings*. London: Chatto & Windus, 2004.

Stater, Victor. *The Political History of Tudor and Stuart England: A Sourcebook*. London: Routledge, 2002.

Strong, Roy. *Coronation: A History of Kingship and the British Monarchy*. London: HarperCollins, 2005.

Struthers, Jane. *Royal London*. London: New Holland, 2005.

Szarmach, Paul E., M. Teresa Tavormina, and Joel T. Rosenthal, eds. *Medieval England: An Encyclopedia*. New York: Garland, 1998.

Talbot, Godfrey. *The Book of the Royal Family*. Feltham, UK: Country Life, 1983.

Taylor, Antony. *"Down with the Crown": British Anti-Monarchism and Debates about Royalty since 1790*. London: Reaktion, 1999.

Taylor, John A. *British Monarchy, English Church Establishment, and Civil Liberty*. Westport, Conn.: Greenwood Press, 1996.

Thomas, David A. *Royal Admirals, 1327–1981*. London: Andre Deutsch, 1982.

Tittler, Robert, and Norman Jones, ed. *A Companion to Tudor Britain*. Malden, Mass.: Wiley-Blackwell, 2009.

Tomlinson, Richard. *Divine Right: The Inglorious Survival of British Royalty*. London: Abacus, 1995.

Usilton, Larry W. *The Kings of Medieval England, c560–1485: A Survey and Research Guide*. Lanham, Md.: Scarecrow, 1996.

*Voices out of the Air: The Royal Christmas Broadcasts, 1932–1981*. London: Heinemann, 1981.

Wagner, John A. *Bosworth Field to Bloody Mary: An Encyclopedia of the Early Tudors*. Westport, Conn.: Greenwood Press, 2003.

———. *Encyclopedia of the Hundred Years' War*. Westport, Conn.: Greenwood Press, 2006.

———. *Encyclopedia of the Wars of the Roses*. Santa Barbara, Calif.: ABC-CLIO, 2001.

Wallace, Ann, and Gabrielle Taylor. *Royal Mothers: From Eleanor of Aquitaine to Princess Diana*. London: Piatkus, 1987.

Waller, Maureen. *Sovereign Ladies: The Six Reigning Queens of England*. London: John Murray, 2006.

Warwick, Christopher. *Two Centuries of Royal Weddings*. London: A. Barker, 1980.

Weir, Alison. *Britain's Royal Families: The Complete Genealogy*. London: Pimlico, 2002.

Whitlock, Ralph. *Royal Farmers*. London: Michael Joseph, 1980.

Williams, Ann, Alfred P. Smyth, and D. P. Kirby. *A Biographical Dictionary of Dark Age Britain: England, Scotland and Wales from c500–c1050*. London: Seaby, 1991.

Williams, Chris, ed. *A Companion to Nineteenth-Century Britain*. Malden, Mass.: Blackwell, 2004.

Williamson, David. *Brewer's British Royalty*. London: Cassell, 1996.

———. *Debrett's Kings and Queens of Britain*. London: Webb & Bower, 1986.

Winton, John. *Captains and Kings: The Royal Family and the Royal Navy, 1901–1981*. Denbigh, UK: Bluejacket, 1981.

———. *The National Portrait Gallery History of the Kings and Queens of England*. London: National Portrait Gallery, 1998.

Wormald, Jenny, ed. *Scotland: A History*. Oxford: Oxford University Press, 2005.

Wrigley, Chris, ed. *Companion to Early Twentieth-Century Britain*. Malden, Mass.: Wiley-Blackwell, 2009.

# About the Author

**Kenneth J. Panton** is professor emeritus at the University of Southern Mississippi, where he was dean of the Honors College. A graduate of the University of Edinburgh and King's College, University of London, he taught at London Guildhall University before moving to the University of Southern Mississippi to lead the country's largest British Studies program, taking 200 graduate and undergraduate students to the United Kingdom every summer. His publications include four previous books for Scarecrow—the two-volume *Historical Dictionary of the United Kingdom* (coauthored with Keith A. Cowlard), the *Historical Dictionary of London*, and, most recently, and again with Keith Cowlard, the *Historical Dictionary of the Contemporary United Kingdom.* Now retired, he spends part of the year tramping the hills in his native Scotland and part in less undulating Mississippi.